Tractor-Trailer
Truck Driver Training

FOURTH EDITION

Tractor-Trailer Truck Driver Training

ALICE ADAMS

DELMAR
CENGAGE Learning·

Australia • Brazil • Japan • Korea • Mexico • Singapore • Spain • United Kingdom • United States

**Tractor-Trailer Truck Driver Training,
Fourth Edition**

Alice Adams

Vice President, Technology and Trades
  Professional Business Unit:
  Gregory L. Clayton

Director, Professional Transportation Industry
  Training Solutions: Kristen L. Davis

Development: Dawn Jacobson

Product Manager: Katie McGuire

Director of Marketing: Beth A. Lutz

Senior Marketing Manager: Jennifer Barbic

Senior Production Director: Wendy Troeger

Production Manager: Sherondra Thedford

Senior Content Project Manager: Cheri Plasse

Senior Art Director: Benj Gleeksman

Cover Photo: @ Jon Feingersh,
  Getty Images Inc.

© 2013, 2006, 2003, 1997 by Professional Truck Driver Institute, Inc. All graphics and illustrations (unless otherwise indicated) © Cengage Learning. All Rights Reserved.

ALL RIGHTS RESERVED. No part of this work covered by the copyright herein may be reproduced, transmitted, stored or used in any form or by any means graphic, electronic, or mechanical, including but not limited to photocopying, recording, scanning, digitizing, taping, Web distribution, information networks, or information storage and retrieval systems, except as permitted under Section 107 or 108 of the 1976 United States Copyright Act, without the prior written permission of the publisher.

> For product information and technology assistance, contact us at
> **Cengage Learning Customer & Sales Support, 1-800-354-9706**
> For permission to use material from this text or product,
> submit all requests online at **www.cengage.com/permissions**
> Further permissions questions can be emailed to
> **permissionrequest@cengage.com**

Library of Congress Control Number: 2012930208

ISBN-13: 978-1-111-03648-5

ISBN-10: 1-111-03648-9

Delmar
Executive Woods
5 Maxwell Drive
Clifton Park, NY 12065
USA

Cengage Learning is a leading provider of customized learning solutions with office locations around the globe, including Singapore, the United Kingdom, Australia, Mexico, Brazil, and Japan. Locate your local office at **www.cengage.com/global**

Cengage Learning products are represented in Canada by Nelson Education, Ltd.

To learn more about Delmar, visit **www.cengage.com/delmar**

Purchase any of our products at your local bookstore or at our preferred online store **www.cengagebrain.com**

Notice to the Reader

Publisher does not warrant or guarantee any of the products described herein or perform any independent analysis in connection with any of the product information contained herein. Publisher does not assume, and expressly disclaims, any obligation to obtain and include information other than that provided to it by the manufacturer. The reader is expressly warned to consider and adopt all safety precautions that might be indicated by the activities described herein and to avoid all potential hazards. By following the instructions contained herein, the reader willingly assumes all risks in connection with such instructions. The publisher makes no representations or warranties of any kind, including but not limited to, the warranties of fitness for particular purpose or merchantability, nor are any such representations implied with respect to the material set forth herein, and the publisher takes no responsibility with respect to such material. The publisher shall not be liable for any special, consequential, or exemplary damages resulting, in whole or part, from the readers' use of, or reliance upon, this material.

PTDI Disclaimer Notice To The Reader

The sale, distribution, or use of this or any other publication by a truck driver training program should not be construed to mean that the training program has been certified by the Professional Truck Driver Institute, Inc. (PTDI) or that an application for course certification is pending. Users are responsible for independently determining whether any such certification exists.

Anyone may use the PTDI curriculum standards as well as purchase and use PTDI-copyrighted materials. However, no entity may indicate that it is meeting or exceeding PTDI standards if it has not gone through the certification process and attained PTDI course certification.

Printed in the United States of America
4 5 6 7 17 16 15

Contents

3

Control Systems 57

4

Vehicle Systems 86

5

Transportation Technology 123

6

Vehicle Inspections 140

7

Basic Control 181

8

Shifting 201

9

Backing and Docking 222

10

Coupling and Uncoupling 237

11

Sliding Fifth Wheels and Tandem Axles 255

12

Preventive Maintenance and Servicing   273

13

Recognizing and Reporting Malfunctions   292

14

Communication   316

15

Visual Search   333

16

Space Management   351

17

Speed Management   366

18

Night Driving   384

19

Extreme Driving Conditions   399

20

Skid Control 427

21

Hazard Awareness 443

22

Railroad Crossings   464

23

Emergency Maneuvers   480

24

Accident Procedures   496

25

Handling Cargo 517

26

Cargo Documentation 550

27

Special Rigs   577

28

Hours of Service   604

29

Trip Planning   619

30

Transportation Security   640

31

Driving International Routes   657

32

Hazardous Materials 677

33

Public Relations and Job Search 706

34

Driver Health, Safety, and Security 728

35

Whistleblower Protections for Professional Drivers 757

36

Compliance, Safety, Accountability (CSA) 776

Preface

As you are reading this, more than five million professional tractor-trailer drivers are moving the economy of North America up and down the highways of three countries every day of the year. These professionals include men and women of all ages and all ethnicities as they supply the food, clothing, furniture, medicines and medical supplies, electronics, household goods, and the various elements that go into the manufacture of every consumable item necessary for living healthily and comfortably in today's world.

Without professional drivers, this continent's economies would fail, with little ability to make progress in any area, including medical research, communications, and other technologies that now save labor and time in our everyday lives.

Here's the point: Often without realizing it, the entire North American population—every man, woman, and child—depends on the knowledge, skills, and commitment of professional drivers for their very lives, not to mention their comfort and well-being.

So, it is a huge responsibility to sit behind the wheel of a tractor-trailer, to drive this continent's roadways, and to be on time with delivery of every cargo—and the men and women who have chosen careers as driving professionals have dedicated themselves to learning and performing their jobs as safely and efficiently as possible.

As you use this textbook to prepare for your career as a professional driver, do not lose sight of the generations of drivers who have brought the profession to where it is today. As you take your place behind the wheel of a tractor-trailer rig, remember those dedicated individuals who spent countless, lonely hours in the freezing cold or blistering heat on the road, driving vehicles without heat or air conditioning, loading and unloading shipments onto makeshift docks in all kinds of weather, without the communications technology and improvements commonly found on tractor-trailer rigs today.

Unlike earlier eras of the transportation industry, where anyone could drive and any driver was expendable, today's focus is not only on getting the job done but getting it done safely, with the driver's health, lifestyle, and security as top priorities.

As you take this giant step into a new career offering new opportunities, the gratitude of an entire continent goes with you. You will soon join the ranks of elite professionals, a strong and dedicated fraternity with proud traditions—a well-trained and skilled group of experts who see their first priority as the safe and efficient movement of goods from origin to destination and, ultimately, to the end user.

This textbook has been designed to help make your transition from where you are now to where you hope to be as a professional driver as easy and as efficient as possible. Yours will be an important job. Do it safely and do it well. This continent, your family, friends, and neighbors are depending on you, every hour you are on the job.

You are joining a time-honored profession and, in doing so, taking on a responsibility that is essential to this continent's future.

Good luck and safe driving!

A NOTE TO THE INSTRUCTOR

As veteran classroom teachers and college instructors, the authors and reviewers of *Tractor-Trailer Truck Driver Training*, **4th Edition** are familiar with the challenges and demands of molding a classroom of inexperienced individuals into the transportation professionals they want to become. It is not an easy task, but with time, study, and practice, many of the new students who come into your classroom will leave as the next generation of professional drivers, ready to take the seats of retiring veterans and a dwindling number of skilled professionals.

To assist you in this task, we have compiled a textbook, supplementary materials, and Instructor Resource to provide you with numerous tools and a comprehensive, turnkey curriculum to use as you train tractor-trailer drivers. Because of the strong growth of cross-border trade and transportation, this new edition of *Tractor-Trailer Truck Driver Training* includes an all-encompassing look at the North American continent—its transportation regulations and its similarity and differences across borders.

As you are well aware, the entire North American continent depends on dedicated, well-trained driving professionals to move its economy forward—and you are key to the continued quality of life everyone strives for. As we understand, this is a huge and demanding task, which is why we offer the following, in addition to the features outlined in Features of the Text section:

Supplements

Used in conjunction with this textbook, the following supplements provide a comprehensive, turnkey curriculum for tractor-trailer driver training.

Tractor-Trailer Truck Driver Training Instructor Resource.

The Instructor Resource provides everything an instructor needs to support classroom teaching. This all-in-one CD contains an Instructor's Guide with overviews of each chapter, suggested learning activities, discussion starters, and answers to all workbook review questions. The CD also contains PowerPoint presentation slides, a computerized test bank, an image library, and digitized video clips.

Tractor-Trailer Truck Driver Training Video Series.

Created in cooperation with the Professional Truck Driver Institute, Inc. (PTDI), these videos can be used as part of the Trucking: Tractor-Trailer Truck Driver training system or as part of an existing driver training program.

Acknowledgments

The development and publication of this book was made possible by many individuals. Special thanks to Alice Adams for her tireless effort updating, revising, and expanding this fourth edition.

We also thank the following reviewers for their valuable contributions:

Marlene Dakita–Certification Coordinator, Professional Truck Driver Institute

Doug DeGrow–Instructor, Kim Richardson Transportation Specialists

Roy Donning–Direction of Education, American Institute of Technology

Don Hess–Chairman, Transportation Programs, John Wood Community College

Yvette Lagrois–President of Truck Training School Association of Ontario, Vice President of Ontario Truck Training Academy

Robert McClanahan–Director, Transportation and Safety Education

John Moore–Ruhl Forensic, Inc.

Robert More–CSP, CDS, CDT, Insurance Industry Loss Control

Gail Swinger–ABF Freight System, Inc.

Bob Watkins–Consolidated Safety Services, Inc.

David Wehman–Truck Driving Program Coordinator, Baker College of Flint

Thank you to the following for supplying us with many great photos for this edition:

5th Wheel Institute

Baker College of Cadillac

Baker College of Flint

Canadian Centre of Occupational Health and Safety

Center for Employment Education (CEE)

Delaware Tech

Don Hess

Erik Berthelsen–1826 Photography

Port of Montreal

Prime Inc.

Qualcomm

SAGE Schools

Star Trailers, Inc.

Sunbury Transport Limited

Redoubt Reporter

Rob Ahlers

The Trucker

Professional Truck Driver Institute (PTDI)

Since its inception in 1986, Professional Truck Driver Institute (PTDI) has become the nation's foremost advocate of standards and professionalism for entry-level truck driver training. The purpose of PTDI is to advance commercial motor vehicle (CMV) driver training, proficiency, safety, and professionalism by promoting high-quality truck driver training courses and by verifying and publicly attesting to their quality.

As it evaluates courses, PTDI looks at much more than curriculum. As an objective third party, PTDI verifies that the school is following voluntary minimum standards as determined by the industry in areas such as administration, instructor qualifications, facilities, equipment, record keeping, graduation requirements, and employment rates.

When it comes to the curriculum itself, PTDI verifies that it consists of skills training in at least five key areas, referred to as "units." They include basic operation, safe operating practices for basic operation, advanced operating practices, vehicle systems and reporting malfunctions, and nonvehicle activities. Also, PTDI makes sure that students are spending specified amounts of time in the classroom, in the lab, and behind the wheel of a CMV.

To learn more about PTDI, visit www.ptdi.org.

PTDI and Delmar: Partners in Improvement

PTDI and Delmar have partnered to bring you comprehensive print, computer-based training (CBT), and Web-Based Training (WBT) products that incorporate the curriculum requirements of the Professional Truck Driver Institute. The chapters in *Tractor-Trailer Truck Driver Training* align very closely, and even go beyond, PTDI's basic curriculum units, as evidenced by a comparison of this textbook's table of contents to the PTDI curriculum overview on the next page. The number of classroom/lab and behind-the-wheel (BTW) hours required by a PTDI-certified course are also shown in the overview.

PTDI Basic Curriculum Units & Minimum Hours of Training

Unit	Classroom & Lab[*][^]	BTW Range & Street[*][•]
1 Basic Operation	18 (22)	24 (29)
1.1 Orientation[#]		
1.2 Control Systems[#]		
1.3 Vehicle Inspections		
1.4 Basic Control		
1.5 Shifting		
1.6 Backing and Docking		
1.7 Coupling and Uncoupling		
2 Safe Operating Practices for Basic Operation	8 (10)	17 (20)
2.1 Visual Search		
2.2 Vehicle Communication		
2.3 Speed Management		
2.4 Space Management		
3 Advanced Operating Practices	14 (17)	3 (4)
3.1 Night Operation		
3.2 Extreme Driving Conditions		
3.3 Hazard Perception		
3.4 Emergency Maneuvers/Skid Avoidance		
3.5 Skid Control and Recovery		
3.6 Passive (Unmarked or Uncontrolled) Railroad Crossings		
4 Vehicle Systems and Reporting Malfunctions[#]		
4.1 Identification and Maintenance		
4.2 Diagnosing and Reporting Malfunctions	6 (7)	0 (0)
5 Non-Vehicle Activities[#]		
5.1 Handling and Documenting Cargo		
5.2 Environmental Issues		
5.3 Hours of Service Requirements	43 (52)	0 (0)
5.4 Accident Procedures		
5.5 Managing Life on the Road/Personal Resources		
5.6 Trip Planning		
5.7 Interpersonal Communication Skills		
Discretionary Hours[+][#]	15 (17)	0
Total	104 (125) +	44 (53)

Total Hours Classroom/Lab + BTW Range/Street **148 (178)**

* Total of range and street behind-the-wheel (BTW) must equal
   at least 44 (53) hours per student.

• Hours are expressed as 60 and (50) minute hours.

+ Discretionary hours are discussed in the PTDI Curriculum Standards & Guidelines.

Units is non-driving subjects so driving time is not awarded.

^ Note: 15% of required classroom/lab hours may be adjusted among units.

See *www.ptdi.org/standards* for the elements within each unit as well as all requirements to have a PTDI-certified course.

Features of the Text

Objectives

Objectives are listed at the beginning of each chapter. They provide clear direction to students as to what they should understand when they have completed the chapter.

OBJECTIVES

When you have completed this chapter, you should be able to:

- Have a working knowledge of the history and evolution of truck transportation in North America.
- Be aware of the importance of the traditions behind truck transportation as well as its place in the economic strength of this continent.
- Understand the responsibility professional drivers assume each day they get behind the wheel of a truck.
- Have an introduction to some of the legislation establishing rules and regulations for the North American trucking industry.
- Be able to describe some of the professional behaviors required of today's drivers and the importance of this behavior on and off the road.

Introduction

The Introduction follows the Objectives in each chapter. It gives a summary of the content that will be covered in the chapter and the key concepts and topics that will be taught.

INTRODUCTION

As you read this first chapter of *Tractor-Trailer Truck Driver Training*, **4th edition,** you beginning an adventure that will change your life and the lives of others—your family, y coworkers, your supervisors and many, many people you will never meet. However, you ties as a professional driver will impact and improve the lives of hundreds of thousands of cons across the street and around the country, as you go about your day-to-day activities. Think abou

It is the hope of the publisher, author, and designers that *Tractor-Trailer Truck Driver Training* edition will open the door to knowledge and discovery that will help you achieve not only your sional goals but your personal goals, as well. We believe this book is your best source of informa instruction. Therefore, as you work through each chapter, you will be provided with basic know important skills, and a true opportunity to succeed.

This book is also the most important guide to professional driving available and can be used as ence as you move up the ranks in the transportation industry.

As the professional driver you are studying and training to be, you stand on the shoulders of pio who faced untold challenges in the early days of the commercial trucking industry. Your forebea this business often sat on orange crates to drive early-model trucks, and used technology that is years away from the comforts and conveniences today's drivers have at their fingertips.

In addition, the demand for professional drivers, which had decreased somewhat in the early pa 21st century, is now expanding. This demand for more drivers, coupled with the increasing cros

66   CHAPTER 3

STOP!
The trailer **brake control** valve should not be used to slow the rig or hold the rig when it is parked. Improper use could result in a jackknife.

▶ Figure 3-12
Foot brake control.

▶ Figure 3-13
Trailer air supply valve.

INTERESTING FACT

By 1912, a number of higher-priced trucks were equipped with air brakes. The Sauer 6-1/2 ton was typical. Compressed air and gas or electric and explosive gas, were used for starting purposes.

Parking brake control valve—a yellow, diamond-shaped push-pull knob that allows the driver to engage the parking brake. The parking brake should be used only after the rig is stopped. It should ALWAYS be engaged before the driver turns off the engine and/or leaves the cab. If the driver fails to set the parking brake, the rig could roll, even on a level surface.

Trailer air supply valve—a red, octagonal-shaped button that, in the open position, supplies air to the trailer brakes. In the closed or pulled out position, it shuts off the air supply to the trailer. The trailer air supply valve needs to be closed (pulled) when the tractor is not connected to a trailer (**see Figure 3-13**).

STOP!
NEVER use the trailer air supply valve as a parking brake. If you do so, loss of air will occur.

CAUTION!
When the air supply drops to 20 to 45 psi (138 to 310 k), the valve closes automatically. This stops the flow of air and protects the tractor's air supply. The trailer's air supply valve triggers the emergency relay valve that puts on the trailer brakes.

Color Blocks

There are green, yellow, and red color blocks throughout the book that emphasize workplace safety and highlight key concepts. The green "Go!" blocks highlight information that makes the student "ready to go" once he or she has a clear understanding of it. Yellow "Caution!" blocks highlight information on concepts or techniques that, for reasons of safety, require the student to exercise caution when putting them into practice. Red "Stop!" blocks draw the students' attention to the most serious safety concerns.

Interesting Facts

Interesting Facts have been included to give the learner a glimpse of how the transportation industry has developed and grown over the decades—from the first wagons and ox carts to today's sleek and powerful tractor-trailer rigs.

INTERESTING FACT

The Buffalo two-and-one-half-ton truck, introduced in 1921, had unusual features to adapt to unusual road conditions. It had two 3-speed gearsets mounted in tandem to provide a gear with a countershift in between for power take-off and a low speed of one mile (1.6 km) in seven and three-tenths hours for extremely hard pulls. Two gearshift levers were mounted in front of the driver. One was used normally and the other could be brought in under heavy load. The low gear ratio allowed driving down the steepest hill without brakes.

▶ *Driver Dan*

▶ *Lisa Cruise*

Cartoons

Cartoons appear throughout the book, adding humor and visual interest, while at the same time providing tips to learners and reinforcing concepts presented. These characters are named Driver Dan, Lisa Cruise and Jake Brake.

▶ *Jake Brake*

Summary

The summary appears at the end of each chapter prior to the list of Key Terms. It can be used to review the chapter and stimulate discussion.

Key Terms

Key Terms from each chapter are listed at the end of chapters. This list can be used as a quick review of the most important terms or concepts presented.

Additionally, Freightliner distributes, markets, and merchandises XM Satellite Radio through its fleet-owner relationships, its dealer organization, and its network of 160 TravelCenters of America. XM radios were first offered in Freightliner's new models of Freightliner, Sterling, American LaFrance trucks, and Thomas Built buses, beginning in 2001. Some trucking companies also offer Satellite Radios to their drivers as a benefit. It provides the driver with static free, often commercial free music, as well as up to the minute weather and traffic conditions.

SUMMARY

In this chapter, you have been able to review some of the technology now available in the transportation industry in North America. Some drivers simply use cell phones to keep in touch with dispatchers as well as home and family while they are on the road. Others use QualComm products, not only for communication but also for business transaction, tracking and reports, and to access other wireless information. Laptop computers, built-in computers, and wireless telecommunications are also available in some of today's trucks.

The bottom line in transportation across North America is that knowledge of wireless communications products and the ability to use a computer are fast becoming skills required of today's professional truck drivers.

KEY TERMS

BlackBerry	Electronic onboard recording	Satellite radio
Cellular phones	(EOBR)	Social networking
Global positioning system (GPS)	Pick-up and delivery (P&D)	Technology
Laptop computer	Qualcomm	Walkie-talkie

Day in the Life Stories

Day in the Life stories appear at the end of many chapters throughout the book. These stories are written by truck drivers and industry leaders, showcasing career beginnings, highlights, memorable moments, and how driving experiences can shape both lives and careers.

A DAY IN THE LIFE...

Jake Brake ~ ABC Transport Inc., Vice President

My name is Jake Brake, and I am currently the Executive Vice President and Chief Operating Officer of ABC Transport Inc. I "happened" into the trucking industry in 1984 at the age of 19. I remember my first day like it was yesterday... I was thrown the keys to a 1971 two-stick Mack and literally told to figure it out. I received a 15-minute tutorial in the driver's seat of the truck and left to my own devices. Having spent a lot of time on the farm growing up, I was used to the "figure it out" learning environment and I enjoyed the challenge and the sense of accomplishment. I found learning to drive the truck and maneuvering about was actually easy for me and I remember thinking to myself, this was going to be a pretty easy and fun job—I got one of the two right, and it wasn't the "easy" part!

> **There is a big difference between being able to drive a truck and being a truck driver...**

There is a big difference between being able to drive a truck and being a truck driver, and I found that out the hard way. I spent seven years on the road running regional and long haul and I can't tell you how many times I encountered an issue or learned something new and said to myself, "Boy, I wish I knew that before right now!" I never understood how a business like trucking, which is critically dependent on drivers and would entrust them with hundreds of thousands of

dollars worth of equipment and liability, would be too busy to invest any time or energy into teaching someone what to do and how to do it. This has stuck with me my entire career.

I moved into dispatch in 1991, just as our company embarked on an aggressive growth strategy. In five short years we grew from 18 trucks to almost 400, and although those were extremely challenging times, I consider myself extremely fortunate to have experienced this. We were a small company transitioning to big business and in the process I was able to touch and learn all aspects of our trucking operations. As our company grew, so did my opportunities and responsibilities. I have never forgotten where I came from and how difficult it was to "break into the business." I try to stay on top of things that are changing and remain focused on making things better for others. My background as a driver makes it easy to relate to our drivers and to collaborate with them to build a better company. I am active on our Driver Advisory Board and I still make time to meet and deal with drivers every single day. I have also learned that in order to look after our drivers, we have to hire and train the best people and give them a true understanding of the support we need to provide our fleet. What I have not been able to glean from the generosity and patience of people working within our industry, I have supplemented with formal education. Today I am responsible for all aspects of our operation, overseeing our Dispatch and Operations, Equipment and Maintenance, Systems and Technology, Safety, Driver Development, and Human Resources. This is a fascinating and exciting industry and I cannot imagine what else I would be doing with my life. This is not about trucks, it is about people—and the only thing you really need to know is what you don't know and where to go for help. What I like most about this industry is that it is full of kind and generous people that are passionate about their careers and eager to help make a difference!

82

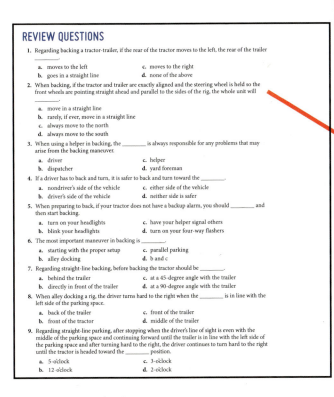

REVIEW QUESTIONS

1. Regarding backing a tractor-trailer, if the rear of the tractor moves to the left, the rear of the trailer _____.
   a. moves to the left
   b. goes in a straight line
   c. moves to the right
   d. none of the above

2. When backing, if the tractor and trailer are exactly aligned and the steering wheel is held so the front wheels are pointing straight ahead and parallel to the sides of the rig, the whole unit will _____.
   a. move in a straight line
   b. rarely, if ever, move in a straight line
   c. always move to the north
   d. always move to the south

3. When using a helper in backing, the _____ is always responsible for any problems that may arise from the backing maneuver.
   a. driver
   b. dispatcher
   c. helper
   d. yard foreman

4. If a driver has to back and turn, it is safer to back and turn toward the _____.
   a. nondriver's side of the vehicle
   b. driver's side of the vehicle
   c. either side of the vehicle
   d. neither side is safer

5. When preparing to back, if your tractor does not have a backup alarm, you should _____ and then start backing.
   a. turn on your headlights
   b. blink your headlights
   c. have your helper signal others
   d. turn on your four-way flashers

6. The most important maneuver in backing is _____.
   a. starting with the proper setup
   b. alley docking
   c. parallel parking
   d. b and c

7. Regarding straight-line backing, before backing the tractor should be _____.
   a. behind the trailer
   b. directly in front of the trailer
   c. at a 45-degree angle with the trailer
   d. at a 90-degree angle with the trailer

8. When alley docking a rig, the driver turns hard to the right when the _____ is in line with the left side of the parking space.
   a. back of the trailer
   b. front of the tractor
   c. front of the trailer
   d. middle of the trailer

9. Regarding straight-line parking, after stopping when the driver's line of sight is even with the middle of the parking space and continuing forward until the trailer is in line with the left side of the parking space and after turning hard to the right, the driver continues to turn hard to the right until the tractor is headed toward the _____ position.
   a. 5-o'clock
   b. 12-o'clock
   c. 3-o'clock
   d. 2-o'clock

Review Questions

Multiple-choice Review Questions appear at the end of each chapter. The review questions will help measure students' knowledge of each chapter, determining which areas of study they thoroughly understand and which areas need further review.

Supplemental Learning Activities

Optional, supplementary learning opportunities invite students to take a closer look at a topic or to encourage exploration and exposure to additional information through research, guest speakers, and off-site experiences.

SUPPLEMENTAL LEARNING ACTIVITIES

1. A pro driver will tell you, "Never apply power as you go over the crest of a hill." Give three reasons this is a good rule to remember. (Hint: Especially if you can't see what's going on ahead.)

2. What is the most dangerous part of driving a big rig going down a hill with a heavy load? In small groups, discuss and come up with one or two scenarios that show why this statement is true.

3. In rural areas across North America, "country" intersections tend to be more narrow than city intersections. As a professional driver, in 100 words or less, describe what this means to you.

4. Look up the meaning of rpm and write a one-page report, demonstrating that you understand what rpm is all about.

5. When shifting from neutral to first gear and you hear "grinding," what does this mean, and what should you do to get the transmission to drop into gear? Discuss as a group and report to the class. Take no more than 10 minutes.

Website References

Each chapter ends with websites and references, provided for learners seeking more insight or in-depth information about topics and concepts presented in the chapter.

FOR MORE INFORMATION

PTDI—Record and Maintain House of Service Requirements, Page 28, Click on Skill Standards
www.ptdi.org/standards

FMCSA Hours of Service Regulations
www.fmcsa.dot.gov/rules-regulations/truck/driver/hos/fmcsa-guide-to-hos.pdf

Sleep Apnea Disorder Information
sleepapneadisorder.info

Ontario Hours of Service
www.e-laws.gov.on.ca/html/regs/english/elaws_regs_060555_e.htm

Department of Justice Canada—Hours of Service Regulations
laws-lois.justice.gc.ca/eng/regulations/SOR-2005-313/

Appendices

At the end of the book, a series of appendices has been provided. These include several expansive explanations to concepts introduced in the chapters. There's also a Trouble shooting Guide to identify equipment problems and a Glossary, which includes definitions for terms found at the end of each chapter. These appendices are included to serve as learning tools. Additionally, the listing of state and Canadian trucking associations has been added to offer new driving professionals information about their home state or province professional associations as well as serve as an information resource for states and provinces in which they will drive.

APPENDIX A

Troubleshooting Guide

Find out your company's rules for drivers doing any type of repairs to their equipment. Find out what they expect of you. Follow your company's policy. Do *not* do any type of repair work unless you have been authorized to do so.

Whatever you do, safety first—everywhere and always. And, if you see someone doing something that is unsafe or attempting something in an unsafe manner, don't hesitate to step up and say something. You may save a life . . . and remember, the most important thing is to get home safely after every run.

Warning. Before you do anything regarding troubleshooting, always put on personal protective equipment including safety glasses, boots, safety vest, hat and gloves. Know what you're doing, and if you don't have the experience or training, leave these activities to the trained technicians. Nothing—time tables, traffic or even pride—is worth injury or your life.

If You See...	System Affected	What to Look For	What to Do
1. Ammeter shows continuous maximum charge	Electrical	Short circuit in wiring	Disconnect battery terminal until short has been repaired
		Points in voltage regulator or cutout sticking	Have mechanic repair
2. Ammeter shows discharge with motor running	Electrical	Loose connection or short in wiring	Tighten connection
		Battery installed wrong	Have checked by a mechanic
		Burned out or improperly adjusted generator or alternator	Have replaced or repaired by mechanic
		Loose or broken alternator	Replace or tighten belt
3. High engine temperature	Cooling	Low water level	Shut off engine, allow to cool to normal, add water
		Frozen radiator	Cover radiator, run motor slowly, add water as needed
		Broken fan belt	Replace fan belt
		Slow water or oil circulation	Have checked and repaired by mechanic
		Defective fan clutch or shutters	Have checked and repaired by mechanic
		Blocked radiator	Have checked and repaired by mechanic
		Defective thermostat or radiator hose suction side	Have checked and repaired by mechanic

789

1 An Introduction to Trucking

© GWimages/www.Shutterstock.com

OBJECTIVES

When you have completed this chapter, you should be able to:

■ Have a working knowledge of the history and evolution of truck transportation in North America.

■ Be aware of the importance of the traditions behind truck transportation as well as its place in the economic strength of this continent.

■ Understand the responsibility professional drivers assume each day they get behind the wheel of a truck.

■ Have an introduction to some of the legislation establishing rules and regulations for the North American trucking industry.

■ Be able to describe some of the professional behaviors required of today's drivers and the importance of this behavior on and off the road.

INTRODUCTION

As you read this first chapter of *Tractor-Trailer Truck Driver Training,* **4th edition,** you are beginning an adventure that will change your life and the lives of others—your family, your coworkers, your supervisors and many, many people you will never meet. However, your abilities as a professional driver will impact and improve the lives of hundreds of thousands of consumers, across the street and around the country, as you go about your day-to-day activities. Think about that!

It is the hope of the publisher, author, and designers that *Tractor-Trailer Truck Driver Training,* **4th edition** will open the door to knowledge and discovery that will help you achieve not only your professional goals but your personal goals, as well. We believe this book is your best source of information and instruction. Therefore, as you work through each chapter, you will be provided with basic knowledge, important skills, and a true opportunity to succeed.

This book is also the most important guide to professional driving available and can be used as a reference as you move up the ranks in the transportation industry.

As the professional driver you are studying and training to be, you stand on the shoulders of pioneers who faced untold challenges in the early days of the commercial trucking industry. Your forebearers in this business often sat on orange crates to drive early-model trucks, and used technology that is light-years away from the comforts and conveniences today's drivers have at their fingertips.

In addition, the demand for professional drivers, which had decreased somewhat in the early part of the 21st century, is now expanding. This demand for more drivers, coupled with the increasing cross-border traffic expected in the next decade, will translate into more trucks on this hemisphere's highway systems. Therefore, you and your contributions as a transportation professional will become part of this important—and ongoing—tradition.

INTERESTING FACT

Few realize that motorized trucks were being built before the automobile in North America. In fact, motorized truck hauling began around 1890 in this country.

So, be proud you have chosen this industry. You will become a professional driver, one of the elite—and your efforts every time you take your place behind the wheel of a tractor-trailer are essential to the growth and economic health of our country. Moreover, what you contribute each day to this proud profession impacts the quality of life available to all of us in North America.

As mentioned earlier, professional drivers provide the momentum behind North America's economy. Therefore, *Tractor-Trailer Truck Driver Training,* **4th edition** emphasizes safety in every chapter and provides information about how you can maintain your physical and emotional health throughout your career. In addition, this book offers tips and information about how to safely handle the demands and responsibilities of professional driving **(see Figure 1-1).**

There are many organizations within the trucking industry. One of the largest is the American Trucking Associations, which manages the industry's "Good Stuff. Trucks Bring It." image campaign (www .trucksbringit.com). The purpose of this program is to emphasize to the general public the important role that trucking plays in everyday life **(see Figure 1-2).**

© SPb photo maker/www.Shutterstock.com

▶ Figure 1–1

Professional drivers help keep the economy moving.

There are organizations that represent all segments and interests within the trucking industry: motor carriers, drivers, trainers, insurance, regulators, shippers, and others. Many of these trucking-related associations, alliances, and councils are listed in Appendix C of this book.

The Truckload Carriers Association (TCA), which represents the interests of truckload companies and the communities they serve, either hosts or co-hosts numerous programs that support professional drivers. They include Best Fleets to Drive For, Driver of the Year, Highway Angel, Trucking's Top Rookie, and Trucking's Weight Loss Showdown. The association also manages the TCA Scholarship Fund, which helps trucking professionals associated with its member companies finance college educations for themselves and their family members (**see Figure 1-3** and www.truckload.org).

The slogan of the Canadian Trucking Alliance emphasizes the importance of trucking in Canada: "If you have it, a truck brought it!"

Consider this: The entire North American continent—every city and town, every citizen, every business, profession, and household—depends on professional drivers every day. Without you and others who will fill the seats of drivers who are retiring in large numbers, no one can continue to enjoy the quality of life they enjoy today.

Yes, your new adventure as a professional driver will not only change your life but it also will provide the opportunity to make a difference for your country, its citizens, and their future (**see Figure 1-4**).

Approximately 16 million trucks operate in the United States and Canada today. Of this number, two million are Class 8 vehicles—tractor-trailers. One in every nine drivers is an independent owner-operator.

The trucking industry is the most significant contributor to North America's economy, growth, and prosperity. Every aspect of life on this continent is impacted every day by millions of men and women who climb behind the wheel to pick up and deliver commodities and products from origin to destination.

Everything we wear, eat, use, and need is transported by trucks. The same is true for businesses, industry, farms, construction, government, medical communities, and schools. Trucks haul the vital products to keep the wheels of industry turning and the nation's economy moving. Without the knowledge and skills of professional truck drivers, this nation could not and would not be as great as it is or can become (**see Figure 1-5**).

When trucks are movin' . . . our economy is groovin'!

Courtesy of American Trucking Associations

Figure 1-2

Courtesy of TCA

Figure 1-3

© Cengage Learning 2013

FACTS YOU NEED TO KNOW ABOUT TRUCKING

- The U.S. trucking industry is made up of more than 227,930 for-hire carriers and more than 282,485 private carriers; 96 percent of these carriers have fewer than 20 trucks.
- The Canadian trucking industry is a $55 billion industry and is made up of more than 671,000 trucks registered in Canada.
- The North American trucking industry employs 9 million people throughout the continent's economy in jobs related to trucking activity, excluding self-employed owner-operators and contractors.
- According to the U.S. Department of Labor, there are 3.39 million truck drivers working in the U.S.
- According to the 2001 census compiled by Statistics Canada, there were close to 300,000 Canadians employed as truck drivers, representing 1.7 percent of Canada's total workforce.
- According to the American Transportation Research Institute, in 2008, trucks hauled nearly 54 percent of the goods (in terms of value) between the U.S. and Canada, and over 63 percent between the U.S. and Mexico.
- In 2008, U.S. trucks carried 68.8 percent of all freight—10.2 billion tons.
- Commercial Class 8 trucks (vehicles weighing over 33,001 pounds) logged 128.4 billion miles (206.6 billion km) in 2007, the equivalent of making over 136,301 cross-country trips per day.
- The average daily run for a long-haul, over-the-road truck driver in North America is almost 500 miles (805 km).
- A majority of long-haul, over-the-road truck drivers will drive, on average, 100,000 to 110,000 miles per year.
- Commercial truck taxes average close to $18,000 per year.
- By 2020, the North American freight transportation industry will carry 18.8 billion tons of freight, generating $1.3 trillion in revenue, representing a 68.5 percent increase over 2008 revenues of $794.9 billion.

Information Courtesy American Trucking Assocations - Trucking Industry Facts 2010, the American Trucking Research Institute and Statistics Canada

▶ **Figure 1–4**

Courtesy of Delaware Tech, M. Lee Derrickson

▶ **Figure 1–5**

Professional drivers impact the economy with the wide variety of products they haul.

THE U.S. TRUCKING INDUSTRY: A BRIEF HISTORY

Although the modern truck transportation industry had its true beginnings in the late 1800s, the idea of self-powered devices to carry goods dates back to 130 B.C. when Hero of Alexandria envisioned such an apparatus powered by steam. The poet Homer mentioned self-moved vehicles in his legendary *Iliad* and the genius Leonardo da Vinci was intrigued enough with this same concept to experiment with primitive models.

But it was in 1769 that Capt. Nicholas Joseph Cugnot (pronounced ku-*no*), a French military officer, designed a three-wheeled cannon carriage that was steam-driven. This is considered to be the first, true prototype for the modern automobile.

From that time on, various inventive individuals began tweaking this basic concept—including familiar names such as Carl Benz and Gottleib Daimler. In 1790, Frenchman Charles Dallery successfully built a steam-driven carriage and by the early 1870s, Nathan Reed of Massachusetts and Apollo Kinsley of Connecticut introduced steam-driven vehicles in the United States **(see Figure 1-6)**. Less than a century later, the brothers Charles E. and J. Frank Duryea rolled out the first gasoline-powered vehicle in the United States, built from a second-hand carriage and a one-cylinder engine.

As the inventors worked to perfect their designs, horses continued providing the power to move people and cargo from one place to another. This had been their main duty for more than 4,000 years. In 1912, for example, there were 25 million work horses in the United States, pulling everything from carriages and wagons to delivery vehicles and multipassenger carts, the forerunners of modern buses **(see Figure 1-7)**.

In Detroit, Max Grabowsky had begun building trucks around 1900. Changing his company's name to the Rapid Vehicle Company (which later became part of General Motors), he organized the REO Motor Car Company, which produced the 1913 REO Democrat Wagon, used by Garrett Freight Lines Inc., in Pocatello, Idaho.

In 1911, Capt. Alexander E. Williams of North Carolina, a West Point graduate, published an article in the *Infantry Journal* about the need for motor trucks for the Army. But the Army felt it was ahead of the curve,

▶ **Figure 1–6**

A 1903 Gardner-Serpollet.

▶ **Figure 1–7**

Twenty-mule-team wagons in Death Valley.

INTERESTING FACT

In 1859, Thomas White invented a small, hand-operated single-needle sewing machine. In 1894, he was ready to diversify, and his son, Rollin, invented a flash boiler for steam cars. In 1900, the first White truck was built.

for it already owned 12 of the 25,000 trucks in the entire country— three in San Francisco, one at Ft. Sam Houston, Texas, one at West Point, and seven in Manila. Most of the Army brass believed nothing could ever replace the horse.

While on special assignment, Williams came across an advertisement for a four-wheel-drive truck developed and manufactured by the Four Wheel Drive Auto Company of Clintonville, Wisconsin. The company driver, Frank Dorn, took Williams through a demonstration that sold the vehicle and the concept. The car was driven through mud holes, sandpits, across plowed fields and, to cinch the deal, up the steps of the local Lutheran church.

Williams' report was so enthusiastic that the quartermaster general purchased one of the vehicles at a price of $1,940 for further testing. The car was shipped to Fort Myer, Virginia, where it was fitted with a cargo box and readied for initial testing over a 1,500-mile (2,414 km) distance.

Not prone to jump into the "unknown" too quickly, the Army decided to field test several motor vehicles. Heavier trucks did somewhat better on this test, since the tendency of the troops to overload the vehicles did not affect the larger trucks as greatly as it did the lighter trucks. The off-road performance was still not all it could have been, but there was little doubt in anyone's mind at the completion of the march that the truck, as it developed and improved, would eventually replace the horse and mule for military transport.

INTERESTING FACT

Because the military didn't have the money to purchase more trucks, money was contributed by the private sector and vehicles were donated by manufacturers.

At the outbreak of World War I, the utility of motor vehicles in military situations was almost immediately confirmed. This belief was further underscored when a French general loaded Renault taxis with all available troops. The movement was so rapid and unexpected, it caught the Germans unaware and shook their confidence enough to disengage, allowing for an Allied victory.

After World War I, trucking became its own industry. After the war, all the results were in. Motorized trucks had proven their worth. Horses could travel only 20 miles (32 km) in a day. Trucks could go 80 miles (129 km). That meant expanded markets for fresh produce and dairy products from American farms. It also meant more stores could carry fresh meats and freshly-caught seafood in addition to the corned beef, smoked sausages, and cured hams consumers had to settle for in cities and towns too far from fresh sources. Even the earliest trucks could triple or quadruple delivery speeds— speeds that tripled and quadrupled the mealtime selections in American homes (see Figure 1-8).

As trucks became more powerful and chassis more streamlined, the worldwide mindset began to envision more uses—and manufacturers were building special models for specific purposes. As early as 1916, the concept for a ready-mix concrete carrier was progressing from the drawing board to an operational model.

Courtesy of Library of Congress, LC-USW3-054178-D

▶ Figure 1-8
Early motorized delivery truck.

Key to this age of transportation innovation were the drivers—called "teamsters" as their team-and-wagon predecessors had been called. Without these rugged and determined individuals behind the wheels and tillers of those early trucks, the industry would have never gained momentum.

Think about it, the roads were primitive and rutted. Hours were long and pay was meager. Early trucks ran on hard rubber tires and the operator's comfort had not been given a thought. Arms were broken by motor crank backlash, and it would be years before models were totally enclosed to protect drivers against the weather.

Pneumatic tires had surpassed hard rubber tires by 1926, saving millions of dollars in road repairs due to the pounding administered by rubber tires. These new tires provided drivers a welcomed air-cushioned ride.

> **INTERESTING FACT**
>
> To generate heat in the winter, teamsters took the kerosene lamps they used for rear lights and put them by their feet. For many, death by asphyxiation was less frightening than death by freezing.

In 1903, the Team Drivers' International Union and the National Teamsters of Chicago organizations joined together to become the International Brotherhood of Teamsters—and this was not the first drivers' union. As far back as 1850, draymen formed an organization in San Francisco, but it wasn't until 1899 that Samuel Gompers organized Team Drivers' International.

As more trucks were manufactured and more drivers were needed, the drivers' union became larger and a more powerful part of the emerging motor transportation industry. Soon, the unions had jurisdiction over all teamsters and their helpers, chauffeurs, men employed on horses, harness, carriages, or automobiles as well as those working in and around stables and garages.

After World War I ended, one of the positive by-products of the war was an experienced pool of well-trained truck drivers and truck mechanics. The surplus trucks from the military were quickly snapped up by companies eager to convert from horse and mule teams to mechanized horsepower, so plenty of truck-driving jobs were available.

Ultimately, in one single generation, the truck transportation industry was conceived, born, and grew into a powerful force in this nation's economy. The powerful 18-wheelers you will be driving over today's highways are the great-grandchildren of those early, clumsy delivery wagons that emerged in the early 20th century **(see Figure 1-9).**

By 1925, close to 3 million trucks were in use on American highways and byways.

Over the last 100-plus years, many events, innovations, and changes have impacted truck transportation as an industry. But thanks to the intrepid men and women on the front lines—the drivers behind the wheels—the industry has prospered and improved, not only in technology and efficiency but also in capacity and service **(see Figure 1-10).** As a result, the entire economy of North America as well as the way of life was transformed—and that transformation continues today.

▶ **Figure 1–9**

A tractor is used to pull one or more vehicles such as semi-trailers, tankers, or carhaulers.

HISTORIC MILESTONES IN EARLY TRUCK TRANSPORTATION

1923: New roads generate new taxes. As a result of increased truck and bus transportation in the U.S., more than 26,000 miles (41,843 km) of new roadways were opened under the Federal Road Aid program and 25 states now charged gasoline tax.

1927: More trucks began using power brakes, a trend developing because of more traffic and a need for safety.

1929: A new trend, called "door-to-door delivery", emerged to trucking's speed and efficiency. This replaced the last of the horse-drawn wagons in many cities.

1929: The economic collapse caused by the stock market puts the brakes on the growth of truck transportation, but only for a short while.

1932: As truck traffic increased, regulations began to be priorities in cities and states. By 1932, the Federal Motor Carrier Act had passed, giving the Interstate Commerce Commission authority over trucks and buses that used the nation's highways. The trucking industry pointed out that, of the 3.5 million trucks and buses in use, 86 percent were privately owned and should not be subject to control by a public agency. This same year, the American Association of State Highway Officials adopted the first recommendations about vehicle size and weight limits.

1933: A new voice was added to the discussion when the American Farm Bureau Federation spoke out against higher gas taxes and restriction on truck development. Three states discussed legislation prohibiting tractor-trailers on their highways, but changes in truck design and lighter materials used in manufacturing trucks side-stepped these legislative threats.

That same year, the American Highway Freight Association and the Federal Truck Association merged to become the American Trucking Associations.

1935: Work continued on the diesel engine. A primary feature was lower fuel cost, although few diesel repairmen were available. Yet, because of a growing demand, the diesel engine in trucks, especially long-haul trucks, eventually became a reality. Soon after, diesel fuel, once tax-free, was taxed in 33 states.

1936: The concept of hauling freight long distance was begun by Keeshin Transcontinental Freight Lines in Los Angeles. Spacing terminals every 200 miles (322 km) along the route to Chicago created a 224-hour round trip to cover 4,900 miles (7,886 km). The transportation industry embraced the new concept of weight distribution and more than 42 states spoke up in favor of tractor-trailers versus four-wheel trucks.

1937: This year, traffic safety was emphasized by the founding of the Automotive Safety Foundation by leaders in the automobile, truck, accessory and finance industries. The foundation spent a half-million dollars in this initial year promoting safety. Supporting this emphasis on safety, all trucks were required to have two methods of braking, mandated to carry tire chains, fire extinguishers, red flags, and flares. All trucks were also required to be manufactured with safety glass and to attach fuel tanks so they weren't projecting beyond the side of the truck. Specific lighting requirements were also enacted, as were requirements for windshield wipers, mirrors, and reflectors.

1938: A closely-coupled, or cab-over, model was introduced this year. This design reduced truck length, shortened the wheelbase and made handling easier. Refrigeration also improved, making way for hauling more perishables.

1939: As World War II became a possibility, mobility was a key word among military forces on both sides of the battle. The Gramm Trailer Division introduced vacuum-operated trailer brakes, featuring automatic brake-lock in case of break-away while Mack Trucks introduced the automatic clutch and synchromesh transmission on its CM bus.

▶ Figure 1–10

A BRIEF HISTORY OF CANADA'S TRUCKING INDUSTRY

For centuries, the preferred way to travel in Canada was by water. European settlers, with their oxen and horses, were the first to establish a network of roads. In 1606, the French explorer Samuel de Champlain built Canada's first road, a rough trail running for 16 km (10 mi) in Nova Scotia. By 1734 a rough highway had been established between Montréal and Québec City **(see Figure 1-11).**

▶ **Figure 1-11**

Historic photo of early Canadians using waterways for transportation.

By the 1850s, railroads began linking communities and soon became Canada's most vital transportation tool. However, people and goods still had to be transported between rail terminals and boat docks to reach their final destinations.

Since the time of Canada's settlement, teamsters have played a crucial role in the country's growth. With the arrival of oxen and horses pulling wagons and carts, someone was needed to drive the teams of animals—hence the term "teamster," someone who could handle the team. Those early teamsters are the direct ancestors of today's truck drivers.

In 1896, the first commercial trucks were introduced in Germany. Two years later, Robert Simpson, a department store owner in Toronto, bought Canada's first truck, an electric delivery wagon manufactured by the Fischer Equipment Company of Chicago.

Parker Dye Works, owner of Canada's first electric vehicle, also purchased Canada's first gasoline-powered truck from the Winton Motorized Carriage Company of Cleveland, Ohio. Alfred Pratt also drove this vehicle, using a tiller instead of a steering wheel as he sat on top of the engine.

Canada's early trucking industry's growth was confined to cities because the roads were paved. North America's first long-distance run occurred between New York and Los Angeles in 1911. Canada's first interprovincial run happened two years later when two drivers from the Canadian Motor Company delivered a Federal truck loaded with mattresses and bedsprings, originating in Winnipeg with the destination in Regina. The trip took four days to complete. Today that same 582-km (361 mi) trip would require six to seven hours.

Beginning in the early 1900s, truck drivers took courses at truck factories to learn how to operate the vehicles. They often were mechanics and engineers, and they carried tools in case the truck broke down. On average, these early teamsters worked 50 to 70 hours a week and made approximately $12 total for their effort.

World War I established the usefulness of the truck, and thousands of Canadian men learned to drive during the war. This made it possible for individuals to have a start as truck owners as they entered the motor transport industry.

INTERESTING FACT

The second truck in Canada was a Canadian-made electric vehicle built by the Still Motor Company of Toronto. Alfred J. Pratt was hired to drive the vehicle because he was a mechanical and electrical engineer and carried his tools with him—a good practice because the Still broke down regularly.

(Continues)

A BRIEF HISTORY OF CANADA'S TRUCKING INDUSTRY (continued)

During the 1930s, refrigerated trailers were introduced. This meant fresh produce could be shipped farther and could reach more people. To support the longer routes, sleeping cabs were introduced. These early berths were far from comfortable—they were very cramped and were often called "suicide boxes" (see Figure 1-12).

Canada's entrance into World War II in 1941 placed considerable strain on the country's trucking industry and Parliament eventually declared truck drivers to be "essential to the prosecution of the war." This meant truck drivers could not be drafted into military service.

© Cengage Learning 2013

Figure 1-12
Early sleeper cab.

During World War II, Canada experienced its first driver shortage. To combat the shortage, women were given the opportunity to get behind the wheel but were limited to driving buses and light delivery vehicles. While women worked side by side with their male counterparts in factories, driving heavy trucks was not considered to be women's work and remained the exclusive domain of men.

INTERESTING FACT

Until the Lord's Day Act in 1972, Sunday trucking was not permitted and only perishable items could be moved by road. Drivers caught not obeying the law could be given jail time.

TRUCK DRIVING IN AND OUT OF MEXICO

The United States made a new trucking agreement with Mexico in early 2011, making it easier for trucking companies in Mexico to do business in the United States.

Truckers in Canada already have similar benefits, so extending the same benefits to Mexican firms furthers the provisions of the NAFTA agreement, which opened the border between the U.S and Mexico for international delivery by trucks into border states.

A permanent agreement, which is part of the current pilot study being conducted jointly between the U.S. and Mexico, requires Mexico to lift tariffs and for the U.S. to allow certified drivers to cross the border.

THE NORTH AMERICAN TRUCKING INDUSTRY TODAY

Like the early days of this industry, manufacturers and merchandisers of all kinds rely on trucks for the pick-up and delivery of goods. Why? Because no other form of transportation can deliver goods door to door. Goods carried by any other method of transportation—airplane, train, or ship—reach their final destination or end user by truck (see Figure 1-13).

With the implementation of computer, satellite, and GPS technology in trucks, the trucking transportation industry continues to

INTERESTING FACT

It's amazing to realize that more than 80 percent of all communities in North America today depend solely on the trucking industry to deliver all their fuel, medicine, food, clothing, and other consumer goods.

increase productivity and bring new opportunities for professional drivers.

The trucking industry—which includes auto-transport companies as well as municipality fleets of trucks, garbage packers, and snowplows—continues to be the lifeblood of North America's economy and provides the infrastructure for the massive distribution system that supports the high quality of life available on much of this continent today.

HOW THE U.S. TRUCKING INDUSTRY IS REGULATED

▶ Figure 1-13
Professional truck drivers transport the basic necessities of life as well as the luxuries.

As you may already know, any common carrier transporting cargo by truck in **interstate** (moving cargo from one state to another) or foreign commerce must first receive authority from the **U.S. Department of Transportation (DOT).** Each carrier also must file the rates it charges to haul freight with the DOT. Contract carriers and private carriers do not have to file rates—and this is just the beginning of the industry's regulation.

The trucking industry is highly regulated by city, state, and federal laws, codes, and regulations. These requirements establish certain standards that trucking companies, owners, and drivers must meet. Federal laws regulate commerce that crosses state lines. State laws regulate **intrastate** commerce (within each state). County, city, town, and village governments regulate routes and speed limits as well as truck loading and parking zones.

As a professional driver, you will be expected to know and understand the regulations that affect your employer and how you perform your day-to-day job as well as how your industry operates in intrastate and interstate commerce. A good starting place for this knowledge is to know how the regulation of the transportation industry has developed and evolved over the decades.

The Motor Carrier Act of 1935

The Motor Carrier Act of 1935 gave the federal government's **Interstate Commerce Commission (ICC)** the authority to regulate interstate truck and bus companies, known collectively as **motor carriers.** The ICC could decide which companies could become motor carriers, what services they could offer, and what rates they could charge.

The Motor Carrier Act was one of several laws enacted during the 1930s that brought a number of American industries under government regulation. Many believed that an unregulated marketplace had led to the Great Depression of 1929 or otherwise harmed the public. The ICC believed tight control over motor carrier operations and rates was necessary to maintain the stable transportation industry.

INTERESTING FACT

The Motor Carrier Act of 1935 divided motor carriers into two categories: **common carriers,** which offered their service to the public generally, and **contract carriers,** which had agreements with one or only a limited number of customers.

The Commercial Motor Vehicle Safety Act of 1986 (CMVSA/86)

The **Commercial Motor Vehicle Safety Act of 1986 (CMVSA/86)** was passed to improve highway safety by ensuring that drivers of large trucks and buses are qualified to operate large vehicles. The secondary goal of the act was to remove unsafe and unqualified drivers from the highways (**Figure 1-14**).

The CMVSA/86 applies to:

- Interstate drivers and carriers
- Intrastate drivers and carriers
- **Commercial Motor Vehicle (CMV)** drivers who drive vehicles with a **gross vehicle weight rating (GVWR)** of more than 26,000 pounds (11,793 kg)
- Drivers of vehicles carrying 16 or more passengers (including the driver)
- Drivers of any vehicles transporting hazardous materials requiring placards

▶ Figure 1–14

CMVSA/86 was passed to improve highway safety.

This act allowed the states to retain their right to issue a driver's license. However, it establishes minimum national standards that must be met when licensing commercial motor vehicle drivers. In addition, the law makes it illegal to have in one's possession more than one commercial driver's license.

The legislation places requirements on the commercial motor vehicle driver, the employing motor carrier, and the states themselves. As a result of CMVSA/86, since 1992, all drivers are required to have a **Commercial Driver's License (CDL)** to operate a commercial motor vehicle. Each state is required to administer both a knowledge test and a skill test.

The CMVSA/86 requires drivers to notify their employers and the state that issued the CDL within 30 days of conviction of any traffic violation (except parking violations) and provide every employer with information about all driving jobs held during the past 10 years. The FMCSR requires drivers to notify their employers at once if their CDL is suspended, revoked, or canceled, even though the CMVSA/86 does not require this.

Commercial Driver's License

- Creates one-year disqualifying offenses for (1) driving a CMV with a revoked, suspended, or canceled CDL or driving while disqualified, and (2) conviction for causing a fatality through negligent or criminal operation of a CMV. Lifetime disqualification is *required* for multiple violations or convictions.

- Disqualifies drivers for up to 30 days without pay if their operation of a CMV would create an imminent hazard.

- Establishes criteria for disqualifying holder of CDL for (1) conviction of a serious offense involving a vehicle that is not a CMV that resulted in license suspension or revocation, or (2) conviction of a drug- or alcohol-related offense involving another type of vehicle.

- Expands the list of traffic violations for which a CDL holder can be disqualified to include:
  - Driving a CMV without obtaining a CDL
  - Driving a CMV without a CDL in possession
  - Driving without a required endorsement

- The act makes the federal medical qualification certificate part of the commercial driver's license requirements.

- The act requires departmental study of feasibility and merits of having medical review officers (MROs) or employers report positive drug tests of CDL holders to the licensing state and requires prospective employers to check with the state.

- The act paves the way for the development of a uniform system to transmit data among the states on convictions for violations of traffic control laws by CDL holders.

This completes the process begun by the CDL program establishing one accurate and complete license for each driver.

- States are required to:
    - Request driver's record from another state issuing the driver's license before issuing or renewing the CDL
    - Request information on underlying violation when reporting disqualification, revocation, suspension, or cancellation of a CDL
    - Include information on all violations of motor vehicle traffic control laws committed by CDL holders in the driver's record
    - Record information on traffic violations received from other states in a driver's record; states may not allow information on violations to be masked or withheld from the CDL holder's record
    - Notify the licensing state of violation by CDL holders within 10 days after violations are committed
    - Check with the National Driver Register and the Commercial Drivers License Information System (CDLIS) before issuing any motor vehicle operator's license.
- States are prohibited from issuing special licenses or permits to CDL holders.

The Motor Carrier Safety Improvement Act of 1999 (MCSIA/99)

The purposes of the Motor Carrier Safety Improvement Act of 1999 are to:

- Establish a **Federal Motor Carrier Safety Administration (FMCSA)**
- Reduce the number and severity of large-truck-involved crashes through more CMV and driver inspections and carrier compliance reviews
- Stronger enforcement, expedited completion of rules and sound research and effective CDL testing, record-keeping, and sanctions

Some of the key provisions of the MCSIA/99 are:

Establishment of the Federal Motor Carrier Safety Administration, Effective January 1, 2000

- Established within the Department of Transportation.
- Provides for the development of a long-term strategy to improve CMV, operator, and motor carrier safety. This annual plan and schedule are followed up by a progress assessment semiannually, which is reported to Congress every year.
- Establishes a Commercial Motor Vehicle Safety Advisory Committee, made up of representatives from motor carriers, drivers, safety advocates, manufacturers, safety and law enforcement officials from border states, and others. This committee shall provide advice to the Secretary of Transportation on commercial motor vehicle safety regulations and other matters related to the FMCSA.
- Provides for department-wide safeguards against conflicts of interest in research.

The USA PATRIOT Act

Commonly called the Patriot Act, the **USA PATRIOT Act** was passed by the U.S. Congress and signed into law by President George W. Bush on October 26, 2001. The title of the act stands for **U**niting and **S**trengthening **A**merica by **P**roviding **A**ppropriate **T**ools **R**equired to **I**ntercept and **O**bstruct **T**errorism Act of 2001.

The original USA PATRIOT Act was valid only until 2005. An extension of the act was voted and signed into law by President Bush in 2007.

The purpose of the USA PATRIOT Act, in general, is to deter and punish terrorist acts in the United States and around the world, to enhance law enforcement investigatory tools, and to maintain the safety of the general public.

One industry finding itself specifically impacted by this act is the trucking industry. As an example, professional drivers who transport hazardous materials must now undergo a security-threat assessment. This assessment is designed to track more closely the movement of hazardous materials within the United States. Drivers who apply for, renew, or transfer a hazardous materials endorsement on their commercial driver's license (CDL) must undergo fingerprinting, background checks, and an immigration check, according to the Department of Licensing.

The trucking industry is not the only industry affected by the increased requirements. Universities, trade schools, libraries, automobile dealers, real estate businesses, and flight schools are also affected by the demand for increased information now required for background checks and other associated costs.

U.S. FEDERAL AND STATE REGULATING AGENCIES
The Federal Motor Carrier Safety Administration

The Federal Motor Carrier Safety Administration (FMCSA) was established as a separate administration within the U.S. Department of Transportation on January 1, 2000. FMCSA's primary focus is on reducing accidents, injuries, and fatalities involving large trucks and buses **(see Figure 1-15).** Headquartered in Washington, DC, FMCSA employs a staff of 1,000 in 50 states and the District of Columbia.

© iStockphoto/wendellandCarolyn

▶ **Figure 1–15**

Several trucks traveling in traffic where drivers have to follow many safety practices.

To achieve its mission, FMCSA is tasked with the following:

- Developing and enforcing data-driven regulations that balance motor carrier safety with industry efficiency (See Chapter 36 on Compliance, Safety, Accountability.)
- Harnessing safety information systems, focusing on higher-risk carriers in enforcing safety regulations
- Targeting educational messages to carriers, commercial drivers, and the public
- Partnering with federal, state, and local enforcement agencies, the motor carrier industry, safety groups, and organized labor on efforts to reduce bus- and truck-related crashes

Key programs of the FMCSA are:

Federal Motor Carriers Safety Regulations (FMCSR)—develops, maintains and enforces federal regulations that promote safety, productivity, and new technologies. Regulations establish safe operational requirements for drivers, commercial vehicles, carriers, and equipment.

Hazardous Materials Regulations (HMR)—enforces regulations designed to ensure the safe and secure transportation of **hazardous materials** and focus, specifically, on classification of hazmat, proper packaging, employee and driver training, hazard communication, and operating requirements.

Commercial Driver's License Program—develops, monitors, and ensures compliance with commercial driver licensing standards for drivers, carriers, and states.

Motor Carrier Safety Identification and Information Systems—provides safety data, including state and national crash statistics, analysis, and detailed motor carrier safety performance data to the public as well as industry.

Motor Carrier Safety Assistance Program (MCSAP)—provides states with financial assistance to hire staff and implement strategies to enforce FMCSR and HMR. Implementation strategies include roadside inspections and the review of motor carriers' compliance with FMCSR and HMR. The goal is to detect and correct CMV safety defects, CMV driver deficiencies, and unsafe motor carrier practices BEFORE they become contributing factors in crashes, injuries, and hazardous materials incidents.

Other Federal Regulatory Agencies

The **Pipeline and Hazardous Materials Safety Administration (PHMSA)** regulates and classifies hazardous materials. It also sets standards for shipping containers, shipping documents, marking, labeling, and placarding **(see Figure 1-16).**

Hazardous materials are also regulated by the **Environmental Protection Agency (EPA),** the **Nuclear Regulatory Commission (NRC),** and the **Occupational Safety and Health Administration (OSHA).** OSHA also inspects facilities and works to protect the health and safety of workers in transportation and many other industries.

The **National Transportation Safety Board (NTSB)** investigates accidents and offers solutions to prevent future accidents.

The **Department of Homeland Security (DHS)** is also tasked with maintaining a safe and secure environment for professional drivers and workers within the transportation industry. In 2005, a $21 million grant from DHS launched the American Trucking Associations' "Highway Watch" program, training professionals to identify and report safety and security concerns from our nation's expansive highway system. The program also helps prepare carriers and professional drivers to respond in the event they or their cargo is the target of terrorist attack.

Figure 1-16

Placards help fire and emergency personnel identify dangerous cargo in the event of an accident or spill.

State Regulations

Every state in the union has laws and rules for the regulation of the transportation industry and commercial motor vehicles. Each state's **Department of Transportation (DOT)** as well as the **Department of Motor Vehicles (DMV)**—and in some states, representatives of the trucking association—usually assist in making these laws, some of which are the following:

- Decide maximum loads various CMVs may carry
- Decide maximum lengths, widths, and weights of **Commercial Motor Vehicles (CMVs)**
- License professional drivers, including the testing required to issue a Commercial Driver's License (CDL)
- Collect road and fuel taxes
- Set minimum insurance requirements

HOW THE CANADIAN TRUCKING INDUSTRY IS REGULATED

Over the past several years, there has been a continuous trend toward the reduction of economic regulation of Canada 's truck transportation industry in favor of increased regulation of the industry's safety operating practices. Canadian carriers are now required to meet the operational standards established under the **National Safety Code (NSC),** introduced in 1987.

Since that time, these standards have continued to evolve in order to increase their effectiveness.

Canada's NSC is designed to assist commercial carriers to remain in compliance with local, national, and international rules for operating commercial vehicles. To date, each province and territory has implemented NSC through its own legislation.

Developed by the **Canadian Council of Motor Transport Administrators (CCMTA),** the NSC standards were developed to achieve the following objectives: (1) establish uniform safety regulations and enforcement across Canada, (2) improve commercial vehicle and driver safety on Canadian cross-border highways, and (3) ensure that, subsequent to economic impacts on the regulations in the 1980s, there is no compromise in the level of truck and bus safety.

The NSC is made up of 16 individual standards, subject to periodic review and updating by CCMTA to enhance the effectiveness of these standards and to respond to new regulatory issues.

NSC Standards Include:

1. Single driver's license——–A driver can have only one driver's license at one time.
2. Knowledge and performance tests for drivers—Drivers are required to take both written and practical tests.
3. Driver examiner training—Testing requirements are consistent across Canada.
4. Classified driver's licensing system—Licenses are classified according to weight and vehicle type.
5. Self-certification standards and procedures—Specific training elements are required for commercial licenses.
6. Medical standards for drivers—Drivers are required to meet medical standards to operate commercial vehicles.
7. Carrier and driver profiles—NSC collects data on companies and drivers.
8. Short-term suspension—A member of the law can issue a short-term suspension of a license.
9. Hours of service—Working hours are restricted.
10. Cargo (load) securement—Loads are to be secured according to certain requirements.
11. Commercial vehicle maintenance and inspection standards—Standards are specified for maintenance and inspection of all commercial vehicles.
12. CVSA (Commerical Vehicle Safety Alliiance) on-road inspections—The CVSA specifies levels of severity of inspections that can be performed.
13. Trip inspections—Guidelines for driver inspection of the vehicle ensure it is safe for the road, from start and during route.
14. Safety rating—Companies are rated on how they perform against national safety codes.
15. Facility audits—Guidelines specify how inspections will be conducted during on-site visits.
16. First aid training—NSC specifies what type of first aid training is required for trucking companies, and when.

NOTE: For in-depth information about each of these 16 standards, please see www.ccmta .ca/english/producstandservices/publications/publications.cfm#NSC.

Truck transportation safety in Canada is a shared responsibility between the Canadian government and the governments of the provinces and territories. The federal government is responsible for extraprovincial truck and bus travel. However, most of this has been delegated to the provincial and territorial-governments through the Motor Vehicle Transport Act **(see Figure 1-17).** The provinces and territories are solely responsible for the regulation of truck and bus travel.

Figure 1-17

Professional drivers need to know the regulations and responsibilities while driving through the ten provinces and three territories.

COMMERCIAL MOTOR VEHICLES

During your career as a professional driver, you may be required to drive any number of commercial vehicles, including special-use rigs as well as standard tractor-trailer rigs. The following terms and descriptions will help acquaint you with the wide variety of commercial motor vehicles.

The Truck Tractor

Truck tractor—or **tractor,** used to pull one or more vehicles (often trailers) **(see Figure 1-18).** Tractors may pull semi-trailers, flatbeds, tankers, lowboys, livestock trailers, or other vehicles.

Conventional tractors—house the engine under the hood and provide a smoother ride because the driver sits between the front and rear wheels. The conventional cab's longer wheelbase sometimes makes maneuvering into tight spaces more difficult **(see Figure 1-19).**

Straight trucks—single-unit vehicles with engine, cab, and cargo compartment on the same frame **(see Figure 1-20).** Like the truck tractor, the straight truck has a front axle and one or more rear axles.

Figure 1-18

Tractor with trailer attached is one of the various types of rigs a commercial driver might drive.

© Cengage Learning 2013

▶ **Figure 1–19**

A conventional tractor.

© iStockphoto/WoodyUpstate

▶ **Figure 1–20**

A straight truck.

Front axle—the steering axle on a commercial motor vehicle.

Rear axle—powered and is called the **drive axle.**

Two-axle truck with a single drive axle—a truck or tractor with only one axle in the rear **(see Figure 1-21).** The wheelbase of the single-drive axle tractor is usually shorter, which allows easier turning in small spaces. However, the shorter wheelbase also limits the amount of weight the truck can carry.

Tandem—(two axles) to accommodate and carry heavier loads when an additional axle is needed. This addition lengthens the wheelbase **(see Figure 1-22).** Some tandems have only one drive axle. This nondriven axle, which is mounted behind the drive axle, is called the **tag axle.** When the nondriven axle is mounted ahead of the drive axle, it is called the **pusher axle.**

Twin screws—term used to describe the **tandem axle tractor,** which has two drive axles. These give the truck more traction on slippery surfaces in extreme conditions.

Drive shaft—runs between the differential of the front drive axle and the differential of the rear drive axle. Many twin screws also have a differential lock to distribute power evenly to each axle. The differential lock is used only in slippery conditions and at low speeds.

Duals—wheels and tires mounted on each end of the axle. A single-driven axle tractor with dual wheels on the rear axle has 10 wheels **(see Figure 1-23).**

Super singles—used by some fleets instead of duals. The super single is a large, single tire that has less rolling resistance than duals,

© Cengage Learning 2013

▶ **Figure 1–21**

A two-axle truck with a single drive axle.

© Cengage Learning 2013

▶ **Figure 1–22**

Tandem axle configuration.

Figure 1-23

A dual axle tractor.

resulting in better fuel economy because they weigh less than two traditional tires, and they accommodate heavier loads.

Wheel identification—how each wheel on a tractor is identified (**see Figure 1-24**). When reporting a tire problem to maintenance or a dispatcher, use these identifications and be sure to call each wheel by its proper name.

Trailers

Trailer—a vehicle built for hauling cargo (**see Figure 1-25**). As motorized trucks became more popular, trailers were developed. The increased use of trailers provided momentum for a standard fifth-wheel configuration for interchangeable use on tractors or trailers.

By the 1930s, it was common to see trailers used in tandem with motor trucks . . . and by the end of that decade, the semi-trailer had made its place as an integral part of the modern trucking industry.

Coupling—connecting a tractor to a trailer.

Semi-trailer—rests on a "fifth wheel" mounted over the rear axle of the tractor (**see Figure 1-26**). A semi-trailer can be made into a full trailer by coupling it to the fifth wheel on a **converter dolly (see Figure 1-27)**. The dolly is hooked onto the rear of another trailer. Putting a dolly on a semi-trailer makes it a **full trailer**.

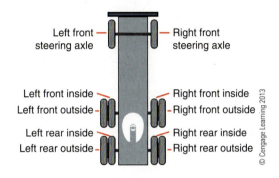

Figure 1-24

Tractor wheel identification.

INTERESTING FACT

Mack manufactured a four-wheel trailer in 1929 in five- and 10-ton capacities, and Freuhauf Company introduced its "Flyer" trailer about this same time, adding an automatic locking device, allowing coupling and uncoupling in 30 seconds, according to the manufacturer.

Figure 1-25

Trailers are vehicles designed to haul cargo.

Semi-trailers come in many different shapes and sizes. Some of them are pictured in **Figure 1-28**.

Fifth wheel—has locking jaws in its center into which the trailer's **kingpin** fits **(see Figure 1-29).** This connects (or couples) the tractor and trailer together, with the fifth wheel serving as the pivot point between the two. The fifth wheel also bears the weight of the front of the semi-trailer.

© Cengage Learning 2013

▶ **Figure 1–26**

A semi-trailer has axles only at the rear of the trailer. The front of the trailer is supported by the tractor. In order to stand independently, the trailer's landing gear is used.

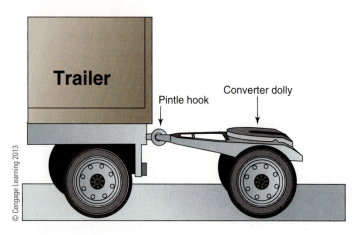

© Cengage Learning 2013

▶ **Figure 1–27**

A semi-trailer is made into a full trailer by coupling it to the fifth wheel on a converter dolly.

© Cengage Learning 2013

▶ **Figure 1–28**

Different types of semi-trailers.

(a)

(b)

© Cengage Learning 2013

▶ **Figure 1–29**

Fifth wheel and kingpin.

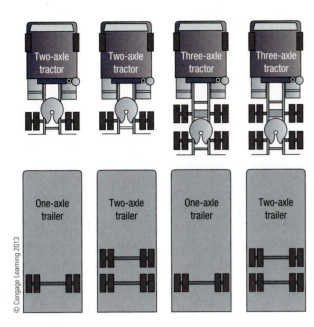

Figure 1–30

Combination vehicles.

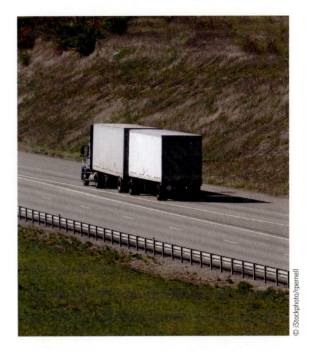

Figure 1–31

A standard double is a rig that pulls two 28-foot (8.53 m) semi-trailers.

When a trailer is added to a tractor or a straight truck, it is called a **combination vehicle** or **combination rig.** Some of the many types of combination vehicles are pictured in **Figure 1-30.** Combination rigs have many different arrangements of wheels and axles.

Other types of combination vehicles are:

Rocky Mountain doubles—a rig with two trailers. The tractor has three axles to make a rig with a total of seven axles. Rocky Mountain doubles are not allowed to run in some states.

Standard doubles—a rig consisting of a single-axle tractor pulling a 28-foot (8.53 m) semi-trailer and a 28-foot trailer. These rigs are not legal in some states **(see Figure 1-31).**

Turnpike doubles—a rig consisting of a tandem axle tractor pulling a 48-foot (14.63 m) semi-trailer and a 48-foot trailer. These rigs are not legal in some states.

18-wheeler—the most familiar rig on North American highways today, the 18-wheeler consists of a 10-wheeled tractor and a semi-trailer with eight wheels. An 18-wheeler has five axles.

INTERESTING FACT

On February 18, 2006, an Australian-built Mack truck with 112 semi-trailers, weighing 2.8 million pounds and more than 4,836 feet long, pulled a load 328 feet to set the world's record for the longest road train (multiple loaded trailers) ever pulled with a single prime mover—a tri-drive Mack Titan (see Figure 1-32).

BECOMING A PROFESSIONAL DRIVER

Successful truck drivers always drive responsibly and act in a professional manner, whatever the situation. These solid professionals:

■ Know their jobs and are responsible for each and every detail

■ Are accountable for their driving and their actions

■ Know the laws, rules, and regulations that govern their industry

- Have a positive attitude
- Learn new skills continually
- Practice safety at all times, never taking risks that endanger themselves, their equipment, or others on the road
- Make responsible, independent judgments
- Know and understand the equipment they use
- Maintain clean, dependable vehicles

▶ **Figure 1–32**

A sample of a road train.

Why Does Truck Driving Require Professionals?

The transportation industry has continued to develop and evolve, and more skills than ever before are required of professional drivers. No longer is the job of a professional driver merely to guide a vehicle down the highway. Today's driving professionals must be knowledgeable of the laws, rules, and regulations, understand and use the evolving and expanding technological tools found on today's rigs, and be able to consistently communicate with any variety of customers. Before sliding behind the wheel of a tractor-trailer for the first time, these professionals must meet the increasing requirements of their profession—physically, intellectually, and reasonably.

Professional drivers must:

- Master specialized knowledge, specific skills, and attitudes resulting from a combination of intense preparation, training, and experience
- Be aware of, and understand, the regulations, practices, and procedures of the industry
- Meet the profession's requirements, including licensing, physical examination, and testing of the required knowledge and skills

Professional tractor-trailer drivers must rank above-average in the following areas:

Physical and mental abilities—meets government, industry, and company standards and requirements.

Skills—is qualified by training, experience, and desire to operate specific vehicle types, such as tractor-trailer, tankers, etc.

Safety standards—understands and practices safe driving methods, obeys the laws, and is an expert. Therefore, he or she is safer in all highway situations than the average driver. While driving, the professional driver maintains a sharp focus on the highway environment, reading clues and working to avoid hazards or accidents.

Tolerance and courtesy—can accept negative behaviors and blatant road rage from other drivers without becoming involved or attempting to get even. He or she cooperates with other road users regularly and maintains constant contact with company dispatchers.

Efficiency—delivers cargo on time and works courteously with others while obeying laws, rules, and regulations. Professional drivers realize their success comes only when schedules are met, keeping in mind his/her own well-being, fuel efficiency, and other operational factors.

Knowledge—knows government regulations and follows industry requirements for driving tractor-trailers and handling cargo. The professional driver maintains current knowledge of rule changes and new regulations that impact the industry and his/her profession (**Figure 1-33**).

Professional drivers understand *they ARE the trucking industry* in the eyes of the consumer and the motoring public. Because of the industry they represent, driving professionals realize they must always perform at higher levels than the average driver.

They also understand that driving well is only part of the job. They also must conduct themselves in a courteous and professional manner, practicing the highest levels of skills and safety on the road, at the dock, at the truck stop and wherever they are. Further, professional drivers know they must continually improve their skills and knowledge of the equipment and the technology they use, day to day, in their jobs.

A new generation of well-trained, skilled, and responsible drivers is critical to improving highway safety across the nation. As carriers hire the next generation of drivers, they will be looking for individuals who will represent the best of the profession—men and women who consistently exhibit courtesy, common sense, a high level of knowledge and skills, and expertise in safety in every situation.

▶ **Figure 1-33**

Professional drivers need to know how to handle cargo and check to make sure their load is secure.

PROFESSIONAL DRIVERS AND SAFETY

At the dock, in the yard, on the highway, and in every aspect of his or her personal life, safety is the tractor-trailer driver's greatest value. While priorities will change from day to day, the values we hold do not. Safely is how the tractor-trailer driver will complete every priority. The North American transportation industry's ultimate goal is to make a profit. If a driver can not move cargo from one point to another without damage to the equipment or cargo and without injury to the driver or those sharing the roadway, he or she will incur significant costs, wiping out any potential profit, and possibly losing money.

Professional driving is integral to this continent's economy—and because it is among the most dangerous and demanding jobs in transportation today. The number one cause of accidental fatalities, not to mention the millions of disabling injuries, in the United States is motor vehicle incidents. Motor carriers seek to hire individuals who consistently meet the highest safety standards. To achieve this high level of skill and expertise, professional drivers must not only thoroughly know the vehicles they operate but they also must have the skill and training necessary to operate these vehicles safely in every environment (**see Figure 1-34**).

INTERESTING FACT

In the aftermath of the terrorist attacks on the United States on September 11, 2001, truck drivers became the nation's lifeline, keeping the wheels of commerce turning. Professional drivers displayed not only a can-do attitude but also a high level of commitment to their industry and a strong loyalty to their country as they served in the face of this tragedy.

▶ **Figure 1-34**

Professional drivers must consistently meet the highest safety standards.

© Cengage Learning 2013

▶ **Figure 1-35**

Professional drivers are trained to drive safely in good and bad weather.

TRAINING AND INSTRUCTION

As recently as a half-century ago, truck drivers had little more than on-the-job training. However, professional drivers of today are required to prepare themselves for their careers by earning their CDL and by enrolling in training that will ensure their safe handling of their tractor-trailer rig in all situations. The more driving skills gained from training classes and other learning opportunities, the more knowledge the professional driver will gain from on-the-job learning experiences, formal training classes, and one-on-one time with mentors and instructors.

A significant portion of a professional driver's preparation and training will be devoted to identifying individual skills as well as strengths and weaknesses behind the wheel. Once an individual realizes a weakness, that's a signal to spend additional time and attention in order to master that area. It's also imperative for students who need additional training to ask the instructor for help.

Training also enables new drivers to understand the capabilities and limitations of the tractor-trailer, in both excellent and hazardous weather and driving conditions **(see Figure 1-35).**

Driving experience in a formal educational environment, such as a driving range, permits drivers to identify hazards and learn how to respond to these hazardous situations with the guidance of an instructor. By identifying these training hazards before they become "live situations," drivers preparing to enter the profession can learn to control many safety factors they will encounter in real-time, over-the-road experiences.

INTERESTING FACT

The world's first road traffic death involving a motor vehicle is alleged to have occurred in August 1869. An Irish scientist, Mary Ward, died after falling out of her cousin's steam car and being run over by it. Because of ongoing efforts among drivers, carriers, trucking associations and federal, state, and provincial agencies to improve safety throughout North America, the number of crashes involving tractor-trailer rigs has declined dramatically, as have the number of deaths.

Yes, emergencies happen—even to the most experienced among us. Usually, these emergency situations happen quickly, depending on road conditions, traffic, or the unsafe actions of other drivers. In these instances, the professional driver—regardless of experience—should have the ability to analyze the situation and determine the best and safest action.

According to recent safety statistics, most CMV driving professionals tend to have more accidents during the early months of their careers. Some of these accidents are due to lack of specific training or experience behind the wheel. For this reason, many carriers now offer new drivers the opportunity to ride with experienced drivers so they can gain further skills in their first few months on the job. This provides new drivers with a wealth of additional knowledge and experience before occupying the driver's seat for the first time.

In addition, improved vehicles, improved safety training, and more safety technology as well as formal education are all focused on making our highways the safest in the world. Moreover, one of the continuing priorities for all professional drivers is to promote courtesy over the road. Carriers are also working to make North America's highways the safest for their employees and the jobs they do every day.

As a new professional driver, your role in this "big picture" is to read and learn as much as you can, ask questions of your instructors, practice what you're learning, and make it your personal priority to make the roadways even safer for yourself, those sharing the road, and the proud industry and profession you represent.

SUMMARY

With this chapter, you launched your preparation and study toward becoming a professional driver. Learning this information is the first step toward your understanding the North American trucking industry, how it began, and how it operates. In this introductory orientation, you learned how the industry developed and grew in the early days in North America. You also learned the names and responsibilities of agencies in the United States, Canada, and Mexico that are given the responsibility to regulate and optimize the safety and well-being of those involved in trucking transportation service. You also learned the types of carriers and where they legally operate; the variety of tractor-trailer rigs; and requirements and responsibilities for professional drivers. In addition, you learned the importance of the emphasis the trucking industry places on safety. We encourage you to use this chapter as a foundation for your personal development as a professional driver, understanding the characteristic traits and values necessary to be a success behind the wheel and in your new career.

KEY TERMS

Canadian Council of Motor Transport Administrators (CCMTA)
Combination vehicle or rig
Commercial driver's license (CDL)
Commercial motor vehicle
Commercial Motor Vehicle Safety Act of 1986 (CMVSA/86)
Common carrier
Contract carrier
Converter dolly
Conventional tractor
Coupling
Department of Homeland Security (DHS)
Department of Motor Vehicles (DMV)
Department of Transportation (DOT)
Drive axle
Drive shaft
Duals
18-wheeler

Environmental Protection Agency (EPA)
Federal Motor Carrier Safety Administration (FMCSA)
Federal Motor Carrier Safety Regulations (FMCSR)
Fifth wheel
Front axle
Full trailer
Gross Vehicle Weight Rating (GVWR)
Hazardous materials
Interstate carrier
Interstate Commerce Commission (ICC)
Intrastate carrier
Kingpin
Motor Carrier Safety Assistance Program (MCSAP)
Motor carriers
National Safety Code (NSC)
National Transportation Safety Board (NTSB)
Nuclear Regulatory Commission (NRC)

Occupational Safety and Health Administration (OSHA)
Pipeline and Hazardous Materials Safety Administration (PHMSA)
Pusher axle
Rear axle
Rocky Mountain doubles
Semi-trailer
Standard doubles
Straight truck
Super singles
Tag axle
Tandem
Tandem axle tractor
Tractor
Trailer
Truck tractor
Turnpike doubles
Twin screws
Two-axle truck with a single drive axle
U.S. Department of Transportation (DOT)
USA PATRIOT Act

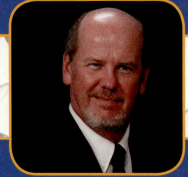

A DAY IN THE LIFE...

Ray Haight – Transrep Inc., CEO

As a driver there are those experiences, or golden moments, that came along once in awhile. I've had more than a few. One I remember was when I was on my way to Sacramento. I was quite young at the time and had been trucking for a couple three years. I was in Nevada on I-80 when I woke up before dawn; I had an egg, got cleaned up and was down the road before the sun broke through. For the next hour I was as close to perfection as a driver can imagine. I came off a high plain and could see the road straight ahead of me for miles—not a car or another truck in sight. My driver's side window was down with my arm hanging out. The temperature was perfect as a bright red sun broke through the morning over my shoulder onto the road and the rockcut around me. I had a soft country tune playing on the stereo that still let me hear the rhythmic sound of the engine as it powered me effortlessly through the desert, and all was right with the world.

I also recall 33 years ago loading out of London, Ontario, headed to Texas when I saw a pretty little girl on a tow motor sliding skids onto a trailer. I was preoccupied all the way to Texas and back and finally worked up the nerve to ask her out. My wife Connie and I celebrated 34 years of marriage in 2011. The moral is, keep your eyes wide open, driver, you never know what you might find on the dock and some of it's pretty damn good.

These are just a few of the many memories that stand out for me in my 10 years of driving, memories that people in other jobs won't come close to and I wouldn't trade for the world.

> ## "This is a great industry full of fantastic people and I am fortunate to be able to call many of them my friends."

This is a great industry full of fantastic people and I am fortunate to be able to call many of them my friends.

Times are tough right now, no doubt, but life is what you make of it no matter what direction you go in. Focus on what's good and not what might go wrong from time to time. Believe me, if you do, you will be able to draw on those golden memories forever. I hope you have a have a great career in the best industry in the world.

REVIEW QUESTIONS

1. The American Trucking Associations, the largest trade association for the trucking transportation industry, has adopted a slogan. What is it?

    a. You got it, a truck brought it!

    b. Good stuff! Trucks Bring it!

    c. We go fast and we go big!

    d. Trucks rock!

2. The North American trucking industry employs well over 10 million people throughout the economy in jobs related to trucking activity. This means the trucking industry not only supplies goods but also generates _____.

    a. business

    b. new business

    c. jobs

    d. military supplies

3. A Class 8 vehicle is _____.

    a. a refrigerated truck

    b. a bob-tail

    c. a straight truck

    d. a tractor-trailer

4. The _____ gave the federal government's Interstate Commerce Commission (ICC) the authority to regulate interstate truck and bus companies, known collectively as "motor carriers."

    a. Interstate Commerce Commission Bill

    b. Patriot Act

    c. Motor Carrier Act of 1935

    d. Hatch Act

5. The device connecting a tractor to a trailer is called a _____.

    a. drive axle

    b. fourth wheel

    c. dual wheel

    d. fifth wheel

6. Canadian carriers are now required to meet the operational standards established under the *National Safety Code* (NSC), introduced in 1987, consists of how many individual standards?

    a. 10

    b. 14

    c. 16

    d. 20

7. Single-unit vehicles with engine, cab, and cargo compartment on one frame are called _____.

    a. straight trucks

    b. A-frames

    c. singles

    d. one-haulers

8. Looking to the future, economists project that by 2020, more trucks carrying more tons of freight, combined with _____ will put a strain on the U.S. highway system.

    a. our growing pattern of consumption

    b. our growing manufacturing sector

    c. our growing human population

    d. our growing cross-border trade

9. A holder of a commercial driver's license can be disqualified from professional driving for (1) conviction of a serious offense involving a vehicle that is not a CMV that resulted in license suspension or revocation, or (2) _____.

    a. conviction of felony theft

    b. a drug- or alcohol-related incident

    c. more than 20 parking tickets

    d. not passing the over-the-road test involving another type of vehicle.

10. Driving experience in a formal educational environment, such as a driving range, permits drivers to identify hazards and _____.

    a. learn routes to avoid hazards

    b. how to make citizen arrests

    c. how to respond to these hazardous situations

    d. how to gear the truck

11. Canada's *National Safety Code* was designed and developed by the _____.

    a. Commercial Motor Transport Group
    b. American Trucking Associations
    c. Canadian Council of Motor Transport Advisors
    d. Canadian Driver's League

12. For carriers and drivers originating in either Mexico or Canada, when they cross into the United States, they should have _____.

    a. a license from their country of origin
    b. an ATA ID license
    c. a CDL
    d. a picture ID and a copy of driving record

13. Cross-border trucking in North America swung into high gear with _____.

    a. NAFTA (North America Free Trade Agreement)
    b. the Montreal Accords
    c. the Patriot Act
    d. the Mexico City Trade Compromise

14. The term "professional driver" has gained popularity in the truck transportation industry because _____.

    a. more education and skills are now needed
    b. highways are of better quality
    c. trucks are easier to drive
    d. trucks are equipped with more technology

SUPPLEMENTAL LEARNING ACTIVITIES

1. Construct a time line of the history of U.S. or Canadian trucking.

2. Look up at least one of the early truck manufacturers based in Canada or the United States and find out what made their products popular in their time.

3. Discuss the challenges faced by early truck drivers. Divide into groups and identify at least five conditions early drivers faced that have been addressed in modern times and no longer exist.

4. In 100 words or less, describe the importance of regulation for the transportation industry today. Who does it benefit?

5. On a map, plot the first cross-continental truck route in either Canada or the United States.

6. Contact a trucking association to find out how they help the trucking industry.

FOR MORE INFORMATION

American Trucking Associations Campaign—Learn information about the "Good Stuff! Trucks Bring it!" campaign
www.trucksbringit.com

Federal Motor Carrier Safety Administration (FMCSA)—Find information about FMCSA's safety programs and the most up-to-date listing of rules and regulations
www.fmcsa.dot.gov

Bureau of Labor Statistics—Search transportation for information about occupations
www.bls.gov

NSC Standards—Learn details about the National Safety Code
www.ccmta.ca/english/producstandservices/publications/publications.cfm#NSC

2 The Commercial Driver's License

© Cengage Learning 2013

OBJECTIVES

When you have completed this chapter, you should be able to:

■ Be familiar with the requirements for passing the U.S. and Canadian Commercial Driver's License (CDL) exam.

■ Understand the Canadian operating requirements, who needs this document, and where it is needed.

■ Understand why every licensed professional driver should be proficient in the skills tested as requirements for passing the CDL.

■ Know and understand the efforts made by the Federal Motor Carriers Safety Administration to help professional drivers remain safe on U.S. highways.

■ Be aware of the penalties for major violations of CDL guidelines.

INTRODUCTION

Driving a commercial motor vehicle (CMV) in North America comes with huge responsibilities.

First of all, you must be able to operate a CMV in such a way that you keep yourself, your load, and others sharing the highway safe. But that's just the beginning. Driving a CMV also requires special skills and knowledge. Most drivers must obtain a **Commercial Driver's License (CDL)** through their home state or province. NOTE: It is illegal to have a license from more than one state. In addition, special endorsements may be required if you or your company drivers will be driving any of the following vehicles:

- a tractor with trailers
- a tractor with tank trailer
- a semitruck carrying hazardous materials
- a passenger vehicle

In the United States, those driving certain CMVs also are required to demonstrate that they have the required skills and knowledge to operate these vehicles safely and within the law. When they earn the commercial driver's license, this certifies that the driver has the necessary skills, is physically capable of driving a CMV, and has been judged as qualified to operate that vehicle **(see Figure 2-1).**

▶ **Figure 2–1**

A driver using three points of contact to enter the truck cab.

INTERESTING FACT

Motor vehicle and driver licensing was begun in Chicago in 1899. Driver's fee was $3 for the first year and $1 to renew. A Board of Examiners of Operators of Automobiles was assembled to determine the qualifications of persons wanting to be licensed.

Early in the history of U.S. trucking transportation, no special license was needed to drive a commercial motor vehicle. Therefore, anyone licensed to drive a car in any of the states or the District of Columbia could legally drive a truck or a bus. Additionally, some commercial vehicle drivers could obtain driver's licenses from more than one state, hiding or spreading convictions among several driving records. This allowed them to continue driving a truck by moving from one state to another.

STOP!

If any driver violates the CDL requirements, the federal penalty is a civil penalty of up to $2,500 or, in aggravated cases, criminal penalties of up to $5,000 in fines and/or up to 90 days in prison. An employer is also subject to a penalty of up to $10,000 if he or she knowingly uses a driver to operate a CMV without a valid CDL.

COMMERCIAL MOTOR VEHICLE SAFETY ACT OF 1986

The Commercial Motor Vehicle Safety Act of 1986, mentioned in the previous chapter, was signed into law on October 27, 1986. The goal of the act is to improve highway safety by ensuring that drivers of large trucks and buses are qualified to operate those vehicles and to remove unsafe and unqualified drivers from the highways **(see Figure 2-2)**. The act retained the state's right to issue a driver's license, but established minimum national standards that states must meet when issuing CDLs.

The Vehicle Safety Act of 1986 addresses problems and safety issues that existed prior to 1986 by:

- making it illegal for CDL holders to possess more than one license
- requiring states to adopt knowledge and skills testing to ensure that individuals required to have a CDL are qualified to operate heavy trucks and buses
- establishing minimum licensing standards and information requirements for the CDLs that states issue

If you operate a commercial vehicle, the Department of Motor Vehicles (DMV) or Department of Public Safety (DPS) will require you to carry a Commercial Driver's License (CDL).

Courtesy of The Trucker

▶ **Figure 2-2**

Law enforcement officer conducting a roadside inspection.

NOTE

The act does not require drivers to obtain a separate federal license; it merely requires states to upgrade their existing testing and licensing programs, if necessary, to conform to the federal minimum standards.

INTERESTING FACT

Driving commercial motor vehicles, which are primarily tractor-trailers, requires advanced skills and knowledge above and beyond those required to drive a car or other light-weight vehicle. Before implementation of the Commercial Driver's License (CDL) Program in 1986, licensing requirements for driving larger vehicles and buses varied from state to state.

© Cengage Learning 2013

▶ *"Rocking my new CDL! This makes even ME look good!"*

GO!

Between 1986 and 2005, according to FMCSA, more than 8 million drivers passed the knowledge and skills tests and obtained a CDL. Approximately 11 percent of these CDL drivers, between 1992 and 1996, have been disqualified at least once.

THE DRIVER AND THE U.S. COMMERCIAL DRIVER'S LICENSE

The Federal Motor Carrier Safety Administration (FMCSA) has developed and issued standards for the testing and licensing of CDL holders. These standards require states to issue CDLs to certain CMV drivers only after the driver passes **knowledge tests** and **skills tests** administered by the state and related to the type of vehicle the driver expects to operate.

Drivers are required to obtain and hold a CDL if they operate in interstate, intrastate, or foreign commerce if they drive a vehicle that meets any of the classifications of a CMV described below.

Classes of License

The federal standard requires states to issue a CDL to drivers according to the following license classifications:

Class A—Any combination of vehicles with a GVWR of 26,001 or more pounds (11,794 kg) provided the GVWR of the vehicle(s) being towed is in excess of 10,000 pounds (4,536 kg)

Class B—Any single vehicle with a GVWR of 26,001 or more pounds, or any such vehicle towing a vehicle not in excess of 10,000 pounds GVWR

Class C—Any single vehicle, or combination of vehicles, that does not meet the definition of Class A or Class B, but is either designed to transport 16 or more passengers, including the driver, or is transporting material that has been designated as hazardous under 49 U.S.C. 5103 and is required to be placarded under subpart F of 49 CFR Part 172 or is transporting any quantity of a material listed as a select agent or toxin in 42 CFR Part 73

Endorsements and Restrictions

Drivers who operate special types of CMVs also need to pass additional tests to obtain any of the following endorsements on their CDL in addition to the basic knowledge test. These include:

- T — Double/Triple Trailers (Knowledge Test only)
- P — Passenger (Knowledge and Skills Tests)
- N — Tank Vehicle (Knowledge Test only)
- H — Hazardous Materials (Knowledge Test and TSA Threat Assessment)
- X — Combination of Tank Vehicle and Hazardous Materials
- S — School Bus (Knowledge and Skills Tests)

A driver must take the skills test in a motor vehicle that represents the type of motor vehicle that the driver applicant operates or expects to operate as defined by the vehicle classifications just described (**see Figure 2-3**). While these classifications are general for the class of vehicle, additional requirements exist for the passenger and school bus endorsements.

To obtain a passenger endorsement, the driver must test in a passenger vehicle. To obtain a school bus endorsement, the driver must test in a passenger vehicle equipped with school bus features (lights, signs, etc.).

If a driver possesses a Class A CDL, but obtains his or her passenger or school bus endorsement in a Class B vehicle, the state must place an M restriction indicating that the driver can operate only Class B and C passenger vehicle or school buses.

If a driver possesses a Class B CDL, but obtains his or her passenger or school bus endorsement in a Class C vehicle, the state must place an N restriction indicating that the driver can operate only Class C passenger vehicle or school buses.

INFORMATION REQUIRED ON THE CDL

It is the responsibility of each state to determine the license fee, the license renewal cycle, most renewal procedures, and the age, medical, and other driver qualifications of its intrastate commercial drivers. However, if you drive interstate routes, you *must* meet federal driver qualifications (49 CFR 391).

▶ **Figure 2-3**

Drivers must take additional tests in order to obtain additional endorsements on their CDL.

Commercial Driver's License Document

While FMCSA sets the minimum standards that states must meet regarding CDLs, administration of the CDL program and issuance of the license itself remains the exclusive function of the states.

States may determine the application process, license fee, license renewal cycle, renewal procedures, and reinstatement requirements after a disqualification provided that the federal standards and criteria are met. States may exceed the federal requirements for certain criteria, such as medical, fitness, and other driver qualifications.

Per federal **regulations,** all CDLs must contain the following information:

- The words "Commercial Driver's License" or "CDL"
- The driver's full name, signature, and mailing address
- The driver's date of birth, sex, and height
- Color photograph of the driver
- The driver's state license number
- The name of the issuing state
- The date of issuance and expiration of the license
- The class(es) of vehicle that the driver is authorized to drive
- Notation of the "air brake" restriction, if issued
- The endorsement(s) for which the driver has qualified

NOTE

The Social Security number must be provided on the application, but it does not need to be printed on the CDL.

States may issue learner's permits for purposes of behind-the-wheel training on public highways as long as the learner's permit holder is required to be accompanied by someone with a valid CDL appropriate for the class and type of vehicle being operated **(see Figure 2-4).**

Further, the learner's permits can be issued for only limited time periods. The permit holder cannot operate a commercial motor vehicle transporting hazardous materials as defined in §383.5. The permit holder must have a valid operator's (non-CDL) driver's license, or have passed such vision, sign/symbol, and knowledge tests as the state issuing the learner's permit ordinarily administers to applicants for operator (non-CDL) drivers' licenses.

Courtesy of Lew Grill of the SAGE Schools

▶ **Figure 2-4**

Instructor and student on a practice course getting behind-the-wheel training.

Nonresident Commercial Driver's License

In certain circumstances, states are permitted to issue a CDL to an individual who is not domiciled within its jurisdiction. If doing so, the word "Nonresident" must be prominently displayed on the CDL, but does not have to be contiguous with "Commercial Driver's License" or "CDL". A Social Security number is not required on the license.

Nonresident CDL means a CDL is issued by a state under either of the following two conditions:

■ To an individual domiciled in a foreign country, other than Mexico and Canada, if the person obtained the license from a state that complies with the testing and licensing standards required for CDL drivers

■ To an individual domiciled in another state while that state is prohibited from issuing CDLs, if the person obtained the license from any state which elected to issue nonresident CDLs and which complies with the testing and licensing standards required for CDL drivers

Exemptions

Each state must exempt from the requirements of 49 CFR 383 individuals who operate CMVs for military purposes. This exception is applicable to active duty military personnel; members of the military reserves; members of the National Guard on active duty, including personnel on full-time National Guard duty, personnel on part-time National Guard training, and National Guard military technicians (civilians who are required to wear military uniforms); and active duty U.S. Coast Guard personnel. This exception is not applicable to U.S. Reserve technicians.

A state may, at its discretion, exempt firefighters, emergency response vehicle drivers, farmers, and drivers removing snow and ice in small communities from the CDL requirements, subject to certain conditions. The use of this waiver is limited to the driver's home state unless there is a reciprocity agreement with adjoining states (**see Figure 2-5**).

© iStockphoto/appleuzr

▶ **Figure 2-5**

Emergency response vehicle.

CANADIAN DRIVER'S LICENSE REQUIREMENTS

In Canada, age and other requirements for obtaining a commercial motor vehicle driver's license vary, according to province. In order to drive in or through any of the Canadian provinces, CMV drivers must be licensed to drive in that province. Although the process for obtaining a CMV license from any of the Canadian provinces is similar to obtaining a CDL in the United States, the main objective is the same: to keep drivers, their rigs, their cargos, and those sharing the highway safe. Here is a listing of some of the Canadian license requirements for CMV drivers by province. For more in depth information please visit - www.servicecanada.gc.ca/eng/subjects/cards/drivers_licence.shtml

Alberta

- Class 4: This permit allows the operator to drive a taxi, ambulance, or bus with seats for up to 24 passengers. Minimum learning or licensing age is 18.

- Class 3: This permit allows an operator to drive a single motor vehicle with three or more axles, or a motor vehicle with three or more axles pulling a trailer with one or more axles (assuming the trailer does not have airbrakes).

- Class 2: This permit allows an operator to operate any bus, in addition to the vehicles permitted by holders of class 3, 4, and 5 permits. Minimum learning or licensing age is 18.

- Class 1: This permit allows an operator to operate any motor vehicle except a motorcycle. Minimum learning or licensing age is 18.

British Columbia

- Class 4 (Commercial license): Permits the holder to operate taxis, limousines, ambulances, special buses used to transport people with disabilities and other special vehicles; also permits the holder to operate vehicles in Class 5. Minimum age: 19.

- Class 3 (Commercial license, heavy trucks): Permits the holder to operate trucks with more than two axles, including dump trucks and large tow trucks; also permits the holder to operate vehicles in Class 5. Minimum age: 18.

- Class 2 (Commercial license, buses): Permits the holder to operate buses, including school buses, special activity buses and special vehicles; also permits the holder to operate vehicles in Classes 4 and 5. Minimum age: 19.

- Class 1 (Commercial license, semi-trailer): Permits the holder to operate semi-trailer trucks; also, permits the holder to operate all motor vehicles or combinations of vehicles except motorcycles. Minimum age: 19.

Manitoba

- Class 4: Permits the holder to operate taxis, ambulances, other emergency vehicles, buses with a passenger capacity of 10–24, and school buses with a capacity of 10–36 ; also permits the holder to operate vehicles in Class 5. Minimum age: 18.

- Class 3: Permits the holder to operate trucks with more than two axles, including dump trucks and large tow trucks; also permits the holder to operate vehicles in Class 4 and 5. Minimum age: 18.

- Class 2: Permits the holder to operate buses with a seating capacity of over 24, and school buses with a seating capacity of over 36; also permits the holder to operate vehicles in Classes 3, 4, and 5. Minimum age: 18.

- Class 1: Permits the holder to operate semi-trailer trucks; also permits the holder to operate all motor vehicles or combinations of vehicles except motorcycles. Minimum age: 18

New Brunswick

- Class 5: Permits the holder to drive any motor vehicle including any vehicle from Class 9; any two-axle motor vehicle except an ambulance, a taxicab or a bus; any three-axle motor vehicle, other than a truck,

(Continues)

CANADIAN DRIVER'S LICENSE REQUIREMENTS (*continued*)

of a type designed for use in the construction, maintenance, and repair of highways, whether or not the vehicle is to be so used; and to tow a towed vehicle that is registered up to and including 4,500 kg gross vehicle mass behind a motor vehicle or motor home referred to herein but not equipped with air brakes.

■ Class 4: Permits the holder to drive any vehicle from Class 5; an ambulance; a taxicab; and a bus with a capacity of less than 25 passengers.

■ Class 3: Permits the holder to drive any motor vehicle that the holder of a Class 5 license may operate; two-axle motor vehicle towing a towed vehicle, the towed vehicle being registered for over 4,500 kg (9,921 lbs) gross vehicle mass but not equipped with air brakes; motor vehicle with three or more axles; and motor vehicle with three or more axles, towing a towed vehicle not equipped with air brakes.

■ Class 3/4: Permits the holder to drive any motor vehicle that the holder of a Class 3 or 4 license may operate.

■ Class 2: Permits the holder to drive any motor vehicle that the holder of a Class 3, 4, or 5 license may operate, and a bus with a capacity of more than 24 passengers.

■ Class 1: Permits the holder to drive any motor vehicle that the holder of a Class 2, 3, 4, or 5 license may operate; truck tractor; truck tractor towing a semi-trailer; truck tractor towing a semi-trailer and a trailer; any truck towing a trailer equipped with air brakes; a truck tractor towing a trailer equipped with air brakes; and a truck.

All applicants for Class 1, 2, 3, and 4 must have completed the Graduated License Program and have a completed medical.

In addition to a class, a driver's license may be endorsed with a letter to expand on the types of vehicles that can be driven by the holder of the license. The endorsements are as follows: A — valid for all motorcycles; B — valid for school bus; C — valid for motorcycle and school bus; D — valid for motorcycle with engine size exceeding 50 cubic centimeters, but not exceeding 550 cubic centimeters; E — valid for vehicles equipped with air brakes; F — valid for vehicles equipped with air brakes.

Newfoundland and Labrador

■ Class 5: Permits the holder to operate all motor vehicles with less than two axles and combination of vehicles where the towed vehicle doesn't exceed 4,500 kg (9,921 lbs). A minimum of one year with a Class 5 license is required before one can apply for a commercial class license.

■ Class 4: Permits the holder to operate taxis, ambulances, all Class 5 motor vehicles, and buses up to 24 passengers.

■ Class 3: Permits the holder to operate trucks with three or more axles.

■ Class 2: Permits the holder to operate buses over 24 passengers.

■ Class 1: Permits the holder to operate semi-trailer trucks.

Nova Scotia

■ You must be at least 16 years old. After successfully completing a multiple choice road theory test and an eye vision test, a driving permit is issued which allows the learning driver to drive on roads accompanied by someone with full valid driver's license whose blood alcohol content (BAC) is less than 0.05.

■ Class 7 or 8 licenses: the learner's stage of the system lasts for 6 months, which may be reduced to 3 months if a recognized driver education or training program is taken. Operating conditions at this stage include:

    ■ No passengers, except an experienced driver who holds at least a Class 5 license; and, zero blood alcohol level for the learning driver. Suspensions will delay graduation to the newly licensed driver stage by the minimum time requirement; that is, 3 months if a recognized driver education or training program was taken, 6 months if not.

In Nova Scotia, drivers are licensed according to the type(s) of vehicle(s) they are qualified to drive.

- Class 4: For driving smaller buses, vans seating under 24 passengers for compensation, taxis, and ambulances
- Class 3: For driving vehicles or vehicle-trailer combinations weighing greater than 14,000 kilograms (30,865 pounds)
- Class 2: For driving large buses, over 24 passengers
- Class 1: For driving semi-trailers and tractor-trailer combinations

Ontario

- Class F: Permits the holder to operate regular bus, maximum of 24-passenger capacity; and ambulances. Can also operate vehicles in Class G.
- Class E: Permits the holder to operate school-purposes bus, maximum of 24-passenger capacity. Can also operate vehicles in Classes F and G.
- Class D: Permits the holder to operate any truck or motor vehicle combination exceeding 11,000 kg (24,251 lbs) provided the towed vehicle is not over 4,600 kg (10,141 lbs). Can also operate vehicles in Class G.
- Class C: Permits the holder to operate any regular bus with designed seating capacity for more than 24 passengers. Can also operate vehicles in Class D, F, and G.
- Class B: Permits the holder to operate any school-purposes bus with designed seating capacity for more than 24 passengers. Can also operate vehicles in Class C, D, E, F, and G.
- Class A with Condition R: Drivers with a restricted Class A license condition are prevented from operating a motor vehicle pulling double trailers or a motor vehicle pulling a trailer with air brakes.
- Class A: Any tractor-trailer or combination of motor vehicle and towed vehicles where the towed vehicles exceed a total gross weight of 4,600 kilograms (10,414 lbs). Can also operate vehicles in Class A with Condition R, D, and G.

Prince Edward Island

- If you are 16 years or older, you may apply for an Instruction Permit. An instruction permit allows you to drive under supervision to receive instruction. This type of license is valid for 2 years. Testing requirements for a driver's license are a written or oral exam, and road sign, driving, and vision tests. A novice driving or driver education course is required for first-time drivers. An eye test is required if your license is expired more than 1 year. The classes of license that can be obtained with appropriate training and required testing are as follows:
- Class 7: Authorizes a person to drive a motor vehicle requiring a Class 5, 6, or 8 driver's license without holding such a license if the person is receiving instruction in the operation of the motor vehicle and is accompanied by another person who holds a valid driver's license of the class required for the vehicle.
- Class 6: Authorizes a person to drive any motor vehicle which the holder of a Class 8 and 9 may operate, and any motorcycle.
- Class 5: Authorizes a person to drive any motor vehicle which the holder of a Class 8 and 9 may operate; any motor vehicle not exceeding 14,000 kg (30,865 pounds) gross mass, except an ambulance, taxi, motorcycle, bus, or a truck-tractor; any motor vehicle not exceeding 14,000 kg gross mass towing a vehicle which does not exceed the gross mass of 4,500 kg.
- Class 4: Authorizes a person to drive any motor vehicle which the holder of a Class 5, 8, and 9 may operate; any ambulance, any taxi, and any bus with a capacity of fewer than 25 passengers.
- Class 3: Authorizes a person to drive any motor vehicle which the holder of a Class 5, 8, and 9 may operate; any motor vehicle exceeding 14,000 kg gross mass, but not including a truck-tractor towing a

(Continues)

CANADIAN DRIVER'S LICENSE REQUIREMENTS (*continued*)

semi-trailer; any truck-trailer combination exceeding 14,000 kg (30,865 pounds) gross mass; any truck tractor without a trailer; and any special mobile equipment.

- Class 2: Authorizes a person to drive any motor vehicle which the holder of a Class 3, 4, 5, 8, and 9 may operate; any bus with a capacity of more than 24 passengers, including a school bus.

- Class 1: Authorizes a person to drive any motor vehicle which the holder of a Class 3, 5, 8, and 9 may operate; any truck-tractor; any truck-tractor towing a semi-trailer; any truck-tractor towing a semi-trailer and a trailer.

Quebec

- A Class 1 license authorizes its holder to drive a combination of vehicles, i.e.: a double-axle road tractor with a net weight of 4,500 kg (9,921 lbs) or more hauling one or more trailers or semi-trailers and a triple-axle road tractor hauling one or more trailers or semi-trailers. It also authorizes driving a truck covered by Class 3 hauling a trailer or semi-trailer whose net weight is 4,500 kg (9,921 lbs) or more and which is only used to transport equipment, tools or furnishings as part of its permanent equipment.

NOTE

A road tractor is a motor vehicle that does not have cargo space and that is permanently equipped with a fifth wheel.

Also authorized is driving a truck covered by Class 3, hauling any trailer or semi-trailer other than those described above, with a net weight of 2,000 kg (4,409 lbs) or more. Class 1 also authorizes the holder to operate all other types of road vehicles, except for motorcycles.

- **Class 1 License—Basic requirements**

- Applicants must have fewer than 4 demerit points entered on their driving record; not have had their driver's license suspended or revoked during the 2 previous years as the result of accumulating demerit points or a driving-related Criminal Code offence; pass the SAAQ's vision test; submit a satisfactory medical report; pass the knowledge test and two road tests.

- **Class 1 License—Experience required**

- Applicant must have 36 months cumulative experience as a holder of a Class 5 probationary license or Class 5 driver's license (passenger vehicle) or, 24 months cumulative experience if he or she has completed the following training:

  - the truck driving training program which leads to the Diploma of Vocational Studies issued by the Ministère de l'Éducation, du Loisir et du Sport; or

  - a 300-hour driving course on the public roadway for heavy vehicles covered by Class 1. This program must include at least 40 hours of driving given by a heavy vehicle driving school AND a professional internship for the number of hours needed to complete the required 300 hours. Applicants must have either of these programs recognized by the SAAQ, which may request certain documents such as the learner's daily logs as well as those of the accompanying rider in the case of the 300-hour program.

Length of the Learning Period

- The applicant must have held a Class 1 learner's license for 3 months, or 1 month if the applicant meets one of the following requirements:

  - Applicant is registered in the truck driving training program which leads to the Diploma of Vocational Studies issued by the Ministère de l'Éducation, du Loisir et du Sport and has successfully completed all mandatory sections of the program required to drive on the road without an accompanying rider; or is aged 25 or over; or has 60 months cumulative experience as a holder of a Class 5 license; or holds a Class 2 or 3 driver's license.

Saskatchewan

- Class 5: Holder must have successfully completed the requirements and held a Probationary Driver's License for 24 months. This license allows you to operate the following types of vehicles:
  - Passenger vehicle, or any double-axle truck or road tractor with a net mass of less than 4,500 kg (9,921 lbs)
  - Tool vehicle: motor vehicle, other than a vehicle mounted on a truck chassis, in which the work station is contained within the driver's compartment (for the purposes of this definition, a truck chassis is a frame equipped with the combination of mechanical components required for a vehicle that is manufactured for the purpose of transporting people, goods, or equipment)
  - Service vehicle: vehicle equipped to supply, repair, or tow road vehicles
- Class 4C: Taxicab : Requirements:
  - Must have held a Probationary Class 5 License for a minimum of 12 months
  - Understand, speak and read French
  - Pass a test on regulations governing transportation by taxi
- Class 4B: Small Bus or Minibus (Less than 25 passengers):
  - Must have 1 year of experience with a Class 5 license
  - School Minibus: An additional "certificate of competence" is required
- Class 4A: Emergency Vehicle:
  - Have 2 years experience under a probationary license or Class 5 driver's license, or
  - Currently hold a probationary license or Class 5 driver's license AND have passed an emergency vehicle driving course recognized by the SAAQ
- Class 3: Straight-Body Truck: Requirements:
  - Must have 24 months cumulative Class 5 experience
  - Must have fewer than 4 demerit points on record
  - Must not have had license suspended or revoked during the previous 2 years as the result of accumulating demerit points or a driving-related Criminal Code offense
  - Must pass the SAAQ's vision test
  - Must submit a satisfactory medical report
  - Must pass the knowledge test
  - Must pass both road tests. (Pretrip inspection test and heavy vehicle road test)

The Professional Driver and the Ontario Operating Records

The Commercial Vehicle Operator's Registration (CVOR) system and the Carrier Safety Rating (CSR) program were developed by the Ministry of Transportation as part of an ongoing commitment to road safety in the province of Ontario.

This guideline is for operators of commercial motor vehicles in Ontario. This includes trucks that have a registered gross weight of over 4,500 kilograms (9,921 lbs), and buses that can carry 10 or more passengers. Owners/operators of these vehicles must apply for, obtain, and renew a **Commercial Vehicle Operator's Registration (CVOR) certificate.**

Each carrier is responsible for monitoring its CVOR record and the performance information it provides, including violation rates, thresholds, audit scores, and resulting Safety Rating. The carrier should identify and address problem areas in order to improve its commercial motor vehicle safety performance.

(Continues)

CANADIAN DRIVER'S LICENSE REQUIREMENTS *(continued)*

The CVOR system is part of the **Carrier Safety Rating (CSR) program.** The Ministry of Transportation monitors carriers and assigns each a Safety Rating based on several factors: collisions, inspections, and convictions, as well as the results of facility audits.

To operate in Ontario, carriers must follow the laws and regulations that apply to the operation of trucks and buses, which include, but are not limited to:

- The Highway Traffic Act
- Transportation of Dangerous Goods Act
- Public Vehicles Act
- Motor Vehicle Transport Act
- Compulsory Automobile Insurance Act
- Fuel Tax Act

The CVOR system tracks the on-road safety performance of the following vehicles:

- Trucks that have a gross weight or registered gross weight over 4,500 kg (9,921 lb)
- Buses that have a seating capacity of 10 or more passengers

The goal of the CVOR system is to improve road safety for all users of Ontario highways by having an effective monitoring and intervention system for all carriers. Poor performance may result in the loss of privileges to operate commercial motor vehicles.

Vehicles that Require a CVOR. A CVOR certificate is required for commercial vehicles that are:

- Plated in Ontario
- Plated in the USA
- Plated in Mexico

NOTE

For-hire operators of buses, including motor coaches and school/school purpose vehicles, may also require an operating authority under the Public Vehicles Act and Motor Vehicle Transport Act. Contact the Ontario Highway Transport Board at (416) 326-6732 for more information.

Vehicles that are plated in other Canadian provinces or territories (not Ontario) do not need a CVOR certificate. They require a safety fitness certificate from the province or territory in which the vehicle is plated.

Exemptions. Carriers that operate certain types of vehicles do not need a CVOR certificate. These vehicles include:

- A truck or bus that is plated in another Canadian jurisdiction
- A truck with a registered gross weight (RGW) and a gross weight of 4,500 kg or less (9,921 lb), whether towing a trailer or not
- A truck or bus leased by an individual for 30 days or less to move his or her personal goods, or to carry passengers at no fare
- An ambulance, fire apparatus, hearse, casket wagon, mobile crane, or tow truck
- A truck or bus operating under the authority of a dealer plate or an in-transit permit
- A bus used for personal purposes without compensation
- A motor home used for personal purposes
- A pickup truck used for personal purposes

CVOR Responsibilities. A CVOR operator (carrier) is the person who is responsible for the operation of a commercial motor vehicle. The carrier is responsible for:

- The conduct of the driver
- The mechanical safety condition of the vehicle
- The shipping of goods or passengers in the vehicle

Carriers are responsible for all the drivers and vehicles in their operation. Examples of these responsibilities include:

- Employing qualified and licensed drivers
- Monitoring the safety performance of drivers, including hours of service
- Resolving driver safety issues when they are identified
- Keeping vehicles in good, safe condition at all times
- Ensuring load security
- Ensuring daily and annual/semiannual inspections are completed
- Keeping records on file (e.g., vehicle repairs, kilometres traveled per year, annual inspection reports, etc.)
- Notifying the Ministry of changes such as name, address, telephone numbers, fleet data, kilometric travel, and changes in corporate officers, etc.

CVOR Documentation Required at Roadside. The CVOR certificate identifies the carrier and contains a unique nine-digit identification number. A copy of the certificate must be carried in each commercial motor vehicle operated under the CVOR and surrendered, upon request, to an MTO Enforcement Officer or police officer for inspection purposes.

Out of Province. For a commercial motor vehicle registered in another jurisdiction operating in Ontario and where the carrier is not required to register for a CVOR Certificate, the motor vehicle permit for that vehicle may be substituted for a CVOR certificate. All vehicles registered in Ontario, prorated into Ontario, and for-hire carriers are required to register for CVOR certificates.

Lease/Contract. Where a lease or contract is involved, the lease or contract must identify the vehicle and the lessee's CVOR number. Documented proof of the lease or contract must also be carried in the vehicle. If the vehicle is being leased for personal use only, for less than 30 days, no CVOR certificate is required.

An owner/driver operating under contract with a licensed carrier is not considered to be a licensed carrier and is therefore required to obtain an Owner/Driver or Single/Source Authority certificate. In this situation, owner/drivers are still required to obtain their own CVOR certificate, but they operate under the CVOR number of their contractual employer.

For more information about the CVOR system and the Carrier Safety Rating program, go to the Ministry's website at www.mto.gov.on.ca or contact MTO Carrier Sanctions and Investigation Office.

In addition, a state may issue a restricted license and waive the CDL knowledge and skills testing requirements for seasonal drivers in farm-related service industries and may waive certain knowledge and skills testing requirements for drivers in remote areas of Alaska. A state can also waive the CDL hazardous materials endorsement test requirements for part-time drivers working for the pyrotechnics industry, subject to certain conditions.

THE U.S. MOTOR CARRIER IMPROVEMENT ACT OF 1999

In July 2002, the Federal Motor Carrier Safety Administration released new rules covering the commercial driver's license that went into effect September 30 of that same year (**see Figure 2-6**). The new rules—which became part of the Motor Carrier Safety Improvement Act of 1999—include tougher penalties on drivers and states that did not comply with the act.

The results from these new rules were fewer CDL-related fatal crashes and fatalities because of the additional CMV operators—and CDL holders, specifically—who are suspended or disqualified for violation of the disqualifying **offenses** and serious traffic violations covered under this rule.

The new rules stated that a commercial driver can now be disqualified if the driver's noncommercial license has been canceled, revoked, or suspended as a result of convictions for traffic violations when driving a passenger vehicle or motorcycle. **Disqualification** can also occur if the driver has committed drug- or alcohol-related offenses while driving a passenger vehicle, motorcycle, snowmobile, ATC, or light watercraft (**see Figure 2-7**).

States failing to comply with FMCSA's 2002 guidelines on issuing licenses and maintaining proper legal databases risk losing federal funding as well as the right to issue CDLs.

▶ Figure 2–6

It is important to be familiar with the most current CDL rules.

▶ Figure 2–7

Commercial drivers can be suspended or disqualified for certain violations and offenses.

CAUTION!

New disqualifying offenses include driving a commercial vehicle with a suspended or revoked CDL and causing a fatality through negligent driving in either a CMV or a passenger vehicle.

THE STATES
Certifications and Record Checks

When an individual applies for a CDL, or attempts to renew or update his or her CDL, the state must perform a check of its own database, the Commercial Driver's License Information System (CDLIS), and the National Driver Register (NDR), to ensure the driver is not disqualified and does not possess a license from more than one jurisdiction.

STOP!

If the driver possesses a license from another jurisdiction, the state must require the driver applicant to surrender his or her driver's license issued by that state before issuing a new license.

The state also must request the complete driving record of the applicant from all jurisdictions where the driver was previously licensed in the past 10 years.

RULES ADDED IN 2012

Effective January 30, 2012, for each operator of a commercial motor vehicle required to have a commercial driver's license, the current licensing states must:

- Require drivers to certify the type of operation the driver expects to conduct and post the driver's self-certification to the driver history record
- Retain the original or a copy of the medical certificate of any driver required to provide documentation of physical qualification for three years beyond the date the certificate was issued
- Post the information from the medical examiner's certificate within 10 business days to the CDLIS driver record

Within 10 calendar days of receiving information from FMCSA regarding issuance or renewal of a medical variance for a driver, the state must update the CDLIS driver record to include the medical variance information provided by FMCSA.

"Hmmm ... not sure if my basket weaving experience would help in this job. That's too bad ... I wonder if my square dancing skills would be considered helpful. They certainly have taught me how to move in tight spaces, avoid stepping on toes, and keep my partner smiling. Sounds like great customer service skills to me!"

Within 10 calendar days of the driver's medical certification status expiring or a medical variance expiring or being rescinded, the state must:

- Update the medical certification status of that driver as "not certified"
- Notify the CDL holder of his or her CDL "not-certified" medical certification status and that the CDL privilege will be removed from the driver license unless the driver submits a current medical certificate and/or medical variance, or changes his or her self-certification to driving only in excepted or intrastate commerce (if permitted by the state)

- Initiate established state procedures for **downgrading** the license (The CDL downgrade must be completed and recorded within 60 days of the driver's medical certification status becoming "not certified" to operate a CMV.)

For persons applying for a hazardous materials endorsement, states now require compliance with the standards for such endorsement specified in Transportation Security Administration requirements, and provide proof of citizenship or immigration status.

CAUTION!

A lawful permanent resident of the United States requesting a hazardous materials endorsement must additionally provide his or her Bureau of Citizenship and Immigration Services (BCIS) alien registration number.

If a state determines, in its check of an applicant's license status and record prior to issuing a CDL, or at any time after the CDL is issued, that the applicant has falsified information or any of the required certifications, the state shall at a minimum suspend, cancel, or revoke the person's CDL or his or her pending application, or disqualify the person from operating a commercial motor vehicle for a period of at least 60 consecutive days.

CDL KNOWLEDGE AND SKILLS TESTS

States develop their own tests, which must meet the minimum federal standards provided for in Subpart G and H of 49 CFR Part 383. Model driver and examiner manuals and tests have been prepared and distributed to the states to use, if they wish. For more information about 49 CFR Part 383, go to www.fmcsa.dot.gov/.

- Each basic knowledge test—the test covering the areas referred to in 49 CFR 383.111 for the applicable vehicle group—shall contain at least 30 items, exclusive of the number of items testing air brake knowledge.
- To pass the knowledge tests (general and endorsement), applicants must correctly answer at least 80 percent of the questions.
- To pass the skills test, applicants must successfully perform all the required skills (listed in 49 CFR 383.113 through 49 CFR 383.123). The skills test must be taken in a vehicle representative of the type of vehicle that the applicant operates or expects to operate. Depending on the type of passenger vehicle used in the skills test, the following restrictions must be added to the license: "except Class A bus" or "except Class A and Class B bus."
- If you have moved from another state, you will be required to surrender your driver's license issued by another state.

CDL Skills Tests

If you pass the required knowledge tests, you are then eligible to take the CDL skills and performance tests. There are three types of CDL skills tests:

- Pretrip inspection test
- Basic controls skills test
- Behind-the-wheel road test

You must take these tests in the type of vehicle for which you wish to be licensed.

Pretrip Inspection Test

The purpose of the **pretrip inspection test** is to determine if you know whether your vehicle is safe to drive. During this test, you will be asked to conduct a pretrip inspection of your vehicle and/or explain to the examiner what you would inspect and why. You must demonstrate that you have a predetermined or set routine for effectively conducting a pretrip inspection (**see Figure 2-8**). You and your vehicle must pass the pretrip inspection test before you are allowed to take the behind-the-wheel road test.

"So, you're telling me that one little bump to the back of a police cruiser during the road test is considered grounds for failure? Oh, com' on!!!!"

Basic Controls Skills Test

The **basic controls skills test** includes up to seven exercises to evaluate your basic skills for controlling a commercial motor vehicle. These exercises are marked out by lines, traffic cones, or other boundaries and may include moving the vehicle forward, backing, parking, and turning maneuvers. The examiner will explain how each exercise should be done. You will be scored on how well you control the vehicle, how well you stay within the exercise boundaries, and how many pullups you make. (A pullup is when you pull the vehicle forward in order to correct your position and continue the exercise.) The basic controls skills test may include any or all of the following exercises:

NOTE

More warehouses and distribution centers are requiring workers and drivers to wear high-visibility vests in the yard. It is important to be knowledgeable of these rules.

- **Measured right turn**—Drive forward and make a right turn around a cone, marker, or curb. Your right rear tires should come as close as possible to the marker without touching it.

- **Forward stop**—Drive forward between two lines (the alley) and stop as close as possible to a stop line at the end of the 100-foot-long (30.5 m) and 12-foot-wide alley (3.7 m). After you stop, the examiner will measure the distance between the bumper and the stop line.

- **Straight-line backing**—Tests your ability to back straight without touching or crossing boundary lines in an alley that is 100 feet long (30.5 m) and 12 feet wide (3.7 m). The examiner will check if you touch or cross the boundaries. Pullups will be counted as errors (**see Figure 2-9**).

- **Alley dock**—Involves backing into an alley stall from the left side to simulate docking. The examiner will watch for pullups or crossing boundary lines or markers. When you stop at the end of the exercise, the distance between the rear of your vehicle and the stop line or dock marker will be checked.

Figure 2-8

Pretrip inspection determines if you know whether or not your vehicle is safe to drive.

▶ **Figure 2-9**

A driver will be tested on their straight-line backing ability.

■ **Parallel park (sight side)**—Involves parking in a space that is to your left. The space will be 10 feet (3.1 m) longer than your vehicle. The examiner will check for pullups, hitting cones, and touching or crossing boundary lines. When you toot your horn at the end of the maneuver, the examiner will record the distance your vehicle is from the back, front, and curb lines.

■ **Parallel park (blind side)**—In this exercise, the parking space is on the right side of your vehicle. The routine is the same as the sight-side parallel park.

■ **Backward serpentine**—Requires backing around cones or markers, beginning and ending with markers on the left side. The serpentine layout is a row of three cones. You are to back around the three cones in a serpentine or snakelike manner without striking the cones or markers. One correction or pullup is usually allowed. In some tests, you are allowed to exit your vehicle to check your position.

CAUTION!

A failure on any part of the skills test may cause you to fail the complete test, or points may be deducted for each error. Make sure you know how the examiner is going to score the test before you attempt the exercises.

▶ **Figure 2-10**

A drive test is performed after completing the written knowledge tests.

Behind-the-Wheel Test

Once you have completed the written knowledge tests, you are ready for the **behind-the-wheel test,** also known as the drive test. It is the test where you show your ability to drive in traffic **(see Figure 2-10).**

In this test, you demonstrate your safe driving skills over a route chosen by the examiner. As you drive, you must follow instructions given by the examiner. You must take the road test in the type of vehicle for which you intend to be licensed.

STOP!

Since safety is paramount, if you cause an accident or do not obey traffic laws during the test, you automatically fail the test. Other errors, such as striking a curb with your trailer tandem, or making a turn without confidence, may also result in a failed drive test.

During the test, you will drive over a preplanned course. The examiner will score certain driving performances in each location. Your application fee generally entitles you to several attempts at passing the behind-the-wheel test, which includes the following maneuvers and locations:

- Left and right turns
- Driving city business streets
- **Intersections**
- **Railway crossings**
- Left and right curves
- Two-lane rural or semirural roads
- Freeways or expressways
- **Downgrades**
- **Upgrades**
- Downgrade stopping
- Upgrade stopping
- Underpass or low clearance bridge
- Before downgrade
- Other railway crossing

These tests and their specified locations offer a wide variety of traffic situations. They also require certain driving tasks to be done properly **(see Figure 2-11)**. For instance, during each of the right turns, the examiner may grade your:

- Speed
- Position and lane usage—such as starting in the wrong lane, ending in the wrong lane, swinging too wide, or swinging too short
- Mirror checks
- Signaling
- Canceling signal
- Gear changes
- Traffic checks

The behind-the-wheel course is planned so that certain tasks or maneuvers are scored only at selected locations during the test. You may make 10 right turns during the test drive, yet only four of the turns will be used as scoring locations.

▶ Figure 2-11

The behind-the-wheel test examines your ability to perform various maneuvers in a variety of traffic situations.

The examiner will not deduct points for a maneuver that is performed improperly if this occurs at a location other than the preselected location for the maneuver to be performed.

STOP!

There is one exception—an error that is grounds for immediate failure (GFIF) will be scored anywhere along the test drive course. Each state has its own special GFIF. When one of these errors is made, the test is stopped immediately.

Any traffic violations, of course, would be grounds for immediate failure. Some examples of these violations include:

- An accident during the test drive that involves property damage/personal injury
- Refusal to perform any maneuver that is part of the test
- Any dangerous action in which an accident is prevented by the actions of the examiner or others
- Passing another vehicle stopped at a crosswalk while yielding to a pedestrian
- Passing a school bus with red lights flashing while bus is loading or unloading
- Making or starting a turn in the wrong lane in traffic conditions
- Running through a red light or stop sign. This also applies if the examiner stops you from running a red light or stop sign
- Being unable to operate vehicle equipment properly or, after a short distance on test course, it becomes apparent that you are dangerously inexperienced

Third-Party CDL Skills Testing

A state may authorize **third-party skills testing,** that is, a person (including another state, an employer, a private driver training facility, or other private institution, or a department, agency, or instrumentality of a local government) to administer the skills tests, if the following conditions are met:

- Tests must be the same as those given by the state.
- The third party has an agreement with the state containing, at a minimum, provisions that:
    - Allow the FMCSA, or its representative, and the state to conduct random examinations, inspections, and audits without prior notice
    - Require the state to conduct on-site inspection at least yearly
    - Require that all third-party examiners meet the same qualification and training standards as state examiners

At least annually, state employees must evaluate the programs by taking third-party tests as if they were test applicants, or by testing a sample of drivers tested by the third party and then comparing pass/fail rates.

Each state has the right to take prompt and appropriate remedial action against the third-party testers in the event that the third party fails to comply with state or federal standards for the CDL testing program, or with any other terms of the third-party contract.

Exemption of Skills Testing Requirements

States have the option to exempt certain individuals with **good driving records** from the skills testing requirement (commonly referred to as "grandfathering"). The state shall impose conditions and limitations to restrict the applicants from whom a state may accept alternative requirements for the skills test described in 49 CFR 383.113. Such conditions must require at least the following:

- Driver has a current license at time of application; and driver has a good driving record and previously passed an acceptable skills test

    or

- Driver has a "good driving record" in combination with certain "driving experience"

"Good Driving Record" under This System in the United States

A "good driving record" means that a driver can certify that, during the 2-year period immediately prior to applying for a CDL, he or she:

- Has not had more than one license
- Has not had any license suspended, revoked, or canceled

- Has not had any convictions in any type of motor vehicle for a major disqualifying offense defined in 49 CFR 383.51(b)
- Has not had more than one conviction for any type of motor vehicle for a serious traffic violation defined in 49 CFR 383.51(c)
- Has not had any violation of state or local law relating to motor vehicle traffic control arising in connection with any traffic accident, and has no record of an accident in which he or she was at fault

Driving Experience

Driving experience means the driver can certify and provide evidence that:

- He or she is regularly employed in a job requiring operation of CMV, and either:
  - Has previously taken and passed a behind-the-wheel skills test in a representative vehicle for that applicant's driver's license classification, or
  - Has operated a representative vehicle for at least 2 years immediately preceding application for a CDL

OTHER REQUIREMENTS

To participate in the national CDL program, states must also meet other requirements related to commercial driver's license holders and motor carriers.

Penalties

A driver who is convicted of violating an out-of-service order shall be subject to a civil penalty of not less than $2,500 for a first conviction and not less than $5,000 for a second or subsequent conviction, in addition to disqualification under FMCSR 383.51(e).

An employer who is convicted of a violation of an out-of-service order shall be subject to a civil penalty of not less than $2,750 nor more than $25,000.

An employer who is convicted of a violation of a federal, state, or local law or regulation, pertaining to railroad-highway grade crossings must be subject to a civil penalty of not more than $10,000.

Commercial Driver's License Information System

States must be connected to the Commercial Driver's License Information System (CDLIS) and the National Driver Register (NDR) in order to exchange information about CDL drivers, traffic convictions, and disqualifications. A state must use both the CDLIS and NDR to check a driver's record, and the CDLIS to make certain that the applicant does not already have a CDL. The state shall notify the operator of the CDLIS of the issuance, transfer, renewal, or upgrade of a license within the 10-day period beginning on the date of license issuance.

Blood Alcohol Concentration Standards

The FMCSA has established 0.04% as the blood alcohol concentration (BAC) level at or above which a CDL commercial motor vehicle operator who is required to have a CDL is deemed to be driving under the influence of alcohol and subject to the disqualification sanctions in the federal regulations. Most states have established a BAC level of 0.08% as the level at or above which a person operating a noncommercial motor vehicle is deemed to be driving under the influence of alcohol **(see Figure 2-12)**.

Employer Notifications

Within 30 days of a conviction for any traffic violation, except parking, a driver must notify his or her employer, regardless of the nature of the violation or the type of vehicle which was driven at the time.

▶ Figure 2-12

Professional drivers should not have even one drink while on the job and going behind the wheel.

▶ Figure 2-13

A driver is required to notify his/her employer of any traffic violations within 30 days.

If a driver's license is suspended, revoked, canceled, or if the driver is disqualified from driving, his or her employer must be notified. The notification must be made by the end of the next business day following receipt of the notice of the suspension, revocation, cancellation, lost privilege, or disqualification.

Employers may not knowingly use a driver who has more than one license or whose license is suspended, revoked, or canceled, or is disqualified from driving. Violation of this requirement may result in civil or criminal penalties (**see Figure 2-13**).

Notification of Previous Employment

All employers shall request, and all person's applying for employment as a commercial motor vehicle operator shall provide, employment history information for the 10 years preceding the date the application is submitted. The request shall be made at the time of application for employment.

VIOLATIONS

A **violation** is an action that is contrary to driving laws or rules. This section describes how they are incurred.

Major Violations While Operating a Motor Vehicle

- Being under the influence of alcohol as prescribed by state law
- Being under the influence of a controlled substance
- Having an alcohol concentration of 0.04 or greater while operating a CMV
- Refusing to take an alcohol test as required by a state or jurisdiction under its implied consent laws or regulations
- Leaving the scene of an accident
- Using the vehicle to commit a **felony** involving the manufacturing, distribution, or dispensing a controlled substance
- Driving a CMV when, as a result of prior violations committed operating a CMV, the driver's CDL is revoked, suspended, or canceled, or the driver is disqualified from operating a CMV
- Causing a fatality through the negligent operation of a CMV, including but not limited to the crimes of motor vehicle manslaughter, homicide by motor vehicle, and negligent homicide
- Using the vehicle in the commission of a felony involving manufacturing, distributing, or dispensing a controlled substance

Serious Violations While Operating a Motor Vehicle

- Speeding excessively, involving any speed of 15 mph (24 km/h) or more above the posted speed limit
- Driving recklessly, as defined by state or local law or regulation, including but, not limited to, offenses of driving a motor vehicle in willful or wanton disregard for the safety of persons or property
- Making improper or erratic traffic lane changes
- Following the vehicle ahead too closely
- Violating state or local law relating to motor vehicle traffic control (other than a parking violation) arising in connection with a fatal accident
- Driving a CMV (as defined in Part 383) without obtaining a CDL
- Driving a CMV without a CDL in the driver's possession
- Driving a CMV without the proper class of CDL and/or endorsements for the specific vehicle group being operated or for the passengers or type of cargo being transported

Railroad Highway Grade Crossing Violations While Operating a CMV

- The driver is not required to always stop, but fails to slow down and check that tracks are clear of an approaching train
- The driver is not required to always stop, but fails to stop before reaching the crossing, if the tracks are not clear
- The driver is always required to stop, but fails to stop before driving onto the crossing
- The driver fails to have sufficient space to drive completely through the crossing without stopping
- The driver fails to obey a traffic control device or the directions of an enforcement official at the crossing
- The driver fails to negotiate a crossing because of insufficient undercarriage clearance

Violation of Out-of-Service Order While Operating a CMV

Violating a driver or vehicle out-of-service order transporting hazardous or nonhazardous materials or while operating a vehicle designed to transport 16 or more passengers, including the driver.

Disqualifications

Disqualifications apply to CDL holders and persons required to have a CDL:

Using a CMV or non CMV in the commission of a felony involving manufacturing, distributing, or dispensing a controlled substance will result in a disqualification for life, without the possibility of reinstatement.

Disqualification for major offenses—The first violation for a major violation, in a CMV or a non-CMV, results in a 1-year disqualification or a 3-year disqualification if transporting hazardous materials required to be placarded. The second violation for a major violation, in a CMV or a non-CMV, results in a lifetime disqualification. The driver may be eligible for reinstatement under certain conditions after 10 years.

Disqualification for serious traffic violations—The first violation for a serious violation does not result in a disqualification. A second serious violation within 3 years, results in a 60-day disqualification, and a third serious violation within 3 years, results in a 120-day disqualification. Serious disqualifications must be served consecutively. All serious violations in a CMV are included. Serious violations in a non-CMV must not be included, unless it results in the revocation, cancellation, or suspension of the CDL holder's license or non-CMV driving privileges.

Disqualification for railroad-highway grade crossing (RRHGC) offenses, while operating a CMV—The first violation of an RRHGC results in a disqualification of not less than 60 days. The second violation, within 3 years, results in a disqualification of not less than 120 days. The third and subsequent violations, within 3 years, results in a disqualification of not less than 1 year.

Disqualification for violating out-of-service orders (OOSO), while operating a CMV—Category 1 describes a driver who was transporting placarded hazardous materials or operating a vehicle designed to transport 16 or more passengers. Category 2 describes drivers not in Category 1.

Category 1—The first violation results in a disqualification of no less than 180 days or more than 2 years. The second and subsequent violations within 10 years, results in a disqualification of no less than 3 years or more than 5 years.

Category 2—The first violation results in a disqualification of no less than 180 days or more than 1 year. The second violation within 10 years, results in a disqualification of no less than 2 years or more than 5 years. The third and subsequent violations result in disqualifications of no less than 3 years or more than 5 years.

If a CDL holder is disqualified from operating a CMV, the state may issue him/her a license to operate a non-CMV. Drivers who are disqualified from operating a CMV cannot be issued a "conditional" or **"hardship"** CDL or any other type of limited driving privileges to continue driving a CMV.

NOTE

If you have a hardship license, then you're most likely under the age of 18—the minimum required to obtain a CDL. There is no "hardship CDL". Hardship licenses cover only regular passenger vehicles and, in some states, motorcycles. If your job depends on having a CDL and you have been disqualified from operating a CMV, there is no way to obtain a "hardship CDL."

For disqualification purposes, convictions for out-of-state violations will be treated the same as convictions for violations that are committed in the home state. Convictions and disqualifications for 60 days or longer that a driver receives outside his or her home state are transmitted to the state of record (SOR) so that the convictions and disqualifications can be applied to the driver's history record (DHR).

Implied Consent to Alcohol Testing

Any person who holds a CDL is considered to have consented to alcohol or controlled substance testing as is required by any state or jurisdiction. The driver shall not be under the influence of alcohol or a controlled substance. He or she should not have any measured alcohol concentration or detected presence of alcohol while on duty or operating, or in physical control of a commercial motor vehicle. Consent for testing is implied by driving a commercial motor vehicle.

CDL from a Decertified State

A CDL issued by a state prior to the date the state is notified by the administrator that the state is prohibited from issuing CDLs, will remain valid until its stated expiration date.

ONCE YOU HAVE A CDL

Drivers who have earned a CDL are held to a higher standard than other drivers. These standards include reporting any involvement in an accident to your employer, whether it involves a CMV or a personal vehicle.

Within 30 days of a conviction for any traffic violation, except parking, a driver must notify his or her employer, regardless of the nature of the violation or the type of vehicle that was driven at the time.

If a driver's license is suspended, revoked, canceled, or if the driver is disqualified from driving, his or her employer must be notified. The notification must be made by the end of the next business day following receipt of the notice of the suspension, revocation, cancellation, lost privilege, or disqualification.

Employers may not knowingly use a driver who has more than one license or whose license is suspended, revoked, or canceled, or is disqualified from driving. Violation of this requirement may result in civil or criminal penalties.

> **STOP!**
>
> For conviction while driving a CMV, drivers must be disqualified and lose their privilege to drive.

REASONS CDL DRIVERS CAN BE DISQUALIFIED

Following are reasons a driver with a CDL can be disqualified:

- Two or more serious traffic violations within a 3-year period, including excessive speeding, reckless driving, improper or erratic lane changes, following the vehicle ahead too closely, and traffic offenses in connection with fatal traffic accidents (90 days to 5 years)
- One or more violations of an out-of-service order within a 10-year period (1 year)
- Driving under the influence of a controlled substance or alcohol
- Leaving the scene of an accident, or using a CMV to commit a felony (3 years)
- Any of the 1-year offenses while operating a CMV that is placarded for hazardous materials (life)
- Second offense of any of the 1-year or 3-year offenses; or using a CMV to commit a felony involving manufacturing, distributing, or dispensing controlled substances
- States have the option to reduce certain lifetime disqualifications to a minimum disqualification period of 10 years if the driver completes a driver rehabilitation program approved by the state

"Yes we are all okay. Well … everyone except for KITT"

- If a CDL holder is disqualified from operating a CMV, the state may issue him or her a license to operate non-CMVs. Drivers who are disqualified from operating a CMV cannot be issued a "conditional" or "hardship" CDL or any other type of limited driving privileges to continue driving a CMV

For disqualification purposes, convictions for out-of-state violations will be treated the same as convictions for violations that are committed in the home state. The CDLIS will ensure that convictions a driver receives outside his or her home state are transmitted to the home state so that the disqualifications can be applied.

SUMMARY

The Commercial Driver's License (CDL) is a license required in the United States to operate any type of vehicle that has a gross vehicle weight rating (GVWR) of 26,001 lb (11,793 kg) or more for commercial use. This includes but is not limited to tow trucks, tractor-trailers, and buses. In Canada, the counterpart to the CDL is the Commercial Motor Vehicle (CMV) license, which can be obtained in any province and is required to drive through each of the provinces. The goal of Canada's CMV license is the same as the CDL in the U.S.—to keep drivers, their rigs, their cargoes and those who share the roadways safe. Training for the CMV license in Canada is obtainable from accredited schools.

The Commercial Motor Vehicle Safety Act of 1986 was designed to improve highway safety by ensuring that truck drivers and drivers of tractor-trailers and buses are qualified to drive Commercial Motor Vehicles (CMVs), and to remove drivers who are unsafe and unqualified from the highways. Under this act, the federal government established minimum requirements that must be met by states when issuing a CDL.

In this chapter you learned the requirements for acquiring and retaining a CDL. You also learned about the violations and disqualifications that can affect holders of CDLs.

Although formal training is not required to obtain a CDL, training may be obtained by completing a qualified CDL training program through a truck driving school. These training programs specialize in teaching potential truck drivers the necessary skills and knowledge to properly and safely operate a truck. The overall purpose of these training schools is to help truckers-to-be pass the CDL knowledge and skills tests as well as advanced driving techniques such as skid avoidance and recovery and other emergency actions for situations such as a break-away trailer and hydroplaning.

There are a number of licensed CDL training schools around the United States, and many trucking companies operate their own schools as well.

KEY TERMS

Alley dock
Backward serpentine
Basic controls skills test
Behind-the-wheel test
Carrier Safety Rating (CSR) program
Commercial Driver's License (CDL)
Commercial Vehicle Operator's Registration (CVOR)

Disqualification
Downgrade
Driving experience
Felony
Forward stop
Good driving record
Hardship
Intersection
Knowledge tests
Measured right turn

Offense
Parallel park
Pretrip inspection test
Railway crossing
Regulations
Skills test
Straight-line backing
Third-party skills testing
Upgrade
Violation

REVIEW QUESTIONS

1. If you pass the CDL knowledge test, then are you are allowed to take the _____ tests.

   a. skills and driving
   b. general usage

   c. instruments
   d. all of the above

2. In the United States and Canada, who sets the minimum standards for licensing and testing commercial drivers?

   a. state/province where testing is done
   b. county where the testing is done
   c. city where the testing is done
   d. federal government

3. According to the Commercial Motor Vehicle Safety Act of October 26, 1986, states must make certain their CDL requirements _____.

   a. are more difficult than federal standards
   b. are printed in at least three languages
   c. are the same as federal standards
   d. are priced at the federal rate

4. Regarding possession of a CDL, a driver must _____.

   a. have a license for each state in which he or she plans to drive
   b. have a license from the state where a load originates
   c. have no more than one license
   d. have a license from the state that is the destination of a load

5. For a first offense of driving a CMV and having an alcohol concentration of 0.04 or greater, a driver will lose the CDL for _____.

   a. 6 months
   b. 1 year
   c. 2 years
   d. 2 months

6. To legally operate a combination vehicle where the combined GVWR is 26,001 pounds (11,794 kg) or more and the GVWR of the vehicle(s) being towed is over 10,000 pounds (4,454 kg), you must have a _____.

   a. Class B CDL
   b. Class C CDL
   c. Haz Mat Endorsement
   d. Class A CDL

7. Which of the following CDL knowledge tests must be taken by all applicants?

   a. passenger bus
   b. general knowledge
   c. combination vehicle
   d. hazardous materials

8. Which of the following is not one of the required CDL skills and performance tests?

   a. pretest inspection
   b. adjusting the fifth wheel
   c. basic control skills
   d. behind-the-wheel road test

9. Which of the following is not one of the required exercises on the basic control skill test?

   a. measured right turn
   b. straight-line backing
   c. backward serpentine
   d. emergency stop

10. During the behind-the-wheel road test, if you cause an accident or do not obey a traffic law, _____.

    a. you may automatically fail the test
    b. the examiner will take 10 points off your test score
    c. the examiner will discuss the situation with you, but you will not fail the test
    d. b and c

11. The Commercial Vehicle Operator's Registration is required for all vehicles plated on the North American continent and is required for any vehicles operating in the Canadian province of _____.

    a. Quebec
    b. British Columbia
    c. Ontario
    d. Saskatchewan

12. The second major violation committed in a CMV or a non-CMV results in _____.

    a. a lifetime disqualification
    b. a six-year suspension of your CDL
    c. losing your CDL for six months
    d. six months of community service

13. If you plan to drive in the province of Ontario in Canada, you must hold _____.

    a. a license issued by the nation of Canada

    b. a visitor's license if you hold a CDL

    c. a license issued by the province of Ontario

    d. a license with a NAFTA endorsement

14. If a driver's license is suspended, revoked, canceled, or if the driver is disqualified from driving, his or her employer must be notified, after the driver receives notice of suspension, revocation, or cancelation of the CDL _____.

    a. within 30 days

    b. by the end of the next business day

    c. within 7 business days

    d. within 5 business days

15. If you hold a CDL, this implies that you consent to _____.

    a. to keep up with new regulations

    b. stop smoking

    c. exercise regularly

    d. be tested for the presence of alcohol in your system

16. A CMV driver is required to _____ if railroad track crossing is not clear.

    a. flash the tractor's brake lights

    b. stop before proceeding

    c. sound the tractor's horn

    d. slow to 5 mph (8 km/h) before crossing

SUPPLEMENTAL LEARNING ACTIVITIES

1. Invite one or more law enforcement officers to class to discuss out-of-service procedures, driving under the influence, and other violations that could cost a professional driver his or her license.

2. Discuss what students may expect when they take their CDL knowledge and skills tests. If you haven't had this experience yourself, invite someone who has.

3. If you have copies of previous CDL knowledge tests, pass them out and have students look them over, and then answer any questions.

4. If any of the endorsement tests are available, distribute these so students may see what they look like.

5. Ask students to work in groups and put together a 200-word paper on their feelings about driving in other countries. They may include differences in regulation, safety issues, communication, and geographical likenesses and differences.

FOR MORE INFORMATION

FMCSA Commercial Driver's License Program
www.fmcsa.dot.gov/registration-licensing/cdl/cdl.htm

Information on driver's licenses for each province or territory
www.servicecanada.gc.ca/eng/subjects/cards/drivers_licence.shtml

Drivers licenses are issued by the provincial governments in Canada
canadaonline.about.com/od/driverslicence/Drivers_Licences_in_Canada.htm

More information about 49 CFR Part 383
fmcsa.dot.gov

3 Control Systems

© iofoto/www.Shutterstock.com

OBJECTIVES

When you have completed this chapter, you should be able to:

■ Identify, read, and describe the role and function of engine controls, primary vehicle controls, and secondary vehicle controls.

■ Name, locate, and describe the control functions for (1) starting the engine, (2) shutting down the engine, (3) steering, (4) shifting, (5) accelerating, (6) braking, and (7) parking.

■ Identify and locate the controls for lights, signals, windshield wipers/washers, suspension, coupling, and cab comfort.

■ Describe the acceptable operating range for the fuel, oil, air, cooling, exhaust, and electrical/electronic systems.

■ Discuss how checking these systems often can help you spot problems early.

INTRODUCTION

If you have ever seen the command capsule of a spacecraft or the cockpit of an airplane, you know there is a vast difference between these control consoles and the dashboard of your personal vehicle. Because the workload of a big rig is much different than that of a smaller vehicle, the controls and instrumentation will also be different (**see Figure 3-1**).

As you learn more about professional driving, you will understand the importance of knowing the function of all controls and instruments found in the cab of a commercial vehicle. Unlike your personal vehicle, tractor-trailer rigs have numerous and unique systems, controls, and instruments that will become important tools to use in your new profession. The purpose of this chapter is to introduce the basic controls and functions of today's tractors and straight trucks.

© Cengage Learning 2013

▶ **Figure 3-1**

Instrument panel.

VEHICLE CONTROLS

Let's begin with the basics and build from there. The three types of controls found on big rigs are:

- **Engine controls**—start the engine and shut it down
- **Primary vehicle controls**—provide driver with control of vehicle
- **Secondary vehicle controls**—assist driver with vision, communication, comfort, and safety but do not affect the vehicle's power

Engine Controls

Engine controls start the engine and shut it down. Engine controls do not control movement. Although they are similar in most vehicles, differences depend on the type of engine, manufacturer, type of fuel used, and starter mechanism.

Engine Control Switch

Starts the engine. Because the engine switch works much like a gate through which the electrical current must pass before the engine cranks, it must be in the "on" position for the engine to start.

Starter Button

Some trucks may have a **starter button.** To start the engine in this type of vehicle, turn the key to the "on" position and push the starter button. Be patient! Normal cranking time is five seconds, or sometimes less.

Other Engine Controls

Engine stop control knob—used in some diesel engines to shut off the engine. Operates by pulling out the knob and holding it until the engine stops.

Computerized idle timer—as a function of the engine's electronic controls, it will shut down the engine in a prescribed amount of time after the truck has come to a complete halt.

Emergency engine stop control—shuts down the engine. Use this control in emergency situations only. Many companies insist that it be reset by a trained technician after each use.

Cruise control—enables the driver to maintain a constant speed without having to depress the accelerator (**see Figure 3-2**).

"With all these electronic controls and pretrip rules, you'd think I was getting ready to fly a 747."

Courtesy of Don Hess

▶ Figure 3–2

Cruise control is available in most newer trucks.

MANDATED SPEED LIMITERS IN ONTARIO AND QUEBEC, CANADA

According to the MTO (Ministry of Transportation of Ontario) website, electronically limiting truck speeds will promote a cleaner environment, safer roads and a stronger economy in Ontario and Québec.

Starting January 1, 2009, most large trucks driven in Ontario will be required to use electronic speed limiters that cap their speed at a maximum of 105 kilometers per hour (65 miles per hour).

Studies conducted by the federal government, through Transport Canada, have demonstrated environmental, safety and cost saving benefits of speed limiters. Ontario and Québec are now working together to jointly launch and implement speed limiter regulations.

Several transportation companies have already limited their vehicles' speed to 105 km/h (65 mph) or less in response to the many benefits of speed limiters.

(Continues)

MANDATED SPEED LIMITERS IN ONTARIO AND QUEBEC, CANADA (*continued*)

According to Ontario's Ministry of Transportation, the speed limiters were mandated for a number of reasons. Studies conducted by the federal government, through Transport Canada, as an example, demonstrated environmental, safety, and cost-saving benefits of speed limiters. Ontario and Québec are now working together to jointly implement speed limiter regulations. Several transportation companies have already limited their vehicles' speed to 105 km/h (65 mph) or less in response to the many benefits of speed limiters.

There also are environmental, safety, and cost benefits from mandating the use of speed limiters. Reducing the speed of a vehicle will result in lower fuel consumption that helps reduce greenhouse gas emissions and saves money on fuel purchases. As well, the risk of collision is reduced when driving at lower speeds.

Further, according to the Ministry of Transportation, setting truck speed limiters at 105 km/h (65 mph) on all heavy trucks in Ontario would save about 100 million liters (26.5 million gallons) of fuel a year—the equivalent of 280,000 tons of greenhouse gas emissions according to the results of the 2007 Transport Canada study.

Roads and signage are designed for maximum driver safety if the posted speed limits are observed. Speed limits are set based on scientific calculations of human capabilities (visual perception, reaction time, shock resistance) and vehicle performance (braking, adherence, etc.). The safety of road users is at risk if the speed limit is exceeded.

Drivers expose themselves to a number of dangers by exceeding speed limits. Driving at higher speeds induces major stress that results in driver fatigue and loss of concentration. Speeding makes it more difficult to react to changes, stop suddenly and control the vehicle, and in case of a collision, the higher the speed the more severe the collision.

In addition, setting speed limiters at 105 km/h (65 mph) or less will reduce the operating costs of many transportation companies by reducing fuel consumption and increasing vehicle energy efficiency. For more information please visit www.mto.gov.on.ca/english/trucks/trucklimits.shtml

Primary Vehicle Controls

The **primary vehicle controls** do exactly what their name implies. They allow the driver to control the vehicle. Primary vehicle controls include the clutch pedal, transmission control, accelerator, steering wheel, and brake control. As a professional driver, you must not only know where these controls are found in the cab of a truck but also how to operate them **(see Figure 3-3).**

Clutch Pedal

To start the engine or to shift gears, you must use the **clutch pedal.** There are four basic pedal positions **(see Figure 3-4):**

1. **Disengaged**—the pedal is pushed within a few inches/centimeters of the floor. When the pedal is in this position, the engine and drive train are separated. The clutch must be disengaged to start the engine and/or to shift gears.

2. **Free play**—this is the amount of pedal movement possible without engaging or disengaging the clutch. It should be between 1/2 and 2-1/2 inches (1.3 to 6.4 cm). Free play is necessary in preventing excessive wear on the clutch.

© iofoto/www.Shutterstock.com

▶ **Figure 3-3**
Primary vehicle controls.

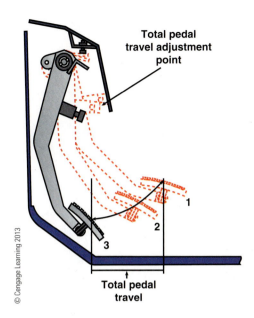

Total pedal travel adjustment point

Total pedal travel

© Cengage Learning 2013

▶ **Figure 3-4**

The three basic clutch pedal positions are (1) engaged, (2) free play, and (3) disengaged.

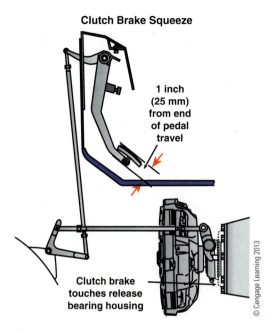

Clutch Brake Squeeze

1 inch (25 mm) from end of pedal travel

Clutch brake touches release bearing housing

© Cengage Learning 2013

▶ **Figure 3-5**

Mechanics of the clutch brake.

3. **Engaged**—the pedal is fully released. The driver is not applying any pressure. The word *engaged* means the engine and drive train are connected and moving together.

4. **Clutch brake**—most transmissions use a clutch brake to stop and control the speed of the transmission input shaft and countershaft. The clutch brake is used to engage only the first gear or the reverse gear when the vehicle is stopped. It works when the pedal is within 1 or 2 inches (2.5 to 5.1 cm) from the floor, depending on the adjustment (**see Figure 3-5**).

STOP!
If the clutch pedal is not operating properly, the transmission or drive train can be severely damaged.

Transmission Controls

Transmission controls vary, depending on the different types of transmissions. Some tractors have manual transmission with both a clutch and a gear lever. All gear changes are manually controlled by the driver.

Some tractors have semiautomatic transmissions, which include a clutch and gear lever, but some of the gear changes are controlled by an onboard computer. In recent years, more trucks are on the highway with fully automatic transmissions—with just a gear lever and no clutch. All gear changes are controlled by computers or by hydraulics on these vehicles.

Controls Found on a Manual Transmission Gear Lever. Typically, a range selector lever on the front of the gear lever allows you to switch between ranges. The lever is in the down position for the low range (usually the bottom four or five gears) and in the up position for the high range (the top four or five gears).

Splitter Valve. Some transmissions—like the 13-speed or 18-speed Eaton Fuller—use a **splitter valve** to split gears into overdrive (**see Figure 3-6**). This valve is controlled with a button on top of the gear shift knob.

Automatic Transmissions

More commercial motor vehicles today are equipped with automatic transmissions. Following are some basic suggestions for driving tractors or trucks with automatic transmissions. For the purposes of this instruction, the Eaton Fuller Automated Mechanical Transmission is used.

Proper Startup. To start a truck or tractor equipped with an automatic transmission, the following steps are suggested (**see Figure 3-7**):

1. Make sure the shifter is in neutral "**N**" and the parking brake is set.

2. Depress the clutch pedal and turn the ignition key to "on."

3. Wait for the service light on the shifter to go out and a solid "**N**" appears on the gear display.

4. Start the engine and let out the clutch pedal to register proper input speed. If the proper input speed is not registered, the engine will not shift into the initial starting gear.

5. Always return shifter to "**N**" before turning engine off (**see Figure 3-8**).

Selecting the Starting Gear. Once the engine has been properly started, the next step is to select the starting gear. The following steps are suggested:

1. Select "D," "H" for manual mode, or "L" for low mode.

2. Depress the clutch pedal. A solid number on the gear display indicates that the gear is fully engaged. If flashing down arrows appear on the gear display, this indicates the input shaft has not slowed enough to get into gear.

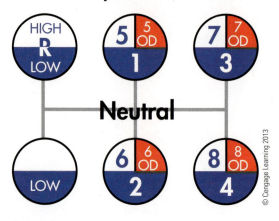

Controls and Operation of a 13-Speed Eaton Fuller

© Cengage Learning 2013

▶ **Figure 3-6**

Diagram of a manual transmission.

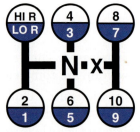

With the auto-range feature, the actual number of conventional lever shifts is half that of conventional ten-speeds. The range shift is triggered automatically at "X" location as the operator moves the lever toward the third rail.

When starting in first gear, preselect the next gear with the splitter button, release the throttle, and accelerate when you are in gear.

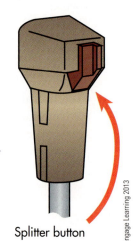

Splitter button

© Cengage Learning 2013

▶ **Figure 3-7**

Controls and operation of Eaton Fuller Super Ten.

▶ **Figure 3-8**

A driver's hand on the shifter.

Courtesy of Baker College of Flint

3. Continue to depress the clutch pedal until the arrows are off. If down arrows are off and the gear number continues to flash slowly, let up on the clutch pedal to fully engage the gear **(see Figure 3-9)**.

4. Depending on how your vehicle is programmed, you can select different starting gears while in "D" or "H" (manual) by using up and down buttons. Remember to choose the correct starting gear for your load and grade.

5. Let out the clutch.

Available Gears.
"H" Manual Mode

1. Can be selected while moving or from a stop.
2. Must use the up and down buttons to shift.
3. Shifter will "beep" if shift cannot be completed due to engine rpm and road speed.

"L" Low Mode

1. Can be selected while moving or from a stop.
2. Selecting "low" from a stop engages and maintains first gear.
3. Selecting "low" while moving will allow for downshifts only and downshifts will be performed at a higher rpm.

"R" Reverse Mode

1. Selecting "reverse" from "neutral" will engage "low reverse" and an "R" will appear on the gear display.
2. Transmission models with multiple reverses must use the up and down arrows to select other reverse gears. Remember to select the proper reverse gear for your load and grade condition.
3. All reverse gears can only be engaged at less than 2 mph (3 km/h).

Proper Shutdown Procedure.

1. Remember to depress the clutch when stopping the vehicle.
2. Before shutting the vehicle off, you must select "neutral" on the shifter and make sure a solid "N" is on the gear display.
3. Turn the key off, release the clutch pedal, and set the parking brake.

Courtesy of Lew Grill of the SAGE Schools

▶ Figure 3-9

A driver's foot on the clutch pedal to engage the gear.

CAUTION!

It is very important that you DO NOT shut the truck off or stall the engine while the transmission is in gear. This will cause the transmission to lock in gear and the engine will not restart.

TIP

Tips for Drivers—Automatic Transmissions

The following general suggestions are provided by Eaton Fuller regarding the Automated Mechanical Transmission:

1. The clutch is only needed at startup, when selecting a starting gear, and when stopping. "D," "H," or "L" can be selected at any speed.

2. When first starting the engine after changing loads, AutoShift needs to adapt to the changing conditions of the vehicle. If the transmission holds a gear while in "D," simply push the "up" button and the shift will be completed. This may have to be done several times before the transmission "remembers."

3. "H" should be used when you want to control the shifts, such as moving around the yard, going up a grade, or in poor traction situations.

4. "L" should be used anytime you want to maximize the engine brake, such as going down a long grade or when coming to a stop.

5. The service light will come on and go off during power-up (see Figure 3-10). If the service light comes on and stays on or comes on while you are driving, the transmission (Auto-Shift) has detected a fault in the system. Note the conditions when this occurs—hot/cold, wet/dry, on a grade/flat terrain—and get the vehicle to a service facility. Some faults prevent the transmission from shifting into other gears.

Courtesy of Don Hess

▶ Figure 3-10

If service light stays on after power-up, or while driving, get vehicle to a service facility.

Shifting Tips for Professional Drivers

■ Always select an initial starting gear that provides sufficient reduction for the load and terrain.

■ In order to shift from a higher starting gear to a lower starting gear, press the service brakes (e.g., "3," press brakes—3rd gear start).

■ For normal driving, place the shift lever in "D." You should not have to move the shift lever again unless driving conditions change **(see Figure 3-11).**

■ For manual control of upshifts, place lever in "3," "2," or "1." When upshift is desired, move gear selector to "D" and then back to "3," "2," or "1."

- Under severe conditions, for the best operation and increased transmission cooling when driving up a long, steep grade, move the gear selector to "3," "2," or "1" from "D." Select proper gear before starting uphill.

- To increase downshift points for optimal uphill driving, move the shift lever into "3," "2," or "1."

- Never coast with the gear shift lever in the neutral position.

- To inhibit upshifts during downhill driving and for optimal engine braking, move the gear selector to "3," "2," or "1." There will be no further upshifts, except to protect engine from overspeeding. The gear selector can be moved at any speed.

- For maximum downhill engine braking, move the gear selector to "1," depress the service brake, and operate the vehicle below 3 mph (5 km/h).

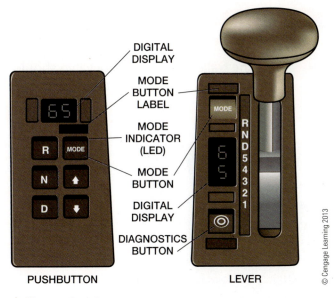

▶ **Figure 3-11**

For normal driving, place the shift lever in "D."

- When driving through adverse conditions, such as deep sand or mud, move the gear selector to "3," "2," or "1." To engage these gears while moving, the vehicle must be slowed to less than 3 mph (5 km/h).

- When parking the vehicle, move the shift lever to "N" and set the parking brake. If you stop on an incline, for safety reasons, block the wheels.

- There is a speed limit on reverse engagements, yet the driver can effectively rock the vehicle by moving the shift lever from reverse to drive and drive to reverse.

Other Controls

Fuel pedal—controls the amount of fuel entering the combustion chamber. Controls the vehicle's road speed (mph, km/h). Push the fuel pedal down to increase **speed** and ease off to reduce speed.

Steering wheel—used to determine direction of the rig. The steering wheel of a CMV is 6 to 12 inches (15.2 to 30.5 cm) larger across (diameter) than the steering wheel of a car. The larger size gives the turning leverage needed to control big rigs.

Three Types of Brake Controls

Air brake controls—used to slow or stop the rig. The air brake control system is complex and involves several separate controls.

Foot brake control valve—also called the foot valve, service brake or treadle valve—operates the service brakes on both the tractor and the trailer. When pushed in, it supplies air pressure to all tractor and trailer service brake chambers (**see Figure 3-12**).

Trailer brake control valve—also called the hand valve, trolley valve, or independent trailer brake—operates the service brakes on the trailer only and should only be used in special situations.

INTERESTING FACT

Truck air brakes were invented in the 1870s by George Westinghouse, who also invented railcar airbrakes. Air brakes are used on larger trucks to bring them to a stop when loaded heavily. Typical cars and other smaller vehicles use brakes that work by hydraulics. Hydraulic brake systems use compressed liquid in order to operate. Air brakes use compressed air, which is much more powerful, an aspect needed when stopping vehicles that are heavily loaded like tractor and trailers.

Courtesy of Lew Grill of the SAGE Schools

© Cengage Learning 2013

▶ **Figure 3-12**

Foot brake control.

▶ **Figure 3-13**

Trailer air supply valve.

INTERESTING FACT

By 1912, a number of higher-priced trucks were equipped with air brakes. The Sauer 6-1/2 ton was typical. Compressed air and gas or electric and explosive gas, were used for starting purposes.

Parking brake control valve—a yellow, diamond-shaped push-pull knob that allows the driver to engage the parking brake. The parking brake should be used only after the rig is stopped. It should ALWAYS be engaged before the driver turns off the engine and/or leaves the cab. If the driver fails to set the parking brake, the rig could roll, even on a level surface.

Trailer air supply valve—a red, octagonal-shaped button that, in the open position, supplies air to the trailer brakes. In the closed or pulled out position, it shuts off the air supply to the trailer. The trailer air supply value needs to be closed (pulled) when the tractor is not connected to a trailer (**see Figure 3-13**).

STOP!

NEVER use the trailer air supply valve as a parking brake. If you do so, loss of air will occur.

CAUTION!

When the air supply drops to 20 to 45 psi (138 to 310 kPa), the valve closes automatically. This stops the flow of air and protects the tractor's air supply. The trailer's air supply valve triggers the emergency relay valve that puts on the trailer brakes.

Trailer emergency relay valve—activates when the air supply is lost, as with severed air line(s) or diaphragm failure. The spring brake will remain locked/parked until the chambers are caged with a caging tool and/or air supply lines are replaced or repaired and the air supply is restored.

Air Brake Components

Air can be compressed—squeezed into a very small space. Therefore, the smaller the space, the more pressure (or resistance) air has. Heavy CMVs require a more complex and powerful braking system than ordinary cars or trucks and air brakes are used as a way to gather the power of compressed air to control the momentum of these vehicles, braking both the tractor wheels and the wheels of the trailers.

In an **air brake system,** this pressure is used to increase the braking force. The compressed air can multiply the force of mechanical braking many times.

The air brake system, which may be differently configured, depending on the manufacturer, is made up of several parts (**see Figure 3-14**):

- Compressor
- Brake chambers
- Drain cocks
- Treadle valve
- Tractor parking brake
- Quick-release valve

- Governor
- One-way check valves
- Air pressure gauge
- Independent trailer brake
- Glad hands
- Relay valve

- Air reservoirs
- Safety valves
- Low-pressure warning signal
- Air application pressure gauge
- Tractor protection system
- Emergency relay valve

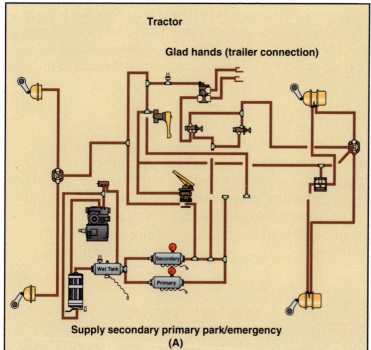
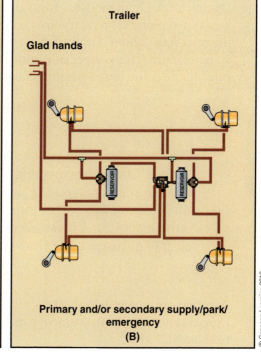

© Cengage Learning 2013

▶ Figure 3-14

(A) Schematic tractor's air brake system; (B) schematic of trailer's air brake system.

Descriptions of Air Brake Components

Compressor. Squeezes air into small space. This, in turn, increases the force the air exerts. Compressors may operate using belts and pulleys or shafts and gears, but they always are run by the engine. However, even though the compressor runs when the engine is running, it is not always pumping. The compressor pumps—or compresses—air until the pressure of the air in the reservoir reaches 125 pounds per square inch (psi) or 862 kilopascal (kPa). Then pumping stops until it is needed again.

Governor. Regulates the compressor to maintain desired pressure. As the pressure approaches its maximum (125 psi/862 kPa), the inlet valves are held open—and this releases air. When pressure drops below 100 psi (690 kPa), the governor closes the inlet valve to let the compressor build air pressure again.

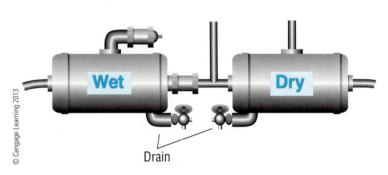

Drain

Figure 3-15

Air reservoirs hold the compressed air supply for the air brake system.

Air reservoirs. Hold the compressed air supply. There are three tanks: wet tank, dry tank, and trailer reservoir. The tank size varies, depending on how many tanks there are in the size of the brake chambers. The wet tank receives the hot, moist air from the compressor and delivers it to the dry tank. The trailer reservoir is near the trailer brake chambers. Compressed air held in this tank is ready for both normal and emergency use **(see Figure 3-15).**

One-way check valves. Prevents air from flowing back into the compressor from the reservoirs. When air flows back, the brakes will not work. This valve is located between the compressor and the wet tanks on the tractor. Two of the valves are used, the second one is located between the wet and dry tanks.

Safety valves. Keep the air pressure from rising to a dangerous level. There is one valve in each air tank that opens and releases air when pressure reaches 150 psi (1034 kPa). This lowers the pressure in the system.

Drain cocks. Drain moisture from air brake system reservoirs. When air is compressed, it becomes hot. When it reaches a reservoir, it cools, expands, and releases moisture. This moisture condenses in the reservoir—and if it is not removed, the moisture can cause rust or ice formation leading to system failure. This is especially critical during the winter months, as moisture will freeze in the line causing the entire brake system to fail.

STOP!

Drain moisture from your air brake system daily by driving your rig onto a level surface. Chock the wheels for safety. Allow all the air to escape from the system so the moisture can drain out. Drain the wet tank first to avoid drawing moisture further into the air system and other tanks. NOTE: Most trucks are equipped with air dryers to remove moisture. These also should be drained daily. If the moisture looks other than clear (e.g., rusty or oily), have the system checked by a qualified air brake mechanic.

Air pressure gauge. Tells you how much air pressure is in the system in "pounds per square inch." This gauge is found on the instrument panel. NOTE: Normal operating range is between 90 and 120 psi (621 and 827 kPa).

Low-pressure warning alarm. Tells you when the air pressure has dropped below 60 psi (414 kPa). A red warning light will turn on, a buzzer will sound, or both will happen. If one or both of these warning signals occurs, put on your brakes (you'll still have enough pressure). If you do not stop at once, you may lose more pressure, and the spring brakes will apply between 20 and 40 psi (138 and 276 kPa). The cause of the low air pressure must be identified and corrected before you continue your trip.

Air application pressure gauge. Shows the amount of air pressure being applied to the brakes. When the brakes are not in use, the gauge will read, "0 psi/kPa" **(see Figure 3-16).**

Treadle valve. Controls air that operates the brakes. The treadle valve is also called the "foot brake." The further down this pedal is pushed, the more air is sent into the system. Letting up on this pedal releases the brakes by letting the air exhaust from the brakes.

Independent trailer brake. Hand valve that regulates the airflow to the trailer unit only and puts on the brakes. It is often called the "trolley valve" and is normally on the right side of the steering column.

Glad hands. Connect the service and emergency air lines of the tractor to the trailer. These connections are secure when the glad hands lock. An O-ring seals the coupling to prevent air loss. Because it is important to keep the O-ring damage free, check for dirt and sand before connecting the air lines. When airlines are unhooked, they should be sealed to keep out dirt. Covers, protection plates, or dead-end (dummy) couplers may be used. They will keep the air lines from dropping down onto the driveshaft and being torn off. You will have much less risk of brake failure if you keep the air lines clean.

Quick-release valve. Makes up for brake lag on a long wheelbase vehicle. When you brake, the distance between the brake pedal and the brake chambers is a factor. The greater this distance, the longer it takes before the brakes are applied. This means the rear trailer brakes will not apply as soon as the tractor brakes. The relay valve speeds up the action of the trailer brakes.

Emergency brake valve. Relays air from the trailer air tank to the brake chambers. If there is a break in the lines between the tractor and trailer, the valve sends air from the trailer reservoir to the brake chambers. This is part of the emergency brake system and activates automatically. You can also put on the trailer brakes in an emergency with the cab-mounted emergency relay valve. The emergency relay valve also can help release the trailer brakes quickly.

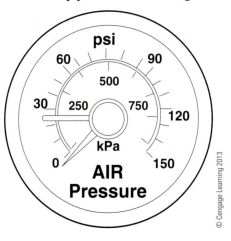

Air Application Gauge

▶ Figure 3-16

The air application gauge shows the amount of air pressure applied to the air brakes.

How Air Brakes Function

1. The brake pedal opens a valve that allows compressed air from a reservoir through air hoses to the front and rear tractor brake chambers, where a series of mechanical devices clamp the brake linings onto the brake drum, creating friction to slow the truck.

2. At the same time, air is sent to the tractor protection valve to the trailer brake chambers.

3. The air compressor pressurizes the air drawn from the reservoir.

4. The governor controls the pressure, releasing excess pressure through a safety valve.

5. A series of air pressure valves and brake valves control the precise amount of brake pressure, including the treadle valve (brake pedal) under the driver's foot.

6. When the brake pedal is released, air escapes to the foot valve, or relay valve, in the tractor into the quick release, or relay valve, in the trailer.

7. A heavy truck's foundation, or mechanical, brakes include such standard brake parts as drums and linings, along with a brake chamber that converts air pressure into braking force.

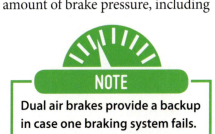
NOTE
Dual air brakes provide a backup in case one braking system fails.

Antilock Brake Systems (ABS)

An **antilock brake system (ABS)** is a safety system allowing the wheels on a motor vehicle to maintain traction with the road surface. This is directed by driver's steering inputs while braking, preventing the wheels from locking up (ceasing rotation) and, therefore, avoiding skidding or jackknifing and loss of vehicle stability, allowing the driver to maintain steering in panic stops **(see Figure 3-17).**

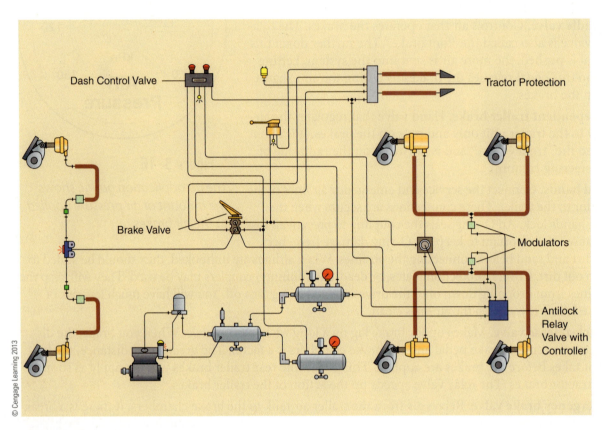

Dash Control Valve

Tractor Protection

Brake Valve

Modulators

Antilock Relay Valve with Controller

© Cengage Learning 2013

▶ **Figure 3-17**
Antilock brake system (ABS).

CAUTION!

An ABS generally improves vehicle control and decreases stopping distances on dry and slippery surfaces. However, on loose surfaces—like gravel or snow-covered pavement—an ABS can significantly increase braking distance, even though it still improves vehicle control.

Recent versions not only prevent wheel lock under braking, but also electronically control the front-to-rear brake bias. This function, depending on its specific capabilities and implementation, is known as electronic brake force distribution (EBD), traction control system, emergency brake assist, or electronic stability control (ESC).

ABS works because special sensors monitor wheel speed at a rate of 100 times per second. If the system detects that any wheel is over-braked for existing conditions, the electronic control unit signals a valve that will reduce braking forces at that wheel until the threat of a skid is eliminated.

FMCSA 393.55 addresses antilock brake systems on U.S. vehicles as follows:

a. **Hydraulic brake systems.** Each truck and bus manufactured on or after March 1, 1999 (except trucks and buses engaged in drive-away-tow-away operations), and equipped with a hydraulic brake system, shall be equipped with an antilock brake (ABS) system that meets the requirements of Federal Motor Vehicle Safety Standard (FMVSS) No. 105.

b. **ABS malfunction indicators for hydraulic braked vehicles.** Each hydraulic braked vehicle subject to the requirements of paragraph (a) of this section shall be equipped with an ABS malfunction indicator system that meets the requirements of FMVSS No. 105.

c. **Air brake systems.** (1) Each truck tractor manufactured on or after March 1, 1997 (except truck tractors engaged in drive-away/tow-away operations), shall be equipped with an antilock brake system that meets the requirements of FMVSS No. 121. (2) Each air-braked commercial motor vehicle other than a truck tractor, manufactured on or after March 1, 1998 (except commercial motor vehicles engaged in drive-away/tow-away operations), shall be equipped with an antilock brake system that meets the requirements of FMVSS No. 121. (a) for trucks and buses, S5.2.3 for semi-trailers, converter dollies and full trailers.

d. **ABS malfunction circuits and signals for air-braked vehicles.**

1. Each truck tractor manufactured on or after March 1, 1997, and each single-unit air-braked vehicle manufactured on or after March 1, 1998, subject to the requirements of paragraph (c) of this section, shall be equipped with an electrical circuit that is capable of signaling a malfunction that affects the generation or transmission of response or control signals to the vehicle's antilock brake system. (2) Each truck tractor manufactured on or after March 1, 2001, and each single-unit vehicle that is equipped to tow another air-braked vehicle, subject to the requirements of paragraph (c) of this section, shall be equipped with an electrical circuit that is capable of transmitting a malfunction signal from the antilock brake system(s) on the towed vehicle(s) to the trailer ABS malfunction lamp in the cab of the towing vehicle, and shall have the means for connection of the electrical circuit to the towed vehicle. The ABS malfunction circuit and signal shall meet the requirements of FMVSS No. 121. (3) Each semi-trailer, trailer converter dolly, and full trailer manufactured on or after March 1, 2001, and subject to the requirements of paragraph (c)(2) of this section, shall be equipped with an electrical circuit that is capable of signaling a malfunction in the trailer's antilock brake system, and shall have the means for connection of this ABS malfunction circuit to the towing vehicle.

In addition, each trailer manufactured on or after March 1, 2001, subject to the requirements of paragraph (c)(2) of this section, that is designed to tow another air-brake equipped trailer shall be capable of transmitting a malfunction signal from the antilock brake system(s) of the trailer(s) it tows to the vehicle in front of the trailer. The ABS malfunction circuit and signal shall meet the requirements of FMVSS No. 121.

e. **Exterior ABS malfunction indicator lamps for trailers.** Each trailer (including a trailer converter dolly) manufactured on or after March 1, 1998, and subject to the requirements of paragraph (c)(2) of this section, shall be equipped with an ABS malfunction indicator lamp which meets the requirements of FMVSS No. 121.

INTERESTING FACT

The ABS was first developed for aircraft use in 1929 by the French automobile and aircraft pioneer, Gabriel Voisin. These systems use a flywheel and valve attached to a hydraulic line that feeds the brake cylinders. The flywheel is attached to a drum that runs at the same speed as the wheel. In normal braking, the drum and flywheel should spin at the same speed. However, if a wheel were to slow down, then the drum would do the same, leaving the flywheel spinning at a faster rate. This causes the valve to open, allowing a small amount of brake fluid to bypass the master cylinder into a local reservoir, lowering the pressure on the cylinder and releasing the brakes. The use of the drum and flywheel meant the valve only opened when the wheel was turning. In testing, a 30 percent improvement in braking performance was noted, because the pilots immediately applied full brakes instead of slowly increasing pressure in order to find the skid point. An additional benefit was the elimination of burned or burst tires.

Components of ABS

There are four main components to an ABS: speed sensors, valves, a pump, and a controller (**see Figure 3-18**).

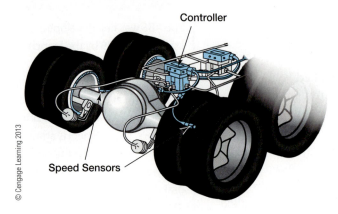

Controller

Speed Sensors

© Cengage Learning 2013

Figure 3-18

Basics of an ABS system.

Wheel speed sensors. The anti-lock braking system needs some way of knowing when a wheel is about to lock up. The speed sensors, located at each wheel—or in some cases in the differential, provide this information.

Valves. There is a valve in each brake's brake line controlled by the ABS. On some systems, the valve has three positions:

- In position one, the valve is open; pressure from the master cylinder is passed right through to the brake.
- In position two, the valve blocks the line, isolating that brake from the master cylinder. This prevents the pressure from rising further should the driver push the brake pedal harder.
- In position three, the valve releases some of the pressure from the brake.

Pump. Since the valve is able to release pressure from the brakes, the pump brings the pressure back up when a valve reduces pressure in a brake line.

Controller. The controller is an electronic stability control (ESC), which receives information from each individual wheel speed sensor. In a turn, if a wheel loses traction, the signal is sent to the controller and the controller will then limit the brake force and activate the ABS modulator, which turns the braking valves on and off.

TIP

Driving with ABS

1. With ABS, you do not have to brake any differently. If necessary, ABS automatically modulates braking while the driver maintains brake pressure.

2. Do not pump the brakes—ABS will control braking for you.

3. Even though your vehicle is equipped with ABS, you should avoid taking unnecessary risks. Be cautious and use good driving skills such as maintaining adequate distances between you and the driver ahead.

4. Use your mirrors to watch your trailer during emergency braking if your vehicle is equipped with ABS. Apply your brakes as necessary to keep your vehicle in line. Tractor ABS will help prevent jackknifing but it will not keep the trailer from swinging out of control.

5. Only if your trailer has ABS will you maintain control when applying your brakes as necessary, to keep your rig in your traffic lane. Trailer ABS will prevent trailer swing but it will not keep your tractor from jackknifing.

GO!

The most sophisticated systems have added two additional sensors to help the system work: a steering wheel angle sensor and a gyroscopic sensor. The theory of operation is simple: when the gyroscopic sensor detects that the direction taken by the vehicle does not coincide with what the steering wheel sensor reports, the ESC software will brake the necessary wheel(s), so that the vehicle goes the way the driver intends.

Engine Brakes and Retarders

Engine brakes and retarders slow the rig without using the service brake system. Their function is to keep the rig operating at a reasonable speed. Many towns and cities restrict the use of retarders because of the noise. There are four types of auxiliary brakes or retarders:

1. **Engine brake (see Figure 3-19)**—most widely used retarder. Operates by altering valve timing and turns the engine into an air compressor. The engine brake can be operated by hand with a switch on the dash or automatically when the foot is moved from the fuel pedal.

2. **Exhaust brake**—simplest form of retarder. Operates by keeping the exhaust gases from escaping. The exhaust brake builds up back pressure in the engine. It is manually controlled by an on/off switch in the cab. It is controlled automatically by a switch on the accelerator or clutch.

3. **Hydraulic retarder**—a type of drive line retarder that is mounted on the drive line between the engine and the flywheel or between the transmission and drive axles. The retarder can be turned on by hand with a lever in the cab or automatically engaged by an accelerator switch on the floor.

4. **Electric retarder**—uses electromagnets to slow the rotors attached to the drive train. It can be turned on or off by a switch in the cab.

> **Figure 3-19**
> *Engine brake.*

CAUTION!

The use of retarders are restricted in certain areas and are not allowed in populous areas.

Interaxle Differential Lock Control

Interaxle differential lock control (or power divider) locks and unlocks rear tandem axles. Unlocked, the axles turn independently of one another on a dry surface **(see Figure 3-20)**. In the locked position, power to the axles is equalized to help keep the wheels without traction from spinning. This position is used on slippery roads.

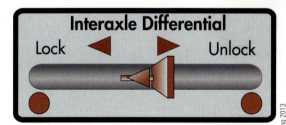

> **Figure 3-20**
> *Interaxle differential in the normal position.*

STOP!

The interaxle differential lock control should *never* be engaged or disengaged while wheels are spinning. The control should be locked before wheels begin to spin.

Secondary Vehicle Controls

Secondary vehicle controls do not affect the rig's power or movement, but play important roles in assisting with safety issues (**see Figure 3-21**).

- **Vision**

  Lights

  Windshield wipers

  Defroster

- **Communication**

  Horns

  Radio

  Lights (headlights, brake lights, four-way flashers)

- **Comfort**

  Seat position

  Air vents

  Air conditioner and heater

- **Safety**

  Seat belts

  Door locks

Other controls not related to driving include those for fifth-wheel lock assembly. Most of these controls are similar to those found in automobiles. Others are found only in tractor-trailer rigs. The number and function of the secondary controls may vary with the design of the truck or tractor.

▶ **Figure 3–21**

Secondary vehicle controls play an important role in driver safety.

GO!

Federal Motor Carrier Safety Regulation 392.16 Use of Seat Belts states:

A commercial motor vehicle that has a seat-belt assembly installed at the driver's seat shall not be driven unless the driver is properly restrained with it.

Seat Belts and Seat-Belt Laws in the United States

All CMV drivers must use a **seat-belt** assembly to be properly restrained when driving the vehicle (**see Figure 3-22**).

According to the National Highway Traffic Safety Administration (NHTSA), death and injury from traffic accidents continue to be among the most serious public health problems facing our country. Motor vehicle injuries constitute 99 percent of nonfatal transportation injuries and 94 percent of transportation deaths. In 2010 the National Highway Traffic Safety

▶ **Figure 3–22**

All CMV drivers must obey all seat-belt laws.

Administration reported the lowest number of motor vehicle related fatalities (32,788) in the United States since 1949. This decline can be attributed to increased seat-belt use along with better designed vehicles. In an effort to save lives, the first seat-belt laws were federal laws, passed in January 1968, requiring all vehicles, except buses, to be fitted with seat belts.

In 2010, more than 32,000 people were killed in vehicle crashes across the United States. Annually, approximately 5,000 of those victims are killed in crashes involving large trucks and 100,000 are injured. Although less than 20 percent of the fatalities in such crashes are occupants of the truck, the truck occupant is often killed in situations that may be preventable had the occupant been wearing a safety belt.

All trucks are now equipped with safety belts. Although they will not prevent accidents, safety belts have been found to often be the difference between life and death when accidents occur.

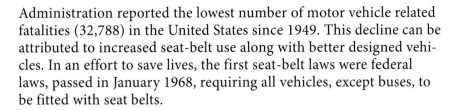

INTERESTING FACT

There are two types of seat-belt laws in the United States, primary and secondary. As of 2010, no federal seat-belt laws exist and individual state governments decide upon the laws. In 1998 Congress passed the Transportation Equity Act for the 21st Century (TEA-21) that contained grant money for states to start new seat-belt laws, child passenger protection, and traffic enforcement programs. All states except New Hampshire have a safety-belt law requiring adults to wear seat belts. Additionally, all 50 states have seat-belt laws requiring children to be in a safety restraint or belt.

SEAT BELTS AND SEAT-BELT LAWS IN CANADA

In 1989, the Council of Ministers Responsible for Transportation and Highway Safety began working to achieve a 95 percent seat-belt use rate by the end of 1995. In response, the CCMTA developed and implemented the National Occupant Restraint Program (NORP) in 1989. Since that time, according to a 2010 report, the number of unbelted, fatally/seriously injured vehicle occupants fell to 85.5 percent killed in 2007 and 76.4 injured during that same period.

A 2007 NORP study, involving 92,440 vehicles and 121,986 occupants in communities, with populations less than 10,000 and more than 1,000, found seat-belt usage totaled 93.1 percent, up from 91.1 percent. According to the same study, seat-belt usage rates at or above the Canadian national average (92.5%) were found in the provinces of Ontario (92.8%), Saskatchewan (93.5%), Prince Edward Island (97.9%), Québec (93%) and British Columbia (94.8%).

Fines for nonuse of seat belts vary across the provinces, ranging from a low of $60 to a maximum of $2,000.

VEHICLE INSTRUMENTS

Scanning the dashboard of a truck or tractor **(see Figure 3-23),** you will immediately notice a number of gauges and meters. These instruments keep you informed about the condition of your rig and its parts. They will also warn you of possible problems and may help avoid major difficulties.

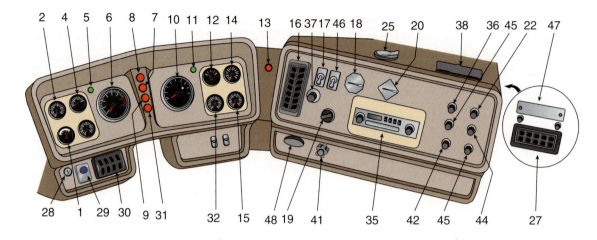

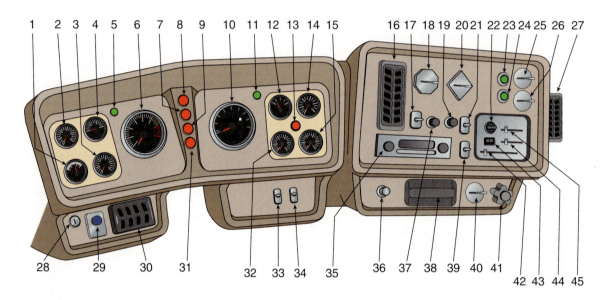

Figure 3–23

Vehicle instrument panel.

1. Battery voltmeter gauge	17. Headlight switch	33. Cargo lamp switch
2. Engine oil pressure gauge	18. Trailer air supply valve knob	34. Heated mirror switch
3. Optional component gauge	19. Wiper/washer control knob	35. Radio
4. Engine coolant temperature gauge	20. System park brake valve knob	36. Cigar lighter
5. Left-hand turn signal indicator	21. Spot light switch	37. Instrument panel rheostat switch
6. Engine tachometer gauge	22. Heater/AC blower motor knob	38. Ash tray
7. High temperature/low water indicator	23. Interdifferential differential indicator	39. Driving lamp switch
8. Headlight hi-beam indicator	24. Interwheel differential indicator	40. Air slide 5th wheel control lever
9. Low air pressure indicator	25. Interdifferential differential control lever	41. Hand throttle control knob
10. Speedometer gauge	26. Interwheel differential control lever	42. Panel, floor, defroster, control lever
11. Right-hand turn signal indicator	27. Heater/air conditioner diffuser	43. Air conditioner ON/OFF switch
12. Fuel gauge	28. Ignition key switch	44. Fresh/recirculating air control lever
13. Preheater indicator	29. Starter pushbutton	45. Heat/cold control lever
14. Dual air pressure gauge	30. Heater/air conditioner diffuser	46. Marker interrupter switch
15. Optional component gauge	31. Low oil pressure indicator	47. Radio power supply
16. Heater/air conditioner diffuser	32. Optional component gauge	48. Engine stop control knob

As you learn the skills of a professional driver, you will want to:

■ Understand the purpose and function of each instrument

■ Understand the information each instrument provides; for example, temperature and pressure gauges can indicate improper or unsafe operating conditions that may damage your rig

- Take action to correct a problem when you notice an improper reading on one or several gauges
- Know when your rig has reached the correct range of operation; for example, a professional driver will know the correct readings necessary for required air pressure, oil pressure, and water temperature

Each vehicle's instruments are divided into two categories:

- **Basic instruments**—to monitor the vehicle's various systems
- **Warning devices**—warning lights or audible signals that indicate when certain systems are malfunctioning or have reached a danger point

Basic Instruments

Speedometer—like that in an automobile, the speedometer in a truck or tractor displays road speed in miles per hour and kilometers per hour **(see Figure 3-24).**

Odometer—indicates how many miles the rig has been driven.

INTERESTING FACT

In 1913, 68 motor truck manufacturers fitted their vehicles with speed governors to limit speeds. Up until the 1950s, truck speeds rarely were capable of going more than 45 or 50 mph (72 or 80 km/h). The interstate highway system, constructed by the mid-1950s, was a major reason trucks began traveling at faster speeds.

▶ **Figure 3–24**
Speedometer.

Courtesy of Jennifer Pierson, Prime Inc.

GO!
FMCSR 393.82 requires that every bus, truck, and truck-tractor be equipped with a speedometer indicating vehicle speed in miles per hour (km/h), which shall be operative with reasonable accuracy.

Tachometer—displays engine speed in revolutions per minute (rpm). The tachometer, or tach, is a guide that indicates when to shift gears. It also assists the driver in using the engine and transmission effectively during acceleration and deceleration.

Fuel gauge—indicates how much fuel is in the fuel tanks. Since the gauge is not always accurate, the driver should check tanks visually before each trip and at all stops.

Voltmeter—measures voltage output of the battery. The meter needle should be between 13.0 and 14.5 volts during normal operation. Higher-than-normal voltage may cause damage or otherwise shorten a battery's life.

Ammeter—measures how much the battery is being charged or discharged. Under normal operating conditions, the ammeter should read as follows

Engine off—0

Engine starts—needle jumps to the charge side and flutters

Engine warmed—reading drops back to 0 or slightly on the charged side

A consistently high reading indicates the battery may be ready to fail. Continuous discharge means the battery is not receiving a charge from the alternator or generator.

A number of conditions may cause these abnormal readings:

- The voltage regulator is not working properly.
- A bare wire is causing a short circuit.
- The alternator is defective.
- There are loose or worn belts.

Air pressure gauge—the air brake system is activated by air pressure. The air pressure gauge indicates the amount of air pressure in the tanks. Air pressure should start building as soon as the engine starts and continue until the maximum pressure is reached, usually around 120 psi (827 kPa). In normal operation, when the air pressure drops to 90 psi (621 kPa), the air compressor will automatically build back to 120 psi (827 kPa). The air compressor governor controls the operation.

CAUTION!

If the air pressure drops to 60 psi (414 kPa) while driving, the low-pressure warning alarm light will turn on. At 20 to 45 psi (138 to 310 kPa), the tractor protection valve will close and shut off the air supply to the trailer. Shutting off air supply to the trailer triggers the emergency relay valve, which puts on the trailer's brakes.

Low air pressure can result from air leaks, failure of the compressor or compressor governor control, broken or kinked air lines, or an open air tank petcock.

STOP!

If you have a loss of air pressure, stop your rig at once. Locate the source of the problem and have it repaired immediately. Do not operate your rig without adequate air pressure!

Oil pressure gauge—indicates the oil pressure within the vehicle's lubrication system, in place to keep metal engine parts from overheating while protecting them from wear. If pressure is lost, some trucks have an automatic shutdown mechanism. Lost pressure means there is not enough lubrication in the system. If this continues, the engine can be destroyed within a very short period.

Oil pressure should register within seconds of ignition. It should then rise slowly to the normal operating range. "Normal range" will depend on the type of vehicle and the engine rpm.

INTERESTING FACT

Gulf Oil Company was the first petroleum company to distribute free road maps.

CAUTION!

You should stop and check the oil level if pressure does not register or if it fluctuates rapidly at ignition. You should also stop if a loss of pressure occurs. Causes of low oil pressure include lack of oil, oil leaks, and oil pump failure. If the oil level is adequate and there are no leaks, the problem may be the oil pump, a clogged oil line, or a filter.

Other Gauges

The number and types of gauges on a vehicle will vary. The only gauges required by law are the speedometer and the air pressure gauge.

Air brake application gauge—indicates in pounds per square inch (psi)/kilopascal (kPa) the amount of air pressure used when the brake pedal or the hand brake is applied. This gauge can also indicate the status of the vehicle's brake adjustment.

Coolant temperature gauge—shows the temperature of the coolant in the engine block. The cooling system protects engine parts against destruction from heat produced by the burning of fuel in the combustion chamber, rapid movement, and friction. The normal operating range is between 170 and 195°F (76.7 and 90.6°C) or the range specified for that particular vehicle.

STOP!

If the coolant temperature gauge registers above the normal range, the engine may be overheating. SHUT DOWN THE ENGINE AT ONCE! Overheating may be caused by (1) not enough engine oil, (2) loose or broken fan belt, (3) malfunctioning fan clutch or control, (4) a blocked radiator, (5) a broken thermostat, coolant pump, or radiator shutter, (6) a severe load—attempting to pull too much or too hard, or (7) the winter front may need to be removed. Remember! Low fluids, oil, or coolant may result in engine shutdown and possibly permanent damage to the engine.

Engine oil temperature gauge—indicates the temperature of the engine oil. Normal operating range is between 180 and 225°F (82.2 and 107.2°C), about 20 to 60 degrees higher than the coolant temperature. High oil temperature causes the oil to thin, which decreases oil pressure. Engine oil temperatures, however, can run as high as 250 to 265°F (121 to 129.4°C) for a short period without damaging the engine, but NEVER operate the engine above the safe operating range.

Exhaust pyrometer gauge—indicates the temperature of the gases in the exhaust manifold. If these gases become too hot, they can damage the turbocharger. Maximum safe operating temperatures may be indicated on the pyrometer name plate.

Gear box temperature gauge—indicates the temperature of the lubricant in the transmission. Normal readings range from 150 to 200°F (65.6 to 93.3°C). A high reading may indicate a low oil level.

Axle temperature gauge—indicates the temperature of the lubricant to the front and rear drive axles. Normal readings range from 150 to 200°F (65.6 to 93.3°C). This reading does not vary when the rig is loaded. Higher readings, up to a range between 230 and 250°F (110 to 121.1°C), are acceptable for short periods. Readings for both drive axles should be within 10 degrees of each other. Generally, the forward rear axle will run hotter than the rear axle.

CAUTION!

Axle temperature gauge readings above the normal range can mean bad bearings or a flat tire.

Warning Devices

Most commercial vehicles are equipped with warning lights and signals to indicate when the rig's fuel, air pressure, or operating temperature has reached a danger point. Some of these warning signals are built into the dash of the tractor. They will signal when there is a problem. When a warning signal occurs, immediately stop the rig **(see Figure 3-25)**.

You should become familiar with the following warning devices:

- **Low air pressure warning alarm**—audible or lighted signal when there is low pressure in the air brake system.

- **ABS warning lamp for trucks and tractors**—usually located on the dashboard or instrument cluster, the warning lamp will come on during the bulb check at vehicle ignition and then will turn off if the warning lamp is functioning properly. If the lamp remains on during vehicle operation, this may signal that ABS is not operating. If ABS is not operating, the vehicle will retain normal braking but without the benefits of ABS.

- **ABS warning lamp for trailers**—usually located on the "road side" near the rear of the trailer, the ABS warning lamp is amber.

- **Automatic traction control (ATC) warning lamp**—will come on at vehicle ignition and will remain on until brake pedal is applied. The lamp will turn off and remain off until a low traction event is encountered. If the vehicle's drive wheels lose traction during acceleration, the ATC lamp will turn on and begin flashing rapidly. The ATC lamp will also flash rapidly when ATC is functioning to assist the driver in accelerating the vehicle.

- **Coolant level alarm**—lights when the coolant level starts dropping, indicating a possible leak.

- **Oil level alarm**—lights when the oil level becomes too low for normal, safe operation.

▶ **Figure 3-25**

Warning lights indicate potential problems.

- **Coolant temperature warning**—lights when the operating temperature is too high for safe operation.
- **Pyrometer warning**—lights when exhaust temperatures are too high.
- **Differential warning**—flashes when the interaxle differential is in the locked position.

STOP!

No matter how well you can read and work with your vehicle's instruments, remember: instruments are not always accurate. Be aware that instruments can malfunction. Readings may not be accurate. Know when it's best to pull over rather than keep going without adequate information to drive your rig safely.

SUMMARY

In this chapter, you were introduced to the control systems, secondary systems, and warning devices for your rig. You now know what the gauges should read for safe operation. As a professional driver with safety as a personal priority, you understand the importance of using a seat belt at all times. Warning devices were also reviewed in this chapter, as was the need to pay immediate attention to any warning lights or signals from these monitors.

INTERESTING FACT

In 1913, a severe driver shortage—the first of many to plague the truck transportation industry in North America—developed, due to inexperience or a shortage of people with driving skills. Adding to this problem was that skilled drivers often lacked mechanical knowledge of their vehicles. This increased the costs of maintaining the equipment.

KEY TERMS

Air brake application gauge
Air brake system
Air pressure gauge
Ammeter
Antilock brake system (ABS)
Axle temperature gauge
Brake controls
Clutch brake
Clutch pedal
Computerized idle timer
Coolant level alarm
Coolant temperature gauge
Coolant temperature warning
Cruise control
Differential warning
Electric retarder
Emergency engine stop control
Engine brake
Engine controls

Engine oil temperature gauge
Engine stop control knob
Exhaust brake
Exhaust pyrometer gauge
Foot brake control valve
Fuel gauge
Fuel pedal
Gear box temperature gauge
Hydraulic retarder
Interaxle differential lock control
Low air pressure warning alarm
Odometer
Oil level alarm
Oil pressure gauge
Parking brake control valve
Primary vehicle controls
Pyrometer warning
Seat belt
Secondary vehicle controls

Speed
Speedometer
Splitter valve
Starter button
Seat belt
Steering wheel
Tachometer
Trailer air supply valve
Trailer brake control valve
Trailer emergency relay valve
Transmission control
Voltmeter

A DAY IN THE LIFE...

Robert Penner – Bison Transport Inc., Vice President

My name is Robert Penner and I am currently the Executive Vice President and Chief Operating Officer of Bison Transport Inc. I "happened" into the trucking industry in 1984 at the age of 19. I remember my first day like it was yesterday . . . I was thrown the keys to a 1971 two-stick Mack and literally told to figure it out. I received a 15-minute tutorial in the driver's seat of the truck and left to my own devices. Having spent a lot of time on the farm growing up, I was used to the "figure it out" learning environment and I enjoyed the challenge and the sense of accomplishment. I found learning to drive the truck and maneuvering about was actually easy for me and I remember thinking to myself, this was going to be a pretty easy and fun job—I got one of the two right, and it wasn't the "easy" part!

> ## "There is a big difference between being able to drive a truck and being a truck driver . . ."

There is a big difference between being able to drive a truck and being a truck driver, and I found that out the hard way. I spent seven years on the road running regional and long haul and I can't tell you how many times I encountered an issue or learned something new and said to myself, "Boy, I wish I knew that before right now!" I never understood how a business like trucking, which is critically dependent on drivers and would entrust them with hundreds of thousands of dollars worth of equipment and liability, would be too busy to invest any time or energy into teaching someone what to do and how to do it. This has stuck with me my entire career.

I moved into dispatch in 1991, just as our company embarked on an aggressive growth strategy. In five short years we grew from 18 trucks to almost 400, and although those were extremely challenging times, I consider myself extremely fortunate to have experienced this. We were a small company transitioning to big business and in the process I was able to touch and learn all aspects of our trucking operations. As our company grew, so did my opportunities and responsibilities. I have never forgotten where I came from and how difficult it was to "break into the business." I try to stay on top of things that are changing and remain focused on making things better for others. My background as a driver makes it easy to relate to our drivers and to collaborate with them to build a better company. I am active on our Driver Advisory Board and I still make time to meet and deal with drivers every single day. I have also learned that in order to look after our drivers, we have to hire and train the best people and give them a true understanding of the support we need to provide our fleet. What I have not been able to glean from the generosity and patience of people working within our industry, I have supplemented with formal education. Today I am responsible for all aspects of our operation, overseeing our Dispatch and Operations, Equipment and Maintenance, Systems and Technology, Safety, Driver Development, and Human Resources. This is a fascinating and exciting industry and I cannot imagine what else I would be doing with my life. This is not about trucks, it is about people—and the only thing you really need to know is what you don't know and where to go for help. What I like most about this industry is that it is full of kind and generous people that are passionate about their careers and eager to help make a difference!

REVIEW QUESTIONS

1. Which of the following is not an element of the primary vehicle control system?

   a. clutch pedal

   b. seatbelt

   c. transmission control

   d. steering wheel

2. Which of the following is not a part of the engine control system?

   a. engine control switch

   b. starter button

   c. emergency engine stop control

   d. clutch pedal

3. Canada's speed limiter ruling for Ontario and Québec mandates a speed limiter on heavy trucks, whether originating in Canada or elsewhere, set at _____.

   a. 121 km/h/75 mph

   b. 100 km/h/62 mph

   c. 105 km/h/65 mph

   d. 110 km/h/68 mph

4. Which of the following is not an accurate statement regarding the clutch brake?

   a. It stops or controls the speed of the transmission input shaft and countershaft.

   b. It is used to engage only the first gear or the reverse gear when the vehicle is stopped.

   c. The clutch brake is used in emergency situations to stop the vehicle.

   d. It works when the pedal is within 1 or 2 inches (2.5 or 5.1 cm) of the floor, depending on its adjustments.

5. For a tractor with a manual transmission, the gear changes are controlled by _____.

   a. manual positioning

   b. hydraulics

   c. treadle positioning

   d. an onboard computer

6. Which of the following is not a correct statement regarding the trailer supply valve?

   a. In the open position it provides air to the trailer brakes.

   b. In the closed position it shuts off the air supply to the trailer.

   c. It is to be closed when there is no trailer.

   d. It is a safe procedure to use this valve to activate the parking brakes.

7. Which of the following slows the rig by altering the valve timing, which turns the engine into an air compressor?

   a. engine brake

   b. exhaust brake

   c. hydraulic retarders

   d. electric retarders

8. When the air supply to the trailer is lost, _____.

   a. the vehicle may safely be driven to a service center

   b. the trailer emergency relay valve is activated

   c. the driver may safely complete the assigned trip without repairs

   d. the driver should make repairs and continue the assigned trip

9. The interaxle differential lock control _____.

   a. is used to equalize power to the axles to help keep the wheels without traction from spinning

   b. is used to lock the rear wheels so an unauthorized person cannot drive the vehicle

   c. should be activated after the wheels start spinning

   d. should only be used at high speeds on interstate highways

10. The trailer brake control valve, also known as the independent trailer brake, _____.

    a. should be used to hold the rig when parked

    b. is to be used when stopping at stop signs and traffic lights

    c. operates the service brakes on the trailer only

    d. is located outside of the cab, near the front of the fifth wheel, and indicates when the trailer brakes are activated

11. Regarding the gauges and meters on a tractor dashboard, which of the following is not a true statement?

    a. It is important for a professional driver to understand the function and purpose of each gauge and instrument.

    b. It is important for a professional driver to understand the information each instrument provides.

    c. It is important for a professional driver to take action to correct a problem when an improper reading is registered on one or several of the gauges.

    d. Since modern tractors have computers to monitor all systems, it is not important for a driver to check the gauges and meters of the vehicle after the trip starts.

12. Which of the following gauges are not required by law?

    a. fuel and tachometer   c. ammeter and oil pressure

    b. odometer and voltmeter   d. speedometer and air pressure gauge

13. Regarding the air pressure gauge, which of the following is a correct statement?

    a. It indicates the amount of pressure in the tires of the drive wheels.

    b. It indicates the amount of pressure in the tanks.

    c. It indicates the average of the amount of pressure in the trailer wheels.

    d. It indicates the speed of the wind the rig is heading into.

14. While you are driving, if the air pressure drops below _____ psi/kPa, the air pressure warning alarm will activate.

    a. 70/483   c. 60/414

    b. 88/607   d. 65/448

15. In Canada, fines for nonuse of seat belts can range from _____.

    a. $100 to $1,000   c. $500 to $5,000

    b. $60 to $2,000   d. $1,000 to $2,000

16. If the coolant temperature gauge registers above the normal range, the driver should _____.

    a. shut down the engine at once

    b. reduce the speed of the vehicle and continue trip

    c. reduce the speed of the vehicle and drive to the nearest repair facility

    d. increase the speed of the vehicle to force more air through the radiator to cool the engine

SUPPLEMENTAL LEARNING ACTIVITIES

1. Visit a nearby truck stop and drive through the parking lot, noticing the exterior condition of carriers or independent truckers. Which appear to be well-kept? Which appear to have layers of road grime? What, in your estimation, is the relationship between a clean, outwardly well-kept vehicle and the safety of that vehicle—or is there a relationship? Write what you see in a 100-word report.

2. In a small group, discuss the importance of knowing the mechanics behind your vehicle's systems. Name three scenarios in which knowledge of mechanical systems and their functions would contribute to your safety and that of your rig and your cargo, save time, or save money. Bring your ideas to the class.

3. In a 100-word report, discuss the impact of high fuel prices on the transportation industry and what drivers, in your opinion, can do to soften the impact of high fuel prices.

4. Many states in the United States and some provinces in Canada have laws or initiatives regarding engine idling. What, in your opinion, are the main issues of engine idling? Discuss in your small group and report to the class.

5. Antilock braking systems first appeared on railcars. As a group, list the advantages of ABS and report to the class.

FOR MORE INFORMATION

Professional Truck Driver Institute Standards
www.ptdi.org/standards/index.aspx

PTDI—Read and Interpret Control Systems, Page 7, Click on Skills Standards
www.ptdi.org/standards

4

Vehicle Systems

© risteski goce/www.Shutterstock.com

OBJECTIVES

When you have completed this chapter, you should be able to:

- Expand your understanding of, and the vocabulary required for, the various vehicle systems.

- Describe and explain the function and relationships between vehicle systems.

- Locate and explain how the frame, axles, wheels and their parts, engine, drivetrain, and brakes operate.

- Understand the function of roll stability systems and how it impacts rig performance.

- Understand the relationships of the previously discussed systems.

INTRODUCTION

A tractor-trailer rig is made up of multiple systems, and while each of these systems and their individual parts perform unique and specific jobs, they must all work together—much like the organs and systems of the human body work together in a healthy human being **(see Figure 4-1).**

As an example, if a tractor is to work efficiently and effectively, each of its systems must work individually and as a group in order for the tractor to pull its cargo down the road **(see Figure 4-2).**

With the addition of electronics to some of the tractor-trailer rig's systems, the systems must work efficiently and effectively both as a group and individually to provide a more comfortable ride, easier operation, and safer transit for the driver, the rig, and its cargo.

This chapter will explore each of these parts and systems and will discuss:

- The reason for each of the rig's systems
- The function of the major parts of each system
- The relationship of each system to safe and economical operation

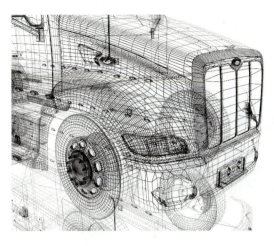

▶ **Figure 4-1**

A tractor-trailer is made up of many parts and systems.

© ArchMan/www.Shutterstock.com

FRAME, SUSPENSION SYSTEMS, AND AXLES

Frame

The **frame** is the infrastructure around which the rest of the rig is assembled. It is the backbone, so to speak, of the truck tractor and many trailers. Engine mounts are attached to the frame and hold the engine in place. The body of the tractor is connected to and strengthened by the frame. The frame supports the suspension system, which in turn supports the axles.

The frame consists of two steel rails and cross members that run the entire length of the vehicle **(see Figure 4-3).** Lightweight tractors have aluminum rails. Tractors that haul oversized or overweight loads usually

▶ **Figure 4-2**

The various systems on a tractor-trailer must work together to perform effectively.

© Cengage Learning 2013

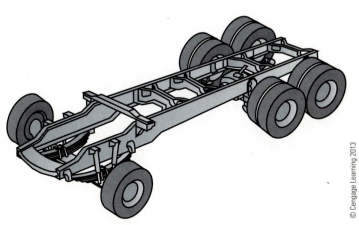

▶ **Figure 4-3**

The frame includes two steel rails that run the length of the vehicle.

© Cengage Learning 2013

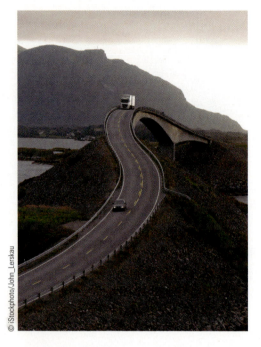

have extra-strength steel rails. Cross members connect the two rails and provide strength and support to the frame. Directly or indirectly, the frame is connected to every other system of the tractor.

Suspension System

The **suspension system** supports, distributes, and carries the weight of the truck. This system is made up of springs and spring hangers. The front and rear axles are attached to it and the frame rests on it. As the ground changes, this system allows the axles to move up and down, independently, without seriously affecting the cargo. By securing the suspension system at several points along the frame, the stress and shocks from the road can be evenly distributed **(see Figure 4-4).**

▶ **Figure 4-4**

A good suspension system supports the load and transmits full engine and braking power to the chassis frame.

A good suspension system should be able to support the load as well as the chassis frame. It should hold the axles securely to ensure correct driveline alignment and should cushion the ride for the driver and cargo, whether the trailer is empty or loaded.

The two types of suspension systems are spring leaf suspension and air bag suspension systems. **Spring leaf suspension** systems consist of narrow metal strips of varying lengths that are bolted together and attached to frame hangers. Heavy-duty systems commonly use the "stack" or "multileaf" spring. Tapered leaf springs are used for lighter weight, tandem axle vehicles. The **air bag suspension** system uses bags of air placed between the axle and the frame. Widely used on trailers, air bag suspension is also used on truck tractors, in which air pressure comes from the tractor's **air compressor.** Some systems have valves, allowing the driver to adjust air pressure for specific loads. Frame height can also be changed for different loads.

NOTE

Many vehicles use a combination of the spring and air bag suspension systems.

Shock absorbers reduce the motion of the vehicle body as the wheels move over uneven surfaces **(see Figure 4-5).** A shock absorber operates like a piston in a cylinder with a hole in it. Since liquid is almost impossible to compress, liquid is forced through the tiny hole as the shock is compressed. The liquid resists the pressure and smoothes out the ride.

An electronically controlled air suspension system (ECAS) is usually compatible with both the antilock braking system and automatic **traction** system.

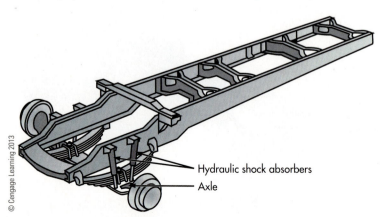

Hydraulic shock absorbers
Axle

▶ **Figure 4-5**

Shock absorbers reduce the motion of the vehicle as the wheels move over uneven surfaces.

The ECAS maintains an accurate leveling of chassis height through the use of the sensor, **electronic control unit (ECU)**, and a solenoid valve. The ECU uses sensor information to determine vehicle chassis height. If the height needs to be adjusted, the ECU controls pressure within the airbags by actuating a solenoid valve. In this way, the ECAS is able to quickly adjust chassis height to a predetermined normal level. This automatic function can occur while the vehicle is in motion or stable.

The ECU also provides ECAS with self-diagnostic and reprogramming capabilities. Detected component or system failures are stored in the ECU's memory and can be retrieved using a diagnostic controller that allows the setting of preset normal, upper, and lower levels as well as other parameters **(see Figure 4-6)**.

NOTE

Traction is defined as "The act of drawing or pulling, especially the drawing of a vehicle or load over a surface by motor power, pulling power, as of an engine and adhesive friction, such as a tire on a road.

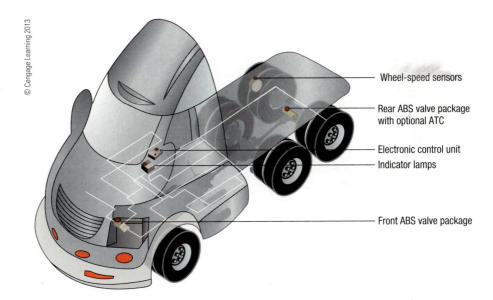

Wheel-speed sensors

Rear ABS valve package with optional ATC

Electronic control unit

Indicator lamps

Front ABS valve package

© Cengage Learning 2013

▶ **Figure 4-6**

Electronically controlled air suspension system (ECAS).

Air Springs

Air springs for trucks and trailers protect cargo, provide constant level hauling, and deliver long, trouble-free service. They also offer a quiet, cushioned ride that makes for better protection from shock and vibration for the cargo and less fatigue for the driver. Also, because there's less vibration, truck, trailer, and bus bodies last longer than with steel springs **(see Figure 4-7)**.

Features

- Improves vibration damping in both loaded and unloaded conditions
- Broadens types of loads available for transport, including electronic equipment where air suspensions are required by the shipper
- Protects hinges, lights, rivets, and all vehicle hardware

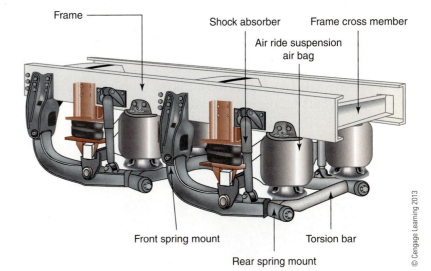

Frame

Shock absorber

Frame cross member

Air ride suspension air bag

Front spring mount

Rear spring mount

Torsion bar

© Cengage Learning 2013

▶ **Figure 4-7**

Air springs.

- Provides greater degree of durability and longer warranty periods from suspension manufacturers
- Increases need for greater axle excursion
- Increases load capacities being transported

Axles

Axles connect the wheel to the rest of the tractor-trailer and support the weight of the vehicle and its cargo. While all axles support the weight of the vehicle, different types of axles perform special functions:

Front tractor axle—connects the steering mechanism and the brakes.

Rear tractor axle—the power or drive axle. This axle transfers power from the engine and drivetrain to the wheels.

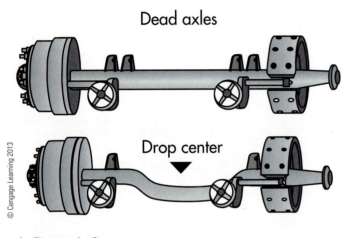

© Cengage Learning 2013

▶ **Figure 4-8**

The drop-center axle design allows space for the driveshaft.

Along with trailer axles, the tractor axle also serves as a connecting point for the brakes. All axles are either dead or live.

A **dead axle** is not powered. It receives or houses the wheel, supports vehicle weight, and provides a place to connect the steering mechanism and brake components. Most dead axles are straight but some have a drop-center design that allows space for the driveshaft **(see Figure 4-8)**. Some are I-beam construction, whereas others consist of a hollow tube or box. Examples of dead axles include **ordinary trailer axles, converter dolly axles, multiple axle assembly, lift axle, variable load suspension (VLS) axles,** and **sliding tandems.**

The main task of the dead axle can be described in one word: *weight*. A tractor-trailer truck can legally "scale" more weight on a set of tandem axles, compared to a single-drive axle. In addition, a dead axle does not weigh as much as a live axle, and therefore allows the rig to haul more freight.

CAUTION!

Dead axles are not common, and, in fact, most professional drivers prefer other drive train configurations. Why? Because when a rig gets mired in the mud or snow, it is much easier to recover it with two drive axles than with a single axle.

The **live axle (see Figure 4-9),** since it is powered, supports the vehicle's weight and sends power to the wheels. Because the live axle is hollow, the gears and axles can transmit through this space to the wheels.

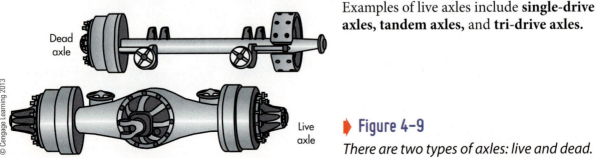

Examples of live axles include **single-drive axles, tandem axles,** and **tri-drive axles.**

© Cengage Learning 2013

▶ **Figure 4-9**

There are two types of axles: live and dead.

ENGINES

The engine provides the tractor's power and there are many types of engines. Those who want to know in depth about engines and how they work should take a mechanic's training course; however, all professional drivers should know something about how engines operate and the types of engines commonly used in truck transportation **(see Figure 4-10).**

Engines are fueled by diesel fuel or gasoline. Engines used in truck tractors are **internal combustion engines,** which means the engine burns fuel inside closed chambers. These chambers are called *cylinders* and serve as the "heart" of the engine. These cylinders are where the engine's power is generated to turn the wheels that run the tractor and pull the trailer.

Engine Location

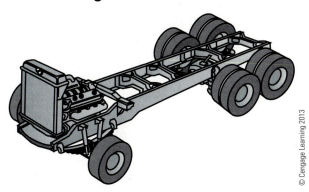

▶ **Figure 4-10**

Engines come in many types to perform various tasks.

Figure 4-11 shows a four-stroke gasoline engine. Key parts of the engine include the **crankshaft,** one or more **camshafts** (magenta and blue), and **valves.** There are one or more **cylinders** (grey and green), and for each cylinder there is a **spark plug** (darker grey), **a piston** (yellow), and a **crank** (purple). A single sweep of the cylinder by the piston in an upward or downward motion is known as a stroke, and the downward stroke that occurs directly after the air–fuel mix in the cylinder is ignited is known as a power stroke. The four phases of operation (intake, compression, power, exhaust) take place in separate locations.

The **engine block** is a large block of steel with holes, or cylinders, drilled through it. Think of a cylinder as a coffee can. One end of the can is sealed shut. The other end is open. A piston fits snugly against the cylinder wall, but it can move up and down. When fuel burns within the cylinder (**combustion**), it creates the expansion that forcefully moves the piston. A rod attached to the piston moves with it. Since the rod is connected to a crank, it turns the crank. The up-and-down movement of the piston is converted into the circular motion of the crankshaft. This circular, or rotary, motion is the force that moves the wheels, which in turn move the vehicle.

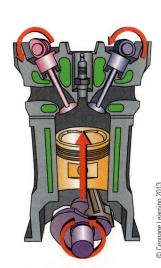

▶ **Figure 4-11**

A typical four-stroke engine.

Fuel alone will not power an internal combustion engine. In the case of the **diesel engine,** fuel injectors rather than carburetors, such as those found in automobiles, supply fuel to the cylinders, and the air that causes combustion is supplied by an **air intake system.** The extreme compression of the fuel and air mixture in the cylinder by the piston squeezes it so much that the diesel fuel ignites. Once the fuel has burned, it is forced out of the cylinder through exhaust valves and manifolds.

COMPUTER MANAGEMENT SYSTEMS

Today, all new medium- and heavy-duty truck systems are managed by computer. Electronically managed engines cost more than their hydromechanical counterparts but last much longer, make vehicles easier to drive, require less maintenance, and produce much better fuel mileage.

Within a 10-year period (between 1987 and 1997), truck engine management systems sold in North America went from almost 100 percent hydromechanical management to almost 100 percent management by electronics.

The Environmental Protection Agency emission requirements, which triggered the introduction of computerized engine controllers and have driven their evolution, have brought additional benefits of fuel economy and much greater engine longevity.

Most tractors now use computers to manage engine and other system functions. These functions are cybernetically controlled. **Cybernetics** is the science of computer control systems that send messages to the systems they control and report degree of functioning to the driver.

Onboard vehicle computers are referred to as engine/electronic control modules (ECM) or electronic/engine control units (ECU). These computers normally contain a microprocessor, data retention media and, usually, the output or switching apparatus.

With the widespread use of electronics in vehicle systems, current systems can be read by most electronic service tools, which makes diagnostic and servicing procedures much more efficient.

Thanks to computerized electronics, any truck engine management system can be programmed to the preferences of the owner regarding governors, cruise control, road speed limit, critical shutdown sensors, peak braking power, idle speed, and other options.

Management systems for current vehicle systems tend to be classified by the degree of control they have over the fueling pulse. **Full authority systems** use electronic fuel injectors or electronic unit pumps. The term *full authority* indicates that the electronic engine control unit has full control of the fueling pulse.

Even with the continued advancements of new technology, it's not time to hang up your tool belt just yet.

© Cengage Learning 2013

Partial authority systems are ECM-managed systems in which an existing hydromechanical fueling apparatus has been adapted for computerized control. These are rapidly becoming obsolete and are not used in new systems.

FUEL SYSTEM

The **fuel system** sends fuel to the engine. In newer models, fuel management is handled by computerized elements of the system. Computers also regulate the amount of fuel in the system and how much is injected into the cylinders.

The pump moves the fuel from the tank through the filtering system and into the injector. Usually the pump delivers more fuel than is needed, so a pipe returns the extra fuel to the tank.

Just before the fuel reaches the injector, a filter cleans it. Even a small speck of debris or dirt can ruin an injector, so the fuel can never be too clean. Because foreign matter, such as debris or dirt, can cause much damage to the engine and its operation, there is often another filter between the tank and the pump.

The computer figures the right amount of fuel and injects it into the cylinder at exactly the right time and at the right pressure. The amount of fuel needed varies because of power needs. Because most engines are now computerized, their power and the amount of fuel used is optimized and much more efficient than older models.

Fuel Tanks

The **fuel tanks** are containers designed to hold the truck's fuel. Most larger trucks have two fuel tanks, strapped to each side of the frame.

Fuel tanks are vented to maintain equal pressure on the inside and outside. The vent hole is usually in the filler pipe cap or at the top of the tank.

The fuel cap area must be kept clean at all times. The fuel filler cap and the neck of the tank should be completely clean before removing the cap. This will keep dirt and other foreign particulates out of the fuel system.

If the tank is under the chassis, use *great care* when cleaning the cap to keep dirt from getting into the fuel system.

Fuel Filters

Filters in the fuel system, **fuel filters,** clean the fuel as it goes from the entry tube of the tank, through the tank and fuel lines, and into the fuel injectors. A coarse filter is the first dirt block; a finer filter is next; finally, a filter/water separator protects the injector jets and engine from water, rust, and other contaminants.

CAUTION!

This final filter—a filter/water separator—is the most important one to remember in the fuel system, because water can seriously harm the fuel system by encouraging rust and corrosion.

Fuel System Heaters

Trucks driven in cold weather should have **fuel system heaters.** The three types of fuel system heaters available are:

1. Units that heat the fuel in the tank
2. Inline heaters that heat the fuel when it is going from the tank to the injector system
3. Filter heaters that heat the fuel filters which, in turn, heat the fuel as it passes through the injection system

When a truck is driven in severely cold weather, all three types of fuel system heaters may be needed. Chemical additives can also be used to prevent the fuel from gelling and to keep wax crystals from forming. As the temperature drops, gelling can occur while driving, causing your unit to stall. It is important to know forecast temperature on your route at least 24 hours in advance so you can plan appropriately. Some chemicals even clean the injectors and improve the fuel.

Diesel Fuel

Diesel fuel offers the following advantages over gasoline. It has a low vaporizing rate and does not create an explosive air–fuel mixture when it is accidentally spilled or leaked. This is an important factor when hauling highly volatile fluids or explosives.

The "cetane number" of diesel fuel indicates the quality of the fuel, showing the amount of time needed for the fuel to ignite the hot air in the combustion chamber of the cylinder. Cetane numbers generally range from 30 to 60. The higher the number, the faster the fuel will ignite.

If the cetane number is too low, the engine will be difficult to start. There may be "knocking" and puffs of white smoke from the exhaust. If it continues, harmful deposits can collect in the cylinders.

A negative characteristic of diesel fuel is that it creates wax crystals in cold weather. These crystals make starting and operating the engine difficult. In the high-tech market of fuel additives, however, new products are now available that provide the following advantages:

- Reduce fuel consumption
- Prevent diesel fuel from gelling in extremely cold temperatures
- Reduce engine maintenance costs and increase the life of a diesel engine
- Reduce fuel emissions, particulates, and exhaust smoke released into the atmosphere from diesel engines

AIR INTAKE AND EXHAUST SYSTEMS

The air intake and exhaust systems ensure that the engine has enough fresh air to process so that the tractor runs properly. The importance of these systems cannot be overstressed. Fresh air is needed constantly in the engine's air supply system **(see Figure 4-12).**

Function of Air Intake and Exhaust System Parts

The air intake system delivers fresh air to the cylinders and an air cleaner removes dirt, dust, and water from the fresh air. Clean air flows into the intake manifold (a pipe with an equal number of outlets and cylinders). Each outlet from the manifold is an intake port for a cylinder. Valves regulate the flow of air into the cylinders. Keep the air cleaner clean so it can function at its best. In dusty or rainy weather, check the air cleaners daily.

Air Intake System

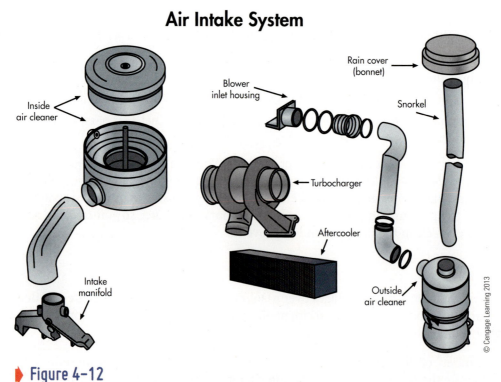

▶ **Figure 4-12**

Fresh air is vital for use in the engine's air supply system.

After combustion occurs in the engine, the **exhaust system** expels used gases. Exhaust valves open in each cylinder. A stroke of the piston expels the used gases through ports in the exhaust manifold. The gases pass through the exhaust pipe and a muffler. The muffler quiets the noise and the gases are discharged from the vehicle through a vertical stack or tailpipe.

The **pyrometer,** found on some instrument panels, measures the temperature of the exhaust gases. This temperature may be anywhere from 600 to 1,000 degrees F (315.5–537.8°C). The normal operating range varies from truck to truck. It is important that this temperature does not get too high, especially on long grades or mountain roads, because it may damage the engine. If the pyrometer temperature becomes too high, downshift. You also may need to completely stop the vehicle and allow the engine to cool down before proceeding.

The turbocharger converts the power received from the exhaust gases into power that can be used by the engine.

The **aftercooler** cools the intake air from the turbocharger and returns it to a safe temperature level.

LUBRICATION SYSTEM

The **lubrication system** distributes oil to the parts of the engine. The film of oil between the moving parts keeps them from rubbing together; instead, they ride or slide on the oil. This reduces friction between part surfaces **(see Figure 4-13).** By keeping friction to a minimum, you increase engine efficiency and extend the life of the parts.

Oil is not pumped directly to the many engine parts that require lubrication. Instead, the "splash method" is used as the bearings and many other rapidly moving engine parts throw off oil. With the constant motion, a fine oily mist reaches those parts not included in the pressure line of the system.

Oil absorbs the heat created from movement of the engine parts and cleans the engine by removing dirt, carbon, and worn metal. The biggest particles settle to the bottom of the **oil pan** while the smaller ones are filtered out.

Another vital function of the lubrication system is to prevent loss of pressure between the pistons and the cylinder wall by forming an oil seal between these parts. Without this seal, when pressure is lost, power is also lost.

Finally, engine oil absorbs shocks by forming a cushion between the surfaces subjected to shocks. For example, each time

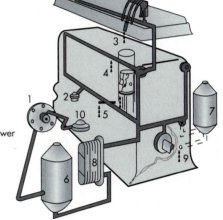

(a) Typical Lubricating System

1. Oil pump
2. Oil fill tube
3. Dipstick
4. Rocker and drain
5. Cam pocket drain
6. Oil drain from blower or turbocharger
7. Full-flow oil filter
8. Bypass oil filter
9. Oil cooler
10. Drain to oil pan
11. Oil pickup screen

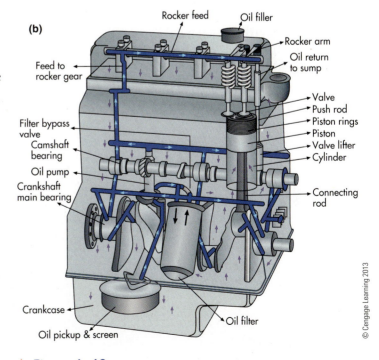

© Cengage Learning 2013

▶ **Figure 4-13**

The lubricating system distributes oil to parts of the engine to reduce the wear and tear caused by friction.

ignition occurs in the combustion chamber, a sudden force hits the piston. This, in turn, sends the force through a **wrist pin,** connecting rod, and crankshaft. Oil helps absorb the shock of these parts as well as reduce noise and wear and tear.

> **CAUTION!**
>
> Every Pretrip Inspection should include checking the oil with the dipstick, usually found at the side of the engine. To properly and accurately check the oil, the engine should be cold.

Oil changes—should be part of the tractor's regular maintenance schedule, recommended at 10,000–15,000 mile (16,000-24,000 km) intervals.

Oil filters—another way to extend the life of an engine is to regularly change oil filters. As the oil circulates through the engine, doing its work of cooling the engine and reducing friction between its parts, it collects dirt, grime, and small bits of metal that must be removed before they cause damage. Oil filters strain out these impurities.

Three types of oil filtering systems are:

1. **Full-flow systems**—in which all oil leaving the oil pump passes through the oil filter. Using the "one-pass" method, all contaminates must be filtered out during this one trip through the filter.

2. **Bypass systems**—or part-flow systems, filter a small amount (about 10 percent) of the oil flow. It is normally used with the full-flow system. It filters excess oil that does not go through the bearings but is normally returned to the oil pan. The flow of oil through the bypass filter is controlled by an opening.

3. **Combination of full-flow and bypass systems**—considered the best type of filtration system, oil from the full-flow filter goes into the bearings and oil from the bypass filter returns to the oil pan.

Centrifugal filter—a type of bypass filter in which the oil entering the permanent housing spins the filter at high speed. This forces the dirt and particles out of the oil for more efficient cleaning. It is used in addition to other oil filters.

Dipstick—a device used to indicate the oil level in the engine. The dipstick is marked in increments— "low" or "add"—but this can vary from one manufacturer to the next (**see Figure 4-14**).

▶ **Figure 4-14**

The dipstick will tell you if the oil level is low.

To use the dipstick to accurately measure the oil level in the engine, complete the following steps:

1. Park the unit on a level surface and turn off the engine.
2. Using gloves, remove dipstick from housing and wipe it thoroughly with a clean utility rag.
3. Insert the clean dipstick in the shaft where it was housed, withdraw it again, and the level of the oil will be indicated on the dipstick with an oily film.
4. If the oil level is at the "low" or "add" mark, add oil before driving the rig again. Follow manufacturer's recommendations to use proper oil for the truck you are driving.

STOP!

If, when checking the oil levels in the engine, the oil mark is too high on the dipstick or you notice a light foam, check immediately for possible coolant leak.

COOLANT SYSTEM

Heat is the basis of the internal combustion engine. However, intense heat can quickly destroy an engine, so a **coolant system** is needed to keep the temperatures down **(see Figure 4-15)**.

As coolant circulates through the engine block and cylinder head, it keeps the engine cool. Remember to think about the engine block as a solid block of steel into which large holes or cylinders have been drilled, although the block is actually a lot more complex than that. In addition to the cylinder holes, the block is honeycombed with a channel that comes very close to all the cylinders. This channel is called the **water jacket.** Here is how it works:

- Coolant flows through the jacket, picking up heat as it goes.
- The channel then takes the coolant to the radiator and in the radiator.
- The coolant flows through small, thinwalled tubes surrounded by air. This cools the coolant before it is pulled into the pump and back into the engine.
- When the coolant enters the water jacket, the process is repeated and the coolant is again cooled.

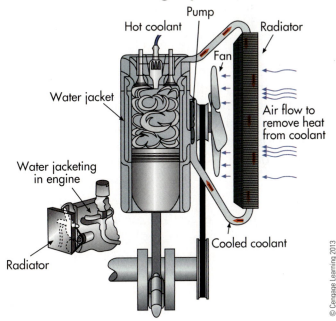

Cooling System

© Cengage Learning 2013

▶ **Figure 4–15**

The cooling system regulates the heat in an internal combustion engine.

The filler neck is located in the upper tank of the **radiator.** The **radiator cap** is placed at the top of the filler neck. To the side of the filler neck is an overflow tube that allows excess water or pressure to escape the radiator.

CAUTION!

It is important to keep the radiator filled with the proper amount of coolant.

Too much coolant will flow out when too much pressure builds inside the radiator. If pressure is excessive, it raises the radiator cap from the filler neck and excess coolant and water will boil out and overflow the tube.

When the pressure drops, the cap falls back into place and stops the flow of coolant.

Note, low fluids may cause engine shutdown or prevent engine from starting.

STOP!

Water should not be used in the cooling system because if it is used alone, it can cause rust or other damage to the system and engine. Commercial antifreeze works better and should be changed annually.

NOTE

The pressure cap will allow the coolant to reach a higher-than-usual boiling point. For this reason, the cap needs to be tested at each preventive maintenance check.

Following are terms related to the coolant system:

Coolant—fluid that circulates within the system, absorbing heat from the engine. It then takes the heat to the radiator for cooling. The coolant then returns to the engine for repeat performance. This coolant is also used to heat the cab through a heater core.

Thermostat—a valve in the water jacket located at a point where the coolant leaves the engine. Until the engine runs long enough to heat the coolant, the thermostat is closed. When the engine reaches normal operating temperature, usually 180 degrees F (82°C), the thermostat opens and the coolant moves into the radiator.

Radiator—the largest part to be found in the cooling system, the radiator consists of upper and lower tanks, the core, the tube, connections for hoses, and a filler cap. The cap also maintains pressure on the coolant, which is important, because the higher the pressure, the higher the boiling point of the cooler.

Fan belt—a belt from the engine that drives the fan. The belt must be checked for slack, cracks, or worn spots. The fan belt should be tightened or replaced as needed. A shroud, or cowling, protects the fan belt and directs airflow. Many engines have fan clutches that disengage the fan when it is not needed. The fan can reactivate at any time, which can cause serious injury.

CAUTION!

A leaking radiator cap can cause the entire coolant system to operate improperly.

ELECTRICAL SYSTEM

The **electrical system** on your tractor is a complex and important system. Without electricity, you could not start your engine, run your lights, or utilize your instruments and gauges. Therefore, it is important to understand this system because it serves many purposes. Following are some basics of the electrical system:

- An electron is a tiny particle carrying a negative charge of electricity.
- Electrical flow produces electrical current—and some materials carry this electrical current to its purpose better than others.
- A good electricity conductor is a material whose electrons can be easily moved. Copper wire is such a conductor and it is used frequently to move electrical charge from its source to its point of use. Because rubber is not a good conductor of electrical current, copper wire is usually surrounded with rubber insulation.
- Insulated wires bring electrical current where electricity is needed to operate.
- Terminals are the connecting devices between the electrical wires and the part where electricity is needed. They connect wires to the components.
- There is also a main terminal where the wires start. This same main terminal contains the system circuit breakers and fuses.

The electrical system consists of four parts:

1. Charging circuit
2. Cranking circuit
3. Ignition circuit
4. Lighting and accessory circuit

Charging Circuit

The seven parts of the **charging circuit** are:

1. Battery
2. Alternator or generator
3. Voltage regulator
4. Ammeter
5. Voltmeter
6. Electrical wires
7. Battery cable

The charging circuit produces electricity to keep the battery charged and runs the electrical circuits.

Battery

The black boxes called **batteries** work very hard, converting chemical energy into electrical energy **(see Figure 4-16)**. Once this occurs, batteries supply power to the rest of the vehicle's electrical system.

▶ Figure 4-16
The battery supplies power to all the vehicle's systems.

The parts of the battery include:

- **Case**—to neatly hold all the parts together.
- **Vent caps**—on top of the battery, these allow gas buildup to escape. You remove the vent caps to check the battery, and you may find them clogged and needing to be cleaned from time to time. Because the liquid in these batteries is a strong acid, proper personal protective equipment and training is needed to safely service these batteries.
- **Individual cells**—there are dry-charged, wet-charged, and maintenance-free batteries. Dry-charged batteries have no fluids in them when they leave the factory, and the dealer adds water to the battery when it is sold. The wet-charged battery has fluid in it when it leaves the factory. These two types must be checked for fluid levels when you do a pretrip inspection.
- **Cell connectors**—these are the transports of the electricity from the cell to the power supply.
- **Terminal posts**—the two posts are located on top of the battery and have a positive post (the larger one) and negative post.

CAUTION!

Electricity can be dangerous if you do not exercise extreme care when you are working around it. Following are some tips about working around batteries safely:

- Disconnect battery ground strap before you begin any electrical or engine work.
- Connect the ground strap last when you install a new battery.
- Never lay metal tools or other objects on the battery.
- Never hook up the battery backwards—make sure to connect the positive cable to the positive terminal post. Connect the negative cable to the negative post. (The positive cable clamp and terminal are usually larger than the negative cable clamp and terminal.)
- Be careful when handling batteries. Battery acid is corrosive.
- Do not lean too close to the battery when adding water, as any splash could get into your eyes.
- Keep fires away from batteries. If you are a smoker, save your cigarette until after you have finished working under the hood.

Alternators and Generators

The **alternators** and **generators** recharge the battery when it loses electricity. The electricity generated can be used by the battery and electrical systems. Most systems today use alternators.

When the engine is running, the alternator is creating electricity. Through computerized control systems, the electricity used for operating—except for starting the engine, which comes from the battery—is provided by the alternator.

Ammeter

The gauge on the instrument panel used to indicate the amount of charge or discharge the battery is receiving from the generator is called the **ammeter.** It should read "zero" when the engine and the electrical system are off. Starting the engine will move the needle from zero to the charge side. Once the engine is on and warm, the needle should drop back to zero. It is also normal for it to read slightly on the charging side.

Voltmeter

The **voltmeter** shows whether the battery is charging properly. This gauge can be identified by the word *volts* on the lower portion of the gauge as well as a picture of the battery. There are three segments of this gauge, each showing a different condition. The far left segment (red) shows undercharging. The middle (green) segment shows normal battery condition. The far right segment (also red) indicates overcharge. A pointer shows which condition the battery is in at the moment.

CAUTION!

If the voltmeter shows a continuous undercharging or overcharging condition, there is a problem in the charging system.

Voltage Regulator

The **voltage regulator** controls the voltage produced by the alternator. The regulator keeps the battery voltage from getting too high, and thus prevents the battery from overcharging. It also keeps other electrical parts from burning themselves out.

Cranking Circuit

The **cranking circuit** sends electricity from the battery to a small starter motor gear **(see Figure 4-17).** By activating the starter switch, the driver puts the ignition system into motion.

Ignition Circuit

In a **gasoline engine,** the **ignition circuit** provides sparks for each cylinder to ignite the fuel–air mixture. An ignition circuit is not needed for diesel trucks because the compression of the air-fuel mixture causes it to ignite.

Lighting and Accessory Circuit

The lighting and accessory circuits send electrical power to:

- Lights (headlights, tail lights, turn signals, running lights)
- Horns
- Instrument lights (speedometer, odometer, gauges, etc.)
- Windshield cleaners (wipers, washers)

Cranking System

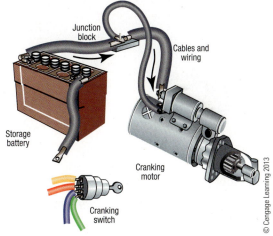

▶ **Figure 4-17**

The cranking circuit sends electricity from the battery to a small starter motor.

GO!

The detachable electrical connection, working between the tractor and the trailer in combination, supplies power from the tractor's power plant to the trailer, where it powers the trailer's lights and anything requiring DC power on the trailer. The ABS is an example of a system requiring DC power.

Straight trucks do not have detachable electrical connections.

DRIVETRAIN

The **drivetrain** takes power generated by the engine and applies it to the tractor's drive wheels. As the wheels turn, the rig moves. The drivetrain has five main parts (**see Figure 4-18**):

1. Clutch
2. Transmission
3. Driveshaft
4. Universal joints
5. Differential

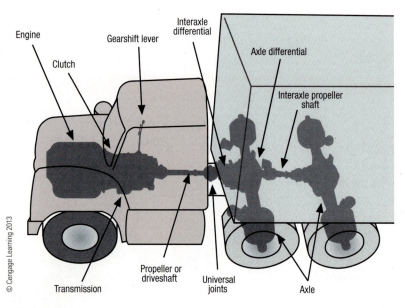

© Cengage Learning 2013

▶ **Figure 4–18**

The main components of the drivetrain.

These five parts perform four basic functions:

1. Connect the engine (source of power) to and disconnect it from the drivetrain.
2. Modify the torque (twist) and engine speed (rpm) produced by the engine to allow the vehicle to operate at its best.
3. Carry the power of the engine to the rear axle and drive wheels.
4. Change the direction of the torque to propel the rear wheels.

The following describes the result of putting various parts of the power train into action. This is an overview, not a complete and detailed explanation.

Clutch Location

© Cengage Learning 2013

Engine   Clutch   Transmission

▶ **Figure 4–19**

The clutch connects or disconnects the engine from the rest of the power train.

Clutch

The clutch is used to connect or disconnect the engine from the rest of the power train (**see Figure 4-19**). One of the primary jobs of the clutch is to help the driver easily shift gears. The main parts of the clutch include:

- Clutch housing
- Flywheel
- Clutch disc(s)
- Pressure plate
- Release assembly
- Clutch brake
- Controls

On most trucks, there are three plates that can be pressed together (engaged) or pulled apart (disengaged). The middle plate (called the clutch disc) is the "driven member." It is connected to a shaft leading to the transmission. The other two plates are "driving members" and connect to the engine.

A spring forces the two driving members toward each other, squeezing them against the middle plate until they all turn together as one unit. When the plates are together, the clutch is "engaged." When the plates are apart, the clutch is "disengaged."

The engine flywheel is the first driving member. It has a smooth surface where it squeezes the driven plate. The other driving member is called the pressure place and is made of heavy cast iron that is smooth on one side. It is fastened to the cover, which is bolted to the flywheel so they can all turn together. This disc can slide forward and away from the driven plate.

The driven plate, or clutch disc, is a flat disc of steel with a friction facing on each side. The plate is fastened by grooves, or slots, called **splines** to a shaft connected to the transmission. The disc fits into the grooves of the shaft so that the plate and shaft turn together and the plate can slide forward and backward on the shaft.

The clutch disc is softer than the other plates and because of this, it will be worn out before damage can occur to other parts of the drivetrain. When a clutch "goes out," it is usually the clutch disc that must be replaced. Riding or resting a foot on the clutch can cause excessive wear and premature clutch failure.

> **CAUTION!**
> To prevent excessive wear or damage, clutches should be adjusted. Locate the access hole where you can make this adjustment.

There are two types of mechanical clutches:

1. **Direct clutch control**—consists of manually operated assembly made of levers, rods, and springs connecting the pedal to the clutch release mechanism. Conventional tractors often use such a clutch.
2. **Cable-operated clutch control**—uses a cable to replace part of the linkage.

ROLL STABILITY SYSTEMS

In 2008, more than 11,000 rollovers and 4,000 jackknifes occurred on U.S. highways alone.

By mid-2011, the potential for regulation of commercial vehicle stability moved into the "Notice for Proposed Rulemaking (NPRM)" phase. This will be followed by tests for medium truck and bus stability control standards on ESC for these and other vehicles, weighing over 10,000 lb (4,535 kg). GVWR will be conducted and, if all results warrant, the NHTSA will decide whether to require ESC on these vehicles, anticipated in 2014.

Roll stability offsets the tendency of a vehicle (or tractor-trailer combination) to tip over while changing direction. This typically occurs while the vehicle is turning. Tipping is usually caused by vehicle height, load offset, road adhesion, suspension stiffness, frame stiffness, and track width of the vehicle.

When necessary, roll stability systems take action to slow the vehicle as quickly as possible, allowing the driver to regain control and avoid rollover. Full stability systems go a step further by providing additional performance to help avoid loss of control situations.

By maintaining a vehicle's stability during both oversteer and understeer situations, the driver's intended path continues to be followed, and loss-of control situations are minimized.

Electronic stability control (ESC) is a computerized technology that improves a vehicle's stability by detecting and minimizing skids. When ESC detects loss of steering control, it automatically applies the brakes to help "steer" the vehicle. Braking is automatically applied to counter oversteering or understeering.

Some ESC systems also reduce engine power until control is regained. ESC does not improve a vehicle's cornering performance; instead, it helps to minimize the loss of control.

The Meritor WABCO SmartTrac family of Stability Control Systems, used here as an illustration, integrates Meritor WABCO's active safety systems technologies into products available to North American (Canada, the United States, and Mexico) truck operators. WABCO's technology is designed for such vehicles as commercial trucks/tractors and trailers, construction, fire and rescue, bus and coach, and military, using advanced electronic control units (ECUs) with enhanced capabilities.

The company's electronic stability control (ESC) combines roll stability control (RSC) with the added capability of yaw or rotational control. ESC can assist the driver in reducing the risk of vehicle instability while in a slippery curve or taking an evasive action, reducing the potential for jackknifing and driftout conditions through select braking of the tractor and application of the trailer brakes. If loss of stability is detected, tractor-trailer speed is reduced through engine control and application of the engine brake and tractor and trailer foundation brakes **(see Figure 4-20)**.

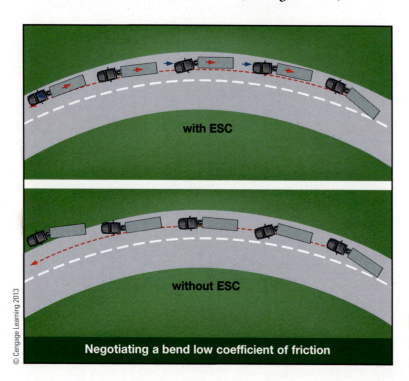

© Cengage Learning 2013

with ESC

without ESC

Negotiating a bend low coefficient of friction

▶ **Figure 4-20**
ESC can assist the driver in reducing the risk of vehicle instability.

The Meritor WABCO Roll Stability Control delivers a high level of tractor rollover stability while helping fleets realize improved performance, ease of maintenance, and minimized operating costs associated with vehicle downtime/replacement, cargo replacement, and insurance. RSC is an active vehicle safety system that assists drivers in maintaining control of the vehicle by continually monitoring conditions that can lead to a rollover, and it automatically intervenes if a high rollover risk is detected.

The company's RSSplus is the next generation of Meritor WABCO's roll stability support system for trailers, and incorporates ABS performance, key safety features, and improved roll avoidance. RSSplus helps the driver maintain trailer and overall vehicle stability. The system simultaneously monitors trailer wheel speed, lateral acceleration, and suspension pressure or spring deflection. The company maintains that if the vehicle approaches its rollover threshold, RSSplus automatically applies the trailer brakes as needed to help the driver bring the vehicle under control.

Bendix Corporation also offers a full-stability solution, Bendix ESP, widely available for the commercial vehicle market. The company states that full-stability technology is more comprehensive than roll-only stability and that its full-stability systems address both roll and directional stability. While roll-only options function on dry surfaces, full-stability systems recognize and mitigate conditions that could lead to rollover and loss-of-control situations sooner on dry surfaces and in a wider range of driving and road conditions, including snowy, ice-covered, and slippery surfaces.

No advanced safety technology replaces the need for a good driver, safe driving practices, and ongoing driver training. But while technology won't make a bad driver a good driver, it might help a good driver avoid a bad situation.

How Roll Stability Systems Work

During normal driving, ESC works in the background to:

- Continuously monitor steering and vehicle direction.
- Compare the driver's intended direction (determined through the measured steering wheel angle) to the vehicle's actual direction (determined through measured lateral acceleration, vehicle rotation (yaw), and individual road wheel speeds).
- Intervene only when it detects loss of steering control, that is, when the vehicle is not going where the driver is steering. This may happen, for example, when skidding during emergency evasive swerves, understeering or oversteering during poorly judged turns on slippery roads, or hydroplaning.
- Estimate the direction of the skid, and then apply the brakes to individual wheels asymmetrically, opposing the skid and bringing the vehicle back in line with the driver's commanded direction.
- Reduce engine power or operate the transmission to slow the vehicle down if driver loses control.
- Inform the driver when the system intervenes so the driver knows the vehicle's handling limits have been approached.
- Activate a dashboard indicator light and/or alert tone (typically). Some intentionally allow the vehicle's corrected course to deviate very slightly from the driver-commanded direction, even if it is possible to more precisely match it.

All ESC manufacturers emphasize the same point stated earlier—that the system is not a performance enhancement nor a replacement for safe driving practices, but rather a safety technology to assist the driver in recovering from dangerous situations. Generally, ESC works within inherent limits of the vehicle's handling and available traction between the tires and road. A reckless maneuver can still exceed these limits, resulting in loss of control. For example, in a severe hydroplaning scenario, the wheels that ESC would use to correct a skid may not even initially be in contact with the road, reducing its effectiveness (**see Figure 4-21**).

▶ Figure 4-21

ECS is a safety technology to help assist the driver in recovering from dangerous situations.

ABOUT SMARTTRAC™ STABILITY CONTROL SYSTEMS WITH MULTIFUNCTION ELECTRONIC CONTROL UNITS

The benefits of roll stability control and electronic stability control are described in product information from Meritor WABCO:

In July 2009, Meritor WABCO Vehicle Control Systems introduced SmartTrac™, a group of proven anti-lock braking, automatic traction control, and stability control systems for commercial vehicles. SmartTrac uses advanced electronic control units with enhanced capabilities, to help North American truck operators with more options to meet their operational needs.

At that time, SmartTrac stability control systems were available as a factory-installation option at several truck, tractor and trailer OEMs. Meritor products include anti-lock braking systems (ABS), automatic traction control (ATC), and stability control systems, designed for vehicle applications.

Electronic Stability Control (ESC) (released in 2005 by Meritor WABCO) combines Roll Stability Control (RSC) with the added capability of yaw or rotational control. ESC can reduce the risk of the vehicle instability while in a slippery curve or taking an evasive action, preventing jack-knife and drift-out conditions through select braking of the tractor and application of the trailer brakes. If loss of stability is detected, tractor-trailer speed is reduced through engine control and application of the engine brake, tractor and trailer foundation brakes.

Roll Stability Control (RSC) provides the highest value of vehicle rollover stability with the fewest components, maintenance requirements and lowest cost. It continually monitors conditions that can lead to a rollover and can automatically de-throttle the engine and apply the engine brake, and drive and trailer axle foundation brakes to reduce tractor-trailer speed when lateral acceleration limits are about to be exceeded. Currently, the company has systems in 60,000 vehicles.

RSSplus™ is an advanced two-modulator valve, trailer only, stability control system that integrates with the trailer's anti-lock braking system. The system simultaneously monitors trailer wheel speed, lateral acceleration and suspension pressure. If the vehicle approaches its rollover threshold, RSSplus automatically applies trailer brakes as needed in order to reduce the risk of rollover and help bring the vehicle under control. RSSplus is an ideal solution for retrofit applications for fast implementation of stability control protection.

Monitoring and telematics: Communicating over the tractor's data bus, status messages can be relayed to an on-board computer with telematics capabilities. Fleet managers at home can correlate stability control and braking events with precise time and location data. This data can be used to proactively address at risk events so they don't turn into crashes.

Improved diagnostics and event recording: The SmartTrac family of ECUs can capture data about braking and stability control events and create a record of accurate, detailed information that fleet managers can use to identify trends and build more effective driver training programs.

THE DIFFERENCE BETWEEN BASIC AND ENHANCED ROLL STABILITY SYSTEMS

As part of an ongoing FMCSA effort to encourage voluntary adoption of onboard safety systems, FMCSA has taken a close look at roll stability control systems and has found commercial vehicle stability systems are not all the same. Major differences exist between **roll-only (basic)** and **full-stability (enhanced)** systems. These differences are based on three factors:

1. Information collected by sensors—The driver's ability to access information regarding vehicle dynamics and to compare them with driver and tension is critical to the operation of the stability system. More information means more tools for the system to determine what's happening and to deliver an earlier and more proactive response.

2. ECU intelligence to process sensor data—Processing data collected from the vehicle's brake and stability system sensors allow the ECU to determine and implement an appropriate response to the situation.

3. The system's ability to deliver an intervention that will maintain the vehicle's stability—These interventions are essential in helping the driver maintain control of the vehicle. The main purpose of all stability systems is to use the vehicle's brakes to reduce speed and help avoid rollovers as quickly as possible. In the event of a jackknife or other loss-of-control scenario, the system will redirect the vehicle along its intended path.

Both roll-only (basic) and full-stability (enhanced) systems use a **lateral acceleration** sensor, but only a full stability system uses the **yaw** sensor, which measures the directional stability of the vehicle, plus the steering angle sensor, which measures the driver's steering intent for the vehicle.

Lateral acceleration creates a force at the center of gravity, pushing the vehicle horizontally while the friction between the tires and the road opposes that force. If the lateral force is great enough, one side of the vehicle may begin to lift up off the ground, creating the potential for the vehicle to roll over.

Yaw stability, which is also called directional stability, is the vehicle's ability to follow a driver's steering input. Factors that influence yaw stability include wheelbase, suspension, steering geometry, weight distribution from front to rear, and vehicle tracking while the truck is moving. If friction between the road's surface and the tractor's tires is not sufficient, one or more of the tires can slide. This may cause the vehicle to spin out. These events are referred to as either "understeer" or "oversteer."

TRAILER-BASED ROLLOVER SYSTEMS

Some trailer-based rollover systems have distinct advantages over tractor-based rollover stability systems. Why? One advantage, as described by the the manufacturer of the Haldex Trailer Rollover Stability (TRS) System, is that the tractor—with its relatively low center of gravity height—effectively separates the driver from the trailer due to the decreased tractor roll motion.

As a result, the driver often remains unaware of the rollover instability at the trailer and fails to take corrective actions in a timely manner, or often overcompensates with erratic steering. In fact, most driver steering movement is amplified by the time it reaches the trailer. Therefore, it is not surprising that most drivers are unaware of rollover conditions until it's too late.

A study, published by American Society of Mechanical Engineers and written by the University of Michigan in 1999, concluded that "a driver's awareness of rollovers on vehicles depends on vehicle type, load position and torsional stiffness of the trailer. Torsionally flexible trailers result in poor roll feedback to the driver, especially on flatbed trailers. Since the tractor has a relatively low center of gravity height, it effectively separates the driver from the trailer due to the decreased tractor roll motion.

"The driver often remains unaware of the rollover instability at the trailer and fails to take corrective actions in a timely fashion. However, if the trailer is monitored and an accurate and timely warning is issued regarding an impending rollover threat, it is possible to avoid some rollover incidents," researchers found.

ABS, Traction Control, and Full-Power Brake System

Several roll stability systems can be installed in tandem with ABS. MICO Inc., for example, offers a full-power brake system with ABS and traction control to provide added control for multiwheeled vehicles operated both on- and off-highway. The system enhances vehicle stability while decreasing stopping distances and improving acceleration under low traction conditions. As many as eight wheels can be controlled independently of the others, which makes the system easily adaptable to four-wheeled, six-wheeled, and eight-wheeled vehicles, according to the company.

The electronic control unit (ECU) monitors wheel speed and brake line pressures with sensors. When wheel lock-up or wheel slip conditions exist, the electronic control unit determines the current needed at the electrohydraulic control valves to improve the operator's control of the vehicle. System status outputs are provided to light ABS and low traction lamps for operator warning and to meet on-highway regulations.

In addition to controlling outputs, the embedded program in the electronic control unit allows it to communicate via CAN (controller area network) with a laptop computer running Windows 2000 or XP. Communication between the electronic control unit and the laptop requires a USB-to-CAN dongle and Diagnostic Interface Software on the laptop.

TRANSMISSION

The **transmission** is a box of gears located behind the clutch. The box is usually fastened to the clutch housing **(see Figure 4-22).** The clutch and transmission look like an extension of the engine.

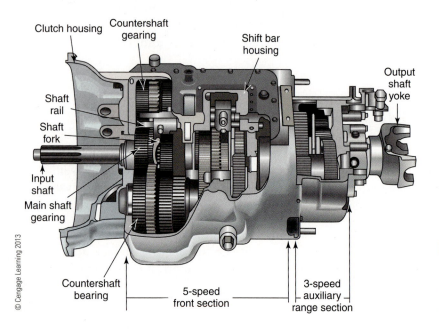

© Cengage Learning 2013

▶ Figure 4-22

The transmission is a box of gears usually attached to the clutch housing.

The transmission adjusts the power generated by the engine so it provides the right speed and torque for the job. For example, when a loaded rig moves from a stopped position, a great deal of power is needed. The driver uses the gears in the transmission to provide the needed combination of power, torque, and speed. The transmission then sends, or transmits, the power from its source—the engine—to the drive, or powered axles. This is the power that propels the vehicle.

The gears in the transmission help control the speed and power of the rig. The engine can be kept at a relatively constant speed. The rig, however, can be moved either slowly or rapidly with much the same power output. Once underway, the rig needs less power to keep it going than it needed to start rolling. Gears make this possible.

DRIVESHAFTS AND UNIVERSAL JOINTS

Behind the transmission is a propeller called the driveshaft. The driveshaft is a steel shaft that runs from the transmission to the rear of the vehicle. Usually, the driveshaft is hollow.

At each end (front and rear) of the shaft are the universal joints, or U-joints. They are called universal joints because they can move in almost any direction. They are usually constructed of two U-shaped pieces set at right angles and are fastened together by cross arms of equal length. As the driveshaft spins, it transfers the twisting motion back to the rear axle. The U-joints let the driveshaft change its angle of operation.

The U-shaped pieces (yokes) pivot on the arms of the cross. Since they are two pivots, the shaft can be at an angle and still transmit power. The U-joints do not have to be in a straight line. This is very important, because they become somewhat misaligned with each bump in the road. The rear axle moves up and down with the wheels while the transmission moves very little. The U-joints let the propeller shaft turn, even though its two ends are shifting in relation to one another.

DIFFERENTIAL

The two types of differentials on trucks today are the differential and the interaxle differential. The **differential** divides the drive axle in half, allowing each to spin independently. It performs two specific tasks: (1) It transmits power from the driveshaft to the axles. (2) Because it divides the drive axle into two independent halves, each axle half may turn at a different speed, which allows each wheel to rotate independently. This facilitates cornering and reduces tire wear.

There are several types of differentials, but our focus is on the major components of the typical differential. These components include the **drive pinion gear,** the **ring gear,** and four **spider gears.**

The drive pinion gear is connected to the end of the driveshaft and drives the ring gear. Attached to the ring gear are four spider gears, which mesh with gears on the ends of the drive axle halves. Each of the spider gears can rotate freely and each axle gear meshes with all four spider gears. This accomplishes the transfer of power from the ring gear through the spider gears and into the drive axle halves.

DIFFERENTIAL CASE HALVES

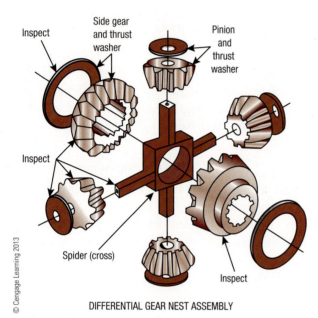

Inspect

Side gear and thrust washer

Pinion and thrust washer

Inspect

Spider (cross)

Inspect

© Cengage Learning 2013

DIFFERENTIAL GEAR NEST ASSEMBLY

▶ **Figure 4–23**

The drive pinions rotate with the spider gears when a tractor-trailer is driving in a straight line and both wheels are turning at the same speed.

The pinion and ring gears accomplish two tasks:

1. They turn the torque (force) of the pinion shaft at right angles so the wheels can turn and drive the vehicle.

2. They can reduce speed and increase torque because the pinion gear is much smaller than the ring gear.

If your rig is traveling in a straight line down the highway and both wheels are turning at the same speed, the drive pinions are rotating with the spider gears (**see Figure 4-23**). When the rig maneuvers through a turn, the inside wheels slow and, as one axle half begins spinning at a lower speed, the spider gears begin rotating, allowing the axle halves to spin at different speeds to accommodate the turn without scrubbing the tires.

The **interaxle differential** divides the two axles, allowing each to turn independently of the other. The interaxle differential is used on tandem rear-drive axle trucks and is sometimes called the "power divider."

WHEELS

Tires are mounted on wheels and the wheel connects the tire to the axle. The three types of wheels are:

1. Spoke or open—called "Dayton" tires and becoming more rarely seen on today's highways.

2. Budd or stud piloted

3. Unimount or hub piloted

Spoke wheels are made of two pieces. They are heavy and difficult to align and balance. Spoke wheels clamp onto wheels with wheel clamps; and if these are not installed properly, the wheel will soon be "out of round." That means it will wobble when it rolls. Disc or stud-piloted wheels are commonly called Budd wheels and are made of aluminum or high-tensile steel. Alignment is simpler because these wheels can be fastened together with six, eight, or 10 wheel studs. Unimount or hub-piloted wheels are often called hub-mount wheels; they center on the hub at the center hole or bore of the wheel.

CAUTION!
The interaxle differential should not be engaged while the vehicle is in motion.

MOUNTING SYSTEMS

The two types of mounting systems are stud piloted and hub piloted. A stud-piloted system uses the studs on the wheel hub to guide and center the wheel. Wheels with the stud-piloted mounting system are often called stud-mount wheels. Stud-piloted wheels are designed to be centered by the nuts on the studs.

Hub-piloted mounting systems use the actual wheel hub to guide and center the wheel. Hub-piloted wheels are used with two-piece flange nuts, which contact the disc face around the bolt hole and do not rely on contacting the bolt hole **chamfer** to function properly. Hub-piloted wheels generally have straight-through bolt holes with no chamfers. This feature provides a visual way of identifying hub-piloted wheels. It is important to use the proper components for each type of mounting and to fit the wheels to the proper hubs.

STOP!

The two types of mounting systems cannot be intermixed.

Wheels are fastened by two methods—ball seat and flange nuts. Ball-seat nuts clamp the wheel on by seating to a tapered part of the stud hole. Flange nuts clamp onto the flat surface and provide more even clamping torque. These two types cannot be intermixed.

TIRES

Although often taken for granted, tires are a critical part of the rig because they provide traction, reduce vibration, and absorb shock. It is important to have good tires—not tires that are good *enough*, but tires that have good tread, are adequately inflated, and are checked frequently for wear and tear (**see Figure 4-24**). Tires must provide traction in all kinds of weather. They also have to be in shape to transfer braking and driving force to the road.

The three types of tires are:

1. Radial (**see Figure 4-25**)
2. Bias ply (**see Figure 4-26**)
3. Belted bias (**see Figure 4-27**)

▶ Figure 4-24

Regularly inspect tires for wear and tear.

© Cengage Learning 2013

Radial
Body cords run perpendicular across the tread, belt piles run circumferentially around the tire under the tread.

© Cengage Learning 2013

▶ **Figures 4-25**

Cross section of a radial tire.

Bias ply
Body cords run diagonally across the tread.

© Cengage Learning 2013

▶ **Figures 4-26**

Cross section of a bias-ply tire.

Belted Bias
Body cords run diagonally across the tread. Belt piles run circumferentially around the tire under the tread.

© Cengage Learning 2013

▶ **Figures 4-27**

Cross section of a belted bias tire.

GO!

All tires have *plies*—separate layers of rubber-cushioned cord. Plies make up the body of the tire and are tied into bundles of wire called bead coils. Plies can be bias, belted bias, or radial.

Bias-ply tires have plies that are placed at a criss-crossed angle. This makes the sidewall and the tread very rigid.

Belted bias tires have plies that cross at an angle with an added layered belt of fabric between the plies and the tread. Belts make the tread more rigid than bias-ply tires and the tread will last longer, because the belts reduce tread motion when the tire is running.

Radial tires have plies that do not cross at an angle but are laid from bead to bead, across the tire. Radial tires have a number of belts and their construction means the sidewalls have less flex and less friction, which requires less horsepower and saves fuel. Plus, radial tires hold the road, resist skidding, and give a smoother ride than the bias types.

STOP!

Never mix radial and bias-ply tires on the same vehicle—or put tires of different sizes or construction on the same axle.

Other Tire Terms

Bead coils and beads—bead coils form the bead, the part of the tire that fits into the rim. Bead coils provide the hoop strength for the bead sections, so the tire will hold its shape when being mounted on a wheel.

Sidewalls—layers of rubber covering, connecting the bead to the tread. Sidewalls also protect the plies.

Tread—part of the tire that hits the road. Treads are designed for specific jobs such as extra traction and high speed. Tires on steering axles should be able to roll and provide good traction. Drive tires must provide good traction for braking and acceleration. Tires for trailers should roll well. Drive wheel position tires need maximum traction in all conditions.

Inner liner—the sealing material that keeps air in the tire.

Load rating—refers to the strength of the tire. This can be rated from A to Z—with Z being the strongest. The maximum load rating is shown in pounds. FMCSR 393 does not permit a tire to be used that cannot support the load, and the load rating makes certain you have the right tire.

Hump—pattern of tire wear that has the same appearance as a cupped hand—the hump at the edge or higher part of the cup.

Tie bars and fillets—are design factors, not wear patterns. A *sipe* is a cut across the tread to improve traction.

Retread—a worn tire that has the old tread layer removed and a new tread layer applied.

CAUTION!

"If the tire fails in the drive position, the vehicle won't overturn," says Harvey Brodsky, managing director of the Tire Retread Information Bureau (TRIB). "Other tires can carry the load. If the tire fails on the steer position, someone could die."

Federal Motor Carrier Safety Regulations do not prohibit nail hole repairs in the tread area of a steer tire. Neither do the tire industry's own standards, although they limit the number of allowable nail hole repairs in a steer tire to one. No bead area repair is acceptable.

According to the "Industry Recommended Practices for Tire Retreading & Tire Repairing," a tire cannot be used on the steer axle of a long-haul truck if it has been previously retreaded.

TREAD DESIGN AND WHEEL POSITION

For highway use, the two truck **tire tread** designs are rib and lug.

Rib tread has grooves in the tire tread that run parallel to the sidewalls. Tires with rib-type tread can be used any-where on the rig and are designed for highway speeds. They are recommended for the front wheels of tractors and large straight trucks for high-speed, long-haul service. They help the driver maintain control of the vehicle and avoid skids **(see Figure 4-28)**.

Lug tread has deep grooves in the tire shoulders that run perpendicular to the sidewalls. These tires are best for the drive wheels. In high-torque road service, they wear bet-ter, have greater traction, and have higher rolling

▶ Figure 4-28

A tire with a rib tread.

© Cengage Learning 2013

resistance than rib types. If you operate in cold weather, it may be wise to use rib tires on the drive wheels for greater fuel efficiency **(see Figure 4-29)**.

Figure 4-29

A tire with lug tread.

NORMAL TIRE INFLATION

Tires must be inflated correctly for the rig to perform at its best **(see Figure 4-30)**. Normal (cold) tire pressure is 100–105 psi (690-724 kPa).

Maximum pressure is designated in pounds per square inch (psi) or kilopascals (kPa) on cold tires driven less than 1 mile (1.6 km). This is why you should check tire pressure before you drive—and do not check tire pressure by kicking or thumping them! Tires have come a long way since your great-grandpa's day, when kicking actually told you something. Tire pressure should be checked weekly—and more often on long trips. Use a tire gauge and measure tread depth with the proper instrument. Check FMCSR 393.75 for regulations regarding normal tire inflation.

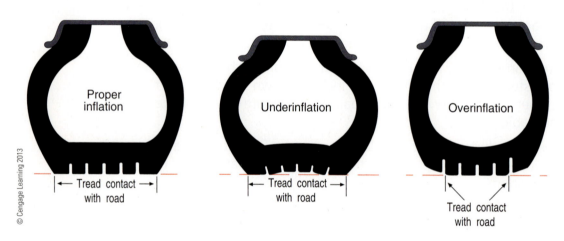

Figure 4-30

Properly inflated tires make a rig easier to handle and have a longer road life than under- or overinflated tires.

If tire pressure increases more than 10 to 15 psi (69 to 103 kPa) during normal operation:

- Tires may be underinflated
- Rig may be overloaded
- Tires may not be the right size
- Combination of the above

Whatever the cause, be sure to correct the problem immediately.

Underinflation

Underinflation increases tread wear and reduces tire life. When the temperature increases in an underinflated tire, it can cause the tread to separate from the body or belt ply of the tire.

If a tire is found to be 20 to 25 percent of normal psi/kPa, it is considered underinflated and should be inspected for cuts or holes.

When a tire is underinflated, it can flex excessively. As this soft tire travels over the road, it builds up heat, which weakens the tire's body cords. If this continues, the body cord deteriorates and may catch fire, due to high internal temperatures.

STOP!

A study by the Federal Motor Carrier Safety Administration found that 7.08 percent of all tires were underinflated by 20 psi (138 kPa) or more. Only 44 percent of tires tested were within 5 psi (34 kPa) of prescribed tire pressure.

Underinflated tires also make a rig difficult to control. This is a dangerous situation in and of itself, but it is especially dangerous in extreme conditions or emergencies.

If you are driving on dual tires and one is underinflated or flat, a fire can result; however, the other tire will carry the load until you are able to stop the truck.

Air Balancing Systems

Newer trucks have air balancing systems—systems that regulate air to the tires and automatically ensure proper inflation.

These balancers extend tire life 25 to 50 percent, prevent cupping, help tires run cooler, solve vibration problems, and automatically balance your tires and wheels while you drive. Most models start working at 20 to 22 mph (32 to 35 km/h) depending on wheel diameter. This occurs long before vibration due to imbalance, which is at speeds in excess of 35 mph (56 km/h).

How Heat Affects Tire Rubber

A tire can become very hot during a long-distance trip involving high-speed driving. Driving in warm weather can also create unusually high tire temperatures. Heat can affect tire tread bonding and may be associated with an increased rate of tread separation. When tires are hot, they are more easily damaged when they rub against a curb, railroad track, or pit rail guide because rubber softens.

CAUTION!

Remember: If you have just had a tire changed, stop after driving for a while and make sure nuts have not loosened.

Tread Life

Because conditions vary, no one can exactly predict the life of the tire tread. Quality of the tire, how the vehicle is handled, tire inflation, load distribution, and care of the tire will all affect the life of the tread. Average tread life for any tire on the market today has been calculated by each manufacturer. This is good information for the driver because it serves as a guide. If the driver shifts gears smoothly and is generally responsible, he or she may be able to get greater-than-average tread wear. On the other hand, the driver can cut tread life in half by speeding, braking sharply, running over debris, maintaining improper air pressure, and running over curbs.

FMCSR 393 provides information about the legal minimum tread depth on a tire. According to this portion of the law, a motor vehicle cannot use tires that:

- Have fabric exposed through tread or sidewalls
- Have less than 4/32 inch of tread measured at any point in a major tread groove on the front axle
- Have less than 2/32 inch of tread measured at any point in a major tread groove on all other axles
- Have front tires that have been **recapped** or **regrooved** if tires have load capacity equal to or greater than 8.25-20 eight-ply tire

STEERING SYSTEMS

To control your rig, the steering system must be working properly, which is accomplished by checking the parts often to ensure smooth operation (**see Figure 4-31**).

The steering system allows the driver to make the necessary maneuvers to move the truck from point A to point B. Maneuvers may include turning corners, moving around barriers, and entering and exiting highway ramps—without slipping, sliding, or rolling over.

The steering system begins with the **steering wheel**—the hand control of the wheels connected to the steering axle. Between the steering wheel and the steering axle are the parts that make steering possible:

1. The steering wheel is connected to the steering column and translates the driver's movements to the steering system. When the steering wheel turns, the steering column turns in the same direction.

2. This motion continues through the U-joint to the **steering gear shaft.** From there, the driver's motion continues through another U-joint to the **steering gear box.**

3. The steering gear box is also called "the steering sector." It changes the rotating motion of the steering column to a back-and-forth motion on the **Pitman arm.**

4. The Pitman arm is a lever attached to the steering gear box, and a **drag link** joins the Pitman arm and the steering lever.

5. The steering lever turns the front wheels left and right when the Pitman arm pulls it back and forth. The steering lever connects to the steering knuckle (the moveable connection between the axle and the wheel, which allows the wheels to turn left or right).

6. There is a steering knuckle at the end of each axle. Each contains the seals, bushings, and bearings that support the vehicle's weight. The steering knuckles translate the motion from the driver to the cross-steering lever and the cross-steering tube (the tie rod).

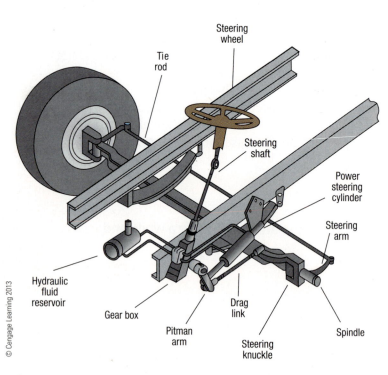

© Cengage Learning 2013

▶ **Figure 4-31**

The steering system gives the professional driver control of his or her rig.

7. Spindles, which are parts of the steering axle knuckles, are inserted through the wheels. Spindles are also called stub axles and are attached to the kingpin.

8. The **tie rod** holds both wheels in the same position. As the left wheel turns, the right wheel follows in the same direction. A kingpin in the steering knuckle gives each wheel its own pivot point.

Wheel Alignment

Manufacturers build the following alignment features into the front end of the rig. They may be changed as needed.

Caster—the amount of tilt measured in degrees—is the caster of an axle. The axle should have a positive caster, meaning it should tilt forward. When set in this manner, the vehicle has a natural tendency to go straight and will also recover from turns more rapidly. Positive caster means easier steering.

Camber—is the degree of tilt at the top of the tires. At its best, the truck's wheels need a positive camber to support the load. When the vehicle is heavily loaded, the tires are straight, relative to the road.

CAUTION!
Other alignment tendencies are often the result of wear and tear. Most noticeable are "toe-in" and "toe-out."

Toe-in means the front wheels are closer together at the front than they are in the rear.

Toe-out means the front wheels are farther apart than the wheels at the rear.

If a vehicle has a **power steering** system, it uses hydraulic pressure or air pressure to assist making the turn, which requires less strength on the part of the driver. Power steering provides greater control of a vehicle with less physical effort. Power steering also reduces driver fatigue because it is less physically demanding. Power steering allows the vehicle to absorb road shocks more and also makes the vehicle easier to maneuver in difficult situations.

When hydraulic pressure assists steering a vehicle, a hydraulic unit replaces the steering gear box and a hydraulic pump is added to the engine to supply the pressure used to help turn the wheels. With hydraulic pressure to help turn the wheels, when the steering wheel is turned to the right, the hydraulic valve senses it, opens, and fluid pressure helps turn the wheels to the right.

COUPLING SYSTEMS

The **coupling system** connects the tractor to the trailer **(see Figure 4-32).** Coupling systems have two main parts—the fifth wheel and the trailer kingpin. Correctly coupling the tractor to the trailer is one of the major responsibilities of every professional driver.

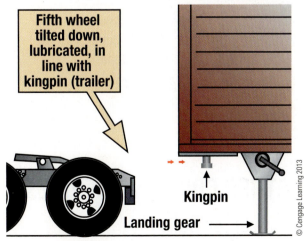

Fifth wheel tilted down, lubricated, in line with kingpin (trailer)

Kingpin

Landing gear

© Cengage Learning 2013

▶ **Figure 4-32**

The coupling system includes the tractor's fifth wheel and the trailer's kingpin.

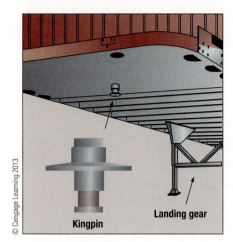

© Cengage Learning 2013

► Figure 4–33

Close-up of a trailer's kingpin and landing gear. Different kingpin settings affect the hookup.

Fifth Wheel

Not really a wheel, the **fifth wheel** is a flat disk on the tractor. The kingpin **(see Figure 4-33)** of the trailer fits into the jaws and is held by the fifth wheel. This link allows the tractor to pull the trailer. There are several types of fifth wheels, appropriate for various types of loads:

Fixed-mount fifth wheel is the most common type. It is secured in a fixed position behind the cab. It has three parts—the top or base plate, the bracket subassemblies, and the frame mounting members. The top plate includes the locking mechanism and bears much of the stress of coupling. The bracket subassemblies hold the top plate in place. The frame mounting members are usually structural steel angles bolted to the fifth wheel.

Sliding (adjustable) **fifth wheel** slides backward and forward but can be locked into place to adapt to different loads. The sliding type increases the flexibility of the total rig. The sliding fifth wheel helps the rig conform to state laws regarding vehicle length and distribution of weight over the axles. Sliding fifth wheels may be locked into place in two ways:

1. Pins fit into matching holes in the slider track and hold it in place.
2. A plunger fits into a row of slotted holes in the base to keep it from moving.

The slider can be adjusted automatically or by hand.

Fifth Wheel Slack Adjusters

The slack adjuster on a fifth wheel adjusts the kingpin locking mechanism so it will fit snugly around the kingpin. Slack adjusters are used on most mechanical locking mechanisms. Compression locking mechanisms reduce problems with slack.

Kingpins

Kingpins are attached to the upper fifth-wheel plate, which is underneath the front of the trailer. The kingpin is usually a 2-inch steel pin that is locked into the jaws of the fifth wheel to couple the tractor to the trailer. It is made of high-strength steel **(see Figure 4-34).**

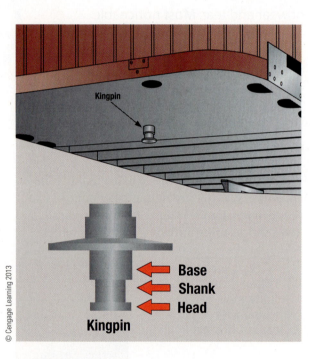

© Cengage Learning 2013

► Figure 4–34

The kingpin.

OTHER COUPLING DEVICES
Converter Dolly

There are two types of **converter dollies:** conventional and jifflox (universal). A **conventional converter dolly** is used to change semi-trailers into full trailers when the dolly becomes the front axle of the trailer. A **jifflox converter dolly** is hooked behind the axle of a single axle tractor to convert it to a tandem axle tractor. The tractor can then pull a loaded trailer.

Trailer Landing Gear

When not coupled with a tractor, a trailer needs support for its front end. The landing gear supports the trailer when it is not coupled with a tractor **(see Figure 4-35)**. The landing gear is usually hand-cranked and will have skid feet. Landing gears will not resist pressure from the side, front, or rear. They are only a means of stationary support and not designed to raise or lower the trailer.

▶ **Figure 4–35**

Trailer on its landing gear.

© Cengage Learning 2013

SUMMARY

The major systems you should be familiar with after studying this chapter are the frame, suspension, axles, engine, ECS, fuel, exhaust, lubrication, electrical, coolant, brake, steering, and coupling. As a professional driver, you need to understand the relationships between the different vehicle systems. It is important to know how the frame, axles, wheels and their parts, engine, drivetrain, and brakes operate. Roll stability systems were also reviewed, and an explanation of how these systems impact the rig's performance was provided.

KEY TERMS

Aftercooler
Air bag suspension
Air compressor
Air intake system
Alternators
Ammeter
Axles
Battery
Belted bias tires
Bias-ply tires
Bypass system
Cable-operated clutch control
Camber
Camshaft
Caster
Centrifugal filter
Chamfer

Charging circuit
Clutch
Combination full-flow/bypass
   system
Combustion
Conventional converter dolly
Converter dollies
Converter dolly axle
Coolant
Coolant system
Coupling/uncoupling system
Crank
Cranking circuit
Crankshaft
Cybernetics
Cylinders
Dead axle

Diesel engine
Differential
Dipstick
Direct clutch control
Drag link
Drive pinion gear
Driveshaft
Drivetrain
Electrical system
Electronic control unit (ECU)
Electronic stability control (ESC)
Engine block
Enhanced roll stability
Exhaust system
Fan belt
Fifth wheel
Fixed-mount fifth wheel

Frame
Fuel filters
Fuel system
Fuel system heater
Fuel tank
Full-flow system
Full-stability systems
Gasoline engine
Generators
Ignition circuit
Interaxle differential
Internal combustion engine
Jifflox converter dolly
Kingpin
Lateral acceleration
Lift axle
Live axle
Lubrication system
Lug tread
Multiple axle assembly
Oil change
Oil filters
Oil pan

Ordinary trailer axle
Partial-authority systems
Piston
Pitman arm
Power steering
Pyrometer
Radial tires
Radiator cap
Recap
Regroove
Retread
Rib tread
Ring gear
Roll-only stability safety valves
Roll stability
Shock absorbers
Single-drive axles
Sliding fifth wheel
Sliding tandem
Spark plug
Spider gears
Splines
Spoke wheels

Spring leaf suspension
Steering gear box
Steering gear shaft
Steering wheel
Suspension system
Tandem axles
Thermostat
Tie rod
Tire tread
Toe-in
Toe-out
Traction
Transmission
Tri-drive axles
Universal joints (U-joints)
Valves
Variable load suspension (VLS)
   axle
Voltage regulator
Voltmeter
Water jacket
Wrist pin
Yaw (directional stability)

REVIEW QUESTIONS

1. The frame of a tractor functions as all but one of the following. Which of these statements is incorrect? _____

   a. The frame is the backbone of the tractor.

   b. Engine mounts are attached to the frame.

   c. The body is connected to and strengthened by the frame.

   d. Axles are directly connected to the frame.

2. The suspension system functions as all but one of the following. Which one? _____

   a. It distributes the load evenly.

   b. It distributes and carries the weight of the truck.

   c. It provides ergonomic comfort for the driver.

   d. The front and rear axles are attached to it.

3. The axles perform all but one of the following tasks. Which task is not accurately stated? _____

   a. They connect the wheels to the rest of the trailer-tractor.

   b. They support the weight of the vehicle.

   c. All axles perform the same function.

   d. They support the weight of the vehicle and cargo.

4. Rear tractor axles may also be referred to as _____.

   a. drive axles

   b. torque axles

   c. carbon axles

   d. suspension axles

5. When describing live axles, it is inaccurate to say _____.

   a. it is a power axle

   b. it is not hollow

   c. it supports the vehicle's weight

   d. it sends power to the wheels

6. The rear axle is _____.
   a. powered
   b. the connecting point to the brake
   c. the stabilizing axle
   d. powered by an additional engine located at the rear of the tractor

7. A plunger that fits snugly against the cylinder wall and that can move up and down the wall is known as a _____.
   a. crankshaft
   b. carburetor
   c. connecting rod
   d. piston

8. In a diesel engine, the extreme _____ of the fuel–air mixture in the cylinder by the piston squeezes it so much that the diesel fuel ignites.
   a. regression
   b. compression
   c. heat
   d. cold

9. In a gasoline engine, the fuel–air mixture is ignited by _____ from the spark plug.
   a. an electrical spark
   b. compression
   c. heavy gas
   d. none of the above

10. The main purpose of roll stability systems is _____.
    a. to maintain a tire's momentum.
    b. to stabilize fuel usage.
    c. to offset the vehicle's tendency to tip over.
    d. to stabilize the rig's couplings.

11. In a diesel engine, the fuel heating system does what?
    a. It creates friction to generate heat line.
    b. It passes fuel through a boiler.
    c. It returns fuel to the fuel tank via a fuel return.
    d. It collects wax crystals and melts them to warm it.

12. The aftercooler cools the intake air from the _____ to a safe temperature.
    a. exhaust system
    b. turbocharger
    c. fuel tank
    d. air intake system

13. The most important function of the lubricating system is to distribute oil to _____ friction between the surfaces of the engine parts.
    a. increase
    b. filter the water in the cooling
    c. the cooling system to reduce the
    d. reduce

14. The _____ system distributes oil to parts of the engine to reduce the wear caused by friction.
    a. lubricating
    b. air filter
    c. support
    d. exhaust

15. While the battery provides the energy to start the engine and is used for extra energy when needed, the _____ furnishes all other electrical needs.
    a. exhaust system
    b. fifth wheel
    c. alternator or generator
    d. cranking circuit

16. The _____ takes the power generated by the engine and applies it to the tractor's drive wheels.
    a. freight train
    b. drivetrain
    c. generator
    d. fifth wheel

17. The driver uses the _____ to connect or disconnect the engine from the rest of the drive (power) train.
    a. fifth wheel
    b. lubricating system
    c. clutch
    d. ammeter

18. At each end of the driveshaft are located the _____, which can move in almost any direction.
    a. transmissions
    c. universal joints
    b. drive pinion gear
    d. multiple gear housings

19. When a tractor maneuvers around a corner, the outside wheels rotate faster than the inside wheels, which is made possible because of the _____.
    a. differential
    c. driveshaft
    b. universal joints
    d. fifth wheel

20. The interaxle differential should remain _____ at all times on normal roads in good weather.
    a. locked
    c. at the terminal
    b. unlocked
    d. in the trailer

SUPPLEMENTAL LEARNING ACTIVITIES

1. Using toy trucks on a cardboard roadway, demonstrate a jackknife and a tip-over. Explain how roll-only and full-stability systems operate to help avoid these situations. Use posters to illustrate your points, if necessary.

2. In 100 words or less, discuss as a group why it is important to know how the various systems on a tractor-trailer rig work together. Give three scenarios about how this information would assist a driver who is over-the-road.

3. Look up FMCSR 393.75 for regulations regarding normal tire inflation and discuss, as a class, why these regulations are necessary.

4. As a review, discuss what you, as a professional driver, should do when getting out of the cab. Would you use a different routine when getting out of your tractor's cab at a truck stop, compared to being parked on a street with your passenger door on curbside and the driver's door opening onto the street?

5. One of the most common causes of injury or death for cyclists is "**dooring**," when the driver of a passenger vehicle or CMV opens a door into the path of an oncoming bicycle. Many states have explicit laws against dooring (including California, Illinois, Wisconsin, and Massachusetts). It is the driver's responsibility to look before opening the door, and some drivers may be fined for failing to do so. Also note that the California and Illinois laws include further prohibitions against leaving doors open toward traffic longer than required to enter or exit the vehicle.

6. Prepare a truck with some underinflated tires and some overinflated tires. Have the class try and determine which tires are not properly inflated without the use of a pressure gauge.

FOR MORE INFORMATION

PTDI—Check and Maintain Vehicle Systems and Components, Page 17, Click on Skills Standards
www.ptdi.org/standards

FMCSA Commercial Vehicle Tire Condition Sensors—Search for Tire Condition Sensors to view PDF
www.fmcsa.dot.gov

FMCSA Benefits and Costs of Roll Stability Control Systems—Enter search for Roll Stability Control Systems
www.fmcsa.dot.gov

5 Transportation Technology

© Christian Lagerek/www.Shutterstock.com

OBJECTIVES

When you have completed this chapter, you should be able to:

- Explain technology that is being used in today's trucking transportation industry.

- Understand the applications of some of this technology and its benefits.

- Make decisions regarding your personal purchase of additional technology to assist you in your goal of becoming a professional truck driver.

INTRODUCTION

Like every other area of our society, the truck transportation industry in general—and professional drivers in particular—continue to use new generations of information technology as it becomes available, as they've done for decades (**see Figure 5-1**). When truckers were over-the-road, to check in with the dispatcher required pulling over when they could find a pay phone and depositing a bunch of quarters—and the days of "Breaker, Breaker 1-9" and the Citizens Band (CB) radio are barely visible in history's rearview mirror. While they are still used, they've been replaced by broadband, wi-fi, BlueTooth, and cellular technology, not to mention **global positioning systems (GPS)** monitoring, laptops, Facebook, and Twitter.

▶ Figure 5-1

Professional drivers have been using information technology for decades.

INTERESTING FACT

The CB Radio was invented in 1945. Al Gross, the inventor, also invented the walkie-talkie. When CB radios were improved to 40 channels in 1977 and prices began decreasing, more users—particularly motorists and big rig drivers—used their CBs to tell other highway users where to find the cheapest gas during the nationwide oil shortage.

Today, as **technology** has saturated the public at large, many more people understand the value of computer applications, communications, wireless technology, and GPS to streamline performance, record keeping, and the daily transactions required in transportation (**see Figure 5-2**).

In many companies, when new drivers come on board, a portion of their probationary training is dedicated to learning the operation and application of high technology to their daily routines—from collections to vehicle maintenance, communication, and the transmission of data about a load. For the owner-operator, the Internet has become more valuable, not only from a weather and road-conditions information perspective but also because more independents are relying on the Internet to identify their next load.

The human resources and recruiting function of many industry members also has been translated to computers and the Internet. Every year, scores of drivers are introduced to job prospects through Internet sites.

Another example, aligning with the new Compliance, Safety, Accountability 2010 (CSA 2010) guidelines, is the inthinc™ Technology Solutions recently released touch-screen driver interface, designed to improve trucking safety. The device, which works in tandem with the company's WaySmart Commercial Driving Safety Program, can provide driver alerts, vehicle locator and diagnosis services, as well as fleet management capabilities.

Without a doubt, today's new professional driver must be as savvy about technology as most white-collar workers, and lack of this knowledge may slow down career progress. Computer literacy is quickly becoming as important as driving the rig itself.

The purpose of this chapter is to provide an overview of today's transportation technology and its application to the day-to-day routine of the professional driver.

▶ Figure 5-2

All new drivers must be trained and knowledgeable in all the technology currently available to them.

A BRIEF HISTORY OF TRUCKING TECHNOLOGY

1910–1920: In the early years of trucking, the only focus was transporting goods from point of origin to end user. This often required navigating primitive roads and driving long hours at a time.

1930: Professional drivers were now required to document every hour they were on the clock, using pen and paper to log in their activity. Many resented having to report how they had spent each 15-minute increment.

1950: By now, Route 66 and the Interstate Highway System were well underway, so big rigs could be driven at higher speeds. However, this was also the time the first federal maximum gross vehicle limits for trucks were adopted, thus piling one more regulation and one more report on the trucking industry.

1970: Using CB radios as their means of communication, truckers relayed information to each other about weather and road conditions, traffic congestion, police officers, transportation authorities, road construction, detours, and more. The tachograph—which functioned as a clock and a speedometer— also came into use in the '70s. Using a mechanical stylus, it recorded a truck's speed and whether it was moving or parked and held drivers accountable for the use of their time.

Mounted in the cab, the tachograph's mechanical stylus recorded the truck's speed and whether it was moving or stationary. The information was displayed on a circular piece of paper that rotated throughout the day. Every 24 hours the driver put in a new sheet and turned in the marked-up sheet.

For the first time, drivers were truly held accountable for how they spent their time.

1980s and 1990s: With deregulation came a dramatic increase in the number of trucking companies— and in the competition. These decades also saw the rise in the industry's performance-driven culture, one based on improving all aspects of performance, including driver performance, vehicle performance, idle time, on-time deliveries, and compliance performance. Data gathering was initially tedious and time-consuming.

However, by the end of the 1980s, technological advances improved efficiencies with affordable on-board computers. At the end of each shift or trip, drivers pulled the data from their trucks, using data-storage software to be uploaded to a PC in the company's office. And because onboard computers made it easy for drivers to complete and submit their logs, these professionals were actually free to do what they'd always done best—drive and deliver.

2000: With mobile communications technology—cell phone tower communications, satellite-based relays, and wi-fi—at the forefront, North America's trucking industry began making advances toward performance excellence:

- Global positioning systems (GPS) made routing and scheduling easier.
- Data from drivers and their rigs became instantly accessible.

2010 and beyond: As technology continues to advance, carriers now have the means to create data models that increase their insights into today and tomorrow. Four advances in this direction impact routing, dispatch, proof of delivery, and trailer automation.

In addition, the Federal Motor Carrier Safety Administration (FMCSA) Compliance, Safety, Accountability 2010 (CSA 2010) initiative and its Advanced Notice of Proposed Rulemaking on electronic onboard recording devices means more change is headed toward the North American transportation industry. While experts can only guess about the future, fleets that employ technology for compliance and performance will lead their industry.

ABOUT QUALCOMM®

Many major carriers equip their fleets with **Qualcomm** mobile fleet management systems. The following information will give you some insight into this company and its services (**Figure 5-3**).

Courtesy of Qualcomm

▶ **Figure 5–3**

Major carriers are using wireless equipment.

Qualcomm's first commercial product was the OmniTRACS® mobile information system, a satellite-based vehicle location tracking and data messaging service used by the trucking industry to manage fleets. This product was introduced in 1988 and paved the way for a whole range of fleet management products that have been widely adopted throughout the transportation and logistics industry. Following after the OmniTRACS system, Qualcomm now offers the Mobile Computing Platform, designed to offer the right solution to fleets with a variety of different operational profiles and needs.

Since its beginnings, Qualcomm has grown by developing and applying advanced technologies for wireless telecommunications products and services. A main focus has been the commercial transportation industry where Qualcomm products have increased efficiency and lowered costs.

As an example, Qualcomm platforms and applications enable drivers to communicate with dispatchers and fleet managers. These same products monitor vehicle locations and help drivers protect their cargo and provide superior customer service while they are on the road. In addition, Qualcomm develops solutions that not only help improve operations and reduce costs, but also help secure and protect drivers and cargo.

Among Qualcomm's mobile technology applications developed for the transportation industry are the following:

Qualcomm's In-Cab Scanning—provides carriers a comprehensive document management solution that enables enhanced customer satisfaction, improves productivity, and reduces operating expenses. No more wasted time making extra stops and paying fees to copy, scan, fax, or mail documents. This end-to-end service enables drivers to scan and transmit documents from the cab of their truck directly into the customer through web services integration. In-Cab Scanning also

Courtesy of Qualcomm

helps improve customer and driver satisfaction by reducing manual errors associated with rekeying important information, including trip and mileage reports, bills of lading, timesheets, receipts, and other critical customer information (**Figure 5-4**).

In-Cab Navigation—including Maptuit NaviGo or ALK CoPilot Live Truck — provides increased driver safety, optimizes drivers' time on the road, reduces accidents and out-of-route miles, and improves efficiency and on-time deliveries. In-Cab Navigation gives drivers turn-by-turn directions, and helps improve the bottom line.

CSA Safety Performance Service—is a comprehensive set of tools, enabling fleets to proactively manage and remediate performance issues related to CSA's scoring methodology. It helps fleets identify and remediate

▶ **Figure 5–4**

In-cab scanning tool.

performance issues before they negatively impact compliance, plus increases driver safety, reduces accidents, incidents, and bad inspections, and increases knowledge and awareness across the organization.

Critical Event Reporting—is an automatic vehicle-monitoring capability that enables safety and fleet managers to manage the safety behavior of their drivers in near real-time. It continuously monitors fleet vehicles for critical events such as hard braking, vehicle yaw and pitch motions, and driver-initiated alerts while providing driver/truck ID, time/date, position/location, hours-of-service (HOS) compliance, and on-board vehicle sensor and device information such as parking brake status, speed, hard braking deceleration rate, and motion stability for potential jackknife or rollover (**see Figure 5-5**).

Courtesy of 5th Wheel Training Institute (1-888-647-7202)

▶ **Figure 5-5**

Critical event reporting continuously monitors fleet vehicles for critical events.

ONBOARD RECORDERS

On September 30, 1988, the Federal Highway Administration published a final rule (53 FR 38666) to allow motor carriers, at their option, to use certain **electronic onboard recording (EOBR)** devices to record their drivers' records of duty status in lieu of the required handwritten records of duty status. This provision is now codified at 49 CFR 395.15. Many motor carriers employing that technology found that their compliance with the hours-of-service regulations improved. For more information, visit www.fmcsa .dot.gov/, search for automatic onboard recording devices.

FMCSR 395.15 reads, in part, as follows: "Authority to use automatic onboard recording device—A motor carrier may require a driver to use an automatic onboard recording device to record the driver's hours of service."

Information required with use of EOBR includes a driver's hours of service chart, electronic display, or printout showing the time and sequence of duty status changes including the driver's starting time at the beginning of each day. Along with using the EOBR to record hours of service, the driver shall have in his or her possession records of duty status for the previous 7 consecutive days available for inspection while on duty. These records shall consist of information stored in and retrievable from the automatic onboard recording device, handwritten records, computer-generated records, or any combination thereof.

INTERESTING FACT

In March 2011, when the trucking ban was lifted between the United States and Mexico, terms of the agreement stipulated that all Mexican trucks would be required to have electronic onboard recorders to track compliance with hours-of-service and related laws, according to the White House. In addition, the Department of Transportation will review drivers' records, ensure that they all understand English, and require that they are tested for drugs.

However, the FMCSA also realizes new technologies are emerging and the narrowly crafted onboard recorder provision is becoming obsolete.

Before considering changes to the rule, the FHWA found it prudent to demonstrate the effectiveness of more recent technology for ensuring compliance with the hours-of-service regulations.

The FHWA also hopes to demonstrate the safety and economic advantages to the motor carrier industry when the technology is used to reduce the prescriptive paperwork and record-keeping requirements of the hours-of-service regulations (49 CFR, part 395). Should the results of the pilot prove to be positive and the safety potential of the involved technologies confirmed, the agency will consider proposing revisions to the FMCSR.

As of February 2011, the Federal Motor Carrier Safety Administration proposed to amend the Federal Motor Carrier Safety Regulations (49 CFR §385, 390, and 395) to require certain motor carriers operating commercial motor vehicles and interstate commerce to use electronic onboard recorders (EOBRs) to document their drivers' hours of service. With this proposal all motor carriers currently required to maintain Records Of Duty Status (RODS) for hours of service (HOS) record-keeping would be required to use EOBRs to systematically and effectively monitor their drivers' compliance with HOS requirements.

Additionally this proposal set forth the supporting documents that all motor carriers currently required to use Records Of Duty Status would still be required to obtain and keep as required by section 113(a) of the Hazardous Materials Transportation Authorization Act. It explains, however, that although motor carriers subject to the proposed GOP requirements still need to retain some supporting documents, they would be relieved of the requirements to retain supporting documents to verify driving time. FMCSA also proposed to require all motor carriers—both RODS and timecard users—to systematically monitor their drivers' compliance with HOS requirements.

According to the proposed amendment, motor carriers would be given three years after the effective date of the final rule to comply with these requirements.

TRACKING DEVICES

Loss prevention and security in any business is an important topic, especially in challenging economic conditions. The truck transportation industry is faced with the additional prospect of losses that can be incurred by theft and misuse of trucks and trailers in a fleet.

The best method for preventing losses is vigilance, being proactive, and outfitting trucks and their cargoes with GPS tracking devices. These are different from the GPS navigation systems that trucking fleets use to help drivers get the best route information **(see Figure 5-6)**.

GPS tracking devices provide real-time feedback to an end user, including location, direction of travel, speed, and geofencing (sending alerts when an asset breaches a preset boundary on a map). These devices have become invaluable because they can be used to monitor asset movement in real-time, which helps fleet operations manage routes and driver activity all from one single PC screen.

If an asset is stolen, the person monitoring this type of activity can know it in an instant and provide the location to law enforcement, who can then recover the asset in mere hours, versus days, weeks, months, or maybe even never.

Another reason GPS tracking is a valuable tool for the trucking industry is because most insurance companies will provide a reduction in

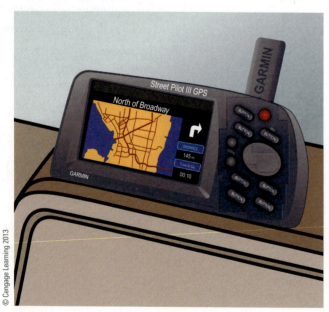

▶ Figure 5-6

Global positioning system (GPS).

insurance premiums for fleets that employ these devices. GPS tracking also makes sense as a loss prevention tool because maintaining a tight grip on business operations is mandatory if the trucking industry is going to survive in a challenging economy.

In March 2011, Morey Corp. unveiled a new tracking device that combines GPS and cellular tracking technology for use in track-and-trace applications where a consistent power source is not available.

The Trax MT-10 Asset Tracker, a telematics-based solution, includes a rugged enclosure designed to IP67/66k standards that is able to withstand extreme shock, vibration, and temperature stresses. It also offers wireless communications via cellular modem, location tracking via GPA, motion detection, over-the-air programming, and internal antennas. The device is powered by a field-replaceable battery.

"According to our tracking systems, this is where the load is currently."

Particularly in tight economies, carriers and companies are seeking straightforward, cost-effective solutions for better asset management. This tracking device was designed to create major improvements in visibility and control of business critical assets, which ultimately translates into better corporate performance.

Later, in the summer of 2011, a new plug-and-play device from Mentor Engineering was introduced to give fleets a quick, affordable way to implement vehicle tracking and baseline telematics. The new ME10 offers automatic vehicle location using an integrated GSM model and GPS.

The device provides real-time tracking and also will plug into a vehicle's OBDII port to monitor items such as mileage and fuel usage. Essentially, the new device is plug-and-play because, within minutes, a fleet manager can have GPS tracking enabled on a vehicle without the headaches of a several-hour installation or needing to take a vehicle out of service. It's also a great option for temporary workers or leased vehicles because there is zero installation impact on the vehicles.

GLOBAL POSITIONING SYSTEMS AND THE FHWA

The Federal Highway Administration believes global positioning system (GPS) technology and many of the complementary safety management computer systems currently being used by motor carriers provide at least the same degree of monitoring accuracy as the EOBRs allowed by the Federal Motor Carrier Safety Regulations, 49 CFR 395.15.

Accordingly, the FHWA announced a voluntary program under which a motor carrier with GPS technology and related safety management computer systems could enter into an agreement with the FHWA to use such systems in a pilot demonstration project to record and monitor drivers'

INTERESTING FACT

The **global positioning system (GPS)**, developed in 1973 by the U.S. Department of Defense, is a space-based global navigation satellite system (GNSS) designed to provide location and time information in all weather, anywhere on or near the Earth, where there is an unobstructed line of sight to four or more GPS satellites. It is maintained by the United States government and became freely accessible by anyone with a GPS receiver in 2007.

hours of service in lieu of complying with the handwritten records of duty status requirement of the FMCSR, 49 CFR 395.8 (**see Figure 5-7**).

Consistent with current initiatives in reinventing government and regulatory reform, the project is intended to demonstrate whether the motor carrier industry can use the technology to improve compliance with the hours-of-service requirements in a manner that promotes safety and operational efficiency while reducing paperwork requirements.

▶ Figure 5–7

A rig with GPS technology.

ELECTRONIC PAYMENT

For four decades, Comdata has been at the forefront of payment innovations, developing the concept of electronic payments for transportation, and in the process, launching the Comdata Card a payment solution that helped drive an industry. Today their products help manage financial transactions of all kinds.

Comdata revolutionized the trucking industry in 1969 with the Comchek® paper draft, the first specialized form of payment to transfer money and information over the road safely, securely, and accurately. This paper draft has grown into an impressive group of funds distribution services, all based on providing a one-card solution for fuel and purchasing.

Today, Comdata offers integrated financial solutions that are changing the way companies manage data, pay employees, process transactions, and manage spending on key business purchases. These solutions help save money, grow revenue, streamline operations, and minimize financial risks.

One such service is the Comdata Fleet Card, an easy-to-use gas card that helps control drivers' expenses and increase fuel efficiency. The card allows fleet managers to monitor spending at the individual level by setting purchasing limits and tracking spending patterns such as grade of fuel, fueling frequency, time of fueling, or fuel location.

FUEL MANAGEMENT AND REPORTING

Several other companies offer a discount fuel network that includes discounts and data monitoring, providing reports that help pinpoint problems and track fuel usage.

Jack Lee, founder and chairman of 4Refuel Canada LP emphasizes, "You can't manage what you don't measure."

Consider this scenario: 10 trucks spend 30 minutes each day getting fuel. This totals up to 1,250 hours spent fueling trucks, which is lost revenue because those 10 trucks weren't on the road. The cost? Try close to $200,000 in lost revenues each year. As the fleet grows, lost revenues increase.

How to win this battle?

Lee's company, 4Refuel Canada LP, is a long-established provider and the only national company to bring fuel onsite. They've also introduced service standards, safety training, environmental protection, and a national certification program for all their operators as well as technology that automates reporting so carriers can manage fuel costs in only a few clicks.

COMMUNICATION

Satellite Communication

Volvo Trucks introduced Volvo Link™, its unique satellite-based communications system, integrated into each truck and available for models 2000 and newer. It is now standard equipment on all new Volvo trucks and integrates vehicle communication to any fleet in the United States and Canada. These powerful tools also maximize uptime and improve efficiency, promote better fleet communication, increase vehicle and fleet productivity, improve safety, and reduce operational costs.

Truck data can be accessed through any PC to monitor the performance of both truck and driver, 24/7. The services supported by Volvo Link are designed to help manage performance issues.

Volvo Link offers reporting to include mileage, fuel utilization, engine idle time, and engine running time. Each feature is easily customizable to every user's needs (see **Figure 5-8**).

▶ Figure 5–8

Volvo Link.

Onboard Laptop Computers

Many companies now provide **laptop computers** as a means of communication and business management for professional drivers. Independents often use at least one laptop onboard to schedule loads, plan trips, get up-to-the-minute reports on road conditions, send and receive e-mail, and communicate with consignors and consignees regarding pickups and deliveries.

Much of today's drivers' paperwork is done via computer and many trucks are now equipped to support wireless access and Internet ports so that drivers can do business during their off-the-road time.

A good laptop—one that is sturdy and easy to use—can save a driver valuable time and, at the same time, keep him or her connected with family members and friends while on the road (see **Figure 5-9**).

▶ Figure 5–9

A good laptop can save a driver valuable time.

Cell Phones

Cellular phones, as a concept and an alternative to landlines, began in 1947 when researchers looked at crude mobile phones and realized that by using small cells (range of service areas) with frequency reuse they could increase the traffic capacity of mobile phones; however, the technology to do it was nonexistent at that time. That same year, AT&T asked the Federal Communications Commission to allocate a large number of radio spectrum frequencies so that widespread mobile telephone service could become feasible and AT&T would have an incentive to research the new technology. Because of the FCC's decision to limit the frequencies, however, only 23 phone conversations could occur simultaneously in the same service area—not a market incentive for research.

In 1968, the FCC increased the frequencies allocation, increasing the capacity of the airwaves for more mobile phones. AT&T Bell Labs proposed a cellular system to the FCC of many small, low-powered broadcast towers, each covering a cell a few miles in radius, collectively covering a larger area. Each tower would use only a few of the total frequencies allocated to the system, and as cars moved across the area, their calls would be passed from tower to tower.

In 1979, the first commercial cellular telephone system began use in Tokyo and in 1983, the first American commercial phone for analog cellular service was offered in Chicago, by Ameritech. In spite of incredible demand, it took cellular phone service 37 years to become commercially available in the United States. By 1987, cellular phone users exceeded 1 million, crowding the airways.

Along with the ability to allow mobile users to communicate through the use of phone numbers, today's cell phones also make it possible to access computers, send text messages to other cell users, and to take and transmit photographs, connect to the Internet, and send e-mails.

Today, with few exceptions, all professional truck drivers carry either personal or company-provided cell phones to keep in touch with dispatch and families and to use in emergency situations. Just look around. Pay phones are few and far between, especially when compared to the days where truckers had to find pay phones to check in with dispatch. The cell phone has not totally replaced the citizens band radio but has become yet another communications tool for the professional driver and the trucking transportation industry.

STOP!

Effective Jan. 3, 2012, the Federal Motor Carrier Safety Administration issued a new rule, banning the use of hand-held cell phones while interstate truck drivers and bus drivers are operating their vehicles. Through the Pipeline and Hazardous Materials Safety Administration, drivers hauling hazardous materials within a state are also included in the ban. The new ruling is the next step in an ongoing process to save lives and prevent injuries on North American highways. Drivers who violate the rule are subject to a fine of up to $2,750 for each offense and disqualification from operating a CMV for multiple offenses.

INTERESTING FACT

The first pager-like system was used in 1921 by the Detroit Police Department, but the first time the term *pager* was used was in 1959. A small radio receiver that delivered a radio message individually to those carrying the device, the first pager was Motorola's Pageboy I, introduced in 1974. It had no display and could not store messages, but it was portable and notified the wearer that a message had been sent.

Pagers

Dedicated radio frequency (RF) devices, pagers, make it possible for the user to receive messages on a specific broadcast frequency over a special network of radio base stations.

By 1980, there were 3.2 million pager users worldwide. Pagers had a limited range, and were used in on-site situations (e.g., medical workers within a hospital). And by 1990, wide-area paging had been invented and over 22 million pagers were in use. By 1994, there were over 61 million pagers in use in the United States alone. Today, companies—particularly those with local pick up and delivery (P&D) operations—use pagers to maintain communication between their headquarters and customer job sites. Most, however, have switched to cell phone usage.

Walkie-Talkies

A new technology was adopted for peacetime use when U.S. police departments began using "call boxes." In 1963, beat officers began to use the **walkie-talkie,** a miniature two-way radio. With 1.4 watts of power, the radio had a range of 10 miles (16 km), weighed less than 2 pounds (0.9 kg), could attach to an officer's belt, and gave officers instant contact with the radio dispatcher and patrol cars (**see Figure 5-10**). By 1967, call boxes were obsolete.

Today, walkie-talkie service is available from coast to coast and across borders. Through direct connections, users can speak to base dispatchers, friends, and families almost anywhere within the network available for the particular device being used.

Citizens Band Radios

In 1958, the first CB radio was used in the United States. By the early 1970s, fuel shortages and the introduction of a 55 mph (89 km/h) speed limit made the CB indispensable to those who made their living on the road. Drivers used CBs to locate fuel and get advance warning of speed traps, hence the adoption of codes and slang to avoid the ears of the highway patrol, often also fitted with CBs.

▶ Figure 5-10

Walkie-talkie service is available from coast to coast and across the borders.

INTERESTING FACT

In 1940, the first handheld two-way radio—called "The Handy Talkie"—was designed by Motorola for the U.S. Army's Signal Corps.

Due to the popularity of the CB with professional drivers and other travelers, the original 23 channels were expanded to 40 in 1976. That year, more than 10 million CBs were sold in the U.S. The introduction of 80-channel CB rigs sparked a renewed interest in CBs, and now there are currently 12 mobile (vehicle mounted) sets, two handheld units, and one base set available.

Today, the CB, while not as popular, still has devoted users. Professional drivers get traffic reports and directions, farm workers coordinate work and keep in touch with each other, children share their homework, families and friends keep in touch when traveling, and community groups continue to use CB radios for organizing bicycle races and other cross-country events. They are also used as communication between the shipper and the truck driver informing them of their dock assignment.

CAUTION!
For security reasons, never discuss or text any information about your load, your destination, or next stop on a CB radio or in an Internet chat.

CAUTION!
Remember that cell phone cameras are everywhere and comments/photos tweeted on Twitter or posted on Facebook will follow you forever and beyond, so be very careful of your actions in and out of your rig and your words and pictures on the Internet.

iPhone

A line of Internet- and multimedia-enabled smartphones designed and marketed by Apple Inc., the first **iPhone** was unveiled on January 9, 2007. An iPhone can function as a camera or video camera (video recording was not a standard feature until the iPhone 3GS was released) and a portable media player, and can send texts and receive visual voicemail, and provide wi-fi and 3G Internet connectivity for e-mail and web browsing.

The iPhone 3GS added a compass, faster processor, and higher resolution camera, including video recording at 480p (which refers to the quality of graphic resolution). The iPhone 4 has a rear-facing camera and a front-facing camera (at a lower resolution) for FaceTime video calling and for use in other apps like Skype. This phone was released in June 2010.

BlackBerry®

Developed by Research in Motion (RIM), based in Ontario, Canada, **BlackBerry** provides wireless connectivity as well as access to a wide range of applications on a variety of wireless devices. It combines award-winning devices, software, and services to keep mobile professionals connected to the people, data, and resources that drive their day.

Social Media

The use of social media, such as Facebook and Twitter, among others, is now officially another way of communicating being used by the North American truck transportation industry.

Marten Transport, a premier time- and temperature-sensitive carrier based in Mondovi, Wisconsin, is expanding its social media presence beyond Facebook to include Twitter, YouTube, and a new blog. Dedicated to providing excellent customer service and the best in quality when it comes to time- and temperature-sensitive transportation services to customers nationwide, the company plans to expand their connections with drivers and customers.

Marten Transport is committed to increasing their communication with drivers and customers, and that includes dedicated social media efforts. These efforts include participating in conversations with customers, prospects, and enthusiasts in the industry about current online topics.

SOCIAL NETWORKING FOR TRUCK DRIVERS

A large percentage of long-haul drivers travel with a laptop. This allows them to keep in touch with family friends and also to log on to social media sites. Favorites **social networking** sites include:

TheTruckersReport.com—social media and forum site for professional drivers. Forums allow anyone to post a question, get information on routes or industry news, or talk to other truck drivers from across the continent and around the world.

LifeOnTheRoad.com—a blog that invites blogs, articles, and posts from driver/writers who want to share stories, and opinions on anything and everything.

TruckersForum.net—a site where you can stay current on industry trends, news, jobs, and changes in the law as it impacts the trucking transportation industry.

Facebook—popular social media sites to stay in touch with family and friends, but also other drivers. You'll find truck driver discussion groups and communities on these sites with just a simple search.

Twitter—quickly becoming the hot new social media for truckers. Messages are short, reach is wide, and "tweeting" can be done and/or followed throughout the day. Some drivers even post TwitPics of their journeys around the country.

REGULATORY COMPLIANCE

A number of companies offer electronic regulatory compliance assistance services. These services include a wide range of services, from fuel tax preparation to employment records.

Permitting Services

Through a wide-ranging network, electronic services provide state, provincial, and local permitting, expediting permit needs so drivers can get on the road.

Fuel Tax Services

Fuel tax services electronically track fuel purchases in every state and then fill out necessary paperwork. Fully automated processing of fuel tax reports includes the use of GPS or dispatch data and electronic fueling records.

License Renewals

License renewal services electronically track and manage base state license renewals, IRP and single-state registrations, and IFTA permitting.

Driver Log Auditing

Driver log auditing services electronically maintain driver logs so that carriers can avoid fines and reduce exposure to conditional ratings, including all major and minor violations.

Fleets submit driver logs—including fueling, roadside inspection, and random drug test information—and access any needed data via the Internet within 48 hours, eliminating paper recordkeeping and having access to all DOT compliance data.

Because the system is Internet based, it offers a higher degree of flexibility than traditional paper-based systems. All information is viewable, but only to those individuals authorized to view specific information.

The system offers access to a mountain of log data that can be organized into several key reports or downloaded and customized to fit a fleet's log management conventions. Plus, it offers routine audit trails on regulatory items important to a fleet, including the number and percent of DOT critical log violations; summary reports of missing, duplicated, and/or incomplete logs; and any necessary driver counseling.

Trip Management

Volvo Trucks feature Volvo Trip Manager to track and report data on each vehicle—a software program that tracks and reports performance on each vehicle by providing comprehensive data such as engine usage, fuel consumption, speed, gear usage, and service information—all without the need for additional onboard hardware (**see Figure 5-11**).

▶ **Figure 5-11**

Volvo trucks feature Volvo Trip Manager to track and report data on the vehicle.

InfoMax™ from Mack Trucks is an onboard data logger that records everything management needs or wants to know about the truck—exactly how your trucks are performing, trip and life of vehicle summaries, maintenance and fault information, engine duty cycle, daily driver stop-and-go activities, plus a lot more.

Data are transmitted from vehicle to computer almost instantly, and completely automatically. You get only the data you want as often as you want. This system can be fully customized to fit the needs of your fleet. InfoMax Wireless™ is the first of its kind and a truly innovative use of the very latest in short-range wireless technology. There are no communication fees or licensing agreements. Manual downloading is eliminated, saving time and money. You can access vehicles on your lot anytime, anywhere and reprogram the parameters on all the trucks in your fleet.

Satellite Radio

Beginning in 2001, Freightliner Corp. and XM Satellite Radio developed new integrated wireless information and entertainment services that are compatible with Freightliner's Truck Productivity Computer.

Additionally, Freightliner distributes, markets, and merchandises XM Satellite Radio through its fleet-owner relationships, its dealer organization, and its network of 160 TravelCenters of America. XM radios were first offered in Freightliner's new models of Freightliner, Sterling, American LaFrance trucks, and Thomas Built buses, beginning in 2001. Some trucking companies also offer Satellite Radios to their drivers as a benefit. It provides the driver with static-free, often commercial-free music, as well as up-to-the-minute weather and traffic conditions.

SUMMARY

In this chapter, you have been able to review some of the technology now available in the transportation industry in North America. Some drivers simply use cell phones to keep in touch with dispatchers as well as home and family while they are on the road. Others use QualComm products, not only for communication but also for business transaction, tracking and reports, and to access other wireless information. Laptop computers, built-in computers, and wireless telecommunications are also available in some of today's trucks.

The bottom line in transportation across North America is that knowledge of wireless communications products and the ability to use a computer are fast becoming skills required of today's professional truck drivers.

KEY TERMS

BlackBerry
Cellular phones
Electronic onboard recording (EOBR)
Global positioning system (GPS)

iPhone
Laptop computer
Pick-up and delivery (P&D)
Qualcomm
Satellite radio

Social networking
Technology
Walkie-talkie

A DAY IN THE LIFE . . .

Richard Dearth – Don Hummer Trucking, Professional Truck Driver

As a trucking citizen, I believe that there is always room for improvement and I look forward to learning new things every day. Regardless of how I feel or the day that I am having, I still try to smile and treat everyone with respect.

In an effort to show respect for the environmental impact that trucking has, I attempt to run my truck at slower speeds—such as running 65 mph instead of 75 mph—to get better fuel mileage. I also keep my idling at a minimum to accomplish the same thing.

I have maintained a safe driving record, have a genuine concern for the role the industry plays in the lives of all Americans, and I have a desire to ensure that trucking continues to be a viable option for employment going forward. Freedom of the open road and the independence that I have to structure my days on my schedule, within load demands and hours of service requirements, makes this position a great alternative to other types of repetitive work or the stuffiness of an office environment.

Over the years, I have taken pride in my record as a commercial driver's license holder. Maintaining a safe following distance, ensuring a safe speed, and anticipating actions of other motorists has enabled me to hold a safe driving record. Treating fellow drivers with respect has always been a priority. Little acts of kindness, such as unhooking a trailer for a driver when meeting for a load swap or spotting for a driver when backing into a tight spot, have always been a priority.

Professional drivers do very important work, and while most Americans do not value their efforts, they reap the rewards of the professional driver's hard work through every meal they eat and every purchase they make. Our economy would be seriously impaired if not for the efforts of millions of professional drivers on our nation's highways each day.

". . . this is an exciting way to earn a good living."

Trucking is my way of life and I am proud to have given a significant contribution during my years of service to that way of life. I want the next generation to know that, while there are many sacrifices, this is an exciting way to earn a good living.

REVIEW QUESTIONS

1. Computer literacy for professional drivers is _____.

   a. not important

   b. somewhat important

   c. the most important part of driving the rig

   d. becoming just as important as driving skills

2. _____ introduced its first product in 1988, a satellite-based messaging service used by the trucking industry to manage fleets and develop solutions that not only provide value and help improve operations, but also help secure and protect drivers and cargo.

   a. Macintosh

   b. DataComm

   c. QualComm

   d. Microsoft

3. Federal rules allow motor carriers to use _____ to record their driver's records of duty status.

   a. automatic onboard recording devices

   b. only required handwritten records

   c. driver's memory (no need for a written record)

   d. telephone answering machine recording at driver's home

4. Some motor carriers with _____ technology and related safety management computer systems may use this technology to monitor driver's hours of service.

   a. cell phone

   b. global positioning system (GPS)

   c. walkie-talkies

   d. citizen band radios (CBs)

5. _____ is honored at truck stops and service centers and is the centerpiece to an unmatched group of services that enable transportation businesses and fleets to operate more profitably.

   a. Onboard recorders

   b. Global positioning systems (GPS)

   c. Satellite communications

   d. Electronic payment (credit cards)

6. _____ is integrated into some tractors and allows immediate access to current tractor information and improves the efficiency of operations as well as the productivity of the driver through instant messaging capabilities between the driver and dispatcher and provides 24/7 access to each truck in the fleet.

   a. Satellite-based communications

   b. Cell phones

   c. Electronic payment systems

   d. Global positioning system

7. Many professional drivers use a _____ to schedule loads, plan trips, get up-to-the-minute reports on road conditions, and send and receive e-mail to communicate with family members, friends, and others in the transportation industry.

   a. GPS

   b. onboard recorder

   c. onboard laptop computer

   d. electronic payment card

8. Today, almost all professional truck drivers carry _____ to keep in touch with dispatch and families and to use in emergency situations.

   a. pagers

   b. onboard recorders

   c. cellular phones

   d. GPS

9. _____ provides wireless connectivity as well as telephone service and access to a wide range of applications such as e-mail, corporate data, voice, SMS messages, web-based information, and paging services.

   a. iPods

   b. GPS

   c. iPhones

   d. iPads

10. _____ is/are Internet-based and electronically maintain driver logs so that carriers can avoid fines and reduce exposure to conditional ratings, including all major and minor violations.

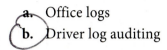

   a. Office logs
   b. Driver log auditing
   c. Dispatcher logs
   d. Shipper logs

SUPPLEMENTAL LEARNING ACTIVITIES

1. Here's the scenario: Your rig just blew a tire. You're in the middle of nowhere, it's night and raining and not much traffic. You have a cell phone and a laptop. Working as a group, decide what's next. Give five steps to get from where you are to back on the road and headed for your destination.

2. Make a list of at least five possible distractions while you're driving. Assume you have a cell phone, an iPod, and an onboard computer.

3. Why is it important to have monitoring equipment on your rig? Working in a group, list five reasons.

4. Write an explanation, in 100 words or less, of how social media can make life on the road easier.

5. In sentences of no more than 25 words each, tell why each of the following has improved a driver's quality of life: (1) Interstate Highway System, (2) CB radios, (3) onboard recorders, (4) GPS, (5) cell phones.

FOR MORE INFORMATION

Technology for Reducing Idling Time
www.transportation.anl.gov/pdfs/TA/74.pdf

Transportation Technology Videos
americanhistory.si.edu/onthemove/themes/story_50_1.html

Transportation Technology Used in Trucks
www.yousigma.com/technologyandarchitectures/transportationtechnologyusedintrucks.pdf

On-Board Recorders Part 395.15
www.fmcsa.dot.gov/rules-regulations/administration/fmcsr/fmcsrruletext.aspx?reg=395.15

6 Vehicle Inspections

© Cengage Learning 2013

OBJECTIVES

When you have completed this chapter, you should be able to:

- Describe a systematic sequence to use in a thorough and complete pretrip inspection.

- Recognize damaged, loose or missing parts, system leaks, and other problems.

- Determine the condition of your rig's critical components, including instruments and controls.

- Explain the importance of correcting malfunctions before beginning each trip.

- Understand and use federal and state regulations for your inspection.

- Perform and explain the steps for en route inspections and perform thorough posttrip inspections, noting actual and suspected component abnormalities or malfunctions.

- Accurately and efficiently complete the Driver's Vehicle Inspection Report (DVIR), or the Canadian Daily Inspection Report.

INTRODUCTION

As a professional driver, safety should be your number one priority, when your rig is being loaded, during your pretrip inspection, on the road, when delivering your cargo, during your posttrip inspection, and every time you climb into or out of the cab **(see Figure 6-1).**

Because today's commercial motor vehicle is more technologically advanced and complex, it requires consistent maintenance and constant attention, and professional drivers must, therefore, learn more skills for optimum performance.

Professional vehicle inspections are not only a way of ensuring safety, but are also mandated by law. Here's what Federal Motor Carrier Safety Administration has to say about vehicle inspections:

Subpart C – Requirements and information for intermodal equipment providers and for motor carriers operating intermodal equipment

§ 390.42 What are the responsibilities of drivers and motor carriers operating intermodal equipment?

a. Before operating intermodal equipment over the road, the driver accepting the equipment must inspect the equipment components listed in § 392.7(b) of this subchapter and be satisfied they are in good working order.

b. A driver or motor carrier transporting intermodal equipment must report to the intermodal equipment provider, or its designated agent, any known damage, defects, or deficiencies in the intermodal equipment at the time the equipment is returned to the provider or the provider's designated agent. If no damage, defects, or deficiencies are discovered by the driver, the report shall so indicate. The report must include, at a minimum, the items in § 396.11(a)(2) –

- Kingpin upper coupling device
- Rails or support frames
- Tie down bolsters
- Locking pins, clevises, clamps, or hooks
- Sliders or sliding frame lock
- Wheels, rims, lugs, tires
- Lighting devices, lamps, markers, and conspicuity marking material
- Air line connections, hoses, and couplers
- Brakes

Each of your rig's systems must be regularly inspected to assure that each part is intact and operating at maximum efficiency. Fluid levels must be frequently checked and refilled when necessary **(see Figure 6-2).** Routine maintenance must be thoroughly and expertly performed.

▶ **Figure 6-1**

Safety is the number one priority for a professional driver.

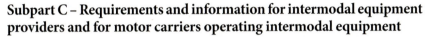

INTERESTING FACT

In 2009, 55 percent of large trucks involved in accidents had at least one mechanical problem in violation of safety regulations and 30 percent had at least one out-of-service problem in violation of safety regulations. The two main causes of mechanical failure were tires and brakes, according to a 2009 study by the University of Michigan based on the Large Truck Crash Causation Study by FMCSA and the National Highway Transportation Safety Administration.

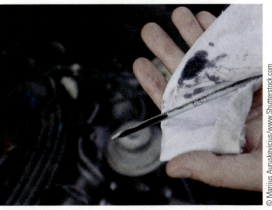

▶ **Figure 6-2**

Check fluid levels frequently and refill as necessary.

GO!

A professional vehicle inspection means not only safety (yours and fellow highway users) but also efficiency. Here's how:

- By avoiding breakdowns during a trip, you save costly road repair service.
- By discovering a problem condition before beginning a trip, you avoid accidents.
- By avoiding breakdowns, you'll have fewer delivery delays, which means increased customer satisfaction.
- By spotting problems before the trip, you'll help cut maintenance costs.

The most critical key, however, to your rig's optimum performance is your timely, step-by-step pretrip, en route, and posttrip inspections.

This chapter will emphasize the critical nature of these inspections and will provide an efficient routine for you to follow each time you check your rig.

CAUTION!

No one in North America has a more dangerous job than a CMV driver, and a professional driver is aware of the importance of safety from the minute he or she steps into the vehicle to the minute he or she steps out of the vehicle—for any reason. The safety of the motoring public is in your hands. A vehicle inspection is the first step toward ensuring the safe operation of your rig.

PRETRIP, EN ROUTE, AND POSTTRIP INSPECTIONS

State and federal laws in the United States and most of the Canadian provinces require that you, the driver, conduct a thorough vehicle inspection each time you take your CMV onto the highway. Drivers may not drive a commercial motor vehicle in the U.S. and Canada without being in possession of a valid inspection report. The three required vehicle inspections are as follows:

- The Pretrip Inspection (See FMCSR 396.13)
- The Enroute Inspection (See FMCSR 392.2)
- The Posttrip Inspection (See FMCSR 396.11)

Federal Motor Carrier Safety Regulations 396 includes the requirement of a vehicle inspection. Further, the FMCSR 392.7 states:

No motor vehicle shall be driven unless the driver thereof shall have satisfied himself that the following parts and accessories are in good working order, nor shall any driver fail to use or make use of such parts and accessories when and as needed:

- Service brakes, including trailer brake connections
- Parking (hand) brake

INTERESTING FACT

In 1966, the Interstate Commerce Commission amended vehicle lighting regulations, making it mandatory for every truck, 80 inches (203.3 cm) or more, to have two headlamps on front, an equal number at each side, two turn signals, two clearance lamps (one at each side), three identification lamps on the centerline of the cab, and a single lamp at the center of the cab.

- Steering mechanism
- Lighting devices and reflectors
- Tires
- Horn
- **Windshield wiper** or wipers
- Rear-vision mirror or mirrors
- Coupling devices

The skills of a professional driver can first be measured in the thoroughness of each of his or her inspection routines **(see Figure 6-3)**. Knowing that the "parts and accessories are in good working order" comes from a thorough vehicle inspection—before going on the road.

Figure 6-3

A driver must thoroughly inspect both the tires and brakes.

GO!

Inspections provide the driver with information about the rig, including:

- Systems and parts that are working properly
- Systems and parts that are not working properly
- Parts that are damaged, loose, or missing
- Systems or parts on the verge of failing
- Systems or parts in danger of failing or malfunctioning

By law, each rig must meet certain performance standards **(see Figure 6-4)**. It is your responsibility for your rig to meet these standards. You will have this knowledge by becoming familiar with the required equipment for your vehicle, how the systems work, how certain damage or defects keep the vehicle from operating properly, and how to load cargo properly.

Figure 6-4

Learning to conduct a thorough inspection may save your life.

GO!

Professional drivers are responsible for knowing how to conduct three types of vehicle inspections:

Pretrip inspection: a systematic check of systems and parts done before each trip, including how the cargo is loaded and/or tied down. These inspections are so important that you should record them in your logbook. During these inspections, look for problems and damage to the vehicle that could cause a breakdown or an accident. Any damage you find must be repaired before the vehicle heads for the highway.

En route inspection: a systematic check of the rig's controls, instruments while driving, and other items such as cargo tie-downs, couplings, tires, and wheels at each stop **(see Figure 6-5).**

Posttrip inspection: a thorough check of the rig at the end of the shift or the end of the trip—or if the trip lasts several days, at the end of each day—and a written **Driver's Vehicle Inspection Report (DVIR)** listing any defect noted or reported to the driver during operation and inspection.

Courtesy of Baker College of Flint

▶ **Figure 6-5**

At each stop, perform systematic check of your rig.

© Cengage Learning 2013

▶ *"All systems inspected, gauges read and joints oiled. Now, let's get this rig to Kansas, Roto!"*

As any veteran driver will tell you, conducting a thorough inspection will ensure your personal safety and the safety of others. Then, by knowledge of your vehicle and its systems, watching gauges for trouble and using your senses (sight, hearing, smell, and feel) to check for any problems that may occur when on the road, you will arrive safely and on time at your destination, along with your load **(see Figure 6-6).**

It is also important that you be able to determine when problems occur while you are operating the vehicle.

Goals of Inspection

- **Goals**
  - To identify
  - A part or system that is malfunctioning or has already failed (or is missing)
  - A part or system that is in imminent danger of failing or malfunctioning
  - A part or system that is all right or is functioning properly
  - The legal requirements for various parts or system conditions
- **Driver Responsibility**
  - Safety of vehicle and cargo
  - Vehicle inspection

- **Basic Reasons**
  - Safety
  - Economy
  - Public relations
  - Legality
- **Three Elements of a Good Inspection**
  - Knowing what to look for
  - Having a consistent way of looking for it
  - Being able to report findings in a technically accurate way so that the mechanics will be able to identify and repair the problems
- **Types of Inspection**
  - Pretrip
  - En route
  - Posttrip

© Cengage Learning 2013

▶ **Figure 6-6**

The pretrip, en route, and posttrip inspections are pivotal to the performance of the rig and to the efficiency and effectiveness of the professional driver.

Aside from the professional driver and those maintenance professionals assigned to maintain rigs, there is one other group that inspects commercial vehicles. These are federal and state inspectors who can conduct an inspection at any time, including on the roadside of the highway or at a weigh station. For these inspections, you either (1) have to stop at an inspection point or (2) the inspector pulls you over to conduct a roadside inspection anywhere in the country.

When these inspections occur, if the vehicle is found to be unsafe in any area, it can be put out of service (OOS) according to **FMCSR 396.9c Motor Vehicle Declared Out of Service.** When you are OOS, you cannot go anywhere until the vehicle is repaired and is safe to go back to the highway. This costs everyone time and money, including customers. For more information regarding new CSA inspection standards, visit www.fmcsa.dot.gov/safety-security/safety-initiatives/mcsap/insplevels.htm.

WHAT MAKES A GOOD INSPECTION GREAT?

Any professional driver will tell you that learning to conduct a thorough vehicle inspection in a specific sequence will make your job easier *and* may save your life and the lives of others **(see Figure 6-7).**

INTERESTING FACT

In 1930, nine state legislatures passed thousands of bills that impacted the vehicle industry. The majority of these bills were directed at the motor truck and motor bus, and were restrictive.

Courtesy of Lew Grill of the SAGE Schools.

▶ **Figure 6-7**

To conduct a thorough inspection you have to have knowledge of your entire rig.

You can conduct a thorough inspection only if you have the knowledge of your rig and its systems. But, more than that, you have to have the desire to operate safely and the discipline to do these inspections to the best of your ability every time. You also have to understand why you want to conduct a thorough inspection and what you are looking for.

CAUTION!

As you learn to perform inspections of tractor-trailer rigs, you should:

- Learn and follow a regular routine. By using the same routine each time you perform an inspection, you will cover the rig front to rear without missing critical points.
- Know what you are looking for.
- Report any problems so mechanics can identify the problem and repair the rig.

What to Look for during a Rig Inspection

As a professional, you must know the following in order to make a thorough inspection:

- If a system is working properly
- When a system or part is in danger of failure or malfunction
- The difference between major and minor defects
- Defects/problems that will make your rig illegal to operate and could cause it to be put out of service during a federal or state roadside inspection

STOP!

The tools needed for a great inspection include a good-quality flashlight, tire pressure gauge, gloves, clipboard, and/or inspection form and good sturdy workboots.

FMCSR 396.3(a)1 requires that every motor carrier systematically inspect, repair, and maintain, or cause to be systematically inspected, repaired, and maintained, all motor vehicles subject to its control. This requirement ensures that parts and accessories are in safe and proper operating condition at all times. These include any additional parts and accessories which may affect safety of operation, including but not limited to, frame and frame assemblies, suspension systems, axles and attaching parts, wheels and rims, and steering systems.

> **FMCSR 396.3 Inspection, repair, and maintenance.**
>
> a. General. Every motor carrier and intermodal equipment provider must systematically inspect, repair, and maintain, or cause to be systematically inspected, repaired, and maintained, all motor vehicles and intermodal equipment subject to its control.
>
> 1. Parts and accessories shall be in safe and proper operating condition at all times. These include those specified in part 393 of this subchapter and any additional parts and accessories which may affect safety of operation, including but not limited to, frame and frame assemblies, suspension systems, axles and attaching parts, wheels and rims, and steering systems.

2. Pushout windows, emergency doors, and emergency door marking lights in buses shall be inspected at least every 90 days.

b. Required records. Motor carriers, except for a private motor carrier of passengers (nonbusiness), must maintain, or cause to be maintained, records for each motor vehicle they control for 30 consecutive days. Intermodal equipment providers must maintain or cause to be maintained, records for each unit of intermodal equipment they tender or intend to tender to a motor carrier. These records must include:

1. An identification of the vehicle including company number, if so marked, make, serial number, year, and tire size. In addition, if the motor vehicle is not owned by the motor carrier, the record shall identify the name of the person furnishing the vehicle;

2. A means to indicate the nature and due date of the various inspection and maintenance operations to be performed;

3. A record of inspection, repairs, and maintenance indicating their date and nature; and

4. A record of tests conducted on pushout windows, emergency doors, and emergency door marking lights on buses.

Code of Federal Regulations 493

c. Record retention. The records required by this section shall be retained where the vehicle is either housed or maintained for a period of 1 year and for 6 months after the motor vehicle leaves the motor carrier's control.

FMCSR 396.9(c) Motor Vehicle Declared Out-of-Service

This regulation states that:

1. Authorized personnel shall declare and mark "out-of-service" any motor vehicle or intermodal equipment which by reason of its mechanical condition or loading would likely cause an accident or a breakdown. An "Out-of-Service Vehicle" sticker shall be used to mark vehicles and intermodal equipment "out-of-service."

2. No motor carrier or intermodal equipment provider shall require or permit any person to operate nor shall any person operate any motor vehicle or intermodal equipment declared and marked "out-of-service" until all repairs required by the "out-of-service notice" have been satisfactorily completed. The term "operate" as used in this section shall include towing the vehicle or intermodal equipment, except that vehicles or intermodal equipment marked "out-of-service" may be towed away by means of a vehicle using a crane or hoist. A vehicle combination consisting of an emergency towing vehicle and an "out-of-service" vehicle shall not be operated unless such combination meets the performance requirements of this subchapter except for those conditions noted on the Driver's Vehicle Examination Report.

3. No person shall remove the "Out-of-Service Vehicle" sticker from any motor vehicle or intermodal equipment prior to completion of all repairs required by the "out-of-service notice."

Canadian drivers must also use a systematic routine for inspecting tractors and trailers.

Fluid Leaks

You may have previous experience with fluid leaks, such as in going out to your personal vehicle and finding puddles of leaking fluid on the driveway or ground under it. You may also know that serious engine damage or breakdowns can occur because of loss of fluids such as coolant or lubricants **(see Figure 6-8).**

During every inspection—pretrip, en route, and posttrip—always check every fluid level, including oil, coolant, and fuel. Your pretrip should begin as you approach the vehicle looking for fluid loss under the vehicle and while you are driving, frequently checking the gauges that monitor these vital fluids.

"Good thing I caught this drip before it dribbled into my on-time delivery."

Figure 6-8

Serious engine damage or a breakdown can occur as a result of the loss of fluid.

Fluid leaks, which could be fuel, oil or coolant, could lead to serious engine damage . . . or worse! Fluid leaks can also be an environmental nightmare.

Careful inspections of each wheel and tire will make blowouts less likely and may prevent accidents as well as costly down-time (**Figure 6-9**).

Figure 6-9

Blown-out tire remnants on a roadway.

Wheels and Rims

Defective wheels or **rims** can cause a tire to come off and cause an accident. Use a lug wrench to check for tightness of lug nuts and look for:

- Cracks or damaged wheels or rims
- Dented or damaged rims or cracks starting at the lug nut holes (**see Figure 6-10**), which can cause tires to lose air pressure or come off the rim on a turn
- Missing spacers, studs, lugs, and clamps
- Damaged or mismatched lock rings

Figure 6-10

Checking for rust around the lug nut holes as well as rust trails will help reduce blowouts and may prevent accidents.

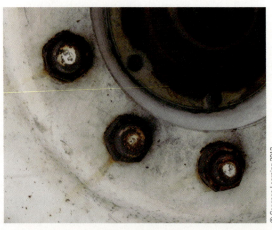

- Welding used to repair wheels or rims, note as defect
- Rust around wheel nuts, check for looseness with wrench
- Out-of-round (oval or egg-shaped) stud or bolt holes on rims
- Hub oil supply and possible leaks

TIRE INSPECTION

Whether you have driven for 2 months or 20 years, you already know that it is dangerous to drive with bad tires. During your inspection:

- Look for worn treads and body ply or belts showing through the tread
- Look for separation of tread or sidewall
- Look for deep cuts or cracks that reveal ply or belt beneath
- Look for damaged or cracked valve stems, or missing stems and valve caps
- If tire is low or flat—or any of the above—get it repaired
- Listen for air leaks and look for bulges (could mean blowout)
- Check inflation pressure with tire gauge (especially during CDL test)
- Check for wear—need no less than 4/32-inch (3.18 mm) tread depth in every major groove on the front and 2/32-inch (1.59 mm) tread depth on other wheels
- Ensure that dual tires are not touching each other or another part of the vehicle
- Make sure all tires are the same size and type (radial and bias-ply tires should not be used on the same axle, which is forbidden in most states)
- Remove regrooved tires on the front of tractors with 8,000-plus-pound front axle rating

Bad Tires

Like every other American traveler, you have certainly driven down a highway and seen the remains of blown or damaged tires, usually commercial motor vehicle tires. Tire defects increase the chances of a blowout and can make any big rig dangerously difficult to handle. In a July 2010 address to the American Truck Dealers board of directors, FMCSA Administrative Director Anne S. Ferro said this as she introduced the new CSA 2010 program: "In the area of vehicle maintenance, most violations we see are with brakes, tires and lighting. The most commonly cited violations we hear about are tires with worn treads; lighting that's either defective or not working at all; and brakes that are out of adjustment or are defective."

INTERESTING FACT

In 1918, Goodyear Tire and Rubber Company announced that all its products would be shipped by truck east of the Mississippi and haul crude rubber on the return trip.

CAUTION!

FMCSR 393.75 states (a) no motor vehicle shall be operated on any **tire** that (1) has body ply or belt material exposed through the tread or sidewall, (2) has any tread or sidewall separation, (3) is flat or has an audible leak, or (4) has a cut to the extent that the ply or belt material is exposed.

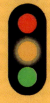

It further states that any tire on the front wheels of a bus, truck, or CMV shall have a tread groove pattern depth of at least 4/32 of an inch (3.18 mm) when measured at any point on a major tread groove, and the measurement shall not be made where tie bars, humps, or fillets are located.

STOP!

Mixing tires with different tread patterns, internal construction and size, especially winter tires, degrades the stability of the vehicle and should be avoided.

© Cengage Learning 2013

"You can never do too much, when it comes to tire inspection."

When checking your tires, remember the acronym ICD:

1. Inflation—100–105 psi (690–724 kPa)
2. Condition—No cuts, rips, or tears
3. Depth—4/32 or 2/32 inches (3.18 or 1.59 mm)

(see Figure 6-11)

Courtesy of Baker College of Flint

▶ **Figure 6-11**

ICD: Inflation – Condition – Depth.

CAUTION!

In February 1999, Transport Canada announced the introduction of a new industry standard to help Canadian consumers identify and buy snow tires that provide a higher level of traction for Canada's harsh winter conditions. This standard is now being implemented by North America's tire manufacturers, and is being monitored by Transport Canada. The tires are marked on at least one sidewall with a pictograph of a mountain and snowflake **(see Figure 6-12).** This design indicates that tires have met specific snow traction performance requirements, and have been designed specifically for use in severe snow conditions. For additional details call Transport Canada's Road Safety Information Line at 1-800-333-0371.

▶ **Figure 6-12**

Tire marking indicating tires have met specific snow traction performance requirements.

© Cengage Learning 2013

Tire Chains

According to another state-by-state requirement in the U.S. and province-by-province in Canada for driving in snow and ice, include **tire chains** in your equipment inspection and be able to mount and remove them in changing weather conditions, as required as seasons change. Check regulations in both your home state/province and other states/provinces where you will be operating. Tire chains are usually required in the mountain regions. Automatic tire chain systems are easy to use and take much less time to install than traditional tire chains. As an aftermarket option, various suppliers and vendors install these on the drive axles.

INSPECTING MUD FLAPS/ SPLASH GUARDS

A common state requirement is that **splash guards (mud flaps)** must be as wide or wider than the tires (**see Figure 6-13**).

- Mud flaps should be no more than 6 inches (15.2 cm) from the ground with vehicle fully loaded. States vary, so be sure to check your state's restrictions.
- Flaps should be mounted as far to the rear of the wheel as possible.

▶ **Figure 6-13**

Generally, mud flaps must be as wide or wider than the tires.

BRAKING SYSTEMS INSPECTION

You must be able to control the stopping and starting of your rig safely. To do so, your **brakes** must be in good operating conditions. Brake violations are among the most common, identified as a result of road-side inspections. Inspect all four wheels in the following manner:

- Check wheel for cracks and hubs for any leaking fluid. Check lugs.
- Check brake lines for worn or weak spots.
- Make sure lines are not kinked or twisted.

Check Air Pressure

You should not be able to hear any air leaks. The sound of air coming from any part of the air brake system means the system is defective and can be dangerous. To check the brake system, follow these steps:

1. Set the brakes (parking and trailer). Start the engine and let air pressure build until the system is fully charged, about 125 pounds per square inch (psi) or 862 kilopascal (kPa).
2. Turn off the engine and release parking brake and trailer brakes (puts air into the spring brake system). After the initial air pressure drop (about 10 to 15 psi/69 to 103 kPa), apply firm and steady

---

INTERESTING FACT

Construction of the 1,390-mile (2237 km) Alaska Highway (also known as the Alaskan Highway, Alaska–Canadian Highway, or ALCAN Highway) began shortly after the bombing of Pearl Harbor for the purpose of connecting the continuous states to Alaska through Canada and was completed in October 1942. This highway is popularly (but unofficially) considered part of the Pan-American Highway, which extends south to Argentina.

pressure (about 90 psi/621 kPa) to the service brake pedal (puts air into the remainder of the system). Hold this for 1 minute.

3. Watch the air pressure gauge. The air pressure should not drop more than:

- 3 psi (21 kPa) in 1 minute for tractor
- 4 psi (28 kPa) in 1 minute for tractor and trailer
- 6 psi (41 kPa) in 1 minute for a tractor and three trailers

Air leaks that can be heard or observed more than the amounts listed should be repaired before the truck or combination is driven, because they are unsafe and violate safety regulations.

STOP! LISTEN!

During any inspection—pretrip, en route, or posttrip—stop moving, stop talking on your cell phone or listening to your iPod, and listen—for air leaks, not just once but several times throughout your inspection. Avoid any distractions while performing an inspection, if someone interrupts you and changes your routine, parts of the inspection can be overlooked.

CAUTION!

FMCSR 393.75 states (a) no motor vehicle shall be operated on any tire that (1) has body ply or belt material exposed through the tread or sidewall, (2) has any tread or sidewall separation, (3) is flat or has an audible leak, or (4) has a cut to the extent that the ply or belt material is exposed.

It further states that any tire on the front wheels of a bus, truck or CMV shall have a tread groove pattern depth of at least 4/32 of an inch (3.18 mm) when measured at any point on a major tread groove, and the measurement shall not be made where tie bars, humps, or fillets are located.

Check Brake Lines

You should not hear any air leaks and should check for air lines that are:

- Not secured properly
- Hardened or swollen
- Chafed or worn so that fabric or steel braid is visible
- Cut or cracked
- Crimped, pinched, or restricted in any way
- Taped or not spliced correctly

Check Air Reservoir

The **air reservoir(s) (see Figure 6-14)** must be attached correctly to the rig. The reservoirs must be bled each day to remove moisture. A good time to bleed them is during the pretrip and posttrip inspections. Moisture is removed from the brake system because if it is allowed to remain, during winter months it will freeze, causing failure to the brake system. Many tractors are not equipped with an air dryer that regularly purges air from the system.

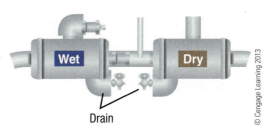

▶ **Figure 6-14**

The air reservoirs should be bled each day.

Check Parking Brakes

- Put your seat belt on.
- Put vehicle in gear and let it move forward slowly.
- Apply parking brake. Vehicle should stop. If it does not stop, get parking brake repaired before your trip.

Check Service Brake

- Go forward about 5 miles per hour (8 km/h).
- Push pedal firmly—if vehicle veers left or right, this could mean brake trouble.
- Any pause before brakes "catch" is another sign of a problem.
- If the brake pedal feels spongy or soft—takes too much time to catch or requires too much effort to push—then the brakes should be checked and repaired before any trip.

STOP!

Most units have redundant systems. Most failures happen over time and can be discovered during the pretrip inspection. Do not operate a unit that you cannot stop.

STEERING SYSTEM INSPECTION

Although this goes without saying, the professional driver must be in control of his or her rig at all times and in all situations. Lack of complete control may be the result of poor maintenance or system malfunction. The **steering system** provides the driver's most immediate control over the direction of a rig, and defects in this system create unsafe situations.

STOP!

Steering system defects may affect total control of the vehicle, and the higher the speed the rig is traveling when steering system problems occur, the more prone you become to a serious accident.

When conducting pretrip, en route, or posttrip inspections of the steering system, look for:

- Bent, loose, or broken parts such as the steering column, steering gear box, tie rods, Pitman arms, and drag link
- Missing nuts, bolts, cotter keys, or other securing devices
- Damaged hoses and pumps
- Proper fluid level in the power steering reservoir
- Air and fluid leaks
- Anything shining to indicate something is loose
- Check the steering wheel for **steering wheel lash (see Figure 6-15),** looseness or play in the steering wheel's movement. (For power steering, if there is more than 5-3/4 inches (14.6 cm) of play, the rig should be placed out of service until this is corrected.)

Steering Wheel Diameter	Manual Steering System	Power Steering System
16 inches or less (40.6 cm)	2 inches (5.1 cm)	4-½ inches (11.4 cm)
18 inches (45.7 cm)	2-¼ inches (5.7 cm)	4-¾ inches (12.1 cm)
20 inches (50.8 cm)	2-½ inches (6.4 cm)	5-¼ inches (13.3 cm)
22 inches (55.9 cm)	2-¾ inches (7.0 cm)	5-¾ inches (14.6 cm)

© Cengage Learning 2013

▶ **Figure 6-15**

Parameters for Steering Wheel Lash (FMCSA 393.209).

To check the steering system:

- Make sure the steering column is securely mounted and the steering wheel is secure, moves easily, and is free of cracked spokes.
- Steering wheel lash or free play (the number of turns the steering wheel makes before wheels move) should be no more than 10 degrees or 2 inches (5.1 cm) on the rim of a 20-inch (50.8 cm) steering wheel according to FMCSR 393. If free play exceeds limits, vehicle will be difficult to steer.
- Check U-joints for wear, slack, damage, or signs of welding repair (not acceptable for U-joint repair).
- Gear box is free of damage, and bolts and brackets are in place and secure.
- Pitman arm is secure.

For vehicles with power steering:

- All parts should be free of damage and in good operating order.
- Belts that are frayed, cracked, or slipping should be replaced or adjusted.
- Look for leaks in lines and tank and make sure tank contains ample power steering fluid.
- If you see missing nuts, bolts, cotter keys, or other damaged parts, replace immediately, as well as damaged, loose, or broken steering column, gear box, or tie rod.

INTERESTING FACT

Francis W. Davis, an engineer of the truck division of Pierce Arrow, in 1926, demonstrated the first power steering system on a truck. Later, military needs during World War II for easier steering on heavy vehicles boosted the need for power assistance on armored cars and tank-recovery vehicles for the British and American armies.

SUSPENSION SYSTEM INSPECTION

The **suspension system** supports the rig's load and maintains axle attachment and alignment. Check the suspension starts as you approach the vehicle, looking to see if one side of the truck looks higher than the other, or is listing. Failure of this system can have tragic results. Check for:

- Cracked or broken torque arms and U-bolts
- Hangers that allow the axle to move from its proper position
- Missing or broken leaves in a spring leaf cluster **(see Figure 6-16).** (The rig will be put out of service if one fourth or more of these leaves are missing. Any broken or missing leaves can be dangerous.)
- Leaking or faulty shock absorbers
- Missing or damaged spring hangers
- Cracked or broken spring hangers
- Damaged or leaking air suspension systems
- Broken leaves or leaves that have shifted and are touching the tires, wheels, frame, or body
- Missing or broken torque rods
- Loose, cracked, broken, or missing frame members
- Check for missing bolts.
- Replace any broken bolts on the frame.
- Check that all bolts and rivets are tight and in place.

© Cengage Learning 2013

▶ **Figure 6–16**

Check of broken or missing leaves in a spring leaf cluster.

CAUTION!

On every inspection, check the vehicle's frame for loose bolts attached to the frame as well as any cracks, sagging, or damage to the frame.

EXHAUST SYSTEM INSPECTION

Faulty **exhaust systems** can lead to harmful—even deadly—gases in the cab or sleeper berth.

- Check for broken, loose, or missing exhaust pipes, mufflers, tailpipes, or stacks.
- Look for loose or broken mountings, missing brackets, bent clamps, or missing or broken nuts and bolts.
- Check to make sure no parts of the exhaust system are rubbing against parts of the fuel system.
- Check for broken, worn, or frayed hoses, lines, and wires.
- With your hand close (but not on it because you will burn yourself) to the exhaust manifold, check for leaks. You will feel them.
- Never patch or wrap the exhaust system. Note any such repair work on your inspection as a defect and have it fixed.

COUPLING SYSTEM INSPECTION

Failure of the **coupling system** (upper or lower **fifth wheel**) can cause cargo damage or serious accidents (**see Figure 6-17).** The coupling system includes saddle mounts, tow bars, kingpins, pintle hooks, and safety **chains** used in tow-away situations. A professional driver should go under the trailer and look into the back of the fifth wheel to make sure the fifth wheel jaws have closed around the shank of the kingpin.

Check for:

- No space between the upper and lower fifth wheel
- Too much slack in the fifth-wheel locking system
- Bends or warping, cracks, or breaks in all parts used to couple vehicles
- Safety chains with broken or twisted links
- Missing pins or other defects in the slide mechanism of the sliding fifth wheel
- Bent, cracked, or worn kingpins
- **Lights,** reflectors, steering, and brakes, which must work on the vehicle when towing or when being towed
- Missing U-bolts, cracked or broken welds, or other defects in the fifth-wheel mounting devices
- More than 3/8-inch (9.53 mm) horizontal movement between the pivot bracket pin and the bracket
- Pivot bracket pin missing or not secured

▶ **Figure 6–17**

Fifth wheel.

© iStockphoto/larryT

INTERESTING FACT

In 1931, General Motors Truck Company manufactured semi-trailers in addition to its truck lines and featured interchangeable parts between the trailers and trucks. A standard fifth wheel could couple with other trailers and adapt other makes of tractors.

CAUTION!

When checking the coupling of a tractor-trailer or inspecting the kingpin of the trailer and the jaws of the fifth wheel, be sure to remove the ignition key from the tractor before crawling under the rig to physically check the coupling.

CARGO INSPECTION

Safely loaded cargo (no room for shifting or falling) should be inspected and the following should be in good working condition (**see Figure 6-18**).

- Tailgate
- Doors
- Cab guard or header board (headache rack)— free of damage and securely in place
- Stakes/sideboards (if necessary)
- **Tarps** tied down and tight
- Spare tire
- **Binders**
- Chains
- **Winches**
- **Braces and support**
- Curbside doors secured and locked

▶ **Figure 6-18**

Cargo should be safely loaded so there is no room for shifting or falling.

Cargo must be loaded without blocking view or impeding driver's arms and legs.

- If you haul sealed loads, then you need security seals on doors.
- If you haul hazardous materials, then you need placards, proper paperwork, and the HazMat Endorsement.

STOP!

Remember: Anything you find on your inspection of the vehicle that is broken or not functioning properly must be repaired before you take the vehicle on the road. Federal and state laws forbid operating an unsafe vehicle.

▶ *"Before we spend the next 10 hours together, I think we should have 'the talk'."*

HOW TO PROPERLY CHOCK YOUR WHEELS

Chocking and blocking wheels prevents accidental or unintended movement of equipment and cargo while workers are inspecting, loading, unloading, hitching, unhitching, or performing service or maintenance.

When chocking, use specially designed truck wheel chocks of the appropriate size and material to securely hold the vehicle. Don't use lumber, cinder blocks, rocks, or other makeshift items to chock. Make it easy to find and use the correct chocking equipment, such as by storing chocks inside trailers or rigs. Chocks also should be available at loading docks.

If you're a professional driver, use special caution when exiting the vehicle. Always face the tractor when exiting. Never face forwarded and never jump from the cab of a tractor. Make sure the brakes are set, the vehicle is at a complete standstill and that it will not roll forward or backward before you exit. If you are performing maintenance or parking the vehicle for an extended period of time, chock the wheels.

To properly chock a free-standing vehicle, place chocks on the left and right rear axle wheels. It is safest to chock both the front and back wheels on both sides of a vehicle. Some vehicle wheels may also need to be chocked at the front and back of each tire.

Ensure that trailers are firmly placed against the loading dock edges and prevent rollaways by using chocks. Place chocks on the left and right wheels that are closest to the loading dock. This placement allows a forklift to push down on the trailer wheels and seat them more firmly against the chock. If only the front axle is chocked, a forklift could push the trailer forward and loosen the chock or cause the wheel to jump the chock. The driver, dock workers, and forklift drivers share the responsibility to ensure that the truck and trailer wheels are properly chocked.

Chocking prevents serious injuries caused by runaway vehicles and accidentally activated machinery.

STEPS FOR A PRETRIP INSPECTION

You have a moral, professional, and legal duty to your employer, other motorists, and yourself to conduct a thorough pretrip inspection of any rig you drive. It takes much longer to learn how to perform a quality pretrip inspection than it takes to do one. After practice and becoming more familiar and more comfortable with this process, you will be able to do a thorough inspection in less than 15 minutes. Drivers who have driven millions of miles safely will say that they owe much to this achievement to doing the same procedures repetitively.

NOTE

Many companies have specific policies on vehicle inspection. Some carriers require drivers to conduct more extensive inspections while other carriers prohibit certain checks. All drivers should establish an inspection procedure that is consistent with company policy.

The secret to making an efficient and accurate inspection is to learn the step-by-step **inspection routine.** If you inspect your rig the same way every time, you will be able to do it quickly and efficiently without a chance of overlooking a key system or part. The seven-step pretrip inspection is, by far, the most used of the routines (**see Figure 6-19**).

In Canada, the term for inspecting a tractor-trailer rig is "circle check." A complete circle check must be performed for the professional driver's rig at the beginning of every shift—this includes checking under the hood as well as all other systems. Note, the circle check varies according to the make and model of each rig as well as the location of the rig's components. At the end of the circle check, the driver will fill out the Daily Vehicle Inspection Report.

Seven-Step Pretrip Inspection Checklist

1. Approach vehicle — look for leaks

2. Check under hood or cab

3. Start engine and check inside cab

4. Check headlights

5. Conduct walkaround

6. Check signal lights

7. Check air brake system

▶ **Figure 6-19**

The secret to an accurate and efficient inspection is to learn a step-by-step routine.

© Cengage Learning 2013

Step 1: Approach the Vehicle

While walking toward the rig, look for signs of damage. Also look for anything that may be in the way when you try to move the vehicle. As you approach the rig, look at the following:

Vehicle posture—a truck sagging to one side may mean flat tires, overloading, shifted cargo, or suspension problems.

Cargo—the trailer or **cargo compartment doors** should be closed and properly fastened. For flatbed trailers and other open cargo compartments, make sure the cargo is not hanging over the side and that restraints can stand 1-1/2 times any pressure from the load **(see Figure 6-20).**

Damaged, loose, or missing parts—check for cracked glass, dents, or missing parts such as fenders, mud flaps, and lights. Check for loose parts such as a fuel tank hanging with unsecured straps.

Leaks—check under the truck for puddles of fresh oil, engine coolant, grease, or fuel. Look for any other signs of leakage and also be sure to listen for air leaks.

▶ **Figure 6-20**

Check cargo restraints to ensure the load is secure.

Courtesy of Baker College of Cadillac

Area around vehicle—look for anything that may be damaged by the rig or will damage your rig as you drive away. Be on the lookout for anything on the ground, such as glass or boards with nails. Look up to check for low-hanging branches, utility wires, and any other overhead objects that may be hit by the tractor or trailer.

Most recent pretrip and posttrip vehicle inspection reports—if items listed affect safety, check to make certain mechanic's certification indicates repairs were made or no repair was needed. Then, inspect these areas yourself to find out what was done about problems noted on last inspection.

Step 2: Check under the Hood

With parking brakes on, check the **engine compartment** to ensure the vehicle has been properly serviced. Look for signs of damage or possible problems with the engine, steering mechanism, and suspension system.

Most tractor hoods are equipped with safety latches and are designed to prevent the hood from falling on the person checking the engine compartment—a particular hazard on windy days. Perform a thorough check of the following:

Fluid levels—check engine oil level (should be above "low" or "add" marks) on dipstick. Check coolant level (should be above "low" mark). Check radiator shutters (if you still have them), remove any ice, and check to see if winter front is open. Inspect the fan to ensure blades are undamaged and hoses and wires are out of the way. Check other fluid levels such as automatic transmission fluid, windshield washer fluid, and engine oil in the makeup reservoir. Be sure all fluids are at the right levels before starting the engine, and that hoses are in good condition.

Leaks—look for leaks such as oil, water, or hydraulic oil in the engine compartment. Check around the entire compartment for grease, soot, power steering fluid, or other signs of fluid leaks. Inspect the exhaust manifold for signs of leakage, and if your rig's main air tanks are under the hood, listen for the hiss of leaking air.

- For windshield washers, check fluid level.
- Automatic transmission? Check fluid level (may do this with engine running).

Check electrical system—make sure the battery is secured and terminals are not corroded. Check for loose electrical wires and check all wires for wear. If your rig has spark plugs, check for secure electrical connections.

Belts and pulleys—inspect alternator, air compressor, and water pump belts for cracks or fraying. Test belts for tension and slippage. If you can slide a belt over a pulley, it is too loose and should be tightened or replaced.

Cooling system—check radiator, shroud, and shutters to make sure they are structurally sound and free or dents or damage. (Newer systems have thermostatic fans that eliminate shutters.) Make sure all parts of the cooling system are properly secured. Check hoses for cracks, breaks, or other damage. Inspect the fan for missing blades and look for hanging wires or hoses that can catch on the blades **(see Figure 6-21).**

Steering system—check steering linkage and gear box closely. Make sure they are secure and look for signs of wear, such as paint that has been rubbed off. If the rig has power steering, make sure these lines are securely connected and there are no leaks. Look for leaking or defective shock absorbers. If the rig has an air suspension system, make sure air bags are not leaking or damaged.

Exhaust system—examine the muffler. Be sure it is securely connected and has no holes, large dents, or is crushed. Make sure all lines and hoses are securely fastened. Report any damage found before your trip. Be sure fuel and electric lines will not come too close to any part of the exhaust system that gets hot.

INTERESTING FACT

In 1905, the major complaint by most truck owners was excessive oil dripping from their vehicles. This problem was more than a mere nuisance. In Washington, DC, for example, truck drivers whose vehicles dripped oil on the streets were taken to police court, fined five dollars, and warned that heavier fines would be levied for repeated offenses.

© Cengage Learning 2013

▶ **Figure 6-21**
Inspect fan.

Braking systems—look for cracked brake drums, missing brake shoes, and missing or disconnected hoses and slack adjusters. Make sure air intake screen for air brakes is not clogged with debris. Open air tank petcocks and drain tanks. Check for oil contamination, but be sure to close petcocks when you have completed this part of the inspection.

Suspension system—check U-bolts, spring pins, spring brackets, and torque arms for cracks, bends, or missing bolts. Check axles for signs of rubbing. If the truck has adjustable axles, make sure all locking pins are in the proper position and fully engaged. Make sure all safety clamps holding locking pins are securely in place. Then check for cracks in the truck's frame and cross members. Check entire suspension system for rust or shiny spots that may indicate excessive wear. Look at all leaf springs for missing, out-of-place, or broken leaves. Leaves sticking out from a leaf spring may touch the tires, rims, or frame.

Step 3: Start the Engine and Check Inside the Cab

After checking the engine, climb into the **cab** and prepare to start the engine. For the professional driver, the cab is a home away from home, of sorts; therefore, it should be kept orderly and clean. Check to make sure:

- All controls and instruments are in working order
- Doors open and close easily and securely
- There are no loose, sagging, or broken parts
- Seats are secured firmly in place
- Front bumpers are secure
- Rear bumpers are firmly on if vehicle is higher than 30 inches (76.2 cm) from the ground (empty).

Perform a thorough check of the following:

Vehicle entry—check that the steps, grab handles and door handles are secure and free of dirt, grease, or ice. Make sure doors latch securely.

Emergency and safety equipment—make sure you have all the required emergency and safety equipment **(see Figure 6-22).**

▶ **Figure 6-22**

Required by law, each truck should have a fire extinguisher and reflective triangles.

Check to see that:

- The fire extinguisher is securely mounted with easy access, which should be checked as part of the inspection. Most vehicles require a 10 B:C rating. Is the nozzle clear and the tip of ring pin in place? Check pressure gauge to be sure needle is in the green area. Make sure the fire extinguisher has not reached its expiration date.

- You know how to use the fire extinguisher.

- There are three reflective emergency triangles (see FMCSR 393.95 for full description and options).

- You have spare fuses and know how to install them, unless your vehicle has circuit breakers.

- You have an accident notification kit (for example, keep a disposable camera in the accident kit to visually record damages) and emergency phone numbers.

Mirrors and glass—always check all windows and panes of glass before you drive **(see Figure 6-23)**. Viewing area must be clean—free of stickers, dirt, discolorations, and only factory tints to reduce glare are allowed.

- Apply only required stickers at the bottom of the windshield, no more than 4-1/2 inches (11.4 cm) into the viewing area.

- Do not allow cracks (longer than 1/4 inch) or 6.35 mm or dings in the glass.

▶ **Figure 6-23**
Check windshield wipers and mirrors.

© Cengage Learning 2013

CAUTION!

When you're outside the cab, if possible, run your hand along the windshield wiper blades to check for worn spots. Rubber should be soft and pliable. When you're inside the cab, check wiper blades for possible damage.

- Make sure mirrors are securely mounted.
- Adjust the seat into a comfortable driving position.
- **Rear-view mirrors** on each side of cab should be adjusted when in the driver's seat. You should be able to see down both sides to the rear of the vehicle. Flat mirrors should be adjusted for longer distance viewing, while the convex mirror should be used for the blind spot just behind the cab. Mirrors should also be clean and free of damage.

Engine startup—once you climb into the cab, look around and inspect the inside area. Put on your seat belt (**see Figure 6-24**). Make sure the parking brake is on and the vehicle is in neutral or park. Start the engine at zero throttle. Do not crank for more than 15 seconds. Listen for any unusual pinging, skipping, or other noises. With the engine running (all readings should register a few seconds after starting the engine), check the following:

▶ Figure 6–24
Driver putting seat belt on.

- Gauges—oil pressure goes to normal in seconds

- Ammeter and voltmeter display readings—needle should jump, flutter, and then register "charge" or "1" for a normal reading

- Coolant temperature—should start "cold" and gradually rise to normal

- Engine oil temp—should rise slowly to normal

- Oil, coolant, and charging circuit warning lights come on and should go off almost immediately (unless a problem exists)

- Low air pressure warning buzzer—should sound until air pressure builds to about 60 psi (414 kPa), then the buzzer or alarm should stop

- Air pressure gauge—should build steadily (Check the time needed for the pressure to build to 125 psi (862 kPa). If it is within 45 seconds, the buildup is adequate. Buildup can take longer with oversized air tanks.)

- Air pressure governor cut-off—should stop between 115 and 125 psi (793 and 862 kPa). If it stops above or below this range, adjustments are needed.

- All controls in working order—check loose or sticking controls, any improper readings or settings

- Mirrors, windshield for defects, problems

- Required **emergency equipment,** including fire extinguisher, triangles, flares, and personal protection gear is in good working order

- Items required by state laws, such as mud flaps and tire chains

NOTE

In trucks with electronically-controlled engines, the needles on all gauges will make a full sweep after ignition. This self-check function ensures that all gauges are working.

CAUTION!

As of 2010, according to the American Transportation Research Institute, 29 states and the District of Columbia, often with several different laws within these states, have instituted anti-idling laws, requiring big rig truck and interstate bus operators to reduce nonessential idling. For more information, go to www.atri-online.org/research/idling/ATRI_Idling_Compendium.pdf.

▶ **Figure 6–25**

Checking for free play or lash in the steering wheel.

Primary Controls—with the engine still running, check the vehicle's main controls:

- **Steering mechanism**—check for **free play** or lash in the steering wheel. Lean out so you can see the left front tire of the truck. While watching the tire, turn the wheel until the tire starts to move **(see Figure 6-25)** for unsafe levels of free play for manual and power steering wheels. If necessary, a driver might open the door to get a clear view of the tire.

- **Clutch**—depress the clutch until you feel a little resistance. For most clutches, 1 to 2 inches (2.5 to 5 cm) of free play is normal. Too much or too little free play can cause difficult shifting, gear clashing, and clutch or transmission damage. To check the clutch brake, push the pedal to the floor. The pedal should stop before reaching the floor.

- **Transmission**—with the clutch depressed, check to see that the transmission allows you to shift freely from neutral into other gears.

- **Gas and brake pedals**—check both pedals for looseness or sticking. Be sure there is no dirt buildup underneath each pedal.

Secondary controls—the following are secondary controls that should be checked prior to beginning each trip to ensure that they are in working order:

- **Defroster**
- Fan
- Horn
- Interior lights
- Turn signals
- High-beam indicator

- Heater and air conditioner
- Lanyard to the air horn
- Windshield washers and wipers
- Dashboard lights
- Four-way flashers
- Steering tilt

Preparing to leave the cab—when air pressure has built to the governor cutout pressure, turn the engine off. If the engine shutoff is the pull-out type, leave it in the pulled-out position until you start the engine again. Put the rig into the lowest forward gear. Set the parking brake. Turn on low-beam headlights and **four-way flashers.**

Step 4: Check Lights and Mirrors

Get out of the cab and go to the front of the rig to check the:

- Low-beam headlights—do they work and are they aligned? (**See Figure 6-26.**)
- Four-way flashers—do both work?

Reach into the cab and switch the lights to high beam.

- Do the high beams work? Are they aligned?
- Inspect mirrors—are they clean? Adjust if necessary.

Step 5: Conduct a Walkaround Inspection

Go back to the cab. Turn off the headlights and four-way flashers. Turn on right turn signal, leave the cab, and begin the walkaround inspection—a 14-point routine (**see Figure 6-27**). During this part of the pretrip inspection, you will be looking at vehicle parts outside the cab. Start with the driver's side of the cab and cover the front and then work down the opposite side. Go over the rear of the vehicle and back to the driver's side of the cab.

General Tips

- Walk around and inspect as you go.
- Clean all lights, reflectors, and glass as you walk around the vehicle.

▶ **Figure 6–26**

Clean and clear headlights.

Walkaround Sequence

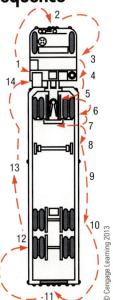

1. Left side of cab area
2. Front of cab area
3. Right side of tractor area
4. Right saddle tank area
5. Coupling system area
6. Right rear tractor wheels area
7. Rear of tractor area
8. Front of trailer area
9. Right side of trailer area
10. Right rear trailer wheels area
11. Rear of trailer area
12. Left rear trailer wheels area
13. Left side of trailer area
14. Left saddle tank area

▶ **Figure 6–27**

Make a copy of this guide and use it as a reference when performing inspections.

Left Side of Cab

- **Driver's door glass**—should be clean and locks in working order.
- **Wheels, rims, and tires**—should be in good condition with no missing, bent, or broken studs, clamps, or lugs. (a) Tires are properly inflated, with valve stem and cap in place. No serious cuts, slashes, bulges, or signs of tread wear. (b) Test lug nuts for looseness (rust streaks coming from the lug nuts also indicate looseness). (c) Hub oil level is good, with no leaks.

CAUTION!

If rims have more than one piece, they are under extreme pressure and can explode from the wheel if damaged, mismatched, or mounted improperly. Always have experts adjust them. These adjustments are regulated by standards set by the Occupational Safety and Health Administration (OSHA).

- **Check for improperly mounted tires and loose or missing lugs**—which can put too much stress on remaining lugs. Look for a rust trail around the lugs. This tells you the lug nuts may be loose. Always use a lug wrench to check lugs.
- **Look for signs of lubricant leaking from wheel seals**—lost lubricant can cause a wheel to lock up. Check the hub oil level.
- **Left front tire**—check air pressure (always use a gauge), general condition, and tread depth (should not be less than 4/32 inch or 3.18 mm). Low **tire pressure** makes the rig hard to handle and can increase the possibility of blowout or tire fire. It also reduces a tire's life. Bald tires or worn out treads cause hydroplaning on wet surfaces.
- **Left front suspension**—check the condition of springs, spring hangers, shackles, U-bolts, and shock absorbers.
- **Left front brake**—check the condition of drum and hoses, and shoes (if they can be seen). Linings should not be less than 1/4 inch (6.35 mm).

▶ Figure 6–28

Check the condition of the front of the cab.

- **Check brake chambers** and slack adjusters.
- **Air tanks**—drain according to specification.

Front of Cab (see Figure 6-28)

- **Front axle**—check for cracks or other problems.
- **Steering system**—check for loose, worn, bent, damaged, or missing parts and test for looseness.
- **License plates**—are on tight and check to make sure all legally required inspection stickers, tax plates, decals, and any placards are in place.
- **Windshield**—should be free of damage and clean. Wipers should be in good working order—check for proper spring tension in wiper arm. Check blades for stiff rubber and that they are secure.
- **Parking, clearance, and identification lights**—should be clean, operational, and the proper color (amber in front and red in rear).
- **Reflectors and red and silver continuity tape**—should be clean and undamaged.
- **Right turn signal light**—must be clean, operating, and the proper color (amber or white in front and red in rear).

> **STOP!**
> The Department of Transportation has mandated many parts of the rear of the trailer be covered with red and silver continuity tape for safety reasons. This includes, at a minimum, bumper and upper corners of the trailer.

Right Front

- **Right side of cab**—check all items as you did for the left front of cab.

Right Saddle Tank Area

- **Right fuel tank**—should be securely mounted with no leaks. Fuel crossover lines are secure, there is adequate fuel in tank for trip, and caps and gaskets are in place and secure.
- **Engine**—check condition of visible parts such as rear of engine with no leaks, transmission not leaking, exhaust system secure and not leaking or touching wires or lines, no cracks or bends in frame and cross members.
- **Driveshaft**—should be in position and secured, both in front and on the rear.
- **Exhaust system**—brackets, pipes, and other parts should be secure and free of leaks. Be sure no fuel lines or wires are in contact with exhaust parts. Look for soot, fluids, or burned areas which indicate leaks.
- **Frame and cross members**—look for bends and cracks in the parts of the frame you need.
- **Air lines and electrical wiring**—check for snagging, rubbing, or wearing.
- **Spare tire carrier**—check for damage and check spare tire/wheel is the right size at proper inflation.
- **Spare tire and wheel**—make sure they are sturdy and strong enough to carry the load and are not damaged. They should be chained.
- **Cargo secure**—cargo is blocked, braced, tied, and chained. Header board secure, sideboards and stakes free of damage and properly placed, canvas or tarp secured to prevent tearing, billowing, or blocking mirrors.
- **Oversized loads**—should have required signs properly mounted and all required permits in driver's pouch.
- **Curbside cargo compartment doors**—check that they are closed and latched with all required security seals in place.

Coupling System

- **Lower fifth wheel**—is it properly lubricated? Is it firmly mounted to the frame? Are any parts missing or damaged? You should be able to see no space between the upper and lower fifth wheels. Be sure the locking jaws are securely fastened around the shank of the kingpin. **Never leave them around the head of the kingpin!** The release arm must be properly seated and the safety latch/lock must be engaged.
- **Upper fifth wheel or apron**—guide plate should be firmly mounted on the trailer frame. Kingpin should not be bent, worn, rusted, or damaged.
- **Air and electrical lines to trailer**—should be in good condition (**see Figure 6-29**). Be sure they are not tangled, snagged, or rubbing against anything. These lines should be free of oil, grease, or damage. The air lines

▶ Figure 6-29

Check air lines to trailer.

© Cengage Learning 2013

must be properly connected to glad hands. (Glad hands are air hose connections between the tractor and the trailer.) Check for leaks. Electrical lines should be firmly attached and locked into place.

- **Sliding fifth wheel (if rig has one)**—should not be worn or damaged. Make sure there are no missing parts. It should be properly lubricated and all lock pins should be locked into place. The in-cab lever should be in locked position. If it is air powered, make sure there are no leaks. The fifth wheel should not be too far forward. If it is, the trailer could hit the cab, the tractor frame, or the landing gear during turns.

STOP!

When checking the coupling of a tractor-trailer or inspecting the kingpin of the trailer and the jaws of the fifth wheel, be sure to remove the ignition key from the tractor before crawling under the rig to check the coupling.

Right Rear Tractor Wheels

- **Dual wheels and rims**—check the condition of wheels, rims, and tires for missing, bent, or broken spacers, studs, clamps, or lugs.
- **Dual tires**—should be evenly matched, of the same type (no mixing of radial and bias types), and properly inflated with valve stems and caps in place. No cuts, bulges, or tread wear. Tires should not be rubbing and should be clear of debris. Wheel bearing/seals should not be leaking.
- **Suspension**—check condition of springs, spring hangers, shackles, and U-bolts. Axle is secure and drive axle(s) not leaking gear oil.
- **Torque rod arms and bushings**—should be in good condition.
- **Shock absorber(s)**—should be working properly.
- **Retractable axle**—check lift mechanism. If air powered, check for leaks.
- **Brakes**—brake drums should be in good condition and hoses checked for wear, rubbing, and so forth.
- **Brake chambers and slack adjusters**—most slack adjusters are self-adjusting. If not, check them on disc S-cam brakes by parking on level ground and turning off the parking brakes so you can move the slack adjusters. Wear gloves. Pull hard on each adjuster you can reach. They should move less than 1 inch (2.54 cm) where the push rod attaches to it. Adjust them or have them adjusted if they move more than 1 inch (2.54 cm). Too much brake slack can make a rig hard to handle.
- **Lights and reflectors**—side-marker lights should be clean and operating; red lights at rear and others are amber. Same for side-marker reflectors.

Rear of the Tractor

- **Rear clearance and identification lights**—should be clean, operating, and red at rear.
- **Reflectors and red and silver continuity tape**—should be clean and red at rear. Tail lights should be clean, operating, and red at rear.
- **Turn signals**—should be operating and the proper color (red yellow or amber at rear).
- **License plates**—should be present, clean, and secure.
- **Splash guards**—should be properly fastened, undamaged, and not dragging or rubbing tires.
- **Air and electrical lines**—should be secure, undamaged, and not rubbing on any other part of the equipment.

- **Cargo**—should be properly blocked and braced, tied, and chained.
- **Tailboards**—should be up and secure. End gates should be free of damage and secured in stake sockets.
- **Canvas or tarps**—should be secured to avoid billowing, tearing, blocking rear-view mirror, or covering rear lights.
- **Overlength or overwidth loads**—have all signs and additional flags/lights in proper position and have all required permits.
- **Rear doors**—check that they are closed and locked.

Front Area of Trailer

- **License/registration holder**—should be in place, contain the current registration, and be firmly mounted with the cover closed.
- **Header board**—should be undamaged and securely mounted.
- **Canvas or tarp (if applicable)**—should be damage free, securely mounted, and secured to the carrier.
- **Clearance and ID lights**—should be in working order, the proper color, clean, and in good condition.
- **Reflectors**—should be clean and damage free.

Right Side of Trailer

- **Front trailer support (landing gear or dolly)**—should be fully raised with no parts bent, damaged, or missing **(see Figure 6-30)**. The crank handle should be present, properly secured, and in low gear if possible. If the crank handle is power operated, there should be no air or hydraulic leaks.
- **Spare tire carrier or rack**—should be in good condition, secure enough to carry the load, and the load should be chained.
- **Spare tire and wheel**—make sure they are sturdy and strong enough to carry the load and not damaged. They should be chained.
- **Lights and reflectors**—side-marker lights should be clean, operating, and the proper color (red at rear; others amber). Same for side-marker reflectors.

▶ **Figure 6-30**
Inspect the trailer.

- **Frame and body**—frame and cross members should be free of bends, cracks, traces of rust, and damage. There should be no missing cross members.
- **Cargo**—should be properly blocked, braced, tied, and chained. Sideboards and stakes should be in good condition and secure. Canvas and tarps should be properly tied down to prevent water damage, blowing, or blocking the driver's view.
- **Doors**—should be secure and in place.

Right Rear Trailer Wheel Area

- **Dual wheels and rims**—check the condition of wheels, rims, and tires for missing, bent, or broken spacers, studs, clamps, or lugs.
- **Dual tires**—should be evenly matched, of the same type (no mixing of radial and bias types), properly inflated with valve stems and caps in place. Check for cuts, bulges, or tread wear. Tires should not be rubbing and should be clear of debris. Wheel bearing/seals should not be leaking.

- **Suspension**—check condition of shock absorbers, torque rod arms, and bushings. Check springs, spring hangers, shackles, and U-bolts to make certain they are in good condition. The axles should be secure and drive axle(s) should not be leaking gear oil.

- **Check brake chambers and slack adjusters**—inspect all brake chambers, making sure everything is connected and is in good working order. Where you can see them, check to make sure brake drums are free of cracks, rust, and wear. Brake shoes should be evenly adjusted. Although most slack adjusters are self-adjusting, check those that are not by parking on level ground and turning off the parking brakes so you can move the slack adjusters. Wear gloves. Pull hard on each adjuster you can reach. They should move less than 1 inch (2.54 cm) where the push rod attaches to it. Adjust them or have them adjusted if they move more than 1 inch (2.54 cm). Too much brake slack can make a rig hard to handle.

▶ Figure 6–31

Inspect the back of a trailer with the lights on.

Rear of Trailer

- **Lights and reflectors**—side-marker lights should be clean, operating, and red at rear and others amber; same for side-marker reflectors **(see Figure 6-31)**.

- **Frame and body**—frame and cross members should be free of bends, cracks, traces of rust, and damage. There should be no missing cross members.

- **ICC underride prevention bumper**—should be in place and in good condition.

- **License plates**—should be in place, current, and securely attached.

- **Splash guards**—should be undamaged and securely attached.

- **Cargo**—should be properly blocked, braced, tied, and chained. Sideboards and stakes should be in good condition and secure. Canvas and tarps should be properly tied down to prevent water damage, blowing, or blocking the driver's view.

- **Doors**—should be secure and in place.

Left Rear Trailer Wheel Area

- Inspect the same things you inspected on the right, except the air tanks.

Left Side of the Trailer

- Inspect the same items you inspected on the right side.

Left Saddle Tank Area

- Check the same items you checked on the right side tank area, except the spare tire. Also check:
  - **Battery box**—see that it's firmly mounted to the vehicle and cover is in place.
  - **Battery** (if not mounted in the engine compartment)—be sure it will not move and the case is not broken or leaking.

Step 6: Check Signal Lights

- Return to the cab.
- Turn off all lights.

- Walk around the vehicle.
- Check the left front and rear of the tractor.
- Check the left rear trailer turn **signal (or identification) lights.** Make sure they are clean, the right color, and in working order.
- Check tractor and trailer stop lights.

Step 7: Check the Air Brake System

- Return to the cab.
- Turn off all lights.
- Make sure you have all trip manifests, permits, and required documents.
- Secure all loose articles in the cab so they will not be in the way while you are driving or become missiles in case of accident.
- Fasten your **seat belt (see Figure 6-32).**

▶ **Figure 6-32**

Once you have completed your pretrip inspection, buckle up and you're ready to go.

GO!

The air brake system check is sometimes combined with the air loss check and the cab check. Now you are ready to test the air brake system. Be sure to check each item carefully.

Low-Pressure Alarm and/or Light

Start "fanning" off the air pressure by rapidly applying and releasing the treadle valve. At approximately 60 pounds (27 kg), the low air pressure warning alarm should sound and/or the light should go on.

Tractor Protection Valve

Continue to fan off the air pressure. Emergency spring brakes should apply at no less than 20 pounds (9 kg) and no more than 45 pounds (20 kg). This action must cause the trailer brakes to lock. If they do not, there is a defect in the system **(see Figure 6-33).**

Air Pressure Buildup

With the engine at operating rpm, the pressure should build from 85 to 100 psi (586 to 690 kPa) within 45 seconds in dual air systems. If air tanks are larger than minimum, buildup time can be longer and still be safe. In single air systems, pressure should build from 50 to 90 psi (345 to 621 kPa) within 3 minutes with the engine idling at 600 to 900 rpm.

Parking and Trailer Hand Valve Brakes

1. Set (lock) the tractor spring brakes and release trailer spring brakes. Then tug against the brakes by slowly releasing the clutch and feeling the tractor tug against the trailer.
2. Set the trailer and the tractor spring brakes, then tug.
3. Release all spring brakes, apply the **trailer hand valve brake**, and tug against the trailer service brakes. Move the truck forward, disengage the clutch, apply the service brake, and stop evenly.

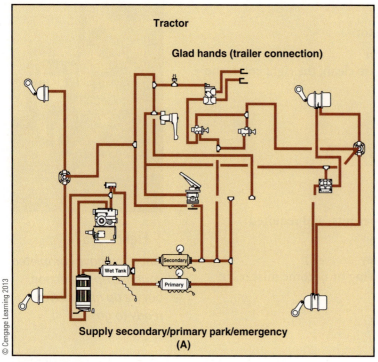

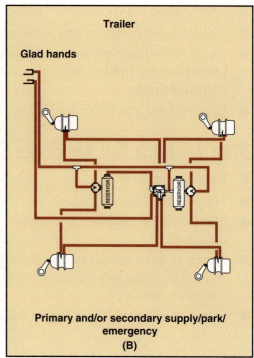

Tractor

Glad hands (trailer connection)

Wet Tank

Secondary

Primary

Supply secondary/primary park/emergency
(A)

Trailer

Glad hands

RESERVOIR

RESERVOIR

Primary and/or secondary supply/park/
emergency
(B)

© Cengage Learning 2013

▶ **Figure 6-33**

Air brake system.

CAUTION!

If the trailer is empty, it is possible to pull it with the brakes locked, but this causes undue wear. The fifth wheel can also be pulled out from under the trailer if it is not properly latched during this maneuver.

Too Much Slack in the Fifth Wheel

Put on the trailer brakes. Then carefully rock the tractor into first gear (low gear). Listen and feel for too much slack at the kingpin's locking jaws. If there seems to be too much slack, have it inspected by a mechanic. Be sure the clutch is working properly during this procedure.

Brake System Balance and Adjustment

In an off-street area, build the vehicle speed up to 5 to 7 miles per hour (8-11 km/h). Put on the service brakes sharply **(see Figure 6-34).** Note if the rig is pulling to one side or the other. If the stopping rate or the adjustment of the brakes does not feel right, have a mechanic check it right away. **Do not drive the rig until you are certain the service brakes are working properly.**

About 5 MPH

© Cengage Learning 2013

▶ **Figure 6-34**

Testing the service brakes.

EN ROUTE AND POSTTRIP INSPECTIONS

En Route Inspections

En route inspections are required by the Federal Motor Carrier Safety Regulations (FMCSR) and should be conducted every time you stop your vehicle.

FMCSR 392.9—En Route Inspections

According to this ruling, a driver may not operate a commercial motor vehicle unless:

- The commercial motor vehicle's cargo is properly distributed and adequately secured.
- The commercial motor vehicle's tailgate, tailboard, doors, tarpaulins, spare tire, and other equipment used in its operation, and the means of fastening the commercial motor vehicle's cargo, are secured.
- The commercial motor vehicle's cargo or any other object does not obscure the driver's view ahead or to the right or left sides (except for drivers of self-steer dollies), interfere with the free movement of his/her arms or legs, prevent his/her free and ready access to accessories required for emergencies, or prevent the free and ready exit of any person from the commercial motor vehicle's cab or driver's compartment.

Drivers of CMVs must:

- Make sure he/she has complied with the provisions of this section before driving that commercial motor vehicle.
- Inspect the cargo and the devices used to secure the cargo within the first 50 miles (80 km) after beginning a trip and cause any adjustments to be made to the cargo or load securement devices as necessary, including adding more securement devices, to ensure that cargo cannot shift on or within, or fall from the commercial motor vehicle.
- Reexamine the commercial motor vehicle's cargo and its load securement devices during the course of transportation and make any necessary adjustment to the cargo or load securement devices, including adding more securement devices, to ensure that cargo cannot shift on or within, or fall from, the commercial motor vehicle.
- Reexamine and make any necessary adjustments when the driver makes a change of his/her duty status, the commercial motor vehicle has been driven for 3 hours, or the commercial motor vehicle has been driven for 150 miles (241 km), whichever occurs first **(see Figure 6-35)**.

▶ **Figure 6-35**

Conduct a walk around to inspect your vehicle every 3 hours or 150 miles (241 km).

FMCSR 397.17—Required Inspections While Hauling Hazardous Materials

According to FMCSR 397.17, the driver must examine each tire on a motor vehicle at the beginning of each trip and each time the vehicle is parked.

If a tire is found to be flat, leaking, or improperly inflated, then the driver must have the tire repaired, replaced, or properly inflated before the vehicle is driven. However, the vehicle may be driven to the nearest safe place to perform the required repair, replacement, or inflation.

If, as the result of an examination, a tire is found to be overheated, the driver shall immediately have the overheated tire removed and placed at a safe distance from the vehicle. The driver shall not operate the vehicle until the cause of the overheating is corrected.

GO!

Each time you stop to inspect your vehicle en route, check the:

- **Tires**—check air pressure and temperature.
- **Brakes**—check adjustment and temperature.
- **Cargo**—check doors and make sure cargo is secure.
- **Coupling device**—check to make sure attachments are secure (remove the key from the ignition before checking coupling).
- **Lights**—check lights at sunset and at every stop if driving at night.

CANADIAN REQUIREMENTS FOR EN ROUTE INSPECTIONS

Whenever the professional driver is driving a commercial motor vehicle, he or she is required to monitor the condition of that vehicle for any major or minor defects. If, while driving, a defect is detected, the driver is required to report this to the carrier by any means possible. The driver must also make note of the defect on the inspection report. He or she may continue to drive the vehicle, but only if a minor defect has been detected. If a major defect is identified, the driver is not allowed to continue his or her trip.

Posttrip Inspection

After every trip, you will be required to:

- Drain moisture from the air tanks and fill fuel tanks as instructed by your employer.
- Identify any problems found during the en route inspection, such as unusual noise and vibrations.
- Inspect rig to further identify or locate problems and to locate any developing problems.
- Identify and diagnose the source of problems (this is covered in a later chapter).
- Complete an accurate and readable Driver's Vehicle Inspection Report (DVIR) **(see Figure 6-36).**

▶ **Figure 6-36**

It is important to perform a thorough inspection routine.

Reporting Findings

Inspections have no meaning unless you take action. As a professional driver, you are required to:

- Report findings to your supervisor and/or maintenance department, as your employer directs.
- Report any problems you find to your mechanics.
- Prepare an accurate and readable Driver's Vehicle Inspection Report (required by law) for each rig you drive through your workday or during your shift.

DRIVER'S VEHICLE INSPECTION REPORT (DVIR)

A written Driver's Vehicle Inspection Report at the end of a trip is required by law for companies in interstate or foreign commerce (FMCSR 396.11). This report must cover the following:

- Service brakes, including trailer brake connections
- Parking brake
- Steering mechanism
- Lights and reflectors
- Windshield wipers
- Rear-view mirrors
- Wheels and rims
- Tires
- Horn
- Coupling devices
- Emergency equipment

The **Driver's Vehicle Inspection Report (see Figure 6-37)** serves as a record of what the driver finds during inspections of the rig. The law requires that one copy of the report be kept in company files for at least 3 months. Another copy must be kept in the vehicle until the next DVIR is completed. This will tell the next driver about defects or problems, which should be repaired by this time. As a professional driver, you must, by law, review the previous driver's report and sign it if safety-related defects are listed.

Driver's Vehicle Inspection Report

Check Any Defective Item and Give Details Under "Remarks,"

DATE ____________________

TRUCK/TRACTOR NO. ____________

- ☐ Air Compressor
- ☐ Air Lines
- ☐ Battery
- ☐ Brake Accessories
- ☐ Brakes
- ☐ Carburetor
- ☐ Clutch
- ☐ Defroster
- ☐ Drive Line
- ☐ Engine
- ☐ Fifth Wheel
- ☐ Front Axle
- ☐ Fuel Tanks
- ☐ Heater
- ☐ Horn
- ☐ Lights
  - Head - Stop
  - Tail - Dash
  - Turn Indicators
- ☐ Mirrors
- ☐ Muffler
- ☐ Oil Pressure
- ☐ Electronic On-Board Recorder
- ☐ Radiator
- ☐ Rear End
- ☐ Reflectors
- ☐ Safety Equipment
  - Fire Extinguisher
  - Flags-Flares-Fusees
  - Spare Bulbs & Fuses
  - Spare Seal Beam
- ☐ Springs
- ☐ Starter
- ☐ Steering
- ☐ Tachograph
- ☐ Tires
- ☐ Transmission
- ☐ Wheels
- ☐ Windows
- ☐ Windshield Wipers
- ☐ Other

TRAILER(S) NO.(S) ____________

- ☐ Brake Connections
- ☐ Brakes
- ☐ Coupling Chains
- ☐ Coupling (King) Pin
- ☐ Doors
- ☐ Hitch
- ☐ Landing Gear
- ☐ Lights—All
- ☐ Roof
- ☐ Springs
- ☐ Tarpaulin
- ☐ Tires
- ☐ Wheels
- ☐ Other

Remarks: ____

☐ CONDITION OF THE ABOVE VEHICLE IS SATISFACTORY

DRIVER'S SIGNATURE ________________________________

☐ ABOVE DEFECTS CORRECTED

☐ ABOVE DEFECTS NEED NOT BE CORRECTED FOR SAFE OPERATION OF VEHICLE

MECHANIC'S SIGNATURE ________________ DATE ________

DRIVER'S SIGNATURE ________________ DATE ________

Courtesy of the US Department of Transportation, Federal Motor Carrier Safety Administration.

Figure 6-37

Driver's Vehicle Inspection Report.

THE DAILY INSPECTION REPORT

In Canada, once the driver has completed the inspection of the vehicle, he or she must complete the Daily Inspection Report, which indicates any findings of major or minor problems.

Required information for each of these reports includes:

- Motor carrier's name
- Date and time of inspection
- License plate number and jurisdiction of the vehicle
- City, town, village, or highway where inspection was completed
- Statement by inspector or driver that a thorough inspection was conducted on this vehicle
- Legibly printed name of the person conducting the inspection
- Odometer reading at time of inspection
- Statement of major/minor defects found or that no defects were found

STOP!

It bears repeating: Drivers may not drive a commercial motor vehicle in Canada without being in possession of a valid inspection report.

DAILY INSPECTION SCHEDULES IN CANADA

In Canada, drivers and inspectors are required to inspect commercial vehicles using the appropriate schedules. Trucks, tractors, and trailers are inspected using Schedule 1. Schedule 2 is for buses. Schedule 3 is to be used daily to inspect motor coaches and Schedule 4 is to be used for 30-day or 12,000-km (7,500 mi) inspections of motor coaches.

Carriers must supply drivers with copies of the appropriate schedules for each commercial vehicle and the driver is to carry a copy of the schedule in the cab of the commercial vehicle, presenting it when requested by enforcement officers. Drivers may not drive or draw a commercial vehicle not inspected within the last 24 hours.

Schedules identify the components and systems to be inspected and classify defects as "major" in column 3 and "minor" in column 2. All defects must be reported. Minor defects must be repaired prior to the next inspection while major defects must be repaired before the vehicle can be driven.

SUMMARY

Upon completing this chapter, you should be able to describe ways to make a thorough, careful, and accurate pretrip inspection. You should also be able to explain the importance of correcting vehicle malfunctions quickly and should have a working knowledge of federal regulations for inspections. You should also be able to explain the purpose and procedures for en route and posttrip inspections.

Ultimately, besides inspections being a regulated requirement, your knowledge of your vehicle systems, along with being able to perform a thorough inspection of your rig will save lives—and this in itself is a responsibility not to be taken lightly.

KEY TERMS

Air reservoir
Binders
Braces and supports
Brakes
Cab
Cargo compartment doors
Cargo securement devices
Chains
Checklist
Coupling system
Defrosters
Driver's Vehicle Inspection
   Report (DVIR)
Emergency equipment

Engine compartment
En route inspection
Exhaust system
Fifth wheel
FMCSR Part 396.9c Motor
   Vehicle Declared Out of
   Service
Four-way flashers
Free play
Inspection routine
Lights
Posttrip inspection
Pretrip inspection
Rear-view mirrors

Rims
Seat belts (safety belts)
Signal (or identification) lights
Splash guards (mud flaps)
Steering system
Steering wheel lash
Suspension system
Tarps
Tires
Tire chains
Tire pressure
Trailer hand valve brake
Winches
Windshield wipers

REVIEW QUESTIONS

1. The best way to check for loose lugs is to _____.

    a. look for rust around the lug nuts
    b. rely on the mechanic when the rig is given its annual inspection
    c. use a lug wrench
    d. use your hand

2. Which of the following is the best method to check tire pressure?

    a. Kick the tires.
    b. Use a tire gauge.
    c. Rely on the semiannual rig inspection by a mechanic.
    d. Look at the stance of the rig.

3. To check steering wheel play (lash) on a rig that has power steering, the engine _____.

    a. need not be running
    b. needs inspection
    c. needs to be warmed up
    d. must be running

4. Regarding the buildup of air pressure as reflected by the air pressure gauge, if the buildup of air pressure is okay (adequate), the time needed for the air pressure to build from 85 to 100 psi (586 to 690 kPa) is _____.

    a. not important
    b. within 45 seconds
    c. Air pressure should not go over 95 psi (655 kPa)
    d. 2 to 3 minutes

5. Rust around the lugs is most often a sign _____.

    a. the lugs are loose
    b. the rims are bent
    c. the rig has been driven in ice and snow
    d. for the shop to be concerned with

6. When inspecting the tractor rear dual tires, which of the following is not a true statement?

   a. Valve stems and caps should be in good condition.

   b. All tires should be the same size and type.

   c. *Thumping* a tire with a tire iron is an accurate method to check for proper air pressure.

   d. Nothing should be stuck between the tires.

7. For a vehicle with a power steering system and a 20-inch (50.8 cm) steering wheel, if steering wheel lash is _____, the vehicle will be considered out of service.

   a. 5-1/4 inches (13.3 cm) or greater   c. 3 to 5 inches (7.6 to 12.7 cm)

   b. 2 to 4 inches (5.1 to 10.2 cm)   d. 4 to 5 inches (10.2 to 12.7 cm)

8. During an inspection, according to Canadian law, if a minor defect is detected, it may be corrected prior to the next inspection. If a major defect, according to the schedule, is found, the CMV is to be _____.

   a. driven at speeds slower than normal   c. taken out of service

   b. driven only if needed   d. driven by veterans only

9. The proper way to inspect the air tanks for oil is _____.

   a. to check the oil level to see if the oil level has gone down

   b. to have a mechanic check for oil as this is not a driver responsibility

   c. to drive to the nearest shop and have the engine tanks checked by a mechanic

   d. to open the petcocks and allow the tanks to drain

10. After the air brake system is fully charged, with the engine off, the parking brake and trailer brakes released, and firm pressure (about 90 psi/621 kPa) applied to the service brake pedal for 1 minute, for a tractor and trailer the air pressure drop should be _____.

    a. zero   c. no more than 15 psi (103 kPa)

    b. tested by a mechanic   d. no more than 4 psi (28 kPa)

11. According to FMCSR, the steering wheel play (lash) in a tractor with a manual steering system and a 20-inch (50.8 cm) steering wheel should be _____.

    a. checked daily by a certified mechanic

    b. between 4 and 5 inches (10.2 and 12.7 cm)

    c. no more than 2-1/2 inches (6.4 cm)

    d. no more than 1-1/2 inches (3.8 cm)

12. According to FMCSR, a driver must stop to examine the cargo securing devices _____ after the start of a trip.

    a. within 50 miles (81 km)   c. between 100 and 150 miles (161–241 km)

    b. at some time   d. after 12 hours or 300 miles (483 km)

13. According to FMCSR, if you are hauling hazardous material and your vehicle has dual tires on any axle, you must check the tires _____.

    a. only at the beginning of the trip

    b. only at the end of the trip

    c. only after each 300 miles (483 km) of the trip

    d. before beginning a trip and each time you stop during a trip

14. The tractor protection valve should automatically go from the *normal* to the *emergency* position when the air pressure is _____.

    a. no less than 20 pounds (9 kg) and no more than 45 pounds (20 kg)

    b. normal

    c. at more than 100 pounds (45 kg)

    d. at 75 pounds (34 kg)

15. You must stop and do an en route walkaround safety inspection _____.

    a. each 100 miles (161 km) of a trip

    b. every 4 hours of a trip

    c. every 150 miles (241 km) or 3 hours (whichever comes first) during a trip

    d. every 400 miles (644 km) or 8 hours (whichever comes first) during a trip

16. For most clutches, _____ inches of free play is normal.

    a. 0   **c.** 4 to 5

    b. 1 to 2   **d.** 6 or more

17. In Canada, a driver may not drive a commercial vehicle not inspected within the last _____ hours.

    a. 10   **c.** 24

    b. 18   **d.** 36

SUPPLEMENTAL LEARNING ACTIVITIES

1. In 200 words or less, explain why a thorough pretrip inspection and a completed and implemented Driver's Vehicle Inspection Report is a good insurance policy for every driver.

2. In a small group, discuss what could, hypothetically, change on a vehicle, with the driver or with cargo between the pretrip inspection and the en route inspection. Make a list of at least 10 possibilities.

3. Whether your rig includes an open trailer or a closed one, what could, hypothetically, happen to cargo during a trip and why is it important to know this as a professional driver? Discuss this in your group and report back to class.

4. In 100 words or less, describe the steps you would take if a rig you were driving was declared out of service.

5. Go to www.fmcsa.dot.gov/safety-security/safety-initiatives/mcsap/insplevels.htm and read about the new driver rating system initiated by the Federal Motor Carrier Safety Administration in the new CSA program. List the seven rating categories and, in no more than three sentences, discuss your opinions.

FOR MORE INFORMATION

PTDI—Perform Vehicle Inspections, Page 9, Click on Skills Standards
www.ptdi.org/standards

FMCSA Preventive Maintenance and Inspection Procedures, search for Preventive Maintenance and Inspection Procedures
www.fmcsa.dot.gov/

CSA Inspection Standards, search for North American Standard Driver/Vehicle Inspection Levels
www.fmcsa.dot.gov/

California Commercial Driver Handbook Truck or Combination Vehicle Inspection Guide
dmv.ca.gov/pubs/cdl_htm/sec10_trkguide.htm

CDL Pre-Trip Inspection and Skills Evaluation Score Sheet
dmv.ca.gov/forms/dl/dl65prt1.pdf

CCOHS Vehicle Start-Up, the Circle Check
www.ccohs.ca/oshanswers/safety_haz/landscaping/vehicle.html

7 Basic Control

© iStockphoto/BanksPhotos

OBJECTIVES

When you have completed this chapter, you should be able to:

■ Enter and exit a tractor cab safely.

■ Show how to safety test a trailer hookup.

■ Explain the correct way to put a rig in motion.

■ Describe the correct way to stop a rig.

■ Describe the skills needed to back a rig in a straight line.

■ Explain the correct procedures for making right and left turns.

INTRODUCTION

As you have already learned, professional driving involves more than simply driving a tractor-trailer up and down the highway, and it's very different from operating your personal vehicle.

As you also have already learned, professional driving means mastering a number of basic and advanced skills. Once you become a professional driver, you'll continue to learn skills to make you better at the job you do, day in and day out **(see Figure 7-1)**.

Of course, the first step toward mastering these skills is learning the correct way to perform certain tasks and maneuvers, beginning with reading about them. The next step is to take what you have learned from this book and your classroom discussions and go to the driving range for practice, practice, practice.

Any veteran professional driver will tell you that you'll continue to master and polish driving skills as you gain more hands-on experience with the tractor-trailer rig and the job of professional driving itself. Professional drivers also will tell you that becoming a professional means spending time practicing and polishing each skill you learn. In other words, once you "get it," keep on working because that's how you *really* understand and can use the skill in any situation **(see Figure 7-2)**.

▶ **Figure 7–1**

Getting a feel for basic control and practicing these skills is the next step toward becoming a professional driver.

▶ **Figure 7–2**

Professional drivers continue to master and polish driving skills.

STOP!

A professional driver never turns the ignition key to his/her rig to begin a trip without knowing that rig's clearances, specifically the total length of the rig, height of the trailers (loaded and unloaded), weight (loaded and unloaded), and the clearance height of the undercarriage.

ENTERING AND EXITING THE CAB SAFELY: A "MUST READ"

We'll call him Eddie. He drives for a beverage company. Everybody on his route loves Eddie, even looks forward to his twice-a-week visits. He likes his job and always seems happy. Eddie's also been driving for the company since the late 1990s, so he knows his stuff. His driving record is unblemished when it comes to safety. He's had a fender-bender while backing his rig, but damage was minimal.

Now Eddie's company is pushing for a better bottom line. Territories have been consolidated and drivers have been laid off. Eddie feels fortunate he's still on his route, but it's been expanded and he's making one-third more deliveries in the same amount of time he's always had every day. Eddie said he's rushed, which means he doesn't have the time he used to have to "catch up" with his customers.

Last Friday didn't start out the best for Eddie. He got up late, had a spat with his wife about not hearing the alarm, and rushed to the plant. Loaders seemed to be moving at half-speed, so he was late getting started on his route.

Driving downtown was particularly challenging. Finding spots to park and unload product was difficult. At one point, he parked in a laundry's customers-only parking spots, nosing his truck into a semi-parallel position. Always good at multitasking, Eddie was readying to get out of the cab and retrieving the customer's invoice from his on-board printer—and this particular invoice always took much longer to print because of the variety of products on the order.

There! Printing finished, so Eddie opened the door as he tore the invoice from the printer—just in time to impede a car traveling in the two-way traffic's right lane. The car's driver, swerving to avoid the tractor's door now in his path, collided head-on with another vehicle.

Three passengers in the car were transported to the hospital, two in critical condition. Emergency responders performed CPR on one of them at the scene.

Eddie's boss required him to complete his route that day. The accident investigation is ongoing.

HOW TO SAFELY ENTER AND EXIT A CAB

The cab of a tractor-trailer is usually large, high off the ground, and may be difficult to enter safely, especially for shorter drivers. Climbing into a big rig cab can also be dangerous, particularly during wet or icy weather. Why? Because improper or careless movements during entry could result in a fall and injury. In brief, this is not the time to multitask. Your entire attention should be focused on entering and exiting the cab safely—it's a requirement of the Federal Motor Carrier Safety Administration (see FMCSR 399.207, Truck and truck-tractor access requirements.) As the first portion of the general rule states:

> Any person entering or exiting the cab or accessing the portion of a high profile COE truck or truck-tractor shall be afforded sufficient steps and handholds, and/or deck plates to allow the user to have at least 3 limbs in contact with the truck or truck-tractor at any time. This rule applies to intermediate positions as well as transition between intermediate positions.

Professional drivers should follow the steps below as a general habit to avoid injury, and during testing for a commercial driver's license to avoid losing safety points:

1. Always check the steps and handles of the cab for grease, fuel, oil, slick mud, or ice. Clean off all residue before entering the cab. Keep all entry steps as clean as possible to eliminate slipping and injury.
2. Wear footwear appropriate to your work and the weather. This does not mean flip-flops. Also, wear high-visibility clothing.

Courtesy of Jennifer Pierson, Prime Inc.

▶ **Figure 7-3**

Three points of contact can be described as either two arms and one foot or two feet and one arm.

3. Maintain a minimum of three points of contact between your body and the cab at all times during entry. Focus on your entry, always facing the tractor, avoiding distraction, which may result in injury (**Figure 7-3**).

4. Place one foot on the step while keeping the other foot securely on the ground. Grip the handle on the inside of the door with one hand and the handle on the exterior cab frame with the other. Notice the three points of contact—two hands and one foot.

5. Move your lower foot to the top step, pulling your body up with your arms if necessary. There are still three points of contact.

6. Bring your rear foot to the top step. Both feet are now on the top step, so you may release one handle and still maintain three points of contact.

7. Slide or step into the cab and release the remaining handle, because you are now safely inside.

To exit the cab safely, use the following steps:

1. Exit the truck by climbing out backward, as if you were using a ladder.

2. Maintain three points of contact at all times.

3. Never jump out of the cab.

CAUTION!

Use the three-point stance when you're taking your Commercial Driver's License Skills Test. Some states may count failing to enter and exit the cab safely as an error.

INTERESTING FACT

In 1918, Standard Trucks featured high-door cabs, which offered protection to drivers in cold weather. The doors on the AB models slid sideways while those on the AC models slid vertically.

START, WARM-UP, AND SHUTDOWN ROUTINES

We call them "routines"—**start routine, warm-up routine, and shutdown routine** because there are specific, routine steps to follow when starting and/or shutting down an engine. Take the time to learn each step and these routines will serve you well.

STOP!

Before starting the engine, always check the trailer coupling (described in Chapter 10, "Coupling and Uncoupling").

Starting the Engine

Starting the Four-Cycle Engine

1. Apply the parking brake.
2. Release the throttle (take foot off fuel pedal) and depress the clutch. Make sure the transmission is in neutral.
3. Turn on the ignition/switch key.
4. If the engine does not start in 10 to 15 seconds, then turn the starter off, wait 60 seconds, and try again.
5. Ease your foot off the clutch.
6. Check readings on all gauges and meters.

Engine Warm-up

Engine warm-up is the period of time after starting the engine and before moving your rig that prepares the engine to do its job. Always use a low RPM level to warm up the engine, between 800 and 1,000 RPM. During warm-up, gauges in your tractor will indicate when the engine is operating within its specified range.

By warming up your engine, you:

- Allow the engine to reach a beginning operating temperature by idling (Remember, however, that excessive **idling** wastes fuel and can cause unnecessary wear and tear on the engine.)
- Circulate oil and build oil pressure to proper levels
- Reach a favorable clearance between moving parts
- Increase coolant temperature, build up air pressure, and lubricate moving parts

Engine warm-up is complete when water temperature reaches anywhere from 170 to 195 degrees F. To achieve this temperature range, it will be necessary to move your rig at a low RPM, shifting into the next highest gear and proceeding slowly.

"Looks like your engine is good and warm!"

STOP!

The results of not warming up the engine properly will damage any parts not properly lubricated.

CAUTION!

During engine warm-up, keep all acceleration smooth and easy, avoiding high RPMs. Rapid acceleration or over-revving the engine during the warm-up period causes damage to crankshaft and bearings over time.

Shutting Down the Engine

Engine shutdown is the period of time after stopping the rig until the engine is turned off. Shutting down the engine requires a cooling-off period to prevent damage to engine parts. Turbo chargers are one of the main reasons for this suggested cool down period. Many states now have regulations regarding how long semitrucks can idle. These new laws are in force as a part of clean air environmental initiatives.

Follow these basic steps for engine shutdown:

1. Depress the clutch and shift into neutral.
2. Release the clutch.
3. Let the engine idle, allowing it to cool down—idling time is determined by cargo being hauled and length of trip.
4. Turn off the key switch/ignition.
5. If engine has stop control, move it to the "off" position to cut off the fuel flow from the injectors.

CAUTION!

Cooling down the engine is as important as the engine warm-up. During the **cool down period,** coolant and oil will flow at reduced temperatures and allow heat built up in the engine to dissipate.

STOP!

Most newer trucks require only a few minutes of idling. Excessive idling causes unnecessary engine wear, wastes fuel (you may miss getting a fuel bonus), and pollutes the air.

Automatic Shutdown/Startup Systems

All electronic diesel engines are capable of shutting down the engine after a set time period. The following are examples of this technology:

IDLE SMART from BBW Inc.—a programmable, electronic control system that monitors temperatures inside and outside the truck. It automatically starts the engine, increases engine speed for maximum efficiency, monitors system, heats or cools the cab, idles down the engine, and shuts the engine off.

The ICON system from Cummins Engine Company Inc.—automatically controls engine starting and stopping for the purposes of reducing excess idle time and maintaining engine temperatures. It has three modes of operation: engine, cab comfort, and mandatory shutdown. Under engine mode, the system monitors engine oil and battery voltage. If either drops below a set level, the engine is automatically started. Under cab comfort mode, a cab thermostat starts and stops the engine to maintain the desired temperature. Under mandatory shutdown mode, the engine will shut down after 5 or 15 minutes.

Temp-A-Start from TAS Distributing Inc.—the original start/stop technology for truck diesel engines introduced in the 1980s and licensed to Detroit Diesel and Cummins Engine Company. The system provides driver comfort and reduced service calls while eliminating unnecessary idling. Temp-A-Start is a mandatory engine shutdown that also turns off all electrical accessories controlled by the ignition switch. It monitors battery voltage and, when a low voltage condition occurs, it will start the engine and charge up the batteries. In engine mode (the default mode) Temp-A-Start monitors engine temperature and starts the engine when oil temperature drops to 55 degrees F and shuts the engine off when oil temperature reaches 135 degrees F. In zero degree weather, Temp-A-Start typically will run the engine for 2.2 hours during a 10-hour period for a 78 percent off-time.

PUTTING THE VEHICLE INTO MOTION—AND STOPPING

Moving a tractor-trailer rig is vastly different from moving an automobile. That should come as no surprise. But, to address this difference, professional drivers must learn an array of skills in making moving a tractor-trailer rig look as easy as moving a personal vehicle.

Three specific steps should always be followed before moving your rig:

Step 1: Test the Tractor-Trailer Hookup

Each time you hook up a trailer you must test the coupling. There are two tests—one for rigs with independent brake control and one for rigs without independent brake control.

To Test Rigs with Independent Trailer Brake Control (Trolley or Hand Valve)

1. Release tractor brakes, depress clutch, and shift into lowest forward gear.
2. Apply the independent trailer brake.
3. Release the clutch to the friction point.
4. Gently pull forward against the locked trailer brakes.
5. Depress clutch.
6. Repeat the entire procedure to ensure proper coupling.

To Test Rigs without Independent Trailer Brake Control (Trolley or Hand Valve)

1. Release tractor brakes, depress clutch, and shift into lowest forward gear.
2. Move trailer protection valve from "normal" to "emergency."
3. Release clutch to friction point.

CHAPTER 7

4. Pull forward gently against the locked trailer brakes.
5. Depress clutch.
6. Repeat the entire procedure.

CAUTION!

Test your rig's hookup at every stop you make—during your shift or during the day.

Step 2: Putting the Tractor–Trailer into Motion

Moving your rig smoothly and with a sense of ease requires much practice and experience in the driver's seat. Remember, there is no substitute for practice **(see Figure 7-4).**

Use the following steps when putting your rig into motion:

1. Release tractor and trailer parking brakes.
2. Push clutch all the way down and shift into lowest gear.
3. Let out clutch slowly as you begin to depress the fuel pedal.
4. When vehicle begins moving, slowly increase engine RPMs to increase the rig's speed.
5. Do not rest your foot on the clutch pedal.
6. When the vehicle is in motion with the clutch fully engaged, take your foot off the clutch and prepare to shift into another gear or stop **(see Figure 7-5).**

▶ **Figure 7-4**

There is no substitute for practice when it comes to learning to drive your rig.

▶ **Figure 7-5**

Basic vehicle maneuvers require skill and coordination between the use of the fuel pedal and the clutch.

Clutch

Fuel pedal

TIP

Tips for Professional Drivers

■ Always engage clutch slowly to avoid slippage.

■ When starting on an upgrade, shift into the lowest forward gear, slowly release clutch, and as the clutch engages, slowly accelerate and release the parking and trailer brakes.

■ Allow for brake lag.

Step 3: Stopping the Tractor-Trailer

Stopping your rig smoothly is also a skill learned from much practice behind the wheel. To stop a rig smoothly, take the following steps if you are driving a manual transmission. If you are operating a vehicle equipped with an automatic transmission, follow your instructor's recommendations.

1. Push down the brake pedal.

2. Control the pressure so the rig comes to a smooth, safe stop.

3. Downshift as you stop. Do not coast for longer length than the vehicle, which in most cases is approximately 70 feet (21.3 m).

4. If driving a manual transmission, do not push in the clutch until the engine rpm is almost to idle.

5. When you have stopped, select a low gear.

6. If you have stopped properly, there should be no nose rebound or bouncing in the cab.

BACKING IN A STRAIGHT LINE

Backing maneuvers are covered in detail in Chapter 9, but basic information is given here to help you prepare for **straight-line backing.**

STOP!

Never begin backing your vehicle without first getting out of the cab, walking to the back of the rig and making certain you have a clear path. If you have a co-driver, have him or her help you back, but YOU should—personally—get out of the cab to check your clearance. Use the GOAL principle: **G**et **O**ut **A**nd **L**ook.

1. **Position the vehicle** by moving forward until the tractor and trailer are aligned and the front wheels are straight. Make sure the area is clear **(see Figure 7-6).**

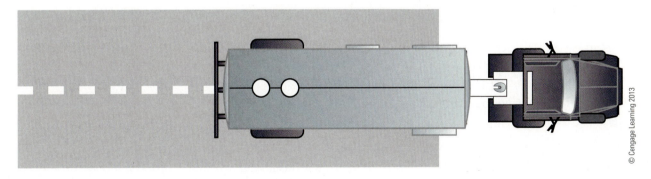

© Cengage Learning 2013

▶ Figure 7-6

A diagram of straight-line backing.

2. **Shift into reverse gear** and back slowly, using idle speed. Do not ride the clutch or brake pedals.

3. **Turn on warning flashers** to communicate with others your intended maneuver.

4. **Use both mirrors constantly** to check behind the rig while backing. Be aware of pedestrians and other vehicles. Many experienced drivers recommend opening both windows while backing to allow you to see better without possible glares; it also gives you the ability to hear anyone around.

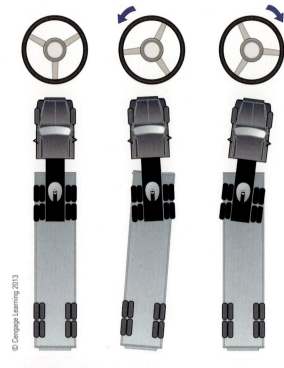

▶ Figure 7-7

Steering wheel positioning in relation to drift in a straight-line backup.

5. **Do not oversteer.** The best way to keep your vehicle on course is not to oversteer.

6. **Correct drifting** (**drift** is when your tractor and your trailer get out of alignment and "drift" in different directions). To correct drift, turn the steering wheel toward the drift as soon as it occurs. If you catch the drift right away, it requires very little movement of your steering wheel to correct it (**see Figure** 7-7).

7. **Use the push–pull method to keep the trailer in a straight line.** When the trailer gets bigger in the mirror, push the steering wheel toward that mirror. Then, immediately pull the steering wheel back to straighten out the rig. The biggest error in using the push–pull method is not returning the steering wheel to a straight position.

8. **Start again.** If your rig is getting too far out of alignment, it is easier to pull forward and start again. Stop, pull forward, realign your rig, and try it again.

GO!

The key to backing your rig in a straight line is to recognize what direction the trailer is drifting and make the necessary adjustments immediately. **Use both outside mirrors** to help you make these steering adjustments, and **use four-way flashers** to communicate what you're intending to do.

TURNING A COMMERCIAL VEHICLE

This section describes basic turning maneuvers. Keep the following basics in mind while making turns (**see Figure 7-8**):

- Know your vehicle—length, width, and clearances required
- Allow for **tailswing,** which occurs when the trailer has a long overhang behind the rear-most axle.
- Allow for off-tracking.
- Plan ahead.

Off-Tracking in Tractor-Trailer Rigs

Off-tracking is what happens when you turn your rig and the rear wheels do not follow the same path as the front wheels of the rig. The rear wheels follow a shorter path; and the more distance between the front wheels and the rear wheels—and the sharper the turn—the more the rear wheels off-track. Keep off-tracking in mind when making turns or taking curves (**see Figure 7-9**).

Tractor-Trailer Truck Tracking Characteristics

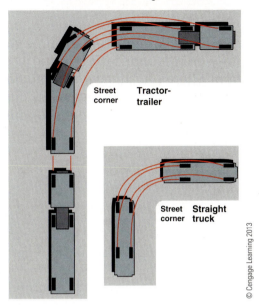

Street corner

Tractor-trailer

Street corner

Straight truck

© Cengage Learning 2013

Off-Tracking Vehicle Path

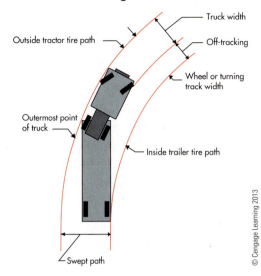

Outside tractor tire path

Truck width

Off-tracking

Wheel or turning track width

Outermost point of truck

Inside trailer tire path

Swept path

© Cengage Learning 2013

▶ Figure 7–8

Professional drivers know their rigs and how they will respond to each maneuver.

▶ Figure 7–9

In off-tracking, the rear wheels of the rig do not follow the same path as the front wheels.

Two key factors determine the off-tracking of the trailer:

- **The distance between the kingpin and the rear trailer wheels.** The greater the distance between the kingpin and the rear trailer wheels, the more the off-tracking.

- **The amount of sideways drag of the rear tires.** Sideways drag of the rear tires increases with the number of tires. The more sideways drag, the more off-tracking. Tandem axles have more sideways drag and greater off-tracking than a single rear axle **(see Figure 7-10).**

Low-Speed Off-Tracking

In low-speed off-tracking, each axle tracks inboard of the axle in front of it. A typical low-speed off-tracking accident involves the trailer sideswiping a car at an intersection.

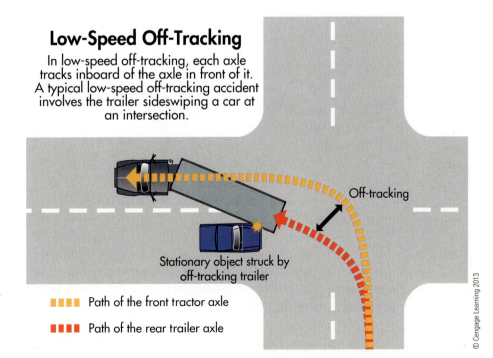

Off-tracking

Stationary object struck by off-tracking trailer

▬▬▬ Path of the front tractor axle

▬▬▬ Path of the rear trailer axle

© Cengage Learning 2013

▶ Figure 7–10

In low-speed off-tracking, each axle tracks inside the path of the axle in front of it.

Making Right Turns

Making a successful right turn requires planning, practice, and patience as well as good judgment, driving at the proper speed, and good control of your rig. Most right turns are tighter than the turning radius of your rig **(see Figure 7-11)**. To make a turn safely around the corner without hitting a curb or other objects, you will need to use more traffic lanes than you would if you were driving your personal vehicle. At the same time, you do not want to obstruct traffic. If the turn is sharp, you should be going slower than usual to make the turn cleanly. If you cannot turn and clear the corner using the space available, then choose an alternate route. Sometimes, by continuing straight ahead for a block or two, you can find space enough to make the turn without hitting the curb or other objects.

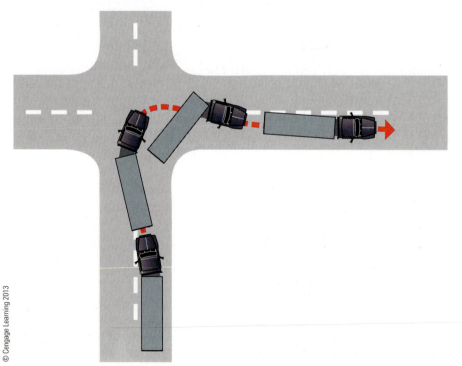

▶ **Figure 7–11**

Most right turns require extra room because they are tighter than the turning radius of your rig.

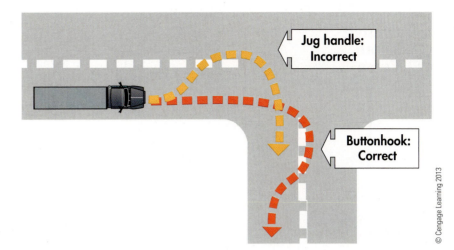

▶ **Figure 7–12**

Jug handle turns are a sloppy and dangerous way to make a right turn.

What Is a Buttonhook Turn?

A **buttonhook turn** will allow you to clear the corner without problems, but you should always use caution because you are crossing into another lane when you make the turn **(see Figure 7-13).**

Use the extra space in front of you in this manner:

1. Approach the intersection in the right lane.
2. If the lane width allows, position your rig about 4 to 5 feet (1.2 to 1.5 m) from the curb, creating as much space to the right of your rig as possible.
3. Turn on your right turn signal.
4. Scan the intersection, watching for a break in the traffic.
5. Proceed straight ahead until the trailer tires will clear the corner in a hard right turn.
6. Turn hard to the right.
7. Finish the turn in the right lane.
8. Cancel your turn signal.

Buttonhook

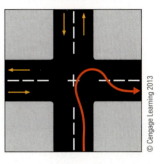

▶ **Figure 7–13**

Buttonhook turns allow safe right-turn maneuvers.

CAUTION!

Regardless of the difficulty of the turn, as a professional driver, you must always yield to motorists, cyclists, and pedestrians.

What Is a Jug Handle Turn?

A **jug handle turn** is a sloppy and dangerous way to make a right turn (check out the jug handle turn diagram in Figure 7-12) for the following reasons:

1. You gain little if any advantage, because the trailer tires do not have time to move away from the curb.
2. If you signal right but move left, as you must do in a jug handle turn, you confuse traffic and someone behind you may even try to squeeze between the trailer and the curb.

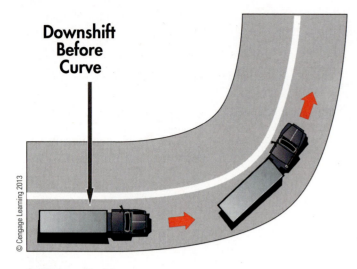

Downshift Before Curve

© Cengage Learning 2013

▶ **Figure 7-14**

Planning ahead means shifting into the proper gear before a turn or a curve.

Now, follow these steps to successfully complete a right turn:

1. Signal in advance to let other drivers know your intentions.
2. Adjust your speed as you approach the intersection. This enables you to speed up slightly as you make your turn.
3. Slow down and shift to the proper gear before entering the turn. In this way, you can keep both hands on the steering wheel during the turn itself (**see Figure 7-14**).
4. Pull your rig farther into the intersection than you would your personal vehicle to avoid running over the curb during the turn, due to off-tracking.
5. Make the turn, turning the steering wheel right and speeding up slightly for a smooth turn.
6. Watch the right mirror for the position of the trailer wheels and to locate other traffic. Then check to the front and left side of your rig.

GO!

A good rule of thumb when making a right turn is to pull about one-half the length of the rig past the corner point of the intersection before beginning the turn. Keep the wheels of your rig straight before turning.

Common Errors When Making Right Turns

Common errors in making right turns include:

- Approaching the intersection too fast
- Not downshifting before the turn
- Shifting gears while turning
- Not allowing for off-tracking of the trailer
- Not getting far enough into the intersection before making the turn

Making Left Turns

Plan ahead before making a left turn just as you would for a right turn. Follow these steps:

1. Slow down as you approach the intersection or prepare to make a left turn.
2. Position your rig in the left turning lane, being as far to the right in the left turn lane as possible and prepare to turn into the left lane.
3. If there are two left turn lanes on the road, use the outside (lane farthest to the right) lane.
4. Put the rig into the correct gear to make the turn.
5. Keep wheels straight.

6. Watch your left mirror during the turn.

7. After turning, turn the steering wheel back to the right to straighten your wheels.

Common Errors in Making Left Turns

Common errors in making left turns include approaching the intersection too fast, shifting gears while turning, and choosing the wrong lane from which to make your turn.

Highway Curves

Position yourself carefully before taking a highway curve **(see Figure 7-15)**. To take a right curve, keep the front of your vehicle toward the center of the lane, or the rear of the trailer may run off the road during the curve. To take a left curve, keep the tractor as close to the outer (right) edge of the lane as possible, to prevent the trailer from running over the center line. This is important when there is opposing traffic. On a ramp where the traffic is one way, the driver should drive on the outermost portion of the curve.

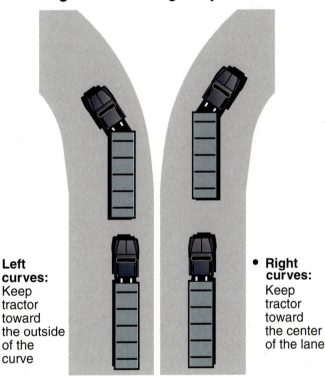

Right and Left Highway Curves

© Cengage Learning 2013

- **Left curves:** Keep tractor toward the outside of the curve

- **Right curves:** Keep tractor toward the center of the lane

▶ Figure 7-15

Maneuvering highway curves requires planning and correctly positioning your vehicle in the traffic lanes.

POSITIVE LOCKING DIFFERENTIAL—WHAT IS IT AND WHAT DOES IT MEAN TO YOU?

The **positive locking differential** dramatically increases traction. With spider gear differentials, the wheel that has the least amount of traction typically gets full power, which isn't good for a stuck truck. Positive locking differentials send power to the wheel that has the most traction, enabling escape from almost any situation.

RANGE PRACTICE

After you have learned the correct methods for operating and maneuvering your rig, your instructor may take you out for driving range practice (**see Figure 7-16**).

You will be expected to:

■ Start, warm up, and shut down the engine.

■ Put the rig into motion and accelerate smoothly.

■ Come to a smooth stop.

■ Back in a straight line.

■ Make turns correctly from the proper position.

To meet these goals, you will need other skills, such as:

■ Coordinated use of the accelerator and clutch

■ Knowing the proper method for putting on air brakes

■ Coordinated use of all controls to drive forward or back in a straight line

■ Understanding off-tracking, or the path the trailer takes as the entire rig takes curves or makes turns

All of these driving skills can be mastered with driving range practice. As you practice, using care in operating your rig will bring you success as a professional driver and value to your future employers.

© Cengage Learning 2013

▶ Figure 7-16

Practice on the driving range will help you master the skills you need to become a successful professional driver.

INTERESTING FACT

By 1922, the advantages of truck transportation over horse-drawn wagons continued, dramatically demonstrating cost savings. This was due, in part, to the drop in truck prices beginning in 1920. Quicker service, reliability, durability, and lower prices widened the gap between trucks and horse teams.

SUMMARY

Upon completing this chapter, you are now prepared to explain routines for starting, warming up, and shutting down your tractor. You also know the steps in testing a trailer hookup and can explain how to put your rig in motion smoothly and then stop your rig just as smoothly. You are also familiar with how to back your rig in a straight line, make turns, and take curves while being aware of your off-tracking. Remember, too, that learning and mastering all of these skills require practice, guidance from experienced professional drivers, and patience with yourself. Rome was not built in a day—and good professional drivers continue to polish the skills you are now learning. As someone once said, "You'll learn something new every day!"

KEY TERMS

Buttonhook turn

Control routines—start, warm-up and shutdown

Cool-down period

Drift

Engine shutdown

Engine warm-up

Idling

Jug handle turn

Off-tracking

Positive locking differential

Starting routine

Straight-line backing

Tailswing

A DAY IN THE LIFE . . .

Danny Smith – Big G Express Inc., Professional Truck Driver

Being a professional driver—not just any job. Having been in the trucking industry for 31 years, I cannot begin to imagine another career. In the beginning, I hauled milk from Tennessee to Florida in trucks with no air conditioning or spring ride suspension. Today I am fortunate to drive the most state-of-the-art equipment available. I have traveled in 48 states and parts of Canada. Why would anyone want another job!!!

Being a professional driver demands that I maintain a safe driving record, which is necessary to be recognized as a top driver. I am proud to have over 2 million accident-free miles. To continue this record, I read current legislation concerning trucking industry changes, rules, and regulations. On the road, I endeavor to observe all drivers to prevent accidents.

One of my favorite activities is sharing experiences with other drivers. Frequently I will chat with a driver to exchange ideas and convey any information I have that is pertinent. When I meet a new driver, I mentor the driver to utilize the many resources available at our company as well as trucking industry publications. As our paths cross and I reconnect with the driver, I want him or her to know that I am available to help whatever the need is.

At my company, Big G Express, my opinions and suggestions are always valued. When the company is going to purchase new equipment, I am asked for my viewpoint. Frequently after using the product, I will suggest ways to improve the system and they are usually implemented. As a driver representative on the Safety Committee, I am able to share my perspective of safety issues and concerns. Most recently I have been asked to serve on the ESOP Employee Committee to represent my fellow drivers. This committee meets to answer questions, advance knowledge and awareness about the ESOP Program.

> " **One of my favorite activities is sharing experiences with other drivers.** "

One aspect I have not mentioned is my family. They are totally supportive of my career and encourage me to be the best I can be. This career has allowed me to send both of my girls to an excellent private college enabling them to be productive, self-sufficient adults.

REVIEW QUESTIONS

1. Which of the following is not part of the recommended routine for the startup of a four-cycle diesel engine?

    a. Apply the parking brake.   c. Pump the fuel pedal.
    b. Operate the starter.   d. Check the instruments.

2. Which of the following does not happen during engine warm-up?

    a. The air compressor inflates the tires to the correct pressure.
    b. The engine reaches a beginning operating temperature.
    c. The cylinder walls are coated with film of oil.
    d. The coolant temperature increases.

3. In exiting the cab, at any time, it is extremely important to _____.

    a. check that the tach is under 30 RPMs   c. stay focused on one task at a time
    b. check the on-board computer   d. make sure you have dispatcher's number
                                                    on your cell phone

4. One of the most common errors while making right turns is _____.

    a. signaling too far ahead of turn   c. braking too far ahead of turn
    b. oversteering   d. approaching the intersection too fast

5. When warming up the engine, which instrument is not necessary to check?

    a. coolant temperature   c. oil temperature
    b. oil pressure   d. trailer air brake

6. When approaching a curve (not a corner), make certain to _____.

    a. keep the vehicle in the middle of the lane
    b. increase RPMs
    c. keep vehicle to the right
    d. keep vehicle to the left

7. When a trailer is hooked up to a tractor, a test of the coupling must be made _____.

    a. every time coupling takes place   c. once a week by a mechanic
    b. once a week   d. annually

8. When putting a tractor-trailer with a manual transmission into motion, when the clutch is slowly engaged (let out), the accelerator is _____.

    a. ignored   c. slightly depressed
    b. fully depressed   d. depressed halfway down

9. Which of the following is a correct statement regarding stopping a tractor-trailer with a manual transmission?

    a. Coast to a stop in neutral.   c. Fully depress the clutch.
    b. Always downshift one gear.   d. There should be nose rebound and bouncing
                                           of the cab.

10. When attempting to back in a straight line, to correct drifting, the driver _____.

    a. turns the steering wheel toward the direction of the drift
    b. turns the steering wheel away from the drift
    c. does not turn the steering wheel
    d. steers away from the drift and brake

11. Regarding using the push–pull method to keep a trailer in a straight line, when the trailer gets bigger in a mirror, the driver _____.

    a. turns the top of steering wheel away from that mirror and immediately pulls the steering wheel back to straighten the rig out
    b. turns the steering wheel two revolutions toward that mirror
    c. turns the steering wheel two revolutions away from the mirror
    d. pushes the steering wheel toward that mirror and immediately pulls the steering wheel back to straighten the rig out

12. Before backing, leave the cab and physically check _____.

    a. air lines
    b. tires
    c. area around rig, top to bottom, too
    d. coupling

13. If you are making a left turn on a two-lane highway, it's always safer to use _____.

    a. your four-way flashers
    b. the right-most lane
    c. both lanes
    d. the center stripe

14. Since most right turns are tighter than the turning radius of a tractor-trailer rig, in a right turn, to make it safely around a corner without hitting the curb, a driver must _____ than he or she would in a car.

    a. turn more sharply
    b. begin turning sooner
    c. pull farther into the intersection
    d. apply brakes sooner

15. When making a left turn in a tractor-trailer rig, a driver should position the rig as far to the _____ in the left turn lane as possible.

    a. left
    b. middle
    c. Position in the lane is not important.
    d. right

16. When entering or exiting the cab, it is important to maintain _____ points of contact.

    a. 0
    b. 1
    c. 2
    d. 3

17. You should test your rig's hookup _____.

    a. at every stop you make
    b. only at the beginning of your trip
    c. every hour
    d. after 100 miles (161 km)

SUPPLEMENTAL LEARNING ACTIVITIES

1. Divide into small groups and spend 10 minutes thinking of and writing as many reasons as possible to avoid multitasking while driving, backing, or parking a rig. For ideas, read the scenario at the beginning of this chapter. Discuss your reasons in class.

2. For classroom discussion: Why should professional drivers-to-be have experience making turns in rigs of various lengths? What type of rig do you think would be the most difficult for turning?

3. Almost every textbook chapter on Vehicle Control emphasizes maneuvering a rig smoothly, while turning, going from low to high speeds and gearing down from high to low speeds. In 100 words or less, describe why "smooth" is an important descriptive word in professional driving. What are the consequences if maneuvers are not made "smoothly"?

4. Knowing clearance requirements of your rig is necessary information you must have before every trip, whether you drive over-the-road or city pick-up-and-delivery. In a group, come up with at least two consequences of not knowing your rig's clearance, and why it's not a good idea to "guess."

5. Throughout your training, you'll hear cautions about "speed." As a professional driver, how can "speed" ruin your day? Give three examples and be ready to discuss.

FOR MORE INFORMATION

PTDI—Exercise Basic Control, Page 10, Click on Skill Standards
www.ptdi.org/standards

PTDI—Manage and Adjust Vehicle Speed, Page 15, Click on Skill Standards
www.ptdi.org/standards

Controlling Sway
www.timberman.com/RIG/sway.htm

8 Shifting

© Krivosheev Vitaly/www.Shutterstock.com

OBJECTIVES

When you have completed this chapter, you should be able to:

- Describe gear-shifting patterns for various transmissions.

- Know when to shift gears—depending on speed, road conditions, and terrain.

- Demonstrate methods of shifting through all the gears of conventional transmissions.

- Demonstrate double-clutching and timing the shift for a smooth and fuel-efficient performance.

- Understand rpm and mph (km/h) for proper gear selection and downshifting.

- Discuss shifting with automatic and semiautomatic transmissions.

- Understand the operation of electronic synchronized and nonsynchronized transmissions.

- Be aware of common shifting errors and the results of these errors, and how improper use can damage a rig.

INTRODUCTION

Many professional driving students—like you—may dread learning to shift gears, thinking it will be the most difficult of all the new skills you have to learn. Common sense tells you shifting gears in a commercial motor vehicle could be more difficult than shifting gears in your personal vehicle. But, like most professional driving skills, shifting becomes less intimidating and less difficult with practice and more practice, along with time and patience.

This chapter will provide clear definitions and good hands-on knowledge of the skill, plus tips, to help you increase and improve your skills behind the wheel.

This chapter also introduces you to the differences in shifting patterns. It explains clutch and fuel pedal control and how to coordinate hands, eyes, feet, sound, and feel to handle the various transmissions found in today's tractor-trailer rigs.

This information and your time on the driving range or behind the wheel will help you master the skills you need to drive a tractor-trailer rig professionally. The information you learn now will serve as a handy reference later. Smooth shifting is a pro skill that takes time and experience to master. More importantly, you will understand that proper gearing evolves from classroom learning, behind-the-wheel practice, and your instructor answering questions you may have.

SHIFT CONTROLS

When you drive a manual transmission **(see Figure 8-1)**, the controls used in shifting are the fuel pedal, gearshift lever, and clutch. Operation of these controls requires coordination and careful timing. When you push down the clutch, you separate the engine from the transmission. This is the only time it is safe to shift gears: when the engine and transmission are separated.

The controls used in shifting are as follows:

- **Fuel pedal**—controls the flow of fuel to the engine and governs the speed of the engine. This information is certainly not new, but it is important to remember because engine speed and shifting are closely related.

- **Gearshift lever**—selects a gear and determines how the engine speed is transferred into road speed. For example, at a specific engine speed, placing the transmission in a low gear will provide a lot of power to the engine but does not impact road speed, because in a low gear, the power of the engine can be multiplied 10 to 15 times. In a high gear, a high road speed can be attained but actual available power is reduced.

- **Clutch**—transfers power from the engine to the transmission, thus allowing you to shift gears. **Remember!** It is only safe to shift gears when the clutch separates the engine from the transmission.

▶ Figure 8-1

Driving a manual transmission requires the use of the fuel pedal, the gearshift lever, and the clutch. Shifting becomes less intimidating with practice.

Thinkstock Images

UNDERSTANDING SHIFTING: THE DIFFERENCE BETWEEN TORQUE AND POWER

Torque is the twisting force that the engine exerts on the drive-line to make the wheels turn. It's the "holding power" of the engine. As you start up a grade, your truck speed will slow slightly, and engine power decreases, but at the same time, engine torque increases and drags the truck up the grade.

Power is the engine's ability to accelerate the truck. Engine power increases when the engine's rpms are raised.

GO!
All engines have more torque at lower rpms, and less torque at higher rpms.
All engines have less power at lower rpms, and more power at higher rpms.

If you don't want to accelerate the truck, maintain the current gear. The torque will increase as the engine rpm decreases and the holding power of the engine will be maximized without a gear shift.

Remember! When you hold a gear, you'll get the most torque out of the engine.

If you don't downshift when the rpm is low, the engine can handle the torsional forces but the drivetrain can't. So, when you downshift, the engine gains more rpm, and the whole process repeats as the engine either holds its rpm or continues to drop rpm while torque increases once again.

GO!
Fuel efficiency is achieved when the engine finds its "sweet spot." The sweet spot is usually midway between the rated torque rpm and the rated power rpm. For example, some rigs get their best fuel efficiency on flat land when the rpms are around 1,500.

NONSYNCHRONIZED TRANSMISSIONS

Nonsynchronized transmissions are those that require "synchronizing," or bringing to the same speed, the teeth of the driving gear and the driven gear. When this is done properly, there is no grinding or clashing of the gears.

Double-clutching is a skill used by professional drivers that allows them to control the engine rpms and to shift gears smoothly. In other words, double-clutching is the art of using the engine rpms to control the speed of the transmission input shaft between gears to match gear speed. When it is time to upshift, the transmission input shaft is turning the same speed as the engine. To engage the next upshift gear, the engine rpms must be lower and the transmission input shaft must also be turning slower rpms to match the gears inside the transmission. Following are the steps to double-clutching and shifting in the simplest form, beginning with **upshifting**:

Upshifting

1. Take foot off fuel pedal.
2. Push clutch pedal down to disengage clutch. Be careful not to engage clutch brake.
3. Move gearshift lever to neutral.
4. Release clutch pedal, engaging clutch.
5. When proper rpm for next gear is reached, push clutch down again, being careful not to engage clutch brake.
6. Move gearshift lever to next higher gear.
7. Release clutch pedal, taking foot off clutch and engaging clutch and transmission.
8. Accelerate.

"Once I get this shifting down, NASCAR will be knocking on my door."

CAUTION!

The clutch should be pushed down 2 to 3 inches (5.1 to 7.6 cm), or just past the free play. It is not necessary to push the clutch all the way to the floor as you would in your standard-transmission personal vehicle.

INTERESTING FACT

The Buffalo two-and-one-half-ton truck, introduced in 1921, had unusual features to adapt to unusual road conditions. It had two 3-speed gearsets mounted in tandem to provide a gear with a countershift in between for power take-off and a low speed of one mile (1.6 km) in seven and three-tenths hours for extremely hard pulls. Two gearshift levers were mounted in front of the driver. One was used normally and the other could be brought in under heavy load. The low gear ratio allowed driving down the steepest hill without brakes.

Downshifting

1. Take foot off accelerator.
2. Push down clutch.
3. Move gearshift lever to neutral.
4. Release clutch.
5. Accelerate enough to match engine rpm with road speed to avoid clashing gears.
6. Push down clutch.
7. Shift to next lower gear.
8. Release clutch.

Be sure to maintain correct engine speed throughout this procedure (**see Figure 8-2**). **Downshifting** too early can result in the vehicle having too much speed for the next lower gear. This can cause the engine to rev beyond its operating range and to stress its parts. Downshifting too early may prevent rapid acceleration, if needed.

In both cases, the clutch uses the engine rpms to get the transmission input shaft to the proper rpm for the next shift point, so that the gears easily mesh.

Split Shifting

Veteran professionals say **split shifting** is a way to save time and shifting, and is commonly used depending on the "lay of the land" and how much weight you're trying to move.

If you're hauling a lot of weight, use your 13 as a 9 unless you're starting uphill. At that point, you'll use the splitter on the low side and this will put you into 12th gear. Then, move the splitter to the high side as soon as you've gained some momentum.

If you see you're having a hard time pulling the weight, it's better to go through all the gears, and a good percentage of the time, the only split you'll need is from 13 to 12 while on an uphill grade.

Additionally, a 15 or 18 gear transmission is no different. Experts say you can shift a 15 like a 10 (which is without the splits) or an 18 like a 9 (also without splits)—and where they come into their own is when running hills with heavy loads.

Key Elements of Shifting

Fuel pedal: Controls fuel to engine

Clutch: Controls connection between engine and transmission

Gearshift lever: Allows driver to select gears in transmission

- Match engine speed (rpm) to road speed

- Shift smoothly to avoid clashing gears

- Shift by the tachometer
  — Upshift when engine rpm approach top of manufacturer recommended rpm
  — Avoid overspeeding

  — Downshift when engine speed approaches low range of manufacturer recommended rpm

  — Avoid lugging

- Variety of rpm/gearshift patterns

- Learn rpm/shift pattern of vehicle you drive

© Cengage Learning 2013

▶ **Figure 8–2**

Proper shifting techniques come from behind-the-wheel practice.

The new "auto" 13s and 18s will go through all the gears, which is usually not a problem. Seasoned professionals say you can skip shift an "auto" if taking off on a downhill.

Bottom line, getting into the top gear as quickly as possible and then maintaining a reasonable speed may result in slightly better fuel mileage. Remember, however, that the length of time spent going through all the gears as opposed to getting into the highest gear for whatever the load requires will not result in significant fuel savings.

Jake Brake and Clutching

There is much debate among drivers about whether or not to use the **jake brake** during shifting. (The "jake brake" is a compression release engine brake, which is an engine braking mechanism installed on some diesel engines. When activated, it opens exhaust valves in the cylinders after the compression cycle, releasing the compressed air trapped in the cylinders, and slowing the vehicle.)

If the gear shift results in large rpm drops, or if the shift is on a steep grade that results in rapid truck speed loss, then use of the jake brake may very well help you to grab that next gear quicker. In this situation, the truck speed is falling rapidly, and the engine rpms are falling normally, so during the double clutch, the engine rpms are yanked lower by the jake brake. This might be helpful to get that next gear in place during a slow and steep grade climb.

Discuss this with your instructor.

▶ **Figure 8–3**

The speedometer and tachometer are necessary tools for shifting gears.

When you reach the top of the speed range for a given gear, it is time to upshift. When you reach the bottom of the speed range for a given gear, downshift.

Tachometer

The **tachometer** displays the engine speed in revolutions per minute (rpm). Just as there is a road speed range for each gear, there is an rpm range for each gear. Upshifting and downshifting are coordinated with rpm ranges the same as they are with road speed ranges (**see Figure 8-4**).

Governor

The **governor** prevents the engine from revving too much while downshifting. It also reduces the fuel supply to the engine when the maximum rpm is reached. In electronic engines, this is controlled by a computer chip or module.

Clutch Brake

A clutch has three phases—free play, working, and **clutch brake.** The clutch brake stops the gears from turning. To engage it, push the clutch pedal all the way to the floor. This prevents the gears from clashing when shifting into low or reverse.

AIDS TO SHIFTING

The speedometer and the tachometer are necessary tools for shifting gears (**see Figure 8-3**).

Speedometer

While speed ranges often vary with the type of transmission, it is important for you to know the road speeds that correspond to each gear. A professional driver must learn the speed ranges for each specific rig and then upshift or downshift as needed.

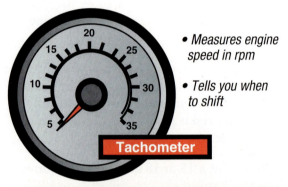

- Measures engine speed in rpm
- Tells you when to shift

Groundspeed and Gear		
Examples of specific gear-to-groundspeed relationships for a nine-speed transmission		
Gear	mph at 1,300 rpm	mph at 1,800 rpm
Low	0	4
1	4	7
2	7	10
3	10	14
4	14	19
5	19	26
6	26	38
7	38	53
8	53	65 *
* Governor set at 1,640 rpm		

▶ **Figure 8–4**

The tachometer indicates engine speed in rpm.

STOP!

Use the clutch brake only when the vehicle is completely stopped (**see Figure 8-5**).

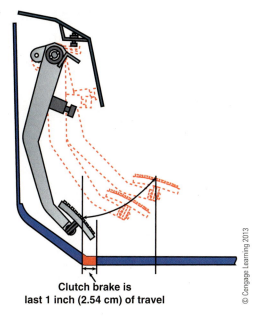

**Clutch brake is
last 1 inch (2.54 cm) of travel**

▶ **Figure 8–5**

*The clutch brake stops gears from
turning.*

▶ **Figure 8–6**

*It is important to have synchronizing skills when
shifting.*

Synchronizing Skills

Although depressing/engaging the clutch twice on each shift is a big part of handling a nonsynchronized transmission, it is not the main shifting event. The key skill—the one requiring special shifting—is **synchronizing** (bringing to the same speed) the teeth of the mating gears (driving and driven gears) **(see Figure 8-6).** When gears are synchronized, there is no grinding or clashing of the gears.

The three ways to determine engine speed are by:

- Reading the tachometer
- Listening to the rpm
- Feeling this speed in the tractor

It is true that some drivers think they are using engine rpms to tell them when to shift when, in fact, they are using their actual sense of the rpms. A veteran driver in a nonsynchronized transmission rig uses his or her sense of rpms to know when to shift, and needs three basic skills to properly shift this type of rig:

1. The ability to identify engine rpm
2. Knowing the correct rpm the engine should be turning
3. The ability to bring engine to correct rpm for each task

How does the driver control the tooth speed of the driving gear?

1. After depressing the clutch, shift into neutral.
2. Then release the clutch to allow engine rpm to drop on upshift or speed up on downshift.
3. This also adjusts tooth speed of the next driving gear to the speed/rpm of the engine.

How does the driver know how much to increase or decrease engine speed?

1. Always read manufacturer's recommendations first if available.
2. A good rule of thumb is when changing gears, change the rpm by 25 percent, which is about 500 rpm, although some transmissions differ from this rule.

GO!

As long as shifts are started at the same rpm, synchronizing rpm will be the same for each shift, which makes shifts a matter of timing and coordination.

What about the synchronizing rpm in more complex shifts?

1. Shifts may be started at various rpms, which means rpms to synchronize the next gear will also vary.
2. On upgrades, the rig loses speed during shifts, so start shift a little earlier than you would on flat ground.
3. On downgrades, speed increases.

UNDERSTANDING THE MEANING OF RPMS— REVOLUTIONS PER MINUTE

Revolutions per minute (rpm) is a measurement of how fast the engine's internal components are spinning. An engine makes its optimum power at a certain rpm, and the closer the rpm is to that, the faster it can accelerate.

The harder you press the fuel pedal, the faster the rpm will climb, so the higher the rpm the more fuel you're going to burn. The gauge that measures rpm is a tachometer, which is usually placed right next to the speedometer. The job of a tachometer is to show, using rpms, how hard the engine is working. Driving at highway speeds at the highest gear possible while using the lowest possible rpms will save fuel.

Typically, there are approximately 300 rpms between gears on a tractor. As a professional driver, it's important to know the time it takes to shift. Here's how to obtain this data: Bring rpms up to 1,200 while your rig is in neutral. Then, measure the time it takes for the rpms to decrease to 900 when you remove your foot from the fuel pedal. That's usually about one second, which means the entire process of shifting should take one second. In double-clutching, the clutch is used twice within this timeframe—so practice, practice, practice.

GO!

Any change in vehicle speed occurring during shifting will affect synchronizing rpm. Experience and practice will teach new drivers to deal with each variation.

Another shifting skill required for a nonsynchronized transmission—along with upshifting and downshifting—is called "finding" or "hitting a gear." This occurs when a vehicle is rolling in neutral and the driver must get the transmission into proper gear. This is usually worked out by either mathematics or a sense or feel of matching the mph (km/h) with the gear or rpm necessary. In general, however, there is only one possible gear for each possible mph (km/h). Most drivers use their "sense of feel," where they feel the speed, recall where the stick should be, and then simply put the stick in front of that gear position.

GO! A SUMMARY OF SHIFTING SKILLS

Good shifting technique is the sign of a seasoned professional driver. These skills include:

- Good timing and coordination
- Shifting without forcing, raking, or grinding the gears
- Never riding the clutch pedal
- Always using the clutch to shift
- Selecting the proper gear for the best fuel economy
- Anticipating change in terrain or traffic

A driver needs to know:

- What gear the vehicle is in at any given time
- The top speed and rpm for each gear
- That downshifting at too high a speed causes damage to internal gears
- That automatic transmissions have a longer "coast-down" time than **manual transmissions,** which means you will need to slow down earlier or use the service brakes until the downshift occurs
- The top mph (km/h) and maximum/minimum rpm for each gear
- About changes in terrain or traffic and what gear will be needed next

What happens if you shift into too low a gear by mistake? You will know immediately because you will hear the engine running too fast (faster than normal). This can damage the clutch, engine, transmission, or drive shaft, and it can cause you to lose control of the vehicle.

What is lugging and what can happen if it occurs? **Lugging** occurs when the driver fails to downshift when the engine speed starts to fall below the normal operating range. In this condition, the tractor produces too little power and begins struggling or lugging. This type of strain can cause engine overheating, damage to the drive train, and stress on most of the rig's systems. It can also shorten the life of all the drivetrain components.

What is progressive shifting? **Progressive shifting** means shifting before you reach the maximum rpm for the gear your rig is in. Progressive shifting allows you to take the most advantage of the engine's power and save fuel at the same time. It is recommended that all drivers learn this technique, explained in **Figure 8-7.**

How is it done? Here are the steps:

1. Think how the engine should feel at that speed and gear.
2. With clutch engaged, throttle up or down until engine feels right.
3. Then push the stick.

It may drop right into gear; but if it does not, generally the best next move is to go to a higher gear.

1. If rpms are too high, grinding noise will be high pitched.
2. If rpms are too low, grinding noise will be deep and hollow.

Progressive Shifting

Technique used with some engine/transmission combinations

- Shift much like automobile
- Gradually increase
- No need to accelerate to governor unless maximum power required

- Available in some engine/transmission combinations
- Use only if engine and company policy allow

- Advantages
  - Reduces equipment wear
  - Lowers noise level
  - Saves fuel

Example:
rpm requirements for progressive vs. standard techniques
10 speed transmission gear split/1,900 rpm
Gross HP (required for 70,000 lbs. (31,745 kg) and 94 sq. ft. (87329 sq. cm) frontal area)

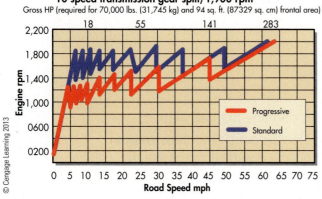

© Cengage Learning 2013

▶ **Figure 8–7**

Progressive shifting allows the driver to take full advantage of the engine's power.

3. When engine is close to proper rpm, stick vibrations are larger and farther apart.

4. When correct rpm is reached, stick will begin to fall into gear, so disengage the clutch and push stick into place.

5. Then release clutch and speed up.

Finding the synchronizing rpm under all possible shifting conditions is needed to handle a nonsynchronized transmission.

CAUTION!

Newer computerized engines are usually set up for progressive shifting. When you accelerate, the engine will "flatten out" at a lower rpm. When you feel this no-power mode, or flattening out, select the next higher gear.

Shifting Procedures

When shifting, shift when the engine reaches cruising rpm instead of the maximum rpm set by the governor or computer. In power gears, shift at the lowest rpm possible without lugging the engine. When downshifting, shift as soon as the rpm reaches peak torque (1,300 rpm on most engines—but check operating manual to make sure). Progressive shifting is advised by many companies because it reduces equipment wear, lowers the noise level, saves fuel, and allows smoother shifts.

SHIFTING PATTERNS AND PROCEDURES

In this section, we will look at the shift patterns of common transmissions: Spicer Pro-Shift Seven Speed, Eaton Fuller Nine Speed, Eaton Fuller Super Ten, Rockwell Ten Speed, and Eaton Fuller Thirteen Speed.

Spicer Pro-Shift Seven Speed

The **Spicer Pro-Shift Seven Speed** is a constant mesh (nonsynchronized) twin-countershaft transmission with a single-range operation. This particular transmission does not have a high and low range and there is not a splitter.

Shift Pattern

The Spicer Pro-Shift Seven Speed transmission uses a simple no-repeat shift pattern, starting at the bottom left and working up through the gears to seventh gear at the bottom right (**see Figure 8-8**). No range selectors or splitters are needed for any of the shifts.

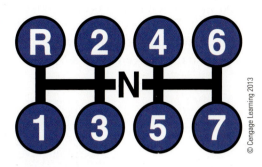

▶ Figure 8-8

The Spicer Pro-Shift Seven Speed shift pattern.

Upshifting

1. Depress the clutch.
2. Move the gear down and the shift lever as far left as possible for first gear.
3. To shift to second, double-clutch, move the lever up and slightly to the right.
4. Shift up through the next five gears, using normal double-clutching technique and follow the standard "H" pattern.

Downshifting

1. Shift from seventh to sixth gear by double-clutching, moving the lever straight forward, and matching the engine speed to the road speed before shifting.
2. Use the same procedure for all future downshifts, following the "H" pattern back down to first gear.

Eaton Fuller Nine Speed

The **Eaton Fuller Nine Speed** transmission is a constant mesh (nonsynchronized) twin-countershaft transmission with high- and low-range operation.

Shift Pattern

The low range has five forward gears, low through fourth. The high range has four gears, fifth through eighth. The range control lever must be lifted or lowered to reach the high or low gears.

Upshifting

1. Depress the clutch.
2. Assure the range lever is down (in the low range).
3. Move the shift lever to first gear.
4. When shifting from second through fourth gear, double clutch.
5. To shift from fourth to fifth gear (low to high range), lift the range control lever up before moving the gear lever.
6. Shift from fifth through eighth gear using normal double clutching.

Downshifting

1. Shift from high range through fifth gear by double clutching, making sure you match engine speed to road speed before shifting.
2. To shift from fifth to fourth gear, push the range control lever down before moving the gear lever.
3. Shift from fourth through first gear by double clutching, making sure you match engine speed to road speed before shifting.

Instead, there are five gear positions that are split, reducing gear lever movements by half. For example, you start in first gear at the bottom left. Then, preselect the next gear with a splitter button located on the gearshift. To engage the gear, release the throttle to break torque and then accelerate again when you are in gear. You only need to move the gear lever from second to third, fourth to fifth, sixth to seventh, and eighth to ninth (**see Figure 8-9**).

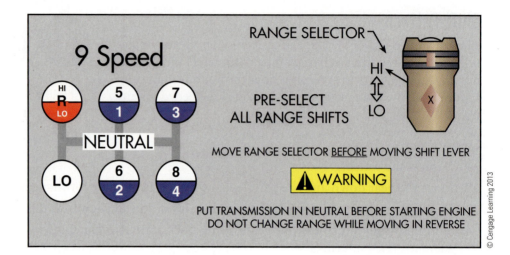

▶ **Figure 8-9**

The Eaton Fuller Nine Speed shift pattern.

Eaton Fuller Super Ten Speed

The **Eaton Fuller Super Ten Speed** transmission is used with three different types of shifts:

> **Button-Only Shift**—a gear ratio change that occurs by moving the shift button (**see Figure 8-10**).

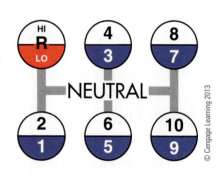

▶ **Figure 8-10**

The Eaton Fuller Super Ten Speed shift pattern.

Upshifting

Used for gear changes first to second, third to fourth, fifth to sixth, seventh to eighth, and ninth to tenth.

1. Accelerate through the current gear, when the next gear is desired.
2. Preselect by moving the shift button forward, immediately break torque by releasing the fuel pedal and depressing the clutch pedal.
3. Allow the engine rpm to decrease to provide synchronous shifting for the next desired gear.
4. The shift will complete when the engine rpm has decreased to the proper speed.

Downshifting

1. As vehicle is decelerating and a downshift is required, with the fuel pedal still applied, preselect by moving the shift button rearward, immediately break torque by releasing the fuel pedal, depressing the clutch pedal, and increase engine rpms to provide synchronous shifting for the desired gear.
2. The shift will complete when the engine rpm has increased to the proper speed.
3. Do not attempt to downshift at two-engine speed (generally above 1,400 rpm).

> **Combination Button/Lever Shift**—a gear ratio change that occurs by moving both the shift button and shift lever

TIP

Use the tachometer to determine when the shift completes.

Upshifting

1. Accelerate. The current gear, when the next gear is desired.
2. Preselect by moving the shift button rearward, immediately brake torque by releasing the fuel pedal and depressing the clutch pedal.
3. Using proper double-clutching techniques, move the shift lever to the next desired gear position.

Downshifting

1. Used for gear changes ninth to eighth, seventh to sixth, and so forth, as the vehicle decelerates and a downshift is required.
2. With the fuel pedal still applied, preselect by moving the shift button forward, immediately releasing the fuel pedal and depressing the clutch pedal.
3. Using proper double-clutching technique, move the shift lever to the next desired gear position.

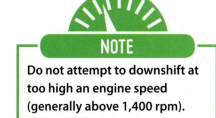

NOTE

Do not attempt to downshift at too high an engine speed (generally above 1,400 rpm).

Lever Only Shift—this shift occurs when the shift lever is moved without moving the shift button. It results in a skip of a full gear ratio and should be used only when the vehicle is bobtail or lightly loaded.

Upshifting

1. With the shift button back—first to third, third to fifth, fifth to seventh, and seventh to ninth. With the shift button forward—second to fourth, fourth to sixth, sixth to eighth, and eigth to tenth.
2. Accelerate to the current gear, when the next gear is desired.
3. Using normal double clutching technique, move the shift lever to the next desired gear position.

Remember! Lever only shifts SKIP an entire gear ratio and will require the engine rpm to decrease twice the amount of a normal shift.

Downshifting

1. With the shift button back—ninth to seventh, seventh to fifth, fifth to third, and third to first. With the shift button forward—tenth to eighth, eighth to sixth, sixth to fourth, fourth to second.
2. As the vehicle decelerates and a downward shift is required, break torque by releasing the fuel pedal and depressing the clutch pedal.
3. Using normal double clutching techniques, move the shift lever to the next desired gear position.

Remember! Do not attempt a lever-only downshift at too high an engine speed (usually above 1,000 rpm).

The Rockwell Ten Speed

The **Rockwell Ten Speed** is a constant mesh (nonsynchronous) twin-countershaft transmission with high- and low-range operation (see Figure 8-11).

Upshifting

1. Depress the clutch.
2. Make sure the range lever is down (low range).
3. Move gear lever to first gear at the bottom left.
4. Shift up through fifth gear, using the double-clutching technique.
5. To shift from fifth to sixth, lift the range control lever up before moving the gear lever.
6. As the gear lever passes through neutral, the transmission pneumatically (with air assist) shifts to high range.
7. Shift from sixth to tenth gears, using the double-clutching technique.

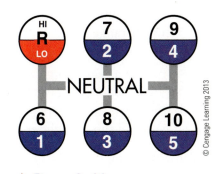

▶ Figure 8–11

The Rockwell Ten Speed shift pattern.

Downshifting

1. Shift down from tenth to sixth, using the double-clutching and engine and road speed matching.
2. To shift down from sixth to fifth, push the range lever down before moving the gear lever.
3. As the gear lever passes through neutral, the transmission pneumatically shifts to low range.
4. Shift down from fifth to first using the double-clutching technique and engine and road speed matching.

Eaton Fuller Thirteen Speed

The **Eaton Fuller Thirteen Speed** is a constant mesh (nonsynchronized) twin-countershaft transmission with high- and low-range operation as well as a splitter on high-range gears.

Shift Pattern

The transmission has five gears in the low range, including a low over low gear. High range has four direct ratios as well as another four overdrive ratios. Overdrive can be engaged in high range with a splitter switch. The shift pattern is a basic double "H." You begin in first gear at the top left (**see Figure 8-12**). Then move through the "H" to fourth. Flip the range lever up, move to fifth and repeat the pattern.

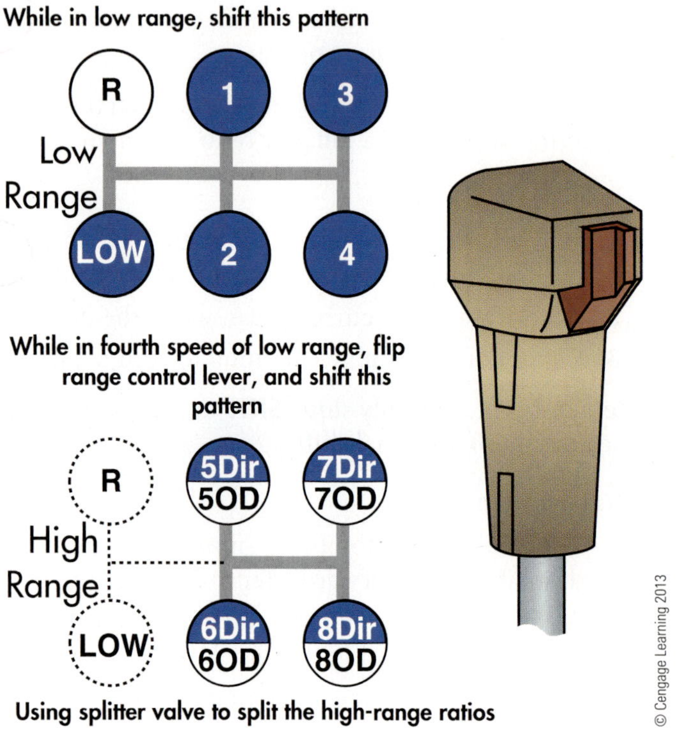

Shifting Procedures

Upshifting

1. Depress the clutch.
2. Make sure the range lever is down (low range).
3. Move the gear lever to first gear (use the low–low only if you are starting from a steep grade with a heavy load).
4. Shift up through fourth gear, using the double-clutching technique.
5. To shift from fourth to fifth, lift the range control lever up before moving the gear lever.
6. As the gear lever passes through neutral, the transmission pneumatically shifts to a higher range.

▶ **Figure 8–12**

Controls and operation of the Eaton Fuller Thirteen Speed.

7. Shift from fifth through eighth using normal double-clutching.
8. To split a gear in high range (go from direct to overdrive), flip the splitter switch, release the fuel pedal, depress and release the clutch, and accelerate again.
9. To shift from overdrive to direct drive in the next higher gear, move the gear level into the next gear and flip the splitter switch just before your foot comes off the clutch.

Downshifting

1. To split down from overdrive to direct in the same gear, flip the splitter switch forward and release the fuel pedal. Then depress and release the clutch and accelerate again.
2. To shift down from direct in one gear to overdrive in the next lower gear, flip the splitter switch to overdrive and make a normal downshift.
3. To shift from fifth direct to fourth, push the range lever down, double-clutch, and make a normal downshift.

SHIFTING SEMIAUTOMATIC TRANSMISSIONS

Some newer **semiautomatic transmissions** use electronic controls to help the driver shift gears. They are essentially manual transmissions, with a clutch and a similar-looking gear lever, but some of the gears are automated. This section looks at how to operate these transmissions and the shift patterns for three types of transmissions—the Eaton Fuller Top 2, the Spicer AutoMate-2, and the Rockwell Engine Synchro Shift (ESS).

Eaton Fuller Top 2

The **Eaton Fuller Top 2** uses the control module of an electronically controlled engine to automatically change the top two gears. It comes in two versions: the Super Ten Top 2 (a 10-speed) and the Super Thirteen Top 2 (a 13-speed). Both are twin-countershaft nonsynchronized transmissions with low-inertia technology that disconnects the back box during compound shifts.

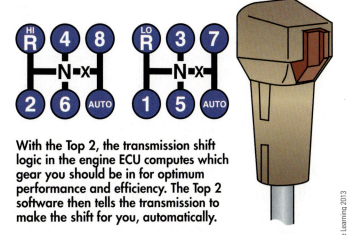

With the Top 2, the transmission shift logic in the engine ECU computes which gear you should be in for optimum performance and efficiency. The Top 2 software then tells the transmission to make the shift for you, automatically.

When starting in first gear, preselect the next gear with the splitter button, release the throttle, and accelerate when you are in gear.

© Cengage Learning 2013

▶ **Figure 8-13**

Controls and operation of the Eaton Fuller Super Ten Top 2.

Shift Pattern

The Super Ten Top 2 (**see Figure 8-13**) has the same shift pattern as the standard Super Ten, and the Super Thirteen Top 2 has the same change pattern as the Eaton Fuller Thirteen Speed. With both transmissions, the top gear position is marked "A." Once the gear lever is in this position, all upshifts and downshifts between the top two gears are automatic.

Shifting Procedure

- Both transmissions are operated as normal nonsynchronized transmissions in all gears but the top two.
- Automatic mode can be changed only when the vehicle is traveling over 40 mph (64 km/h).
- With the Super Ten Top 2, you change normally to eighth, then double-clutch and move into the "A" position.
- With the Super Thirteen Top 2, you shift normally to eleventh, then double-clutch and move into "A."
- While in the "A" position, the engine and transmission work together to change, up or down, when needed. When a shift point is reached, the engine speed automatically changes to match road speed and the change is made—all without driver input.
- You can delay an upshift by applying more throttle, or delay a downshift by easing off the throttle.
- With the engine brake on, the electronic controls automatically extend governed engine speed by 200 rpms to help maintain the lower gear on a downgrade.

Spicer AutoMate-2

The **Spicer AutoMate-2** is a 10-speed transmission that uses electronic controls on the transmission to automatically change the top two gears. It is available in direct-drive and overdrive versions.

Shift Pattern

The AutoMate-2 has a familiar 10-speed shifting pattern. First gear is at the bottom left, second is up and to the middle, third is straight down, and so on. When you reach fifth, you flip the range lever up and come back to the bottom left, then up and to the middle for seventh, and straight down for eighth. Once the lever is moved to that position, the transmission automatically senses road and engine speed and changes up to tenth and back down to ninth when necessary.

Shifting Procedure

- The AutoMate-2 is operated as a normal nonsynchronized transmission in the bottom eight gears. First, use the clutch and then change, up or down, by manually matching the road and engine speeds (**see Figure 8-14**).

- Vehicle must be traveling over 38 mph (61 km/h) to engage the automatic mode.

- When reaching eighth gear, double-clutch and move to the "A" mode.

- No driver input is needed to change gears in ninth and tenth. The transmission automatically senses when a change is needed and then adjusts the engine speed (no matter where the driver has the throttle) and makes the change.

- Upshifts in the "A" mode can be delayed by applying more throttle, and downshifts can be delayed by easing off the throttle.

▶ **Figure 8-14**

The Spicer AutoMate 2 shift pattern.

Rockwell Engine Synchro Shift

The **Rockwell Engine Synchro Shift (ESS)** uses engine electronic controls to automatically synchronize the engine speed to the road speed during shifts in all gears. The system reads the input and output speeds of the transmission, the neutral position of the gear lever, and the position of the special Shift Intent Switch on the side of the gear knob. The engine controller processes the information and sends a message to the fuel control system to automatically increase or decrease the engine speed to synchronize with the road speed during shifting. In essence, this turns a nonsynchronized box into a synchronized one. The driver has the option of turning the system off and operating the transmission as a fully manual box.

Shift Pattern

ESS is fitted to either the Rockwell Nine Speed or the Rockwell Ten Speed manual transmissions. It allows the driver to move through the standard shifting pattern. Both transmissions are nonsynchronized boxes with range-change shift patterns (**see Figure 8-15**).

Shifting Procedure

- To begin, the driver turns the ESS switch on the side of the gear knob to the "on" position.

- The clutch pedal is depressed, first gear is selected, and the clutch is released. Then, the clutch is used again only when bringing the vehicle to a complete stop.

- To shift up, the driver puts the Shift Intent Switch on the side of the gear knob in the "up" position.

- At the appropriate engine speed (around 1,500 rpm), the driver applies light force on the shift lever toward neutral while in gear. The transmission should allow a shift to neutral.

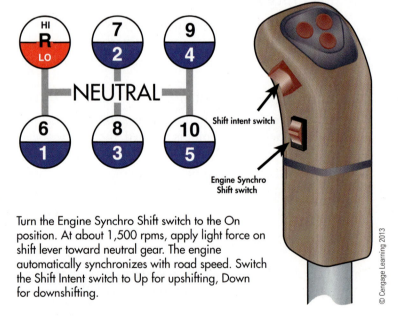

Turn the Engine Synchro Shift switch to the On position. At about 1,500 rpms, apply light force on shift lever toward neutral gear. The engine automatically synchronizes with road speed. Switch the Shift Intent switch to Up for upshifting, Down for downshifting.

▶ **Figure 8-15**

Controls and shift patterns for the Rockwell Engine Synchro Shift.

- The engine automatically synchronizes with the road speed and allows the driver to move to the next gear without touching the throttle or the clutch.

- Downshifting is similar, except the driver must put the Shift Intent Switch in the "down" position before making the shift. The engine automatically increases its speed to match the road speed for a smooth shift.

- While in the ESS mode, the range control function is automated, so the driver does not have to flip from low to high or high to low.

- Any time the driver uses the clutch while the vehicle is moving or turns the ESS switch off, the transmission reverts back to fully manual operation and the driver must use the clutch and throttle to shift gears.

SHIFTING FULLY AUTOMATIC TRANSMISSIONS

Fully **automatic transmissions** use a torque converter instead of a clutch to transfer power. These converters provide a fluid coupling instead of the hard frictional coupling provided by a clutch. Newer transmissions also may have lockup functions that lock the converter when the transmission is in top gear. This provides a solid coupling and improves fuel mileage.

Many automatic transmissions use a lever to change gears (**see Figure 8-16**) but newer models with electronic controls use buttons instead of levers. To select a gear position on these models, simply push a button.

Range Selector Positions

Neutral (N)—used for starting, standing still, and parking the vehicle. The parking brake should be set when the vehicle is standing or parked.

Reverse (R)—used to back the rig. There is one gear in the reverse range. The vehicle must come to a complete stop before shifting into reverse. A reverse warning signal sounds when the vehicle is placed in reverse (**see Figure 8-17**).

Neutral
Use when starting, standing, or parking
Reverse
Vehicle must be completely stopped before using
2-5 or Drive
All normal driving conditions
2-3 / 2-4
Lower range for load types and driving conditions
2
When pulling through mud, snow, or up steep hills
1
Creeper gear for off-highway use

© Cengage Learning 2013

▶ **Figure 8-16**

Controls and shift procedures for a fully automatic transmission.

CAUTION!

Never coast in neutral, as this will damage the transmission and could cause you to lose control of the vehicle. A commercial motor vehicle cannot be out of gear longer than the length of the unit.

2–5 or Drive—used for all normal driving conditions, Drive or 2-5 starts in second and shifts up to third, fourth, and fifth as the vehicle accelerates. Downshifting is automatic as your speed slows.

2–3 / 2–4 Lower range—lower range gears provide greater engine braking and for some road conditions as well as certain cargo and traffic conditions make it desirable to restrict automatic shifting to the lower gear. When the need for this range ends, shift back to high range (Drive or 2–5).

Figure 8-17

A warning signal sounds when a vehicle is placed in reverse.

Figure 8-18

Low gear is used when driving through mud, snow, or up a steep incline.

2/Low gear—this gear is used for pulling through mud or snow or driving up a steep grade **(see Figure 8-18)**. It provides the most engine braking power. The lower range (2–3/2–4) will not upshift above the highest gear unless the engine governor speed for that gear is exceeded.

1/Creeper Gear—this gear is for off-highway use. It provides the greatest traction. Never make a full power shift from creeper gear to a higher range.

Upshifting and Downshifting with an Automatic Transmission

Upshifting Using the Fuel Pedal

- The pressure of the foot on the fuel pedal influences automatic shifting.
- When the fuel pedal is fully depressed, the transmission automatically shifts up to the recommended speed for the engine.
- When the fuel pedal is partially depressed, upshifts occur sooner and at a lesser engine speed.
- Either method provides the accurate shift spacing and control needed for maximum performance.

Downshifting

- Occurs automatically **(see Figure 8-19)**.
- The transmission prevents downshifting when engine speed is too high.

Figure 8-19

Downshifting occurs automatically in an automatic transmission.

STOP!

Watch your rpms very closely when you are on a slope. Gravity will drag your truck and can get the engine moving too fast or too slow, possibly damaging it.

SUMMARY

In this chapter you learned how to shift properly and safely. You also learned a variety of shift patterns and the safe and effective operation of each. The following guidelines apply to every kind of shift:

1. Know the shift pattern of the vehicle.
2. Start the rig in the lowest gear.
3. Use the clutch brake properly.
4. Upshift smoothly.
5. Downshift at the precise point and time required.
6. Use double-clutching.
7. Avoid snapping or riding the clutch.
8. Use the tachometer and speedometer to time shifts.
9. Avoid lugging or revving the engine.
10. Do not force the transmission into gear.
11. Avoid overloading the rig.

KEY TERMS

Automatic transmission
Clutch
Clutch brake
Double-clutching
Downshifting
Eaton Fuller Nine Speed
Eaton Fuller Super Ten Speed
Eaton Fuller Thirteen Speed
Eaton Fuller Top 2
Fuel pedal

Gearshift lever
Governor
Jake brake
Lugging
Manual transmission
Nonsynchronized transmission
Power
Progressive shifting
Rockwell Engine Synchro
   Shift (ESS)

Rockwell Ten Speed
Semiautomatic transmission
Split shifting
Synchronizing
Tachometer
Torque
Upshifting

REVIEW QUESTIONS

1. Which of the following is not a control used in shifting a manual transmission?

   a. clutch
   b. accelerator
   c. fifth wheel
   d. gearshift lever

2. When shifting, your essential tools will be _____.

   a. fuel pedal and brake
   b. brake and tachometer
   c. speedometer and tachometer
   d. odometer and tachometer

3. The key skill in smooth, appropriate shifting is called _____.

   a. organization
   b. synchronization
   c. fuel efficiency
   d. optimization

4. Three ways to determine engine speed are listening to rpms, feeling the speed of the tractor, and
_____.

   a. idling the engine
   b. checking the speedometer

   c. reading the tachometer
   d. feeling the vibration of the clutch

5. Lugging occurs when _____.

   a. engine speed falls below normal operating range without downshifting
   b. lugnuts rust on drive axle tires

   c. you shift before reaching maximum rpm for the gear your rig is in
   d. you shift to take advantage of engine's power

6. The clutch brake _____.

   a. stops the vehicle
   b. stops the clutch from functioning

   c. stops the gears from turning
   d. is used to stop the vehicle only in a clutch (an emergency)

7. On upgrades, your rig will lose speed during shifts, so start shifting _____ as you would on flat terrain.

   a. much later
   b. much earlier

   c. at about the same time
   d. a little earlier

8. You can always tell if your rpms are too high when you shift because you will hear a _____ grinding.

   a. sort of interrupted
   b. bumpy

   c. low-pitched
   d. high-pitched

9. When downshifting, after the gearshift lever has been moved to neutral and the clutch has been released, _____.

   a. apply the brakes
   b. increase the rotation of the fifth wheel

   c. both a and b
   d. accelerate enough to match the engine rpm with the road speed

10. Shifting gears before a rig reaches the maximum rpm for the gear the rig is in, is called _____.

    a. regressive shifting
    b. progressive shifting

    c. lugging
    d. throttling

11. In a vehicle with an automatic transmission, when the fuel pedal is depressed, the transmission automatically _____.

    a. shifts up to the recommended speed for the engine
    b. shifts down and then up to speed
    c. gauges the amount of fuel needed to run the engine
    d. shifts into neutral until more fuel is supplied

12. In a truck with an automatic transmission, the transmission prevents downshifting when engine speed is _____.

    a. uneven
    b. too low

    c. too high
    d. sporadic

13. With both the Super Ten Top 2 and the Eaton Fuller 13 Speed, the top gear position is marked _____.

    a. 1
    b. A

    c. D
    d. 1-A

14. The Rockwell Engine Synchro Shift (ESS) uses _____ to automatically synchronize the engine speed to the road speed during shifts in all gears.

    a. a specific downshift pattern   **c.** engine sensors that decelerate

    b. engine and tire sensors   **(d.)** engine electronic controls

15. Newer computerized engines are usually set up for _____ shifting, so when you accelerate, the engine will "flatten out" at a lower rpm.

    (a.) progressive   **c.** retrograde

    b. high rpm   **d.** alternating

16. When the fuel pedal is partially depressed, upshifts occur sooner and at a _____ engine speed.

    a. greater   **c.** standard

    (b.) lesser   **d.** varying

SUPPLEMENTAL LEARNING ACTIVITIES

1. A pro driver will tell you, "Never apply power as you go over the crest of a hill." Give three reasons this is a good rule to remember. (Hint: Especially if you can't see what's going on ahead.)

2. What is the most dangerous part of driving a big rig going down a hill with a heavy load? In small groups, discuss and come up with one or two scenarios that show why this statement is true.

3. In rural areas across North America, "country" intersections tend to be more narrow than city intersections. As a professional driver, in 100 words or less, describe what this means to you.

4. Look up the meaning of rpm and write a one-page report, demonstrating that you understand what rpm is all about.

5. When shifting from neutral to first gear and you hear "grinding," what does this mean, and what should you do to get the transmission to drop into gear? Discuss as a group and report to the class. Take no more than 10 minutes.

FOR MORE INFORMATION

PTDI—Execute Shifting, Page 11, Click on Skill Standards
www.ptdi.org/standards

How to Shift a Tractor-Trailer
www.ehow.com/how_5505283_shift-tractor-trailer.html

How to Double Clutch a Tractor-Trailer
www.ehow.com/how_4852957_double-clutch-tractor-trailer.html

9 Backing and Docking

© iStockphoto/Publicimage

OBJECTIVES

When you have completed this chapter, you should be able to:

■ Understand and describe the procedures for backing and parking.

■ Know how to prepare for backing maneuvers, including proper mirror adjustments.

■ Explain the principles of reverse steering when backing an articulated vehicle.

■ Avoid the hazards of backing.

■ Understand the importance of a helper while backing and how to use one safely.

■ Know basic maneuvers for parking at docks in various positions and conditions.

INTRODUCTION—BACKING PRINCIPLES AND RULES

Backing a 48-foot (14.6 m), or longer, trailer into position easily and without problems is always satisfying to a professional driver. It's an accomplishment to have these skills and one you, as a new professional, must practice to master and develop. But, as any experienced driver will tell you: Try not to back your rig any more than necessary, even if it means driving around the block or coming into a docking area from an alternate direction **(see Figure 9-1)**. **Backing is one of the most common crash types.**

However, before getting into the cab to back a vehicle on your own, there are some principles and rules you should know. This chapter contains information you need to know to back a rig safely and efficiently. Studying it will help you master this necessary skill.

▶ **Figure 9-1**

Experienced drivers tell you not to back your rig any more than necessary.

STOP!

Make sure you know your vehicle's clearances—How high is your tractor? Your trailer? Are there overhead clearance issues? How long is your rig? How wide? What about your undercarriage? How high off the ground is it?

Steering Principles

Proper backing technique is necessary to know and use for the safe and efficient operation of a tractor-trailer rig in all situations and under all conditions. Unless enough time and attention are devoted to mastering this skill, maneuvering the rig can become very difficult.

Most drivers feel comfortable backing a personal vehicle. A car has two axles. In most cars, the front axle is used for steering and the rear axle has fixed wheels that cannot steer. They simply follow the direction the car is headed.

The technique used to back a tractor-trailer is much different from that used to back a car or pickup truck. Backing a tractor-trailer is more complicated because the rig is made up of two units. The tractor steers both vehicles. The trailer—with its fixed wheels—depends on the tractor for direction. In other words, the tractor steers the trailer **(see Figure 9-2)**.

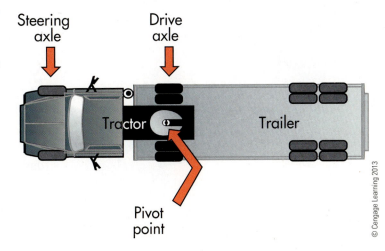

▶ **Figure 9-2**

To learn backing techniques, new drivers should first be familiar with the parts of their rig involved in backing.

STOP!

Check your mirrors and adjust them to give you the best views possible of each side of your rig. This is also the time to get out of your tractor, remember the GOAL principle—Get Out And Look—and check the space on each side, front and back, and top and bottom of your rig to make sure all areas are clear. Roll down your windows. Turn on your warning flashers to begin backing, even if your rig is equipped with a backup beeper. Then, right before you move into reverse gear, sound your horn for safety.

GO!

Think "slow" for every step in the backing and/or docking process! Backing and/or docking is a very precise set of maneuvers. Don't get in a hurry. Easy does it, as they say. Use the skills you've learned and remember, there's no time clock, so take the time you need to show the professional skills you know.

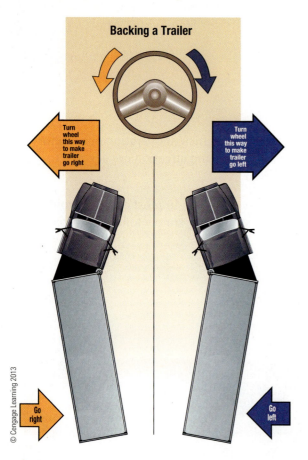

© Cengage Learning 2013

▶ Figure 9-3

When the tractor moves in one direction when backing, the trailer moves in the opposite direction.

So, now the technique starts to get difficult. The rear tractor axle becomes the trailer's steering axle. When you are backing the rig and the tractor moves in one direction, the front of the trailer moves in the same direction, which forces the rear of the trailer in the opposite direction.

When you turn the steering wheel to the right, the rear of the trailer goes left. When you turn the steering wheel to the left, the rear of the trailer goes right **(see Figure 9-3).** The amount of turning the trailer does is proportional to the angle created between the trailer and the tractor. As the angle becomes greater, the more the trailer will pivot and the less movement to the rear there will be.

SAFETY RULES WHEN BACKING

Because you cannot see directly behind your vehicle, backing should always be considered a dangerous **maneuver.** Common sense dictates that you should avoid backing when possible. For example, when you park your rig, try to park so you will be able to pull forward when you leave.

Even though you can reduce the need to back your rig by planning ahead, almost everyone who drives professionally will have to back at times. When you do have to back your rig, there are a few rules to remember:

■ Avoid backing if possible.

■ Adjust your mirrors for the best possible view of both sides of your rig.

■ Rolling down your windows, regardless of weather conditions, helps eliminate glare or reflection on the mirrors.

■ Inspect your intended path before backing your rig.

▶ *Two (or three) heads are better than one when it comes to backing and docking.*

■ Also check the entire space around your rig, top, bottom, front, back, and both sides.

■ Use a helper to signal your path.

■ Use four-way warning flashers and sound your horn before putting your rig in reverse. This communicates your intentions to those working in the area.

■ Back and turn toward the driver's side when possible.

■ Always watch your mirrors—and don't be adverse to doing pullups. These maneuvers help you maintain a wider view of your backing path in your mirror.

Avoid Backing Whenever Possible

On the road, it is sometimes impossible to avoid backing, but when the opportunity arises, always park your rig so you can pull forward when you leave the location.

Adjust and Clean Your Mirrors

To get the best view, make certain your mirrors are adjusted to provide the most expansive view of your rig. You should only be able to see a thin sliver of the vehicle and trailer on the inside edge of both the flat and convex mirrors. Properly adjusted mirrors should give the best viewing in all situations. And, in bad weather, make certain they are clean for your best visibility. Dirty mirrors in bright sunshine can cause glare.

Inspect Your Intended Path

Whether you will be backing in a straight line or backing and turning, inspect your path as you approach the area where you'll be backing. Get out and walk around your rig. Check the clearance of the path your vehicle will make. Ensure that the road, parking area, or docking areas will be able to support your vehicle. Look for low clearances such as low-hanging wires or debris and roof overhangs. Check for debris in your path, other parked vehicles, or any debris that could move into your path. Is your path sloping down to the dock? Get a mental picture before you begin backing (**see Figure 9-4**).

▶ **Figure 9-4**

Inspect your path before backing. Get out and walk around your rig before backing.

Also check the space around your rig. Make certain there are no low-hanging tree branches, electrical wires, or building overhangs that may be blocking your path. What about undercarriage clearance? Also check each side of your rig to make certain there's nothing to block the path you'll take to back your rig.

Use a Helper to Signal Your Path

Use a helper or spotter any time you have to back your rig. You cannot see behind your rig and there are blind spots in the mirrors. A helper is always needed for **blind-side** backing. The helper should stand in front of the truck so the driver can have a clear view of the helper's signals. Hearing the helper's spoken directions is often difficult. Therefore, before you begin the backing maneuver, work out hand signals so you will understand when the helper wants you to stop in order to back your rig safely. Remember that even though you are using a helper, the driver is always responsible for any problems **(see Figure 9-5).**

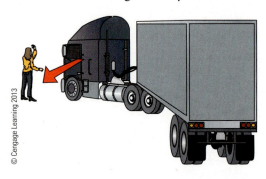

© Cengage Learning 2013

▶ **Figure 9-5**

Whenever possible, use a helper when backing.

Use Your Four-Way Flashers and Horn

Use four-way warning flashers and sound your horn three times before putting your rig in reverse. **This communicates your intentions to those working in the area.** Once you have inspected your intended driving path, get back into your cab and turn on your four-way flashers. If your truck is not equipped with a backup alarm, blow your horn two or three times before you begin backing. Check both mirrors and the front of your rig constantly throughout the maneuvers.

Back and Turn toward the Driver's Side Whenever Possible

When you have to back and turn, try to back toward the **driver's side** of the vehicle. You will have a better view and you will also be able to avoid the dangers of backing to your blind side.

If you back toward the driver's side, you can watch the rear of the vehicle by looking out of the side window and by using your left window and your left mirror. In a tractor with a box trailer, you can only see the side of the trailer in your right mirror during blind-side backing. Do not become focused on one mirror. Always use both mirrors and scan from mirror to mirror several times while backing.

Avoid backing into the street when possible. Back into an alley, instead, so that you can drive out forward. If you must back into the street, **driver-side backing** allows you to block off the whole street and protect other drivers who might otherwise try to pull around you before you get into position. When possible, try to get a helper to watch your blind side by standing in front of the truck. Other vehicles may try to get around you.

When you know you will have to back your rig, plan ahead so you can use driver-side backing. This may mean going around the block to put your vehicle in the correct position. The added safety and ease of operation is well worth the extra driving.

GENERAL BACKING RULES

The general rules to remember every time you back your rig are:

- Start in the proper position.
- Back slowly.

- Avoid distractions.
- Constantly check behind your vehicle.
- Start over when necessary.

Start in the Proper Position

The most important maneuver when you are backing your rig is to begin with the proper setup. Position is everything **(see Figure 9-6).**

Position your rig properly before beginning to back. Reach the right position by moving forward. When you think the vehicle is in the right position, stop and secure it. Get out and check your position from the front, rear, and both sides. Try to limit the distance of the pullup. The farther you pull up, the farther you must back up. Use a helper or spotter when possible.

Back Slowly

Use the lowest reverse gear and idle back slowly. Be patient. If possible, stay off the brakes and fuel pedal and avoid riding the clutch.

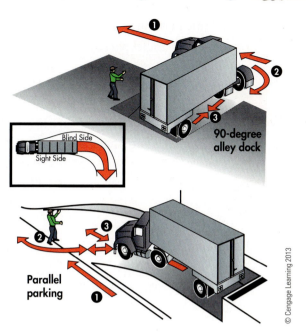

▶ Figure 9–6

Examples of backing maneuvers: 1-Setup, 2-Back in, Pull out, 3-Straighten and adjust.

Avoid Distractions

This is no time to be talking on your Bluetooth, texting, or even listening to your radio. Backing and/or docking require your total attention and concentration on doing what you know is the best and safest backing procedure. Turn off defrosters, radios, and roll down the window so you can better hear audible warnings. With the radio off, you as a driver are more likely to hear someone who might be trying to get your attention.

Constantly Check behind Your Vehicle

Backing a tractor-trailer rig is usually done with mirrors. You should know what the trailer looks like in the mirrors at all times. Use both mirrors and do not become focused on one mirror, and use minimal steering correction. It takes 8 to 12 feet (2.4 to 3.7 m) for the trailer to react to the driver's direction. Be patient and go slowly.

Start Over Whenever Necessary

If the trailer gets out of position, pull straight forward and start over. It is better to pull forward and try again than continue to back blindly.

BASIC BACKING MANEUVERS

There are eight basic backing skills. You should be able to perform all of these safely and efficiently:

- Straight-line backing
- Offset backing to the right
- Offset backing to the left
- Alley-dock backing
- 90-degree alley dock

CHAPTER 9

- Straight-line parking
- Conventional parallel parking
- Sight-side backing

> ### CAUTION!
> Before backing, make sure your mirrors are properly adjusted. **G**et **O**ut **A**nd **L**ook! (GOAL) to avoid an accident. Once you release the clutch and begin backing, try rolling at a continuous safe, slow speed until you complete the maneuver or need to reposition.

Straight-Line Backing

Straight-line backing is the easiest backing maneuver to perform and also serves as a basis for all other backing maneuvers. The point where the tractor and trailer are connected becomes the **pivot point** for your vehicle (**see Figure 9-7**).

A pivot point on your rig (a point of **articulation**) is extremely sensitive to movement. If you have the tractor-trailer perfectly aligned and you hold the steering wheel so the wheels are pointing straight ahead, when you begin to move back, rarely will the entire rig move in a straight line. Usually, the trailer will begin to drift either left or right.

The key to backing your rig in a straight line is to recognize what direction the trailer is drifting and make the necessary adjustments immediately. **Use both outside mirrors** to help you make these steering adjustments.

To correct the drift, turn the top of the steering wheel toward the drift. It takes very little movement of the steering wheel to correct the drift, if you adjust early. Do not oversteer and overcorrect (**see Figure 9-8**).

Steps in Straight-Line Backing

Turning toward right mirror corrects right drift

Backing straight

Turning toward left mirror corrects left drift

1. Position vehicle properly and check path
2. Back as slowly as possible
3. Constantly check behind with mirrors
4. Use push-pull method of steering
   - When the trailer gets bigger in one mirror, turn the steering wheel toward that mirror to correct the drift

© Cengage Learning 2013

▶ **Figure 9-7**

Backing in a straight line is the easiest of all backing maneuvers.

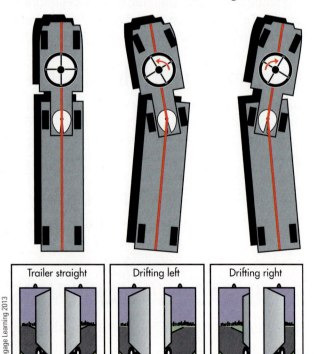

© Cengage Learning 2013

▶ **Figure 9-8**

Use your mirrors to watch for and correct trailer drift when backing.

When the trailer begins to respond to your correction, begin turning the wheel in the opposite direction to remove the initial correction. Depending on the length of the trailer, it takes 8 to 12 feet (2.4 to 3.7 m) for the trailer to respond. Shorter trailers react faster than longer trailers.

Be patient! Think your moves through carefully. If you find the trailer has gone too far out of line, pull forward and position for another try.

STOP!

Any time you're backing and want to make corrections, do this only after your trailer has entered the space. If it isn't in the space and you need to make corrections, it's better to pull up and begin the backing maneuver again.

Offset Backing to the Right

Offset backing to the right is used when there is not enough space for straight-line backing. First, line up your vehicle directly in front of the lane to the left of the empty lane on the right. Pull up as much as possible. Use your mirrors and check from your window often. Then, by turning your wheel to the left, begin angling your rig so that it points to the left-hand edge of the lane to the right.

NOTE

If you don't have a good point of reference, put on your parking brake and get out of the cab to see where you are.

If you need to pull up and start the maneuver again, don't let this frustrate you. Just think of this as a challenge and there are concrete buildings on each side of your target lane. Slowly continue backing, correcting periodically and turning the wheel to the left until you have eased your rig into position in the new lane **(see Figure 9-9).**

Offset Backing to the Left

This maneuver is the same as the above, except you position your rig to the right of the empty lane, as though you were going to straight-line back **(see Figure 9-10).**

Then, using your mirrors and your driver's side window, begin slowly backing your rig and turning your steering wheel to the right. Pull up when needed, leave the cab and check and correct as you slowly steer to the right, positioning your rig into the lane to the left of your starting position.

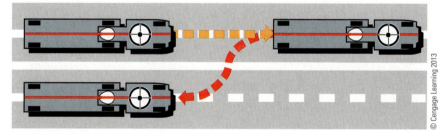

▶ **Figure 9-9**

Offset backing to the right.

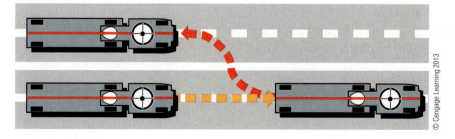

▶ **Figure 9-10**

Offset backing to the left.

Alley–Dock Backing

Alley-dock backing is required at freight docks when the driver must back in from the street or when the driver must back the rig into a space between two vehicles. The steps include:

1. Pull forward in a straight line near the space at the dock. You should be about 3 to 5 feet (0.9 to 1.5 m) out from other parked vehicles. When the front of the trailer is in line with the left side of the parking space, turn hard to the right **(see Figure 9-11).**

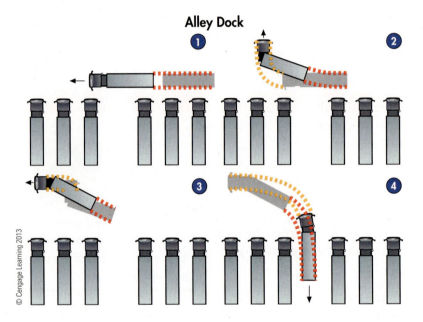

Alley Dock

▶ **Figure 9–11**

When alley docking a rig, turn hard to the right when the front of the trailer is in line with the left side of the parking space.

2. While continuing to move forward at a speed of about 3 to 5 miles per hour (5 to 8 km/h), when the tractor is at the 12-o'clock position, straight away from the parking space, turn to the left.

3. Keep moving in this forward position until the trailer is near a 45-degree angle. When the tractor is at a slight angle to the left of the trailer and the parking space can be seen from the driver's window, straighten the steering tires and stop.

4. Set your brakes and get out of the cab. Your tractor tandem should be about 12 to 15 feet (3.7 to 4.6 m) in front of the left side of the parking space. Be sure the steering tires are straight. Get back into the cab and start backing. Straighten out the rig as you enter the space and watch the direction of the rear tandem. Correct drift as needed. Check for drift using side mirrors and a helper if one is available.

CAUTION!

Always check both mirrors for room on each side when alley docking. Do not rely on one mirror to guide you.

90-Degree Alley Dock

Although the 90-degree alley dock is least desired, it is one you should know. To begin, approach from the right, parallel to the dock, and drive a distance past the door of the dock. Keep your rig at least 6 feet (1.8 m) from the fronts of rigs and/or trailers already docked. This allows you plenty of room to swing the nose of your rig as you start your 90-degree turn.

Now, put on your parking brake (four-way flashers are still on) and walk to the back of your rig for two reasons: (1) you need a point of reference for your final approach; and (2) you need to open the doors of your trailer. Once docked, there will be no room to open them.

Line up your trailer for the backing-up maneuver. If you are fortunate enough to be able to perform a straight backing-up maneuver into the dock, pull your rig forward until the trailer is directly behind the tractor and lined up squarely with the dock. Most docks will require an angled backing-up maneuver. In this case, pull your tractor forward until the back of your trailer is about 20 feet (6.1 m) past your docking slot. The driver's side of your rig must be facing the dock.

- Press in the clutch and put the tractor in reverse.
- Turn the steering wheel all the way to the left. If you wait until after you are rolling to turn the steering wheel, it will take some time and distance before the tractor begins to turn.
- Let the clutch out slowly. Do not press down on the accelerator. Backing should only be done at idling speed. Watch both mirrors as you begin to move back.
- Turn your wheel gradually to the right to straighten the rig as you approach the dock.
- Press the clutch in when you get to within 10 feet (3.1 m) of the dock. Hitting the dock at idling speed can damage dock plates, as well as your trailer. Feather the clutch as you approach the dock, and brake as necessary.
- Back the trailer firmly onto the dock. Set the trailer brakes and chock your trailer's wheels.

Straight-Line Parking

Straight-line parking requires the following steps:

1. Pull forward in a straight line near the parking space. You should be about 3 to 5 feet (0.9 to 1.5 m) out from the other parked vehicles.
2. Stop when your line of sight is in the middle of the parking space. Look out your right window for a reference point that is within a line of sight and even with the middle of the parking space (**see Figure 9-12**).

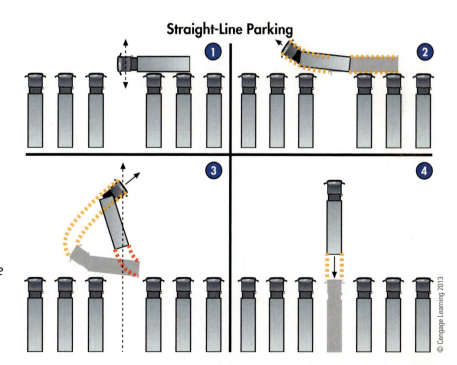

Straight-Line Parking

▶ Figure 9-12

Before beginning a straight-line parking maneuver, pull the rig forward about 3 to 5 feet (0.9 to 1.5 m) from other parked vehicles.

© Cengage Learning 2013

3. Continue moving forward. When the front of the trailer is in line with the left side of the parking space, turn hard to the right. Keep turning to the right until the tractor is headed toward the 2-o'clock position.

4. Straighten the steering tires and pull forward until the rig is in front of the parking space. Set your brakes and get out of the cab. Be sure the trailer is directly behind the tractor. The rig should be directly in front of the parking space. Get back into the cab and start backing.

Conventional Parallel Parking

Parallel parking is required when you need to bring your rig alongside a curb or a dock. The following will help you accomplish this sometimes difficult maneuver:

1. Make certain your rig can fit into the parallel space.

2. You should begin with your rig 2 to 3 feet (0.6 to 0.9 m) from other parked vehicles. Pull forward in a straight line near the parking space. Stop when the rear tandem axles of the trailer are about 8 feet (2.4 m) in front of the parking space (**see Figure 9-13 - Position 1**).

3. Set your brakes and get out of the cab. Be sure your rig is in a straight line and is 2 to 3 feet (0.6 to 0.9 m) away from other parked vehicles. Check to be sure the rear tandem axles of the rig are 8 feet (2.4 m) in front of the parking space.

4. Get back into the cab and begin backing with the steering wheel turned to the left. The angle between the left side of the tractor is about 12 to 15 degrees away from the front of the trailer.

5. Turn hard to the right and continue backing until the tractor and the trailer are in a straight line (**see Figure 9-13 - Position 2**).

   Continue backing until the front of the trailer is even with the front of the parking space (**see Figure 9-13 - Position 3**).

6. Turn hard to the right and continue backing until the trailer is parallel inside the parking space. The tractor should be at an 85- to 90-degree angle to the left. Leave the tractor in this position for an easier exit (**see Figure 9-13 - Position 4**).

Parallel Parking

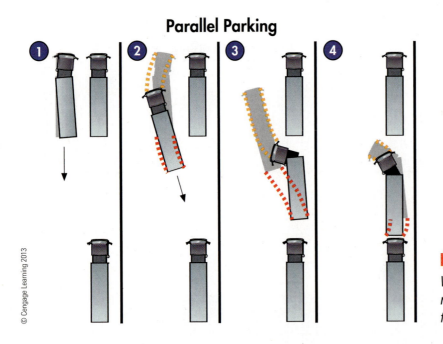

▶ **Figure 9-13**

When parallel parking, pull the rig 2 to 3 feet (0.9 to 1.5 m) from other parked vehicles.

Sight-Side Backing

In lining up your rig for backing maneuvers, it is always safer to use the sight-side, or the driver's side, whenever you can—and if this means driving around the block, the extra mileage is worth it, safety-wise. Blind-side backing is simply the opposite, and you must be able to see and process information provided by your rig's convex mirror.

DOCKING TIPS

1. Always set your parking brake, and get out of your cab and open the doors of your trailer before completing the docking maneuver.

2. Never ram the dock. Ease up to the dock as easily as you can.

3. Be on the lookout for impeding posts or walls.

4. Backing a 53-foot (16.15 m) trailer up to a dock takes patience, time, and skill. Never be in a hurry.

5. Keep checking your mirrors. There's never "too many times."

6. Open your window and turn off your radio—for concentration and so you can hear what's going on outside.

7. Before putting your rig in reverse to begin backing, turn on your four-way flashers and honk your horn.

8. Don't ride the clutch.

SUMMARY

In this chapter, you learned the step-by-step procedures for backing a tractor-trailer safely and efficiently. You also learned that tractor-trailer combinations have different backing characteristics from those of your personal vehicle. How to proceed with alley-dock backing and parallel parking were also explained.

KEY TERMS

Alley-dock backing
Articulation
Blind-side
Driver's side

Driver-side backing
Maneuver
Offset backing
Parallel parking

Pivot point
Straight-line backing
Straight-line parking

© Cengage Learning 2013

A DAY IN THE LIFE...

Phil Johnson – Marten Transport, Ltd., Professional Truck Driver

I was first exposed to the trucking industry by my dad. He was an engineer for the Ford Motor Company helping with the design of trucks. He would point out those trucks while we were driving and explain to me what the trucks were used for. I remember at 10 years old sitting on his lap as he was teaching me to drive. From that point on I knew this was something I enjoyed and wanted to do for a living. My first experience driving a tractor-trailer came while I was in the Marines at 17 years old, hauling jet fuel to jets out on the runway and equipment to the field. After completing a civilian truck driving course, I started driving local. With five years of driving behind me, I was ready for the road. For the next 28 years, my career has been pulling a flat bed, dry van, over-dimensional loads, bulk tank along with tanker, and refrigerated loads. There isn't an interstate north, south, and east or west, which I haven't driven on, along with the entire country of Canada. I have lost track of all the secondary roads. Presently, I have been employed with Marten Transport for the past 24 years, having driven 3 MILLION SAFE MILES for Marten Transport, and I also worked in the office as a Driver Manager. The time I spent in the office gave me the ability to see the trucking industry from both sides. I received the Truck Load Carriers Association Highway Angel, and received runner-up for the Georgia Motor Trucking Association "Driver of the Year" for 2002.

For an employee to be recognized for doing his or her job means that they are not only just doing their job well, but doing it in a manner that shows they take pride in their work. Truck driving isn't a 9 to 5 job. It's a way of life. I was told, back when I started driving in the Marines, that I was a natural. My gunnery sergeant said there wasn't anything I couldn't drive. Although I have worked in other jobs, I have found that for the 31 years I have been driving, I have felt mostly at home behind the wheel. Passing on what I have learned over the years, as a Driver Trainer, has earned me a lot of respect from other drivers and I don't take that lightly. When I am not driving, I put that same passion for my job in other aspects of my life.

Truck driving isn't a 9 to 5 job.

Before my wife passed away, she was asked if she kept a honey-do list for me. She laughed and said she didn't need one for me because I put more on myself than she ever could. I take pride in doing things not just well, but to the best of my ability. I want to be remembered as someone who cared for others as much as he cared for himself.

REVIEW QUESTIONS

1. Regarding backing a tractor-trailer, if the rear of the tractor moves to the left, the rear of the trailer _____.

   a. moves to the left
   b. goes in a straight line
   c. moves to the right
   d. none of the above

2. When backing, if the tractor and trailer are exactly aligned and the steering wheel is held so the front wheels are pointing straight ahead and parallel to the sides of the rig, the whole unit will _____.

   a. move in a straight line
   b. rarely, if ever, move in a straight line
   c. always move to the north
   d. always move to the south

3. When using a helper in backing, the _____ is always responsible for any problems that may arise from the backing maneuver.

   a. driver
   b. dispatcher
   c. helper
   d. yard foreman

4. If a driver has to back and turn, it is safer to back and turn toward the _____.

   a. nondriver's side of the vehicle
   b. driver's side of the vehicle
   c. either side of the vehicle
   d. neither side is safer

5. When preparing to back, if your tractor does not have a backup alarm, you should _____ and then start backing.

   a. turn on your headlights
   b. blink your headlights
   c. have your helper signal others
   d. turn on your four-way flashers

6. The most important maneuver in backing is _____.

   a. starting with the proper setup
   b. alley docking
   c. parallel parking
   d. b and c

7. Regarding straight-line backing, before backing the tractor should be _____.

   a. behind the trailer
   b. directly in front of the trailer
   c. at a 45-degree angle with the trailer
   d. at a 90-degree angle with the trailer

8. When alley docking a rig, the driver turns hard to the right when the _____ is in line with the left side of the parking space.

   a. back of the trailer
   b. front of the tractor
   c. front of the trailer
   d. middle of the trailer

9. Regarding straight-line parking, after stopping when the driver's line of sight is even with the middle of the parking space and continuing forward until the trailer is in line with the left side of the parking space and after turning hard to the right, the driver continues to turn hard to the right until the tractor is headed toward the _____ position.

   a. 5-o'clock
   b. 12-o'clock
   c. 3-o'clock
   d. 2-o'clock

10. Regarding parallel parking, when the trailer is parallel inside the parking space, the tractor should be _____.

    a. at an 85- to 90-degree angle to the left
    b. at an 85- to 90-degree angle to the right
    c. parallel to the parking space
    d. neither a, b, nor c

11. Using a helper while backing allows him or her to watch _____.

    a. the trailer's off-tracking   c. the space around your rig
    b. your blind side   d. the dolly

12. Important docking tips include _____.

    a. don't ride the clutch   c. turn on your four-way flashers
    b. check your mirrors   d. all of the above

SUPPLEMENTAL LEARNING ACTIVITIES

1. Using toy tractor-trailers, demonstrate the difference between a 90-degree alley dock and offset backing to the left. Make certain your "toy" environment is as realistic as possible.

2. In small groups, discuss the pros and cons of using a spotter or helper during backing maneuvers. What five safety instructions would you give if you were a driver using a helper?

3. Go to a local truck stop and, using a video camera or cell phone, video tractor-trailer rigs backing into parking spaces. Bring the video to class and critique the driver's technique.

4. Ask a professional driver to visit your class and talk about how he or she learned backing maneuvers. Make certain there's plenty of time for questions at the end of the driver's talk.

5. Visit a freight dock. Take photos of the outside of the dock. Bring them to class and discuss what you find. In your community, who's dock is in the best shape? The worst? And why?

FOR MORE INFORMATION

PTDI—Back and Dock Tractor-Trailer, Page 12, Click on Skill Standards
www.ptdi.org/standards

Backing a Tractor-Trailer
www.tpub.com/content/engine/14081/css/14081_176.htm

Backing Up Tractor-Trailer Rigs
www.gonefcon.com/trucktcom/backing.htm

10 Coupling and Uncoupling

© Cengage Learning 2013

OBJECTIVES

When you have completed this chapter, you should be able to:

- Demonstrate the correct way to safely and efficiently couple a tractor with a trailer.
- Demonstrate the correct way to safely and efficiently uncouple a rig.
- Describe the controls used when coupling or uncoupling a rig.
- Explain the hazards of coupling and uncoupling a rig improperly.

INTRODUCTION

Coupling is the driver's responsibility prior to every trip (**see Figure 10-1**).

As you know by now, a **tractor** and a **trailer** are separate and independent units until they are brought together and joined, coupled, or hooked together. Well-practiced skills in coupling tractors and trailers are a vital part of the professional driver's tool box—not only knowing the step-by-step approach to joining a tractor and a trailer or multiple trailers, but understanding the process and the components needed for coupling as well as how to accomplish it efficiently and safely.

The best way to learn coupling is a 15-step approach that protects you and others from injury and your vehicle and cargo from damage. Use this same sequence each time you couple a rig. For uncoupling your rig, use the 11-step approach, also shown in **Figure 10-2.**

▶ **Figure 10-1**

Coupling correctly is extremely important.

Coupling	Uncoupling
Step 1: Inspect fifth wheel and kingpin	Step 1: Position the vehicle
Step 2: Check surrounding area and secure trailer	Step 2: Secure the vehicle
Step 3: Position the tractor	Step 3: Lower landing gear
Step 4: Back slowly into position	Step 4: Disconnect air lines and electrical cord
Step 5: Secure the tractor	Step 5: Release fifth-wheel latch
Step 6: Check the trailer height	Step 6: Lower air suspension
Step 7: Connect the air lines	Step 7: Pull tractor partially clear
Step 8: Supply air to the trailer	Step 8: Secure tractor
Step 9: Start the engine and lock trailer brakes	Step 9: Inspect trailer supports
Step 10: Back under the trailer	Step 10: Pull tractor clear
Step 11: Check the connection	Step 11: Reinflate air suspension
Step 12: Secure the vehicle	
Step 13: Inspect the coupling	
Step 14: Connect electrical cord and check air lines	
Step 15: Raise trailer landing gear	

▶ **Figure 10-2**

A quick checklist for coupling and uncoupling.

> **STOP!**
>
> Trying to couple or uncouple a rig without knowing these sequences can be dangerous, not only when your rig is in the yard, but on the road as well—and every professional driver's number one priority is going home safely after every shift.

> **CAUTION!**
>
> Typical hazards in coupling or uncoupling a rig include:
>
> 1. When the tractor is not secured, brake lines can be damaged.
> 2. When trailer brakes are not functioning, the trailer can be pushed into an obstruction.
> 3. When the ground is not firm for uncoupling, the trailer can fall and be damaged.
> 4. When trailer wheels are not **chocked,** the trailer may roll or be pushed into an obstruction and be damaged.
> 5. When climbing on the tractor during coupling, the driver could fall because of slippery surfaces.
> 6. If the driver works under an unsupported trailer (no jackstand or tractor under the trailer's nose) he or she could be injured if the landing gear collapses and the trailer drops to the ground.

THE COUPLING SEQUENCE

The Federal Motor Carrier Safety Administration requires all professional drivers to be qualified in the 15-step **coupling** operation.

Step 1: Inspect the Fifth Wheel

To make the safest connection possible, inspect the **fifth wheel** and the trailer's kingpin.

- Look for any damaged, loose, or missing parts. Be sure to check the kingpin for bends, breaks, or severe rust.
- **Locking jaws** should be open (**see Figure 10-3**).

Fifth Wheel

1. **Coupler arm**

2. **Release handle and safety latch**

3. **Locking jaws**

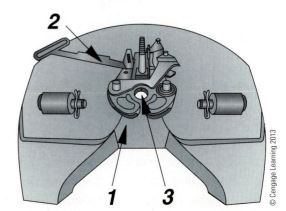

▶ Figure 10-3
Major parts of the fifth wheel.

© Cengage Learning 2013

Grease Retention Groove

© Cengage Learning 2013

▶ Figure 10-4

The fifth wheel must always have a coating of grease in the retention groove to ensure smooth movement when turning, particularly in cold weather. Without grease, the trailer will not properly pivot and this will cause accidents.

- Check to see that the fifth wheel is tilted downward toward the rear of the tractor.
- The fifth wheel should also be greased. Lack of proper lubrication could mean steering problems that result from friction between the tractor and trailer (see Figure 10-4).
- Safety release handle should be in the automatic lock position.
- Slider locks should be in place.
- The fifth-wheel position should allow coupling without allowing the rear end of the tractor to strike the landing gear.

Step 2: Inspect the Area

Be sure area around the rig is clear of all debris and hazards.

- There should be enough space in which to maneuver the tractor.
- Check the cargo to make certain it is braced well and will not move when the trailer is coupled with the tractor.
- If the trailer is equipped with spring brakes, make sure these brakes are applied before coupling begins.

Step 3: Position the Tractor

The tractor should be placed squarely in front of the trailer. Never back at an angle. The wrong approach by the tractor can push the trailer back, forward, or sideways. This could break the **landing gear** and cause the trailer to fall **(see Figure 10-5).**

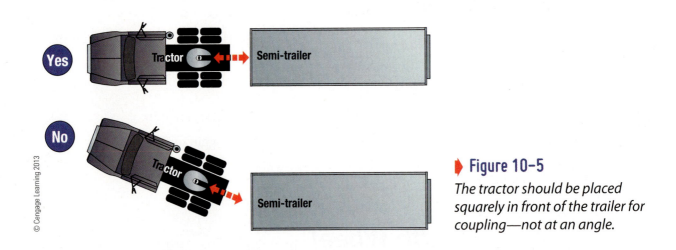

© Cengage Learning 2013

▶ Figure 10-5

The tractor should be placed squarely in front of the trailer for coupling—not at an angle.

- If the situation calls for you to back at an angle, get out of the cab frequently and check the alignment between the fifth wheel and the kingpin.
- To properly line up your tractor and trailer, use the outside edge of your tires and the edge of the trailer or guide points. In doing so, the tractor, outside edge of the drive axle tires, and the edge of the trailer form a straight line, if the trailer is 8 feet (2.4 m) wide.
- If the trailer is 8.5 feet (2.5 m) wide, the tractor drive axle tires should be 1-1/2 to 3 inches (3.8 to 7.6 cm) inside the outer edge of the trailer **(see Figure 10-6).**

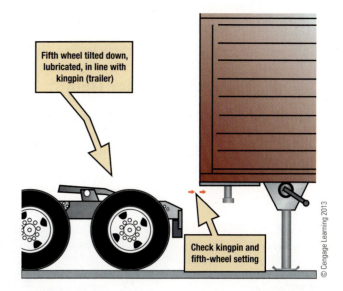

▶ **Figure 10-6**

Proper positioning of the tractor and trailer to begin coupling.

GO!

Pulling up directly in front of the trailer is preferred in all cases, but if you have to "angle in," check as often as necessary to make sure the throat of the fifth wheel is aligned with the kingpin.

Step 4: Back Slowly into Position until the Fifth Wheel Just Touches the Trailer

Back slowly toward the nose of the trailer and stop just before the fifth wheel reaches the trailer.

- ■ If your tractor has air bags, dump the air at this point.
- ■ You should be close enough to compare the fifth-wheel height with the height of the trailer.

CAUTION!

If you are unfamiliar with the tractor and trailer, stop and exit the truck to check the distance from the trailer **(see Figure 10-7).**

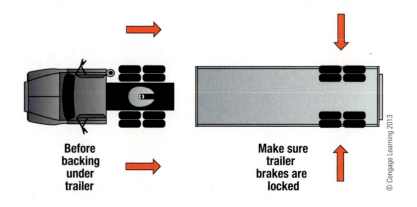

▶ **Figure 10-7**

Always check to make sure trailer brakes are locked before attempting the coupling procedure.

Step 5: Secure the Tractor

Shift into neutral, put on the parking brakes, and exit the cab.

Step 6: Check the Trailer Height

Inspect the height of the trailer nose compared to the fifth wheel. The nose should be slightly higher than the back of the fifth wheel. To couple properly, the nose of the trailer should touch the middle of the fifth wheel **(see Figure 10-8).** You may raise or lower the fifth wheel, using the tractor's adjustable air suspension, if available.

▶ **Figure 10–8**

Inspect the height of the trailer nose compared to the fifth wheel. The nose should be slightly higher than the back of the fifth wheel.

The other option is to crank the landing gear, although this may be difficult with a loaded trailer.

- If the trailer is too low, the tractor may collide with it, causing damage.
- If the trailer is too high, it may ride up and over the fifth wheel, colliding with the cab.

Step 7: Connect the Air Lines

When the height of the trailer is correct, you are ready to connect the tractor's air lines to the trailer. There are two air lines running from the tractor to the trailer, called the "service" and "emergency" lines. **Glad hands** are used to connect the air lines **(see Figure 10-9).**

Take the glad hands and electrical cord and attach them—red on red and blue on blue—with the red on the driver's side and the blue on the passenger's side.

For the trailer's brakes to work correctly, the air lines must be connected correctly. Match the plug to the connector, but do not force it if it does not fit. Sometimes the tractor's connectors do not match, so use a converter if necessary. Firmly seat the plug in the receptacle. Put on the safety catch or latch to keep them from accidentally separating.

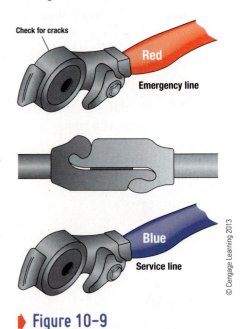

▶ **Figure 10–9**

Connect the service and emergency air lines.

Step 8: Supply Air to the Trailer

After the air lines have been connected and secured, get back into the cab. With the truck engine off, push in the **trailer air supply valve** to supply the trailer brakes with air. Listen for escaping air. If you hear a leak or if the air pressure gauge registers excessive loss of air, correct the problem at once. You will notice air leaking if you connected the air lines incorrectly.

STOP!

A professional driver will perform an audible air leak test and confirm the brake lights are operating properly before the unit can be safely driven.

Step 9: Release the Tractor's Parking Brake and Put on the Trailer Brake

You are now ready to back the tractor under the trailer, using the following steps:

- Start the truck engine.
- Put the truck into gear.
- Release the tractor's parking brake.
- Apply the trailer brakes.

Step 10: Back under the Trailer

Using the lowest reverse gear, back the tractor slowly under the trailer. You should feel or hear the **kingpin** lock into the fifth wheel **(see Figure 10-10).** Do not hit the kingpin too hard. This could bend the kingpin, buckle the upper plate, jump the pin and cause the trailer to hit the tractor, push the trailer away from the tractor, or damage cargo in the trailer.

▶ **Figure 10-10**
Kingpin locking fifth wheel.

CAUTION!

Do not accelerate while backing under the trailer.

Step 11: Test the Connection

Test the connection by pulling the tractor gently forward in low gear while the trailer handbrake is on **(see Figure 10-11).** As soon as resistance to forward motion is felt, disengage the clutch. Accelerate just enough to keep the engine from stalling. Then test the connection again.

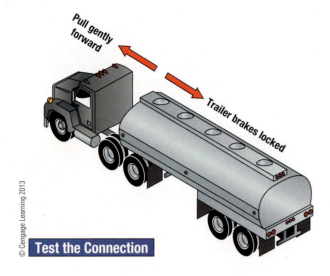

Pull gently forward

Trailer brakes locked

Test the Connection

© Cengage Learning 2013

▶ **Figure 10–11**

Test the hookup by gently pulling the tractor forward in low gear while the trailer hand brake is on.

Step 12: Secure the Vehicle

When you are sure of a solid hookup, apply the parking brake. Turn off the engine, put the key in your pocket, and get out of the cab.

Step 13: Inspect the Coupling

You will now need to go under the trailer and, by using a flashlight, get a good look at the coupling (**see Figure 10-12).** Check to see that the following have been done:

Courtesy of Baker College of Cadillac

▶ **Figure 10-12**

Inspecting the coupling.

- Fifth-wheel jaws have engaged the shank of the kingpin and not the head. If the jaws are closed around the head, the trailer will bounce the kingpin out of the jaws.

- Jaws should be closed and locked. The safety catch should be over the locking lever.

- The upper fifth-wheel plate should be in full contact with the lower trailer plate. There should be no gap between the trailer apron and the fifth-wheel plate. If there is a space between the two, stop and fix the problem before doing anything else. NOTE: The space may be due to uneven ground surface. If this is the case, move the rig to flat ground and check again.

- Be sure to inspect the coupling each time you stop the truck, once you get on the road, especially when leaving a truck stop or rest area.

STOP!

Never crawl under your rig without putting the ignition keys in your pocket. This will prevent anyone from accidentally moving the rig while you are conducting a coupling inspection.

Step 14: Connect the Electrical Cord and Check Air Lines

Plug the electrical cord into the trailer, then fasten the safety catch. Be sure neither the electrical cord nor the air lines are damaged. These must not hit any moving parts of the rig.

Step 15: Raise the Landing Gear

You are now ready to raise the landing gear **(see Figure 10-13).** Most crank handles have a low speed and a high speed. Use the low speed to start raising the landing gear. Switch to high speed when the trailer weight is off the landing gear. Keep cranking until the landing gear is fully raised—and make sure both legs of the landing gear go up.

Landing Gear

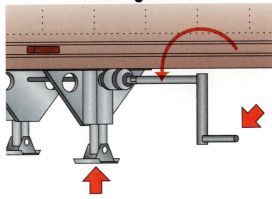

- Check clearance between rear of tractor frame and/or mudflaps and landing gear.
- Use low range to begin raising landing gear.
- Once free of weight, switch to high gear.
- Crank until fully raised.
- Safely secure crank in holder in low gear.
- Check clearance between top of tractor drive wheels and nose of trailer.

© Cengage Learning 2013

▶ **Figure 10-13**

Raise the landing gear.

STOP!

Never drive your rig with the landing gear partly raised. It can snag on railroad tracks, dips in the road, and on other obstacles. Make sure the crank handle is tightly secured to prevent damage to other vehicles or injury to pedestrians.

STEP-BY-STEP UNCOUPLING PROCEDURE

Step 1: Position the Vehicle

To prepare to **uncouple** your rig, place the tractor directly in line with the trailer on level ground to keep from damaging the landing gear when pulling the tractor from under the trailer. Make sure the surface where you plan to uncouple the trailer is level and also will support the weight of the rig **(see Figure 10-14).**

© Cengage Learning 2013

▶ *"Sooo . . . this is what they meant by 'coupling' and 'uncoupling'—and I thought they were talking about speed-dating."*

▶ **Figure 10-14**

Rig with tractor inline with trailer.

CAUTION!

Blacktop will soften in hot weather, making the surface unstable.

Step 2: Secure the Vehicle

Place the tractor protection valve in the emergency position. This cuts off the air supply between the tractor and the trailer. Make certain you have backed tightly against the kingpin. If not, it will bind and will not release properly. Put on the tractor's parking brake and exit the cab.

▶ **Figure 10-15**

As a professional driver you must learn how to safely lower the landing gear.

Step 3: Lower the Landing Gear

Inspect landing gear for rust and damage. Inspect the ground to verify you can lower the landing gear without the foot pads sinking while supporting the trailer's weight. Then lower the landing gear until both legs touch the ground. **Make sure both legs come down!** If one touches the ground but not the other, find a more level location to drop the trailer (**see Figure 10-15**).

Step 4: Disconnect and Store the Air Lines and Electrical Cable

Carefully disconnect the air lines and electrical cable. Place the air line glad hands on the dummy couplers behind the cab. Hang the electrical cable down to avoid moisture on the plug and store in its holder. Secure the lines against snagging, scraping, cuts, or other damage.

Step 5: Release the Fifth-Wheel Latch

To release the fifth wheel, raise the release handle lock pin and pull to the open position. On a single axle tractor, this usually is not hard. On tandem axle tractors, however, the release handle is sometimes hard to reach. If it is difficult to reach, use a pull handle or hook.

Step 6: Lower the Air Suspension

If your rig has air suspension, as on most modern trucks, when back in the cab flip the switch so the air is removed from the air suspension and the tractor is lowered. This prevents the end of the tractor from popping up when later pulling clear.

Step 7: Pull the Tractor Partly Clear of the Trailer

Get back into the cab and release the parking brake, leaving the tractor protection valve in the set position. In the lowest possible forward gear, pull the tractor forward—releasing the parking brakes—until the fifth wheel begins to clear the trailer apron plate. As you pull the tractor forward, the service brakes are holding the trailer in position until it uncouples from the tractor. Stop the tractor while its frame is still under the trailer. This will keep the trailer from falling if the landing gear collapses or sinks.

> ### CAUTION!
> As you pull the tractor slowly forward, use your driver's side mirror to watch and see that, as the tractor moves forward, the trailer slides down and settles on the ground. Once this occurs, stop the tractor. You should be only a few inches from the trailer.

Step 8: Secure the Tractor

Set the tractor parking brakes. Exit the cab.

Step 9: Inspect the Trailer Supports

Be sure the landing gear is supporting the trailer and is not damaged.

Step 10: Now, Pull the Tractor Clear of the Trailer

Release the parking brake. Check the area ahead of the tractor and pull the tractor slowly away from the trailer. Uncoupling is now safely completed.

Step 11: Reinflate the Air Suspension System

After pulling the tractor away from the trailer, reinflate the air bags (if this applies to your rig).

> ### GO!
> Use the following memory aid (LAPD) to help you remember how to begin the uncoupling procedure:
>
> L = Lower the landing gear
> A = Air lines and electrical lines disconnected
> P = Pull and release arm
> D = Deflate Air Ride Suspension system

COUPLING TWIN TRAILERS

Step 1: Secure the Second or Rear Trailer

If the second trailer does not have spring brakes, drive the tractor close to the trailer, connect the emergency line, charge the trailer air tank, and disconnect the emergency line. This will set the trailer emergency brakes if the slack adjusters are correctly adjusted. Chock the wheels.

CAUTION!

For safe handling on the road, the more heavily loaded semi-trailer must always be in the first position behind the tractor. The lighter trailer should be in the rear.

A converter gear or dolly is a **coupling device** of one or two axles and a fifth wheel by which a semi-trailer can be coupled to the rear of a tractor-trailer combination forming a double bottom rig.

Step 2: Position the Converter Dolly in Front of the Second or Rear Trailer

- Release the dolly brakes by opening the air tank petcock. (Or, if the dolly has spring brakes, use the dolly parking brake control.)
- If possible, wheel the dolly into position by hand so it is in line with the kingpin (**see Figure 10-16**).
- Or, use the tractor and first semi-trailer to pick up the converter dolly:
    - position combination as close as possible to converter dolly
    - move dolly to rear of first semi-trailer and couple it to the trailer
    - lock pintle hook
    - secure dolly support in raised position
    - pull dolly into position as close as possible to nose of the second semi-trailer
    - lower dolly support
    - unhook dolly from first trailer
    - wheel dolly into position in front of second trailer in line with the kingpin

Courtesy of Baker College of Cadillac

▶ **Figure 10-16**

When possible, wheel the converter dolly into position by hand.

Step 3: Connect the Converter Dolly to the Front Trailer

- Back first semi-trailer into position in front of the dolly tongue.
- Hook dolly to front trailer:
    - lock pintle hook
    - secure converter gear support in raised position

Step 4: Connect the Converter Dolly to the Rear Trailer

- Lock trailer brakes and/or chock wheels.
- Make sure trailer height is correct. (It must be slightly lower than the center of the fifth wheel so the trailer is raised slightly when the dolly is pushed under.)
- Back converter dolly under rear trailer.
- Raise landing gear slightly off ground.
- Test coupling by pulling against pin of rear trailer.
- Check coupling and locking jaws.
- Connect safety chains, air hoses, and electrical cords.
- Close converter dolly air tank petcock, and shut-off valves at rear of second trailer.
- Open shut-off valves at rear of first trailer and on the dolly, if so equipped.
- Raise the landing gear completely.
- Charge trailers and check for air at the rear of the second trailer by opening the emergency line shut-off.

UNCOUPLING DOUBLE TRAILERS

Uncouple Rear Trailer

- Park rig in a straight line.
- Apply parking brakes.
- Chock wheels of the second trailer.
- Lower the landing gear of the second semi-trailer enough to remove some weight from the dolly.
- Close air shutoffs at rear of the first semi-trailer and on the dolly, if so equipped.
- Disconnect all dolly air and electric lines and secure them.
- Release dolly brakes.
- Release converter dolly fifth-wheel latch.
- Slowly pull tractor, first semi-trailer, and dolly forward to pull dolly out from under rear semi-trailer.

Uncouple Converter Dolly

- Lower dolly landing gear.
- Disconnect safety chains.
- Apply converter gear spring brakes or chock wheels.
- Release pintle hook on first semi-trailer.
- Slowly pull clear of dolly.

CAUTION!

Never unlock the pintle hook with the dolly still under the rear trailer. The dolly tow bar may fly up, possibly causing injury, and making it very difficult to recouple.

COUPLING AND UNCOUPLING TRIPLE TRAILERS

Couple Second and Third Trailers

- Couple second and third trailers using the method for coupling **doubles**.
- Uncouple tractor and pull away from the second and third trailers.

Couple Tractor/First Semi-trailer to Second/Third Trailers

- Couple tractor to first trailer. Use the method already described for coupling tractor-semi-trailers.
- Move converter dolly into position and couple first trailer to second trailer using the method for coupling doubles. **Triples** rig is now complete.

Uncouple Triple Trailer Rig

- Uncouple third trailer by pulling the dolly out, then unhitching the dolly, using the method for uncoupling doubles.
- Uncouple remainder of rig as you would any double-bottom rig using the method already described.

COUPLING AND UNCOUPLING OTHER COMBINATIONS

The methods described so far apply to the more common tractor-trailer combinations. However, there are other ways of coupling and uncoupling the many types of truck-trailer and tractor-trailer combinations that are in use. There are too many to cover in this handbook. Learn the right way to couple the vehicle(s) you will drive according to the manufacturer and/or vehicle owner.

Inspecting Doubles and Triples

There are more items to inspect on a combination vehicle than on a single vehicle (**see Figure 10-17**). Many of these items are simply more of what you would find on a single vehicle.

However, there are also some new items to check.

ADDITIONAL ITEMS FOR WALKAROUND INSPECTION

Coupling System Areas

- Fifth-wheel (lower):
    - securely mounted to frame
    - no missing, damaged parts
    - properly greased
    - no visible space between upper and lower fifth-wheel
    - locking jaws around the shank, not the head of the kingpin
    - release arm properly seated and safety latch/lock engaged
- Fifth wheel (upper):
    - glide plate securely mounted to trailer frame
    - kingpin not damaged

▶ **Figure 10-17**

A professional driver has to remember there are more items to inspect on a combination vehicle.

- Air and electric lines to trailer:
  - electrical cord firmly plugged in and secured
  - air lines properly connected to glad hands, no air leaks, properly secured with enough slack for turns
  - all lines free from damage
- Sliding fifth-wheel:
  - slide not damaged or parts missing
  - properly greased
  - all locking pins present and locked in place
  - if air powered—no air leaks
  - fifth wheel not so far forward that tractor frame will hit landing gear, or cab hit the trailer, during turns

Landing Gear

- Fully raised, no missing parts, not bent or otherwise damaged
- Crank handle in place and secured
- If power operated, no air or hydraulic leaks

Double and Triple Trailers

- Shut-off valves (at rear of trailers, in service and emergency lines):
  - rear of front trailer(s): OPEN
  - rear of last trailer: CLOSED. (Glad hands should be covered to protect from debris.)
  - converter dolly air tank drain valve: CLOSED
- Be sure air lines are supported and glad hands are properly connected.
- If spare tire is carried on converter gear (dolly), make sure it is secured.
- Be sure pintle-eye of dolly is in place in pintle hook of trailer(s).
- Make sure pintle hook is latched.
- Safety chains should be secured to trailer(s).
- Be sure electrical cords are firmly in sockets on trailers.

WHAT YOU NEED TO KNOW ABOUT LONGER COMBINATION VEHICLES (LCVs)

LCV types include:

- Triples: Three 28.5-foot (8.7 m) trailers; maximum weight up to 129,000 pounds (58,513 kg)
- Turnpike Doubles: Two 48-foot (14.6 m) trailers; maximum weight up to 147,000 pounds (66,678 kg)
- Rocky Mountain Doubles: One 40 (12.2 m) to 53 (16.2 m) foot trailer (though usually no more than 48 feet) and one 28.5-foot (8.7 m) trailer (known as a "pup"); maximum weight up to 129,000 pounds (58,513 kg)
- In Canada, a Turnpike Double is two 53-foot (16.2 m) trailers and a Rocky Mountain Double is a 50-foot (15.2 m) trailer with 24-foot (7.3 m) "pup"

(Continues)

WHAT YOU NEED TO KNOW ABOUT LONGER COMBINATION VEHICLES (LCVs) *(continued)*

Regulations on LCVs vary widely from state to state. No state in the U.S. allows more than three trailers without a special permit. Reasons for limiting the legal trailer configurations include both safety concerns and the impracticality of designing and constructing roads that can accommodate the larger wheelbase of these vehicles and the larger minimum turning radii associated with them.

Most states restrict operation of larger tandem trailer setups such as triple units, the Turnpike Double (twin 48–53 ft/14.6–16.2 m units) or the Rocky Mountain Double. (a full 48–53 ft/14.6–16.2 m unit and a shorter 28 ft (8.5 m) unit).

In general, these types of setups are restricted to tolled turnpikes such as I-80 through Ohio and Indiana, and specific Western states. Tandem setups are not restricted to certain roads any more than a single setup.

Some form of LCVs are currently allowed on designated routes in Alaska, Arizona, Colorado, Florida, Idaho, Indiana, Iowa, Kansas, Massachusetts, Michigan, Missouri, Montana, Nebraska, Nevada, New York, North Dakota, Ohio, Oklahoma, Oregon, South Dakota, Utah, Washington, and Wyoming. Oversize/Overweight vehicles may be allowed by local jurisdictions in California for certain vehicles and loads.

CAUTION!

LCVs are known in the transportation industry as "wiggle wagons," mainly because they can be challenging to pull. Wind can flip the third trailer without any warning to the driver. "Trips," as triple trailers are also known, also can't be backed, so drivers must always make certain they can drive these rigs forward. Doubles can be backed for a short distance sometimes, but trips never. Extra space must be allowed for turning as each trailer cuts tighter through the turn.

SUMMARY

In this chapter, you reviewed the steps necessary to couple a trailer to a tractor, uncouple a rig, use the controls needed to couple or uncouple a rig, and how to test the connection.

KEY TERMS

Chock	Glad hands	Trailer
Coupling	Kingpin	Trailer air supply valve
Coupling device	Landing gear	Triples
Doubles	Locking jaws	Uncoupling
Fifth wheel	Tractor	

REVIEW QUESTIONS

1. It is the _____ responsibility to couple the tractor and trailer correctly for any trip.

    a. dispatcher's

    b. technician's

    c. foreman's

    d. driver's

2. When positioning the tractor for coupling with a 8-1/2 foot (2.6 m) wide trailer, the tractor drive axle tires should be approximately _____.

    a. 1-1/2 to 3 inches (3.8 to 7.6 cm) inside the outside edge of the trailer

    b. 1-1/2 to 3 inches (3.8 to 7.6 cm) outside the outside edge of the trailer

    c. in line with the tires of the trailer

    d. 12 inches (30.5 cm) inside the outside edge of the trailer

3. During the coupling process, when inspecting the height of the trailer nose compared to the height of the fifth wheel, the nose of the trailer should be _____ than the back of the fifth wheel.

    a. lower

    b. slightly higher

    c. 2 feet (0.6 m) higher

    d. 3 feet (0.9 m) higher

4. During the coupling process, when supplying air to the trailer, if you hear an air leak or the air pressure gauge registers excessive loss of air, then you know you _____.

    a. have not connected the electrical lines correctly

    b. have not connected the air lines correctly

    c. the trailer is not in line with the tractor

    d. the nose of the trailer is too high compared with the fifth wheel

5. During the coupling process, when backing under the trailer, the driver stops when the _____ is felt or heard to lock into the fifth wheel.

    a. nose of the trailer

    b. landing gear

    c. kingpin

    d. driveshaft

6. When inspecting a successful coupling, the driver should see the jaws of the fifth wheel closed and locked around the kingpin with the safety catch _____.

    a. over the locking lever

    b. behind the locking lever

    c. over the rear tires of the trailer

    d. over the rear axle of the tractor

7. To test the tractor and trailer connection (hookup), the driver _____.

    a. drives forward 20 to 30 feet (6.1 to 9.1 m) with all brakes off

    b. drives forward 20 to 30 feet (6.1 to 9.1 m) with all brakes on

    c. gently pulls the tractor forward in low gear while the trailer hand brake is on

    d. lets the mechanic test the connection

8. When preparing for uncoupling, the tractor _____.

    a. can be at any angle with the trailer

    b. should be placed directly in line with the trailer on any surface as the landing gear will support the trailer on any kind of surface

    c. should be placed directly in line with the trailer on level ground

    d. with the trailer attached should be driven to the shop for the mechanic to do the uncoupling

9. When performing the uncoupling procedure, after the fifth-wheel latch has been released and the tractor is being pulled forward, the driver _____.

   a. drives to the technician's shop for the completion of the uncoupling process

   b. drives the tractor at least 15 feet (4.6 m) from the trailer to ensure the tractor is clear of the trailer

   c. drives forward at least 3 feet (0.9 m) and then backs at least 5 feet (1.5 m) to ensure the trailer is on firm ground

   d. drives forward and stops the tractor while the frame is still under the trailer

10. Which of the following is not an element of the memory aid LAPD, which helps the driver remember how to start the uncoupling procedure?

    a. lower landing gear

    b. pull forward and then back

    c. air lines and electrical lines disconnected

    d. pull and release arm or release pin

11. A set of triple trailers and a tractor will weigh in the vicinity of _____.

    a. up to 200,000 pounds/90,718 kg

    b. up to 229,000 pounds/103,872 kg

    c. up to 129,000 pounds/58,513 kg

    d. up to 150,000 pounds/68,039 kg

12. LCVs are often called "wiggle wagons" because _____.

    a. the long configuration resembles a worm or caterpillar

    b. there is movement among trailers

    c. couplings aren't secure

    d. they are challenging to pull

SUPPLEMENTAL LEARNING ACTIVITIES

1. Why, as a professional driver, would you take the time to walk around your rig before you uncoupled or coupled your tractor to a trailer? Make a list as a group and be ready to discuss.

2. Discuss, in your group, why a professional driver will test the coupling connection of his or her rig while still in the yard, not on the roadway. Give at least three reasons and share them with the class.

3. Ask permission to watch a professional driver couple or uncouple a rig. Use a checklist of your own design to determine if the driver did or did not follow a safe sequence. Discuss what you observed with the class.

4. Discuss the importance of properly chocking wheels. If any members of your group have visited a freight dock, describe what the chocking blocks look like. (It will be interesting to hear what materials and/or items are commonly used to chock wheels.)

5. Remember, every step of every process has been designed to keep the driver and those working around a dock or a rig safe. Discuss how being in a hurry and not taking enough time to learn and follow each process can only sabotage safety.

FOR MORE INFORMATION

PTDI—Couple Trailer, Page 12, Click on Skill Standards
www.ptdi.org/standards

California DMV—Coupling and Uncoupling
dmv.ca.gov/pubs/cdl_htm/sec7.htm

Coupling & Uncoupling
www.newbiedriver.com/abcsupdates/couplinguncoupling.htm

11

Sliding Fifth Wheels and Tandem Axles

© Kevin Norris/www.Shutterstock.com

OBJECTIVES

When you have completed this chapter, you should be able to:

- Describe the function of the sliding fifth wheel or trailer tandem axles.
- Explain the effects of the sliding fifth wheel or trailer tandem action on overall length, maneuverability of the rig, and off-tracking.
- Explain the correct way to slide the fifth wheel of a tractor with a trailer attached.
- Explain the hazards of sliding the fifth wheel or trailer tandem axles improperly.

▶ **Figure 11–1**

A tractor-trailer can have one or both; a sliding fifth wheel on the tractor and a sliding tandem axle on the trailer.

INTRODUCTION

Many tractor-trailer rigs have a **sliding fifth wheel** on the tractor and **sliding tandem axles** on the trailer. Tractor-trailers can have either one or both of them **(see Figure 11-1).**

The sliding fifth wheel can adjust the overall length of the tractor-trailer, adjust the turning radius of the vehicle, and adjust and balance the weight of each of the axles. The sliding tandem axles on the trailer can adjust the off-tracking of the trailer, adjust the turning radius of the vehicle, and adjust and balance the weight on each of the axles of the trailer.

Wheels and axles have similar effects on both the tractor and the trailer—and their positions are important for the driver to understand if he or she wishes to safely and legally haul a load.

In addition, professional drivers should be able to slide the tandems because many of today's loading docks now require the trailer tandems to be positioned all the way to the rear of the trailer before the fork truck is allowed to load or unload them.

CAUTION!

On every trip and with every load, the driver is responsible for:

- Legal gross vehicle weight
- Overall length of the vehicle
- Amount of weight per axle
- Rig's maneuverability and ability to turn safely
- Knowing all state and local laws/restrictions

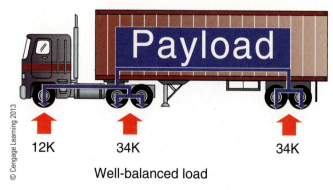

12K   34K   34K

Well-balanced load

▶ **Figure 11–2**

When a trailer is coupled to a tractor, some of the weight is transferred to the tractor.

The purpose of this chapter is to help you learn how to slide the fifth wheel and the trailer tandem axles. You will also learn some of the basic reasons for making these adjustments to the rig.

SHIFTING WEIGHT

When a trailer is coupled to a tractor, some weight of the trailer is transferred to the tractor through the connection with the fifth wheel **(see Figure 11-2).** If the payload is evenly distributed in the trailer, standard trailer axle and fifth-wheel settings will properly distribute the weight on each axle.

Some trailers have sliding tandem axles to transfer weight to the tractor if the payload in the trailer is not evenly distributed. The amount of the weight transferred to the tractor can be adjusted by sliding the tandem axles on the trailer toward the rear. This will increase the amount of weight on the drive and steering axles of the tractor (**see Figure 11-3**).

By sliding the trailer tandems forward, you can shift weight off the tractor (**see Figure 11-4**). This causes the weight behind the trailer's tandem axles to actually tip the weight off the tractor. Shifting the weight decreases the amount of weight on the drive and steering axles of the tractor.

Some tractors have a sliding fifth wheel. This can adjust the length of the tractor-trailer and balance, or shift, some of the weight from the trailer to between the steer axle and drive axles of the tractor. By sliding the fifth wheel on the tractor forward, you can transfer weight to the steer axle and also shorten the overall length of the rig.

INTERESTING FACT

Progress in power, strength, maneuverability, and durability by 1958 generated emphasis on increasing the use of lightweight materials like aluminum, fiberglass, and plastics in building tractors and trailers. Every time a pound/kg of weight was subtracted from the rig's structure, the vehicle could carry one more pound/kg of cargo to hold down the cost of delivering products.

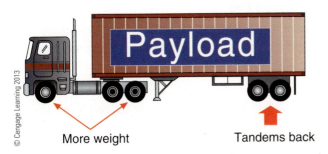

More weight   Tandems back

▶ Figure 11–3

Sliding tandems to the rear increases weight on the drive and steering axles.

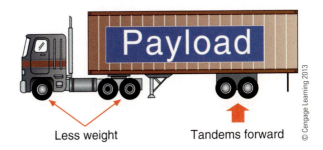

Less weight   Tandems forward

▶ Figure 11–4

Sliding tandems forward shifts weight off the tractor.

▶ *"Calculating sliding fifth-wheel positions? Go figure!"*

▶ **Figure 11-5**

More weight on the steer axle makes the tractor more difficult to steer and maneuver.

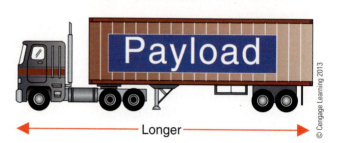

▶ **Figure 11-6**

Sliding the fifth wheel toward the rear increases total length of the tractor and reduces weight on the steer axle.

If you slide the fifth wheel on the tractor toward the rear, you can reduce the amount of weight on the steer axle, but you will also increase the total length of the tractor **(see Figure 11-6).** If too much weight is shifted off the steer axle, the steering will feel light and you will not have as much control over the steering. Shifting too much weight off the steer axle can also make the rig overweight on the drive axles.

As mentioned earlier, at night, your headlights will be aimed at the sky instead of the road ahead. As you can see, the positions of the fifth wheel and the trailer tandem axles have a lot to do with the weight per axle and handling of the rig **(see Figure 11-7).**

▶ **Figure 11-7**

Distribution of weight has a teeter-totter effect.

THE BRIDGE FORMULA

To achieve the maximum legal weight on each axle, you need to know the **Bridge Formula** (also known as the Federal Bridge Formula and Bridge Formula B). It is a mathematical formula used by professional drivers in the U.S. and the Department of Transportation to determine the appropriate maximum gross weight for a CMV, based on number of axles and spacing of those axles.

The Bridge Formula became necessary to prevent heavy vehicles from damaging roads and bridges and was developed to prevent stress to highways and bridges caused by trucks hauling heavy loads **(see Figure 11-8).** All trucks operating on U.S. interstate highways and some state highways must comply with the Bridge Formula.

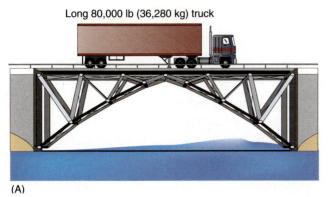
Long 80,000 lb (36,280 kg) truck

(A)

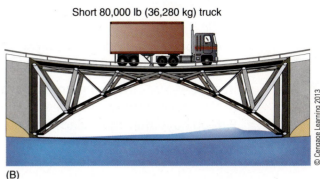
Short 80,000 lb (36,280 kg) truck

(B)

© Cengage Learning 2013

▶ **Figure 11–8**

Bridge Formula illustration.

The solution, provided by the Bridge Formula, links allowable weights to the number and spacing of axles.

Axle spacing is as important as axle weight in designing bridges. In Figure A, the stress on bridge members as a longer truck rolls across is much less than that caused by a short vehicle as shown in Figure B, even though both trucks have the same total weight and individual axle weights. The weight of the longer vehicle is spread out, while the shorter vehicle is concentrated on a smaller area.

STOP!

Deteriorating U.S. Infrastructure Make Bridge Formula Particularly Important

In August 2007, the collapse of the Interstate 35W Mississippi River bridge in Minneapolis brought renewed attention to the issue of truck weights and bridge stress. Slightly more than a year later, in November 2008, the National Transportation Safety Board determined several reasons for the bridge's collapse, including faulty and aging elements in the bridge as well as inadequate inspections, and the extra weight of heavy construction equipment combined with the weight of rush hour traffic.

As early as 1998, the Federal Highway Administration (FHWA) had expressed concern over bridges on the I-35 corridor due to an expected increase of international truck traffic from Canada and Mexico.

In 2007, U.S. truck traffic was estimated to have increased 216 percent after 1970, shortly before the federal gross weight limit for trucks was increased by 30,000 pounds (13,605 kg). Research shows that increased truck traffic (and therefore, increased stress) shortens the life of bridges.

Smaller bridges have a weight limit (or gross weight load rating) indicated by a sign posted in a visible position in front of the bridge (hence the reference to a "posted bridge"). These are necessary when the weight limit of the bridge is lower than the federal or state gross weight limit for trucks.

Driving a truck over a bridge that is too weak to support it usually does not result in an immediate collapse. The bridge may develop cracks and these, over time, can weaken the bridge and cause it to collapse. Most of these cracks should be discovered during mandated inspections of bridges.

While the number varies from year to year, as many as 150 bridges can collapse in a year. About 1,500 bridges collapsed between 1966 and 2007, and most of those were the result of soil erosion around bridge supports.

In special cases involving unusually **overweight trucks** (which require special permits), not observing a bridge weight limit can lead to disastrous consequences. Fifteen days after the collapse of the Minneapolis bridge, a heavy truck collapsed a small bridge in Washington State.

In the U.S., CMVs are required to pass through weigh stations, located at the borders of most states and some large cities. These weigh stations are run by state DOTs, and CMV-weight and size enforcement is overseen by the FHWA. Weigh stations check each vehicle's gross weight and axle weight using a set of in-ground **truck scales,** and are usually where a truck's compliance with the formula is checked. Also note, in some states semi-trailers longer than 50 feet shall not have a wheel base of less than 37.5 ft and not more than 40.5 ft + 6 inches measured from the kingpin coupling to the center of the rear axle or the center of the rear axle assembly.

Compliance with Bridge Formula weight limits is determined by using the following formula:

$$W = 500\left[\frac{LN}{N-1} + 12N + 36\right]$$

W = the overall gross weight on any group of two or more consecutive axles to the nearest 500 pounds (266.7 kg)

L = the distance in feet between the outer axles of any group of two or more consecutive axles

N = the number of axles in the group under consideration

In addition to Bridge Formula weight limits, federal law states that single axles are limited to 20,000 pounds, and axles closer than 96 inches apart (tandem axles) are limited to 34,000 pounds. Gross vehicle weight is limited to 80,000 pounds (23 U.S.C. 127).

NOTE

To test your skills, go to the Federal Highway Administration's Bridge Formula Weights Calculator at www.ops.fhwa.dot.gov/freight/sw/brdgcalc/calc_page.htm.

Under the formula rules, tractors must have a minimum **outer spread** (distance between the center of the front axle and the center of the rearmost axle) of 14 feet to scale the maximum 46,000 pounds (12,000 pounds on the steer axle, 34,000 pounds on the tandems). This distance is not affected when you slide the fifth wheel forward or back, but two other distances are affected—the **inner bridge** (between the center of the rearmost axle and the center of the leading trailer axle) and the **outer bridge** (between the center of the forward tractor tandem and the rearmost trailer axle).

Sliding the fifth wheel or a trailer slider will change these distances and may affect your legal load-carrying capacity. For example, a five-axle tractor-trailer must have an outer bridge of at least 51 feet to haul the maximum allowable 80,000 pounds.

MANEUVERABILITY AND OFF-TRACKING

The **maneuverability** and **off-tracking** of the tractor-trailer are affected by the position of the trailer tandems and the position of the fifth wheel. When you slide the fifth wheel to the rear of the tractor, the overall length of the vehicle increases. The distance between the steer axle and the kingpin also increases along with the distance to the trailer tandem axles.

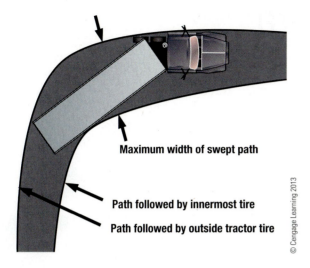

Figure 11-9

Off-tracking in a 90-degree turn.

(within figure) Maximum width of swept path

Path followed by innermost tire

Path followed by outside tractor tire

Figure 11-10

The position of the tandem axles of the trailer affects the amount of space needed to turn.

When you turn, the greater the distance between the steer axle and the pivot point (kingpin) of the trailer, the further the trailer will off-track. The swept path of the trailer will increase, so you will need more space to make a turn (**see Figure 11-9**).

The position of the tandem axles of the trailer also affects off-tracking and the space needed to turn. When you slide the tandem axles all the way to the rear, the distance between the kingpin and the real axle wheels increases. The overall length of the vehicle does not change, but the amount of space needed to turn increases (**see Figure 11-10**).

When the tandem axles are all the way back, trailer off-tracking increases, and so does the swept path of the vehicle. The sharper the turn, the more the rear wheels will off-track (**see Figure 11-11**). When you slide the tandem axles forward and the distance between the kingpin and the rear axles decreases, the rig is easier to maneuver. There is also less trailer off-tracking, which is helpful when making deliveries.

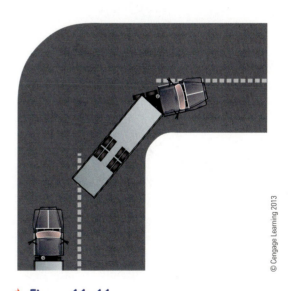

Figure 11-11

The sharper the turn, the more the rear wheels will off-track.

CAUTION!

Be careful when the tandem axles are all the way forward because there will be a trailer overhang. This overhang becomes critical in tight turns, as it results in the rearmost portion of the trailer swiveling past what would otherwise be its normal range, and can strike objects and vehicles.

THE FIFTH WHEEL

The two types of fifth wheels are fixed (stationary) fifth wheels and sliding fifth wheels. A **fixed-mount fifth wheel** is usually mounted directly on the **frame rails** of the tractor by a bracket assembly (**see Figure 11-12**). The bracket assembly allows the fifth wheel to rock up and down. The stationary fifth wheel is placed to get the best weight distribution between the tractor's steer axle and the drive axle(s) of a properly loaded trailer.

GO!

Weight adjustments are made by sliding the tandem axles of the trailer.

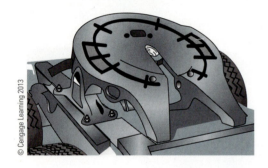

▶ **Figure 11–12**

A fixed, or stationary, fifth wheel.

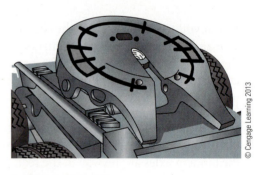

▶ **Figure 11–13**

A sliding fifth wheel.

Sliding fifth wheels are attached to the sliding bracket assembly (**see Figure 11-13**). The sliding bracket assemblies can be attached to a base that has a sliding rail assembly built into it. The base is then attached to the frame rails of the tractor. Then, the fifth wheel and sliding bracket assembly are attached directly to the frame rails.

The fifth wheel has a locking device that holds the sliding assembly in place. The two types of locking assemblies are manual release and air-operated release:

Manual release—allows you to release, or unlock, the sliding mechanism by pushing or pulling a release handle (**see Figure 11-14**). This release handle may be on the driver's side of the fifth wheel or directly in front of the fifth wheel. When the handle is pulled to the unlock position, the locking pins are released from the locking holes or notches on the mounting base or sliding rail assembly.

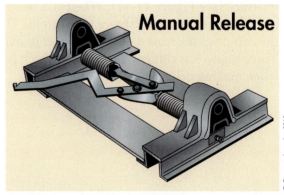

Manual Release

▶ **Figure 11–14**

Manual release allows you to unlock the fifth wheel with a release handle.

CAUTION!
Keep your feet out of the tire path and use free hand to brace balance.

Air-operated release—lets you release the locking device on the sliding fifth wheel by moving the fifth-wheel release lever in the cab to the "unlocked" position. When the lever is in the unlocked position, air is forced against a piston on the fifth-wheel locking device. The piston forces the locking pins to release from the locking holes or notches on the mounting base or sliding rail assembly (**see Figure 11-15**).

SLIDING THE FIFTH WHEEL

Sliding the fifth wheel is not a difficult procedure, but it should be done on a level surface, off the road, and away from hazards.

1. Be sure to set the trailer parking brake before getting out of the cab—for any reason. This will keep the tractor from rolling.

2. The trailer must be properly connected to the locked fifth wheel and the kingpin, and locked in place.

3. The air and electrical lines should be connected to the trailer.

4. If the trailer has a sliding tandem axle, it should be locked into place.

5. Test the connection to the trailer, gently pulling forward with the trailer brake on. If you have just made the connection to the trailer, look at the connection to be sure the fifth-wheel jaws are locked around the kingpin of the trailer, then crank up the trailer's landing gear.

6. Place the fifth-wheel release handle or lever in the "unlocked" position. Then, put on your trailer brakes, either by pulling down on your trailer brake hand valve (if you have one) or by pulling out the red trailer air supply valve.

7. Release the tractor brake valve. With your tractor brakes released and your trailer brakes engaged, you are ready to slide the fifth wheel.

   If you want to slide the fifth wheel forward—put the tractor into reverse.

   If you want to slide the fifth wheel back toward the rear of the tractor—use low gear and ease the tractor forward or backward gently. You may get some resistance from the sliding assembly when you do this (**see Figure 11-16**).

▶ **Figure 11-15**

An air-operated release unlocks the fifth wheel by a release lever in the cab.

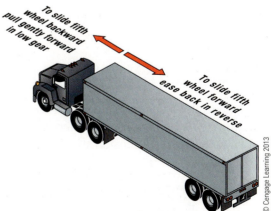

▶ **Figure 11-16**

When sliding the fifth wheel, you may have some resistance from the sliding assembly.

If the fifth wheel has not been moved for quite some time, you may experience what is called **binding.** Look at the fifth-wheel locking pins first to make sure they have unlocked and that the fifth wheel is free to slide. Pressure on the pins may be holding them in place.

If the pins appear to be stuck or binding, you can usually free them by gently rocking the tractor. Corrosion, dirt, or grime may have gotten into the mechanism, causing it to lock. You may have to clean some of the road grime off the mechanism so it can work correctly. You may also want to lower the landing gear. It can help relieve binding and stress, allowing the fifth wheel to move easier.

Once you have moved the fifth wheel to where you want it, place the fifth-wheel release lever or handle in the locked position. With the trailer brakes still on, gently tug or push against the trailer. This will let the fifth-wheel locking pins unseat themselves.

Set the tractor brakes. Look at the fifth-wheel slider to make sure it is properly locked into place—and remember, you have just changed your overall length. This will make a difference in your ride, weight distribution, and maneuverability.

CAUTION!

Quick Review—Sliding the Fifth Wheel

1. Make sure the tractor is properly coupled to the trailer.
2. Place the fifth-wheel release in the unlocked position.
3. Set the trailer brakes, using the hand valve or by pulling the red trailer air supply valve.
4. Release the tractor brake or parking brake system.
5. Ease the tractor gently in the opposite direction in which you want to move the fifth wheel.
6. Place the fifth-wheel release in the locked position.
7. With the trailer brakes still set, gently tug or push against the trailer to seat the locking pins.
8. Set the tractor brakes and visually check that the fifth-wheel slider is properly locked into place.
9. Remember you have just changed the rig's overall length, and that means the ride, weight distribution, and maneuverability will be different.

TRAILER TANDEM AXLES

Not all trailer axles are tandem axles. A light-duty trailer may have just one axle, and that axle is usually stationary. Trailers with high-rated cargo-carrying capacity usually have tandem axles. All trailer axles are attached to a suspension system and subframe (**see Figure 11-17**).

One-axle trailer   Tandem-axle trailer

© Cengage Learning 2013

▶ **Figure 11-17**

Light-duty trailers may have only one axle, while trailers with high-rated carrying capacity usually have the tandem axles.

Trailer tandem axles can be grouped into two categories: fixed (stationary) and sliding.

Fixed tandem axle assemblies—include the suspension and subframe. The assembly is usually mounted directly on the frame rails of the trailer. The fixed (stationary) tandem axle assembly is placed to produce the best weight distribution between the tractor and the trailer. Weight adjustments between the tractor and trailer are then made by moving or shifting the load inside the trailer.

Sliding trailer tandem axle assemblies—are also mounted directly on the frame rails of the trailer. The difference is the subframe assembly allows the trailer axles and suspension to **slide,** or move, along the frame rails of the trailer. The part of the subassembly that slides is called the tandem axle slide. There is one slide on each side of the trailer **(see Figure 11-18).**

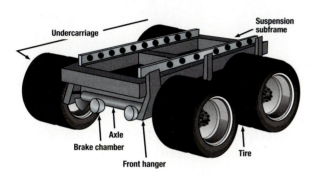
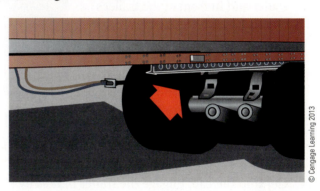

▶ Figure 11–18

The part of the subassembly that slides is called the "tandem axle slide."

There are evenly placed holes along the length of the slide. These holes are designed to seat four locking pins that are attached to a locking lever or handle called the **locking lever.** You engage the locking lever manually. There is no in-cab control switch. At the ends of the sliding rails are stops that keep the assembly from coming apart when you slide the axles.

Sliding the Trailer Tandem Axles

Sliding the trailer tandem axles is similar to sliding the fifth wheel. This also should be done off the road and on a level surface, away from hazards.

1. The trailer should be properly connected to the fifth wheel.
2. The kingpin should be locked into place.
3. The air and electrical lines should be connected to the trailer.
4. The sliding fifth wheel and the trailer's sliding tandem axle assembly must also be locked.
5. If you get out of the cab for any reason, be sure to set the tractor parking brakes. This will keep the tractor from rolling.

CAUTION!

Entry level drivers should be extremely careful when sliding trailer tandems. An older trailer is going to require additional attention and care, due to rusty tandem sliding mechanisms.

Additionally, because many shippers require the driver to slide the tandems all the way to the rear of the trailer prior to loading, new drivers should make certain they learn how to properly and safely slide the tandems to prevent/avoid damage.

6. Now you are ready to test the connection to the trailer by gently pulling forward with the trailer brake in the "on" position.

7. If you have just made the connection to the trailer, look at the connection to make sure the fifth-wheel jaws are locked around the kingpin of the trailer. Then raise the landing gear of the trailer.

8. Locate the locking lever, which is usually on the driver's side of the trailer and in front of the trailer's wheels. The lever is usually inside the lever guide that serves as a support. Some units have a safety lock on the locking lever to keep it from bouncing up and down while traveling **(see Figure 11-19)**. Placing wheel chocks both in front and behind the trailer tandems helps secure the trailer from moving.

▶ **Figure 11–19**

The pin or lug control lever is usually on the driver's side of the trailer, just in front of the trailer wheels.

9. Get into the cab. Engage the trailer brakes by either pulling down the trailer brake hand valve or pulling out the red trailer air supply valve. You now have your tractor brakes released and your trailer brakes engaged and are ready to slide the tandem axles.

CAUTION!

The lever controls four locking pins, two on each side of the trailer. Lift and pull this lever toward you until the grooves on the lever line up with the slot on the lever guide. Then slip the lever into the sideways slot. The slot will hold the lever in the unlocked position. Make sure the lever is firmly seated in the slot. Once the sides are unlocked, it is important to make sure all four locking pins are completely out of the holes on the slides **(see Figure 11-20).** If all pins are not out of the holes, you will have to repeat the unlocking procedures.

Due to a combination of being moved infrequently and road grime, the pins can sometimes be very difficult to release. Application of a cleaner/lubricant, such as WD-40, followed by tapping on the pin ends with a hammer may help loosen the pins up, and allow them to release. Having one person tap on the pin ends while a second pulls the release is also useful.

▶ **Figure 11–20**

Once you have unlocked the slides, make sure all four locking lugs are completely out of the holes in the slides.

10. If you are going to slide the tandem axles forward, put the tractor into reverse. If you want to slide the tandem axles toward the rear of the trailer, use low gear. With the tractor in gear, ease the tractor forward or backward gently.

11. Once you have moved the sliding tandem axle into position, follow these steps:
    - Put on the parking brakes.
    - Climb out of the truck.
    - Get back into the tractor.
    - Release the tractor brakes.
    - With trailer brakes left on, and tractor brakes released, gently move the rig forward or backward so that the pins will lock into the next set of holes.

12. When you move the sliding tandem axle, you change axle dimensions and will have a difference in your ride, weight distribution, and maneuverability (**see Figure 11-21**).

13. Decide how you want to set up your rig for loading before it is actually loaded. It is easier to make adjustments on an empty unit than on a loaded one. Even though it may be difficult in the beginning, you need to be skilled in anticipating the needs of each load.

← Tandems back
More off-tracking

→ Tandems forward
Overhang

© Cengage Learning 2013

◆ **Figure 11-21**

When you move the sliding tandem axles, you change axle dimensions and will have a difference in your ride, weight distribution, and maneuverability.

CAUTION!

Quick Review: Moving the Sliding Tandem Axle

1. Make sure the tractor is properly coupled to the trailer.
2. Set the tractor brakes.
3. Lift and pull the locking lever until the grooves slip into the sideways slot on the lever guide. This will disengage the locking pins.
4. Check to make sure all four pins are retracted properly.
5. Set the trailer brakes by pulling out the red trailer air supply valve or pulling down the trailer brake hand valve.
6. Release the tractor brakes by pushing in the yellow parking brake valve.
7. Ease the tractor forward to slide the tandem backward. Ease the tractor backward to slide the tandem forward.
8. Reset the tractor brakes by pulling out the yellow parking brake valve.
9. Release the locking lever. Place it into the locked position.
10. Release the tractor brakes.
11. With the trailer brakes still set, gently tug or push against the trailer to seat the locking pins.
12. Reset the tractor brakes.
13. Look at all four pins to make sure they are firmly seated through the holes of the tandem axle slides. Make sure the locking lever has remained locked and is secured.
14. Inspect the trailer air supply lines and make sure they are not hanging down.

STOP!
Always move the rig very gently and slowly when sliding the tandems to a new position. Moving too quickly can cause the tandems to shear the safety stops, and allow the tandems to slide out from underneath the trailer!

Remember—you have just made changes that will affect the handling of your rig.

How you adjust your fifth wheel and axle depends on a combination of factors, including the following:

- Distribution of weight
- Overall length laws
- Legal axle weight laws
- Bridge weight laws
- Handling stability
- Maneuverability
- Preventing damage to cargo

CAUTION!
Sliding the fifth wheel to adhere to load limits should be considered a complex process in which the driver must consider binding mechanisms, differing vehicle designs, and challenging topography.

INTERESTING FACT

In 1950, the Twin Company introduced a new concept for a freight-hauling truck with their Fageol Super Freightliner. This vehicle was, basically, a trailer fitted with a single-driving axle, under-floor engine and transmission. An unusual steering arrangement had the front axle pivoting on a platform around a fifth-wheel kingpin. This arrangement allowed use of dual wheels on the front axle.

DRIVER TIP

A good way to keep track of important information about how to balance loads is to keep a notebook on each customer, describing how you set up your rig for each load as well as directions for getting to the dock, phone numbers, and who to talk to. Also note days and hours of operation, when they ship, and whether an appointment is needed. Then you will be able to set your rig before it is loaded.

CAUTION!
To prevent the trailer from sliding into the cab or the tandems from sliding out from under the trailer, be sure to check the fifth-wheel stop plates and the stop bars, welds, and brackets of the trailer slides to be sure they are intact.

SUMMARY

In this chapter, you have learned the reasons for sliding the fifth wheel or the trailer tandem axles. You have also learned that doing this will change the distribution of weight as well as the overall length of the rig, the ride, maneuverability, and off-tracking of the trailer wheels. Correct ways to slide the fifth wheel and the tandem axle assembly have been explained and illustrated. Finally, you have an understanding of the hazards created when these procedures are not done properly.

KEY TERMS

Air-operated release
Binding
Bridge Formula
Fixed-mount fifth wheel
Frame rails
Inner bridge
Locking lever

Maneuverability
Manual release
Off-tracking
Outer bridge
Outer spread
Overweight trucks
Slide

Sliding fifth wheel
Sliding tandem axle
Sliding trailer tandem
   axle assemblies
Truck scales

A DAY IN THE LIFE...

Daniel Poorman – Gordon Trucking Inc., Professional Truck Driver

I have been a professional truck driver for 24 years and have worked for Gordon Trucking since 1992. While employed with Gordon Trucking I have logged 2,748,762 accident-free miles. My achievements were recognized on two different occasions as the Company Driver of the Month and when I won the title of Washington State's Driver of the Year with the Washington Trucking Association in 2002.

> ❝ **I gained all my experience from my dad.** ❞

I gained all my experience from my dad. He, also, won the title of Washington State's Driver of the Year in 1989 and I am proud to follow in his footsteps. He retired from trucking after 36 years of driving. I teamed with him the first two years of my career and learned how to become a successful truck driver. He taught me the importance of safety and patience.

I continually guide other drivers in safe practices and completed the Washington State Highway Watch Training Program in 2001 to be certified to identify and accurately report unsafe motorists, incidents of road rage, road hazards, changing road conditions, and to correctly direct medical response teams to scenes of accidents. In addition, I give driving tests to potential company drivers to review their driving skills and safety habits.

Like my father, I have always set high standards for myself and am very dedicated to my job and discipline of safety. I never miss a day of work, have never caused a load to be late, and I am always volunteering to take on extra work. I make sure I am always doing my job safely and attend additional safety classes outside my company. I do what I can to protect the environment by keeping my truck well maintained, keep idling to a minimum and my speed and R.P.M.s down to reduce fuel consumption. I take pride in my appearance and the appearance of my truck. I want to represent my company and the trucking industry well. I know people "judge a book by the cover" and the first impression needs to be a good one.

I give to the community by giving to the local businesses and supporting the school fundraisers. I have held fundraisers for our local music school and organized community garage sales for charity. I also donate regularly to our local food bank.

I am in it for the long haul!

REVIEW QUESTIONS

1. Which of the following can a sliding fifth wheel not influence?

   a. the overall length of the tractor-trailer

   b. the turning radius of the vehicle

   c. the weight on each of the axles

   d. the center of gravity of the trailer

2. Which of the following can sliding tandem axles on a trailer not influence?

   a. driver reaction time

   b. off-tracking of the trailer

   c. turning radius of the vehicle

   d. the balance of the weight on each of the axles on the trailer

3. Sliding tandem axles to the rear _____ the weight on the drive and steering axles.

   a. decreases

   b. has no effect on

   c. increases

   d. neither a, b, nor c

4. Which of the following is not a result of sliding the fifth wheel of a tractor forward?

   a. Less weight will be transferred to the steer axle.

   b. More weight will be transferred to the steer axle.

   c. The overall length of the vehicle will be shortened.

   d. The turning radius of the vehicle will be shortened.

5. The Bridge Formula is a national formula to adjust _____ designed to protect the country's roads and bridges.

   a. total payload weight

   b. maximum legal weight on steer axles

   c. maximum legal weight on each axle

   d. maximum legal vehicle weight

6. When turning your rig, the greater the distance between the steer axle and the pivot point (kingpin) of the trailer, _____.

   a. the less off-tracking there will be

   b. off-tracking is not affected

   c. the further the trailer will off-track

   d. neither a, b, nor c

7. For a rig with a fixed (stationary) fifth wheel and a properly loaded trailer, weight adjustments are made by _____.

   a. adding additional air pressure to all of the tires

   b. sliding the tandem axles of the trailer

   c. reducing the air pressure in all of the tires

   d. adjusting the center of gravity

8. Regarding sliding the fifth wheel, which of the following characteristics of the rig will not change?

   a. the overall length

   b. weight distribution

   c. maneuverability

   d. the weight on the rear axles

9. Regarding trailers with stationary tandem axles, which of the following is not a correct procedure for adjusting the weight between the tractor and trailer?

   a. moving the load inside the trailer

   b. shifting the load inside the trailer

   c. increasing the air pressure in the trailer tires

   d. a and b

10. Federal law states that _____ consecutive axles may not exceed the weight computed by the Bridge Formula even though single axles, tandem axles, and gross vehicle weights are within legal limits.

    a. no more than three

    b. at least four

    c. two or more

    d. half the total of

11. If you want to slide the fifth wheel forward _____.

    a. put on the brakes and shift down to neutral

    b. move the kingpin to the left and move the tractor forward

    c. put the tractor in reverse

    d. disconnect the air lines and put the tractor in neutral

12. If too much weight is shifted to the steer axles, all of the following will occur EXCEPT: _____.

    a. the tractor will be hard to steer

    b. the lights may not be aimed properly

    c. the rig will be easier to control

    d. the rig may be overweight on the steer axle

SUPPLEMENTAL LEARNING ACTIVITIES

1. Invite a seasoned professional to speak with the class and ask, specifically, about the best ways to release "binding" or move a "stuck" fifth wheel platform.

2. A hands-on exercise—sliding the fifth wheel—should be used to demonstrate the differences as well as reasons to slide the fifth wheel.

3. As an exercise, go to bridges in your area and inspect for erosion around the bridge footings, any rusted, cracked, or broken supports. It would also be interesting to call the city or county engineer's office to find out the last time the bridge you inspected was officially inspected as well as if any bridges in your area have been found to be unsafe. Report your findings to the class.

4. Discuss safety measures to be used when working to slide tandem axles or sliding the fifth wheel. Also, list the safety equipment needed to keep these tasks safe.

FOR MORE INFORMATION

Freight Management and Operations
www.ops.fhwa.dot.gov/freight/

Moving the Fifth Wheel on Your 18-Wheel Tractor-Trailer
www.truck-drivers-money-saving-tips.com/fifth-wheel.html

Council of Ministers—A detailed description of legal weights per axle and for various tractor-trailer configurations across North America
www.comt.ca/english/programs/trucking/NAFTA%20Side%20by%20Side%20Update%20May%202001.pdf

12 Preventive Maintenance and Servicing

© Baloncici/www.Shutterstock.com

OBJECTIVES

When you have completed this chapter, you should be able to:

- Know and understand the different types of maintenance.

- Find, identify, and know the basic function of the following vehicle components: frame, suspension, axles, engine, fuel system, lubrication system, cooling system, electrical system, drive train, brake systems, wheels, bearings, rims and tires, steering system, and coupling system.

- Correctly note problems or indications of possible problems for various systems on a Driver's Vehicle Inspection Report (DVIR).

- Know how to perform various simple maintenance procedures safely.

- Know your responsibilities in maintaining your rig, and which repairs are to be handled only by qualified technicians.

- Understand the inspection, repair, and maintenance requirements as stated in the Federal Motor Carriers Safety Regulations.

INTRODUCTION

Most major motor carriers today realize that newer, well-maintained, and clean equipment is a necessity for attracting the best professional drivers, instilling confidence in customers and conducting business in the safest and most efficient manner. Professional drivers also realize that rigs that are well maintained will do the job much more effectively and efficiently than those that are neglected **(see Figure 12-1).**

To keep a rig in good shape, a driver must know how to inspect that vehicle and all its parts. A vehicle that is not well maintained may break down, making it difficult to make pick-up or delivery appointments **(see Figure 12-2).** Moreover, breakdowns occurring over the road add to the professional driver's stress levels while making it difficult to perform the job in a timely, cost-effective manner.

© Baloncici/www.Shutterstock.com

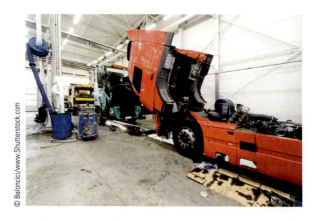

Figure 12-1

A well-maintained rig is necessary to do a safe and efficient job.

© Cengage Learning 2013

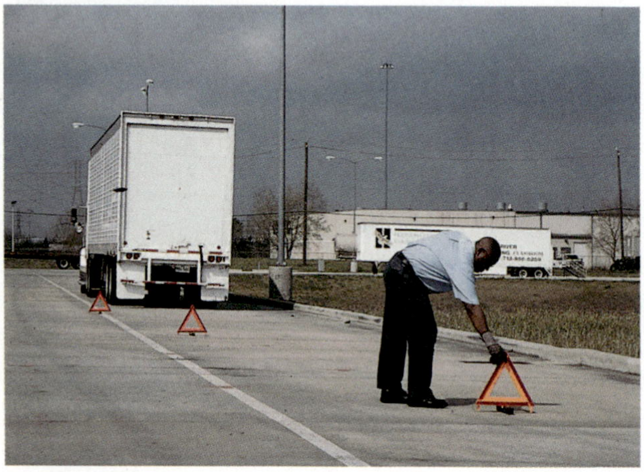

Figure 12-2

Reflective triangles should be correctly placed by driver, and removed after repairs have been made and before starting to drive again.

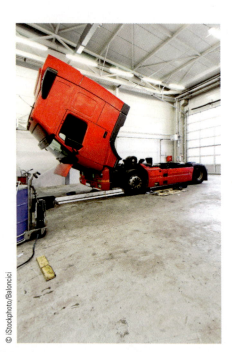

While some routine servicing tasks can be done by the driver, most service and repair work today should be done by trained maintenance personnel. When someone who is trained for the job does the servicing and maintenance, the cost is less and it takes less time. If someone who is not trained attempts to work on the rig, it is possible that the work will not be done correctly and, in some cases, if faulty work is done, more damage may be caused. Work not done by professional maintenance personnel may also result in accidents, injuries, or death. In every case, good, routine maintenance eliminates downtime, highway breakdowns, and other problems on the road **(see Figure 12-3).**

© iStockphoto/Baloncici

Figure 12-3

Most service and repair work today should be done by trained maintenance personnel.

This chapter is written with three goals in mind:

1. To teach the basic checks and servicing needed for the engine and vehicle
2. To show you how to perform some basic preventive maintenance and simple emergency repairs
3. To emphasize that drivers are not expected to be mechanics. Drivers should not try to do any maintenance or repair work unless they have been taught to do it and have experience repairing it under the guidance of a trained individual (**see Figure 12-4**).

PREVENTIVE MAINTENANCE

Preventive maintenance (PM) is the servicing done at regular intervals on a tractor and trailer. By servicing the tractor regularly, many costly emergency repairs can be avoided and small problems can be fixed before they develop into larger ones (**see Figure 12-5**).

In many fleets, even the most routine maintenance is performed by a maintenance department, a dealer, an independent garage, or a truck leasing company. Drivers are not permitted to do any maintenance work. Other carriers, however, require the driver to perform certain minor maintenance tasks as part of his or her job. Independent owner-operators generally do more maintenance than those who drive company-owned vehicles.

TYPES OF MAINTENANCE

There are three types of maintenance:

- Routine servicing
- Scheduled preventive maintenance
- Unscheduled maintenance and repair

Routine Servicing

Routine servicing can be done by drivers. These tasks include the following:

- Adding fuel
- Checking and adding oil
- Adding coolant
- Draining moisture from fuel and air systems

Scheduled Preventive Maintenance

Scheduled preventive maintenance is servicing based on time or mileage since the last maintenance. Most fleets have a regular preventive maintenance schedule, although it is the driver's responsibility to inform the shop of repairs that are needed or failures that occur between scheduled inspections.

▶ **Figure 12-4**

Regular, routine maintenance eliminates downtime and other problems on the road.

▶ **Figure 12-5**

Preventive maintenance helps avoid costly emergency repairs.

Most preventive maintenance is often set up under four schedules.

Level A—at 15,000 to 25,000 miles/24,000 to 40,000 kilometers—may be combined with level B services.

Includes:

- Grease job
- Oil change
- Filter change
- Checking all fluid levels

Level B—same as level A but more involved. If combined with level A, approximately every 15,000 miles/24,000 kilometers; if not combined, typically every 25,000 miles/40,000 kilometers.

Includes:

- All of level A
- Inspection and maintenance of key components such as lubricating water pump shaft

Level C—conducted every 100,000 to 120,000 miles/160,000 to 192,000 kilometers.

Includes:

- All level A and level B maintenance
- Engine tune-up
- Detailed inspection of all major components
- Road test

Level D—conducted at 500,000 to 750,000 miles/800,000 to 1,200,000 kilometers.

Includes:

- All of level A, level B, and level C
- Rebuilding parts
- Alternator
- Replace all engine drive belts

© Cengage Learning 2013

▶ *"A qualified technician might be able to shed some light on that rattling noise."*

Unscheduled Maintenance and Repair

Unscheduled maintenance and repair occurs when unexpected breakdowns or emergencies require immediate maintenance and includes the following:

- Breakdowns en route or on deliveries
- Repair of accident damage
- Problems found and listed during a driver's pretrip or posttrip inspection report

FEDERAL MOTOR VEHICLE INSPECTION AND MAINTENANCE REQUIREMENTS

All professional drivers must learn what the **Federal Motor Carrier Safety Regulations (FMCSR)** require and then must meet these requirements. Every motor carrier, its officers, drivers, agents, representatives, and employees directly concerned with inspection or maintenance of commercial motor vehicles must comply and be conversant with these rules.

FMCSR Part 396 requires professional drivers to do the following:

Part 396 Inspection, Repair, and Maintenance:

1. The report must list any condition that the driver either found or had reported to him that would affect safety of operation or cause a breakdown. If no defect or deficiency is reported or found, the report should state this.

2. The driver must sign the report in all cases.

3. Before dispatching the vehicle again, a carrier shall ensure that a certification has been made as to any defect or deficiency, that they have been corrected, or state those deficiencies that do not require immediate correction. Carriers must keep the original posttrip inspection report and the certification of repairs for at least three months from the date of preparation.

4. Before starting out, the driver must be satisfied that the motor vehicle is in safe operating condition. If the last vehicle inspection report notes any deficiencies, the driver must review and sign to acknowledge that necessary repairs have been completed.

Periodic Inspection

Every commercial vehicle, including each segment of a combination vehicle, requires periodic inspection that must be performed at least once every 12 months. The original or a copy of the periodic inspection report must be retained by the motor carrier for 14 months from the report date. Documentation (report, sticker, or decal) of the most recent periodic inspection must be kept on the vehicle.

DRIVER'S VEHICLE INSPECTION REPORT (DVIR)

Results of the posttrip inspection must be entered on an official **Driver's Vehicle Inspection Report (DVIR) (see Figure 12-6).** The form must be completed even if no defects are found. The driver must make an accurate report of everything found on the posttrip inspection. Then, after accurately and legibly completing the form, the driver must sign and date the document. The report must then be delivered to the supervisor.

Driver's Vehicle Inspection Report

Check Any Defective Item and Give Details Under "Remarks,"

DATE _____

TRUCK/TRACTOR NO. _____

☐ Air Compressor
☐ Air Lines
☐ Battery
☐ Brake Accessories
☐ Brakes
☐ Carburetor
☐ Clutch
☐ Defroster
☐ Drive Line
☐ Engine
☐ Fifth Wheel
☐ Front Axle
☐ Fuel Tanks
☐ Heater

☐ Horn
☐ Lights
    Head - Stop
    Tail - Dash
    Turn Indicators
☐ Mirrors
☐ Muffler
☐ Oil Pressure
☐ Electronic On-Board
    Recorder
☐ Radiator
☐ Rear End
☐ Reflectors
☐ Safety Equipment
    Fire Extinguisher
    Flags-Flares-Fusees
    Spare Bulbs & Fuses
    Spare Seal Beam

☐ Springs
☐ Starter
☐ Steering
☐ Tachograph
☐ Tires
☐ Transmission
☐ Wheels
☐ Windows
☐ Windshield Wipers
☐ Other

TRAILER(S) NO.(S) _____

☐ Brake Connections
☐ Brakes
☐ Coupling Chains
☐ Coupling (King) Pin
☐ Doors

☐ Hitch
☐ Landing Gear
☐ Lights—All
☐ Roof
☐ Springs

☐ Tarpaulin
☐ Tires
☐ Wheels
☐ Other

Remarks: _____
_____
_____
_____
_____
_____
_____

☐ CONDITION OF THE ABOVE VEHICLE IS SATISFACTORY

DRIVER'S SIGNATURE _____

☐ ABOVE DEFECTS CORRECTED
☐ ABOVE DEFECTS NEED NOT BE CORRECTED FOR SAFE OPERATION OF VEHICLE

MECHANIC'S SIGNATURE _____ DATE _____

DRIVER'S SIGNATURE _____ DATE _____

Courtesy of the US Department of Transportation, Federal Motor Carrier Safety Administration.

Figure 12-6

Driver's Vehicle Inspection Report.

Importance of Preventive Maintenance

Failure to perform preventive maintenance can increase the cost of operation. For example, breakdowns on the road may include these extra costs:

- Cargo transfer charge
- Late delivery charge
- Expensive road services such as towing and out-of-town repairs
- Driver expenses while not driving, such as food and lodging

▶ **Figure 12-7**

A poorly tuned engine means longer trip time.

© Baloncici/www.Shutterstock.com

Operating Costs

Vehicles that are poorly maintained cost more to operate; for example, fuel costs are higher. A poorly tuned engine gets fewer miles/kilometers per gallon and requires longer trip times than a highly tuned engine (**see Figure 12-7**). A breakdown on the road can result in an accident. Of course, this adds to expenses and decreases trip efficiency. The extra costs can include repairing the damage, lost work time, medical expenses, and increased company insurance rates.

BASIC SERVICE AND ROUTINE MAINTENANCE

Drivers should understand and perform basic servicing and routine maintenance, such as:

- Inspect and change engine fluids, certain filters, lights, and fuses
- Drain moisture from air reservoirs and fuel systems

Checking and Changing Engine Fluids, Filters, Lights, and Fuses

This section will discuss the correct maintenance procedures for the following:

- Fuel filter
- Oil level and oil filter
- Coolant level and coolant filter
- Battery fluid level, if applicable
- Power steering fluid level
- Air filter element
- Lights and bulbs
- Fuses and circuit breakers

Checking the Fuel Fluid Level

1. Park the rig on level ground.
2. Open fuel cap.
3. Check the fuel level. Make sure it matches the gauge reading in the cab.

Changing the Fuel Filter Element

1. Use gloves that will not absorb the fuel. This is a messy job.
2. If you use a filter wrench to remove the old **fuel filter,** be sure to use it at the bottom of the filter so you will not crush the filter shell **(see Figure 12-8).**
3. Turn the fuel filter element counterclockwise until it comes off the base.
4. Clean the surface of the seal on the filter base. Be sure to always remove the old seal and use a new one.
5. Wipe off any fuel that may have spilled when you took off the filter.
6. Fill the new filter with clean fuel.
7. Screw the filter onto the base until the seal touches the base.
8. Tighten the filter one-half turn.
9. Start the engine. Check for leaks.
10. Discard the old filter element according to EPA standards.

Courtesy of Baker College of Flint

▶ **Figure 12-8**

Changing the fuel filter element.

Replacing the Filter

The following method of replacing the filter is general in nature. There are many types of fuel filter systems. To find the correct way to replace your filter, read the manufacturer's instructions.

1. Turn off the fuel supply from the fuel tanks.
2. Place a container under the filter.
3. Open the drain cock in the filter housing base.

4. Drain the filter.

5. Remove the filter body with the element. If you use a filter wrench, be sure to use it at the bottom of the filter so you will not crush the filter shell.

6. Discard the filter element according to EPA guidelines.

7. Clean the housing.

8. Close the drain cock.

9. Install the new filter in the housing.

10. Fill the housing with clean fluid.

11. Install the filter housing containing the new filter element with a gasket. Always use a new seal.

12. Lubricate with fuel or engine oil and tighten.

13. Open the fuel line shut-off valve.

14. Start the engine.

15. Check for leaks.

Draining the Fuel Filter

To drain a fuel filter:

1. Locate the filter and water separator.

2. Remove the drain plug at the bottom of the filter.

3. Allow the water to drain.

4. Replace the drain plug.

Checking the Oil Level

To check the oil level, follow these steps:

1. Park the vehicle on level ground.

2. Shut off the engine.

3. Wait a few minutes for the oil to drain down.

4. Find the dipstick and remove it.

5. Wipe it clean and replace it.

6. Pull it out again.

7. Check the oil level.

The oil level should be between the "full" and the "add" marks. Do not over-fill or drive when the oil level is below the "add" mark. Be careful not to overfill when you need to add oil (**see Figure 12-9**).

Typical Lubricating System

1. Oil from main gallery
2. Oil fill tube
3. Rocker and drain
4. Cam pocket drain
5. Oil drain from blower or turbocharger
6. Full-flow oil filter
7. Bypass oil filter
8. Oil cooler
9. Drain to oil pan
10. Oil pick-up screen

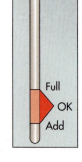

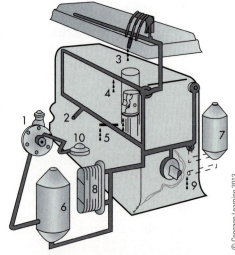

© Cengage Learning 2013

▶ Figure 12-9

Be careful not to overfill when adding oil.

Changing the Oil Filter

Changing the **oil filter** on a tractor is a messy but important task. It is far harder than changing a car's oil filter. Like fuel systems, what is right for changing the filter on one system may be wrong for another type of system.

CAUTION!

Change filters only after you have been trained and checked out by your supervisor or mechanic.

To change an oil filter, follow these steps:

1. Remove the drain plug from the bottom of the filter housing.
2. Drain the oil.
3. Remove the filter housing that contains the filter element. Most filters today are one piece and disposable.
4. Discard the old filter according to EPA standards.
5. Fill the new filter element with clean oil and install it.
6. Secure the housing.
7. Replace the drain plug.
8. Start the engine.

Checking the Coolant Level

To check the **coolant** level, follow these steps:

1. Shut off the engine.
2. Wait until the engine is cool.
3. Put on thick gloves to protect your hands.
4. Remove the radiator cap carefully. Turn the cap slowly to the first stop. Step back while pressure is released from the cooling system.
5. When all of the pressure is released, press down on the cap and remove it.
6. Look at the level of the coolant.
7. Do not add water.
8. Add coolant if needed. Ask maintenance for specific instructions.

GO!

Many tractors now have sight-glasses or see-through containers for checking coolant levels. If your rig has one, you will not need to go through the previous routine to check the coolant level. If the coolant level becomes too low, you simply add coolant to the reservoir.

Changing the Coolant Filter

To change the **coolant filter,** follow these steps:

1. Shut off the engine.
2. Wait until the engine is cool.
3. Put on thick gloves. Do not handle a hot filter with your bare hands.
4. Turn the filter element counterclockwise to remove it.
5. Replace it with a new filter element and a new cover gasket.
6. Start the engine.
7. Check for leaks.

Checking the Battery Fluid Level

CAUTION!

Be very careful when checking the level of the **battery fluid.** Follow these safety rules **(see Figure 12-10).**

1. Protect your eyes with safety goggles or glasses.
2. Protect your hands because batteries contain substances that can burn your skin.
3. Do not smoke because batteries give off explosive gases.

Courtesy of 5th Wheel Training Institute (1-888-647-7202)

▶ **Figure 12–10**

Follow the safety rules when checking battery fluid.

Some batteries are maintenance free and do not need to have the level of the fluid checked. Others are not and must have the level of the fluid in the battery checked. Follow these steps to check the battery fluid level:

1. Open battery caps.
2. Check the fluid level.
3. If the battery needs fluid, use distilled water.
4. Fill to the bottom of the split ring in the cell filler well.

Checking the Power Steering Fluid Level

With the engine running at normal operating temperature, turn the steering wheel back and forth several times to stabilize the **power steering fluid** level. To check the fluid level, follow these steps:

1. Turn off the engine.
2. Remove the dipstick.
3. The fluid should be between the bottom of the dipstick and the full mark.
4. If fluid is needed, add enough to raise the level to the full mark but do not overfill.

Changing the Air Filter Element

Dust, dirt, grease, and grime can get into an engine when you change the air filter. Be careful to keep the area as clean as possible. On air cleaners with a restriction indicator, change the element or clean it when the indicator shows "red." On tractors or trucks that have an air filter restriction gauge, consult a mechanic for information on when to change the element.

To change the **air filter element,** follow these steps:

1. Remove the end covering from the housing.
2. Make sure hands are clean.
3. Remove filter element.
4. Inspect the end cover and gasket surfaces for dents or possible air leaks.
5. Check the outlet tube to be sure it is clean and undamaged.
6. Check the filter element for wear.
7. Replace the element if it is damaged.
8. If the filter is not damaged, clean with compressed air. NOTE: OSHA does not permit cleaning with compressed air in excess of 30 psi (207 kPa).

    Always blow the air in the opposite direction of the normal cleaner flow. Some filters should not be blown out. If your unit does not have an indicator or air filter restriction gauge, find out how often to replace it.
9. Wipe away any dirt in the filter housing.
10. Install the filter element.
11. Replace the end cover and secure.

STOP!
When driving in winter weather conditions it is possible for snow or ice to accumulate around the air intake for the air filter(s), and may cause the engine to lose power, over heat, or even stop. Always check the air intake when driving in heavy snow each time you stop for a break.

CAUTION!
Always handle the filter element carefully to keep dirt from shaking loose onto the clean side of the filter system **(see Figure 12-11).**

Courtesy of Baker College of Flint

▶ Figure 12–11

Always change the air filter carefully to avoid getting dirt on the clean filter.

Changing a Bulb in a Headlight or Clearance Light

To change a headlight bulb or a clearance light, follow these steps:

1. Park the rig and turn off the engine.
2. Remove the trim ring from the burned-out light.
3. Unfasten the mounting screws.
4. Disconnect and remove the light from the socket. The bulb may be hot, so handle carefully.
5. Clean any dirt or bugs off the socket area.
6. Plug in the new headlight bulb.
7. Test the light to see if it works properly.
8. Fasten the mounting screw.
9. Make sure the new light is clean.

CAUTION!

New halogen style headlights are very high temp and are extremely sensitive to any grease and oils that could be transferred from the driver's hand into the light bulb. These greases and oils greatly reduce the life expectancy of the bulb. Do not touch the glass portion of the new bulb.

STOP!

Do not touch the headlight adjusting screws when you are changing the bulb!

Changing Fuses and Resetting Circuit Breakers

Fuses—always use a **fuse** that is the right size and has the same amp rating as the fuse it replaces (**see Figure 12-12**).

▶ **Figure 12–12**
Closeup of fuse box.

Courtesy of Baker College of Flint

To change a fuse, follow these steps:

1. Check the fuse and clip holder to be sure they are clean and do not have any burrs.
2. If the holder is dirty, touch up the contact points with a coarse cloth.
3. Gently but firmly snap the new fuse into the clip holder.
4. Make sure there is a good connection between the fuse ends and the fuse holder.

   Circuit breaker—To reset the **circuit breaker,** follow these steps:

1. Remove the circuit breaker cover panel.
2. Flip the circuit breaker switch back to reset it.
3. Replace the panel.

Some circuit breakers reset themselves.

CHECKING TIRE AIR PRESSURE

As a professional driver, you should *never* change tires. Allow only qualified mechanics with proper tools and safeguards to change tires because this is extremely dangerous.

To check air pressure:

1. Make sure tires are cool before you check the air pressure.
2. Remove the valve stem cap.
3. Place the air gauge over the valve stem opening.
4. Read the inflation pressure from the gauge.
5. Compare the tire's pressure with the correct pressure listed on the sidewall of the tire.
6. Replace the valve stem cap.

STOP!
A tire that is 20 pounds below recommended psi/kPa should not be reinflated by the driver. This task is dangerous and could cause serious injury or death.

DRAINING THE AIR RESERVOIRS

If your air tanks have drain valves, drain the **air reservoirs** as follows:

1. Park the truck on level ground.
2. Open the draincocks by twisting the valve on the bottom of the tank.
3. Allow all of the air pressure to escape. The air pressure gauge will read 0 psi/kPa. This will let the moisture drain out **(see Figure 12-13).**
4. Close the valve.

▶ **Figure 12-13**
When air pressure gauge reads "0 psi/kPa," moisture will drain from air reservoirs.

CAUTION!

Drain the wet tank first to prevent moisture from being drawn further into the air system and other tanks.

ADJUSTING THE TRACTOR-TRAILER BRAKES

Some carriers require their drivers to make minor brake adjustments. Drivers must be certified to adjust brakes and, when asked to do so, must follow company policy. Many tractors and trailers now have automatic slack adjusters, but these also need to be checked regularly for proper adjustment.

Learn what type of braking system your rig has, and know what your employer expects from you as a driver regarding keeping the brakes in proper working order. For your personal safety and the safety of those who share the road, be sure any person who works on your brakes is qualified for the specific braking system on your rig **(see Figure 12-14).**

WITHIN AN INCH OF YOUR LIFE

IF BRAKE SLACK EXCEEDS ONE INCH, YOU COULD BE DRIVING A "KILLER TRUCK".

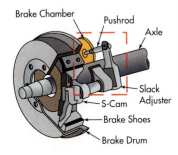

THIS IS THE MOST IMPORTANT INCH OF YOUR LIFE.

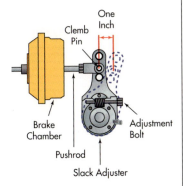

BRAKES SHOULD BE CHECKED BEFORE EACH TRIP AND MORE FREQUENTLY IN HILLY AREAS.

TRUCKERS! Poorly adjusted brakes could cost you time and money with out-of-service violations, jeopardize your safety and that of others due to impaired stopping ability, and even cost you your life. The only way to be sure that your vehicle's brakes are properly adjusted is to physically check each wheel on a regular schedule. It is difficult for you to sense, simply from pedal feel, that your brakes are out of adjustment. Under normal braking conditions, your brakes may respond satisfactorily, but under a hard panic stop you may find that you are unable to stop in time.

HOW TO CHECK

Before checking or making adjustments, be sure that your vehicle is parked on a level surface with the wheels blocked, spring brakes released, and the engine shut off. The following measurements are for *Type 30 air chamber brakes only*. For other types, check with your mechanic, supervisor, or manufacturer.

One-person method: (1) Pull the chamber pushrod to its limit by hand or by prying with a short pry bar. (2) Measure from the clevis pin to the chamber face at both full retraction and at full extension. The difference between the measurements is the pushrod travel or slack. One-half inch (12.7 mm) is correct, and the *MAXIMUM ALLOWABLE TRAVEL IS ONE INCH* (25.4 MM) (one-person method).

Two-person method: Make the same measurements described in the one-person method, but with brakes fully applied and with brakes released. Because of the considerable stretching and bending of various parts when using the two-person method, the *MAXIMUM ALLOWABLE TRAVEL IS TWO INCHES* (50.8 MM) for Type 30 air chamber brakes.

HOW TO ADJUST

Brake adjustment, or "taking up the slack," is done by first making sure the brakes are released, then turning the adjusting bolt on the slack adjuster arm: (1) Depress the spring locking sleeve with a wrench. (2) Tighten the bolt until solid resistance is met. This indicates that the brake linings are touching the drum.

NOTE: Most adjusting bolts require a normal clockwise turn to "set up" the brakes, but some require a counterclockwise turn. Be alert for any outward movement of the chamber pushrod and slack adjuster arm while the adjustment bolt is being turned. This movement means you are turning in the wrong direction.

(3) Restore running clearance by backing off the adjustment between one-quarter and one-half a turn. Re-check the pushrod travel. Proper adjustment leaves one-half an inch, or 12.7 mm. (4) Check each brake drum or rotor for excessive heat soon after the brakes have been adjusted. An extra-hot brake drum means that you have adjusted the brakes too tightly.

For both this type and other types of brake systems, always check with the manufacturer for proper maintenance and adjustment procedures. If you are not comfortable with these procedures, ask your mechanic or supervisor.

© Cengage Learning 2013

 Figure 12–14

Have a qualified person regularly inspect your brakes.

CANADIAN VEHICLE INSPECTION STATIONS

Like U.S. weigh stations, vehicle inspection stations are located along Canadian highways, and when the adjacent signs signal the inspection station is open, the professional driver is required to stop for an inspection.

Vehicles and loads are checked for weight, height, length, width, and axle spacing.

STOP!

Canadian Ministry of Transportation officers or members of the Royal Canadian Mounted Police (RCMP) also check registration permits and licenses to make certain that a "for hire" carrier has authority to be carrying the goods they are hauling.

Driver's licenses are also checked for validity and to assure the driver has the proper class license for the vehicle he or she is driving.

During these inspection stops, drivers are required to produce documents to assure they meet regulations and legislative requirements, such as log books documenting hours worked, daily trip inspections, current medical card, and proof of commercial vehicle operator registration.

STOP!

Any time a police officer or ministry officer directs a driver to drive to an inspection station, the driver must comply and must assist with the inspection if requested. Inspections may be conducted on the side of any Canadian highway at any time.

Commercial motor vehicles are subject to safety checks for brakes, lights, couplings, and other systems.

Drivers refusing to proceed to a weigh scale are guilty of an offense and may be fined anywhere from $200 to $1,000. The driver's license may also be suspended for 30 days. Drivers refusing to redistribute or remove part of a load or make arrangements to do so, or any drivers who obstruct weighing, measuring, or inspection are guilty of an offense and may be fined $100 to $200.

The Canadian Annual Inspection Certificate

Carriers or independent operations are required to have every vehicle and trailer inspected each year by a licensed motor vehicle inspection mechanic. The mechanic must check to ensure that each vehicle and trailer complies with all maintenance requirements. Component performance standards must be detailed in the applicable regulations and schedules of the Highway Traffic Act.

If the vehicle/trailer meets these standards and requirements, the motor vehicle inspection mechanic completes an inspection certificate. The certificate is issued with a corresponding decal, which indicates the vehicle type and the month and year of the inspection. The mechanic then places the decal on the outside lower left corner of the windshield or left side of the truck cab or the outside surface of the front side of the trailer, semi-trailer, or trailer converter dolly.

> ### STOP!
> Drivers in Canada also are responsible for ensuring that the vehicle they are driving is fit for highway use. As part of your daily inspection routine, verify that the date on the inspection certificate decal on each piece of equipment is still valid.

SUMMARY

In this chapter, you learned what types of maintenance are needed for the various systems on your rig. You learned that preventive maintenance keeps the need for unscheduled or emergency maintenance to a minimum. The types of reports that you, as a professional driver, will be expected to fill out and turn into your carrier's maintenance department were described. You also read about how to do certain basic routine maintenance and servicing, and you understand that, under no circumstances, should you ever attempt to change a tire on your rig.

KEY TERMS

Air filter element
Air reservoir
Battery fluid
Circuit breaker
Coolant
Coolant filter
Driver's Vehicle Inspection
  Report (DVIR)

Federal Motor Carrier Safety
  Regulations (FMCSR)
Fuel filter
Fuse
Oil filter
Power steering fluid
Pre-employment Screening
  Program

Preventive maintenance (PM)
Routine servicing
Scheduled preventive
  maintenance
Unscheduled maintenance
  and repair
Vehicle Condition Report
  (VCR)

REVIEW QUESTIONS

1. To keep a rig in good shape, a driver must know how to _____.

   a. inspect the vehicle and all its parts
   b. change a tire
   c. change the oil
   d. adjust the brakes

2. Preventive maintenance is _____.

   a. repairs to a rig as needed
   b. repairs to the trailer as needed
   c. the inspection done by a driver before the rig is driven
   d. the servicing done at regular intervals

3. Which of the following is not a type of maintenance?

    a. routine servicing

    b. scheduled repairs

    c. the driver's pretrip inspection

    d. unscheduled repairs

4. Regarding federal motor vehicle inspection and maintenance requirements, which of the following is not a Federal Motor Carrier Safety Regulation (FMCSR) that a driver must meet?

    a. Perform a pretrip inspection.

    b. Couple tractor to trailer.

    c. Review the last daily vehicle inspection report.

    d. Sign the last inspection report and confirm mechanic has completed any needed work on the rig.

5. Which of the following is not a requirement of a driver regarding a Driver's Vehicle Inspection Report (DVIR)?

    a. The report must be completed even if no defects are found.

    b. If defects are found in the posttrip inspection, the DVIR must be delivered to the head mechanic.

    c. The driver must make an accurate report of everything found.

    d. The DVIR must be signed and dated by the driver.

6. Regarding basic servicing and routine maintenance, which of the following should a driver not do?

    a. Inspect and change engine fluids and certain filters.

    b. Change a tire/wheel.

    c. Drain moisture from air reservoirs.

    d. Inspect and change lights and fuses.

7. Regarding checking the coolant level, which of the following is not a correct statement?

    a. Shut off the engine.

    b. Wait until the engine is cool.

    c. Remove the radiator cap very carefully.

    d. Add water if the coolant level is low.

8. Regarding changing a bulb in a headlight, which of the following is not a correct step?

    a. Turn off the engine.

    b. Clean any dirt or bugs off the socket area.

    c. Fasten the mounting screw.

    d. Always change the headlight adjusting screws because the vibration of the vehicle will cause them to get out of adjustment.

9. Regarding checking the air pressure in the tires of a rig, which of the following is not a correct statement?

    a. Place the air gauge over the stem opening.

    b. Compare the reading with the pressure listed on the sidewall.

    c. The tires should be hot to get a true valve reading.

    d. Replace the valve stem cap.

10. Regarding draining the air reservoirs, which of the following is not a correct statement?

    a. Chock the wheels.

    b. Open the draincocks.

    c. Allow the air pressure to escape.

    d. Park the rig on a hill with the front of the rig pointing downhill so the water will run out of the tanks.

11. Documentation (report, sticker, or decal) of the most recent periodic inspection must be kept _____.

    a. with the driver's papers

    b. on the vehicle

    c. by the company

    d. on the driver

12. If you are assigned a vehicle that had deficiencies noted on the DVIR by the driver who brought it in from Phoenix yesterday, before taking it on your assigned run, you must _____.

    a. decline to drive it

    b. assume repairs have been done

    c. find driver, have him/her sign report, saying repairs have been made

    d. inspect and sign report, saying vehicle is safe to drive

13. Posttrip inspection reports must be kept on file at least 3 months. The _____ keeps the reports.

    a. driver who signed report

    b. carrier for the maintenance department

    c. State Department of Transportation

    d. mechanic who usually works on specific vehicle

SUPPLEMENTAL LEARNING ACTIVITIES

1. Breakdowns on the road are costly, both in time and money. Divide the class into teams. Assign each team a common problem causing a breakdown on the road and have team members survey a number of mechanics in your area regarding repair costs plus towing charges plus time required to repair problem. Have them bring their findings back to the class. Problems could be: shredded tire, poorly-functioning brakes, light system problems, oil alarm warning (when oil level becomes too low for safe operation), pyrometer warning (when exhaust temperatures are too high), load distribution, and others.

2. Ask an experienced professional driver to visit the class to discuss the importance of careful inspection and consistent vehicle maintenance. Ask about their experiences of handling breakdowns on the highway.

3. Write a 100-word report about the dangers associated with vehicle batteries and necessary safety precautions.

4. With the class in groups, role play a professional driver's call to dispatch because of a breakdown or an out-of-service order. Assign a specific problem to each group without letting the other groups know and have those groups guess—from the driver's description of what happened—the type of problem that has occurred.

5. Discuss, as a class, the importance of rig and cargo security when pulled over by a mechanical problem. What precautions should the professional driver take?

FOR MORE INFORMATION

PTDI—Check and Maintain Vehicle Systems and Components, Page 17, Click on Skill Standards
www.ptdi.org/standards

Commercial Vehicle Safety Alliance—Roadcheck
www.cvsa.org/programs/int_roadcheck.php

U.S. DOT Roadcheck 2011
fastlane.dot.gov/2011/06/roadcheck-2011.html

13 Recognizing and Reporting Malfunctions

© K. Miri Photography/www.Shutterstock.com

OBJECTIVES

When you have completed this chapter, you should be able to:

■ Know when vehicle systems and parts are not working correctly.

■ Use the senses of sight, sound, feel, and smell to detect problems.

■ Discuss the importance of the professional driver being able to completely and accurately describe to maintenance personnel how the vehicle is functioning.

■ Safely start a vehicle with a dead battery or without air pressure if it has an air starter.

■ Know the procedures in reporting a malfunction.

■ Complete a Driver's Vehicle Inspection Report.

INTRODUCTION

Tractor-trailer drivers are not expected to be mechanics. Most companies have a policy that clearly describes what repairs and adjustments may and may not be done by drivers (see Figure 13-1). This chapter will help you understand what is generally expected of a driver. You will learn about common mechanical problems, how to identify them, and what to do if they occur.

In some cases, the correct action will be to adjust a simple part. In other cases, you will be told to move on to the nearest mechanic or call the company maintenance department for instructions.

You will learn how to use common sense and apply what you know. You also will learn to do only what you are capable of doing, be concerned about safety, and follow company policies (see Figure 13-2).

▶ Figure 13-1

As a professional driver you may perform certain simple repairs and adjustments to your vehicle.

DRIVER RESPONSIBILITY

- Know company maintenance policy
- Identify sources of problems
- Diagnose and fix simple problems when policy permits
- Report symptoms correctly

▶ Figure 13-2

Knowing your exact responsibilities will make you more efficient and effective in your job.

DIAGNOSING AND REPORTING MALFUNCTIONS

Many new trucks have electronic controls that detect problems and sound buzzers or flash warning lights. From these warnings, drivers can often diagnose a problem. Although you are not expected to become a mechanic, you should be knowledgeable enough of the various systems to find the source of the problem. This section will discuss how to gather information and report it to the mechanic. If this is done correctly, the mechanic can usually pinpoint the problem and come to the site with proper tools and parts.

Driver Awareness

Driver awareness is vital. In Chapter 8 on shifting, the ability to sense the engine's rpms was mentioned. This same awareness, using the senses and intuition, is also necessary in being able to diagnose a rig's problems (see Figure 13-3).

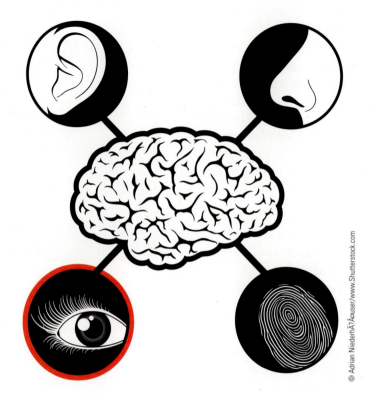

▶ **Figure 13–3**

Driver awareness is vital.

© Adrian NiederhÄ?Äœuser/www.Shutterstock.com

GO!

Familiarize yourself with all gauge indicator positions during normal operations. With this knowledge, if one gauge indicator is in a position that is different from normal, you'll immediately notice it during routine scans of your instruments.

Seeing

- Look at the instrument gauges and exhaust smoke.
- Look for fluid leaks, damaged tires, and missing wheel lugs.
- A good flashlight is an essential tool in seeing defects, especially in poorly lit environments.

Hearing

- Listen for any unusual engine noises, air leaks, or other sounds.
- Listen to the rhythm of the tires on the pavement as well as road sounds.
- Listen for the typical sounds occurring when increasing or decreasing speed, turning the wheels, and/or applying the brakes.

Feeling

- Feel for vibrations, thumps, and swaying that is not normal for your truck.
- Feel the rhythm of tires on pavement.

Smelling

- Be aware when you smell diesel fuel, smoke, other fumes, or burning rubber.

Report any symptoms or irregularities to your service department. By using your senses, you can notice a defect before it develops into a breakdown, a costly repair, or an accident.

Intuition

■ Some people call it "a feeling." Others call it "a hunch," but many professional drivers, especially those with experience often know, intuitively, when something isn't exactly right with their vehicle. This intuition, when coupled with one of the senses, help a driver know when a system is getting ready to fail.

GO!

If you understand the electronic diagnostics on your tractor, you may be able to help the mechanic pinpoint the problem that needs repair.

Early Detection of Malfunctions

By using your senses and noticing symptoms and irregularities early, you can cut repair costs. Problems that are found and fixed in their early stages can prevent major damage from occurring. This means repairs will be minor and the vehicle will spend less time in the shop while operating more efficiently.

If you work for a company, your supervisor will be impressed with your efficiency and production **(see Figure 13-4)**. If you own the truck, you will be able to drive more and spend less for repairs.

EARLY DETECTION OF MALFUNCTIONS

Early detection of malfunctions results in:

■ Lower maintenance expense   ■ Longer vehicle life

■ Minimum downtime   ■ Lower operating costs

■ Fewer accidents

© Cengage Learning 2013

▶ **Figure 13-4**

Using your senses and your experience can help head off major problems and damage.

When problems are noticed early and corrected, there is not as much chance for equipment failure or accidents. The tractor will probably last longer and, most importantly, your chances of being stranded down the road will be reduced.

STOP!

As a professional driver, you will learn and develop a wide variety of skills. However, you cannot adjust your rig's air brakes unless you have completed an approved air brake adjustment course or you are a certified mechanic.

Driver Responsibility

Your company should have a **maintenance policy,** and you should know what they expect from you. You will not have to be an expert, but you should be able to identify the sources of **malfunctions** and diagnose and fix simple problems. How much you are allowed to do and what you do will depend on the company maintenance policy.

STOP!

Do not try to fix any problem unless the maintenance policy permits and you have specific training to do so.

Maintenance Technician Responsibility

The technician should:

- Learn about system failures from reading driver reports or listening to driver descriptions.
- Diagnose the causes of the problem.
- Correct any malfunctions and/or replace any defective parts.
- Ensure the problem or failure has been fixed before releasing the truck for further use.

Driver and Technician Joint Responsibility

Drivers and technicians must work together if the company is to benefit. A driver can be very helpful by knowing the rig and reporting all problems—large or small—as soon as they become obvious. The technician can make sure all problems are fixed as soon as possible. When drivers and technicians work closely together, they can prevent serious damage to the equipment.

Troubleshooting

As a driver you need to know:

- About your vehicle's systems
- Where the systems are located
- The parts of each system
- Where the parts are located
- How each system works
- How all systems work together

Understanding how a system works is the first step to realizing when it is not functioning properly or is in danger of failing. A vehicle will, in most cases, alert you to trouble by warning signals, such as:

- Sharp drop in fuel mileage
- Erratic gauge readings
- A temperature gauge that is too high or too low
- A thump, bump, whine, grind, or rattle

If you know how your vehicle's systems work, you can notice the danger signals more easily. You will be better able to trace a problem to its source, or report your findings to a qualified technician.

Detection of Problems

When you notice a symptom, stop the truck as soon as possible (or as soon as the seriousness of the problem dictates). Then think about the problem thoroughly before starting to **troubleshoot.** Start with the most likely cause of the problem, keeping the following points in mind:

- You are not a technician or a mechanical expert.
- You should not try to do a technician's job.
- If you cannot identify the exact source of the trouble—actually see the part that is broken or malfunctioning—do not try to guess.
- Carefully describe the problem when you report it. Report what you checked and what you found, observed, smelled, and so on. Include the "what," "when," and "where" and any other information you may have.

Reporting Requirements

The first required step is to report the symptoms of the problem as soon as possible.

Written report—The **Federal Motor Carrier Safety Regulations (FMCSR)** require drivers to submit a **Driver's Vehicle Inspection Report (DVIR)** for each trip or 24-hour period within a trip. Include any problems in this report. Drivers also must review the previous DVIR to verify all problems have been corrected before beginning the next use of the equipment.

STOP!
A DVIR must be submitted for each power unit and each trailer and converter used in a 24-hour period.

Oral report—it often saves time to discuss any problem you have detected with the mechanic, depending on company policy. This gives the mechanic an opportunity to ask questions about your written report and helps in understanding the details of the problem.

Limitations—report only the facts about the symptoms and what your troubleshooting found, but avoid guessing. The mechanic's job is to use the details you supply to solve the problem.

Driver's Vehicle Inspection Report

Each carrier and transportation company has its own DVIR forms. The data the driver supplies should be accurate so that the maintenance department can locate problems quickly and easily **(see Figure 13-5).**

If there are no problems, your report should verify that fact. If problems have occurred, you should:

- Check the appropriate place on the form to show what system or part was involved, if you know.
- Describe the symptoms and troubleshooting in as much detail as possible.
- Discuss the problem with the technician in person, by e-mail or by phone, whatever company policy requires.

Useful Items for the Remarks or Comments Section
- Symptoms
  A description of the way the problem appears to the driver.
  How did it start?
  Did it start suddenly or gradually?

Driver's Vehicle Inspection Report

Check Any Defective Item and Give Details Under "Remarks,"

DATE _____

TRUCK/TRACTOR NO. _____

☐ Air Compressor	☐ Horn	☐ Springs
☐ Air Lines	☐ Lights	☐ Starter
☐ Battery	Head - Stop	☐ Steering
☐ Brake Accessories	Tail - Dash	☐ Tachograph
☐ Brakes	Turn Indicators	☐ Tires
☐ Carburetor	☐ Mirrors	☐ Transmission
☐ Clutch	☐ Muffler	☐ Wheels
☐ Defroster	☐ Oil Pressure	☐ Windows
☐ Drive Line	☐ On-Board Recorder	☐ Windshield Wipers
☐ Engine	☐ Radiator	☐ Other
☐ Fifth Wheel	☐ Rear End	
☐ Front Axle	☐ Reflectors	
☐ Fuel Tanks	☐ Safety Equipment	
☐ Heater	Fire Extinguisher	
	Flags-Flares-Fusees	
	Spare Bulbs & Fuses	
	Spare Seal Beam	

TRAILER(S) NO.(S) _____

☐ Brake Connections	☐ Hitch	☐ Tarpaulin
☐ Brakes	☐ Landing Gear	☐ Tires
☐ Coupling Chains	☐ Lights—All	☐ Wheels
☐ Coupling (King) Pin	☐ Roof	☐ Other
☐ Doors	☐ Springs	

Remarks: _____
_____
_____
_____
_____
_____
_____
_____
_____

☐ CONDITION OF THE ABOVE VEHICLE IS SATISFACTORY

DRIVER'S SIGNATURE _____

☐ ABOVE DEFECTS CORRECTED
☐ ABOVE DEFECTS NEED NOT BE CORRECTED FOR SAFE OPERATION OF VEHICLE

MECHANIC'S SIGNATURE _____ DATE _____

DRIVER'S SIGNATURE _____ DATE _____

▶ **Figure 13–5**

Driver's Vehicle Inspection Report.

If it came on gradually, over what period of time—several minutes, hours, days?

When did it appear?

■ Conditions

What were the conditions when the symptoms occurred?

How long had you been driving?

Was the weather hot or cold?

What type of cargo and vehicle weight were you carrying?

How far did your troubleshooting go?

What did you find?

Example

A driver notices the braking response time is getting slower and the vehicle pulls to the right when the brakes are applied.

It came on gradually during the first morning of the trip.

The weather was mild and clear.

The cargo was a max load of vegetables.

Troubleshooting consisted of checking tires, suspension, and brakes.

Results

Tire inflation is okay.

There are no broken or bent springs, shock absorbers, and so on.

Problem must be brakes or front-end alignment.

Driver called dispatcher for aid.

Dispatcher told driver to bring truck in at once for servicing.

Troubleshooting Guide

You will find a troubleshooting guide in the appendix. It is organized by sense; that is, it lists the signals picked up by your senses and the kinds of problems these may indicate.

The following are examples of two signals or symptoms. One is something you can hear, such as a dull thud; the other is something you can see, such as a gauge reading.

Noise: A dull thud—a sound you hear when you turn the wheels of the tractor. What caused the problem?

Possible Systems Involved	**Possible Causes**
1. Tires	Flat tire
2. Wheels, rims, lugs	Loose wheel or tire lugs
	Rock between duals

Proper Action

1. Stop as soon as you find a safe place.
2. Decide the logical starting point for your troubleshooting. Start with the simplest reason first. In this case, do you have a flat tire? If you do not have a flat tire, you might need to tighten the lugs or remove a rock from between the tires.

STOP!
Do not—for any reason—try to remove the tire from the rim.

Something you see: Gauge reading—your ammeter shows a continuous maximum charge. (**See Figure 13-6**).

▶ Figure 13-6
Gauges often indicate a problem.

© iStockphoto/Difydave

Possible Systems Involved

1. Electrical

Possible Cause

Short circuit in wiring

Proper Action

1. Disconnect the battery terminals until the short is repaired by a mechanic.

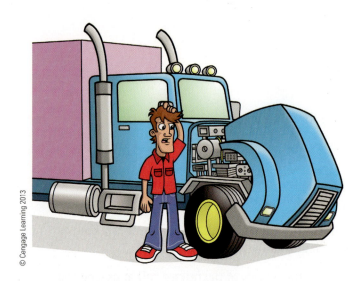

© Cengage Learning 2013

▶ *"Huh . . . the circuit breaker keeps tripping. I wonder if there is an 'app' I can download for that?"*

PROBLEM-SOLVING EXERCISES

Following are 12 problems. After your instructor has set the scene, discuss and troubleshoot the following problems. Follow these three steps when solving each problem:

1. **Identify** the systems that may be involved.
2. **Trace** the problem toward its source.
3. **Decide** the best course of action.

Following the problems, the solutions are presented. The systems that may be involved are identified. The possible source of the problem is noted. The best course of action is discussed. Compare these solutions with the class discussion. Was anything important overlooked?

Courtesy of Don Hess

▶ **Figure 13-7**

Properly adjusted mirrors are very important.

Problem One

Each time you stop, the tractor is bumped or pushed by the trailer.

— Trailer air
— Trailer Brakes

Problem Two

Your mirrors are adjusted properly but you can see more of one side of the trailer than the other (called trailer dog-tracking) **(see Figure 13-7).**

— Rear axle alignment
— Trailer Brakes

Problem Three

Your coolant temperature suddenly rises and the oil pressure is falling fast.

— loss of oil

Problem Four

The trailer sways too much when you make turns.

— Fifth wheel not locked
— Tandem not locked

Problem Five

The low-air warning buzzer keeps sounding for a split second at a time. *-slow leak in gladhand* *- water on air tanks*

Problem Six

The circuit breaker for the trailer's running lights keeps tripping. *- short*

Problem Seven

When you make sharp turns on slippery road surfaces, the steering wheel is turned but the tractor continues moving straight ahead. In other words, the tractor does not turn fully in response to the turning of the steering wheel. *- tires* *- moving too fast* *- power steering loss*

Problem Eight

When coupling the tractor to the trailer, the tractor protection valve opens. There is a severe loss of air pressure. *- hole in svc line to trailer*

Problem Nine

You hear a loud snap or click when you first start and move the truck. *- seized brakes* *- kingpin loose*

Problem Ten

You notice exhaust odor in the cab. *- exhaust damage*

Problem Eleven

As you drive, you notice the ammeter registers discharge or there is a low reading on the voltmeter. *- alternator fail*

Problem Twelve

Excessive smoke is coming from the exhaust pipe (**see Figure 13-8**).

Solutions

Problem One: Each time you stop, the tractor is bumped or pushed by the trailer.

Possible Systems Involved

- Trailer air brakes
- Coupling

Possible Causes

- Slow timing of the trailer brakes (driver cannot adjust the brake timing between tractor and trailer)
- Air line connections between tractor and trailer
  - Loose glad hand connections
  - Worn or missing O-ring
- Air lines from glad hands to brake chambers
  - Holes or cracks in the line
  - Kinked hose
- Brake chambers
  - Air leaks
  - Slack adjuster

▶ Figure 13-8

Watch for smoke from the exhaust pipe.

© iStockphoto/dossup1

- Fifth-wheel locking mechanism loose
- Fifth-wheel slack adjuster needs adjusting
  - More than one-half inch (25.4 mm) of horizontal movement between upper and lower halves will cause the unit to be put out of service

Proper Actions

- Stop at first safe place and pull truck off the road.
- Check for causes.
- Call the maintenance department and report problem. Be sure details are correct.

Problem Two: Your mirrors are adjusted properly but you can see more of one side of the trailer than the other (**see Figure 13-9**).

▶ **Figure 13-9**

Although your mirrors are adjusted properly, you can see more of one side of the trailer than the other.

Possible System Involved

- Axles

Probable Causes

- Tractor is not aligned properly.
- Sliding tandems
  - Lock pins that hold tandems in place are not in holes
  - Lost pins
  - Pins have jarred loose
- Axles are not aligned properly.

Proper Actions

- Slow down at once.
- Find a safe place to pull off the road.
- Locate problem areas.
- If you have sliding tandems:
  - Make sure lock pins are in place in holes opposite each other.
  - Replace pins if they are missing.
  - If pins are loose or need to be replaced, ask a trained technician to do this.
- If you have fixed tandems:
  - Call maintenance department immediately.

Problem Three: Your coolant temperature suddenly rises and the oil pressure is falling fast (**see Figure 13-10**).

▶ **Figure 13-10**

Coolant temperature is rising and oil pressure is falling.

Possible System Involved

- Lubrication

Probable Causes

- Low oil level due to:
  - Lost drain plug
  - Oil filter not properly secured or tightened
  - Broken oil line
  - Blown gasket

Proper Actions

- Pull off the road at once.
- Stop and turn off engine.
- Check engine oil level. CAUTION: Engine is very hot.
- Check all probable causes.
- Check for oil leaks in the engine compartment and under the truck.
- Call maintenance for assistance—be accurate in details and description of problem.
- Do not restart your engine, unless instructed by the maintenance department.

Problem Four: The trailer sways too much when you make turns (**see Figure 13-11**).

Possible Systems Involved

- Suspension
- Tires

Probable Causes

- Cargo has shifted
- Broken or loose shock absorbers
- Broken or shifted spring or spring hanger
- Underinflated or flat tires

Proper Actions

- Slow down at once.
- Find a safe place and pull off the road.
- Check out possible causes.
- If cargo has shifted, move it back into position, if possible, and secure it. This will probably require help, even a fork truck to correct the problem.
- If problem is shock absorber, call your maintenance department.
- If problem is flat tire, call for help.

Problem Five: The low-air warning buzzer keeps sounding for a split second at a time (**see Figure 13-12**).

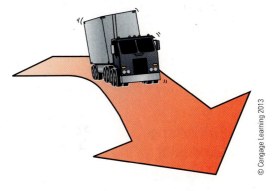

▶ **Figure 13-11**

Excessive trailer sway may indicate that cargo has shifted.

▶ **Figure 13-12**

A severe leak of disconnected air line may cause periodic low-air buzzer warnings.

Possible System Involved

- Air brakes

Probable Causes

- Severe air leak
- Loose compressor belt
- Ruptured air line
- Disconnected air line
- Petcock open on air reservoirs
- Malfunctioning compressor
- Loose glad hand connections
- Worn or missing O-ring on glad hand
- Blown brake chamber diaphragm

Proper Actions

- Stop at once.
- Park your rig.
- Locate problem.
- Call for assistance.
- Have problem corrected before resuming your trip.

Problem Six: The circuit breaker for the trailer's running lights keeps tripping.

Possible System Involved

- Electrical

Probable Causes

- Exposed or hanging wire (the insulation may have worn off, exposing bare wire)
- Broken ground wire

Proper Actions

- Stop your truck at the first safe spot off the road.
- Turn engine off. Check out the problem.
- Call maintenance or dispatch.
- Tape any bare, exposed wire, if permitted.
- Locate and reset circuit breaker.
- Drive to first truck stop and have electrical system checked by qualified mechanic.

Problem Seven: When you turn sharply on slippery road surfaces, the steering wheel is turned but the tractor continues moving straight ahead (see **Figure 13-13**).

Possible System Involved

- Steering

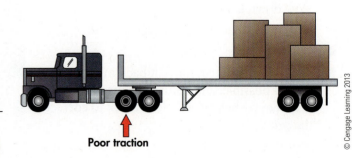

Poor traction

© Cengage Learning 2013

▶ **Figure 13-13**

Poor traction may be caused by a lightly loaded steering axle.

Probable Causes

- Steering axle too lightly loaded
- Fifth wheel in need of grease
- Fifth wheel iced up

Proper Actions

- Slow down at once and look for a safe place to pull off the road.
- Move the load to get more weight on the fifth wheel.
- If your truck has a sliding fifth wheel, move the fifth wheel forward.
- Grease fifth wheel.
- Remove ice from fifth wheel.
- If rig does not have a sliding fifth wheel but has sliding tandems on the trailer, move the tandems to the rear to put more weight on the fifth wheel by transferring weight to the steering axle.

CAUTION!

This is usually a problem on tandem axle tractors with a short wheelbase. Tandems are a short distance behind the steering wheel and tend to take control of the vehicle, preventing it from moving straight ahead.

Problem Eight: When coupling the tractor to the trailer, the tractor protection valve opens. There is a severe loss of air pressure (**see Figure 13-14**)

Possible System Involved

- Air brakes

Probable Causes

- Glad hands are not seated properly or they have a bad O-ring.
- Air lines are crossed. Service line is connected to the emergency line, and emergency line is connected to service line.
- Trailer air tank petcock is open.
- Broken air lines.

▶ **Figure 13-14**

Crossed air lines may cause a severe loss of air pressure.

Proper Action

- This problem must be found and corrected before you drive from the yard.

Problem Nine: You hear a loud snap or click when you first start and move the truck.

Possible System Involved

- Drive train

Probable Causes

- Loose U-joint
- Excessive wear on U-joint or differential

Proper Actions

- Be very careful when you put the truck into motion.
- Proceed to the nearest mechanic or call dispatch/maintenance.
- Have the drive train checked by a qualified mechanic.

Problem Ten: You notice exhaust odor in the cab.

Possible System Involved

- Exhaust

Probable Causes

- Loose connection in the exhaust system
- Cracked or broken exhaust pipe
- Leaking muffler
- Rusted exhaust system
- Cracked exhaust manifold

Proper Actions

- Open all cab windows.
- Stop at next truck stop/mechanic.
- Have exhaust system checked and repaired by qualified technician as soon as possible.

Problem Eleven: As you drive, you notice the ammeter registers discharge or there is a low reading on the voltmeter.

Possible System Involved

- Electrical

Probable Causes

- Loose or broken alternator belt
- Loose wiring connection
- Inoperable generator or alternator
- Generator or alternator not adjusted correctly
- Defective voltage regulator

Proper Actions

- Do not shut off the engine.
- Pull off the road at first safe spot.
- Look for any obvious cause:
  - Missing belt (keep hands away from moving belts, pulleys, etc.)
  - Loose connections
  - Bare insulation or a worn wire
  - Short circuit in the wiring
- Go to first available technician and get assistance in correcting the problem **(see Figure 13-15).**

 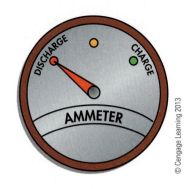

 **Figure 13-15**

When the ammeter registers discharge or there is a low reading on the voltmeter, go to the first available truck stop for a mechanic's assistance.

Problem Twelve: Excessive smoke is coming from the exhaust pipe. (**see Figure 13-16**).

Possible Systems Involved

- Exhaust
- Fuel
- Turbo malfunction

Probable Causes

- Dirty air cleaner
- Poor grade fuel
- Return fuel line blocked, bent, or squeezed together
- Fuel pump malfunction
- Engine overfueled

NOTE

These are only some of the more common problems. There are a number of other possibilities.

 **Figure 13-16**

Smoke coming from the exhaust pipe may signal a dirty air cleaner, an overfueled engine, or a frozen turbine. Shut down immediately.

Proper Actions

- If you smell oil from the turbo and/or see oil coming from the turbo, pull over in a safe spot and shut down immediately.
- Call maintenance department/dispatch for instructions.

Troubleshooting Summary

A good troubleshooter knows his or her vehicle and its systems thoroughly, uses common sense, knows the company maintenance policy, does not attempt to make repairs for which he or she has not been trained, and keeps good records.

EMERGENCY STARTING PROCEDURES

In this section, you will learn the safe way to start a truck that has a dead battery. If a truck has an air starting system and has lost air pressure, it will also have to be manually started. The correct method is explained in this section.

Jump-Starting Dead Batteries

There are three things to remember when you **jump-start** a dead battery:

1. Observe all safety rules.
2. Prepare the truck.
3. Attach jumper cables properly.

Observe All Safety Rules – See Figure 13–17

- Shield your eyes or wear safety goggles.
- Do not smoke.
- Make sure the batteries of both vehicles are negatively grounded and carry the same voltage (use a 12-volt battery to charge a 12-volt battery).

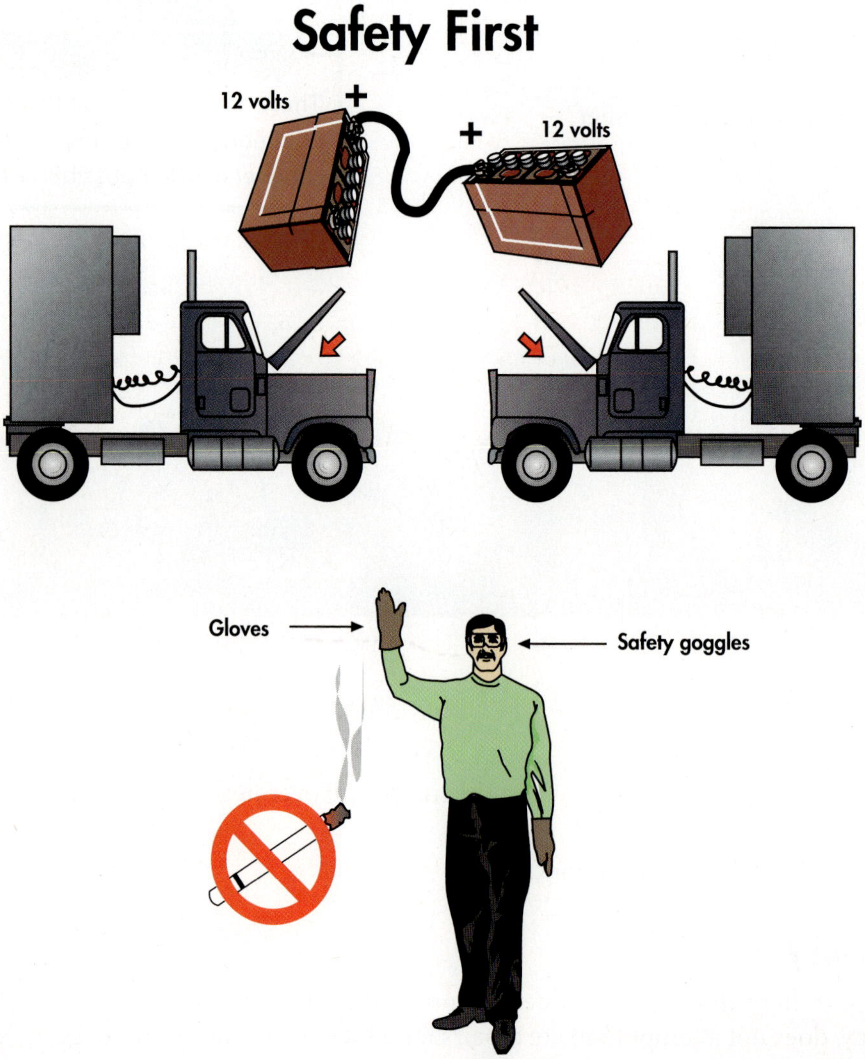

Safety First

12 volts +   + 12 volts

Gloves → ← Safety goggles

▶ Figure 13–17

Safety is your top priority when starting a truck with a dead battery.

- Keep all battery fluids away from skin and clothing.
- Never jump-start a battery if the battery fluid is frozen.

Prepare the Truck

- Align the vehicles so the jumper cables will reach without strain. Do not allow the vehicles to touch each other.
- Set the parking brake.
- Shift into neutral.
- Add distilled water to dead battery, if needed.

Attach Jumper Cables Properly

- Clamp one cable to the positive (1) pole of the dead battery.
- Clamp the other end of the cable to the positive pole of the booster battery.
- Connect the second cable to the negative (2) pole of the booster battery.
- Attach the other end of the cable to the stalled truck's frame, engine block, or other metal part as a ground.
- Start the booster truck—always start the booster engine first.
- Start the disabled truck.
- Remove the battery cables in reverse order.

STOP!

Do not attempt to jump-start a battery unless you are qualified to do so. Modern semi-tractors utilize sensitive electronic components and applying too much amperage could destroy expensive parts. Drivers need to know what they are doing before attempting this type of maintenance procedure.

PROCEDURE FOR STARTING A VEHICLE WITH A DEAD BATTERY

Because dead batteries on the road cost you time and money, an important skill is knowing how to properly and safely jump-start your rig. Carelessness or not knowing how to jump-start your truck's battery can do damage to the vehicle or be more dangerous for bystanders than jump-starting a personal vehicle, simply because you're dealing with a much larger battery and more electrical power.

You also could permanently damage your engine if proper precautions are not taken. There are two ways to jump-start any vehicle: using a battery charger, or using a second vehicle. It is important to buy a quality battery charger/jumper cables with durable, strong cables and proper voltage rather than dealing with dangers that come with using poor quality accessories.

(Continues)

PROCEDURE FOR STARTING A VEHICLE WITH A DEAD BATTERY (*continued*)

Equipment Needed:

- Safety glasses
- Battery charger with proper voltage—such as a Rescue Booster Pack 2020 (capable of starting 12- and 24-volt batteries), Cobra CJIC-250 Jump Starter Powerpack or RoadPro RPAT715 Jumpstart Powerpak, to name a few—and durable cables, or
- Jumper cables 15- to 20-feet (4.6 to 6.1 m) long and a minimum of 2-gauge thickness and
- Second vehicle with a battery of equal voltage (most big rigs have 24-volt batteries)

Procedure:

1. Put on safety glasses or goggles. If someone is helping you, make certain they have safety goggles, too.
2. Identify the starter terminals of your vehicle. If there is any dust or rust, remove this before connecting any cable.
3. Turn off all electrical utilities, such as the radio or video player, in your vehicle before you connect the cable to your vehicle.
4. Make sure the vehicle ignition is off and brakes are on.
5. Connect the end of "+" (positive) of the cable to "+" (positive) terminal of your rig's battery.
6. If using a second vehicle, attach the other "+" (positive) end of the cable, to the "+" (positive) terminal of the secondary battery. Then attach one end of "−" (negative) cable to "−" (negative) terminal of the secondary battery.
7. Find a metal plate that is secure, not painted, and without rust, such as the engine manifold, compressor bracket of air conditioner, or alternator bracket. Connect the other end of the "−" (negative) cable to that metal plate.
8. Start the battery charger or second vehicle. Allow second vehicle or charger to run for two minutes.
9. Start the dead semitruck. It should start. If not, check the connections thoroughly and wait for two to three minutes and start your rig again.
10. Disconnect the cables in the reverse order from which you placed them. Turn off charger or second vehicle. Allow semi to run for 15–20 minutes to fully charge the battery.

INTERESTING FACT

Although Alessandro Volta in Italy is usually credited with being the inventor of the modern battery (silver-zinc), the first evidence of batteries comes from archaeological digs in Baghdad, Iraq. This first "battery" was dated to around 250 B.C. and may have been used in simple operations to electroplate objects with a thin layer of metal. The so-called Baghdad Battery consisted of a clay jar with a stopper made of asphalt. Sticking through the asphalt was an iron rod surrounded by a copper cylinder. When filled with vinegar—or any other electrolytic solution—the jar produced about 1.1 volts.

Starting Trucks That Have Air Starters

To start a truck that has an **air starter** requires fewer safety precautions. It is never a good idea, however, to smoke when inspecting or working on a vehicle.

To prepare the vehicle, align the truck with the charged air supply. Hook up the air line properly. When using a compressor, follow these steps:

1. Hook up the air line from the compressor to the glad hand of the disabled truck's air reservoir.
2. Fill the reservoir.
3. Start the disabled tractor's engine.

When you are using another tractor, supply air in this way:

1. Hook up the air line from one reservoir to the other.
2. Start the booster tractor's engine.
3. Fill the empty air reservoir of the disabled tractor.
4. Start the disabled tractor's engine.

SUMMARY

In this chapter, you learned the driver's responsibilities in maintaining and servicing his or her vehicle. You also know that a trained mechanic should provide most repairs. This chapter described how to troubleshoot and report malfunctions. As a professional driver, you may at some time in your career have a vehicle that will not start. Remember to follow safe and correct emergency starting procedures.

KEY TERMS

Air starter
Driver awareness
Driver's Vehicle Inspection
   Report (DVIR)

Federal Motor Carrier Safety
   Regulations (FMCSR)
Jump-starting

Maintenance policy
Malfunction
Troubleshoot

A DAY IN THE LIFE...

Reuben Dupsky Jr. – Fremont Contract Carriers Inc., Professional Truck Driver

I was bitten by the truck driving bug when I enlisted in the Army upon graduation from high school and drove military support vehicles. Upon completion of service to our country in 1970, I helped with the family farm operation while the whole time dreaming of getting back into a truck and driving. I decided to take the leap and for the past 35 years, have had the opportunity to live my dream by driving over 4 million accident-free miles. I take great pride in my profession and feel I am a strong and confident leader for Fremont Contract Carriers (FCC) by promoting safe driving amongst my peers. I am well known for my willingness to assist colleagues in any task and provide advice and mentoring to those drivers that are new to the industry as well as veteran drivers. I contribute my success to the core values of hard work, dedication, and treating each and every person that I meet with mutual respect and trust. I have built a reputation for excellence and commitment to customer service in my 10+ years at FCC. The confidence that I have obtained throughout my years of driving inspires me to be an advocate for the industry by promoting responsibility for the profession amongst drivers. I am a member of the company Accident Review Committee and have also recently participated in an insurance industry conference providing insight to the industry on the true inner workings of the trucking industry from a driver's perspective.

I am well known in the local trucking community for my passion and generosity to the Special Olympics organization. I am a true advocate in supporting the mission that this organization represents while always working toward my personal goal of making a positive difference in the lives of these special individuals. I enjoy being a positive role model while helping shape the lives of these individuals and giving them inspiration to reach for their dreams each and every day.

> ## " I take great pride in my profession . . . "

I try to pass on my wisdom of the industry to the younger generation through community educational opportunities with the local schools and also through my truck driving diary blog. My goal is to change the public's overall perception of the trucking profession and to inspire our youth to become involved in the industry.

REVIEW QUESTIONS

1. Which of the following is not true regarding expectations of most tractor-trailer drivers?

    a. They are to follow company policy regarding repairs to the rig.

    b. They are to follow company policy regarding adjustments to the rig.

    c. They are to be driver-mechanics.

    d. a and b

2. Although a professional driver is not expected to become a technician, he or she should be _____.

    a. knowledgeable enough of the various systems to find the source of a problem

    b. able to repair a flat tire

    c. able to repair the electrical system

    d. able to repair the fuel system

3. When a driver uses his or her seeing, hearing, feeling, and smelling to collect clues regarding the operation of the rig, the driver is said to be using his or her _____.

    a. reaction time

    c. brake lag time

    b. senses

    d. intuition and senses

4. Which of the following is not a typical result of an early detection of a malfunction of your rig?

    a. lower maintenance expenses

    c. fewer accidents

    b. increased downtime the rig

    d. longer vehicle life

5. Which of the following is not a driver's responsibility regarding maintenance and/or repairs of a rig?

    a. Know the company expectations.

    c. Diagnose/repair simple problems.

    b. Identify sources of malfunctions.

    d. Make repairs to fuel system.

6. Which of the following is not an expectation of a driver regarding troubleshooting the systems of a rig?

    a. Know where the systems are located.

    c. Replace old system with new one.

    b. Know the parts of each system.

    d. Know how all systems work together.

7. Regarding a driver's involvement with a rig, if one is searching out the source of a problem and attempting to solve it, one is said to be _____.

    a. troubleshooting

    c. backtracking

    b. double-clutching

    d. sharpshooting

8. As a professional driver, if your rig experiences a sharp drop in fuel mileage, erratic gauge readings, temperature gauge readings too high or too low, or a thump, bump, whine, grind, or rattle, this should alert you to the fact that _____.

    a. you are driving into a strong wind

    c. your rig needs a tune-up

    b. you are experiencing a strong crosswind

    d. one or more systems is in danger of failure

9. When reporting the results of your troubleshooting to the company technician, which of the following will least help a technician find and resolve the problem?

    a. When I brake, I hear a different kind of noise than I usually hear.

    b. My clearance lights sometime blink when I turn to the right.

    c. I think I hear a rubbing sound coming from the right side of my trailer.

    (d.) I hear a funny sound coming from the front of the truck.

10. If Melissa drives rig A for deliveries from 8 A.M. to 11 A.M. and drives rig B for deliveries from 1 P.M. to 3 P.M., according to FMCSR, how many Driver's Vehicle Inspection Reports (DVIRs) must she fill out for the day?

    a. one for rig A only

    (b.) one for rig A and one for rig B

    c. one for rig B only

    d. none since Melissa did not drive either rig for 8 hours

11. Before actually jump-starting your rig, all but _____ is required.

    a. putting on safety goggles

    b. turning off ignition and setting brake

    (c.) opening air valves and draining petcocks

    d. turning off radio, TV, other electricals

12. After jump-starting your rig, it is important to _____.

    a. note the jumpstart on the DVIR

    b. reset your brakes ✗

    c. allow rig to run for 15 minutes

    d. replace spark plugs at nearest truckstop

    A + C ?

13. A DVIR must be submitted for every power unit and each trailer and converter used in a(n) ____-hour period.

    a. 8   c. 16

    b. 12   (d.) 24

14. A Driver's Vehicle Inspection Report is required by the _____.

    a. National Highway Safety Administration

    b. World Wide Web

    c. National Transportation and Agency

    (d.) Federal Motor ~~Transportation~~ Safety Administration

    Carrier

SUPPLEMENTAL LEARNING ACTIVITIES

1. Find a battery pack and practice jump-starting a dead battery.

2. Find out about the myth of not storing batteries on the floor and who first coined the term "battery." Is the myth, in your opinion, correct or incorrect?

3. Discuss how human behavior often interferes with human safety. Talk about people who think they are "bullet-proof" when it comes to following safety rules of such procedures as jump-starting a truck. Do you know any of these people?

4. Discuss why saving time is never a good excuse for not following proper safety regulations. Discuss personal experiences that prove this is true.

5. When it is your responsibility to complete and file a DVIR, pretrip and posttrip, how could "skimping" on doing a thorough check after a trip put a colleague's life in jeopardy?

FOR MORE INFORMATION

PTDI—Diagnose and Report Malfunctions, Page 18, Click on Skill Standards
www.ptdi.org/standards

Driver's Vehicle Inspection Report
www.fmcsa.dot.gov/rules-regulations/administration/fmcsr/fmcsrruletext.aspx?reg=396.11

How to Jump-Start a Big Rig Using the Rescue 2000
www.youtube.com/watch?v=_fLV3Jb62oo

© iStockphoto/MCCAIG

OBJECTIVES

When you have completed this chapter, you should be able to:

- Know and understand the importance of using signals.

- Know ways to minimize distracted driving.

- Explain why good communications help avoid collisions and traffic violations.

- Describe how to send and receive communications.

INTRODUCTION

Professional drivers are some of the most visible users on our highways today, and those who share the highways with big rigs tend to criticize some of the professional driver's practices. This means it's up to you—the pro—to drive responsibly, drive defensively, and anticipate what other drivers might do and if you can compensate for their actions. In driving responsibly, being able to **communicate** with your fellow highway drivers is an extremely important skill.

If our travel as a professional driver and your operation of a commercial motor vehicle is to be safe and efficient, you must stay in constant communication with others on the road.

Does this mean you should communicate with everyone, using a cellular telephone or a CB radio?

Absolutely not! But it does mean you, as a professional driver, must signal your next move through traffic, and at the same time, be alert to the messages coming from other drivers, pedestrians, and cyclists.

So, what is good communication on the highway, anyway?

INTERESTING FACT

In 1938, 31 states required direction signals when trucks were so loaded that hand signals could not be seen. That same year the Teleoptic Company introduced turn signals that were controlled by a switch mounted to the gearshift ball handle.

It is a professional skill that requires knowledge, foresight, experience, and understanding of the driver's needs as well as the needs of others on the road **(see Figure 14-1)**. In its simplest form, communication on the highway is helping each other get down the road and helping each other get jobs done.

How does good communication occur on the highway?

In addition to using turn signals and emergency flashers when necessary, good communications from your tractor also incorporate the horn and your speed—letting other highway users be aware of your presence, your position, and your intentions.

Should drivers of other vehicles automatically know when a big rig pulls behind them, in front of them, or beside them—because the rig is so big?

▶ **Figure 14-1**

Good communication on the highway helps you get down the road and get the job done.

This may be difficult to believe, but some people do not realize you are there because they are not paying close attention. They may be thinking about dinner tonight, a sore tooth, or a personal problem. They may be talking on the phone or listening intently to the music playing at that moment. Therefore, when you communicate your presence by letting others know where you are, you may be helping everyone avoid an accident down the road.

EYE CONTACT

There are mixed opinions about making eye contact with a fellow driver, especially if the other person sees eye contact as a threat. However, when you're making a tight turn or moving slowly into an intersection, it is a good idea to check the vehicles around you to make certain the drivers are aware of your

▶ **Figure 14-2**

A driver must carefully watch other drivers at all times.

presence and have seen you signal your intent. Eye contact is a good way to confirm they've received your communication (**see Figure 14-2**).

ROAD RAGE

One situation occurring on America's highways today is **road rage.** Professional drivers tell of days when they have seen or been involved in a dozen or more of these dangerous incidents. According to psychologist Arnold Nerenberg, road rage occurs in North America as many as 2 billion times every year.

Road rage can be defined as anything from aggressive driving, to criminal behavior, to simply bad driving. One law enforcement officer defines road rage as "an event occurring when drivers are running out of time and running out of options." Another highway veteran calls road rage "a problem of sharing—conflict between the law-abiding road user and people who cut in and out, trying to beat the traffic." And some would point out that road improvements have not kept up with the increasing motor vehicle traffic, yet another factor contributing to road rage.

Because road rage has surpassed epidemic proportions, professional drivers must be constantly aware of how his or her "communication" of their rig's presence or their intentions are perceived. Honking the horn too often, following too closely, or cutting off a driver at a ramp or turnoff may spike the opportunities for road rage.

So, take care in how you communicate with others using the same roadway. Be aware of how important it is to let others know your whereabouts and your intentions, and never overdo signals or flashing lights, speed, or use inappropriate methods to communicate your plans to maneuver your rig.

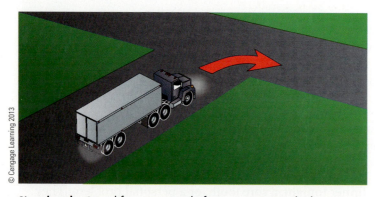

Signal early: Signal for some time before you turn. It is the best way to keep others from trying to pass you when it is not safe to pass.

Signal continuously: Do not cancel the signal until you have completed the turn.

Cancel your signal after you have turned: Turn off your signal if you do not have self-cancelling signals.

▶ **Figure 14-3**

Using signals correctly communicates your next maneuver to others sharing the road.

SIGNAL YOUR INTENT TO OTHER DRIVERS

Even though you know where you are and where you are going at any given time while on the roadways, other highway users do not know. Remember the concern you felt when a bicyclist was in your lane on the highway? The best way to let others know your intent to change lanes, turn, or slow down is to signal before you do it; and there are rules to observe for signaling when driving a rig.

Why do these special rules exist? Because of the size of the rig, your blind spots while driving a rig, and the space you require for turning. The rules help you do everything you can to let others know what you intend to do (**see Figure 14-3**).

SIGNALING

Part of safe driving is letting drivers around you know what you will do next. You can communicate your intentions by using your turn signals, and it's generally required by law whenever you make a turn or change lanes. Signaling to other drivers, those in front of you and those behind your rig, that you are planning to turn, means you're communicating your intention to change lanes or directions. Communicating to other drivers is not only an effective tool in preventing accidents, but it is also part of your job as a professional driver.

Signaling for Turns

The three rules to follow when you signal before making a turn are:

1. Signal early
2. Signal continuously
3. Cancel your signal

Signal early—as you know, the size of your rig makes it hard for you to see another driver who is about to pass you or who may already be doing so. The best way to keep others from trying to pass when you are ready to make a turn is to give advanced warning. **Put on your turn signal early.**

CAUTION!

The general rule of thumb is to turn on the turn signal one-half block before an intersection or about 500 feet (152.4 m) from the intersection on the open highway. According to the FMCSR, you must signal at least 100 feet (30.5 m) in advance of your maneuver.

State laws vary from 100 to 500 feet (30.5 to 152.4 m). Keep in mind these legal requirements are minimums—100 feet (30.5 m) may not be far enough in advance for some traffic or weather conditions.

Signal continuously—you may find that after turning on your signal, you must stop and wait for a safe break in the traffic. Keep your signal on to tell everyone what you are going to do.

Cancel your signal—when you have completed the turn, cancel your signal. Do not cancel the signal until you have completed your maneuver.

Stopping at stop signs—when making a right turn at a red light or stop sign, you must come to a full stop. The law doesn't specify how long you need to remain stopped, but your rig must cease moving forward, or risk a fine.

NOTE

Unlike automobiles, few trucks are equipped with self-canceling turn signals.

CAUTION!

An entry-level commercial vehicle driver should avoid making a right turn on a red traffic light. A tractor trailer takes considerably more time and room to successfully navigate a turn, so "right turn on red" should be avoided by new drivers if possible.

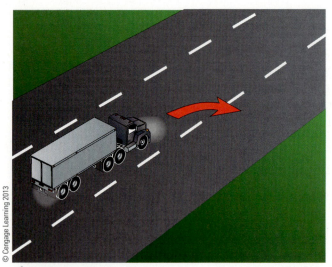

Changing Lanes:
- Check traffic to the front and rear, especially in your blind spot.
- Signal the lane change.
- Do not tailgate while waiting to change lanes.
- Make a smooth lane change, maintain your speed, and allow the correct distance between all vehicles.
- Cancel your signal.

▶ **Figure 14-4**

Following these steps when changing lanes helps maintain roadway safety.

Changing lanes—lane changes require the same early warnings that you signal when making turns. They also need one more signal—the motion of your vehicle. Once you begin your lane change, pause for a few seconds as you enter the new lane. This will catch the attention of those who did not notice your earlier signal and will give them a chance to react **(see Figure 14-4).** You must signal at least 100 feet (30.5 m) before making your move . . . and at a speed of 60 mph (96 km/h), that's going to be about 1.2 seconds. Indicate your intentions to other drivers to give them as much time as they need to know what you're doing.

Merging between vehicles—most professional drivers give themselves, at least, a four-second gap between vehicles when they're merging, and more if the space is available.

GO!

One good way to remember to cancel the signal is to connect it in your mind with the upshift. After completing the turn, speed up, cancel the signal, and upshift. This routine will soon become a habit.

SIGNAL YOUR INTENTIONS IN THESE SITUATIONS

Slowing Down—Warn drivers behind you when you see you'll need to slow down. A few light taps on the brake pedal—enough to flash the brake lights—should warn following drivers. **Use the four-way emergency flashers for times when you are driving very slow or are stopped.**

Highway users expect vehicles ahead of them to keep moving. Any time you slow suddenly, you should give the drivers behind you some type of warning. *Communicate your intent.* A few light taps on the brake pedal—enough to flash the brake lights without exhausting your air supply—should be enough.

Warn other drivers in any of the following situations:

Trouble Ahead—The size of your vehicle may make it hard for drivers behind you to see hazards ahead. If you see a hazard that will require slowing down, warn the drivers behind by flashing your brake lights or, better yet, activating your emergency flashers as you slow.

Tight Turns—Most car drivers don't know how slow you have to go to make a tight turn in a large vehicle. Give drivers behind you warning by braking early and slowing gradually so they will be prepared for you to slow your rig.

(Continues)

SIGNAL YOUR INTENTIONS IN THESE SITUATIONS (continued)

Stopping on the Roadway—Car and bus drivers sometimes stop in the road to unload cargo or passengers, or to stop at a railroad crossing. Other drivers are forced to stop in a traffic lane when others behind them may not expect it. Sometimes the reason for stopping may be a railroad crossing. Other times, you may have to stop your rig to back into a driveway, or you may come to a stop because your rig is experiencing mechanical difficulties. Give the drivers following you as much warning as possible. Warn drivers behind you by flashing your brake lights. Don't stop suddenly.

Driving Slowly—Drivers often do not realize how fast they are catching up to a slow vehicle until they are very close. If your rig is being slowed by hills or heavy cargo, let other drivers know you are going slowly by turning on your four-way flashers until you are able to resume normal highway speeds.

STOP!

Do Not Direct Traffic

As a professional driver, your job is to manage your rig, not to tell other drivers what to do. Some drivers mean well as they try to help others by signaling when it is safe to pass, but what they fail to realize is that if their "help" causes an accident, they could be held liable for the damage. Signal only to tell others what *you* plan to do with your own rig. Leave directing traffic to the police or highway patrol **(see Figure 14-5).**

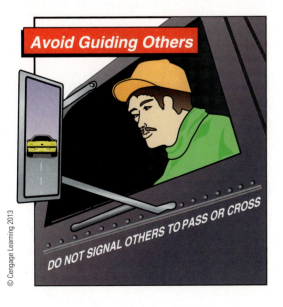

© Cengage Learning 2013

INTERESTING FACT

In 1971, the Bureau of Motor Carrier Safety initiated new rules involving driver qualifications and the National Highway Safety Bureau changed its name to the National Highway Traffic Safety Administration.

▶ Figure 14–5

Remember that your job is to be a professional driver, not to direct traffic.

Overtaking Other Vehicles

When you overtake other highway users such as an automobile, another rig, a bicyclist, or a pedestrian, it is best to assume that they do not see you; and if they do not see you, there is also a chance they will suddenly move into your path. Before overtaking them, signal that you are there by tapping lightly on the horn. Avoid loud blasts that may startle them, causing them to swerve into your path.

Signal any time you overtake and pass pedestrians or cyclists. Obviously you cannot signal every time you overtake another vehicle, but it is a good idea to do it when possible, especially when you approach a driver who is signaling a lane change or starting to pull into your path. Especially when approaching pedestrians and cyclists from behind, a couple of taps on the electric horn button on your steering wheel will usually warn them without startling them, as air horns might.

▶ **Figure 14–6**

It is often difficult to see or be seen at dawn or dusk.

When It Is Hard to See

It is hard to see at dawn or dusk **(see Figure 14-6).** It is also difficult to see in rain, fog, snow, at night, or during cloudy days, particularly when a driver is fatigued or right after eating a heavy meal.

A rig can be as difficult to see as any other vehicle on the roadway. If you are having trouble spotting oncoming vehicles, assume other drivers are having a tough time seeing you. Turn on your lights and use your headlights to identify your rig as it goes down the highway.

At the Side of the Road

Anytime you pull off the road and stop, turn on your four-way flashers **(see Figure 14-7).** This is especially important at night when a driver who has not seen you decides to pull off the road in the same spot.

▶ **Figure 14–7**

Any time you pull your rig off the road, use your emergency flashers.

USING FOUR-WAY FLASHERS AND REFLECTIVE TRIANGLES

Four-way flashers are so called because they flash both sides of the front and rear of the vehicle.

According to FMCSA 392 - 2 Subpart C - Stopped Commercial Motor Vehicles:

Whenever a commercial motor vehicle is stopped upon the traveled portion of a highway or the shoulder of a highway for any cause other than necessary traffic stops, the driver of the stopped commercial motor vehicle shall immediately activate the vehicular hazard warning signal flashers and continue the flashing until the driver places the required warning devices.

The flashing signals shall be used during the time the warning devices are picked up for storage before movement of the commercial motor vehicle. The flashing lights may be used at other times while a commercial motor vehicle is stopped in addition to, but not in lieu of, the required warning devices.

(b)   Placement of warning devices—

1. General rule. Except as provided in paragraph (b)(2) of this section, whenever a commercial motor vehicle is stopped upon the traveled portion or the shoulder of a highway for any cause other than necessary traffic stops, the driver shall, as soon as possible, but in any event within 10 minutes, place the warning devices in the following manner:

    i. One on the traffic side of and 4 paces (approximately 3 meters or 10 feet) from the stopped commercial motor vehicle in the direction of approaching traffic;

    ii. One at 40 paces (approximately 30 meters or 100 feet) from the stopped commercial motor vehicle in the center of the traffic lane or shoulder occupied by the commercial motor vehicle and in the direction of approaching traffic; and

    iii. One at 40 paces (approximately 30 meters or 100 feet) from the stopped commercial motor vehicle in the center of the traffic lane or shoulder occupied by the commercial motor vehicle and in the direction away from approaching traffic.

2. Special rules—

    i. Fusees and liquid-burning flares. The driver of a commercial motor vehicle equipped with only fusees or liquid-burning flares shall place a lighted fusee or liquid-burning flare at each of the locations previously specified.

    There shall be at least one lighted fusee or liquid-burning flare at each of the prescribed locations, as long as the commercial motor vehicle is stopped. Before the stopped commercial motor vehicle is moved, the driver shall extinguish and remove each fusee or liquid-burning flare.

NOTE

Fusees are rarely used today and have been replaced by reflective safety triangles.

    ii. Daylight hours. Except as provided in paragraph (b)(2)(iii) of this section, during the period lighted lamps are not required, three bidirectional **reflective triangles,** or three lighted fusees or liquid-burning flares shall be placed as specified in paragraph (b)(1) of this section within a time of 10 minutes.

    In the event the driver elects to use only fusees or liquid-burning flares in lieu of bidirectional reflective triangles or red flags, the driver must ensure that at least one fusee or liquid-burning flare remains lighted at each of the prescribed locations as long as the commercial motor vehicle is stopped or parked.

    iii. Business or residential districts. The placement of warning devices is not required within the business or residential district of a municipality, except during the time lighted lamps are required and when street or highway lighting is insufficient to make a commercial motor vehicle clearly discernable at a distance of 500 feet (152.4 m) to persons on the highway.

(Continues)

USING FOUR-WAY FLASHERS AND REFLECTIVE TRIANGLES (continued)

iv. Hills, curves, and obstructions.

If a commercial motor vehicle is stopped within 500 feet (152.4 m) of a curve, crest of a hill, or other obstruction to view, the driver shall place the required warning signal in the direction of the obstruction to view a distance of 100 to 500 feet (30.5 to 152.4 m) from the stopped commercial motor vehicle so as to afford ample warning to other users of the highway.

v. Divided or one-way roads.

If a commercial motor vehicle is stopped upon the traveled portion or the shoulder of a divided or one-way highway, the driver shall place the required warning devices, one warning device at a distance of 200 feet (61 m) and one warning device at a distance of 100 feet (30.5 m) in a direction toward approaching traffic in the center of the lane or shoulder occupied by the commercial motor vehicle. He/she shall place one warning device at the traffic side of the commercial motor vehicle within 10 feet (3.1 m) of the rear of the commercial motor vehicle.

vi. Leaking, flammable material. If gasoline or any other flammable liquid, or combustible liquid or gas seeps or leaks from a fuel container or a commercial motor vehicle stopped upon a highway, no emergency warning signal producing a flame shall be lighted or placed except at such a distance from any such liquid or gas as will assure the prevention of a fire or explosion.

Whenever a commercial motor vehicle is stopped upon the traveled portion of a highway or the shoulder of a highway for any cause other than necessary traffic stops, the driver of the stopped commercial motor vehicle shall immediately activate the vehicular hazard warning signal flashers and continue the flashing until the driver places the required warning devices.

The flashing signals shall be used during the time the warning devices are picked up for storage before movement of the commercial motor vehicle. The flashing lights may be used at other times while a commercial motor vehicle is stopped in addition to, but not in lieu of, the required warning devices.

CAUTION!

If you must drive slowly, alert following drivers by turning on your emergency flashers if it is legal. Laws regarding the use of flashers differ from one state to another. Check the laws of the states where you will drive.

CAUTION!

Remember: Don't Direct Traffic! Some drivers try to help out others by signaling when it is safe to pass. Never, never use your left turn signal to tell following motorists it is safe to pass. In some areas, it is against the law. Moreover, you could cause an accident and be liable for damages.

COMMUNICATING YOUR PRESENCE

Other drivers may not notice your vehicle, even when it's in plain sight. Let them know you're there to help prevent accidents.

- **When Passing.** Whenever you are about to pass a vehicle, pedestrian, or bicyclist, assume they don't see you. They could suddenly move in front of you. When it is legal, tap the horn lightly or, at night, flash your lights from low to high beam and back. And drive carefully enough to avoid a crash even if they don't see or hear you. Be careful when flashing your lights at another truck you intend to pass, as some drivers might take that as a signal that it's OK to move over in front of you!

- **When It's Hard to See.** At dawn or dusk or in rain or snow, you need to make yourself easier to see. If you are having trouble seeing other vehicles, other drivers will have trouble seeing you. Turn on your lights. Use the headlights, not just the identification or clearance lights. Use the low beams; high beams can bother people in the daytime as at night.

- **When Parked at the Side of the Road.** When you pull off the road and stop, be sure to turn on the four-way emergency flashers. This is important at night. Don't trust the taillights to give warning. Drivers have crashed into the rear of a parked vehicle because they thought it was moving normally. If you must stop on a road or the shoulder of any road, you must put out your emergency warning triangles within 10 minutes.

- **When Backing.** Use your four-way flashers any time you're backing unless it is against the policies of your yard or a customer's dock.

USING CELL PHONES SAFELY

Not that many years ago, a **cell phone** was an unheard-of space-age gadget **(see Figure 14-8).** Cell phones are everywhere now and have been recognized as a major distraction for drivers. The evidence linking cell phone use to accidents is so compelling that an increasing number of countries, and U.S. cities, have actually made it illegal to drive while talking on the phone. In the U.S. as of January 1, 2012 drivers of CMV's can only use a cell phone utilizing "Hands Free" technology. Regardless of where you are or what state you are in – drivers cannot talk on the phone with one hand and drive a commercial motor vehicle with the other. Effective January 3, 2012, Federal Motor Carrier Regulations ban the use of cell phones while truck and bus drivers are behind the wheel. This law supersedes all state laws.

Cell phone conversations and/or sending or receiving text messages while driving is also illegal in all provinces.

Even if you think you are watching the road, you are actually just steering the vehicle by force of habit, and using your logic and reasoning brain for your non-driving activities. This means that if you

▶ **Figure 14-8**

Using a cell phone can be a distraction; use only if absolutely necessary.

CAUTION!

Any activity you perform in your cab, whether you're moving or not, could be considered a distraction—from eating a burger, drinking coffee, or unwrapping a stick of gum. Your 100 percent concentration is required any time you're in the driver's seat—and caution runs a close second to concentration.

had to make a sudden decision (for instance, if traffic suddenly stopped in front of you on the freeway) you would have to take time to "reengage" your decision-making brain and would not be able to react as quickly as if you had been paying full attention to the road.

Commercial and private drivers have come to depend on the flexibility and convenience cell phones offer, but as a professional driver, your safety is important and it is compromised by a cell phone call. In fact, many carriers have now instituted cell phone use policies. Be sure you know what your employer allows.

AVOIDING DISTRACTED DRIVING

In this era of cellular communications, wi-fi, iPads, on-board computers, and GPS, distractions in the cab are inevitable. In this section, we'll examine the possible distractions you, as a professional driver, should know about and avoid.

There are three main types of distraction:

- Visual—taking your eyes off the road
- Manual—taking your hands off the wheel
- Cognitive—taking your mind off what you're doing

Distracted driving is any nondriving activity a person engages in that has the potential to distract him or her from the primary task of driving and increase the risk of crashing (**see Figure 14-9**). While all distractions can endanger drivers' safety, **texting** is the most alarming because it involves all three types of distraction—visual, manual, and cognitive (or thinking about what you're reading or texting).

Other distracting activities include:

- Using a cell phone
- Eating and drinking
- Talking to passengers
- Grooming
- Reading, including maps
- Using a PDA or navigation system
- Watching a video—yes, it's possible with smartphones.
- Changing the radio station, CD, or Mp3 player.
- Using a CD radio

▶ Figure 14-9
Texting can endanger a driver's safety.

Because distracted driving has become so hazardous on today's highways around North America, a number of researchers have conducted studies that revealed the following:

- 20 percent of injury crashes in 2009 involved reports of distracted driving (NHTSA).
- Of those killed in distracted-driving-related crashed, 995 involved reports of a cell phone as a distraction (18% of fatalities in distraction-related crashes) (NHTSA).

- In 2009, 5,474 people were killed on U.S. roadways and an estimated additional 448,000 were injured in motor vehicle crashes that were reported to have involved distracted driving.

- The age group with the greatest proportion of distracted drivers was the under-20 age group—16 percent of all drivers younger than 20 involved in fatal crashes were reported to have been distracted while driving (NHTSA). And since you're not in this age group, don't think you're in the clear. You share the highways with these young drivers and should be alert to fellow drivers who are driving distracted.

- Drivers who use handheld devices are four times as likely to get into crashes serious enough to injure themselves (Insurance Institute for Highway Safety).

- Using a cell phone use while driving, whether it's handheld or hands-free, delays a driver's reactions as much as having a blood alcohol concentration at the legal limit of 0.08 percent (University of Utah).

Driver distraction presents a serious and potentially deadly danger and comes in various forms, such as cell phone use, texting while driving, eating, drinking, lighting a pipe or a cigarette, flicking ashes in an ashtray and talking with passengers, as well as using in-vehicle technologies and portable electronic devices. There also are other less obvious forms of distractions including daydreaming or dealing with strong emotions, such as having an argument with a spouse, manager, or dispatcher while you're on the road.

While these numbers are significant, they may not state the true size of the problem, since the identification of distraction and its role in a crash can be very difficult to determine using only police-reported data. New data sources are available to provide more details on the type and presence of driver distraction.

- The proportion of fatalities reportedly associated with driver distraction increased from 10 percent in 2005 to 16 percent in 2009. The portion of drivers reportedly distracted at the time of the fatal crashes increased from 7 percent in 2005 to 11 percent in 2009.

- The under-20 age group had the highest proportion of distracted drivers involved in fatal crashes (16%). The age group with the next greatest proportion of distracted drivers was the 20- to 29-year-old age group—13 percent of all 20- to 29-year-old drivers in fatal crashes were reported to have been distracted.

- Of those drivers reportedly distracted during a fatal crash, the 30- to 39-year-old drivers were the group with the greatest proportion distracted by cell phones. Cell phone distraction was reported for 24 percent of the 30- to 39-year-old distracted drivers in fatal crashes.

- Light-truck drivers and motorcyclists had the greatest percentage of total drivers reported as distracted at the time of the fatal crash (12% each). Bus drivers had the lowest percentage (6%) of total drivers involved in fatal crashes that were reported as distraction-related.

- An estimated 20 percent of 1,517,000 injury crashes were reported to have involved distracted driving in 2009.

- During NHTSA's 100-Car Naturalistic Driving Study, driver involvement in secondary tasks contributed to more than 22 percent of all crashes and near-crashes recorded during the study period.

Many states and provinces include a category for cell phone/electronic equipment distraction on police accident report forms. Recently proposed federal legislation would require states to collect these data in order to qualify for certain federal funding.

Many local municipalities have passed their own distracted driving bans. However, some states prohibit local municipalities from enacting such laws.

CELL PHONE, TEXTING LAWS IN THE CANADIAN PROVINCES

As of July 2011, distracted driving legislation had been enacted in all Canadian provinces, with restrictions similar to those being adopted in the United States.

Many Canadian provinces have active laws against use of handheld cell phones and/or text messaging while driving.

Here's an update on the current specifics of the provinces and territories:

- New Brunswick's distracted driving law took effect June 6, 2011. The law prohibits drivers from using handheld cell phones and texting devices.

- Alberta's law targeting distracted driving took effect Sept. 1, 2011, covers PDAs and other handheld electronic communications devices. Also prohibited were personal grooming, noncommercial use of CB radios, writing, drawing, sketching, and use of certain video screens.

- The Yukon Territory's ban on drivers' use of cell phones and "similar electronic devices" went into effect April 1, 2011. Fines run up to $250 with a possible 3 points against the driver's license.

- The Northwest Territory's House was expected to consider a ban on handheld electronic devices in August 2011. One minister held that distracted driving laws were not needed because many areas were without cell phone coverage.

- Prince Edward Island's ban on the use of handheld electronic devices went into effect January 23, 2010. Fines range from $250 to $400 plus 3 points against the license.

- Saskatchewan's ban on talking and texting on handheld cell phones became law January 1, 2010. Violators are to be fined $280 and will receive 4 demerit points. Regina, Saskatchewan, police say they wrote almost 500 tickets for cell phone use in 2010. Thirty-one warnings were handed out as well. A Saskatchewan poll taken in September 2009 indicated that 60 percent of residents "strongly support" bans on cell phone use and text messaging by drivers. Saskatoon's police chief has called for cell phoning and texting to be outlawed for motorists.

- British Columbia's bans on handheld cell phone use and text messaging while driving became law January 1, 2010, with fines of $167.

- Quebec's ban on the use of a cell phone or another handheld device with a telephone function while driving has been in effect since April 1, 2008.

- Manitoba's ban on drivers' use of handheld cell phones and texting devices went into effect July 15, 2010. The fine is $191, the transportation ministry said. A public education campaign began in September 2009.

- Ontario's law against text messaging and using handheld cell phones while driving went into full effect in February 2010. Ontario police handed out 45,975 tickets to distracted drivers in the period from February 1, 2010 (when active enforcement began), to December 31, 2010. Fines of $155 didn't kick in until February 1. A year after enforcement of the province's handheld electronic devices ban, Toronto police say they're citing about 40 motorists a day. Ontario's law officers have cited more than 20,000 motorists for distracted driving infractions in the seven months since full enforcement of its law began in February 2010.

> **NOTE**
>
> The Canadian Automobile Association is convinced that driving while using a hands-free cell phone is no safer than driving with a handheld cell phone. It's pushing the provincial governments to expand their bans. The market research company Angus Reid says 88 percent of Canadians surveyed were supportive of a ban on use of handheld cell phones by car drivers. 77 percent said this prohibition would make the country's roads and highways much safer.

How to Avoid Distracted Driving

Without a doubt, distracted drivers pose a deadly risk to everyone on the road. As a professional driver, your job becomes two-pronged: (1) To be aware of distracted drivers on the roadway with you and (2) to remain focused and undistracted in your own driving.

1. **Turn it off.** Turn your phone off or switch to silent mode before you get into your rig.

2. **Spread the word.** Set up a special message to tell possible callers you are driving and you'll get back to them as soon as possible.

3. **Pull over.** If you need to make a call, pull over to a safe area first.

4. **X the Text.** Don't ever text and drive, surf the web or read your e-mail (or anything else) while driving. It is dangerous and against the law in most states and provinces.

5. **Know the law.** Familiarize yourself with province, state, and local laws before you get in your rig. Some states and localities prohibit the use of handheld cell phones. As of January 2012, U.S. CMV drivers cannot use a handheld cell phone, they must use "hands free."

6. **Prepare.** Review maps and directions before you start to drive. If you need help when you are on the road, pull over to a safe location to review the map/directions again.

7. **Focus on the task at hand.** Refrain from smoking, eating, drinking, reading, and any other activity that takes your mind and eyes off the road.

▶ *"Distracted? I thought I was multitasking !? Not wise for this job."*

© Cengage Learning 2013

SUMMARY

In this chapter, you learned the importance of communicating with other road users. You learned that communication is key to highway safety. The correct ways to signal a turn or lane change, slowing down, and overtaking another road user were explained. You also now know how to place warning devices correctly if you must stop your truck by the side of the road—and, finally, you learned that truck drivers have a responsibility to continually communicate with the driving public—wherever you go.

KEY TERMS

Cell phones	Distracted driving	Road rage
Communication	Reflective triangle	Texting

REVIEW QUESTIONS

1. When a professional driver signals his or her next move and at the same time is alert to the messages coming from other drivers, pedestrians, and cyclists, the driver is said to be _____.

    a. driving slow

    b. driving fast

    c. needing rest

    d. communicating with others on the road

2. Aggressive driving, criminal behavior, or bad driving can be defined as _____.

    a. good conduct

    b. road rage

    c. good driving

    d. safe driving

3. Which of the following is not considered distracted driving?

    a. signaling a turn

    b. drinking a cup of coffee

    c. changing radio stations

    d. answering a call from your dispatcher

4. Distracted driving in 2009 was the cause of _____ percent of vehicular accidents in the U.S.

    a. 30

    b. 20

    c. 10

    d. more than 50

5. To communicate an intent to slow suddenly, the professional driver _____.

    a. taps the brake pedal lightly a few times to flash the brake lights

    b. flashes the clearance lights

    c. flashes the headlights

    d. turns on the emergency flashers

6. Which of the following is not a good practice when overtaking a pedestrian or a bicyclist?

    a. blast your air horn loud and long to teach them not to use the highway

    b. a light tap on the air horn

    c. a light tap on the electrical horn

    d. at night, flash the lights with the dimmer switch

7. Any time a professional driver must pull off and stop at the side of the road, to warn other drivers, the _____ should be turned on.

    a. clearance lights

    b. left turn signal

    c. head lights

    d. four-way flashers

8. If a driver is forced to stop on or near the road, reflective triangles must be put out within _____.

    a. 30 minutes

    b. 5 minutes

    c. the first hour

    d. 10 minutes

9. If a driver is forced to stop on an undivided highway, to give overtaking drivers plenty of warning, a reflective triangle must be placed _____ behind the rig on the shoulder or in the lane in which the rig is stopped.

    a. 10 feet/3.1 meters

    b. about 50 feet/15.2 meters

    c. about 100 feet/30.5 meters

    d. 1 mile/1.6 kilometers

10. If a driver is forced to stop on a one-way divided highway, to give overtaking drivers plenty of warning, a reflective triangle must be placed about _____ behind the rig.

    a. 50 feet/15.2 meters   **c.** 75 feet/22.9 meters

    b. 200 feet/61 meters   **d.** 80 feet/24.4 meters

11. As of June 2011, _____ of the Canadian provinces/territories have laws against using cell phones while driving.

    a. 7   **c.** 10

    b. 9   **d.** 11

12. Ways to avoid distracted driving include all but which of the following:

    a. Pull over.

    b. Tell people you'll call when you're parked.

    c. Turn off cell phone.

    d. Wear dark-colored clothing.

13. Good communication on the highway includes _____.

    a. using turn signals   **c.** your position on the road

    b. your driving speed   **d.** all of the above

SUPPLEMENTAL LEARNING ACTIVITIES

1. A survey conducted in 2010 found that 71 percent of people between the ages of 18 and 49 admit they text or talk on the phone while driving. Unfortunately, these tasks can often end in tragedy. How long does it take to read a text? In five seconds and traveling at 40 miles per hour (64 km/h), your personal vehicle travels approximately the length of a football field. Try to determine how long the following tasks might take: (1) Looking up a cell phone number from your contacts. (2) Looking in the mirror and fluffing up your hair. (3) Reading a 10-word text. (4) Lighting a cigarette. (5) Opening a soft drink. Now, translate this time—using 5 sec × 40 mph/64 km/h = 100 yards/91.4 m—to determine how far your personal vehicle would travel while your eyes are off the road.

2. Discuss your personal experiences with people you know who have had accidents while texting or talking on their cells—whether in a parking lot, a city street, or on the highway.

3. Talk about emotional distractions with a small group—events that happen before you get behind the wheel, such as an argument with a friend, a fight with a spouse, or a reprimand from a boss. How would you think these emotional moments would distract your concentration and affect your driving? Make a list and be prepared to discuss these in class.

4. Is cell phone usage/texting an addiction? Make your arguments, why or why not, in a 100-word report.

5. List as many distractions as you can, inside and outside of the cab while driving. The learner with the longest list wins!

FOR MORE INFORMATION

Highway Watch Program: Infrastructure—Transportation—The Highway Watch Program
www.domesticpreparedness.com/

Trucker CB Communications
www.truckercountry.com/trucker-communications.html

Sections of the Canadian Highway Traffic Act, Ontario
www.e-laws.gov.on.ca/html/statutes/english/elaws_statutes_90h08_e.htm#BK120 and www.e-laws.gov
.on.ca/html/regs/english/elaws_regs_900596_e.htm

15 Visual Search

© topora/www.Shutterstock.com

OBJECTIVES

When you have completed this chapter, you should be able to:

- Explain the different types of mirrors as well as their adjustments and how to use them effectively.
- Know the relationship between speed and sight distance.
- Describe the professional driver's responsibility to other drivers.
- Learn the visual search patterns and importance for straight driving, changing speed or direction, and for entering or crossing traffic.
- Understand visual search patterns and scanning procedures.

INTRODUCTION

To become a safe and efficient driver, it is important to learn how to be constantly aware of the environment—what is going on around your rig at all times **(see Figure 15-1)**. Sound strange? Keep reading!

Imagine having a view of your rig from a few hundred feet above. Notice the space on all sides of the rig—front, back, sides, and top. This is the **external environment**—the environment you will constantly need to see, hear, feel, and sense when driving.

There is also an **internal environment**—the environment inside the cab of the tractor—where the driver must be constantly aware of the conditions in which he or she has to work **(see Figure 15-2).**

▶ **Figure 15-1**

Constantly be aware of the environment around your rig.

▶ **Figure 15-2**

The interior environment of the cab also impacts how a driver feels and reacts to outside factors.

Why is the internal environment important? Because the cab's environment has a great impact on how the driver feels, how quickly the driver is fatigued, and how well the driver can react to factors on the outside of the cab. Is the temperature too hot or too cold? Are there exhaust fumes filtering into the cab? Does the chatter of the CB distract? Is the music too loud and too chaotic? All of these factors impact how you drive. These environments also change every second your rig is rolling, so you are constantly adjusting your awareness of what is around you.

As you study this chapter, you will learn what you need to know to be constantly aware of your environment and how to respond and drive through each situation.

THE DRIVER'S VIEW

Think about what you are able to see from behind the wheel of a big rig. The view from the tractor's cab is much different from the view you have when you are behind the wheel of your personal vehicle. Obviously, you can see a greater distance ahead because you are sitting above the traffic. In some cases, you can see over the traffic, which is to your advantage! **(See Figure 15-3).**

▶ **Figure 15-3**

The view from the tractor's cab is very different than from a personal vehicle.

On the flip side, you cannot see as well to the sides and rear of your rig as you can when you are driving your personal vehicle. In the cab of a tractor, it is difficult to see the right side of the tractor-trailer and along the drive wheels on both sides. It is also difficult for a driver to see smaller vehicles that are driving close around a big rig.

Ultimately, the driver must be able to get a clear, complete, and accurate picture of the outside environment. Of course, there are existing blind spots that cannot be eliminated unless the driver does a vehicle walkaround before getting into the truck and makes the needed adjustments. For example, blind spots exist in the front of the tractor and at the rear of the trailer. To be eliminated, these must be observed and cleared by the driver just as he or she would make sure the direction the truck is going is clear before starting the engine.

FOCUSING ON THE ROAD AHEAD

While most of this discussion may seem obvious, it is important to explore the responsibilities of a professional driver as he or she takes to the road. Without question, looking down the road as well as watching the road directly ahead and to the back and sides of your rig makes you aware of the environment around the truck **(see Figure 15-4).** Steering toward an imaginary target or a reference point in the center of your lane of travel keeps you in your lane and aware of any possible problems ahead. Having a target will keep you and your vehicle centered in your lane.

© Andrey Tirakhov/www.Shutterstock.com

▶ **Figure 15-4**

A professional driver should always focus on the road ahead, and around.

Veteran truckers will tell you: A good rule of thumb is to have a target at least the distance you'll travel in the next 12 to 15 seconds. Another name for this is **"eye lead time."** In city driving, 12 seconds equals about one block ahead. On the open highway, 12 seconds ahead is about a quarter mile (0.4 km).

CAUTION!

If you cannot look ahead one block in the city or a quarter mile (0.4 km) on the highway, slow down and be extra alert.

Looking as far ahead as possible will give you time to:

- Identify any problems ahead
- Prepare for these problems
- Decide how you can drive defensively around the problem
- Check anything that could keep you from making any changes in speed, direction, lane, etc.
- Take the right action to keep you and others around you safe

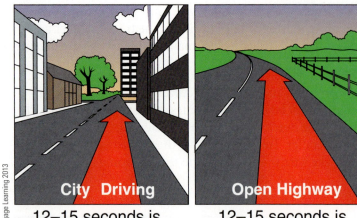

City Driving — 12–15 seconds is about 1 block

Open Highway — 12–15 seconds is about 1/4 of a mile

© Cengage Learning 2013

▶ **Figure 15-5**

Looking down the road gives the driver time to avoid hazards.

Looking ahead 12 to 15 seconds and having enough visual lead time will allow you the ability to react efficiently and safely, save fuel, and save time, because you will have fewer close calls, near misses, or accidents **(see Figure 15-5)**.

- **Safety**—by looking ahead, you will see hazards early enough to avoid them.

- **Fuel**—by looking 12 to 15 seconds ahead, you can adjust smoothly and avoid quick speed adjustments, which require more fuel.

- **Time**—spotting situations early will help you avoid being trapped behind turning vehicles, getting stuck in the wrong lane, or missing your exit.

SIGHT AND DECISIONS

One of your most valuable tools as a professional driver is your eyesight—your vision—and the most important thing you can do to help you see better is to have regular eye examinations and wear corrective lenses if you need them.

Remember: Normal eyes are at their peak performance when a person is in their teens. Vision begins to decline around age 15. So, if you have not yet experienced any noticeable changes in your vision, be aware that it will happen. Watch for warning signs, such as blurry objects far away and difficulty judging distance at night.

Age-related changes in your eyesight may include poor vision in dim light, difficulty seeing in glare conditions and reduced peripheral vision. As they occur, these changes require more time to effectively search the traffic scene.

As a professional driver, you rely on your good vision in many more ways than just seeing down the roadway. Did you know, for example, you gather most of the information you need to drive safely from the information you receive from your eyes—and about 90 percent of the decisions you make are based on what you see **(see Figure 15-6).** For this reason it is very important to also keep windows and mirrors clean. Windshield wipers must also be in good condition.

What you are able to see without obstruction is called your "line-of-sight." The best conditions for visual search are when your line of sight

Courtesy of 5th Wheel Training Institute (1-888-647-7202).

▶ **Figure 15-6**

Ninety percent of the decisions you make while driving are based on what you see.

around all sides of your vehicle is not obstructed. When you can see well ahead, behind, and along each side, you can identify hazards, predict the conditions you might encounter, and prepare to execute your driving maneuvers.

When and wherever you drive, be aware of the quality of your line-of-sight. Look far ahead at the center of your path of travel and practice an orderly search pattern by moving your eyes. FOCUS quickly and keep your eyes moving. To ensure you can detect hazards in all directions, do not stare at anything or in any one direction for more than a fraction of a second.

SCANNING AND THE VISUAL SEARCH

Although it is important to have 12 to 15 seconds of visual lead time as you drive, be careful not to spend all of your time staring at the roadway ahead. Why? Because it is also important to know what is going on around your rig—to the sides, the back, and even on top of your rig.

Once you have chosen a reference point on the road ahead, make a **visual search** and scan around the rest of your rig.

Conduct your visual search pattern without interruption: search ahead, your mirrors, search ahead, check the dashboard, and continuously repeat this cycle. As you conduct your visual search, make a conscious attempt not to be distracted.

The routine looks like this:

Look 12 to 15 seconds ahead of the rig and on both sides of the roadway ahead. Now quickly look away from your reference point ahead and scan both sides and in back of the rig before returning to the reference point.

Let us review the routine:

- Pick a reference point 12 to 15 seconds ahead and look at both sides of the road between your rig and that reference point.
- Now quickly look to either side—using your mirrors—and to the back of your rig before picking up the reference point.

When **scanning,** look for anything that can affect your travel path (**see Figure 15-7**):

- People—on foot and in cars
- Traffic signs
- Debris on the highway
- Signals
- Slick spots or potholes in the road
- Intersections
- Merging lanes
- Road shoulders

© Cengage Learning 2013

"Cleaning your shades doesn't just make you look cool . . . it makes you a visionary!"

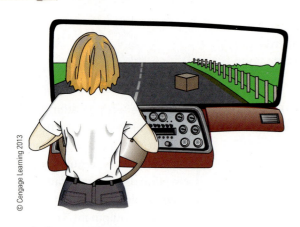

▶ **Figure 15–7**

Visual scanning gives the driver time for defensive action.

- Construction zones
- School zones
- Stopped vehicles
- Emergency situations

A 12-to-15-second visual control search will give you time to identify a place or places to which you can steer, on or off the road, if a potential problem situation develops into a threatening situation. The 12-to-15-second visual control zone also allows time to decide where to go if you cannot steer where you intended. Being able to identify alternate paths also becomes critical if you are in a situation where you may be struck from the rear.

CAUTION!

As you scan, always look for **escape paths**—places you can use to avoid a crash. In many instances the space between you and the vehicle in front of you will be an escape path. Make sure you leave adequate following distances at all times. Once you become accustomed to the visual search and scanning pattern, you will also learn how to pick and choose what you look for, depending on traffic and your driving environment.

CAUTION!

The following are clues that you are not looking far enough ahead when you drive:

- You make frequent quick stops.
- In traffic, you often find yourself boxed in a slow-moving lane. This indicates you have not spotted problems well enough in advance to avoid them.

INCREASE THE SCOPE OF YOUR VISUAL SEARCH ROUTINE

Once you have mastered the routine above, try adding a few more points to your visual search:

- Adjust any type of mirrors you'll use to increase the scope of your visual search.
- Maintain a minimum 12–15-second eye lead time.
- Scan both sides of the road, using quick glances to see any nearby vehicles and other activity.
- Check mirrors for hazards—and always check mirrors when changing speed or direction.
- Check instrument panel frequently in your visual search.
- Look ahead as far as possible on turns and curves.

- Check to the side before turning or changing lanes.
- Monitor overtaking traffic so you'll know about vehicles behind and in your blind spots.
- Avoid diverting your attention from the roadway ahead of you.
- Check all intersections and crossings, using proper technique.

THE VISUAL SEARCH AT NIGHT

Although we will go into this topic in depth in a separate chapter on night driving, it is important to continue your visual search, even as daylight drifts into darkness.

At night, as you might expect, your vision is impaired and driving safely becomes more difficult. Your depth and distance perception are decreased, you have a low ability to distinguish colors, eye muscles fatigue from exposure to bright daylight, and your eyes' ability to recover from glare is decreased. If you are driving facing the sun at dusk or dawn, you may need glasses to reduce glare. However, as we will state several times in this chapter, sunglasses should never be worn at night when driving.

Remember, the faster you are traveling, the longer it takes to stop. If you are traveling so fast that you cannot see past the location where you would come to a complete stop, you are "overdriving your headlights." If you overdrive your headlights, and you see an obstacle in your path, you will not be able to stop before you hit that obstacle.

In curves, your headlights are pointing straight ahead, not into the curve. Slow down and try to search into curves beyond the illuminated path to the best of your ability. Reducing your speed will help.

If an oncoming vehicle has its high-beam lights on, flash your high beams once to signal that its headlights are blinding you. If the driver does not switch to low beams, look at the white lane markings to the right to maintain your lane position. Check oncoming traffic with quick glances.

NOTE

Smaller straight trucks might have this type of equipment, but it will not be found on larger equipment.

If someone's headlights are on behind you, you may want to switch your mirrors to the night setting. This setting is designed to reduce glare but might affect your ability to judge the distance of traffic behind you. If the setting does not help, look for a place to safely pull over and let the driver pass.

One More Thing to Remember

It is just as important to be seen as it is to see. You share the road with many drivers who have declining vision, so be aware that many drivers may not see you clearly even though you can see them.

Never assume other drivers see you or that they will see you and stop in time to avoid hitting you.

Scanning and Driving into Intersections

After stopping at an intersection, know how to look at this environment before moving into and across the traffic lanes. The following guidelines should help:

- Move your rig forward slowly, giving other drivers a chance to see you and to understand your intentions. The slow, controlled speed will also allow you to stop again before pulling into the path of cross traffic.
- Look to the left, then to the right, and then straight ahead. Then look left again as you begin to move forward.

GO!

The reason for using this order of scanning is:

■ The first lane you cross carries traffic from the left; until this lane is clear, you cannot move forward.

■ If the right lane is also clear, you can safely begin to move forward.

■ At this point, the second look to the left ensures that there are no changes from that direction.

■ Even if driving onto a one-way road, you need to be aware of pedestrians and cyclists. Moreover, crashes have occurred when a driver went the wrong way down a one-way road.

■ You can now go through the intersection, but be aware of blind spots.

From your seat in the cab, you can see behind you only in your left and right side-view mirrors. Check these mirrors when you scan and search. It is important to check them before you slow down, stop, or change lanes or direction.

Visual search is one of the most critical components in driver safety and efficiency. A **systematic search** begins with a walkaround of the vehicle every time it is driven, paying close attention to the space in front and at the rear of the vehicle.

The only way to eliminate front and rear blind spots is to first be aware that they are there. The driver sitting behind the steering wheel *always* has a blind spot directly in front of the vehicle that can range a distance of 30 to 50 feet (9.1 to 15.2 m). A blind spot existing directly behind a vehicle can range a distance of 200 feet (61 m).

CAUTION!

Imagine an 8-foot-wide (2.4 m) trailer, multiplied by the 200-foot (61 m) distance, could equal 1,600 feet (487.7 m) of blind space. So, *always begin a visual search before entering the vehicle.*

**Field of Vision
Using a Plane Mirror**

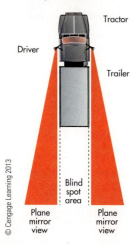

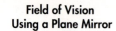

FIELD OF VIEW

You have the largest **field of view** in your left side-view mirror. The closer the mirror is to you, the larger the image. The larger the image, the bigger the field of view. Images will appear similar to those in the side-view mirror of your personal vehicle (**see Figure 15-8**).

▶ **Figure 15-8**

The plane mirror gives the driver the best view of the rear of the trailer and roadway behind but it leaves blind spots.

© Cengage Learning 2013

THE "NO ZONE"

The **"no-zone"** refers to the blind-spot areas around large commercial vehicles, or the areas where cars are so close to the truck or bus that the driver's ability to stop or maneuver safely is restricted.

Although this program was implemented several decades ago, many professional drivers still refer to the "no-zone." In conjunction with the enactment of the Intermodal Surface Transportation Efficiency Act, Congress directed the Federal Highway Administration (FHWA) (now under the direction of the Federal Motor Carrier Safety Administration [FMCSA]) to educate the driving public about how to safely share the road with trucks and buses. In response, FMCSA introduced the "No-Zone" or "Share the Road" Program in 1994.

The goal of the campaign was to educate motorists about how to safely share the road with trucks and buses, specifically by increasing awareness of the no-zones—danger areas like blind spots, around commercial vehicles, in which cars "disappear" from the view of the truck or bus driver. No-zones are areas where crashes are more likely to occur. Educating drivers about the no-zones may reduce deaths, injuries, and property damage from these kinds of crashes.

Why do you need to know about the no-zone?

Knowing about the no-zone areas around large vehicles will help you to steer clear of unsafe situations involving large vehicles and help reduce crashes **(see Figure 15-9).**

▶ **Figure 15–9**

No-zones are areas where crashes are more likely to occur.

There are more than 250,000 crashes involving cars and trucks every year. Many could be avoided by keeping these important points in mind:

- Large vehicles have much more sizable blind spots than cars do.
- Large vehicles also have deep blind spots directly behind them. If you are driving behind a truck or bus and you can't see one of its side-view mirrors, the driver can't see you.
- At times, truck and bus drivers need to swing wide to the left to make a right turn. Don't cut in between the vehicle and the curb or the shoulder to the right.
- Large vehicles cannot stop as quickly as cars. When passing, look for the whole front of the vehicle in your rear-view mirror before pulling in front of the truck or bus.
- After passing, don't slow down.

More about the no-zone:

In mid-August 2011, the Colorado State Patrol initiated a new safety campaign called TACT—Ticketing Aggressive Cars and Trucks.

In 2011, no-zone violations were a leading cause of the 968 crashes in Colorado between cars and trucks. Fifty of those accidents resulted in fatalities.

A no-zone violation is classified as following too close.

How do you stay out of the no-zone?

Keep enough distance behind the truck so the side-view mirrors are visible. That way you know the trucker can see you. If you're so close to the truck that you can't spot those mirrors, you're in the no-zone and could be ticketed by the patrol.

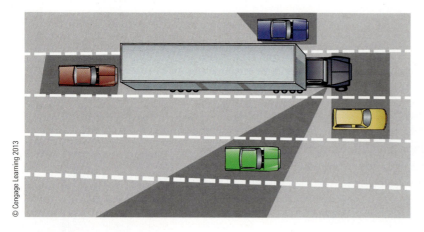

▶ **Figure 15–10**

Large blind spots are to the right, left, rear, and in front of the rig.

What About Those Blind Spots?

Blind spots behind a tractor-trailer can conceal large or multiple vehicles, which is one reason many trucks carry warnings about not following too closely. These warnings—"If you can't see my mirrors, I can't see you"—are necessary, in part, because the driver's position in the cab is higher. Tractor-trailers not only have large rear-quarter blind spots, but there are also large blind spots to the left, right, and front of the rig **(see Figure 15-10).**

Additional equipment that can help eliminate blind spots are **"fish-eye mirrors"** or "bubble mirrors," which are part of or adhered to the side-view mirror. These mirrors can bring blind spots into view, but their optical properties impart a great deal of distortion so as to make it difficult to judge distances. Ideally the convex and flat mirrors should be independently adjustable. The two mirrors are designed to show images from different locations. In addition, the location where a bubble mirror is affixed to a flat mirror is a "valuable" spot on the mirror. "Aspheric" mirrors allow blind spots to be eliminated while minimizing distortion by enlarging the field of view by 1.4 to 1.7 times. Panoramic rear-view mirrors widen the rear-view field.

Rear bumpers of large vehicles—particularly heavy mining equipment—can be fitted with rear-view cameras, allowing a better view from behind. These are most useful in tractor-trailers, which cannot see from behind while backing without these cameras.

Field of Vision Using a Convex Mirror

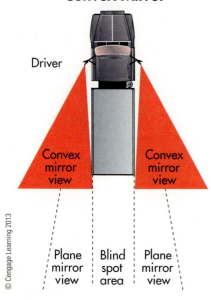

▶ **Figure 15–11**

Convex mirrors are curved to give a wide-angle view.

MIRRORS

The two types of side-view mirrors are plane (flat) and convex (curved).

- The flat mirror, **plane mirror** or **West Coast mirror** gives the most accurate view of the rear of the trailer and the roadway behind. It does not give a wide view and it can leave blind spots along the length of the rig **(see Figure 15-11).**
- **Convex mirrors** are curved to give you a wide-angle view. They are best used for side close-ups because they provide a much wider field of view.

Convex mirrors eliminate most, but not all, of the blind area created by the plane mirror. The images you see, however, will be smaller and will appear farther away than they really are. With plane mirrors, the blind areas are too large. Using only the convex mirror creates too much distortion, so it is best to have both plane and convex mirrors on your rig. Many rigs have this combination because it gives drivers the best possible side and rear vision **(see Figure 15-12).**

© Cengage Learning 2013

Combination of Plane/Convex Mirror

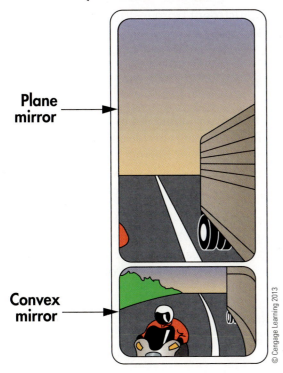

Plane mirror

Convex mirror

© Cengage Learning 2013

Field of Vision While Making a Right Turn

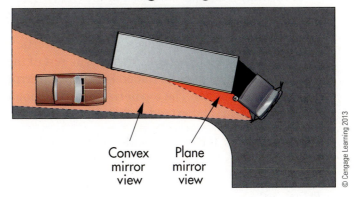

Convex mirror view

Plane mirror view

© Cengage Learning 2013

▶ **Figure 15-12**

Combination plane/convex mirrors provide the best rear and side vision.

▶ **Figure 15-13**

The convex mirror gives a wider field of vision when making a right turn.

GO!

Remember that blind spots will still be there, even when using both convex and plane mirrors. Always adjust your mirrors and check both to have the best possible visual of your rig.

A **fender mirror** is mounted on the fender of the tractor. Drivers use the fender mirror because it requires less eye movement and does not interfere with your view of the road ahead.

Wide-angle (convex) fender mirrors let you see a wide field of vision when you are making right turns. This is particularly helpful in making a tight turn. The view of the road is similar to what you see with a convex side mirror but with less distortion (**see Figure 15-13**).

Adjusting Mirrors

Every driver should adjust both the left and right mirrors on the tractor to get an accurate view of the sides and rear of the rig—before beginning each trip. All mirrors should be adjusted to show some part of the vehicle, such as the trailer body, tires, and so on. This will give the driver a good **point of reference** for judging the position of everything around the rig. For best effect, adjust mirrors when the rig is straight.

> **GO!**
>
> Some rigs have motorized mirrors. These allow adjustment from inside the cab. They can also be used to get a wider view when needed and can then be returned to normal positions.

For left-side mirrors, plane mirrors, the inside vertical edge of the mirror (about 3/4 to 1 inch/1.90 to 2.54 cm) should show the trailer's body. The remaining part will show what is beside and behind the trailer. The range of view to the side will be about 15 feet (4.6 m). For convex mirrors, the inside vertical edge of the mirror should show part of the trailer. The top horizontal edge should show a view overlapping that of the plane mirror by about 5 feet (1.5 m) and going back to the end of the trailer.

For right-side mirrors, plane mirrors, the inside vertical edge of the mirror (about 3/4 to 1 inch/1.90 to 2.54 cm) should reflect the trailer's body. The rest of the mirror will show what is on the side (for about 15 feet/4.6 m) and behind the trailer. For convex mirrors, the inside vertical edge of the mirror should reflect part of the trailer. The top horizontal edge should show a view overlapping that of the plane mirror by 5 feet (1.5 m) and extend to the end of the trailer.

For fender mirrors, the convex fender mirrors on both the right and left side should be adjusted so you can see the trailer's tires, curbs, and other objects when turning **(see Figure 15-14).**

Distortion of Convex Mirrors

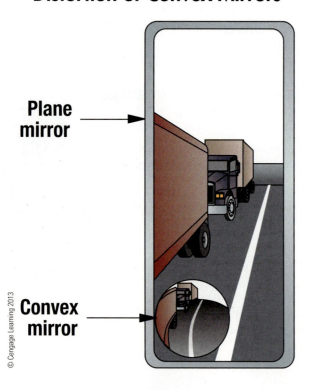

Plane mirror

Convex mirror

© Cengage Learning 2013

▶ **Figure 15–14**

Be aware of the distortion of convex mirrors.

Seeing to the Rear

Checking your rig's mirrors is a part of scanning and searching. Be sure to check the security of your load as well as the tires (looking for blowouts or fire). In addition, your mirror checks can tell you if there are any hazards around your rig as well as what is beside or behind the rig. To review FMCSA's Standard 111 regarding rear-view mirrors go to www.fmcsa.dot.gov

Using Mirrors When Making Lane Changes

Before making any sudden changes in speed or direction, always check the traffic behind you.

Changing lanes—always use the plane and convex mirrors when changing your path of travel. Be aware that there are blind spots behind and to each side of your rig.

It is important to make many checks to be sure of the traffic around you and remember it takes longer to check the rear when driving a rig than it does when you are driving a car. Properly checking the left mirrors takes almost 1 second. Checking mirrors on the right takes approximately 1.5 seconds.

Before checking your mirrors, make certain it is safe to look away from the front of the rig. At 55 mph (88 km/h), you travel 80 feet (24.4 m) in 1 second. Keep enough space between yourself and the vehicle traveling in front of you. Avoid taking chances. If there is not enough space or time, delay the lane change (**see Figure 15-15**).

Turning corners—when coming to a corner where you want to turn, check your side-view mirrors before slowing your rig for the turn. Then check them again as you are turning.

INTERESTING FACT

The rear-view mirror's earliest known mention was by Dorothy Levitt in her 1906 book, *The Woman and the Car*, which noted women should "carry a little hand-mirror when driving" so they may "hold the mirror aloft from time to time in order to see behind while driving in traffic," thereby inventing the rear-view mirror before it was introduced by manufacturers in 1914. The earliest known rear-view mirror mounted on a motor vehicle appeared in Ray Harroun's Marmon racecar at the inaugural Indianapolis 500 race in 1911, although Harroun claimed he got the idea from a horse-drawn vehicle with a rear-view mirror in 1904.

Checking to Sides and Rear

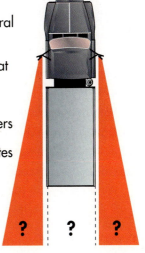

- Check mirrors several times a minute
- Be especially alert at
  - Intersections
  - Shopping centers
  - Construction sites
  - School zones

© Cengage Learning 2013

▶ Figure 15-15

Remember, it takes longer to check the rear of your rig than it does to check the rear of your personal vehicle.

CAUTION!

After completing the turn, check the mirrors again to make sure your rig is not entangled with or dragging anything and that your rig has not damaged anything.

SOME REVIEW TIPS ABOUT THE VISUAL SEARCH AND SCANNING

■ Develop the habit of observing the ground for changes in road traction conditions and for shadows that might indicate hidden hazards, such as children between parked cars. This practice will also help you judge the speed of other vehicles.

■ When changing lanes, check for traffic behind you, glance in your rear-view and side mirrors to make sure no one is preparing to pass you. Also, before you change lanes, glance over your shoulders to check the blind areas to be certain no one is near the left- or right-rear corners of your vehicle. Install larger side mirrors to reduce this blind spot.

■ Whenever you have to back your vehicle, check behind it before getting in. Children or small objects are hard to see from the driver's seat. Back up slowly because your vehicle is much harder to control and stop while you are backing.

■ Bright light at night reduces your vision and makes driving difficult and dangerous. Using the night setting on your rear-view mirror may help, but it may hamper your ability to judge the distance of traffic behind you.

■ At night, when there is no opposing traffic, use your high beams whenever possible to illuminate your path. Be sure to turn off your high beams if there is opposing traffic or when you see tail lights of vehicles ahead. If an approaching driver refuses to switch his high beams to low, you should locate the white marker and use it to guide you.

■ Do not overdrive your headlights: Never drive so fast that you do not have time to stop to avoid hitting something just beyond your lights. If you over-drive your headlights, and you see an obstacle in your path, you will not be able to stop before you hit that obstacle.

■ To help you see better in low-light conditions: Give your eyes a chance to adjust to darkness, especially after entering the dark from a brightly lit room. Give your eyes at least 30 seconds to adjust to the darkness while your engine is warming up. Keep in mind, it does not have to be pitch black for light levels to be inadequate.

■ Allow your eyes time to adjust to other low-light conditions such as twilight, fog, or haze.

■ Use all available light. If you are driving in the city, use low-beam headlights and stick to well-lit streets.

■ Make sure you get full use of your headlights. If you think your headlamps are not projecting light far enough ahead, have them checked and adjusted if necessary.

■ Keep headlights clean. Dirty lenses can cut the amount of light your headlights emit by as much as 90 percent.

■ Wear sunglasses during the day so your eyes are rested if you have to drive at night.

■ Do not smoke while you drive. In addition to creating a smoke screen, smoking reduces night vision. It also makes the windshield dirty.

■ One of the most overlooked, yet one of the most critical things related to vision, is keeping all the windows in your truck clean. The inside of the windshield and side windows is just as important as the outside. Make a habit of cleaning the windows inside and out regularly. You may find that in the summer, bugs cause the windshield to need daily cleaning, while in the winter, operating mostly with rolled-up windows causes the inside glass to need to be cleaned weekly.

SUMMARY

In this chapter, you learned how to systematically search the driving environment around your rig. You learned the value of looking ahead and planning for hazards. You now know the correct methods of crossing an intersection and making lane changes using visual search techniques, and you understand the differences between the reflected images in convex and plane mirrors. You are also aware of the importance of adjusting your mirrors before every trip so that you will have maximum visibility when you are on the road.

KEY TERMS

Convex mirror
Escape paths
External environment
Eye lead time
Fender mirror
Field of view

Fish-eye mirror
Internal environment
No-zones
Plane mirror or West Coast
  mirror
Point of reference

Scanning
Systematic search
Visual search

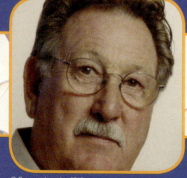

© Cengage Learning 2013

© Cengage Learning 2013

A DAY IN THE LIFE...

Tom and Karen Moore – Tom Moore Transportation, Team Drivers

After over 10 years and more than 1.2 million accident-free miles we still like each other. As team drivers we entered the industry after a variety of careers—as a legal secretary and running our own successful photography and racing businesses. We made the decision to change careers and enter the trucking industry over 10 years ago and haven't looked back. We got our CDLs, and became a one-truck business team, under our own authority pulling a flatbed—and are loving it. There is never a dull day.

Over the years this career has allowed us to experience the entire country and we have seen some very memorable things. The variety of the loads we haul make every day an adventure and we do it together. Every day we encounter new things and meet new people. While one of us drives, the other rests and then we switch. We are a team in every sense of the word.

We have had the privilege of watching the armadillos in Texas, moose in Maine, as well as mountain lions and big horned sheep. We have the ability to deliver needed cargo to every corner of the country taking in the sights and enjoying every opportunity that presents itself along the way.

One of our most memorable loads was delivering a windmill to a dairy farmer to allow him to power his family's dairy farm. We completed this trip during a blizzard in the roads of Montana. While this might not sound like the best job to some people, we were thrilled to be able to deliver needed equipment in a safe, on-time manner.

We take great satisfaction in the business we have built over the years. We are proud to have driven this many years and remain ticket and accident free. We understand the importance of safety in being on the road every day. We always take extreme pride in our log books and the great reputation we have earned for doing a great job.

> ## As team drivers we entered the industry after a variety of careers . . .

We took off our other hats after experiencing our previous careers and are happy every day to be a great trucking team! And while we are pretty sure we will never be rich, we truly feel our lives are rich with experience and adventure.

Trading in the high heels and business suits was a good decision.

What a learning experience this has been.

REVIEW QUESTIONS

1. Regarding visual search, the space on all sides of the rig a driver constantly needs to see, hear, feel, and sense when driving is called _____.

   a. the internal environment
   b. added space
   c. the external environment
   d. total stopping distance

2. The visual search pattern that helps a driver know what to look at, what to look for, and where to look is called _____.

   a. systematic seeing
   b. blind spot
   c. automatic seeing
   d. visual acuity

3. Looking at a target (point) at least the distance the rig will travel in 12 to 15 seconds is called _____.

   a. adjustment time
   b. eye lead time
   c. following distance
   d. reaction distance

4. The process of looking ahead of the rig 12 to 15 seconds, looking on both sides of the roadway ahead, and scanning both sides and in back of the rig should happen every _____.

   a. 5 miles (8 km/h)
   b. 6 to 8 seconds
   c. 30 seconds
   d. 1 mile/1.6 km

5. Regarding scanning and the visual search, the places that a driver can use to avoid a crash are called _____.

   a. safety zones
   b. construction zones
   c. exit ramps
   d. escape paths

6. Regarding scanning and driving into intersections, the general guidelines state: look to the left, then to the right, then straight ahead, and then _____ again.

   a. right
   b. straight ahead
   c. left
   d. behind the rig

7. Which of the following provides the driver the most accurate view of the rear of a trailer and the roadway behind it?

   a. plane (flat) mirror
   b. concave mirror
   c. convex mirror
   d. fish-eye mirror

8. Which type of mirror is best for side close-up views?

   a. plane mirror
   b. flat mirror
   c. fish-eye
   d. convex

9. Adjusting the mirrors to show some part of the rig will give the driver a point of reference for _____.

   a. checking the back doors of the trailer
   b. determining the speed of other images
   c. determining the width of the blind spot
   d. judging the position of the other vehicles

10. The "no-zone" refers to the blind spot areas around large commercial vehicles, or the areas where
_____.

    a. cars are so close to the truck/bus, the driver cannot see them. ✓

    b. other vehicles are not allowed

    c. the headlights of other vehicles blind the driver

    d. accidents happen most often

A ≠ D?

SUPPLEMENTAL LEARNING ACTIVITIES

1. Find out as much as you can about FMCSA's "No-Zone" campaign, including why it was developed, and how it continues to impact drivers across North America. Report to the class.

2. Practice the visual search. Ask a veteran driver to come and discuss how he or she conducts a visual search, and its importance, with your class.

3. Review FMCSR Standard 111. Then, discuss it with your instructor and the class.

4. Write a 100-word essay on the importance of undistracted scanning and visual search while driving.

5. Compare and contrast the flat, convex, and fish-eye mirrors and the unique uses of each.

FOR MORE INFORMATION

PTDI—Perform Visual Search, Page 14, Click on Skill Standards
www.ptdi.org/standards

Concave and Convex Mirrors and Lenses
faculty.virginia.edu/teach-present-bio/LightRefraction.html

16 Space Management

© Konstantin Sutyagin/www.Shutterstock.com

OBJECTIVES

When you have completed this chapter, you should be able to:

- Explain the safest following distance for driving in different conditions.

- Show the importance of maintaining distance between your rig and other vehicles when driving defensively.

- Describe how you, as a professional driver, can control your space on the roadway.

- Prevent the dangers of clearance and overhead obstructions.

- Explain the correct procedures for making turns.

- Manage space when driving through intersections.

INTRODUCTION

Just what does it take to become a professional driver in America's trucking industry? Some would say a citation-free, accident-free record. Others would say vehicles and cargos reaching their destinations without incident or damage. Obviously both of these statements are true, but it takes more than a clean record and a well-handled load.

In fact, a professional driver's highest achievement may be managing the space around his or her vehicle at all times (**see Figure 16-1**). Why? Because professional drivers make it their business to understand that the size and weight of large commercial vehicles create unique challenges that can be managed by exercising good judgment and employing defensive driving techniques. They know the importance of maintaining a safe following distance, how excessive speed can jeopardize their ability to maintain control of their vehicle, the need to yield the right-of-way and how to compensate for blind spots. These skills assist professional drivers in keeping themselves out of danger and preventing danger to other road users.

Veterans define **space management** as "maintaining a cushion of air around the vehicle in every environment." For the purposes of this book, we define it as "maintaining enough space around your rig to make every trip smooth, comfortable, and above all, uneventful" (**see Figure 16-2**).

THE IMPORTANCE OF SPACE MANAGEMENT

▶ **Figure 16-1**

Managing the space around your vehicle at all times is one sign of a skilled professional.

Space Cushion

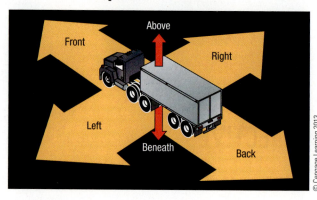

▶ **Figure 16-2**

Maintaining a cushion of air around your vehicle in every environment is good space management.

When driving a big rig, you need space around your vehicle at all times—in front, to the sides, and to the rear. When emergencies happen on the road, this same space gives you time to adjust.

Other vehicles may stop unexpectedly or turn in front of you. You may need space to change lanes, but you will continually need to check your mirrors and maintain this very important space around your rig. This process takes time, and time requires space.

Professional drivers are concerned with space in all directions—ahead, behind, to the sides, and above and below the rig. You also need to be aware of the space necessary for turning, crossing the roadway, and entering traffic.

To have the space you need when something goes wrong, whether it is mechanical problems, problems caused by debris on the roadway, or other drivers, you need to continue to manage the space around your rig at all times. This, of course, is true of all those using the highway, but it is especially important for professional drivers who are driving big rigs, because they take up more space and they need a great deal more space for every maneuver.

SPACE AHEAD

It does not take an experienced driver to realize that the most important space around a rig is the space ahead. This is the amount of space you need to stop your rig in any situation and for any reason. Experience and accident records indicate the vehicle most likely to be hit by a tractor-trailer rig is the one in front of it—and the most common cause of these collisions is that the rig has been following too closely.

If the vehicle ahead is lighter than your rig, it can stop faster and in less space. So, if the small sedan ahead suddenly puts on its brakes, it can stop

"Hey there big rig, just checking to make sure you have all the elbow room you need"

before you have completed your braking process. If that same small sedan begins to slow down and you—the driver of the rig that is following—fail to notice it, by the time you realize what is happening and decide to put on your brakes, you have used up most or all of the space that separates your rig from that little sedan.

The lesson here is, if you are following too closely, you may not be able to avoid hitting the vehicle in front of you.

How Much Space Do You Need to Be Safe?

How much space should you put between your rig and the vehicle in front of you? A good rule of thumb is that you need 1 second for each 10 feet (3.1 m) of your rig's length **(see Figure 16-3)**. That means if you are driving a 40-foot (12.2 m) rig, leave at least 4 seconds of time between your front bumper and the vehicle ahead of you. In a 60-foot (18.3 m) rig, you will need 6 seconds of space between you and that vehicle traveling in front of yours **(see Figure 16-4)**.

Heavy Vehicle Formula
For timed interval following distance

- 1 second required for each 10 feet (3.1 m) of vehicle length at speeds under 40 mph (64 km/h)
- Above 40 mph (64 km/h) use same formula, then add 1 second for the additional speed

40 foot (12.2 m) truck (under 40 mph/64 km/h) = 4 seconds

50 foot (15.2 m) truck (above 40 mph/64 km/h) = 6 seconds

60 foot (18.3 m) truck (under 40 mph/64 km/h) = 6 seconds

▶ **Figure 16-3**

Determine adequate following distances based on the length of your rig. Keep in mind that distances should increase when conditions are less than favorable due to poor visibility, snow, ice, rain, etc.

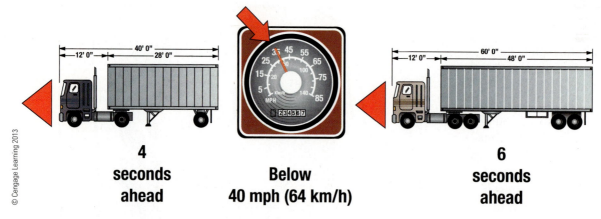

4 seconds ahead

Below 40 mph (64 km/h)

6 seconds ahead

▶ **Figure 16–4**

Adequate distance between your rig and the vehicle in front of you is measured in seconds.

CAUTION!

The "following" times mentioned above should be increased when driving in less favorable conditions, such as heavy traffic, poor visibility, high winds, snow, ice, rain, slick roads, or when experiencing mechanical problems.

GO!

To measure adequate following distance, note when the rear end of the vehicle ahead passes a mile marker, building, or other landmark. Then count off the seconds: 1-1000, 2-1000, 3-1000, and so on, until the front of your rig reaches the same spot. Compare your count with the rule of 1 second for every 10 feet (3.1 m) of your rig's length.

▶ **Figure 16–5**

You should have at least four seconds of space between your rig and the vehicle in front of you.

If you are driving a 40-foot (12.2 m) rig and count less than 4 seconds, you are following too closely. Drop back. Then count again. Until you have at least 4 seconds of space between your rig and the vehicle you are following, you are in danger and so are all other road users around you (**see Figure 16-5**).

For speeds above 40 mph (64 km/h), add 1 second to the basic amount of space needed:

Example: 50-foot (15.2 m) rig traveling at 48 mph (77 km/h):

■ Basic amount of space needed = 5 seconds (50/10 = 5)

■ Above 50 mph (80 km/h), add 1 second

■ Total following distance needed = 6 seconds (5 rig lengths = 1 speed over 40 mph (64 km/h) = 6)

For bad weather, poor visibility, or poor road conditions, you should add at least 1 more second:

Example: 60-foot (18.3 m) rig with poor visibility traveling at 55 mph (89 km/h):

- Basic amount of space needed = 6 seconds (60/10 = 6)
- Above 40 mph (64 km/h), add 1 second
- Poor visibility, add 1 more second
- Total following distance needed = 8 seconds (6 rig lengths + 1 speed over 40 mph (64 km/h) = 1 weather = 8)

NOTE

The times listed here are absolute minimums to ensure seeing time, thinking time, reacting time, and braking time.

USE EXTRA CAUTION DURING INCLEMENT WEATHER

Adjust your speed to match road conditions at all times. Driving on a wet or icy roadway can increase stopping distance significantly. Be prepared for other drivers who might lose control of their vehicles. Remember, the roadway can be extremely slippery immediately after it begins raining, when road oils are brought to the surface. Use your mirrors to monitor traffic on both sides and to the rear of the vehicle—and leave yourself a way out whenever possible!

SPACE BEHIND

As you know, you cannot completely control the space behind your rig because you cannot control drivers who approach your rig from behind on the highway. You can, however, do a number of things to have more control over this area:

1. Stay to the right.
2. Be careful when changing lanes.
3. Expect **tailgating** (when another vehicle follows your rig too closely to have adequate time to stop).
4. Respond safely to tailgaters.

- **Stay to the right**—sometimes going uphill or when a load is very heavy, a rig cannot keep up with other traffic. At these times, it is best to use the special truck lanes or stay as far to the right as possible. In some states, however, driving on the shoulder of the road is illegal. When going uphill, do not try to pass a slower vehicle unless it can be done quickly. Being caught behind two trucks that are side by side is annoying to other drivers and could bring on a case of severe road rage.

- **Changing lanes**—the length of the tractor-trailer makes it hard to judge whether a lane change can be made safely. Here are a few suggestions to make lane changes safer and easier:

  - When in doubt, leave plenty of space between you and other vehicles.

  - Wait a little longer before pulling in front of a vehicle you have passed.

  - On a multilane road, there is no need to rush your return to the right-hand lane **(see Figure 16-6).**

  - Do not always trust the signals of other drivers. They may have good intentions, but you really have no idea what they are going to do.

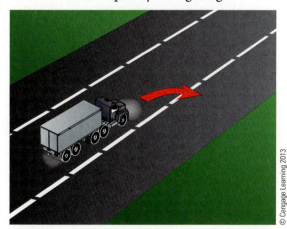

▶ **Figure 16-6**

When changing lanes, leave plenty of space between your rig and other vehicles.

- **Anticipate tailgating**—in large vehicles, it is difficult to know when you are being tailgated. A good rule is to expect to be tailgated under the following conditions:

  - When you are traveling slowly (**see Figure 16-7**)—drivers trapped behind a slow-moving vehicle tend to edge up too close, even though some states have minimum following distances.

  - Bad weather—many drivers follow large vehicles closely in bad weather, especially when visibility is poor or at night.

- **Respond safely to tailgaters**—if you find yourself being tailgated, these actions may help reduce the chance of an incident:

  - Reduce your speed slowly—this may encourage the tailgater to pass you (**see Figure 16-8**).

  - Avoid quick changes—if you have to slow down or turn, signal your intentions early and make the change very slowly.

  - Increase your following distance—create more space in front of your rig. This will help you avoid the need for making quick changes.

  - Do not speed up—tailgaters often tend to stay close, no matter your speed.

  - It is better to be tailgated at a low speed than at a high speed.

  - Avoid tricks—do not turn on your headlights or flash your brake lights to shake up the tailgater. You could make the situation worse by angering or confusing the driver following you.

▶ **Figure 16-7**

Be aware of being tailgated.

▶ **Figure 16-8**

When being tailgated, the vehicle behind you has a reduced view of the road ahead.

KNOW HOW LONG IT WILL TAKE YOU TO STOP YOUR RIG

Stopping distance can be determined by taking four factors into account:

1. Perception time
2. Reaction time
3. Brake-lag time
4. Time it takes to stop the vehicle once the brakes have engaged

It will easily take you 3 seconds to recognize the hazard, react, and apply the brakes.

Using this formula, at 60 mph (97 km/h) your vehicle will travel approximately 255 feet (77.7 m) before brakes engage. Then add an additional 200 feet (61 m) after the brakes begin to slow you down, bringing your total stopping distance to 455 feet (138.7 m)—or seven times the length of an average tractor-trailer. Remember that stopping distance increases significantly with higher speeds.

SPACE TO THE SIDES

The wider your vehicle, the less space it has to the sides. To protect yourself on both sides, manage your space with care by keeping your rig centered in your lane. Avoid driving alongside other vehicles. Overtake and pass carefully.

Staying Centered in Your Lane

There is usually little more than a foot (0.3 m) between the sides of your trailer and the edges of the lane in which you are driving. Keeping your rig centered is important for safety.

CAUTION!

Keep as much space as possible to the sides of your rig. Keep your rig centered in your lane when meeting, passing, or being passed by other vehicles.

Do not move to the right because of an approaching vehicle. This maneuver may put you too close to the other side of your lane. Also avoid any oncoming vehicles if they move over into your lane.

CAUTION!

Visually scan your mirrors often to be sure your trailer has not drifted out of line. If it has, get in front of it and pull it back into the center of your lane.

Traveling beside Others

Two dangerous situations can develop any time you travel alongside other vehicles:

1. Another driver may change lanes suddenly and turn directly into your rig.
2. You may need to change lanes and find there is no opening, so you remain trapped in your present lane.

GO!

The best way to avoid potentially dangerous situations is never travel in a pack of vehicles. Maintain space to the side, ahead of, and behind your rig. Find an open spot where you have the road pretty much to yourself. When there are no open spots, stay alert to the traffic around you and be aware of their blind spots. If you have to travel near other vehicles, stay out of their blind spots by dropping back or pulling ahead.

▶ **Figure 16-9**

Hitting objects overhead is a major cause of damage to tractor-trailer rigs.

SPACE OVERHEAD

Hitting overhead objects is a major cause of damage, both to rigs and damage done by them **(see Figure 16-9).**

Make sure you have enough clearance overhead at all times. In residential areas, for example, professional drivers must be on the lookout for phone and cable lines as well as power lines.

Most overhead collisions are with low-hanging wires, marquees, signs, and air-conditioning units. Check the heights of any overhead structures before driving under them. If you have any doubt about clearance, slow down and drive very carefully. Keep in mind, a modern air ride trailer will "hop" if not fully loaded. For example, this hopping effect will cause a 13.6 foot (4.15 m) van trailer to bounce, and a bridge marked at 13.7 foot (4.18 m) or 13.8 foot (4.20 m) could cause damage to the top of a trailer. This damage could be avoided by slowing down on rough roads underneath bridge overpasses.

Never rely on posted heights at bridges or overpasses. Repaved roads or packed snow may reduce the clearance space indicated.

The weight of your rig also affects its height. The fact that you were able to drive under a bridge fully loaded does not mean you will clear the same bridge when your trailer is empty or lightly loaded.

Sometimes your rig may tilt to the side of the road because of the road's high crown or different levels of paving. When this occurs, you may not clear signs, trees, or other objects alongside the road. If this is a problem, try to drive a little closer to the center of the road.

SPACE BELOW

Many drivers overlook the importance of maintaining adequate space beneath their rigs. That space can be "squeezed" when a vehicle is heavily loaded and the springs are compressed, making the vehicle ride lower. When you are driving low-bed equipment, there may not always be enough clearance beneath the rig. The following situations may create a space problem beneath your rig:

Railroad tracks—often extend several inches/centimeters above the surface of the road. This is often a problem on dirt roads and in unpaved yards where the surface of the track wears away.

Soft surfaces—make sure any surface will hold the weight of your rig before driving onto that surface. One way to lose clearance is to sink down until the truck frame is resting on the surface.

Shopping center parking lots—many lots are not made for heavy trucks and often erode, or holes are created in the pavement as the result of repeated shopper use. If you have a shopping center delivery, check ahead to make sure the surface of the parking lot can handle your loaded rig.

Unpaved surfaces—dirt surfaces will usually support your rig in good weather; however, after a rainstorm, the dirt can quickly become muddy muck. Check before driving onto unpaved surfaces, especially if they are covered with gravel or grass. They may not be as firm as they look.

Excavated areas—can be dangerous, especially for big rigs. They may be covered with planks that cannot bear the weight of your rig. Sometimes they are filled in with loose dirt. Use care when you have to drive near road work or construction.

Parking lots entrances with lowered water drainage—can be hazardous because landing gear may get hung up.

SPACE FOR TURNS

Having enough room to the sides of your rig when you turn is important **(see Figure 16-10)**. Because your rig has a wide turning radius and needs space for off-tracking, there is a tendency to **sideswipe** other vehicles or turn over objects during turns.

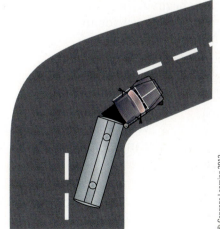

▶ Figure 16-10

Having enough space to turn your rig is sometimes difficult.

© Cengage Learning 2013

Right Turns

Because most right turns have a tight turning radius, you have to swing wide for a successful turn. Timing is key, so stay to the right as long as possible if you have to swing out to the left to make your turn. Otherwise, the driver of the vehicle following you may not realize you are planning to turn and will try to pass you on your right.

When making a right turn:

- Approach the intersection in the right lane.
- Turn on your right turn signal at least 100 feet (30.5 m) before turning.
- Swing left just as you approach the intersection, if you need the room.
- Turn sharply to the right.

If the turn is particularly sharp or difficult, swing out into the street you are about to enter. Watch your off-tracking to avoid running over the curb or grassy areas, which may hide things such as sprinkler heads. Return to the right lane as soon as possible.

GO!
When making a right turn, remember! It is better to travel a few blocks farther and make three right turns to get on a street you want than to endanger others because of a tight turn.

Left Turns

When you make a left turn, be sure you reach the center of the intersection before turning left. If you turn too soon, the side of the trailer, as it off-tracks, may hit an object or a vehicle waiting to enter the intersection.

The choice of lanes is very important in a left turn. If there are two turning lanes, use the right lane. If you begin in the left lane, you will have to swing out in order to make the turn. A driver on your right may not expect you to turn and may drive into the side of your rig.

CAUTION!
When making a left turn, keep traffic in the next lane on the "left side" where you can see it best. A vehicle to your right may be difficult to see.

SPACE TO CROSS OR ENTER TRAFFIC

Drivers new to the profession often do not allow for the size and weight of their rigs when they cross or enter into traffic **(see Figure 16-11).**

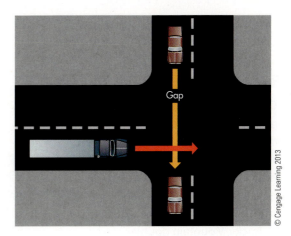

▶ **Figure 16-11**

Keep the size and weight of your rig in mind when crossing an intersection.

CAUTION!

Remember the following when crossing or entering traffic:

■ Because your rig accelerates slowly, it requires more space than a smaller vehicle, so you need a much larger gap to cross or enter traffic than you would need for your personal vehicle.

■ Acceleration varies with the weight of a vehicle. Allow more room and more time to accelerate if you have a heavy load.

■ Before starting to cross a street, think about the length of your rig. Make sure there is enough space for you to clear the intersection completely when you cross.

■ Also be mindful of "stale green lights"—which are traffic devices that have been green for an unknown amount of time and could change to yellow very soon.

YIELDING RIGHT-OF-WAY

Managing the space around your rig means more than monitoring your own driving. The speed other vehicles are traveling and their relationships to you are important factors and should be considered in every decision you make while you are driving. For example, when crossing an intersection, make sure there is adequate room for you to clear the intersection without impeding traffic. Depending on the size and weight of your vehicle, it may take 8 to 10 seconds or more to clear an intersection. In that time, a vehicle traveling 55 mph (89 km/h) may travel 550 to 800 feet (167.7 to 243.8 m). If an intersection proves to be too hazardous to make a safe left turn, making a series of right turns may offer a safer alternative.

In addition, be especially careful when passing other vehicles on the two-lane road. The gap between you and an oncoming vehicle could be closing at a rate that exceeds 100 mph (161 km/h). Also, always make sure the vehicle you're passing is not planning to turn left at an upcoming intersection. Also, watch for other vehicles that may be entering the highway from cross roads or driveways.

In Canada, road trains are more commonly referred to as long combination vehicles (LCVs), extended length vehicles (ELVs), or energy efficient motor vehicles (EEMVs). Four types of LCVs are permitted: turnpike doubles, triples, Rocky Mountain doubles, and Queen City triples, which consist of a tractor unit pulling one semi-trailer up to 16.2 meters (53 ft) long and two shorter "pup" trailers up to 9.8 meters (32 feet) long. Queen City triples are permitted only between the cities of Saskatoon and Regina, Saskatchewan. These are the longest combinations allowed in North America on public highways (see Figure 16-12).

Figure 16-12
Long combination vehicle (LCV).

SUMMARY

In this chapter, you learned the importance of managing the space around your tractor-trailer. There should always be adequate space in front of it, behind it, to both the right and the left side, and above and below the vehicle.

You also learned the types of hazards you may encounter if you fail to manage these spaces correctly, and you learned how to convert time into distance, thus being able to decide if you are a safe distance from other road users.

The types of road surfaces that may present a danger were described and you also learned how to make both right and left turns correctly and how to enter or cross traffic safely.

KEY TERMS

Sideswipe   Space management   Tailgating

REVIEW QUESTIONS

1. Maintaining enough space around a rig to make every trip safe, while being considerate of the "no-zone," is called _____.

    a. distance management   c. space management
    b. good fuel economy   d. stopping distance

2. When things go wrong on the road, _____ gives you time to adjust.

    a. space   c. the mechanic
    b. the dispatcher   d. speed

3. Of all the space around a rig, the space _____ is the most important.

    a. behind   c. over
    b. under   d. ahead

4. Regarding the space needed between your 60-foot (18.3 m) rig traveling at 39 mph (63 km/h) and a vehicle in front of your rig, you will need _____ of space between the two vehicles.

    a. 60 seconds   c. 39 feet (11.9 m)
    b. 39 seconds   d. 6 seconds

5. Regarding the space between vehicles, if the rig is traveling at a rate of 40 mph (64 km/h) or over, how much time is added when figuring space?

    a. 1 second for each 10 mph (16 km/h) over 40 mph (64 km/h)
    b. 1 second
    c. 5 seconds
    d. 1 second for each 10 foot (3.0 m) of length of the rig

6. For a 60-foot (18.3 m) rig traveling 55 mph (89 km/h) in the rain, how many seconds of space will the driver need?

    a. 8 seconds   c. 60 seconds
    b. 55 seconds   d. 6 seconds

7. If you, as a professional driver, find you are being tailgated, which of the following is not a recommended action?

    a. Slowly reduce the speed of the rig.   c. Increase the speed of the rig.
    b. Increase your following distance.   d. Avoid quick changes in direction.

8. Regarding space for turns, because of their wide turning radius and _____, rigs frequently sideswipe other vehicles or run over objects during turns.

    a. out-tracking   c. over-tracking
    b. off-tracking   d. in-tracking

9. Regarding right turns, if the driver has to swing to the left for the turn, the driver should stay to the right as long as possible so _____.

    a. there will not be too much loss of speed by the rig
    b. other drivers will not try to pass the rig on the right
    c. other drivers will not attempt to pass on the left side of the rig
    d. federal law requires all right turns by rigs be made out of the left lane so traffic will flow smoothly

10. Regarding crossing or entering traffic, acceleration varies with the weight of the load, therefore _____ if the rig has a heavy load.

    a. more room and more time is needed
    b. less room and less time is needed
    c. room and time do not increase
    d. speed should be increased by 16 percent

11. When entering and clearing an intersection, which may take 8–10 seconds, a vehicle traveling 55 mph (89 km/h) may travel a maximum of _____.

    a. 1,000 feet/304.8 m   c. 250 feet/76.2 m
    b. 800 feet/243.9 m   d. 450 feet/137.2 m

12. As a professional driver, especially when hauling a heavy load, expect tailgating _____.

    a. on rural roads   c. on freeways
    b. on hills   d. in city driving

13. Don't take a chance on getting hung on a railroad crossing. If you have any questions about clearing the rails, always _____.

    a. get out and measure the clearance
    b. call the dispatcher and get his or her best guess
    c. call a fellow driver and ask about clearance
    d. none of the above

14. Always keep in mind a modern air ride trailer will "hop" if not fully loaded, making it necessary to _____.

    a. slow down on rough roads underneath bridge overpasses
    b. check the height of overhead structures before driving under them
    c. drive carefully when near any overhead structures
    d. all of the above

SUPPLEMENTAL LEARNING ACTIVITIES

1. Invite a local law enforcement officer from the traffic division to discuss the topics of tailgating and other space management issues. Be sure to have questions about local "hot spots" where space management can be an issue for professional drivers.

2. Invite a psychologist to talk to the class about "road rage," its causes and what, as a professional driver, you can do to avoid being a victim of drivers with road rage.

3. Write a 100-word essay on a personal experience you have had with road rage.

4. In small groups, list as many hazards as you can think of that would occur above a CMV. Do the same for hazards that could be found below the rig. Share these with the class.

5. Discuss with the class anticipated space management issues for triples, turnpike doubles, and Rocky Mountain doubles.

FOR MORE INFORMATION

PTDI—Manage and Adjust Vehicle Space Relations, Page 15, Click on Skill Standards
www.ptdi.org/standards

FMCSA Defensive Driving Tips for CMV Drivers
www.fmcsa.dot.gov/facts-research/research-technology/report/FMCSA-RRR-09-003.pdf

Keys To Safety
thekeystruckers.com/keys-to-safety/

17 Speed Management

© Konstantin Sutyagin/www.Shutterstock.com

OBJECTIVES

When you have completed this chapter, you should be able to:

- Explain the relationship between speed and stopping distance, hydroplaning, causes of accidents, the driver's ability to control the rig, and the rig's fuel economy.

- Know how to properly use cruise control.

- Discuss the effect of speed on the rig's weight, its center of gravity, and its stability.

- Show how the driver's available sight distance and the road surface conditions affect choosing a safe speed.

INTRODUCTION

Speed limit laws, which date back to 1901, have traditionally been the responsibility of the states. During the oil shortage of 1973, Congress directed the U.S. Department of Transportation to withhold highway funding from states that did not adopt a maximum speed limit of 55 mph (89 km/h). The National Research Council attributed 4,000 fewer fatalities to the decreased speeds of 1974, compared with 1973, and estimated that returning the speed limit on rural portions of the interstate highway system to pre-1974 levels would result in 500 more fatalities annually, a 20 to 25 percent increase on these highways.

As concerns about fuel availability and costs faded, however, speeds began to gradually climb on U.S. highways and by the mid-1980s, a majority of the vehicles across the U.S. highway system were traveling at speeds that exceeded 55 mph (89 km/h). In 1987, Congress allowed states to increase speed levels on rural interstates to 65 mph (105 km/h).

In 1995, the National Highway System Designation Act repealed the maximum speed limit and allowed states to set their own speed limits. Many states quickly raised speed limits on both urban and rural interstates as well as limited access roads. As of 2011, 34 states had raised speed limits to 70 mph (113 km/h) or higher on some roads.

Often, conditions and traffic will require professional drivers to move at speeds significantly under the maximum speed limit. Likewise, it is important to understand that even when road and weather conditions are perfect, it isn't necessary to travel at the maximum speed limit. Many companies restrict drivers to a specific maximum speed regardless of conditions. In North America, many trucks are equipped with governors to assure operations at speeds under maximum limits.

INTERESTING FACT

Early Romans marked the wheels of their chariots and counted the revolutions, estimating distance traveled and average daily speed. Nautical speed data were recorded in the 1500s by an invention called the chip log, a line knotted at regular intervals and weighted to drag in the water. The number of knots let out in a set amount of time would determine the speed of the craft, hence the nautical term "knots" still applied today.

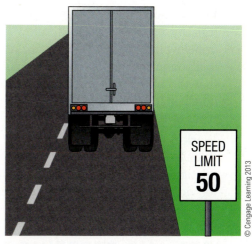

▶ Figure 17–1

As a professional driver, it is your job to know the speed limits of the states and provinces in which you travel.

INTERESTING FACT

The speedometer was invented by the Croatian Josip Belušić in 1888, and was originally called a velocimeter. It is a gauge that measures and displays the instantaneous speed of a land vehicle. Now universally fitted to motor vehicles, they started to become available as options in the 1900s, and as standard equipment from about 1910 onward.

As a professional driver, it is your job to know the speed limits of each of the states and provinces in which you travel, but more importantly it is also your job to know the principles of speed management and how to adjust your speed to fit each traffic and road condition you encounter (**see Figure 17-1**).

As the driver of a big rig, you must use not only your knowledge and your skills as a professional driver, but also your best judgment while in traffic. As any veteran driver will tell you, there is no place for individuals who do not look at professional driving as just that—a profession.

SPEED MANAGEMENT TERMINOLOGY

Basic speed rule—requires vehicle operators to drive at a speed that is reasonable and prudent. As a corollary to this rule, state laws usually provide that every person shall drive at a safe and appropriate speed when approaching and crossing an intersection or railroad grade crossing, when approaching and going around a curve, when approaching a hill crest, when traveling upon any narrow or winding roadway, and when special hazards exist with respect to pedestrians or other traffic or by reason of weather or highway conditions.

Minimum speed rule—prohibits a person from operating a motor vehicle at such a slow speed as to impede the normal and reasonable movement of traffic. In order to avoid a possible conflict with the basic speed rule, the law normally provides that a slow speed is permissible when reduced speed is necessary for safe operation or in compliance with law.

Racing on the highway—is usually defined as driving any vehicle in any race, speed competition or contest, drag race or acceleration contest, test of physical endurance, exhibition of speed or acceleration, or for the purpose of making a speed record.

Reckless driving—is normally defined as driving any vehicle in willful or wanton disregard for the safety of persons or property. Note that speed is not necessarily a factor in this offense.

Statutory speed limit—is one specifically provided for under a state's traffic code (rules of the road). Such limits may vary by highway type (e.g., interstate) or by location (e.g., urban district). State laws may require that these limits be posted.

Posted (maximum) speed limit—even though specific speed limits may have been established via legislation, state laws usually allow either state or local authorities to set highway speed limits above or below the statutory ones. Prior to taking such action on any portion of a highway, the law normally requires that governmental authorities conduct a study to determine the safe speed limit for that part of the highway. State laws may also allow such authorities to specify different speed limits on all or selected highways (or portions thereof) either for various times of the day or for various types of vehicles (e.g., trucks).

Work zone speed limits—nighttime roadwork has increased over the last few years and will continue to grow out of necessity. While there are reduced traffic volumes at night, the safety issues relating to traffic control are a major concern. Lower speed limits and extremely high traffic fines for violation of these speed limits are strictly enforced.

SPEED AND STOPPING DISTANCE

Speeding is defined as exceeding, or driving faster than, the legal or posted speed limit. You also speed when you drive too fast for current road, traffic, and weather conditions. The phrase "driving too fast for the conditions" is harder to define specifically, but it is just as important.

According to the National Highway Traffic Safety Administration, the Federal Highway Administration, and the Federal Motor Carrier Safety Administration, speeding is one of the major causes of crashes, deaths, and injuries on U.S. highways. Speeding has consistently been a contributing cause in approximately 30 percent of all motor vehicle crashes over the last 10 years. The approximate cost of accidents resulting from speeding is more than $30 billion a year.

In a report published by the NHTSA in July 2011, the early estimate of motor vehicle traffic fatalities for the first quarter of 2011 was 6,618. The projected 30 percent of those fatalities caused by speeding totaled 2,206.

Speeding reduces a driver's ability to steer safely around curves or objects in the roadway, extends the distance necessary to stop a vehicle, and increases the distance a vehicle travels while the driver tries to react to a dangerous situation.

The physics of speeding involves the concept that the higher the travel speed, the greater the risk of serious injury or death in a crash. Vehicles and their occupants in motion have kinetic energy that is dissipated in a crash. The greater the energy that must be dissipated, the greater the chances of severe injury or death.

When the vehicle you are driving is a tractor-trailer rig, it is important to realize the weight of your load becomes stored energy and adds momentum, particularly when you are attempting to stop or turn your vehicle.

Motor vehicle crashes are complex events with multiple causes, and individuals have a wide range of tolerance to injury, but the amount of energy that must be dissipated, and thus the probability and severity of injury in a crash, is related to a vehicle's speed at impact. The laws of physics tell us that crash severity increases disproportionately with vehicle speed. A frontal impact at 35 mph (56 km/h), for example, is one third more violent than a crash at 30 mph (48 km/h).

Managing speed is a big part of driving safely and a major responsibility for professional drivers. The faster you go, the less time you have to react to what is happening around you, and there is no question that conditions can change in a split second (**see Figure 17-2**).

▶ Figure 17-2

Managing speed is a critical part of driving safely.

INTERESTING FACT

GPS devices are positional speedometers, based on how far the receiver has moved since the last measurement. The GPS's positional accuracy, and therefore the accuracy of its calculated speed, is dependent on the satellite signal quality at the time. Speed calculations will be more accurate at higher speeds, when the ratio of positional error to positional change is lower. The GPS software may also use a moving average calculation to reduce error.

GO!

It's a good idea to drive at or below the speed limit. An easy conversion is that 100 km/h is approximately equal to 60 mph, so if you see 100 km/h posted, drive at around 55 mph (89 km/h). In the U.S. it's common to "push" the speed limits; in Mexico it's advisable to hold back a little. This will mean driving through some small towns at 15 mph (24 km/h). A good rule of thumb is five under the speed limit.

CAUTION!

The faster you go, the longer it will take you to stop. It takes more than eight times the distance to stop a vehicle going 50 mph (80 km/h) than it does a vehicle going 15 mph (24 km/h).

Figure 17-3 provides an explanation of the distance it takes to stop a tractor-trailer on dry pavement. Remember, these distances are not exact. The three distances are:

- **Driver reaction distance**—the distance your rig travels from the time you identify a hazard to the time you apply your brakes.
- **Vehicle braking distance**—the distance your rig travels from the time you apply pressure to the brake pedal until the rig stops.
- **Total stopping distance**—the driver reaction distance plus the vehicle's braking distance.

The weight of the rig, how the brakes are working, and the weight of the load also figure into the braking distance.

Miles per Hour /Kilometers per Hour	How Far the Rig Will Travel in 1 Second	Driver Reaction Distance	Vehicle Braking Distance	Total Stopping Distance
15/24	22 ft./6.7 m	17 ft./5.2 m	29 ft./8.8 m	46 ft./14.0 m
30/48	44 ft./13.4 m	33 ft./10.1 m	115 ft./35.1 m	148 ft./45.1 m
45/72	66 ft./20.1 m	50 ft./15.2 m	260 ft./79.5 m	310 ft./94.5 m
50/80	73 ft./22.3 m	55 ft./16.8 m	320 ft./97.5 m	375 ft./114.3 m
55/89	81 ft./24.7 m	61 ft./18.6 m	390 ft./118.9 m	451 ft./137.5 m

© Cengage Learning 2013

▶ **Figure 17-3**

Stopping distances.

There is no speed that will always be a safe speed. Speed must be adjusted to the conditions. Those conditions change often during the trip—even a short trip **(see Figure 17-4).**

© Cengage Learning 2013

▶ **Figure 17-4**

Empty trucks need greater stopping distances because an empty vehicle has less traction. The brakes, tires, springs, and shock absorbers on heavy vehicles are designed to work best when the vehicle is fully loaded.

DRIVING ON VARIOUS ROAD SURFACES

To steer your rig to a stop, under any conditions, you need **traction.** Traction is created by the friction of tires making contact with the road **(see Figure 17-5).** Sometimes traction is defined as the "grip" of the tires on the road.

Some road surfaces keep tires from having good traction. When this occurs, slow down to maintain control of your rig.

Slippery Surfaces

It takes longer to stop a rig when the road surface is slippery due to rain, ice, or snow. It is also harder to turn your rig in these conditions because the tires lose their grip on the road's surface. If you are to maintain control of your rig, slow down when the road is slippery. This is called managing your speed.

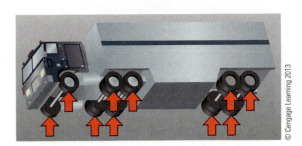

If your rig has antilock brakes, do not expect to stop faster than you would with other brakes. Antilock brakes only allow you to stay in control when braking your rig.

▶ **Figure 17–5**

The points of friction (traction) between the tires and road are small.

How much you should slow down depends on the conditions and your own confidence about handling your rig. If the surface is wet, you should reduce your speed by at least one fourth. If you are driving 55 mph (89 km/h), slow to at least 40 mph (64 km/h).

STOP!

Professional drivers should avoid the risk of driving in snow or icy road conditions if possible.

Identifying Slippery Surfaces

Because it is often hard to know when a road is slippery, get as much information as you can from your dispatcher, Internet road information, or global positioning system. Larger carriers that utilize satellite-based communication devices will often send a message to drivers in the path of potentially bad weather, updating them on road closures and traffic delays. Drivers should always check local weather and traffic before entering large metropolitan areas.

You should also look for certain clues to help you identify "bad spots."

Shaded areas—when the sun begins to melt ice and snow, shaded areas of the road stay icy long after open areas are clear. This is especially true around bridges and trees.

Bridges—because air can circulate over and under bridges, these structures tend to freeze more quickly than other parts of the road. Be careful when the temperature is around 32 degrees F (0 degrees C). When the ice begins to melt, bridges will be wet and even more slippery.

Black ice—is a thin layer of ice, clear enough to let you see the road beneath. This condition makes the road appear wet. Any time the temperature is below 32 degrees F (0 degrees C) and the road looks wet, watch out for patches of black ice.

▶ *"Black ice? Nope, I've never heard of it. Of course, I'm from the south so the only ice I am familiar with is in my snowcones!"*

▶ Figure 17-6

Not seeing tire spray could be a good indication you are driving on black ice.

Rainy days—when the temperature is near or below freezing, look for ice beginning to form on your vehicle. An easy way to check for ice is to open the window and feel the front of the mirror. If you feel ice accumulating on the front of the mirror, the road surface is probably getting icy too.

Just after rain begins—when rain begins to fall after a period of dry weather, it mixes with dirt, grease, grit, oil, and other road debris to make the road slippery. For the first 15 minutes of a rain, the road will be very slick. On hot days, this is a problem on asphalt roads because the oil in the asphalt tends to rise to the surface, called **bleeding tar.**

As the rain continues, the mixture is washed away. In heavily forested areas, where there are leaves on the road, the leaves become very slippery even after the rain has stopped because all of the oil and water are trapped between the forest debris and the surface of the road.

Hydroplaning

When water and slush collect on the roadway, your tires may lose contact with the road's surface. This loss of traction is called **hydroplaning.** It is much like waterskiing. A thin film of water separates the tires from the road and your rig simply slides along on top of the water. Under these conditions, you lose much of your ability to steer, brake, or control the rig.

Your rig can hydroplane on even the thinnest layer of water. Usually hydroplaning occurs when you are traveling at higher speeds, but it can also happen at speeds below 30 mph (48 km/h), depending on how much water is on the road and the condition of your tires (**see Figure 17-7**).

▶ Figure 17-7

When your rig hydroplanes, do not brake but gradually lower speed.

TAKING CURVES SAFELY
Center of Gravity

To maintain safety for themselves and those around them, professional drivers learn to adjust their speed to the conditions of the road and the weather at all times. This becomes even more important when you are driving a big rig.

How high your **center of gravity** is will determine your speed when you drive a curve (**see Figure 17-8**). One layer of crates of equal weight will keep the center of gravity lower than the same number of crates stacked on top of each other in an 8-foot (2.4 m) stack. The higher the load is stacked, the higher the center of gravity— and the higher the center of gravity, the more likely the rig will be to tip over during turns (**see Figure 17-9**).

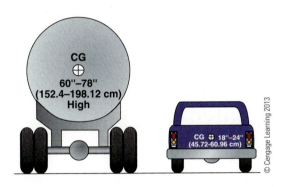

▶ **Figure 17-8**

Your center of gravity helps determine safe speeds on curves.

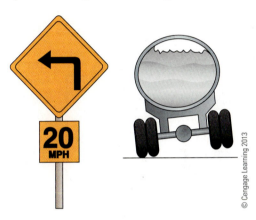

▶ **Figure 17-9**

The higher the center of gravity, the more likely your rig will tip over.

How the load is secured is also important because a shifting load can cause serious control problems for the driver (**see Figure 17-10**).

Adjusting Your Speed

If you need to reduce speed for a curve, brake prior to entering the curve, and gently accelerate out of the curve. Braking while moving through a curve increases the centrifugal pull on your rig, and can cause a rollover. Taking a curve too fast can cause you to lose control of your rig. This happens in one of two ways: (1) The steer tires lose traction and continue straight ahead, called a **skid;** or (2) the tires may keep their traction, but momentum will not allow the rig to turn, which can cause a rollover.

▶ **Figure 17-10**

It is important to properly secure your load. A shifting load can cause serious control problems.

If you downshift before entering a curve, slow down enough before you shift. This will allow you to speed up when you need to. Then, you can speed up slightly in the curve to help keep your rig stable. Once you are through the curve, bring your rig back up to a safe speed that is appropriate to road conditions and terrain.

CAUTION!

The speeds posted for curves are the safe speeds for automobiles driving in good weather. To be safe, drive your truck slower than the posted curve speed. To minimize the effects of centrifugal forces on curves, stay as far to the outside of the curve as possible.

NOTE

When approaching a curve, watch your speedometer as you slow to a safe speed. After driving at a high speed for a long period of time, your body may be fooled into thinking you have slowed down enough when, in actuality, you may still be traveling at a rate of speed too high to be safe as you enter the curve.

DRIVING ON HILLS

Gravity affects speed on upgrades and downgrades. On upgrades, your rig is working against gravity. To maintain speed, you must increase pressure on the fuel pedal. Going downhill, your vehicle is working with gravity to increase your speed. Be careful to slow your rig to a safe speed to keep it under control.

THE SAFE USE OF CRUISE CONTROL ON YOUR RIG

According to a report by Road Safe America, an organization dedicated to making U.S. highways safer, the use of cruise control causes the driver to be less engaged and slower to react. Well-managed fleets of trucks set their speed governors slightly slower if the driver chooses to use cruise control, to adjust for this lost reaction time.

Road Safe America strongly believes that the only type of cruise control that is safe to use on a heavy commercial vehicle is adaptive cruise control with active braking. This type of cruise control sets both speed and the distance between the front of the truck and the vehicle it is following.

Sensors cause the truck to slow down if the vehicle it is following slows down, and active braking will actually stop the truck safely without any action from the driver.

Cruise control is designed for normal road conditions. It doesn't know when the pavement is slippery. Under slick conditions, you need to be in complete control and monitoring road conditions. You're more likely to notice hydroplaning if you are not relying on the cruise control.

With some vehicles, it is possible that the wheels will actually spin faster when the cruise control is on and the car hits a slippery spot. When the tires make contact with firm road again, the vehicle can skid or lose control.

On most vehicles, the cruise control is disengaged by tapping on the brake. In an emergency, this adds a fraction of a second to your response time as well as increases the risk of the braking action itself causing a loss of control on a slippery road.

STOP!

Do not use cruise control when driving on any slippery surface, such as a rain-slick, wet road, ice, or sand.

WORK ZONE DRIVING SAFETY

While it is desirable to maintain normal speeds, restrictions around highway and roadway construction zones sometimes necessitate reduced speed limits. Lane width reductions, severe alignment changes, workers exposed to high-speed traffic, and other conditions may indicate the need for a reduced speed limit (**see Figure 17-11**).

▶ **Figure 17-11**

Many construction zones necessitate reduced speed limits.

Whether or not the speed limit is reduced, adequate enforcement is important to ensure that posted speed limits are obeyed. And be aware—breaking traffic laws in work zones means harsh fines and, in some cases, the loss of driving privileges.

CAUTION!

In all cases, drivers should be aware of current conditions in night work zones so that they can seek alternate routes and/or adjust their driving behavior as necessary.

HOW FAR CAN YOU SEE?

When you are driving, you are constantly adjusting your **field of vision,** and in order to do so, you must also adjust your speed to accommodate how far you can see ahead in order to drive safely on various roadway surfaces and in various weather conditions.

Driving at 45 mph (72 km/h), you will need 310 feet (94.5 m) to stop your rig. If, because of fog, rain, or snow, you can only see ahead 100 feet (30.5 m), then you are automatically placing yourself in a dangerous situation. Imagine a stalled vehicle on the roadway, just beyond your field of vision.

CAUTION!

A general guideline is that you should always be able to stop within the distance you can see ahead (**see Figure 17-12**).

Effect of Speed on Sight Distance

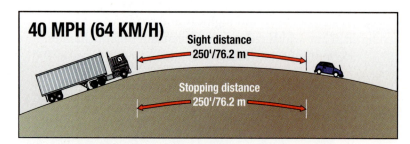

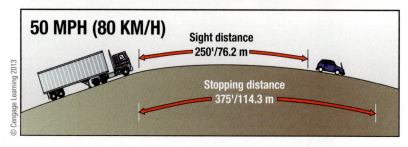

© Cengage Learning 2013

▶ **Figure 17–12**

Your field of vision often requires adjustments in your speed.

Night Driving

Apply the same general field-of-vision guidelines to night driving. Low beams let you see about 250 feet (76.2 m) ahead. If you drive faster than 40 mph (64 km/h) at night with low beams, you will not be able to stop in time to keep from hitting something that suddenly appears on the road in front of you (**see Figure 17-13**).

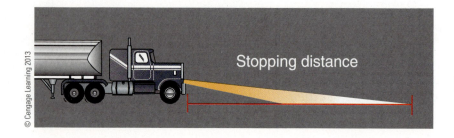

▶ **Figure 17–13**

Low beams allow you to see about 250 feet/76.2 meters ahead.

Bad Weather

Heavy rain, sleet, fog, and smog can greatly reduce your visibility.

CAUTION!

Poor weather conditions also limit what you can see ahead to just a few feet/meters beyond the hood of your rig. To regain better vision of the roadway ahead, slow down as much as necessary to drive safely.

Remember, when it is hard for you to see other vehicles, other drivers also have difficulty seeing you.

Speed and Field of Vision

Your field of vision includes everything you can see in front of you and to the sides while looking straight ahead. The faster you go, the less you can see to the sides.

> **CAUTION!**
>
> As your speed increases, your field of vision decreases. To see something clearly, you must stop your eyes from moving and fix them on the object you want to see.

Remember this when you are looking at cross traffic or at the scene around you. Moving eyes do not see clearly. You cannot react to what you do not see, and you cannot see an object if you are not looking at it.

SPEED AND TRAFFIC

The safest speed in traffic is usually the same speed as other vehicles **(see Figure 17-14).** Accidents happen more often when vehicles are traveling at different rates of speed. As a rule, it is best to blend with other traffic.

Adjust your speed to match that of others while still obeying traffic laws. Some drivers try to save time by speeding, but, of course, this never pays because speeding is risky and often leads to accidents, and when there is other traffic, you usually cannot save more than a couple of minutes in an hour of driving. Bottom line, it is simply not worth the extra risk to speed.

The following may occur if you drive faster than the traffic surrounding you:

▶ **Figure 17–14**

Go with the flow. The safest speed in traffic is the same speed as the other vehicles.

- You will have to pass many other vehicles and each time you change lanes to pass, there is a risk of an accident.
- You tire faster, as driving fast takes a greater toll on the human body and often causes fatigue.
- You will be more likely to attract the attention of law enforcement personnel in the area.
- You will waste fuel and increase the wear and tear on your brakes (going with the flow is not only safer but also easier and cheaper).

INSTANT SPEED MONITORING IN THE U.S.

More U.S. cities are installing cameras to apprehend traffic law violators. Instantaneous speed cameras measure the speed at a single point. There also are a variety of other technologies to measure your speed now being used:

- Radar speed guns use a microwave signal that is directed at a vehicle; the Doppler effect is used to derive its speed.
- LIDAR speed guns utilize the time of flight of laser pulses to make a series of time-stamped measurements of a vehicle's distance from the laser; the data are then used to calculate the vehicle's speed.
- Sensors embedded in the roadway in pairs, for example electromagnetic induction or Piezo-electric strips a set distance apart.

- Infra-red light sensors located perpendicular to the road (e.g., TIRTL, which is **The Infra-Red Traffic Logger**, more commonly known simply by the acronym **TIRTL**), a multipurpose traffic sensor that can be used as a traffic counter, speed sensor, red light camera sensor, heavy vehicle tracker, over-height vehicle sensor, rail crossing sensor, and network management system.

Maximum Posted Speeds in the U.S.—2011

There are speed limits for various types of roads in the 50 states and the District of Columbia. If a state has different speed limits for commercial trucks, they are listed separately. See www.motorists.org/speed-limits/state-chart for more detailed information.

In many states, the maximum speed limit that state or local authorities can establish depends on whether the road is a rural or urban interstate, a noninterstate limited-access highway, or another type of road. Limited-access highways are multiple-lane roads with restricted access via exit and entrance ramps, rather than intersections. The limited-access highways that make up the national interstate highway system are divided into urban and rural sections, based on population density figures from the U.S. Census Bureau. The designations may be adjusted by state and local governments to reflect planning and other issues.

As stated earlier in this chapter, speed limits have traditionally been the responsibility of the states. In the mid-1970s, however, Congress established a national maximum speed limit by withholding highway funds from states that maintained speed limits greater than 55 mph (89 km/h). The requirement was loosened for rural interstates in 1987 and completely repealed in 1995. As of today, 34 states have speed limits of 70 mph (113 km/h) or higher on some portion of their roadway systems.

SPEED LIMITS IN THE CANADIAN PROVINCES

Since 1977, Canadian speed limits have been posted in kilometers per hour (km/h). They were previously in miles per hour (mph) when Canada used the English system of measurement. A sign reads "MAXIMUM XX", such as "MAXIMUM 80" for 80 km/h (50 mph). A minimum speed sign reads "XX MINIMUM", such as "60 MINIMUM" for 60 km/h (37 mph).

Typical speed limits are:

- 15–20 km/h (9–12 mph) at mall entrances
- 30–50 km/h (19–31 mph) within school and playground zones
- 40–50 km/h (25–31 mph) on residential streets within cities and towns
- 50–80 km/h (31–50 mph) on major arterial roads in urban and suburban areas
- 70–90 km/h (43–56 mph) on major arterial roads, arterial highways and at-grade expressways
- 80–110 km/h (50–68 mph) on grade-separated expressways/freeways

Note that where more than one limit is given per road, it usually indicates a difference between provinces; however, within provinces, different roads of the same classification have different speed limits **(see Figure 17-15)**.

▶ Figure 17–15

There are different speed limits depending on the type of road you are driving on.

© iStockphoto/gratomlin

For example, in Alberta and Nova Scotia, some freeways have a limit of 100 km/h (62 mph), while others have a speed limit of 110 km/h (68 mph). The general speed limit on rural highways in Prince Edward Island is 80 km/h (50 mph), except on the Trans Canada Highway where the maximum can range up to 90 km/h (56 mph).

In Ontario, all freeways have a maximum speed limit of 100 km/h (62 mph) except for a few rare cases where it's 80 km/h–90 km/h (50–56 mph). Starting January 1, 2009, most large trucks driven in Ontario were required to use electronic speed limiters that cap their speed at a maximum of 105 km/h (65 mph). Studies conducted by the federal government, through Transport Canada, have demonstrated environmental, safety, and cost saving benefits of speed limiters. Ontario and Québec are now working together to jointly launch and implement speed limiter regulations.

From the Ministry of Transportation of Ontario website:

"In any proceeding under this section and in the absence of evidence to the contrary, proof that a commercial motor vehicle was driven on a highway at a speed equal to or greater than the speed prescribed for the purpose of this subsection is proof that the vehicle was not equipped with a speed-limiting system that was activated and functioning as required." (Ontario Highway Traffic Act)

Stated in the HTA (Ontario) R.S.O. 1990 subsection 68.1 (9):

Speed limits are generally lower in Ontario and Quebec on comparable roads than in other Canadian provinces.

Examples of this disparity include rural two-lane highways in Ontario which have a standard speed limit of 80 km/h, while comparable roads in other provinces have standard speed limits of 90–100 km/h. In rural western Ontario, however, some two-lane roads have speed limits of 90 km/h.

In British Columbia, a review of speed limits conducted in 2002 and 2003 for the Ministry of Transportation found that posted limits on investigated roads were unrealistically low for 1309 km and unrealistically high for 208 km. The reports recommended to increase speed limits for multi-lane limited-access highways constructed to high design standards from 110 km/h to 120 km/h. As described in that report, the Ministry is currently using "… *Technical Circular T-10/00 […] to assess speed limits. The practice considers the 85th percentile speed, road geometry, roadside development, and crash history.*"

In most Canadian provinces, as in most other locales, speed violation fines are double (or more) in construction zones, although in Ontario and Alberta this only applies if workers are present in the construction zone.

In Ontario speeding fines double in areas identified as "Community Safety Zones" as well as in "school zones."

In Ontario as of September 2007, drivers caught speeding 50 km/h (31 mph) over the posted speed limit face a $2,000–$10,000 fine, 7-day vehicle impound, 7-day license suspension, and 6 demerit points.

SPEED LIMITS IN MEXICO

The first maximum speed law for Mexico was created in 1903 by then president Porfirio Díaz. It established a maximum of 10 km/h (6 mph) for small and crowded streets, and 40 km/h (25 mph) elsewhere. Current speed limits are:

- 10 km/h (6 mph) in parking lots and residential areas
- 60 km/h (37 mph) in streets with no speed limit
- 60–80 km/h (37–50 mph) on urban arterial roads

(Continues)

SPEED LIMITS IN MEXICO (continued)

■ 80 km/h (50 mph) in avenues with no speed limit

■ 70–90 km/h (43–56 mph) on rural two-lane roads

■ 90 km/h (56 mph) on two-lane highways

■ 90–100 km/h (56–62 mph) on major highways inside cities

■ 100 km/h (62 mph) on major highways leaving or approaching towns or cities

■ 110 km/h (68 mph) on major highways

No Mexican highway allows going up to 110 km/h (68 mph), but speed limit is enforced generally only above 130 km/h (81 mph).

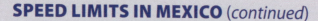

SUMMARY

Now that you have completed this chapter, you learned the critical importance of speed management and heeding speed limits. You understand and can explain the relationship of speed to stopping distance, hydroplaning, fuel economy, and accidents. You also learned how speed affects your ability to control the rig; and, because you have completed this chapter, you can now discuss the effect of speed on the rig's weight and center of gravity as well as a rig's loss of stability. Finally, you also can show how the driver's available sight distance and road surface conditions affect choosing a safe speed.

KEY TERMS

Black ice
Bleeding tar
Center of gravity
Driver reaction distance
Field of vision

Gravity
Hydroplaning
Managing speed
Skid
Speeding

The Infra-Red Traffic Logger
  (TIRTL)
Total stopping distance
Traction
Vehicle braking distance

A DAY IN THE LIFE...

© Cengage Learning 2013

Bradley Chapdelaine – Dart Transit Company, Professional Truck Driver

In the past 26 years, I've found that trucking is more than a career to me—it's my passion. There are days that everything goes right, and days that everything goes wrong. But I stick with it because it's what I love to do.

Being an owner operator and working for yourself means putting in extra effort to make sure everything you do is professional. If you treat others with respect, they will treat you the same. That's how I see it when I work with Dart, my customers, and other owner operators. I am polite and courteous with everyone I come in contact with. And if someone needs help, I am more than happy to give my time.

To me, safety is the most important part of being a professional driver. I have driven 3.5 million accident-free miles. Every day I use past experiences and what I've learned about safe driving, and make sure I am always putting safety above everything else. A huge part of being safe is doing a thorough pretrip inspection on the truck and trailer. I always check the equipment before driving it.

I've been with Dart since 1999. Basically, I look at it like all trucking companies are the same. The only difference is the personnel that Dart has. It's one of the reasons I'm still here. It just feels like family. That kind of relationship is important because family is everything to me. My fiancée Jessica and my son Bradley are my life away from trucking.

I am a huge believer in giving back to the community. One of the ways I get involved each year is with the World's Largest Truck Convoy, an event that raises money for Special Olympics. Truck drivers from all over come together for the Convoys. For the past 10 years, I've helped organize, recruit drivers, and raise extra money for Special Olympics. Being part of that long line of trucks driving down the road and seeing all the athletes cheering you on gives you a warm feeling. This year, Special Olympics Minnesota appointed me "Ambassador for Special Olympics." As Ambassador, I support Special Olympics events throughout the year and speak at events. This year I did this with one of the athletes, Bobby Kimber.

> **" I've found that trucking is more than a career to me – it's my passion. "**

Each year, I also deliver toys for "Toys for Tots," which collects toys around Christmastime and gives them to less fortunate families. I volunteer to pick up the toys at warehouses and deliver them to armories where the families come to pick them up. It's great to see the smiles on the parents' faces who go home with gifts they wouldn't otherwise be able to give their kids.

REVIEW QUESTIONS

1. Regarding speeding, which of the following is the most complete answer: A driver is said to be speeding when the driver is driving too fast for current _____.

    a. road conditions
    c. weather conditions
    b. traffic conditions
    d. a, b, and c

2. Which of the following is not an element of total stopping distance?

    a. driver experience
    c. brake lag distance
    b. perception distance
    d. driver reaction distance

3. The distance a rig travels from the time a driver identifies a hazard until the brakes are applied is known as the _____.

    a. vehicle braking distance
    c. brake lag distance
    b. perception distance
    d. driver reaction time

4. _____, sometimes called "grip," is created by the friction of tires making contact with the road.

    a. Reaction time
    c. Traction
    b. Speed
    d. Stopping distance

5. In an emergency, when you release cruise control, this adds approximately _____ to your reaction time.

    a. 5 seconds
    c. 2 seconds
    b. 10 seconds
    d. 1 second

6. After snow and/or ice collects on a roadway or bridge and it begins to melt, bridges and shaded areas _____.

    a. may be more slippery than other areas
    c. will be best for speeding
    b. will be dry before the other areas of the roadway
    d. will provide more traction than dry areas

7. A thin layer of ice that looks wet and is clear enough to let the driver see the road beneath is called _____.

    a. road slick
    c. ice pack
    b. black ice
    d. stopping distance

8. The higher the center of gravity, _____ during turns.

    a. the more stable the rig will be
    c. the more likely a rig will tip over
    b. the more a driver may speed
    d. a and b

9. If a driver takes a curve too fast, with the tires keeping their traction, and momentum will not allow the rig to turn, the result will be _____.

    a. a skid
    c. a and b
    b. a safe turn
    d. a rollover

10. In traffic, the safest speed is usually _____.

    a. faster than other vehicles
    c. slower than other vehicles
    b. the same speed as other vehicles
    d. two times the speed of the slowest vehicle

11. Cruise control is designed for _____ road conditions.

    a. normal
    c. snowy
    b. slippery
    d. any of the above

SUPPLEMENTAL LEARNING ACTIVITIES

1. Ask a veteran driver and a driver with one year or less behind the wheel to come to your class to discuss speed management. Have a list of questions to ask them, and compare/contrast their answers.

2. Divide the class into groups and then have each group list 10 reasons why using cruise control is not a safe idea in conditions involving rain, ice, sleet, or fog. Discuss as a group.

3. Write a 100-word report about how speed contributes to more than 30 percent of highway deaths each year.

4. Speeding is never a good idea, whether you are driving your personal vehicle or a big rig. Find the penalty for speeding violations in your state and three neighboring states.

5. Canadian provinces usually charge points against a driver's license when speed limits are violated. Discuss the importance of avoiding these penalties.

FOR MORE INFORMATION

PTDI—Manage and Adjust Vehicle Speed, Page 15, Click on Skill Standards
www.ptdi.org/standards

Safety Impacts on Differential Speed Limits on Rural Interstate Highway
www.fhwa.dot.gov/publications/research/safety/04156/index.cfm

FMCSA Large Truck Crash Causation Study
www.fmcsa.dot.gov/facts-research/research-technology/analysis/fmcsa-rra-07-017.htm

National Motorists Association State Speed Limit Chart
www.motorists.org/speed-limits/state-chart

© Gilles Lougassi//www.Shutterstock.com

OBJECTIVES

When you have completed this chapter, you should be able to:

- Describe how and when to use high-beam headlights in night driving.

- Know the factors that most affect night driving—the driver, the road, and the rig.

- Know the impact of headlight glare on safe driving and how it affects driver's ability to see and drive.

- Know state/provincial laws covering how headlights and auxiliary lights are used.

- Understand the importance of adequate sleep for safe night driving.

INTRODUCTION

Think about the last time you drove between the hours of dusk and dawn. You probably stopped around 6 P.M. or later and had a good meal. Then you climbed into your personal vehicle and hit the road.

Unfortunately, the first several hours after a meal are the ones where you will find yourself less alert and more fatigued than any other time—but there you were, after a heavy meal, driving down the highway (probably going 60 to 70 mph/97 to 113 km/h) and feeling full and drowsy. FYI—drowsiness makes driving more difficult because it dulls concentration and slows reaction time.

That evening meal—that one factor alone—makes driving at night more difficult and dangerous than any other time of the day. Why? Because eating a heavy meal makes you want to fall asleep.

Why else is night driving so dangerous?

One obvious answer is darkness. Ninety percent of a driver's reaction depends on vision, and vision is severely limited at night. Depth perception, color recognition, and peripheral vision are compromised after sundown. We also tend to look only as far ahead as our headlights give us the ability to see. This tends to give the driver less time to react to hazards that would be seen during the daylight hours.

Traffic death rates are three times greater at night than during the day, according to the National Safety Council. Yet many of us are unaware of night driving's special hazards or effective ways to deal with them.

Night driving problems require special attention from the professional driver in the form of changes for the following:

- Inspection routines
- Scan and visual search
- Communication
- Speed control
- Space management

This chapter discusses how to meet the special demands of driving safely at night (**see Figure 18-1**).

▶ Figure 18-1

Pay special attention when driving at night.

NIGHT DRIVING FACTORS

Why is night driving demanding?

First and foremost, because of the lack of daylight, it is more difficult to see at night. This isn't rocket science, but it is a factor you must always consider when you drive at night. Bottom line, your field of vision is limited at night.

Because there is less light and your vision is decreased, in order to see possible road hazards, you must be closer to them—which means less time to react and less space to maneuver defensively.

Not being aware of this simple fact causes more than one-half of all traffic accidents occurring between the hours of dusk and daylight (**see Figure 18-2**).

© SergeyDV/www.Shutterstock.com

▶ **Figure 18–2**

Your field of vision is limited when there is less light.

CAUTION!

The following are quick reference rules for driving at night.

Beyond using courtesy and common sense, remember:

■ Never overdrive your headlights. Always keep them clean and aimed properly. Use them at dusk and dawn. Check your headlights regularly to be sure they are clean and the lenses are clear. The acrylic/plastic headlight lenses common in modern vehicles tend to get cloudy over time. There are kits that can be used to restore clarity to the lenses, or ask your shop to restore them. Driving with cloudy lenses significantly reduces headlamp output and effectiveness.

■ Bright lights must be dimmed 500 feet (150 m) before meeting an oncoming vehicle or 300 feet (91 m) before passing a vehicle.

■ If street or freeway lights cause glare, dim your dashboard lights and use your sun visor. Avoid using any other light inside your vehicle.

■ Roadway signs are more difficult to see at night.

■ Use edge lines and center lines of the roadway as guides.

■ Do not stop on the roadway. If you must stop, carry and use your four-way flashers and place your safety triangles on the roadway.

The four main factors that contribute to night driving problems are:

1. Driver
2. Road
3. Vehicle
4. Weather

The Driver

NOTE

Some carriers provide drivers with orange reflective vests to make them more visible when conducting safety inspections or securing loads during the hours between dusk and dawn.

As a professional driver, you should be aware of the factors that affect your driving at night. These factors include vision, glare, fatigue, inadequate sleep, and lack of experience. The most important factor, however, is your concentration and focus.

Vision—becomes more difficult at night. Your eyes need time to adjust to the change between daylight and darkness, but even after they adjust, your eyes cannot see as well at night as they can during the day. Objects are harder to identify, you cannot see as well to the sides of the rig, and your field of vision is severely limited at night.

Glare—often causes temporary blindness from oncoming headlights and other lights. As you may also realize, recovering from glare takes time. Unfortunately, while your eyes recover, you and your rig continue moving down the highway.

When meeting oncoming vehicles with bright headlights, look up, beyond and slightly to the right of the oncoming lights.

CAUTION!

Cut down on glare by following the rules of the road for vehicle lights:

- Use low-beam headlights within 500 feet (150 m) of the oncoming vehicle or when following a vehicle within 200 feet (60 m).
- On country roads, switch to low beams when you come to a curve or hilltop so you can see oncoming headlights and won't blind oncoming drivers. If you don't see headlights, switch back to high beams.

Fatigue—is always a concern when you drive, but it is more of a concern at night. Why? Because you do not see as clearly when you are tired and cannot react as quickly to what you see. As you become less alert, you are slower to see hazards and react even more slowly to avoid them.

Fatigue while driving can be a killer. It happens frequently on long drives, especially long night drives. You may have recognized some warning signs of fatigue, such as back tension, burning eyes, shallow breathing, inattentiveness, and any kind of erratic driving such as drifting, abnormal speed, tailgating, or failure to obey traffic signs.

Relieve fatigue by stopping and walking around your rig. If you still feel fatigued, stop and take a nap.

Inadequate sleep—often figures as a major problem with night driving. Consider this familiar scenario: You have been on the road a while. The highway seems endless. The cab's interior is warm and you are tired. You stare straight ahead, at miles and miles of road, as you start to feel your shoulders sag and your eyes slowly close.

Abruptly, you open your eyes, jerk up in your seat. You have started to drift out of your lane, or maybe even off the road. You steer back into the lane, take a few deep breaths, and realize, fearfully, what just happened. You were asleep.

- Thirty-seven percent of drivers have nodded off for at least a moment or fallen asleep while driving at least once in their driving career.
- Eight percent have done so in the past 6 months.

An obvious cause of fatigue is lack of sleep, also called "sleep deprivation." Without 7 or 8 hours of sleep the night before a trip, you are courting fatigue. Get enough rest, and do not start a trip late in the day. Long-distance driving is hard work, and you need to be fresh and alert.

The only solution to inadequate sleep is *sleep*. Find a safe, guarded rest area, truck stop, or service station. Even a 20-minute nap may refresh you enough to get to a hotel or motel. (This is an emergency maneuver. Do not try it as a common driving technique.)

Safe driving demands your full attention. If you feel your eyelids getting heavy, then your next actions may not simply determine whether you will stay awake, but whether you will stay alive.

▶ *"Early birds might get the worm, And night owls might be wise, But when it comes to driving safe … Being well-rested is the most important prize!"*

Lack of experience—as a professional driver and the problems of reduced vision, glare, and fatigue add up to the fact that new drivers have higher nighttime accident rates than more experienced drivers. In view of these statistics, learn to adjust your speed, space management, and driving techniques to match the demands of driving at night.

Laws covering the use of headlights—High-beam headlights are called "brights" in the U.S. and Canada. Some American states and Canadian provinces have a law saying that whenever weather conditions require that you need to use the windshield wipers, you should also switch on the headlights. For example, the Oct-98 printed edition of the Illinois Driver's Manual "Rules of the Road" says: "Your headlights must be on when operating your wipers. Parking lights are not acceptable." Along with Illinois, headlights when wipers are on are also required in Delaware, Indiana, Kentucky, Louisiana, Maine, Maryland, Minnesota, Missouri, New Jersey, New Mexico, New York, North Carolina, Oregon, Pennsylvania, Tennessee, Virginia, and West Virginia.

In Texas and Vermont, laws require headlights on from 1/2 hour before sunset to 1/2 hour before sunrise. In Alaska, headlight use is required on certain highways.

Some stretches of roads have signs indicating that headlights should be switched on, even during the day. This is presumably because the road is frequently subject to mist and fog. In fine weather most motorists ignore these signs. A good example of this is a tunnel; signs are usually posted that instruct drivers to use their headlights for safety.

Road Conditions Affecting Night Driving

Several conditions affect night driving:

1. Weather
2. Fog
3. Low-level light at night
4. Changes in levels of light
5. Knowledge of the road
6. Other road users and their actions
7. Drivers under the influence of alcohol or drugs

Weather—whether it's a humid, sultry night where no position is comfortable or you're in the middle of a blizzard, weather is always a major factor in night driving **(see Figure 18-3).** Fog, for example, is probably the least expected and the most frequent "surprise" road condition. Remember to use low beams and to reduce your speed in these conditions.

Driving in wet weather can also be equally demanding, not only because you are at a much higher risk of skidding or being unable to stop quickly, but you must also contend with the glare that comes from wet, rainy roads. Be prepared by lowering your speed and being alert for hazards in the road or erratic drivers around you.

Fog—Fog is a thin layer of cloud, usually hovering at ground level. Fog can reduce driver visibility, resulting in driving conditions that are difficult. Avoid driving in fog if at all possible. Check weather forecasts throughout your trip. If there is a fog warning, delay your trip until it clears. If a delay is not possible—or if you get caught in fog and visibility is decreasing—move to a safe parking area to wait until the fog clears.

▶ **Figure 18-3**
Driving in different weather conditions can be demanding on a professional driver.

PROFESSIONAL DRIVING SAFETY TIPS FOR FOGGY CONDITIONS

■ Slow down gradually and drive the speed that best suits weather and road conditions.

■ Make sure your vehicle's full lighting system is on.

■ Use low beams. High beams reflect off the moisture droplets in the fog, making it harder for you to see.

■ If you have fog lights on your vehicle, use them in addition to your low beams.

■ Use pavement markings to help guide you; use the right edge of the road as a guide rather than the center line.

■ Increase your following distance; you will need extra distance to stop safely.

■ Keep looking as far ahead as possible—and be patient. Avoid passing, changing lanes, and crossing traffic.

■ Look and listen for hazards that may be ahead.

■ Keep windows and mirrors clean. Use your defrosters and wipers to maximize your vision.

■ Never speed up suddenly, even if the fog seems to be clearing. It's possible you'll find yourself in more fog.

■ Watch your speed at all times. Aside from slowing because of foggy conditions, don't speed up to pass another vehicle in fog or to put distance between you and a closely following vehicle.

TIP

Professional Driving Safety Tips for Foggy Conditions

■ **Slow down gradually and drive the speed that suits weather and road conditions.**

■ **Make sure your vehicle's full lighting system is on.**

■ **Use low beams. High beams reflect off the moisture droplets in the fog, making it harder for you to see.**

Low-level light at night (low beam headlights)—usually comes from the headlights of vehicles on the road. Headlights are useful for a short and narrow path directly ahead of your vehicle. However, it is useful to remember that headlight beams do not bend around corners.

© Cengage Learning 2013

▶ **Figure 18-4**

Be alert for obstacles when working in darkened delivery areas and loading docks.

Changes in levels of light—causes you to continually adjust your eyes to different types and degrees of light. Flashing lights (and especially flashing neon lights) distract as much as they illuminate. Traffic signals are often hard to see against a background of other lights in towns and cities. Going through a business district in the rain, for example, can be difficult because of the extra glare created by the wet road surfaces. Your rig also may need extra stopping distance in this situation.

Poorly lit work areas—even if your driving skills at night are top notch, you must constantly be alert for obstacles in your work area if you have to deliver a load at night. Be aware of every step you take on a dark dock or a poorly lit delivery area. Safety should always be your first concern when working at night **(see Figure 18-4).**

Knowledge of the road—be extra alert on roads you have never driven before. Do not take even familiar roads for granted, however. Your view of the road will not be the same at night, so situations on the same road will also change.

Other road users—pedestrians, joggers, bicyclists, and animals (that are more active at night than in daylight), cannot see—or react—any better than you can at night. They also cannot be seen as well at night as they can during the day. All are hazards you need to be aware of and should be looking for when you drive at night **(see Figure 18-5).**

© Shutterstock/Tony Campbell

▶ **Figure 18-5**

Hazards in the road cannot be seen as well at night as during the day.

INTERESTING FACT

Since 1993, about 4,700 wild animals are reported killed on British Columbia highways each year. In 2002, deer represented about 77 percent of the wild animals killed on British Columbia highways. Over the last 10 years, about 80 percent of wildlife collisions involved deer. Bear-related vehicle collisions peak in September in the north parts of the province and in October in the south parts.

Drivers under the influence of alcohol or drugs—are always out there. Despite the efforts of Mothers Against Drunk Drivers and law enforcement agencies, there are always people driving under the influence. Your chance of meeting one of these folks increases after sundown. Keep this in mind when driving past roadside taverns and businesses such as liquor stores, strip clubs, or ballrooms and dance halls.

Driving Your Vehicle at Night

As a professional driver, it is your responsibility to make sure your rig is safe for night driving **(see Figure 18-6).**

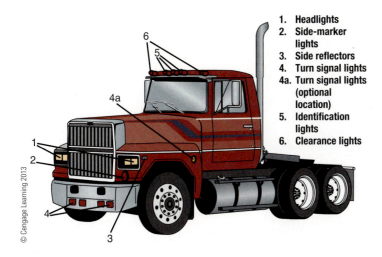

1. Headlights
2. Side-marker lights
3. Side reflectors
4. Turn signal lights
4a. Turn signal lights (optional location)
5. Identification lights
6. Clearance lights

© Cengage Learning 2013

▶ **Figure 18-6**

Your rig should be equipped with the proper tools to make driving at night less difficult.

Be sure to check the following:

- Headlights
- Auxiliary lights
- Daytime running lights

- Turn signals
- Windshield
- Mirrors

Headlights

Your tractor's headlights are your first and best source of light on the road after sundown. They are also your rig's main signal of its location to other road users. Be sure your headlights are clean and properly adjusted at all times.

It goes without saying—the distance you can see ahead at night is much less than it is during the day. Low-beam headlights light a path of about 250 feet (76.2 m) ahead of your rig (less than the length of a football field). High beams light 350 to 500 feet (106.7 to 152.4 m) ahead (**see Figure 18-7**).

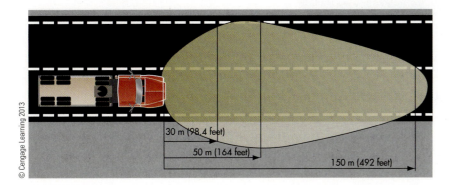

© Cengage Learning 2013

30 m (98.4 feet)
50 m (164 feet)
150 m (492 feet)

▶ **Figure 18-7**

Illustration showing symmetrical high-beam illumination of road surface.

INTERESTING FACT

The earliest headlamps were fueled by acetylene or oil and were introduced in the late 1880s. Acetylene lamps were popular because the flame was resistant to wind and rain. The first electric headlamps were introduced in 1898 and were optional. Two factors limited the widespread use of electric headlamps: the short life of filaments in the harsh environment, and the difficulty of producing dynamos small enough yet powerful enough to produce sufficient current.

Your **sight distance** is limited to the range your headlights provide. You must drive at a speed that allows you to stop within your sight distance. If your speed is greater than this, you are **overdriving** your headlights (**see Figure 18-8**). Driving within your headlights or sight distance is your best bet for avoiding crashes with objects or other road users (**see Figure 18-9**).

Low-beam headlights show the road about 250 feet (76 m) ahead

And you need 250 feet (76 m) to stop at 40 mph (64 km/h)

▶ **Figure 18–8**

Never overdrive your headlights or sight distances.

▶ **Figure 18–9**

Slow down so you can stop in the distance you can see ahead.

Auxiliary Lights

When all lights are working, big rigs are easily visible and *usually* can be seen by other road users (**see Figure 18-10**), but never *assume* they see you, just because you're a big rig.

1. Turn signal lights
2. Backup lights
3. Rear reflectors
4. Tail lights
5. Turn signal lights
6. Stop lights
7. License plate lights

▶ **Figure 18–10**

Auxiliary lights on your rig make it easier for others to see you at night.

The following **auxiliary lights** must be cleaned regularly and kept in working order:

- Auxiliary lights
- Reflectors (also called "conspicuity tape")
- Clearance lights
- Identification (ID) lights
- Tail lights
- Brake lights

Daytime Running Lights

Daytime running lights (DRLs) are headlights that are lit whenever a vehicle is running. A low-cost method to reduce crashes, they are especially effective in preventing daytime head-on and front-corner collisions by making it easier to see vehicles, particularly as they approach from far away.

Laws in Canada require vehicles to operate with lights on during the daytime. Canada requires vehicles made after December 1, 1989, to be equipped with DRLs.

There are currently no state laws requiring the use of 24-hour low-beam headlights. However, research suggests a potential reduction in daytime multiple vehicle crashes—especially head-on and front-corner collisions—with the 24-hour use of low-beam headlights.

Turn Signals

Turn signal lights are key signals to other drivers of your intentions. How well you communicate with other drivers depends on your turn signals (**see Figure 18-11**). Turn signals that are not working or dirty do not allow you to signal your intent on the highway, and will increase your risk for accidents.

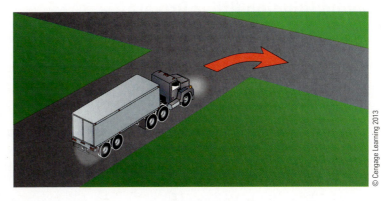

▶ **Figure 18–11**

Turn signals assist in communicating with other roadway users at night.

Windshield

A clean windshield is a must for safe driving during the day or night (**see Figure 18-12**). If a clean windshield shuts out 5 percent of the available light, think about how much light is blocked by a dirty windshield, plus it can cut your ability to see and relate to traffic. Clean the outside and inside of your windshield before each trip so that you can see as well as possible.

Mirrors

Mirrors help you see what is going on around you. Unless you can see the other vehicles, you cannot relate to them. Be sure to keep your mirrors clean, and properly adjust them before each trip and after each stop.

NIGHT DRIVING PROCEDURES

Before attempting to drive at night, the first step is to prepare yourself and your rig.

If you wear glasses, make certain you have regular, annual checkups and testing to keep your lens prescription up to date. Also make certain your glasses are clean. Dirty or scratched lenses increase the effects of glare.

▶ **Figure 18–12**

A clean windshield and wipers that function are a must for safe driving at night.

CAUTION!

Be sure to travel with a pair of sunglasses to wear during the day, particularly when you have to drive at night. Wearing sunglasses during the day will decrease the amount of time your eyes will need to adjust to the darkness of night; but, NEVER wear sunglasses at night.

The next step of your preparation for driving at night is to plan your route. Know where the rest stops are located. Think ahead about any known hazards or construction areas along your route. Know the locations for unlighted areas of the road, exit ramps, and construction areas. Then, always expect changes—and keep your eyes open for these.

Check all lights on your rig during your pretrip inspection. Clean all lights and mirrors, and replace lights that are not working. Never go on the road with a malfunctioning light.

Avoid Blinding Other Drivers

Headlight glare from oncoming and following vehicles can be a problem for every driver on the highway.

The FMCSR state that a driver must dim his headlights 500 feet (150 m) before encountering an oncoming vehicle. This regulation not only meets all state laws, but it also makes sense to be considerate on the highway. If your headlights make it hard for an oncoming driver to see, then you and your rig are also in danger.

Dim your headlights before they impair the vision of other drivers. Although not required by the FMCSR, you should also dim your headlights 300 feet (91 m) before overtaking another vehicle. In addition to eliminating a road rage situation, this action also complies with most state laws.

Avoid Blinding Yourself

To facilitate night driving, keep your cab as dark as possible. Adjust your instrument panel lights to a low level, yet make sure they are bright enough to read easily.

CAUTION!

Keep the dome light off! The brighter the inside of the cab, the harder it is for you to see the roadway ahead, and destroy your "night vision".

Use high beams when safe and legal to do so

© Cengage Learning 2013

Use high-beam headlights only when it is safe and legal to do so. Many drivers make it a habit to always drive with low beams at night, but this can seriously cut down their vision. Always try to give yourself the best night vision **(see Figure 18-13).** Take advantage of headlights from the vehicles ahead to spot hazards, and let road signs and reflectors act as visual guides.

▶ **Figure 18-13**

Use high beams when they will not impact the visual field of oncoming drivers.

NIGHT DRIVING ADJUSTMENTS

To drive safely at night, the driver must modify some basic daytime driving techniques.

Communicating—make sure you signal to reduce speed, stop, or turn in plenty of time. It is wise to signal earlier than you would during daylight conditions. Check to make sure your tail lights, backup lights, and turn signals are in working order before each trip and before leaving each stop.

Signal your presence because eye contact is not possible at night. Light use of the horn can be helpful. Never hurt the vision of others by using your headlights to signal a lane change or other maneuver.

Space—because you cannot see as well or as far at night, you need more time to react to events around your rig. Get the needed time by increasing the space around your rig (**see Figure 18-14**). Increase your following distance at night by at least 1 second more than the normal daytime following distance.

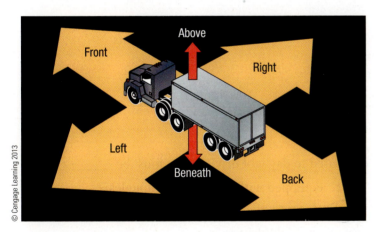

▶ **Figure 18-14**

Managing the space around your rig is more crucial at night.

Speed—adjust your rig's speed to keep the stopping distance within your sight distance. Do not overdrive your headlights. A lower speed is needed to keep from hitting objects when they suddenly come into view. If you do not adjust your speed to nighttime conditions, you will have too little time and too little space to safely react to hazards (**see Figure 18-15**).

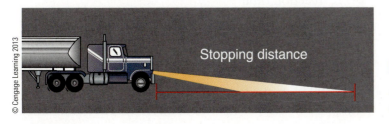

TIP

Night Driving Safety Tips: A Review

- Prepare your vehicle for night driving. Keep headlights, tail lights, signal lights, and windows (inside and out) clean.

- Have your headlights properly aimed. Mis-aimed headlights blind other drivers and reduce your ability to see the road.

- Don't drink and drive. Not only does alcohol severely impair your driving ability, it also acts as a depressant. Just one drink can induce fatigue.

- Avoid smoking when you drive. Smoke's nicotine and carbon monoxide hamper night vision.

- If there is any doubt, turn your headlights on. Lights will not help you see better in early twilight, but they'll make it easier for other drivers to see you. Being seen is as important as seeing.

- Reduce your speed and increase your following distances. It is more difficult to judge other vehicle's speeds and distances at night.

- Don't overdrive your headlights. You should be able to stop inside the illuminated area. If you're not, you are creating a blind crash area in front of your vehicle.

- When following another vehicle, keep your headlights on low beams so you don't blind the driver ahead of you.

- If an oncoming vehicle doesn't lower beams from high to low, avoid glare by watching the right edge of the road and using it as a steering guide.

- Make frequent stops for light snacks and exercise. If you're too tired to drive, stop and get rest.

- If you have mechanical trouble, pull off the road as far as possible. Warn approaching traffic at once by setting up reflecting triangles near your vehicle and 300 feet (91 m) behind it. Turn on flashers and the dome light. Stay off the roadway and get passengers away from the area.

▶ **Figure 18-15**

Appropriate speeds keep your rig's stopping distances within your sight distance.

Observe night driving safety as soon as the sun goes down. Twilight is one of the most difficult times to drive, because your eyes are constantly changing to adapt to the growing darkness.

SUMMARY

In this chapter, you learned the many differences between driving during daylight hours and driving from dusk to dawn. You learned that inspection routines must be altered and that communication with other drivers must be done by signaling because you do not have eye contact with them at night.

You also learned that you must slow down so that you will be able to stop within the distance you can clearly see ahead. The reasons for allowing more space around your rig and between you and other highway users were explained.

Finally, you learned that adequate sleep is immensely important for safe night driving and that changes while driving at night are made for safety reasons. As a responsible professional, you will want to create the safest road conditions possible for yourself and for other drivers.

KEY TERMS

Auxiliary lights
Fatigue
Glare

Low-level light
Overdriving
Sight distance

Turn signal lights
Vision

REVIEW QUESTIONS

1. In order to see possible hazards at night, compared to daylight driving, you must be _____.
   a. farther from hazards
   b. equipped with bifocals
   c. equipped with night-vision goggles
   d. closer to objects/hazards

2. Regarding night driving, the factor that most affects night driving is _____.
   a. vision
   b. concentration and focus
   c. glare and reaction time
   d. fatigue and sleep deprivation

3. Lack of experience driving a rig and the problem(s) of _____ add(s) up to the fact that new drivers have higher nighttime accident rates than more experienced drivers.
   a. vision, glare, and fatigue
   b. stopping distance
   c. brake lag time
   d. center of gravity

4. After sundown, when driving past taverns, liquor stores, or similar businesses, the chances of _____ increases.
   a. stopping distance
   b. meeting a driver under the influence of drugs or alcohol
   c. reaction time
   d. brake lag time

5. The range of vision your headlights provide is your _____ distance.
   a. stopping
   b. reaction
   c. sight
   d. brake lag

6. At night if one is driving at such a speed that the rig cannot be stopped within the driver's sight distance, then the driver is said to be overdriving _____.
   - **a.** the brake lag time
   - **b.** the driver's reaction time
   - **c.** his headlights
   - **d.** the center of gravity of the trailer

7. Auxiliary lights, such as marker and clearance lights on a rig, _____.
   - **a.** make it easier for others to see your rig at night
   - **b.** because of the glare they produce, make it more difficult for others to see your rig at night
   - **c.** increase reaction distance
   - **d.** increase brake lag time

8. The FMCSR state that a driver must dim his or her headlights _____ before encountering an oncoming vehicle.
   - **a.** 500 yards (457.2 m)
   - **b.** 1,000 feet (304.8 m)
   - **c.** 1,000 yards (914.4 m)
   - **d.** 500 feet (152.4 m)

9. Regarding lights inside the cab of a rig at night, the _____ the inside of a cab, the harder it is to see outside.
   - **a.** darker
   - **b.** brake lag time increases if it is darker inside the cab
   - **c.** brighter
   - **d.** a and b

10. Regarding space around your rig, at night a driver should increase his or her following distance by at least _____ more than normal daytime following distance.
    - **a.** 10 seconds
    - **b.** 1 second
    - **c.** 1 minute
    - **d.** 15 seconds

11. When daytime driving in most Canadian provinces, it is important to remember to _____.
    - **a.** stop on flashing red before turning
    - **b.** use four-way flashers
    - **c.** use daytime running lights
    - **d.** turn on low beams 1/2 hour before dusk

12. In Canada, the metric system is used and mileage signs are expressed in kilometers. How do you convert kilometers to miles? A kilometer is a metric length unit. A mile is an imperial length unit. Keep in mind that one mile is a longer distance than one kilometer. A kilometer is equal to 0.621371192 miles. You can multiply the number of kilometers in question by the conversion factor, or you can use one of the many online calculators available for conversions. How many miles is 50 kilometers?
    - **a.** 25.025 miles
    - **b.** 31.069 miles
    - **c.** 55.10 miles
    - **d.** 100.025 miles

13. When driving during foggy conditions it is best to use _____.
    - **a.** low beams
    - **b.** high beams
    - **c.** daytime running lights
    - **d.** auxiliary lights

14. High beams should be used to aid the driver in seeing better _____.
    - **a.** on major highways
    - **b.** on darker country roads
    - **c.** when approaching another vehicle
    - **d.** none of the above

15. One obvious cause of driver fatigue is _____.

   a. sleep degradation   c. sleep apnea
   b. sleep deprivation   d. sleep deterioration

16. An adequate amount of sleep for the average individual is _____ hours.

   a. 5–7 hours   c. at least 4 hours
   b. at least 6 hours   d. 7–8 hours

SUPPLEMENTAL LEARNING ACTIVITIES

1. Examine the pros and cons of using daytime running lights (DRLs). Divide into groups and then discuss your answers with the class.

2. After eating a big lunch, your body experiences what is known as "the afternoon apathy syndrome." What is this syndrome and why does it make driving immediately after lunch more dangerous than driving before lunch?

3. If you found yourself in an expanding stretch of fog, what would be your first inclination? Write a 100-word essay on safety measures to take.

4. Talk in small groups about why animals are more apt to dart into the path of traffic during severe droughts.

5. If you could do one thing to prepare your vehicle for night driving, what would you do and why? Discuss this in small groups. Reach a consensus in your class.

FOR MORE INFORMATION

PTDI—Identify and Adjust to Difficult and Extreme Driving Conditions, Page 20, Click on Skill Standards
www.ptdi.org/standards

Tips for Safe Night Driving—Road & Travel Magazine
www.roadandtravel.com/safetyandsecurity/safenightdrivingtips.htm

Hub Pages—Night Driving Tips
hubpages.com/hub/Night-Driving-Tips

FMCSA—Driver Fatigue
www.fmcsa.dot.gov/about/outreach/education/driverTips/Driver-fatigue.htm

19 Extreme Driving Conditions

© iStockphoto/stockstudioX

OBJECTIVES

When you have completed this chapter, you should be able to:

- Realize the effects of rain, wind, snow, and ice on your ability to control your rig.

- Understand the causes of skidding and jackknifing and how to avoid them.

- Perform special inspections for various extreme driving conditions.

- Show the effects of ice, snow, water, mud, and debris on your rig's brakes.

- Perform various extreme weather driving procedures.

- Understand the impact of cold weather on fuel.

- Demonstrate the best ways of driving in mountainous terrain.

INTRODUCTION

The words **extreme driving conditions** are familiar to every driver, and you have probably heard them many times, but what do they really mean?

Figure 19-1

A professional driver must know how to drive safely in extreme driving conditions.

"Extreme" means the worst. The term *extreme* refers to the most difficult of anything—extreme sports, extreme poverty, extreme—the worst you can find in any category. So, what are the worst driving conditions? That means driving when it is cold, wet, icy, dry, hot, snowing, high winds, or foggy conditions. Driving in mountain ranges and across the desert is also considered extreme driving conditions.

Be aware: you cannot learn how to drive in all of these extreme conditions by reading a book or sitting in a classroom. On the other hand, before you encounter extreme driving conditions of any type, it may be good to have some tips and other information under your belt **(see Figure 19-1)**. You never know when it will come in handy, so keep reading, and read carefully.

EXTREME WEATHER

Knowing your way around your rig, including its parts and its systems, is the first step in preparing yourself for driving in extreme conditions. Reduced **traction** and poor **visibility** are two major safety hazards that occur in extreme conditions. Less traction increases the stopping distance and decreases the driver's ability to control the rig. Reduced visibility means you will not see hazards as quickly and you will have less time to respond to anything up ahead.

Vehicle Checks

Be sure both you and your rig are ready and equipped to drive into extreme weather conditions. If you are not ready or are unsure, then stay put. Make a thorough pretrip inspection **(see Figure 19-2)**. Your pretrip inspection should include a check of the following:

Coolant level and antifreeze concentration—make sure the coolant system is full because a low coolant level affects operation of the heater and defroster as well as engine performance. Make sure the concentration of antifreeze is appropriate for the conditions you expect to encounter.

Heating equipment—a poorly heated cab can reduce your performance efficiency. Check the heater hose for wear as well as the controls and fans. Also check window defrosters.

Wipers/washers—check for cracks, collapsed areas, and loose clamps. Make sure reservoir is full and fluid is not frozen. In cold weather, add winter blend washer fluid and make sure wipers are in top shape and working order. Washer fluid can be flammable. Don't smoke while dispensing or checking the fluid.

Tires—check mountings and look for flaws on sidewalls or treads. Check air pressure with tire pressure gauge. Make sure tires are properly inflated and tread depth is safe. Use a depth gauge to check the tread depth at three points around the tire. The tread on a new truck tire can be as deep as 15/32 inch (11.91 mm). Most, if not all, tires have wear bars molded into the tread area. When these bars are flush with the tread, the tire is at 2/32 inch (1.59 mm). Tires must have enough traction to easily push the rig over wet pavement or through snow.

SPECIAL EXTREME WEATHER CHECKLIST FOR PRETRIP INSPECTION

- Coolant and antifreeze
- Heater/defroster
- Wipers/washers
- Tires
- Chains
- Brakes
- Horn
- Steering mechanism
- Lights and reflectors
- Windows and mirrors

- Hand and toe holds
- Radiator shutters and winter fronts
- Exposed wiring and air lines
- Fuel tank
- Engine and exhaust systems
- Coupling devices
- Interaxle differential lock
- Emergency equipment
- Weather reports and road conditions

© Cengage Learning 2013

▶ **Figure 19-2**

Extreme weather conditions will change your pretrip inspection priorities.

Chains—some states/provinces/territories require chains during certain periods of the year. As a professional driver, it is your responsibility to know about the varying chain laws in each state/province. Carry the correct number of chains and make certain they are in working order. Watch for broken hooks, worn or broken cross links, and bent or broken side chains.

Brakes—they should apply pressure equally and at the same time. If one wheel stops turning before the others, it may cause a skid or other handling problem. Check brake linings for ice, which can cut the braking power. Finally, drain the moisture from tractor and trailer air tanks, because an accumulation of frozen moisture will prevent air from getting to the brakes, resulting in the feeling that a particular brake doesn't work properly.

Lights and reflectors—make sure the lights and reflectors are free of mud or dirt, not broken or bent. How well you see and how well others see you depends on the lights and reflectors on your rig being clean and in top shape.

Radiator, shutter, and winter front—remove any ice from the winter front, which can keep shutters from opening and cause the engine to overheat. If the engine overheats, then you may need to adjust the shutters or opening sizes on your winter front. Close them if the engine is too cold.

Wiring and air lines—be sure all wiring and lines are properly supported and remove any ice or snow before and during the trip. Buildup can cause lines to sag and eventually snap.

Fuel tank—be sure the fuel tank is full before you begin a trip. If extreme weather is expected, top off your tank frequently. Beware of low-quality fuel that can gel in cold weather. It is wise to fill the tank at the end of the trip to reduce moisture buildup. Follow company

INTERESTING FACT

Tire chains were invented in the early 1900s by Harold D. Weed in Canastota, New York. Weed noticed that every winter, drivers would wrap rope around their tires to increase traction on muddy roads. Weed's experience and expertise led him to believe he could improve on this simple idea. He sought to make a traction device that was more durable and would work with snow as well as mud and soon developed functional tire chains made of metal. These chains were considerably more durable than the rope and could be securely fastened to the vehicle's tires.

NOTE

Shutters are found on older model tractors and are rapidly disappearing on any new models.

GO!

Many modern tractors come equipped with an **air dryer,** which routinely removes any moisture from the air system. An air dryer is a valuable tool for keeping the air system clean.

procedures regarding anti-gel and/or winter fuel conditioning chemicals. Drain water from the bottom of the fuel tank. Ice buildup on a crossover line can freeze or break the line between fuel tanks.

Engine and exhaust system—keep exhaust connections tight to prevent carbon monoxide from leaking into the rig.

Coupling devices—make sure the fifth wheel is coated with a winter-grade lubricant to prevent binding. This also will help steering on icy or wet slippery roads.

Interaxle differential lock—is used on vehicles with tandem rear axles. The differential lock is controlled by a lever or push–pull control valve on the instrument panel. This feature can be in only two positions—lock or unlock—as indicated. Normally the valve should be kept in the unlock position. Use the lock position only when you approach conditions where one or both wheels of an axle may slip. The valve locks the differential and causes it to act as a "through drive," transmitting power equally to both axles. Avoid unnecessary use of differential lock since it will result in tire wear and axle strain. **Caution:** You should not lock or unlock the differential lock when the wheels are actually spinning **(see Figure 19-3).**

Emergency equipment—have proper clothing, extra food, water, gloves, an extra blanket or two, a fully-charged cell phone, and a 12-volt DC charger when driving into extreme weather. You should also have a scraper, snow brush, small folding shovel, triangles, and a fire extinguisher.

Weather reports and road conditions—through your dispatcher and electronic sources, you can receive the Weather Channel, NOAA weather radio, 5-1-1 phone, and Internet services offered by local radio and television stations. These are reliable sources for current weather information. Mountain passes have additional information sources, and truck stops on either side of major passes have pass

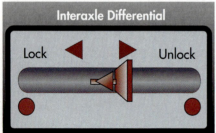

© Cengage Learning 2013

Lock
Wheels have to be locked before driving on a slippery surface and before they start to spin.

Unlock
Normal position.

▶ **Figure 19-3**

If your rig has an interaxle differential lock, operate it according to directions in the owner's manual.

© Cengage Learning 2013

▶ *"I knew I forgot something when I left the terminal!"*

boards at the fuel desk. Local authorities fax current conditions for posting on the board. Some states such as Oregon have live road cams of the passes showing at the truck stops. Idaho broadcasts pass conditions on CB channel 19.

Tire Chains

Tire chains are a must for driving in snow, ice, or extreme winter conditions, mainly because they prevent skidding and increase your rig's pulling and braking power. Chains can increase traction by as much as 500 percent. Chains should be mounted according to the law of the region in which you're traveling.

When to Use Chains

Many states have specific rules about when to use chains. Some states require that chains be carried in the truck during certain months. Other states have laws that indicate where chains must be installed on the rig. In some western states, the locations of tire chains on the rig will vary from region to region. It is the professional driver's job to know these regulations.

A chain control area is a highway area where it is illegal to drive without chains. Checkpoints are usually set up ahead of these areas, where trucks are stopped to see that the proper number of chains are on board. If not, the inspector will not allow the rig into the chain control area. This could mean costly downtime.

When you see the warning "Chains advised," you have the choice of whether to drive using tire chains. Be extremely careful in these areas. There can be large fines if you spin out, jackknife, or block the highway because you did not have snow chains.

Snow Chain Laws in the United States

Chain laws vary from state to state. Some states have outlawed the use of tire chains because of the wear and tear they cause on their highways. Heavy-snow states, however, have strict laws regarding carrying and using tire chains and impose penalties on truckers who are not equipped with the right number and right-sized tire chains. The following is a listing of general laws regarding tire chains:

Alabama—Tire chains, or metal studded or safety spike tires of reasonable proportions may be used when required for safety because of snow, rain, or other slippery conditions.

Alaska—It is permissible to use tire chains because of snow, ice, or other conditions that may cause a vehicle to skid.

Arizona—Permissible when required for safety because of snow, ice, or other conditions tending to cause a vehicle to skid. If a mountain pass or other roadway is posted, vehicles must use chains because of immediate weather conditions, then the vehicle must chain-up or stop until the posting is lifted.

Arkansas—Chains of reasonable proportions may be used on any vehicle when required for safety. Pneumatic tires with flat-headed studs projecting 1/16 inch (1.59 mm) or less beyond the tread may be used on trucks up to 6,000 lb (2,721 kg) in weight when required for safety on ice or snow.

California—Required to be equipped with tire traction devices when entering a signed restricted area. For more information, go to Caltrans' website at www.dot.ca.gov/hq/traffops/trucks/trucksize.

Colorado—When the chain law is in effect, drivers will see signs along the roadway indicating which vehicles should chain-up. In some areas of the state, lighted variable message signs will also alert drivers of the chain-up information. Metal chains must consist of two circular metal loops, one on

---

INTERESTING FACT

In 1979, Hyok Lew of Colorado patented a tire chain design, featuring chains arranged in either a zig-zag or diamond-shaped pattern. These chains attached to the tire with a star-shaped tie cord and provided better traction and easier installation than Weed's design. In his patent description Lew claimed that spreading sand and salt on roads to deal with snow and ice "is not only economically wasteful but also harmful to the environment." He believed that by making reliable tire chains available to all drivers, this practice could be reduced or altogether eliminated.

each side of the tire, connected by not less than nine evenly spaced chains across the tread. Commercial vehicles having four or more drive wheels must chain four wheels. Dual tire chains are acceptable. For more information, go to CDOT's website at www.cotrip.org/winterdriving/chainregs.htm.

Connecticut—Studded tires and any other nonskid devices may be used from November 15–April 30.

Delaware—No tires used on the highways of Delaware may have on their peripheries any blocks, studs, flanges, cleats, or spikes or any other protuberances of any material other than rubber that project beyond the traction surface, except that studded tires are permitted from October 15 to April 15.

Georgia—Safety spike metal studs may be used when conditions demand them. A set of chains is also permissible for all vehicles likely to encounter conditions requiring chains.

Idaho—Permissible to use tire chains. There are times when chains are required. Signs will be posted "Chains required beyond this point" when the road is snow-covered or icy.

Illinois—Tire chains of reasonable proportion will be legal when required for safety because of snow, ice, or other conditions causing vehicles to skid.

Indiana—When required for safety because of snow, ice, or other conditions, tire chains of reasonable proportions may be used on the highways. From October 1 to May 1, tires in which ice grips or tire studs of wear-resisting materials have been inserted may be used.

Iowa—Permissible upon any vehicle when required for safety because of snow, ice, or other conditions tending to cause a vehicle to skid.

Kansas—Permissible upon any vehicle when required for safety because of snow, ice, or other conditions tending to cause a vehicle to skid.

Kentucky—Permissible when icy road conditions exist.

Louisiana—Permissible upon any vehicle when required for safety because of conditions tending to cause a vehicle to slide or skid.

Maryland—In case of declared snow emergency, chains will be required on certain designated highways. Studded snow tires are not allowed on vehicles having a registered gross weight of more than 10,000 pounds (4,536 kg).

Massachusetts—Studded tires are permissible in Massachusetts between November 1 and May 1.

Michigan—Permissible only when snow is on the ground.

Minnesota—Permitted when road conditions (ice and snow) require tire chains. Studded pneumatic tires are not allowed on Minnesota registered vehicles.

Mississippi—Permissible upon any vehicle when required for safety because of snow, ice, or other conditions tending to cause a vehicle to skid.

Montana—Chains are permissible from October 1 until May 31, but not mandatory unless the department determines they are required and notices are posted. They are then required on one set of drive axles.

Nebraska—Permissible upon any vehicle when required for safety because of snow, ice, or other condition tending to cause a vehicle to slide or skid.

Nevada—Requires operators of all vehicles of more than 10,000 pounds/4,536 kg (GVW) to install chains when chains or snow tire requirements are in effect. Vehicles over 10,000 pounds/4,536 kg (GVW) are permitted in chain control areas when equipped with chains or Automatic Traction Devices (ATD) on drive axles. Studded snow tires are permitted between October 1 and April 30. For more information, go to NDOT's website at www.nevadadot.com/business/trucker/.

New Jersey—May be fitted with tire chains of reasonable proportions when roads, streets, and highways are slippery, because of rain, snow, ice, oil, manner of construction, or other reason; provided, however, that no tire chains shall be used at any time on improved highways when highway conditions do not make such use necessary for the safety of life or property. No person shall use any tire chains so constructed or installed as to be likely to be thrown so as to endanger any person or property.

New Mexico—Permissible upon any vehicle when required for safety because of snow, ice, or other conditions tending to cause a vehicle to skid.

New York—Tire chains are required when a snow emergency has been declared.

North Carolina—Permissible upon any vehicle when required for safety because of snow, ice, or other conditions tending to cause a vehicle to slide or skid.

North Dakota—Tire chains may be used when necessary. Pneumatic tires with metal stubs projecting to 1/16 inch (1.59 mm) above the tread surface may be used between October 15 and April 15.

Ohio—Permissible when there is ice and/or snow on the roadway where you are driving or in the immediate vicinity, if you deem it necessary.

Oklahoma—Permissible upon any vehicle when required for safety because of snow, ice, or other conditions tending to cause a vehicle to skid.

Oregon—Tire chains are required when conditions demand because of snow, ice, or other inclement weather and signs are posted. For more information, go to ODOT's website at www.tripcheck.com/pages/.

Pennsylvania—One set of chains or snow tires is required when vehicles are likely to encounter any adverse weather conditions that may require chains. They must consist of not less than five cross chains and must not project more than 1 inch (2.54 cm) on the outside surface of the wheel.

Rhode Island—Tire chains of reasonable proportions are permitted on any vehicle when required for safety because of ice, snow, or other conditions tending to cause a vehicle to skid.

South Carolina—Vehicles likely to encounter conditions requiring chains must carry them and have them ready for use.

South Dakota—Permissible upon any vehicle when required for safety because of snow, ice, or other conditions tending to cause a vehicle to slide or skid. The secretary of transportation may restrict public travel upon any state trunk highway system to four-wheel drive vehicles or motor vehicles equipped with tire chains.

Tennessee—Permissible to use on any vehicle when required for safety because of snow, ice, or other condition tending to cause a vehicle to skid. Must carry one set of tire chains for all vehicles likely to encounter conditions requiring them.

Texas—May be used when required for safety because of a condition that might cause the vehicle to skid.

Utah—Vehicles likely to encounter conditions requiring chains must carry sets for at least one driving wheel on each side. Signs will designate when chains are required.

Virginia—Permissible when required for safety because of snow, ice, or other conditions tending to cause a vehicle to slide or skid. Vehicles blocking traffic due to lack of tire chains may be fined.

Washington—The chain requirements are effective when the department of transportation has posted signs marked "Chains required." On certain routes sufficient tire chains must always be carried on the vehicle from November 1 to April 1. The number of chains required varies, depending on the number of axles and vehicle configuration. At least two extra chains must be carried on the vehicle. For more information, go to WSDOT's website at www.wsdot.wa.gov/commercialvehicle/chain_req.htm.

West Virginia—It shall be permissible to use tire chains of reasonable proportions upon any vehicle when required for safety because of snow, ice, or other conditions tending to cause a vehicle to skid.

Wisconsin—May be used when required for safety because of snow, ice, or other conditions tending to cause a vehicle to skid.

Wyoming—May be required when the superintendent or his authorized representative determines that travel is sufficiently hazardous due to snow, ice, or other conditions.

No chain laws—Washington, D.C., Florida, Hawaii, Maine, Missouri, New Hampshire, and Vermont.

Snow Chain Laws in the Canadian Provinces

Alberta—Allowed when conditions warrant.

British Columbia—Vehicles in the mountains must be equipped with snow tires or chains from November 1 to April 30.

Manitoba—Permissible upon a motor vehicle where required for safety.

New Brunswick—May also be carried in the vehicle for use in ice and snow conditions.

Newfoundland—Required on drive wheels when there is snow or ice on the surface of the highway.

Nova Scotia—Permissible upon any vehicle when required for safety because of snow, ice, or other conditions tending to cause a vehicle to slide or skid.

Ontario—Permissible to use tire chains.

Prince Edward Island—Permissible to use tire chains.

Québec—The Minister of Transport may authorize, under the conditions and for the period he determines, the use of certain types of nonskid devices for such road vehicles as he may designate.

Saskatchewan—Required when conditions warrant.

DRIVING IN BRITISH COLUMBIA

Winter roads in British Columbia can be challenging, even for the most experienced professional drivers. Rapid changes in elevation and weather can make highway conditions unpredictable.

A driver who starts a trip in sunshine may face stretches of ice, heavy snowfall, or packed ice before reaching his/her destination. Tire chains are an important part of any driver safety kit.

British Columbia's ministry of transportation and infrastructure post signs advising where and when to use tire chains for traction and safety. These say, "Use winter tires or carry chains beyond this point, October 1 through April 30." When you see these signs, you must be ready to install chains or have proper winter tread tires before proceeding. Should you go beyond that point without the proper equipment, you may be subject to fine.

There are many types of chains on the market, so it's important to know which type is right for you and how to use them.

Single chains—have two outer rails with cross-links between them. They are generally used on steering and trailer axles and cover only one wheel. Do not use single chains for uphill traction on drive wheels with dual tires.

Duals and triples (3 side rails)—designed to fit over dual drive tires. The center rail between the dual tires gives extra strength and traction.

Cable chains—wrap around the tire, but are generally not used on commercial vehicles.

There are two rules that serve as reliable guidelines when choosing truck tire chains:

- Chains with cross-links that are equipped with V bars in the links generally provide more starting, stopping, and cornering traction and those with straight cross-links.

- Ladder-style ring chains will generally perform better in deep snow (more than 8 inches or 20.32 cm) than the ladder-style cable chains.

Case-hardened steel chains are good. The best of these chains have a tungsten tip, which is harder. Most good winter traction products have steel hoops or other features, such as side tighteners that make them easier to install on vehicle tires. Some tighteners also ensure chains remain properly fitted, eliminating the need to stop and retighten them.

When using linked chains, always inspect each chamber for installation to remove any tangles or twists. Links chains may break prematurely if you drive on twisted links, drive at speeds greater than 50 km/hour (31 mph) for prolonged periods of time, drive for extended periods on bare pavement, or spin your tires excessively.

About ABS and ATC—Automatic brake systems (ABS anti-lock) and automatic traction control (ATS) systems can improve traction. However, snow banks and heavy snowfall make tire chains necessary, even with these systems.

Safety When Installing Chains

Never forget your personal safety, the safety of your rig, and the safety of others when putting on tire chains. In many states, "chain-up" areas are provided for this task and some have Department of Transportation officers on site to make certain your chains have been installed properly **(see Figure 19-4)**.

When you are installing your chains, make certain you are in a safe and secure place, away from highway traffic. Note the following when preparing to put on snow chains:

- Pull well off the road.
- Park on a level, solid surface.
- Be careful because walking can be difficult on a snowy or icy surface.
- Be sure to put the chains on, right side out.
- Be sure to put a chain on the left rear trailer tire to help hold the trailer on the highway.

How to Install Chains

Many professional drivers prefer to have an experienced installer put on tire chains. However, the following steps provide a general guideline:

▶ Figure 19–4

Exercise caution when installing your chains.

1. Put on your vehicle's emergency brake to make sure it does not roll or slide.
2. Wear heavy gloves.
3. The tighter the chains are installed, the longer they and the tires will last.
4. Check inflation pressure before installing chains.
5. Lay the chains flat on the ground so that each side is parallel. Make sure there are no twists in the chain links and the wire locks are on the outside.
6. Drape the chains up and over the top of each tire, keeping the J-hook on the inside. Make sure the smooth side of the cross-member hook ends are facing away from the tire.
7. Release the emergency brake and move rig forward slowly until the wire lock is roughly axle high.
8. Apply the emergency brake.
9. Hook up the outer side chains by tugging firmly on both ends of the outer side chain to remove slack.
10. Thread the wire lock through a link.
11. Fasten the J-hook by inserting it through the side cross link from the other end of the side chain. Pull the slack toward the outside edge of the tire.
12. Drive one-quarter mile (approx. 1/2 km) and retighten as necessary to remove slack.

STARTING YOUR ENGINE IN COLD WEATHER

In the winter, all engines are more difficult to start. The lower the temperature, the more difficult it is. Big rigs are no exception. There are, however, certain devices that can be helpful in getting an engine started, even in the coldest weather:

NOTE

Most motor carriers do not recommend or allow ether on their units because it causes over-revs and blown engines when not used correctly.

- Special starting substances, like ether or ether-based fluid
- Glow plugs
- Preheaters

Ether

Ether has a very low flash point. It ignites easily, even in subzero temperatures. Since it is such a high-energy fuel, using ether has a few drawbacks. If not used properly or used too often, ether can damage the engine by cracking cylinder heads, breaking pistons, or snapping connecting rods.

CAUTION!

Ether is highly flammable. If you spill any on your clothing, change immediately. Stay away from open flames, matches, cigarettes, or hot exhaust pipes and heaters. They could cause your clothing to ignite.

Ether is packaged in aerosol cans, pressurized cylinders, driver-controlled injection systems, or capsules. These can be applied manually and automatically.

Aerosol spray cans, capsules, and pressurized cylinders are used manually. The capsules can be placed in a special holder attached to the air cleaner. Each capsule is good for one start. They also require only one person to start the engine.

Aerosol spray cans and pressurized cylinders require two people to start the engine. One person sprays ether into a rag in front of the air cleaner while the other person starts the engine. Be cautious, however, because too much spray may cause flashback fire or engine damage.

Automatic injection systems need only for the driver to start the engine. Ether is put into the engine in one of two ways. The driver turns on a switch in the cab and ether is injected into the engine, or ether is injected automatically when the engine is started.

The automatic injection system should not be used with aerosol ether.

Glow Plugs

Glow plugs are simply electric heating elements that warm the air coming into the engine from the air intake. They can be mounted in the intake manifold or in each combustion chamber. On diesel engines, they are sometimes located in the precombustion chamber. They raise the temperature in the chamber and it is the hot, compressed air that ignites the fuel. This usually takes about 60 seconds.

STOP!

Never use ether and glow plugs at the same time!

Preheaters

Preheaters keep the engine warm while parked for the night. Of the two types, in-block and immersion, most of the preheaters used are the in-block type. They fit into the freeze plug holes in the lower water jacket. The other end of the preheaters heats the coolant to approximately 160 degrees F (71 degrees C), which is near normal operating temperature. The coolant circulates through the engine and keeps it warm. The immersion type of preheater is used on off-highway construction vehicles and mining equipment.

GO!

When starting an engine in winter, do not apply any foot throttle to the engine while cranking. Leave your foot completely off the accelerator pedal until the engine is running on its own for at least 15 seconds before applying any throttle. Even then, it should be applied very moderately. Revving a cold engine may cause extreme engine damage.

AN ENGINE THAT WILL NOT START

If your engine will not start when you use starting aids, check to be sure the engine is getting fuel. To do this, check your rear-view mirror to see if vapor or smoke is visible from the exhaust stack. Check the fuel tanks and the fuel lines to be sure they are not blocked by ice or gelled fuel, and check the fuel tank vent.

STOP!

Do not crank the engine if it is not getting fuel. This will only run down the battery. Never crank the engine more than 15 seconds at a time. If the engine is getting fuel and still will not start, check the electrical system. If the rig has an electrical starter, remember the battery does not operate at full capacity in cold weather. The battery must be in the best possible condition. Check for the following:

- Corrosion on the terminals
- Loose connections
- Cracks in the cables
- Moisture in the cables

If the rig has an air starter, the engine will not start unless there is an air supply. If there is no air, the air supply can be restored from another tractor or an air compressor.

BAD WEATHER OPERATING HAZARDS

The two major hazards when driving in bad weather are reduced visibility and reduced traction (**see Figure 19-5**).

Reduced Visibility

When ice and snow build up on windows and mirrors, your visibility is reduced and you cannot see the driving environment around you as well. When this happens, you must stop and clean windows and mirrors. Do not drive with your side- or rear-view mirrors blocked. All lights and reflectors should also be free of ice, snow, mud, and dirt. Stop and clean them when needed. Some states will issue a citation

PRIMARY HAZARDS

Reduced visibility

Reduced traction

■ Road surface

— Different surfaces, different degrees of traction

— Be aware of changing conditions

■ Speed

— Speed magnifies mistakes

— Determine the speed at which the wheels roll without spinning

— Adjust speed to changing road surfaces and conditions

© Cengage Learning 2013

▶ **Figure 19–5**

The two major driving hazards in bad weather are lower visibility and less traction.

for a dirty windshield. Even when your windows, lights, and reflectors are clean, your visibility is sometimes limited by rain, snow, or fog. Slow down and drive carefully.

STOP!

Sometimes visibility can be almost zero. This happens at night in heavy snow, a downpour, or dense fog. Driving is not safe under these conditions. Stop and wait until your visibility improves before continuing.

Reduced Traction

As you will recall, the definition for *traction* is the grip, or friction, created between your rig's tires and the pavement. Different surfaces offer different amounts of traction. Some states use asphalt for roads that reduce spray and hydroplaning when wet. If there is ice or packed snow, about 80 percent of your traction is lost.

Slippery roads due to rain, sleet, ice, or snow will cause drive wheels to spin easily. This often results in less traction and, therefore, less control of the rig. As you drive, be aware of changing conditions. To check traction, periodically put on your brakes.

Proper tire inflation, tread, and weight on the drive wheels provides better traction and better control of your rig.

Speed is another factor in the traction equation. As the rig's speed increases, traction decreases. When traction is poor—for any reason—slow down until you have the rig well under control.

If the road is wet, reduce your speed by one-fourth. If you are driving 55 mph (89 km/h), slow to 40 mph (64 km/h). On packed snow and icy surfaces, stop your vehicle. Do not attempt to drive on these extremely dangerous surfaces. If you are forced to drive on snow or ice, cut your speed to about one-third the normal speed, or around 18 mph (29 km/h).

Remember—these are only general guidelines. Your exact speed should be determined by how much control you have of your rig. If that requires going slower than the general guidelines, go slower.

The following are also factors for determining a safe speed:

- Weight of rig
- Type of rig
- Condition of tires
- Type of road surface
- Temperature
- Type of precipitation

It is important to mention black ice in this section. Black ice is so clear you can see the road surface beneath it. It usually is difficult to spot but is often found on bridges, in dips in the road, beneath overpasses, in shaded areas, and on the lower sides of banked curves.

Black ice is also hard to spot at night. If a driver is not aware of black ice, it can be very dangerous.

When driving in sleet, check the front of your mirror for ice. If there is buildup of ice on the front of your mirror, then there is probably ice on the road and the safest option is to park your truck.

Skidding

The four basic causes for **skidding,** when tires lose traction on the road, are:

1. Driving too fast
2. Overacceleration
3. Overbraking
4. Oversteering

Driving too fast for road conditions causes most of the serious skids. Drivers who adjust their driving to the conditions do not overaccelerate and do not have to overbrake or oversteer because of too much speed.

Overbraking means braking too hard for the surface conditions. Excessive use of the service brakes is one cause of overbraking. Suddenly releasing the fuel pedal can also cause a braking effect that throws the rig into a skid. Skids also can be caused by using the engine brake incorrectly or downshifting to a gear lower than the speed requires. Drivers tend to overbrake when they drive too fast for the conditions, do not look far enough ahead, or do not leave enough following distance.

Oversteering occurs when a driver tries to round a turn too fast and turn the steering wheel too quickly. The drive wheels naturally want to continue to move straight ahead. Then, there is too little grip between the tires and the road. The result is a skidding trailer and a tractor-trailer jackknife. (Please see Chapter 20 for additional, in-depth information.)

Jackknifing

When the drive wheels lose traction, they cause the tractor-trailer to skid. This skid can result in a **jackknife.** Be careful not to make things worse by putting on the brakes or adding power in a skid **(see Figure 19-6).** Some of the causes of skidding and jackknifing are:

- Overacceleration
- Overbraking
- Oversteering
- Speed too fast for conditions

▶ **Figure 19-6**

When drive wheels lose traction, they can cause the tractor-trailer to skid.

STOP!

Although this chapter makes suggestions about driving in hazardous conditions, the only true way to stay safe when icing conditions are present or expected: **Slow Down! Keep speeds below 45 mph (72 km/h)** or simply *stay home*. No tire tread pattern, driver skill/technique, antilock brake, or traction control system can overcome the laws of physics regarding the coefficient of friction between rubber and ice. The only true way to mitigate the danger is to reduce speed. New tires, sandbags, and low-speed practice in parking lots will not prevent or prepare a driver for loss of control at highway speeds, which is the cause of the vast majority of road icing fatalities and major damage/injury crashes.

DRIVING IN BAD WEATHER

Professional drivers soon learn that trips in bad weather take longer than driving the same distance under good weather and road conditions. To emphasize the importance of reducing speeds in bad weather, a total of 22 people were killed in traffic accidents over a two-day period, December 15–16, 2010, in freezing rain and icy roads across Missouri, North Carolina, Illinois, Alabama, Mississippi, South Carolina, Georgia, and Kansas.

This section focuses on driving on slippery surfaces and the problem with wet brakes.

Driving on Slippery Surfaces

Take the following precautions on slippery surfaces:

- Start slowly. At the beginning of your trip, take your time so you can get a feel for the road. Do not hurry.

- Adjust your turning and braking to the conditions. Make turns as gradually as possible. Avoid braking any harder than necessary. Do not use the engine brake, if possible **(see Figure 19-7)**.

- Check your mirrors for the trailer when you brake, to be sure it is not drifting to one side. You can prevent a jackknife by acting when there is still time to recover.

- At night, if your trailer's lights begin to show in your mirror, it may mean the trailer is jackknifing.

- Adjust speed to the conditions. Do not overtake and pass other vehicles unless you have to, and slow to a safe speed.

- Watch far enough ahead to flow with the traffic, to help you avoid the need to change speeds rapidly.

- Take curves and turns at slower speeds than usual. Brake before curves. Be sure you are in the right gear before you enter a curve. Speed up slightly in the curve.

- As it gets warmer, ice melts and becomes more slippery. Slow down even more, if necessary.

- Avoid driving beside other vehicles, and stay out of packs and caravans.

Gentle pressure on brakes

© Cengage Learning 2013

▶ **Figure 19-7**

If your rig has antilock brakes, apply them and hold for safest stop.

- Maintain longer following distance.
- When traffic ahead looks congested, fall back. Stop, if necessary, and wait for traffic to thin out.
- Plan ahead for stops. Avoid panic stopping.
- Do not pump antilock brakes. Apply them and hold to provide the safest stop.

Wet Brakes

When you drive in heavy rain or deep standing water, the brakes will get wet. Then the linings may slip on the drum or disc and cause uneven braking. The final result can be loss of brakes, wheel lockup, veering from one side of the lane to another, or a jackknife.

Avoid standing water when possible; however, if you must drive through water, follow these steps:

1. Slow down.
2. Shift to a lower gear.
3. Place your left foot lightly on the brake.
4. Increase engine speed (rpm).
5. Accelerate through the water.

After you are out of the water, do the following:

1. Stay in low gear.
2. Keep your left foot on the brake.
3. Increase rpm to prevent stalling.
4. Keep light pressure on the brakes for a short distance to dry them out.
5. Release the brakes.

Check the rear of your rig to make sure no one is following too closely. Then, make a test stop to be certain your brakes are working properly.

Summary: Bad Weather Operation

All drivers and rigs have limits. As a professional driver, one of your duties is to know these limits and adjust your driving to the changing conditions. The best way to avoid accidents in bad weather is to adjust your speed, braking, steering, and space cushion. When it is too dangerous to drive, stop and wait until conditions improve and are safe for driving.

A Vehicle That Becomes Stuck

The best advice concerning a stuck vehicle is— DON'T GET STUCK! **(See Figure 19-8.)** You can sometimes keep from getting stuck by smarter driving.

▶ **Figure 19-8**
Best advice—don't get stuck.

STOP!

Stay away from situations that can cause a rig to get stuck, such as soft dirt on the roadside, deep snow, mud, ice, and slippery highways.

When in doubt, avoid any unknown or suspicious surfaces. Be alert when you leave the main road to make a delivery or when you pull off the road for rest, repair, or a vehicle check.

Freeing a Stuck Rig

To free a stuck rig, follow these steps:

1. Do not spin the drive tires or rock back and forth. These actions will dig the vehicle in more. On ice, spinning the wheels will cause heat. This will warm the ice under the tires and reduce traction by about 50 percent.

2. Use traction aids—dig under the front of the drive wheels and scatter sand or gravel in their path.

3. Lock the interaxle differential (if your rig has one).

4. Use a low gear, such as second or third gear. This will keep the wheels from spinning by reducing the force and applying it smoothly.

5. Start with the steering wheels straight ahead. If you have to start with the wheels turned, accelerate gently. Turn the steering wheel back and forth gently (less than 1 inch/2.54 cm) to prepare a path for the wheels.

6. As you begin to move, accelerate gently and smoothly. Ease off the accelerator if you start to slide.

GO!

Avoid:

- Soft berms
- Deep snow
- Muddy roads

When stuck:

- Do not spin wheels
- Use traction aids
- Lock interaxle differential
- Place in lower gear
- Accelerate gradually

When using a tow truck, remember:

- You are responsible for your vehicle and your cargo.
- Maintain control of the operation.
- Stay informed during all steps of the towing operation.

Towing

If your efforts to free your rig fail, call a tow truck. Remember that you are responsible for the equipment and the cargo, so you should be available to help supervise the towing operation.

Agree on a procedure before the operation is underway (**see Figure 19-9**).

Ask questions before the operation begins to free your rig, such as:

- In what direction will the tow truck pull the rig?
- In what direction should you steer, if this is needed?
- When is the tow truck to stop?

▶ **Figure 19-9**

A professional driver is responsible for the equipment and cargo.

If Your Rig Breaks Down in a Remote Area

If your rig breaks down in a remote area or you are stranded in a remote area because of bad weather conditions, stay in your cab. Being out in the wind and cold can be dangerous. Put on extra clothing to stay warm. Do not try to hike for help. You may not make it or may become disoriented in heavy snow or rain. Stay with your rig so you can move it if it needs to be towed out of deep snow or mud.

If you must leave your rig for any reason, attach a note to the steering wheel stating the time you left the rig and which direction you went.

> **CAUTION!**
>
> If your rig is stuck but the engine is operational, do not allow exhaust fumes to collect in the cab. Keep a window open slightly.

Surviving in Cold Weather

1. Before beginning your trip, check the current road conditions and weather forecasts. Make certain you know what weather is expected for the area in which you will be driving.
2. Smart professionals are always prepared for emergencies when bad weather is expected by carrying a supply of drinking water, candy bars, fruit, blankets, extra clothing, and toilet paper.
3. Follow other vehicles from a safe distance.
4. Always prefit your chains to your vehicle's tires before they are needed.
5. Always set your vehicle parking brake before installing chains.
6. Be aware of the potentially dangerous icy areas, such as shiny spots, bridges, and overpasses. Approach them with caution. They are usually the first areas to be icy, and often this ice is not visible—which is why it's called "black ice."
7. Snow and ice are most slippery when the road surface temperatures are at the freezing point (32°F or 0°C). Roads are also slippery if there have been sharp changes in temperatures that have resulted in ice formation.
8. Be prepared for changing conditions. Keep your survival kit handy, as well as blankets, appropriate clothing, and, of course, water.

DRIVING IN HOT WEATHER

In hot weather, it is particularly important for your rig to be in top condition and you to be prepared for the worst conditions. Watch the following areas carefully while driving in hot summer weather:

Vehicle inspection—an important driver preparation task. You are the one who will be out on the highway with your rig, so make sure you know how to deal with severe heat. Also make certain your rig, its systems, and all its equipment can stand the heat.

Tires—check mounting and inflation (**see Figure 19-10**). If you are hauling hazmat, inspect tires every 2 hours or 100 miles (161 km); if you are not hauling hazmat, inspect tires every 3 hours or

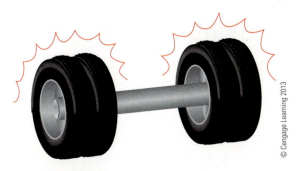

▶ **Figure 19-10**

In hot weather, check tires, mounting, and inflation to guard against blowouts or fire.

© Cengage Learning 2013

150 miles (241 km). An increase of 10 to 15 psi (69 to 103 kPa) is common. Check the heat of the tire with the back of your hand. If the tire pressure increases more than 15 psi (69 kPa) or the tire becomes extremely hot when you test it, stop driving. The tire could blow out or catch fire. Let the tires cool off.

STOP!

Never bleed air from tires when they are hot. Let them cool and then recheck the pressure.

Engine lubrication—oil helps cool the engine. Keeping the oil at the proper level is mandatory at all times, but particularly in hot weather. Check the oil level before you start each trip and often while en route. Check the oil temperature gauge regularly.

Engine coolant system—although big and powerful, engines are also quite delicate. They need heat to run, but too much heat can damage them quickly. The engine coolant system is vital to proper engine operation and should be kept full and clean. Also watch your water temperature gauge (**see Figure 19-11**).

Some types of engines tend to run warmer than others, so always carry extra coolant. If you must add coolant, allow the engine to cool first. Then run the engine at high enough rpm to circulate the fluid. Very carefully remove the coolant reservoir cap with a heavy rag. Keep your face and body clear because the coolant may spray. Add new coolant slowly.

Engine belts—check belt tension. Then check for fraying, cracking, or wear. Slipping belts can cause the fan or water pump to stop operating, which will result in an overheated engine.

Hoses—check for cracks, fraying, and kinks. Be sure hoses do not collapse when the engine accelerates. Coolant must circulate freely to keep the engine operating at peak performance and the right temperature.

© Cengage Learning 2013

▶ **Figure 19-11**

In warm weather, check your water temperature gauge often.

DRIVING IN THE DESERT

To some people, the desert contains a unique beauty. To others, it is a vast expanse of sand and rock. Regardless, the desert does have certain characteristics all professional drivers should know and understand (**see Figure 19-12**).

Washes—these are secondary roads often built through dry riverbeds. During heavy rains, these roads, or washes, can flood quickly. When it looks like rain, get to the main road as soon as possible.

© iStockphoto/MCCAIG

▶ **Figure 19-12**

The desert has certain unique characteristics.

Bleeding tar—tar used to pave roads comes to the surface in hot weather. Spots where tar is bleeding can become very slippery. Watch for these areas and avoid them when possible.

High speeds—often happen unintentionally after driving over long, flat desert roads for long periods of time. Keep an eye on your speedometer.

Vehicle breakdown—when breakdowns occur in remote areas, do not leave your vehicle. Use your dispatcher or your cell phone to communicate your position and your situation. Sit under the trailer, out of the sun, while awaiting help to arrive. Drink plenty of fluids if they are available to avoid dehydration.

MOUNTAIN DRIVING

Mountain driving is different from other driving conditions, and there are a number of considerations to keep in mind when driving through mountainous terrain. First, you and your rig must deal with gravity—the force that pulls objects toward the center of the earth. Gravity also changes normal driving patterns **(see Figure 19-13)**. No matter whether you are going uphill or down a grade, the pull of gravity is so severe, you must adjust your driving.

▶ **Figure 19-13**

Mountain driving is different from other driving conditions.

> **CAUTION!**
> Failing to make adjustments in your driving style while driving in the mountains can make your trip more difficult and more tiring. You also may damage your rig.

When you climb a grade, gravity adds to the weight of the load. This pulls the rig down and takes more horsepower to move the rig. It is also difficult to pass other vehicles when climbing a hill.

When you go downhill, gravity pulls the rig forward **(see Figure 19-14)**. This increases forward momentum. If the grade is steep, gravity can pull the vehicle off the road on curves, bumps, or loose gravel.

Inspections

Before driving in the mountains, it is important to inspect the following to maintain a high level of safety:

- Check the air brake system carefully.
- Make sure the compressor can maintain full reservoir pressure.
- Be sure the pressure drop when brakes are fully applied is within normal limits.
- Look for ice buildup on service brakes.
- Check for correct adjustments on slack adjusters.
- Listen for air leaks—check when brakes are both on and off.
- Make sure glad hands and air lines are secure.
- Check brake drums for overheating, but do not touch the drum. Hold the back of your hand close to the drum. Some heat is normal, but high heat is not.
- Be sure the trailer supply valve is working.

TRUCKS
GEAR
DOWN

FOR
NEXT
5 m/
8 km

ALLOW ENGINE COMPRESSION
AND FRICTION TO HELP
SLOW YOUR VEHICLE

© Cengage Learning 2013

▶ **Figure 19–14**

In mountain driving, gravity requires adjustments to normal driving patterns.

When Driving on Upgrades

Shifting—when rpm falls, downshift to the next lower gear. Gravity cuts your speed during the downshift. Complete the shift quickly before the rpm reaches the bottom of the range. Downshift until you reach the gear necessary to maintain the rpm.

Position—drive upgrades with patience. Move your rig to the far right truck lane. Stay in this lane and do not try to pass if you cannot do so quickly and safely.

CAUTION!

Remember, a slow uphill truck creates a negative reaction about the entire transportation industry in the minds of other road users. Other drivers may lose patience and make reckless moves. Don't be tempted to follow their lead.

STOP!

Most states and some provinces require vehicles to use four-way flashers when driving at speeds under 40 mph (64 km/h).

Watch your gauges—pulling a heavy load on a long grade can cause overheating. Check the coolant and water temperature gauges often. Shift a few hundred rpm earlier than the lowest rpm for that gear to help compensate.

When Driving on Downgrades

When driving on a downgrade, watch for signs showing the angle and length of the grade. These will help you decide on the correct speed while going downhill. Never go faster than the posted minimum speed. Talk with other drivers who have made the same downhill runs before because they often have helpful suggestions.

Because gravity plays such a big role in mountain driving, allow for the pull of gravity on your rig when going downhill. Make sure your brakes are properly adjusted. Check the traffic pattern in your mirrors, especially to the left and to the rear.

STOP!

Downshift before you start down the hill. NEVER downshift while going downhill because you will not be able to get into a lower gear while traveling at a high speed. You may not be able to shift at all; and if that happens, you will lose all braking capacity from the engine.

If you try to force an automatic transmission into a lower gear at a high speed, you can damage the transmission; and if you damage the transmission, you will lose all engine braking.

When you are in the right gear, your engine will not race. Be sure your speed is not too fast for the total weight of your vehicle and its cargo, length of the grade, steepness of the grade, road conditions, and weather.

Use your engine as the primary way to control your speed. The braking effect of the engine is greatest when it is near the governed rpm and the transmission is in a lower gear. Save your brakes until you really need them.

STOP!

Never shift into neutral and coast, because it is both illegal and unsafe.

If you use your brakes too often, then they may get hot and fade. You will have to apply them harder to get a braking effect. If you keep using them, then they may fail completely and you will be without brakes.

The American Association of Motor Vehicle Administrators makes the following recommendation:

"Once the vehicle is in the proper low gear, the following braking technique is suggested:

1. Apply the brakes just hard enough to feel a definite slowdown.
2. When speed has been reduced approximately 5 mph or 8 km/h below your safe speed, release the brakes. Brake application should last about 3 seconds.
3. When your speed has increased to your safe speed, repeat steps 2 and 3."

For example, if your safe speed is 40 mph (64 km/h), do not put on the brakes until you reach 40 mph (64 km/h). Then brake hard enough to reduce your speed to 35 mph (56 km/h). Release the brakes and repeat as often as you need to until you reach the end of the downgrade.

NOTE

There are two schools of thought regarding downhill braking: (1) "fanning" the brakes as described here, or (2) even, steady pressure on the brake pedal all the way down. The second approach seems to predominate, and is the way most schools teach downhill braking. When driving steep grades, professional drivers almost always perform a "brake check" or take a "safety break to analyze the safest approach" at the top of the hill.

GO!

Upgrades:

- Downshift until you find a gear that will maintain rpm.
- Position vehicle in the right lane.
- Do not pass.
- Turn on four-way flashers if speed drops to 40 mph (64 km/h).

Downgrades:

- Never downshift while descending.
- Use a low gear.
- Go slowly.
- Use close-to-rated engine speed to maximize drag.
- Use engine brake or other auxiliary braking device to help keep brakes cooler and more effective.
- Use snubbing method when braking.
- Turn on your four-way flashers.

AUXILIARY BRAKES AND SPEED RETARDERS

Auxiliary brakes and **speed retarders** reduce the rig's speed without using the service brakes. This saves wear and tear on the brakes. The retarders help control the rig on long grades. They can often keep the rpm within a safe range. If not, the service brakes will have to be used to keep the rig under control.

Types of Auxiliary Brakes and Speed Retarders

The four basic types of auxiliary brakes and speed retarders are as follows:

- Engine brakes
- Exhaust brakes
- Hydraulic retarders
- Electric retarders

Engine brakes—eliminate the engine's power stroke and convert the engine to an air compressor for braking purposes. Compressed air is expelled and slows the piston movement.

Exhaust brakes—back exhaust gases into the engine to create 40 to 50 psi (276 to 345 kPa) of pressure to slow piston movement. Exhaust brakes may be controlled by an on–off switch in the cab. Other types operate with an automatic switch that is turned on by releasing the fuel pedal and turned off by depressing the clutch pedal.

Hydraulic retarders—are mounted between the engine and the transmission. They can be adjusted manually to different levels of operation. The higher the setting, the more effective their performance. They have a treadle valve and may have a clutch switch.

Electric retarders—are mounted in the drive line and slow the driveshaft rotation with an electromagnet that can be turned on or off. There is no in-between setting.

Operation and Control

Because these devices can be noisy, be sure you know whether they are permitted in the area where you are driving. You will also need to know which gears they may be used with, as well as the proper rpm for their use and what kinds of weather you may use them in. Speed retarders are useful any time the service brakes are used continuously, usually in the mountains or on long downhill grades.

ESCAPE RAMPS

Escape ramps are designed to stop a vehicle safely without injuring people or damaging cargo **(see Figure 19-15).** They are built to stop most commercial vehicles traveling at 55 mph (88 km/h) about 450 feet (137.2 m) into the ramp. Stopping feels like a hard lock wheel stop on dry pavement.

Ramps either sink the rig in loose gravel or sand or send it up an incline. The grade may be as much as 43 percent. Either way, damage to the rig and cargo is limited to minor scratches, nicks, lost battery covers, and other minor problems.

The four basic types of ramps are:

■ **Gravity ramps**—have a loose material surface, such as pea gravel. The grade is usually from 5 to 43 percent.

■ **Sand piles**—are mounds or ridges built high enough to drag the undercarriage of the rig. Sand piles are from 85 to 200 feet (25.9 to 61 m) long.

■ **Arrester beds**—are masses of loose materials (usually pea gravel) arranged in flat beds from 300 to 700 feet (91.4 to 213.4 m) long.

■ **Combination ramp and arrester bed**—rely on the loose surface material to stop the rig. They have a grade of 1.5 to 6.7 percent and are from 500 to 2,200 feet (152.4 to 670.6 m) long.

▶ **Figure 19-15**

Escape ramps are available on mountain roads or continuous grades.

CAUTION!

If you find yourself having braking problems on a grade, remember the following:

■ First tighten your seat belt.

■ You can use an escape ramp.

■ Try to enter the ramp squarely and not at an angle.

■ Escape ramps save lives and cargos.

■ You probably will have to pay to have your rig towed back to the highway.

■ When in doubt, use the ramp.

DRIVING IN HIGH WINDS

Whether driving in a mountainous region or across the flatlands, high winds can have a definite impact on your rig, your speed, and your control of your vehicle. It isn't unusual to see headlines that read: "High winds topple 18-wheeler" or "High winds blow 18-wheeler off the road."

Be aware that, in some parts of North America, high winds can be accompanied by blowing dust—sometimes to the extent that visibility is cut to only a few feet/meters.

In dangerous weather, all drivers should exercise increased caution to assure their own safety and the safety of others on the road. Unfortunately, not all drivers take responsibility for their actions and can cause accidents in bad weather.

In any case, the following tips serve as a minimum guideline for the precautions you should take when high winds are encountered:

1. **Slow down.** Reducing your speed will make you less likely to drift off course if a sudden gust of wind comes along.
2. **Keep both hands on the wheel.** Higher winds can put you off course, particularly on open stretches of road, when passing over bridges, and when passing gaps in vegetation.
3. **Be aware of other high-profile vehicles, RVs, and motorcycles.** High winds make driving more difficult for every vehicle on the highway, but particularly tractor-trailer rigs and motorcycles. Take care when passing other high-profile vehicles and watch out for motorcyclists who may be swept off course by the wind.
4. **Avoid driving a high-profile vehicle.** These include trucks, buses, recreational vehicles (RVs), and campers. Towing trailers is also especially dangerous when wind speeds are high.
5. **Watch for flying debris and debris in the road.** You should be driving slowly enough that you can either stop before hitting the debris or drive around the debris.
6. **Beware of other weather conditions.** Often, high winds are accompanied by heavy rains and storms. Be prepared to meet more serious weather conditions down the road and watch out for wet or slippery areas that can cause skids or hydroplaning.

SUMMARY

In this chapter, you learned that driving in adverse conditions differs greatly from driving in good weather and on good roads. You also learned that rig inspection procedures in extreme driving differ from normal inspection routines.

You learned how to become aware of possible bad weather conditions and what you should do when you encounter or anticipate them. You also learned several methods for starting an engine in cold weather and what to do if your tractor will not start.

You learned how to avoid skids and how to dry out the truck's brakes should they become wet. You also learned your responsibility should your rig become stuck and require towing. The hazards of driving in hot weather and in the desert were explained.

Finally, you learned that driving in the mountains takes special skills and you learned about auxiliary braking systems, the best way to drive on downgrades, and the use of escape ramps.

KEY TERMS

Air dryer	Emergency equipment	Jackknife
Arrester beds	Engine brakes	Sand pile
Auxiliary brakes	Escape ramp	Skidding
Bleeding tar	Exhaust brakes	Speed retarders
Combination ramp and arrester bed	Extreme driving conditions	Tire chains
	Gravity ramp	Traction
Electric retarders	Hydraulic retarders	Visibility

A DAY IN THE LIFE...

Robert Stewart – Interstate Distributor Co., Professional Truck Driver

As an owner/operator, I do my best to portray myself and fellow truck drivers in a positive way. Some things may appear to be minor, such as a clean truck, good manners and personal appearance, or more important matters such as charity events or courtesy on the highway. A motorist will remember the truck that cut them off long before they will remember the truck that made room for them to enter the freeway. I also treat my customers like gold, since they can make or break you. I'm proud that I have never had a non–weather-related service failure or a complaint from a customer. My company has learned that I can be counted on to help out with turning a load or helping to cover a less-than-desirable load. When freight volume spikes I stay out for extended periods or hire on a team driver to capitalize on this. Not only is this beneficial to myself, but it also helps the company.

Safety is of utmost importance to me. I am very proud of my 2.5 million-plus safe miles hauling everything from explosives to toilet paper. I do detailed route planning to new customers since statistics prove wrong turns are asking for trouble. Since I run in all climates in all 48 states, staying informed of weather and road conditions also pays for safety.

I have helped several drivers new to my occupation. Some of these drivers were my trainees when I was a driver trainer. One trainee became one of my best friends. Some are friends or relatives just getting started, and having second thoughts about their choice. I reassure them that they need to give it time, not to expect too much too fast. This occupation is not for everyone, but is very rewarding if you put forth a good effort.

> " **Safety is of utmost importance to me.** "

In the '90s my wife and I were "Trucker Buddies" for several years, corresponding with a kindergarten class in Mercer Island, Washington. Although no longer active in Trucker Buddies, we enjoyed the program and loved our yearly visits to the school, usually with a safety mural trailer. For the past several years we have been participating in the "World's Largest Convoy for Special Olympics." The amount of funds raised has risen every year and the enjoyment of the disabled participants in this event is something my wife and I look forward to every year.

REVIEW QUESTIONS

1. Conditions such as cold, wet, heat, wind, snow, fog, or mountain ranges are called _____.

   a. all-weather driving conditions   c. multi-gear driving conditions

   b. extreme driving conditions   d. high-level driving conditions

2. One of the two major safety hazards caused by driving in extreme weather that increases stopping distance and decreases the driver's ability to control a rig is _____.

   a. less traction   c. brake lag time

   b. increased traction   d. increased center of gravity

3. A low coolant level in the cooling system affects the _____.

   a. brake lag time   c. center of gravity

   b. operation of the heater and defroster   d. efficiency of the brakes

4. Regarding the vehicle check for extreme weather driving, the tread depth of the front (steering) tires are considered worn out at _____.

   a. 1 inch (25.4 mm)   c. 2/32 inch (1.59 mm)

   b. 1/2 inch (12.7 mm)   d. 3 inches (76.2 mm)

5. When checking the brake balance as part of the extreme weather checklist, the brakes should _____.

   a. apply more pressure on the front wheels

   b. apply more pressure on the drive wheels

   c. apply more pressure on the trailer wheels

   d. all apply pressure equally and at the same time

6. Regarding fuel selection in extreme weather (cold), a driver should beware of low-quality fuel because it _____.

   a. gets poor mileage per gallon   c. causes longer brake lag time

   b. has a tendency to explode   d. can freeze (gel) in the fuel lines and filters

7. Broadcasting on 162.40 to 162.55 MHz, the _____ broadcasts constant, updated forecasts from many locations around the country.

   a. National Public Radio   c. FMCSR Radio

   b. National Weather Radio Service   d. American Trucking Associations

8. When a rig is going uphill in heavy wet snow, tire chains increase the pulling power of the drive wheels by _____.

   a. increasing the traction of the drive wheels   c. decreasing the traction of the drive wheels

   b. increasing the traction of the trailer wheels   d. increasing the reaction time of the driver

9. Single chains, made for single tires, are to be used on _____.

   a. the left front tire of the tractor only   c. the outside tire of dual wheels

   b. steering or trailer axles   d. the right inside tires of the trailer only

10. Regarding starting your engine in cold weather, the lower the temperature, _____.

   a. the harder engines are to get started   c. the greater the traction

   b. the easier engines are to get started   d. the more quarts of ether should be poured into the air cleaner

11. When attempting to start an engine, never crank the engine more than _____ at a time.

    a. 1 minute

    b. 30 seconds

    c. 2 minutes

    d. 15 seconds

12. Which of the following is not a major hazard when driving in bad weather?

    a. less visibility

    b. less traction

    c. lower cab temperature

    d. lower center of gravity

    C + D?

13. Proper tire inflation, tread depth, and weight on the drive wheels provide _____ and better control of a rig.

    a. a higher center of gravity

    b. better traction

    c. lower center of gravity

    d. less traction

14. Regarding driving on curves and turns on slippery surfaces, which of the following is not a recommended practice?

    a. speed up slightly in the turn or curve

    b. shift to the correct gear before entering a curve or turn

    c. reduce speed during a curve or turn

    d. brake before a turn or curve

15. The best advice regarding stuck vehicles is _____.

    a. do not spin the wheels

    b. place in higher gear

    c. do not get stuck

    d. use traction aids

16. If a tow is needed, who is responsible for the rig?

    a. driver of the tow truck

    b. dispatcher

    c. service technician

    d. driver of the rig

17. Regarding mountain driving, the force that pulls objects toward the center of the earth and affects a rig going uphill as well as downhill is called _____.

    a. gravity

    b. traction

    c. friction

    d. center of gravity

18. Regarding driving on downgrades, which of the following is the correct procedure for shifting?

    a. Upshift before starting down the hill.

    b. Downshift once you are on the downgrade.

    c. Downshift before starting down the hill.

    d. Upshift once you are on the downgrade.

19. Regarding driving on downgrades, according to the American Association of Motor Vehicle Administrators' Model CDL Manual, once a vehicle is in the proper low gear and the brakes have been applied hard enough to feel a definite slowdown, _____.

    a. when the speed has reduced to approximately 5 mph (8 km/h) below the safe speed, release the brakes until speed increases to the safe speed, then repeat for the remainder of the hill

    b. shift to a lower gear until the rig reaches a safe speed, then shift again to a lower gear; repeat for the remainder of the hill

    c. shift to a higher gear and then apply the brakes until a safe speed is reached, then shift to a higher gear again; repeat for the remainder of the hill

    d. continue to apply the brakes down the remainder of the hill

20. Auxiliary brakes and speed retarders _____.

    a. reduce a rig's speed without using the service brakes

    b. reduce the rpm of the engine and increase power to the drive wheels

    c. are used in emergencies only

    d. along with electric retarders reduce the amount of electricity needed to operate the rig

21. When the drive wheels lose traction, they cause the tractor-trailer to skid and this situation can be made worse by _____.

    a. calling the dispatcher   c. putting on the brakes

    b. checking the tach   d. none of the above

22. Some of the causes of skidding and jackknifing are _____.

    a. overacceleration   c. overbraking

    b. oversteering   d. all of the above

SUPPLEMENTAL LEARNING ACTIVITIES

1. Divide into groups. Ask those in each group who have been stranded on a highway because of weather or a breakdown in bad weather to help compile a list of dos and don'ts. Report back to the class.

2. Discuss driving a private vehicle on icy, slick roads. From your reading and class instruction, compare the precautions necessary to drive a tractor-trailer on icy roadways.

3. If you could put together a survival kit for all-weather survival, limited to a 12 × 12-inch (30 × 30-cm) container, what would you include? Work as a group and come up with the best possible collection of needed items.

4. Find several different types of tire chains and display them for the class. Discuss how to "chain-up" for winter driving. If possible, demonstrate how to put on tire chains with a spare tire brought to the classroom or on the driving range.

5. In an essay of 100 words, describe what you would do, as a professional driver, if you found yourself on a flooded or washed-out highway. Look up incidents on the Internet where trucks became stranded in flooding conditions, such as Hurricane Irene (2011) on the East Coast or Hurricane Katrina (2005) on the Gulf Coast.

FOR MORE INFORMATION

PTDI—Identify and Adjust to Difficult and Extreme Driving Conditions, Page 20, Click on Skill Standards
www.ptdi.org/standards

PTDI—Deal with Environmental Issues, Page 24, Click on Skill Standards
www.ptdi.org/standards

Weather Channel—Driving Safety Tips
www.weather.com/activities/driving/drivingsafety/drivingsafetytips/snow.html

Washington State Department of Transportation—Guide for Cold Weather Driving
www.wsdot.wa.gov/winter

20 Skid Control

© steve estvanik/www.Shutterstock.com

OBJECTIVES

When you have completed this chapter, you should be able to:

- Show how skid control can prevent accidents.
- Explain vehicle control factors including traction, wheel load, and force of motion.
- Understand the causes of skidding.
- Illustrate a tractor-trailer jackknife, front-wheel skid, and an all-wheel skid.
- Describe the ways to recover from a skid if it is detected early enough.
- Know the operating characteristics of ABS and non-ABS brakes.

INTRODUCTION

When any vehicle skids, the driver loses control. Skids occur when tires lose their grip on the road. What many professional drivers do not know is that they can prevent most skids, and, in fact, it is much easier to prevent a skid than to correct one.

Typically, a skid happens when your vehicle's wheels slide out of control on the slick roadway. They can involve the front, rear, or all wheels—and may cause a vehicle to jackknife.

Most skids are caused by driving too fast for road or traffic conditions. *Or they may be caused by sudden, hard braking, going too fast when cornering, or entering the roadway or accelerating too quickly.*

If your vehicle begins to skid, steer the vehicle in the direction you want to go, being careful not to oversteer. In icy conditions or skidding in a straight line, step on the clutch or shift to neutral.

▶ Figure 20–1

Skids can happen at any time but are more common on slippery roads.

Skids can occur because of one of the following four driver mistakes. The most common is trying to quickly change speed (overacceleration). The next most common cause of a skid is trying to change direction too quickly (oversteering). The other two reasons skids occur are overbraking (braking too hard and locking up the wheels or using the speed retarder when the road is slick) and driving too fast, which results in the most serious skids.

Most skids happen when the road is slippery due to rain, snow, and ice (**see Figure 20-1**). Loose material on the pavement—like gravel or wet leaves—can also make the road slippery and interfere with traction. Because most skids are caused by a sudden change in speed or direction, professional drivers must always be aware of the weather conditions and the road's surface and adjust their speeds based on these factors.

In this chapter, you will learn about skids, how skids happen, how they can be prevented, and how to make corrections and recover control, once the vehicle begins to skid. Hands-on experience should be practiced only on a special driving range or skid pad, never on the open road.

▶ *"I'm singin' and dancin' in the rain . . ."*

VEHICLE CONTROL FACTORS

When the vehicle control factors are not in balance, a skid will occur. Factors that affect control of the vehicle include traction, wheel load, and force of motion.

Traction

The two types of **traction** are as follows:

- **Rolling traction**—the friction of one surface rolling over another; for example, the friction of a rolling tire moving over the road in the same direction the rig is moving.
- **Sliding traction**—the friction of one surface sliding across another. This occurs when other forces acting upon surfaces are greater than the traction between them. This can happen whether the wheels are locked or turning.

Tires may slide in any direction when they lock up from too much braking. Too much **centrifugal force** (outward force) also may cause tires to slide sideways, even though they are turning.

Wheel Load

Wheel load is the downward force of weight on a tire. The greater the load on the tire, the better the traction. Wheel load is determined by the weight of the vehicle plus the weight and distribution of the load.

Notably, while wheel load may increase the downward force and the amount of tread touching the pavement, wheel load may not actually improve the traction. For example, if there is ice or snow on the road surface, there is still a lack of adequate traction, and skidding can occur.

Some tractor-trailer drivers have the misconception that a heavier wheel load will guarantee better traction on slippery surfaces, but this is not true.

Force of Motion

The **force of motion** of the rig is determined by its weight and speed. The heavier the rig and its load and the faster it travels, the greater the force that moves that rig. To keep the rig under control, the professional driver must avoid skids.

CAUSES OF SKIDS

There are several reasons a truck will begin to skid, but the two basic causes are changes in speed and changes in direction (**see Figure 20-2**).

Change in Speed

A sudden change in speed can result from either too much braking or speeding up too fast. If the forces of motion are greater than the traction of the tire against the pavement when you brake, instead of stopping, the rig will skid. Make a conscious effort to periodically check your speed—do not trust your instincts.

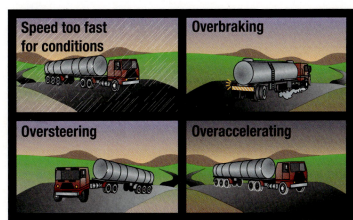

▶ **Figure 20-2**

All professional drivers need to understand the most common causes of skids.

Locked wheels can cause a skid

© Cengage Learning 2013

▶ **Figure 20-3**

Wheels can lock when you apply brakes too hard, downshift too much, or suddenly slow down.

Skids involving speed may be from braking or acceleration. Braking skids can result in:

■ Wheel lockup

■ Tire slides

Both of these conditions increase the rig's stopping distance and cause the driver to lose control (**see Figure 20-3**).

Wheel Lockup

Wheel lockup happens because you:

■ Put on the service brakes, exhaust brakes, or speed retarder too hard

■ Downshift too much

■ Slow suddenly

You lose control when the locked wheels slide and the rig skids out of control. The skid may be straight ahead, sideways, or a jackknife. The unit will be out of control until you, the driver, correct the problem, or a collision occurs.

Tire Slides

Tire slides occur when the forces from weight and acceleration of the rig are greater than the ability of the tires to maintain traction. Wheel lockups and tire slides increase the rig's stopping distance. And remember—sliding tires do not slow a vehicle as well as rolling tires.

Spinning tires occur when the force from acceleration on the drive wheels is greater than the ability of the tires to provide traction. The wheels spin, but the vehicle does not move. The spinning continues until the driver stops accelerating. The rear of the tractor may also move in a sideways spin, called a **power skid.**

Slowing too fast may also cause a skid. If the rig has moved onto ice and the driver suddenly recognizes the problem, he or she may quickly react by removing his or her foot from the accelerator. This reaction may reduce the wheel speed too fast and cause a skid; so if possible, slow before reaching any icy spots on the road.

CAUTION!
Remember, the major cause of skidding is a sudden change in either speed or direction.

Change of Direction

Changing the direction of your steering too quickly can cause the rolling tires to lose their friction with the road surface. When this happens, the rig continues in the direction it has been moving instead of changing to follow the direction of the steering wheels.

When a vehicle makes a turn, centrifugal force makes it keep going in the same direction. As a result, the vehicle tends to slide outward in a turn.

If the rate of speed or the sharpness of the turn is too great, centrifugal force exceeds traction. This causes the tires to skid sideways. A new driver may put on the brakes suddenly, which causes the tires to lock up and makes the skid worse because the driver has even less control.

> **CAUTION!**
>
> When you brake your rig too hard, you will cause a skid. You also need to know that when you speed up too quickly, you can also cause a skid because you increase the wheel speed to a point where the tires cannot provide traction. The result is a **jackknife.**

PREVENTING SKIDS

In any situation, it is always better to prevent a skid than to try to recover once a skid occurs. Safe driving practices can help prevent skids. ABS, which was discussed in Chapters 3 and 4, stands for "antilock braking system." This technological breakthrough has gone far to eliminate tractor-trailer jackknifes. We will talk more about ABS later in the chapter.

The following tips may help you avoid skid situations:

- Adjust your speed before entering curves to reduce your chances of a cornering skid.
- Drive within your sight distance to reduce the need for sudden stops and the possibility of a braking skid.
- Maintain enough following distance so you will not have to make a quick stop.
- Do not drive too fast on slick surfaces.
- Adjust your speed to the surface and weather conditions and to the curvature of the road.
- Do not overbrake.
- Do not suddenly downshift.
- Use the brake limiting valve correctly.
- Inspect the air and brake systems before and during each trip. All wheels should start stopping at the same time. If they do not, a skid can result when you brake your vehicle.
- Inspect tires, front wheel alignment, and suspension system.
- Load cargo properly.

TRACTOR-TRAILER SKIDS

Tractor-trailer skids are grouped according to what happens to the rig as a result of the skid. The four major types of skids are:

1. Trailer jackknife
2. Tractor jackknife
3. Front-wheel skid
4. All-wheel skid

Trailer Jackknife

A trailer jackknife is caused by too much braking or cornering. In either case, the trailer tires skid because they become locked. The force that locks them overcomes the traction with the surface of the road (see **Figure 20-4**). It is much more common to have a trailer jackknife than a tractor jackknife, and ABS

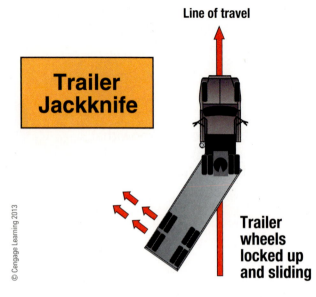

Line of travel

Trailer Jackknife

Trailer wheels locked up and sliding

© Cengage Learning 2013

▶ **Figure 20–4**

A trailer jackknife is caused by excessive braking or sharp cornering.

has made great strides in attempting to curb the number and severity of these types of accidents. Also, roll stability indicators give drivers warning that the equipment is near the threshold where an accident is more likely.

NOTE

Overbraking is the number one cause of trailer jackknife and can be avoided by slowing down before entering curves and turns.

- **Overbraking**—caused by putting on the footbrake too hard or not using the trailer brake correctly. The trailer brake should not be used for stopping the entire rig. Sometimes the driver is forced to use the brakes excessively because of a mechanical problem, such as:

  - A faulty air system that sends too much pressure to the trailer wheels
  - Not adjusting the brakes on the trailer equally, called cam-over
  - Worn trailer brake linings that cause a brake seizure

- **Excessive cornering**—if a rig enters a curve too fast for the surface conditions, the tires may lose traction, causing the rig to jackknife or skid out of control.

CAUTION!

Always adjust your speed—to the road conditions and to the curve—before you enter a curve. This will help you avoid a jackknife.

When entering curves, ease off the fuel pedal and then accelerate through the second half of the curve. Never accelerate into a curve, only out of one. This is done so the tractor pulls the trailer through the curve rather than allowing the trailer to push the tractor through the curve.

STOP!

Be sure to always inspect the air system and brakes before and during every trip.

Tractor Jackknife

A tractor jackknife (also called a **drive-wheel skid**) occurs when the tractor drive wheels lose traction **(see Figure 20-5).**

This happens because of:

- Wheel lockup
- Overacceleration
- Trailer override

When any of these three conditions occur, the drive wheels have less traction than the front wheels, so they try to overtake the front wheels. As a result, the rear of the tractor tends to swing out—and as it does, the tractor pulls the trailer outward. Then, the trailer pushes the tractor outward and a jackknife results.

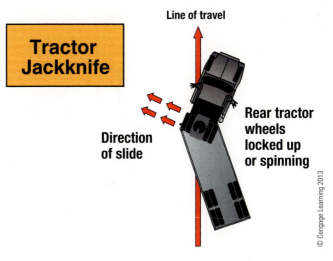

Figure 20-5

A tractor jackknife occurs when the tractor drive wheels lose traction.

If a drive-wheel skid occurs on ice or snow, it can be easily managed by taking your foot off the accelerator. (If road conditions are very slippery, push in the clutch.) Otherwise, the engine will keep the wheels from rolling freely and regaining traction.

Wheel lockup—occurs for the following reasons:

- Putting on the brakes too hard
- Downshifting on a slippery road surface
- Sudden release of fuel pedal on a slippery surface with retarder on
- Load imbalance (drive wheels too lightly loaded)
- Faulty brakes
- Poor tread on the drive tires

Overacceleration—occurs when too much pressure for the gear and vehicle speed is placed on the fuel pedal, which causes a power skid. Most power skids occur while driving on a slippery surface, the rig has an engine with high horsepower (high torque), or the trailer is heavily or improperly loaded.

Trailer override—when you brake, the cargo may push the trailer against the tractor. This forces the tractor out of line and creates a jackknife. Trailer override most likely will occur if the pavement is slippery, the trailer is not loaded properly, or the cargo is not distributed correctly or secured properly. It can also occur if the rig is taking a curve or making a rapid lane change.

The best way to prevent a tractor jackknife is to avoid the following:

- Overbraking
- Overaccelerating
- Sudden downshifts
- Sudden turns
- Incorrect loading

Front-Wheel Skid

Front-wheel skids happen when you lose front-wheel traction **(see Figure 20-6).** The rig continues to move forward but you cannot steer it.

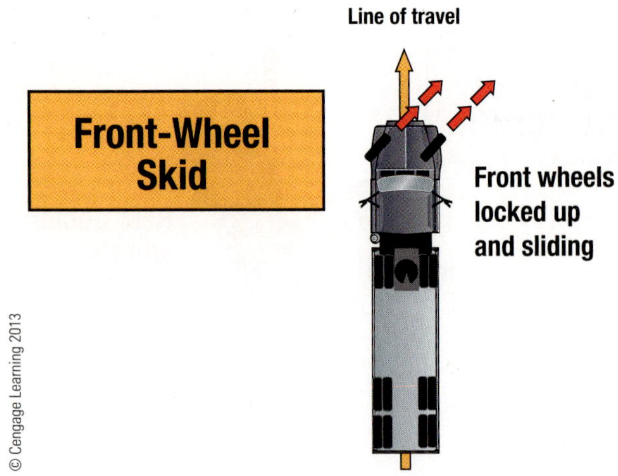

Line of travel

Front-Wheel Skid

Front wheels locked up and sliding

© Cengage Learning 2013

▶ **Figure 20-6**

Front wheel skids occur when your front wheels lose traction.

The rig also may move sideways or fail to round a curve. Front-wheel skids are usually caused by:

■ Too big a load on the fifth wheel (this happens when cargo is not properly loaded and it shifts forward when you brake your rig)

■ Too much speed

■ Not enough front tire tread

■ Hydroplaning

■ Oversteering in combination with any of the above mentioned reasons

■ Malfunction of the brake system

■ Worn brake linings or other brake defects

■ A dry fifth wheel

Front wheel skids can be prevented by:

■ Slowing your speed when driving on slippery pavement (caused by rain, snow, sleet, ice, or fog)

■ Loading cargo correctly

■ Inspecting tires, front-wheel alignment, and suspension system—and having any problems you find corrected

■ Using good braking techniques

All-Wheel Skid

When all wheels lock and do not roll, your rig will lose traction. It stops rolling and starts to slide. The rig often continues in a straight line without traction; and, without traction, the driver loses control **(see Figure 20-7).**

The major causes of this kind of skid are excessive speed and overbraking on a slippery surface. In cases of overbraking, one set of wheels generally locks up before the others. In some cases, even light brake pressure causes the wheels to lock up.

To prevent all-wheel skids:

■ Allow plenty of stopping distance

■ Control your speed

■ Do not brake too much on slippery surfaces

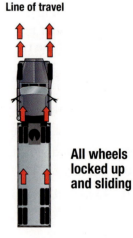

Line of travel

All-Wheel Skid

All wheels locked up and sliding

© Cengage Learning 2013

▶ **Figure 20-7**

The major causes of all-wheel skids are excessive speed or overbraking on slick roads.

Summary of Skid Prevention

As discussed earlier in this chapter, preventing skids is a priority task for professional drivers. You learned that controlling your rig comes from managing your speed; and the space around your rig is also a priority, especially when driving in extreme conditions.

Most skids result from sudden changes in speed or direction. Overbraking and oversteering as well as fast acceleration or deceleration cause the sudden changes that often result in skids.

Skidding usually occurs on slippery surfaces. To prevent skidding:

- Avoid quick braking and quick turns on slippery pavement.
- If you must turn or brake your rig, do no more than is absolutely necessary.

WHAT IS THRESHOLD BRAKING?

Threshold braking will bring you to a reasonably quick, controlled stop in your own lane, even in icy conditions. It involves braking as hard as you can without locking up or skidding your wheels, as follows:

- Press down on the brake pedal, getting as much brake power as possible.
- If you sense your wheels locking up, release the brake pressure slightly and reapply.
- Continue breaking until you have brought your vehicle to a complete stop.
- Don't pump the brakes.

ANTIJACKKNIFE DEVICES

Antijackknife devices are made to restrict trailer swing and prevent damage to the rig; however, these devices do not prevent skidding. There are two basic types of antijackknife devices:

- Fifth-wheel devices
- Cable devices

  Fifth-wheel antijackknife devices—are automatic and restrict the rotation of the kingpin. This prevents a collision between the trailer and the cab. They are mounted on the tractor and can be used with any type of trailer.

  Cable antijackknife devices—are mounted to the trailer and connected to the tractor. They are activated by hard braking and keep the trailer and tractor in line.

ANTILOCK BRAKES

As you already read about in earlier chapters, **antilock braking systems (ABS)** are electronic systems that monitor and control wheel slip during vehicle braking. ABS can improve vehicle control during braking, and reduce stopping distances on slippery road surfaces by limiting wheel slip and minimizing lockup. Rolling wheels have much more traction than locked wheels. Reducing wheel slip improves vehicle stability and control during braking since stability increases as wheel slip decreases.

ABS can be applied to nearly all types of vehicles and can be successfully integrated into hydraulic and airbrake systems.

Some vehicles also use a traction control system in conjunction with ABS. Traction control helps the ABS improve vehicle traction by minimizing wheel slip on the drive axle during acceleration. If one wheel on the drive axle starts to slip, the traction control automatically brakes the wheels slightly, transferring engine torque to the wheels with better traction. If all drive wheels start to slip, the traction control system may also reduce engine power **(see Figure 20-8)**.

The National Highway Traffic Safety Administration (NHTSA) requires that ABS be installed on commercial air-braked truck tractors built on or after March 1, 1997, and on other air-braked vehicles such as trucks, buses, trailers, and converter dollies built on or after March 1, 1998. This same mandate applied to all hydraulically-braked trucks and buses with gross vehicle weight ratings of more than 10,000 pounds manufactured after March 1, 1999.

These requirements specify that ABS on truck tractors and full trailers must control the brake pressures to at least one front axle and one rear axle. The ABS on semi-trailers and dollies must control at least one axle of the vehicle. Additionally, the ABS on tractors must control one rear axle with two modulator valves so that the brake pressure on one end of the axle is independent of the brake pressure on the other end.

When used properly, an ABS is a safe and effective braking system. ABS allows the driver to maintain directional stability, control over steering, and in some situations, to reduce stopping distances during emergency braking situations, particularly on wet and slippery road surfaces. To gain this safety advantage, drivers must learn how to operate their ABS correctly:

NOTE

Since antilock brake systems lose their effectiveness with "pumping" the brakes, stab braking may not be the skid-recovery technique of choice. This is because it actually reduces the effectiveness of the tractor brakes and increases the braking power coming from the trailer. This situation sets up your rig for a trailer skid or the inability to come to a stop as soon as necessary. Controlled braking is the correct technique in this type of skid.

- An antilock braking system works with the regular or foundation brakes on your vehicle. ABS simply keeps your base brakes from locking up.

- In vehicles not equipped with ABS, the driver can manually pump the brakes to prevent wheel lockup.

- In vehicles equipped with ABS, the driver's foot remains firmly on the brake pedal, allowing the system to automatically pump the brakes.

- When your brakes lock up on wet and slippery roads or during a panic stop, you lose steering control and your vehicle can spin. Rear wheel ABS prevents wheel lockup so that your vehicle stays in a straight line.

- Antilock systems use electronic controls to read wheel speed and prevent the brakes from locking up the wheels under hard braking. This feature increases driver control during braking but does not necessarily shorten stopping distances.

- Antilock brakes are most effective when you hit the brake pedal and hold it down.

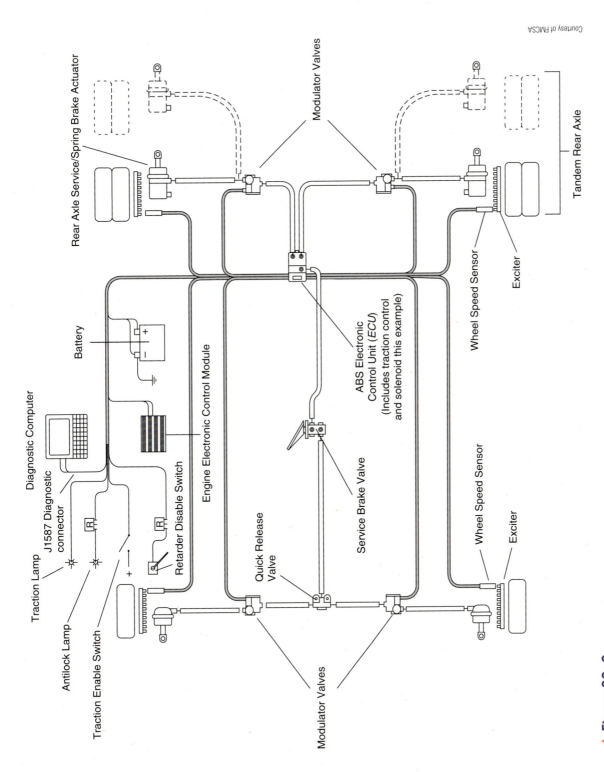

Courtesy of FMCSA

Figure 20-8
Schematic of tractor ABS.

FEATURES AND BENEFITS OF ANTILOCK BRAKING SYSTEMS

1. **Control of steering, drive, and trailer wheels:** increases steering ability and vehicle stability during braking. Reduces possibility of jackknifing and trailer swing.

2. **Traction control:** an optional feature that controls excessive wheel spin during acceleration, reducing the possibility of power skids, spins, or jackknifes.

3. **Fail-safe electrical, electronic system:** if the electrical/electronic system fails, the ABS is shut off, returning the vehicle to normal braking. On some systems, the ABS is only shut off at the affected wheels.

4. **Self-diagnosing system:** built-in system makes maintenance check quick and easy.

5. **ABS malfunction indicator lamp:** informs the driver or technician that an ABS fault has occurred. The warning lamp may also transmit link code information. It does not signal all possible faults.

CAUTION!

Drivers unfamiliar with antilock braking are often surprised by the vibration that happens the first time they brake hard in an emergency. It is a good idea to practice using emergency braking under controlled conditions with a qualified instructor. This will familiarize you with what to expect so you can react quickly and effectively in an emergency.

SKID RECOVERY

Almost all tractor skids are corrected by the same techniques:

1. Disengage the clutch.
2. Get off the brakes.
3. Countersteer.

Most skids happen when you try to change speed too quickly for the conditions. Remove your foot from the brake pedal to reduce skidding. Then you can more easily gain control of the direction the rig is going. Do not put on the independent trailer brake.

STOP!

If the trailer has started to jackknife, putting on the trailer brake will only make the situation worse!

If overbraking resulted from downshifting, depress the clutch quickly and then use the ABS. If overacceleration has caused the skid, you should ease off the fuel pedal. Then depress the clutch pedal to remove engine power from the drive wheels.

Corrective Steering

In a tractor jackknife, corrective steering is needed to put the tractor back on course (see Figure 20-9). Steer toward the direction the rig is moving. Steer in the line of travel.

Oversteering—on a slippery surface, when you lose control of your steering and traction, you must oversteer (turn beyond the intended path of travel). Unless you oversteer, you will not be able to regain control of your rig.

Countersteering—when you try to correct a skid, little traction makes the rig slow to respond. As the rig resumes the correct course, the driver must countersteer early. Do this to avoid a new skid (see Figure 20-10). Continue countersteering until the rig is on a straighter path. Each countersteering movement should get smaller until the rig is going straight again. If a new skid happens because you countersteered too late, the rig may turn beyond the intended path and spin out. Although it may not spin out the first time you countersteered too late, each correction may make the situation worse until a spinout occurs.

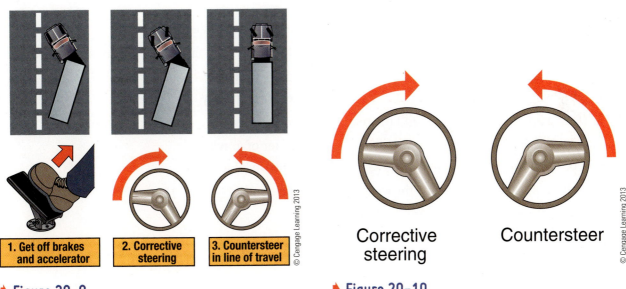

| 1. Get off brakes and accelerator | 2. Corrective steering | 3. Countersteer in line of travel |

© Cengage Learning 2013

Corrective steering   **Countersteer**

© Cengage Learning 2013

▶ Figure 20-9

When a tractor jackknife occurs, corrective steering can often put the tractor back on course.

▶ Figure 20-10

Countersteering will help you avoid a new skid.

Braking to a Stop

Once a vehicle is on a straight path, you can brake to a stop. It is best to brake lightly and steadily. If the vehicle is equipped with antilock brakes, a light, steady application of the brake is best.

SUMMARY

In this chapter, you learned the types of skids and what can be done to prevent them. You also learned there are ways to recover from each type of skid in order to prevent damage to your rig and injury to yourself or others. The conditions that cause skids were also discussed.

KEY TERMS

Antilock brake
  system (ABS)
Cable antijackknife devices
Centrifugal force
Countersteering
Drive-wheel skid

Fifth-wheel antijackknife
  devices
Force of motion
Jackknife
Oversteering
Power skid

Rolling traction
Sliding traction
Tire slides
Traction
Wheel load
Wheel lockup

REVIEW QUESTIONS

1. When vehicle control factors are not in balance, _____.

    a. the vehicle will be overweight
    b. the brakes control the vehicle more efficiently
    c. a skid will occur
    d. the fifth wheel will balance the weight of the tractor and the trailer

2. Regarding vehicle control factors, which of the following is not a factor that controls the vehicle?

    a. traction
    b. wheel load
    c. age of vehicle
    d. center of gravity

3. The "grip" between the tires and the road surface is known as _____.

    a. friction
    b. traction
    c. center of gravity
    d. centrifugal force

4. Wheel load is determined by the weight of the vehicle and _____.

    a. the weight and distribution of the load
    b. the weight of the load
    c. the center of gravity of the load
    d. b and c

5. Antilock braking systems monitor and control _____.

    a. braking time
    b. wheel slip
    c. friction
    d. brake reaction time

6. Which of the following is *not* a condition that can produce a skid?

    a. overbraking
    b. oversteering
    c. overaccelerating
    d. excessive traction on drive axle tires

7. When the force from acceleration on the drive wheels is more than the tire's ability to provide traction, _____ occurs.

    a. a power skid
    b. a gravity skid occurs
    c. a trailer jackknife
    d. an antigravity skid occurs

8. Regarding changes of direction, if the rate of speed or sharpness of a turn is too great and the rig slides outward, centrifugal force of the rig exceeds _____.

    a. the braking force of the rig
    b. the traction of the tires
    c. oversteering
    d. countersteering

9. In any situation it is always better to _____ than to try to recover once a skid occurs.

   a. drive faster to increase force of gravity

   b. countersteer

   c. increase the rig's center of gravity

   d. prevent skids

10. In a trailer jackknife, which is caused by excessive braking or sharp cornering, the trailer wheels _____.

   a. decrease traction   c. a and b

   b. increase friction   d. lose direction

11. A tractor jackknife (drive-wheel skid) occurs when the tractor drive wheels _____.

   a. increase traction   c. lose traction

   b. increase friction   d. a and b

12. Which of the following is not a cause of front-wheel skids?

   a. loss of front wheel traction   c. too big a load on the fifth wheel

   b. increased traction   d. too much speed

13. Which of the following is *not* one of the best ways to prevent all-wheel skids?

   a. Reduce the time on slippery areas by driving faster.

   b. Allow plenty of stopping distance.

   c. Do not brake too much on slippery surfaces.

   d. Control your speed.

14. Most skids result from _____.

   a. sudden changes in speed   c. sudden changes in the fifth-wheel alignment

   b. sudden changes in direction   d. a and b

15. Regarding skid recovery, which of the following is not one of the techniques used to recover from a skid?

   a. Increase the speed of the rig.   c. Get off the brakes.

   b. Disengage the clutch.   d. Countersteer.

16. Antilock braking systems (ABS) are electronic systems that can _____.

   a. improve vehicle control during braking

   b. reduce stopping distances on slippery road surfaces

   c. minimize lockups

   d. all of the above

SUPPLEMENTAL LEARNING ACTIVITIES

1. If possible, obtain a video or simulator time so that learners will have an opportunity to see skids, wheel slips, and the use of ABS.

2. Discuss the importance of undistracted driving in situations where roadways are slick or icy.

3. Invite a veteran driver to your class to discuss driving in conditions that could cause a rig to skid or jackknife. "War stories" are permitted.

4. Discuss why reducing wheel slip improves vehicle stability. Refer to the document found at www.fmcsa.dot.gov/documents/fhwa-abs.pdf.

5. Discuss why hard braking in icy conditions is not a good idea. Ask for input from learners who have experience driving on ice, snow, or rain-slick roadways.

FOR MORE INFORMATION

Antilock Braking Systems
www.fmcsa.dot.gov/documents/fhwa-abs.pdf

Why Does a Tractor Trailer Jackknife?
www.cartaste.com/transport-safety/article-4-08022.html

Tractor Trailer Jackknife
www.marules.com/docs/expertreports/ExpertReport_TractorTrailerJackknife.pdf

How to Avoid Jackknifing
auto.howstuffworks.com/auto-parts/towing/vehicle-towing/maneuvers/how-to-avoid-jackknifing.htm/printable

21 Hazard Awareness

© iStockphoto/olaser

OBJECTIVES

When you have completed this chapter, you should be able to:

■ Recognize possible hazards early and determine when the road or your surroundings may pose a danger.

■ Explain the various dangerous road conditions, such as slippery surfaces, uneven surfaces, curves, soft surfaces, and sloping roads.

■ Describe common highway threats to safety, such as debris, obstructions to visibility, and crosswinds.

■ Know the consequences of using the engine braking system or trailer brake on a slippery highway.

■ Recognize clues that tell you when other road users may be a possible hazard.

INTRODUCTION

As a professional driver, you must have skills in a number of areas, but the majority of your skills are focused in two areas: (1) your vehicle and (2) dealing with the driving environment.

The driving environment includes the roadway and its condition, weather, buildings, people, signs, trees, and animals (**see Figure 21-1**). To operate safely at all times, you must be familiar with this environment and the possible changes that may occur as you drive from one area to another.

Some of what you will see along the roadway will be friendly, such as wide shoulders, emergency ramps, and climbing lanes. Some elements of the environment will be neutral, such as signs, stores, and homes along the roadway. Other elements, however, will be dangerous, such as drunken or ill drivers in other vehicles, crosswinds on a mountain pass, heavy sleet or snow, high winds, low bridges, wires, and trees.

The purpose of this chapter is to assist you in becoming aware of the driving environment and the clues it offers to help you drive safely. As a professional driver, part of your job is to recognize and interpret these clues so that you can adjust your driving and continue your trip in a safe, economical manner.

▶ **Figure 21–1**

You must be familiar with your driving environment in order to operate safely.

WHAT IS A HAZARD?

As you probably know, a **hazard** is any condition or road user (another vehicle and driver, cyclist, pedestrian, or animal) that could create a possible danger to you, your cargo, and your rig. *Possible* is the key word, because these elements may or may not become a hazard and a danger on the road.

Either way, you should be aware of the possibilities. For example, the brake lights of the vehicle ahead as it approaches an exit ramp could signal a possible danger (**see Figure 21-2**). You do not know what that driver intends to do. When a driver's brake lights go on, this may signal that the driver is unsure about his or her exit. At the last minute, the driver of that vehicle could change his or her mind and veer back into your lane.

▶ **Figure 21–2**

Seeing a vehicle's brake lights is a clue indicating a possible hazard.

If this happens, that vehicle is no longer a hazard. It is now a danger, because you will have to react by either clearing the lane or using your brakes. What if there is not enough room in the next lane for you? What about the "slosh factor"—or "surge"—if you are driving a tanker (**see Figure 21-3**).

This example brings a laser focus on the whole idea of recognizing hazards. A driver who did not understand the vehicle was a hazard would not respond until it started to change lanes, and then his or her response might have been to brake suddenly or to rapidly change lanes. Both maneuvers could easily cause an accident. To have enough time to react, ensure that you have adequate "eye lead time."

▶ Figure 21-3

Tanker drivers must be aware of the "slosh factor" when stopping abruptly.

▶ Figure 21-4

Commentary driving helps you become more aware of your environment and the activities of other drivers on the highway.

COMMENTARY DRIVING AND HAZARD PERCEPTION

Before continuing our discussion about hazards and how to recognize them along the highway, it is important for you to understand the skill of "commentary driving."

Commentary driving is making comments about what you see as you drive. During the on-street part of your instruction, you may be asked to try this exercise. It will help you identify hazards and will let your instructor know what you are seeing and how you react to what you see.

In commentary driving, you do not discuss what you see at length. Your job is to see and identify any possible hazard, using brief statements such as "truck in front of me . . . could stop quickly without warning." Such statements make you aware of a possible hazard (**see Figure 21-4**).

This simple example makes commentary driving sound really easy. Depending on the situation, however, commentary driving may not be as easy as it sounds. Seeing and talking about a car beside the road sounds like an easy thing to do, but when you add the tasks of professional driving, commenting can become very demanding.

Commentary driving has its boosters and its naysayers. Some people like the procedure, some do not. Even though it may seem difficult at first, you will find that it helps you become a professional driver who is more aware of the surrounding environment and the activities of those vehicles sharing the highway with you.

NOTE

If your instructors use commentary driving, it is very important to comment on your observations, as this helps them understand whether or not you're looking far enough ahead, and if you are correctly perceiving hazards.

Guidelines for Commentary Driving

The following steps are required for commentary driving:

1. Identify in your mind any hazard—object, road condition, or road user—that is a possible threat to your safety. Identify and describe only those hazards to which you are prepared to respond.

   Example: Something in the road. Looks like a box. Could be wood. Need to change lanes.

© Cengage Learning 2013

▶ *"Like a bridge over troubled water ..."*

2. Describe the hazard as concisely as possible—what and where it is.

   Example: Child in the street on the left

   Pavement in the shade of that bridge

3. Use only a few words to describe what makes it a hazard.

   Example: Child is looking the other way

   Pavement might be slippery

4. In a conflict situation (where a crash is possible), describe only the vehicle or object in conflict with your rig.

   Example: Car in my lane

   Bicyclist with back toward me in my lane

   Wind blowing debris across the road

5. When the object, road condition, or person is not a hazard, say nothing.

LEARNING TO RECOGNIZE HAZARDS

Learning to recognize hazards is much like learning to read—we first see how letters look and sound, and then we begin to pick out whole words. The words soon fit together into sentences and those single letters we learned in the beginning now have meaning.

You learn to recognize hazards much the same way. When driving, it is difficult to see every detail in the environment that surrounds you. As a professional driver, however, you must train yourself to become acutely aware of everything going on around you. Often, you only see **clues** about what is happening, then you begin fitting these clues together as you go down the highway.

Hazards—when clues are seen—are usually fairly easy to figure out and then you can decide your response. Unfortunately, professional drivers learn to recognize these clues because of close calls, near misses, other drivers' stories, or accidents.

In the previous situation, for example, the car's brake lights were a clue. The car ahead was slowing down or stopping. The driver sees the brake lights and either responds or prepares to respond. Seeing and knowing what the brake lights mean is recognizing a hazard. Though the vehicle slowing down is not a direct threat to your safety, you must be aware that it remains a possible hazard.

SOURCES OF CLUES

Clues to hazards can be found around your rig in every driving environment. There are three types of clues:

■ Road conditions
■ Appearance of other road users
■ Activities of other road users

Road Conditions

Road conditions are a major factor in tractor-trailer accidents because of the following:

1. Big rigs travel more miles/kilometers and in more bad weather than most other vehicles.
2. Big rigs are less stable because of a higher center of gravity, their size, and their weight. These factors make them tip over more easily than most other vehicles on the highway.
3. Big rigs require longer stopping distances than most other vehicles on the highway.

Road characteristics that can be hazardous to tractor-trailer rigs include surface conditions, shape, and contour. Road surfaces can also be hazardous if they are slippery, soft, sloping, uneven, or littered with debris.

Slippery Surfaces

Sometimes it is difficult to tell if a road is going to be slippery. The following sections describe some of these conditions (**see Figure 21-5**).

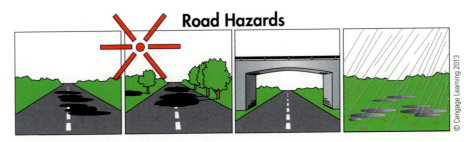

▶ **Figure 21-5**
Road conditions signal possible hazards.

Wet weather—in wet conditions, many surfaces may be more slippery than they look. Patches of oil dripped from passing vehicles is very slippery just after it starts to rain. Painted or paint-striped areas, railroad tracks, and construction plates also can be slippery (**see Figure 21-6**).

Cold weather—in cold weather conditions, look out for black ice, shaded areas, and bridges. Black ice is a thin, clear coating of ice that makes the road appear wet. Shaded areas on the highway can freeze in wet weather when the rest of the roadway is dry. Bridges, both the traveled surface and the roadway below a bridge, tend to freeze more quickly than the rest of the roadway. Also look out for "refreeze"—snow that was warmed up during the day melting onto the roadway, then freezes at night, causing icy patches.

▶ **Figure 21-6**
In wet weather, many surfaces become slick and dangerous.

Hot weather—in hot weather conditions, oil may come to the surface of an asphalt road and make it slippery. When driving on an asphalt road, be very careful when it starts to rain. The water mixes with this surface oil and reduces traction, causing the surface to become very slippery until the oil is washed away (**see Figure 21-7**).

INTERESTING FACT

From January 5 to 10, 1998, Canada and parts of the U.S. experienced one of the most devastating ice storms in history, experiencing temperatures of −10 degrees C (14 degrees F) and a total water equivalent of precipitation that exceeded 85 mm (3.3 inches) in Ottawa, 73 mm (2.8 inches) in Kingston, 108 mm (4.3 inches) in Cornwall, and 100 mm (3.9 inches) in Montreal. Most of this precipitation came in the form of freezing rain and ice pellets mixed with snow. Ice reached a thickness of up to 10 cm (3.9 inches) after six days.

▶ **Figure 21-7**
A slippery roadway requires more stopping distance for a big rig.

Using the Engine Brake on Slick Surfaces

A braking feature of tractor-trailer rigs is the engine brake, which could be either a compression brake (usually shortened to "jake brake") or an exhaust brake. The use of compression brakes alone, however, produces a loud and distinctive noise, and owing to noise pollution, some local municipalities have prohibited or restricted the use of engine brake systems inside their jurisdictions, particularly in residential areas (**see Figure 21-8**).

NOTE

Often a professional driver can apply the motor brake and not have to apply the traditional foot brake. Using a motor brake saves heat-sensitive brakes from possibly overheating, which could lead to brake failure.

**HEAVY VEHICLES
PLEASE NO
ENGINE BRAKES
NEXT 5 m / 8 km**

▶ **Figure 21-8**
Some locations have prohibited or restricted use of engine brake systems.

The main advantage to using the jake brake instead of conventional brakes is that a truck can travel down a long grade without overheating its wheel brakes. Some vehicles can also be equipped with hydraulic or electric retarders, which have an advantage of near silent operation.

STOP!

Tractor-trailer rigs are more difficult to drive in snow and ice since the trailer loses traction more easily than a straight truck. Using the retarder and/or engine brake only worsens the situation, making the composition more prone to jackknifing. A tractor-trailer is more likely to jackknife on ice because of the semitrailer weighing significantly more than the tractor.

Soft Surfaces

Some surfaces such as asphalt, construction areas, and soft shoulders will not bear the weight of a fully loaded rig. On very hot days, some asphalt roadways may become soft, and your rig may sink into it. In construction zones, surfaces that cover filled-in sewer trenches and septic tanks are seldom strong enough to hold the weight of a truck. Graded shoulders also may become very soft after a heavy rain or when the snow thaws. In these conditions, there is a danger your rig may sink or turn over.

Sloping Surfaces

A curve that is not properly banked is a hazard. The wheels of your rig are more likely to slide on the curve, so you must take these curves at a slower speed. Learn to recognize when a curve is not properly banked. Roads that are high in the middle and low on each side (sometimes called "high crown" roads) are worse than flat roads. On curves, a wrong-way slope can cause severe front-end dip, front wheel lockup, or loss of control.

Debris

No matter the size of your vehicle, debris on the road is always a hazard. A small box may contain heavy material that can cause control problems or damage to your tires or the rig itself. If a box does not move with the wind, think of it as a hazard. A pile of rags and paper or cloth sacks can also be hazards because they may contain cement or another hard substance. If you hit them, you can damage tires, wheel rims, air lines, electrical lines, or fuel crossover lines.

INTERESTING FACT

A tractor's compression release engine brake, frequently called a jake brake or Jacobs brake, is an engine braking mechanism installed on some diesel engines. When activated, it opens exhaust valves in the cylinders, releasing the compressed air trapped in the cylinders, and slowing the vehicle. Although *jake brake* properly refers to the Jacobs brand of engine brakes, the term has become a generic trademark and is often used to refer to engine brakes or compression release engine brakes in general. The name is derived from the manufacturer, Jacobs (of drill chuck fame), and was patented 1962–1965 by Clessie Cummins.

CAUTION!

Another hazard clue is pavement that drops off near the edge of the road. This can cause the top of the trailer to hit objects, such as signs or tree limbs hanging near the road.

Uneven Surfaces

Bumps in the road can hang up a low trailer and damage the undercarriage or tear off the dolly wheels. Try to avoid driving through puddles. Often seemingly small puddles can disguise deep potholes that can make you lose control of your rig and cause damage to your equipment, such as your suspension or your tires.

Contour of the Road

The shape or contour of the road can create hazards. The most common problems result from curves that restrict visibility. Another common problem is the crosswinds that occur around curving terrain (**see Figure 21-9**).

> **Curvature**—is the amount of curving the earth does in your line of sight. Trees, power lines, or buildings can be clues to a curving road before you reach the actual curves. Are they in a straight line? Do they go up and down toward the horizon?

The **curvature** of expressway ramps can be dangerous for all drivers, but they are even more difficult and dangerous for tractor-trailer drivers. Curving, downhill ramps are especially difficult because the weight and high center of gravity of a rig work with the **centrifugal force** that automatically pulls your rig to the outside of the curve to make holding onto the road more difficult (**see Figure 21-10**).

> **Restrictions to visibility**—many road characteristics restrict the driver's vision. Be prepared for these situations:

- At sunrise or sunset, you can be faced with extreme glare at the crest of a hill. It may help to lower your visor and put on your sunglasses.

- At night, as you approach a hilltop, lights from the other side of the highway warn of oncoming traffic. Be ready for headlight glare and protect yourself by looking to the right edge of the road.

- When approaching a tunnel in daylight, remember your eyes adjust slowly to changes in light. To increase your scanning ability, take off your sunglasses and to increase your visibility, turn on your headlights before entering the tunnel. Do the same when you enter a warehouse or dark alley on a sunny day (**see Figure 21-11**).

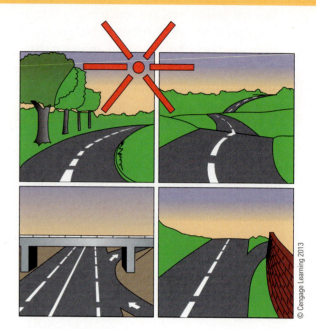

© Cengage Learning 2013

▶ **Figure 21-9**

The shape or contour of the road can create a driving hazard.

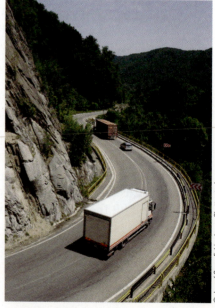

© Jozsef Szasz-Fabian/www.Shutterstock.com

▶ **Figure 21-10**

The force that attempts to push a vehicle off the road in a curve is centrifugal force.

▶ **Figure 21-11**

When approaching a tunnel during the day, take off your sunglasses and turn on your low beams.

© Cengage Learning 2013

INTERESTING FACT

A runaway truck ramp, runaway truck lane, emergency escape ramp, or truck arrester bed is a traffic device that enables vehicles that are having braking problems to safely stop. First appearing in the 1960s, usually in mountainous areas, these ramps are long, sand- or gravel-filled lanes adjacent to a road with a steep grade. The deep gravel allows the truck's momentum to be dissipated in a controlled and relatively harmless way, allowing the operator to stop it safely. By 1990, there were reportedly 170 runaway ramps in 27 (mostly western) states. Current data are scarce, but a 1981 NHTSA study noted that there had been 2,450 runaway-truck incidents that year, with 2,150 of those involving the use of ramps.

Crosswind areas—on windy days, you can be hit with a violent **crosswind** when moving from a protected area into an open area. A sudden crosswind can cause you to lose control of your rig, so look for the absence of trees, hills, or other protection when you come out into the open after driving in protected terrain. Crosswinds can be an extreme hazard to professional drivers hauling livestock—and if you're deadheading a livestock trailer, use extreme caution in high winds.

Highway Construction Zones

Increased infrastructure spending and funding for road construction have led to a significant increase in the number of highway construction projects around North America. The safety of road users and workers is a concern on roads and highways throughout Canada, the U.S., and Mexico.

In the U.S., 667 fatalities resulted from motor vehicle crashes in work zones in 2009. The number of injuries in highway construction sites are even higher.

According to the Federal Highway Administration (FHWA) the annual number of persons killed in motor vehicle crashes in work zones in the U.S. has increased 45 percent over the last 10 years. The majority of these fatalities are drivers or occupants; however, 15 percent are nonmotorists—including pedestrians, bikers, and construction workers (**see Figure 21-12**).

▶ **Figure 21-12**

A professional driver has to be aware of the hazardous challenge of driving in a construction zone.

The Risks to Road Safety at Construction Zones

Road construction zones present a hazardous challenge for professional drivers, as well as construction workers and pedestrians. This hazard is brought about by high speed limits, impatient drivers, and widespread traffic congestion. To this we can add heat, driving stress, and long stretches of highway under construction—creating a perfect storm for extreme driving hazards.

The construction zones—also called "cone zones"—are those portions of the highways marked by cones, barrels, and signs where road construction is taking place. Some work zones might have a speed-monitoring device to alert motorists of their speed prior to entering the work zone. Even though they are marked and signposted as areas where motorists must slow down and drive with extra caution, many drivers speed up to get through the construction area as quickly as possible.

The main causes of deaths and injuries at construction zones are:

- Speeding traffic—the number one cause of death and injury in highway construction work zones.
- Inadequate sign posting and lighting, and drivers failing to notice road workers.
- Drivers do not pay attention to work zone signs or flaggers indicating they should slow down or come to a stop.
- Drivers are distracted by cellular phone calls, conversations, and activities at the roadside and are not merging properly.
- Drivers are driving up to where merging ends and then try to force themselves in, and if the other driver doesn't let them get in, they enter the work zone and endanger the lives of workers.

National and state-enacted awareness campaigns are one way to convey the message that out on the road, orange-clad workers and orange cones mean "slow down." But, drivers should also be encouraged to follow the rules of the road through construction zones across the country.

Traffic enforcement is a principal way to improve safety around these zones. Many states in the U.S. and provinces in Canada have greatly increased penalties for speeding through work zones. Tough new measures are implemented to encourage drivers to slow down and avoid the potentially deadly consequences of reckless driving through work zones.

CAUTION!

In the U.S. and Canadian provinces, signs saying "Speeding Fines Double" in construction zones mean what they say. Obey the speed limits—and also make room for emergency vehicles when they share the roadway.

SAFETY TIPS FOR DRIVING INTO HIGHWAY CONSTRUCTION ZONES

Safety professionals recommend several precautions to help make construction zones safer for everyone:

- When approaching a construction/maintenance zone, exercise caution and slow down.
- Observe warning and caution signs before entering a construction zone.
- Observe these posted signs until you see the one that says you've left the work zone.
- Turn on your lights to make your vehicle more visible.

- "Expect the unexpected" is a golden rule when traveling through construction zones.
- Avoid abrupt driving maneuvers.
- Always be aware that vehicles ahead of you may stop unexpectedly.
- Maintain a safe following distance. Rear-end collisions are one of the most common types of construction zone accidents.
- Drivers should slow to the posted speed and move to the proper lane as instructed.
- Traffic and road conditions may dictate an even slower speed.
- Keep up with the traffic flow. Motorists can help maintain traffic flow and posted speeds by merging smoothly and not slowing to "gawk" at road work and equipment and crews.
- Obey road crew flaggers! The flagger knows what is best for moving traffic safely in the work zone. A flagger has the same authority as a regulatory sign, so you can be cited for disobeying his or her direction.
- Drivers should not wait until the last minute to merge to the correct lane.
- Use correct merging techniques when changing lanes—use your indicators.
- Narrow lanes and restricted shoulders make construction zones a common place for lane-change accidents.
- Regular traffic lanes are often shifted to temporary lanes and shoulders that may not provide the stability regular traffic lanes offer.
- Stay alert for aggressive drivers. If another motorist is aggressively jockeying for position, drivers should let him or her move on. Challenging another driver encourages road rage and endangers the safety of other motorists and workers in the area.
- Avoid distracting activities. Remaining alert for unexpected hazards is critical when traveling through construction zones. Talking on a cell phone, tuning the radio, eating, reading, or other similarly distracting activities can quickly lead to an accident.
- Watch for construction equipment and workers. Construction equipment entering and exiting a work zone without warning, equipment extending into traffic, and construction crews and flaggers working dangerously close to moving traffic are a few of the hazards to expect.
- Stay alert for obstacles and debris. Construction equipment, signs, and barriers may be located close to the edge of the roadway. Debris from work projects, especially dust, dirt, and gravel, may cause added disruption.
- Be patient, cautious, and courteous. Remember, the work zone crew members are working to improve the road—and your driving experience.

Appearance of Other Road Users

Drive defensively! While no driver can watch every move of every other road user, he or she can drive so that if the other driver makes a dumb or dangerous move, an accident can be avoided.

CAUTION!

Other drivers are really not bad drivers, but they are not educated in the hazards of operating near a CMV and are sometimes careless. Anytime you share the roadway, be alert to other users. It makes good sense!

It also makes sense to watch for clues that tell you other road users may be ready to do something unexpected. For example, you must be ready to deal with another driver's sudden change of speed or direction. Among the clues to watch for are obstructed vision, distraction, confusion, slow travel, impatience, and impairment.

Obstructed Vision

People who cannot see the road well are a serious hazard to other drivers. This section discusses clues that identify drivers who may have obstructed vision.

Vehicles with limited visibility—include vans, loaded SUVs, and cars with obstructed rear windows. These drivers may have limited ability to see the road around them. Drivers of rental trucks and recreational vehicles are often not familiar with their limited vision. Be alert for these drivers.

Sometimes vehicles are partly hidden by a blind intersection. You can see the other vehicle, but you know the other driver cannot see you. This is a defensive driving situation. A good example is when you enter an intersection with the intention of turning left. If oncoming traffic in the lane nearest to you is stopped to let you turn, you may not be able to see vehicles passing to the right of the stopped vehicles. They, of course, are a hazard if you turn in front of them. In these situations, the height of your cab can be helpful but it does not prevent other roadway users from being hidden from your view.

The vision of drivers of delivery trucks is sometimes blocked by packages or vehicle doors. Drivers of step vans, postal vehicles, and local delivery trucks may leave their vehicles in a hurry, often double-parking in the roadway. Watch out for these drivers.

Parked vehicles—people in parked vehicles should always be considered a hazard. You never know when a driver may open the door and climb out of the vehicle in front of you. Watch for movement inside the vehicle, exhaust, and brake and reverse lights. Parked vehicles may also move out into your lane without signaling.

When police units or emergency units are along the side of the road, move as far left as possible as soon as you can. Slow down if you can do it safely, because anything can happen. Someone may even run out or be pushed into traffic lanes.

CAUTION!

States such as Kansas issue citations for not moving to the far left for emergency or law enforcement vehicles stopped by the side of the road.

Distraction

If a driver is looking at, thinking about, or reacting to anything else, he or she may not see your rig. This is a distracted driver (**see Figure 21-13**). A driver can attend to only those parts of the driving environment he or she can see, hear, or sense. Therefore, help other drivers see and pay attention to you and your rig. The following are some common clues that signal a distracted driver.

Distracted Drivers

▶ **Figure 21-13**

Cell phones, crying children, and driving an unfamiliar road can distract a driver.

© Cengage Learning 2013

Lack of eye contact—road users looking elsewhere—at children, at a roadmap, or other distractions—may not be aware of your rig and may pull into your path. Always try to make eye contact with others, although positive eye contact is no guarantee they are aware of you. Pedestrians and cyclists may often assume you will yield or give them room. A light tap on the city horn may help establish eye contact.

> **CAUTION!**
> Some states have pedestrian right-of-way rules. Be aware of these when you drive in multiple states.

Talkers—people talking to others in their vehicle have already taken their full attention away from the driving environment. They may not be aware of your rig, so stay alert!

Workers—highway construction, road repair, and utility workers often are not concerned about traffic. They may think someone else is directing traffic. Delivery people may be distracted by their work or their schedules, especially if they are loading and unloading. The presence of road repair equipment or delivery trucks is a clue for the professional driver to remain on high alert **(see Figure 21-14)**.

Vendors—a vendor's vehicle, such as an ice cream van or taco wagon, is a clue to a hazard. People seem to forget there is traffic when they deal with a neighborhood street vendor. They walk or run across streets and roads without paying attention. Ice cream trucks and small children are also a dangerous combination.

© Cengage Learning 2013

▶ **Figure 21-14**

Highway construction sites and workers around those sites often present a hazard.

Objects appearing from the side—a baseball, basketball, or other object appearing in the street usually means a child is following, so be prepared to stop.

Disabled vehicle—a vehicle being worked on beside a road or street is always a hazard. Drivers changing a tire or looking under the hood are usually not thinking about traffic—so always be on the alert when passing a breakdown on the highway.

People talking on cell phones—do not always have their minds or attention on their driving or what is happening around them. Be particularly careful around these drivers. They are often driving on autopilot.

People texting—be aware of people texting, looking at their GPS, or changing channels on their radios. They are distracted and are not paying full attention to the road.

School bus—slowing or stopping school buses almost always mean children are on the move. They may come out from in front of or behind the bus. From either side of the road, expect the unexpected and know state laws concerning school buses.

Toll booths—always check ahead as well as in your rear-view mirrors for pedestrians at toll booths. These may be drivers who have gotten out of their cars or toll booth employees who fail to realize the danger of walking near tractor-trailers.

Confused Drivers

Confused drivers are those driving more slowly than the rest of the traffic. They may be visiting the area or just driving through, but they tend to stop or change direction without warning (**see Figure 21-15**).

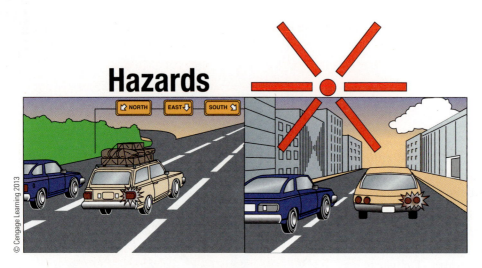

Figure 21-15
Confused drivers present big hazards. Look for clues.

Clues that a driver may do something unexpected include:

- Cars topped with luggage
- Cars pulling a camping trailer
- An RV, with or without a tow vehicle
- Cars with out-of-state or out-of-country license plates
- Unexplainable actions such as stopping in mid-block, changing their minds about taking a certain exit at the last minute, changing lanes for no apparent reason, or backup lights suddenly going on
- Slow driving, frequent braking, or stopping in the middle of an intersection
- Driver obviously looking for street signs, looking at maps, or searching for house numbers

Slow Travel

Motorists who do not travel at the normal speed are a hazard. Sometimes it is difficult to judge how fast you are closing in on or overtaking a vehicle. Following it too closely can create a problem. Identifying a slow driver early can prevent an accident. Clues that help identify slow-moving vehicles include:

- Underpowered vehicles such as a subcompact, extremely old vehicle, recreational vehicle, or any vehicle towing a house trailer or other heavy load
- Farm or construction equipment, such as tractors or bulldozers
- Mopeds or other smaller motorcycles
- Vehicles with the slow-moving vehicle symbol—an orange triangle with red sides. At night this symbol may look like an orange blob.
- Vehicles signaling a turn into an alley, driveway, shopping center, or those turning left that pause for oncoming traffic.

Impatience

Impatient drivers often view all trucks as slow moving. Because they do not want to be caught behind a tractor-trailer, they may recklessly try to get in front of you—at all costs. Watch for impatient drivers who overtake and pass you and then cut back into your lane too quickly. They may even slow down after making the pass.

At intersections, be alert for drivers who pull out before it is safe. They are trying to avoid waiting until you and your rig pass through.

A commercial vehicle driver whose income depends on speed sometimes becomes impatient. They see you and your rig as getting in the way of the job they are trying to do. A taxi driver, messenger, delivery driver, or any other worker behind schedule can be a hazard. Keep your eyes open for these drivers.

Impaired Drivers

While you may meet an impaired driver at any time, you are more likely to meet one late at night **(see Figure 21-16)**. Common forms of impairment are being **under the influence** of alcohol or drugs, or being fatigued.

Clues to a driver being under the influence are:

- Weaving across the lanes
- Running off the right side of the road
- Going over the curb while turning
- Stopping at a green light or sitting too long at a stop sign with no crossing traffic in the vicinity
- Driving with the window open in cold weather
- Erratic speed—too fast or too slow or changing speeds often
- Throwing materials out of the window
- Acting unusually happy or extremely depressed

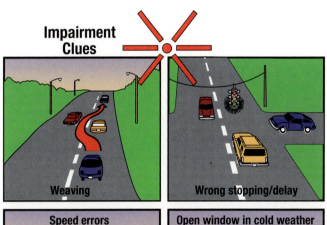

▶ Figure 21-16

You are more likely to meet an impaired driver late at night.

These clues may not mean that a driver is impaired, but your job is to be alert for such clues and to stay out of the way of impaired drivers. If the clues you see are strong enough, you may want to contact authorities. Remember, though, you are only reporting unusual or strange behavior. Do not suggest that the other driver may be impaired, because that is for the authorities to decide. Sometimes strange, erratic driving is the result of other conditions.

Drivers who are drowsy or suffering from fatigue often provide a number of clues, including:

- Weaving across lanes
- Running off the right side of the road or crossing the center stripe
- Erratic speeds—slowing down and then speeding up

Be aware that these clues could mean more than fatigue or drowsiness. Stay out of the way of these drivers.

CAUTION!

Anytime you see another highway driver driving recklessly, weaving across lanes, driving erratically, or speeding up and then slowing down, drive defensively. Stay out of this driver's way, a safe distance behind, or pull off the road if it is possible to do so.

Activities of Other Road Users

Any road user can be a hazard. Clues to these hazards can often be seen in their activities. Examples include:

- Movement by the driver
- Movement of the vehicle
- Buttonhook turns by other rigs and other drivers

- Activities around buses and taxis
- Pedestrians and cyclists
- Conflicts

Movement by the Driver

Before making an erratic move or doing something dangerous, a driver will often make some sudden movement. Watch the heads, bodies, and vehicles of other drivers.

Head movement—looking to the side means the driver plans to change direction. Drivers usually look in the direction they are going to turn. A turn of the head, therefore, may warn of a possible turn of the vehicle. A driver looking in the rear-view mirror may also signal that he or she is planning to make a lane change.

Body movement—drivers often straighten up just before turning to brace themselves for the turn and to get better control of the steering wheel.

Vehicle movement—drivers often edge across a lane in the direction of an intended turn. This sideways or lateral movement may be a clue for an impending lane change.

Buttonhook—big-rig drivers, because of the length of their rigs, often make a **buttonhook** turn when they need to make a tight, right turn. They often swing wide to the left to gain turning space before they make a right turn. Other drivers do this too. Be on the lookout for buttonhook maneuvers and do not try to pass a vehicle on the right that has swung out to the left just before coming to an intersection.

Buses and Taxis

Passengers leaving buses may cross the highway from the front or the back of the bus. In some cases, they may not be able to see your rig as they make a decision to cross the road. Therefore, it is up to you to be aware of the hazards.

A taxi that is reducing speed is a clue to a possible hazard. Another possible hazard is a taxi driver looking for passengers or following a passenger's directions. These drivers often act in ways that create hazards. Slow driving, U-turns, quick stops, and changes in direction are common. Pass taxis carefully because passengers may leave a taxi from either side as soon as the taxi stops. Also be on the alert for pedestrians running to catch a taxi.

CAUTION!

Always be prepared to stop quickly on city streets with bus and taxi traffic.

Pedestrians and Cyclists

Pedestrians and cyclists can be a hazard for many reasons (**see Figure 21-17**).

Watch for people on the sidewalk, shoulder of the road, or on the road itself.

- They may travel with their backs to traffic.
- They are sometimes careless.
- Their vision may be limited by their clothing or something they are carrying, such as a hat pulled too low or an umbrella.
- They may not realize they have moved directly in your path.
- They may be on the phone, texting, or otherwise distracted.

Pedestrian Hazards

▶ **Figure 21-17**
Closely watch pedestrian traffic.

Be aware that children are easily distracted. They tend to act without thinking or looking around them. When kids are playing, they often do not think about the traffic.

Emergency Areas

Accident **scenes** and hospital emergency areas are dangerous for all drivers because of curious Lookie Lous and rubberneckers. This is also true in slow-moving traffic. People become stressed because they have been slowed down and are trying to see the reason for the traffic delay, which distracts them from watching the road. Beware of cell phone users in emergency areas and on the highway in general. Without question, you cannot pay attention to a phone conversation and watch the road carefully at the same time.

Conflicts

A **conflict** occurs when a vehicle is on a collision course with an object or another road user. Other road users become a problem for the professional driver when you have to make a sudden change in direction or make a sudden stop. Such actions can damage your rig or cargo. Being able to see and understand conflicts early is an advantage (**see Figure 21-18**). You can then plan what you will do and can often avoid the conflict.

Obstructions

A few common obstructions are:

- The end of a lane
- A barricade
- Slow-moving or stalled traffic
- A disabled vehicle
- An accident on the roadway

Collision Conflicts

▶ **Figure 21-18**
A conflict occurs when one vehicle is on a collision course with another vehicle or object.

Obstructions may be in your lane or another lane. If the obstruction is in your lane, you must see the hazard in time to avoid conflict with it. If the obstruction is in a lane going the same direction as yours or is in an opposing lane, you must watch for other road users who may move into your path (**see Figure 21-19**).

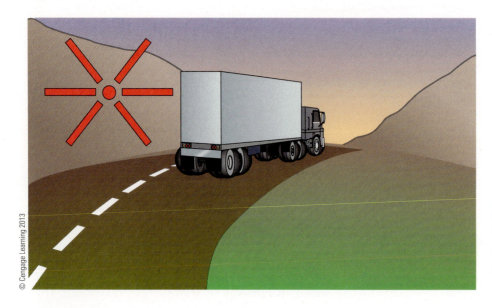

© Cengage Learning 2013

▶ **Figure 21-19**

Whether on the open road or a winding mountain road, always be alert for obstructions.

Merging

Certain merge situations may force another vehicle into your path. Examples would include a car entering a freeway, pulling out of a driveway or side street, or moving out of a parallel parking space.

Intersections

When streets or roads come together, conflicts can develop. Other road users may not stop or yield the right of way. They may be in your blind spot or hidden by shrubbery, signs, or buildings. Road users in conflict with you and your rig may come from the right, left, or the opposite direction. At times, you may even find yourself in conflict with more than one road user. The bottom line is be aware, be alert, and be ready to react.

SUMMARY

In this chapter, you learned that your ability to blend with other highway users depends on how well you can see and understand your surrounding environment and the clues provided by other highway users. You learned that the road environment includes the roadway, the curvature of the road, the surface condition, and the immediate area around the road.

You also learned that as a professional driver, you must watch for and interpret the intentions and actions of the drivers around you, as well as watch for clues to guide you and to help pinpoint possible hazards.

Finally, you learned that driving is a social act because it involves you, other drivers, and every object in your immediate environment. Your success as a professional driver depends on how well you identify and interpret potential hazards and how quickly you can react by adjusting your driving or your position on the road.

KEY TERMS

Buttonhook	Curvature	Scene
Centrifugal force	Hazard	Under the influence
Crosswind		

A DAY IN THE LIFE . . .

© Cengage Learning 2013

Jimmy McSwain – Sunco Carriers, Professional Truck Driver

I come from a trucking family. Fresh out of high school, at 18 years old I started driving. I give a big thank you to Commercial Carrier Corporation, in Auburndale, Florida, for allowing me to start in this career. I started driving within the state of Florida. At 21, I moved to another division and started driving the long haul in my very own first truck, a 1970 Freightliner. I traveled through the entire 48 continental states hauling a wide variety of loads. One of my most memorable loads was driving on I-70 from Denver, Colorado, to Grand Junction. I was driving a truck weighing 40 tons, which was not equipped with a Jake Brake. I was traveling down over a-one-mile downgrade, relying solely on the foot brake—to say the least, it was a fairly scary ride.

In 1992 I made a change and came over to Sunco Carriers, where I still am today. This allowed me to drive runs over the 15 southeastern states—from Texas to Virginia and down to Florida, which is where I call home. Today I am running regional freight throughout the state of Florida, which again allows me to be closer to home, on shorter runs.

As an independent contractor, I have always taken tremendous pride in my occupation, myself and the company I represent. My dedication, conscientious driving habits and commitment to the industry is of the highest caliber. I have learned that taking responsibility and applying yourself is the most important part of achieving success.

My appearance, as well as my equipment is always neat and clean. I feel my polite and courteous attitude extends not only to my fellow contractors, shippers, receivers, vendors, and clients, but to all I come in contact with. I currently have in excess of 3.5 million consecutive miles of driving without a preventable accident and with no moving violations and have received numerous safety awards.

My fellow operators and co-workers at Sunco Carriers know I am always available to help with any problem or concern and I always take into consideration their feelings without concern for personal sacrifice. I also make sure to treat all new contractors with respect, compassion, and understanding. It is my hope that with my 33 years of experience and the way I handle myself in all situations, I will have a positive effect on the trucking industry.

> ## I have learned that taking responsibility and applying yourself is the most important part of achieving success.

I feel I exhibit the initiative, drive, commitment, and professionalism. I am truly grateful for the opportunities that been provided to me and allowed me to achieve financial independence and success. I believe I am an excellent example of what a person can achieve in this industry with integrity and hard work! After 33 years I am still trucking!

REVIEW QUESTIONS

1. Any condition or road user that could create a "possible" danger in your path can be categorized as a _____.

   a. catastrophe
   b. hazardous material
   c. hazard
   d. mechanical failure

2. Regarding clues, drivers learn to recognize clues to possible hazards, interpret the clues, and _____.

   a. react in a safe and responsible manner
   b. always increase the speed of the rig to avoid the hazard
   c. always slow the rig
   d. increase the traction of the tires by increasing the speed

3. The force that pushes a vehicle off the road in a curve is called _____.

   a. traction
   b. centrifugal force
   c. friction
   d. center of gravity

4. Curving expressway ramps that are downhill are especially bad for rigs because the weight and the _____ of the rig work with centrifugal force to pull the rig to the outside of the curve.

   a. friction
   b. traction
   c. high center of gravity
   d. a and b

5. If another driver is looking at, thinking about, or reacting to anything else, _____.

   a. this driver would be of no danger to you as these are characteristics of safe drivers
   b. his or her brake lag time will increase
   c. the center of gravity of his or her vehicle will increase
   d. he or she may not see your rig

6. When a driver sees a slowing or stopped school bus, which of the following cannot be expected?

   a. Children are on the move.
   b. Children may come out from behind the bus.
   c. Children may come out from in front of the bus.
   d. Children will exit the bus and yield to all oncoming traffic.

7. As a professional driver, when are you most likely to meet an impaired driver?

   a. at high noon
   b. late at night
   c. on Sunday in front of a church
   d. 3 o'clock in the afternoon

8. Regarding activities of other road users, before doing something hazardous a driver often _____.

   a. makes some sudden movement of his or her body
   b. increases the traction of his or her rig
   c. increases the friction of the tires
   d. b and c

9. When a vehicle is on a collision course with an object or another road user, a(n) _____ is said to occur.

   a. conflict
   b. increased amount of traction
   c. increased amount of friction
   d. increased brake lag time

10. A sign that a driver is new to the area or possibly confused would be _____.

    a. a vehicle weaving over the road

    b. a dealer's tag rather than a license plate

    c. luggage in a rack on top of the vehicle

    d. a foreign license plate

11. Using the retarder and/or engine brake only worsens the situation when driving on slick roadways because it makes the vehicle more prone to _____.

    a. jackknifing

    b. increasing speed

    c. sliding off the road

    d. skidding

12. The number one cause of fatalities in highway construction zones is _____.

    a. drivers texting

    b. drivers speeding

    c. drivers who are "under the influence"

    d. inexperienced drivers

13. If you hit debris on the road, you risk damaging _____.

    a. tires and wheel rims

    b. air lines and electrical lines

    c. fuel cross-over lines

    d. all of the above

14. A sudden crosswind can cause _____.

    a. sudden dizziness

    b. off-tracking of your rig

    c. loss of control of your rig

    d. none of the above

SUPPLEMENTAL LEARNING ACTIVITIES

1. Try to find videos of tractor-trailers using runaway or escape ramps of different types. After viewing these videos, discuss the pros and cons of each type of ramp.

2. Divide into small groups and discuss your personal experiences with distracted drivers. List the various types of distractions and how these can be avoided by professional drivers.

3. Look at the laws or regulations regarding "jake" brakes in your own community. Then, look at the rules for engine retarders in your state and one adjacent state. Are there any differences in these three sets of regulations or laws?

4. Go to your state's Department of Transportation website and find data regarding highway work site injuries and fatalities. Find the main reason these incidents have occurred. Then, apply this information to your own professional driving.

5. Write a 100-word essay on what, in your personal driving experience, is the more formidable hazard on your community's or state's roadways today. What, if anything, is being done to prevent this hazard?

FOR MORE INFORMATION

PTDI—Identify Potential Driving Hazards and Perform Emergency Maneuvers, Page 19, Click on Skill Standards
www.ptdi.org/standards

Alberta's Traffic Safety Amendment Act—2005
www.saferoads.com/drivers/constructionsfty_faq.html

British Columbia's Laws, as of Aug. 2011
www.bclaws.ca/EPLibraries/bclaws_new/document/ID/freeside/96318_05

Tractor-Trailer Driving Tips
www.ehow.com/way_5610919_tractor-trailer-driving-tips.html

22 Railroad Crossings

© Cengage Learning 2013

OBJECTIVES

When you have completed this chapter, you should be able to:

- ■ Identify active and passive railroad crossings, and their dangers.
- ■ Understand the physical characteristics of a railroad crossing and how to cross safely.
- ■ Identify common driver distractions and limited visibility affecting safety at crossings.
- ■ Know and explain "best practices" for drivers at railroad crossings.

INTRODUCTION

Most professional drivers are well versed on the nation's highway systems—where to expect construction and where to be ready to avoid other hazards. As a professional driver, however, you must also think about how much rail traffic travels the nation's railways every day of the year.

Train traffic means hazardous railroad crossings and there are literally thousands criss-crossing the country.

America's landscape is dotted with more than 280,000 public and private highway–rail grade crossings. In recent years, roughly 300 to 400 deaths have occurred annually at the nation's grade crossings, a statistic that has received significant attention from transportation agencies.

According to available statistics, when motorists disregard signs, lights, bells, and gates at railroad crossings, a collision involving a vehicle and a train is 40 times more likely to result in a fatality than a collision involving another vehicle.

Ruling to Prevent Crossing Collisions

Guidelines for professional drivers and motor carriers are in place in an effort to decrease railroad crossing accidents. With these guidelines, reckless truckers who tempt fate at railroad crossings by trying to beat oncoming trains stand to lose their commercial driver's license, and their employers could face fines up to $10,000.

These guidelines cover convictions of federal, state, or local laws dealing with five types of offenses:

- Failing to make a required stop before railroad tracks
- Failing to slow down and check for a train
- Getting caught on the track for lack of sufficient space to clear the crossing
- Failing to obey a railroad signal or the directions of an official at a crossing
- Getting hung up on the tracks because of insufficient ground clearance

Drivers convicted of violating one of these offenses will lose their Commercial Driver's License (CDL) for at least 60 days for the first offense. Subsequent convictions written within a 3-year period would result in a 120-day suspension for the second offense and a 1-year suspension for a third offense.

Motor carriers whose drivers break crossing laws are subject to the fines if it can be proven that they authorized or encouraged the drivers to ignore the regulations. Carriers may also be fined if they fail to take actions to prevent further offenses.

In the year 2000, according to the Federal Railroad Administration, there were 3,500 collisions at **highway–rail grade crossings** in the United States. These collisions resulted in 425 deaths and 1,219 injuries. An additional 463 pedestrians died in 1999, walking on or along tracks (**see Figure 22-1**).

Today, more than nine times a week, a truck with a trailer and a train collide. There are many more near-hits in addition to these collisions. Nearly half of all collisions occur at railroad crossings equipped with properly functioning automatic warning devices (flashing lights with bells or gates with lights and bells).

▶ Figure 22-1
Follow all guidelines when at a railroad crossing.

▶ *Using caution at railroad crossings always puts you on the right track!*

When you think about railroad crossings, also think about this: An 18-wheeler going 50 miles an hour (80 km/h) needs the length of a football field to stop. It takes a train, traveling at the same speed, more than 1-1/2 miles (2.4 km) to come to a halt, which is why professional drivers pay particular attention to railroad crossings, both marked and unmarked. Understand, too, that a train is at least 3 feet (almost 1 m) wider than the tracks—and that your view of an oncoming train is going to be distorted because you are looking down the tracks.

More recently, it has been noted that most collisions involving vehicles and trains occurred when the vehicle ran into the side of the train as it crossed the intersection. Studies show that these collisions occur because of the driver's inattention, overdriving his or her headlights, or driving while stressed or fatigued and thus being too distracted to notice the train.

According to the Federal Motor Carrier Safety Administration regulations:

Every motor vehicle shall, upon approaching any railroad grade crossing, make a full stop not more than 50 feet (15.2 m), nor less than 15 feet (4.6 m) from the nearest rail of such railroad crossing, and shall not proceed until due caution has been taken to ascertain that the course is clear; except that a full stop need not be made at:

■ A street car crossing within a business or residence district of a municipality.

■ A railroad grade crossing where a police officer or a traffic control signal (not a railroad flashing signal) directs traffic to proceed.

■ An abandoned or exempted grade crossing which is clearly marked as such by or with the consent of the proper state authority, when such marking can be read from the driver's position.

All such motor vehicles shall display a sign on the rear reading, "This Vehicle Stops at Railroad Crossings" (**see Figure 22-2**).

▶ **Figure 22-2**
Railroad crossing sign on the back side of a tractor-trailer.

RAILROAD CROSSINGS IN MEXICO

A stop sign at a railroad crossing (Ferrocarril Crucero) means yield to oncoming trains. Some crossings are marked with flashing red lights while others have lights, crossing barriers, and white crossbucks **(see Figure 22-3).**

Courtesy of Angel Zaragoza Zavala

▶ **Figure 22–3**

Ferrocarril Crucero means yield to oncoming trains.

BRITISH COLUMBIA'S LAWS REGARDING RAIL CROSSINGS

185 (1) When a driver is approaching a railway crossing at a time when

　a. a clearly visible electrical or mechanical signal device gives warning of the approach of a railway train,

　b. a crossing gate is lowered or a flagger is giving a signal of the approach or passage of a railway train, or

　c. a railway train is approaching and is within approximately 500 m/1,640 ft of a crossing or by reason of its speed or nearness to the crossing is an immediate hazard and emits an audible signal or is visible, the driver must stop the vehicle within 15 m/50 ft but not less than 5 m/16 ft from the nearest rail of the railway, and must not cause or permit the vehicle to proceed until he or she can do so safely.

(2) A person must not drive a vehicle through, around or under a crossing gate or barrier at a railway crossing while the gate or barrier is closed or is being opened or closed.

(3) If a stop sign is erected at a railway crossing, a driver approaching the railway crossing

　a. must stop his or her vehicle

　　i. no closer than 5 m/16 ft, and

　　ii. no farther than 15 m/50 ft from the nearest rail of the railway, and

　b. must not proceed until he or she can do so safely.

(Continues)

BRITISH COLUMBIA'S LAWS REGARDING RAIL CROSSINGS (continued)

(4) Except at a railway spur line or an industrial track in a business or residence district, the driver of

   a. a bus carrying passengers for compensation,

   b. a school bus carrying a child,

   c. a vehicle carrying explosive substances or any poisonous or flammable substance as cargo, or

   d. a vehicle used to carry flammable liquids or gas, whether or not it is then empty, approaching a railway crossing that is not protected by gates or railway crossing signal lights, unless otherwise directed by a flagger, must

   e. stop his or her vehicle

      i. no closer than 5 m/16 ft, and

      ii. no farther than 15 m/50 ft from the nearest rail of the railway,

   f. remaining stopped, must listen and look in both directions along the railway for an approaching train, and for signals indicating the approach of a train, and

   g. must not proceed until he or she can do so safely.

(5) When a driver has stopped in accordance with this section, the driver must

   a. cross the railway tracks in a gear that he or she will not need to change while crossing the tracks,

   b. not shift gears while so crossing, and

   c. not stop with a part of the vehicle on or over the tracks.

(6) Despite this Act, the driver of a vehicle approaching the track of a railway must proceed with caution to avoid a collision between the vehicle and an approaching train.

OPERATION LIFESAVER—U.S.

In Idaho, in 1972, Operation Lifesaver came into being when the national average of collisions at highway–rail grade crossings exceeded 12,000 annually. This nonprofit, nationwide public education program is dedicated to ending crashes, injuries, and fatalities at intersections where roadways meet railways. Operation Lifesaver began as a 6-week public awareness campaign launched by Idaho Governor Cecil Andrus, the Idaho Peace Officers, and Union Pacific Railroad as a one-time, one-state initiative.

During the campaign's first year, Idaho's crossing-related fatalities dropped by 43 percent and, when the Operation Lifesaver campaign was adopted by Nebraska the next year, that state's collision rate was reduced by 26 percent. Today Operation Lifesaver programs are active in all 50 states across the U.S. with free presentations available to address highway–rail safety issues (see oli.org/state_coordinators/ for state contact information). Specific safety tips for professional drivers are included in these presentations with additional materials at oli.org/training/professional-drivers. It is estimated that more than 10,000 lives and 40,000 injuries may have been prevented through this national outreach program working with community, state, and federal safety leaders and volunteers. A free interactive program for professional drivers is also available at oli.org/prodriver (see Figure 22-4).

Courtesy of Operation Lifesaver

▶ Figure 22-4

OPERATION LIFESAVER—CANADA

Every year in Canada approximately 300 collisions and trespassing incidents occur at highway–railway crossings and along railway tracks resulting in the death or serious injury of nearly 130 people. Virtually all of these incidents could be avoided.

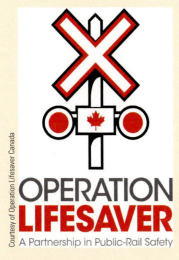

Courtesy of Operation Lifesaver Canada

▶ Figure 22–5

Railway companies and government agencies have long been concerned about the needless loss of life and rail-related injuries. In 1980, Roger Cyr, the first National Director of Operation Lifesaver in Canada began the new program with little more than a desk, materials from the U.S. program, and his Rolodex of railway contacts. This led to railway companies joining forces with the federal, provincial, and municipal governments in Canada to build lasting and aggressive programs to improve railway-related safety. The result was that by 1988, all provinces were participating in Operation Lifesaver **(see Figure 22-5).** For more information, visit www .TrainToDrive.net.

Operation Lifesaver saves lives by educating Canadians about the hazards surrounding rail property and trains. Its mission is to prevent collisions between trains and motor vehicles. It also works to prevent trespassing incidents that lead to serious injury or death. It works with the rail industry, government, police, unions, the media, other organizations, and the public to spread the word.

ACTIVE VERSUS PASSIVE RAILROAD CROSSINGS

An **active railroad crossing** usually attracts high traffic and is marked with the familiar white crossbuck with flashing lights or the crossbuck with flashing lights and a gate. These active warning devices activate only when a train is approaching the crossing, or intersection.

Almost two-thirds of all railroad crossings in the United States, however, are **passive railroad crossings,** which means they are marked with advance warning signs, pavement markings, and crossbucks, but there are no gates and no flashing lights. It is, therefore, up to you—the professional driver—to look both ways and to make certain no train is coming before you proceed **(see Figure 22-6).**

So let's talk about how a professional driver, even the most experienced, might ignore rail crossing warnings, try to outrun a train and end up stuck on the tracks—or worse, yet, a victim of a truck–train collision. On any day, at any time in your driving career, you will fit one of three driver profiles: (1) the content driver, (2) the sad driver, or (3) the conflicted driver.

Content Driver

In this scenario, the content driver is satisfied with his life. There is more happiness than sadness, there are few problems, and life is balanced and seems good.

How does this state of mind translate into driving behavior?

You are rested and ready to do a good job behind the wheel. You drive with skill and confidence. You know and obey the laws, you maintain your rig in top shape, and your skill level is higher than average, not only in handling your rig on the highway but also in your relationships with coworkers, shippers, and consignees. You are proud of the job you do, you take care of yourself, and you are achieving your career and life goals at a solid clip **(see Figure 22-7).**

DRIVER BEHAVIOR AT PASSIVE RAILROAD CROSSINGS

Highway–rail grade crossing collisions and casualties at public and private crossings for all highway users

Year	Collisions	Fatalities	Injuries
2009	1,920	247	738
2008	2,428	290	988
2007	2,776	339	1,058
2006	2,941	369	1,070
2005	3,066	359	1,053
2004	2,623	368	931
2003	2,597	299	918
2002	2,709	316	866
2001	2,843	386	1,038
2000	3,502	425	1,219
1999	3,489	402	1,396
1998	3,508	431	1,303
1997	3,865	461	1,540
1996	4,257	488	1,610
1995	4,633	579	1,894
1994	4,979	615	1,961
1993	4,892	626	1,837
1992	4,910	579	1,969
1991	5,386	608	2,094
1990	5,713	698	2,407

From the Federal Railroad Administration Office of Safety Analysis 2009 Report.

▶ **Figure 22–6**

Highway–rail grade crossing information from 1990 to 2009.

Sad Driver

When you are performing within the sad driver scenario, your outlook on life is shaded. You may not be sad to the point of depression, but you fail to see much of the good that life has to offer. Your relationships may not be on the best footing, you may have financial problems, or you may be at a point in life where nothing seems to be going right.

You may have some health concerns, you do not have time to do what you need to do, and you always seem to be behind schedule. Because of nagging problems you do not always sleep well at night and spend much of your rest tossing and turning in your sleeper.

Your rig has had a string of mechanical problems, your relationship with your foreman or supervisor has not been going well and, bottom line, you are just not happy with yourself, others, or life in general.

When you drive, although your knowledge and skill level are high, you are sometimes careless on the highway. You become angry with other drivers, you do not like the way the eggs were prepared at breakfast, and you think the truckstop overcharged you the last time you fueled your rig.

You like driving but may not like your employer. Your appearance has changed from its usual professional standard and you have gained weight. You have several goals to pursue at this moment, but you lack motivation to obtain the goals.

You may see what is in front of you, but you are not fully aware of your total environment. You may tend to tailgate the vehicle in front of you, not because you are being malicious, but because you are just not paying attention like you usually do.

Conflicted Driver

In the conflicted driver scenario, you are unhappy to the point of depression. Your relationships with others are terrible. You have just broken up with your partner, you have money problems, and you may be drinking when off duty.

You dislike your job, you think your rig is falling apart, and you get angry with the way other people drive. Because of your level of seniority, you think you get the worst runs, have to unload more often than your fellow drivers, and, physically, you feel terrible most of the time because you cannot sleep as well in the sleeper as you once did.

You feel bad about yourself and others. When you drive, you are more aggressive and less consider-

© mangostock/www.Shutterstock.com

▶ **Figure 22–7**

Content, proud drivers perform the best work.

ate than usual. You take unnecessary chances on the road, try to beat the odds when possible, and push the limits when you have the opportunity.

Your appearance is as sloppy as your driving. You have withdrawn from most of your relationships. You lack goals and motivation to achieve.

When you drive, your mind wanders. You feel sorry for yourself and you think about other people in other places. More than once, you have had to maneuver quickly to avoid a collision. You are doing your job but your appearance is more like that of a zombie than a human being.

Truthfully, any driver who is conflicted for more than a week should seek special help in sorting out his or her problems. This driver may have just experienced a personal loss such as the death of a family member or a divorce. This driver could have recently filed for bankruptcy or have problems with alcohol or other substance abuse.

Whatever personality you take on each day—from contented to sad or conflicted—it will have an impact on how you handle rail crossings and every other part of your driving experience. Be aware of your mood and how it impacts your performance—and if you're sad or conflicted, it's probably in your best interest not to get behind the wheel that day.

DRIVER DISTRACTIONS AND PASSIVE RAIL CROSSINGS

Because your life outside your work has a direct impact on how you perform each day, your attitude—happy, sad, or conflicted—does a lot to distract you from what you do as a driver. For example, if you feel happy, you will see the warning signals at an active rail crossing and be alert for trains at passive rail crossings. If you feel sad, you may not automatically stop at a highway–rail grade crossing; and if you are in a conflicted state, you may not even notice you are rolling over a railroad crossing.

WARNINGS TO HEED

The following warnings are important to recognize:

Crossbuck sign—is one of the oldest warning devices. It is a white regulatory, X-shaped sign with the words "Railroad Crossing" in black lettering. These signs are usually positioned alongside the highway prior to a railroad crossing, on the right-hand side of a public roadway on each approach to the highway–rail grade crossing, when possible. The crossbuck sign signals all vehicles approaching the crossing to yield and is required at all public highway–rail grade crossings **(see Figure 22-8)**.

▶ **Figure 22-8**

Crossbuck signs are one of the oldest railroad warning devices.

Advance warning sign—is a round yellow warning sign (minimum of 36 inches (91.4 cm) in diameter) with a black "X" and "R-R" located alongside the highway in advance of the crossing. It serves to alert the motorist that a crossing is ahead. The advance warning sign is usually the first sign you see when approaching a highway–rail grade crossing. The distance of the sign from the track is dependent on the posted highway speed, but should not be less than 100 feet (30.5 m) in advance of the nearest rail. This distance will allow the vehicle's driver ample time to comprehend and react to the sign's message by slowing down, looking, listening, and being prepared to stop if a train is approaching.

Cantilevers—are structures sometimes used to locate the flashing light signals over one or more lanes of vehicular traffic. Some states require the signals to be placed over the center of each lane. Other states mandate the signals be located to the right of the lane. Cantilevers are being used in increasing numbers because several states have required roadside installation to be set back farther from the roadway surface.

Flashing light signals—are regulatory devices installed on a standard mast or cantilever which, when activated, display red lights flashing alternately. The number of flashes per minute for each incandescent lamp is between 35 and 55. Each lamp is illuminated the same length of time. Flashing light signals indicate the approach of a train, and require a complete stop by the professional driver **(see Figure 22-9)**. When a train is approaching the highway–rail grade, the flashing light signals are activated. These flashing signals are mandatory when gates are used to stop traffic at a highway–rail grade crossing. When both the gate and the flashing light signals are activated, the gate arm light nearest the tip is illuminated

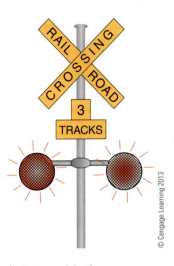

continuously and the other two lights flash alternately in unison with the flashing light signals. These signals are found at all types of public highway–rail grade crossings. They normally are placed to the right of the approaching highway traffic on all roadway approaches to a crossing.

Standard bell—a device, which, when activated, provides an audible warning that may be used with flashing light signals and gates. A standard bell is most effective as a warning to pedestrians and bicyclists. The bell is usually activated when the flashing light signals are operating. In some cases, the bell stops ringing when the lead end of the train reaches the crossing or when gate arms descend to within 10 degrees of the horizontal position. A new technology being used by most railroads is the electronic bell, with a volume that can be adjusted to various levels, depending on the location.

Standard warning gate—a device that was first introduced in 1936, the standard gate assembly is an active traffic control device used with flashing lights **(see Figure 22-10).** The device consists of a drive mechanism and a fully reflectorized red and white striped gate arm with lights. In the "down" position, these gates extend across the approaching lanes of highway traffic about 4 feet (1.2 m) above the top of the pavement. In its normal upright position—when no train is approaching or occupying the crossing—the gate arm should be either vertical or almost vertical. A standard warning gate is normally accompanied by a crossbuck sign, flashing light signals, and other passive warning signs.

▶ **Figure 22–9**

Flashing light signals.

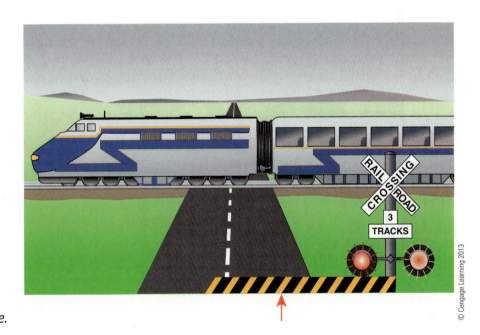

▶ **Figure 22–10**

Standard warning gate.

Four-quadrant gate—compared to a standard gate assembly, these have an additional pair of dual gate arms. These gate arms are lowered on each side of a bidirectional crossing. Potential gate violators are prevented from driving around the gates because the intersection is entirely sealed off. Operating like the standard gate and the long-arm gate, the four-quadrant gate restricts motorists from entering a highway–rail grade crossing by lowering the gate arm when the presence of a train is detected.

Barrier gates—a fairly new warning gate technology that locks into a post when in the down position. This feature disallows vehicles from driving around them at a crossing. When a vehicle attempts to drive through the gate, the cables grab it like a net to prevent it from attempting to cross. These cables are designed to catch a pickup truck traveling up to 50 miles an hour (80 km/h) and stop it with a soft landing, causing no harm to the driver or passengers. There are currently only a few locations where a barrier gate is being used.

Surfacing—the highway–rail grade crossing surface usually consists of pavement or other highway and rail surface materials on the approaches and crossover points with the railroad track. As the vehicle moves across the highway–rail grade crossing, the material on which its tires roll is commonly referred to as a crossing surface. This surface must carry the train or highway vehicle and transmit the wheel loads to the foundation structure. The surface of the roadway at the crossing is an important aspect of the highway–rail grade crossing. If the crossing surface is uneven, rough, or littered with exposed and protruding spikes, attention is on the surface rather than the warning signals (**see Figure 22-11**).

▶ **Figure 22-11**

Crossing surfaces provide an even surface for vehicles to pass over the railway tracks.

Median barriers—consist of a prefabricated mountable island. The island is placed in the center of the roadway leading up to the highway–rail grade crossing. Used at several crossings around the country, a key advantage to median barriers is they are a proven low-cost investment with a high rate of safety return.

Intelligent Transportation Systems (ITS)—these are applications of electronics, communications, and information processing products and services used to solve surface transportation problems such as safety issues at grade crossings. ITS projects are developed with the following goals: increased safety, increased efficiency, improved mobility, increased productivity, and conserving energy while improving the environment.

ITS projects have been implemented across the country in several metropolitan areas.

OTHER DEVICES

Following are additional signals, signs, and warnings:

Yield sign—this sign assigns right of way. Vehicles controlled by a yield sign need to avoid interference with other vehicles, including trains, which are given the right of way.

"Do Not Stop on Tracks" sign—a black and white regulatory sign placed at a crossing when an engineering study or experience determines there is a high potential for vehicles stopping on the tracks (**see Figure 22-12**).

Stop sign—a red regulatory stop sign with lettering intended for use where motor vehicle traffic is required to stop. This sign can be added to the crossing, requiring all vehicles to come to a complete stop before crossing the railroad tracks.

"Tracks Out of Service" sign—this sign is for use at a crossing in lieu of the crossbuck when a railroad track has been abandoned or its use discontinued.

Parallel track signs—diamond-shaped yellow advance warning signs located on roadways to the railroad tracks indicate the road ahead will cross tracks. These signs are intended to warn motorists making a turn that there is a highway–rail grade crossing immediately after the turn.

DO NOT STOP ON TRACKS

▶ **Figure 22-12**

Black and white regulatory sign.

"Low Ground Clearance" warning sign—a new advance symbol sign for railroad grade crossings is a warning where conditions are sufficiently abrupt to create hang-ups of long wheelbase vehicles or trailers with low ground clearance. Based on research conducted by the Federal Highway Administration, which tested the new sign with New York's professional driver population, this sign may be used at these special locations (**see Figure 22-13**).

Multiple track crossing signs—these signs indicate the number of tracks crossing the highway–rail grade crossing and will be placed on the post below the crossbuck.

RR lettering—these white **pavement markings** are set into the surface of or applied to the pavement in advance of the crossing, which is for the purpose of advising, warning, and guiding traffic (**see Figure 22-14**).

© Cengage Learning 2013

▶ **Figure 22-13**
Low ground clearance warning sign.

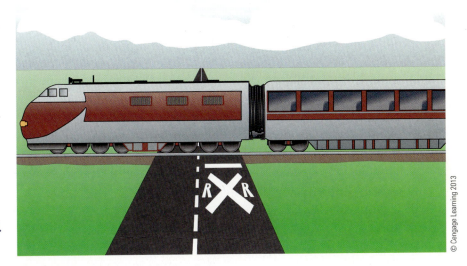

© Cengage Learning 2013

▶ **Figure 22-14**
RR lettering.

WHAT EVERY DRIVER NEEDS TO KNOW ABOUT RAILROAD CROSSINGS

Drivers should stay alert at places where the roadway crosses railroad tracks. These highway–rail grade crossings are a special kind of intersection—a highway–rail intersection. If possible, plan your route to avoid crossing railroad tracks.

Be aware that local and state laws may be more restrictive than the following reminders:

- As a professional driver, you should expect a train to come through a highway–rail grade crossing at any time.

- You should be aware that a train's size and weight, combined with other factors, create an optical illusion. This makes it virtually impossible for you to judge the speed and distance of an oncoming train from the crossing, so never try.

Approaching the Crossing

- Never ignore flashing lights, bells, closing gates, or stop signs.
- Look up and down the track and test your brakes.
- Be certain to check for a train. Roll down your windows; turn off fans and radios; listen for warning signals.

Stopping Safely at Highway—Rail Intersections

At 80,000 pounds (36,287 kg), pulling a 53-foot (16.2 m) trailer, a typical rig on a level road with good surface conditions requires at least 14 seconds to clear a single track and more than 15 seconds to clear a double track (see Figure 22-15).

▶ **Figure 22-15**

Take the proper precautions—allow sufficient time for your rig to safely cross railway tracks.

Keeping this in mind, the following precautions are suggested when coming to a highway–rail intersection:

- Stop no closer than 15 feet (4.6 m) and no farther than 50 feet (15.2 m) from the nearest rail.
- Never stop on the tracks, and never enter a crossing unless you have enough space to fully clear the tracks.
- If you are a Hazmat driver, with a placarded load or you have just unloaded a placarded cargo, you must always stop—loaded or unloaded—before proceeding to drive through a highway–rail intersection.
- Never try to drive around lowered gates. If you suspect a signal malfunction, call local law enforcement, the railroad, 911, or the 1-800 number posted on the warning device.
- If there is a line of traffic at a traffic light and you may have to stop on a railroad track, a good rule of thumb is never stop, even if you do not see a train coming.
- Check for traffic from behind while stopping gradually. Use a pull-out lane, if available.
- Turn on four-way flashers; leave on until following traffic has stopped safely.
- To better hear the train, roll down the window and turn off the stereo, CB, and fans.
- While stopped, look carefully in each direction for approaching trains, moving head and eyes to see around obstructions such as mirrors and windshield pillars.
- Never race a train to a crossing.
- If a train is stopped nearby, do not cross the tracks for any reason. It is illegal and also dangerous. Many railroad crossings have multiple tracks and you may not see another train—because of the stopped train—about to cross the intersection.

Resuming Travel

- Before resuming and after the signals have stopped flashing, make sure there is enough room on the other side of the tracks for the entire rig to clear the tracks, including any trailer overhang.
- If you stopped in a pull-out lane, signal and pull back onto the road when there is a safe gap in traffic. Expect traffic in other lanes to pass you.
- Use the highest gear that will let you cross the tracks without shifting.
- If the red lights begin to flash after starting over tracks, KEEP GOING. Lights should begin flashing at least 20 seconds before the train arrives at crossing.

Special Situations

All professional drivers, no matter what their cargo, should be aware that certain rigs can get stuck on raised railroad crossings:

- Low slung units, such as lowboys, car carriers, moving vans, and possum-belly livestock trailers
- Single-axle tractors pulling a long trailer with its landing gear set to accommodate a tandem-axle tractor

If You Get Stuck or Hung on Tracks

If you are crossing raised railroad tracks and your rig gets caught on the tracks, first get out of the truck and away from the tracks. Check signposts or signal housing at the crossing for emergency notification information. Then call 911 as soon as possible, giving the location of the crossing. To give emergency teams the best possible location, use all identifiable landmarks, especially the DOT number if one is posted.

RAIL SAFETY TIPS FOR EMERGENCY RESPONSE VEHICLE DRIVERS

- A train always has the right of way. Plan routes allowing drivers and other crew members clear views down the railroad tracks in both directions.
- Know which railroad controls the tracks and have emergency numbers for them at dispatch centers. This is especially important if there is more than one railroad operating in your community.
- If a train is blocking an intersection you must use, contact your emergency dispatcher or the local railroad office.
- Don't place emergency vehicles on tracks and expect a train to be able to stop quickly enough to avoid a collision.
- To stop a train, contact the railroad. Use all available reference points, checking signal housing for DOT crossing number, to give exact locations. If known, supply railroad mile posts, road name, crossroads, and town.
- When fighting long-term brush or structure fires, contact the railroad to obtain clearance to move ballast stones and feed hoses under the tracks. Doing so allows both safe, effective firefighting and train passage.

SUMMARY

In this chapter, you gained insight into the dangers of railroad crossings as well as the number of accidents involving tractor-trailers and trains every year. You also learned about "smart streets and road" projects and what they offer in the way of safety for drivers. Finally, you now understand the importance of practicing safety at all times when you cross railroad tracks, the hazards of getting stuck or hung on the tracks, and how to maintain the safety and security of your rig and your cargo when crossing railroad tracks.

KEY TERMS

Active railroad crossings
Advance warning sign
Crossbuck sign
Highway–rail grade
  crossing

Low Ground Clearance
  warning sign
Parallel track signs
Passive railroad crossings

Pavement markings
Tracks Out of Service sign

REVIEW QUESTIONS

1. A railroad crossing that is marked with the familiar white crossbuck sign with flashing lights or a crossbuck with flashing lights and a crossing gate is known as a(n) _____ railroad crossing.

   a. passive
   b. active
   c. inactive
   d. impassive

2. A railroad crossing that is typically marked with advance warning signs, pavement markings, and crossbucks, but with no gates or flashing lights, is known as a(n) _____ crossing.

   a. passive railroad
   b. active railroad
   c. inactive railroad
   d. low priority railroad

3. A low ground clearance sign warns drivers that _____.

   a. water may cover the tracks
   b. a railroad crossing is at the top of the next hill
   c. the road approach to the railroad crossing is very bumpy
   d. low-clearance trucks may get hung on the tracks

4. A railroad crossing where the crossbuck lights are flashing requires _____.

   a. that the driver speed up to avoid a long delay for a train
   b. a complete stop by the rig
   c. that the driver turn around and find another route to the destination
   d. that the driver slows for tracks under construction

5. Yellow diamond-shaped parallel track signs located in roadways close to railroad tracks indicate _____.

   a. two or more railroad tracks ahead that are parallel
   b. the tracks ahead are parallel to an adjacent interstate highway
   c. the road ahead will cross tracks
   d. that after a right or left turn, the rig will be on a road that is parallel to an adjacent railroad

6. As a professional driver, you should expect a train to come through a highway–rail grade crossing _____.

   a. on a regular schedule
   b. only at night
   c. at any time
   d. only in the mornings

7. At 80,000 pounds (36,287 kg) and pulling a 53-foot (16.2 m) trailer, a typical rig on a level road with good surface conditions requires _____ to clear a single track.

   a. at least 14 seconds
   b. 5 seconds
   c. at least 1 minute
   d. 44 seconds

8. Regarding resuming travel after stopping at a railroad crossing, a professional driver will make sure there is enough room on the other side of the tracks for the entire rig to clear the tracks, including the train's overhang, which is _____ wider than the rails on both sides.

   a. 6 feet (1.8 m)
   b. 1 foot (0.3 m)
   c. at least 3 feet (0.9 m)
   d. 10 feet (3.0 m)

9. If you are transporting chlorine or any placarded hazardous materials, or driving a cargo tank used for hazardous materials, whether loaded or empty, you are required to _____.

   a. stop at highway–rail intersections
   b. stop only at crossings with a signal
   c. stop only at rail crossings within cities
   d. b and c

10. When you are stopped at a railroad crossing and look down the track at an approaching train, you will experience an optical illusion that makes a train appear _____.

   a. nearer than it really is

   c. farther away and traveling more slowly than it really is

   b. to be going faster than it really is

   d. a and b

11. If your vehicle gets hung on a railroad track, the first thing you must do is _____.

   a. call your dispatcher

   c. get out of your vehicle and away from the tracks

   b. call 911

   d. flag down a fellow driver for help

12. If you drive an emergency response vehicle, who has the right-of-way at a rail crossing?

   a. common traffic

   c. an oncoming train

   b. a loaded emergency vehicle

   d. only police or fire vehicles

SUPPLEMENTAL LEARNING ACTIVITIES

1. Divide into teams of two. Then divide your city, town, or community into sections and each team should make a physical survey of their assigned section, identifying active and passive rail crossings in that section. Make a report to the class.

2. Invite an emergency responder to speak to the class. Ask about rail crossings and what they typically do when a train is crossing their path to an emergency.

3. Divide into groups. Then, go to the Operation Lifesaver website and find at least five factoids you think are valuable enough to present to the class. That website for the U.S. is oli.org and for Canada the website is www.operationlifesaver.ca.

4. With a cell phone camera, take photos of at least five different types of rail crossing signs. Show these to the class, telling what message each sign conveys.

5. Invite an experienced professional driver to speak to the class. Ask the driver about rail crossings and any close calls they may have experienced on rail crossings.

FOR MORE INFORMATION

Operation Lifesaver—Canada
www.operationlifesaver.ca and www.TrainToDrive.net

Operation Lifesaver—U.S.
oli.org

U.S. DOT Compilation of State Laws Regarding Railroad Crossings
www.fra.dot.gov/rrs/pages/fp_2305.shtml

Highway–Rail Grade Crossing Safety Regulations
www.fmcsa.dot.gov/about/outreach/railcrossing/railregs.htm?printer=true

U.S. DOT—Railway-Highway Grade Crossing
safety.fhwa.dot.gov/xings/

CDC—Railroad Crossing Safety for Emergency Responders
www.cdc.gov/niosh/docs/2003-121/

23 Emergency Maneuvers

© Cengage Learning 2013

OBJECTIVES

When you have completed this chapter, you should be able to:

- Think ahead to avoid possible driving emergencies.

- Know the safest maneuver to avoid an impending collision.

- Describe the safest ways to make quick stops and quick turns off the road, and how to safely return to the highway.

- Understand how the tractor and trailer react to evasive steering.

- Know how the braking systems work and how to safely bring your rig to a complete stop.

- Explain the safest ways of dealing with brake failure and blowouts.

INTRODUCTION

In a perfect world and an ideal road environment, vehicles of all types—cars, vans, trucks, motorcycles, buses, and bicycles—should maintain adequate space between themselves and other road users **(see Figure 23-1)**. This would not only be a safe environment for everyone, but it also would help each user avoid any problems. The cold, hard reality, however, is that this does not always happen.

When you slide behind the wheel of any vehicle, you can make mistakes and, unknowingly, create an emergency. In fact, anything can happen at any time in traffic. The professional driver is aware of this possibility and can, in most cases, avert accidents. However, sometimes the driver has no ability to control the situation.

▶ Figure 23-1

In an ideal road environment, vehicles of all types should allow adequate space between themselves and others on the road.

This chapter should help you prepare for, recognize, and respond to possible emergency situations on the roadway. Before we get into the specifics, however, the following tips may assist the professional driver when making emergency maneuvers:

1. If you see an obstacle in your path, often the best maneuver is to steer around it to try to miss it. Stopping is not always the best option because (1) you may not have enough room to stop, and (2) sometimes a quick stop may cause the tractor-trailer rig to flip or jackknife **(see Figure 23-2)**.

2. Once you have steered around whatever was in your path, you will turn the wheel back in the other direction. This is called **countersteering** and you must be prepared to steer in the opposite direction. A speedy reaction time is important in this maneuver.

3. When turning to miss an obstacle, do it quickly and do not apply your brakes, as you could skid out of control.

4. In most situations, steering to the right will move you and your rig out of harm's way. If

▶ Figure 23-2

Sometimes a quick stop may cause the tractor-trailer to jackknife.

you are blocked on both sides, moving to the right is the best choice, because you will avoid moving into the oncoming traffic or causing anyone to move into the opposite lane.

5. If you have to leave the paved roadway to avoid a crash, try to keep the wheels on one side of the vehicle on the pavement for better traction. As you return all wheels to the pavement, try to do it sharply as to minimize tire damage and maximize control.

6. If your brakes fail, downshift to the lowest gear possible and try to pump the brakes. With hydraulic brakes, you can often build enough pressure to stop the vehicle. The emergency brake is another option, but be sure to press the release button or pull the release lever at the same time you pull the emergency brake. If nothing works, find an escape ramp or turn uphill. This will sometimes slow your vehicle.

7. If your tires fail (if you notice thumping, vibration, or if steering feels tight), stop as soon as possible. To maintain control of your vehicle, hold the steering wheel firmly and stay off the brake until the vehicle has slowed. Then pull off the road and stop.

8. Professional drivers always allow themselves more space to stop than the average driver. This precaution is especially important in an emergency situation when the CMV must stop unexpectedly or swerve to miss an obstacle.

AVOIDING EMERGENCIES

The best way to handle an emergency is to avoid it in the first place. This may sound simple, but most emergencies happen when drivers make mistakes. These mistakes often create unsafe situations, which brings us to the first rule of the road: If we do not practice **defensive driving,** then accidents will occur.

Professional drivers reduce the chance of accidents by using their knowledge and the skills gleaned from this book, and learning to recognize possible emergencies and react to them in order to avoid a problem.

There are a number of practices professional drivers can use to reduce the chances of an emergency:

- Thorough vehicle inspection
- Regular and disciplined visual search
- Recognizing hazards
- Communication
- Speed management
- Space management
- Excellent night driving skills and tactics
- Well-practiced skills in driving during extreme operating conditions
- Maintaining good health, good vision
- Observing safety practices

In the FMCSA's Large Truck Crash Causation Study conducted by the University of Michigan's Center for National Truck and Bus Statistics, it was found that a large percentage of all vehicle accidents could have been avoided with the proper driving techniques. Though an escape route or "out" was usually available, most drivers hit their brakes and let their vehicles skid out of control, according to the study. Panic braking is a result of habit. Drivers tend to put on the brakes anytime there is an emergency or difficult situation.

EMERGENCY MANEUVERS

Six types of emergency maneuvers are reviewed in this section:

1. **What to do when skidding occurs**—regaining control of your vehicle
2. **Evasive steering**—steering out of an emergency situation
3. **Off-road recovery**—using the roadside as an escape path and then safely returning to the highway
4. **Emergency stopping**—stopping quickly while keeping the vehicle under control
5. **Handling brake failure**—stopping the truck when you lose your brakes
6. **Blowout**—maintaining control when a front tire blows

What to Do When Skidding Occurs

Whenever your tires lose traction, a skid can result. The obvious move is applying the brakes, but braking often causes other problems.

Oversteering can also cause skidding, so avoid turning the wheels more than the vehicle itself can turn.

Driving too fast is one of the most common reasons a vehicle goes into a skid. Manage your speed, matching it with road and weather conditions.

Another common reason a rig will skid is when the rear wheels lose traction from overbraking or overaccelerating.

When you skid because of ice or snow, simply take your foot off the accelerator and push in the clutch.

When the rear wheels skid, it is usually a result of overbraking and the wheels locking.

To correct a drive wheel braking skid, take your foot off the brake, allow the wheels on the rear to roll, and if you are on icy roads push in the clutch to let the wheels turn freely.

If the vehicle begins to slide sideways, steer in the direction you want the vehicle to go—and turn the wheel quickly. As a vehicle corrects its course, the tendency is to keep on turning. So, unless you turn your wheel the other way quickly, you may start skidding again. Don't worry about the trailer at this point. Keep your eyes looking up and out, steering in the direction you want the vehicle to go.

Front wheel skids occur, usually when driving too fast, because of worn front tires, or overweight on the front axle. In a front wheel skid, the best maneuver is to let the vehicle slow down. Stop turning or hard braking. Slow as quickly as possible without skidding.

Technologies Assist in Preventing Skids, Jackknifes

Antilock brakes—an **antilock brake system (ABS)** can significantly reduce the tendency for a tractor-trailer to jackknife because the ABS controls tire slip to maximize braking force while maintaining a high level of the lateral, or side, force to keep the vehicle under directional control. During pretrip inspection you should identify if the tractor and/or trailer are equipped with ABS and if the system is functioning properly.

TT600 Jackknife Control System—is controlled by a dash-mounted module, which can engage the limiting device by a single switch. This device limits the jackknife articulation angle to 26 degrees while driving. A light on the module indicates when it's engaged. In this mode, the rig is now safe from jackknife and can bring to bear all the steering and braking control necessary in any driving situation. Adequate range for the articulation of the tractor and trailer remains for all normal road maneuvers, including a double lane change or obstacle avoidance. In the instance of a panic stop, a pneumatic cushion effect stops the truck from slamming to a halt within the articulation limit. This safety mechanism prevents damage or undue stress to the tractor-trailer. A buzzer sounds before you reach the turn articulation limit, allowing you to disengage the unit in seconds with a single switch for backing and docking.

Landscan III—is a product for tractor-trailers that gives drivers early warning that there is jackknifing during a braking operation. The driver will know because of the distinct sound that the truck is sliding left or right. This will save the driver valuable time so he or she can react to the skid of the tractor or trailer and regain control of their vehicle.

Bendix Wingman—another technology used to make drivers aware of potential danger is the Bendix Wingman. This lets the driver know when the angle between the tractor and trailer increases to a point that a jackknife is possible. The Wingman also informs the driver concerning the roll stability of the CMV.

STS Accident Control and Antijackknife System—controls articulation of the trailer in excess of 14 degrees by mechanically limiting the amount of rotation of the tractor relative to the trailer in emergency stop situations. This system empowers drivers with the ability and confidence to use the full braking and steering capabilities of the tractor-trailer without the fear of losing control, rollover, or jackknifing.

Evasive Steering

Evasive steering is a safe way to get out of or avoid an emergency situation **(see Figure 23-3)**. It reduces the chances of an accident, reduces the severity of the accident, and allows the use of possible escape routes. *Reducing the chance of an accident* by turning your truck is the best evasive maneuver. Turning can be accomplished more quickly than stopping your rig. Often you can turn far enough to avoid the emergency. *Reducing the severity of the accident* occurs when you use evasive steering because you will, in almost all cases, avoid a head-on collision. With the size, weight, and height of a truck, a head-on or rear-end collision is likely to be fatal. *Using possible escape routes* should always be an option, whether it is a formal escape route, another lane, or the road's shoulder. If a lane is available, a quick lane change is often the best escape route. If there is not a lane available, the shoulder of the road is sometimes a suitable escape.

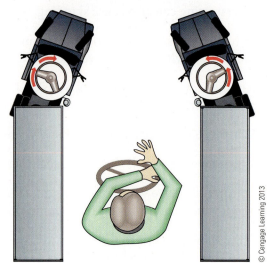

▶ Figure 23-3

Evasive steering is a safe way to avoid an emergency situation.

© Cengage Learning 2013

CAUTION!

Always be aware of any unusual or special characteristics of your load. Loads that can easily move or shift, such as liquids in tankers or suspended meat, require drivers to keep greater following distances and to avoid sudden steering wheel movements.

If there is a choice between a collision and trying an evasive action, trying to evade the collision is usually safer, but a sharp turn of the steering wheel can often cause a rollover. Using other evasive actions is usually safer.

If you are hauling a stable load and your rig has a low center of gravity, you have the best chance of avoiding an accident when using an evasive action. Firm traction on the road or shoulder offers added safety.

General Procedures for Evasive Steering

■ When using evasive steering, turn the steering wheel as little as possible to avoid the emergency. Turn quickly. Be sure to use correct braking while turning. Countersteer once you have passed the emergency.

CAUTION!

Countersteering means turning back toward your intended path of travel.

- To turn as quickly as possible, hand-over-hand steering is best. Placing the hands at 9 o'clock and 3 o'clock positions lets the wheel turn 180 degrees without releasing either hand. If you always drive with your hands in this position, you will be ready if a quick turn is needed. Remember, speed magnifies: the higher the speed, the less you turn the wheel.

- Brake before turning. If possible, avoid braking in a turn. By braking before the turn, you can make a sharper turn and decrease the chance of a rollover or a jackknife.

- After making an evasive turn, be ready to countersteer immediately. Do it smoothly to keep your rig from going out of the escape path or off the road. Timing is very important. Begin to countersteer as soon as the front of the trailer clears the obstacle.

CAUTION!

Every state has seat-belt laws, so you should always drive with them locked in place. When you turn the steering wheel of a rig quickly, you can slide out from under the wheel and lose control, which is another reason for wearing your seat belt at all times.

Evasive Driving in Specific Situations

Different evasive techniques are needed in different situations. Common situations involve an oncoming vehicle, a stopped vehicle, or a merging vehicle.

Oncoming Vehicle. Probably the most common of the emergencies you will encounter, an oncoming vehicle is also one of the most frightening (**see Figure 23-4**). Another vehicle comes toward you from the opposite direction usually due to driver error, because the driver is impaired or experiencing a health emergency. In any event, you must try to prevent a collision. The best move is usually to try and move to your right. A blast of your horn may startle the oncoming driver into corrective action.

Stopped Vehicle. Problems from this occur in two ways:

- You may be following the car ahead too closely and then suddenly the car stops.
- You come over the top of a hill to find a stopped vehicle in your lane.

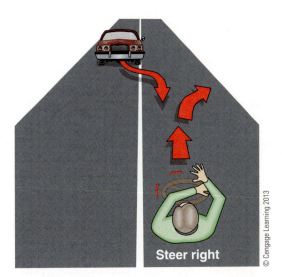

Steer right

© Cengage Learning 2013

▶ **Figure 23-4**

An oncoming vehicle in your lane is one of the most frightening and potentially most dangerous emergencies.

STOP!

Remember! Leaving the road on the right is always better than a head-on collision.

Steering to the left is usually a bad move because the other driver may try to correct by pulling back into his or her lane, and you will still be on a collision course.

When you encounter an oncoming vehicle or a stopped vehicle, there are three possible evasive actions:

1. If the lane to your left is clear, you can turn into that lane and avoid the obstacle. This move is usually better than a swerve to the right because it prevents sideswiping a vehicle on your right. The height of the cab allows you to see if the oncoming lane is clear (**see Figure 23-5).** This is one emergency situation in which it can be safe to turn left into an oncoming lane.

2. If you are driving along a clear shoulder with a good surface, you can swerve to the right. Sideswiping another vehicle on a shoulder is rare.

3. If you are in one of the middle lanes of a multilane road, move into whichever lane is clear. Otherwise, evade to the right. If there is a vehicle in the right lane, it is better to force it over than to force another vehicle into an oncoming lane.

Merging Vehicle. A merging vehicle can create an emergency situation in the following ways (**see Figure 23-6**):

- Another vehicle may try to change lanes and move into your lane.
- Another vehicle may try to merge onto the highway without yielding to you.
- A vehicle may pull out from a side street, driveway, or parking space.
- Another road user—such as a pedestrian or cyclist—may enter the highway.

▶ **Figure 23-5**

The height of the cab lets you see the oncoming lane when maneuvering out of an emergency situation.

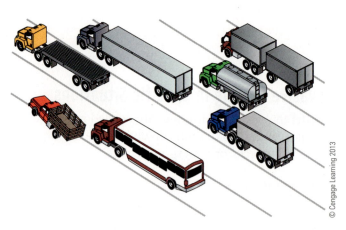

▶ **Figure 23-6**

An accident waiting to happen: A merging vehicle in your lane.

CAUTION!

Common sense tells you that blasting your horn can—and usually does—startle the other driver or individual. Sometimes, a blast on your horn will frighten the other driver to the point that he or she will veer into your lane or make a sudden stop. If this happens, you may be required to do more evasive steering to avoid the problem.

Some drivers think using the horn will annoy other drivers, and formal studies about driver behavior find this to be exactly the case. In an emergency situation, however, annoying other drivers by using your horn is better than a collision.

Stopping Instead of Evasive Steering

A quick stop is always safer than an evasive turn because there is no risk of a collision with a vehicle you did not see—but only if you have room to make a quick stop. Such a stop also is not likely to cause a jackknife or a rollover.

When evasive steering is not possible, braking is your only option. Even if you cannot bring your rig to a full stop, the impact of the collision will not be as hard, and both vehicles may have less damage. There will also be less chance for injury or death. Activate your four-way flashers to warn traffic behind you.

Your ABS makes it possible to brake and make an evasive turn at the same time without losing control of your rig.

Off-Road Recovery

When the area beside the road provides the best escape path, it may be either the right shoulder of the road or the shoulder of the median strip. Most drivers try to avoid leaving the road (**see Figure 23-7**) because staying on the road is a well-ingrained habit. Some drivers fear the shoulder will not support the rig, or they may have heard stories of a crash when the roadside is used for evasive action. The truth, however, is that most roadside crashes occur because drivers are distracted or fall asleep. Keep in mind that many evasive actions are successful and do help avoid accidents. Unfortunately, these successes are never reported.

Sometimes drivers wait too long to leave the road. Successful **off-road recovery** means the driver must leave the road at once when the problem occurs. Most accidents that result from using the roadside are caused by the driver's poor technique. Generally, off-road recovery is safe when the roadside is wide enough and firm enough to handle the rig and the driver uses good judgment and strong technique in controlling the vehicle.

> **Off-road recovery procedure**—as soon as you see a need to leave the road to avoid a collision, remember to brake before turning and avoid braking in the turn unless your rig has anti-lock brakes. Also, turn as little as possible.
>
> Is the roadside clear? Decide when and how to countersteer, and how to handle the wheel drop that happens when wheels leave the road (**see Figure 23-8**).
>
> **Brake before turning**—when you plan to leave the road, slow down as much as possible. Brake to control your rig.
>
> **Turn as little as possible**—keep one set of tires on the pavement, if possible, because you will be able to maintain control of your steering. Traction is also better on the pavement because gravel and dirt reduce traction. Reduced traction causes skids. Turn as little as possible on the roadside and maintain as straight a course as possible.

Off-Road Recovery

- **Reduce speed**
- **Avoid braking within the turn**
- **Minimize turning**
- **Point of return decisions**
- **Return to roadway techniques**

© Cengage Learning 2013

▶ **Figure 23-7**

Most drivers try to avoid steering their rigs off the road.

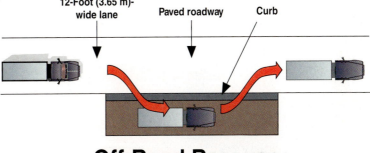

12-Foot (3.65 m)-wide lane   Paved roadway   Curb

Off-Road Recovery

■ Gravel area

■ Curb with a 5- to 6-inch (12.7 to 15.24 cm) drop to gravel

© Cengage Learning 2013

▶ **Figure 23-8**

Using good techniques and skills can help avoid accidents in emergencies.

Returning to the highway—when your rig leaves the road, do not try to return to the highway too quickly. Grasp the wheel firmly and think about steering straight ahead. Stay on the roadside and allow the engine compression to stop the rig. Put on the brakes only when you have slowed enough to stop safely. Signal and check your mirrors before returning to the highway.

If there is a telephone pole, sign, parked vehicle, or other obstacle in your path, stay off the road until your view is clear. Then turn back sharply onto the road. Attempting a gradual return to the roadway may cause you to lose control of your rig and go into a skid. The skid may make your rig cross over into an oncoming lane, jackknife, or roll over. Turning sharply lets you countersteer and decide the point where you will return to the road.

Countersteering—means when you return to the road, turning quickly as soon as your right front wheel rides up onto the surface of the road. Both turning back on the road and countersteering should be done as a single steering move.

When wheels drop off the road—do not try to return the wheel to the road at once. Instead, come to a complete stop before attempting to return to the road. Follow the same procedure as you do for an off-road recovery. If the path ahead is clear, let the vehicle slow to a complete stop and then return to the road when it is safe.

Emergency Stopping

By using your brakes properly, you can maintain control of the rig and shorten the distance required in emergency stopping. By hitting your rig's antilock brakes hard and holding down the brake pedal, the system's electronic controls will ensure the wheels do not lock.

If a vehicle pulls in front of you and you are going to overtake it quickly at your present speed, you can steer to the left or right (evasive steering) and brake quickly.

If oncoming traffic and vehicles on the right prevent evasive steering, you have no choice but to brake quickly.

Handling Brake Failure

Well-maintained brake systems rarely fail completely. Several devices are designed for handling brake failure and preventing accidents. Keep your cool and you can usually bring your rig under control and to a safe stop.

Brakes usually fail because of lack of air pressure, air blockage, brake fade, or mechanical failure (**see Figure 23-9**).

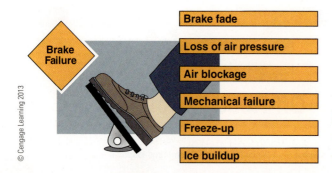

> **Figure 23-9**
>
> *Well-maintained brake systems rarely fail. Those that do fail do so for these reasons.*

Loss of air pressure—when a leak occurs in the system, a warning buzzer sounds when air pressure gets too low. When this happens, stop at once. Why? At 60 psi (414 kPa), you'll be alerted that the air pressure is dropping and then between 20 and 45 psi (138 to 310 kPa) the tractor protection valve will force out the parking brake and the trailer protection valve.

STOP!

If you do not stop when you hear the low pressure warning sound, you may lose more air from the system and your brakes will fail so that you cannot stop your rig.

A built-in safety system automatically puts on the brakes when the air loss reaches a critical level. This happens while there is still enough air in the system to stop the rig. However, if the air loss is too fast, the air supply may be used up before the rig is stopped. Nothing is 100 percent guaranteed.

The independent trailer brake valve will not put on the trailer brakes because they also depend on the air system. If the rig has spring-loaded parking brakes, the brakes will come on automatically when the air pressure fails. They will generally stop the truck unless it is on a steep downgrade.

CAUTION!

Independent trailer brakes can fade to a point where they are ineffective in stopping your rig.

Air blockage—occurs when air is kept from reaching the brakes. A common cause is water freezing in the air system.

Brake fade—occurs when the brakes overheat and lose their ability to stop the truck on a downgrade **(see Figure 23-10)**.

Mechanical failure—occurs when some part of the braking system does not work. Usually, this will not affect all the brakes at the same time, and the rig can be stopped.

What to Do When Brake Failure Occurs

If your brakes fail, you must reduce speed as much as possible and find an escape path and follow it.

▶ Figure 23-10

When driving a long, steep downhill stretch, professional drivers should always be prepared for brake failures.

Reduce speed—if your brakes fail and your rig is on a level surface, try to downshift to allow the engine to serve as a brake to slow the rig. It also raises the revolutions per minute (rpm) and increases the air pressure. Keep downshifting until your rig is moving slowly enough so you can stop it with the spring-loaded parking brake.

Find an escape path—by looking for an escape route at once. Do not wait to see if the rig can be stopped. If you do so, you may go past the only available escape path. Safe escape paths include:

- Side road (particularly one that runs uphill)
- Open field (even though you may damage the undercarriage of your tractor)
- Runaway vehicle escape ramp

Other Things You Can Do

Create drag—to slow down, rubbing tires along the curb or sliding your truck down a guardrail may help. In open country, you may be able to drive into heavy brush or small bushes. Remember that the main idea is to prevent serious damage to your rig and serious injury to you and others by avoiding a collision with other vehicles. Firm steering control is essential using this technique.

Inspect the brakes—after escaping an emergency. Pull over to the side of the road and do not return to the highway until your brakes are working properly. This may require road service. Some drivers foolishly try to nurse their rigs to the closest technician, but this is not recommended because of the danger and risk involved.

Blowout

A **blowout** occurs when a tire suddenly loses air. This can happen because the tire may be worn to the point that it is too thin to hold air, has a crack in the tire casing, or is damaged from debris, potholes, curbs, nails, and so on. Blowouts can often be prevented by thorough pretrip inspections and proper braking. This close inspection is extremely important during all inspections—pretrip, en route, and posttrip **(see Figure 23-11).**

▶ Figure 23-11

A blowout occurs when a tire suddenly loses air.

What Happens When a Tire Blows Out?

Steering problems are your first concern because the rig may veer to the side. A blowout to the rear tractor tires may produce a vibration in the cab. This can cause the rear of the tractor to pull in the direction of the air loss. Trailer tire blowouts can generally be identified by handling difficulties or by the sound of the tire blowing out. If it is an outside tire, you may be able to see it in your mirrors.

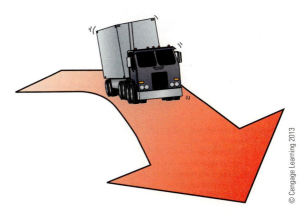

Front Tire Blowout

The front tire blowout usually occurs with a loud bang. Remember, however, a tire can also deflate without a sound. Grasp the steering wheel tightly so it will not be jerked from your hands. You may have steering problems **(see Figure 23-12).** You want to keep the rig from veering off to the side. Speed up to stop the side force and regain control. Then bring the vehicle to a gradual and controlled stop.

Having to grasp the wheel tightly in an emergency is one reason to hold the steering wheel at the 9 o'clock and 3 o'clock positions at all times. When placing your hands on the wheel at these positions, your thumbs should be facing up. The force of a blowout can break a thumb wrapped around the wheel or under a wheel spoke.

▶ **Figure 23-12**

A front tire blowout will cause steering problems.

NOTE

When the blowout occurs, by speeding up at once, you can keep the rig moving in a straight line. Slow down gradually when you have the rig under control.

CAUTION!

Braking after a front tire blowout is dangerous because it shifts weight to the front of the vehicle and makes steering more difficult **(see Figure 23-13).** After the engine has slowed down the rig, it is then safe to gently apply the brakes and pull off the road.

▶ **Figure 23-13**

Braking after a front tire blowout is dangerous because it shifts the weight to the front of the vehicle, making it difficult to steer.

Rear Tire Blowout

A rear tire blowout is not as dangerous as a blowout of a front tire. You usually will not feel any pull on the steering wheel but the truck may pull to the side of the flat. When this occurs, do not brake at once. Let the rig slow down gradually. Then brake slowly and pull off the road before gently braking the rig to a stop. Be sure to check inside and adjacent tires for damage.

When a blowout occurs, have the tire (or tires) changed as soon as possible. Check for any damage the blown tire may have caused, including the following:

- Air lines and other adjacent parts
- Wheel rim
- Fire
- Damage to other vehicles

SUMMARY

In this chapter you learned how to avoid some of the common driving emergencies. You were shown how to steer evasively, how to recover when the rig goes off the road, and how best to stop in an emergency. You also learned what to do in the event of a potential head-on collision as well as the reasons for brake failure and what to do when that occurs. Tire blowouts were described and techniques for dealing with them were provided. The best way to handle an emergency is to avoid one—through proper vehicle maintenance, regular and thorough inspections of your rig, and your defensive driving skills.

KEY TERMS

Air blockage	Countersteering	Off-road recovery
Antilock brake system	Defensive driving	Retreads
Blowout	Emergency stopping	
Brake fade	Evasive steering	

A DAY IN THE LIFE . . .

Jeanette Simpson – Independent Owner Operator

Born in Australia and now a U.S. citizen, I entered the trucking industry in 1999, from dock worker, to company driver and now owner operator. During my twelve years driving over the road, I have developed many strong connections.

I have worked closely with business contacts, using suggestions from a corporate viewpoint, together with my understanding and experience from a driving viewpoint to assist in the development of a profit and loss program, which I share with others to help grow their business. A manager at a trucking company implemented a replica of my own operations and uses it as an example in class for newly leased owner operators.

I have been presented with the opportunity to speak to my peers on profit and loss, customer service, and driver support. I have received several quality service awards. I share my experiences with my peers, explaining the importance of being a "team player."

Continuing safety awareness is an integral part of my business plan and with the implementation of CSA 2010, this has become even more important. I pride myself on the ability to remain calm in situations, giving me the ability to think things through and apply the necessary steps to complete the task at hand. I feel that this is important as this contributes greatly to the safe operation of my equipment.

My success is a direct reflection of the outstanding support that I have received from my colleagues, brokers, customers, and corporate. By following the few tips that I have demonstrated, success can be achieved by all who follow these guidelines and implement them into their own practice.

One must understand that in all endeavors there is success, disappointment, and situations that require a positive attitude. Continual effort and dedication to the proposition requires that one must accept these as part of our ability to be successful.

> **"Showing integrity and courtesy is essential when dealing with the public in general."**

We as drivers have one of the largest visual networks in the country. Showing integrity and courtesy is essential when dealing with the public in general. I believe that I have the necessary skills and attitude to perform my job admirably.

REVIEW QUESTIONS

1. When one drives in such a manner as to avoid or get out of problems that may be created by other drivers, one is said to be using _____.

   a. offensive driving
   b. negative driving
   c. defensive driving
   d. the center of gravity of the rig

2. Evasive steering, off-road recovery, emergency stopping, and handling brake failure are types of _____.

   a. emergency maneuvers
   b. nonemergency maneuvers
   c. center of gravity utilization
   d. b and c

3. After making an evasive turn and the front of the trailer clears the obstacle that caused the evasive turn, the driver should _____.

   a. counterattack
   b. countersteer
   c. utilize counter gravity
   d. utilize counter traction

4. When a vehicle stops in your lane, if you are driving in the middle lane of a multilane road and none of the adjacent lanes are clear and a stopped vehicle is too close to avoid a collision, you should _____.

   a. evade to the left
   b. hit your brakes
   c. evade to the right
   d. speed up

5. Regarding off-road recovery procedures, if a driver brakes in the turn when leaving the roadway, the brakes could lock and may cause a _____.

   a. brake lag
   b. high center of gravity
   c. reaction time
   d. skid

6. If you are forced to make an emergency stop, the act of putting on the brakes with a steady pressure just short of wheel lockup is called _____.

   a. stab braking
   b. controlled braking
   c. counter braking
   d. reaction time braking

7. If you've lost air pressure in the air system, if a leak has occurred in the air system, and a warning buzzer sounds, the driver should _____.

   a. drive to the next truck stop
   b. continue driving and call the dispatcher
   c. continue driving and call the company mechanic
   d. stop at once

8. Which of the following is not a procedure to utilize if the brakes fail?

   a. reduce the speed of the rig
   b. downshift if on a downgrade
   c. find an escape path
   d. create drag

9. Braking immediately after a front tire blowout is dangerous because it _____, making it difficult to steer.

   a. shifts weight to the front of the vehicle
   b. shifts weight to the rear of the vehicle
   c. shifts weight to the rear of the trailer
   d. shifts weight to the front of the trailer

10. When there is a rear tire blowout, the truck may _____.

    a. pull to the side opposite the flat   **c.** pull to the side of the flat

    b. increase the friction of the front tire   **d.** a and b

11. After escaping an emergency, the first thing a professional driver should do is _____.

    a. call dispatch and report the near-miss   **c.** inspect brakes

    b. drive to the next garage   **d.** continue your trip to stay on schedule

12. If your rig is out of control because of an evasive maneuver, the best way to alert fellow road users is _____.

    a. nothing—avoid a collision   **c.** give three blasts on your horn

    b. turn on four-way flashers   **d.** tap your brakes

13. To help avoid a collision know your possible escape options, which include _____.

    a. a formal escape route   **c.** the shoulder of the road

    b. another open lane   **d.** all of the above

14. The best maneuver to avoid a head-on collision is to _____.

    a. leave the road to the left   **c.** stay in your lane

    b. leave the road to the right   **d.** none of the above

SUPPLEMENTAL LEARNING ACTIVITIES

1. Using a simulator or toy trucks, demonstrate the physics of a jackknife and an evasive maneuver.

2. Find some videos of jackknife or emergency maneuvers and try to analyze what the driver intended to do to avoid a collision.

3. Using your textbook, demonstrate the proper positioning of your hands on a steering wheel and how to best protect your hands in case of a steering wheel whip or other problem during emergency maneuvers.

4. Ask a professional driver to come speak to the class about his or her experiences with emergency maneuvers. Feel free to ask the driver questions at the end of the presentation.

5. In a 100-word essay, describe the action you would take if your rig is forced off the roadway because of an emergency maneuver, and the safest way to reenter the roadway traffic.

FOR MORE INFORMATION

PTDI—Identify Potential Driving Hazards and Perform Emergency Maneuvers, Page 19, Click on Skill Standards
www.ptdi.org/standards

FMCSA—Required Knowledge and Skills, Search Required Knowledge
www.fmcsa.dot.gov

FMCSA—Preventive Maintenance and Inspection Procedures, Search Preventive Maintenance
www.fmcsa.dot.gov

24 Accident Procedures

© David Gilder/www.Shutterstock.com

OBJECTIVES

When you have completed this chapter, you should be able to:

- Explain the responsibilities of a professional driver and the correct procedures to be followed at the scene of an accident.

- Detail the information required for an accident report.

- Know how to protect an accident scene.

- Describe the equipment and procedures necessary to address an accident that results in a fire.

- Know what special skills and reports are needed when hazardous materials are involved in an incident.

INTRODUCTION

Like any major industry, accidents sometimes occur in the transport of cargo from point of origin to point of delivery. It could be as minor as a dented fender or as major as a total loss of the rig. It could include having freight scattered across the highway or spillage of a hazardous chemical.

When an accident does occur—whatever the severity—the professional driver should know his or her responsibilities, including what to do immediately as well as what is not required and should not be done **(see Figure 24-1).**

This chapter will explain the professional driver's responsibilities at the scene of the accident and in protecting equipment, cargo, and human life. This discussion will include what to do about your rig, how to report an accident, how to protect yourself and others, and how to prevent a fire or control a fire if one ignites. It will also cover what equipment to use, how to act safely, what you must do to stay within the law, and how to report an accident.

▶ Figure 24-1

When an accident occurs, the professional driver should know his or her responsibilities.

What to Keep with You at All Times in Case of an Accident

1. Keep a camera, preferably a digital one. Do not depend on a camera in your cell phone; most people do not know how to print or save the pictures, and the quality is not the best. Most companies have an accident reporting kit in their trucks that includes a camera. Once you turn the camera in to the company, it is doubtful that you will have access to those pictures again. They are better than nothing, but add your own tools to make sure that you can record and document ALL the information and evidence at the accident scene, including witnesses and law-enforcement contact information.

2. A tape recorder to record any statements you hear by the other driver, witnesses, or law enforcement. This includes your statements to law enforcement or rescue personnel.

3. A tape measure, preferably a 100-foot (30.5 m) one.

4. A couple cans of orange or white spray paint to mark points of reference such as impact, direction of travel, etc.

5. It also is recommended that all drivers carry a well-stocked first aid kit and know how to use it. Think about reading a book about first aid or sign up for a first aid course. These skills could make the difference between life and death in an accident. Although you want to get all the facts regarding the crash as soon as possible, the first priority is to ensure prompt first aid and medical treatment for you and any and all crash victims.

NOTE

If you are using a film camera (not a digital), make sure to use the whole roll of film to document the conditions and positions of pertinent objects at the time of the crash.

GUIDELINES FOR CANADIAN DRIVERS INVOLVED IN AN INJURY ACCIDENT

If you are a driver who has been involved in a collision, you must stay at the scene and give all possible assistance. If you are not personally involved in a collision (and if company policy allows), you should stop to offer help if the police or other help has not yet arrived.

(Continues)

GUIDELINES FOR CANADIAN DRIVERS INVOLVED IN AN INJURY ACCIDENT (*continued*)

In a collision with injuries, possible fuel leaks, or serious vehicle damage, stay calm and follow these steps:

1. Call for help or have someone else call. By law, you must report any collision to the police when there are injuries or damage to vehicles or other property exceeding $1,000.

2. Turn off engines (including refrigeration, if applicable) and engage four-way flashers. Set up warning signals or flares and have someone warn approaching drivers.

3. Do not let anyone smoke, light a match, or put flares near any vehicle in case of a fuel leak. If the vehicle is on fire, get the occupants out of harm's way and make sure bystanders also are well out of the way. If there is no danger of fire or explosion, leave injured people where they are until trained medical help arrives.

4. If you are trained in first aid, treat injuries in the order of urgency, within the level of your training. For example, clear the person's airway to restore breathing, use rescue breathing, or stop bleeding by applying pressure with a clean cloth.

5. If you were not trained in first aid, use common sense. For example, people in collisions often go into shock. Cover the person with a jacket or blanket to reduce the effects of shock.

6. Stay with the injured until help arrives.

7. Disabled vehicles on the road may be a danger to you and other drivers. Do what you can to make sure everyone involved in a collision is kept safe.

GUIDELINES FOR CANADIAN DRIVERS AFTER A NONINJURY ACCIDENT

Follow these steps in a collision where there are no injuries:

1. If the vehicles can be moved, move them as far off the road as possible—this should not affect the police officers' investigation. This is especially important on busier high-speed roads where it may be dangerous to leave vehicles in the driving lanes. If you cannot move the vehicles off the road, set up warning signals or flares far enough away to give other traffic time to slow down or stop.

2. Call police (provincial or local, depending on where the collision takes place). By law you must report any collision to the police where there are injuries or damage to vehicles or property exceeding $1,000.

3. Give all possible help to police or anyone whose vehicle has been damaged. This includes giving police your name and address, the name and address of the registered owner of the vehicle you are driving, the vehicle plate and permit number, and the liability insurance card.

4. Get the names, addresses, and phone numbers of all witnesses.

5. If the damage is less than $1,000, you are still required by law to exchange information with anyone whose vehicle has been damaged. However, the collision does not have to be reported to the police.

6. Contact your insurance company as soon as possible if you intend to make a claim.

WHEN AN ACCIDENT OCCURS—U.S. DRIVERS

When an accident occurs, there are federal laws and company policies to guide the professional driver, both at the scene and in reporting the incident.

Steps to Take at the Scene of an Accident

Drivers should:

1. Stop immediately.
2. Compose yourself—and if you need to be treated for injuries, don't refuse help from first responders.
3. Follow company procedures to the letter. This should be part of your orientation training, but if this information is not available, be sure to ask.
4. Protect the scene to prevent further accidents.
5. Notify proper authorities.
6. Remember, diesel fuel makes the road slippery if spilled.
7. Provide reasonable assistance to injured persons.
8. Protect injured persons, not moving them unless they are in danger of additional injury (trained medical emergency personnel should move them, reducing the chance for further injury).

NOTE

Diesel fuel also causes considerable damage to the environment when it is allowed to seep into the ground. Professional drivers should do everything possible to contain the spill. Many carriers provide their drivers with spill kits that contain absorbent towels used to soak up as much of the spilled fuel as possible.

Get the following information from others involved in the accident:

■ Name and address of drivers
■ Name and address of motor carrier, if any other commercial vehicles were involved
■ Vehicle registration or license plate number
■ Driver's license number and state issuing it
■ Name and address of insurance companies and policy numbers

Give the following information to the other persons involved in the accident:

■ Your name and address
■ Name and address of your carrier
■ Your vehicle registration or license plate number
■ Your driver's license number and state issuing it
■ Name and address of the company insuring your rig and the policy number

Report the accident to your company as soon as possible.

■ You can expect to be tested for drugs or alcohol in your system after the accident. It is the carrier's responsibility to ensure the driver is tested for drugs or alcohol if someone dies as the result of the accident, if someone is injured and must receive treatment away from the scene, or if the vehicle is damaged so much it must be towed from the scene and the driver of the commercial vehicle receives a citation for a moving violation.

■ Carriers must make sure their drivers know the rules for drug testing.

■ Common sense, the company's policy, and the law provide a guide for all drivers after an accident has occurred. Companies often provide guidelines for drivers after an accident (**see Figure 24-2**).

© Cengage Learning 2013

▶ **Figure 24-2**

The driver is responsible for the safety of others and for protecting the scene.

These guidelines include:

1. Shut off engine and turn on four-way flashers.
2. Call for help—police and ambulance, if needed—and protect injured from further injury.
3. Protect the scene to prevent further accidents.
4. Stay calm and courteous at all times.
5. Notify the company.
6. Remain on the scene until the company releases you to leave.
7. Provide required identification when requested.
8. Collect facts (e.g., required ID of those involved, names/phone numbers of witnesses).
9. Say nothing about who is at fault. Do not offer to pay damages, and do not accept payment from anyone involved.
10. Make sure any spilled cargo has been cleared before leaving the scene.
11. Check your rig to make sure it is in a condition to be driven again.
12. File a complete accident report.
13. Expect a drug test if accident is DOT reportable.

Colliding with an Unattended Vehicle

If a commercial motor vehicle hits an unattended vehicle, the driver should stop and make a reasonable effort to locate the driver of the other vehicle. If he or she cannot be located, the CMV driver must leave a note on the other vehicle where it will be easily seen. The note should contain the driver's name and address as well as the name and address of the carrier. The note should be attached in such a way that it will not blow away or fall off. It should be placed where the driver can see it easily, because if it appears there was no note, you could be charged with a hit-and-run offense.

GO!

Use your cell phone to take and send photos of the scene to the company's safety department, showing damage to your rig or other vehicles.

NOTE: When taking photographs, focus on the vehicles, skid marks, damage to vehicles, and position of the vehicles. It is not your job to take photos that include accident victims.

CAUTION!

Drivers need to know their company's policy regarding taking any photos at the scene of an accident. And only take photos after making sure the scene—and any victims—are protected and assisted, law enforcement has been notified, and you have reported the accident to the company.

Accidents While Transporting Hazardous Materials

A professional driver with a cargo of hazardous materials should be aware that any accident can be dangerous. Always check shipping papers prior to beginning the trip to know what class of hazardous material and the approximate amount you are hauling.

The driver must make sure shipping papers for hazardous materials are within easy reach throughout the trip and are readable. Placards must show the product's name or be empty. In 2001, placards with slogans such as "Have a nice day!" or "Drive safely" were outlawed.

If you are hauling hazardous materials and have an accident, you should:

- Check for any leaks or if any cargo has been spilled and assume it is hazardous material. Do not allow anyone to walk or drive through the spills.
- Keep onlookers away **(see Figure 24-3).**
- Stay upwind of any spills. Do not allow anyone to eat, drink, or smoke in the area.
- Advise emergency responders about hazardous materials involved and allow them to check the shipping papers. Always check to be sure papers are legible when you accept a shipment.

▶ **Figure 24-3**

Keep onlookers away and stay upwind of any spills.

- Set out warning devices to protect the scene.
- Notify local authorities. Be sure they understand the truck is transporting hazardous materials. Tell them the classes and quantities on board.
- Contact the motor carrier. Make sure the carrier understands hazardous materials are involved and whether there has been a spill. If the accident is near water, inform the carrier of this situation as well.
- Follow the company's policy regarding the driver's responsibilities at the scene of the accident.

Accident Reporting When Hazardous Materials Are Involved

When a vehicle transporting hazardous materials is involved in an accident, additional reports must be made. Usually the carrier handles these reports, based on the information given by the driver. The driver should not handle any of this reporting except in the following circumstances:

- The driver is an owner and operator.
- The driver cannot contact the motor carrier for whom he or she is driving.
- The shipper's instructions require reporting by the driver.
- The authorities at the scene request that the driver make a report.

Emergency Procedures

Because the laws are constantly changing, always check with your employer before you begin a trip in which you are hauling hazardous materials. Learn what you must do if there is an accident or spill **(see Figure 24-4).**

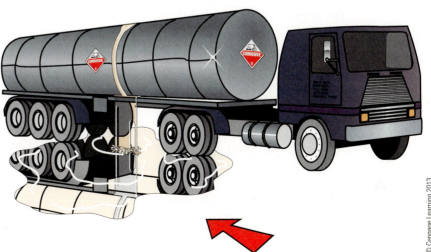

▶ **Figure 24-4**

The driver is responsible for preventing further accidents or injury.

You may need to notify some of the following agencies (**see Figure 24-5**):

U.S. Coast Guard National Response Center—helps coordinate emergency forces in response to chemical hazards. Their number is 1-800-424-8802.

Canadian Transport Emergency Centre (CANUTEC)—tells emergency responders the steps they need to take in mitigating the aftermath of a hazardous materials incident. These services are available 24 hours a day. CANUTEC can be reached by calling 613-996-6666; in an emergency, call collect. Or cellular in Canada only, help can be accessed by calling *666. For information, call 613-992-4624 (collect).

Chemical Transportation Emergency Center (CHEMTREC)—provides callers with a real person. An automated response is not used, and whenever there is an emergency, this Emergency Center has a good reputation for informing emergency responders in the U.S. what they need to know to make the proper notifications. Their 24-hour number is 1-800-424-9300 (emergency calls only). You can call 1-800-226-8200 for general information.

When you call CHEMTREC or CANUTEC, be sure to include:

- Your name and a call-back number
- Name of the motor carrier and the unit number
- Name of the consignee
- Name of the shipper or manufacturer
- Description of the accident scene

National Response Center—must be notified if there is an accident that results in any of the following:

- A fatality
- An injury requiring hospitalization
- Property damage of $50,000 or more
- Fire, breakage, spillage of contamination from radioactive materials or disease-causing agents
- Situation presenting a continuous danger to life
- Discharge of a hazardous substance
- Public evacuation lasting 1 hour or more
- Major transportation artery closed or shut down for 1 hour or more

Centers for Disease Control and Prevention—should be contacted if the load involved in an accident or a spill contains a disease-causing agent. The 24-hour emergency response hotline is 1-770-488-7100.

National Response Center
(800) 424-8802

CHEMTREC
(800) 424-9300

Canadian CANUTEC
(613) 996-6666

© Cengage Learning 2013

▶ **Figure 24-5**

If you are hauling hazardous material, you need to know and understand what assisting agencies do and what they cannot do.

For more specific information about reporting accidents involving hazardous materials, refer to 49 CFR Section 171.15. Federal laws also require filing a written **Hazardous Materials Incident Report** (Form 5800.1 Rev. 6-89) for any unintended release of hazardous materials (with limited exceptions). This report must be filed within 30 days and the driver must report any such release and give the necessary information to the supervisor for preparing this report. For more specific information, refer to 49 CFR Section 171.16.

How to Protect the Scene

The professional driver—or someone acting for him or her—should warn oncoming traffic to prevent further accidents. To do this, the driver must know the types of warning devices to be used to protect the scene and how to place warning devices quickly and correctly.

Types of Warning Devices to Protect the Scene of an Accident

FMCSR 393.95 requires reflective **emergency triangles** to be carried on all current commercial vehicles **(see Figure 24-6).** The triangles are useful warning devices because they can be used during the day or at night, are self-illuminating at night, and have an orange border that is easy to see during the day-time and can be used more than once. They can be used on any vehicle with any cargo.

Placing Warning Devices

The reason for using warning devices is to signal approaching vehicles of a problem and to guide them around the scene. Properly placed warnings are those that can be easily seen and do not confuse other motorists **(see Figure 24-7).**

When setting up triangles, it is best to walk well off the road and hold the triangle in front of you so that approaching traffic can see it. This will make you more visible and will help protect you from being hit by oncoming traffic.

When you stop your rig, follow these steps:

1. Turn off your engine.
2. Turn on the four-way flashers as a warning to traffic.
3. While the flashers are on, put out the emergency warning devices. This should be done within 10 minutes of stop-ping your rig.
4. After warning devices have been placed, turn off the four-way flashers to save the battery.
5. When you are ready to start again, turn on the four-way flashers.
6. Pick up the emergency warning devices and put them back in the cab.

▶ **Figure 24-6**
Emergency triangles are required safety equipment on all rigs.

▶ **Figure 24-7**
Emergency triangles are placed to warn approaching traffic of a problem.

STOP!

Do not jeopardize your own safety when trying to retrieve emergency triangles in heavy traffic. Triangles can be replaced, but you cannot.

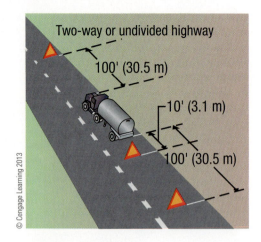

▶ **Figure 24–8**

Placement of warning devices on a two-lane highway.

Always place warning reflectors at least 100 feet (30.5 m) from the accident or disabled vehicle (**see Figure 24-8**). On a two-lane highway, place one triangle on the traffic side within 10 feet (3.1 m) of the rear of the truck. Another device should be placed about 100 feet (30.5 m) from the truck, in the center of the traffic lane or where the truck is stopped. Another device should be placed 100 feet (30.5 m) from the front of the truck.

On one-way or divided highways, place one device no more than 10 feet (3.1 m) from the rear of the truck, then one 100 feet (30.5 m) and one 200 feet (61 m) from the truck toward approaching traffic. Place them in the center of the lane or on the shoulder where the truck is stopped (**see Figure 24-9**).

In business or residential districts, use emergency devices when there is not enough light to give oncoming drivers a view of your truck from 500 feet (152.4 m) away.

On a hill or curve, place the rearmost triangle at a point where oncoming motorists will have adequate warning before your truck comes into view (**see Figure 24-10**).

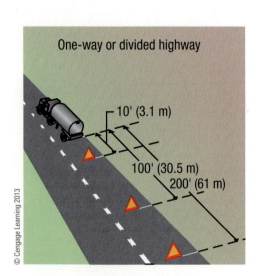

▶ **Figure 24–9**

Placement of warning devices on a divided highway.

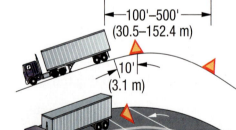

If line of sight view is obstructed due to a hill or curve, move the rearmost triangle to a point back down the road so warning is provided.

▶ **Figure 24–10**

On a hill, warning devices are placed up to 500 feet (152.4 m) from the accident site.

Managing the Accident Scene

If an accident occurs, it is your duty to:

- Call the police and ambulance (if necessary)
- Assist and protect the injured
- Conduct yourself properly and calmly
- Call your company for instructions
- Complete accident report

- Use accident packet
- Diagram the accident and take photos
- Identify witnesses
- Provide proper identifications and information
- Remain at the scene until all requirements are met

Call 911 for an ambulance—if an ambulance is needed. Give the exact location, but remember—most modern emergency response centers not only have caller ID, but they also can locate you from your cell phone transmission. However, if this technology is not available and you are not familiar with the area, ask others at the scene if they can help determine the location. Use a cell phone or the CB emergency channel, find someone with a cell phone, or send someone to call for help if cell phones are not available.

Assist the injured—after stopping and protecting the scene, your first priority is to help anyone who is injured, but know your limitations:

- Do not try to do anything you are not trained to do.
- Do not move the injured unless they are in danger.
- Avoid doing anything that could bring additional liability.
- Insist that anyone who claims injury get medical help because a doctor's record is the best protection against future claims. If a person refuses treatment, be sure to report this.

Conduct yourself properly—an accident can be an emotional experience. Much depends on keeping your cool. Remain calm and in control, even if others try to blame you. Do not debate right or wrong or admit that you are at fault.

STOP!

Remember that legal liability for what happened will be determined later, sometimes much later. What you say or do at the scene can affect the final decision about liability. **Do not offer or accept money and do not sign any type of release.** The only paper you should sign is a traffic citation from a law enforcement officer. At every point, follow company policy to the letter.

Call the company for instructions—take the following steps when calling your company for instructions:

- Tell them whether or not you are injured.
- Report any damage to the truck and cargo.
- Ask for help, if needed; for example, you may need another rig or a crew to transfer cargo.
- Be sure to report what you are hauling so they can make any special arrangements needed.
- Get instructions from your supervisor as to whether you should continue the trip or return to the terminal.

Use accident packet—most companies provide drivers with **accident packets** to assist in handling their responsibilities at the scene of an accident. Check this packet during your pretrip inspection. (For a sample, go to www.thehortongroup.com, search for accident packet.)

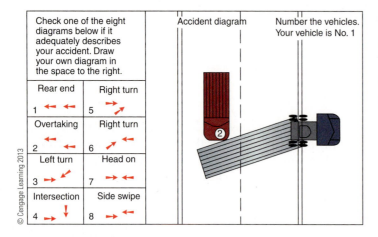

Check one of the eight diagrams below if it adequately describes your accident. Draw your own diagram in the space to the right.	
Rear end 1 ← ←	Right turn 5 ↗ ↘
Overtaking 2 ← ←	Right turn 6 ↗ ←
Left turn 3 → ↗	Head on 7 → ←
Intersection 4 → ↓	Side swipe 8 → ←

© Cengage Learning 2013

▶ **Figure 24–11**

Include a diagram of the accident in your accident report.

Accident packets usually contain:

- Basic instructions for handling the scene of the accident
- Preliminary accident report or memo
- Witness cards

    Draw a diagram—if possible, photograph the scene before any vehicles are moved, or draw a diagram of the scene, showing the position of vehicles before, during, and after the accident **(see Figure 24-11).** Include a description of the damage to other vehicles and property as well as an estimated amount of property damage, if possible.

    Witnesses and witness cards—try to get witnesses who can verify the vehicles' positions, speed, use of turn signals, skid marks, and so on. Sometimes drivers of cars near you can verify your speed. If your company supplies an accident packet, use the witness cards to get names and addresses. If no one volunteers as a witness, record the license plate numbers of possible witnesses. Note addresses of nearby buildings from which someone may have seen the accident.

Remain at the scene—do not leave the scene until your carrier instructs you to do so. Be sure you have given all the required information to authorities and others involved in the accident.

If there is a cargo spill, remove the unbroken packages as safely as possible. Clean up contents of broken or leaking packages as soon as possible. If you are hauling hazardous material, you will need specialized cleanup. Do not handle the product unless you have been trained to do so and have the necessary special equipment.

Give your rig a pretrip-type inspection to see if it is safe to drive **(see Figure 24-12).** If it is unsafe, call a mechanic to make repairs or a tow truck to remove the rig from the scene.

By law, every accident must be reported, regardless of how bad it is. Leaving the scene of an accident is a major traffic violation. A conviction for leaving the scene of an accident while driving a commercial motor vehicle will result in losing your CDL for one year in addition to any other penalties imposed.

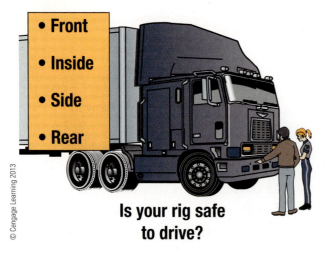

- **Front**
- **Inside**
- **Side**
- **Rear**

Is your rig safe to drive?

© Cengage Learning 2013

▶ **Figure 24–12**

Before leaving the accident scene, inspect your rig to ensure that it is safe to drive.

NOTE

As noted, leaving the scene of an accident has many undesirable consequences. Often a driver might leave the scene of an accident because of his or her alcohol level, illegal drug use, or other type of criminal behavior. Often these drivers are eventually located and the ramifications are often more severe for leaving than if they had stayed.

Drivers often face criminal charges for leaving the scene of an accident. Technology has advanced to such a level that cameras are everywhere and drivers may not be aware that others have seen the accident and could use the camera function of their cell phone to record an event.

STOP!

Failure of a driver to report an accident to the motor carrier will almost always result in the driver losing his or her job and will make it even more difficult to get another job. The driver will also be subject to prosecution.

Importance of driver's information—be very careful when you get information at the scene of an accident **(see Figure 24-13)**. This information will affect everything that occurs as a result of the accident. Your information is needed by the company to prepare the required reports for the carrier's insurance company, state agencies, and the U.S. DOT, if required.

Sample Supervisor's Investigation Report

COMPANY Safe Company Trucking	TERMINAL OR DIVISION Tenth Street Terminal
DRIVER M. Peachy	TYPE OF VEHICLE IDENTIFYING NO. Single Truck
LOCATION OF ACCIDENT *(Street, town, state)* Tenth Street Terminal Yard	DATE AND TIME OF ACCIDENT February 6, 200X 8AM

NO. OF PERSONS INJURED AND EXTENT OF PROPERTY DAMAGE *(Company and other)*

No injuries.

Left rear fender (apx. $50.00 damage)

No damage to truck, bumper contacted car.

DESCRIPTION OF ACCIDENT   *(State in detail what occurred just before, and at the time of the accident)*

Truck rolled away from loading dock, no chocks were placed at rear

wheels. Truck was not in gear, parking brake was not securely set.

(Truck brakes were out of adjustment.) Truck rolled apx. 10 feet (3.1 m) and

struck rear fender of parked car in yard. Car was parked illegally

in yard.

UNSAFE CONDITION   *(Describe unsafe conditions such as faulty brake, light, etc. contributing to accident)*

No chock blocks on truck.

Brakes out of adjustment.

UNSAFE ACT *(Describe the unsafe action of driver as turning from wrong lane, speeding, failing to signal, etc.)*

Brakes not secured when parked. Truck not in gear.

Car parked in truck area.

REMEDY *(As a supervisor, what action have you taken or do you propose taking to prevent a repeat accident)*

Check truck dock for chocks. Require chocks at loading dock and stops.

Driver issued warning. Keep private vehicles out of loading area.

SUPERVISOR *R.Ray*	REVIEWED AND APPROVED BY	DATE REPORT PREPARED February 8, 200X

(Use reverse side for sketch and additional detail)

© Cengage Learning 2013

▶ **Figure 24-13**

The driver's information affects everything that occurs as a result of the accident.

The driver's information helps the company determine legal obligations. The company also needs to update the driver's record and to reach an equitable settlement if there are claims.

What the driver tells the company may also be used to find measures that can be taken to prevent similar accidents in the future. Additionally, this information may be used to assess the company's overall experience and trends in accidents.

Summary of Accident Reporting Requirements

Unless the professional driver is an owner-operator, he or she does not prepare the reports for the insurance company or the state or federal agencies; however, the driver should understand the state and federal reporting requirements, as follows:

State reporting requirements—every accident resulting in a fatality or personal injury must be reported to state authorities. Each state has its own limit for reporting property damage accidents. The limit amounts range from $50 to $2,000. The driver involved in a property damage accident should be sure to check with the police about reporting requirements.

Federal reporting requirements—a motor carrier operating in interstate or foreign commerce must report accidents to local authorities if they result in:

- Fatalities
- Injury requiring treatment away from the scene
- Disabling damage to one or more vehicles requiring the vehicles to be towed from the scene

Local authorities are responsible for notifying the U.S. DOT. An accident does not have to be reported to the DOT if it only involves getting on or off a vehicle or loading or unloading cargo, unless the incident releases hazardous material, and then it *must* be reported.

NOTE

Carriers will often conduct an accident review board, which is made up of management and senior drivers. The driver involved in an accident will be asked to explain what occurred and the events that took place leading up to the accident. The accident review board will then make a ruling as to if the accident was chargeable or nonchargeable. Also they will rule if the accident was preventable or nonpreventable. For example, an accident where a tractor-trailer hit a deer would be viewed as nonchargeable and not preventable. However, most accidents are eventually deemed chargeable and preventable.

Accidents and the Professional Driver

A professional driver works hard to maintain an accident-free driving record. Carriers also place a high priority on accident-free miles—in commercial vehicles and their own personal vehicles—often awarding drivers who have clean driving records.

The FMCSR requires interstate motor carriers to annually review the record of each driver. This includes an evaluation of each driver's accident record and number of traffic violations.

Every accident costs the carrier money, even though the driver may not be to blame. If the driver is at fault in any way, the cost to the company is much greater.

Usually, a reconstruction of the incident, along with testimony from the drivers and witnesses to the incident, will help decide whether an accident could have been prevented. In most cases, this ruling is more than just a question of whether the truck driver was issued a citation. These facts, observations, and other materials are used to decide if the driver failed to take any action that could have prevented the accident.

Under the trucking industry's standards, an accident is considered preventable if the driver did anything that contributed to it or if the driver did not try to avoid it.

GIVING FIRST AID

First aid is immediate and temporary care given to an accident victim until professional help arrives. To administer first aid, you should have training, such as that offered by the American Red Cross course, "Essential First Aid and CPR," so you can be of help if needed in an emergency **(see Figure 24-14).**

As a professional driver, if an accident occurs and you are one of the first on the scene, then offer help. If help is already on the scene, you do not need to stop. If your help is not needed, your stopping will only add to the congestion at the scene of the accident.

▶ Figure 24-14

To administer first aid, you need proper training.

Limitations

A person's ability to help is limited by company policy and the state's laws for limits they place on you. Learn about each state's "Good Samaritan" laws, which protect a person giving reasonable first aid. Learn also about each state's requirements for persons who are trained in first aid and cardiopulmonary resuscitation (CPR).

Basic Principles of First Aid

It is important to stay calm in an accident situation. Do not move anyone who is injured unless there is danger to that person from fire, heavy traffic, or other serious threat. Take the following steps:

- Get help by calling police and ambulance.
- Keep onlookers back.
- Make the victims comfortable.
- Keep the injured warm.
- Never give water or other liquids to an unconscious or partially conscious person.
- Talk calmly to the victim and get the victim's permission to help.
- Never discuss the extent of a victim's injuries.

First Aid Summary

It is best to get training from the American Red Cross or other agency before you need to give first aid. If you have to give first aid, know your limits, know the state and federal laws for treating victims, and follow company policy.

When an accident happens you may, initially, feel confused and "out-of-it" as far as what has happened. Be aware that seeking medical help for yourself, if needed, is extremely important.

FIRES AND FIREFIGHTING

It is always better to prevent a fire than to have to extinguish one. Ways to prevent fires and methods for putting them out will be discussed in this section.

While fires occur in only a small percentage of truck incidents, such incidents usually cause property damage, severe injuries, and fatalities.

All professional drivers have the responsibility of putting out a vehicle fire. The first priority, in this situation, is protecting your life and the lives of others. Then try to save the vehicle and its cargo.

What Causes Fires?

Fires can start after accidents, as a result of a fuel spill or the improper use of flares. There is also the possibility of a tire fire.

Underinflated tires and dual tires that touch create friction enough to cause fires. On some trucks, there is also a strong possibility of electrical fires, usually coming from short circuits caused by damaged insulation or loose wires.

Carelessness is one of the major causes of vehicle fires, with behaviors such as smoking around the fuel pump, improper fueling, and loose fuel connections. There is also the possibility of flammable cargo and cargo not being properly sealed, ventilated, or loaded, which can cause a fire.

> **CAUTION!**
>
> All of these reasons make it very important to make a complete pretrip inspection of electrical, fuel, and exhaust systems, plus tires and cargo.

To burn, a fire needs fuel, a source of heat, oxygen, and a chemical chain reaction **(see Figure 24-15).** If you remove one of these elements, there will be no fire. You can put out a fire by cooling it to the point that it will not burn; and you can usually do this by putting water on the fire or smothering it, which cuts off the supply of oxygen. Water should not be put on every fire, so it is important for you to know what kind of fire you are dealing with. You can also put out a fire by using a gas or powder. The powder releases a gas that, when heated, smothers the flames. Certain agents such as Halon and some dry chemicals extinguish fires by interrupting the chain reaction.

Different Types of Fires

The four different types or classes of fires are **(Figure 24-16):**

Class A—a fire involving ordinary combustibles such as wood, paper, and cloth.

Remove Any Side of the Tetrahedron

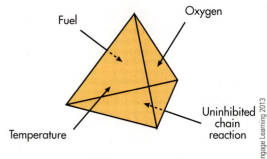

And There Is No Fire

▶ **Figure 24–15**

If you remove one of the required elements, a fire will not burn.

Classes of Fires

A. Wood, paper, ordinary combustibles
Extinguish by cooling and quenching
Use: water or dry chemicals

B. Gasoline, oil, grease, other greasy liquids
Extinguish by smothering, cooling, or heat-shielding
Use: carbon dioxide or dry chemicals

C. Electrical equipment fires
Extinguish with nonconducting agents:
Carbon dioxide or dry chemicals
Do not use water

D. Fire in combustible metals
Extinguish by using specialized extinguishing powders

Fire Extinguisher Type	For	Class of Fire
Regular dry chemical		B,C
Multipurpose dry chemical		A,B,C, or B,C
Purple-K dry chemical		D
KCL dry chemical		B,C
Dry powder special compound		D
Carbon dioxide (gas)		B,C
Halogenated agent (gas)		B,C
Water		A
Water with antifreeze		A
Water, loaded stream style		A,B
Foam		B, some use on A

▶ **Figure 24–16**

Different types of fires require different fire extinguishers to be brought under control.

Class B—a fire involving flammable (or combustible) liquids and gases such as gasoline, diesel fuel, alcohol, paint, acetylene, and hydrogen.

Class C—a fire in live electrical equipment. You must put these fires out with something that does not conduct electricity. After the electricity source has been cut off, extinguishers suitable for Class A or Class B fires may be used.

Class D—a fire in combustible metals, such as magnesium and sodium. These fires can be extinguished only with special chemicals or powder.

Putting Out Different Types of Fires

Different fires must be put out using different methods. For example, using a stream of water on a burning liquid or a water-reactive hazardous material will make the situation worse. On other types of fires, such as a burning tire, water is needed to cool the burning material even though smothering may temporarily control visible flames.

FIRE EXTINGUISHERS

FMCSR Part 393.95 requires that professional drivers always carry a fire extinguisher. Part 393.95 also requires that the fire extinguisher in your truck be inspected every two years **(see Figure 24-17)**. If a vehicle transports hazardous material, the fire extinguishers must have a UL rating of 10B:C or more.

When fighting fires, know the type of fire you are fighting. Most **fire extinguishers** are marked by a letter or a symbol to indicate the classes of fires for which they can be used. Every tractor or truck with a gross vehicle weight rating (GVWR) of 10,001 pounds (4536 kg) or more must have a fire extinguisher. The extinguisher must be checked as part of the pretrip inspection.

Most trucks carry a 5-pound (2.2 kg) fire extinguisher—it's the law. These can put out Class B and C fires. If the vehicle is hauling hazardous materials that are placarded, then a 10-pound (4.5 kg) B:C fire extinguisher filled with a dry chemical is required. When squeezing the handle on this kind of extinguisher, a needle punctures an air pressure cartridge inside the tank, and released air pressure forces the powder out of the tank. This powder travels through the hose and nozzle and onto the fire, thus extinguishing the fire by smothering it.

To use the extinguisher, aim it at the base of the fire. The base of the fire is the problem, not the flames themselves **(see Figure 24-18)**. Know how to use the fire extinguisher in your truck. When using the extinguisher, stay as far from the fire/flames as possible. Position yourself with your back to the wind. Continue dousing the fire until whatever is burning has cooled. The presence of smoke or flames is not important. Make sure the fire is completely out so it will not start again.

© iStockphoto/gerisima

▶ **Figure 24-17**

Professional drivers should always carry a fire extinguisher.

• **Aim at Base of Flames**

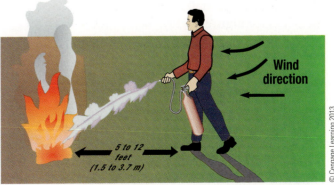

Wind direction

5 to 12 feet
(1.5 to 3.7 m)

▶ **Figure 24-18**

To put out a fire, aim the extinguisher at the base of the flames and spray back and forth.

© Cengage Learning 2013

CAUTION!

Keeping in mind that caution is most important, it may also be helpful to know that fires have been made worse by drivers who do not know what to do. Follow these steps for successful and safe firefighting:

1. Get the vehicle off the road and stop in the nearest safe place. Park in an open area, away from buildings, trees, brush, and other vehicles. DO NOT PULL INTO A SERVICE STATION!
2. Use your CB or cell phone to notify police, highway patrol, or 911. Be sure to give your location.
3. Keep the fire from spreading, so before trying to put out the fire, do what you can to keep it from traveling elsewhere.
4. For engine fires, turn off the engine. Avoid opening the hood. Aim the fire extinguisher through the radiator louvers or from beneath the vehicle.
5. Keep the doors shut if the cargo is on fire. Opening the doors will feed the fire with air from outside.
6. Use water on burning wood, paper, or cloth, but not on electrical fires because you could get shocked. Do not use water on a gasoline fire, because it will feed and spread the flames.
7. A burning tire should be cooled, so you will need to bathe it with a lot of water. If no water is in the area, throw sand or dirt on the flames.
8. Use the right kind of fire extinguisher.

ADDITIONAL INFORMATION ABOUT TRUCK FIRES

If your tractor-trailer should catch fire, immediately drive it to the nearest, safest place and stop. Stay as far away from buildings as possible. Get help, and if the tractor can be unhooked from the trailer safely then do so to help stop the spread of the fire.

Tire Fires

Tire fires usually occur because the air pressure in the tire is too low. Tires that are low or flat flex too much, which causes heat to build up inside the tire. When it gets hot enough, the surface will burst into flames. You can control the flames with a fire extinguisher, but large quantities of water must be poured on the tire to cool it down. Then the fire can finally be put out. Tires can easily re-ignite because heat builds up between the plies (**see Figure 24-19**).

▶ Figure 24-19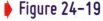

Tire fires can be extinguished with a fire extinguisher and a large quantity of water.

Tire fires can be prevented by checking to be sure the tires are properly inflated. Tires can be checked best by using a truck tire gauge. It is the only way to be sure the air pressure is balanced for dual tires. Because of the nature of their cargo, drivers transporting hazardous materials are required to check the tires every 2 hours or after each 100 miles (161 km) of travel.

Cargo Fires

Cargo fires often become unmanageable, especially if they ignite in a closed van. You may not know there is a fire until smoke seeps out around the cargo doors. To keep the fire smoldering instead of burning, keep the doors closed. This will limit the oxygen reaching the fire.

Stop in a safe location and get help. Let the fire department open the cargo doors to lessen flare-up. If you can safely do so, remove the undamaged cargo before firefighters put water on the fire. Better yet, check your carrier's safety policy for what they require in case of a fire.

Fuel Fires

Any truck crash creates a great risk for fire, particularly if the fuel tank is ruptured or a fuel line breaks. The leaking fuel may be ignited by sparks from the accident or other source (**see Figure 24-20**). The truck's fire extinguisher may not control a fire from a large fuel spill. Although diesel fuel does not burn as easily as gasoline, it will burn if it gets hot enough.

▶ **Figure 24-20**

In an accident, leaking fuel may be ignited by sparks from another source.

© Cengage Learning 2013

If you find any fuel leaks during a pretrip inspection, correct them before starting your trip. Be sure the caps are secure on the fuel tanks. When you refuel, do not smoke or allow others to smoke around you. Metal-to-metal contact must be maintained between the nozzle and the fill pipe.

Federal law states it is unlawful to fill any fuel tank to more than 95 percent of its capacity. This prevents spills when the fuel expands as it warms. If the cargo is hazardous material, a person must control the flow of fuel when the truck is being refueled.

Electrical Fires

Electrical fires can happen when the insulation on wiring is worn or frayed. If the bare wires touch each other or other metal parts of the truck, a fire can result. In an accident, damaged wiring can short circuit and cause a fire. If you can safely disconnect the battery when there is an electrical fire, this will remove a source of heat.

Making Safety a Habit

Always check your rig and your cargo, pretrip and en route, including the tires, wheels, and truck body, for signs of heat. Always fuel the vehicle safely and be careful with any part of the vehicle that usually creates heat or flame. While driving, check gauges and other instruments often. Use mirrors to look for signs of smoke; and if any system is overheating, fix it before you have a bigger problem.

SUMMARY

In this chapter, you learned how a driver should react in case of an accident: what information to obtain, what information to give others involved in the accident, and what subjects not to discuss. The requirements for hazardous material spills were outlined. The types of fires and ways of fighting them were also discussed. You also learned there are different types of fire extinguishers and how they are used in different types of fires.

KEY TERMS

Accident packet
Canadian Transport Emergency
    Centre (CANUTEC)
Centers for Disease Control and
    Prevention
Chemical Transportation
    Emergency Center
    (CHEMTREC)

Class A fire
Class B fire
Class C fire
Class D fire
Emergency triangles
Fire extinguisher
First aid

Hazardous Materials Incident
    Report
National Response Center
U.S. Coast Guard National
    Response Center

REVIEW QUESTIONS

1. If you are involved in an accident, which of the following is not a correct action?

   a. Stop immediately.

   b. Leave the scene of the accident because you have a scheduled delivery.

   c. Protect the scene to prevent further accidents.

   d. Notify proper authorities.

2. If a driver of a rig hauling hazardous materials has an accident, which of the following is not a correct action?

   a. If oil, diesel fuel, fuel, or any other flammable substance spills on the highway, soak up as much as possible so the highway will not be slick.

   b. Do not allow anyone to walk or drive through any spill.

   c. Keep onlookers away.

   d. Stay upwind of any spills.

3. If a Canadian driver is involved in an accident involving hazmat, the _____ must be notified.

   a. U.S. Coast Guard National Response Center

   b. CHEMTREC Emergency Center

   c. CANUTEC

   d. National Response Center

4. What type of warning device must be carried on all commercial vehicles?

   a. emergency triangles   c. handheld flashlight

   b. fuses   d. a, b, and c

5. When setting up warning devices (triangles) so you can be seen by oncoming traffic, the triangles should be carried _____.

    a. behind you   **c.** in front of you

    b. at your side in your right hand   **d.** at your side in your left hand

6. Regarding placement of warning devices on a hill or curve, the rearmost triangle should be placed _____.

    a. 500 feet/152 meters from the rear of your rig

    b. 1,000 feet/305 meters from the rear of your rig

    c. one-half mile (2-1/2 km) from your rig

    d. where oncoming motorists will receive adequate warning before coming upon your rig

7. Regarding handling an accident scene, after stopping and protecting the scene, a professional driver's first priority is to _____.

    a. call a lawyer

    b. call the dispatcher

    c. be aware of your limitations, but help anyone who is injured

    d. regardless of your knowledge of first aid, administer first aid to all injured persons

8. Since every accident in the U.S. must be reported regardless of how bad it is, a conviction for leaving the scene of an accident while driving a commercial motor vehicle will result in losing your CDL for _____.

    a. six months

    b. six months if you are at fault

    c. no time if not your fault

    d. one year in addition to any other penalties imposed by state law

9. Regarding federal requirements for motor carriers operating in interstate or foreign commerce, which of the following is not an incident that must be reported to local authorities?

    a. a fatality

    b. an injury requiring only treatment at the scene of the accident

    c. an injury requiring treatment away from the scene of the accident

    d. disabling damage to one or more vehicles requiring the vehicle to be towed from the scene

10. As a professional driver, if your tractor-trailer should catch fire, you should _____.

    a. stop immediately

    b. drive to the nearest truck stop and report the fire

    c. drive to the nearest fire station

    d. immediately drive it to the nearest safe place and stop

11. As part of your emergency supplies, in case of accident, you should carry all but which of the following?

    a. measuring tape   **c.** digital camera

    b. cans of white or orange spray paint   **d.** mop and broom

12. The fire extinguisher carried in your rig should be inspected _____.

    a. every six months   **c.** every five years

    b. every two years   **d.** once every year

SUPPLEMENTAL LEARNING ACTIVITIES

1. Invite a first responder from a local hazmat team to speak to your class about how tractor-trailer accidents involving hazmat are conducted.

2. Without using your notes, list the steps to be taken whenever a tractor-trailer is involved in an injury accident. At the end of this exercise, compare your list with other learners and discuss.

3. Invite a CPR or first aid trainer to your class and become certified in CPR or basic first aid.

4. Ask your instructor to bring several different types of fire extinguishers to class, and learn how to operate them.

5. Federal law prohibits filling a tractor-trailer fuel tank more than 95 percent full. Write a 100-word essay about why this law exists.

FOR MORE INFORMATION

PTDI—Deal with Accident Scenes and Reporting Procedures, Page 23, Click on Skill Standards
www.ptdi.org/standards

Canadian Emergency Response Guidebook
www.tc.gc.ca/eng/canutec/new-222.htm

Example of a Trucker's Accident Packet
www.thehortongroup.com/Files/86365175-6df5-f5d6-b78e-342151174129.pdf

FMCSA's "Smart Roadside Initiative"
www.fmcsa.dot.gov/facts-research/art-technology-smart-roadside-for-commercial.htm

25 Handling Cargo

© Cengage Learning 2013

OBJECTIVES

When you have completed this chapter, you should be able to:

■ Specify importance and responsibility for checking and handling cargo safely.

■ Describe the methods of containing and securing cargo.

■ Identify state and federal regulations that control how cargo is shipped.

■ Know procedures for loading and unloading cargo.

■ Explain the distribution of weight when loading cargo.

■ Describe special handling that certain materials require.

INTRODUCTION

Professional truck drivers today are required to have many more skills than simply driving a truck down a highway. To call yourself a "professional," you must also have the ability and the knowledge to properly handle and load cargo in such a way as to avoid damage in transit **(see Figure 25-1).**

Professional drivers also know that properly loaded cargo will add to the operating efficiency of any rig. Freight that is improperly loaded may not only be damaged in transit but also could be a danger to the driver and to other highway users. An overloaded truck or a load that is improperly loaded or secured presents an enormous threat to safety, on or off the highway, and because of this possibility, the FMCSR has set specific methods for securing cargo and specific vehicle weight limits for rigs.

In addition, FMCSR 392.9 states that the professional driver must assure himself/herself that the cargo loading techniques for every load have complied with securement regulations before he/she drives that commercial motor vehicle. If the driver has some question regarding the way cargo has been loaded and/or the safety factors involved, he or she has the option of not accepting the load (See Whistleblower guidelines in Chapter 35 for more details.)

▶ **Figure 25–1**

Professional drivers must know how to properly handle and load cargo to avoid shifting or damage in transit.

SAFETY FIRST WHEN LOADING OR UNLOADING TRUCKS AND TRAILERS

In most cases, forklifts are used to load and unload trucks and trailers, except for tankers, dumpers, and livestock haulers—and this operation is considered extremely dangerous. The forklift operation considered to be the most dangerous occurs when the forklift is moving from the stability of the concrete floor of a warehouse or dock to an unstable truck or trailer. Not only may the vehicle be unstable, but the means of going from the warehouse or dock into the vehicle (by way of a dock plate) can be hazardous.

Any veteran driver can probably tell stories of experienced freight-handlers either being severely injured or losing their lives, due to a loading or unloading accident.

The following rules are considered best practices and should be adhered to at all times:

1. **Set the brakes:** Be sure that the brakes are set on the vehicle to be unloaded. This could range from air brakes or spring-loaded brakes on larger semi-trailers to hand brakes on other vehicles. Generally the driver of the over-the-road truck will be the person who sets the brakes. But, as with all other rules listed here, it is the forklift operator's responsibility to check that the brakes have been set and all other safety rules have been carried out.

2. **Secure the vehicle to the dock:** It's a good idea to secure the vehicle to the loading dock by the use of wheel chocks or a mechanical dock locking system. By using wheel chocks or a dock-lock system, the trailer or truck is prevented from moving forward whenever the operator drives the forklift into the trailer to pick up or deposit a load. This rocking motion caused by the forklift's braking action can cause semitrailers and other trucks to creep forward, even if the vehicle brakes are set.

NOTE

Some shippers and customer terminals require drivers to slide trailer tandems all the way to the rear, as a safety precaution for fork truck drivers prior to entering the trailer.

3. **Install the dock board or plate:** After the vehicle restraint system is in place, install and check the **dock board**. This metal plate serves as a ramp between the dock or warehouse floor and the trailer floor. After installation of the dock board, the forklift operator should walk out on it to make certain that it overlaps the trailer sufficiently and that the trailer is square with the unloading area so that the dock board fits uniformly onto the trailer **(see Figure 25-2).**

4. **Check the condition of the trailer floor:** Once the dock plate is secure, and before driving into the trailer, the forklift operator should check the condition of the floor of the vehicle to be driven onto. If the floor of the trailer has weak, rotten, or otherwise unsafe areas on it, do not drive on it! Many accidents, including injuries and fatalities, have occurred because the forklift operator did not check the trailer's floor condition prior to driving into it.

▶ **Figure 25-2**

Installing and checking the dockboard.

A lightweight **pallet jack** may have to be used to load or unload trailers if the truck or trailer floor conditions warrant that the heavier forklift stays out of the trailer.

5. **Determine if the semi-trailer is still attached:** If the tractor has been removed and the trailer is to be loaded or unloaded, place supports or jackstands under the nose of the trailer to prevent it from upending. Upending can occur if a heavy load is being placed in the nose of the trailer that has the tractor removed.

6. **Check the lighting:** To be sure that there is adequate lighting before driving into a semitrailer or other vehicle. If the light is poor, turn on and position the loading dock lights. If the lift truck has lights, turn them on also.

CARGO SECUREMENT REGULATIONS

On September 27, 2002, FMCSA revised its regulations concerning protection against shifting and falling cargo for commercial motor vehicles (CMVs) engaged in interstate commerce. These rules became effective January 1, 2004.

These cargo securement standards are based on the North American Cargo Securement Standard Model Regulations. They reflect the results of a multiyear comprehensive research program to evaluate U.S. and Canadian cargo securement regulations; the motor carrier industry's best practices; and recommendations presented during a series of public meetings.

These regulations require motor carriers to change the way they use cargo securement devices to prevent articles from shifting on or within, or falling from, CMVs. In some instances, the changes may require motor carriers to increase the number of tie-downs used to secure certain types of cargos. However, the rule generally does not prohibit the use of tie-downs or cargo securement devices currently in use. Therefore, motor carriers were not required to purchase new cargo securement equipment to comply with the rule.

The intent of the regulations is to reduce the number of crashes caused by cargo shifting on or within, or falling from, CMVs operating in interstate commerce, and to harmonize to the greatest extent practicable U.S., Canadian, and Mexican cargo securement regulations.

The cargo securement rules apply to all cargo-carrying CMVs (as defined in 49 CFR 390.5) operated in interstate commerce **(see Figure 25-3).** This includes all types of articles of cargo, except commodities in bulk that lack structure or fixed shape (e.g., liquids, gases, grain, liquid concrete, sand,

▶ Figure 25–3

New cargo securement rules apply to cargo-carrying commercial vehicles operated in interstate commerce, such as hauling grain.

▶ *"What do you mean I can't secure my cargo with duct tape?"*

gravel, aggregates) and are transported in a tank, hopper, box, or similar device that forms part of the structure of a commercial motor vehicle.

Requirements for Securement Devices

Securement rules require that all devices and systems used to secure cargo to or within a vehicle must be capable of meeting the performance criteria. All vehicle structures, systems, parts, and components used to secure cargo must be in proper working order when used to perform that function with no damaged or weakened components that could adversely affect their performance. The cargo securement rules cite manufacturing standards for certain types of **tie-downs** including steel strapping, chain, synthetic webbing, wire rope, and cordage.

FMCSA's updated rules reference the November 15, 1999, version of the National Association of Chain Manufacturers (NACM) Welded Steel Chain Specifications. FMCSA also notes that, generally, the working load limits of the updated version are the same as those in the 1991 publication.

The updated rules required that motor carriers replace tie-down devices purchased prior to January 1, 2004. If the tie-downs satisfied the old rules, the devices should also satisfy these rules.

Cargo Securing and Handling Devices

- **Dolly**—also called hand truck, two wheeler, stack truck, trolley, trolley truck, or bag barrow. A dolly is an L-shaped box-moving handcart with handles at one end, wheels at the base, with a small ledge to set objects on, flat against the floor when the hand truck is upright. The objects to be moved are tilted forward, the ledge is inserted underneath them, and the objects allowed to tilt back and rest on the ledge. Dollies are fabricated from many different types of materials: tube steel, aluminum tube, and high-impact plastics. Most commercial hand trucks that are used for beverage and food service deliveries are rugged and very lightweight.

- **Cargo nets**—can be made of any number of fibers. Used with hooks or other types of tie-downs to secure large loads on flatbeds or in box trailers. Usually lightweight and easy to handle.

- **Slings**—a strap, chain, or other material used to hold cargo items securely that are to be hoisted, lowered, or suspended.

- **Rug poles**—or "carpet poles" are used to transport rolls of carpet. Poles can be any length but are generally 2-3/4 inch (7 cm) diameter, made of a variety of high-strength material, rotateable, replaceable, and most have a tapered tip. Many have the capacity to be attached to lift trucks.

■ **Johnson bars**—a generic term related to any long lever acting as a fulcrum or cheater bar, especially on warehouse docks with tools to leverage cargo upon casters or hand trucks. It also may be referred to as a "pry lever bar."

Proper Use of Tie-Downs

The regulations require each tie-down to be attached and secured in a manner that prevents it from becoming loose, unfastening, opening, or releasing while the vehicle is in transit **(see Figure 25-4).** All tie-downs and other components of a cargo securement system used to secure loads on a trailer equipped with rub rails

▶ **Figure 25-4**
As a professional driver you are responsible for properly tying down your cargo.

must be located inboard of the rub rails when practicable. Edge protection also must be used when a tie-down would be subject to abrasion or cutting at the point where it touches an article of cargo. The edge protection must resist abrasion, cutting, and crushing.

Front End Structures on CMVs

FMCSA rules concerning front-end structures or headerboards have changed the applicability of the requirements to cover CMVs transporting cargo where the cargo is in contact with the front-end structure of the vehicle. By contrast, the old rules required certain vehicles to be equipped with front-end structures, regardless of whether the devices were used as part of a cargo securement system.

Headerboards—located at the front end of the load, are also called headache racks and protect the driver from the freight shifting or crushing in an accident or a sudden stop. Front-end headerboards protect the driver who is carrying these kinds of loads.

General Rule

Cargo must be firmly immobilized or secured on or within a vehicle by structures of adequate strength, **dunnage** (loose materials used to support and protect cargo) or **dunnage bags** (inflatable bags intended to fill space between articles of cargo or between cargo and the wall of the vehicle), **dunnage boxes,** shoring bars, tie-downs, or a combination of these.

Cargo Placement and Restraint

Articles of cargo that are likely to roll must be restrained by **chocks,** wedges, a cradle, or other equivalent means to prevent rolling. The means of preventing rolling must not be capable of becoming unintentionally unfastened or loose while the vehicle is in transit. Articles of cargo placed beside each other and secured by transverse tie-downs must be:

1. Placed in direct contact with each other
2. Prevented from shifting toward each other while in transit

Minimum Working Load Limit for Cargo Securement Devices and Systems

The total working load limit of any securement system used to secure an article or group of articles against movement must be at least one-half the weight of the article or group of articles. The total working load limit is the sum of one-half the working load limit of each tie-down that goes from an anchor point on the vehicle to an attachment point on an article of cargo; and the working load limit for each tie-down that goes from an anchor point on the vehicle through, over, or around the cargo and then attaches to another anchor point on the vehicle.

OUT-OF-SERVICE CRITERIA FOR LOAD MANAGEMENT

The following are points covered by roadside inspectors regarding how cargos are loaded and those loading errors that could cause a rig to be put out of service:

- Spare tire or portion of load/dunnage could fall from vehicle.

- Fitting for securing container to container chassis solely via corner fittings (for intermodal freight) is improperly latched.

- 25 percent or more of type/number of tie-downs required by FMCSR 393.102 are loose or missing.

- 25 percent or more of required type or number of tie-downs are defective.

- Chain is defective if working portion contains knot or damaged, deformed, or worn links. Clevis-type repair link, if as strong as original link, is okay.

- Wire rope is defective if working portion contains kinked, birdcaged, or pitted section; over three broken wires in any strand; over two broken wires at fitting; over 11 broken wires in any length measuring six times its diameter (e.g., with 0.5-inch (1.3 cm) thick rope, more than 11 broken wires in any 3-inch (7.6 cm) section); repairs other than back or eye splice; or discoloration from heat or electric arc.

- Fiber rope is defective if working portion contains burned or melted fibers, except on heat-sealed ends; excessive wear, reducing diameter 20 percent; any repair (properly spliced lengths are not considered a repair); or ineffective (easily loosened) knot used for connection or repair.

- Synthetic webbing is defective if working portion contains a knot; more than 25 percent of stitches separated; broken or damaged hardware; any repair or splice; overt damage; severe abrasion; cumulative for entire working length of one strap, cuts, burns, or holes exceeding width of 3/4 inch (1/9 cm) for 4-inch-wide (10 cm) webbing, exceeding width of 5/6 inch (2 cm) for 3-inch-wide (7.6 cm) webbing, or exceeding width of 3/8 inch (1 cm) for 1-3/4-inch-wide (4.4 cm) or 2-inch-wide (5 cm) webbing. Multiple defects confined to one strand of a strap are not cumulative (just measure largest single defect in that strand).

- Load binders or fittings that obviously are cracked, worn, corroded, distorted, or discolored from heat or electric arc.

- Evidence of wire rope slipping through cable clamp.

- Anchor point on vehicle displays: distorted or cracked rails or supports, cracked weld, or damaged or worn floor rings.

Minimum Number of Tie-Downs

The cargo securement system used to restrain articles against movement must meet the minimum tie-down requirement **(see Figure 25-5)**. This requirement is in addition to complying with rules concerning the minimum working load limit. When an article of cargo is not blocked or positioned to prevent movement in the forward direction, the number of tie-downs needed depends on the length and weight of the articles. (See FMCSR 393.5–393.135 regarding cargo securement and tie-down regulations.)

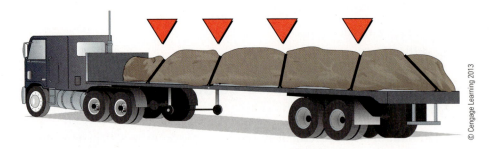

© Cengage Learning 2013

▶ **Figure 25-5**

Cargo should have at least one tie-down for each 10 feet (3.1 m) of cargo. Make sure you have enough tie-downs to meet this need. No matter how small the cargo is, there should be at least two tie-downs holding it.

There must be one tie-down for articles 5 feet (1.5 m) or less in length, and 1,100 pounds (499 kg) or less in weight; two tie-downs if the article is one of the following:

1. At or less than 5 feet (1.5 m) in length and more than 1,100 pounds (499 kg) in weight
2. Greater than 5 feet (1.5 m) but less than 10 feet (3.1 m), regardless of weight

When an article of cargo is not blocked or positioned to prevent movement in the forward direction, and the item is longer than 10 feet (3.1 m) in length, then it must be secured by two tie-downs for the first 10 feet (3.1 m) of length, and one additional tie-down for every 10 feet (3.1 m) of length, or fraction thereof, beyond the first 10 feet (3.1 m). For example, if an article is blocked, braced, or immobilized to prevent movement in the forward direction by a headerboard, bulkhead, other articles that are adequately secured, or other appropriate means, then it must be secured by at least one tie-down for every 10 feet (3.1 m) of article length, or fraction thereof.

Special Rule for Special-Purpose Vehicles

Generally, the basic rules concerning the minimum number of tie-downs do not apply to a vehicle transporting one or more articles of cargo such as machinery or fabricated structural items (e.g., steel or concrete beams, crane booms, girders, and trusses, etc.) which, because of their design, size, shape, or weight, must be fastened by special methods. However, any article of cargo carried on that vehicle must be secured adequately to the vehicle by devices that are capable of meeting the performance requirements and the working load limit requirements.

Commodity-Specific Securement Requirements

FMCSA has adopted detailed requirements for the securement of logs, dressed lumber, metal coils, paper rolls, concrete pipe, intermodal containers, automobiles, light trucks and vans, heavy vehicles, equipment and machinery, flattened or crushed vehicles, roll-on/roll-off containers, and large boulders.

Logs—the rules for the transportation of logs are applicable to the transportation of almost all logs **(see Figure 25-6)** with the following exceptions:

1. Logs that are unitized by banding or other comparable means may be transported in accordance with the general cargo securement rules.
2. Loads that consist of no more than four processed logs may be transported in accordance with the general cargo securement rules.
3. Firewood, stumps, log debris, and other such short logs must be transported in a vehicle or container enclosed on both sides, front, and rear and be of adequate strength to contain them. Longer logs may also be transported in an enclosed vehicle or container.

▶ **Figure 25-6**

Pole trailers carry long narrow loads, such as logs, poles, timbers, girders, or concrete beams.

Dressed lumber and similar building products—the rules in this section apply to the transportation of bundles of dressed lumber, packaged lumber, and building products such as plywood, gypsum board, or other materials of similar shape. Lumber or building products that are not bundled or packaged must be treated as loose items and transported in accordance with the general cargo securement rules. The term *bundle* refers to packages of lumber, building materials, or similar products that are unitized for securement as a single article of cargo.

▶ **Figure 25-7**

Cargo must be secured to prevent shifting or falling during transit.

▶ **Figure 25-8**

Intermodal container.

▶ **Figure 25-9**

Auto carrier.

Metal coils—the rules in this section apply to the transportation of one or more metal coils that, individually or grouped together, weigh 5,000 lb (2,268 kg) or more **(see Figure 25-7)**. Shipments of metal coils that weigh less than 5,000 lb (2,268 kg) may be secured in accordance with the general cargo securement rules.

Paper rolls—the rules for securing paper rolls are applicable to shipments of paper rolls that, individually or together, weigh 5,000 lb (2,268 kg) or more. Shipments of paper rolls that weigh less than 5,000 lb (2,268 kg), and paper rolls that are unitized on a pallet, may either be secured in accordance with the rules in this section or the general cargo securement rules.

Concrete pipe—the rules in this section apply to the transportation of concrete pipe on flatbed trailers and vehicles and lowboy trailers. Concrete pipe that is bundled tightly together into a single rigid article with no tendency to roll, and concrete pipe loaded in a sided vehicle or container, must be secured in accordance with the general rules.

Intermodal containers—the requirements for intermodal containers cover the transportation of these containers on container chassis and other types of vehicles. Intermodal containers are freight containers designed and constructed to permit them to be used interchangeably in two or more modes of transportation **(see Figure 25-8)**. Cargo contained within intermodal containers must be secured in accordance with the general cargo securement rules or, if applicable, the commodity-specific rules.

Automobiles, light trucks, and vans—this portion of the new standards applies to the transportation of automobiles, light trucks, and vans that individually weigh 10,000 lb (4,536 kg) or less. Vehicles which individually are heavier than 10,000 lb (4,536 kg) must be secured in the same manner as heavy vehicles, equipment, and machinery **(see Figure 25-9)**.

Heavy vehicles, equipment, and machinery—these requirements are applicable to the transportation of heavy vehicles, equipment, and machinery that operate on wheels or tracks, such as front-end loaders, bulldozers, tractors, and power shovels and that individually weigh 10,000 lb (4,536 kg) or more. Vehicles, equipment, and machinery lighter than 10,000 lb (4,536 kg) may be secured in accordance with these rules; the rules for automobiles, light trucks, and vans; or the general freight requirements **(see Figure 25-10)**.

Flattened or crushed vehicles—the transportation of vehicles such as automobiles, light trucks, and vans that have been flattened or crushed is covered by these requirements. The transportation of automobiles that are flattened or crushed in a crash or accident, as opposed to being intentionally flattened or crushed in preparation for transportation to recycling facilities, is not subject to these requirements. However, vehicles damaged in a crash or accident are subject to the general cargo securement requirements.

Roll-on/roll-off or hook-lift containers—these rules apply to the transportation of roll-on/roll-off or hook-lift containers. A hook-lift container is a specialized container, primarily used to contain and transport materials in the waste, recycling, construction/demolition, and scrap industries, which is used in conjunction with specialized vehicles in which the container is loaded and unloaded onto a tilt frame body by an articulating hook arm. Hoist-type equipment should be considered separate and distinct from roll-on/roll-off equipment. Containers transported on hoist-type equipment must be secured in accordance with the general securement rules.

Large boulders—the rules in this section are applicable to the transportation of any large piece of natural, irregularly shaped rock weighing in excess of 11,000 lb (5,000 kg) or with a volume in excess of 70 cubic feet (2 cubic meters) on an

▶ **Figure 25-10**
Trucks are used to haul heavy equipment such as bulldozers and front-end loaders.

▶ **Figure 25-11**
A cargo of boulders requires heavy-duty chains for securement.

open vehicle, or in a vehicle whose sides are not designed and rated to contain such cargo. Pieces of rock weighing more than 220 lb (100 kg), but less than 11,000 lb (5,000 kg) must be secured, either in accordance with this section or in accordance with the general cargo securement rules, including (1) rock contained within a vehicle which is designed to carry such cargo; or (2) secured individually by tie-downs, provided each piece can be stabilized and adequately secured. Rock which has been formed or cut to a shape and which provides a stable base for securement must also be secured, either in accordance with the provisions of this section or in accordance with the general securement rules (**see Figure 25-11**).

IMPORTANCE OF HANDLING CARGO PROPERLY

Without a doubt, carrying goods safely and efficiently is the backbone of this nation's trucking industry. Americans rely on trucks to carry goods from manufacturers to the retail outlet in the shortest time possible. This reliance also includes delivering the merchandise safely and in the best condition.

Today's tractor-trailer rigs are designed to safely carry maximum payloads built of strong, lightweight materials. To make good use of this equipment, professional drivers know how to protect their vehicles—and their cargo—from costly damage.

FMCSR 393 states that no person shall drive a commercial motor vehicle unless the vehicle's cargo is properly distributed and adequately secured. No company, by law, should ever allow you to drive your vehicle unless the cargo is properly distributed and adequately secured.

The only protection you and your company have against liability for cargo claims is your professionalism and your skill as a professional driver. All too often most preventable cargo claims result from inadequate concern or effort on the part of the driver.

ACCEPTING AND LOADING FREIGHT

When you accept freight for your trailer, you become responsible for safely delivering the load in good condition (**see Figure 25-12**).

Always inspect cargo for:

- The condition of the packages
- Any leaky contents
- Broken pallets or torn shrinkwrap
- The proper container for the material
- Proper quantities as listed on the shipping documents
- Compatibility with the other freight
- Identification marks and addresses
- Weight: will the rig be overweight?
- Identification of any hazardous materials
- Any packages marked "glass" or "fragile"

Bring any damage or inaccurate counts to the shipper's attention at once. Usually there is a company policy on accepting such shipments. Contact your supervisor when in doubt about accepting any shipment.

Loading Cargo

Always put the tractor in gear and put on the parking brake when loading or unloading. Never attempt to load freight on your trailer without the proper tools. Some common tools for loading cargo are described in the sections that follow.

Forklifts—are used for loading pallets or heavy objects (**see Figure 25-13**). Occupational Safety and Health Administration (OSHA) laws require that forklift operators become certified on the individual type of forklift they operate. Never operate a forklift for which you are not certified.

▶ **Figure 25-12**

The driver is responsible for delivering his or her load in good condition.

▶ **Figure 25-13**

Operate only forklifts on which you have been personally trained and certified. It is an OSHA (Occupational Safety and Health Administration) regulation.

Pallet jacks—are used for loading palletized cargo. They are similar to the forklift, only smaller. Use the same safety rules as when operating a forklift:

- Do not operate unless you are qualified to do so.
- Make sure the equipment is rated to handle the load.
- Check your overhead clearance.
- Operate the equipment carefully.
- Use dockboards to bridge between the loading dock and the trailer.
- Do not damage the freight with the equipment.
- Do not raise freight higher than necessary.
- Avoid tilting the load. You might drop the freight.
- Do not damage the trailer.

INTERESTING FACT

The first forklift was introduced to the United States in 1917 by Clark, a Michigan axle manufacturing company. Originally the forklift resembled a tractor with a detachable platform. With additional manufacturers, the forklift soon became battery operated. As time passed, more manufacturers of forklifts began to compete to bring new specifications to the invention. For example, the 1960s brought about the introduction of electronic controls, and in the 1980s Toyota and Nissan were some of the top sellers of forklifts.

PREPARING THE WORK AREA FOR USING A FORKLIFT FOR LOADING/UNLOADING

NOTE: Some terminals, warehouses, and docks have special procedures for loading and unloading. Make sure you are familiar with any site-specific rules for loading/unloading.

- Set the vehicle's brakes up.
- Chock the vehicle's wheels.
- Install fixed jacks to support a semi-trailer that is not coupled to a tractor to prevent it from upending.
- Post signs warning not to move a vehicle.
- Check that the height of the vehicle's entrance door clears the forklift height by at least 5 cm (2 in.).
- Make sure floors can support the combined weight of the forklift and the load.
- Inspect interior of a vehicle for the following: trash, loose objects, and obstructions; holes or weak floors; poor lighting; and low overhead clearance.
- Install anti-slipping material in any area that could be a hazard because of weather conditions.
- Ensure that docks and dock plates are clear of obstructions and not oily or wet.
- Protect gaps and drop-offs at loading docks.
- Use dock levelers.

What should you do to load (unload) vehicles using a forklift truck?

- Keep forks pointed downhill when traveling without a load on a ramp.
- Keep forks pointed uphill when traveling with a load on a ramp **(see Figure 25-14).**

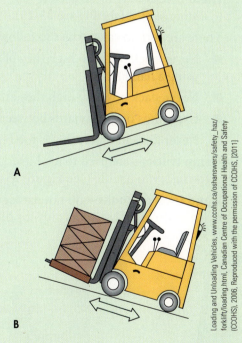

Loading and Unloading Vehicles, www.ccohs.ca/oshanswers/safety_haz/forklift/loading.html, Canadian Centre of Occupational Health and Safety (CCOHSI), 2006, Reproduced with the permission of CCOHS), [2011]

▶ **Figure 25-14**

Professional drivers should be aware of proper and safe forklift operations for uphill and downhill loading or unloading situations.

(Continues)

PREPARING THE WORK AREA FOR USING A FORKLIFT FOR LOADING/UNLOADING *(continued)*

■ Stay clear of edges of docks, rail cars, or ramps. Have edges clearly marked.

■ Do not tow or push railway cars or trucks with a forklift.

■ Do not operate forklifts inside vehicles for long periods without ventilation.

■ Make sure that the dock plate is properly secured and can support the load before driving over it. (Load weight should be clearly marked.)

■ Drive carefully and slowly over the plate. Do not spin wheels.

Source: Information provided by the Canadian Centre for Occupational Health & Safety.

Cranes and hoists—are often used to load cargo. Watch for the following details to avoid injury or cargo damage:

■ Check the load rating of winches, cables, chains, and so on.

■ Never exceed the rated load.

■ Do not stand under raised cargo.

■ Provide protection in case the chain or cable breaks and whips around.

■ Never drop freight on your trailer.

Hand trucks—are often used to carry small loads from the trailer to a storage area **(see Figure 25-15).**

There are certain safety rules to follow when using them:

■ Never stack boxes so high they obstruct your vision when using a hand truck.

■ Never stack boxes so high they are apt to topple over.

■ Use ramps or dockboards between the trailer and the dock.

■ Never load an object that is too big for the hand truck.

Carton truck   Utility truck

© Cengage Learning 2013

▶ **Figure 25–15**

Hand trucks make carrying small loads easier.

Drum trucks—are used to load drums. Secure the locking strap and do not try to move a drum that is too heavy to handle **(see Figure 25-16).**

Hand tools or hooks—do not damage the outside packaging when using these tools. Learn to identify fragile cargo. Use tools only for the purpose for which they were designed.

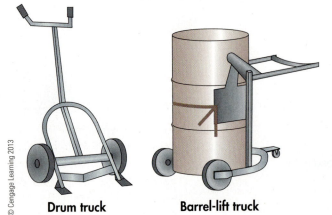

© Cengage Learning 2013

Drum truck   **Barrel-lift truck**

▶ **Figure 25–16**

Use a drum truck to move a drum too heavy to lift.

FUNDAMENTALS IN HANDLING CARGO

The following steps should be used in handling cargo:

Step One: Inspecting and Securing Cargo

1. The inspection process begins while cargo is being loaded.
2. It continues as part of your pretrip inspection—checking for overloads, poorly distributed and balanced weight, and cargo that is not properly secured.
3. Check again after you have driven 25 miles (40 km) from the originating dock or terminal, which is a federal regulation, so adjustments are needed.
4. Check again every 3 hours or every 150 miles (241 km) that you drive.
5. Check every time you take a break during your trip.

Step Two: Loading Cargo

Before loading, look at the floor of the trailer and make certain there are no nails, splinters, or other obstacles that could damage the cargo. In vans, make certain the floor and walls are clean and dry.

As any cargo is loaded onto a trailer, the weight of the total cargo must be evenly distributed between all the axles.

It is the driver's responsibility not to overload the vehicle. Check the legal weight limit where you are, because all states have maximum gross vehicle and axle weights. As you review legal cargo weights, it is important to know the following terms:

Gross vehicle weight (GVW)—is the total weight of a single vehicle and its load.

Gross combination weight (GCW)—is the total weight of a powered unit, its trailer, and its load, such as a loaded tractor-trailer.

Gross combination vehicle weight rating (GCVWR)—is the maximum specified by the manufacturer for a specific combination of vehicles and their loads.

Center of gravity—is the point where weight acts as a force; it affects the vehicle's stability.

Axle weight—weight transmitted to the ground by one axle or one set of axles. Axle weight is not how much axles themselves weigh; axles support the vehicle and its load.

Tire load—maximum weight a tire can carry safely at a certain tire pressure. This information is stamped on the side of the tire. If tires are overinflated or underinflated, this rating may no longer apply and, thus, an underinflated or overinflated tire may not carry the same load safely that it could with the right inflation pressure.

Suspension systems—all have a manufacturer's weight/capacity rating. The manufacturer states how much weight these parts can carry safely.

Coupling device capacity—all coupling devices are rated by the manufacturer for the weight they can safely carry.

Bridge weight—because bridges can handle only so much weight at any one point, some states have bridge laws—a formula used to determine how much weight is put on any point of the bridge by any group of axles, like one set of tandems. If the vehicle has more than one set of tandems, the formula takes into account how close the sets of axles are to each other. The resulting maximum axle weight for axles that are closer together may be lower for each axle in the group.

INTERESTING FACT

The first 4-direction wooden shipping pallet was devised by Robert Braun in 1945. In 1948, Sullivan Stemple made a wooden pallet that was compatible with forklifts.

▶ **Figure 25-17**

Heavy load.

© Cengage Learning 2013

Balancing the Load

Some people in the trucking business have a sixth sense about how to achieve a balanced load. Others follow a specific formula and still others simply learn from experience.

Distribute the weight of the cargo over all axles and remember the center of gravity factor. You should put the load's center of gravity where it has the most support.

The height of the vehicle's center of gravity is important for safe handling of that vehicle. If cargo is piled high on or in the trailer or if heavy cargo is on top, this high center of gravity will cause the rig to tip over. This is especially true on curves or if you have to suddenly swerve to avoid an accident or a hazard.

It is best to distribute the weight of the load over all axles and keep the center of gravity as low as possible. Load the heaviest parts of the cargo under the lightest parts **(see Figure 25-17).**

Picture your empty vehicle sitting on level ground. Remember that the weight should be distributed over all the axles, including the front axles under the cab. Draw a line from wheel to wheel. When the center of gravity is over the center of this rectangle, the vehicle will be most stable.

Importance of Balanced Weight

- A poorly balanced load will make the vehicle tough to handle and unsafe.
- Too much weight on the steering axle makes the vehicle difficult to steer and can damage the steering axle and tires.
- Underweight front axles can make the steering axle weight too light, creating problems in steering safely.
- Too little weight on the driving axles indicates poor traction (in bad weather it will be difficult for the truck to keep going).
- If the center of gravity is too high, the possibility of rollover increases.
- If the center of gravity is too high on a flatbed load, it will shift to the side and may fall off.

STOP!

Oversized loads usually require special permits, may be allowed on certain roads only at certain times, and may be asked to take "irregular" routes rather than usual interstate routes. Some oversized loads are required to have escorts, either those provided by the carrier (a pilot car) or the police.

Step Three: Securing Cargo

Proper loading is an important part of moving freight safely and efficiently from one point to another. Securing the cargo is equally important for the same reasons: safety and efficiency.

Following are step-by-step guidelines for properly securing all types of loads:

In the Cargo Compartment

- **Bracing** is a method that prevents movement of the cargo in the trailer or any other cargo compartment. When you brace a load, you use various elements to steady the load, from the upper part of the cargo to the floor. You also place braces on the walls of the compartment to minimize movement (**see Figure 25-18**).

- **Blocking** is another method, used in front, in back, and/or on the sides of a piece of cargo to keep it from sliding in the trailer. Blocking is usually shaped to fit tightly against and around the cargo and then is secured to the deck of the trailer to prevent the cargo from moving (**see Figure 25-19**).

- **Load locks** are long poles that stretch from wall to wall in a trailer. These should be at the rear of the load to prevent cargo from falling. Place one at the top and another halfway down.

NOTE

Because loaded locks put pressure on the walls or roof of a trailer, the walls and roof tend to give. Load locks have been known to fall because other load locks have affected the fit of the load lock. Beware of possible falling load locks during installation.

▶ **Figure 25-19**

Time taken to correctly block and brace cargo prior to departure will save valuable time later.

Action Load Locking Bars for Vans

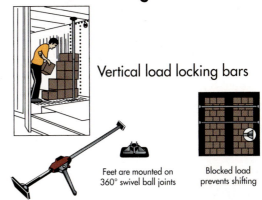

Vertical load locking bars

Feet are mounted on 360° swivel ball joints

Blocked load prevents shifting

Horizontal load locking bars

Horizontal load locking hoops
(Slip over the ends of lock bars above)

© Cengage Learning 2013

▶ **Figure 25-18**

Federal regulations (FMCSR 393.100) set standards for securing cargo with various devices.

Material blocked and braced in a van trailer

Right

Wrong

© Cengage Learning 2013

CAUTION!

When loading pallets, make certain the pallets do not lean. Each should be placed tightly against the one ahead or in front of it. Leave space between rows of pallets and between pallets and the walls of the trailer.

On the Flatbed Trailer

- Tie-downs are used to keep cargo from moving in closed trailers and flatbed trailers without sides. This secures the cargo, preventing it from shifting and/or eventually falling off the trailer. To use tie-downs to secure cargo, they must be of the right type and the right strength. Tying down a mammoth turbine with kite string will not secure the cargo.

CAUTION!

As a rule, the combined strength of all cargo tie-downs must be strong enough to lift one-and-one-half times the weight of the cargo that is to be tied down.

- Proper tie-down equipment includes ropes, straps, and chains.
- Tension devices used in tie-downs include winches, ratchets, and cinching components.
- All tie-downs regardless of material should be attached correctly to the vehicle, using hooks, bolts, rails, and rings (**see Figure 25-20**).

Type	Advantages	Disadvantages
Nylon rope	Easily installed and adjusted	Stretches and becomes loose
Wire rope	Very strong	Difficult to handle
Web (nylon) straps	Strong, lightweight, easily adjusted	May become frayed or cut by sharp edges
	May be used with ratchet or winch assemblies	Sunlight rots nylon fiber
	Inexpensive and easy to store	May not be used to secure steel machinery or certain metal products
Steel straps	Good for securing boxes on pallets or wooden crates on vehicle	No means of adjustment during transport
		Vibration can cause failure
		Straps over 1 inch wide (2.5 cm) need two pairs of crimps
		May cut into cargo and become loose
Hooks and chains	Strong and durable	May damage cargo if too tight
	Readily available	Not of equal strength for rated load
	Hooks may be replaced and easily checked	

© Cengage Learning 2013

▶ **Figure 25–20**

Evaluation of tie-down devices.

- According to the new securement standards, the following applies to all tie-downs:
    1. Tie-downs and securing devices must not contain knots.
    2. If a tie-down is repaired, it must be repaired in accordance with the applicable standards or the manufacturer's instructions.
    3. Each tie-down must be attached and secured in a manner that prevents it from becoming loose, unfastening, opening, or releasing while the vehicle is in transit.
    4. All tie-downs and other components of a cargo securement system used to secure loads on a trailer equipped with rub rails, must be located inboard of the rub rails whenever practicable.
    5. Edge protection must be used when a tie-down would be subject to abrasion or cutting at the point where it touches an article of cargo. The edge protection must resist abrasion, cutting, and crushing.

CAUTION!

Each tie-down, or its associated connectors or attachment mechanisms, must be designed, constructed, and maintained so the driver of an intransit commercial motor vehicle can tighten them. However, this requirement does not apply to the use of steel strapping.

MANUFACTURING STANDARDS FOR TIE-DOWN ASSEMBLIES

An Assembly	Must Conform to Component of
Steel strapping[1,2]	Standard Specification for Strapping, Flat Steel and Seals, American Society for Testing and Materials (ASTM) D3953-97, February 1998[4]
Chain	National Association of Chain Manufacturers' Welded Steel Chain Specifications, November 15, 1999[4]
Webbing	Web Sling and Tie Down Association's Recommended Standard Specification for Synthetic Web Tie Downs, WSTDA-T1, 1998[4]
Wire rope[3]	Wire Rope Technical Board's *Wire Rope User's Manual*, 2nd edition, November 1985[4]
Cordage	Cordage Institute rope standard: 1. PETRS-2, Polyester Fiber Rope, 3-Strand and 8-Strand Constructions, January 1993[4] 2. PPRS-2, Polypropylene Fiber Rope, 3-Strand and 8-Strand Constructions, August 1992[4] 3. CRS-1, Polyester/Polypropylene Composite Rope Specifications, 3-Strand and 8-Strand Standard Construction, May 1979[4] 4. NRS-1, Nylon Rope Specifications, 3-Strand and 8-Strand Standard Construction, May 1979[4] 5. C-1, Double Braided Nylon Rope Specifications DBN, January 1984[4]

[1]Steel strapping not marked by the manufacturer with a working load limit will be considered to have a working load limit equal to one-fourth of the breaking strength listed in ASTM D3953-97.

[2]Steel strapping 1 inch (25.4 mm) or wider must have at least two pairs of crimps in each seal and, when an end-over-end lap joint is formed, must be sealed with at least two seals.

[3]Wire rope which is not marked by the manufacturer with a working load limit shall be considered to have a working load limit equal to one-fourth of the nominal strength listed in the manual.

[4]See 393.7 for information on the incorporation by reference and availability of this document.

The law also specifies:

1. The minimum number of tie-downs required to secure an article or group of articles against movement depends on the length of the article(s) being secured.

2. When an article is not blocked or positioned to prevent movement in the forward direction by a headerboard, bulkhead, other cargo that is positioned to prevent movement, or other appropriate blocking devices, it must be secured by at least:

   ■ One tie-down for articles 5 feet (1.5 m) or less in length, and 1,100 lb (500 kg) or less in weight.

   ■ Two tie-downs if the article is 5 feet (1.5 m) or less in length and more than 1,100 lb (500 kg) in weight or longer than 5 feet (1.5 m) but less than or equal to 10 feet (3.1 m) in length, irrespective of the weight.

   ■ Two tie-downs if the article is longer than 10 feet (3.1 m), and one additional tie-down for every 10 feet (3.1 m) of article length, or fraction thereof, beyond the first 10 feet (3.1 m) of length.

   If an individual article is required to be blocked, braced, or immobilized to prevent movement in the forward direction by a headerboard, bulkhead, other articles that are adequately secured, or an appropriate blocking or immobilization method, it must be secured by at least one tie-down for every 10 feet (3.1 m) or article length, or fraction thereof.

3. Special rule for special-purpose vehicles. The rules in this section do not apply to a vehicle transporting one or more articles of cargo such as, but not limited to, machinery or fabricated structural items (e.g., steel or concrete beams, crane booms, girders, and trusses) which, because of their design, size, shape, or weight, must be fastened by special methods. However, any article of cargo carried on that vehicle must be securely and adequately fastened to the vehicle.

Fundamentals of Cargo Securement

International cargo securement rules are applicable to the transportation of all types of articles of cargo, except commodities in bulk that lack structure or fixed shape (e.g., liquids, gases, grain, liquid concrete, sand, gravel, aggregates) and are transported in a tank, hopper, box, or similar device that forms part of

WORKING LOAD LIMITS (WLL), CHAIN

	WLL in kg (lbs)				
Size mm (inches)	Grade 30 Proof	Grade 43 High Test	Grade 70 Transport	Grade 80 Alloy	Grade 100 Alloy
7 (1/4)	580 (1,300)	1,180 (2,600)	1,430 (3,150)	1,570 (3,500)	1,950 (4,300)
8 (5/16)	860 (1,900)	1,770 (3,900)	2,130 (4,700)	2,000 (4,500)	2,600 (5,700)
10 (3/8)	1,200 (2,650)	2,450 (5,400)	2,990 (6,600)	3,200 (7,100)	4,000 (8,800)
11 (7/16)	1,680 (3,700)	3,270 (7,200)	3,970 (8,750)		
13 (1/2)	2,030 (4,500)	4,170 (9,200)	5,130 (11,300)	5,400 (12,000)	6,800 (1,500)
16 (5/8)	3,130 (6,900)	5,910 (13,500)	7,170 (15,800)	8,200 (18,100)	10,300 (22,600)

Chain Mark Examples					
Example 1	3	4	7	8	10
Example 2	30	43	70	80	100
Example 3	300	430	700	800	1000

Synthetic Webbing

Width mm (in)	WLL kg (lb)
45 (1-3/4)	790 (1,750)
50 (2)	910 (2,000)
75 (3)	1,360 (3,000)
100 (4)	1,810 (4,000)

Wire Rope (6 × 37, Fiber Core)

Diameter mm (in)	WLL kg (lb)
7 (1/4)	640 (1,400)
8 (5/16)	950 (2,100)
10 (3/8)	1,360 (3,000)
11 (7/16)	1,860 (4,100)
13 (1/2)	2,400 (5,300)
16 (5/8)	3,770 (8,300)
20 (3/4)	4,940 (10,900)
22 (7/8)	7,300 (16,100)
25 (1)	9,480 (20,900)

Manila Rope WLL

Diameter mm (in)	WLL kg (lb)
10 (3/8)	90 (205)
11 (7/16)	120 (265)
13 (1/2)	150 (315)
16 (5/8)	210 (465)
20 (3/4)	290 (640)
25 (1)	480 (1,050)

Nylon Rope WLL

Diameter mm (in)	WLL kg (lb)
10 (3/8)	130 (278)
11 (7/16)	190 (410)
13 (1/2)	240 (525)
16 (5/8)	420 (935)
20 (3/4)	640 (1,420)
25 (1)	1,140 (2,520)

Polypropylene Fiber Rope WLL (3-Strand and 8-Strand Constructions)

Diameter mm (in)	WLL kg (lb)
10 (3/8)	180 (400)
11 (7/16)	240 (525)
13 (1/2)	280 (625)
16 (5/8)	420 (925)
20 (3/4)	580 (1,275)
25 (1)	950 (2,100)

Double Braided Nylon Rope WLL

Diameter mm (in)	WLL kg (lb)
10 (3/8)	150 (336)
11 (7/16)	230 (502)
13 (1/2)	300 (655)
16 (5/8)	510 (1,130)
20 (3/4)	830 (1,840)
25 (1)	1,470 (3,250)

Polyester Fiber Rope WLL (3-Strand and 8-Strand Constructions)

Diameter mm (in)	WLL kg (lb)
10 (3/8)	250 (555)
11 (7/16)	340 (750)
13 (1/2)	440 (960)
16 (5/8)	680 (1,500)
20 (3/4)	850 (1,880)
25 (1)	1,500 (3,300)

Steel Strapping WLL

Width × thickness mm (in)	WLL kg (lb)
31.7 × 0.74 (1-1/4 × 0.029)	540 (1,190)
31.7 × 0.79 (1-1/4 × 0.031)	540 (1,190)
31.7 × 0.89 (1-1/4 × 0.035)	540 (1,190)
31.7 × 1.12 (1-1/4 × 0.044)	770 (1,690)
31.7 × 1.27 (1-1/4 × 0.05)	770 (1,690)
31.7 × 1.5 (1-1/4 × 0.057)	870 (1,925)
50.8 × 1.12 (2 × 0.044)	1,200 (2,650)
50.8 × 1.27 (2 × 0.05)	1,200 (2,650)

the structure of a commercial motor vehicle. The commodity-specific rules take precedence over the general requirements of this section when additional requirements are given for a commodity listed in those sections.

General—cargo must be firmly immobilized or secured on or within a vehicle by structures of adequate strength, dunnage or dunnage bags, shoring bars, tie-downs, or a combination of these.

Cargo placement and restraint—cargo likely to roll must be restrained by chocks, wedges, a cradle, or other equivalent means to prevent rolling. The means of preventing rolling must not be capable of becoming unintentionally unfastened or loose while the vehicle is in transit.

Articles or cargo placed beside each other and secured by transverse tie-downs must either be placed in direct contact with each other or be prevented from shifting toward each other while in transit.

Minimum strength of cargo securement devices and systems—the total working load limit of any securement system used to secure an article or group of articles against movement must be at least one-half times the weight of the article or group of articles. The total working load limit is the sum of:

- One-half of the working load limit of each associated connector or attachment mechanism used to secure a part of the article of cargo to the vehicle, and
- One-half of the working load limit for each end section of a tie-down that is attached to an anchor point.

Covered Cargo: What You Should Know

In the past, when you have seen an 18-wheeler pulling big cargo pieces on a flatbed trailer, you probably thought it was covered to keep it clean. According to regulations, cargo is covered for two reasons: (1) to protect people from spilled cargo, and (2) to protect the cargo from the weather. In some states, the cargo must be covered to prevent spills. Find out what the covering rules are in the states where you will be running.

Tarps

Tarps (tarpaulins) are used to protect cargo **(see Figure 25-21).** Tarps are used to cover most freight and are tied down with rope, webbing, or elastic hooks. Be sure to have enough tarps to cover a load measuring $8 \times 14 \times 42$ feet ($2.4 \times 4.3 \times 12.8$ m).

Spill Protection
- To protect public
- To meet state law requirements

Cargo Protection
- To prevent corrosion or other weather damage
- Company can be liable for ruined cargo
- Use tarp when needed
- Make sure tarp does not leak
- Make sure tarp is tied properly so it will not tear or leak

© Cengage Learning 2013

▶ **Figure 25–21**
Cargo covers.

STOP!

Remember, it is always better to buy protection with tarping than to pay a damage claim.

Worn tarps or tarps with holes offer little or no protection. Make sure to inspect your tarps regularly to ensure that they will be functional when needed. If you do not have enough tarps to protect your load, contact your supervisor.

In some states, the cargo must be covered to prevent spills. Find out what the covering rules are in the states where you will be running.

To tarp a load—lift the rolled-up tarp to the top of the front racks; then, unroll it over the bars to the back of the truck bed. Pull it tight. Tie it to cross bars on the rack. If the tarp is placed over the cargo tightly and evenly, it will not flap (**see Figure 25-22).**

To tarp a load that is uneven or of irregular shape—place the tarp on the cargo after the tie-down assemblies are tight. Then tie down the tarp to prevent wind and weather damage. Longer ropes may be needed to tie down irregular configurations. Overlapping the front will help keep wind and weather out.

To "smoke tarp" a load on a flatbed—cover the front part of the load to keep exhaust from smokestacks from discoloring the load.

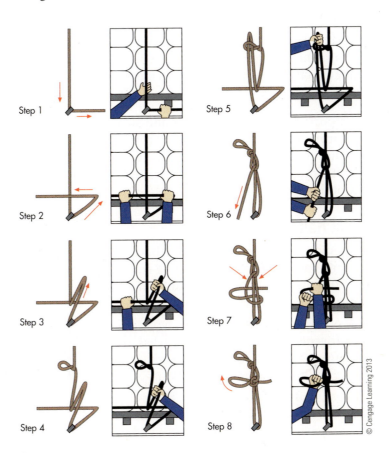

© Cengage Learning 2013

▶ **Figure 25-22**

Truckers draw hitch.

While on the road, professional drivers check the covering on a load every 150 miles (241 km) of driving or more frequently. When a cover pulls free, uncovers the cargo, and is flapping in the wind as your trailer pulls down the highway, you should stop and reattach it immediately so that the cover will not fly off and block your vision or someone else's.

Never secure tarp edges to the outside of the trailer rub rail. This allows grime and moisture to seep under the tarp.

CAUTION!

Winds can be dangerous when installing tarps, so always:

1. Consider the wind direction.
2. Consider the strength of the wind or expected gusts.
3. Secure tarps in a sequence that minimizes risks.
4. Get help and avoid injury.

Loading Flatbed Loads

If a crane or forklift is to be used in placing or unloading a heavy piece of freight, place loose packing material (called dunnage) under the load. This will allow the forklift at the receiving dock or destination to get under the load without a problem.

Sealed and Containerized Loads

Container traffic—cargo that is placed in a container and sealed to be carried as part of its journey by rail or ship—is a fast-growing component of the U.S. freight business. Some shippers prefer containerized shipments because they are often easier to handle and more secure, especially if the cargo is traveling by ship or rail.

Containers, once they reach port, are loaded onto trucks and are on their way to the end user. Containers may also be transported from manufacturer or shipper from the shipper's location to the loading dock for rail or transocean movement. Some containers have their own tie-downs that attach to a special frame for container loads. Others are loaded onto flatbed trailers and are secured with tie-downs every 2 feet (0.6 m), just like any other cargo.

Cargo Requiring Special Handling

Dry bulk tanks—like liquid tankers, dry bulk tankers have a high center of gravity, which means the driver will use special care, particularly when rounding curves and entering or exiting a freeway by using a freeway ramp. With the dry bulk tanker or any tanker, always drive at a speed well under that posted on curves, ramps, and in any kind of weather.

Swinging meat—a side of beef or any other meat can be extremely unstable, hanging in a refrigerated trailer (reefer). It also has a high center of gravity **(see Figure 25-23)**. Drive under the speed limit and use care on curves, turns, ramps, and in bad weather.

Livestock—hauling live animals such as beef, hogs, horses, sheep, and goats creates the same problems as liquid loads, and adds a few additional challenges. Livestock trailers always have a high center of gravity. Live animals also have a tendency to lean while going around a curve; and this creates a problem similar to the liquid surge found in liquid tanks.

▶ **Figure 25-23**

Cargo, such as meat hanging in a refrigerated trailer, requires special handling.

If you do not have a full load, use portable bulkheads to keep the animals from moving around. The tighter the animals are packed, the less movement.

Remember the "nose factor." When parked in a truckstop or roadside rest area, remember to park downwind or, because of the odor, you will accumulate many enemies.

Step Four: Driving with a Load

The high center of gravity associated with some trailers and the way cargo is loaded has already been covered. Remember when you are loaded and have a high center of gravity to give yourself plenty of time and room to stop, plus drive slowly on curves, entrance ramps, exit ramps, and turns.

When You Are Loaded

- A heavy load gives you better traction, which means you can stop better.
- A light load does not give good traction. You may be able to move faster but it also takes more distance to stop this type of vehicle.
- Poor distribution of cargo weight makes axles too light, which makes it easier to skid.

When You Are Turning

- A loaded trailer puts more weight on the axles, including the steering axle. The heavier the weight on the steering axle, the more difficult the rig will be to steer.
- Too much weight on the rear axles means not enough weight on the steering axle. This decreases steering control.

Driving Banks and Curves

- A load with a high center of gravity will make driving banks and curves more hazardous.
- If the cargo is loaded incorrectly with a high center of gravity, the vehicle will tip on a steep bank or curve. The same will happen if cargo is unbalanced when it is loaded.
- If you are driving a flatbed on a bank or curve and your cargo is not secure, it may shift or fall off on a curve or steep bank.
- If you are hauling hanging sides of meat, suspended from rails in the trailer, the swinging caused by the motion of the trailer may cause a problem. As the meat swings more and more, the sides of meat build momentum, which can make the vehicle very unstable, especially on curves and ramps.
- If you are hauling dry bulk, then you will be driving a tanker that has a high center of gravity because of its design. Sometimes on curves and sharp turns or ramps, the load will shift, creating a dangerous situation.

Driving Upgrades and Downgrades

- A properly secured load will not cause problems, but any time a vehicle is loaded, it will perform differently on upgrades and downgrades (**see Figure 25-24**).
- If the truck is overloaded, it will navigate a hill very slowly. If possible, use a climbing lane. Otherwise, be aware of traffic behind you and other drivers who may be apt to tailgate your vehicle.

▶ **Figure 25-24**

A fully loaded vehicle will perform differently on upgrades or downgrades than on a level highway.

- On a downgrade, the vehicle that is loaded will pick up momentum at a greater rate than the same unloaded vehicle. If your speed on the downgrade becomes excessive, use your brakes; but remember that trying to slow or stop a loaded vehicle going at a high speed on a downgrade may cause brake failure, a common accident and one that is easily prevented.

Dunnage—this softer packing material is often used to secure cargo and keeps water-sensitive cargo from making contact with the trailer floor. When using dunnage, place it in such a manner to support the total weight of the cargo you are securing.

Friction mats—placed on the deck or between cargo, these must provide resistance against forward movement equal to 50 percent of the weight of the cargo resting on it.

Wooden restraints—ash, beech, elm, hickory, hard sugar maple, and oak are used as blocks, braces, chocks, cradles, dunnages, and wedges to prevent rolling or as high-pressure restraints. The wood must be strong enough to withstand being split or crushed by the cargo or tie-down. Their working load limit is required to be 50 percent or greater than the weight of the material to stop it from moving forward.

Step Five: Cargo Responsibilities

The Shipper's Responsibility

Whether the shipper is the originator or the pass-through for a shipment, the shipper is responsible for packing and loading the cargo in a manner that will ensure safe transportation. The shipper is also responsible for determining whether any protective devices are required to ensure safe transport of the shipment.

Once the driver has had an opportunity to size up the load—and if the driver sees the packaging or protective devices for any shipment as inadequate—the driver should call the driver manager or dispatcher for help in resolving the problem. Under no circumstances should the driver argue with the shipper about how they have packaged or loaded the merchandise.

The Driver's Responsibility

Although many drivers do not load or supervise the loading of the trailers they pull, they are still responsible for checking to see that all cargos are properly secured (**see Figure 25-25**).

When loading cargo, the driver is responsible for:

- Preparing the bill of lading if one has not been provided by the shipper
- Counting the cargo—and making sure the count matches the shipper's count (Never assume the count is correct until you have counted the cargo yourself.)

▶ Figure 25-25

When you accept freight, you become responsible for the safe delivery of that shipment.

- Inspecting the cargo (Do not assume preloaded cargo is undamaged. If inspection is not possible, notify the safety department or the dispatcher where you work.)
- Recording the condition of the cargo (If the cargo is in perfect condition or is less than perfect, record it on the bill of lading and notify your dispatcher. When necessary, take photos of the shipment. An accurate description and photos of preexisting damage helps reduce your liability in the event of a claim.)

It is fairly easy to make a visual check if cargo is loaded on a flatbed or open trailer. If an enclosed van has locking security seals, a more creative method for checking the load is required. When you check your cargo, include:

- A visual check of the springs and tires of your tractor and trailer for signs of overloading
- Checking for any sagging or bowing of the trailer, which is also a sign of overload
- Awareness of whether you have enough power to move the rig
- General handling characteristics of the rig
- Checking for any leaks that could indicate damaged cargo
- Figuring the weight of the load by adding all weights shown on shipping papers

If the trailer is an open type or a van without seals or restricted access, the driver is responsible for checking the load for:

- **Weight distribution**—heavy items loaded close together
- Heavy freight loaded high in the trailer or positioned where it could fall on other cargo during transport
- Fragile or hazardous material
- Loose freight not properly secured by holding devices or dunnage
- Materials not compatible
- Regulated or restricted materials

The driver is also responsible for checking all parts necessary for hauling, containing, and protecting cargo. These may include:

- Tailgates
- Tailboards
- Doors
- Headerboards
- Tarps

The Consignee's Responsibility

The consignee (or receiver) of the freight is responsible for unloading, counting, and inspecting cargo. They are then responsible for noting any overages, shortages, or damages on the delivery receipt. To signify they have received the shipment, consignees must also sign your delivery receipt. Do not refuse to allow them to note any cargo damages, shortages, or overages on the delivery receipt.

VEHICLE WEIGHT

Limits on the weight and size of vehicles vary from state to state, and some have lower limits than others. Check the size and weight regulations for each state you will drive through. (Thomson Delmar Learning publishes a handy reference, *Trucking Rules and Regulations,* that lists size and weight regulations by state.)

Violations for your rig being overweight are often expensive and can reflect on your driving record (**see Figure 25-26**).

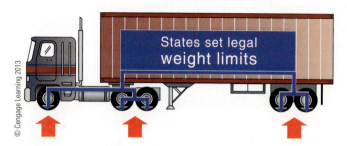

▶ **Figure 25–26**

Each state sets its own weight and length load limits.

NOTE

Most carriers stress that their drivers are personally responsible for every "Over Weight" ticket. If a driver is unsure if the cargo is legal, he or she needs to weigh the vehicle to see if the load is over gross, or if it is misloaded and the trailer tandems need to be slid in order to comply with each state's individual weigh laws.

Inspection officials are permitted to detain an overweight vehicle and may make the driver off-load the cargo or redistribute the weight, in addition to charging the driver with a fine.

STOP!

A rig that is detained for an overload results in great expense for the trucking company. It also means a late delivery to the customer.

Weights are usually checked in the following ways:

Individual wheel weight—usually checked by state or local officials with a portable scale that measures the load on each wheel. Wheel weights are then checked against the permitted load for each tire.

Axle weight—also checked with a portable scale. The weight of each wheel on an axle is recorded. The weights are then added to find the axle weight. At weigh stations, drive each set of axles onto the scale to measure the axle weight.

Combined axle weight—tandem or triple axles can have a different weight per axle as compared to a single axle. To find the total combined axle weight, add the weights of all the axles. You can also find the total weight by driving the entire rig onto the scale platform.

Gross vehicle weight (GVW)—is the total weight of a straight truck and its load.

Gross combination vehicle weight rating (GCVWR)—is the total weight of a tractor, trailer, and load. Local or state officials may check the GCVWR by weighing each wheel or axle individually and adding the total or by having you drive the entire rig onto the platform scale to be weighted as a unit.

More restrictions are placed on short, heavy rigs for wheel, axle, and gross weights, because the total load is distributed over a shorter surface. This increases the stress placed on bridges and other highway structures.

STOP!

If you pull a heavy cargo in an intermodal container on a short trailer or chassis, you may exceed the weight limit for some bridges. Always know your gross vehicle weight.

Some states are testing "smart" weigh stations that electronically weigh trucks that pass over a set of specially-designed sensors.

These types of weigh-in motion sensors are imbedded in the road surface. States use these data to see if a truck is close to the allowable maximum weight. This type of technology is placed in the roadbed prior to arriving at the fixed weigh station and gives personnel working there prior knowledge regarding trucks that are close to their gross weight. These trucks and their loads are then inspected more closely.

Manufacturers' warranties and liabilities may be affected if you exceed the rated weight for each of your rig's components. Limits include the following:

- Tires—maximum load at specified inflation
- Suspension system—maximum for spring assembly
- Axle weight—rated weight for single or combination
- Fifth wheel—maximum pull weight
- GCVWR—recommended gross weight

DISTRIBUTION OF WEIGHT

If cargo weight is not distributed properly, the rig will be harder to handle. Distribution of weight on a tractor depends on the location of the fifth wheel:

- With a single rear axle, the fifth wheel should be slightly in front of the axle.
- With a tandem rear axle and a stationary fifth wheel, weight should be slightly in front of the tandem center line.
- With a tandem rear axle and a sliding fifth wheel, the last notch of the slider adjustment should be just ahead of the tandem center line.

With a movable fifth wheel, move it forward and the load shifts more to the steering axle(s). Move it back and the load shifts to the tractor drive axle(s).

The rig will handle differently, depending on the way you distribute the weight. When the load is moved forward, the rig will handle more easily and will allow for better cornering. If too much weight is shifted forward, you can lose traction on the rear axles and steering will be difficult.

CAUTION!

When you move a load forward, be careful not to exceed the legal weight limits for the front axle.

Weight shifted too far back causes light steering with poor control. It can also overload the drive axles **(see Figure 25-27)**.

Distribution of weight in a trailer is just as important. Distribute the weight of the cargo as evenly as possible between the trailer's rear axle(s) and the tractor's drive axle(s) **(see Figure 25-28)**.

If you are pulling double trailers, center the weight on the converter dolly.

When you load the trailer, be sure to:

- Find out the total weight of the load.
- Load half in front and half in the rear, if possible.

Weight Distribution on Tractor and Trailer

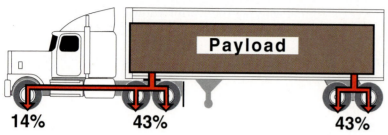

14%   43%   43%

Example of a Well-Balanced Load

Tractor
- Distribute weight properly over axles
- Weight distribution depends on position of fifth wheel
  - Single axle - slightly forward of center line
  - Tandem axle
    - Stationary - just ahead of center line
    - Sliding - last notch of slider adjustment
    - Fifth wheel moved forward
      - More of load shifted to front axle

Trailer
- Divide load evenly between front and rear
- Adjust load to meet axle weight limitations
  - Heavy freight on bottom
  - Properly distributed

▶ **Figure 25–27**

It is the driver's responsibility to see that each load is balanced and weight is distributed evenly over all axles.

▶ **Figure 25–28**

Too much weight on the steering axle can damage the axle and tires and cause hard steering.

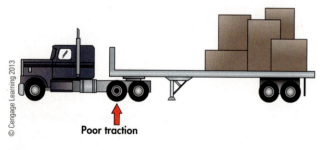

Poor traction

▶ **Figure 25–29**

How cargo is loaded will impact the rig's overall reaction.

- Spread the load evenly over the floor from side to side to prevent shifting.
- Keep heavy freight as low as possible to help keep the rig's center of gravity low.
- Spread out any heavy cargo to prevent concentrated stress on the trailer's floor (**see Figure 25-29**).
- Do not load heavy objects where they can fall on other freight.
- Move the heavy freight as needed to keep the weight evenly distributed after part of the cargo has been unloaded (**see Figure 25-30**).

- The weight can be adjusted in trailers with sliding rear axles by moving the axle.
- Slide the axle forward to shift more weight to the trailer axle and off of the tractor drive axle.
- Slide to the rear position to shift the most weight to the tractor drive axle.

With sliding axles or fifth wheels, be aware of the bridge formula laws that dictate axle spacing. On interstate highways and some state routes, you are required to have certain axle spacing to haul maximum allowable weights.

High Center of Gravity

Some vehicles have a high center of gravity **(see Figure 25-31),** as discussed earlier in this chapter. This means the weight is carried high off the road. Such rigs are top-heavy because they carry hanging loads such as meat, or they carry tiered loads such as livestock or liquid loads in bulk, such as milk or gasoline. These high-center-of-gravity rigs require special skills in handling, loading, and unloading.

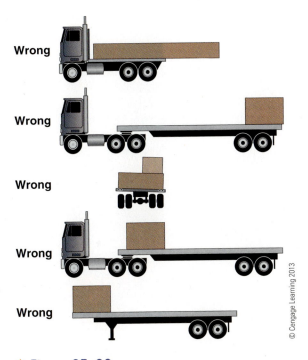

Wrong

Wrong

Wrong

Wrong

Wrong

© Cengage Learning 2013

▶ **Figure 25–30**

Examples of improper weight distributions.

© Cengage Learning 2013

▶ **Figure 25–31**

Tankers have a higher center of gravity.

SUMMARY

In this chapter, you learned why it is important to handle cargo properly. You also learned the professional driver's responsibilities for handling various cargos. You discovered there are laws regarding the way cargo is shipped and how it must be secured. You also know the importance of weight limits and distribution of weight when handling cargo.

KEY TERMS

Axle weight
Blocking
Bracing
Bulkhead
Center of gravity
Chocks
Combined axle weight
Dock board, dock plate

Drum truck
Dunnage
Dunnage bag
Dunnage box
FMCSR 393
Forklift
Gross combination vehicle
    weight rating (GCVWR)

Gross vehicle weight (GVW)
Hand truck
Headerboard
Individual wheel weight
Pallet jacks
Tarps
Tie-downs
Weight distribution

© Cengage Learning 2013

A DAY IN THE LIFE…

Freddie Bell—Epes Transport, Professional Truck Driver

I have been around trucks just about my entire life. My dad drove for many years and I learned everything I know about being safe from him. I started my driving career by driving for my uncle to the west coast. I did this for 6 years and received safe driving awards from that company. I then went to another company and received their Driver of the Year award as well as numerous safety awards.

I have been employed with Epes Transport for 14 years. In all those many years and miles, I have never been involved in a collision, service failure, or had a negative report on a roadside inspection. I have received the company's highest honor of "Top Achiever," which is given for providing on-time service without accidents or out-of-service hours because of service violations for each of the past 13 years. I consider myself a true professional and have been praised by those I work with for my attitude, commitment, and professionalism on and off the road.

I am currently a Lead Driver at one of Epes Transports dedicated operations and am well-respected by both my customers and peers. I oversee several drivers on an account that we have at RJR. I oversee the daily operations for the loads and keep up with the equipment. My professionalism and upbeat attitude are just two of the things I feel make me an asset to the organization as well as the industry.

I try to express safe driving habits with other drivers on a daily basis. I have also done some work in the community to help move disaster relief equipment for the NC Baptist Men's Association. The community I live in had a brush fire and I was one of the first there to help keep the fire from reaching some homes.

When not on the road I enjoy the beach, touring historical cities, and camping with my wife of 15 years, Kelly, and my daughter Brittany. I also love attending NASCAR events with my dad.

> **"I have always strived to be the safest and most courteous driver that I can be . . ."**

I enjoy the work I do daily and feel like I am really making a positive impact on the great industry that I have been involved with for many years. I have always strived to be the safest and most courteous driver that I can be and am constantly looking for ways to help others be safe too.

REVIEW QUESTIONS

1. Properly handling and loading cargo that will avoid damage in transit and add to the operating efficiency of the rig is the responsibility of the _____.

   a. dispatcher
   b. professional driver
   c. shipper
   d. receiver

2. Regarding cargo distribution and securement, FMCSR Section 392 states in part that if the vehicle's cargo is not properly distributed and adequately secured, _____.

   a. the driver cannot be required to drive the load
   b. the driver can decide if he or she drives the load
   c. if the dispatcher says the load is okay the driver must drive
   d. if the shipper says the load is okay the driver must drive

3. FMCSR require drivers of tie-down loads to inspect the load _____.

   a. within the first 25 miles (40 km)
   b. only at the beginning of the trip
   c. each 100 miles (161 km) of the trip
   d. within the first 50 miles (80 km)

4. The North American Securement Standards Model Regulations were developed by _____.

   a. Canada
   b. U.S. and Canada
   c. Mexico, U.S., and Canada
   d. U.S.

5. A device that protects the driver from the freight shifting or crushing him or her during a sudden stop and/or accident is called a _____.

   a. high center of gravity
   b. backboard
   c. headboard
   d. friction board

6. A friction mat placed on the deck or between cargo must provide resistance against forward movement equal to _____ percent of the weight of the cargo resting on it.

   a. 50
   b. 30
   c. 20
   d. at least 20

7. The one responsible for packing and loading cargo in a manner that will ensure safe transportation is the _____.

   a. driver
   b. receiver
   c. shipper
   d. dispatcher

8. Once a driver has an opportunity to evaluate a load, and if the driver sees that packaging or protective devices for the shipment are inadequate, the driver should _____.

   a. have the customer make corrections
   b. call the driver manager or dispatcher
   c. accept the load as the customer presents it
   d. call the federal transportation agency, as inadequate packaging or protective devices is a violation of federal law

9. The one responsible for seeing that all cargos are properly secured and that the cargo's weight is evenly distributed over all axles is the _____.

   a. shipper
   b. loader of the cargo
   c. dispatcher
   d. driver

10. If your tractor is attached to an enclosed van with locking security seals, which of the following is not a recommended method to check the enclosed cargo?

    a. Conduct a visual check of the springs and tires of the rig for signs of overloading.

    b. Quiz the shipper regarding the securing methods of shipping papers.

    c. Know the general handling characteristics of the rig.

    d. Figure the weight of the load by weight and adding all the weights shown on the cargo.

11. If your tractor is attached to an open-type trailer or van without seals or restricted access, which of the following is the driver not responsible for?

    a. waterproof packing of the freight
    b. weight distribution
    c. heavy freight loaded high in the trailer
    d. regulated or restricted materials

12. When hauling cargo, you must stop within the first 50 miles (80 km) of your trip and then _____ to check your load and all securing devices.

    a. once daily
    b. 30 minutes before delivery
    c. every 3 hours or 150 miles (241 km) thereafter
    d. every 5 hours or 200 miles (322 km) thereafter

13. Cargo that is likely to roll, whether loaded in open or closed trailers, should be secured by _____.

    a. tie-downs
    b. straps
    c. chocks
    d. dunnage

14. The gross combination vehicle weight rating (GCVWR) is the _____.

    a. total weight of the tractor and trailer
    b. total weight of the tractor, trailer, and load
    c. amount of weight allowed on any interstate highway
    d. amount of weight allowed on most bridges

15. When focusing on the weight distribution of a load, which of the following is an example of a well-balanced load?

    a. The rear axles of the tractor will have two times the weight of the axles of the trailer.

    b. All axles, including the steering, will have the same weight on them.

    c. The rear axles of the tractor and the axles will have the same amount of weight on them.

    d. The steering axle will have the most weight on it.

16. Before loading, look at the floor of the trailer and make certain there are no _____.

    a. nails or splinters
    b. holes or rotten boards
    c. obstacles that could damage the cargo
    d. All of the above

17. When using a hand truck to load cargo, which of the following rules should not be followed?

    a. Never stack boxes so high they obstruct your vision when using a hand truck.

    b. Never load a mix of boxes, pallets, and canisters.

    c. Use ramps or dockboards between the trailer and the dock.

    d. None of the above.

18. Firewood, stumps, log debris, and other such short logs must be transported on _____.

    a. a special logging truck

    b. a vehicle or container enclosed on both sides, front, and rear, and of adequate strength

    c. a drop-deck trailer

    d. none of the above

SUPPLEMENTAL LEARNING ACTIVITIES

1. Visit a freight dock or warehouse and observe trailers being loaded or unloaded. Once you return to class, report on what you saw.

2. Ask a veteran loader or warehouse personnel to speak to the class about challenges as well as gratifying parts of the job.

3. Ask the manager of an irregular route carrier to speak to the class. Ask him or her about the largest load they've carried as well as the steps to haul one load from point A to point B. Ask, in particular, about permits, hours of operation, and other areas that differ from common carrier hauling.

4. Write a 100-word report on dock and warehouse injuries that occur while loading or unloading freight. Highlight the most frequent causes of injuries/fatalities around dock/warehouse operations and what is being done to avoid these.

5. Divide into groups and discuss the various driver responsibilities regarding the load they will haul. Make a list—from memory if possible—of what the driver is responsible for when it comes to the load he or she will haul.

FOR MORE INFORMATION

FMCSA Cargo Securement
www.fmcsa.dot.gov/rules-regulations/truck/driver/education-material.htm

FMCSA Development of North American Standard for Protection Against Shifting and Falling Cargo
www.fmcsa.dot.gov/cargosecurement.pdf

OSHA Worker Safety Series Warehousing
www.osha.gov/Publications/3220_Warehouse.pdf

FMCSA Cargo Securement Rules
www.fmcsa.dot.gov/rules-regulations/truck/vehicle/cs-policy.htm

Oregon Motor Carrier Transportation Load Securement
www.oregon.gov/ODOT/MCT/SAFETY.shtml#Load_Securement

26

Cargo Documentation

© s_oleg/www.Shutterstock.com

OBJECTIVES

When you have completed this chapter, you should be able to:

- Check the shipping documents to verify the cargo, quantity to be shipped, and compliance with the law.

- Know how to complete and distribute freight bills, cargo manifests, bills of lading, and other required forms.

- Understand the legal terms of a shipping contract.

- Explain how drivers can protect themselves and their companies from loss claims.

INTRODUCTION

The **documentation** that accompanies shipments serves many purposes. Its most important use is to provide an accurate record of the cargo (**see Figure 26-1**). In some cases, it also serves as a contract for transportation services. As a professional driver, you must be able to understand the terms and content of the shipping documents and your legal responsibilities.

▶ **Figure 26-1**

Documentation must be accurate because it often serves as a record of the cargo.

How important is your understanding of cargo documentation?

If you do not understand how to properly prepare and handle the papers that document the freight you haul, you may:

- Be liable for civil or criminal penalties if there is a cargo loss or shortages
- Suffer damage to your reputation as a professional driver
- Be fired from your job
- Endanger the health and safety of many by not communicating the dangers of a hazardous materials load

DEFINITION OF TERMS

To better understand certain words used by the shipper, carrier, or the person to whom delivery is made, you will need to know specific terms and exactly what they mean. The following terms have specific meanings when referring to the trucking industry:

Shipper (consignor)—person or company offering the goods for shipment

Receiver (consignee)—person or company to whom goods are being shipped or consigned

Motor carrier—the person or company in the business of transporting goods; in this chapter, *carrier* may mean:

- **Private carrier**
- **For-hire carrier**
  - **Common carrier**
  - **Contract carrier**
  - **Exempt commodity carrier**

Freight forwarder—a person or company that arranges for the transport of freight.

Originating (pick up) carrier—the carrier that first accepts the shipment from the shipper.

Connecting carrier—any carrier that transports freight to an interchange location and then transfers the cargo to another company to continue transport of the shipment.

Delivery (terminal) carrier—the carrier that delivers the shipment to the consignee.

Bill of lading (BL)—written contract between the shipper and the carrier for transporting a shipment. This paper identifies all freight in the shipment as well as the consignee, the delivery location, and the terms of the agreement.

Straight bill of lading—contract providing for delivery of a shipment to the consignee. The driver does not need to get a copy from the consignee when the goods are delivered.

International bill of lading—**used in international shipping** to bind the buyer and the supplier in a business agreement that results in mutual satisfaction, a contract, or a document called the bill of lading was introduced in the international shipping business. It is the evidence that binds both the parties in a commitment that a contract exists and it should be fulfilled by every means. The bill of lading contains the following information:

- Shipper, exporter, or the consignor: specifying the correct name and address and it should be totally consistent with credit provisions
- Carrier: specifying carrier's name and address
- Consignee: this is in accordance to the requirements after delivery involving name and address
- Contents of the cargo: the contents of the goods that are being supplied or transported should be mentioned
- The packaging number and number of goods: the number of packages with serial number
- Gross weight: the total weight of the consignment based on freight
- Size: the size of the consignment in volume
- Name of the carrying container, carrier, or vessel
- Ports: the name of ports of loading and discharge
- Freight and documentation billing number

The bill of lading (BL) contract is signed by the carrier/transporter, stating that the consignment is to be delivered in good condition and ensuring that the goods match with the mentioned account. The cargo is then transported at the specified location. The buyer party on the other side can receive the shipment if they comprise the BL, which is sent by the supplier on receiving the payment.

The **international bill of lading** is a contract for the carriage of goods between the shipper and the transportation company. It serves as a receipt issued by the carrier upon taking possession of the goods, and it may serve as a document of title that permits its holder to obtain title to and possession of the goods.

There are two types of bills:

- Straight bill of lading is a nonnegotiable bill of lading that is made in the name of the consignee; an agreement of delivery is made between involved parties.
- Order bill of lading is a negotiable bill of lading that is made in the name of a foreign party or its bank. Possession of goods is given and they bear the endorsement of the exporter.

These transport documents expedite an export shipment from the time of departure to delivery. When freight changes hands from the shipper to the carrier, it is the signature on the bill of lading that signifies that the goods have been received in "good order." That is, the goods are in the same condition as when they left the shipper's facility, or a "clean" bill of lading has been issued. A bill of lading without any comments regarding damage, overage, or underage can play a crucial role in permitting the seller to receive payment for the merchandise **(see Figure 26-2).**

UNIFORM STRAIGHT INTERNATIONAL BILL OF LADING
ORIGINAL – NOT NEGOTIABLE

PLACE PRO-LABEL HERE

SHIPPER'S NUMBER	PURCHASE ORDER NUMBER	ROUTE

RECEIVED, subject to the classifications and lawfully filed tariffs in effect on the date of the issue of this Bill of Lading.
On Collect on Delivery shipments, the letters "COD" must appear before consignee's name or as otherwise provided in Item 430, Sec. 1

SHIPPER OF HAZARDOUS MATERIAL 24 HOUR EMERGENCY PHONE NO.

The property described below, in apparent good order, except as noted (contents and condition of contents of packages unknown) marked, consigned and destined as shown below, which said company (the word company being understood throughout this contract as meaning any person or corporation in possession of the property under the contract) agrees to carry to its usual place of delivery at said destination, if on its own railroad, water line, highway route or routes, or within the territory of its highway operations, otherwise to deliver to another carrier on the route to said destination. It is mutually agreed, as to each carrier of all or any of said property overall or any portion of said route to destination, and as to each party at any time interested in all or any of said property, that every service to be performed hereunder shall be subject to all the conditions not prohibited by law, whether printed or written, herein contained, including the conditions on back hereof, which are hereby agreed to by the shipper and accepted for himself and his assigns.

SHIP DATE:	Through Bill Shipment between U.S. Mexico. Canada?	Will Saia Handle Border Crossing in Laredo?

SHIPPER INFORMATION:		PHONE #:	ULTIMATE CONSIGNEE INFORMATION:		PHONE #:
ADDRESS:			ADDRESS:		
ADDRESS:			ADDRESS:		
CITY	STATE	ZIP CODE	CITY	STATE	ZIP
FREIGHT FORWARDER (On Southbound Shipments):		PHONE #:	U.S. CUSTOM HOUSE BROKER (On Northbound Shipments):		PHONE #:
ADDRESS:			ADDRESS:		
CITY	STATE	ZIP CODE	CITY	STATE	ZIP
SPECIAL INSTRUCTIONS:			BILL TO COMPANY		
			ADDRESS:		
			CITY	STATE	ZIP

No. of Pkgs.	*HM	Palletized or Loose	DESCRIPTION OF ARTICLES, SPECIAL MARKS, AND EXCEPTIONS	CLASS	WEIGHT (in Pounds) (Sub. to Cor)

NOTE (Release valuation on household goods, furniture, and personal effects not to exceed 10 per pound). **TOTAL WEIGHT**

"This is to certify that the materials named above are properly classified, described, packaged, marked, and labeled and are in proper condition for transportation according to the applicable regulations of the Department of Transportation. X
Signature

"Liability for Loss, Damage, or Delay to Cargo Moving Between Mexico and Other Countries" - With respect to any shipment originating outside Mexico with ultimate destination in Mexico, or originating in Mexico with ultimate destination outside Mexico, Saia shall have NO liability, either for itself or for any Mexican Carrier involved in the move, for loss, damage, or delay which occurs within Mexico, or while in the possession of the designated brokers.

SHIPPER HEREBY CERTIFIES THAT HE IS FAMILIAR WITH ALL THE BILL OF LADING TERMS AND CONDITIONS IN THE GOVERNING CLASSIFICATIONS AND THE SAID TERMS AND CONDITIONS ARE HEREBY AGREED TO BY THE SHIPPER AND ACCEPTED FOR HIMSELF AND HIS ASSIGNS. THE TERMS OF THIS BILL OF LADING ARE IN EFFECT EXCEPT DURING TRANSIT WITHIN MEXICO.

FREIGHT CHARGES ARE TO BE PAID BY:

Freight Charges are Prepaid if not otherwise indicated		Ppd / 3rd Prty	Collect
Note: If paid in Pesos, the Mexican Carrier is liable for all collection of freight charges from Shipper or Consignee	US Freight Charges in USD		
	US Freight Charges in Pesos		
	Mexico Freight Charges in USD		
	Mexico Freight Charges in Pesos		

Subject to Section 7 of conditions, if this shipment is to be delivered to the consignee without recourse on the consignor, the consignor shall sign the following statement: The carrier shall not make delivery of this shipment without payment of freight and all other lawful charges.
X
(Signature of Consignor)

Cargo insurance is available on all international shipments at an additional cost. This must be arranged with Mexican Partner Carrier at the time of pickup from Shipper. I hereby request insurance on this international shipment. The insured value is:
$
U.S. Dollars

NOTE - Where the rate is dependent on value, shippers are required to state specifically in writing the agreed or declared value of the property. The agreed or declared value of the property is hereby specifically stated by the shipper to be not exceeding.

PER SHIPPER NAME
SHIPPER SIGNATURE
X
SAIA OR MEXICO PARTNER CARRIER (Driver Signature)
X
DATE & TIME
TOTAL # OF PIECES / UNITS

*Mark with "X" to designate Hazardous Materials as defined in the Department of Transportation Regulations governing the transportation of hazardous materials. The use of this column is an optional method for identifying the hazardous materials on bills of lading per Section 172.20(a)(1)(iii) of Title 49, Code of Federal Regulations. Also, when shipping hazardous materials, the Shipper's certification statement prescribed in Section 172.204(a) of the Federal Regulations must be indicated on the bill of lading, unless a specific exception from this requirement is provided in the Regulations for a particular material.

Figure 26-2
International bill of lading.

"I need to keep these Hazmat shipping papers with me at all times. Oh man, I don't have any pockets in my pjs!"

© Cengage Learning 2013

Order Notify Bill of Lading—a bill of lading that permits the shipper to collect payment before shipping reaches its destination. A driver must pick up the consignee's copy of the BL before delivering the shipment.

Through Bill of Lading—a bill of lading used with shipments transported by more than one carrier that has a fixed rate for the services of all carriers.

Manifest—a list describing the entire shipment on a vehicle.

Packing Slip—a detailed list of packed goods prepared by the shipper.

Freight Bill—a bill submitted by a common carrier for transport services. The freight bill contains much of the same information as the bill of lading. A copy usually serves as a receipt for services when signed by the consignee.

Delivery Receipt—a paper signed by the consignee or an agent of the consignee, accepting the shipment from the driver. The driver keeps the receipt as proof of delivery.

Warehouse Receipt—a paper signed by the driver to prove the shipment was unloaded at a warehouse.

Agent—a person or company acting as the official representative of another, such as a consignee's agent.

Hazardous Materials Shipping Paper—a bill of lading describing hazardous materials by proper shipping name, hazard class, identification number, and the quantity being shipped. This form must be legible.

Hazardous Waste Manifest—a form describing hazardous waste that identifies the shipper, carrier, and destination by name and by identification numbers assigned by the Environmental Protection Agency. The shipper prepares, dates, and signs the manifest. All carriers of the shipment must sign the paper. It also must be signed by the consignee and the driver keeps a copy.

TRANSPORTATION CHARGES AND SERVICES

Transportation charges are the fees for transportation services. They may include payment for the goods shipped. It is important to understand the terminology used about the charges and payments for services. This helps protect you from liability and personal expense.

Usually, the cost for goods in the shipment is agreed upon by the shipper and the customer before the shipment is offered for transport. Sometimes the carrier will also have to collect the payment for the goods being shipped from the receiver and return this payment to the shipper. The shipper and carrier usually agree on the transportation charges before the freight is loaded.

Types of Payment

Prepaid shipments—transportation charges are paid at the shipping point.

Collect-on-delivery (COD) shipments—the driver must collect payment before the cargo can be unloaded **(see Figure 26-3).** The payment may be for the transportation charges only or also include the cost of the goods. The driver must know the company's policy for the types of payment that can be accepted, such as certified check, money order, or cash, as well as how payment should be sent to the office for deposit. Remember, receipts have to be given to the customer and a paper trail needs to be utilized.

Figure 26-3

On COD shipments, the driver must collect payments before the cargo is unloaded.

Order notify shipment—payment for the goods is made when the driver gets a copy of the order notify bill of lading from the consignee. At that point, the driver must get the bill from the consignee before delivering the shipment. In both prepaid and COD shipments, the bill must be signed and sent back to the carrier.

Transportation Rates

Charges for transportation are figured by multiplying the rate by the weight of the cargo and distance the load will be shipped (**see Figure 26-4**). Rates are based on the value of the cargo and services performed by the

Transportation Rates = Rate X Weight of Cargo X Distance Shipped

Figure 26-4

Transportation rates.

NOTE

CODs are often used when a customer is delinquent on paying their past freight bills and the carrier is worried they will not be paid for services completed. CODs are also used in the household goods business. Families are often asked to settle up on all freight charges before any personal effects are removed from the trailer. You will see very few COD shipments.

NOTE

Many carriers are now using smartphone technology, downloaded with apps that allow drivers to copy the bill signed by the consignee and then to send it back to the home terminal for billing. This eliminates "snail mail" and lag time between delivery and billing.

STOP!

It is important to understand that weights appearing on the freight bill may be either true weights or estimated weights. If the weight is estimated, there could be a significant difference between the true and estimated weights—sometimes by as much as 1,000 pounds (454 kg). Professional drivers should never depend on stated weights as being accurate—and since drivers are ultimately responsible for knowing the correct weight of their loaded equipment, it is always necessary to verify this weight as accurate.

NOTE: A stated weight on a bill of lading will not excuse the driver from operating an overweight CMV.

carrier. Since deregulation in the 1980s, freight charges have fluctuated widely to accommodate the demands of the shipper. Much like today's airlines, which have also been deregulated, and varying ticket prices, the same has occurred with freight charges.

The value of the cargo used for rate purposes is either the actual value of goods shipped as shown on the bill of lading, or the value shown on the BL is set by the shipper as the limits of carrier liability (**see Figure 26-5**).

▶ **Figure 26–5**

The value shown on the bill of lading limits the carrier's responsibility.

Services to be performed by the carrier are based on special handling requirements and **tariffs.** Tariffs are lists of services common carriers perform for the public and the rates charged for them.

Services and Surcharges

Rates for services and surcharges, or additional charges, are negotiated between the shipper and the carrier before the carrier accepts the shipment. Surcharges may include those charges for special services to be performed by the driver when delivery is made, such as inside delivery, storage, or other charges. An example is a "fuel surcharge," which is designed to fluctuate as the price of fuel increases and/or decreases.

Trucking companies often enter into long-term agreements with their regular customers and most of these agreements allow carriers to make additional charges in cases when fuel prices spike. This particular surcharge has saved many smaller trucking firms from going out of business because they had to absorb high fuel prices.

GO!

It is important for the driver to know the meanings of the terms describing certain services. The services should be clearly stated in the bill of lading.

Inside delivery—indicates freight is to be delivered inside the building rather than unloaded at the curb.

Tailgate delivery—the freight is unloaded and delivered at the tailgate (back) of the truck.

Helper service—a helper is to be provided for loading or unloading freight. The bill of lading specifies who will pay for the helper.

Residential delivery—the BL will specify the address and method for collecting payment if the shipment is going to a residence.

Dunnage and return (DR) charges—when the weight of the dunnage is listed on the bill of lading. If shipper wishes it to be returned, this will be stated on the bill of lading.

Storage and delay (S&D) charges—an additional amount to be paid to the carrier if delivery is postponed by the consignee or shipper, or if a shipment must be stored before it can be delivered. These terms are stated on the bill of lading.

Detention time or demurrage—detaining a vehicle beyond a given time. Payment is made to the carrier when the delivery is delayed. Typically driver/equipment detention starts two hours after the stated appointment time. Once the driver is held beyond this two-hour window the customer is charged accordingly. Usually drivers are compensated for their time beyond the two-hour customary time limit. Most drivers are paid by the mile/kilometer and make no revenue when the truck isn't moving.

NOTE

Detention time is used as an incentive to hurry the shipper—to get the truck driver loaded and on the road. Plus, the Hours of Service (HOS) clock usually does not stop once the driver arrives at a customer and, therefore, the driver runs the risk of being in violation of the federally mandated HOS and not able to continue driving.

CABOTAGE

Cabotage is the transport of goods or passengers between two points in the same country. Originally starting with shipping, cabotage now also covers aviation, railways, and road transport.

Commonly used as part of the term "cabotage rights," cabotage means the right of a company from one country to trade in another country. Economically, cabotage regulations that limit trade to domestic carriers constitute a form of protectionism.

Recent Changes to Canadian Cabotage Rules

As of early September 2011, the Canada Border Services Agency (CBSA) issued a new Customs Notice on the point-to-point move of domestic freight in Canada by foreign-based motor carriers, commonly referred to as "cabotage."

Both Canada and the U.S. have nearly identical cabotage rules and only permit such movements in very narrowly defined circumstances. However, the U.S. has been more zealous in making sure foreign carriers don't drive equipment point-to-point on their soil, according to an article appearing in the September 8, 2011, edition of "Today's Trucking.com."

The notice does not mean a change in the rules, which have been in place for more than 10 years, but the Canadian Trucking Alliance sees it as a reminder of the rules and perhaps a signal that CBSA will be paying closer attention to foreign carrier operations in Canada.

CBSA plans to conduct postcompliance verification and has said it will issue sanctions against violators.

CTA said this move will finally equal the playing field between Canadian and U.S. cross-border haulers.

"The rules are, quite frankly, very complicated—on both sides of the border—so whatever can be done to improve the level of understanding about them is a step in the right direction," said CTA President David Bradley. However, he said there still needs to be a joint approach to modernizing the cabotage rules in both countries, namely by providing more flexibility to foreign carriers when moving empty trailers.

"We're not talking about wide-open cabotage, but I think if anyone were to take a step back and look at the situation, and see different rules for trucks and the people who drive them, and restrictions on something as simple as re-positioning an empty trailer, they would realize that this is an area that is crying out for reform."

The CTA and its counterparts at the American Trucking Associations even appealed to the EPA that changing the archaic empty trailer movement rules would be environmentally beneficial, but to no avail. Until the policy is relaxed, however, "it is imperative there be a level playing field in terms of compliance with the law," Bradley said.

The rules governing trucking cabotage generally forbid domestic hauls by foreign truckers, except when the move is "incidental to the international traffic of the imported or exported goods."

The rules governing trucking cabotage are set out in federal legislation known as the Customs Tariff, under which the domestic movement of goods by foreign trucking equipment is generally forbidden, except when the move is "incidental to the international traffic of the imported or exported goods." Customs Notice 11-014 clarifies the meaning of "incidental" as follows:

■ Only one incidental (domestic) move is permitted per international trip.

■ The move must follow a route consistent with the international route of the imported or exported goods.

■ Domestic goods can be carried as part of a re-positioning move, but only if the vehicle is en route to pick up a scheduled load for export from Canada, and the drop off point of the goods is in a direct line to the pick-up of the export load.

It is also vitally important to understand that the clarification issued by CBSA only covers trucking equipment. Foreign drivers, who fall under the authority of Citizenship and Immigration Canada, are forbidden from making point-to-point domestic moves unless they have obtained a temporary work permit.

Cabotage Information for Mexico–Domiciled Motor Carriers
Based on information provided by the Federal Motor Carrier Safety Administration, July 2007

According to the U.S. Department of Transportation, **international transportation** means cargo transported by Mexico-domiciled motor carriers and commercial motor vehicles from a foreign country to the United States, with no loading in the United States, or from the United States to a foreign country, with no loading in the United States **(see Figure 26-6).**

Domestic cargo is cargo loaded in the United States and delivered to a location within the United States.

▶ **Figure 26-6**
Tractor-trailer driving in Mexico.

The following are regulations governing point-to-point transportation of cargo in the United States:

49 CFR 365.501(b)—prohibits Mexico-domiciled motor carriers from providing point-to-point transportation services, including express delivery services, within the United States for goods other than international cargo.

49 CFR 392.9(a)—prohibits Mexico-domiciled motor carriers from operating beyond the scope of their operating authority. Operating authority issued to Mexico-domiciled motor carriers is limited to the transportation of international cargo.

49 CFR 123.14—prohibits point-to-point transportation of domestic freight with some exceptions. These regulations are enforced by the United States Department of Homeland Security.

8 CFR 214.2(b)(4)(i)(E)(1)—prohibits foreign drivers from performing point-to-point domestic transportation in the United States. The regulations are enforced by the United States Department of Homeland Security.

Cabotage Enforcement/Citing Violations

In the event that you and your rig are stopped for inspection by an enforcement officer checking for cabotage violations, here is what you should expect:

- The enforcement officer will look for domestic point-to-point deliveries on your driver's log book or record of duty status.
- The enforcement officer will check the bills of lading or other delivery documents in your possession.
- The enforcement officer also will check any other available records and will question the driver concerning all transportation services provided while in the country.
- If a cabotage violation is discovered, expect the following:

  1. The enforcement officer will conduct a driver/vehicle inspection and complete the driver/vehicle inspection report.
  2. The enforcement officer will document on the inspection report and sign the driver for a violation of 49 CFR 392.9a(a)—operating beyond the scope of an operating authority.
  3. The enforcement officer will place the vehicle out-of-service as provided on the North American Standard Out-of-Service Criteria.
  4. The enforcement officer will obtain documentation of the violation (log book, shipping documents, driver statements, etc.)
  5. The enforcement officer will provide the documentation to the FMCSA Division Administrator, through the appropriate chain of command, in the state where the inspection occurred. To find the Division Administrator of the state, go to www.fmcsa.dot.gov. Then click on Contact Us, then on Field Officers on the left **(see Figure 26-7).**

© iStockphoto/inhauscreative

▶ Figure 26-7

Enforcement officers provide documentation to the FMCSA Division Administrator.

NOTE

- A Mexico-domiciled motor carrier can transport cargo loaded in the United States for delivery to a point in Canada. This is considered transportation of international cargo.
- A Mexican driver may enter the United States with an empty tractor to pick up a trailer for delivery to Canada or Mexico.
- A Mexican driver may deadhead a trailer from one location to another within the United States, provided the deadhead trailer is either the one the driver came in with or the one he or she is departing with. The driver may not haul an empty trailer from one location in the United States to drop it off at another location in the United States.
- A foreign driver may perform associated functions such as loading and unloading cargo that is necessary to international trade. Loading and unloading that is merely incidental to the primary purpose of transporting goods into or out of the United States is permitted.
- A Mexican driver may drop the trailer and bobtail to another location to pick up a trailer for return to Mexico. However, the driver must deliver the picked-up trailer to Mexico. The driver may not reposition trailers in the United States.
- A U.S. carrier may employ a nonimmigrant foreign driver if the driver is engaged only in the international delivery of goods and cargo to or from the United States. The foreign driver must have an established foreign residence that he or she does not intend to abandon. The foreign driver may not engage in any domestic carriage of goods without employment authorization to work in the United States.

U.S. COMMERCIAL VEHICLE SIZE AND WEIGHT PROGRAM

Authorization of the "Dwight D. Eisenhower System of Interstate and Defense Highways" (the Interstate Highway System) in the 1950s created an interest in preserving the integrity of highways built with federal funds. Federal interest in the nation's highway system also extends to ensuring the safety, productivity, and mobility of freight commerce.

The national Vehicle Size and Weight Team, a part of the Federal Highway Administration's (FHWA's) Office of Freight Management and Operations, oversees state enforcement of heavy truck and bus size and weight standards in the United States. Additionally, staff in each of FHWA's 52 Division Offices provide one-on-one support to individual states, the District of Columbia, and Puerto Rico. Washington Headquarters and Division Office staff also assist with policy questions, clarifications, reporting requirements, training, and other related program and administrative issues.

Standards center on a commercial vehicle's weight, length, and width. Specific details of the standards are listed below.

Commercial Vehicle Weight Standards

National weight standards apply to commercial vehicle operations on the Interstate Highway System, an approximately 40,000-mile (64,374 km) system of limited access, divided highways that span the nation. Off the Interstate Highway System, states may set their own commercial vehicle weight standards.

Federal commercial vehicle maximum standards for a single axle CMV on the Interstate Highway System are:

Single Axle:	20,000 pounds (9,072 kg)
Tandem Axle:	34,000 × 2 pounds (15,422 × 0.9 kg)
Gross Vehicle Weight:	80,000 pounds (36,287 kg)

Federal commercial vehicle maximum for a steer axle CMV are:

Steer Axle:	12,000 pounds (5,443 kg)
Tandem × 2:	34,000 × 2 pounds (15,422 × 0.9 kg)
Gross Vehicle:	80,000 pounds (36,287 kg)

Bridge Formula Weights

The Bridge Formula was introduced in 1975 to reduce the risk of damage to highway bridges by requiring more axles, or a longer wheelbase, to compensate for increased vehicle weight. The formula may require a lower gross vehicle weight, depending on the number and spacing of the axles in the combination vehicle.

Commercial Vehicle Size (Length and Width) Standards

National vehicle size standards apply on what is known as the National Network of Highways. The National Network includes: (1) the Interstate Highway System and (2) highways, formerly classified as Primary System routes, capable of safely handling larger commercial motor vehicles, as certified by states to FHWA. The total National Network system is about 200,000 miles (321,869 km). (See the following table for specific limits.)

FEDERAL COMMERCIAL VEHICLE SIZE LIMITS ON THE NATIONAL NETWORK

Overall vehicle length	No federal length limit is imposed on most truck tractor-semi-trailers operating on the National Network.
	Exception: On the National Network, combination vehicles (truck tractor plus semi-trailer or trailer) designed and used specifically to carry automobiles or boats in specially designed racks may not exceed a maximum overall vehicle length of 65 feet (19.8 m), or 75 feet (22.9 m), depending on the type of connection between the tractor and trailer.
Trailer length	Federal law provides that no state may impose a length limitation of less than 48 feet (14.6 m) (or longer if provided for by grandfathered rights) on a semi-trailer operating in any truck tractor-semitrailer combination on the National Network. (Note: A state may permit longer trailers to operate on its National Network highways.)
	Similarly, federal law provides that no state may impose a length limitation of less than 28 feet (8.5 m) on a semi-trailer or trailer operating in a truck tractor-semi-trailer-trailer (twin-trailer) combination on the National Network.
Vehicle width	On the National Network, no state may impose a width limitation of *more or less* than 102 inches (259 cm). Safety devices (e.g., mirrors, handholds) necessary for the safe and efficient operation of motor vehicles may not be included in the calculation of width.
Vehicle height	No federal vehicle height limit is imposed. State standards range from 13.6 feet (4.1 m) to 14.6 feet (4.5 m).

Penalties for Noncompliance with Federal Standards

Weight Standards: A state is subject to loss of its *entire* National Highway System apportionment if its laws or regulations establish weight limits for commercial motor vehicles operating on the Interstate Highway System that are either higher or lower than federal weight standards. The only exception relates to changes affecting established "grandfather" limits; although a state may not set weight limits above a grandfathered maximum, it may set them below the maximum, provided such a limit is not below the corresponding federal standard.

Size Standards: A state that violates federal statutes on commercial vehicle size, or the implementing regulations, is subject to a civil action in federal district court for injunctive relief, in accordance with 49 U.S.C. 31115, "Enforcement." The action will be brought by the Department of Justice on behalf of FHWA.

Reporting Requirements: Each year, states must provide the FHWA with both a plan and a certification of accomplishment of planned size and weight enforcement activities. Failure to certify, or inadequately enforce all state laws affecting maximum size and weight on Federal-Aid highways, *despite the provision of certifying documents to FHWA*, can result in a 10 percent reduction of all Federal-Aid highway funds to the state for the next fiscal year.

CANADIAN COMMERCIAL VEHICLE WEIGHT AND SIZE REGULATIONS

Similar to the United States, where weight regulations are controlled by individual states, the provinces in Canada control the weight regulations applied to commercial motor vehicles and their cargoes.

In Ontario, commercial vehicle weights are broken into two categories:

■ **Category one is "Gross Vehicle Weight" (GVW).** The gross vehicle weight number is determined when the owner registers the vehicle with the Ministry of Transportation. The Ministry takes into account such factors as number of tires, size of tires, number of axles, axle spreads, and the amount of weight the owner wishes to carry. Once the weight has been determined, it is placed on the ownership of the vehicle.

■ **Category two is the "Manufacturer's Registered Gross Vehicle Weight" (MRGVW).** The manufacturer of the vehicle determines the gross vehicle weight. Once determined, this information is placed on the door frame of the vehicle.

NOTE

Canada and the United States have many reciprocal agreements, i.e., you may drive in any Province or State as long as you hold a valid driver's license in your province or state. United States' and Canada's weight regulations also are similar.

Vehicle Weight and Dimension Reforms in Ontario

During the period 2000 through 2010, Ontario introduced a four-phase overhaul of the Vehicle Weight and Dimension (VW&D) regulations. The main purpose of the reforms was to cause a migration to vehicles that are designated as Safe, Productive, and Infrastructure-Friendly (SPIF). These reforms address excessive damage to provincial and municipal roads and bridges and are expected to reduce the numbers of tractor-trailer collisions, while maintaining industry productivity.

Regulations governing SPIF vehicles are more straightforward, in order to improve compliance and enforcement. Characteristics of SPIF vehicles are carefully prescribed and include that the vehicles must be:

■ Equipped with fixed axles, or a combination of fixed and self-steering axles, that do not need to be raised for cornering;

■ Able to automatically distribute weight over all axles to minimize infrastructure wear;

■ Tested against national performance targets to ensure satisfactory stability and control and reduced risk of rollovers and jackknifes;

Industry productivity is maintained by allowing similar payloads as those for previous vehicles.

Each phase of the reform project dealt with a different grouping of vehicles. There was a need to group the various types of vehicles and deal with them separately because of complex technical, economic, and operational issues. Vehicle groupings and implementation dates were as follows:

1. Non-dump light semi-trailers (3 axles or less), implemented in January 2001.

2. All dump semi-trailers, implemented in January 2003.

3. Heavy semi-trailers (4 axles or more) and double trailers, implemented in January 2006.

4. Trucks, truck-trailers, buses, and remaining vehicles, implemented in July 2011.

The amended Ontario Regulation 413/05 of the Highway Traffic Act titled, "Vehicle Weights and Dimensions—for Safe, Productive and Infrastructure-Friendly Vehicles" is available through the e-laws web site: www.e-laws.gov.on.ca/html/regs/english/elaws_regs_050413_e.htm

Non-SPIF vehicles, excluding 53 feet (16.2 m) semi-trailers and other long tractor-trailer combinations, can legally operate in Ontario at reduced gross vehicle weights under what is now a VW&D two-tier system.

How Do These Changes Affect Operation of Vehicles or Vehicle Combinations?

According to the Ministry of Transportation 2001, Ontario:

> The starting point is to determine whether or not a vehicle or combination qualifies as SPIF. SPIF vehicles are referred to in the regulation as "Designated Combinations."
>
> To qualify as SPIF, the vehicle or combination must meet the description and dimensional limits set out in one of the 31 schedules of the regulation as well as any Preconditions listed in Sections 5 to 14. If your vehicle qualifies as a designated SPIF combination, its allowable weights are as described in the Weight Limit Chart of the Schedule. Please refer to www.e-laws.gov.on.ca/html/regs/english/elaws_regs_050413_e.htm.
>
> If the vehicle or combination does not qualify as SPIF, non-SPIF reduced weights are applicable, as described in Section 21. If the vehicle or combination is grandfathered, allowable weights on aggregate and non-aggregate vehicles continue to be determined separately as described in Section 22.
>
> The decision chart, found at www.mto.gov.on.ca/english/trucks/vwd/questions-and-answers.shtml, can be used to aid in the determination of your SPIF compliance.

BASIC SHIPPING DOCUMENTS

A bill of lading is a contract between a shipper and a carrier. It lists all the goods in the shipment and any special handling requirements or conditions for transportation. It is a legally binding document that is regulated by federal law.

There are several different types of bills of lading that serve the following purposes:

- Identifies the type and quantity of freight being shipped
- Shows the ownership of the goods
- States the value of the freight in case of loss or damage
- Establishes the rates and freight charges
- Serves as a legal contract
- Identifies the point of origin of the shipment and where it is being shipped
- States the methods of payment for all charges
- Serves as a permanent record of the transactions

Uniform Straight Bill of Lading

The most common type of bill of lading is the **uniform straight bill of lading.** It is a contract that the parties cannot change. The goods must be delivered to the consignee or an authorized representative **(see Figure 26-8).** There are usually three copies:

- Copy 1—original copy sent to the consignee
- Copy 2—shipping order copy is carrier copy
- Copy 3—memorandum copy is shipper copy

(To be Printed on White Paper)

UNIFORM STRAIGHT BILL OF LADING

ORIGINAL-NOT NEGOTIABLE-Domestic

Shipper's No. _____
Agent's No. _____

_____ Carrier _____ (SCAC)

RECEIVED, subject to the classifications and tariffs in effect on the date of the issue of this Bill of Lading.

From _____ Date _____ , 20 _____

At _____ Street _____ City _____ County _____ State ____

The property described below, in apparent good order, except as noted (contents and condition of contents of packages unknown) marked, consigned, and destined as shown below, which said company (the word company being understood throughout this contract as meaning any person or corporation in possession of the property under the contract) agrees to carry to its usual place of delivery at said destination, if on its own railroad, water line, highway route or routes, or within the territory of its highway operations, otherwise to deliver to another carrier on the route to said destination. It is mutually agreed, as to each carrier of all or any of said property over all or any portion of said route to destination and as to each party at any time interested in all or any of said property, that every service to be performed hereunder shall be subject to all the conditions not prohibited by law, whether printed or written, herein contained, including the conditions on the back hereof, which are hereby agreed to by the shipper and accepted for himself and his assigns.

Consigned to _____

Destination _____ Street _____

City _____ County _____ State _____ Zip _____

Routing _____

Delivering Carrier _____ Vehicle or Car Initial _____ No. ____

Collect On Delivery _____ and remit to: _____

_____ Street _____ City _____ State

C.O.D. charge } Shipper ☐
to be paid by } Consignee ☐

No. Packages	Kind of Packages, Description of Articles, Special Marks, and Exceptions	*Weight (Subject to Correction)	Class or Rate	Check Column

Subject to Section 7 of conditions, if this shipment is to be delivered to the consignee without recourse on the consignor, the consignor shall sign the following statement: The carrier shall not make delivery of the shipment without payment of freight and all other lawful charges.

_____
(Signature of consignor)

If charges are to be prepaid write or stamp here "To be Prepaid."

_____

Received $ _____
to apply in prepayment of the charges on the property described hereon.

_____
Agent or Cashier

Charges advanced:
$ _____

*If the shipment moves between two ports by a carrier or by water, the law requires that the bill of lading shall state whether it is "Carrier's or shipper's weight."

Note -Where the rate is dependent on value, shippers are required to state specifically in writing the agreed or declared value of the property.

The agreed or declared value of the property is hereby specifically stated by the shipper to not be exceeding _____ per _____

_____ Shipper _____ Agent

Per _____ Per _____

Permanent address of Shipper: Street _____ City _____ State _____

© Cengage Learning 2013

▶ **Figure 26-8**

Uniform straight bill of lading.

A uniform straight bill of lading **(see Figure 26-9)** will have the:

1. Carrier's name
2. Shipper's name
3. Date goods were accepted by the carrier
4. Number of items in the shipment and a description of each

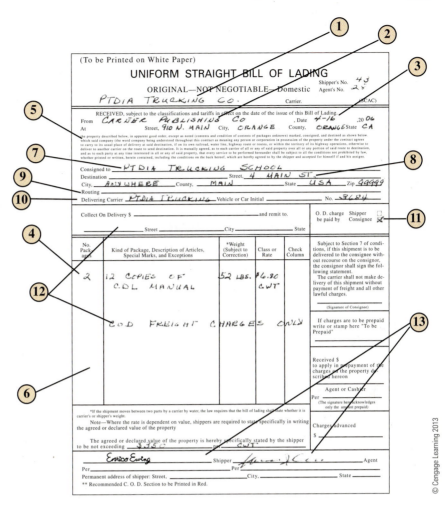

► **Figure 26–9**

The uniform straight bill of lading must contain specific information about the shipment.

5. Condition of the packages or goods in the shipment
6. Space for the driver to note damage, shortages, or improper packing
7. Name of the consignee
8. Address to which the shipment can be delivered
9. Routing, if more than one carrier will transport cargo
10. Identification of connecting carriers, if any are necessary
11. Freight charges and method of payment, such as COD or prepaid
12. Special handling services
13. Signatures of the shipper and the driver as agents for the carrier (the bill is not valid without signatures)

Contract information will be detailed on the back of copy 2 in case the driver must check for specific duties on delivery.

Order Notify Bill of Lading

An order notify bill of lading is a special type of BL. Ownership of the shipment can be transferred by the valid sale of this document. There will be three copies:

- Copy 1—original copy (yellow)
- Copy 2—shipping copy (blue)
- Copy 3—memo copy (white)

The information describing the freight in the shipment will be the same as that needed for the uniform bill of lading.

The driver must check the back of the yellow page (original) to make sure it is signed by the shipper and any bank or financial institution that has paid the shipper. If there is any question about the validity or proper preparation of the order notify bill of lading, contact the financial department or billing agent for your company.

The driver must not deliver any part of the shipment unless he or she has the original copy (copy 1) of the bill. After delivery, the original copy of the bill is given to that consignee. The holder of the order notify bill of lading is the legal owner of the freight.

Household Goods Bill of Lading

A **household goods bill of lading** is used by moving companies for their shipments. This bill serves as a legal contract between the shipper and the carrier. The household goods bill of lading lists the carrier and the customer and is a combined bill of lading, freight bill, and a record of the items in the shipment. It also states their appearance, their condition, and how they are packaged.

Legal requirements for weighing a load with a household goods bill of lading differ from those of ordinary freight.

Freight bills are prepared by the carrier from the bill of lading (**see Figure 26-10**). Drivers are mainly concerned with copy 1 of the BL, which serves as the delivery receipt copy. The driver must have the consignee sign the bill, showing that he or she accepts the shipment after it is unloaded.

The freight bill will tell the driver if the carrier charges are prepaid or if there is a COD charge due on delivery. Freight bills are usually preprinted with **pro numbers** (progressive numbers). These numbers are in front of the freight bill numbers. Often the driver will have to identify the bill by its pro number. Sometimes drivers refer to cargo manifests as "pro bills" or "pro sheets" because the manifest lists all freight bills (**see Figure 26-11**).

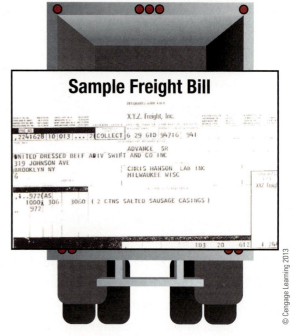

▶ **Figure 26-10**

Freight bills are prepared by the carrier from the bill of lading.

Other Documents

Invoice—a bill from the shipper listing the goods, prices, and total due. This may be mailed to the consignee, or the driver may have to give it to the consignee if the freight comes as a COD shipment.

Packing slip—a list of the total parts packaged in a shipment. The responsibility of opening packages and checking the contents against the packing slip belongs to the consignee.

DRIVER'S SIGNATURE AND RESPONSIBILITY

The driver's signature on a shipping document puts that driver and his or her company on the line (**see Figure 26-12**). NEVER sign a shipping document unless you completely understand all the terms and conditions. Be sure you compare all descriptions with the freight offered for loading.

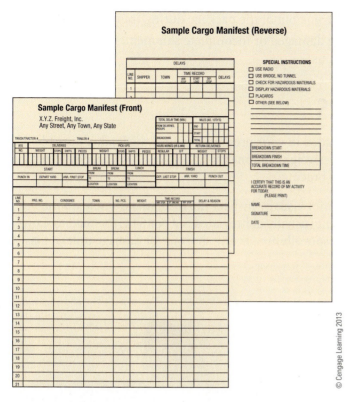

▶ Figure 26–11

Drivers refer to cargo manifests as "pro bills" or "pro sheets" because the manifests list all freight bills.

▶ Figure 26–12

Never sign a shipping document unless you completely understand the terms and conditions.

The driver's signature on a bill of lading means:

- You and your company are legally responsible for fulfilling all the terms and conditions of the contract.
- You and your company agree to the methods and rates of payment for the services you stated.
- You and your company are responsible for delivering the articles in the quantities listed in good condition to the consignee.
- You have inspected the shipment and found all items to be in good condition. The count is also correct.
- You have noted any shortages, damages, or mistakes before signing the bill.

As a professional driver, protect your reputation and your job in the following manner:

- Never take the word of someone else for the freight count or the condition of the shipment. Always count the cargo yourself.
- Always observe the loading of cargo to ensure all pieces are loaded.
- Check the descriptions on the packages against the bill of lading.
- Learn to quickly and correctly count palletized packages.
- Check the address on the freight against the delivery address of the consignee to avoid loading the wrong cargo.
- Handle fragile goods properly when you load them. If they are loaded by others, watch for any rough handling and breakage.
- Never load or permit someone else to load leaking packages or drums. The leakage could damage other freight.

- Note freight that is poorly packaged and could come out of the package during transport.
- Know the policies of your company for refusing damaged or incomplete shipment. If you accept these for shipment, it could result in freight claims.

PREVIOUSLY LOADED TRAILERS

Before signing a bill of lading for a shipment not loaded in your presence, inspect the load, if possible. Check the bill of lading for incompatible freight, overweight shipments, and so on. Also check the general appearance of the load for proper blocking and bracing.

If the trailer is sealed with a security seal or you cannot visually inspect the load, make a note on the bill of lading that reads "shipper's weight, load, and count (usually abbreviated SLC or STC for 'Said to Contain')." This releases you and your company from responsibility for any shortage or damage unless it is caused by an accident.

Security Seals

For trailers that are equipped with **security seals** by the shipper:

- Record the serial number of the seal on all copies of the bill of lading. This is usually preprinted on the BL, but the driver should always verify that the serial number on the seal corresponds with the one printed on the BL **(see Figure 26-13).**
- Note on the bill of lading "shipper's weight, load, and count."
- Check the seal to be sure it is properly locked. The serial number must match the number noted on the bill of lading.
- Have the consignee sign for the shipment on delivery BEFORE breaking the seal.
- If the seal is broken en route—for inspection by law enforcement officials—obtain their signature(s), badge number(s), and department(s) and get a replacement seal.
- If the seal is broken en route by someone other than an enforcement official, notify your dispatcher or supervisor at once.

Courtesy of Don Hess

▶ **Figure 26-13**

For trailers with security seals, record the serial number of the seal on all copies of the bill of lading.

DELIVERY OF FREIGHT

When you deliver freight, remember—you are responsible for the shipment until it is accepted by the consignee:

- Make sure delivery is to the proper consignee.
- Obtain the correct signature on freight bills, bills of lading, receipts, or other documents before unloading the shipment.
- Collect COD payments before unloading cargo.
- Obtain the properly signed order notify bill of lading before you unload the shipment.

- Check to be sure the entire consignment is delivered.
- Any differences, shortages, or changes in the method of payment should be reported to your dispatcher or supervisor before you release the shipment to the consignee.
- Know your company policy on freight delivery problems.

INTERMODAL FREIGHT TRANSPORT

Intermodal freight transport is the transportation of freight in an **intermodal container** or **vehicle,** using multiple modes of transportation (rail, ship, and truck), without any handling of the freight itself when changing modes.

This method reduces cargo handling, and so improves security, reduces damages and losses, and allows freight to be transported faster. Reduced costs over road trucking is the key benefit for intracontinental use. This may be offset by reduced timings for road transport over shorter distances.

Intermodal transportation goes back to the 18th century and predates the railways. Some of the earliest containers were those used for shipping coal on the Bridgewater Canal in England in the 1780s. Coal containers (called "loose boxes" or "tubs") were soon deployed on the early canals and railways and were used for road/rail transfers (road at the time meaning horse-drawn vehicles).

Wooden coal containers used on railways go back to the 1830s on the Liverpool and Manchester Railway. In 1841 Isambard Kingdom Brunel introduced iron containers to move coal. By the outbreak of the First World War, the Great Eastern Railway was using wooden containers to trans-ship passenger luggage between trains and sailings.

The early 1900s saw the first adoption of covered containers, primarily for the movement of furniture and intermodal freight between road and rail. A lack of standards limited the value of this service and this in turn drove standardization. In the U.S. such containers, known as "lift vans," were in use from as early as 1911.

When containers were first standardized in the United Kingdom by the Railway Clearing House in the 1920s, this allowed both railway-owned and privately-owned vehicles to be carried on standard container flats. By modern standards these containers were small, being 1.5 or 3.0 meters long (5 or 10 ft), constructed of wood with a curved roof and insufficient strength for stacking. From 1928 the London, Midland, and Scottish Railway offered "door to door" intermodal road/rail services using these containers. This standard failed to become popular outside the United Kingdom.

Truck trailers were first carried by railway before World War II, an arrangement often called "piggyback," by the small Class I railroad, the Chicago Great Western in 1936. The Canadian Pacific Railway was a pioneer in piggyback transport, becoming the first major North American railway to introduce the service in 1952.

In the United Kingdom the big four railway companies offered services using standard RCH containers that could be craned on and off the back of trucks. Moving companies such as Pickfords offered private services in the same way.

NOTE

Upon arrival, the driver reports to the delivery office and surrenders all paperwork relating to the load. Do not break the trailer seal without permission. Customers should be given the opportunity to personally inspect that the trailer has not been tampered with while in shipment. In most instances, the customer will not release paperwork until after the cargo is completely unloaded and the driver is free to leave.

INTERESTING FACT

Pallets made their first major appearance during World War II, when the United States military assembled freight on pallets, allowing fast transfer between warehouses, trucks, trains, ships, and aircraft. Because no freight handling was required, fewer personnel were required and loading times were decreased.

In the 1950s, a new standardized steel intermodal container based on specifications from the United States Department of Defense began to revolutionize freight transportation. The International Organization for Standardization (ISO) then issued standards based upon the U.S. Department of Defense standards between 1968 and 1970.

▶ Figure 26-14

Crane loading semi-trailers onto large cargo ship.

Intermodal Transportation Today

Container ships are used to transport containers by sea. These vessels are custom-built to hold containers. Some vessels can hold thousands of containers. Their capacity is often measured in TEU or FEU. These initials stand for "twenty-foot equivalent unit," and "forty-foot equivalent unit," respectively. For example, a vessel that can hold 1,000 40-foot (12.2 m) containers or 2,000 20-foot (6.1 m) containers can be said to have a capacity of 2,000 TEU. In 2007, the largest container ships in regular operation are capable of carrying in excess of 15,000 TEU **(see Figure 26-14).**

Onboard ships are typically stacked up to seven units high.

A key consideration in the size of container ships is that larger ships exceed the capacity of important sea routes such as the Panama and Suez canals. The largest size of container ship able to traverse the Panama Canal is referred to as Panamax, which is presently around 5,000 TEU. A third set of locks is planned as part of the Panama Canal expansion project to accommodate container ships up to 12,000 TEU in the future, comparable to the present Suezmax.

This expansion project on the Panama Canal is scheduled to be completed by 2014, making it able to handle the larger container ships. Once this happens, ports along the eastern seaboard will have access to these large ships, ultimately cutting down on shipping time and cost from manufacturers overseas.

In mid-2011, the cost to ship a loaded oil container from China to the U.S., with a rate of $100 per barrel was $5,000. As the price of oil increases, shipping costs increase.

Trucking is frequently used to connect the "linehaul" ocean and rail segments of a global intermodal freight movement. This specialized trucking that runs between ocean ports, rail terminals, and inland shipping docks, is often called **drayage,** and is typically provided by dedicated drayage companies or by the railroads.

In the first half of 2010, U.S. container ports handled a total of 110 million metric tons of containerized cargo, 17 percent higher than the 95 million metric tons handled in the same period in 2009.

On a typical weekday in 2009, U.S. container ports handled an average of 68,000 TEUs of freight, up from 37,000 TEUs per day in 1995, but down from the peak of about 78,000 in 2007.

Containers carry a wide variety of commodities—from sweaters, blouses, and flat-screen televisions to computer equipment and wood and paper products. During the first half of 2010, America's container ports handled over $256 billion worth of containerized cargo imports weighing more than 62 million metric tons. They also handled exports worth over $100 billion and weighing 48 million metric tons.

In 2009, U.S. ports handled $474 billion containerized imports. The top imported commodities by value in 2009 were print machinery, television and electronics, and motor vehicle parts and accessories. By weight, the leading imported commodities were furniture, bananas, and worked monumental or building stones.

In 2011, Canadian National Railway announced capacity improvements to accommodate growing container volumes at its largest intermodal terminal in Canada. Located in the prime logistics area of Greater Toronto, the Brampton Intermodal Terminal (BIT) is touched by more than 60 percent of the railway's systemwide intermodal traffic.

Other improvements include creation of about 25 percent more ground space for international containers by staging CN containers offsite; purchasing five new cranes in 2011; and increasing the labor force by about 10 percent in 2011.

BIT's intermodal volumes through the end of April rose by 12 percent from a year earlier. In 2010, CN's total intermodal volumes increased by 17 percent to 1.4 million units while intermodal revenues climbed by 18 percent to $1.6 billion Canadian **(see Figure 26-15)**.

Figure 26-15

Intermodal volumes continue to increase.

INTERLINE FREIGHT

Pick up freight from an **interline carrier** in the same way you would from a shipper. Deliver freight to an interline carrier as if it were a consignee:

- Always inspect the shipment for damage or shortages.
- Compare the bill of lading with the freight.
- Do not sign freight bills, bills of lading, or receipts until you note any shortages or damages and they are signed by an interline carrier.
- Make sure you thoroughly understand any special services and the method of payment.
- Get signatures and receipts before you release the shipment to the connecting carrier.
- If there is an equipment interchange with the connecting carrier, know the policy of your company. Always follow the established procedures.

Remember, you are responsible not only for the freight but also for making sure the trailer is within legal limits. Check the weight of the shipment on the papers so you will not accept an overloaded trailer.

HAZARDOUS MATERIALS AND WASTE

Hazardous materials shipments must be specially labeled, prepared, handled, documented, and placarded.

Communication of hazards in transportation is vital to public health and safety **(see Figure 26-16)**. If there is an accident or spill, police, fire, and emergency crews must be able to quickly recognize the presence of these materials.

As a professional driver, you must know how to recognize hazardous materials shipments and be aware of the dangers of each hazard class.

Figure 26-16

All hazmat shipments must be specially labeled, prepared, handled, documented, and placarded.

The Shipper's Responsibilities

By federal law, the shipper is required to:

- Train all employees involved in hazmat functions
- Identify all hazardous materials by hazard class
- Properly pack the material in the correct packaging
- Prepare the shipping papers, listing—in this order—the proper shipping name, hazard class, identification number, and packing group
- State the total quality or volume of the material
- Properly label each package with the correct hazard class label if one is required
- Mark each package with the proper shipping name and identification number for the contents
- Provide placards for the carrier
- Provide the emergency response telephone number

The Driver's Responsibilities

By federal law, drivers are required to:

- Check the bill of lading for hazardous material cargo
- Make sure the shipping papers are complete and accurate
- Check the shipping papers to make sure the shipper's certification form is signed (**see Figure 26-17**)
- Check the packages for proper labeling and marking
- Check compatibility and segregation requirements for the materials
- Observe the special handling and loading requirements
- Properly placard vehicle as required on all four sides (**see Figure 26-18**)
- Make certain shipping papers are within driver's reach or on the driver's seat if the driver has left the truck (**see Figure 26-19**)
- Comply with FMCSR

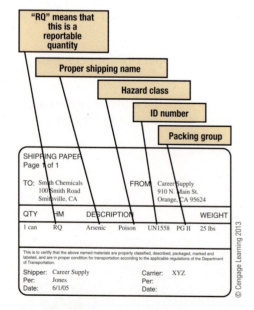

▶ **Figure 26-17**

Hazmat shipping papers itemize the contents of a hazmat cargo and serve to inform drivers of any special handling requirements.

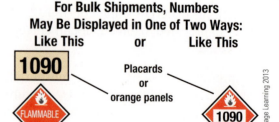

▶ **Figure 26-18**

There are two ways of displaying numbers on bulk shipments.

HAZARDOUS MATERIALS SHIPPING PAPERS

KEEP THIS ENVELOPE VISIBLE AND ACCESSIBLE

- While Drving - papers must be within driver's reach with seat belt fastened.
- In Driver's Absence From Unit - Papers must be on driver's seat or in pouch on driver's door.

Date	Vehicle No.	Dispatched By	Classification of Hazardous Materials on Vehicle	Weight	Type of Placard	Applied By

IN CASE OF SPILL OR OTHER EMERGENCY CALL _____

Mark the location of each class of Hazardous Materials loaded
onto the vehicle on the Diagram below.
BEFORE GIVING TO DRIVER

DRIVER'S INSTRUCTIONS ON REVERSE SIDE OF ENVELOPE

© Cengage Learning 2013

▶ **Figure 26-19**

Hazmat shipping papers must be within the driver's reach or on the driver's seat if the driver has left the truck.

SUMMARY

In this chapter, you learned the importance of cargo documentation: bills of lading, freight bills, cargo manifest, invoices, packing slips, and hazardous materials shipping papers. The responsibility of the shipper and the driver were explained. How to accept a load for shipment and the correct way to deliver it were described.

NOTE: It is important to always remember that when you pick up or deliver a load, you are representing your company as well as the company whose products or goods you are hauling or delivering. Often times the truck driver is the only person affiliated with a company the shipper or receiver actually sees or meets. Dressing and acting professionally are always important, but especially so when picking up or delivering the load.

KEY TERMS

Agent
Bill of lading (BL)
Cabotage
Collect-on-delivery (COD) shipments
Common carrier
Connecting carrier
Contract carrier
Delivery (terminal) carrier
Delivery receipt
Detention time or demurrage

Documentation
Domestic cargo
Drayage
Dunnage and return (DR) charges
Exempt commodity carrier
For-hire carrier
Freight bill
Freight forwarder
Helper service
Household goods bill of lading

Inside delivery
Interline carrier
Intermodal container
Intermodal freight transport
International bill of lading
International transportation invoice
Invoice
Manifest
Order notify bill of lading
Order notify shipment

Originating carrier
Packing slip
Prepaid shipments
Private carrier
Pro numbers
Receiver (consignee)

Residential delivery
Security seals
Shipper (consignor)
Storage and delay (S&D)
   charges
Straight bill of lading

Tailgate delivery
Tariff
Through bill of lading
Transportation charges
Uniform straight bill of lading
Warehouse receipt

REVIEW QUESTIONS

1. Cabotage is the transport of passengers or goods between _____ in the same country.

   a. port and railroad
   b. three cities
   c. three points
   d. two points

2. The consignee is _____.

   a. the person or company that offers the goods for shipment
   b. the person or company that is transporting the goods
   c. the person or company to whom the goods are being shipped
   d. the person or company that checks the load for hazmat items

3. A bill of lading is _____.

   a. a written contract between the shipper and the carrier for transporting a shipment
   b. a verbal contract between the shipper and the carrier for transporting a shipment
   c. a detailed list of packed goods that is prepared by the shipper
   d. a paper signed by the consignee or an agent of the consignee accepting the shipment from the driver

4. The most common type of bill of lading, which is a contract that the parties cannot change and requires that the goods must be delivered to the consignees or an authorized representative, is a(n) _____.

   a. original bill of lading
   b. nonuniform bill of lading
   c. order notify bill of lading
   d. uniform straight bill of lading

5. The responsibility for opening packages and checking the contents against the packing slip belongs to the _____.

   a. driver
   b. consignee
   c. person packing the trailer
   d. dispatcher

6. If you are asked to tow a trailer that is sealed with a security seal or you cannot visually inspect the contents, what should you do to release you and your company from responsibility for any damage unless the damages are caused by accident?

   a. Insist the shipper make the contents of the trailer available to you for a visual inspection.
   b. Make a note on the bill of lading: "shipper's weight, load and count."
   c. Accept the load but notify the Federal Transportation Commission that the shipper is in violation of federal regulations.
   d. Take the trailer as if you had inspected the contents.

7. Which of the following is not a shipper's responsibility regarding hazardous material and waste?

    a. Determine the route the rig should take to make the delivery.

    b. Train all employees involved in hazmat functions.

    c. Identify all hazardous materials by hazard class.

    d. Provide the emergency response telephone numbers.

8. Which of the following is not a responsibility of the driver regarding transporting hazardous material and/or waste?

    a. Check the bill of lading for hazardous material cargo.

    b. Check the packages for proper labeling and marking.

    c. Check FMCSR for route to take to make the delivery.

    d. Observe the special handling and loading requirements.

9. Placards are diamond-shaped signs that _____.

    a. indicate the increase in total stopping distance because of the characteristics of the load

    b. indicate the center of gravity of the load

    c. tell the hazard class of the shipment

    d. tell the driver the location of the delivery site

10. When receiving shipping papers from a shipper, the professional driver should make certain _____.

    a. hazardous materials are hazard listed in purple ink.

    b. hazmat are palletted together.

    c. hazardous materials are marked with class.

    d. hazmat are marked in indelible ink.

11. On an order notify bill of lading, the driver must check the back of the first (yellow) copy to make sure it is _____.

    a. date stamped

    b. signed by the shipper

    c. signed by the carrier

    d. all of the above

SUPPLEMENTAL LEARNING ACTIVITIES

1. Ask a local shipper for several copies of uniform bills of lading for the class to study. Make copies of the uniform BL in your book and fill them out for the following shipment: two 10-gallon drums of fertilizer, 50 cases of household cleaner, 90 cases of pillow cases, and 60 cases of hair color. Note any hazardous materials and find their hazard class.

2. Go to a dock or warehouse and observe the back-office operation, i.e., where bills are created and drivers are dispatched. Write a report about what you learned.

3. Write a 150-word report on "cabotage." In your report, discuss the impact of cabotage laws on domestic and foreign shipping companies.

4. Divide into groups, discuss and list the driver's responsibilities for documentation of a load of freight. From the list, pick one or two responsibilities you judge to be most important. Discuss these with the entire class.

5. Divide into two teams and have one person give out shipping documentation terms to the teams. These terms are found at the front of the book. The team getting the most terms correct will win.

FOR MORE INFORMATION

PTDI—Handle and Document Cargo, Page 22, Click on Skill Standards
www.ptdi.org/standards

Cabotage Rules for Canadian Drivers in the U.S.
www.fmcsa.dot.gov/intl-programs/intl-programs.htm

U.S. Customs and Border Protection
www.cbp.gov

FHWA's Office of Freight Management and Operations—Information on CMV Weight and Size Regulations in the U.S.
www.ops.fhwa.dot.gov/freight/sw/index.htm

Highway Traffic Act—Canadian Truck Weight and Size Laws
www.e-laws.gov.on.ca/html/regs/english/elaws_regs_050413_e.htm

© Cengage Learning 2013

OBJECTIVES

When you have completed this chapter, you should be able to:

- Identify common special rigs.

- Understand the function, operating characteristics, size, special features, and hazards of special rigs.

- Know the special skills and training needed to operate some rigs.

- Be aware of various types of cargos that are hauled and driving skills required.

- Safely tarp and untarp cargo on a flatbed trailer.

INTRODUCTION

A special rig is any combination vehicle differing from the standard tractor and 48- to 53-foot (14.6 to 16.2 m) dry freight trailer van with five axles and 18 wheels (**see Figure 27-1**). In this section, we will describe many of the common special rigs and the special skills needed to drive them (**see Figure 27-2**).

▶ **Figure 27–1**

Special rigs are any combination vehicle differing from the standard tractor and 48- to 53-foot (14.6 to 16.2 m) dry freight trailer with five axles and 18 wheels.

Special Purpose Vehicles

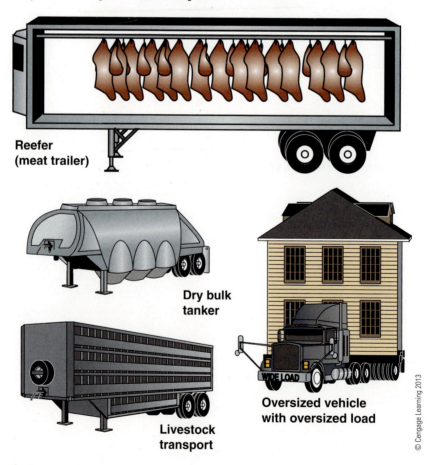

Reefer
(meat trailer)

Dry bulk
tanker

Oversized vehicle
with oversized load

Livestock
transport

▶ **Figure 27–2**

Special rigs are designed to haul specialized loads and require special driving skills.

> **CAUTION!**
>
> Because special rigs require special handling skills, professional drivers who drive them should be specially trained, either in school or by the employer.

▶ *"They said I was going to drive a special rig. This certainly is 'special' alright!"*

The following information is intended only to familiarize you with the unusual nature and driving requirements associated with some of the more common special rigs.

Among special rigs used commonly today are those:

- With more than one point of **articulation,** or **multiarticulation (see Figure 27-3)**
- That are **overlength**, **overheight**, **overwidth**, or **oversize**
- With a low ground clearance
- With a high center of gravity, when loaded
- With load stability problems
- That are used for special cargos
- That require special handling

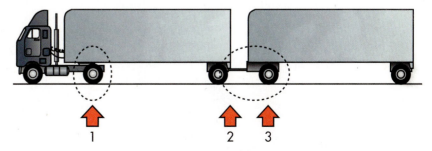

▶ **Figure 27-3**

A typical tractor-trailer rig has one joint. Twin trailers have three articulation joints.

The three articulation points of a twin trailer combination
1. Tractor fifth wheel and lead trailer kingpin connection
2. Lead trailer pintle hook connection with dolly tow bar
3. Dolly fifth wheel and rear trailer kingpin connection

© Cengage Learning 2013

The word *articulate* means "consisting of segments separated by joints." A multiple-articulation rig is one with several parts connected by joints. A typical tractor-trailer has just one joint—the connection at the kingpin and the fifth wheel between the tractor and the trailer.

> **CAUTION!**
> Steering a special rig can be affected by dry (lacking lubrication) fifth wheels on the tractor and dolly.

LONGER COMBINATION VEHICLES

Rigs with more than one trailer are known as longer combination vehicles (LCVs). They include:

- Twin trailers
- Rocky Mountain doubles
- B-trains
- Triple trailers

▶ **Figure 27–4**

A double trailer.

Twin Trailers

These rigs are also known as doubles, or sets **(see Figure 27-4).** The two basic types of twin trailers are **standard doubles** and **turnpike doubles.**

Standard Doubles

Standard doubles use two semi-trailers. The second trailer is converted into a full trailer by using a **converter dolly** (a set of wheels with a fifth wheel) **(see Figure 27-5).** The second semi couples with the fifth wheel at the converter. Most converters have a draw bar with one eye that connects to the pintle hook on the back of the first trailer. These are known as A-dollies. Some converters have a set of two parallel eyes that hook into two pintle hooks on the back of the first trailer. These are known as B-dollies. A rig with an A-dolly is also known as an A-train and a rig with B-dollies can be called a C-train **(see Figure 27-6).**

▶ **Figure 27–5**

Single axle converter dolly.

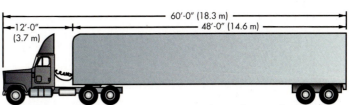

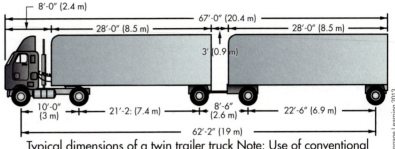

Typical dimensions of a tractor–semi-trailer with a 48-foot (14.6 m) semi-trailer

Figure 27–6

Trailer lengths vary and each combination requires special techniques in handling.

Typical dimensions of a twin trailer truck Note: Use of conventional tractor adds 3 to 7 feet (0.9 to 2.1m) to total length.

© Cengage Learning 2013

LONGER COMBINATION VEHICLES IN CANADA

- Ontario's LCV program consists of "turnpike doubles" generally operating on a primary LCV network of "freeway-style" highways and to and from approved origin/destination locations in close proximity to the primary network.

- The program has been developed cooperatively with Québec to ensure free movement of LCVs between the two jurisdictions.

- Participating carriers, drivers, and vehicles are held to higher standards than other trucking operations to enhance highway safety. LCVs operate under carefully developed controls and are closely monitored.

- The program is a private sector initiative led by the Ontario Trucking Association (OTA) and Private Motor Truck Council of Canada (PMTC). These associations are responsible for identifying highways for inclusion in the primary network, appropriate rest/emergency stop locations and undertaking all necessary engineering assessments or route modifications. Road authority consent must be obtained for any nonprovincial routes.

- The OTA and Québec Trucking Association (QTA) are also responsible for adapting the Canadian Trucking Alliance (CTA) LCV driver training program for Ontario/Québec operations and overseeing issuance of LCV Driver and Instructor certificates required for LCV operations in Ontario.

- Participating carriers are responsible for issuance of LCV Driver Certificates after ascertaining the driver meets specified qualifications, training, and experience.

- Participating carriers must enter into a Memorandum of Understanding (MoU) with the Ministry of Transportation Ontario MTO signifying that the carrier accepts responsibilities as outlined in this document.

- MTO will issue permits to qualifying carriers for operation on the primary LCV network and specified off-network routes to approved origin/destination locations.

British Columbia restricts LCV operation to the Coquihalla Highway (formerly a toll road) between Hope and Merritt, with the exception of B-doubles (mainly used for hauling wood chips).

(Continues)

LONGER COMBINATION VEHICLES IN CANADA (continued)

Alberta allows LCV operation on most major highways. The Queen Elizabeth II Highway between Calgary and Edmonton carries the majority of turnpike doubles and triples. Theoretically, these vehicles could be used on Highway 16 as far west as Hinton and Highway 43 as far north as Valleyview, but are rarely used on these routes. LCV operation north and west of Edmonton is limited to Rocky Mountain doubles, since the road is undivided north of Valleyview. The destination of most Rocky Mountain doubles is Yellowknife in the Northwest Territories.

The Northwest Territories allows LCVs of up to 31 m (101.7 ft) in length. These vehicles are restricted to specific destinations in Hay River and Yellowknife. LCVs do not operate north of Yellowknife **(see Figure 27-7)**.

Saskatchewan restricts LCVs to divided highways but appears to allow them to use undivided sections of those highways.

NOTE

Prospective LCV drivers in Alberta and NWT must have held a license for legal length articulated vehicles for two years (five years in the Northwest Territories). They may have no more than two moving offenses recorded within three years and may not have any vehicle-related criminal code violations. They are required to pass a PDIC (professional driver improvement course) every four years. They are required to pull an LCV at least once a year in order to keep their LCV license.

Courtesy of Sunbury Transport Limited

▶ **Figure 27-7**
Longer combination vehicle in Canada.

Identifying Characteristics.   Doubles have three points of articulation:

- First trailer kingpin and the fifth wheel
- Pintle hook and eye
- Converter dolly fifth wheel and the kingpin of the second trailer

Other Major Characteristics.   Trailer lengths for doubles vary from 26 to 28 feet (7.9 to 8.5 m) with overall lengths from 65 to 75 feet (19.8 to 22.9 m). Trailers may be vans, flatbeds, tankers, cargo, or others.

Special Handling Skills.   Driving doubles requires some special handling techniques:

- Always hook the heavy trailer as the lead trailer.
- Always avoid backing. This vehicle is not designed for the backing maneuver.
- Steering must be smooth. Jerking or whipping the steering wheel may cause the second trailer to overreact **(see Figure 27-8)**.
- Do not brake while negotiating a curve. This will cause the second trailer to dip.
- Be aware of the rig's greater length when passing other vehicles, changing lanes, or crossing intersections and railroad tracks.

- You cannot make tight turns with these closely coupled vehicles.
- Try to avoid bumps, potholes, and other road hazards. These can cause the tops of the trailers to bump each other.
- Be aware where your wheels are tracking. It is harder to stay in your lane when making turns with doubles.

Special Requirements. A professional driver must have a doubles/triples CDL endorsement. A driver must also have specialized knowledge and skills to safely drive double rigs. These rigs may be used in many states but are prohibited in others. Check the regulations for each state in which you will be driving doubles for the maximum allowed lengths and weights.

A quick steering move could flip a trailer

▶ **Figure 27–8**

Steering a set of trailers should be smooth because jerking or whipping the steering wheel may cause the second trailer to overreact.

GO!

Check each state's regulations to make sure you have the required permits before driving doubles in those states.

During pretrip and en route inspections, the driver must inspect the following:

- The drawbar and pintle hook articulation
- Safety chains
- Light cords
- Air line hookup
- Valve positions

More difficult coupling and uncoupling procedures must also be mastered.

Turnpike Doubles

Commonly used on turnpikes in eastern states, turnpike doubles typically have nine axles. Some midwestern state turnpikes (including the Indiana and Ohio Toll Road) allow drivers to legally haul "turnpike doubles."

Identifying Characteristics.

- Trailer lengths of 40 to 53 feet (12.2 to 16.2 m)
- Overall rig length of 100 feet (30.5 m) or more
- Usually equipped with high-powered engines and multiple-gear transmissions

Other Major Characteristics and Handling. Turnpike doubles have the same handling characteristics as standard doubles. The longer trailers, for example, require more room for maneuvering.

Trailers are 26 to 28 feet (7.9 to 8.5 m) long, and the overall length of the rig is 100 feet (30.5 m) or more (as allowed in some states). These trailers may be vans, flatbeds, tankers (used mostly in the western states), or various types of cargo trailers.

Special Requirements. A doubles/triples endorsement is required on the CDL for these rigs. Professional drivers are required to have more skill and more knowledge when driving turnpike doubles **(see Figure 27-9).** If a special permit is held, turnpike doubles can be used on certain toll roads. For more information, see individual state regulations. Inspection procedures are basically the same as those used for standard doubles. Toll road authorities sometimes require special, more demanding inspection routines.

© Cengage Learning 2013

▶ **Figure 27-9**

Turnpike double: A three-axle tractor pulling two tandem-axle semi-trailers—nine axles in all.

Rocky Mountain Doubles

Rocky Mountain doubles are larger than standard doubles but smaller than turnpike doubles. The lead trailer is typically longer than the second trailer.

Identifying Characteristics

Semi-trailers are 40 to 50 feet (12.2 to 15.2 m) long. Full trailers are 26 to 29 feet (7.9 to 8.8 m) long. Many van and refrigerated trailers come standard at 53 feet (16.2 m) and are commonly used as the lead trailer. The rig's overall length is 80 to 100 feet (24.4 to 30.5 m), sometimes longer.

Other Major Characteristics and Handling

Rocky Mountain doubles have the same handling characteristics and require the same driving skills as standard doubles, but the long lead trailer requires extra space for maneuvering. Trailers may be vans, flatbeds, or tankers.

Special Requirements

Professionals driving Rocky Mountain doubles must have a doubles/triples endorsement on their CDL. More knowledge and driving skills are also required.

Special permits are needed to operate Rocky Mountain doubles, and they are most commonly permitted on limited access roads in the western U.S. and western Canada.

B-Trains

A **B-train** is a rig with two semi-trailers pulled by a tractor. The first trailer has two or three axles on the rear of the trailer body. The second or third axle extends beyond the rear of the trailer body and under the nose of the second semi-trailer. A fifth wheel is mounted above the second axle, which removes the need for a converter. The second semi-trailer couples to the first semi, using the fifth wheel. This arrangement eliminates one point of articulation **(see Figure 27-10).**

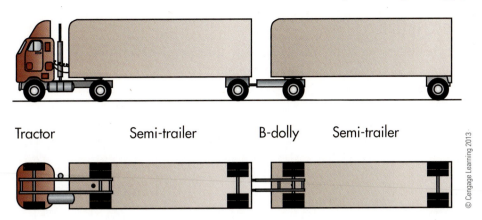

▶ **Figure 27-10**

A B-train is composed of a tractor towing two semi-trailers. The trailers have an extended frame with a fifth wheel for attaching the next trailer, made of a B-dolly and semi-trailer.

Tractor   Semi-trailer   B-dolly   Semi-trailer

Identifying Characteristics

Combinations with one tractor and one semi-trailer have one point of articulation. Doubles have three; B-trains have two.

When a semi-trailer has tandem axles, they are usually located all the way under the trailer. In B-trains, the second axle extends beyond the rear of the first semi-trailer.

Other Characteristics

The trailers and overall length vary depending on the state or province in which they are driven. For example, there may be two 40-foot (12.2 m) trailers or one 40-foot (12.2 m) trailer and one 27-foot (8.2 m) trailer. The trailers may be vans, tankers, flatbeds, dumps, and so on.

B-trains have been used in Canada for many years but they are now being seen more frequently in the U.S. They carry many types of cargo.

A C-train is composed of a tractor-trailer semi-trailer towing one or more full trailers made of a B-dolly and semi-trailer.

Special Handling

In addition to the safe driving practices for regular combinations are a number of special handling points for B-trains:

■ Backing is difficult and should be avoided; however, B-trains are easier to back than regular doubles.

■ Steer smoothly—jerking or whipping the steering wheel causes the second trailer to overreact.

■ Driver must be aware of the rig's greater length when overtaking and passing other vehicles, changing lanes, and crossing intersections and railroad crossings.

■ Driver must remain aware of tracking to be able to stay in the proper lane when driving curves.

Special Requirements

Driving a B-train requires special training, skills, and knowledge. A doubles/triples endorsement is needed on the CDL. With special permits, these rigs may be driven on certain roadways only. For more information, see each state's requirements.

Triple Trailers

Other names for **triple trailer** rigs are triples, triple headers, triple bottoms, or triple sets.

Description

Triple trailers are combination rigs with three semi-trailers pulled by a tractor. The second and third semis are converted to full trailers by converters. They are connected by drawbars and pintle hooks (**see Figure 27-11**).

© Cengage Learning 2013

▶ **Figure 27-11**

Triples—or triple trailers.

Identifying Characteristics

Similar to doubles, triples have a number of connection points—five to be exact. There are three king-pin and fifth-wheel connections and two eye-and-pintle hook connections. The length of each trailer is 26 to 28 feet (7.9 to 8.5 m).

Other Major Characteristics

Characteristics are about the same as they are for doubles. Trailer lengths are 26 to 28 feet (7.9 to 8.5 m), and overall length of the rig varies, up to 100 feet (30.5 m), depending on state regulations. Trailers may be flatbeds, tankers, boxes (used mostly in the western U.S.), or any type of cargo trailers. Some Midwestern state turnpikes allow drivers to legally haul triple trailers. Examples include the Indiana and Ohio Toll Road.

Special Requirements

Professionals who drive triples must have the doubles/triples endorsement on their CDL and are required to have different skills from those who drive doubles. The drivers must also have more driving skills. Special permits are needed when using certain highways. Check each state's requirements and regulations before driving triples in those states.

SPECIAL TRAILER TYPES

These trailers are used for oversized loads, and include lowboys, drop frames, flatbeds, and open-top vans. They have multiple wheels and axles, depending on the vehicle, cargo weight, and state laws.

Many of these special trailers have **outriggers** to support oversized loads. Converter dollies may be attached in the usual way or to the cargo itself to distribute the weight over more axles and to support larger loads.

These rigs are used for hauling various types of large, overweight loads including:

- Equipment for power plants
- Nuclear reactors
- Industrial dryers
- Generators
- Oil field equipment
- Heavy construction equipment

Special Requirements

Special training, additional skills, and specialized knowledge are needed by the professional driver who drives rigs using special trailer types. As an example, a doubles/triples endorsement is required on the CDL in order to drive these special rigs. With special permits, these rigs may be operated on certain highways, often at designated times of the day. For more information, see each state's laws and regulations.

Examples of Special Trailer Types

Two-axle double drop deck low bed with outriggers—this rig has a double-top frame and two rear axles. Outriggers are attached to each side of the trailer. When they are extended, they support wider loads (**see Figure 27-12**). This type of trailer is used to haul oversize loads, machinery, and construction equipment, often referred to as over dimensional loads.

▶ **Figure 27–12**

Two-axle double drop deck low beds often use outriggers to support oversize loads.

Five-axle removable gooseneck low bed with detachable two-axle dolly—this low-bed frame has three rear trailer axles. A two-axle dolly is attached to the rear of the trailer. The detachable **gooseneck** lets the trailer rest on the ground when loading heavy equipment such as bulldozers, front loaders, and backhoes (**see Figure 27-13**).

▶ **Figure 27–13**

Five-axle removable gooseneck low bed with detachable two-axle dolly.

Double deck trailer—provides rear entry loading of livestock or other cargo to both levels (**see Figure 27-14**).

▶ **Figure 27–14**

Double deck trailer with two levels.

Two-axle float—this rig has a flatbed frame with two rear axles and no landing gear. It is used mainly in the oil fields for hauling drilling equipment **(see Figure 27-15).**

▶ **Figure 27–15**
Two-axle float.

Four-axle removable gooseneck low bed with outriggers—this rig has a low-bed frame, four rear trailer axles, and a detachable gooseneck. This allows the trailer to rest on the ground for loading heavy equipment such as bulldozers and cranes. For wide loads, outriggers may be attached **(see Figure 27-16).**

▶ **Figure 27–16**
Four-axle removable gooseneck low bed with outriggers.

Multiwheel low-bed trailer with jeep dolly—this rig has a low-bed frame and two rear trailer axles **(see Figure 27-17).** A two-axle dolly is attached to the trailer using the actual cargo. One end of the cargo rests on the dolly; the other end rests on the trailer. A two-axle jeep dolly can be attached to the fifth wheel. The fifth wheel is between the tractor and the trailer.

▶ **Figure 27–17**
Multiwheel low-bed trailer with jeep dolly.

▶ **Figure 27–18**
Low-clearance vehicle.

LOW-CLEARANCE VEHICLES

The two types of low-clearance vehicles are drop deck and double drop deck **(see Figure 27-18).**

The **double drop deck** drops close to the ground. The **single drop deck** drops about half that distance. Both drop far enough behind the kingpin plate to keep the tractor hookup from hitting the trailer drop. Be sure the fifth wheel is not too far forward. The tractor frame must not hit the trailer drop and the rear wheel must not hit the trailer on sharp turns.

Drop decks haul heavy, oversized cargos or larger, space-demanding loads **(see Figure 27-19).**

Special Requirements

Low-clearance vehicles are similar to other special rigs in their requirements for special training, added skills, and knowledge needed by drivers. With special permits, these rigs may be operated on certain highways. For specific guidelines and other information, check individual state or province regulations and requirements.

Lowboys or Flatbeds

Low beds are also known as flatbeds or lowboys. They haul heavy equipment such as bulldozers, cranes, or earth movers. They also haul oversized items such as equipment for power plants, boilers, and generating stations. They may have as many as four axles and 24 wheels. These trailers can have bottom clearance problems at railroad crossings, curbs, and large potholes and require special skills for driving and maneuvering.

▶ **Figure 27-19**
Double deck vehicle, generally known as an autohauler.

▶ **Figure 27-20**
Single drop trailer.

Warehouse or furniture vans are the most commonly used vans in the household goods moving industry. The drop-in frame provides a greater load capacity. For instance, a drop of 27 inches (68.6 cm) gives a trailer an additional 3,000 cubic feet (85 cubic meters) of cargo space. Generally, these vehicles are easy to load by hand because of the drop; however, the wheel housing can be a problem if a forklift is used.

Electronics vans are designed to handle delicate electronic equipment. They have air ride or soft ride suspension to protect fragile loads. Now they are also used to haul high-bulk, low-weight items such as clothing, potato chips, and plastics; but these vans have a smaller drop (21 inches/53.3 cm) than a warehouse van. They also have smaller (15 inch/38.1 cm) wheels, which make room for a flat floor with no wheel wells. The drawback is that these vans provide less space for cargo and cause more heat buildup in the brake drums and tires.

Single Drop Low Bed

This low-bed design is also known as the flatbed. These can haul higher loads without going over the legal height limits **(see Figure 27-20).** Bottom clearance problems are not as bad as those of the double drop frames **(see Figure 27-21).** These trailers can have many axles and wheels, depending on type and weight of load.

Single Drop Warehouse Van

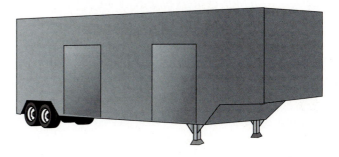

Single Drop Low Bed

▶ **Figure 27-21**
Low beds are designed to carry higher loads, and bottom clearance problems are not as frequent.

Warehouse, furniture, or electronics vans can have either a single drop frame or double drop frame design.

HIGH CENTER OF GRAVITY IN VEHICLES

As the name suggests, the bulk of the weight of the cargo in these rigs is high in the load. The **center of gravity,** therefore, is farther from the road's surface. This makes the trailer more likely to roll over when taking a curve **(see Figure 27-22).**

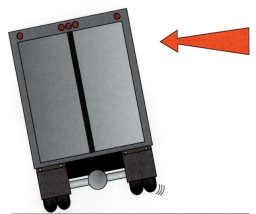

Dry Bulk Tankers

The shape of the semi-trailer varies but is usually cylindrical. It may be high at each end and slope to a center bottom discharge gate. Trailer lengths vary. The high center of gravity requires careful speed control, particularly on curves.

Dry bulk tankers haul such items as flour, sugar, powdered milk, ground limestone, cement, fly ash, and plastic pellets. These rigs are usually loaded through openings in the top. They are unloaded by a blower from the tractor or through the bottom of the tanker.

Liquid Cargo Tankers

Milk tankers are rarely used for other cargos. These **smooth-bore tanks** do not have **baffles** or **bulkheads.** Their smooth linings must be kept very clean. These rigs can be difficult to handle because they must be driven with partial loads. As deliveries are made and the cargo is reduced, handling characteristics change **(see Figure 27-23).**

The smooth interior of the tanks and partial loads make driving challenging **(see Figure 27-24).** Drivers should accelerate slowly, avoid braking turns, and turn only at safe speeds.

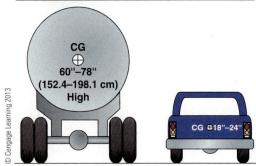

▶ **Figure 27-22**

Trailers with high centers of gravity are more likely to roll over on a curve.

▶ **Figure 27-23**

Liquid cargo tanker.

▶ **Figure 27-24**

When driving tankers, accelerate slowly, avoid braking turns, and turn at safe speeds.

UNSTABLE LOADS

The two common types of unstable loads are:

- Liquid in tankers
- **Livestock** or carcasses, sometimes called "swinging meat"

It usually takes the first 100 to 200 miles (161 to 322 km) of a trip for swinging meat to interlock and stabilize.

Liquid Tanker

Liquid tankers are used to transport liquid cargo such as gasoline, asphalt, milk, orange juice, or lique-fied gases **(see Figure 27-25).** The tanker itself may be hot, cold, or pressurized. The type of tanker used will depend on the cargo it carries.

The semi-trailers of these liquid tanker rigs are usually oval, circular, or square. The load/unload mechanism may or may not be connected to the tractor **(see Figure 27-26).**

The number and lengths of compartments vary. There may be one compartment or many. Some contain *baffles* (walls with holes to reduce surge) or *bulkheads* to prevent liquid from surging, front to back. Handling these vehicles can be very difficult. **Surging loads** create an unstable vehicle.

Examples of Tankers

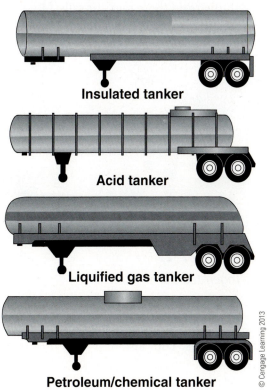

Insulated tanker

Acid tanker

Liquified gas tanker

Petroleum/chemical tanker

© Cengage Learning 2013

© Cengage Learning 2013

▶ **Figure 27–25**
Liquid tanker.

▶ **Figure 27–26**
Tankers transport various types of liquid cargo: hot, cold, and pressurized.

Petroleum or chemical tankers have one to five compartments and may or may not have baffles. Their capacity can be as high as 9,500 gallons (35,961 liters).

Acid tank rigs have a small-diameter tank with outside stiffener rigs and a variety of linings or baffles. They are sometimes insulated and carry up to 6,000 gallons (22,712 liters) of liquid.

Liquid gas tankers are designed for high pressure and carry butane, propane, oxygen, hydrogen, and other gases in a liquefied state.

Insulated tankers carry heated material. Steel tankers can carry materials as hot as 500 degrees F (260 degrees C). Aluminum ones carry loads up to 400 degrees F (204 degrees C).

Special Requirements for Driving Liquid Cargo Tankers

There are special requirements for liquid cargo tanker drivers and every driver must be familiar with the characteristics and handling requirements of these vehicles. Because of the tanker's high center of gravity, much practice and experience is required before driving a tanker on the open road.

Refrigerated Trailer

There are two types of reefers:

- Nose mount
- Belly mount

Nose mount trailers have the refrigeration unit at the upper front of the trailer (**see Figure 27-27**). In **belly mount** trailers, the unit is under the trailer.

Both are box-type semi-trailers. Some have racks or rails suspended from the roof. Beef, pork, and lamb are hung from these racks or rails. Others have separate compartments. Some cargo can be kept frozen while other cargo is only cooled. These units have slotted floors and canvas ducts in the ceiling to let air or gas circulate (**see Figure 27-28**).

▶ **Figure 27-27**
Refrigerated trailer—"reefer."

Refrigerated Semi-trailer

▶ **Figure 27-28**
"Reefers" carry loads requiring controlled, cooler temperatures.

Refrigeration units have their own engines and may be powered by gasoline, diesel fuel, or liquefied petroleum gas. They also have their own fuel tanks, which are located beneath the trailer unit. Generally, the floors, sides, and roofs are thickly insulated (**see Figure 27-29**).

Refrigerated trailers, or reefers, that have rails attached to the trailer roof from which to hang meat, present a special problem because the high-hanging meat raises the vehicle's center of gravity.

Loosely packed, swinging meat loads create dangerous stability problems. Swinging meat is more of a handling problem than sloshing liquid in a tanker. Safe handling procedures are vital.

▶ **Figure 27–29**

Refrigerated haulers have their own engine and fuel tanks separate from the tractor.

INTERESTING FACT

The first refrigerated car to carry fresh fruit was built in 1867 by Parker Earle of Illinois, who shipped strawberries on the Illinois Central Railroad. Each chest contained 100 pounds (45 kg) of ice and 200 quarts (189.3 liters) of strawberries. It wasn't until 1949 that a refrigeration system made its way into the trucking industry by way of a roof-mounted cooling device, patented by Fred Jones.

GO!

It takes 100 to 200 miles (161 to 322 km) for hanging meat to stabilize. Stepping on the brakes a few times will help slide the hooks forward. Do this before adjusting sliders for weight distribution.

Some modern meat processing plants complete the entire process at one location and the final product is boxed and easily palletatized. These reefer models have steel floors with ribs for ventilation.

Special Requirements for Driving Reefers

Special training, additional skills, knowledge, and experience are all needed by the professional driver before driving reefers. For more information, check each state's or province's laws.

Before driving a reefer, carefully inspect each trailer for holes in the walls, ceiling and ducts, doors, and door gussets. Also check the fuel level, the reefer's engine coolant, and oil and refrigerant levels (**see Figure 27-30**). En route, the driver should monitor the operation of the reefer unit.

NOTE: Vehicles designed to transport meat should be marked for food use only to prevent cross contamination by other cargos.

▶ **Figure 27–30**

Before a trip, a driver must inspect the refrigeration unit for holes in the walls, ceilings, and doors and check the fuel, coolant, oil, and refrigerant levels of the reefer unit.

SPECIAL CARGO VEHICLES

Any rig designed to haul one certain type of cargo is special. For example, a tanker designed to transport edible cargo should not carry any loads that cannot be eaten.

Pole Trailer

A **pole trailer** carries long, narrow cargo. It may be telescoped—made longer or shorter—to fit the load. Cargo may be poles, timbers, logs, steel girders, or concrete beams **(see Figure 27-31)**.

The load-carrying bed consists of two U-shaped cradles (bunks) connected by a steel pole (reach). The reach is the part that can be lengthened or shortened. Some rigs do not have a reach. If this is the case, the load becomes the body. Sometimes a straight truck is used as the tractor and the front bunk of the trailer is mounted on the flatbed of the truck body.

Autotransport Trailer

The autotransport trailer hauls cars, SUVs, and pickup trucks. It can carry six full-size cars or up to 10 subcompacts. Sometimes another car is mounted on the rack above the tractor. A rear ramp can be raised or lowered to allow cars to be driven on and off the transport **(see Figure 27-32)**.

Pole Trailer

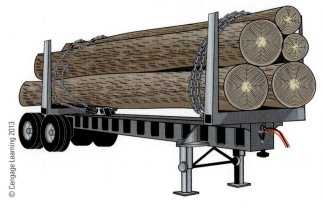

▶ Figure 27-31
Pole trailers carry long, narrow loads, such as logs, poles, timbers, girders, or concrete beams.

▶ Figure 27-32
Auto transporter.

SPECIAL HANDLING VEHICLES

These rigs have special handling problems because of visibility, location of the steering axle, and so on.

Low Cab Forward

The cab is in front of the engine on this small diesel, used for city pickup and delivery. A heavy-duty diesel may be used as a combination city and short-distance haul rig.

Snub Nose Tractor

The engine extends back into the cab of the snub nose tractor, which is otherwise a conventional tractor. It is often used for close-clearance city work **(see Figure 27-33)**.

▶ **Figure 27-33**
City pickup and delivery truck.

© Anton Foltin/www.Shutterstock.com

Yard Spotter Trucks

Sometimes known as a cab-beside-engine, the yard tractor is a heavy-duty diesel most frequently used as a yard horse. Its job is to shuttle, or transfer, trailers from one part of the yard to another.

Dromedary Tractor

The dromedary tractor has a cargo body mounted just behind the cab and ahead of the fifth wheel. Its cargo space—or drom box—may be loaded from the rear or through side doors.

HOW TO SAFELY TARP AND UNTARP A LOAD ON A FLATBED TRAILER

Not every state in the U.S. has a mandatory truck tarp law for hauling product such as asphalt, sand, and aggregate, but every state does have littering laws that require haulers of refuse to cover their loads in order to prevent garbage from littering the roadways.

An exposed load, be it of gravel, rocks, or lumber, is a hazard to motorists, creates more litter along the sides of roads, and adds more dust to the air. The easiest way to cover the load in any truck is with a tarp; vinyl, polyethylene, and mesh are all used. Truck tarps, however, are cut specifically for certain load and bed sizes, with flatbed and dump trucks being the two general options.

Any time you tarp or untarp a load, be certain you have access to and use the right safety equipment. This includes a pair of steel-toe boots with good traction control and ankle support, well-fitting gloves, a high-visibility vest, hat, long pants, and safety glasses **(see Figure 27-34)**.

INTERESTING FACT

Chattanooga, Tennessee, mechanic Ernest Holmes got a call from his old business school professor, John Wiley, in 1916. Wiley and his son had been driving when their Model T veered off the road and flipped upside down in a creek bed. Holmes came to help, but it took him eight hours and six men to retrieve the car from the creek bed. Searching for a better solution, Holmes modified a 1913 Cadillac, adding a crane and pulley system and a pair of outriggers to stabilize it while it was lifting and pulling other vehicles—creating the first tow truck in the U.S.

▶ **Figure 27–34**

Having all personal safety equipment is extremely important.

Before learning how to safely cover a load with a tarp, it is important to be familiar with the various types of tarps and their uses:

A lumber tarp—25 feet (7.6 m) long by 24 feet (7.3 m) wide. Also is called a tarp with "8-foot (2.4 m) drops." The 8-foot (2.4 m) drops refers to the trailer's width, which is 8 feet (2.4 m) across, so if this tarp is centered on the load, there will be 8 feet (2.4 m) of material hanging down on each side. These kinds of tarps are good for lumber, wall board, trim molding, and other "tall" loads. When you're ready to secure the bottom edge of the tarp, you don't have to roll up 4 feet (1.2 m) of tarp along the bottom. Think of making a twin bed with a king sheet.

Some lumber tarps come with either a flap at the front end or a "boxed end."

Most lumber tarps, regardless of boxed or flapped, have three rows of "D" rings, starting along the bottom edge and going up every 12 inches (30.5 cm) or so, running the length of the tarp and across the flap or box. This is so you can roll up excess at the bottom and still secure the tarp.

Flap tarps—If a tarp has a flap, the flap is generally 12 feet (3.7 m) wide, and 8 feet (2.4 m) tall, sewn across the front middle of the tarp, allowing it to be folded down over the front of the load. These styles of tarps are usually 12 inches (30.5 cm) wide and can be placed across the front of the load and then wrapped around the corners of the load to keep wind, rain, and debris from getting under the tarps. This style also prevents "parachute tarps"—a term describing when wind gets under the tarp, causing the tarp to bulge out like a parachute full of air. "Parachuting" is a safety issue and should be avoided.

A "boxed end" tarp—where the sides of the flap are sewn to the front of the tarp, with the front flap edges sewn to the side drop front edges. Imagine this type of tarp to be similar to a "fitted" bed sheet (without the elastic around the bottom). These tarps are helpful in some ways, especially if you regularly haul the same sized load, because there is no need to manipulate the front flap to fit the load or to use a bungee cord. It is already sewn on, and is water and air tight.

Steel tarps—are usually 24 feet (7.3 m) long by 12 feet (3.7 m) wide. Used with the 8-foot (2.4 m) wide trailer, this tarp only has 2-foot (0.6 m) drops on each side. Steel, being heavier, is usually the shortest load on the trailer, so the driver may not need 8 feet (2.4 m) of tarp material to roll up. This is why the short-sided tarp is often used, mainly because it works well with sheet steel and rebar. There is no flap on the front and it usually has two rows of "D" rings, sewn along all four edges. Steel tarps are also good to use with a load of crated material and only need a top cover to keep dirt or wetness off of the load.

Smoke tarps—are usually 12 feet (3.7 m) by 12 feet (3.7 m) with two rows of rings. Smoke tarps are used on the top front of a load to keep exhaust smoke off of the load, or if you have a load of pipe (steel or PVC) and you don't want the wind whistling through the load. They can also be used for loads where only very small items need a cover, but not the whole load.

Bag tarps—are tarps sewn into a bag-shape to go over loads, such as steel coils. (Bag tarps are also called "coil tarps.") Bag tarps are used to go over individual coils, have several rows of rings, and come in various sizes.

Glass tarps—are usually made of a very heavy weave or knitted material (think fishnet) that go over crates of glass. They are not water tight, but are mainly used to protect the load from road debris.

Custom-made lumber tarps—custom-made lumber tarps have 4-foot (1.2 m) drops, but have a second set of "clip-ons" that are 4 feet (1.2 m) tall, and are however long their main tarp is. Made this way, if they only need 2 or 4 feet (0.6 or 1.2 m) of drop, they have it with the one tarp, but if they need 8 feet (2.4 m), they clip a piece on that extends the drop to 8 feet (2.4 m). Instead of carrying two full sets of tarps, they only have to carry one with the extenders. The top edge of the extension has clips that clip onto the lowest edge of the "D" rings on the main tarp. While these custom tarps save a lot of room and are easy to use, they are rather pricey.

OSHA SAFETY GUIDELINES FOR TARPING AND UNTARPING

When working with a load of tarped freight, one of the most important safety precautions is protecting yourself from falling, whether adjusting, removing, or applying a tarp from the top of your load. If you are working at a company facility, your employer must provide an appropriate fall protection system or method. You also must receive training on how to use it, according to OSHA guidelines. If you are working at a shipper's facility, that shipper is responsible for providing fall protection when you come on site and need to tarp a load.

When on the road it may be difficult or impossible to use fall protection. Situations when fall protection may not be possible include vehicle inspections, service work, roadside repairs, and construction sites. Use safe work practices when fall protection systems are not available.

If you need to get on a load to adjust, remove, or apply a tarp:

- Wear nonskid shoes.
- Use a ladder to get to the top of your load.
- Don't lift with your back when you position the tarp.
- Look for gaps and cracks on the top of the load so that you won't trip over them when you're unrolling the tarp.
- Stay as close to the center line of the load as possible when you are unrolling the tarp.
- Make sure the tarp meets the deck and that the tie-downs are not worn or damaged.
- Roll tarps properly when you put them away. A loosely rolled part of the tarp is difficult to handle when being used to tarp the next load.

When Possible:

- Go to a truck stop or another safe area—don't just pull to the side of the road.
- Position an unrolled tarp from the end of the load. This will allow you to push the tarp while rolling.
- Get a forklift operator to load your tarps for you—or to help you retrieve tarps when you're ready to tarp another load.

HOW TO TARP A LOADED FLATBED TRAILER

Before pulling the tarp across the load, make certain the load is arranged properly. First, ensure the load's weight is distributed evenly across the trailer to make it easier to pull and steer. Arranging the load with wind resistance in mind is also important. The more wind hitting a load, the harder it is to pull and the more stress is put onto the cover itself. The single biggest reason tarps tear while enroute to its destination is improper loading, so when loading, try not to have anything high and wide standing over and above the truck.

Select the right tarp to cover the load. Polyethylene and canvas tarps do not stand up to the abuse of the wind and/or the elements of nature, so after the first mile of your trip, you can expect tearing. Therefore, it is important to select heavy vinyl tarps with a weight of at least 18 ounces (510 grams) that is UV treated and waterproof. These tarps are 10 times stronger than the typical blue poly covers.

Choose a tarp style that has heavy, well-attached grommets. The sewing of the fabric's edges will also make a big difference out on the road. Look for hems/edges that have two rows of sturdy stitches that go through multiple layers of the material.

Courtesy of Don Hess

Once the flatbed is loaded and you have chosen your tarps, ask a fork truck operator to lift the tarps to the top of the load to begin tarping. Help is necessary because tarps often weigh 80 pounds (36 kg) **(see Figure 27-35).**

▶ **Figure 27-35**

Forklift lifting tarp to top of loaded flatbed.

STOP!
Know the load surfaces and where the holes are to prevent falling. Also, NEVER walk backward when tarping or untarping a load.

Use a ladder to access the load when placing the tarp. But, before climbing the ladder, inspect it—side rails and rungs—to make certain it is in good repair. Never take this for granted. Also, make certain the ladder will reach 3 feet (0.9 m) above the height of the load and that the rungs provide solid, non-slip footing.

To cover the load, stretch the tarp across the load and ensure there is an equal length on both sides. Use sturdy rubber tie-downs to attach the cover to the trailer and start strapping in the centers. When you get to the corners, fold the excess underneath before strapping it down to prevent the wind from catching the edges.

When you are on top of the load and working near the edge, it is safest to get down on your hands and knees.

Next, use wide nylon ratchet straps to tie both the tarp and the load down to the trailer. If the trailer is equipped with an enhanced ratchet system, run the hook over the load and set the metal bar across to secure the straps. Then lock the ratchet mechanism into place.

Covering a loaded flatbed trailer with a tarp is the most important step in preparing for transport. Exposure to the outside elements and winds encountered while going down the highway has a significant impact, but by loading the flatbed correctly and using high-quality tarps accurately, your load will reach its destination safely **(see Figure 27-36).**

© iStockphoto/kozmoat98

▶ **Figure 27-36**

High-quality tarps protect a driver's load.

HOW TO SAFELY REMOVE A TARP

- Put on personal protective equipment.
- Be sure you know the load and where the holes might be if the load is a mix of items.
- Get help for this activity.
- Remove all tie-downs.
- Grab one corner—any corner—and yank it upward to allow air to get under the tarp.
- Use a steady, balanced pulling motion, much like the one you would use to pull a bucket from a well.
- Once you have the tarp ready to remove, make sure it is aligned so it is flat and square for folding.
- Use proper lifting techniques, or use a fork truck to lift the tarp.
- Remember to use your legs when lifting heavy tarps.
- Work smart as you move the tarp into storage.

SUMMARY

Many of the special rigs described in this section are dangerous in the hands of an untrained driver. All require special instruction and training as well as long experience. Most special rigs also require special permits. Using special care in the loading and unloading, tarping and untarping, and handling of specialized loads is also imperative. As a professional driver, it is your responsibility to develop these skills, know safety precautions, seek help and information from more experienced drivers, and keep safety at the forefront in meeting the requirements of handling specialized rigs and their loads.

KEY TERMS

Articulation
A-train
Baffle
Belly mount
B-train
Bulkhead
Center of gravity
Converter dolly
Double deck trailer
Double drop deck
Dry bulk tankers
Gooseneck

Liquid tankers
Livestock transport
Multiarticulation
Multiwheel low-bed trailer
Nose mount
Outriggers
Overheight load
Overlength load
Oversize load
Overwidth load
Pole trailer
Refrigerated trailer (reefer)

Rocky Mountain double
Single drop deck
Smoothbore tank
Special rig
Standard double
Surging loads
Triple trailer
Turnpike doubles
Two-axle double drop low bed
    with outriggers
Two-axle float

© Cengage Learning 2013

A DAY IN THE LIFE...

Kim Richardson – KRTS Transportation Specialists Inc., President

Let me start by saying that the trucking industry is one of the greatest fraternities in the world. My immediate and extended family has made a great living in this industry.

As a young boy I had a dream, like every other Canadian boy who ever put on a pair of skates—to be a professional hockey player in the National Hockey League (NHL). Although I did not make it to the Big Leagues, I learned so much about life from some great coaches at the hockey arena. This experience taught me to be a team player with a "failure is not an option" attitude. I believe this philosophy has carried through to my current role in the trucking industry.

> **We learned early that establishing relationships is a critical part of business success.**

I come from a family of truckers, which makes me a "trucking brat." Although I did try other career opportunities, I was always in the industry. As a young boy I washed trucks and trailers and remember getting my AZ (CDL) license five days after my 18th birthday. Working in the family business was tough—the expectations were high. As young as 20, I was teaching entry-level drivers and really enjoyed it. Soon I started doing road tests, seminars, and anything related to safety compliance. I enrolled in numerous seminars that focused on improving my skills.

After a number of years in the family business, I was ready to go out on my own. In 1989, with the support of my wife and business partner, Lisa, we founded Kim Richardson Transportation Specialists Inc. (KRTS). From a one-truck-and-trailer operation we certified new entry-level drivers and supplied a number of services to carriers and companies in Canada and the United States. This corporate training became a major part of our business. We learned early that establishing relationships is a critical part of business success. This has helped us to grow to meet the needs of our customers. We increased the size of our fleet and expanded our operation to include a number of training divisions. Today we offer training for tractor-trailer and straight truck, heavy equipment, forklift, 0–8-ton lifting devices, and car training, as well as offering our corporate services to over 250 clients in Canada and the United States.

My career has afforded me many opportunities. I enjoy being a board member of the Ontario Trucking Association Allied Trade Division. My involvement on the board of directors of the Professional Truck Driver Institute and on the membership committee of the Truckload Carriers Association has been of great value both personally and professionally.

In the last few years we have had the opportunity to expand our interests. We founded *The Rear View Mirror,* an industry newspaper that lands on the desks of decision makers in the trucking industry. Another venture has led me to partner with my long-term industry friend and mentor, Ray Haight, who is another "trucking brat." Launching our company, TransRep, has involved us in a new sector of the industry. We feel that these new endeavours are a great fit for KRTS.

My career in the trucking industry has been anything but normal, but that's not a bad thing. We have embraced the opportunities that have come our way, and while not all have been successful, they have all been a learning experience. Remember, victory and success love preparation!

REVIEW QUESTIONS

1. Any combination vehicle that differs from the standard tractor and 48- to 53-foot (14.6 to 16.2 m) dry freight trailer with five axles and 18 wheels is known as a(n) _____.

   a. ordinary rig

   b. B-train

   c. special rig

   d. turnpike double

2. A multiple-articulation rig is one that has _____.

   a. a high center of gravity

   b. several parts connected by joints

   c. poor traction

   d. multiple driver trains

3. Which of the following is NOT one of the special handling techniques required for driving rigs with more than one trailer?

   a. When slowing for a curve, it is better to brake in the curve because it makes the following trailer(s) follow the path of the first trailer.

   b. Always hook the heavy trailer as the lead trailer.

   c. The driver must avoid backing.

   d. The driver must avoid jerking or whipping the steering wheel because this act may cause the following trailer(s) to overreact.

4. Which of the following is not a true statement regarding the special requirements for driving doubles or triples?

   a. Special skills are needed.

   b. Special knowledge is needed.

   c. All states have the same rules and regulations regarding doubles and triples.

   d. Special permits may be needed.

5. Regarding special trailer types used for oversized loads, which of the following is not a correct statement about the use of converter dollies?

   a. The converter dollies may be attached to the load itself.

   b. The dollies distribute the weight over more axles.

   c. They support longer loads.

   d. Reduced air pressure in the tires of the dollies increase the stability of the load.

6. Low-clearance vehicles have which special characteristic?

   a. require no special permits

   b. can haul oversized loads

   c. require no special driving skills

   d. have no load stability problems

7. Which of the following is not a characteristic of high center of gravity vehicles?

   a. The bulk of the weight of the cargo is low in the load.

   b. The bulk of the weight of the cargo is high in the load.

   c. The center of gravity is farther from the road than in a vehicle with a low center of gravity.

   d. The trailer is more likely (than a lower center of gravity vehicle) to roll over when taking a curve.

8. Which of the following is not a correct statement regarding pulling a trailer transporting livestock?

    a. The cargo shifts.

    b. These types of rigs have a permit to drive at least 10 mph (16 km/h) above the speed limit to keep the animals cool.

    c. The balance and stability change when slowing.

    d. When preparing to stop, the driver should tap the brakes lightly to set the animals.

9. The load of a liquid tanker may surge when stopping, starting, and/or changing directions, which creates a(n) _____.

    a. stable vehicle

    b. situation that does not affect the vehicle

    c. unstable vehicle

    d. a and b

10. Refrigerated trailers (reefers) that have rails attached to the trailer roof from which meat is hung _____.

    a. raise the center of gravity of the trailer

    b. lower the center of gravity of the trailer

    c. make the trailer more stable on the turns

    d. make the trailer more stable when stopping

11. When tarping or untarping a load a driver must have all the right safety equipment, some of which include _____.

    a. steel-toe boots

    b. well-fitting gloves

    c. high-visibility vest

    d. all of the above

12. If you are working at a shipper's facility, who is responsible for providing a means to use fall protection when you need to tarp or untarp a load?

    a. the shipper

    b. the employer

    c. the driver

    d. none of the above

SUPPLEMENTAL LEARNING ACTIVITIES

1. Ask a special rig driver (or more than one) to come speak to your class. Have questions prepared ahead of time to learn more about the special driving skills and the professional drivers' own experiences in driving special rigs.

2. Visit a fire department and/or emergency medical service. Ask the drivers to talk about the special skills required for driving emergency vehicles.

3. Think about driving a pole trailer loaded with freshly cut trees along narrow mountain roads. In a small group, think about maneuvering this load. What are the challenges? What are the rewards of driving logs to a lumber mill? Use Internet research for additional information.

4. Driving an auto transport has its advantages, including fairly regular schedules. In a small group, discuss the challenges and the skills required for driving a transport, loaded with new or used vehicles. Use Internet research for additional information.

5. As a refrigerated truck driver, you have a double focus: the mechanical function of the rig and the function of the refrigeration for the trailer. Discuss the challenges as well as the positive aspects of driving a "reefer." Use the Internet to learn more about refrigerated rigs.

FOR MORE INFORMATION

Tanker Driving Jobs
www.ehow.com/about_4795086_tanker-driving-jobs.html

NYS DMV Commercial Driver's Manual—Tank Vehicles
www.nydmv.state.ny.us/broch/cdl/cdl10sec08.pdf

Cattle Hauling Jobs
www.ehow.com/list_6851078_cattle-hauling-jobs.html

Big Rigs Around the World
en.wikipedia.org/wiki/Semi-trailer_truck

Ontario LCV Program
www.mto.gov.on.ca/english/trucks/lcv/program-conditions/overview-and-principles.shtml

Hours of Service

© Timothy Epp/www.Shutterstock.com

OBJECTIVES

When you have completed this chapter, you should be able to:

■ Understand the reasons behind the hours-of-service laws.

■ Know the requirements and rules of Part 395 of FMCSR covering hours of service.

■ Know industry methods for recording hours of service and what information should be included.

■ Understand the effect of fatigue while driving and how best to avoid it.

■ Compute on-duty hours and required rest stops while on the road.

INTRODUCTION

As a professional driver, you have a daily responsibility of maneuvering up to 40 tons (36,280 kg) of loaded equipment in all types of demanding weather, traffic, and road conditions **(see Figure 28-1)**. The hours-of-service laws were designed to help keep you at your best and safest level of performance by regulating the number of hours you can spend on the clock and behind the wheel.

Aside from the fact that drivers and trucks continue to move freight from point A to point B, the motor carrier industry has drastically changed since 1938, when the original **hours-of-service (HOS) regulations** were mandated for truck drivers. Roads are better designed, constructed, and maintained in networks across states, provinces, and countries to provide greater mobility, accessibility, and safety for all highway users—and, because of scientific research, we know more about the capacity of the human body and the impact of each individual's biological clock.

Vehicles also have been dramatically improved in terms of design, construction, safety, comfort, efficiency, emissions, technology, and ergonomics.

Proposed changes for the HOS regulations were under consideration by the Federal Motor Carrier Safety Administration (FMCSA) for several years before a final rule was announced in 2003. Now, these hours of service are once more up for review and revision. The results of this current review were announced in December, 2011 when FMCSA announced the final ruling on hours of service, with the bulk of the rules going into effect on July 1, 2013.

On February 14, 2012, the American Trucking Associations (ATA) stated that they had no choice but to file suit against the Federal Motor Carrier Safety Administration(FMCSA)'sfinalhours-of-service ruling.

The rule, published in the Federal Register last December, upheld the current 11-hour daily driving limit, but did accompany some changes.

According to the FMCSA's website:

- Rest breaks—after June 30, 2013, driving is not permitted if more than 8 hours have passed since end of driver's last off-duty or sleeper-berth period of at least 30 minutes.

- On-duty time "does not include any time resting in a parked CMV. In moving CMV, does not include up to 2 hours in passenger seat immediately before or after 8 consecutive hours in sleeper-berth. Also applies to passenger-carrying drivers," effective Feb. 27, 2012.

▶ Figure 28-1

Federal laws regulate the number of hours a driver can spend on the road.

▶ *On time delivery translates to driver success, no matter what time zone you're in!*

■ "Waiting time for certain drivers at oilfields must be shown on logbook or electronic equivalent as off duty and identified by annotations in 'remarks' or a separate line added to 'grid.'"

But perhaps the biggest change that drivers will endure effective on July 1, 2013, is the 34-hour restart provision which "must include two periods between 1 A.M.–5 A.M. home terminal time." This decision is said to reduce a driver's work week from 82 to 70 hours, which would lead to productivity problems since a reduction would limit a driver's time on the road, which could cause delivery complications and increased rates for shippers (which then trickle down to higher costs for consumers).

As of February 2012, drivers who exceed their hours by 3 or more will face maximum penalties.

More information about hours of service can be found on the Federal Motor Carriers Safety Administration website at www.fmcsa.dot.gov.

HOURS OF SERVICE: A BRIEF HISTORY

The first hours of service for U.S. professional drivers were enforced in 1938. Through the decades, as more information about the work of professional drivers was gathered and considered, new rules were put into place. In every case, hours-of-service regulations were developed to increase the safety of drivers and the welfare of their cargos and fellow highway users.

INTERESTING FACT

In 1962, for reasons it never clearly explained, motor carriers were required to give drivers 8, rather than 9, consecutive hours off-duty each day. These rules allowed for 10 hours of driving and 8 hours of rest within a 24-hour day.

Between 1962 and 2003, there were numerous proposals to change the HOS again, but none were ever finalized. By this time, the ICC had been abolished and regulations were now issued by the FMCSA.

The 2003 changes applied only to property-carrying drivers (i.e., truck drivers), and the most notable change of 2003 was the introduction of the "34-hour restart."

In 2005, the FMCSA changed the rules again, *practically* eliminating the split sleeper berth provision. Drivers are now required to take a full 8 hours of rest, with 2 hours allowed for off-duty periods, for a total of 10 hours off-duty. This provision forces drivers to take one longer uninterrupted period of rest, but eliminates the flexibility of allowing drivers to take naps during the day without jeopardizing their driving time.

In the years since 2005, groups such as Public Citizen Litigation Group, Parents Against Tired Truckers (PATT), Owner-Operator Independent Drivers Association (OOIDA), Citizens for Reliable and Safe Highways (CRASH, which has merged with PATT), and the American Trucking Associations (ATA) have been working to change the HOS again. Each group has its own ideas about what should be changed, and different agendas on why the rules should be changed.

NEW U.S. HOURS-OF-SERVICE RULES—12/22/2011

After many postponements, litigation, and study, new hours-of-service rules were issued as part of FMCSR 49 CFR Part 395. The new HOS rules had been pending since June 2009. As found on www.fmcsa.dot.gov/rules-regulations/topics/hos/index.htm:

The Hours-of-Service regulations (49 CFR Part 395) put limits in place for when and how long commercial motor vehicle (CMV) drivers may drive. These regulations are based on an exhaustive scientific review and are designed to ensure truck drivers get the necessary rest to perform safe operations.

FMCSA also reviewed existing fatigue research and worked with organizations like the Transportation Research Board of the National Academies and the National Institute for Occupational Safety in setting these HOS rules.

The regulations are designed to continue the downward trend in truck fatalities and maintain motor carrier operational efficiencies. Although the HOS regulations are found in Part 395 of the Federal Motor Carrier Safety Regulations, many states have identical or similar regulations for intrastate traffic.

Who must comply with the Hours-of-Service Regulations?

Most drivers must follow the HOS Regulations if they drive a commercial motor vehicle, or CMV. In general, a CMV is a vehicle that is used as part of a business and is involved in interstate commerce and fits any of these descriptions:

- Weighs 10,001 pounds (4,536 kg) or more
- Has a gross vehicle weight rating or gross combination weight rating of 10,001 pounds (4,536 kg) or more
- Is designed or used to transport 16 or more passengers (including the driver) not for compensation
- Is designed or used to transport 9 or more passengers (including the driver) for compensation
- A vehicle that is involved in Interstate *or* intrastate commerce and is transporting hazardous materials in a quantity requiring placards is *also* considered a CMV
- They can be found, in total, at www.fmcsa.dot.gov/rules-regulations/truck/driver/hos/fmcsa-guide-to-hos.pdf

The rule will mainly affect drivers who work more than 70 hours a week on a continuing basis. These drivers are mostly a subset of long-haul truckload drivers. Local drivers and less-than-truckload drivers, who rarely work more than 5 days a week, are unlikely to be affected.

Key Elements of the December 2011 HOS Rule

The goal of this rulemaking is to reduce excessively long work hours that increase both the risk of fatigue-related crashes and long-term health problems for drivers. A rule cannot ensure that drivers will be rested, but it can ensure that they have enough time off to obtain adequate rest on a daily and weekly basis. The objective of this rule, therefore, is to reduce both acute and chronic fatigue by limiting the maximum number of hours per day and week that the drivers can work. On average, the rule reduces a driver's maximum allowable hours of work per week from 82 hours to 70 hours, a 15 percent reduction. The 15 percent reduction in the average maximum allowable hours of work based on the new rule results from the restrictions on the use of the restart period.

1. **Maximum Driving Hours**—FMCSA retained the current 11-hour driving time limit, but placed a limit on the number of consecutive driving hours. No driving may occur if more than 8 consecutive hours have passed since the last break of 30 minutes or more.

2. **Restart**—Any restart period must include two consecutive nighttime periods (from 1 A.M. to 5 A.M.), and must be at least 34 consecutive hours long. Drivers are permitted to use the restart provision only once in any seven calendar days.

3. **14-Consecutive-Hour Day (now called Driving Window)**—The rule retains a 14-consecutive-hour driving window. With a 30-minute rest break, maximum **on-duty time** within the 14 hour window is 13.5 hours. No driving may occur after 14 consecutive hours since coming on duty; nondriving work is allowed past the 14 hour driving window.

4. **Mandatory Rest Break**—Drivers will not be permitted to drive if 8 hours have passed since their last break of 30 minutes or more. (Only one break may be required depending upon timing.)

5. **Off-Duty in a Parked CMV or in Passenger Seat**—The rule allows drivers to record time spent in a parked CMV as **off-duty time.** Also, team drivers would be permitted to record up to 2 hours of time spent in the passenger seat of a CMV in operation as off-duty time, if it is just before or after an 8-hour **sleeper berth** period.

6. **Oilfield Exemption**—Waiting time at an oil well or natural gas site will not count toward calculation of the 14-hour window but must be recorded as off-duty on a paper or electronic log.

7. **Egregious Violations**—A driver who exceeds, and/or a motor carrier that allows a driver to exceed, the driving time limit by 3 hours or more is considered to have committed an egregious violation and be subject to the maximum civil penalties of $2,700 for drivers and $11,000 for motor carriers—for each offense.

8. **Effective Date & Compliance Date**—This rule will be effective in late February 2012, and the oilfield exemption change must be implemented by then. However, interstate motor carriers and drivers will not be required to comply with the remainder of the new rules (restart change, rest break requirement, etc.) until July 1, 2013.

9. **Sleeper Berth Rules**—FMCSA did not propose nor has it adopted any changes to the provisions that cover the use of sleeper berths.

10. **The Problem of Detention Time and Extended Wait Periods**—FMCSA does not have the statutory authority to regulate shippers and receivers.

Figure 28-2 summarizes the differences between the previous HOS Rule and the new HOS Final Rule published in December 2011.

CANADIAN HOURS-OF-SERVICE

Effective January 1, 2007, Transport Canada (www.tc.gc.ca) issued new rules regarding commercial motor vehicle driver hours of service. These regulations are based on NSC Standard #9–Hours of Service, as developed by the Canadian Council of Motor Transport Administrators (CCMTA), the organization responsible for coordinating all matters dealing with the administration, regulation, and control of motor vehicle transportation and highway safety in Canada. The objective of this HOS regulation is to improve motor carrier safety by limiting a driver's hours of work to increase alertness and reduce fatigue.

The rule is consistent with the expectations of CTA, Canada's trucking lobbying group, which worked closely with Transport Canada to develop this regulation. Some highlights of the new rule include:

- Drivers can be on-duty for a maximum of 14 consecutive hours and during that time the driver may drive for a maximum of 13 hours

- After meeting either of these two limits, the driver must have 10 hours off-duty

- Off-duty period must consist of at least 8 consecutive hours, with the remaining 2 hours allowed to be split into no less than half-hour increments

- No more than 16 hours may elapse between 8 consecutive hours of off-duty times

- No less than 10 hours/day off-duty time in a 14-day cycle, a driver may accumulate no more than 120 hours on-duty time, or 70 hours on-duty time without taking at least 24 consecutive hours of off-duty time

- In a 7-day cycle, a driver may be on-duty no more than 70 hours

- A 7-day cycle may be reset after at least 36 consecutive hours of off-duty time, while a 14-cycle may be reset after at least 72 hours.

For more detailed information please visit www.tc.gc.ca/eng/roadsafety/safedrivers-commercialdrivers-hoursofservice-index-110.htm.

Provision	Current Rule	Final Rule – Compliance Date July 1, 2013
Limitations on minimum "34-hour restarts"	None	(1) Must include two periods between 1 A.M.–5 A.M. home terminal time. (2) May only be used once per week.
Rest breaks	None except as limited by other rule provisions	May drive only if 8 hours or less have passed since end of driver's last off-duty period of at least 30 minutes. [HM 397.5 mandatory "in attendance" time may be included in break if no other duties performed]

Provision	Current Rule	Final Rule – Compliance Date February 27, 2012
On-duty time	Includes any time in CMV except sleeper-berth.	Does not include any time resting in a parked CMV. In a moving property-carrying CMV, does not include up to 2 hours in passenger seat immediately before or after 8 consecutive hours in sleeper-berth. Also applies to passenger-carrying drivers.
Penalties	"Egregious" hours of service violations not specifically defined.	Driving (or allowing a driver to drive) 3 or more hours beyond the driving-time limit may be considered an egregious violation and subject to the maximum civil penalties. Also applies to passenger-carrying drivers.
Oilfield exemption	"Waiting time" for certain drivers at oilfields (which is off-duty but does extend 14-hour duty period) must be recorded and available to FMCSA, but no method or details are specified for the recordkeeping.	"Waiting time" for certain drivers at oilfields must be shown on logbook or electronic equivalent as off duty and identified by annotations in "remarks" or a separate line added to "grid."

Courtesy of FMCSA

▶ **Figure 28–2**

Differences between the previous HOS Rule and the new HOS Final Rule published in December 2011.

RECORD OF DUTY STATUS

While your first duty as a professional driver, regarding hours-of-service, is to follow the guidelines to the letter, it is also important to maintain good, legible, and accurate records. The regulations do not describe exactly what your hours-of-service log must look like, but your records must include a 24-hour graph grid, which is shown in the regulations.

The 24-hour graph grid must include the date, total miles/kilometers driven that date, truck or tractor-trailer number, carrier name, main office address, your signature—which certifies all entries are true and accurate—the name of a co-driver if you have one, time zone of

NOTE

Any time you work for more than one motor carrier during a 24-hour period, you must make extra copies and give a copy of your log to each carrier.

For complete log book guidelines, explanations, and examples, go to www.fmcsa.dot.gov/rules-regulations/topics/hos/hos-logbook-examples.htm.

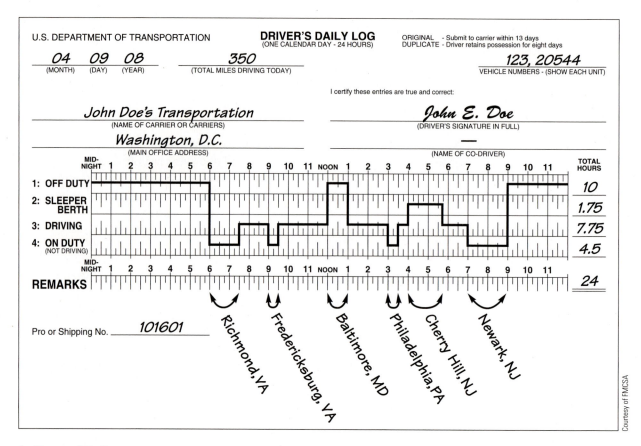

Figure 28-3

Sample of completed driver's log.

your home terminal, total hours, and shipping document numbers (**see Figure 28-3**). There is also a remarks section and this space is used to list the location where a change of duty status occurs as well as explanations of any unusual circumstances or log entries that may require clarification during review. An example of this could be sudden adverse driving conditions.

After you have completed your log, regulations allow you 13 days to get the original copy to your carrier, although your carrier may require that you return it sooner. You must also keep a copy of your completed log for the next seven consecutive days.

GO!

Adverse driving conditions, such as snow, sleet, fog, icy pavement, and other unusual road or traffic conditions, may prevent the driver from completing a scheduled run in the time allowed by the Hours-of-Service law. In such cases, the driver is legally allowed to reach the original destination or a safe place to park the rig and wait for safer driving conditions. Adverse driving conditions must be noted in the "Remarks" section of the daily log. The driver must not have had prior knowledge of the adverse condition.

For the purposes of completing the daily log, "on duty time" means all time from the time a driver begins to work or is required to be in readiness to work until the time the driver is relieved from work and all responsibility for performing work. On duty time shall include:

1. All time at a plant, terminal, facility, or other property of a motor carrier or shipper, or on any public property, waiting to be dispatched, unless the driver has been relieved from duty by the motor carrier;

2. All time inspecting, servicing, or conditioning any commercial motor vehicle at any time;

3. All driving time as defined in the term driving time;

4. All time, other than driving time, in or upon any commercial motor vehicle except time spent resting in a sleeper berth;

5. All time loading or unloading a commercial motor vehicle, supervising, or assisting in the loading or unloading, attending a commercial motor vehicle being loaded or unloaded, remaining in readiness to operate the commercial motor vehicle, or in giving or receiving receipts for shipments loaded or unloaded;

6. All time repairing, obtaining assistance, or remaining in attendance upon a disabled commercial motor vehicle;

7. All time spent providing a breath sample or urine specimen, including travel time to and from the collection site, in order to comply with the random, reasonable suspicion, post-accident, or follow-up testing required by part 382 of this subchapter when directed by a motor carrier;

8. Performing any other work in the capacity, employ, or service of a motor carrier; and

9. Performing any compensated work for a person who is not a motor carrier.

Onboard Electronic Recorders

According to the FMCSA, it is now acceptable to use on-board recorders (OBRs) as a **driver's daily log** to record duty status as long as electronic records include the minimum information required by Part 395.8 of the FMCSR and must be formatted in accordance with the rules. In addition, the driver must adhere to the following:

- Print the log at the completion of each day and sign it. Note that the driver's signature cannot be electronic. The driver must physically sign the log after printing it.

- Be able to print the log for the current 24-hour period on demand.

- Maintain a copy of printed and signed log printouts for the previous 7 consecutive days and have it available for inspection at the request of an enforcement officer.

PENALTIES

Drivers who make false entries on their daily logs, do not prepare a daily log, or drive more than the allowable hours are subject to serious penalties. These laws are enforced by the Department of Transportation and penalties may include:

- Drivers placed out of service (shut down) at roadside until the driver has accumulated enough off-duty time to be back in compliance

- State and local enforcement officials assessing fines

- FMCSA levying civil penalties on driver or carrier, ranging from $550 to $11,000 per violation depending on severity

- Carrier's safety rating downgraded for a pattern of violations

- Federal criminal penalties being brought against carriers who knowingly and willfully allow or require HOS violations

Carriers who do not keep proper records on all drivers are also subject to heavy fines and civil liability if there is an accident because the driver has violated the regulations.

DOT REQUIRES ELECTRONIC ON-BOARD RECORDERS FOR TRUCK AND BUS COMPANIES WITH SERIOUS HOURS-OF-SERVICE VIOLATIONS

April 2, 2010—The U.S. Department of Transportation's Federal Motor Carrier Safety Administration today issued a new rule that will require interstate commercial truck and bus companies with serious patterns of hours-of-service (HOS) violations to install electronic on-board recorders (EOBRs) in all their vehicles. Nearly 5,700 interstate carriers will use EOBRs after the final rule's first year of implementation.

"Safety is our highest priority," said FMCSA Administrator Anne S. Ferro. "In addition to requiring EOBRs for carriers that have already demonstrated a pattern of hours-of-service violations, we will initiate a rulemaking later this year that considers an EOBR mandate for a broader population of commercial motor carriers."

Electronic on-board recorders are devices attached to commercial vehicles that automatically record the number of hours drivers spend operating the vehicle. Driving hours are regulated by federal HOS rules, which are designed to prevent commercial vehicle–related crashes and fatalities by prescribing on-duty and rest periods for drivers.

Under the EOBR final rule, carriers found with 10 percent or more HOS violations during a compliance review will be required to install EOBRs in all their vehicles for a minimum of two years. The rule also provides new technical performance standards for EOBRs installed in commercial motor vehicles, including requirements for recording the date, time, and location of a driver's duty status.

Additionally, carriers that voluntarily adopt EOBRs will receive relief from some of FMCSA's requirements to retain HOS supporting documents, such as toll receipts used to check the accuracy of driver logbooks.

The rule will go into effect on June 1, 2012, to ensure EOBR manufacturers have sufficient time to meet the rule's performance standards and to manufacture products to meet industry demand.

Fatigue Prevention

One of the major reasons for changing the HOS rule was to prevent CMV drivers from becoming fatigued due to their hours of service. For more than a decade, studies have examined driver fatigue, its causes, and ways to prevent it.

Each year, according to the National Highway Traffic Safety Administration (NHTSA), 100,000 police-reported crashes are the direct result of driver fatigue. These drowsy driving–related accidents cause an estimated 1,500 deaths and 71,000 injuries each year **(see Figure 28-4)**.

In some states, such as New Jersey, new laws have been passed, making "driving while drowsy" a criminal offense; and experts say drowsiness and driver fatigue are increasingly viewed as a criminal offense in courtrooms across the country under existing reckless driving and vehicular homicide laws.

Obviously, when you are behind the wheel and begin feeling sleepy, you are in a dangerous situation. That feeling of sleepiness, or fatigue, slows reaction times, decreases awareness, increases aggressiveness (tired, cranky drivers often react differently to other drivers and may be more prone to road rage and speeding), and impairs judgment enough to cause a crash.

A recent survey from the National Sleep Foundation shows that about 50 percent of adult drivers say they have driven a vehicle while feeling drowsy in the past year.

When you think of the term "biological clock," you probably think it is all about women and their child-bearing years. However, each individual has a biological clock that tells the body when it is hungry, when

▶ Figure 28–4

Fatigued or sleep-deprived drivers can lead to accidents involving injury or possible death.

▶ Figure 28–5

Your biological clock tells your body when it's hungry, when it's energetic, and when it's time to sleep (circadian rhythm).

it has energy, and when it is tired **(see Figure 28-5).** The biological clock causes changes in the body's temperature and causes the person to feel wide awake or sleepy.

Twice a day—once in early afternoon (between 2 and 5 P.M.) and once in the early morning (between 2 and 6 A.M.)—your biological clock may make you feel sleepy, too sleepy to operate a vehicle safely.

Research by FMCSA has determined that driver alertness and performance were more consistently related to time of day than time on task. Drowsiness episodes were eight times more likely between midnight and 6 A.M. than at other times during the day.

To avoid driver fatigue, drivers should be aware of their own biological clock and to know which times of the day they are most alert. In addition, drivers should take the responsibility to get enough sleep during off-duty hours.

In many cases, drivers try to battle fatigue with a variety of methods, such as coffee or cola (caffeine), super energy drinks (similar to 5-Hour Energy) or drugs (similar to No-Doz). However, studies have found when a driver is sleep deprived, taking these stimulants only causes drivers to experience "microsleeps," or brief, four- to five-second lapses; these are even more dangerous than fatigue because four to five seconds is plenty of time for a driver to become involved in a crash.

STOP!

Nothing helps more when you're sleepy or feel fatigued than a brief nap—and it's better to stop for a short nap than it is to drive fatigued or drowsy and risk a wreck.

Sleep Apnea

According to the National Institutes of Health, approximately 18 million Americans suffer from some form of sleep apnea (pronounced *AP-ne-ah*), and most don't know they have the problem. About 4 percent of men and 2 percent of women between the ages of 20 and 60 suffer from sleep apnea.

Sleep apnea is a common disorder in which one or more pauses in breathing or shallow breaths occur periodically during sleep. These breathing pauses can last from a few seconds to minutes and may occur 5 to 30 times or more an hour. Typically, normal breathing then starts again, sometimes with a loud snort or choking sound.

Sleep apnea usually is a chronic (ongoing) condition that disrupts sleep and those diagnosed with sleep apnea often move out of deep sleep and into light sleep when breathing pauses or becomes shallow. This results in poor sleep quality that results in tiredness or fatigue during the day. In fact, sleep apnea is one of the leading causes of excessive daytime sleepiness.

This condition often goes undiagnosed because physicians usually can't detect the condition during routine office visits. Also, there are no blood tests for the condition. Most people who have sleep apnea don't know they have it because it occurs only during sleep. A family member and/or bed partner may first notice the signs of sleep apnea.

The most common type of sleep apnea is obstructive sleep apnea. This most often means that the airway has collapsed or is blocked during sleep. The blockage may cause shallow breathing or breathing pauses and often causes loud snoring.

Obstructive sleep apnea is more common in people who are overweight, but it can affect anyone.

Obstructive sleep apnea is an acknowledged problem by the transportation industry and, since 2009, the National Transportation Safety Board has urged mandatory apnea testing and treatment for drivers of trucks, buses, and trains as well as airline pilots and ship captains.

According to the National Transportation Safety Board, sleepiness has played a role in 31 to 41 percent of crashes of commercial vehicles, resulting in 1,500 to 2,000 deaths a year.

A 2007 presentation by the American Trucking Associations noted that most truckers are men (about 92 percent at that time)—and the average body mass index is 31, above the obesity benchmark of 30.

The Federal Motor Carrier Safety Administration for many years has been considering rules on testing for and treatment of sleep apnea, but has not imposed rules yet. An advisory committee for the group, however, heard testimony on sleep apnea in December 2011.

How to Know If You Are Sleep Deprived

Another study by FMCSA found that during their main daily sleep period, drivers slept only about 5 hours, which was 2 hours less sleep than their "ideal" requirement of slightly over 7 hours. The bottom line is that getting enough sleep is essential to a driver's performance behind the wheel (**see Figure 28-6**).

But, here's the caveat—most drivers don't realize that they haven't had enough sleep until they start dozing off behind the wheel. A few danger signals leading up to feelings of heavy fatigue include:

- Eyes close by themselves or go out of focus.
- You have trouble keeping your head up.
- You cannot stop yawning.
- Thoughts are wandering and disconnected.
- You suddenly do not remember driving the last several miles/kilometers.

▶ **Figure 28-6**

Being well-rested is essential to a driver's performance behind the wheel.

- You miss an exit.
- You tend to speed up or slow down.
- You start drifting in and out of your lane.

Most people do not realize that getting less than 7 or 8 hours of sleep in a 24-hour period can lead to chronic sleepiness and can also cause irritability, crankiness, and depression. It also makes it more likely that the driver will fall asleep while driving, and the only way to correct this situation is to get more or better sleep.

The following suggestions may help to avoid driving tired, although the best way to avoid problems with fatigue is to get plenty of good, healthy sleep:

- Before starting your run, get enough sleep—even take a short nap before going on duty.
- If driving alone, try to keep alert by talking on the CB radio. If team driving, talk to your co-driver. If you are both too sleepy to drive, pull over and take a nap.
- Be aware of any feelings of drowsiness and if you are too drowsy to drive, stop and take a nap.
- Schedule breaks to get out of your seat every 100 miles (161 km) or every 2 hours.
- Get fresh air into the cab.

SUMMARY

In this chapter, you learned about the changes being made in the federal hours-of-service laws, why HOS laws exist, and the proposed changes in these laws. You also learned the importance of keeping an accurate daily log, either manually or using an onboard electronic recorder.

The details of the on-duty and off-duty time requirements were explained. The penalties for both drivers and carriers if they fail to abide by these rulings in their operations were outlined. Finally, you learned that a neat and readable log is the result of a driver's professional responsibility and is the product of a positive and professional attitude.

Finally, you learned about driver fatigue, sleep apnea, and the dangers of driving while sleep-deprived or drowsy. Above all else, getting back home safely after every trip is your number one priority. In every activity as a professional driver, safety is job one.

KEY TERMS

Driver's daily log

Hours-of-service (HOS)
  regulations

Off-duty time

On-duty time

Sleeper berth

REVIEW QUESTIONS

1. The hours-of-service laws were designed to _____.

   a. make as much money as the rig can

   b. make the dispatcher's job easier

   c. help keep you at your best and safest level of performance

   d. move cargo from point A to point B as fast as possible

2. In 1995, Congress directed the FMCSA to research a change in the hours-of-service rule, because it was concerned about _____.

   a. freight not moving fast enough

   b. the effect of fatigue as a contributing factor in commercial motor vehicle crashes

   c. stopping distance of rigs

   d. center of gravity of loads

3. The current U.S. hours-of-service ruling requires drivers to take at least _____ hours off between shifts.

   a. 11

   b. 10

   c. 9

   d. 12

4. According to the current U.S. hours-of-service ruling, drive time and _____ of loading/unloading time is included in a 14-hour cycle.

   a. all

   b. 1/2

   c. 1/3

   d. 3/4

5. When does your "biological clock" make you too sleepy to operate a vehicle safely?

   a. three times per day—two times in the afternoon and one time in the early morning

   b. one time per day at about 1:00 P.M.

   c. one time per day at about 10:00 A.M.

   d. twice a day—once in the early afternoon and once in the early morning

6. The best way to avoid driving while sleepy and having problems with fatigue is to _____.

   a. stop and take a short nap

   b. drink coffee or cola (caffeine)

   c. use drugs (No-Doz)

   d. talk on the CB

7. Which of the following activities can extend the 14-hour on-duty period?

   a. off-duty time for meals

   b. the use of a sleeper berth

   c. off-duty time for fuel stops

   d. a and c

8. Driver's daily log entries regarding time entries must be made using the time zone _____.

    a. the rig is currently in   **c.** of the driver's home terminal

    b. of Central Standard Time   **d.** of Eastern Standard Time

9. Which of the following is NOT one of the penalties that may be assessed for false entries by a driver on the daily log?

    a. driver placed out of service at roadside until the driver has accumulated enough off-duty be back in compliance

    b. state and local enforcement officials may assess fines

    c. driver placed out of service, but permitted to drive to the nearest motel for rest until the driver has accumulated enough off duty time to be back in compliance

    d. the carrier's safety rating can be downgraded for a pattern of violations

10. A driver may be declared out of service by any agent of the Department of Transportation if he or she has been on duty too many hours or if _____.

    a. he or she doesn't have daily logs for the previous 7 days

    b. he or she does not have an OBR

    c. he or she appears fatigued and not alert

    d. he or she has not filed a trip plan

11. If you are using an OBR to record your daily log, you must print your driver's daily log every _____.

    a. 7 days   **c.** day

    b. other day   **d.** 2 days

SUPPLEMENTAL LEARNING ACTIVITIES

1. In a group, discuss the possible actions that can be safely taken in the following hypothetical scenario: You are 2.5 hours away from your destination and, in spite of drinking several cups of coffee, you find yourself extremely tired. What steps would you take to get your load safely to your destination?

2. In a group, discuss your own experiences in being sleep-deprived. What happened? What did you do to finally catch up? Would you attempt to drive an 18-wheeler if you were sleep-deprived? Why or why not?

3. Discuss in a group and then make a list of the top five reasons an up-to-date driver's daily log is important (aside from avoiding being put out of service). What are the two top safety reasons to make certain your log book is accurate?

4. Write a 200-word report or discuss in a group the reasons, in your personal opinion, the U.S. hours-of-service regulations for professional drivers have continuously changed since the 1930s. Be specific.

FOR MORE INFORMATION

PTDI—Record and Maintain House of Service Requirements, Page 28, Click on Skill Standards
www.ptdi.org/standards

FMCSA Hours of Service Regulations
www.fmcsa.dot.gov/rules-regulations/truck/driver/hos/fmcsa-guide-to-hos.pdf

Sleep Apnea Disorder Information
sleepapneadisorder.info

Ontario Hours of Service
www.e-laws.gov.on.ca/html/regs/english/elaws_regs_060555_e.htm

Department of Justice Canada—Hours of Service Regulations
laws-lois.justice.gc.ca/eng/regulations/SOR-2005-313/

29 Trip Planning

© Robert Pernell/www.Shutterstock.com

OBJECTIVES

When you have completed this chapter, you should be able to:

- Understand procedures for route planning, including preparing paperwork, route selection, and estimating time, fuel, money, and personal needs.

- Understand planning trip routes using maps and new software, including finding alternative routes.

- Estimate mileage and travel time.

- Describe types of vehicles and cargos most likely to have routing restrictions or special requirements.

- Describe the various types of enforcement procedures.

- Know the types of vehicles, cargos, and routes requiring special permits, and the regulations and procedures to obtaining these permits.

▶ **Figure 29-1**

Professional drivers must have trip-planning skills and knowledge of state laws and regulations affecting drivers.

NOTE

Not only are personal finances to be addressed and determined if adequate, but a professional driver should also take into account toll roads traveled and, if so, how much money will be required. Driving a commercial motor vehicle in the northeastern part of the country could cost considerable monies in order to pay both bridge and turnpike tolls.

NOTE

Not all states have this ability, but the State of Michigan issues an Enhanced Commercial Driver's License. This particular license has the same identification chip also incorporated in a passport card and border agents on both sides will honor this type of identification.

INTRODUCTION

As you become more familiar with safely driving a tractor-trailer rig, you'll also want to learn how to efficiently and effectively plan each trip. Ask any professional and he or she will tell you that strong and well-practiced trip planning skills are essential to your success. These skills include reading and understanding maps, knowing the general size and weight laws of the various states and provinces and understanding permitting, registration, and fuel tax requirements (**see Figure 29-1**). Along with trip-planning skills, the professional driver also must be aware of special regulations to be followed when planning a trip.

Ultimately, a carefully crafted trip plan can save you time and money as well as stress and physical wear-and-tear while setting a safe route for your pick-ups and deliveries.

Another important part of the professional driver's job is to keep accurate records to show compliance with the hours-of-service regulations as well as cargo, fuel tax payments, and registration fees (**see Figure 29-2**).

As a professional driver, you should be able to estimate:

- Mileage from point of origin to destination, road conditions, and weather
- Trip time
- Fuel requirements—how often and where you're going to stop
- Personal financial needs

It is also important to have correct and up-to-date paperwork, the appropriate permits, bills of lading as well as the required licensure, daily driving logs, a Driver Vehicle Inspection Report (DVIR), identification, medical certification and, in the case of all North American drivers who travel across borders, a passport.

▶ **Figure 29-2**

Professional drivers are responsible for keeping accurate records of their trips.

DRIVER TRIP REPORT

State laws require the driver to keep a record of miles driven and fuel purchased in each state for each trip. Failure to submit this report will result in a charge for the determined tax liability.

Departing From _____ City ___ State

Truck/Tractor No _____

Destination _____ City ___ State

Trailer No _____

Mo	Day	Yr	State	Route	Entering Odometer	Toll Miles/km	Weight	Axles
				Starting Odometer Reading (no tenths) -->				
				Ending Odometer Reading (no tenths) -->				

FUEL PLACED IN VEHICLE (Exclude Reefer Fuel)

Mo	Day	Yr	State	Receipt Number	Gallons	Cost	City

Driver Name _____

_____ **Driver Signature**

▶ **Figure 29–3**

Sample driver trip report.

Depending on the carrier, the driver may be involved with all these aspects of trip planning, or perhaps only a few of them. Companies differ in how routes are planned. In many cases, the carrier will use routing software, which considers fuel purchase sites, rest stops, road conditions, and other elements (**see Figure 29-3**).

TYPES OF DRIVING RUNS AND ASSIGNMENTS

Various types of runs are made in the North American trucking industry. Some carriers operate only a single type of run. Others operate a variety. As a professional driver, you may have a choice in the type of run you are assigned.

Many times, the driver will be given specific instructions about which routes to use. These instructions must be followed. In other cases, company management specifies the use of a specific route because it may be the safest or have the best highway conditions. Going off an assigned route without a good reason is a serious violation of company policy and may result in disciplinary measures or termination.

When fuel prices reach the four and five dollar range or higher, companies become extremely careful about their equipment going off route. Next to the loan payment for the equipment, fuel is the second largest expense and companies are very interested in how to cut any additional cost.

Local Operations

Local pick-up and delivery (P&D)—driver operates in and around certain cities, delivering freight to its final destination and picking up freight from shippers. Local P&D may also move freight between nearby points of origin and destinations. Local drivers must know the street system well so that pick-ups and deliveries can be made in the safest, quickest way. The local P&D driver also must know the local traffic patterns in order to avoid areas of congestion and delay when possible.

It is a common practice to deliver all the freight in the trailer in the morning and then make pick-ups during the afternoon and deliver them back to the home terminal in the evening.

Peddle run—a type of local P&D operation. Usually freight is hauled from the terminal to separate destinations in the nearby area. Peddle run drivers also pick up freight along the route and bring it back to the terminal. Because of frequent changes in points to be served, drivers of this type of service may be asked to select their routes because they will know the quickest and safest routes.

Shuttle operations—drivers move empty or loaded trailers between nearby points, such as terminals to customer, drop yards to customer, railheads to customer, and vice versa. The number of trailers a driver can move during a single driving period will depend on the distances involved.

Long-Distance Transport

Long-distance transport involves moving cargo from point of origin to one or more distant destinations **(see Figure 29-4)**.

Several types of operations fall into the general classification, including one in which the

▶ Figure 29-4

Long-distance operations are used for cross-country runs.

© Cengage Learning 2013

long-distance driver will return to the home terminal at the end of 10 hours of driving. In other cases, the driver may be on the road for two days or more at a time. Brief descriptions of several types of long-distance operations follow:

Regular run—the driver operates between the same points on each trip and may not have a regular starting and finishing time for each period of driving.

Open dispatch—the driver goes from point of origin to a distant point. Depending on the driving time and the need to comply with hours-of-service limits, the driver may take another unit to an additional destination. After resting in compliance with the Hours-of-Service ruling, the driver may be given a run heading toward the home terminal or may be dispatched to another point. This cycle may be repeated for several days before the driver returns home.

Regular route—refers to line-haul transport between given origins and destinations using assigned highways. Most less-than-truckload (LTL) fleets are regular route operations **(see Figure 29-5)**.

Irregular route—long-distance transport between a combination of origin and destination points using any suitable route. This type of run is also called **over-the-road trucking**. In this type of operation, the professional driver is most likely to be asked to select a route, although management may set the route to be used and the driver must comply with this route.

Relay run—refers to a trip in which a driver drives for the maximum allowable hours and then goes off duty as prescribed by the hours-of-service laws. Another driver takes the unit on to the next point. This cycle may be repeated several times as the truck is driven from origin to final destination by several different drivers.

Meet and turn—a relay run in which two drivers start driving toward each other from different points and meet at a chosen midpoint. At the meeting place, the drivers exchange complete units or only trailers. Then, each driver goes back to his starting point.

Turnaround run—a driver travels for about 5 hours to a destination and then returns to the home terminal. At the turnaround point, the driver may switch units or trailers for the return trip.

Sleeper operations—the driver of a rig with a sleeper berth can accumulate the required off-duty time as long as he or she meets the hours-of-service standard. The sleeper operation may use a single driver or a two-driver team **(see Figure 29-6)**.

Carriers that use this type of operation travel great distances. It is not uncommon for team drivers to travel in excess of 1,000 miles (1,609 km) in a

▶ **Figure 29-5**
Semitruck going through the Canadian Rockies.

NOTE

An irregular route requires the most trip planning. Professional drivers will be asked to travel routes they may never have traveled before, and fuel mileage and hours of service become extremely important. Drivers will simply be given a delivery appointment, so trip planning is vital.

▶ **Figure 29-6**
Drivers with sleeper rigs can save lodging costs on the road.

24-hour period and can accumulate 5,000 or 6,000 miles (8,047 or 9,656 km) in a week. Shippers who ship high-value cargo will request teams to accommodate their needs and companies will, in turn, pay a premium to drivers who wish to share the driving.

ROUTE SELECTION

There are many types of highways and each type is coded on a map. To make route selection more efficient, a motor carrier road atlas is a good investment, as discussed in the section "Map Reading." Not only will this atlas explain the different colors associated with different types of road, but it will highlight which roads are "truck routes and National Network" and commercial motor vehicles need to stay to these routes.

The various types of highways are described in the following section. They are listed in order of preference to use:

- Interstate routes
- Toll roads
- U.S. numbered routes
- State primary roads
- Primary provincial roads
- Other streets and highways

Interstate routes—usually preferred because they separate opposing traffic, have limited access, and bypass many small towns. Although they are considered the safest highways, drivers must be aware that these popular and much used highways can sometimes be snarled by bad weather or traffic congestion, especially in the urban areas. Drivers should be aware of the growing number of "trucks only" lanes on interstate routes.

Generally, odd-numbered interstates run north and south, while even numbered interstates run east and west. Three-digit interstates that start with an odd number are spurs into a city. Three-digit interstates that start with an even number, go around a city. The second two digits refer to a connecting north/south or east/west interstate.

Toll roads—similar to interstates, these roads require users to pay a toll. In many states, toll roads are part of the interstate system. The decision to use a toll road must be based on many factors in addition to cost. Drivers should also consider:

- Differences in time and distance over alternate routes
- Terrain and traffic
- Road conditions
- The need to go through built-up areas
- The amount of stop-and-go driving
- Wear and tear on the equipment
- Fuel usage

U.S. numbered routes—make up the major through routes. Those that parallel interstates may be good alternatives in case of delays on interstates because of traffic or weather.

State primary routes—are major routes that may be as good as, or even better than, a nearby U.S. numbered highway.

Primary provincial roads—are major Canadian roads that are well maintained and engineered.

Other streets and highways—are often used to reach loading or unloading points. Generally, drivers choose county roads or other routes designated by number or letter. These are the through routes set by the local authorities and are generally better than other local streets to safely handle truck traffic.

Special Situations

Because it is not possible to foresee every problem, professional drivers must learn to approach new situations carefully and to use common sense. Some of the special situations you may find are local truck routes, posted bridges, and restricted routes (**see Figure 29-7**).

Local truck routes—many cities and towns have designated routes for trucks. Although they are not always well marked, the driver must stay on these truck routes to avoid a ticket.

Posted bridges—many bridges have special weight restrictions. Do not cross a bridge if your rig's weight is more than the weight posted. Some fines are as much as $10,000.

Restricted routes—one reason to prohibit trucks from using some roads is a long past history of accidents. Always heed posted prohibitions. If you drive on a restricted road, you may be cited by local law enforcement, be faced with a hazardous condition, or be unable to avoid an accident.

There are other ways to get information about certain routes or get the help you need when planning a trip. Suggested ways include:

- Talking to other truck drivers or local residents about road conditions
- Using local Internet websites for route information, traffic conditions, and suggested alternate routes
- Being familiar with how to utilize a motor carrier road atlas, in case satellite route planning software fails
- If you are near a destination, stopping and calling the shipper or consignee for directions. They will inform you of any local construction that could hinder you from reaching your destination in a timely manner.
- Making inquiries about local conditions at truck stops, firehouses, police stations, or other locations where people may know the information you need
- Looking in a road atlas—many have information on restricted routes, low clearances, etc.
- Using your CB to ask questions about the route

▶ **Figure 29-7**

Professional truck drivers should never drive their CMVs across a bridge that has a weight restriction greater than their rig weights.

MAP READING

Being able to read maps is an important skill for the professional driver. However, because of continually improving software, trip planning can also be done through the use of computer programs with a great deal more information and accuracy.

Part of the professional driver's job is to locate unfamiliar pickup and delivery points. Maps continue to be a good investment because they provide a good backup for the driver who relies on computerized trip planning and/or Global Positioning Systems (GPS). You should purchase an **atlas,** a collection of maps from all U.S. states, Canadian provinces, and Mexican states. These may be purchased in bookstores or truck stops **(see Figure 29-8).**

Local or area map—useful for the local driver because it will detail local streets. Plan to buy a new local map every year, particularly in fast-growing areas.

State map—free state maps are available at many North American border information centers and along interstate highways.

Province map—available at many U.S./Canadian border information centers.

▶ **Figure 29-8**

Map reading is a very important skill for professional drivers to have.

Atlas—a driver expecting to travel extensively throughout the country should consider investing in a carrier or trucker's road atlas. In addition to state, city, and area maps, certain atlases may include the following information:

- Location of permanent scales
- Low underpasses
- Size and weight limits
- Fuel taxes
- Designated routes for operation of twin trailers and 53/103 foot (16.2/31.4 m) semi-trailers or other specialized equipment
- State laws for access to the Designated Highway System
- Driving distances

Pointers for Reading Maps

- In most cases, north is at the top of the map. It is often indicated by an arrow symbol with the letter N or a symbol showing all four points of the compass. In some cases, a map of a small area may be printed with north to one side. North will almost always be shown by some symbol.
- Read the key or legend that explains the symbols and colors used to show the interstates, provincial, federal, state and local routes, rest areas, interchanges, distances, and other important features. Each map also has a distance key, which can be used to gauge total distance, for example it might read 1 inch = 5 miles/km.
- Learn to figure the distance between points by adding the mileage figures shown along the route. Black numbers often refer to short distances between two black dots, these intermediate miles/km calculate distances between intersections. Red numbers refer to longer distances (cumulative miles/km) between two red dots.

Some maps have mileage charts showing approximate distances between principal cities and towns. Driving times are usually for automobiles, so allow more time for trucks. Computerized trip planning software also provides this information automatically.

Learn to use the grid coordinates of a map to locate specific cities or towns. Numbers are printed across the top and bottom of the map. Letters are printed down each side. Most maps have an index and will list the names of cities and their grid coordinates, such as A-10. To find the location, look down from 10 and across from A to find that particular city where the two coordinates intersect.

Figure 29-9

Knowing your average speed and fuel usage is essential.

CALCULATING TRAVEL TIME AND FUEL USAGE

Knowing how to figure the distance, your average speed, and trip time are required for trip planning **(see Figure 29-9).** The driver who wants to track average speed and fuel usage may want to invest in a laptop computer, trip planning software or, at the very least, a calculator.

The following formulas are often used by truck drivers for these calculations:

Distance = Speed multiplied by time
50 mph (80 km) × 9 hours = 450 miles (724 km)
Average speed = Distance divided by time
450 miles (724 km) divided by 9 hours = 50 mph (80 km)
Trip time = Distance divided by average speed
450 miles (724 km) divided by 50 mph (80 km) = 9 hours

KEEPING RECORDS

A driver must carry all up-to-date papers while on duty. Each carrier has its own way of keeping records to meet the information needs of that carrier and to help drivers remain within the law. You must use the record-keeping method your company specifies.

"I thought 'E' stood for 'Excellent.'"

If a driver does not keep the records the company requires, both the driver and the company can be penalized. Not carrying the right papers or keeping necessary records may also cause delays in being paid.

CAUTION!

As a professional driver, it is important to be organized. For example, if you have the only copy of a bill of lading or proof of delivery and this type of documentation is required in order for your employer to bill the customer—and you misplace this document—both you and your employer are likely to not receive payment.

The driver must carry the following documents at all times because law enforcement officers have the right to examine them:

- Driver's license
- Passport or enhanced CDL (such as Michigan's) if traveling between countries
- Current medical certificate (Note: by 2014, this will become part of the CDL.)
- Driver's daily log
- Driver's Vehicle Condition Report

Driver's license—a valid commercial driver's license with all required endorsements

Passport now required for travel between the U.S., Canada, and Mexico—since June 2009, individuals traveling between Canada, the U.S., and Mexico have needed a passport or equivalent travel document. (Some exceptions apply to children's passport requirements.) If you need a passport right away, get a passport within 24 hours with a service such as that at Rushmypassport.com.

Passport requirements have been a complicated and ever-changing issue for U.S. travelers to Canada for the past few years due to the Western Hemisphere Travel Initiative (WHTI), which was introduced in 2004 by the U.S. government to strengthen U.S. border security and standardize travel documentation. Bottom line, for security purposes, Canada will not allow a U.S. citizen into the country who does not have the proper documentation to return home. The same is true for Mexico.

Medical certificate—current and valid health record is needed for the driver; and the driver must be in compliance with any special requirements such as glasses or hearing aids

Driver's daily log—correctly completed and available for the last 7 days as well as the current day

Driver's Vehicle Condition Report—prepare at the end of the trip or tour of duty

Shipping papers—to describe the contents of the freight being hauled

Trip reports—generally include the following data:

- Name of driver
- Terminal
- Vehicle identification
- Departure time from terminal
- Routing instructions
- Address of each stop to deliver or pick up freight
- Times of arrival and departure from each stop
- Quantity of freight handled
- Time of return to terminal
- Beginning and ending mileage (in some cases)
- Space for remarks

CAUTION!

The driver must always comply with company policies when preparing trip reports.

Onboard Recorder

More carriers are now using onboard recording equipment. Some carriers use this equipment to show compliance with hours-of-service rules. If the company for which you work uses such devices, they will train you in how to use them properly so you can maintain your driver's daily log.

Some trucks have recorders installed to control how the truck is operated. Basic information recorded includes:

- Time engine is running
- Whether the truck is stopped or moving
- Speed
- Miles/kilometers driven

Calculating Personal Needs

When planning any trip, drivers should consider their personal needs. These needs include expenses to be met while on the trip, how they will be reimbursed—or if they qualify to be reimbursed by the carrier, and what paperwork must be kept to prove expenses and how forms should be completed. These expenses and who is usually responsible are as follows:

Meals	Driver expense
Lodging	Driver expense
Fuel	Company expense
En route repairs	Company expense
Tolls	Company expense, if authorized
Permits	Company expense
Special fees	Company expense

Each company handles expense reimbursement according to set policy. Find out how your company handles expenses before you begin a trip. Keep copies of all receipts for your personal records. Retain logbooks to document your daily expenses for tax purposes. Truck drivers, who file U.S. taxes, are allowed to expense a pre-diem amount providing they had to spend the entire 24 period in the CMV. This deduction can only be utilized providing they are able to file a schedule "C."

▶ **Figure 29-10**

It is important for drivers to know what type of weather they might encounter to be well prepared.

Be Aware of Weather Conditions

Drivers should know the kind of weather to expect during each trip. They should know when they might encounter extreme weather conditions and carry the right kinds of clothing for any situation. Clothing for working outside the truck during bad weather should also be included. Many drivers also carry blankets, a sleeping bag, and extra food and water in case they are stranded **(see Figure 29-10).**

NOTE

Always check national and local weather conditions. These can be viewed at most modern truck stops, and many clear channel AM radio stations offer both traffic and weather on a regular basis.

TRIP PLANNING SOFTWARE

The market for trip planning software contains scores of choices for today's professional driver. This routing software contains common capabilities, including:

- Geocoding addresses, that is, locating the latitude and longitude by matching the address against data contained in a digital map database
- Determining the best paths through street networks between pairs of geocoded points

- Solving vehicle routing problems, assigning stops to routes and terminals, sequencing stops, and routing vehicles between pairs of stops
- Displaying the results in such a way that dispatchers can communicate results to drivers, loaders, and other personnel

The following trip planning software was chosen at random to illustrate some of the available applications for trip planning purposes.

CoPilot Truck®

ALK Technologies' CoPilot Truck software combines truck routing, mileage, and mapping capabilities with in-vehicle GPS navigation and route guidance to create the first onboard laptop computer navigation system specifically designed for owner-operators, leased-operators, and company drivers.

Data in the newly released CoPilot Truck | Laptop 4 solution include over 7 million miles of U.S. roadways, 31,000 exit numbers, and more than 100 million addresses. Canadian map data cover 830,000 road miles and more than 10 million addresses. Also incorporated are over 3 million points of interest, including truck stops, truck washes, and weigh stations.

ProMiles®

ProMiles, by the ProMiles Software Development Corporation, offers door-to-door addressing along with truck attributes such as designated truck routes, hazardous restrictions, and weight and height restrictions. By combining this functionality with Tele Atlas' detailed routing and addressing content, the new version of ProMiles offers even more solutions to trip planning, incorporating Tele Atlas' turn-by-turn data into its routing and logistics products for street-level routing applications.

ProMiles also offers an electronic logging package. Drivers who become familiar with this type of technology often like and come to rely on this application finding that it cuts down on the amount of time required to complete a traditional paper log.

NOTE

It's important to know that inexpensive and readily available GPS devices, typically sold at most electronics retailers are not meant for commercial use, and shouldn't be relied on. The truck-specific GPS units, such as those mentioned above, take into consideration low clearances, truck routes, weight limits, etc.

PC*Miler®

PC*Miler, also by ALK Technologies, is a point-to-point routing, mileage, and mapping software application which generates detailed reports, routes, mileages, and maps over the entire U.S., Canadian, and Mexican truck-usable highway network. It features the largest and most accurate North American highway database on the market. PC*Miler includes point-to-point distance calculations, including rate determination, driver pay, and instant customer quotes. It also offers routing and optimization, including dispatch and routing, route optimization, trip time and cost estimates, load planning, truck stop routing, and instant rate quotes, and gives detailed driving instructions including trip time and cost reports as well as map quality graphics.

VEHICLE LICENSING AND PERMITS

Every vehicle must have a registration (license) in order to operate. Fees are paid each year and registration plates are issued. The majority of trucks or tractor-trailer combinations weighing more than 26,000 pounds (11,793 kg) will be registered under the **International Registration Plan (IRP)**.

The IRP is a registration agreement among the states and Canadian provinces based on the percentage of miles/kilometers driven by that rig in each state or province. License fees are paid to each state or province in which the vehicle operates. A cab card is issued to the vehicle, stating the IRP areas in which the vehicle is allowed to operate.

In most cases, the company obtains the registration plate, but the driver is responsible for keeping mileage records. The percentage of fees paid to each state depends on the number of miles/kilometers driven in that state compared to the miles/kilometers driven in all states and provinces.

If a truck that has IRP plates plans to operate in a state not shown on the IRP cab card, a trip permit must be obtained. The company is responsible for telling the driver how to obtain these permits, which are usually issued for a given period of time, ranging most often from 24 to 72 hours. Federal laws require all states to be members of IRP.

Permits for Oversize Shipments

There are many rules and regulations governing the transport of oversize loads. For more information, please visit ops.fhwa.dot.gov/freight/sw/permit_report/index.htm.

Fuel Tax Law

Some 48 states in the U.S. and 10 Canadian provinces are part of the International Fuel Tax Agreement (IFTA). Commercial motor vehicles are given one sticker for each tractor and fuel tax is calculated by the motor carrier and payment is submitted to the state in which the motor carrier resides. The state or province, in turn, then settles with each state/province as needed.

The driver must be sure he or she gets receipts for all fuel purchases, although many companies now use computerized tracking of their fuel purchases and drivers are directed to buy from certain fuel companies that provide this tracking information as part of their service.

Weight Distance Taxes

Some states charge a **weight distance tax**—sometimes called a mileage tax, ton–mile tax, or axle tax. These taxes are paid by the carrier and are based on the annual ton mileage **(see Figure 29-11).** The carrier must also file a quarterly report. States often require trucks to be registered for the weight distance tax. Once taxes are paid, the carrier usually obtains a decal or number for the tractor. These taxes are enforced by the state's highway department or transportation department.

FEDERAL LENGTH AND WEIGHT LIMITS

A driver is responsible for staying within federal and state weight and length laws. All states must allow truck combinations of certain weights and lengths to operate on roadways that are part of the **National System of Interstate Highways,** a system also known as the Designated System or **National Network.** Most of these highways are identified with the letter I and the number of the highway, such as I-80 or I-45. Many multilane, divided highways, such as the U.S. routes and turnpikes, are also part of this system.

Many state highways have requirements similar to the following federal weight and size limits, so it is always wise to check the applicable maps or computer data for actual dimensions and weights.

Vehicle Weight

A maximum of 20,000 pounds (9,072 kg) may be carried on any one axle (except steer axles, which are allowed only 12,000 pounds (5,443 kg)) and 34,000 pounds (15,422 kg) on the tandem axle. An overall gross weight of 80,000 pounds (36,287 kg) is allowed on a typical five-axle tractor-trailer. The way the

Mileage Control (Speedometer Mileage Readings)

Destination _____

Date _____ Unit Nos. _____

Driver _____

New Jersey
  Beginning _____
  State Line OUT _____
  State Line IN _____
  Ending _____

New York
  State Line IN _____
  State Line OUT _____

Connecticut
  State Line IN _____
  State Line OUT _____

Pennsylvania
  State Line IN _____
  State Line OUT _____

© Cengage Learning 2013

▶ **Figure 29–11**

The mileage control sheet is used by the carrier to track its mileage taxes.

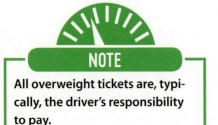

NOTE

All overweight tickets are, typically, the driver's responsibility to pay.

axles are spaced and the number of axles may lower the single and tandem axle limits. Rigs must stay within weight-to-length limits based on the weight of groups of two or more adjacent (following) axles.

The **Federal Bridge Formula** is used to calculate permissible gross loads. Ideally, a typical 80,000-pound (36,287 kg) fixed-axle highway rig should carry 12,000 pounds (5,443 kg) on the front axle and 34,000 pounds (15,422 kg) on each of the tandems. The tractor must have an outer spread (distance between the middle of the front axle and the middle of the rearmost axle) of at least 14 feet (4.3 m). The formula also requires minimum distances between the tractor and the trailer axles (**inner** and **outer bridge**).

Vehicle Length

There is no limit on the overall length of a tractor-trailer on the interstates and other designated highways, but some states do limit lengths. These are typically measured from the center of the trailer tandems. Pay special attention if the trailer is over 48 feet (14.6 m) long. Some states require a permit for this length.

No state can prohibit doubles on the interstate. Longer doubles—more than 28 feet (8.5 m) per trailer—and triple trailer combinations usually operate under special permits.

STATE LIMITS

Unless they are controlled by federal interstate law, weight and size limits vary from state to state. If a driver is not certain about the state's limits, he or she should find out about the limits before entering the state. Dispatchers usually have this information or it can be found in Thomson Delmar Learning's *Trucking Rules and Regulations.* The state police, highway patrol, departments of transportation, and state trucking associations can also provide accurate information.

Professional drivers need to know each individual state's and province's specific access policies and how far a driver may stray from a truck route. The state of Illinois, for example, limits a driver to 1 mile (1.6 km) from the National Network for loads over 73,280 pounds (33,239 kg). Overweight fines can be costly for being between 73,280 and 80,000 pounds (33,239 and 36,287 kg) and all fines are the responsibility of the driver.

When deciding whether a tractor-trailer is within limits, the four key factors to be considered are vehicle weight, the number of axles, vehicle length, and vehicle height and load.

Vehicle weight—many state agencies provide color-coded maps (red, green, purple) that identify load maximums to be carried on various roads. These maps are based on the condition of the road and the weight that can be supported by the bridges. You can weigh your rig at fleet or shipper terminals or on public scales at truck stops. Some public scales will certify weight and even pay overweight if they are wrong.

Number of axles—state bridge laws limit the maximum weight that may be carried. The laws are determined by the number of axles and the distance between them on a rig. While most states have adopted the Federal Bridge Formula to determine axle weight limits and gross weight limits, some states use other means for figuring these limits.

Vehicle length—is regulated by both state and local governments. They also set the maximum load, length, and overhang (the distance beyond support of the load bed) permitted. The legal length may be set in terms of either overall length (from bumper to bumper) or trailer length.

Vehicle height and load—while some states permit vehicle heights of 14-1/2 feet (4.4 m), most restrict heights to 13-1/2 feet (4.1 m). This limit includes the load. Overpasses on most interstates have clearances of 16-1/2 feet (5.0 m) but some are only 13-1/2 feet (4.1 m). Always check on these height limits before starting your trip.

Special Permit Hauling

Loads that are larger than either state or local laws allow will require special permits. You can get these permits from state agencies and police departments. Typical loads requiring these permits include machinery, buildings, and bridge construction girders.

Some permits limit hours of operation, such as before sundown, after sunrise, or during rush hours. They will also specify the routes to be used (**see Figure 29-12**).

Hauling this load requires a special permit

© Cengage Learning 2013

▶ **Figure 29-12**

Special permits often limit the hours of operation and routes used.

Permits may:

- Be limited to specific vehicles
- Require the use of special signs, such as "Oversize Load"
- Require the use of escort vehicles in front of and behind the load
- Require using special lights, such as rotating amber lights
- Specify the route to be followed

Drivers may have to submit their planned route before they can get a permit. If a detour or delay occurs, the driver should call the state or local agency that issued the permit to request a change in time or route.

ROADSIDE ENFORCEMENT

As well as the normal enforcement of traffic laws, there are three other types of controlling activities routinely carried on by the states. Drivers need to be aware of scales, ports of entry, and roadside safety inspections **(see Figure 29-13)**. In many cases, these functions are carried out at a single location.

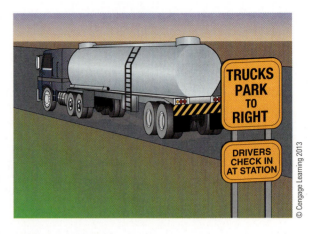

▶ **Figure 29-13**

Be sure to obey all instructions at scales and ports of entry and during roadside inspections.

Ports of Entry

Ports of entry are locations where the driver must stop and prove the carrier has authority to operate in the state. In some cases, the driver may have to buy permits or pay fees **(see Figure 29-14)**. Weighing may also be done at a port of entry. Do not pull onto the scales. Instead, park near the scales and walk up to get your permit. Some states fine drivers if they pull onto the scales without a permit, and sometimes the driver's daily log will be checked for hours-of-service violations and then time-stamped by the person on duty.

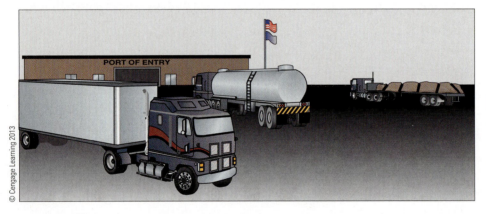

▶ **Figure 29-14**

Observe all signs, follow instructions, and have all paperwork ready for inspection at a port of entry.

Roadside Safety Inspections

Roadside safety inspections are done at scales, ports of entry, or special safety inspection facilities, or a suitably safe area. The driver must show his or her license, medical certificate, driver's logs, and the shipping papers for the load. Inspectors have the authority to inspect cargo, even if it is sealed. If a sealed load is inspected, a new seal will be put on by the inspector, and the driver should record the identification numbers, both of the old seal and the new seal. The driver may be put out of service at once for the following:

■ Hours-of-service violation

■ A vehicle so unsafe it is likely to be involved in an accident or a breakdown

■ Leaking hazardous materials

At the end of the roadside inspection, the driver will be given a copy of the form filled out by the inspector. This form must be turned in to the carrier. If the driver will reach a company facility within 24 hours, the form may be turned in at that time. If not, the driver should mail the form to the carrier.

SUMMARY

This chapter presents the different types of trucking operations and how to plan a trip. You learned about the different types of roads and various trip-planning software. The permits that may be required were explained and methods of reading maps and calculating travel time and fuel consumption were also discussed. Legal weight and length limits were described and planning for personal needs during a trip was also emphasized.

KEY TERMS

Atlas
Average speed formula
Distance formula
Federal Bridge Formula
Inner bridge
International Registration Plan (IRP)
Interstate routes
Irregular route
Local pick-up and delivery (P&D)
Local truck routes

Long-distance transport
Meet and turn
National Network
National System of Interstate Highways
Open dispatch
Outer bridge
Over-the-road trucking
Peddle run
Port of entry
Posted bridges
Primary provincial roads

Regular route
Regular run
Relay run
Restricted routes
Shuttle operations
Sleeper operations
State primary routes
Toll roads
Trip time formula
Turnaround run
U.S. numbered routes
Weight distance tax

A DAY IN THE LIFE...

Larry McCann—Tennant Truck Lines, Professional Truck Driver

© Cengage Learning 2013

I feel it is important to be 100% safe on the road for the company, for the general public as well as for myself and other truck drivers. We need to get the loads through, and I take great pride in doing my part. I always respect other drivers—even when they are too frustrated to show the same common courtesy.

Even if I am on the road, I will keep my recyclable containers and will take them to my home to reprocess. It's not much, but just think of the difference drivers can make if each one did that too. How much better it would be—both the environment as well as our image.

For 52 years, I have kept an eye out on the road and my patience with others while helping out. Part of that helping out includes my fellow truck drivers. Even when they aren't part of Tennant, I try to help them. One time a driver from another company was having trouble with his engine. I figured it was the fuel filter and gave him an extra one I had on-hand. Another time, I helped a driver who ran out of fuel. I didn't ask either of them to pay me for it, just got them on the road again. I know that I'll get paid back by another driver, up the road sometime.

I have helped my company's drivers with receipts, directions, and other small tasks much as my supervisor does for me. We have a great relationship, and he knows he can always count on me and he listens when I've got something to say. And after 52 years of driving trucks, it's nice to have that respect.

I know the best way to make the customer happy is to show up with a good attitude. Truck drivers get a bad rap sometimes, and sometimes they deserve it. I am always courteous, on time, well groomed, and full of patience. That last one is especially important because I have found if I am not having a good day, chances are the customer isn't either. If I show the good qualities of a truck driver, the customer will show their good qualities. If they are having a rough day, I try to help them solve some of their problems—without leaving mine with them.

> " I know the best way to make the customer happy is to show up with a good attitude. "

Whether on the road or at home, I am a good "Citizen" who happens to be a Truck Driver too. And I take pride in both.

REVIEW QUESTIONS

1. Who is responsible for knowing the various state rig size and weight laws and understanding registration and fuel tax requirements?

   a. dispatcher

   b. professional driver

   c. shipper

   d. receiver

2. Moving cargo from a point of origin to one or more distant destinations is known as _____.

   a. long-distance transport

   b. pickup and delivery

   c. long-distance peddle run

   d. distance shuttle operations

3. The usually preferred nontoll roads that separate opposing traffic, have limited access, and bypass many small communities are known as _____.

   a. U.S. numbered routes

   b. state primary routes

   c. interstate routes

   d. local streets

4. To determine the trip time for a specific distance, the professional driver _____.

   a. multiplies gallons used by distance of the trip

   b. divides gallons used by distance traveled

   c. divides distance traveled by time

   d. divides trip distance by average speed

5. Regarding the up-to-date documents that a professional driver is required to have while on duty, which of the following is not required?

   a. driver's license

   b. a complete record of all repairs to the tractor

   c. medical certificate

   d. driver's inspection report

6. The International Registration Plan (IRP) is a registration agreement among the states and Canadian provinces _____.

   a. offering discounts, including discount lottery tickets to drivers of big rigs

   b. offering fuel discounts for professional drivers

   c. offering discounts at national food chains

   d. based on the percentage of miles driven in each state or province

7. The Federal Bridge Formula is used to calculate the _____.

   a. permissible gross loads

   b. weight of the freight load allowed on federal bridges

   c. minimum weight on the steering axle

   d. weight of the freight load allowed on provincial bridges

8. Which of the following is not one of the key factors in deciding whether a tractor-trailer is within state length and weight limits?

   a. vehicle weight

   b. the total stopping distance of the rig at 30 mph (48 km/h)

   c. the number of axles

   d. vehicle length, height, and width

9. Regarding special permit hauling for loads that are larger than either the state or local laws allow, which of the following is typically not one of the restrictions for this type of operation?

   a. limited to specific vehicles

   b. requires using special lights

   c. movement of the load should be at night

   d. requires a specific route

10. During a roadside safety inspection, which of the following is not typically an element of the inspection?

    a. trip plan

    b. driver's log

    c. driver's license

    d. driver's medical certificate

11. To better enforce traffic laws, all but one of the following is used in North America.

    a. scales

    b. port of entry

    c. roadside inspection

    d. border crossings

12. Restricted routes were the result of _____.

    a. too much traffic that slowed truckers

    b. inadequate road strength

    c. a long history of accidents

    d. inadequate lane widths for trucks

13. Maps continue to be a good investment because _____.

    a. they are usually four-color and have pictures and photographs

    b. they provide a good backup for the driver who relies on computerized trip planning

    c. they usually show where truck stops are located

    d. none of the above

14. Loads that are larger than state or local laws allow, require special permits This permit may _____.

    a. specify the route to be followed

    b. require the use of special signage

    c. be limited to specific vehicles

    d. all of the above

SUPPLEMENTAL LEARNING ACTIVITIES

1. Using some of the links below, plan a trip from Montreal to Miami. Make certain you travel the best roads, can make the best time and, of course, in the best weather. Do this in teams of two, and make sure you plan for money and fuel as well as safe and secure stops along the way.

2. Using only a state/provincial map and your past travel experiences, calculate trip time between your current residence and the capitol city of your state/province.

3. Using an atlas, calculate trip time between your current residence and either Montreal, if you live in the U.S., or between your current residence and Washington, DC, if you live in Canada or Mexico.

4. Invite a veteran international driver to speak to your class. Be sure to ask about how he or she plans trips, what software he or she recommends, and any other tips he or she would like to share.

5. In small groups, assemble an all-weather emergency kit that would serve you, as a professional driver, traveling from Miami, Florida, in the U.S. to any point in Nova Scotia during the month of January.

FOR MORE INFORMATION

PTDI—Plan Trips/Make Appropriate Decisions, Page 25, Click on Skill Standards
www.ptdi.org/standards

Trucker Country—Trip Planning Center
www.truckercountry.com/trip-planning.html

CDL Jobs Trip Planning
www.cdljobs.com/tripplanning.htm

Longhauler Maps
www.longhauler-usa.com/bttrmaps.htm

Canadian Permits
www.bclaws.ca/EPLibraries/bclaws_new/document/ID/freeside/30_78

Ministry of Transportation Ontario—Guide to Oversize/Overweight Vehicles and Loads in Ontario
www.mto.gov.on.ca/english/trucks/oversize/guide.shtml

U.S. DOT Federal Highway Administration—Oversize/Overweight Load Permits
ops.fhwa.dot.gov/freight/sw/permit_report/index.htm

30 Transportation Security

© iStockphoto/shotbydave

OBJECTIVES

When you have completed this chapter, you should be able to:

- Understand the reasons and actions to increase security measures within the transportation industry.

- Discuss the professional driver's responsibilities for maintaining security during each trip.

- Identify governmental and other agencies involved in transportation security.

- Identify ways in which you can personally increase the security of your rig and your cargo.

INTRODUCTION

Security has always been a major part of a professional driver's job. Every year, millions of dollars in cargo and equipment are stolen, and while much is recovered, much more disappears. This type of theft, pilferage, and loss is costly to consumers, carriers, and you, the driver.

Prior to **September 11, 2001,** and the destruction of the World Trade Center towers in New York City, most North Americans thought **terrorist activities** happened in some other country, certainly not in their own.

It is now obvious that terrorism is a very real danger in this hemisphere, and will continue to be a concern for years to come.

Historically, motor vehicles of all kinds, particularly trucks—because of their larger capacities—have been used as means of delivery for terrorist activities, and there is every reason to believe that terrorist activities using a truck as a delivery system will continue to be real threats to the safety of people everywhere. Recall in 1983, a 3/4-ton pickup truck loaded with explosives was used to attack the U.S. Embassy in Beirut, Lebanon, killing 83 people. In the horrendous aftermath of the Oklahoma City bombing, it was found the delivery device for the explosives was a rented straight truck. Car bombs are used all over the world today, taking down buildings and destroying lives in their wake.

Since 9/11 and Oklahoma City as well as the experiences of U.S. and NATO forces in Afghanistan and Iraq, trucks of all sizes are now viewed as possible **weapons of mass destruction (see Figure 30-1).** As an example: a B-52 bomber can deliver 2,000 pounds (907 kg) of precision munitions per bomb within 10 meters (32.8 feet) of its target. A tractor-trailer rig has the capacity to deliver 40,000 pounds (18,144 kg) of precision munitions within 10 meters (32.8 feet) of its target.

It is, therefore, the responsibility of all professional drivers to be aware of the possibilities of their rigs being used to perpetrate a terrorist's mission and to prevent the use of their rig and those of their fellow drivers as weapons of mass destruction.

▶ Figure 30-1
Security has always been a major part of a professional driver's job.

THE U.S. DEPARTMENT OF HOMELAND SECURITY

Because the threat of terrorism became a reality in 2001 in this country, the following year the Homeland Security Act established the **Department of Homeland Security** as an executive department of the United States.

Its mission is threefold:

■ Prevent terrorist attacks within the U.S.

■ Reduce the vulnerability of the U.S. to terrorism

■ Minimize the damage and assist in the recovery from terrorist attacks occurring in the U.S.

In a speech delivered in March 2005 to the Security Policy Institute, then Secretary of Homeland Security Michael Chertoff explained:

> "Risk management is fundamental to managing the threat, while retaining our quality of life and living in freedom. Risk management must guide our decision-making as we examine how we can best organize to prevent, respond and recover from an attack. We all live with a certain amount of risk. That means that we tolerate that something bad can happen; we adjust our lives based on probability; and we take reasonable precautions."

U.S. TRANSPORTATION SECURITY ADMINISTRATION

On November 19, 2001, former President George W. Bush signed into law the U.S. **Aviation and Transportation Security Act (ATSA),** which, among other things, established a new **Transportation Security Administration (TSA)** within the U.S. Department of Transportation. This act established a series of challenging but critically important milestones necessary toward achieving a secure air travel system.

The Transportation Security Administration was formed to protect the nation's transportation systems, to ensure freedom of movement for people and commerce. In its capacity as a federal agency, the TSA will continuously set the standard for excellence in transportation security through its people, processes, and technologies.

TRUCKING SECURITY GROWS INTO LARGER ISSUE

Since the events of September 11, 2001, the area of **security** has gained much additional attention, from every level of government. Today's terrorists not only want to topple buildings and kill people, but also cripple entire countries. Experts in terrorism warn that the trucking industry is a ripe target for the next round of terrorist activities.

During an address to the Truckload Carriers Association, Ken Allard—a retired army officer and security and information intelligence analyst for MSNBC cable network—made this assessment:

> "The goal of terrorists is not to destroy our buildings and kill our citizens. They want to destroy our economy and our way of life. Terrorism is a threat to everything we do and to everything we stand for."

James Hall, former chairman of the U.S. National Transportation Safety Board, addressing the same group, said this:

> "The challenge for trucking is to build security into operations in the same way that safety has been promoted. With narrow profit margins and increasing insurance premiums, many executives will question how to pay for increases in security. For instance, federal, state, and local officials have called for new and redundant background checks and identification procedures for transportation employees. If enacted, some of these proposals could bankrupt many trucking companies.
>
> Trucking is vulnerable to terrorists. Added expense along with increased paperwork will do little to relieve that vulnerability, so the first step toward defeating terrorists is to understand the nature of the threat.
>
> Understanding the threat shows that vulnerability is not limited to the security of company facilities, employees or loads. Attacks on customers or suppliers can harm truck lines just as badly as an attack on the company. An attack on infrastructure, such as power supplies or water sources, could severely damage a local economy."

Hall added that no one could afford to adopt security measures that do not work or that ruin the transportation economy in the process. He encouraged carriers and professional drivers to:

- Make plans for alternate communication systems in case of primary telephone or radio network damage
- Test these plans to ensure the backup systems are working at all times
- Use the company safety program to build security awareness throughout the entire company, not just drivers
- Identify key emergency management officials in areas where the carrier operates. Contact these officials and set a procedure for getting in touch with them at any time.
- Drivers and their satellite tracking and communications systems can become the eyes and ears of America (**see Figure 30-2**).

▶ Figure 30-2

Drivers and their communications systems can be the "eyes" and "ears" of America.

FMCSA SUGGESTS MEASURES TO REDUCE SECURITY RISKS

Terrorist threats are real and here to stay. You play a vital role in protecting your family, friends, and countrymen because, since September 11, 2001, your role as a truck driver has become more important. Now more than ever, those who share the roadway with you depend on you to move freight safely and securely, especially if you transport **hazardous materials.** While high valued commodities have always been hijacking targets, shipments capable of mass destruction or environmental damage must now be protected with the utmost care. The North America nation is counting on you.

First Observer Program

Long before 9/11, professional truck drivers worked with local, state, provincial, and national authorities, serving as law enforcement's eyes and ears in spotting and reporting stolen loads, crimes being committed, and possible terrorist activities.

Since 2008, the U.S. First Observer program has helped route this ongoing, eyewitness information that doesn't rise to the level of an immediate emergency from truckers to anti-terrorism agencies. This same program was recently singled out for its successes by the Transportation Security Administration.

The First Observer program has earned honors for its role in advancing the ongoing protection of U.S. transportation systems, including the Transportation Security Agency's Partnership Award.

In presenting the award, TSA officials noted that the Partnership Award "recognizes industry partners or other government employees whose accomplishments and excellence in performance distinctly benefit the interests of the United States and clearly advance TSA's mission to protect the nation's transportation systems while significantly enhancing TSA's ability to achieve its strategic goals: prevent and protect; respond and restore; and achieve organizational effectiveness."

The First Observer program is run by HMS Co., under a contract funded by the Department of Homeland Security and the Federal Emergency Management Agency. First Observer has a call center in the DC area, which is trained to gather information from trucking professionals. For additional information and/or to register for the program, go to www.firstobserver.com or call 888-217-5902.

On the Road

- Be alert when leaving. Criminal surveillance often begins at, or within a mile/km of, your origin.
- Don't discuss your cargo, destination, or other trip specifics on open channels or near people you don't know **(see Figure 30-3).**
- If you believe you are being followed, call for emergency assistance/law enforcement and your dispatcher immediately.
- Avoid being boxed in. Where possible leave room in front and behind your truck.
- Look for vehicles following you, especially if there are three or more people in a car.
- If you believe you are being hijacked, try to keep your truck moving.

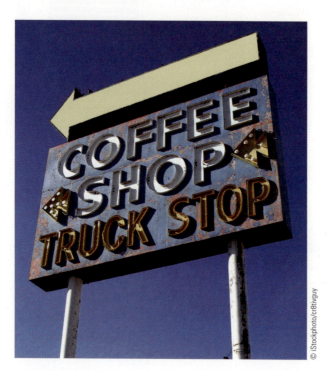

© iStockphoto/cr8tivguy

> **NOTE**
>
> Being "boxed in" means to have traffic on the left and to the rear (close) and following too close to the vehicle ahead of you. The truck driver is traveling in the right lane and has nowhere to go but on to the shoulder in an emergency, and is not in control. A hijacking team might use this tactic to take control of the tractor-trailer.

▶ **Figure 30–3**

When sharing a meal with other people you don't know, be sure not to share trip specifics.

Stopping Your Rig

- Leave your rig in a secure parking lot or truck stop if possible; if not, be certain someone can watch your vehicle.
- If you are team driving, one person should always stay with the rig.
- Never leave your vehicle running with the keys in it; shut off the engine and lock the doors.
- If at all possible, do not stop in "hot spots"—unsafe or high crime areas.
- Always lock the cargo door(s) with padlocks.
- Use seals to prevent and identify tampering.

© Cengage Learning 2013

▶ *"Hey fellas! I'm all for security but this is overkill. Fellas! Fellas?"*

Keeping Your Rig Secure

- Use a battery kill switch.
- Use tractor and trailer brake locking devices.
- Criminals know about electronic tracking systems and how to dismantle them; check your system regularly, and notify dispatch when it's not working.
- If you drop a trailer, use a kingpin lock whenever possible.

GENERAL SECURITY PROCEDURES

Terrorists continue to select soft targets for attack, particularly those that will yield a high casualty count. Examples include residences, recreational and shopping venues, and business buildings and complexes. The Department of Homeland Security also has submitted the following guidelines for trucking transportation general awareness:

General Awareness Procedures

- Review current contingency plans and, if not already in place, develop and implement procedures for:
    - Receiving and acting on threat information
    - Alert notification
    - Terrorist incident response
    - Evacuation
    - Bomb threat
    - Hostage and barricade
    - Chemical, biological, radiological, and nuclear (CBRN)
    - Incident management procedures, accountability
- After implementing plans and procedures, conduct internal training exercises and invite local emergency responders (fire, rescue, medical, and bomb squads) to participate in joint exercises.
- Coordinate and establish partnerships with local authorities and other business/facility owners to develop intelligence and information-sharing relationships.

Security Personnel Procedures for Transportation Facilities

- Arrange for law enforcement vehicles to be parked randomly near entrances and exits.
- Increase the number of visible security personnel where possible **(see Figure 30-4).**
- Institute/increase vehicle, foot, and roving security patrols varying in size, timing, and routes.
- Implement random security guard shift changes.

▶ Figure 30-4

Visibility of security personnel is important near transportation facilities.

- Approach all illegally parked vehicles in and around facilities, question drivers, and direct them to move immediately; if the owner cannot be identified, have the vehicle towed by law enforcement.

- Institute a robust vehicle inspection program to include checking under the undercarriage of vehicles, under the hood, and in the trunk. Provide vehicle inspection training to security personnel.

The Carrier Should

- Ensure all levels of personnel are notified via briefings, e-mail, voicemail, and signage of any changes in threat conditions and protective measures.

- Encourage personnel to be alert and immediately report any situation that appears to constitute a threat or suspicious activity.

- Encourage personnel to take notice and report suspicious vehicles.

- Encourage personnel to know emergency exits and stairwells and the locations of rally points to ensure the safe egress of all employees.

The DHS also invites commercial carriers and others to report information concerning suspicious or criminal activity to local law enforcement, the local FBI Joint Terrorism Task Force, or the Homeland Security Operations Center (HSOC). The HSOC may be contacted via telephone at (202) 282-8101 or e-mail at HSCenter@dhs.gov.

TRANSPORT CANADA'S MOTOR CARRIER POLICY

In Canada, jurisdiction over motor carriers (truck and bus operators) is shared between the federal government and the provinces. However, the federal role is largely one of coordination and facilitation. Federal legislation, the Motor Vehicle Transport Act (MVTA), allows provinces to apply their own rules and regulations to motor carriers in federal jurisdiction, subject to the conditions set in the act.

Motor Carrier Policy is one of two groups within Transport Canada that is directly concerned with matters relating to the MVTA, the other being the Road Safety Group.

Activities

- Monitor and provide policy advice on motor carrier regulatory issues that are not directly related to safety, such as vehicle weights and dimensions (mainly a provincial issue), economic regulation of the intercity and charter bus industry, and the transportation provisions of the *Agreement on Internal Trade*.

- Main source of federal information on the Conditions of Carriage Regulations, which apply only to the conditions of carriage for the movement of goods by truck.

- Shared responsibility for the motor carrier aspects of the North American Free Trade Agreement (NAFTA).

- Monitor developments in Canada–United States–Mexico that could have an impact on Canadian motor carriers.

Canadian Road Security. Transport Canada's road security program is managed by the Surface and Intermodal Security Directorate and encompasses several initiatives including policies and legislative tools governing the security of Canada's international bridges and tunnels (IBTs), and the security for the Transportation of Dangerous Goods (TDG).

International Bridges and Tunnels. The security of international bridges and tunnels in Canada is subject to the International Bridges and Tunnels Act (IBTA), which came into effect in April 2007. The act was introduced to ensure the safety and security of all international bridges and tunnels in Canada, while maintaining the flow of people and goods across these vital trade links.

(Continues)

TRANSPORT CANADA'S MOTOR CARRIER POLICY (continued)

Transportation of Dangerous Goods. Transport Canada is developing a framework for the implementation of the new security provisions in the Transportation of Dangerous Goods Act, 1992. Key security provisions include:

- Providing authorities for creating security regulations, measures, and interim orders; and
- Establishing mandatory requirements with respect to security plans and training in accordance with regulations

If you would like further information, contact Transport Canada by e-mail at sims-stti@tc.gc.ca.

Report all security incidents to 1-866-TC-SECUR / 1-866-827-3287.

Canadians Step up Cargo Security

In August 2011, stakeholders from every level of the Canadian trucking industry—fleet owners, drivers, and representatives from the Canadian Trucking Alliance (CTA)—met with Vic Toews, the federal Minister for Public Safety to discuss, among other issues, cargo crime. One of the outcomes of that meeting was nine steps for professional drivers to take to increase cargo safety.

On the menu: Issues affecting trucking.

1. **Check footprints and follicles:** Conduct background checks of drivers, warehouse employees, and anyone with access to shipment information and other logistics details. Many cargo thefts are "inside jobs." Many carriers are now doing criminal and background checks on personnel and some are conducting hair-follicle testing for drugs, with the premise that those who use drugs are more likely to break other laws.

2. **Get front row seats:** More carriers are now providing security training for all employees as well as educating drivers on how to prevent cargo theft and hijacking. Canada's National Insurance Crime Bureau (NICB) experts believe a driver who knows, understands, and follows security tenets is less likely to have his/her truck targeted for theft.

   As an example, drivers should:

   - Park their rigs in well-lit areas, preferably near the front of the truck stop, near the facilities rather than in a quiet back row.
   - Check to make sure load seals are intact during pretrip and en route inspections.
   - Learn to watch for a vehicle tailing them and what to do if they spot one.
   - Know the required procedure if a theft happens.
   - Not leave the keys in the truck. In 2011, a thief stole a $50,000 tractor-trailer packed with $200,000 in beef. Making a delivery at 3:30 A.M., the driver parked the rig with the key in its ignition and returned 10 minutes later to find the rig had disappeared.
   - Not discuss a load or where it's going on the CB or at truck stops. Controlling information is key. A conversation with a stranger could be a seemingly innocent one over a cup of coffee, which, when combined with other information, reveals a lot about the rig and the cargo **(see Figure 30-5).**

▶ **Figure 30-5**
Always practice safety against theft at truck stops.

© iStockphoto/buzbuzzer

(Continues)

TRANSPORT CANADA'S MOTOR CARRIER POLICY *(continued)*

3. **Avoid red-light districts:** Thieves routinely wait outside known shipping points, such as plants, warehouses, and distribution centers. They then follow trucks, wait for drivers to stop, and then grab the cargo—often in less than five minutes. Drivers can avoid this by going at least 322 km (200 miles) or four hours before stopping, and then using secured lots—and they should avoid cargo theft hot spots, such as freight pick-up or delivery areas and isolated docks.

4. **Lock the lock; walk the walk:** Locks will deter thieves and/or at least slow down those targeting a specific load. Drivers should also be aware of thieves that go down the line, opening trailers and then hooking up to one that contains something in it they like. Kingpin locks, glad hand locks, any of that stuff—there's always a way to defeat it, but if thieves see a driver doing something to protect a load, they may move on to the next trailer.

   In addition to padlocking trailer doors, consider ways to secure unattended trailers, like kingpin locks, and for the tractor, locks for air brake valves and glad hands. There are also devices designed to prevent tampering with cargo seals.

5. **Make computers your friend:** High-value cargos might require high-tech protection. Most tracking and communication systems can remotely disable a truck that has been reported stolen or that travels outside a previously set "geo-fence." For instance, InteliTrailer sells a keyless lock/unlock product operated by smartphone or handheld remote control. It also offers a GPS tracking and disabling system. Magtec makes security systems with features like driver authentication; unattended idle protection; real-time reporting of the state of the vehicle; remote disabling while moving or parked; in-cab panic/emergency buttons; remote lock and unlock, and more.

6. **Make your tracks covert:** Tracking and communications systems, like Skybitz trailer tracking, can keep track of vehicles and help recover lost loads. However, as regular truck and trailer tracking used for productivity has become common, professional thieves have become experts in disabling it. That's why you're seeing more "covert" devices that can be hidden inside a freight pallet or beneath the undercarriage of a trailer. Some are small enough to be hidden inside a pill bottle. Ryder's Anderson points out that these devices are not cheap, so they are only viable in a situation where you will be able to get them back.

   If a driver picks up a load where the shipper has used covert tracking, it's important for the driver to work hand in hand with the shipper because proper response procedures and notification procedures must be in place and everyone should know what they need to do if a theft takes place.

7. **Weekends are top times for theft:** If a driver picks up a load on Friday that the consignee won't accept until Monday, that load will sit over the weekend, the statistically peak times for cargo theft, especially of fully-loaded trailers. Terminal yards should therefore have good fencing and a gate system that's monitored by security staff. If it makes sense, install alarm-surveillance systems. Make sure the perimeter, entrances, building doors, and windows are well-lit. Back trailers up against a solid wall or barrier to prevent door openings. Some carriers employ closed-circuit TV for extra security when high-value loads are parked over the weekend.

   Trip planning is important in finding a secure place to stop. Safe parking for a fee is available from Secure Trailer Parking Network, part of Terminal Exchange Services. Its yards have 24-hour surveillance, plus cross-docking, office space, and service bays. It has more than 125 locations nationwide and is opening more this year. The company also is developing a wireless Internet reservation system.

   Weekends also are top times for human traffickers (smugglers) to look for unlocked trailers so illegal immigrants can ride to freedom. Top locations include U.S. border cities. It is also common for smugglers to try to hire truck drivers to smuggle their human cargos over the border, and from state to state.

(Continues)

TRANSPORT CANADA'S MOTOR CARRIER POLICY (continued)

In 2003, a passerby on U.S. Highway 77, outside of Victoria, Texas, called the police to report a hand, waving a bandana out of a hole in the back of an 18-wheeler. "A flood of human beings" spilled out of the trailer and 18 of the 100 Mexicans, El Salvadorans, Guatemalans, and Hondurans had asphyxiated in the trailer, which was abandoned by three traffickers.

8. **Make your cargo "hard to get":** All these strategies will be effective when used in combination, using the theory that the more barriers you place between the thieves and your cargo, the less cargo theft will occur. Any thief will go for "low-hanging fruit" before they deal with highly-secure loads. And remember, in almost every theft or rig-jacking, there's always one process failure—like a rig parked in an unsecure place, a rig left unattended for a long period of time, or sloppy basic securement.

9. **It's up to you to stay informed—and alert:** Most thieves are smart and are always finding new ways to "beat" security systems. So it's up to the driver to stay informed about current trends, identifying places where stopping should be avoided, or at least where additional security precautions should be taken. Some carriers use information from other fleets to share with their drivers. Others use local law enforcement bulletins as well as information and weekly messages from the FBI, **FreightWatch International,** and **CargoNet.**

WHAT SECURITY IS IMPORTANT?

Security expert Jeff Beatty believes an interruption in North America's commercial transportation system could do untold—if not irreparable—damage to all economies as well as take a tremendous toll on human life.

Beatty suggests food riots could break out if regular shipments were not able to move into grocery stores within several hours after an attack. "This would happen not because the shelves were bare but because the public would be insecure about what was going to happen next," he said, "and, therefore, the cost of a single large truck bomb incident could reach $5 billion—with government response driving the cost up by 10 times."

In devising a security plan, the American Trucking Associations (ATA)—like the Canadian Ministry of Transportation—wanted to deter terrorists and, most importantly, reduce vulnerability and ward off attacks. One of the most important parts of a security plan, according to the ATA, is putting the right person behind the wheel, which can be done with the proper **background checks (see Figure 30-6).**

Other aspects of a security plan include load tracking, cargo security, and employee training—to do their jobs correctly while staying alert to terrorist threats or any unusual activity.

© Cengage Learning 2013

▶ Figure 30–6

One of the most important parts of a security plan is to know who is behind the wheel.

The centerpiece of the ATA security plan is training to:

- Know what to look for and where to be alert
- Look at what is "vulnerable" and what is to be a "likely target"
- Detect operational acts—what terrorists do during their rehearsals; for example, in Oklahoma City, there were 140 "acts" of observing the building, observing traffic patterns, observing likely parking spots, and so forth
- Know your fellow drivers
- Know your neighbors in a parking lot
- Know who is driving what rig

WHAT ELSE CAN BE DONE?
Technical Innovation

Make yourself aware of technical innovations that assist in security:

- Invest in a **cell phone,** satellite tracking, and surveillance systems.
- Look at state-of-the-art seals and locks.
- Ask if access control systems are appropriate.
- Consider tamperproof locking features for fifth wheels, kingpins, and glad hands.
- Consider use of blanket-type alarms that signal when blanket is moved.
- Consider installing **electronic engine controls** that require a code, in addition to a key, to start the vehicle.

Communications

Consider communications as a big piece of any security plan:

- Develop a communications network to share information with others in the industry.
- Develop a means of communication from dispatch/safety offices to vehicle.

Emergencies

While driving in the United States and Canada, call 911 for the following emergencies:

- Life-threatening road conditions
- DWI and erratic driving
- Criminal activities such as assaults, drug activity
- Vehicle accidents, including instances of hit and run
- Medical emergencies
- Unsafe equipment and insecure loads, which may endanger other drivers
- Life-threatening instances of road rage
- Hazmat spills/accidents involving hazmat loads
- Any other life-threatening emergency witnessed by an observant driver

INTERESTING FACT

In 1968, 911 became the national emergency number for the United States. In theory at least, calling this single number provided a caller access to police, fire, and ambulance services, through what would become known as a common public safety answering point (PSAP). The number itself, however, did not become widely known until the 1970s. Conversion to 911 in Canada began in 1972 and most major cities are now using 911.

For nonemergencies, dial 1-855-TRUCKIN (878-2546) when you see:

- Hazardous road conditions—in all weather
- Closed roads/highways
- Abandoned vehicles
- Stolen vehicles
- Unusual trailer issues, such as open trailer doors on a moving vehicle, people inside trailer, etc.
- Broken traffic signals
- Reckless or aggressive driving
- Excessive speed
- Stranded motorists
- Nonthreatening debris on the highway, such as dead animals, wayward orange cones, car parts, and tire treads
- Congestion

Understand that terrorist activities tend to happen in groups, and if one attack occurs then heighten security immediately. Always increase security measures if your nation is engaged in military activity in a foreign country.

Cell Phones

Cell phones give professional drivers the ability to communicate by voice and text messaging almost anywhere, any time, and with anyone—and because pay phones are becoming scarce, it is essential the professional driver is equipped with a reliable cell phone or other electronic communications device **(see Figure 30-7).**

▶ **Figure 30-7**

Cell phones are a necessary communication device for professional drivers.

- A driver can use a cell phone, but as of January 2012, in the U.S. they must be used with "hands free" technology while driving.

- Get to know your phone and its timesaving features, such as speed dial and redial. If you can, memorize the phone's keypad so you can use the speed dial function without taking your eyes off the road.

- If your phone has a 911 location feature, make sure it is turned on. This will allow emergency response to quickly pinpoint your location.

- Position your phone within easy reach and make sure you can answer it without taking your eyes off the road. If you get an incoming call at an inconvenient time, let your voicemail answer it for you.

- Stop any conversations during hazardous driving conditions or high traffic situations. As a professional driver, your first responsibility is to pay attention to the road. Better yet, make it a priority not to talk on cell phones while driving.

- Do not text, take notes or directions, or look up phone numbers or addresses while driving. Most states have passed laws banning texting while driving. Avoid a dangerous situation that could occur because you are reading or writing and not paying attention to the road or other vehicles.

© Cengage Learning 2013

NEW LAWS PROHIBIT TEXTING

The Federal Motor Carriers Safety Administration, as of October 27, 2010, prohibits texting while operating a commercial motor vehicle in interstate commerce and imposes sanctions, including civil penalties and disqualification from operating CMVs in interstate commerce, for drivers who fail to comply with this rule. Additionally, motor carriers are prohibited from requiring or allowing their drivers to engage in texting while driving. FMCSA amends its Commercial Driver's License (CDL) regulations to add to the list of disqualifying offenses a conviction under state or local traffic laws or ordinances that prohibit texting by CDL drivers while operating a CMV, including school bus drivers. Recent research commissioned by FMCSA shows that the odds of being involved in a safety-critical event (e.g., crash, near-crash, unintentional lane deviation) are 23.2 times greater for CMV drivers who engage in texting while driving than for those who do not. This rulemaking increases safety on the nation's highways by reducing the prevalence of or preventing certain truck- and bus-related crashes, fatalities, and injuries associated with distracted driving.

ELECTRONIC SECURITY DEVICES
En Route Security for Yourself and Your Rig

The following suggestions, some of which have been cited previously, are repeated here in an attempt to help you be mindful of maintaining security for yourself, your rig, and your cargos when you're on the road.

- Avoid high-population areas, including downtown or metropolitan areas, tunnels, and bridges. See 49 CFR397.67 at www.fmcsa.dot.gov.
- Ensure that all hazardous materials are delivered as soon as possible.
- Drivers should always lock vehicles when in transit or when vehicles are left unattended.
- Drivers must be aware if a vehicle or vehicles are following their trucks.
- Drivers should also beware of strangers asking inappropriate questions about their rigs or their cargos or destinations.
- Drivers should be suspicious of individuals asking them to stop as a result of an alleged traffic accident. If unsure whether an accident has occurred, drive to a police station or well-lit, busy location before stopping.
- Be cautious about stopping to help stranded motorists or at accident scenes. The better choice would be to call the state police and report the stranded motorists or the accident.
- Do not pick up hitchhikers.
- Do not discuss the nature of your cargo over the CB radio, at coffee shops, truck stops, or elsewhere.
- Be aware of your surroundings at all times.
- Have the means to maintain communication with your company or dispatcher at all times. These means would include cell phones, two-way radios, CBs, and satellite communications systems.
- Be aware of the technology that could help you increase and improve your personal security and the security of your rig and your cargos, such as cell phones, satellite tracking, and surveillance systems.
- Look for state-of-the-art locks and seals.

- Consider installing electronic engine controls that require a code in addition to a key to start the vehicle.
- Consider theft-prevention devices, steering locks, fuel cutoff switches, electrical cutoff switches, and other high-security ignition devices.

As a professional driver, be aware that terrorist activities tend to occur in a series. If new attacks begin, tighten your security because of the possibilities of increased efforts on the part of terrorists.

It is also important to increase security measures when your nation or a neighboring nation is involved in military activities in foreign countries. Your nation's military involvement in a foreign land only invites retaliation from the terrorists bred in that country. It also gives terrorists, in general, a reason to heighten their efforts to attack your nation in as many ways as possible.

Finally, those suspicious activities you would have ignored a couple of years ago now are good reasons to remain vigilant and report what you have observed. Not reporting suspicious activities that may lead to violence and death is more of a problem than reporting activities that may not lead to violence. Law enforcement does not mind following a lead that does not pan out, and it is much worse to miss warning signs that are costly in lives and property.

Remember that terrorism costs more than buildings. It costs lives, national confidence, and our ability to grow as a free nation. Protect yourself at all costs. Protect your rig and your cargo. It is a big part of the job!

SUMMARY

Without a doubt, as a professional driver, your first responsibility remains your personal safety as well as the safety of your rig and its cargo.

In this chapter, you learned the reasons for an increased emphasis in security during loading, over the road, and during unloading. You also learned about certain things to watch for and what to do/who to notify if suspicious activities or situations arise. Finally—and most importantly—you learned the importance of protecting yourself at all costs.

KEY TERMS

Aviation and Transportation
   Security Act (ATSA)
Background checks
CargoNet
Cell phone
Department of Homeland
   Security

Electronic engine controls
FreightWatch International
Hazardous materials
Safe Explosives Act
Security
September 11, 2001
Terrorist activities

Transportation Security
   Administration (TSA)
Weapons of mass
   destruction

REVIEW QUESTIONS

1. Security _____.
   a. is only the responsibility of the dispatcher
   b. has always been a major part of the professional driver's job
   c. is only the responsibility of the receiver of the goods
   d. is only the responsibility of the shipper

2. Regarding the Department of Homeland Security, which of the following is not one of its stated missions?
   a. reduce terrorism worldwide
   b. prevent terrorist attacks within the U.S.
   c. reduce the vulnerability of rigs to terrorism
   d. minimize the damage and assist in the recovery from terrorist attacks that do occur within the U.S.

3. Which of the following is not one of the recommended procedures for increasing security on the road?
   a. Be alert when leaving a location.
   b. Do not discuss your cargo or destination near strangers.
   c. Avoid being boxed in on the road.
   d. If you believe there is a threat of hijacking, stop your rig and lock the doors.

4. If you stop your rig for food, rest, etc., which of the following should you not do?
   a. Talk to your dispatcher while you're still in the dining room.
   b. Stop only where you've stopped before.
   c. Park your rig at a crowded truck stop.
   d. If team driving, always leave one person with the rig.

5. According to the American Trucking Associations (ATA), one of the most important parts of a security plan is _____.
   a. having all professional drivers armed
   b. putting the right person behind the wheel, which can be done with the proper background checks
   c. to lock the rig, if the engine is left running, when the driver is away from the rig
   d. to not take the same route to a destination so hijackers will not know where a rig will be traveling

6. Which of the following is not a centerpiece of the ATA security plan?
   a. Know what to look for and where to be alert.
   b. Look at what is "vulnerable" and what is to be a "likely target."
   c. Know who is driving what rig.
   d. When a driver leaves the rig with the engine running, the doors should be locked.

7. One of the technical innovations that assists in security is installing electronic controls that require a _____, in addition to a key to start the engine.

    a. second key
    b. honk of the horn
    c. code
    d. none of the above

8. Regarding wireless telephone safety, a professional driver's first responsibility is to _____.

    a. pay attention to the road
    b. respond immediately to calls from the dispatcher
    c. respond immediately to calls from the shipper
    d. respond immediately to calls from the receiver of the items shipped

9. Which of the following is not a suggestion made to help drivers maintain security for themselves, their rigs, and their cargos when they are over the road?

    a. Always stop and help at accident scenes.
    b. Consider installing electronic controls required to start the engine.
    c. Do not pick up hitchhikers.
    d. Avoid high population areas, including downtown or metropolitan areas, tunnels, and bridges.

10. As a professional driver, your first responsibility is _____.

    a. to the dispatcher
    b. to the shipper
    c. to the receiver of the goods shipped
    d. your personal safety as well as the safety of your rig and its cargo

11. While driving in Canada and you need emergency assistance, you should first dial _____

    a. Canada 911
    b. your dispatcher
    c. 911
    d. the Canadian consignor or consignee

12. Tracking and communications systems can track trailers and often can _____.

    a. recover stolen keys
    b. identify driver's use of alcohol
    c. identify thieves
    d. recover stolen cargo

SUPPLEMENTAL LEARNING ACTIVITIES

1. In many areas of the country, 9/11 caused a total stoppage of freight movement. How long did this last and what was the result of trucks not rolling? Answer these questions in a 100-word report.

2. In a small group, discuss the outcome of a week-long stoppage of truck transportation in North America. Try to imagine the impact. Then, as a group, make a list of what you consider to be the most significant impact of a week without freight movement.

3. Invite a veteran professional who was driving during 9/11. Ask about his or her thoughts, fears, and what he or she did on this day and the several days that followed.

4. Imagine that your rig becomes boxed in and eventually stopped on a highway by three armed men. Make a list of what you would do first and how you would attempt to protect your load.

5. Make a list of five emergency numbers for a professional driver and put this list in your wallet.

FOR MORE INFORMATION

FMCSA Limiting the Use of Wireless Communication Devices, Search Limiting Wireless Communication
www.fmcsa.dot.gov/

NCTR UCF Intermodal Transportation Safety and Security Issues
www.nctr.usf.edu/jpt/pdf/JPT%208-4S%20Tarr.pdf

Trucking Security from the TSA
www.tsa.gov/what_we_do/grants/programs/tsp/2009/index.shtm

Road Transportation in Canadian Regions
www.tc.gc.ca/eng/regions-road.htm

U.S. DOT FMCSA Safety & Security
www.fmcsa.dot.gov/safety-security/safety-security.htm

OBJECTIVES

When you have completed this chapter, you should be able to:

- Drive with some knowledge about safety and security when entering Canada or Mexico from the United States.

- Describe FAST and the role it plays at the U.S./Canadian border.

- Understand the basics of NAFTA.

- Understand the laws that affect driving in Canada.

- Understand the laws that affect driving in Mexico.

- Report an emergency in either Mexico or Canada.

© Cengage Learning 2013

▶ **Figure 31-1**

The North American Free Trade Agreement (NAFTA) was designed to improve all facets of doing business between the United States, Canada, and Mexico.

INTRODUCTION

When implemented in January 1994, the originators of the **North American Free Trade Agreement (NAFTA)** intended to improve all facets of doing business among the participating countries—Canada, the U.S., and Mexico **(see Figure 31-1).** Their goal was to eliminate almost all tariffs and also targeted barriers to trade, such as import licenses. Although several programs have been attempted, at this writing, trucks from Mexico continue to be held at the border, going only as far as the 20-mile (32-km) limit in border cities. The same is true for U.S. trucks traveling in Mexico.

In April 2011, the Federal Motor Carrier Safety Administration proposed a three-year pilot study in which Mexican and U.S. carriers could offer long-haul service into each country.

The pilot study, consisting of three stages, culminates in permanent authority for U.S. and Mexican carriers to have cross-border operations.

Once the program is in place, Mexico will start to suspend the tariffs it began levying when the U.S. Congress killed an earlier version of the pilot study.

Some of the other details of FMCSA's program include:

- FMCSA is training state and local enforcement officials for the pilot program's requirements.

- Mexican carriers will not be permitted to provide point-to-point transportation of domestic cargo (cabotage) and this requirement will be enforced.

- Mexican trucks would have to comply with post-1998 EPA emissions rules as well as U.S. and Canadian vehicle safety standards.

- Mexican trucks and drivers will have to comply with all U.S. safety rules, size and weight restrictions, vehicle registration requirements, and environmental requirements.

- FMCSA will equip each truck with a GPS device or electronic onboard recorder to track compliance.

FMCSA officials said it found Mexico has rigorous requirements for driver knowledge and skill similar to U.S. requirements, and requires all new drivers to be trained before they are tested. Retraining also is required each time their licenses are renewed—requirements the U.S. does not have. Mexico's physical qualifications for drivers are more specific, more detailed, and stricter than those of the U.S. As an example, Mexico addresses body mass index, cancers and tumors, skin and appendages, and psychiatric and psychological disorders—all of which are not addressed in U.S. DOT physicals.

When all borders are opened and you are driving international routes, it is important to know that all motor carriers operating in NAFTA countries must follow the same federal and state/provincial regulations and procedures that apply to all carriers originating in that country **(see Figure 31-2).**

All safety regulations, insurance requirements, tariff requirements, and payments of taxes and fees apply to anyone operating a truck in that country. Foreign carriers and drivers also must follow Customs, immigration laws, and regulations of the countries in which they are driving.

SUGGESTIONS FOR SECURITY WHEN DRIVING INTERNATIONALLY

Regardless if you drive international routes, one of your first priorities should be to assure your personal security and the security of your vehicle and cargo. Following are suggestions for safe trips in any country, at any time:

1. Never leave your vehicle unlocked, even when you are driving.

2. Keep your doors locked when you are sleeping.

3. Never leave valuables unattended. If possible, lock them in the motel or truck stop safe.

4. If you spend the night at a motel, make certain the door to your room is locked at all times. If you cannot securely lock your door, ask for another room where your door can be locked. Then, for added security, use the night chain or other secondary locking devices.

5. Report all suspicious persons and activities in hallways or parking areas to management.

6. Keep all valuables in your vehicle out of sight.

7. Do not carry large amounts of cash. Use traveler's checks and credit cards as much as possible. If needed, carry cash in a money belt under your clothing.

8. While out walking, remain in well-lighted and traveled areas. Do not take shortcuts through darkened areas.

▶ **Figure 31–2**

Carriers operating in NAFTA countries must follow the federal and state/provincial regulations of the country in which they are driving.

CROSSING INTO CANADA

When NAFTA was passed, it provided a continuity in the efforts by the U.S. and Canada to improve the movement of freight and people over the border. With an average flow of more than $1.9 billion worth of goods across the border into both countries each day, both governments continue to have a huge interest in seeing their neighboring nations continue to enjoy economic stability (**see Figure 31-3**).

Four months after the terrorist attacks on New York and Washington, DC, in 2001, Canada's then-foreign minister, Pierre Pettigrew, and Tom Ridge, director of Homeland Security for the United States of America, co-signed the U.S.–Canada Smart Border Declaration, outlining an action plan to identify and address existing security risks at the border. The plan also attempted to expedite traffic into both countries with new processes at the border into each country.

One year later, a status report on the implementation of this effort showed progress. Specifically, it was reported that the efforts on both sides of the border were steadily improving the smooth flow of traffic crossing the border each day.

▶ **Figure 31–3**

Provencher Bridge.

Facts About Canada

- The population of Canada is 31,485,623 people, approximately one-tenth the population of the United States.
- Québec has the highest annual snowfall with 337 centimeters (132.7 inches).
- The highest point in Canada is Mt. Logan (in the Yukon) at 5,959 meters (19,551 feet).
- In Canada, the infant death rate is lower and the life expectancy is longer than in the U.S.
- Every product in Canada is labeled in English and French.
- Canadians use the metric system as the preferred unit of measure.
- Canada contains almost 10 million square kilometers (3,861,022 square miles) of land and 891,163 square kilometers (344,080 square miles) of water.
- The good news is Canada has more donut shops per capita than the U.S.
- Sports fans in Canada favor hockey and lacrosse.
- St. John's, Nova Scotia, is the wettest area of Canada, receiving 1,482 millimeters of rain each year.
- As of 2012, mail sent from Canada require 61 cents for letters or documents sent within Canada, $1.05 to the U.S., and $1.80 to countries overseas.
- There are $1 and $2 coins—and prices appear to be higher than in the U.S. because of the Canadian monetary system. For exchange rates, visit www.bankofcanada.ca.
- The Trans-Canada Highway is usually two lanes wide. Highway 401 north of Toronto is 16 lanes wide in places.

NOTE

Canada maintains a very strict policy of not admitting (in fact, detaining) American drivers trying to enter the country who may have a criminal record, even if it is decades old. This could be a real problem, and many American drivers, unfamiliar with the policy, are detained every year. Drivers who may have criminal issues in their background can apply for a "minister's waiver" (a Canadian minister is a political minister, not a member of the clergy!), which allows them clearance into Canada.

Crossing the Border into Canada

Any international driver hauling freight into Canada will need the following items and documentation:

1. Valid Commercial Driver's License (CDL)
2. Proof of citizenship—passport, proof of Canadian landed immigrant status (form IMM 1000)
3. Vehicle license and permits, including valid International Fuel Tax (IFT) and International Registration Plan (IRP) permits
4. An enhanced driver's license, if applicable
5. Operating license (also called an operating authority or safety certificate) recognized by each jurisdiction in which you will be traveling
6. Required number of copies of paper work for Canadian Customs

How to Report an Emergency in Canada

- To report an emergency, dial 911 and give your complete number (mobile phone and area code).
- Tell the operator your exact location as precisely as possible. Look for street signs, highway markers, and other landmarks.
- Stay on the phone as long as you are needed for information. Do not hang up until the emergency operator tells you to do so.
- Keep your mobile phone on in case the operator needs to call you back.

Driving in Canada

The speed limits in Canada are posted in kilometers per hour as opposed to miles per hour. The speed limit on most city streets is 50 km/hr (31 mi/hr). On most highways, the speed limit is posted as 100 km/hr (62 mi/hr). Speed limits may vary among the provinces, so keep an eye on the posted speed limit signs. A rule of thumb is to multiply the posted speed limit by 6 and then divide by 10 to convert

the posted kilometers per hour to miles per hour. Drivers must also be aware overhead clearances are listed in meters and not feet and inches. Also bridge weights are not in pounds but use the metric system.

Canadian Monetary System

The **monetary exchange rate** varies from establishment to establishment. As there are no laws enforcing the rate of exchange on foreign currency, it is wise to change your money at a bank or a reputable currency exchange. Banks are generally open 10:00 A.M. to 4:00 P.M., Monday through Friday. An increasing number are open evenings and Saturday mornings.

Because of the fluidity of the exchange rate, check with the bank of your choice once you cross the border to know exactly what a U.S. dollar is worth.

> **NOTE**
>
> Typically, most Canadian businesses accept U.S. currency. U.S. bank credit/debit cards are also honored. Your card account will be billed in U.S. funds, not Canadian.

The Commercial Vehicle Safety Alliance

The rules and guidelines of the **Commercial Vehicle Safety Alliance (CVSA)** are used on all roads across Canada just like they are across the United States **(see Figure 31-4).** Similar to those in the United States, CVSA guidelines are used by inspectors performing roadside inspections of commercial vehicles. If you, your paperwork, or your vehicle do not conform to CVSA guidelines—in the U.S. or Canada—you risk being placed out of service or given a restricted service condition. Both entail hassle, paperwork, fines, and jail time, depending on the severity of your infraction(s).

In Canada, you can be put out of service if you are not of legal age to drive; if you do not have proper license to drive; if you do not pass physical requirements; if you are sick, fatigued, or otherwise impaired; or if you are driving under the influence of drugs or alcohol.

You can also be put out of service if you have exceeded the legal number of hours of service, have an incomplete log or no driving log, or if your vehicle does not pass inspection.

Mechanical problems can include defective brakes, defective coupling devices, defective or missing safety devices, defective exhaust system, defective or missing lighting devices, unsafe loading standards, defective steering mechanisms, defective or inadequate suspension, defective frame, defective or inappropriate tires, wheels, and rims, or insufficient welds, glazing of the windshield, or defective windshield wipers **(see Figure 31-5).**

If your vehicle passes a roadside inspection, a CVSA sticker, which is good for 3 months, will be placed on your vehicle.

▶ **Figure 31-4**

Commercial Vehicle Safety Alliance (CVSA) rules and guidelines are used on roads in Canada and the United States.

▶ **Figure 31-5**

Mechanical problems can result in your being put out of service.

Border Crossings into Canada

To save waiting time and to maintain your projected schedule, know the hours of operations of the **border crossing** you wish to use as well as the hours of operation for the destination where you want to clear Customs.

Nonresident drivers crossing into Canada will need to know when Canadian border crossings are open. For specific information about a particular crossing, call 800-461-9999 or visit the website www.ccra-adrc.gc.ca and find "Customs" by using the A–Z index.

The following provincial border crossings are open 24 hours a day, 365 days a year. All other border crossings provide service from 8:00 A.M. to 5:00 P.M., Monday through Friday.

Alberta	Coutts Crossing
British Columbia	Pacific Highway, Osoyoos, and Kingsgate
Manitoba	Emerson
New Brunswick	Woodstock, St. Stephen
Ontario	Pigeon River, Ft. Francis, Sault Ste. Marie, Sarnia, Prescott, Lansdowne, Ft. Erie, Niagara Falls, Windsor
Quebec	Lacolle, St. Armand-Phillipsburg, Stanhope, Rock Island
Saskatchewan	North Portal

Wait times are usually less than 5 minutes at most crossings, Mondays through Thursdays. On weekends, wait times may be as much as 20 minutes. Periodically, wait times at the Port Huron, Michigan, bridge can be as long as 45 minutes.

GO!

If your load simply takes you through Canada (Ontario, for instance), as opposed to reaching a delivery or pick-up destination there, you will have the border agents simply attach a "seal" to your trailer door and you must then complete a "transit manifest." Upon returning to the United States, your seal is verified that it is intact and you are free to continue.

CLEARING CUSTOMS

1. The first advice to heed in getting through **Customs** at any border is to take your time. Relax, smile, and always be ready for an inspection, and this means having your trailer loaded so it can be inspected easily. To accomplish this, let the shipper know that the shipment needs to be packed to avoid delay at the border.

   If you have waiting time, practice patience, be cordial, and be helpful with inspectors. Remember that it is a serious offense under the Customs Act to leave the border and/or to not report to the compound when requested.

2. Know what your cargo contains so you can answer any questions the Customs inspector may have.

3. Declare all of your personal goods, including prescription drugs, firearms, or pets. Be prepared to pay duty and taxes, depending on your personal declaration of goods.

4. It is unlawful to carry firearms in the cab of your vehicle. Additional weapons such as switchblades, butterfly knives, or mace are either restricted or prohibited. If you have this contraband in your cab, it will be seized and shipped back to your home address at your expense.

CAUTION!

Border Patrol agents have the authority to break any seal and inspect the trailer. Therefore, you should keep extra company seals on hand so that the load can then be resealed once you clear customs. You must also note on the bill of lading that the seal was broken by Customs/Border Patrol agents. The consignee might question why the seal has been tampered with and you should always keep documentation to prove your position. An inspection of your cargo does not carry a cost; if an inspection fee is charged, report this immediately.

One other point to remember is if you attempt to deliver cargo that has not been released by Customs, your truck and cargo may be seized and you will be additionally punished with a sizable fine.

GUIDELINES FOR DRIVERS ENTERING THE U.S.

Government officials from the U.S. and Canada have developed guidelines to assure expeditious movement of goods between their two countries. At each border, commercial trucks have their own lanes, clearly marked and designed to assist rapid clearance of their loads. To assist in the speedy clearance of your cargo, remember the following:

- Have documentation in order and ready for inspection, and make sure your logs are up to date.
- Whatever happens, never argue with a border inspector.
- Have required identification documents available, such as driver's license, hazmat endorsement, passport, birth certificate, or other immigration documents.
- Know exactly what's in your trailer, be able to answer any questions border agents may have, and when crossing into the U.S. be able to speak understandable English. Bottom line, your freight should exactly match your manifest.
- If your load requires faxing information to the border prior to your arrival, make certain this happens.
- PAPS—the Pre-Arrival Processing System assists in reporting cargo to customs officers prior to your arrival at the border. This occurs when the Inward Cargo Manifest (ICM) and necessary supporting documents are faxed to the U.S. Customs broker at least one hour before you and your cargo arrive.
- BRASS—Border Release Advance Screening and Selectivity program is commodity- and customs-broker specific. Instructions include (1) shipper includes BRASS indicator along with shipper invoices. (2) Driver completes U.S. Inward Cargo Manifest. (3) Driver must be FAST-approved and have a valid FAST ID card (explained in the following section). (4) BRASS shipments don't require PAPS, and no paperwork is required to be faxed ahead of your arrival.

CANADIAN DRIVERS CROSSING INTO THE U.S.

Considering that more than 80 percent of Canadian trucking moves north/south, it is not unlikely that a Canadian truck driver will regularly cross the border into the U.S. As a first experience, crossing the border may be stressful and, perhaps a little intimidating, as most border patrols at U.S. borders are fully armed and often use dogs to search cargoes. However, if you have the proper paperwork, both personal and cargo-related, everything should go smoothly and your crossing won't be delayed.

International Registration Plan (IRP)

The International Registration Plan is an agreement between U.S. states and Canadian provinces for registering vehicles traveling into two or more of the jurisdictions. With the exception of Yukon, Northwest Territories, Nunavut, Alaska, and Mexico, all Canadian provinces and U.S. states are members of the IRP program. This program provides for the payment of registration fees for the commercial vehicles based on the distance traveled in each jurisdiction. The unique feature of the IRP is that although registration fees are paid to the various jurisdictions into which the vehicle travels, only one set of license plates and one cab card are issued for each vehicle.

International carriers, under IRP, file applications with their home jurisdiction, which will then issue one permit, cab card, and a set of apportioned license plates per vehicle. These plates are embossed with the letters PRP, which stand

Roses are red,
Violets are blue,
When it comes to smooth border crossing,
Good preparation is your clue!

for Pro Rate Plate and are located down the left side of the plate. These are the credentials you will need to operate in various international jurisdictions. The cab card lists weights that have been requested for each jurisdiction and registration fees are apportioned according to these weights.

The home jurisdiction collects the applicable fees for all jurisdictions and at one time. These fees are calculated and sent to the other IRP jurisdictions. They are based on:

- percentage of distance traveled and each jurisdiction
- vehicle identification information
- maximum weight to be carried in that jurisdiction

The FAST Program

The **Free and Secure Trade (FAST) program** is a joint Canada–U.S. initiative involving the Canada Customs and Revenue Agency, Citizenship and Immigration Canada, the United States Customs Service, and the United States Immigration and Naturalization Service. FAST supports moving preapproved eligible goods across the border quickly and verifying trade compliance away from the border.

It is a harmonized commercial process offered to preapproved importers and carriers, and registered drivers. Shipments for approved companies, transported by approved carriers using registered drivers, will be cleared into either country with greater speed and certainty, and at reduced cost of compliance.

FAST focuses on greater speed and certainty at the border and reduces the cost of compliance by:

- Reducing the information requirements for Customs clearance
- Eliminating the need for importers to transmit data for each transaction
- Dedicating lanes for FAST clearances
- Reducing the rate of border examinations

- Verifying trade compliance away from the border
- Streamlining accounting and payment processes for all goods imported by approved importers (Canada only)

What You Can and Cannot Bring into Canada

Pets

You can bring pet dogs or cats that are 3 months old or older into Canada from the U.S. if you have a certificate from a licensed veterinarian identifying the animal by breed, age, sex, coloring, and distinguishing marks. The certificate must also show the animal has been vaccinated against rabies during the last 3 years. Animal tags are not acceptable and cannot be used as a substitute for this certificate (**see Figure 31-6**).

▶ **Figure 31-6**

You can bring your pet cat or dog into Canada if it is three months or older and you have the proper documentation.

Firearms

Canada has strict laws about **firearms.** If you plan to bring one into the country, you must declare them at Customs when you enter. If you fail to register them, Customs officials have the right to seize your firearms and you will face criminal charges. For more information regarding a specific firearm or any applicable fees, call the Canadian Firearms Center at 1-800-731-4000.

Alcohol

The FMCSA specifically addresses the use of alcohol and illegal drugs for commercial drivers. In Canada, many of the same rules apply. No open containers of beer, wine, or other alcoholic beverages are allowed in the truck. You cannot carry alcohol or illegal drugs in your cab or drive while under the influence of alcohol or illegal drugs.

Canadian officials have the right to test you if they suspect you are driving under the influence of alcohol or illegal drugs. If you test positively, you will be fined and subject to criminal conviction as well as seizure of your vehicle and its cargo.

Driving Time in Canada

Commercial drivers in Canada are allowed to drive 13 hours. Maximum time on duty, including driving time, stands at 14 hours. This requires at least 10 hours off duty before you can return to driving or duty. In any 7-day period in Canada, drivers may be on duty for only 70 hours. During an 14-day period, drivers can be on duty a maximum of 120 hours.

Once in Canada you as a driver are held to the Canadian HOS and no longer bound by FMCSA authority. The same holds true for Canadian drivers here in the United States—they might be Canadian but they are held to U.S. HOS rules.

Necessary Records in Canada

Like the U.S., all commercial drivers in Canada are required to maintain up-to-date logbooks. If a driver fails to keep his or her log current, he or she can lose his or her license to drive, be fined, taken out of service, or face a combination of these penalties. Like the U.S., it is unlawful to maintain more than one daily log or to falsify the daily log.

If you want to use electronic or other mechanical devices to maintain your daily log, this is permissible as long as the device records all required information and you have signed copies of each log generated for the current trip. Required information includes (1) the number of hours spent driving each day, (2) the on-duty hours each day, (3) the total on-duty hours accumulated for the current periods of 7, 8, or 14 days, and (4) the changes of your duty status and when these changes occurred each day.

What Other Documents Are Needed to Cross into Canada? All drivers must also have a current commercial driver's license plus current registrations and licenses for the vehicle. If your trip will involve travel to several provinces, states, or countries, you are also required to have an International Fuel Tax Agreement (IFTA) sticker.

The required registration for the area in which you plan to travel must also be available if you are asked for this documentation. This ensures that your International Registration Plan (IRP) card is current for all areas in which you will be traveling and will prevent you from paying additional registration fees.

▶ **Figure 31–7**

Check with the Mexican customs broker for your shipment to find out the most up-to-date laws and regulations for driving in Mexico.

CROSSING THE BORDER INTO MEXICO

A professional commercial driver who drives in Mexico should remember that he or she is in a foreign country with different laws, customs, and safety standards. The driver also needs to realize that laws and customs are changing in Mexico because of the changing political climate of all of North America, security concerns, and changing NAFTA rules **(see Figure 31-7)**.

Because of these changes, the Mexican Customs broker hired for your shipment will be your best source of current information. The Mexican Customs broker will have the most up-to-date information about the best route to your destination along with the best fuel stops, hotels/motels, and restaurants.

Personal Identification Needed to Enter Mexico. The government of Mexico requires that all U.S. citizens present a passport or passport card. Driver's permits, voter registration cards, affidavits, and similar documents are not sufficient to prove citizenship for readmission into the United States.

Facts About Mexico

- **Official name:** The United Mexican States (or in Spanish, *Estados Unidos Mexicanos*)
- **Geography:** Covers approximately 761,600 square miles (1,972,534 square kilometers)
- **Population:** 113,724,225 (*CIA World Factbook,* January 2012)
- **Capital city:** Mexico City (or *Distrito Federal* in Spanish)
- **Number of states:** Thirty-one and one federal district. Each state is headed by an elected governor
- **Major transportation centers:** Border cities: with connections to major interior cities—Tijuana to Baja California; Nogales to the Pacific Coast; Ciudad Juarez to Chihuahua, Torreon, Monterrey, San Luis Potosi, Mexico City, and Guadalajara; Nuevo Laredo to Monterrey, San Luis Potosi, Mexico City, and Guadalajara; Reynosa and Matamoros to Monterrey, San Luis Potosi, Mexico City, and Guadalajara Interior cities: Chihuahua, Monterrey, San Luis Potosi, Guadalajara, and Mexico City
- **Miles/kilometers of highways (paved):** Total 60,000 miles (96,561 km) of which 4,000 miles (6,437 km) are expressways (estimated 1997)

- **Climate:** Varies from tropical to desert with high rugged mountains, low coastal plains, and high plateaus. Mexico's climate is generally more closely related to altitude and rainfall than to latitude.
- **Economy:** An estimated 40 percent of all Mexican citizens live below the poverty line. Main crops are corn, wheat, soybeans, rice, beans, cotton, fruit, coffee, tomatoes, beef, poultry, dairy products, and wood products.

  Industries include food and beverages, tobacco, chemical, iron and steel, petroleum, mining, textiles, clothing, motor vehicles, and consumer durables.

  Export commodities include manufactured goods, oil and oil products, silver, fruits, vegetables, coffee, and cotton.

  Export partners: USA 88.4 percent, Canada 2 percent. Import partners: USA 68.4 percent, Canada 2.5 percent.
- **Money:** Currency is the Mexican **peso** (MXN). Exchange rate: Mexican pesos per U.S. dollar— $0.0755 as of Oct. 15, 2011.

Mexico's Telephone System

Domestic telephone service offers 12 main lines per 100 persons. Adequate service is available for business and government. The use of cellular telephones is common for much of the domestic service. Internationally numerous satellite Earth stations are giving Mexico improved access to South America, Central America, and much of the United States. Check with your communications provider to determine the availability of cellular telephone service in Mexico.

Reporting an Emergency in Mexico

If you have an emergency while driving, the equivalent of 911 in Mexico is 060, but this number is not always answered. If you are driving on a toll highway, or **cuota,** or any major highway, contact the **Green Angels,** a fleet of trucks with bilingual crews that operate daily. The Green Angels may be reached directly at (01) 55 5250-8221. If you are unable to call them, pull off the road and lift the hood of your truck.

Buying Diesel Fuel in Mexico

Fuel prices in Mexico are government controlled. Prices fluctuate with the economy. There is only one grade of diesel fuel in Mexico and it is sold in liter measures **(see Figure 31-8).** One liter is close to one quart. Four liters equal about 1 gallon. To convert liters to gallons, divide the number of liters purchased by 4 to calculate the number of gallons purchased. Look for the black sign that signals diesel fuel is sold at that location.

▶ **Figure 31–8**

Fuel prices in Mexico are controlled by the government and fluctuate with the economy.

The Language

Of the population over age 15, almost 90 percent can read. The principal language of the country is Spanish, with various regional dialects spoken. English is also spoken, particularly in larger communities.

Holidays in Mexico

Mexico celebrates many holidays. Independence Day is September 16. The Day of the Dead is November 1. If you are driving in Mexico, it is important to know about their national holidays because, in many cases, the holidays signal business closings and thus delivery of freight may be difficult.

Hours of Service in Mexico

To date, there is no governmental limit to the number of hours driven per shift in Mexico.

Safety and Security When Visiting Mexico

To obtain security information before traveling in Mexico, visit the website www.state.gov.

The following recommendations may be helpful:

- Visitors should be aware of their surroundings at all times, even when in areas generally considered to be safe.
- Exercise caution when traveling on all highways in Mexico and use toll (*cuota*) roads, rather than the less secure free (*libre*) highways, when possible. Never hitchhike or accept rides.
- Be wary of persons representing themselves as Mexican police or other local officials.
- Do not hike alone in backcountry areas, or walk alone on lightly frequented beaches, ruins, or trails.

What to Avoid in Mexico. Visitors should avoid demonstrations and other activities that might be deemed political by the Mexican authorities. Mexican constitutional provisions prohibit political activities by foreigners, and such actions may result in detention and/or deportation.

Driving Safety

While in any foreign country, U.S. citizens may encounter road conditions that differ significantly from those in the United States. In Mexico City, in order to cut down on air pollution, authorities restrict traffic. Therefore, vehicles not registered in Mexico are not allowed to drive one day of the week, as follows: The restriction is based on the last digit of the license plate. On Mondays, license plates with the last digit of 5 or 6 cannot drive. On Tuesdays, those with the last digit of 7 or 8 cannot drive. On Wednesdays, vehicles with license plates ending in 3 or 4 are not allowed. On Thursday, no driving for vehicles with license plates ending in 1 or 2. On Fridays, no driving of vehicles with a final digit of 9 or 0 as well as vehicles with temporary license plates. On Saturdays and Sundays, all vehicles may drive. Failure to abide by this schedule may result in a vehicle being impounded as well as fines.

Traffic and Road Conditions

Concerns continue regarding criminal activity on highways along the Mexican border (which includes placement of illegal checkpoints and the murder of persons who did not stop and/or surrender their vehicles).

While in a foreign country, U.S. citizens may encounter road conditions that differ significantly from those in the United States. As an example, public transportation vehicles, specifically taxis and city buses, often do not comply with traffic regulations, including observing speed limits and stopping at red lights.

Driving and Vehicle Regulations

U.S. driver's licenses are valid in Mexico. Mexican law requires that only owners drive their vehicles, or that the owner be inside the vehicle. If not, the vehicle may be seized by Mexican Customs and will not be returned under any circumstances. The government of Mexico strictly regulates the entry of vehicles into Mexico.

Insurance

Mexican insurance is required for all vehicles, including rental vehicles. Mexican auto insurance is sold in most cities and towns on both sides of the border. U.S. automobile liability insurance is not valid in Mexico, nor is most collision and comprehensive coverage issued by U.S. companies. Motor vehicle insurance is considered invalid in Mexico if the driver is found to be under the influence of alcohol or drugs.

Road Emergencies and Accidents

Motor vehicle accidents are a leading cause of death of U.S. citizens in Mexico. Motorists should exercise caution and remain alert on all Mexican roads.

If you are involved in an automobile accident, you may be taken into police custody until it can be determined who is liable and whether you have the ability to pay any penalty. If you do not have Mexican liability insurance, you may be prevented from departing the country even if you require life-saving medical care, and you are almost certain to spend some time in jail until all parties are satisfied that responsibility has been assigned and adequate financial satisfaction received. Drivers may face criminal charges if injuries or damages are serious.

Mexican Toll Roads

Much of Mexico is covered by modern *cuota* toll roads, and most of these are privately owned. They are generally much faster than the free *libre* roads, if the latter run parallel, as the *libre* roads will slow considerably as they pass through small towns and villages.

Using toll roads in Mexico is quite expensive: the tolls range from about 25 to 150 Mexican pesos (approximately $2.50–$15 American dollars) for passenger cars, depending on the section of highway. If you are planning on making a long drive on toll roads, make sure you have plenty of Mexican pesos with you. U.S. dollars and credit cards are NOT accepted on many toll roads, though they may be accepted in some heavily touristed areas (such as Highway 180 in Yucatan). The price goes up only if you're in an RV or towing something. Also, there can be several tollbooths between cities.

Even with the prices of using Mexican toll roads, some are not in conditions one would expect for the price you pay to use them. Some are in need of resurfacing, and will abuse your car if you travel the speed limit (which is normally 110 km/h, or 68 mph). It is a good idea to travel these sections of road under the speed limit to make sure your rig makes it back up north without any suspension or other issues.

If the conditions of the toll road cause damage to your vehicle (including blowouts), insurance is included in the price of the toll (make sure to keep your toll payment receipt). This does not include an accident with another vehicle. (Your Mexican car insurance covers that.) Damage caused to your truck has to be reported immediately at the next tollbooth you come to. It would be a good idea to take note of the kilometer marker where the incident happened, and have all of your papers ready (including toll receipt). If your only loss is a tire, and you're in a hurry, you may not want to bother making a claim since it can take some time. Some very fluent Spanish is also a strong recommendation, since most employees working the toll roads may not speak enough English to process a claim.

A plus for toll roads is that there are clean bathrooms and snack shops at most toll booths. It's a good opportunity to stretch your legs a bit, have a bite to eat, or visit the restroom before continuing on your way.

Country Roads

Once you get off the main highways, it's common to find potholes, dropoffs, dirt roads, and other hazards **(see Figure 31-9)**. The Mexicans brave these in standard passenger cars, but you'll probably be more comfortable in a higher-clearance

▶ **Figure 31–9**

Urban road conditions in Mexico are rated "good," rural roads are rated "fair."

vehicle such as an SUV, especially if you plan to visit hot springs, beaches, camping areas, or other off-the-beaten-path locations.

The Federales

The Mexican Federal Police (Policia Federal, or "Federales") patrol the roads. Unfortunately, the culture of "mordida" (the term for *bribe* in the local slang) still prevails, and as often as not the Federales may be willing to let you off with a warning in exchange for some folding money. However, do not by any means assume that the officer is expecting a bribe—the police are well aware that it is illegal and rarely will ask directly; occasionally an officer might be offended or may even arrest you for offering. As in most places, courtesy and respect are most important. Knowing Spanish is also very useful in these situations, since the police often do not know English.

More About the Green Angels

The Mexican government operates a roadside assistance program called the "Angeles Verdes" or "Green Angels." The green trucks and their operators have the wherewithal to fix many debilitating automobile conditions. In fact, many travelers who have benefited from their services consider them miracle workers: did you know you can fix a leaking radiator with pepper or an egg? Services and information are free; parts or gasoline if necessary must be paid for. You can call the Green Angels for assistance by dialing 078.

Mexican Topes and Vados

In Mexico, they're serious about speed control. "Topes," or speed bumps, often consist of a large steel pipe with small asphalt ramps. When driving cross-country, you will often encounter "vados," or dips. These are generally places where a stream or other feature crosses the road, and often they are severe—slow down and keep your eyes open. Cattle tend to congregate in vados.

Mexico's Mountainous Areas

When on steep, narrow, or single-lane roads, the downhill traffic has the right of way over uphill traffic **(see Figure 31-10).**

If you are going uphill and you see oncoming traffic, pull over to the side of the road, well out of the way, and either slow down or stop. If you are going downhill, use caution as the driver may not be aware of the law.

From a practical standpoint, it is wise to keep an eye out for pullouts. The closest one may be behind you. This tip applies only to some really out-of-the-way roads, as there are few of these old roads left.

▶ **Figure 31–10**

Mexico's mountainous area.

A practical tip for mountain driving is to keep your cool. If you get behind a big truck on a narrow two-lane road, do not try to pass on blind curves. Be patient. Eventually, there will be a pullout or slightly wider section where it will be safe to pass.

Checkpoints

Expect checkpoints along most major and some minor roads manned by the Mexican military, mostly with automatic weapons. You will be asked for driver's license and insurance information. Your vehicle will be searched with varying degrees of scrutiny depending upon your attitude, your load, and how bored they are. They are looking for drugs or weapons, which you should not have with you. They do not expect (or accept) bribes of any sort, but cold nonalcoholic beverages are often appreciated.

At military checkpoints, you will never be asked for identification because the army has no right to do so.

Night Driving in Mexico

Many guidebooks and travelers advise against driving at night. This is excellent advice. When driving the libre roads at night you will likely encounter pedestrian traffic (people on the way to church every night), animals, slow moving traffic, road hazards, and the occasional person who has fallen asleep on the warm road or is simply just sitting there. Driving at night, outside of a municipality, tourist area, or on a toll road is risky and dangerous. There are some Mexicans who (perhaps to save fuel) drive without lights; drunk driving is very common at night.

Driving on a toll road, or *cuota,* is considerably safer than on *libre* roads but can still be hazardous. These roads may be unlit and may sometimes be used by pedestrians and/or bicyclists. Use them with caution.

RESPECT IN MEXICO

- ■ If you're driving behind someone on a two-lane highway, and they signal a left turn without slowing down, they're indicating that it's safe for you to pass. The same signal from someone behind you may indicate they wish to pass.

- ■ If someone driving toward you flashes the lights, it means there may be hazards ahead.

- ■ If you are in a line of traffic on a two-lane federal highway, and the driver ahead of you turns on his hazards, **SLOW DOWN** quickly. Then you will want to leave some room between you and the car ahead of you.

- ■ Flashing hazards while driving means that there is some sort of danger ahead, or a fully-loaded semi is going extremely slow. You can also show this courtesy if you are the first rig in line and you spot a situation that warrants slowing way down (i.e., cattle, debris, or other hazards in the road). Hit your brakes and reach for the hazards at the same time.

For additional information in concerning Mexican driver's permits, vehicle inspection, road tax, mandatory insurance, etc., telephone the Mexican Secretariat of Tourism (SECTUR) at 1-800-44-MEXICO (639-426). You can also consult MexOnline for further information regarding vehicle inspection and importation procedures. For detailed information in Spanish only, visit Mexican Customs' website: Importación Temporal de Vehículos ("Temporary Importation of Vehicles"). Drivers in Mexico are advised to consult with the Mexican Embassy or the nearest Mexican consulate in the United States for additional, detailed information prior to entering Mexico. For travel information for the Baja California peninsula, you can also consult independent websites: Travel to Baja or Discover Baja California.

Legal Problems While in Mexico

In Mexico, U.S. citizens are subject to Mexico's laws and regulations, which sometimes differ significantly from those in the United States and may not afford the protections available to the individual under U.S. law. Americans who commit illegal acts have no special privileges and are subject to full prosecution under the Mexican judicial system. Penalties for breaking the law can be more severe than in the United States for similar offenses. Persons violating Mexico's laws, even unknowingly, may be expelled, arrested, or imprisoned.

Prison conditions in Mexico can be extremely poor. In many facilities, food is insufficient in both quantity and quality, and prisoners must pay for adequate nutrition from their own funds.

Penalties for Drug Offenses in Mexico

Penalties for drug offenses are strict, and convicted offenders can expect large fines and jail sentences up to 25 years. As in the United States, the purchase of controlled medication requires a doctor's prescription. The Mexican list of controlled medication differs from that of the United States, and Mexican public health laws concerning controlled medication are unclear and often enforced selectively.

Further information on bringing prescription drugs into the United States is available from the U.S. Customs Service at the following website: www.customs.ustreas.gov.

The **U.S. Embassy** cautions that possession of any amount of prescription medicine brought from the United States, including medications to treat HIV and psychotropic drugs, such as Valium, can result in arrest if Mexican authorities suspect abuse or if the quantity of the prescription medicine exceeds the amount required for several days' use.

Penalties for Firearms Violations

Do not take any type of firearm or ammunition into Mexico without prior written authorization from the Mexican authorities.

Entering Mexico with a firearm, certain kinds of knives, or even a single round of ammunition is illegal, even if the firearm or ammunition is taken into Mexico unintentionally. Firearms and ammunition of a caliber higher than .22 are considered for the exclusive use of the military and their importation carries penalties of up to 30 years in prison. The Mexican government strictly enforces its laws restricting the entry of firearms and ammunition along all land borders and at airports and seaports.

SUMMARY

In this chapter, you received information about driving safely and securely when entering Canada or Mexico from the U.S. You also learned something about each of these neighboring countries, the requirements to cross the border into Canada, and the documentation required. You learned some of the basics regarding the North American Free Trade Agreement, using the FAST system to clear customs in Canada, and the laws affecting driving in Canada and Mexico. You also learned something about reporting emergencies in both countries; about laws regarding pets, firearms, drugs, and alcohol; and penalties for taking such items into other countries.

KEY TERMS

Border crossing
Commercial Vehicle Safety
  Alliance (CVSA)
Cuota
Customs

Firearms
Free and Secure Trade (FAST)
  program
Green Angels
Monetary exchange rate

North American Free Trade
  Agreement (NAFTA)
Peso
U.S. Embassy

A DAY IN THE LIFE...

Yvette Lagrois

© Cengage Learning 2013

Truck Training School Association of Ontario, President - Ontario Truck Training Academy, Vice President

One in four Canadians works in the transportation industry. With such a diversity of job opportunities, finding the right one is a challenge for all of us. My passion is working with people and developing individuals to reach their potential. I choose to specialize in developing commercial drivers for our roads.

My employment journey started in the insurance industry. Through the eyes of this industry, I observed for 20 years the cost of drivers not reaching their potential in crucial driving decisions on the road. The solution from the insurance world is better loss control. Loss control is preventing losses through education and training. This concept stayed with me over the years.

Dennis Lagrois, my husband, was a professional commercial tanker driver of 25 years and a senior driver trainer. He took pride in developing the skills of new tanker drivers. Dennis was unhappy with the lack of training available to new drivers. We often discussed the issues we both saw. Four years later, Ontario Truck Training Academy was formed. It required both our personal strengths woven together to form a quality entry-level driver training facility. We were not afraid to introduce new training methods and develop new programs. By 2002, state-of-the-art driving simulators (trucks with no wheels) were added to our equipment list as well as a variety of trucks to our fleet. We attracted quality trainers and adopted a co-op management style to encourage our trainers to share their passion with new drivers—transferring decades of over-the-road experiences to the next generation of professional drivers.

As truck training school owners, we could take the time to explain to future professional drivers that they need to make an investment in themselves if

they want fruitful, long-term employment. Adding a Professional Commercial Driving skill opens employment doors but also has financial and legal consequences, if the skill is not mastered. Driver ignorance of the law is no longer an acceptable defense. A student entering the industry must set goals, invest the time to train, and focus on the task of commercial driving in order to meet the industry expectation of a Professional Commercial Driver.

> " **My passion is working with people and developing individuals to reach their potential.** "

In 2010, my advocate role expanded to include President of the Truck Training School Association of Ontario. Being elected by other truck training schools was a great honor. This experience has been an invaluable opportunity to work with government, industry, and other similar-minded truck training schools across the province to promote the next generation of driver training ideals. My lifelong goal is to leave a legacy of safe professional drivers. I want to be instrumental in scoping out new teaching material, new teaching methods, and staying true to the valuable skills required by the companies that hire entry-level drivers. Making a difference one new commercial driver at a time.

REVIEW QUESTIONS

1. Regarding suggestions for safe trips in any country, which of the following is not a correct statement?

    a. Never leave your vehicle unlocked.
    b. Do not leave valuables unattended; lock them in the motel or truck stop safe.
    c. If you've unloaded and your trailer is empty, you don't have to lock your trailer.
    d. Keep all valuables in your vehicle out of sight.

2. When NAFTA was passed, it _____.

    a. provided a continuity in the efforts to increase trade in North America.
    b. focused on restricting trade between North America and Canada.
    c. focused on improving trade between South America and North America.
    d. focused on improving trade between North America and Europe.

3. Canadians use the _____ system to measure speed and fuel.

    a. Arabic
    b. Euro
    c. modified imperial
    d. metric

4. The rules and guidelines of the Commercial Vehicle Safety Alliance are used on all roads across Canada just like they are across _____.

    a. all of Mexico
    b. all of South America
    c. all of Central America
    d. all states in the U.S.

5. The Free and Secure Trade (FAST) supports moving _____ across the border quickly and verifying trade compliance away from the border.

    a. race cars only
    b. preapproved eligible goods
    c. all items manufactured in Europe
    d. any items from South America

6. Which of the following is not a good practice regarding getting through Canadian customs?

    a. Have your trailer loaded so it can be inspected easily.
    b. Be knowledgeable and helpful with inspectors.
    c. Don't declare personal goods.
    d. Know what your cargo contains so you can answer any questions the authorities may have.

7. Regarding commercial drivers in Canada, which of the following is not a correct statement?

    a. Maximum time on duty is 15 hours including driving time.
    b. Drivers are allowed to drive 10 hours in a 24-hour period.
    c. The driver is required to have 8 hours off duty before driving again.
    d. In any 8-day period, drivers may be on duty for only 48 hours.

8. Because of changes in Mexico brought about by such things as changing political climates, security concerns, and changing NAFTA rules, _____ is (are) the best source of information concerning the best route to your destination, best fuel stops, hotels/motels, and so forth.

    a. the Mexican Customs broker hired for your shipment
    b. other drivers
    c. newspapers, magazines, etc.
    d. television news

9. Since fuel in Mexico is sold in liter measures, to convert liters to gallons divide the number of liters purchased by _____.

    a. 6

    b. 10

    c. 4

    d. 2

10. Regarding hours of service in Mexico, which of the following is correct?

    a. Mexican law is the same as U.S. law.

    b. Drivers may drive 15 hours with 9 hours off duty.

    c. Drivers may be on duty 15 hours with 13 hours of driving and 9 hours off duty.

    d. There is no governmental limit to the number of hours driven per shift.

11. If you take arms or munitions into Mexico, you must have _____.

    a. permission from the broker

    b. permission from Customs officers

    c. permission from the government

    d. permission from the shipper

12. The FAST program is _____.

    a. through-lanes designated for preapproved certain trucks

    b. a harmonized process offered preapproved to importers and carriers

    c. certain customs agents checking pre-approved cargos

    d. schools offering three-day training for CMV drivers

13. To report an emergency in Canada, dial 911 and be prepared to:

    a. give your complete phone number

    b. give your exact location

    c. stay on the line as long as needed for information

    d. all of the above

14. To report an emergency in Mexico, _____.

    a. call 060

    b. call the Green Angels at (01) 55 5250-8221

    c. pull off the road and lift the hood of your truck

    d. all of the above

SUPPLEMENTAL LEARNING ACTIVITIES

1. In a group and using the Internet, trace the zigzagging path of Mexican/U.S. trucks and their efforts to do business across the U.S./Mexican border. This began with the signing of the NAFTA treaty in the early 1990s.

2. Write a 100-word opinion about how an international professional driver can best learn necessary information about the road rules in at least two of the three major countries in North America.

3. Invite an international trucker to speak to your class. Ask him or her about the most important lessons learned in his or her international driving experience.

4. Make a quick list about who and where to call if you experience problems in a country other than the country where your company is domiciled. Keep it with you if you will be doing any international driving.

5. If you plan to drive internationally and don't have a passport, find out what's required and obtain one. (See travel.state.gov/passport/forms/ds11/ds11_842.html)

FOR MORE INFORMATION

Mexican Laws and Regulations Available on MTO
mexicotrucker.com/en/translation-of-mexican-laws-and-regulations-available-on-mto

Mexico's Vehicle Height and Weight Standards
mexicotrucker.com/wp-content/uploads/downloads/2010/09/Translated-Mexican-Transport-Rules-and-Regulation.pdf

Transport Canada CANUTEC
www.tc.gc.ca/eng/canutec/

Guide to the Agreement on Uniform Vehicle Weights and Dimensions Limits in Atlantic Canada
www.comt.ca/english/programs/trucking/Guide.PDF

Canadian Trucking: Trucking Regulations
www.articlesbase.com/industrial–articles/canadian-trucking-trucking-regulations-1189440.html

32 Hazardous Materials

© majeczka/www.Shutterstock.com

OBJECTIVES

When you have completed this chapter, you should be able to:

- Understand the various classes of hazardous materials and the rules that apply to handling and hauling hazmat.

- Respond safely if an incident or spill involving hazardous materials occurs, including using the Emergency Response Guide.

- Understand the driver's and carrier's responsibilities when hauling hazardous materials.

- Understand and correctly handle shipping papers involving hazardous materials.

- Understand the environmental impact of your vehicle and its cargo as well as regulations in place to cut down on fuel, equipment, and freight pollution.

INTRODUCTION

The regulations for handling and hauling hazardous materials (called "dangerous goods" in Canada) have changed significantly over the last several years and continue to change. Therefore, job one in the transport of hazardous materials is for the professional driver, carrier, and shipper to remain current in their knowledge of changing hazmat requirements.

Initially, these changes were made to provide for the harmonization of the United States' hazardous materials regulations with international standards in order to facilitate foreign trade and maintain the competitiveness of U.S. goods. The applicability of the hazardous materials regulations was extended to all intrastate shipments of hazardous materials by highway, effective October 1, 1998.

Special agents of the Department of Transportation cannot be denied reasonable access to those areas that fall within the official scope of their duties. The Department of Transportation (DOT) Secretary has delegated this authority to the Federal Aviation Administration (FAA), Federal Motor Carrier Safety Administration (FMCSA), Federal Railway Administration (FRA), Pipeline and Hazardous Materials Safety Administration (PHMSA), and the United States Coast Guard (USCG).

The Government Printing Office has made the Federal Register and 49 CFR available on the Internet. The website for the Federal Register is www.gpoaccess.gov/fr/index.html. The website address for 49 CFR is www.gpoaccess.gov/cfr/index.html. Clarifications of the requirements contained in the Federal Hazardous Materials Regulations and the Motor Carrier Safety Regulations may be found at www.fmcsa.dot.gov/rulesregs/fmcsrhome.htm.

Hazardous materials regulations apply to the transportation of hazardous materials in commerce and their offering to:

1. Interstate, intrastate, and foreign carriers by rail car, aircraft, motor vehicle, and vessel
2. The representation that a hazardous material is present in a package, container, rail car, aircraft, motor vehicle, or vessel
3. The manufacture, fabrication, marking, maintenance, reconditioning, repairing, or testing of a package or container that is represented, marked, certified, or sold for use in the transportation of hazardous materials (49 CFR 171.1[a])

According to the General U.S. Department of Transportation's Hazardous Materials Regulatory Requirements, "No person may offer or accept a hazardous material for transportation in commerce unless that person is registered in conformance with regulations and the hazardous material is properly classed, described, packaged, marked, labeled, and in condition for shipment as required or authorized . . ." (49 CFR 171.2[a])

In the Hazardous Materials Regulations, you'll find three important terms: *person, offeror,* and *commerce.* The word *shipper* is frequently used by industry in place of the word *offeror.* For the purpose of this document only, the term *shipper* and *offeror* are used interchangeably.

These three words—*person, offeror,* and *commerce*—are important in that they define when you are subject to the jurisdiction of the U.S. Department of Transportation. Additionally, you may be subject to the requirements of other federal and/or state laws (**see Figure 32-1**).

© TFoxFoto/www.Shutterstock.com

▶ Figure 32-1

To transport hazardous materials, you will have to pass the hazardous materials endorsement for the CDL.

As noted, hazmat rules required shippers registered as Hazmat shippers with the Department of Transportation and shippers of certain highly hazardous materials to develop and implement written security plans. In addition, all shippers and carriers of **hazardous materials** must ensure that their employee training includes a security component. General awareness hazmat training also is required within 90 days of new hires or at the next recurrent training for existing employees.

Effective January 31, 2005, the Transportation Security Administration (TSA) began requiring background information and fingerprints from applicants trying to obtain Hazmat Endorsement on their CDL.

In compliance with the U.S. Patriot Act, the **Hazmat Threat Assessment Program** established the risk of an individual seeking to transport hazardous materials as being a potential terrorist threat. Under the rules governing the Hazmat Threat Assessment Program, an applicant will be disqualified from holding a hazmat endorsement (HME) if he or she:

- Has been convicted or found guilty by reason of insanity in a military or civilian court for any of the permanently disqualifying crimes
- Has been convicted or found not guilty by reason of insanity in a military or civilian court within the past 7 years for a felony on the list of disqualifying crimes
- Has been released from prison within the past 5 years for any of the disqualifying crimes. Some permanently disqualifying offenses are espionage, sedition, and treason. For additional and specific information, go to www.tsa.gov/what_we_do/layers/hazmat/index.shtm.

Any current hazmat driver who has a disqualifying offense prohibiting the holding of a hazmat endorsement must immediately surrender the HME to the State Department of Motor Vehicles.

To learn more about the Hazmat Threat Assessment Program, visit the Transportation Security Administration's website at www.hazprints.com.

HAULING AND HANDLING HAZMAT IN CANADA

The Transportation of Dangerous Goods Act and Regulations were introduced in Canada in 1985 to protect the motoring public who shared the highways with truckers in the Canadian provinces. This act also was passed to control the potential dangers that could come from the accidental release of dangerous goods during their transport on Canadian highways. The act regulates commercial vehicles used in the transport of dangerous goods as well as drivers who handle dangerous goods.

Part 6 of the Transportation of Dangerous Goods Regulations requires anyone who handles, offers for transport, or transports dangerous goods (the term for "hazmat" in the United States) to hold a valid training certificate, effective Oct. 1, 2009.

At that time, Canada's federal transportation ministry no longer accepted a hazardous materials endorsement as the sole evidence that a driver had completed necessary training.

Additional proof required now is a certificate of training, according to Transport Canada. These certificates, obtained at the completion of required training, must be available to show to inspectors **(see Figure 32-2).**

▶ **Figure 32-2**

According to Transport Canada, drivers must have a certificate of training to show inspectors.

(Continues)

HAULING AND HANDLING HAZMAT IN CANADA *(continued)*

The requirements for U.S. drivers are set out in section 6.3 of Part 6 of the Transportation of Dangerous Goods Regulations. There is no change for Canadian drivers, who are already required to carry a document as described in section 6.4 of the regulation.

Canadian drivers must carry a document that states that the individual has been trained according to 49 CFR, which is the equivalent training required by Canadian legislation.

STOP!

Canadian drivers who have completed this training and have earned a Valid Training Certificate must carry this certificate with them while hauling any hazardous materials.

In the United States, drivers who transport hazmat in quantities that require placards must pass a state-level exam required by section 383.93 of 49 CFR. The state will then add a hazmat endorsement to their commercial driver's license. In Canada, Canadian drivers are not required to have a hazmat endorsement on their driver's license when transporting dangerous goods. However, they are required to have the Valid Training Certificate as well as a FAST Card, a form of identification for the driver. This requirement has been in place since 2006.

An agreement between the U.S. Department of Transportation–Federal Motor Carrier Safety Administration and Transport Canada states that:

- Transport Canada will recognize:
    - the hazmat endorsement of the commercial driver's license;
    - a copy of the certification stipulated in section 172.704(d)(5) of 49 CFR; or
    - a Transportation of Dangerous Goods training certificate issued under Part 6 of the Transportation of Dangerous Goods Regulations.
- The United States will accept a Canadian driver's training certificate in lieu of a hazmat endorsement.
- Canadian transportation of dangerous goods inspectors can request further verification by contacting the Director of Compliance and Response, Transport Dangerous Goods Directorate within Transport Canada.

To find out more, contact your regional Transport Dangerous Goods Office or visit the Transport Dangerous Goods website at www.tc.gc.ca/eng/tdg/safety-menu.htm.

THE HAZMAT CDL ENDORSEMENT, FOR U.S. DRIVERS ONLY

If you plan to transport hazardous materials in quantities that require hazardous materials placards on your vehicle, you must read this chapter carefully because you will need to pass the **hazmat endorsement** for your CDL.

The Commercial Motor Vehicle Safety Act of 1986 made it a requirement that all persons with a hazmat endorsement on their CDL will have to retake the hazmat endorsement test each time they renew their CDL.

> **CAUTION!**
> If you are hauling hazmat and you don't have the hazardous materials endorsement on your CDL, you will be fined and possibly jailed for noncompliance. So, the word is DON'T BREAK THE RULES. These rules are here for your safety and the safety of others.

Focus on Hazardous Materials

Hazardous materials are becoming more and more frequent cargo. Because of the incident in Oklahoma City and the terrorist attacks of 9/11, there have been changes in how hazmat is handled and changes in how it should be hauled. If you regularly haul hazmat cargos, you must know and practice the latest and safest way to handle these kinds of loads.

Some states now ask drivers to retake the hazmat endorsement test every two years. Others do not, so check with your local department of motor vehicles to find out.

Why Special Hazmat Regulations Are Needed

Although it is handled and hauled like other cargo, some hazardous materials can injure or kill people if allowed into the environment. So the reason for the regulations is to lessen the danger.

Hazmat rules exist for drivers as well as for shippers. These rules—called **containment rules**—are very clear about how a material is packaged, loaded, hauled, and unloaded. These procedures assure that hazmat is contained and handled properly and guard against problems of leaking and spillage.

Anyone dealing with hazmat—shippers and carriers—are required to tell drivers and others about the hazardous qualities of the cargo they are carrying. In case of an accident, drivers hauling hazmat must warn motorists and others about the risks in case of an accident or spill.

HM-181 and 126-F Training Guidelines

HM-126-F requires hazmat training (covering HM-181) be provided for all drivers who transport hazmat. This regulation further requires that a record of the driver's training in hazmat be kept on file while that driver is employed with the company and for 90 days after the driver leaves employment.

The record must have (1) the driver's name, (2) most recent training date, (3) description of the training materials used to meet the requirements of the section, (4) name and address of person providing training, and (5) certification that the employee was trained and tested according to regulations.

HM-126-F also requires that all drivers involved in transporting hazmat be trained by the carrier in (1) general awareness, (2) function specific, (3) safety training, and (4) driver training.

To certify that training and testing was conducted, the trainer must teach the general awareness portion of the training from the Hazardous Materials chapter. The Hazardous Materials Regulations (HMR) can be found in parts 171–180 of Title 49 of the Code of Federal Regulations (49 CFR 171–180).

Hazmat Training and Testing

All drivers involved in transporting hazardous materials, according to regulations, receive training and testing. The employer is required to provide this training and to keep a log (record) of this training as long as that employee works for the company and for 90 days after he or she leaves. Regulations also require that employees receive updated hazmat training every two years.

Drivers who haul flammable cryogenic liquids and certain route-controlled quantities of **radioactive material** are required to receive training every two years. These drivers must also, at all times, carry a dated certificate showing the date of training.

If you haul quantities requiring placards in cargo tanks and portable tanks, you must also have training in hazmat every two years.

CAUTION!

Hazmat permits are separate and do not cover hazardous waste materials **(see Figure 32-3)**.

U.S. Department of Transportation **Federal Motor Carrier Safety Administration**	**Combined Motor Carrier Identification Report and HM Permit Application**

REASON FOR FILING (Check Only One)
☐ NEW APPLICATION ☐ BIENNIAL UPDATE OR CHANGE ☐ OUT OF BUSINESS NOTIFICATION ☐ REAPPLICATION (AFTER REVOCATION OF NEW ENTRANT)

1. NAME OF MOTOR CARRIER/HM SHIPPER	2. TRADE OR D.B.A. (DOING BUSINESS AS) NAME

3. PRINCIPAL STREET ADDRESS/ROUTE NUMBER	4. PHYSICAL CITY	5. MAILING ADDRESS (P O BOX)	6. MAILING CITY

7. PHYSICAL STATE/PROVINCE	8. PHYSICAL ZIP CODE +4	9. PHYSICAL COLONIA (MEXICO ONLY)	10. MAILING STATE/PROVINCE	11. MAILING ZIP CODE +4	12. MAILING COLONIA (MEXICO ONLY)

13. PRINCIPAL BUSINESS PHONE NUMBER	14. PRINCIPAL CONTACT CELLULAR NUMBER	15. PRINCIPAL BUSINESS FAX NUMBER

16. USDOT NO.	17. MC OR MX NO.	18. DUN & BRADSTREET NO.	19. IRS/TAX ID NO. EIN# SSN#	20. INTERNET E-MAIL ADDRESS

21. COMPANY OPERATION (*Circle either Registrant, or up to one Carrier and one Shipper Operation*)
☐ A. Interstate Carrier ☐ B. Intrastate Hazmat Carrier ☐ C. Intrastate Non-Hazmat Carrier ☐ D. Interstate Shipper ☐ E. Intrastate Shipper ☐ F. Registrant

22. CARRIER MILEAGE (to nearest 10, 000 miles for Last Calendar Year)   YEAR

23. OPERATION CLASSIFICATION (Circle All that Apply)

☐ Authorized For-Hire	☐ Private Passengers (Business)	☐ U.S. Mail	☐ Local Government
☐ Exempt For-Hire	☐ Private Passengers (Non-Business)	☐ Federal Government	☐ Indian Tribe
☐ Private (Property)	☐ Migrant	☐ State Government Other _____	

24. CARGO CLASSIFICATIONS (*Circle All that Apply*)

☐ GENERAL FREIGHT	☐ MACHINERY,LARGE OBJECTS	☐ COAL/COKE	☐ PAPER PRODUCTS
☐ HOUSEHOLD GOODS	☐ FRESH PRODUCE	☐ MEAT	☐ UTILITY
☐ METAL:SHEETS,COIL,ROLLS	☐ LIQUIDS/GASES	☐ GARBAGE,REFUSE,TRASH	☐ FARM SUPPLIES
☐ MOTOR VEHICLES	☐ INTERMODAL CONT.	☐ U.S. MAIL	☐ CONSTRUCTION
☐ DRIVE AWAY/TOWAWAY	☐ PASSENGERS	☐ CHEMICALS	☐ WATER WELL
☐ LOGS,POLES BEAMS,LUMBER	☐ OIL FIELD EQUIPMENT	☐ COMMODITIES DRY BULK OTHER _____	
☐ BUILDING MATERIALS	☐ LIVESTOCK	☐ REFRIGERATED FOOD	
☐ MOBILE HOMES	☐ GRAIN,FEED,HAY	☐ BEVERAGES	

Courtesy of FMCSA

(Continues)

▶ **Figure 32-3**

Sample Hazmat permit

25. HAZARDOUS MATERIALS CARRIED OR SHIPPED *(Check All that Apply)* C-CARRIED S-SHIPPED B(BULK)-IN CARGO TANKS NB(NON-BULK)-IN PACKAGES

C ☐ S ☐ DIV 1.1	B ☐ NB ☐	C ☐ S ☐ DIV 2.3D	B ☐ NB ☐	C ☐ S ☐ DIV 6.1SOLID	B ☐ NB ☐
C ☐ S ☐ DIV 1.2	B ☐ NB ☐	C ☐ S ☐ CLASS 3	B ☐ NB ☐	C ☐ S ☐ CLASS 7	B ☐ NB ☐
C ☐ S ☐ DIV 1.3	B ☐ NB ☐	C ☐ S ☐ CLASS 3A	B ☐ NB ☐	C ☐ S ☐ HRCQ	B ☐ NB ☐
C ☐ S ☐ DIV 1.4	B ☐ NB ☐	C ☐ S ☐ CLASS 3B	B ☐ NB ☐	C ☐ S ☐ CLASS 8	B ☐ NB ☐
C ☐ S ☐ DIV 1.5	B ☐ NB ☐	C ☐ S ☐ COMB LIQ	B ☐ NB ☐	C ☐ S ☐ CLASS 8A	B ☐ NB ☐
C ☐ S ☐ DIV 1.6	B ☐ NB ☐	C ☐ S ☐ DIV 4.1	B ☐ NB ☐	C ☐ S ☐ CLASS 8B	B ☐ NB ☐
C ☐ S ☐ DIV 2.1	B ☐ NB ☐	C ☐ S ☐ DIV 4.2	B ☐ NB ☐	C ☐ S ☐ CLASS 9	B ☐ NB ☐
C ☐ S ☐ DIV 2.1LPG	B ☐ NB ☐	C ☐ S ☐ DIV 4.3	B ☐ NB ☐	C ☐ S ☐ ELEVATED TEMP MAT	B ☐ NB ☐
C ☐ S ☐ DIV 2.1(METHANE)	B ☐ NB ☐	C ☐ S ☐ DIV 5.1	B ☐ NB ☐	C ☐ S ☐ INFECTIOUS WASTE	B ☐ NB ☐
C ☐ S ☐ DIV 2.2	B ☐ NB ☐	C ☐ S ☐ DIV 5.2	B ☐ NB ☐	C ☐ S ☐ MARINE POLLUTANTS	B ☐ NB ☐
C ☐ S ☐ DIV 2.2A (AMMONIA)	B ☐ NB ☐	C ☐ S ☐ DIV 6.2	B ☐ NB ☐	C ☐ S ☐ HAZARDOUS SUB(RQ)	B ☐ NB ☐
C ☐ S ☐ DIV 2.3A	B ☐ NB ☐	C ☐ S ☐ DIV 6.1A	B ☐ NB ☐	C ☐ S ☐ HAZARDOUS WASTE	B ☐ NB ☐
C ☐ S ☐ DIV 2.3B	B ☐ NB ☐	C ☐ S ☐ DIV 6.1B	B ☐ NB ☐	C ☐ S ☐ ORM	B ☐ NB ☐
C ☐ S ☐ DIV 2.3C	B ☐ NB ☐	C ☐ S ☐ DIV 6.1POISON	B ☐ NB ☐		

26. NUMBER OF VEHICLES THAT CAN BE OPERATED IN THE U.S.

	Straight Trucks	Truck Tractors	Trailers	Hazmat Cargo Tank Trucks	Hazmat Cargo Tank Trailers	Motor Coach	Number of Passengers (including the driver)								
							School bus			Mini-bus	Van		Limousine		
							1-8	9-15	16+	16+	1-8	9-15	1-8	9-15	16+
OWNED															
TERM LEASED															
TRIP LEASED															

27. DRIVER INFORMATION

	INTERSTATE	INTRASTATE	TOTAL DRIVERS	TOTAL CDL DRIVERS
Within 100-Mile Radius				
Beyond 100-Mile Radius				

28. IS YOUR U.S. DOT NUMBER REGISTRATION CURRENTLY REVOKED BY THE FEDERAL MOTOR CARRIER SAFETY ADMINISTRATION?   Yes ☐ No ☐

If Yes, enter the U.S. DOT Number with the revoked registration. _____

29. PLEASE ENTER NAME(S) OF SOLE PROPRIETOR(S), OFFICERS OR PARTNERS AND TITLES (e.g. PRESIDENT, TREASURER, GENERAL PARTNER, LIMITED PARTNER)

1. _____   2. _____
   (Please print Name)   (Please print Name)

30. WHICH OF THE FOLLOWING HAZARDOUS MATERIAL(S) DOES YOUR COMPANY TRANSPORT, CHECK ALL THAT APPLY:

☐ Highway Route Controlled Quantities(HRCQ) of Radioactive materials

☐ More than 25kg (55 pounds) of a Division 1.1, 1.2, or 1.3 material or a Division 1.5 material that requires placarding

☐ For materials that meet the definition of "material poisonous by inhalation" (TIH) as defined in 49 CFR 171.8: More than 1 liter (1.08 quarts) per package of material meeting the definition of a Hazard Zone A TIH material, a material meeting the definition of a Hazard Zone B TIH material in a bulk package (capacity greater than 405 liters [119 gallons]), or a material meeting the definition of a Hazard Zone C or D TIH material in a bulk packaging that has a capacity greater than 13,248 L (3,500 gallons).

☐ Shipments of compressed or refrigerated liquid methane or liquefied natural gas with a methane content of at least 85% in a bulk packaging that has capacity greater than 13,248L (3,500 gallons)

31. IF YOU CHECK QUESTION 30, ARE YOU APPLYING FOR RENEWING A HM SAFETY PERMIT? PLEASE CHECK ONE:

☐ INITIAL   ☐ RENEWAL

(Continues)

▶ **Figure 32–3**

Sample Hazmat permit

| 32. IF YOUR COMPANY DOES NOT HAVE A U.S.DOT NUMBER, HOW MANY ACCIDENTS AS DEFINED IN 49 CFR 390.5 HAS YOUR COMPANY HAD IN THE PAST 365 DAYS? |

| 33. DOES YOUR COMPANY CERTIFY THEY HAVE A SATISFACTORY SECURITY PROGRAM IN PLACE AS REQUIRED IN 49 CFR PART 385, SUBPART E? | ☐ Yes ☐ No |

| 34. IS YOUR COMPANY REQUIRED BY ANY STATE(S) TO HAVE A PERMIT FOR ANY OF THE HAZARDOUS MATERIALS LISTED IN QUESTION 30? | ☐ Yes ☐ No |

35. IF YOUR ANSWER TO QUESTION 34 IS YES, CHECK THE STATE(S) IN WHICH YOU HAVE THE PERMIT

☐ AL	☐ AK	☐ AR	☐ AZ	☐ CA	☐ CO	☐ CT	☐ DC	☐ DE	☐ FL	☐ GA
☐ HI	☐ ID	☐ IL	☐ IN	☐ IA	☐ KS	☐ KY	☐ LA	☐ MA	☐ MD	☐ ME
☐ MI	☐ MN	☐ MO	☐ MS	☐ MT	☐ NC	☐ ND	☐ NE	☐ NH	☐ NJ	☐ NM
☐ NV	☐ NY	☐ OH	☐ OK	☐ OR	☐ PA	☐ PR	☐ RI	☐ SC	☐ SD	☐ TN
☐ TX	☐ UT	☐ VT	☐ VA	☐ WA	☐ WV	☐ WI	☐ WY			

NOTE:

All motor carriers must comply with all pertinent Federal, State, local and tribal statutory and regulatory requirements when operating within the United States. Such requirements include, but are not limited to, all applicable statutory and regulatory requirements administered by the U.S. Department of Labor, or by a State agency operating a plan pursuant to Section 18 of the Occupational Safety and Health Act of 1970 ("OSHA State plan agency"). Such requirements also include all applicable statutory and regulatory environmental standards and requirements administered by the U.S. Environmental Protection Agency or a State, local or tribal environmental protection agency. Compliance with these statutory and regulatory requirements may require motor carriers and/or individual operators to produce documents for review and inspection for the purpose of determining compliance with such statutes and regulations.

36. CERTIFICATION STATEMENT (TO BE COMPLETED BY AN AUTHORIZED OFFICIAL)

I,_____,certify that I am familiar with the Federal Motor Carrier Safety Regulations and/or the Federal Hazardous Materials Regulations.
      (Please print Name)   Under penalties of perjury, I declare that the information entered on this report is, to the best of my knowledge and belief, true, correct, and complete.

Signature _____ Date **11/1/2011** Title _____

Courtesy of FMCSA

▶ **Figure 32–3**

Sample Hazmat permit

© Cengage Learning 2013

▶ **Figure 32–4**

Placards help fire and emergency personnel identify dangerous cargo in the event of an accident or spill.

Hazmat and Special Routing

Sometimes drivers with loads of hazmat are required to take certain routes, and some states require a special permit before certain hazmat is moved. Make sure you know about any special rules regarding hazmat from your state and in the areas in which you will be driving. You can find out from your company's safety official or the local DMV to make certain you comply with all federal and state hazmat regulations. Examples of special routing would be avoidance of tunnels, bridges and heavily populated urban areas. Often hazmat loads are routed around these obstacles to avoid any possible acts of terrorism.

The Importance of Placarding

If you are hauling a hazmat load, you are required to use **placards** on all four sides of your vehicle, letting other drivers know the risk (**see Figure 32-4**). As a professional driver, it is also your job to make sure shipping papers are in the proper place and they must be within hands reach without releasing the seat belt.

> **CAUTION!**
> The responsibility for the proper and lawful handling of hazardous materials is shared among the shipper, the carrier, and the driver.

THE SHIPPER'S ROLE IN HAZARDOUS MATERIAL HANDLING

Anyone sending the hazmat from point A to point B must understand and use hazmat regulations in order to decide the following for each hazmat product:

- Proper shipping name
- Hazardous class
- Identification numbers
- Correct type of packing
- Correct label and marking on the package
- Correct placard(s)

The shipper is also responsible for packing the hazmat properly, labeling it properly, and identifying it properly on the package. The shipper must use the diamond-shaped labels indicating the hazmat within the package. If the label cannot be placed on the package, the shipper must attach a tag or decal, indicating the hazard involved. The shipper must also certify on the shipping papers that the shipment has been prepared according to regulations. The only exception is when the shipper is a private carrier, transporting its own products.

THE CARRIER'S RESPONSIBILITY IN HANDLING HAZARDOUS MATERIALS

The carrier plays a smaller but equally important role. The carrier must:

- Transport the shipment to the proper destination
- Ensure that the shipper has correctly named, labeled, and marked the hazmat shipment
- Report any accident or incident involving hazmat to the proper government agency
- Always park in a safe place

THE DRIVER'S RESPONSIBILITY IN HANDLING HAZARDOUS MATERIALS

The professional driver's first duty in handling a hazmat load is to double-check the shipper and the carrier, making sure the load is properly identified, marked, and labeled if it is hazardous material.

- Verify shipping papers are properly completed.
- The driver must REFUSE to haul any leaking cartons or shipments.
- The driver must communicate the risk by attaching proper placards to the vehicle.
- The driver must deliver products as safely and quickly as possible, following federal and state hazmat regulations.
- The driver is required to keep all hazmat shipping papers in the proper place, within a hands reach without releasing the seat belt.
- Verify or apply proper placards (**see Figure 32-5**).

▶ **Figure 32–5**

This particular trailer is a good example of hauling multiple types of hazardous material at the same time. Each individual type must have its respective hazardous material class and identification number listed.

This is important information, so a review will be helpful. As a driver:

1. You need to be able to recognize you are loading and will be hauling hazardous materials. How do you do that? First look at the shipping papers. Then determine if hazardous materials are being shipped.

2. If hazmat is part or all of the cargo, look to make sure the shipping papers are properly filled out with the shipping name, hazard class, and ID number, listed in that exact order.

3. The driver must also look for highlighted products or the letters X or RQ in the HM column.

4. When accepting a delivery for shipment, the driver must be 100 percent sure the shipping papers are correct, packages are properly labeled, and vehicle is loaded properly and displaying the appropriate placards.

STOP!

If you are not 100 percent certain that the process of identifying, marking, and labeling hazmat materials has been followed TO THE LETTER, you should contact the terminal dispatcher. It is also your responsibility to inspect—AND NEVER ACCEPT DAMAGED OR LEAKING HAZMAT SHIPMENTS.

The driver can protect himself or herself by being knowledgeable of the three main Hazardous Material Lists that shippers, carriers, and drivers are to use. The following lists determine the proper handling of any hazmat load:

- **Hazardous Materials Table**
- List of Hazardous Substances and Reportable Quantities
- List of Marine Pollutants

STOP!

Remember! Before transporting any unfamiliar products or items, look for its name on the three lists. Each list will have the proper shipping name, hazardous class, identification number, and proper labeling required.

If you have any questions about the load, call your dispatcher.

Exercise Caution When Loading Hazmat

The following rules apply when handling Hazmat:

- No smoking at any time, but particularly when loading explosives, oxidizers, or flammables. Never handle these materials around a heat source.
- Never load damaged or leaking packages or containers.
- Never open any packages during transport. If a package breaks open, call your dispatcher immediately.
- No overhangs or tailgate loads for explosives, oxidizing materials, or flammable solids.
- Rules forbid using cargo heaters or air-conditioning unless you know the rules for the cargo you're hauling. If in doubt, check with your company.
- Park and set the brakes.
- Do everything possible to protect the public.

As soon as the shipping papers have been checked and the truck has been properly placarded, there are a few reminders for drivers:

- Never park within 5 feet (1.5 m) of the traveled part of the road if you are hauling any amount of explosives.
- Never park within 300 feet (91.4 m) of a bridge, tunnel, building, or other places where people gather, or by an open fire, when hauling explosives.
- Someone should be in attendance of the vehicle at all times—the shipper, the carrier, or the consignee when hauling any amount of explosives.
- Vehicles can be left unattended on a government-approved safe haven—a location approved for parking unattended vehicles loaded with explosives.

If hauling hazmat but not explosives, you can:

- Park within 5 feet (1.5 m) of the road, only if the job requires it and someone is with the vehicle at all times and that person understands the hazards involved.
- Never uncouple trailer and leave it on a public street.
- If parked along the roadway, set out reflective triangles within 10 minutes.
- Never park within 300 feet (91.4 m) of an open fire.

Performance-Oriented Packaging (POP)

Performance-oriented packaging (POP) is a government term meaning that the packaging used for hazmat must "perform" in such a way to be safe, making it possible to handle and transport the hazmat safely.

These standards require each package be designed and produced so that when it is filled to capacity, sealed, and transported under normal conditions, the package will:

- Have no release of hazmat products
- Not be reduced in strength or seal or other change due to change in temperatures
- Contain nothing itself that could ruin the packaging

For additional information, check HMR Part 173, "Shippers General Requirements for Shipments and Packaging."

To comply with governmental regulations, all packaging must meet the previous requirements and (1) must contain the manufacturer's marking, (2) must be marked with proper shipping name and ID number, and (3) must be tested/approved before use.

THE HAZARD CLASS

The **hazard class** of materials indicates the degree of risks associated with that material. The hazard class has nine categories, found in Part 173 of the HMC and the provisions of Section 172.101.

Do not memorize the classes but be aware of what they are. In the past there were 22 hazard classes, and now there are nine, thanks to the changes made in the new HM-181 regulations. In the past, the description contained letters; the new system uses numbers to define each class.

The Hazard Class Numbering System

The first number indicates the class of the hazardous material, that is, explosives, gases, flammable liquids, flammable solids, oxidizing substances, poisons, radioactive materials, corrosive material, and miscellaneous material. The second number indicates the division. In Class 1.3, for example, the 1 tells you the material is an explosive, and the 3 tells you the division, which is explosive B.

Classes and Divisions of Hazardous Materials

Figure 32-6 lists the classes and the divisions of hazardous materials:

HM-181 CLASSES AND DIVISIONS	
New Classes and Divisions	**Old Classes**
Class 1 (Explosives)	**Explosives**
1.1	Explosive Class A
1.2	Explosive A or B
1.3	Explosive B
1.4	Explosive C
1.5	Blasting Agent
1.6	
Class 2 (Gases)	**Gases**
2.1	Flammable Gas
2.2	Non-Flammable Gas
2.3	Poison Gas
Class 3 (Flammable Liquids)	**Flammable Combustible**
3.1	Flammable Liquid
	Combustible Liquid
Class 4 (Flammable Solids)	**Flammable Solids**
4.1	Flammable Solid
4.2	Flammable Solid/Liquid
4.3	Flammable Solid—dangerous when wet
Class 5 (Oxidizing Substances)	**Oxidizing Substances**
5.1	Oxidizer
5.2	Organic peroxide
Class 6 (Poisons)	**Poisons**
6.1	Poison B
6.2	Etiologic Agents (infectious substances)
Class 7 (Radioactive Material)	**Radioactive Material**
Class 8 (Corrosive Material)	**Corrosive Material**
Class 9 (Miscellaneous Material)	**Other Regulated Material (ORM)**

▶ Figure 32–6

Classes and divisions of hazardous materials

Explosive Classes of Hazardous Materials

An **explosive** is any material, substance, or item (such as an explosive device) designed to operate through an explosive action or through a chemical reaction; or, this material may function in a similar manner, even though it was not designed to explode.

Class 1—Explosives

Division 1.1	Explosives that are a mass explosion hazard—if one goes, they all go, which makes for a bad situation. This type is dangerous, to say the least.
Division 1.2	Explosives that are not a mass explosion hazard but are a projection hazard.
Division 1.3	Explosives that have a fire or minor blast or minor projection hazard, or both, but not a mass explosion hazard.
Division 1.4	Explosive devices with a minor explosion hazard (can contain more than 25 grams of detonating material).
Division 1.5	Insensitive explosives that usually carry a mass explosion hazard but chances are remote. Under normal conditions, this type would make the transition of being on fire and then exploding.
Division 1.6	Explosives without mass explosion hazard. This type has only very insensitive detonating substances and demonstrates little chance of accidental fire or explosion.

Class 2—Gases

Division 2.1	Any material that, at 68 degrees F or 20 degrees C and 14.7 psi (101 kPa) pressure, will ignite when in a mixture of 13 percent or less by volume with air or has a flammable range with air of at least 12 percent, regardless of the lower limit.
Division 2.2	Nonflammable and nonpoisonous compressed gases. This includes compressed gas, liquefied gas, pressurized cryonic gas, and compressed gas, which is in solution. In other words, any material or mixture which exerts an absolute pressure on the packaging of 40 psi (276 kPa) at 68 degrees F (20 degrees C). Any material in this division does not meet the definition of Division 2.1 or 2.4.
Division 2.3	Known to be poisonous and toxic enough to be a hazard to human health, even if adequate data do not currently exist, but have been toxic to lab animals. Scientifically, this type has an LC value not more than 5,000 PPM.

Class 3—Flammable Liquids

Class 3 has no divisions. A flammable liquid is one with a flash point of not more than 140 degrees F (60 degrees C), except for materials meeting the definition of any Class 2 material. This class also includes a mixture having components that have a flash point greater than 141 degrees F (60.5 degrees C) or higher—if it makes up at least 99 percent of the total volume of the mix. Or it could also be a distilled spirit of 140 proof or lower, considered to have a flash point of lower than 73 degrees F (23 degrees C).

Class 4—Flammable Solids

Division 4.1	Flammable solids of three types: (1) wetted explosives that when dry are explosives of Class 1, except those of compatibility group A; (2) self-reactive materials that may undergo—at normal or elevated temperatures—a decomposition that could make them ignite. (This can happen in high transport temperatures or through contamination.) Any solids that are readily combustible can create fire through friction. This material shows a burning rate faster than 2.2 mm per second; and (3) metal powder, which can ignite and react over the test area in 10 minutes or less.

| Division 4.2 | These liquid or solid materials, even in small quantities, ignite within 5 minutes of exposure to air under certain test procedures. |
| Division 4.3 | These materials can become spontaneously flammable on contact with water. This division also contains material that can emit (give off) flammable or toxic gases at a rate of 1 liter per kilogram per hour or greater. |

Class 5—Oxidizing Substances

| Division 5.1 | Because they emit oxygen these materials can cause or increase the combustion of other materials. |
| Division 5.2 | This class includes organic peroxide, a derivative of hydrogen peroxide. |

Class 6—Poisons

| Division 6.1 | This class includes materials that are toxic to humans or so toxic they pose a health hazard during transportation. The class also includes materials presumed hazardous to humans because of laboratory tests; and it includes irritants such as tear gas. |
| Division 6.2 | Infectious substances that may cause disease or death in animals or humans. This includes human or animal excretion, secretion, blood tissue, and tissue components. |

Class 7—Radioactive Material

Radioactive material is defined in 49 CFR 173.403 as any material containing radionuclides where both the activity concentration and the total activity in the consignment exceed the values specified in the table in 49 CFR 173.436 or values derived according to the instructions in 49 CFR 173.433. (See www.fmcsr.dot.gov/rules-regulations/administration/fmcsr/rules.)

Class 8—Corrosive Material

Includes materials that cause destruction/irreversible damage to human skin tissue on contact—either liquid or solid; also has high corrosion rate on steel and/or aluminum.

Class 9—Other Regulated Material

Any material that presents a hazard during transport but is not included in any of the other classes and is subject to hazmat regulations.

HOW TO USE THE HAZARDOUS MATERIALS TABLE

Column 1 has symbols with a specific meaning. These include:

1	Designated proper shipping name and hazardous class must always be shown, even if product does not match hazard class definition.
D	Proper shipping name is appropriate for describing materials for domestic transportation but may not be proper for international transport.
A	Subject to the regulations only when transported by air, unless materials are hazardous substances and hazardous waste.
W	Subject to regulations only when transported by water unless material is a hazardous substance, hazardous waste, or marine pollutant.

Column 2 shows the name of regulated materials in alphabetical order. On this table, the proper shipping names are always shown in regular type. The names shown in italics are not proper shipping names and can be used only with the proper shipping name.

Column 3 is the hazard class or division, and may have the word *forbidden*. When you see *forbidden*, never transport this material. The hazard class for the material is the indicator of what placards to use. To choose the proper placard, you must have three pieces of information:

1. Hazard class for the cargo
2. Amount being shipped
3. Amount of all hazmat in all classes on the vehicle

If you have the words **inhalation hazard** on the shipping papers, you must use a poison placard in addition to the others that are required.

Column 4 shows the **identification number** for each proper shipping name. These ID numbers are preceded by the initials UN or NA. The letters NA are only used in shipments between the United States and Canada. The ID number must also appear on the shipping paper, the package, and the cargo tanks and all other bulk packages.

Column 5 identifies the packing group, which is assigned to the material.

Column 6 shows the hazard label, which shippers must put on packages of hazardous materials. Some products require more than one label. If the word *none* appears, no label is required.

Column 7 lists additional provisions for this material. If you see a column 7 entry, refer to federal regulations for specific information.

Column 8, a three-part column, shows section and numbers covering packaging for hazmat.

Columns 9 and 10 do not apply to highway transport.

WHAT DRIVERS SHOULD KNOW ABOUT SHIPPING PAPERS

The **shipping paper** is a document describing the hazmat the driver will be carrying **(see Figure 32-7).** Every item listed on the shipping paper must show the hazard class. Shipping papers include bills of lading and manifests. Having incorrect or incomplete shipping papers is the most frequent violation found during roadside inspections of hazmat loads.

What Should Be Shown on the Shipping Paper

Each copy of the shipping paper should have numbered pages with the first page indicating the total number of papers for the shipment. The shipping paper should have the proper description of any hazardous material, and the shipper's certificate—signed by the shipper's representative—must also be included. This certificate verifies that the shipment has been prepared according to all applicable regulations.

The Important Uses of Shipping Papers

The shipping paper is used for several purposes, the primary one being to communicate what is being shipped and if there is risk involved. If for some reason the driver is injured or taken ill and unable to speak, the shipping paper would inform the authorities if hazardous materials are included in the cargo.

After the attending officials obtain information regarding the shipment, they can take appropriate action to protect the safety of everyone. This makes the shipping paper a vital part of the shipment and emphasizes why it should be filled out correctly. Lives may be at stake and fast action may be required—there is no time to decipher what the cargo holds.

TC TENNESSEE EXPRESS

www.tcwonline.com

615-255-1122
FAX 615-780-3246
22 Stanley Street
Nashville, Tennessee 37210

TNXP 11/1/04

Date: **STRAIGHT BILL OF LADING – SHORT FORM – Original – Not Negotiable**

SHIP FROM

Name: Pace Chemical Co., Inc.

Address: 810 Atlanta Rd.

City/State/Zip: Atlanta, GA 30010

SHIP TO

Name: ABC Warehouse Co., Inc.

Address: 411 Pine St.

City/State/Zip: Nashville, TN 37210

THIRD PARTY FREIGHT CHARGES BILL TO:

Name:

Address:

City/State/Zip:

SPECIAL INSTRUCTIONS:

Bill of Lading Number: ___123654___

CARRIER NAME: TENNESSEE EXPRESS, INC.

Trader number: ___5342___

Seal number(s): ___2465___

SCACL TNXP

Pro number:

Freight Charge Terms:
(freight charges are prepaid unless marked otherwise)

Prepaid __X__ Collect _____ 3rd Party _____

____ Master Bill of Lading: with attached underlying Bills of Lading
(check)

COD Amount: $ _____
Fee Terms: Collect: _____ Prepaid: _____
Customer check acceptable: _____

Trailer Loaded: Freight Counted:
__X__ By Shipper   __X__ By Shipper
_____ By Driver   _____ By Driver/pallets said to contain
                     _____ By Driver/Places

CARRIER INFORMATION

QTY	TYPE	COMMODITY DESCRIPTION *Commodities requiring special or additional care or attention in handling or showing must be marked and packaged as to assure safe transportation with ordinary care.*	WEIGHT	H.M. (X)
800	cases	Pesticide, Liquid, Toxic, n.o.s.	40000#	X
		class 6.1, un2902, IL		
		(contains pyrethrin)		
		seal #2465 S L + C		
		In case of emergency, call		
		CHEMTREC (24 hours)		
		1-800-424-9300	TOTAL	

NOTE Liability Limitation for loss or damage in this shipment may be applicable. See 49 U.S.C. § 14706(c)(1)(A) and (B).

RECEIVED, subject to individually determined rates or contracts that have been agreed upon in writing between the carrier and shipper, if applicable, otherwise to the rates, classifications and rules that have been established by the carrier and are available to the shipper, on request, and to the terms and conditions set forth on the reverse side heron as well as to all applicable state and federal regulations.

Shipper Signature   Date   11/05/04
This is to certify that the above named materials are property classified, packaged, marked and labeled, and are in proper condition for transportation according to the applicable regulations of the DOT.

Carrier Signature   Pickup Date   11/01/04
Carrier asknowledges receipt of packages and required placards. Carrier certifies emergency response information was made available and/or carrier has the DOT emergency response guidebook or equivalent documentation in the vehicle.
Property described above is received in apparant good order, except as noted.

Shipper Signature
The carrier shall not make delivery of this shipment without payment of freight and all other lawful charges.

Where the rate is dependant on value, shippers are required to state specifically in writing the agreed or desclared value of the property as follows: "The agreed or declared value of the property is specifically stated by the shipper to be not exceeding_____ per _____

Figure 32–7

Example of hazmat shipping paper.

GO!

There are exceptions about how shipping papers are handled. A private shipper carrying its own freight does not need to sign a shipper's certificate.

THE HAZARDOUS WASTE MANIFEST

Any cargo containing **hazardous waste** must be accompanied by a hazardous waste manifest, signed by the driver. This manifest is the responsibility of the shipper; and the driver will treat the hazardous waste manifest as any other shipping paper.

The carrier who accepts the hazardous waste cargo must make certain that the hazardous waste manifest is properly completed and a shipment labeled as hazardous waste may be delivered only to another registered carrier or to a facility authorized to receive and handle hazardous waste.

The carrier must maintain a copy of the hazardous waste manifest for three years following transport. Once delivered to the authorized hazardous waste facility, the facility's operator must sign for the shipment.

When to Use the "Dangerous" Placard

If you have a load requiring a flammable placard and then pick up 1,000 pounds (454 kg) of combustible material, instead of using two separate placards, such as **"flammable"** or **"combustible,"** you will use the **"dangerous" placard.**

The two exceptions are (1) if you have loaded 5,000 pounds (2,268 kg) of hazardous material at one location, you must use the placard for that material; and (2) if the words "Inhalation Hazard" are on the shipping papers, you must use the material's specific placard *and* a "Poison" placard.

Blasting agents (1.6), Oxidizer (5.1), and dangerous placards are not required if the vehicle contains Class 1 explosives and you are using Division 1.1, 1.2, or 1.3 placards.

When the vehicle displays a Division 2.1 Flammable Gas or an Oxygen placard, you do not need to display a Non-Flammable Gas placard if you pick up that material and add it to your load.

STOP!

Displaying the wrong placard is as wrong as not displaying any placard.

Placards are used to communicate with and inform others. Incorrect information is just as harmful as no information and may place rescue personnel in danger.

MIXED SHIPMENTS OF NONHAZMAT AND HAZMAT CARGOS

In the case where you are hauling nonhazardous and hazardous materials, and the shipping papers show a mix of hazardous materials and nonhazardous materials, those items that are hazardous must be marked by:

- Describing the item first
- Highlighting or printing in a different color
- Placing an X before the shipping name in the column marked HM
- Using the letters RQ if the shipment is a reportable quantity

CAUTION!

The description of the hazardous product must include (1) the proper shipping name, (2) the hazmat class or division, and (3) the ID number in that order. Do not use abbreviations. The only abbreviation permitted is for the packaging type and the unit of measure, which can appear on the shipping paper before or after the description.

If the shipment is hazardous waste, the word *waste* must appear before the name of the material being shipped.

Also included must be the total quality and unit of measure (e.g., drums, cylinders, cartons). If the hazmat shipment is a reportable quantity, the letters RQ must be on the shipping paper under HM.

WHEN HAZMAT IS INVOLVED IN AN ACCIDENT

It may be necessary for law enforcement officials to obtain information quickly, so the following also applies to the shipping papers:

- The shipping papers must be tagged or tabbed and placed on top of all other shipping papers. This is the responsibility of the carrier and the driver.
- When the driver is out of the truck, shipping papers must be placed on the driver's seat or in a pouch in the driver's door.
- While driving, the driver must place shipping papers in a pouch in the driver's door or within hands reach when the seat belt is being used.

STOP!

Once the hazmat have been unloaded, it is the driver's responsibility to remove the placards!

HAZMAT EMERGENCIES
The Emergency Response Guidebook

The *Emergency Response Guidebook* (*ERG*, for short) is used by firefighters, police officers, and industry safety personnel and others in the event of an emergency involving hazmat. It was developed jointly by the U.S. Department of Transportation, Transport Canada, and the Secretariat of Communications and Transportation of Mexico (SCT) for use by firefighters, police, and other emergency services personnel who may be the first to arrive at the scene of a transportation incident involving a hazardous material.

The *ERG* is primarily a guide to aid first responders in (1) quickly identifying the specific or generic classification of the material(s) involved in the incident, and (2) protecting themselves and the general public during this initial response phase of the incident. The *ERG* is updated every three to four years to accommodate new products and technology.

When an emergency occurs, police and fire personnel must determine what type of hazmat is involved; and this is accomplished by looking at shipping papers, looking at placards, and getting information from the driver. In some accidents, however, there may be no time to locate shipping papers or talk to the driver. The only thing left is to look at the placards.

Once the type of hazmat is determined, personnel can then take steps to protect life and property, which is one more reason why the right placards are used, the shipping papers should always be accurate, and the driver must be aware of what is being hauled.

To learn how to use the *ERG,* see the video provided about using the *ERG* at www.phmsa.dot.gov/hazmat.

DOT's goal is to place one *ERG* in each emergency service vehicle, nationwide, through distribution to state and local public safety authorities. To date, nearly 11 million copies have been distributed without charge to the emergency response community.

Copies are made available free of charge at www.phmsa.dot.gov/hazmat.

In Canada, contact CANUTEC at 613-992-4624 or via e-mail at canutec@tc.gc.ca for distribution information.

In Mexico, call SCT at 52-5-684-1275.

Copies are also available commercially through the GPO Bookstore and other commercial vendors. For a PC download of the *ERG* and more information from Transport Canada, see www.tc.gc.ca/CANUTEC/en/GUIDE/menu.htm.

Driver's Responsibility in Case of an Accident Involving Hazmat

The following is your responsibility at the scene of an accident involving hazmat:

- Warn people of danger and keep them away.
- If you can do so safely, contain the spill.
- Contact the appropriate emergency response personnel (police, fire, or other emergency responders) and tell them what has happened.

Be prepared to provide the following information to emergency responders:

- Hazmat product's shipping name, hazard class, and ID number
- Extent of the spill
- Location
- When accident/incident happened
- Phone number where you can be reached

Let them hang up first; make sure they have all the information they need. Then contact your dispatcher and follow your instructions.

If a Fire Occurs

Never attempt to fight a hazmat fire unless you have specific training on how to do it. The power unit of a vehicle with placards must have a fire extinguisher with a UL rating of at least 10 BC.

If a Leak or Spill Occurs

First of all, do not touch the material, because certain hazmats can kill you, just by touching them or breathing their fumes. Determine what the hazmat is by looking at shipping papers but do not go near the spill or allow anyone else to go near it. Contact the local authorities and your dispatcher as quickly as possible.

STOP!
If a leak or spill occurs, do not attempt to move the vehicle unless you have to because of safety concerns.

If you are driving and notice something leaking from the vehicle, pull as far off the road as you can, get the shipping papers, and get away from the vehicle. Then send someone for help. Stay away from the truck, but keep it in sight so you can keep others away.

Do not drive to a phone if you spot a leak.

When sending someone for help, write down your location, description of emergency, your name, your carrier's name and phone number, and the shipping name, hazard class, and ID number.

Never smoke or allow smoking around the vehicle.

If you see leakage or damage to a hazmat package while unloading, get away from the vehicle as quickly as possible and contact your dispatcher immediately. Do not touch or inhale the material!

If certain types of hazardous materials leak or spill, the Department of Transportation and the Environmental Protection Agency must be notified. The Hazardous Substances and Reportable Quantities List will tell you if the cargo is a reportable quantity. The product and the amount spilled decides whether it is reportable.

An asterisk (*) next to the name indicates the product also appears on the hazardous materials table.

If there is any size spill of any hazmat, the driver must report the spill to the carrier.

The carrier reports it to the National Response Center, and they have the ability to contact the proper law enforcement agency and the proper containment or cleanup personnel.

The carrier is required to call the National Response Center (NRC) (800-424-8802) if an incident of leakage or spill occurs and:

- Someone is killed
- Someone is injured and requires hospitalization
- Estimated property damage exceeds $50,000
- One or more major roadways is closed for 1 hour or more
- Fire, breakage, spillage, or suspected radioactive contamination occurs
- Fire, breakage, spillage, or suspected contamination of etiologic agents occurs

When calling the NRC, give the following information:

- Name
- Name/address of carrier
- Phone number where carrier can be reached
- Date, time, and location of event
- Extent of injuries, if any
- Class, name, and quantity of hazardous materials involved
- Kind of incident and nature of hazardous material involved
- If a reportable quantity of hazardous substance is involved, name of the shipper and quantity of the hazardous material discharged

CHEMTREC is the acronym for Chemical Transportation Emergency Center, located in Washington, DC. It has a 24-hour toll-free line and has evolved to provide emergency personnel with technical information and expertise about the physical properties of hazardous products. CHEMTREC and the National Response Center work closely together. If you call CHEMTREC at 800-424-9300 or the National Response Center at 800-424-8802, they will notify the other about the problem.

In addition to calling the NRC or CHEMTREC, drivers are responsible to help carriers make a detailed written report. The driver is particularly valuable in completing these reports so it is a good idea for the driver to write out a report as soon as possible, detailing what took place.

CANUTEC—FOR HAZMAT EMERGENCIES

The Canadian Transport Emergency Centre, or **CANUTEC,** provides vital information to emergency personnel responding to transportation accidents involving dangerous goods. CANUTEC also offers information on all aspects of regulatory requirements for the transportation of dangerous goods.

CANUTEC's computerized data bank consists of information on more than 2 million commercial products. CANUTEC also has access to a large number of industry data banks and has communication links with other emergency response centres. This provides the CANUTEC scientists with quick access to a vast national and international resource network. Professional staff are able to provide immediate 24-hour telephone advice on chemical, physical, and toxicological properties and incompatibilities of the dangerous goods; health hazards and first aid; fire, explosion, spill, or leak hazards; remedial actions for the protection of life, property, and the environment; evacuation distances; personal protective clothing; and decontamination. Should on-site assistance be required, CANUTEC can contact various industry or government emergency response plans.

Ensuring air, marine, rail, and road safety, as well as the safe transportation of dangerous goods, is a huge task. Transport Canada develops and enforces safety regulations and standards; tests and promotes safety technologies; and is introducing safety management systems as a reliable and cost-effective way to prevent and manage safety risks in all modes of transportation.

In the event of an emergency involving dangerous goods in Canada, call CANUTEC at 613-996-6666 or ***666 on a cellular phone.**

STOP!

On May 5, 2003, TSA published a rule to secure the transportation of hazardous materials (hazmat), including explosives, by requiring threat assessments for all individuals who apply for, renew, or transfer a Hazardous Materials Endorsement (HME) on their Commercial Driver's License (CDL). On January 25, 2007, TSA modified this rule to include additional disqualifiers and appeal mechanisms. The rule is 49 CFR 1572.

Drivers must undergo a security threat assessment to transport hazardous materials requiring vehicle placards under DOT regulations. This rule does not apply to applicants for holders of a CDL who do not wish to transport hazardous materials. There is a separate rule addressing Canadian drivers hauling explosives into the U.S., and eventually all drivers will have to meet threat assessment and eligibility standards that are comparable to the standards that now apply to Hazmat drivers in the U.S.

OTHER INFORMATION NEEDED WHEN HAULING HAZMAT

Precautions during refueling—always turn off engine before refueling and someone must be in control of the fuel at the nozzle **(see Figure 32-8).**

Where to keep shipping papers en route—they must always be in the pouch on the driver's door or where driver can reach them while seat belt is buckled—and in clear view. Shipping papers for loads containing hazmat should be tagged and on top of all other papers.

Where to keep papers when you leave the rig—they should be placed on the driver's seat or in a pouch inside the driver's side door.

Special inspections for rigs hauling hazmat—other than the pretrip and en route checks, stops are required every two hours or every 100 miles (161 km) to check tires and remove any tires that are overheated. If you have a flat or a tire noticeably leaking, drive only as far as you need to get it fixed.

Directions for hauling chlorine—you should have an approved gas mask in the vehicle and must also know how to use an emergency kit for controlling leaks in dome lid plate fittings on the tank.

What to do when approaching a railroad crossing—no matter what, if you are in a placarded vehicle or carrying any amount of chlorine or have cargo tanks used to transport hazmat (loaded or empty), you must stop no closer than 15 feet (4.6 m) and no farther away than 50 feet (15.2 m). Do not shift gears while crossing. Turn on your four-way flashers when stopping at a railroad crossing **(see Figure 32-9).**

Hazmat route restrictions—some areas of the country require permits and **special routing** for carriers transporting certain materials. As the driver, you must know about these special requirements, so check with your company and always check routes before beginning a trip—you want to be permitted to travel on the roads you will be driving. Fines are costly against both the company and you as the driver.

▶ **Figure 32–8**
Always turn off the engine before refueling.

▶ **Figure 32–9**
When transporting hazardous materials, you must stop no closer than 15 feet (4.6 m) and no farther than 50 feet (15.2 m) at a railroad crossing.

STOP!
Anytime you are hauling explosives (1.1, 1.2, or 1.3), you are required to follow a written route plan. The same is true when hauling radioactive materials: The carrier is responsible for telling the driver that the trailer is loaded with radioactive material.

SECURITY MEASURES FOR HAZMAT LOADS

The FMCSA encourages the following suggestions to prevent any tampering or any security breaches involving loads of hazardous materials:

- Use tamper-resistant or tamper-evident seals and locks on cargo.
- Identify preferred and alternated routing, including acceptable deviations. Make sure routing complies with local routing restrictions.
- If possible, alternate routes to frequent destinations.
- Minimize exposure in downtown or heavily populated areas and expedite the shipment to the final destination.
- Minimize stops en route; if you must stop, select locations with adequate lighting on well-traveled roads and avoid high crime or dangerous areas.
- Use an engine kill switch.
- Use tractor and trailer brake locking devices.
- If trailer is dropped, use a kingpin lock when possible.
- Perform a quick walkaround to check your vehicle for foreign objects after all stops.
- Train drivers on how to avoid hijackings or theft of property. Keep vehicles locked when parked and avoid conversation about route, cargo, and destinations on open channels or with strangers.

TSA HAZMAT CONTACT INFORMATION

TSA HAZMAT Office—571-227-3200

TSA Media Contact—571-227-2829

TSA Contact Center—866-289-9673

Federal Motor Carrier Safety Administration (FMCSA) Media Contact—202-366-8810

NORTH AMERICAN ENVIRONMENTAL CONSIDERATIONS

The North American trucking industry has a significant impact on the environment and has become fully committed to reducing this impact while promoting sustainability. Sustainability means to support or provide for the ongoing existence of something—in this case, our planet Earth.

In the report "Critical Issues in the Trucking Industry–2010," presented by the American Transportation Research Institute in October 2010, environment had moved from number eight in 2008 to number seven in 2010, the highest rank in five years.

Trucks consume up to one gallon of diesel fuel for each hour at idle, using as much as 2,400 gallons of fuel every year per truck. This totals 1.2 billion gallons of diesel fuel consumed every year from idling. On average, each idling truck produces about 21 tons of carbon dioxide (CO_2) and 0.3 tons of nitrogen oxides (NOx) annually.

In an effort to lower emissions and cut down dependency on nonrenewable petroleum resources, Canadian and U.S. governmental agencies are implementing new regulations aimed at reducing truck idling. In addition, many states and provinces are enacting stricter anti-idling rules with more severe penalties for violators. Regulatory agencies at all levels of government are also working with industry parties to foster awareness of the harmful effects of idling and the solutions available from suppliers to combat them.

The increase of anti-idling regulations, federal and state equipment mandates, and ongoing debate on carbon tax cap and trade legislation created concern that compliance costs and basic difficulty exceed benefits.

The emergence of so many new regulations/proposals seeking to reduce emissions and greenhouse gases pave the way for environmental issues and industry concerns to increase over the coming years.

For more information on U.S. state idling regulations, go to www.atri-online.org/research/idling/ ATRI_Idling_Cab_Card.pdf.

For more information on Canadian province idling regulations, go to oee.nrcan.gc.ca.

Despite the fact that it may seem pretty simple to load up a big rig with goods, drive them across the country to their destination, and then unload and get paid before hooking up the next rig, there are a number of concerns, environmental and ethical, facing the shipping industry as a whole, and the over-the-road (OTR) portion in particular.

Environmental issues are indeed a concern among industry leaders, with greenhouse gas emissions apparently having some effect on global climate and the occurrence of pollution-related diseases on the rise.

Environmental protection also includes being knowledgeable of the environmental impact and the safe handling of the various types of hazardous materials being hauled from coast to coast and border to border in North America.

Although a handful of trucking operations are looking into alternative fuel vehicles, such as fleets of bio-diesel trucks, there really hasn't been a lot of headway in this arena. And considering that many truck drivers scrimp and save to buy their own rigs, there are an awful lot of trucks on the road that aren't cor-porately regulated, which makes enacting environmental regulations even more difficult.

The American Transportation Research Institute has also proposed a national standard for truck emis-sions as an alternative to current capital raising initiatives and has also proposed to develop strategies to increase industry awareness and participation in voluntary programs. One example of this effort is the American Trucking Associations' six-point program, Trucks Deliver a Cleaner Tomorrow, Canada's Smart Driver program, and the EPA's Smart Way Transport partnership.

Eventually the price of petroleum may make it impractical to drive diesel-powered vehicles, but until then, they are pumping tons of toxic hydrocarbons into the atmosphere every year.

In an effort to decrease these toxic hydrocarbons, the U.S. Environmental Protection Agency in 2006 implemented revised emission standards for diesel trucks (reducing airborne pollutants emitted by diesel engines), which promise to improve air quality and public health.

> ## CAUTION!
>
> Components of diesel exhaust were confirmed as an animal carcinogen in 1988 by the National Institute for Occupational Safety and Health, and by 2002, the U.S. Environmental Protection Agency (EPA) considered it "likely to be carcinogenic to humans," linked to (among other health effects) lung cancer, chronic bronchitis, and aggravated asthma. It has also been identified as a greenhouse gas. For these and other reasons, alternatives and improvements to standard diesel fuel have been developed.

Starting in June 2006, the EPA began requiring petroleum refiners to begin producing ultra-low sulfur diesel (ULSD) fuel, which has 97 percent less sulfur than the previous low-sulfur diesel fuel. When fuel containing sulfur is burned, sulfur dioxide is produced, a main component of acid rain. ULSD, together with new air pollution control technologies required in trucks (starting with model year 2007), are predicted to reduce harmful emissions by 90 percent. By full implementation, the EPA estimates 2.6 million tons of smog-producing emissions are eliminated each year.

Another environmental impact of the trucking transportation industry comes from road noise—and, strangely enough, noise pollution is often as impactful as air pollution.

In Canada, the federal role in trucking is not as large as it is for air, rail, and marine industries, largely because the roads used by trucks are for the most part maintained by the provinces and territories whose local governments maintain the roads and trucking industry under their jurisdiction. The federal role in Canada is relatively small for a second important reason: since 1954, responsibility for regulation of extra-provincial truck operators has been delegated to the provinces under the Motor Vehicle Transport Act (MVTA).

While motor carrier regulations are broadly similar in the U.S. and Canada, greater coordination between the two countries has occurred as a result of NAFTA. Today, truck engines in both countries meet the same standards. Coordination of regulations is expected to intensify as Mexican trucks are beginning to operate in NAFTA countries.

In an attempt to lower emissions in new truck engines, Environment Canada has authority under the Canadian Environmental Protection Act of 1999 to regulate emission levels for trucks and other vehicles. However, regulation of emission levels for trucks and services is up to the provinces.

Notably, truck engines are considerably cleaner today than they were a decade ago and will become more so with the current timetable for increasing standards. A recent report for the North American Commission for Environmental Cooperation concludes that "by 2020, truck emissions into the environment will be considerably lower than rail in the U.S.–Canada corridors."

In Chapter 15 of the Canada Transportation Act Review, it is noted that the trucking industry in Canada and in the U.S. is large and is growing. For this reason it is increasingly important for every member of the transportation industry to become more aware of the environmental impact of trucks, maintenance facilities, fuels, and cargos, now and into the future.

SUMMARY

In this chapter, you learned about the various classes of hazardous materials and your responsibilities as a professional driver when loading and hauling hazardous materials cargo. You also reviewed your responsibilities of checking and then carrying shipping papers when hauling a hazmat load, as well as what to do when a spill or incident involving hazardous materials occurs. You also learned the security measures necessary when loading hazardous materials and what you should do to maintain the safety of your cargo, your rig, and those around you when handling hazardous material loads. You also learned the environmental impact of your vehicle and its cargo as well as regulations in place to cut down on fuel, equipment, and freight pollution.

KEY TERMS

CANUTEC
CHEMTREC
Combustible
Containment rules
"Dangerous" placard
Explosive
Flammable

Hazard class
Hazardous materials
Hazardous materials table
Hazardous waste
Hazmat endorsement
Hazmat Threat Assessment
    Program

Identification number
Inhalation hazard
Placards
Radioactive materials
Route restrictions
Shipping paper
Special routing

REVIEW QUESTIONS

1. As of January 31, 2005, the Transportation Security Administration (TSA) required _____ from applicants trying to obtain hazmat endorsement on their CDL.

   a. a low center of gravity

   b. background information and fingerprints

   c. less fuel emissions

   d. greater braking efficiency on all rigs

2. According to the Commercial Motor Vehicle Safety Act of 1986, persons with a hazmat endorsement on their CDL have to retake the hazmat endorsement test _____.

   a. each time they renew their CDL

   b. every year

   c. only one time

   d. every 10 years

3. HM-126-F requires that carriers train hazmat drivers in _____.

   a. general awareness

   b. function specific

   c. safety

   d. a, b, and c

4. If you are hauling a hazmat load, you are required to use placards on _____.

   a. the front only

   b. the back only

   c. all four sides of the vehicle

   d. the sides only

5. Regarding the shipper's role in hazardous material handling, which of the following is not required of the shipper?

   a. Pack products properly.

   b. Label products properly.

   c. Certify on the shipping papers that the shipment has been prepared according to regulations.

   d. Notify the receiver of the goods shipping date.

6. Regarding the responsibility in handling hazardous materials, which of the following is not the carrier's responsibility?

   a. Transport the shipment to the proper destination.

   b. Ensure the shipper has correctly named, labeled, and marked the hazmat shipment.

   c. Report accident or incident involving hazmat to proper government agency.

   d. Notify the driver about hazmat shipment.

7. Which of the following is not the driver's responsibility regarding handling hazardous materials?

   a. must haul any leaking cartons labeled *hazardous* if the dispatcher tells the driver to do so

   b. must communicate the risk by attaching proper placards to the vehicle

   c. must deliver products as safely and quickly as possible while obeying federal and state hazmat regulations

   d. required to keep all hazmat shipping papers in the proper place

8. Regarding the driver's responsibility concerning loading and handling of hazardous materials, which of the following is not a correct action?

   a. Never open any packages during transport.

   b. No overhangs or tailgate loads for explosives.

   c. Do everything possible to protect the public.

   d. Smoking is permitted unless loading explosives.

9. Regarding performance-oriented packaging (POP), which of the following is not a required performance standard?

   a. No release of hazmat products during transport.

   b. Biodegradable upon discard.

   c. No reduced characteristics during use.

   d. The package contains nothing that could ruin the packaging.

10. The hazard class of materials indicates _____.

    a. which items should be placed near the top of the load

    b. the required stopping distance for vehicles transporting hazmat

    c. the degree of risk associated with that material

    d. the required center of gravity for hazmat loads

11. Regarding the hazard class numbering system, the first number indicates _____.

    a. the division, such as flammable gas, flammable liquid, flammable solids

    b. the required stopping distance for rigs transporting hazmat

    c. the class of the hazardous material (explosive, gases, flammable solids, etc.)

    d. which items can be mixed in a shipment

12. Regarding the shipping papers for hazardous materials, which of the following is not included?

   a. The route the driver must take.

   b. The proper description of the hazardous material.

   c. The signature by the shipper's representative.

   d. Verification that the shipment has been prepared according to all regulations applicable.

13. In case of an accident involving hazmat, which of the following is not the driver's responsibility?

   a. Warn people of danger and keep them away.

   b. If it can be done safely, contain the spill.

   c. Tell authorities the destination of the goods shipped.

   d. Contact the appropriate emergency response personnel.

14. If you are hauling hazmat merchandise and you notice something leaking from the vehicle, which of the following should you not do?

   a. Pull as far off the road as you can.   c. Keep others away from the vehicle.

   b. Get the shipping papers and get   d. Drive to the nearest fire station.
      away from the vehicle.

15. Regarding security measures for hazmat loads, which of the following is not recommended by FMCSA?

   a. using tamper-resistant or tamper-evident seals and locks on cargo

   b. locking the doors of the tractor and leaving the engine running at a truck stop while you are away from the vehicle

   c. using an engine kill switch

   d. using tractor and trailer locking devices

16. In an effort to lower emissions and cut down dependency on nonrenewable petroleum resources, Canadian and U.S. governmental agencies are implementing new regulations aimed at reducing truck _____.

   a. driving times   c. load sizes

   b. idling times   d. fuel capacity

SUPPLEMENTAL LEARNING ACTIVITIES

1. You are handed shipping papers for a load of mixed hazardous materials. What is the next step? Write a 100-word report on your responsibilities as a driver, transporting a mixed load, or use this question as a focus for your class discussion.

2. Hazmat drivers are instructed to travel with shipping papers nearby at all times. List five reasons this is an important policy, and discuss.

3. During your en route inspection, you notice something leaking from your trailer. What's your next move? Do you try to move your rig from the parking lot at the truck stop? Call CANUTEC or CHEMTREC? Call your dispatcher? Look at your shipping papers? What's next?

4. Placards are important, why? Discuss or write a report of approximately 100 words.

5. If you are planning to earn your hazmat endorsement or foresee hauling hazmat in your career, what do you think are the top five characteristics of a professional driver entrusted with a hazmat load?

FOR MORE INFORMATION

TSA Transportation Worker Identification Credential
www.tsa.gov/what_we_do/layers/twic/index.shtm

Transport Canada—CANUTEC
www.tc.gc.ca/eng/canutec/menu.htm

TSA HAZMAT Endorsement Threat Assessment Program
www.tsa.gov/what_we_do/layers/hazmat/index.shtm

British Columbia—Ministry of Environment
www.gov.bc.ca/env/

British Columbia—Ministry of Transportation and Infrastructure
www.gov.bc.ca/tran/

Environment Canada
www.ec.gc.ca/default.asp?lang=En&n=FD9B0E51-1

FMCSA—Hazardous Materials
www.fmcsa.dot.gov/safety-security/hazmat/hm-theme.htm
www.fmcsa.dot.gov/safety-security/hazmat/complyhmregs.htm

33 Public Relations and Job Search

© iStockphoto/shotbydave

OBJECTIVES

When you have completed this chapter, you should be able to:

■ Understand the importance, responsibility, and results of a professional driver presenting a good image to the public.

■ Explain the importance of good relations with customers.

■ Exhibit appropriate communications skills, including use of interpersonal and technology communications.

■ Describe the proper procedures for applying for a job as a professional driver.

■ Understand reasons a driver candidate can be disqualified from job consideration.

INTRODUCTION

A s has been mentioned numerous times in this book, a professional driver is more than someone who can steer an 18-wheeler down the highway. Far from it. Not only do professional drivers have the skills to handle millions of dollars worth of equipment and cargo, but they also must have many skills beyond those early drivers who sat on boxes to drive their vehicles and learned how to drive by running tractors or farm-to-market loads of produce from the family farm.

Aside from driving skills, technical skills, and a thorough understanding of local, state, provincial, and federal regulations, today's professional drivers also must know how to represent their company well, not only to customers but also to the driving public **(see Figure 33-1).**

They also must know how to communicate effectively and efficiently with maintenance technicians, safety directors, dispatchers, dock personnel, law enforcement, border crossing personnel, customers, and many others—plus today's professional drivers must also be able to present themselves in a professional manner as they conduct job searches and/or interviews for promotions **(see Figure 33-2).** Examples of possible promotions might be load planners (dispatchers), logistics or operations positions as well as employment opportunities within recruiting and the safety department. Having behind-the-wheel-experience is very helpful when dealing with a driver associate. It allows you to relate to what they are experiencing.

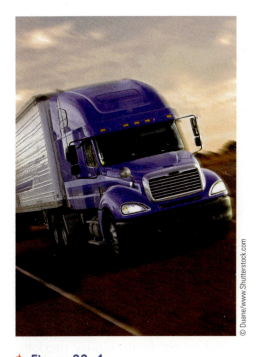

▶ Figure 33-1

Drivers today must know how to represent their company well.

▶ Figure 33-2

Professional drivers must know how to communicate effectively and efficiently.

It's obvious, therefore, that today's professional driver must not only master many skills to be successful but he or she also must continue to polish and update these skills to keep up with an ever-changing transportation industry.

In this chapter, we'll take a look at the skills needed by professional drivers for public relations, interpersonal communications, and the job search.

PUBLIC RELATIONS

Public relations can be defined as how the general public thinks about or views a subject, an issue, or an industry.

Much of what the general public thinks about the trucking industry comes from how they see drivers behave on the road **(see Figure 33-3)**. Thoughtful and courteous tractor-trailer drivers create a positive impact on how the public views the entire industry. On the other hand, one careless or rude truck driver on the highway, at a truck stop, or in a roadside park can immediately create a poor image for the entire industry.

However, when focusing on and promoting the importance of truck transportation as a vital part of our North American economy, the image of professional truck drivers moves to the next level.

If you think about it, tractor-trailer drivers are the front-line public relations team for the carrier they represent and for all the people who work in the transportation industry. Professional drivers are the part of the industry the public sees most often and the image they create is the image the general public remembers—and for this reason, drivers must take ownership of their profession. Often you as the driver are the only face the customer ever sees of your company. You represent the company every time you arrive that their facility. It takes years to build a quality relationship and only a few minutes to destroy years of work.

▶ **Figure 33-3**

The public's perception of the trucking industry comes from the driver behavior they see on the road.

▶ *"Well it's one for the money, two for the show, three to get ready . . ."*

This "ownership" includes completing paperwork accurately, neatly, and on time. It also means taking pride in keeping equipment clean and in good working order—and, perhaps as important as these previous suggestions, making certain personal hygiene is at the highest possible level.

It is human nature for the memory of the public to be a short one. A four-wheeler may have seen a trucker risk his or her life to keep other highway users safe and may have had positive interactions with professional drivers on the highway for years. Then, they may see a truck driver taking chances—perhaps repeatedly changing lanes in heavy traffic or cutting off other drivers on a freeway—and suddenly the positive image becomes a negative.

If the public does not like what they see, they will remember. Some may even complain to a lawmaker and, bottom line, the industry will hear about it in ways that will hurt business and affect earnings and jobs.

In this chapter, we will discuss not only how professional drivers can create positive public relations but also the importance of good employee–employer relations. At the end of the chapter, we discuss the professional driver's job search, qualifications, and recommendations for handling the job interview.

Public Relations and the Professional Driver

How well do you think the general public perceives the trucking transportation industry? How does the general public see the professional driver? In most cases, the relationship between the general public and the trucking industry is determined by how well professional drivers obey the laws and regulations meant to protect road users. Professional drivers can improve the image of the trucking transportation industry by obeying the laws, being courteous, using everyday common sense on the road, at roadside parks, and at truck stops, avoiding being too aggressive behind the wheel or in dealing with other people. At the same time, an improved public image will bring more dedicated drivers to an industry that is respected and valued.

Image of the Trucking Industry

The trucking industry operates under many state and federal laws and regulations. Most of the laws have been made to protect the public. Some pose challenges to the transportation industry:

- High road use taxes
- Laws restricting vehicles from using certain roads
- Lower speed limits for heavy vehicles
- Hours-of-service rules that make it difficult for drivers to get the rest they need

The public's image of the trucking industry heavily influences the creation of laws that affect the industry. This image of the trucking industry and professional drivers—whether accurate or not—often results in legislation that is unfavorable to the industry and decreases profits. These difficulties sometimes mean loss of jobs within the industry.

One driver's thoughtlessness can have a dramatic impact on the entire industry. Therefore, the industry—particularly the American Trucking Associations—but other industry groups as well, has taken steps through programs, such as the America's Road Team, to introduce the public to the industry and to the importance of the jobs being done every day by professional drivers.

Courteous drivers who know and practice safe driving at all times can truly be seen as "knights of the road" by the general public **(see Figure 33-4).**

▶ Figure 33-4

It is important to present a positive image to the public.

Contact with the Public

Professional drivers have numerous opportunities for public contact, which can be either cooperative or abrasive. Drivers must take great care that their conduct and actions create a positive picture of the industry in all situations, whether you are at a truck stop for lunch, communicating with a shipper, or working with dock personnel. Your "publics" are everywhere. Treat everyone with courtesy and respect.

STOP!

All of us have stress in our lives—but THERE IS NO EXCUSE for ROAD RAGE from a professional driver.

▶ Figure 33–5

A neat appearance will gain more respect for the industry.

Every professional driver is responsible for maintaining a positive image while driving—and you do this by obeying the law, making a clean and neat appearance, and sharing the road courteously.

Obeying the law—is first and foremost. Laws are meant to protect every citizen and visitor to this country, and should be obeyed at all times. When professional drivers obey the law, they project the image of true professionals. Obeying the law also cuts down on incidents that make life harder for your fellow drivers, the industry, and yourself.

Making a good appearance—a clean, neat, professional appearance gains respect for drivers and for the industry they represent. Professional drivers should also make it a priority to stay in top physical, mental, and emotional shape (**see Figure 33-5**).

Professional drivers must be sure rigs are in top condition, as well. A good pretrip inspection may prevent an accident or breakdown. A clean, well-maintained vehicle makes the industry look good and illustrates the pride a professional driver feels because he is part of the proud tradition of trucking. Flapping tarps, spilling cargo, and dragging chains or ropes say we belong to a shoddy industry.

Sharing the road—because professional drivers must share roads with the public, conflicts can occur. A few of the actions that create public resentment toward the transportation industry are:

- **Space related**—following too closely or driving in packs that prevent other drivers from passing. If you as a professional driver are following too closely and the driver in the car ahead looks in the rear view mirror and all he or she sees is the grill of a Peterbilt, that makes a statement, and it's not a good one.
- **Speed related**—speeding and cutting in and out of traffic.
- **Going uphill**—attempting to pass another vehicle without enough speed results in two trucks blocking the flow of traffic. You could block an unmarked emergency or police vehicle. The same situation can occur when trucks do not keep to the right and pull over to allow other vehicles to pass. Be careful, and do not pull onto a soft shoulder because your rig could sink, turn over, or throw gravel at vehicles behind you.
- **Passing**—when the truck cuts off other drivers or does not signal his or her intention to pass.
- **At intersections**—never try to bluff your way through intersections. Trucks are large and can frighten some drivers to react in a way that causes an accident. Other drivers do not always leave enough room for a tractor-trailer to make a turn. Keep cool and be aware that many drivers do not always heed red lights. Look both ways after the light turns green, and be sure there are no emergency vehicles approaching.

- **Use of headlights**—not dimming lights when meeting or following other vehicles can be dangerous. Shining high beams into vehicles ahead can confuse the driver and possibly cause an accident. Remember—the posted speed is the maximum you should drive. Remember, too, you are always creating an image.

- **Noise**—using your horn when it is not needed is irritating and often frightening. Mufflers that are damaged or not the right type create unnecessary and irritating noise.

- **Parking incorrectly**—when you block traffic unnecessarily, people may think it is deliberate, which reflects negatively on you, your carrier, and your industry.

- **Improper behavior**—yelling, foul language, and obscene gestures on the streets and highways can also give the trucking transportation industry a black eye. This behavior accomplishes nothing and, if reported, may cause you to lose your job.

© iStockphoto/MCCAIG

▶ **Figure 33-6**

A professional manner on and off the road is the best policy.

You are the professional! The best policy is to act like a professional at all times **(see Figure 33-6)**. Remember, many trucks on the road today have a phone number painted on them that people may call to report both good and bad driving habits.

Make a habit of being clean, neatly groomed, and neatly dressed when on duty. If your carrier prefers uniforms, be sure yours is neat, clean, and pressed. Be courteous and polite and avoid arguments. You represent an entire industry.

CUSTOMER RELATIONS

As far as the general public is concerned, professional drivers ARE the company. As a driver, how you act can lose or gain business for your company. The extra effort it takes to do a good job and present a positive image is well worth the effort, both short-term and long-term. Both you and the company will benefit from good **customer relations.** Remember—it takes years to build a good company relationship with a customer and only a few minutes to destroy it.

NOTE

Good communication between drivers and the sales department goes a long way in furthering good customer relations. Drivers who show up with advertising gifts to give a customer are always viewed positively.

CAUTION!

Remember: How you and your equipment look are important, too—and first impressions count!

Factors that affect your image as seen by the public mean more when the public is a customer. The image you project is the customer's closest view of the company **(see Figure 33-7).**

Company policies and procedures were set up to attract and grow the business. Follow the company policy for cargo and freight documentation and handling, dealing with customers, and dealing with problems.

Tips for Good Customer Relations
• Follow company procedures
• Do not argue or lose your temper
• Be courteous
• Be polite, honest, and helpful
• Always thank the customer
If you give that extra care,
you may get more business!
Remember... the driver has more contact with customers than any other person in the company
© Cengage Learning 2013

Figure 33-7

Good customer relations begin with drivers who conduct themselves professionally at all times.

Drivers who do not follow company policy give the company a bad reputation. Moreover, neglecting company policy can result in the loss of your job. If you have a problem at a customer location or on the road, call the dispatcher. It is the company's job to help you.

A positive attitude is extremely important. What does a positive attitude look like? Check out the following:

- Promptness when picking up or delivering cargo
- Courtesy—to everyone
- Politeness, helpfulness, and honesty at all times
- A sincere interest in doing a good job and taking personal ownership of your profession
- An easy manner—not arguing or allowing yourself to become provoked

CAUTION!

If you, as a driver, have a disagreement with the shipper or receiver about anything at all, do not argue or debate with him or her. This could cost your company a contract. Step back, relax, remove yourself from the conflict or potential conflict, then call your dispatcher. Allow the company to work out the issues while you keep your cool (and your job!)

EMPLOYER–EMPLOYEE RELATIONS

Before you read further, ask yourself this question: If you were running a trucking company, what kind of employees would you want to work for your firm?

Your answer, of course, is that you would want people who work hard, are reliable, responsible, dependable, and will help your company make money.

In this section, we discuss **employer–employee relations** and the requirements of a good employee, attitudes and conduct, and required skills.

Basic Job Requirements

A good attitude is a must for success in finding and holding any job. The general qualifications expected of a professional tractor-trailer driver mandate that a driver must:

- Meet the requirements of federal law, including the medical qualifications and having the correct CDL
- Meet the employer's needs and qualifications as stated in company policy
- Know about the trucking industry and have the attitudes and interests suited to its environment **(see Figure 33-8)**

Do You Want To Drive A Tractor-Trailer?

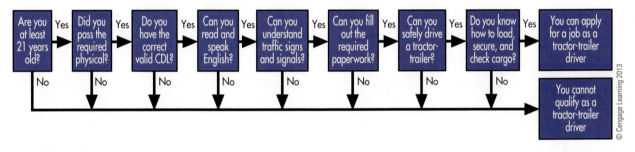

▶ **Figure 33–8**

Basic job requirements for professional drivers.

Requirements of Federal Law

People who apply for professional tractor-trailer driving jobs must meet the U.S. Department of Transportation (DOT) qualifications as stated below:

- Be at least 21 years old (although 18-year-olds are allowed to drive intrastate)
- Be physically qualified according to FMCSR 341.91
- Have a valid CDL
- Be able to read and speak English. New CDL testing requirements do not allow for the use of interpreters for either the knowledge or the skills test. These regulations went into effect July 2011.
- Understand traffic signs and signals
- Be able to fill out required paperwork
- Be able to safely drive a tractor-trailer
- Know and use the correct methods of securing cargo
- Be able to determine if cargo is properly loaded and secured

© Cengage Learning 2013

▶ **Figure 33–9**

Professional drivers need to pass certain tests.

Professional tractor-trailer drivers must also pass certain tests and be able to fill out the applications that are required **(see Figure 33-9).**

- Fill out a job application that meets DOT requirement FMCSR 391.21 (carrier will supply application).
- Take a written test and a road test given by the company (the DOT requires the company to keep the results on file).
- Have passed all the tests needed to earn the CDL:
  - General Knowledge Test
  - Air Brakes Test
  - Combination Vehicles Test
  - Pretrip Inspection Test
  - Basic Control Skills Test and Road Test

Drivers who operate double or triple trailer combinations or tankers or haul hazardous materials must pass additional tests before they can drive these vehicles **(see Figure 33-10).**

Do You Want To Get A CDL That Will Let You Drive A Tractor-Trailer?

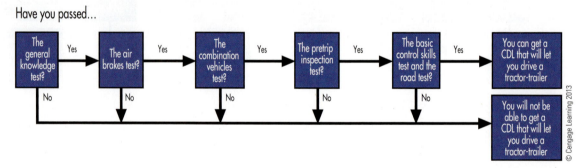

▶ **Figure 30–10**

Requirements to earn a CDL.

Disqualifications

Under FMCSR 391.15, an applicant for a CDL that will allow him or her to drive a tractor-trailer must be disqualified for any of the following reasons:

- Medical reasons
- Loss of license
- Operating a commercial motor vehicle (CMV) while under the influence of alcohol, illegal drugs, or other stimulants
- Transportation, possession, or unlawful use of a Schedule I drug
- Being in an accident that results in injury or death and leaving the scene
- Conviction of a felony involving the use of a commercial motor vehicle

General Qualifications

Professional driver applicants should know something about the various types of vehicles used in the transportation industry (**see Figure 33-11**). They should also be informed about the systems and components of the various vehicles. Applicants should be able to speak the language of the industry and know how to fill out the required paperwork.

A knowledge of state and local traffic regulations and laws must be demonstrated. This includes the basic hazardous materials requirements.

Being able to drive safely and learning to drive the employer's vehicles safely are vital skills. The professional driver also must know how to handle cargo using the correct methods at all times.

▶ **Figure 33–11**

Professional driver applicants should know about the various vehicles used in the transportation industry.

To qualify, an applicant must have a positive attitude toward the trucking industry, the employer, and the job itself. One of the biggest reasons new drivers have difficulty is because they have unrealistic expectations about the job and its requirements.

Every applicant must be willing to follow company policies regarding hours of work, safety rules, and public relations.

Finally, the candidate must have a personality that suits the job. This includes a high level of interest in the job, maturity, safety awareness, enthusiasm, and a responsible work ethic.

Company Policy

Each company has its own policies. Company policy must be followed, even if it differs from what you have learned in school or elsewhere. Find out what is expected during your job interview, and then meet those expectations.

Most carriers have company policies that cover:

- Hours of work and benefits
- Basic work rules
  - Types of supervision
  - Requirements for advancement
  - Discipline, including rules for dismissal
- Safety rules
  - Safety training
  - Safety meetings
  - Safe driving and cargo handling rules

- Vehicle inspection and maintenance requirements
  - Instructions
  - What is expected of the driver
  - Forms to be filled out
- Rules for trips
  - Driving rules for fuel economy
  - Where and when drivers can make fuel and rest stops
  - Reimbursement policy for drivers
  - Use of credit cards
  - Cash advances
- Relations with customers and the public
  - Dress code
  - Conduct expected

What Companies Cannot Require of a Driver

No driver can be required to work in violation of state, federal, or local regulations. Drivers must be provided with a safe place to work and a safe vehicle. No driver is allowed to violate the hours-of-service regulations or safety regulations (**see Figure 33-12**).

Whistleblower Protection Program

The Whistleblower Protection Program provides protection from discrimination for commercial motor carrier industry employees who report information related to commercial motor carrier safety or participate in other protected activities.

Employees of trucking companies, their contractors, and their subcontractors are protected from

▶ **Figure 33-12**

Drivers must record hours of service.

retaliation, discharge, or otherwise being discriminated against for providing information relating to commercial motor safety violations to their employer or to the federal government, or filed, testified, or assisted in a proceeding against the employer relating to any violation or alleged violation of any order, regulation, or standard of the Surface Transportation Assistance Act (STAA) or any other federal law relating to commercial motor carrier safety, or because they are about to engage in any of these actions.

To qualify for protection under the Whistleblower Protection Program, you must:

1. Be or have been an employee as mentioned
2. Be or have been engaged in an activity as mentioned
3. Believe you are being or have been discriminated against by your employer for engaging in an activity as mentioned

For more information please visit fmcsr.gov, or you may contact OSHA at 1-800-321-OSHA (6742).

Drivers and Company Policy

The more a driver applicant knows about a company, the easier it is to get a job interview and do well during the interview. The Internet may be a good source of information about a prospective employer. If possible, know the answers to the following questions in advance:

- Do you have the abilities the employer needs?
- If additional training is available, are you willing to learn?
- Is this a place where you want to work?
- Are the hours, pay, and working conditions going to meet your needs?

Obviously, the greatest chance for a good match is when the company and the applicant agree that their needs will be met through the job.

Finally, applicants' attitude is as important as their knowledge of the company requirements. The key attitudes to have for a successful job search are:

- Loyalty
- Dependability
- Safety mindedness
- Honesty
- Enthusiasm
- Team player
- Good representative for the company

INTERPERSONAL COMMUNICATIONS FOR PROFESSIONAL DRIVERS

Interpersonal communication can be defined in several ways. However, it usually describes who's talking and the relationship between those speaking and listening. Interpersonal communications can involve one-on-one conversations or individuals interacting with many people in a group **(see Figure 33-13)**.

Interpersonal communication is the process that we use to communicate our ideas, thoughts, and feelings to another person.

It's important to understand that our interpersonal communication skills are learned behaviors that can be improved through knowledge, practice, and feedback.

Interpersonal communication includes message sending and message reception between two or more individuals. This can include all aspects of communication such as listening, persuading, asserting, nonverbal communication (sometimes called body language), and more.

Figure 33-13

Interpersonal communication is important for professional drivers.

© iStockphoto/shotbydave

Figure 33-14

Interpersonal communication can also be indirect electronic communications.

As people, we also communicate on different interpersonal levels, depending on who we are including in the communication. For example, if an individual is communicating with a family member, that communication will more than likely differ from the communication used with a friend or significant other.

Interpersonal communication can be accomplished using direct (face-to-face) and indirect (e-mails, telephone calls, voicemail, or text messages) **(see Figure 33-14).** Successful interpersonal communication requires that both the message sender and the message receiver will interpret and understand the message being sent.

The following are four principles of interpersonal communication:

Interpersonal communication is inescapable—We communicate not only through words, but also through tone of voice and through gesture, posture, facial expression, etc. We constantly communicate to those around us. Even when we sleep, we communicate. Remember a basic principle of communication: people judge us by our behavior, not our intent. We can't not communicate. If we choose not to communicate, that communicates something, too.

Interpersonal communication is irreversible—You can't take back something once it has been said. The effect must inevitably remain. Despite the instructions from a judge to a jury to "disregard that last statement the witness made," the lawyer knows that it can't help but make an impression on the jury.

Interpersonal communication is complicated—No form of communication is simple. Even simple requests are extremely complex—because of the listener's attitude, the speaker's hairstyle, tone of voice, posture, facial expression, etc. Think of it this way: whenever we communicate, there are at least six "people" involved: 1) who you think you are; 2) who you think the other person is; 3) who you think the other person thinks you are; 4) who the other person thinks he or she is; 5) who the other person thinks you are; and 6) who the other person thinks you think he or she is.

We don't actually speak in ideas. We speak in symbols, called "words," that stand for ideas. This also complicates communication. Words (our symbols for ideas) do not have inherent meaning. We simply use them in certain ways, and no two people use the same word exactly alike.

Effective interpersonal communication isn't as easy as one might think. In fact, our words many times can be totally misunderstood. To demonstrate just how difficult effective interpersonal communication can be, a Finnish linguist by the name of Wiio came up with the following observations, called "Wiio's Laws":

- If communication can fail, it will.
- If a message can be understood in different ways, it will be understood in just the way that does the most harm.
- There is always somebody who knows better than you what you meant by your message.
- The more communication there is, the more difficult it is for communication to succeed.

Interpersonal communication is contextual—In other words, communication does not happen in isolation. There is:

- **Psychological context,** which is who you are and what you bring to the conversation. Your needs, desires, values, personality, etc., all form the psychological context. ("You" here refers to both participants in the interaction.)
- **Relational context,** which concerns your reactions to the other person—the "mix" they bring to the conversation.

- **Situational context** deals with the psychosocial setting in which you are communicating. An interaction that takes place in a classroom will be very different from one that takes place in a bar.

- **Environmental context** deals with the physical place where you are communicating. Furniture, location, noise level, temperature, season, and time of day, all are examples of factors in the environmental context. A conversation during a ball game will be environmentally different from one at a golf course.

- **Cultural context** includes all the learned behaviors and rules that affect the interaction. If you come from a culture (foreign or within your own country) where it is considered rude to make long, direct eye contact, you will—out of politeness—avoid eye contact. If the other person comes from a culture where long, direct eye contact signals trustworthiness, then we have in the cultural context a basis for misunderstanding.

NOTE

The cardinal rule of communication is that the "message lies with the receiver." In other words, it doesn't matter what the sender (person talking) actually MEANS, what matters is what the receiver THINKS was meant. This may not be fair, but this is the way it is!

TIPS FOR EFFECTIVE INTERPERSONAL COMMUNICATION

Want to improve your interpersonal relationships with others? Improve your skill at interpersonal communication and you will reap the harvest in more successful work relationships. Effective communication is a must at work.

How to Deal with People at Work

If you've worked successfully for more than a couple of years, you've mastered much of the art of interpersonal communication at work. Maybe you've not yet figured out how to deal with your especially difficult coworkers and bosses, but you know how to deal with the everyday people at work.

How to Hold a Difficult Conversation

If you manage people or care about your friends at work, chances are good that one day you will need to hold a difficult conversation. As an example, when people dress inappropriately and unprofessionally for work or their personal hygiene is unacceptable, good communication will help you hold difficult conversations with them.

Provide Feedback That Has an Impact

Make your feedback have the impact it deserves by the manner and approach you use to deliver feedback. Your feedback can make a difference to people if you can avoid a defensive response.

Receive Feedback with Grace and Dignity

Interested in hearing about how others view your work? Make it easy for them to tell you. If they think you'll appreciatively consider their feedback, you'll get lots more. And, that is good.

Overcome Your Fear of Confrontation and Necessary Conflict

Meaningful confrontation is never easy, but conflict is often necessary if you want to stick up for your rights at work. Whether the confrontation is over shared credit, irritating coworker habits, or ineffective approaches, sometimes you need to hold a confrontation with a coworker. The good news is that while confrontation is almost never your first choice, you can—with practice and education—become better and more comfortable with necessary conflict.

(Continues)

TIPS FOR EFFECTIVE INTERPERSONAL COMMUNICATION (continued)

To Drink or Not to Drink?

To drink or not to drink at work-related events is a question every employee has to decide about. Whether the business occasion is lunch during an interview, the company holiday party, or an awards banquet, alcohol is usually an option. Make your decision about how much to drink before you are faced with choices.

How to Adopt Group Guidelines

The members of every team and work group develop particular ways of interacting with each other over time. Effective interpersonal communication among group members and successful communication with managers and employees external to the team are critical components of group functioning. With the potential power of the impact of these interactions on group success, why leave group member interaction to chance? Be aware of and adopt group relationship guidelines or group norms early to ensure group success.

Interpersonal Communication Dynamics

Each of us is a radar machine constantly scoping out our environment. Human beings are sensitive to body language, facial expression, posture, movement, tone of voice, and more. To effectively communicate, these interpersonal communication dynamics must match your words.

Demonstrate Respect at Work

Ask anyone in your workplace what treatment he or she most wants at work. The person will likely top his or her list with the desire to be treated with dignity and respect. You can demonstrate respect with simple yet powerful actions. These ideas will help you avoid needless, insensitive, unmeant disrespect, too.

Why Politics at Work Is Risky

In a workplace that honors diversity, every person's politics, religious beliefs, sexual activities, and opinions about nonwork issues are irrelevant. Therefore, these topics should, for the most part, stay home. Do you agree or disagree about talking politics at work?

The Benefits of Assertiveness

Assertiveness is a skill that not only helps with marriage and interpersonal relationships, but can reduce stress and help you attain more balance at home, at work, and in life. Being assertive is not about being a bully, but it is about standing up for yourself and what you believe to be the right thing to do.

Emotional Intelligence

Have you ever known someone who had poorly developed emotional intelligence (EI)? This is a person who has difficulty understanding the emotions that are communicated in every message. Someone with a low EI capacity is also ineffective at understanding and expressing his or her own emotions.

Have You Held a Difficult Conversation?

Difficult conversations need to occur occasionally at work. These are the conversations you'd rather avoid, but there's no way around difficult conversations. They stretch your interpersonal communication skills and, as the saying goes, "what doesn't kill you makes you strong."

APPLYING FOR A JOB

Generally, when you apply for a job as a professional tractor-trailer driver, you must fill out an application, give references for the prospective employer to check, and provide employment history for the past 10 years. The next step is attending a job interview and being tested . . . and while much of the following sounds like something you've heard before, it's always a good idea to review what you already know about applying for a new job.

The application form is the first impression you make on the potential employer. If your application is completed neatly and is accurate and honest, you will usually make a good impression on the employer. However, whether you meet their requirements is not always easy to tell from the application without also having an interview.

CAUTION!

Avoid leaving blank spaces on the application. Some carriers receive numerous applications per day and do not have time to check incomplete applications.

Documents to Have at Your Fingertips

As a professional driver, you should file and have handy the following documents, even if you're not looking for employment. Care of these documents is a must, as they are the keys to your next job, promotion, or new opportunity:

- Employment history with dates of service up to and including your current employment, for the last 10 years of professional driving employment and past three years of every job, whether you were driving or not. Make sure dates are accurate and that contact information for former employers is updated. If you're not sure of the accuracy of your dates, get your Drive-A-Check (DAC) report. DAC reports are available from HireRight. To receive your report, you must mail in a Consumer Report Request Form, or you can request your free DAC report from HireRight online at www.hireright.com/Disputes/Report.aspx.

  Inaccurate reporting and errors can easily end up on your report and, if not corrected, can negatively affect your ability to get work. DACfix.com is a company dedicated to assisting drivers dispute inaccurate/negative information on their DACs. Contact them at www.DACfix.com or call 800-494-7517.

- If you've had an accident that wasn't your fault that appears on your Motor Vehicle Report (MVR), make certain you have a copy of that accident report so you can show a new employer the details.

- Military records—a copy of your discharge papers (Form DD214). There are sometimes government incentives for companies that hire veterans.

- Copies of truck driving school completion certificate, safe driving awards, or other awards associated with your employment as a professional driver.

- You should also obtain your Pre-employment Screening Program (PSP) Report. Make certain data is correct, as more employers, under CSA, are now looking closely at this report.
- Finally, you should know what is on your MVR. Nobody likes surprises, especially during a job search.

References Are Important

When the potential employer asks for references, you should supply a list of the names and addresses of previous employers. If there are "holes" in your work record, be prepared for questions about what you were doing during those periods, in regard to employment. It is important that you give an accurate account of your previous driving record. Always be honest and truthful **(see Figure 33-15).**

© iStockphoto/MichaelDeLeon

▶ **Figure 33–15**

Always be honest and truthful during an interview.

Next to the road test, the interview is the most important part of finding a job, and you have a chance to sell yourself. The four key rules for a good job interview are:

- Be prepared.
- Know how to act during the interview.
- End the interview on a positive note and thank the person for the time and consideration.
- Do not overstay your appointed time for the interview.

Preparing for the Interview

To prepare for the interview, do the following:

- Learn all you can about the company. Ask current and former employees and visit the corporate website.
- Be ready to ask intelligent questions, such as the following:
    - What are the company policies?
    - What are the chances for training?
    - Is there opportunity for advancement?
- Know your own abilities and limitations. Be realistic.
- Know whether you can drive the kind of vehicle used in this job and handle the cargo.
- Know whether you need extra training.
- Tell the truth—even if it is not always pretty—and this cannot be emphasized enough! It is essential that a potential employee remain honest. If during an interview an employee is dishonest, it is often viewed as an indication that further down the road the same person would also be untrustworthy.
- Make sure you have all the necessary paperwork with you, including the correct license, endorsement, certifications, and letters of reference.
- Be ready for the interview. Be on time or even a bit early. Visit the location a day or so before the interview so you will not get lost or delayed. Dress neatly and be ready to drive if you are asked to take a road test.

How to Act During the Interview

The interview is your chance to sell yourself. Be on time, be polite and courteous, and if you are a smoker, refrain from smoking even if you are invited to do so. When you are asked about your qualifications and experience, present them clearly and honestly. Do not stretch the truth. Be sure the interviewer knows what you have done in the past. Show how your experience and qualifications fit with what the company needs **(see Figure 33-16).**

Most people are a little nervous before and during interviews. Do not let this bother you. Just try and be as relaxed as you can be—and be yourself. Keep a positive attitude about the job. If possible, do a little research on the Internet and find out something about the company's history and mission.

GO!

A good attitude is often what makes the difference in who gets the job! Never be negative about a previous employer.

▶ **Figure 33–16**

Be prepared to be yourself at an interview.

▶ **Figure 33–17**

After the interview, thank the interviewer for his or her time.

Remember, the interviewer's job is to learn about you—to find out who you are and what you are like. Try to answer questions clearly but do not volunteer unnecessary information. Try to keep your conversation focused on the job and why you are the best candidate for that job.

Ask questions. Find out about the company.

End the Interview Well

Thank the interviewer for his or her time and interest. If you are interested in the job, show your interest in the company and the job and repeat how you believe you can meet the company's needs. Ask how and when you will be informed of the company's decision (**see Figure 33-17**).

Remember, you may not get the job. If you do not—and you think the company is a place where you want to work—you may choose to accept a job as a helper or dock worker as a place to begin. By proving your strong work ethic and your interest in becoming a professional driver for the company, you may be considered for the next open position.

© Cengage Learning 2013

▶ **Figure 33-18**

The road test is the most important part of applying for a job.

Tests

Be prepared and well rested before sitting for any written tests or before taking road performance tests. To prepare for the written tests, study the regulations regarding safe driving practices and review the state-prepared handbook and the FMCSRs available at www.fmcsa.dot.gov.

Review safe driving information and procedures learned during your classes. It is also a good idea to purchase the review book *Pass the CDL,* published by Thomson Delmar Learning.

It is also helpful to study the tests at the end of each chapter in this book as a practice review.

The road test is the most important part of applying for a job **(see Figure 33-18).** The test will probably include a pretrip inspection, coupling and uncoupling, backing, parking, and driving in traffic.

Be comfortably dressed and ready for the test. Bring gloves, rags, and driving equipment. Ask about unfamiliar parts or accessories. If you feel you are not yet qualified to drive the rig, do not drive. Never take the risk of driving an unfamiliar vehicle for testing purposes.

Physical Examination

You must have a current and valid doctor's certificate, stating you have passed a physical examination and meet the minimum qualifications for the DOT physical exam. Some potential employers will also request a "preemployment" drug screen in addition to the DOT physical exam. The carrier may refer you to a specific physician or you may get a physical from your family physician.

SUMMARY

In this chapter, you learned that how a professional driver acts has much to do with how the public views the trucking industry as a whole. You also learned how to present a positive image, both on the highway and in other public places. Ways to maintain good public relations were explained in this chapter as well as how to become a professional driver, finding a job, and handling the job interview.

KEY TERMS

Customer relations
Employer–employee relations

Interpersonal communications

Public relations

A DAY IN THE LIFE . . .

© Cengage Learning 2013

David Wehman—Truck Driving Program Coordinator, Baker College of Flint

When thinking about my career I often say, "I can't believe they pay me to do something I really love" and "If you find something you love to do, you'll never work again."

I always wanted to drive a truck. When asked what I wanted for Christmas or a birthday, my request was always "a truck." I often thought a fun afternoon was sitting by a nearby interstate in Ohio and watching the trucks.

In 1979, at the age of 20, I landed my first job within the industry. It was pumping fuel at a truck stop in Monroeville, Ohio. On my first day an owner-operator came in and asked me to check the oil on the tractor. I quickly agreed, but knew I had to tell the truck driver that I didn't know how to raise the hood or check his oil. The owner-operator smiled and said, "C'mon on, I'll help you." Even with a job that only entailed fueling up semis, my love for trucks grew.

One month after turning 21, I completed a tractor-trailer training program and landed my first job as a truck driver with Midwestern Distribution out of Fort Scott, Kansas. The fact that they were paying me, was just icing on the cake. Unbelievably, I had the chance to travel down the same interstate as the one I used to sit at as a young boy. My first job was fulfilling a childhood dream.

I drove for Midwestern Distribution for six months and then hired on with Sam Tanksley Trucking located out of Cape Girardeau, Missouri. My favorite part of Sam Tanksley was their new equipment. I loved the freedom of the road—meeting new people, but mostly I just loved the trucks.

In the early '80s, I took a break from being on the road to serve my country and completed a tour in the U.S. Navy. Afterwards I completed a bachelor's degree in accounting from Cedarville University in 1987. Soon

my degree landed me a job in the accounting field, but I soon realized I couldn't stay at a desk job for long. So again I went back on the road with Davis Cartage Company out of Corunna, Michigan.

It was the perfect job, due to now having a wife and young family at home. Davis Cartage could get me home on most weekends. I was again doing the job I loved. I did take a short break to work in the office at Davis Cartage's Accounts Receivables and Accounts Payable Department. While working this job, I completed my master's degree in business administration in 1993. I also took another short job as the Office Manager for TransNational in Haslett, Michigan.

At this point I had pursued many jobs, but not my ultimate dream of becoming an owner-operator. While working part-time at Baker College as a truck-driving instructor, it allowed me the opportunity to work as an owner-operator. In 2003, I purchased a 1997 Kenworth. For two-and-a-half years, I again would often comment, "I can't believe they are paying me to do this job."

I can't believe they pay me to do something I really love.

Since 2006, I have held many different positions at Baker College and am currently the System Program Coordinator overseeing all truck-driver training.

REVIEW QUESTIONS

1. Regarding public relations, who are the front-line public relations persons for the trucking industry?

   a. the owners of the trucking companies

   b. the professional drivers

   c. the dispatchers

   d. dock personnel

2. In interpersonal communications, ideas are sent and received, using _____.

   a. gestures

   b. text messages

   c. language

   d. symbols

   ALL

3. Regarding contact with the public, most conflicts occur _____.

   a. while sharing the road

   b. because truck is in poor repair

   c. because of road work crews

   d. because of state regulations

4. Regarding good customer relations, the _____ has more contact with customers than any other person in the company.

   a. dispatcher

   b. professional driver

   c. company owner

   d. office manager

5. Which of the following is not a basic job requirement for a professional driver?

   a. meet the requirements of federal law, including the medical qualifications and having the correct CDL

   b. meet the employer's needs and qualifications as stated in the company policy

   c. know all the federal laws regarding the trucking industry

   d. know about trucking's history and have the attitudes and interests suited to its environment

6. According to FMCSR, which of the following will not disqualify an operator of a tractor-trailer rig from driving?

   a. operating a CMV while under the influence of alcohol, amphetamines, or narcotics

   b. being in an accident that results in injury or death and leaving the scene

   c. speeding

   d. conviction of a felony involving the use of a CMV

7. Regarding state, federal, or local regulations, a driver can _____.

   a. not be required to violate these regulations

   b. violate these regulations if told to do so by the dispatcher

   c. violate these regulations if told to do so by the shipper

   d. violate these regulations if told to do so by the owner

8. Which of the following is key to a professional driver's success on the job?

   a. cheerful personality

   b. dependability

   c. good grooming

   d. a and b

9. Regarding opportunities for advancement in the trucking industry, advancements usually come from _____.

   a. other carriers

   b. shippers

   c. hard work and effort

   d. driver training schools

10. When being interviewed for a job, research the company before the interview. Then, if you have questions, it is best to _____.

   a. ask them during the interview
   b. wait until you get the job and then ask questions
   c. look for the answer on the Internet
   d. ask other drivers

11. Interpersonal communication includes sending and receiving messages between two or more individuals. This can include _____.

   a. electronic messages
   b. listening
   c. body language
   d. all of the above

SUPPLEMENTAL LEARNING ACTIVITIES

1. In a role play, make your words say something that doesn't match your nonverbal communications. Start with "I love the way you're dressed" as your spoken message. Also try, "Oh yes sir, I'm happy to move that freight from this door to one 10 doors down."

2. In a 100-word essay, discuss why people, in general, don't like to be confronted with a mistake they've made—and tell how you would soften the conversation with good interpersonal communications skills.

3. In your opinion, why do you think some members of the general public have bad opinions of truck drivers? Share your opinion with a small group and then create a list of the group's top 10 reasons.

4. On a job interview, what are the top five things to remember? Discuss this with the class and practice these in role plays.

5. After a job interview, it is good job search etiquette to write the interviewer a note of thanks. Practice writing this note, as an individual or as a class. Make certain your note is genuine and reflects your sincere appreciation.

FOR MORE INFORMATION

PTDI—Use Effective Communications, Page 26, Click on Skill Standards
www.ptdi.org/standards

Job Search Tips
jobsearch.about.com/cs/jobsearchhelp/a/jobtips.htm

Bureau of Labor Statistics—Job Interview Tips
www.bls.gov/oco/oco20045.htm

Public Relations Tips
www.mindtools.com/CommSkll/FirstImpressions.htm

Professional Driving Careers
www.ehow.com/list_6557208_professional-driving-careers.html

For additional job opportunities (and these are only a few sites of many):

Class A Drivers Jobs
www.classadrivers.com

National Truck Driving Jobs
www.nationaltruckdrivingjobs.com

34 Driver Health, Safety, and Security

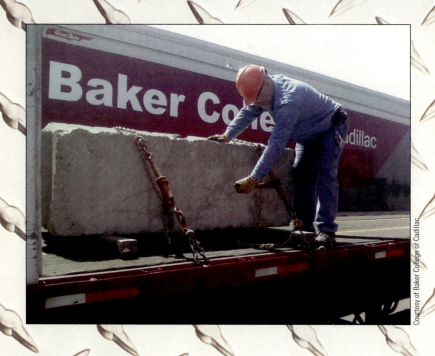

Courtesy of Baker College of Cadillac.

OBJECTIVES

When you have completed this chapter, you should be able to:

- Understand the demands and health requirements of professional driving.

- Describe the causes and cures of fatigue, and how it can affect your ability to drive safely.

- Explain the FMCSR regarding drug and alcohol use.

- Know the benefits of a healthy diet, regular exercise, and plenty of rest.

- Understand the factors and causes of the different types of stress on the job.

INTRODUCTION

A major challenge for every professional driver is that of staying healthy—and "healthy" means more than eating the right diet, getting enough rest, getting exercise a few times a week, and avoiding stress. Staying healthy means doing all of these and anything else you can do, including regular physicals, vision and hearing exams, plus a healthy lifestyle—all to maintain good health, a positive outlook, and time for a satisfying career (**see Figure 34-1**).

▶ **Figure 34-1**

A healthy lifestyle contributes to excellence in job performance.

A 2007 study published in the *Journal of the American Dietetic Association* found 86 percent of an estimated 3.2 million truck drivers in the U.S. are overweight or obese. In 2010, the Healthy Trucking Association of America, an industry organization based in Montgomery, Alabama, conducted a blood pressure screening of more than 2,000 drivers at an annual trucking conference. Twenty-one of those tested were sent directly to a local emergency room and one driver suffered a heart attack on the way to the hospital.

That same year, 2010, heavy truck and tractor-trailer drivers accounted for 13 percent of all fatal occupational injuries, according to preliminary data from the Bureau of Labor Statistics—and a 2010 report from the Federal Motor Carriers Safety Administration found that 87 percent of crashes involving truckers stemmed, to some degree, from driver error. Twelve percent of these crashes occurred because the driver was asleep, in diabetic shock, had a heart attack, or suffered from some other health problem.

As a professional driver, staying healthy means adjusting your lifestyle (your personal habits) to support the demands of your job as a professional driver. For some, hours on the road means making certain **diet and exercise** are in balance. It means making sure you get exercise, no matter where you are on the road—and it means eating at regular times and eating a healthy diet, low in salt and fried foods, and high in protein and other nutrients. A **DOT physical examination** is required that professional drivers must pass every two years (**see Figure 34-2**). If the applicant is on any type of prescribed medication, they will only receive a one year DOT physical.

Nowhere will you find being able to drive down the road, balancing a bag of chips in one hand, a soft drink in your cup holder, and a bag of chocolate cookies on the passenger's seat as a required skill for professional drivers.

Getting enough rest is also paramount to your good health. Today's drivers should avoid fatigue at all costs, and, although it goes without saying, it is worth mentioning that professional drivers should also avoid using alcohol and drugs at all costs on the job or prior to going on the road.

The Federal Motor Carrier Safety Regulations address alcohol, drugs, and fatigue. Knowing what these laws say is mandatory if you want to keep your license and maintain your career and your paycheck.

The purpose of this chapter is to explain these laws and to give you information to help you "be the best you can be" behind the wheel, at home, and in all parts of your life.

NOTE

As a veteran driver pointed out, "Two of the largest hurdles new drivers must face and overcome are having to sleep while someone else is driving or attempting to sleep in a noisy truck stop. Both lead to poor quality of sleep."

PHYSICAL REQUIREMENTS FOR INTERSTATE TRUCKERS

- Vision

  20/40 vision

  Peripheral vision—at least 70 degrees in each eye

  Distinguish red and green

  Eye check every 24 months

- Hearing

  Hear forced whisper at 5 feet (1.5 m)

- Stamina

  To meet job requirements (e.g., loading and unloading)

- Disqualifications

  Loss of limb(s) or disease that limits limbs

Chronic illness that seriously affects driving

Examples:

- Diabetes
- Heart disease
- Alcoholism

- Required physical examination

  Every 2 years

  At carrier's discretion

  After serious injury or illness

- Certification by physician

  Must be carried at all times

  As important as driver's license

© Cengage Learning 2013

▶ Figure 34-2

Professional drivers are required to pass the DOT physical examination AJ65 every 2 years.

OVERVIEW

In 2010, according to reports from the Centers for Disease Control and Prevention, overall U.S. life expectancy dropped a tenth of a year to 77.8. It's down by a fifth of a year in white men and women but up to 70 years for black men—an all-time high, compared to a 2006 life expectancy of 69 years. Canadians born in 2010 may live to celebrate nearly 81 birthdays on average, a Statistics Canada report in February 2010 on life expectancy suggests.

The 2010 Statistics Canada report on births and deaths in Canada also showed life expectancy at birth reached 80.7 years for the three-year period between 2005 and 2007, up 0.2 years from an average of 80.5 between 2004 and 2006. In 1995 to 1997, life expectancy at birth was 78.4—and Canadians over 65, in particular, can expect to live longer.

To determine how professional drivers compared to the U.S. population in general, researchers asked drivers about their lifestyles and their health habits at a trucking transportation convention a few years ago.

The following data gathered from 3,000 North American drivers at an industry trade show tell us much about driver lifestyles **(see Figure 34-3)**.

Traditionally, health habits of professional drivers have not been stellar **(see Figure 34-4)**. In fact, older drivers in the current driver population may be headed, at breakneck speed, toward a collision with serious (and possibly career-ending) health problems.

HEALTH OF U.S. POPULATION COMPARED TO NORTH AMERICAN DRIVERS

Activity	U.S. Population	North American Drivers
Smoking	27%	49%
Obesity (heavy-set)	33%	73%
High blood pressure (hypertension)	26%	33%
Poor eating habits	80%	80%
Exercise regularly	25%	8%

© Cengage Learning 2013

▶ **Figure 34-3**
Population health activities breakdown.

▶ **Figure 34-4**
Health habits make a difference in how you feel and how well you do your job.

▶ **Figure 34-5**
A professional driver must keep his or her truck in good condition so it runs smoothly and ensures a safe trip. The same applies to your body.

How to Change the Current Health Trends

A professional driver knows what has to be done to keep a truck running smoothly and to ensure a safe trip **(see Figure 34-5)**. Each part and each system contributes to keeping the vehicle operating safely.

The same principle is true for the body. To keep the body healthy and running smoothly, the driver must have—or develop—good eating habits, regular exercise, the proper amount of sleep, and a plan to manage stress.

Today, some carriers, industry organizations, and a few truck stops are offering initiatives to help truckers improve their health, stay in shape, and slim down. Carriers are holding seminars on improving health, building on-site gyms, and bringing nutritionists and fitness trainers to work with professional drivers. Some offer financial incentives to employees who stop smoking or lose weight.

The Truckload Carriers Association is working with a clinic, specializing in weight loss, that offers a nutrition and exercise program for the trucking community. An organization called Rolling Strong offers health and wellness programs for truckers across the country. All are working to improve driver health.

DRIVER NUTRITION

Poor Eating Habits Common among Professional Drivers

Long hours behind the wheel, varying work cycles, and being away from home are factors that contribute to poor eating habits for professional drivers; however, these habits can be changed with a little effort (**see Figure 34-6**). Otherwise, you will fall into the same habits as those drivers who now are dealing with health problems such as obesity, diabetes, heart disease, and sleep apnea.

© Cengage Learning 2013

▶ Figure 34-6
Driver preparing for the road.

Try to avoid:

- Eating foods high in fat content (1 ounce of fat contains 2-1/2 times the calories of 1 ounce of protein or carbohydrates)
- Eating fried foods
- Eating breaded fried foods such as fried fish and chicken-fried steak
- Eating gravies and sauces, as most have high fat content
- Eating too much salt
- Not eating enough vegetables and fruits
- Not eating enough foods high in fiber content
- Not drinking enough water
- Snacking on cookies and doughnuts

Helpful Hints for Good Nutrition

To increase your opportunities to look good, feel good, and handle your job efficiently, try to:

- Reduce amount of fast foods
- Avoid fried foods
- Eat roasted or baked meats
- Remove the skin from chicken
- Use nonfat spreads on breads and potatoes
- Take a portable cooler or refrigerator on the road (more economical than restaurants)
- Eat breakfast from your cooler (yogurt, banana, apple, fruit juice)

- Carry snacks in your cooler (fruits, such as apples, bananas, peaches, plums, grapes, raisins; raw vegetables such as celery, carrots, green or yellow squash, bell peppers)
- Drink seltzer, low-fat milk, vegetable juice, ice tea, or water
- Choose a salad bar for one of your daily meals and use nonfat dressings
- Avoid desserts, as many are high in fat content and sugar

WHAT ABOUT EXERCISE?

To keep your body running as smoothly as your rig, you must have a total exercise program. A total exercise program consists of movement, strength training, and development of flexibility.

"I wonder how many laps I have to do around my rig to work off that cheeseburger I ate for lunch?!"

© Cengage Learning 2013

Movement can be any activity that is done briskly, including walking, swimming, playing basketball, rope jumping, mowing the grass, hiking, playing golf, riding a bike, or any number of other activities.

Walking is a good exercise choice for every driver of every age because it requires no special facilities or equipment—only a pair of shoes, an open space, and a professional driver with a desire to stay healthy. If time allows, walk around the truck stop. Maybe even make several trips around.

Effects of Physical Activity on Health and Disease

With a minimum of 30 minutes of exercise per day, you can do much to stay healthy and feel good while on the road. Always get clearance from a physician before beginning an exercise program.

The following is what you can achieve by adding physical activity to your daily routine:

- *Overall mortality:* high to moderate levels of regular physical activity are associated with lower mortality rates.
- *Cardiovascular diseases:* regular physical activity decreases the risk of cardiovascular diseases and prevents or delays the development of **high blood pressure** and reduces blood pressure in persons with hypertension.
- *Cancer:* regular physical activity is associated with a decreased risk of colon cancer.

- *Diabetes:* regular physical activity lowers the risk of developing diabetes.
- *Osteoporosis:* physical activity is essential for maintaining peak bone mass in adults.
- *Falling:* reduces the risk of falling due to increased strength and balance.
- *Obesity:* reduces obesity by increasing the amount of calories used.
- *Mental health:* reduces and relieves the symptoms of stress, makes you look better, and feel better.
- *Low-back pain decreases:* research has shown that strong low-back muscles are less prone to injury.

HOW TO CHOOSE A SAFE, QUIET TRUCK STOP

Getting a good night's rest is imperative if you want to be at your best behind the wheel the next day—and often a good night's rest depends on selecting a safe, quiet truck stop along your route.

According to a survey of more than 2,000 professional drivers, conducted as the "National Truck Parking Survey by UDOT Systems Planning and Programming," both male and female drivers:

- Prefer parking facilities with fuel, food, restrooms, and showers that are safe and convenient.
- Six percent preferred rest areas for quick naps—no more than two hours.
- Ninety percent preferred truck stops for resting, eating, doing laundry, truck repairs, and other activities.
- Preferred "basic amenities" included safe, clean facilities where drivers can eat a meal, take a shower, and get some uninterrupted sleep.
- Ninety-eight percent of the drivers said it was their decision where to park, and 21 percent decide where to stop before starting their trip.

Tips for Staying Safe at Truck Stops—from Veteran Drivers

Depending on the time and place, truck stops may be as safe as your own home or as dangerous as your worst nightmare. Staying safe depends on you—but here are some tips to make it easier:

- Most truck stops are relatively safe. Truck stops around big cities generally are not as safe as truck stops near rural communities.
- According to veteran professionals, you should always watch your back, no matter where you stop.
- You've probably heard of "lot lizards"—or ladies of the evening. But, according to veteran drivers, it's not the lot lizards you have to worry about; it's other types of crime and violence. Usually, you just tell a lot lizard to go away and she leaves you alone.
- Many truck stops now have surveillance of their parking lots. Park in a lighted area and make sure to double-check your locks, particularly when you leave your truck.
- Be aware of your surroundings. Don't leave your truck unattended if at all possible. Dinnertime is when the highest rate of theft occurs—everyone is inside eating and away from their trucks. If you're a team driver, one member of your team should stay in the cab during eating breaks.
- Physical barriers will help secure cargo; air break locks, often called "glad hand" lock, will keep theft down—if they can't drive off, thieves won't be able to move the trailer. Use kingpin locks if trailer and load are separated. Installing a locking bar across the trailer will help.
- Don't discuss your load in the truck stop, on the radio, or anywhere else, especially if you're hauling high-target loads like pharmaceuticals, electronics, or hazmat.
- If you're hauling an empty trailer, be particularly vigilant about keeping the trailer locked so that others cannot hitch a free ride.
- Let people know where you are: your dispatcher, spouse, friends, coworkers, etc. Have an emergency contact and check in with that person often. Someone who hasn't heard from you will look for you.

JOB STRESS

Being a professional driver can be very stressful. Tight schedules, heavy traffic, higher costs of fuel, construction zones, crabby shippers, and aggressive four-wheelers all lead to driver stress. Many drivers also report experiencing a high level of stress involving their families because of the complexities of today's society.

Definition of Job Stress

The National Institute for Occupational Safety and Health (NIOSH), the federal agency responsible for conducting research and making recommendations for prevention of work-related illness and injury, defines **job stress** as:

> The harmful physical and emotional responses that occur when the requirements of a job do not match the capabilities, resources, or needs of the worker.

Causes of Job Stress

Nearly all experts agree that job stress results from the interaction of the worker and the conditions of work. The exposure of stressful working conditions can have a direct influence on workers' safety and health.

The following job conditions may lead to stress:

- *The design of the task:* heavy workloads, infrequent rest breaks, long hours, and hectic and routine tasks.
- *Management styles:* lack of participation by workers in decision making, poor communications in the organization, lack of family-friendly policies.
- *Interpersonal relations:* poor social environment and lack of support or help from coworkers and supervisors. If a driver is a "people person," this could be a real problem. Some companies are addressing this problem by letting family members accompany the driver.
- *Career concerns:* job insecurity and lack of opportunities for growth, advancement, or promotion. Many drivers feel there is little room for advancement or promotion in the industry. Some prefer to work for themselves, buy a rig, and become a contract driver.
- *Environmental conditions:* unpleasant or dangerous physical conditions such as crowding, noise, air pollution, or ergonomic problems. Such factors as aggressive drivers, poor sleeping conditions, heavy traffic, bad weather, miles and miles of construction, diets high in fat content, and lack of exercise lead to stress for the professional driver.

After looking at any of these working conditions, it is obvious that being a professional driver is a very stressful job. Yet, with proper diet, regular exercise, plenty of rest, and maintaining a regular schedule, life on the road can be not only comfortable but also rewarding.

Job Stress and Its Toll on Your Health

Medical authorities tell us there is a relationship between job stress and health and report the following:

> *Cardiovascular disease:* psychologically demanding jobs that allow employees little control over the work process increases the risk of cardiovascular diseases.

> *Musculoskeletal disorders:* it is believed that job stress increases the risk of development of back and upper-extremity disorders.

> *Psychological disorders:* several studies suggest that job stress leads to job burnout.

> *Workplace injury:* there is some indication that stressful working conditions interfere with safe working practices and set the stage for injuries at work.

> *Cancer, ulcer, and impaired immune functions:* some studies indicate a relationship between stressful working conditions and these health problems.

Family Stress

Not only does a professional driver experience stress on the job, but many also have family situations that cause additional stress.

One veteran driver put the impact on stress from work and/or family this way: "I often associate truck driving to a 'coffee pot.' While driving, things tend to percolate/trickle. Possible stress at home, a dispatcher makes a remark you misinterpret and all day long—as you drive—you analyze what was said and often come to wrong conclusions. Then a motorist cuts you off in traffic and you boil over or experience road rage!"

CAUTION!

When the driver is gone for long periods of time, relationships with his or her children will probably change and the significant other that remains at home will have to assume family duties that the driver may have performed. Whatever your family/support system situation, regular communication, patience, and understanding—on both sides of the phone—will make the situation much more enjoyable and less stressful.

© iStockphoto/LivingImages

▶ **Figure 34-7**

Family situations can be a cause of stress for professional drivers.

The professional driver probably will miss many of the children's important events, such as birthdays, school activities, and athletic events (**see Figure 34-7**) or drivers may not be at home to help in the event of illnesses or accidents. Missing the important events in a child's life may cause anger in the child and cause the driver-parent to feel guilty. This then causes stress in the family.

The significant other who remains at home may experience major changes in their role within the family. With the driver gone, the partner must perform all the child-rearing duties such as attending school and athletic events and taking care of the children in the event of illness or accident.

In addition to caring for the children, the partner often has to deal with household emergencies such as stopped-up sewer lines and car repairs. Dealing with these issues sometimes makes the stay-at-home partner frustrated and angry. The driver may feel guilty for not being at home to help with such emergencies. This causes more stress in the family.

Many family therapists say the best thing a family can do to reduce stress is to make a greater effort to communicate.

Some drivers use cell phones and call home each day. Many drivers send e-mail messages daily to the family. Some companies allow significant others and/or children to go on the road with the driver.

What You Can Do About Job Stress

Fortunately, **stress management** strategies continue to be effective in lowering stress on the job.

Most medical experts agree that the following activities help reduce stress:

- Have a balance between work and family or personal life. Depending on your employer, you may opt to drive routes that do not require your being away from home more than a few nights each week. If you do not have this option, try to stay in contact with friends and family members by telephone or e-mail. Skype and Facetime also offer an inexpensive method to do video phone calls. Some companies allow family members to accompany the driver on the road, and this adds to the balance a driver needs between work and personal life.

- Develop a supportive network of friends and coworkers. This is another area that is very helpful to the professional driver, since the driver is on the road so much that there is little time to interact with friends and coworkers.

- A special warning to drivers: With AIDS and the increase of antibiotic-resistant sexually transmitted diseases, it would be to a driver's advantage to avoid any encounters with strangers while on or off the road.

- Eat a low-fat diet mostly of green vegetables, beans, legumes, fruit, rice, pasta, cereals, and low-fat milk and yogurt. This is one area where a professional driver has control. As previously stated, eat breakfast and snacks from foods in your cooler or refrigerator, and avoid fast and fried foods. Have one meal per day from a salad bar. Use the Food Guide Pyramid to help make wise food choices.

- Walk 30 minutes a day, 5 days per week. This is another area where the driver has control. Walking 30 minutes per day will drain stress and make the driver feel better. Some drivers report that their walk done in the morning helps to jump-start their day. Be safety conscious while walking just as you are when you are driving.

- Have a positive outlook and take time to relax. This is another area where the professional driver has control. Many medical authorities think taking time out to relax and having a positive attitude is the most effective way to reduce stress.

ALCOHOLISM AND DRUG ABUSE

It does not require rocket science to understand that drinking, drugs, and driving do not mix. According to the rules and regulations governing professional drivers, those who use alcohol and drugs—particularly while or before they are scheduled to drive—will lose their licenses and their ability to drive professionally (**see Figure 34-8**).

MYTHS AND TRUTHS ABOUT ALCOHOL	
Myth	**Truth**
Alcohol increases mental and physical ability.	Nonsense. It decreases both. A person under the influence of alcohol usually thinks he or she is doing better than they really are.
Some people can drink without being affected.	Not true. Any person who drinks is affected by alcohol. Some persons may be slower to show the effects because of greater body weight or experience.
If you eat a lot before drinking, you will not get drunk.	Not true. Food will slow down the absorption of alcohol, but it will not prevent it.
Coffee and fresh air will help a drinker sober up.	Not true. Only time will help a drinker sober up. Other methods just do not work.
Stick with beer—it is not as strong as wine or whiskey.	False. There is the same amount of alcohol in a 12-ounce glass of 5% beer, 5-ounce glass of 12% wine, or 1-1/2-ounce shot of 80-proof liquor.

© Cengage Learning 2013

▶ **Figure 34–8**

Drinking and driving do not mix.

© Cengage Learning 2013

1 1/2 oz. Liquor   5 1/2 oz. Glass of Wine   12 oz. Can of Beer

▶ **Figure 34–9**

All forms of alcohol have the same effect and can cause you to lose your CDL if you drink and drive.

Besides loss of income or a career, the use of alcohol and drugs also costs users their health.

More than 100,000 Americans die each year as a result of alcohol abuse, and alcohol is a factor in more than half of the country's traffic accidents, homicides, and suicides (**see Figure 34-9**). In purely economic terms, alcohol-related problems cost society approximately $185 billion per year. In human terms, the costs cannot be calculated.

Moderate alcohol use—up to two drinks per day for men and one drink per day for women and older people—is not usually harmful for most adults. A standard drink is one 12-ounce bottle or can of either beer or wine cooler, one 5-ounce glass of wine, or 1.5 ounces of 80-proof distilled spirits. Nonetheless, a large number of people get into serious trouble because of their drinking. Currently, nearly 14 million Americans—one in every 13 adults—abuse alcohol or are an alcoholic **(see Figure 34-10).**

BAC	EFFECTS
.01–.04	Judgment and inhibitions are slightly affected. Drinker is more relaxed, sociable, and talkative. Some risk if drinker drives.
.05–.09	Judgment, vision, and coordination are affected. Behavior changes. Drinker has false sense of security. Serious risk if drinker drives.
.10 and over	Judgment, vision, and coordination are seriously affected. Drinker is not able to drive safely because of dangerously lessened abilities.

© Cengage Learning 2013

▶ **Figure 34–10**

Effects of alcohol on blood alcohol concentration increases.

The toll of alcohol on physical health can range from mild mood changes to complete loss of coordination, vision, balance, and speech. Any of these can signal a temporary poisoning of the system called "acute alcohol intoxication or drunkenness."

For most people, these effects usually wear off in several hours after the person has stopped drinking; however, a .08 percentage of alcohol in the bloodstream is considered by many law enforcement agencies as evidence of intoxication.

Alcohol abuse is defined as a pattern of drinking that results in one or more of the following situations within a 12-month period:

■ Failure to fulfill major work, school, or home responsibilities

■ Drinking in situations that are physically dangerous, such as while driving a car or operating machinery

■ Having recurring alcohol-related legal problems, such as being arrested for driving under the influence of alcohol or for physically hurting someone while drunk

■ Continued drinking despite having ongoing relationship problems that are caused or worsened by the drinking

Although alcohol abuse is basically different from **alcoholism,** many effects of alcohol abuse are also experienced by alcoholics.

A person's physical dependence on alcohol may or may not be obvious to other people. While some chronic alcoholics get very drunk, others exercise enough control to give the appearance of coping with everyday affairs in a near-normal way. However, alcoholism can lead to a number of physical ailments, including hypoglycemia, brain and heart damage, enlarged blood vessels in the skin, chronic stomach inflammation, and the more damaging inflammation of the pancreas.

Alcoholism often causes impotence in men, damage to the unborn child in a pregnant mother, and an increased risk of cancer of the voice box, esophagus, stomach, pancreas, and upper gastro-intestinal tract.

> **CAUTION!**
> The alcoholic's continual craving for alcohol makes halting the use of alcohol extremely difficult. The alcoholic's condition is also complicated by denying that she or he has a serious problem.

Although alcoholism can be treated, a cure is not yet available. In other words, even if an alcoholic has been sober for a long time and has regained good health, he or she remains susceptible to relapse and must continue to avoid all alcoholic beverages. "Cutting down" on drinking does not work. Cutting out alcohol is necessary for a successful recovery.

Drug Abuse

In the year 2000, illegal drug use cost America close to $161 billion, including $110 billion in lost productivity, $12.9 billion in health care costs, and $35 billion in other costs, such as efforts to stem the flow of drugs.

Beyond the raw numbers are other costs to society:

- Spread of infectious diseases such as HIV/AIDS and hepatitis C either through sharing of drug paraphernalia or unprotected sex
- Deaths due to overdose or other complications from drug use
- Effects on unborn children of pregnant drug users
- Other effects such as crime and homelessness

Drug addiction is a complex brain disease. It is characterized by drug craving, seeking, and using drugs that persist even in the face of extremely negative consequences. Drug seeking becomes compulsive, in large part, as a result of the effects of prolonged drug use on brain functioning and thus on behavior. For many people, drug addiction becomes chronic, with relapses possible even after long periods of abstinence.

Each drug has short-term and long-term physical effects; stimulants such as cocaine increase heart rate and blood pressure, whereas opioids such as heroin may slow the heart rate and reduce respiration.

NOTE

Employed drug abusers cost employers about twice as much in medical and worker compensation claims as their drug-free coworkers (information provided by the National Institute on Drug Abuse).

Commonly abused drugs include alcohol, cocaine, club drugs, heroine, inhalants, LSD, marijuana, methamphetamine, ecstasy, nicotine, PCP, prescription drugs, and steroids.

Addiction begins with drug abuse when an individual makes a conscious choice to use drugs, but addiction is not just "a lot of drug use." Recent scientific research provides overwhelming evidence that, at some point, changes occur in the brain that can turn drug abuse into addiction, a chronic relapsing illness. Those addicted to drugs suffer from a compulsive drug craving and usage and cannot quit by themselves. Treatment is necessary to end this compulsive behavior.

Random Drug Testing

FMCSR 382 outlines the purpose and procedure for carriers to establish programs designed to help prevent accidents and injuries resulting from the misuse of alcohol or use of controlled substances by drivers of commercial motor vehicles (see Figure 34-11).

According to this ruling:

- No driver shall report for duty or remain on duty requiring the performance of safety-sensitive functions while having an alcohol concentration of .04 or greater.

- No employer having actual knowledge that a driver has an alcohol concentration of .04 or greater shall permit the driver to perform or continue to perform safety-sensitive functions.

- No driver shall use alcohol while performing safety-sensitive functions. No employer having actual knowledge that a driver is using alcohol while performing safety-sensitive functions shall permit the driver to perform or continue to perform safety-sensitive functions.

▶ Figure 34-11

The Federal Motor Carrier Safety Regulations provide guidelines for establishing programs to help prevent substance abuse-related accidents.

- No driver shall perform safety-sensitive functions within 4 hours after using alcohol. No employer having actual knowledge that a driver has used alcohol within 4 hours shall permit a driver to perform or continue to perform safety-sensitive functions.

- No driver required to take a post-accident alcohol test shall use alcohol for 8 hours following the accident, or until he/she undergoes a post-accident alcohol test, whichever occurs first.

- No driver shall refuse to submit to a postaccident alcohol or controlled substances test, a random alcohol or controlled substances test, a reasonable suspicion alcohol or controlled substances test, or a follow-up alcohol or controlled substances test. No employer shall permit a driver who refuses to submit to such tests to perform or continue to perform safety-sensitive functions.

- No driver shall report for duty or remain on duty requiring the performance of safety-sensitive functions when the driver uses any controlled substance, except when the use is pursuant to the instructions of a licensed medical practitioner who has advised the driver that the substance will not adversely affect the driver's ability to safely operate a commercial motor vehicle.

- No driver shall report for duty, remain on duty, or perform a safety-sensitive function if the driver tests positive or has adulterated or substituted a test specimen for controlled substances.

- No employer having actual knowledge that a driver has tested positive or has adulterated or substituted a test specimen for controlled substances shall permit the driver to perform or continue to perform safety-sensitive functions.

Testing Requirements

Preemployment Testing

Prior to the first time a driver performs safety-sensitive functions for an employer, the driver shall undergo testing for controlled substances as a condition prior to being used. No employer shall allow a driver to perform safety-sensitive functions unless the employer has received a controlled substances test result indicating a verified negative test result for that driver.

Postaccident Testing

As soon as practicable following an accident involving a commercial motor vehicle operating on a public road in commerce, each employer shall test each of its surviving drivers for alcohol.

Return-to-Duty Testing

Return-to-duty testing is a means of enabling employees to come back to work after testing positive for drugs of abuse and subsequently completing an employee assistance program and/or similar **substance abuse** recovery program.

Follow-up Testing

Employees returning to work following treatment for drug and/or alcohol abuse will be subject to unannounced follow-up alcohol and/or controlled substance testing as directed by a substance abuse professional. Employees with a follow-up test result indicating some alcohol concentration shall be subject to disciplinary action including probable dismissal from employment. Employees with a follow-up test result indicating a positive controlled substance result shall be subject to termination from employment.

Random Alcohol and Drug Testing

Every driver shall submit to **random alcohol and controlled substance testing**. The selection of drivers for random alcohol and controlled substances testing shall be made by a scientifically valid method, such as a random number table or a computer-based random number generator that is matched with drivers' Social Security numbers, payroll identification numbers, or other comparable identifying numbers. These tests will be unannounced.

Reasonable Suspicion Testing

An employer shall require a driver to submit to an alcohol test when the employer has reasonable suspicion to believe that the driver has violated the FMCSR. The employer's determination that reasonable suspicion exists to require the driver to undergo an alcohol test must be based on specific observations concerning the appearance, behavior, speech, or body odors of the driver.

An employer shall require a driver to submit to a controlled substances test when the employer has reasonable suspicion to believe that the driver has violated the prohibitions of the FMCSR concerning controlled substances. The employer's determination that reasonable suspicion exists to require the driver to undergo a controlled substances test must be based on specific observations concerning the appearance, behavior, speech, or body odors of the driver. The observations may include indications of the chronic and withdrawal effects of controlled substances.

FOR U.S. DRIVERS, A DOT PHYSICAL IS REQUIRED EVERY TWO YEARS

Regulation 391.43 of the Federal Motor Carrier Safety Administration's regulations outlines the medical examination for professional drivers that must be done every two years.

© iStockphoto/asiseeit

▶ Figure 34-12

The requirement of a DOT physical every two years helps assure that only healthy professional drivers are on the road.

The purpose of the history taken by the examiner and the physical examination conducted by the examiner is to detect the presence of any physical and mental defects. A history of certain defects may be cause for rejection or may indicate the need for making certain lab tests or a closer examination (**see Figure 34-12**).

Defects may be recorded that do not, because of their character or degree, indicate that certification of physical fitness should be denied. However, these defects should be discussed with the driver and he or she advised to take the necessary steps to ensure correction, particularly in the case of neglect it could lead to a condition that could affect his or her ability to drive safely.

MEDICAL CERTIFICATION REQUIREMENTS: A GUIDE FOR COMMERCIAL DRIVER'S LICENSE HOLDERS

NOTE: According to FMCSA, starting January 30, 2012 and no later than January 30, 2014, all CDL holders must provide information to their State Driver Licensing Agency regarding the type of commercial motor vehicle operation they drive in or expect to drive in with their CDL. Drivers operating in certain types of commerce will be required to submit a current medical examiner's certificate to their SDLA to obtain a "certified" medical status as part of their driving record. CDL holders required to have a "certified" medical status who fail to provide and keep up-to-date their medical examiner's certificate with their SDLA will become "not-certified" and they may lose their CDL.

For specific State by State requirements for drivers and information related to how a State is handling the Medical Certification requirements, and to determine who to contact for additional information, click on the following link: www.aamva.org/aamva/DocumentDisplay.aspx?id={687D99D3-FFB5-4B76-BD6F-F5EF54728BE0

What is changing? State driver licensing agencies (SDLAs) will be adding your medical certification status and the information on your medical examiner's certificate to your Commercial driver's license system (CDLIS) record.

What is not changing? The driver physical qualification requirements are not changing.

What are CDL holders required to do?

1. You must determine what type of commerce you operate in. You must certify to your SDLA to one of the four types of commerce you operate in as listed below,

   - **Interstate non-excepted**: You are an Interstate non-excepted driver and must meet the Federal DOT medical card requirements (e.g. – you are "not excepted").

   - **Interstate excepted**: You are an Interstate excepted driver and do not have to meet the Federal DOT medical card requirements.

   - **Intrastate non-excepted**: You are an Intrastate non-excepted driver and are required to meet the medical requirements for your state.

   - **Intrastate excepte**d: You are an Intrastate excepted driver and do not have to meet the medical requirements for your state.

2. If you are subject to the DOT medical card requirements, provide a copy of each new DOT medical card to your state driver licensing agency prior to the expiration of the current DOT medical card.

The following parts should be completed by the medical examiner performing the physical:

Appearance: the examiner is directed to note any overweight, any posture defect, perceptible limp, tremor, or other defects that could be caused by alcoholism, thyroid intoxication, or other illness.

The FMCSR provides that no driver shall use a narcotic or other habit-forming drugs.

Head-eyes: if the applicant wears corrective lenses, these should be used during the visual testing. If the driver habitually wears contact lenses while driving, there should be sufficient evidence to indicate that he or she has good tolerance and is well adapted to their use. The use of contacts should be noted on the record.

Drivers who have lost one eye are not qualified to operate commercial vehicles under existing FMCSRs.

Ears: note any evidence of middle ear disease, symptoms of dizziness, or Meniere's syndrome. When recording hearing, record distance from patient at which a forced whispered voice can first be heard. If an audiometer is used to test hearing, record decibel loss at 500 Hz, 1,000 Hz, and 2,000 Hz.

Throat: note any evidence of disease, deformities of the throat likely to interfere with eating or breathing, or any condition of the larynx that could interfere with the safe operation of a CMV.

Chest and heart: stethoscopic examination is required. Note murmurs and arrhythmias and any past or present history of cardiovascular disease of a variety known to be accompanied by syncope, dypsnea, collapse, enlarged heart, or congestive heart failures. EKG is required when stethoscopic findings so indicate.

Blood pressure: record using a blood pressure cuff. If the blood pressure is consistently above 160/90 mm Hg, further tests may be necessary to determine whether driver is qualified to operate CMV.

Lungs: if lung disease is detected, state whether active or arrested. If arrested, you must give your opinion as to how long it has been arrested.

Gastrointestinal system: note any diseases of the esophagus, stomach, small or large intestine.

Abdomen: note any wounds, scars, injuries, or weakness of muscles of abdominal walls sufficient to interfere with normal function. Any hernia should be noted, including how long it has been present and if adequately contained by truss.

Abnormal masses: if present, note location and if tender, whether applicant knows how long they have been present. If diagnosis suggests the condition may interfere with control and safe operation of CMV, more tests should be made before applicant can be certified.

Tenderness: when tenderness is noted, state where it is most pronounced and the suspected cause. If diagnosis suggests condition may interfere with control and safe operation of CMV, more tests should be made.

Genitourinary: a urinalysis is required. Acute infections of the genitourinary tract noted and indications from urinalysis of uncontrolled diabetes, symptomatic albumin urea in the urine, or other findings indicating health conditions that may interfere with control and safe operation of CMV will disqualify applicant from operating a CMV.

Neurological: pupillary reflexes should be reported for both light and accommodation. Knee jerks are to be reported absent only when not obtainable upon reinforcement and as increased when foot is actually lifted from the floor, following a light blow to the patella. Sensory vibratory and positional abnormalities should be noted.

Extremities: care should be taken to examine upper and lower extremities. Record the loss or impairment of a leg, foot, toe, arm, hand, or finger. Note all deformities, the presence of atrophy, semiparalysis, or paralysis or varicose veins. If a hand or finger deformity exists, determine whether sufficient grasp is present to enable driver to secure and maintain a grip on the steering wheel. If a leg deformity exists, determine whether there is sufficient mobility and strength present to enable the driver to operate pedals properly.

Particular attention should be given to, and a record should be made of, any impairment or structural defect that may interfere with the driver's ability to operate a CMV safely.

Spine: note deformities, limitation of motion, or history of pain, injuries, or disease in cervical or lumbar spine region. If findings dictate, x-ray or other examination should be used to diagnose congenital or acquired defects.

Rectogenital studies: diseases or conditions causing discomfort should be evaluated carefully to determine the extent to which the condition might be handicapping while lifting, pulling, or during periods of prolonged driving that might be necessary as part of the driver's duties.

Laboratory and other special findings: urinalysis is required as well as other tests as medical history and physical findings may indicate as necessary. A serological test is required if applicant has a history of luetic (relating to syphilis) infection or findings indicating the possibility of latent syphilis. Other studies deemed necessary by the examiner may also be ordered.

Diabetes: if insulin is necessary to control a diabetic condition, the driver is not qualified to operate a CMV. If mild diabetes is noted and stabilized by use of a hypoglycemic drug and a diet that can be obtained while the driver is on duty, it should not be disqualifying; however, the driver must remain under adequate medical supervision.

FOR CANADIAN DRIVERS, REGULAR PHYSICALS ARE REQUIRED, ACCORDING TO AGE GROUP

National Safety Code Standard 6 mandates medical standards for Canadian drivers. As it states:

Since a driver's physical and mental condition play a large part in driver and highway safety, all provinces and territories have established the minimum requirements for these tests. They have also designated a need for periodic testing to confirm the driver's continued good health.

While medical requirements vary between jurisdictions, most include the requirements for vision, color perception, hearing, handicaps, and conditions requiring medications, such as diabetes and drug or alcohol problems.

The periodic medical exams vary by age and license class as well, and each jurisdiction uses its own form, which must be completed by a medical professional and filed by the driver.

The timing for medical examinations is summarized below. However, it must be stressed that a driver must confirm the requirements with the licensing authority to which they are applying for a license.

Alberta
* At time of application
* Every 5 years to age 45
* Every 2 years to age 65
* Annually thereafter

British Columbia
* At time of application
* Every 5 years to age 45
* Every 2 years to age 65
* Every year after age 65

Manitoba
* At time of application for class 1 to 4 vehicles
* Every 10 years to age 39
* Every 5 years to age 60
* Every 2 years thereafter

New Brunswick
* At time of application
* Every 4 years to age 45
* Every 2 years thereafter

Newfoundland
* At time of application
* Every 5 years to age 45
* Every 2 years to age 65
* Annually thereafter

Northwest Territories
* At time of application
* Every 3 years to age 45
* Every 2 years to age 65
* Annually thereafter

Nova Scotia
* At time of application
* Every 3 years to age 44
* Every 2 years to age 59
* Annually thereafter

Ontario
* At time of application
* Every 3 years thereafter

Prince Edward Island
* At time of application
* Every 5 years to age 45
* Every 3 years ages 45–65
* Annually after age 65

Quebec
* At time of application
* Every 6 years to age 46
* Every 2 years to age 66
* Annually thereafter

Saskatchewan
* At time of application
* Every 5 years ages 18–45
* Every 3 years ages 46–65
* Every year ages 66 and older

Yukon Territories
* At time of application
* Every 3 years to age 45
* Annually thereafter

▶ Figure 34-13

If found to have a clean bill of health, the examiner will sign a certificate.

The examiner will ask the driver if there is any history of head or spinal injuries, seizures or convulsions or fainting, extensive confinement by illness or injury, heart disease, tuberculosis, syphilis, gonorrhea, diabetes, stomach ulcer, nervous stomach, rheumatic fever, asthma, kidney disease, muscular disease, any other diseases or permanent defect from illness or injury, psychiatric disorder, and any other nervous disorder.

Once the examination and the medical history is complete, the examiner will sign a certificate, stating that the driver has met all requirements and is certified to safely control and operate a CMV (**see Figure 34-13**).

DRIVER SAFETY

The need for **safety equipment** and safe practices while performing nondriving tasks cannot be stressed enough. Many accidents and injuries happen while the professional driver is working around the vehicle or with cargo. These nondriving accidents can be costly in a number of ways. They can even cause a driver to miss paychecks or be out of work for a long period of time.

STOP!

YOU CAN NEVER BE TOO SAFE. SAFETY SHOULD BE A HABIT, ON OR OFF DUTY!

Safety Dress and Proper Equipment

Dressing properly for the job requires the arms, legs, and feet to be covered. Shorts, flip-flops, and tee-shirts are not enough. Heavy denims offer the best protection. In cold weather, wear warm clothing and dress in layers. In warm weather, wear light colors and protect your skin and eyes from the sun's rays.

Protect your hands. Many professional drivers are the victims of hand injuries each year. Typical hazards include sharp steel bands used to tie boxes and crates, nails, broken glass, pointed wire, and irritating or corrosive chemicals.

Avoid wearing jewelry because it can get snagged and cause serious injuries. Always wear gloves when handling cargo or inspecting your rig. Selecting the right gloves is important. Gloves should have a good gripping surface. Hazardous materials or wastes usually require special gloves. Ordinary gloves may trap corrosives. Rubber or latex gloves do not (**see Figure 34-14**).

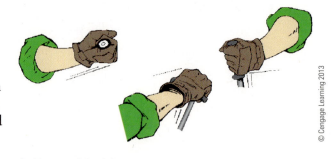

▶ Figure 34-14

Protect your hands.

Protect your eyes. If you require prescription lenses and wear glasses, make sure they are shatterproof. Wear sunglasses to protect your eyes from glare and make certain they are high quality so they will filter out infrared rays. Protective goggles or a face shield may be needed with some cargo; for example, goggles will protect your eyes when dealing with dust, flour, or cinders.

Protect your feet. Safety shoes protect your feet from falling objects. Steel-toed shoes or work boots are best and are required by some trucking companies. Do not wear sandals or flip-flops on the job. The soles of your shoes, if in good condition, will help reduce your risk of falls, and can help with good posture which reduces the risk of soft tissue injuries.

Special Protection Equipment

Circumstances may require special equipment for protection:

- Hard hat protects your head from chains or falling cargo at construction and delivery sites.

- Respirator prevents being overcome by fumes when handling chemical loads and liquefied chemicals. Some chemical loads require a self-contained breather (air supply). Find out what is needed. Take nothing for granted. If such is required you should get specific training regarding its use, and limitations are required by OSHA.

- Splash aprons prevent liquids from splashing on your skin and causing burns.

- Goggles or a face shield prevents severe eye damage from flying particles.

- When handling chemicals, do not wear contact lenses. Fumes can become trapped under them and cause blindness.

- Dust masks prevent respiratory problems when handling dry chemicals or similar loads. Some companies require drivers to be clean shaven with no facial hair so dust masks and face shields will fit tightly.

- Shin guards with heavy metal plates protect the front of the leg and tips of the shoes from rolling steel bars.

- Special coveralls protect the body from corrosives and other hazardous materials.

- Gas masks protect from poisonous gases and other hazardous materials (**see Figure 34-15**).

▶ **Figure 34–15**

Special cargoes require special protective equipment.

Danger Zones

There are many hazards when you work around a tractor-trailer or with cargo (**see Figure 34-16**). A driver can be seriously injured if he or she falls, trips, or gets bumped. A driver must use care when exiting the cab or trailer. Most accidents in the vehicle and cargo **danger zones** can be avoided if the driver makes safety a habit and is aware of these dangers.

Use great care when you are in the following areas:

- Cab
- Coupling and uncoupling area

▶ **Figure 34–16**

There are many hazards working around tractor-trailers. Take care getting out of your cab or trailer.

- Rear end of the trailer
- Cargo area
- Around the vehicle
- Truck stops/truck stop parking lots
- Loading areas

Cab—the height of the cab presents a great danger to the driver. Handholds or steps can become greasy or otherwise slippery. When getting into or out of the cab, look at the surfaces and always use the three-point stance when getting into the cab. Always enter and exit facing the inside of the cab area. Other injuries that are possible in the cab area include:

- Injury from a falling hood if you are looking at or working on the engine
- Thumb injuries from the steering wheel if the proper grip is not used
- Falls from the cab or missteps when entering or exiting

Danger areas

© Cengage Learning 2013

▶ **Figure 34-17**

The coupling and uncoupling area can be dangerous.

Coupling and uncoupling area—the coupling/uncoupling area can be dangerous because of grease and oil (**see Figure 34-17**). If you have to stand on the vehicle to connect the air lines or electric cables, be careful of slippery surfaces, such as the fuel tank or battery box, because these are especially dangerous when wet or covered with ice, oil, or grease. If possible, use surfaces that have been treated with a rout material or that have a ribbed grid plate. Without proper precautions, pulling the release latch handle during coupling or uncoupling is dangerous because you may be thrown off balance and injure your back.

Rear of the trailer—open and close the swinging cargo door with great care to avoid injury or damaging the freight. When you open the door, remember the cargo or load bars may have moved and be resting against it. If it is, the door will pop open from the force of the cargo as soon as the latch is released. If that happens, you could be knocked down and have cargo fall on your back. Be careful when it is windy. The cargo doors can break your fingers and hands or knock you down.

Some drivers have been hurt closing the door because they stood on the trailer dock, grabbed the strap, and jumped to the ground. If the strap breaks or the driver loses grip, he or she can fall to the ground.

Use common sense when using a power lift or tailgate to load or unload heavy cargo. Keep your hands and feet as well as your cargo away from areas of shearing or pinching. Be sure the cargo is secure and will not fall off.

Other problems include:

- Slippery surfaces
- No handhold
- Nails or splinters from the trailer floor

Always used the proper handholds and steps when available, and wear gloves when possible.

Cargo area—various types of trailers and cargos present different types of hazards. For instance, working with a tanker sometimes requires climbing to the top to hook or unhook dome covers. Flatbeds have no sides so there is a danger of falling off while tying down cargo. Open-top vans mean you have to climb up the side to tie down the tarp cover. Working inside a van is dangerous for many reasons:

- You may have to climb in, over, and around cargo to find a piece that is to be unloaded.
- You can be bruised or cut by nails or broken glass.

- You can bump into the sharp edges of cargo.
- Cargo can fall on you when you are climbing around.

Around the vehicle—there are many aspects that can cause injuries. Damaged rigs can cause injury. Tears in the trailer's skin and unrepaired damage to fenders, bumpers, or the hood can cut if you rub against or bump into them.

CAUTION!

When working at night, a flashlight is a must. You cannot couple or uncouple a rig or do a pretrip inspection without light.

Working under a rig is always dangerous. Make sure the vehicle is in the right gear and the auxiliary brake is on. Be sure, too, that the keys are in your pocket so no one can hop into the rig and move it while you are working underneath.

Cleaning the windshield—if possible, use an extension handle on a squeegee when cleaning the windshield of your rig. Then you can stand on the ground rather than having to climb on the tractor. If you must climb to clean it, be careful of slippery surfaces. Keep both feet and one hand securely on the vehicle at all times.

Lifting—because many injuries occur when lifting heavy objects, the following eight steps are recommended (**see Figure 34-18**):

1. Feet should be shoulder's length apart—one alongside and one behind the object.
2. Turn your forward foot in the direction of the movement.
3. Keep back straight.
4. Tuck in your chin.
5. Grip object with your palm and fingers.
6. Tuck in your elbows and arms.
7. Put your body weight directly over your feet.
8. Avoid twisting—a common cause of back injuries.

▶ **Figure 34-18**

Use the correct technique when lifting anything.

CAUTION!

Always wear gloves—they will help your grip and will protect your fingers while guarding against pinching your hands when lifting.

ROADSIDE EMERGENCIES

When you must stop in an emergency, be careful. How, when, where, and under what conditions you stop your rig make a difference between safety and serious problems.

If you park on the shoulder of the road, there is a great chance you could be rear-ended. Pull off the road as far as possible. Look for a truck stop or rest area. Be alert when there is no breakdown lane or adequate area to stop your rig. Rural roads and city streets do not have breakdown lanes.

Check before stopping. Be particularly careful in the dark because you cannot tell what surface is available for stopping your rig. During heavy rain or snow, a road shoulder may be too soft to support the weight of your rig. It could get stuck or could even roll over on a soft surface.

STOP!

Many drivers have been injured while checking a vehicle stuck on an icy or slippery hill. A rig can slide downhill and roll over the driver.

Get out of the cab safely. Many drivers who have stopped properly in an emergency get hurt while leaving the cab. Never jump from the cab. Use the three-point mount and dismount. Do not get out on the driver's side into the path of oncoming traffic. Remember to turn on the four-way emergency flashers. After you safely get out of the cab, put out emergency triangles to warn other drivers of a problem.

More safety reminders—you can never be too careful or too safe. Be especially alert in extreme weather.

- **Cold metal**—in cold weather, always wear gloves. In freezing weather, your hands can stick to cold metal and you can ruin your skin trying to remove them from the cold objects.
- **Hot tires**—you can receive serious burns checking hot tires. Never touch a tire—always place the back of your hand near the tire's surface.
- **Live wires**—if electrical wires land on your rig in a storm, do not move around in the cab or touch anything you are not already in contact with. If you have a cell phone or CB, call for help.

In addition to driving hazards, professional drivers should be aware of the security of themselves, their rigs, and their cargos at all times. Among other hazards are hijacking and robbery. These can usually be avoided best by following company policies. Be aware of high crime areas and know which types of cargos are more likely to be targets. Always keep your cargo doors locked, even when the trailer is empty. It is illegal (per FMCSR) to pick up hitchhikers. Do not carry a gun. It is illegal without a permit and a permit is generally valid only in the state in which it is issued.

CAUTION!

Do not set yourself up for crime. Do not carry a lot of cash. Stay away from dangerous areas. If something looks suspicious, call for help on your cell phone or CB. Stay away from dark, unlighted areas.

LARGE TRUCK CRASHES INCREASED IN 2010

Fatalities in U.S. highway accidents involving large trucks increased 8.7 percent in 2010, the first increase in four years, the National Highway Traffic Safety Administration reported.

A total of 3,675 people died in truck-related accidents in 2010, an increase of 295 from the 2009 total of 3,380, NHTSA said in its annual report.

In addition, the number of people injured in truck-related accidents rose to 19,000 in 2010, from 17,000 in 2009, a 12 percent increase.

At the same time, truck occupant fatalities increased by 6 percent, to 529 in 2010 from 499 in 2009.

"We're still trying to figure out clearly what [caused] this uptick," NHTSA Administrator Davie Strickland said when the report was unveiled in 2011.

American Trucking Associations said that in the 10-year period from 1999 to 2009, the number of large trucks involved in fatal crashes dropped by 35 percent, while injury crashes dropped by 48 percent.

At the same time, the number of registered big rigs rose by more than 3 million, or 41 percent.

CAUSES OF ACCIDENTS

The three main causes of traffic accidents are:

- **Vehicle defects**—mechanical defects, poor maintenance, and poor inspections are common causes of accidents. Parts that are falling or are in danger of falling often do so while the rig is on the road. Overloaded or improperly loaded rigs also lead to accidents.
- **Road or weather conditions**—slippery roads, poor visibility, lack of light (especially at dusk or dawn) and headlight glare, which can lead to momentary blinding. Accidents are also caused by poorly maintained roads and signals. Some examples of this are potholes, stop signs hidden by branches, and exit ramps that are too sharp for heavy-duty vehicles.
- **Driver error**—as a major cause of accidents, driver error can be caused by stress, both on and off duty, lack of good physical condition, and fatigue. By being aware of what is going on around the rig, thinking ahead, and using good judgment, many times a driver can make adjustments before a problem or opportunity for an accident occurs **(see Figure 34-19).**

A driver's errors are usually caused by one or more underlying causes:

- Not being alert or lacking concentration on what is happening around the rig
- Letting your mind wander to other things, such as a cell phone conversation while driving
- Driving while impaired—with impairment caused by illness, alcohol, substance abuse, or prescribed medication that makes you drowsy or interferes with concentration or fatigue **(see Figure 34-20)**

Drive Safely

▶ Figure 34-19

Following too closely is one of many invitations to trouble.

▶ Figure 34-20

Use of alcohol or drugs can lead to traffic accidents, resulting in injury, death, or property damage. It can also lead to arrest, fines, jail sentences, and the end of a driving career.

- Trying to make up for lost time
- Showing off or being too aggressive
- Lack of technical knowledge of the vehicle
- Poor driving skills
- Failing to recognize personal limitations

Driving a tractor-trailer rig is a full-time job, just like piloting an airplane or monitoring delicate equipment. It takes all of your attention at all times. Nobody can drive a problem and a rig at the same time. It is up to you—the professional driver—to park either the problem or the rig.

DRIVER FATIGUE AND SLEEP APNEA

Driver fatigue has been a safety issue of special concern to the transportation industry for more than a decade. Many commercial vehicles run at night, and drivers sometimes have irregular and unpredictable work schedules. Most of their mileage is compiled during long trips on interstate and other limited-access highways.

The CMV's high annual mileage exposure (often five to 10 times that of passenger vehicles) and other factors make the commercial drivers' risk of being involved in a fatigue-related crash far greater than that of noncommercial drivers. This is true, even though CMV drivers represent a relatively small proportion of all drivers involved in fatigue-related crashes.

The following quiz was developed to assess what individuals know about sleep, fatigue, and sleep deprivation. See how you do.

A QUIZ TO DETERMINE HOW MUCH PEOPLE KNOW ABOUT SLEEP AND SLEEP DEBT

1. Coffee overcomes the effects of drowsiness while driving. (T or F)
2. I can tell when I'm going to go to sleep. (T or F)
3. Rolling down my window or singing along with the radio will keep me awake. (T or F)
4. I'm a safe driver so it doesn't matter if I'm sleepy. (T or F)
5. You can stockpile sleep on the weekends. (T or F)
6. Most adults need at least 7 hours of sleep each night. (T or F)
7. Being sleepy makes you misperceive things. (T or F)
8. Young people need less sleep. (T or F)
9. Wandering, disconnected thoughts are a warning sign of driver fatigue. (T or F)
10. Little green men in the middle of the road may mean the driver is too tired to drive. (T or F)
11. On a long trip, the driver should never take a break but try to arrive at the destination as quickly as possible. (T or F)
12. A microsleep lasts 4 or 5 seconds. (T or F)

Driver fatigue quiz answers

1. FALSE. Stimulants are no substitute for sleep. Drinks containing caffeine, such as coffee or cola, can help you feel more alert, but the effects last only for a short time.

2. FALSE. Sleep is not voluntary. If drowsy, you can fall asleep and never even know it. You cannot tell how long you have been asleep.

3. FALSE. An open window or the radio has no lasting effect on a person's ability to stay awake.

4. FALSE. The only safe driver is an alert driver. Even the safest drivers become confused and use poor judgment when sleepy.

5. FALSE. Sleep is not money. You cannot save it up ahead of time and you cannot borrow it. As with money, however, you can go into debt.

6. TRUE. The average person needs 7 or 8 hours of sleep a night. If you go to bed late and wake up early to an alarm clock, you probably are building a sleep debt.

7. TRUE. One warning sign of a drowsy driver is misjudging surroundings.

8. FALSE. Young people need more sleep than adults. Males under 25 are at the greatest risk of falling asleep. Half of the victims of fatigue-related crashes are under 25.

9. TRUE. If you are driving and your thoughts begin to wander, it is time to pull over and take a break.

10. TRUE. Seeing things that are not there is a good indication it is time to stop driving and take a rest.

11. FALSE. Driving, especially for long distances, reveals a driver's true level of sleepiness. To be safe, drivers should take a break every 3 hours.

12. TRUE. During a microsleep of 4 or 5 seconds, a truck can travel 100 yards (91.44 m), plenty of time to cause a serious crash.

Sleep Apnea: Some drivers believe they experience more drowsiness, depending on when they drive, but researchers found no difference in the amount of drowsiness during variously scheduled trip segments. What was apparent was a surprising number of drivers suffered from a condition called **sleep apnea,** a condition caused by automatic cessation of breathing while the driver is asleep. Because this cessation awakens the individual, their sleep is interrupted several times during the night and this often causes fatigue while driving.

Researchers also have reported no significant relationships between driver age and fatigue. There were no consistent differences between older and younger drivers in terms of observed drowsiness, frequency of naps, self-ratings, or driving performance.

Changes in driving performance, measured by increasing variable steering and lane tracking, were found as a result of fatigue. This correlation between drowsiness and degraded driving performance supports the concept of continuous monitoring of driver performance to detect fatigue.

Sleep Apnea is the current "Hot Issue" within the transportation industry. What regulatory guidance might look like regarding sleep apnea and a driver's body mass index (BMI) has been hinted at by FMCSA. Drivers with a BMI greater than 35 (for 6' person, weight would be 258 lbs/117 kgs. or over) would have to be tested for sleep apnea within 60 days. Commercial drivers diagnosed with sleep apnea many not be unconditionally certified medically to receive their CDL's (two year certification) and must utilize a CPAP machine. Estimates are that half of the 3.5 million CDL holders have a BMI greater than 35. These suggestions from FMCSA represent a huge economic price for an industry already burdened with extensive cost, with the cost associated with sleep apnea testing likely being the responsibility of the driver.

▶ **Figure 34–21**

If you are fatigued, pull off in a safe spot and get some sleep.

PROGRESS IN FATIGUE MANAGEMENT

There is no quick fix and no single solution to the fatigue problem. Sleep is the principal countermeasure to fatigue. All drivers require adequate sleep. Drivers must also be afforded the opportunity to obtain adequate sleep on their off hours and encouraged to do so.

Bottom line, when drivers feel fatigued, the best, safest, and only **fatigue management** solution is sleep **(see Figure 34-21).** Pull off the road in a safe and legal place to sleep. Secure your vehicle and get comfortable. Most company policies require calling the dispatcher to let them know you are taking a break because of fatigue.

There are many myths about how to cure fatigue, but sleep is the only cure when fatigued or feeling drowsy behind the wheel. Never push your own personal limits. Take a break and nap before trying to continue your trip.

SUMMARY

In this chapter, you learned about stresses confronting the professional driver as well as suggestions for maintaining balance between work and family. You also learned about the DOT physical and what is expected. You read about the importance of refraining from the use of drugs and alcohol and the penalties for use while on the job. You also learned about the drug testing requirements for professional drivers, including preemployment, random, and postincident testing. Finally, you learned more about driver fatigue, its impact on the transportation industry, and recent findings on sleep deprivation, sleep apnea, and driver fatigue.

KEY TERMS

Alcoholism	Drug testing	Sleep apnea
Cold metal	Fatigue management	Stress
Danger zones	High blood pressure	Stress management
Diet and exercise	Job stress	Substance abuse
DOT physical examination	Random alcohol and controlled	Vehicle defects
Driver error	substance testing	
Driver fatigue	Safety equipment	

REVIEW QUESTIONS

1. A survey of 3,000 professional drivers at a trade show indicated that U.S. drivers' health habits were _____ the U.S. population on average.

   a. worse than

   b. better than

   c. about the same as

   d. ranged from about the same as, to better than

2. While sleep apnea is often associated with overweight and sometimes causes drivers to fall asleep at the wheel, healthy drivers also experience microsleeps or dozing behind the wheel because they _____.

   a. didn't sleep well the night before

   b. drink too much coffee

   c. neglect to get regular exercise

   d. neglect to eat a balanced diet

3. When adding physical exercise to your daily routine, a minimum of _____ minutes of exercise per day will keep you feeling healthy and good while on the road.

   a. 15

   b. 45

   c. 60

   d. 30

4. According to Canada's NSC 6, drivers must be monitored for all but one of the following.

   a. diseases requiring medications

   b. a gain in body weight

   c. color perception

   d. hearing

5. Alcoholism or the abuse of alcohol is considered _____ by the medical community.

   a. a bad habit

   b. an anesthesia for personal problems

   c. an illness

   d. a social disease

6. Procedures designed to help prevent accidents and injuries resulting from the use of alcohol and controlled substances by drivers of commercial motor vehicles mandate that no driver shall perform safety-sensitive functions within _____ hours after using alcohol.

   a. 12

   b. 24

   c. 8

   d. 4

7. According to federal rulings (FMCSR 382), no driver, while having an alcohol concentration of 0.04 or greater, shall _____.

   a. report for duty or remain on duty requiring the performance of safety-sensitive functions

   b. not drive over 50 mph (80 km/h)

   c. not drive, but may load trailers

   d. not drive over 35 mph (56 km/h)

8. Which of the following is the main cause of most highway accidents?

   a. vehicle defects

   b. weather conditions

   c. road conditions

   d. driver error

9. Which of the following is the most effective remedy for fatigue?

   a. exercise

   b. sleep

   c. diet

   d. caffeine

10. A 2007 study published in the *Journal of the American Dietetic Association* found that _____ percent of an estimated 3.2 million truck drivers in the U.S. are overweight or obese.

    a. 35

    b. 47

    c. 86

    d. 75

11. During a microsleep of 4–5 seconds, a rig can travel _____.

    a. 100 feet (30.5 m)

    b. 100 yards (91.4 m)

    c. 200 feet (61 m)

    d. 200 yards (182.9 m)

12. A 2010 report from the National Highway Traffic Safety Administration found fatalities caused by big truck crashes increased by _____ percent over the previous year.

    a. 12

    b. 15

    c. 20

    d. 6

13. Elements of professional driving that can contribute to stress include _____.

   a. high traffic   **c.** tight schedules
   b. construction zones   **d.** all of the above ⦁

14. When it comes to decreasing stress level, the professional can _____.

   a. eat properly   **c.** make time for relaxation
   b. communicate any problems **d.** all of the above ↵

SUPPLEMENTAL LEARNING ACTIVITIES

1. Using a copy of the DOT's driver physical form, write your past medical history, including any surgeries, broken bones, diseases requiring medications and your lifestyle, which includes if—or how often—you use alcohol, tobacco, or drugs. Include in your medical history any medications you take regularly, including aspirin and other over-the-counter drugs. Having your medical history and a list of medications will save time during your physical.

2. Practice a safe, three-point stance when entering the cab of a tractor.

3. Take a good look at your lifestyle. This includes your diet (what you eat regularly), your stress levels, weight, use of tobacco or alcohol and the amount of exercise you get regularly. Pinpoint any area that could be improved and begin working on this now, before you begin your professional driving career.

4. Ask a veteran driver to visit your class. Ask questions regarding the driver's personal safety and lifestyle routines while driving over-the-road. Ask about any hints for healthy living he or she has learned while away from home.

5. Discuss driver fatigue, as a group. What are some good ways to get adequate sleep? What about getting a good night's sleep while away from home? Find some driver fatigue studies on the Internet and report the findings to the class.

FOR MORE INFORMATION

PTDI—Manage Personal Resources While on the Road, Page 27, Click on Skill Standards
www.ptdi.org/standards

FMCSA Drug and Alcohol Program
www.fmcsa.dot.gov/rules-regulations/topics/drug/drug.htm

DOT Office of Drug and Alcohol Policy and Compliance Notice
www.fmcsa.dot.gov/documents/Medical-Marijuana-Notice.pdf

Risk Factors in Professional Driving
www.workhealth.org/OSI%20Index/OSI%20Introduction.html

35 Whistleblower Protections for Professional Drivers

© Gemenacom/www.Shutterstock.com

OBJECTIVES

When you have completed this chapter, you should be able to:

- Understand what situations call for a whistleblower's report.
- Know what coverage a professional driver has and how to go about receiving whistleblower protection.
- Understand the meaning of the Canada Labour Code—Part II.

INTRODUCTION

To the professional driver, following the rules that regulate the transportation industry and observing safety standards means the difference between continuing a career and losing it.

When any professional driver goes out on the road, he or she is automatically held to every transportation rule, regulation, and safety standard, whether it is enforced by city, state, province, or federal regulators. Not observing these rules, regulations, and safety standards not only place professional driving careers in jeopardy, but failure to follow these rules also can compromise the safety of that driver as well as others sharing the same streets and highways.

It also is the responsibility of the professional driver to make judgments regarding whether a truck meets safety standards or a load is within the regulatory guidelines. For example, if a truck is overloaded, if the load is not properly secured, if the load requires special skills the driver may not have (such as the hazmat endorsement on the CDL), or if the vehicle itself does not meet regulatory standards, it is up to the driver to stop at that point and either have these problems corrected or turn down the load.

Unfortunately, some employers expect drivers to look the other way when guidelines are not followed or equipment is substandard. Some employers take the attitude, "It is my way or the highway. If you do not like the loads we give you, go work elsewhere."

With protections in place in the U.S. and Canada, any driver, mechanic, and freight handler at any company has the ability to comply with transportation rules and regulations—and to turn down improper loads or to avoid use of vehicles that do not meet safety standards—without fear of job loss **(see Figure 35-1).**

▶ Figure 35-1

Protection is in place for drivers to turn down jobs, without fear of losing their job.

In the U.S., there are actually two separate whistleblower protections for professional drivers, freight handlers, and other transportation employees:

1. Section 11(c) of the **Occupational Safety and Health Act of 1970 (OSH Act)** authorizes the **Occupational Safety and Health Administration (OSHA)** to investigate employee complaints of **employer discrimination** against employees who are involved in safety and health activities protected under the act.
2. The second whistleblower protection—the Surface Transportation Assistance Act (STAA)—was passed in 1982.

In Canada, protections for professional drivers, freight handlers, and other transportation employees are outlined in Part II of the Labour Code.

OSHA WHISTLEBLOWER PROTECTIONS—WHAT THEY COVER AND HOW TO REPORT VIOLATIONS

Workers who have been discriminated against by an employer have the right to complain to OSHA and seek an OSHA inspection **(see Figure 35-2).** Some examples of discrimination are firing, demotion, transfer, layoff, losing the opportunity for overtime or promotion, exclusion from normal overtime work, assignment to an undesirable shift, denial of benefits such as sick leave or vacation time, blacklisting with other employers, taking away company housing, damaging credit at banks or credit unions, and reducing pay or hours.

Refusing to do a job because of potentially unsafe workplace conditions is not ordinarily an employee right under the OSH Act. (A union contract or state law may, however, give this right, but OSHA cannot enforce it.) Refusing to work may result in disciplinary action by an employer; however, employees have the **right to refuse** to do a job if they otherwise would be exposed to an imminent danger that poses the risk of death or serious injury. Call 800-321-OSHA immediately to report imminent dangers.

How Are Drivers Protected under the OSH Act?

To be protected under the OSH Act, an employee must satisfy several criteria before he or she refuses to perform a job. If a driver believes an employer has treated him or her differently because he or she exercised safety and health rights, contact the local OSHA office right away. Most discrimination complaints fall under the OSH Act, which gives the driver 90 days to report discrimination.

▶ Figure 35–2

Drivers who have been discriminated against can file a complaint with OSHA and seek an OSHA inspection.

GO!

If a driver believes working conditions are unsafe or unhealthful, he or she should call the employer's attention to the problem. If the employer does not correct the hazard or disagrees about the extent of the hazard, the driver also may file a complaint with OSHA.

Refusing to work may result in disciplinary action by the employer; however, employees do have the right to refuse to do a job if they believe in good faith that they are exposed to an imminent danger. "Good faith" means that even if an imminent danger is not found to exist, the worker had reasonable grounds to believe that it did exist.

Imminent danger is defined in the FMCSR as "any conditions or practices in any place of employment which are such that a danger exists which could reasonably be expected to cause death or serious physical harm immediately or before the imminence of such danger can be eliminated through the enforcement procedures otherwise provided by this act."

Before a hazard can be called an imminent danger, the following conditions must be met:

1. There must be a threat of death or serious physical harm. "Serious physical harm" means that a part of the body is damaged so severely that it cannot be used or cannot be used very well.

2. To be considered a health hazard, there must be a reasonable expectation that toxic substances or other health hazards are present and exposure to them will shorten life or cause substantial reduction in physical or mental efficiency. The harm caused by the health hazard does not have to happen immediately.

3. The threat must be immediate or imminent. This means that the driver must believe that death or serious physical harm could occur within a short time, for example, before OSHA could investigate the problem.

If an OSHA inspector believes that an imminent danger exists, the inspector must inform affected employees and the employer that he or she is recommending that OSHA take steps to stop the imminent danger. OSHA also has the right to ask a federal court to order the employer to eliminate the imminent danger.

As a general rule, the driver does not have the right to walk off the job because of unsafe conditions. If the driver does walk off the job and the employer fires or disciplines the driver, OSHA may not be able to protect that driver, so stay on the job until the problem can be resolved.

When Does a Driver Have a Right to Refuse to Do a Task under the OSH Act?

The driver's right to refuse to do a task is protected if *all* of the following conditions are met:

1. Where possible, the driver has asked the employer to eliminate the danger, and the employer failed to do so.
2. The driver refused to work in "good faith." This means that he or she must genuinely believe that an imminent danger exists. The driver's refusal cannot be a disguised attempt to harass the employer or disrupt business.
3. A reasonable person would agree that there is a real danger of death or serious injury.
4. There is not enough time, due to the urgency of the hazard, to get it corrected through regular enforcement channels, such as requesting an OSHA inspection.

When all of these conditions are met, the driver must take the following steps:

1. Ask employer to correct the hazard.
2. Ask employer for other work.
3. Tell employer that he or she will not perform the work unless and until the hazard is corrected.
4. Remain at the worksite until ordered to leave by the employer.

If an employer discriminates against a driver, mechanic, freight handler, or other transportation employee for refusing to perform the dangerous work, contact OSHA immediately **(see Figure 35-3).** Acts of retaliation or discrimination prohibited by OSHA's whistle-blower provisions include assigning undesirable tasks, blacklisting with other companies, evicting from company housing, damaging financial credit, demoting, denying overtime or promotion, disallowing benefits, disciplining, failing to hire or rehire, firing or laying off, intimidating, transferring, reassigning work, and reducing pay or hours.

OSHA Occupational Safety and Health Administration

© Cengage Learning 2013

▶ Figure 35-3

Occupational Safety and Health Administration (OSHA) investigates employee complaints against employer discrimination of employees involved in safety and health activities under the OSH Act.

▶ *"Hey, I love duct tape as much as the next person, but . . ."*

How to File a Whistleblower Complaint with OSHA

1. If a driver believes his or her employer is discriminating against him or her because the driver exercised his or her legal rights, the driver should contact the local OSHA office immediately and within the legal time limit of 90 days. The **whistleblower complaint** may be telephoned, faxed, or mailed **(see Figure 35-4)** to the OSHA office listed on OSHA's website at www .osha.gov.

2. OSHA will conduct an in-depth interview with the driver to determine the need for investigation.

3. If the evidence supports the driver's claim of discrimination, OSHA will request that the employer restore the driver's job, earnings, and benefits.

▶ **Figure 35–4**

Complaints can be telephoned, faxed, or mailed to OSHA.

THE SURFACE TRANSPORTATION ASSISTANCE ACT—WHISTLEBLOWER PROTECTIONS AND HOW TO REPORT VIOLATIONS

When the **Surface Transportation Assistance Act (STAA)** was passed in 1982, it included Section 405 to protect drivers, technicians, freight handlers, and certain other transportation industry employees from retaliation from their employers when they reported safety violations.

Specifically, Section 405 states that an employer is prohibited from firing, demoting, or in any other way discriminating against an employee who:

1. Refuses to operate a vehicle, which fails to meet federal, state, or local safety regulations
2. Reports a violation of vehicle safety requirements
3. Reports that he or she has been exposed to significant hazards
4. Testifies or otherwise participates in safety-related proceedings

STOP!

If you have refused to drive a vehicle that fails to meet safety standards, you believe it would be hazardous to you and your fellow road users, and you have been fired, demoted, or discriminated against in any other way, you have rights under STAA Section 405!

When Do Whistleblower Protections Apply under STAA Section 405?

To be protected by STAA, a worker must be in the private sector and must be a driver, freight handler, mechanic, or someone responsible for the maintenance and inspection of a commercial vehicle. The vehicle must:

1. Have a gross weight of at least 10,001 pounds (4,536 kg)
2. Be designed or used to transport passengers for compensation (excluding taxi cabs or vehicles having capacity of not more than six passengers)
3. Be designed or used to transport at least 15 passengers, including the driver, and not used to transport passengers for compensation
4. Be used to transport hazardous materials in quantities requiring placarding under section 5103 regulations prescribed by the secretary of transportation

To be covered by STAA's whistleblower protections, the worker must also bring the Driver's Vehicle Inspection Report (DVIR) to the attention of an employer, the Department of Transportation, or state or local police. If the worker violates safety regulations by driving the substandard vehicle, he or she is not protected by the law.

If a worker reports an unsafe vehicle or load that does not comply with regulations and the employer does not correct the problem or makes the correction and then disciplines the worker, the worker is protected by STAA.

STOP!

Reporting a safety problem to a union representative, a mechanic, or coworkers is not considered when seeking whistleblower protection. The problem must be reported to the employer, the DOT, or the police.

What Is Considered a Violation of Safety Standards or Federal Regulations under STAA?

Every driver should have his or her own copy of DOT regulations, which should be available from every employer. In particular, health condition violations are very complex and each driver should be familiar with the exact wording of the laws before pursuing a complaint.

The most common violations of regulations or safety standards include:

1. Hours of service (DOT section 395.2). This regulation has been—and will continue to be—strictly enforced by the courts (as written in the STAA) for drivers who refuse a trip or a dispatch that violates hours of service regulations.
2. Refusal to speed to complete a dispatch is also covered and strictly enforced.
3. Failure to have the correct placards for hazmat loads.
4. Lack of safety inspections or uncorrected mechanical problems.
5. Lack of required safety equipment, including lights, falls under these protections. However, DOT rulings say that burned-out clearance lights are not safety violations and that stoplights have reflective qualities that substitute for required reflectors, making the lack of these reflectors a nonviolation.

6. Driver illness. If a driver is ill and unable to work, he or she must present a valid reason for this health condition to the employer and, having done so, the employer cannot demand that the ill driver operate a commercial vehicle.

7. State laws covering overweight vehicles, speeding, and overlength or overheight vehicles are also included in the STAA regulations—and also include local ordinances involving routing or special height and width requirements.

Each situation the driver believes to be a safety violation must be reported to his or her employer and it must be noted that the condition involves a safety issue.

Along with violation of safety regulations, the STAA law not only covers the condition of the truck but also the environment in which the truck is driven, including driver illness, driver fatigue, bad weather, or poor road conditions.

What Are Considered Unsafe, Dangerous Conditions by the STAA Rules?

Weather and Road Conditions

If weather conditions make it unsafe to drive a truck and the driver refuses to drive, he or she is protected under STAA laws. In a court case, the court ruled that driving an empty bobtail on icy roads was unsafe and the driver acted reasonably by refusing to drive. Refusing to drive into bad weather also has been upheld by the courts.

> **CAUTION!**
>
> Remember: The hazardous situation—such as tornados, high winds, or icy roads—must definitely exist, not the driver's fear that bad weather may occur. In cases of bad weather or road conditions, highway patrol travel advisories or other traffic alerts can back up a claim.

But what about situations of dangerous road or weather conditions where others have made it through, but a driver sees the situation as too dangerous and refuses to drive? According to previous court cases, judges have ruled that it was "blind luck" that others made it through and survived while another driver refused to continue.

Two other cases to know about: In one case, the driver believed the load was too heavy to maintain highway speeds. The court ruled that this was an **STAA unsafe condition.** Another driver claimed a co-driver was unsafe and refused to drive with that driver. The court ruled that an unsafe co-driver was an unsafe condition; however, the co-driver's unsafe habits required supporting testimony from other drivers who had driven with that co-driver in the past.

Driver Illness and Fatigue

The driver's health is a major consideration in safely operating a CMV, particularly professional drivers who are pushed to work long hours. To claim illness or fatigue as a reason to refuse a dispatch, however, the driver must give the employer a reason for the fatigue.

If fatigue makes it necessary for the driver to stop by the side of the road for a nap, it is not necessary to inform an employer before stopping—and this stop is also protected by STAA laws. However, the driver must notify the employer afterward about the reason for pulling off the road for a nap.

Drivers who also have had to wait an excessive period of time for dispatch have been upheld by the courts for refusing to go to work because they were suffering from fatigue—if the wait was excessively long and if the driver informed dispatch about his problems with fatigue.

If a driver becomes ill and cannot drive, he or she must specifically report the illness to the employer. A report stating "I do not feel good" is not enough. The driver must be specific, such as "I have a migraine headache that affects my driving."

Do Not Go Home without Telling the Boss!

The common mistake of a driver going home without reporting the unsafe condition to the employer leaves the driver unprotected by STAA laws.

STOP!

If you encounter an unsafe truck or unsafe conditions in your workplace, **never go home without calling in and reporting the specific safety problem to an employer.**

When making this report to an employer, the driver must identify the safety violation (vehicle defects, weather conditions, unsafe road conditions, illness, or fatigue), tell why the condition is unsafe, and be able to verify that the condition existed at the time the driver refused to drive.

Once the report is made, the employer must take an adverse action toward the driver in order for the incident to be covered by STAA's whistleblower protections.

An adverse action could be a warning letter, harassment, lower paying runs, fewer runs, suspension, reassignment of duties, discharge, or loss of money. When bad weather and a need to rest caused one driver to spend the night in a motel, the court made the company pay motel expenses.

Because many of these actions are done in writing, the driver has an easier job of proving they happened. The more difficult part of the task is connecting these actions to having blown the whistle about safety conditions.

How to File an STAA Whistleblower Complaint

In any and every case, professional drivers should carry a camera to document information that could be useful. Drivers are also encouraged to photocopy any Driver's Vehicle Inspection Report (DVIR) or other documents that may be needed to document a case of whistleblower discrimination. Some professionals also carry small notebooks to write specifics of important situations, including witnesses and other information to document violations or questionable events.

1. All complaints must be filed with the federal OSHA regional office in the area in which the driver works. (The telephone number will be listed in the phone book under United States Government, **Department of Labor**—Occupational Safety and Health Administration.)

2. All complaints must be filed within 180 days (including weekends and holidays) from the time of the employer's adverse action. The complaint letter merely asks the driver to describe the unsafe condition, the driver's action, the employer's response, and the driver's contact information.

3. OSHA will investigate within 60 days and may want dates, names, and other available documentation (audiotapes, videotapes, photos, or notes).

4. If the case is found to have merit, OSHA will order the employer to reinstate the driver with back pay. (If the employer does not comply, DOT will provide the driver with an attorney.)

5. If OSHA does not feel the case has merit, the driver is notified by letter and can object to OSHA's findings. In this case, the driver's best alternative is to hire a labor attorney and, within 30 days, send a written objection to the company, the Department of Labor (DOL) Office of Administrative Law Judges, and the regional OSHA director (all of these addresses will be supplied in OSHA's letter of findings).

6. After filing the objection, the administrative law judge will conduct a hearing within 45 days. Drivers are encouraged to have an attorney to represent them at this hearing.

7. During this hearing, the driver is allowed to call witnesses, and these witnesses (which are often coworkers) are protected from adverse actions by the company. The judge will review the evidence and can question witnesses. Decisions are usually made within 30 days from the time the judge receives all requested materials.

Professional Drivers Are Also Protected by OSHA—What's the Difference?

Drivers are also covered by OSHA's Section 11(c)—or its equivalent in states where there is a state OSHA plan. The OSHA Section 11(c) whistleblower protection law only has a 90-day period in which to file a complaint while STAA whistleblower protections offer the advantage of a longer filing period of 180 days.

STAA also allows the worker to hire a private attorney to bring action (and pays attorneys' fees if the discrimination is proven), provides for reinstatement of a fired worker when the DOL determines the complaint has "merit" status, and provides back pay as well as damages. Under OSHA's Sec. 11(c), only the DOL can bring action.

CANADIAN WORKPLACE HEALTH AND SAFETY

The purpose of the **Canada Labour Code—Part II,** Subsection 122.2 is to prevent accidents and injury to health arising out of, linked with, or occurring in the course of employment.

Under Subsection 122.2, preventive measures should consist first of the elimination of hazards, then the reduction of hazards, and finally, the provision of personal protective equipment, clothing, devices, or materials, all with the goal of ensuring the health and safety of employees.

Each year, many Canadians are killed or injured on the job. These tragedies have profound social repercussions and cost billions of dollars.

Knowing the Canada Labour Code and, more importantly, applying the provisions of Part II enables the Canadian government to identify and correct problems that affect health and safety. It is one of the most effective ways to reduce accidents and occupational diseases in the workplace.

The Canada Labour Code applies to employees who work under federal jurisdiction, which encompasses about 10 percent of the Canadian workforce. They are employed in key sectors of the economy, notably air, rail, and highway transport, pipelines, banks, broadcasting and telecommunications, uranium mines, marine transport, and related services.

Some 40 Crown corporations and agencies, Indian reserves, and the entire federal public service are also subject to the code. Enforcement and administration of the Canada Labour Code comes under the responsibility of the Labour Program of Human Resources and Skills Development Canada in partnership with Transport Canada and the National Energy Board.

Transport Canada is responsible for on-board employees in the aviation, marine, and rail sectors under federal jurisdiction, while the National Energy Board is responsible for employees in the oil and gas sector under federal jurisdiction.

(Continues)

CANADIAN WORKPLACE HEALTH AND SAFETY (continued)

Occupational health and safety legislation in the federal jurisdiction has been consolidated under Part II of the Canada Labour Code and applies to the following interprovincial and international industries:

- banks
- railways, highway, and air transport
- ferries, tunnels, bridges, and canals
- telephone and telegraph systems
- pipelines
- radio and television broadcasting and cable systems
- shipping and shipping services
- employment in the operation of ships, trains, and aircraft
- grain elevators licensed by the Canadian Grain Commission, and certain feed mills and feed warehouses, flour mills, and grain seed cleaning plants
- federal public service and persons employed by the public service and about 40 Crown corporations and agencies
- Indian reserves
- exploration and development of petroleum on lands subject to federal jurisdiction

NOTE

Part II of the Canada Labour Code **does not apply** to certain undertakings regulated by the Nuclear Safety and Control Act.

Duties of Employers

Under Section 124 of the code, employers have a general obligation or duty to ensure that the health and safety of every person employed by the employer is protected while they are working.

Also, under Subsection 125.1, employers have specific duties in regard to each workplace they control and every work activity under their authority that occurs in a workplace that is beyond the employer's control.

Duties of Employees

Under Subsection 126.1, the Canada Labour Code, Part II places several obligations on employees, all of which have the goal of preventing occupational related injuries and diseases. Employees have a responsibility to take all reasonable and necessary precautions to ensure their health and safety and that of anyone else who may be affected by their work or activities.

Nobody knows a workplace better than the people who work in it. Part II of the code gives the workplace parties a strong role in the identification and resolution of health and safety concerns.

The provisions of the code are designed to strengthen employers' and employees' self-reliance to effectively deal with occupational health and safety issues and, in so doing, make workplaces safer.

Workplace Health and Safety Committees

Workplace health and safety committees must be established in workplaces where there are 20 or more employees. At least half of the committee members must be employees who do not have managerial functions **(see Figure 35-5)**.

Each workplace health and safety committee is required to meet nine times a year, at regular intervals and during regular working hours. If circumstances make additional meetings necessary, they should be held during or outside regular hours, whatever is required.

There are several powers and duties. The workplace health and safety committee will:

- consider and expeditiously dispose of health and safety complaints;
- participate in the implementation and monitoring of programs for the prevention of workplace hazards;
- participate in the development, implementation, and monitoring of programs to prevent workplace hazards, if there is no policy committee in the organization;

▶ **Figure 35–5**

Workplace health and safety committees must be established in workplaces with more than 20 employees.

- participate in all of the inquiries, investigations, studies, and inspections pertaining to employee health and safety;
- participate in the implementation and monitoring of a program for the provision of personal protective equipment, clothing, devices, or materials, and, if there is no policy committee, participate in the development of the program;
- ensure that adequate records are kept on work accidents, injuries, and health hazards;
- cooperate with health and safety officers;
- participate in the implementation of changes that may affect occupational health and safety, including work processes and procedures, and, if there is no policy committee, participate in the planning of the implementation of those changes;
- assist the employer in investigating and assessing the exposure of employees to hazardous substances;
- inspect each month all or part of the workplace, so that every part of the workplace is inspected at least once a year; and
- participate in the development of health and safety policies and programs, if there is no policy committee.

The committee may request from an employer any information that it considers necessary to address workplace hazards. It has full access to all government and employer reports, studies, and tests relating to the health and safety of employees. Of course, it does not have access to an individual's medical records without the individual's consent.

CANADA OCCUPATIONAL HEALTH AND SAFETY REGULATIONS

Generally speaking, the Canada Labour Code establishes the legislative framework and outlines the duties and responsibilities of the employer and employees pertaining to occupational health and safety.

The Canada Occupational Health and Safety Regulations identifies, in much greater detail, the specific requirements in order to ensure a healthy and safe workplace.

For example, the code requires an employer to ensure that the levels of ventilation, lighting, temperature, humidity, sound, and vibration are in accordance with prescribed standards. This in itself does not offer much guidance, therefore Part VI—Lighting of the Regulation provides the detail on levels of lighting in different workplaces.

A CANADIAN EMPLOYEES' THREE BASIC RIGHTS

Part II of the Canada Labour Code provides an employee with three rights:

- **Right to know**
- **Right to participate**
- **Right to refuse**

Right to Know

Through the provisions of the code, employees have the right to be informed of known or foreseeable hazards in the workplace and to be provided with the information, instruction, training, and supervision necessary to protect their health and safety.

This right to know is strengthened by ensuring that the methods of communication are appropriate for all employees, including employees with special needs.

STOP!

Through health and safety committees or representatives, employees are given the right to have access to government or employer reports relating to the health and safety of employees, but do not have access to medical records of any person except with that person's consent.

Right to Participate

As health and safety representatives or committee members, employees have the right to participate, as well as the responsibility, in identifying and correcting job-related health and safety concerns.

Employers who employ 300 or more employees are required to establish a policy health and safety committee. The purpose of the policy committee is to handle issues that are organization-wide in nature. Because these types of issues go beyond a single workplace, there is a need for a more strategic or global approach for their resolution.

Part II of the Canada Labour Code further provides for employee participation through the use of an internal complaint resolution process.

Right to Refuse

An employee, at work, has the right to refuse dangerous work if he or she has reasonable cause to believe that:

- a condition exists at work that presents a danger to himself or herself;
- the use or operation of a machine or thing presents a danger to the employee or a coworker;
- the performance of an activity constitutes a danger to the employee or to another employee.

In order for an employee to be protected by the code when exercising the right to refuse, the employee must follow the proper procedure.

Right of Redress

The purpose of the right of redress is to protect employers from abuse of the right to refuse and protect employees from arbitrary discipline.

Exercise of the right of redress can occur only after a health and safety officer has deemed that a dangerous situation did not exist.

The burden of proof is upon the employer to prove that the employee had abused his or her right to refuse to the Canadian Industrial Relations Board before disciplinary action can be carried out.

This provision in the code is intended to balance the protection from abuse against the protection from arbitrary discipline.

Training

Under the code, the employer provides, in the prescribed manner, each employee with the information, instruction, training, and supervision necessary to ensure his or her health and safety at work;

- ensure that employees who have supervisory or managerial responsibilities are adequately trained in health and safety and are informed of the responsibilities they have under this Part where they act on behalf of their employer; and
- ensure that members of policy and workplace committees and health and safety representatives receive the prescribed training in health and safety and are informed of their responsibilities.

The employer's managerial representatives should know, first, what their responsibilities are regarding health and safety, and second, how to address health and safety issues in a knowledgeable and informed manner. The increasing complexity of the work organization, the work processes, and work materials requires that managers and supervisors receive the necessary training in health and safety.

Supervisors and managers, who act on behalf of their employer, should be adequately trained in and informed of their responsibilities in safe work practices and procedures, including any procedures, plans, policies, or programs that the employer is required to develop by the provisions of the code.

Specifically, training should cover the duties of the employer, the duties of the employees, the three basic rights of employees, and procedures required by the code, such as the steps to follow in cases of refusal to work, when complaints are filed, and when hazardous occurrences need to be investigated.

Compliance with the code can be achieved through ongoing programs of instruction in the requirements of the legislation and in work practices and procedures specific to the particular workplace.

Methods of instruction can include lectures, films, hands-on demonstrations, and information materials of various kinds. The extensiveness of the training is dependent on the work practices and procedures particular to the workplace. For example, it is important and essential to explain appropriate lifting and carrying techniques and work procedures to supervisors and managers in warehouses.

For workplaces with more and greater hazards, such as grain elevators, rail shops, repair garages, and places where toxic substances are used, it would be necessary to provide supervisors and managers with lengthier, more detailed instruction **(see Figure 35-6).**

With respect to the duties of the employer and of the employees, and the basic rights of the employees, a lecture or an information session would normally be seen as basic training.

▶ Figure 35–6

Some workplaces have greater working hazards.

INTERNAL COMPLAINT RESOLUTION PROCESS

It has been widely held that the workplace parties (employer and employees) are more knowledgeable regarding hazards that may exist in the workplace and have a greater vested interest in dealing with these issues.

The legislative framework establishes a process that allows for a graduated series of investigations to resolve workplace issues while maintaining employment safety. The process allows for the resolution of workplace health and safety issues in a more timely and efficient manner and reinforces the concept of the internal responsibility system.

The process provides the employer/supervisor with the opportunity to address and correct employee concerns without the need to involve the workplace health and safety committee, the health and safety representative, or a health and safety officer.

The first step for the health and safety officer will be to ensure the internal complaint resolution process has been followed.

The health and safety officer will then investigate the matter and:

- may issue a direction to the employer or employee if a contravention to the code is identified;
- may, if the officer considers it appropriate, ask the employer and employee to resolve the matter between themselves; and
- will issue a direction if the officer concludes that a danger exists.

An employee cannot be disciplined for exercising his or her rights or fulfilling a duty under the code as long as the employee has acted in accordance with the code.

SUMMARY

While the rights of all professional drivers, mechanics, freight handlers, and other U.S. transportation employees are actually covered by two whistleblower protections—OSHA and STAA—and the rights of Canadian transportation employees are covered by Part II of the Canada Labour Code, it is the driver's personal responsibility to know and understand these protections and how to report complaints or violations when they occur.

It also is up to the driver to document each incident, to follow the guidelines completely, and to be responsible for notifying employers to report unsafe vehicles or situations.

The driver should also be familiar with the laws provided by the Department of Transportation and the Canada Labour Code regarding vehicular safety as well as determining what comprises unsafe driving conditions.

Finally, it is up to the U.S. driver to file a complaint with either OSHA or STAA and the Canadian driver to follow the internal complaint process as described in the Canada Labour Code, depending on the particular situation and event. It is also the driver's responsibility to provide documentation of the events leading up to refusal to drive a certain vehicle or refusal to work under certain conditions.

In the U.S., the driver may also want to ask for coworker testimony if this is needed, but ultimately, it is up to the professional driver in North America to be informed and to remain informed about rules regarding vehicular safety and the best safety practices.

Updates can be found at www.osha.gov or www.fmcsa.gov, or by reading transportation publications, company newsletters, or going to websites created specifically for driver information.

KEY TERMS

Canada Labour Code—Part II
Department of Labor
Employer discrimination
Imminent danger
Occupational Safety
   and Health Act (OSH Act)

Occupational Safety and Health
   Administration (OSHA)
Right to know
Right to participate
Right to refuse
STAA Unsafe Conditions

Surface Transportation
   Assistance Act (STAA)
Transport Canada
Whistleblower complaint

A DAY IN THE LIFE...

Don Hess—John Wood Community College, Chair Transportation

My name is Don Hess. I'm a Professor of Transportation and Department Chair at John Wood Community College in Quincy, Illinois. My department is responsible for our Truck Driver Training courses and related subjects. Some say trucking "gets into your blood." I think that's true for many, and it certainly is for me. I'll share with you the path that brought me to where I am today.

I began driving 18-wheelers in 1971. In those days, there were very few driving schools. Most drivers learned to drive serving as an apprentice to an experienced driver. I talked a company into letting me work for free as a trainee, until my trainer decided I was ready to test for my Class One license ("CDLs" didn't yet exist). We pulled tankers hauling gasoline, diesel fuel, jet fuel, and other flammables and explosives throughout Southern California. I did that for seven years, then moved to the Midwest and started trucking there.

Over the next 10 years, I pulled swinging beef to the east and west coasts, grain throughout the Midwest, and worked as a heavy equipment operator/driver/superintendent at a highway construction company. Over those 17 or so years driving, I had the privilege of visiting all of the lower 48 states, and since then I've added Hawaii and Alaska. It's a special feeling for me knowing that I've been in all 50 states.

About 1987, I decided to find a way to stay around trucks but be home every night. While I loved trucking, I wanted more home time. I left trucking to finish my degree at the University of Nebraska, then began teaching truck driving. After spending two years teaching, I was hired by my present school to create a new trucking program. And nearly 20 years later, I'm still here. Watching our students learn and grow, and then enter the trucking industry as safe, properly-trained, entry-level drivers is one of the most rewarding things I've ever done.

As one of those drivers, you can help improve our industry. "Back in the day," truck drivers were known as "Knights of the Road." They would stop and help each other, or any motorist broken down on the side of the road. Truckers and nontruckers all had stories to tell about a driver who had helped them or someone else. We were held in high regard everywhere we went. Over the years, a bad element crept into the profession, and stained that polished image. But together, we can fix that.

> **Conduct yourself with pride and professionalism in all you do. I promise you'll never regret it.**

As you make your journey through this noble profession, keep in mind that you represent not just your company, but all of us. Fewer than 2% of the population have earned a Commercial Driver License, making you part of an elite group. Conduct yourself with pride and professionalism in all you do. I promise you'll never regret it. And whether you spend your entire career driving, or eventually choose a different path into dispatching, operations, safety, teaching, or a hundred other possibilities, you'll know you can take pride in the fact that you are part of the network of professionals in the trucking industry that keeps North America running.

REVIEW QUESTIONS

1. The Canada Labour Code—Part II specifies that training should cover the duties of the employer, the duties of the employees, the three basic rights of employees, and procedures required by the code, such as the steps to follow in cases of refusal to work, when complaints are filed and _____.

   a. when unsafe situations need investigation
   b. when employees are unwilling to work
   c. when employees are disruptive
   d. when employees become violent

2. Because of OSHA whistleblower protection, workers who have been discriminated against by an employer have the right to _____.

   a. receive double-time pay for working under dangerous conditions
   b. free meals when working away from their home base
   c. drive 15 hours straight without rest to make up for lost time
   d. complain to OSHA and seek an OSHA inspection

3. Enforcement and administration of the Canada Labour Code comes under the responsibility of the Labour Program of Human Resources and Skills Development Canada in partnership with the National Energy Board and _____.

   a. provincial Transportation ministries   c. Transport Canada
   b. provincial Transport Authorities   d. the Canadian NAFTA board

4. As a general rule, when unsafe conditions are observed by a driver, the best choice of action is to _____.

   a. walk off the job
   b. call the company president
   c. make your point with the dispatcher
   d. stay on the job until the problem can be resolved or you can document the situation

5. If a driver believes his or her employer is discriminating against him or her because the driver exercised his or her legal rights, the driver should contact the local OSHA office immediately or within the legal time limit of _____ days.

   a. 45   c. 30
   b. 60   d. 90

6. To be protected by STAA, if a driver reports an unsafe vehicle or load, the report must be made to _____.

   a. a union representative   c. a technician
   b. the employer, the DOT, or the police   d. a coworker

7. Which of the following workers in the private sector are not protected by STAA?

   a. drivers   c. dispatchers
   b. freight handlers   d. technicians

8. Every driver should have his or her own copy of their rights and regulations, which should be made available by the _____.

   a. state highway patrol   c. federal government
   b. local bookstore   d. driver's employer

9. Regarding STAA law that covers the condition of the truck and the environment in which the truck is driven, which of the following is considered to be an element of the environment covered under STAA law?

    a. driver illness
    b. driver fatigue
    c. bad weather
    d. a, b, and c ✌

10. Which of the following is not a recommended way to document information that could be useful to a professional driver in filing a STAA whistleblower complaint?

    a. Carry a camera to document information that could be useful.
    b. Photocopy any vehicle condition report (VCR) or other documents that may be needed to document a case of whistleblower discrimination.
    c. Tell other drivers about your experiences with your company. ✦
    d. Carry a small notebook to write specifics of important situations.

11. While the rights of all professional drivers, technicians, freight handlers, and other transportation employees are actually covered by two whistleblower protections—OSHA and STAA—if a driver is involved in an incident where he or she may need whistleblower protection, who is personally responsible to know and understand the various whistleblower protections and how to report complaints or violations?

    a. driver ✌
    b. employer
    c. dispatcher
    d. federal government

SUPPLEMENTAL LEARNING ACTIVITIES

1. You are asked to haul an LTL load of mixed commodities. You have some questions about several pallets of nail polish remover and household bleach. You do not have a hazmat endorsement. What do you do next?

2. Your supervisor asks you to pick up a load at a local swimming pool chemical company. When you explain you do not have a hazmat endorsement, the supervisor says, "The trip is only 150 miles. Nothing to worry about." What do you do next?

3. You have been experiencing blinding headaches for two weeks. You've seen a physician and have undergone tests, but so far your physician has not made a diagnosis, but has instructed you not to operate heavy machinery while you're taking the painkillers that have been prescribed. Your boss calls you in for a run, saying two drivers quit on Monday and two more are out with the flu. You're his only possibility. When you explain what your physician has said, he explodes and tells you to show up in 30 minutes, ready to work—or lose your job. What do you do next?

4. You have performed your walk-around/pretrip inspection and filled out the DVIR, noting some leaking fluids, coming from who-knows-where. After the mechanic checks out your truck, he, too, hasn't figured out where the leak is coming from. To stay on schedule, you have to leave the terminal within the next 30 minutes. There are no other tractors available. What do you do next?

5. What does it mean, in Canada Labour Code, when it says, "The burden of proof is on the employee"? Does this mean you need documentation? Witnesses? What?

FOR MORE INFORMATION

Human Resources and Skills Development Canada
www.hrsdc.gc.ca/eng/labour/health_safety/overview.shtml

FMCSA Motor Carrier Employee Whistle Blower Protection
www.fmcsa.dot.gov/rules-regulations/administration/w-blower.htm

FMCSA—Rules and Regulations
www.fmcsa.dot.gov/rules-regulations/rules-regulations.htm

U.S. Department of Labor Whistleblower Protection
www.dol.gov/compliance/laws/comp-whistleblower.htm

U.S. DOT OIG Hotline Complaint Center
www.oig.dot.gov/Hotline

36 Compliance, Safety, Accountability (CSA)

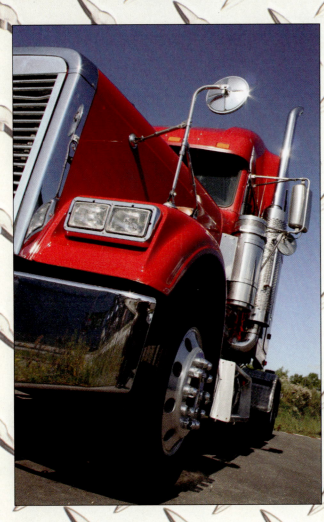

© Benjamin Haas/www.Shutterstock.com

OBJECTIVES

When you have completed this chapter, you should be able to:

- Understand the meaning and purpose of CSA.
- Explore CSA requirements and the responsibilities of a professional truck driver.
- Describe the CSA's measurement tools and how to track a driver's progress.

INTRODUCTION

The U.S. Department of Transportation's Federal Motor Carrier Safety Administration (FMCSA) took a major step toward improving commercial truck and bus safety with its Compliance, Safety, Accountability (CSA) program. When first announced, CSA 2010 stood for Comprehensive Safety Analysis, but when it was finalized the CSA stands for Compliance, Safety, and Accountability.

This program (CSA) replaces the "SafeStat" program that scored/rated only the carrier and had no scoring capability for drivers with the new Safety Measurement System (SMS).

Specifically, CSA is a U.S. government **initiative** to make roads safer by contacting motor carriers sooner before crashes occur. How? By identifying safety problems so correction can take place (**see Figure 36-1),** the details of which are described in this chapter.

▶ Figure 36-1

CSA is a U.S. government initiative to make the roads safer.

A BRIEF HISTORY OF CSA

Since 1986, the **Compliance Review (CR)** has been the primary **intervention** and investigative tool used by FMCSA to compel compliance and determine the safety fitness of commercial motor vehicles and passenger carriers (**see Figure 36-2**). A CR is a comprehensive assessment of a motor carrier's records by one of FMCSA's (or a state's) safety investigators at the carrier's principal place of business.

Data show the comprehensive Compliance Review to be very effective in changing unsafe behavior. However, it is also very time-consuming and labor-intensive. A CR can take a safety investigator up to a week or more to complete, depending on the size of the carrier and the complexity of **violations** found. This can be a problem because the comprehensive CR was, until CSA, the only tool at the disposal of FMCSA's safety investigators to begin the process of compelling improved compliance.

In addition, regulation for determining the safety fitness of motor carriers of property and passengers prior to CSA was tied to the comprehensive CR. Based on the findings of comprehensive CRs, motor carriers were issued a safety rating of Satisfactory, Conditional, or Unsatisfactory. However, these ratings could not change without conducting an additional CR, no matter how far a motor carrier's on-road performance may have slipped. The end result of these limitations was that FMCSA could address the safety deficiencies and rate only a small fraction of the industry—between two and three percent of the carrier population annually.

NOTE

TO DRIVERS DOMICILED AND LICENSED IN CANADA OR MEXICO: When transporting freight through the U.S., drivers are held accountable for their actions through interactive computer collection of data for CSA. Therefore, be aware of the requirements and parameters of this U.S. system.

▶ Figure 36-2

A driver inspecting his rig.

▶ **Figure 36-3**

Members of the CRWG include FMCSA headquarters and field staff.

▶ **Figure 36-4**

The FMCSA's safety mission includes the goal of reducing large truck crashes.

In the face of a growing industry and the government's limited resources, FMCSA senior leadership commissioned a Compliance Review Work Group (CRWG) to develop recommendations for improving the efficiency of the agency's compliance and enforcement program. This was soon after FMCSA became a stand-alone federal agency in 2000. Members of the work group consisted of FMCSA headquarters and field staff. The CRWG's major recommendation was the CSA concept—a more performance-based business model for compelling compliance and determining the safety fitness of motor carriers (**see Figure 36-3**).

In May 2005, the FMCSA Administrator commissioned the CSA team to develop a working business model for the agency, and to facilitate its implementation. Like the CRWG, the CSA team consisted of FMCSA headquarters and field staff, but was expanded to include state partner representatives as these partners are critical to the success of the CSA initiative in improving motor carrier safety.

Throughout the entire process of developing CSA, FMCSA continued to be as transparent as possible. The agency held a total of 11 public listening sessions to seek feedback from partners and stakeholders and continues to consider and incorporate as much feedback as possible.

THE GOALS OF CSA

In a letter to the U.S. Committee on Transportation and Infrastructure, dated June 2010, the Federal Motor Carrier Safety Administration's Administrator Anne S. Ferrero explained CSA as:

> CSA is an improved way for the Federal Motor Carrier Safety Administration (FMCSA) to carry out its important safety mission of reducing large truck and bus crashes, injuries, and fatalities on our nation's highways (**see Figure 36-4**). It is a business model by which the Agency can better target high risk motor carriers for early intervention and achieve improved levels of compliance with Federal safety and hazardous materials regulations. Additionally, through increased operational efficiencies, CSA will enable FMCSA and its State partners to address the safety deficiencies of a much larger segment of the motor carrier industry than we currently do.

CSA represents a great opportunity for FMCSA and its State partners to work to fulfill our obligation to the American people to find new solutions to our safety challenges.

THE CORE PRIORITIES OF CSA

To help prioritize the responsibilities of FMCSA and focus effort and resources on eliminating severe and fatal crashes involving commercial vehicles, FMCSA's priorities include:

- Raise the bar to enter the industry;
- Require operators to maintain high safety standards to remain in the industry; and
- Remove high-risk operators from our roads and highways.

This framework applies to companies, drivers, brokers, and service providers alike. To achieve the best outcome, FMCSA is working to improve its program and rule-development processes, its stakeholder relationships, and the health of the organization.

Although much remains to be accomplished, Ferrero, also a member of the U.S. Senate Subcommittee on Infrastructure Safety and Security and the Senate Committee on Finance, Science, and Transportation, issued a statement on April 28, 2010, that outlined recent improvements in motor carrier safety, which include:

- Total miles/kilometers traveled by all vehicles has grown significantly over the past 10 years, most significantly for large trucks and buses—there has been a 16 percent increase in miles/kilometers traveled by these vehicles from 1998 to 2008. In addition, the number of large trucks and buses registered has increased 17 percent over this time period.
- Even with the continued growth in commercial vehicle traffic, the most recent data available show that U.S. highways experienced their lowest number of fatalities (4,525 in 2008) from crashes involving large trucks and buses since fatal crash data collection began in 1975.
- Fatalities from large truck or bus crashes have dropped for three years in a row, a decline of 15 percent from 2006 to 2008.
- Safety improvements have been realized not only in terms of fatal crashes, but also in injury crashes. In 2008, 113,000 people were injured in crashes involving large trucks and buses, the lowest number of persons injured in these crashes since 1988, the first year of injury crash data collection.

SMS AND BASICS—MAJOR COMPONENTS OF CSA IMPROVE FMCSA'S METHOD OF DOING BUSINESS IN THREE WAYS

1. **The new Safety Measurement System (SMS) will replace the FMCSA's current measurement system, SafeStat.** In measuring a motor carrier's safety performance, **SafeStat** looks at only those roadside violations that result in Out-of-Service Orders, even though many more safety checks are conducted. Also included are certain moving violations and crash reports. None of the violations are weighted based on their relationship to crash risk.

   In contrast, the new SMS looks at all safety violations discovered at roadside, weights each one based on its crash risk, and measures safety performance in seven unsafe behavioral areas, called **BASICs**—Behavior Analysis Safety Improvement Categories. These are:
   (1) Unsafe Driving
   (2) Fatigued Driving (Hours-of-Service)
   (3) Driver Fitness
   (4) Controlled Substances/Alcohol
   (5) Vehicle Maintenance
   (6) Cargo-Related, and
   (7) Crash Indicator

By looking at all of the safety violations and grouping them into more categories related to unsafe behavior, SMS provides a much more comprehensive, robust, and granular view of the specific violations incurred by motor carriers and individual drivers. This enables FMCSA to get a better picture and more readily identify high-risk carriers, as well as other motor carriers, with violations that are not identified today through SafeStat.

SMS shows FMCSA when to begin to intervene with a motor carrier and because of its specificity, enables the agency to apply more efficient interventions. The end result is that under CSA, both motor carriers and drivers will have to be more alert to their roadside safety performance.

2. **The second major component that improves the FMCSA's current way of doing business is the broader array of compliance interventions developed under CSA.** Through CSA, FMCSA has more tools in its toolbox from which to choose in response to a motor carrier's safety performance. These include interventions that are more efficient and less labor intensive than the CR but that are focused on a carrier's specific problems.

The CSA operational model provides a broader array of less resource-intensive interventions to improve compliance. With the new SMS and interventions, this performance-based approach is designed to compel compliance and to remedy on-road performance deficiencies for a greater segment of the motor carrier population than can be reached with comprehensive CRs alone.

For example, for those motor carriers with just one or two deficient BASICs identified by the SMS, FMCSA may conduct an off-site investigation from one of its field offices or an onsite focused investigation. Additionally, FMCSA safety investigators do not have to spend time looking for violations in areas where the data suggest the carrier does *not* have a safety performance problem.

Also, for a motor carrier that has not demonstrated past safety deficiencies, but is beginning to do so, FMCSA will send a warning letter. The warning letter advises the carrier of its deficiency and that corrective action is warranted. Further monitoring of the carrier's performance through roadside data could result in improved compliance or the need for further intervention.

Under CSA, safety investigators are being trained to identify the root cause of the safety deficiency. For example, with hours-of-service violations, the root cause could be training and communication or a lack of internal oversight policies, practices, and procedures on the part of the motor carrier. By taking a few extra minutes with those motor carriers that demonstrate a willingness to correct their safety deficiencies, identifying the root cause not only facilitates quicker corrective action, but corrective action that will be more sustainable over time.

3. **The third major CSA component that will improve the agency's current way of doing business is a new methodology for determining property and passenger carrier fitness.** The new CSA safety fitness methodology would decouple the onsite CR from the safety rating. Thus, FMCSA could propose adverse safety ratings through the new SMS without necessarily having to go onsite to a motor carrier's place of business. This ultimately would allow FMCSA to assess the safety performance of a much larger segment of the motor carrier industry.

In addition to roadside performance, the new methodology would emphasize certain fundamental violations that would immediately trigger a proposed Unfit notice, such as not having a drug and alcohol testing program in place.

The ratings under consideration are Continue Operation, Marginal, or Unfit in contrast to the current ratings of Satisfactory, Conditional, or Unsatisfactory. The new Continue Operation label would allow FMCSA to move away from the Satisfactory label, which has sometimes led to requests for review of safe motor carriers, so that FMCSA could concentrate more directly on motor carriers with safety deficiencies and removing unsafe operators from the road.

Results to date indicate that individual FMCSA and state partner safety investigators in the test group are able to conduct up to 37 percent more investigations. In addition, enforcement actions against individual drivers were higher in the test group, in part because of the specificity with which the new SMS is able to identify violations among drivers as well as carriers. The efficiencies were further demonstrated in the types of investigations that have been conducted in the test states:

- Off-site Investigation—25 percent
- On-site Focused Investigation—45 percent
- On-site Comprehensive Investigation—30 percent

FMCSA continued to remain strong on enforcement throughout the test states. Enforcement actions have been taken as a result of off-site as well as on-site investigations. In addition, the agency continued in the test states to meet its congressional mandate by addressing high-risk motor carriers through on-site CRs. FMCSA also continued to intervene with passenger carriers and certain hazardous materials carriers through comprehensive on-site investigations.

IMPLEMENTATION PLANS FOR CSA

To implement the program, FMCSA has (1) replaced its current measurement system, SafeStat, with SMS; (2) sent warning letters nationwide; and (3) implemented a revised nationwide Inspection Selection System for roadside inspectors that is based on SMS rather than SafeStat. All motor carriers, including high-risk carriers, will be targeted for intervention using the new SMS. In addition, motor carrier safety performance in each BASIC will be publicly displayed in the same manner that the SEAs are displayed under SafeStat today.

With regard to the Crash BASIC, only the raw crash data will be displayed publicly. This is consistent with SafeStat today, because the crash reports do not include information on preventability or accountability. FMCSA will explore the feasibility of using police accident reports to determine accountability before the crash reports are entered into SMS to ensure it has the most accurate information available for assessing carriers' safety fitness.

Now motor carriers will be able to see their violations categorized by BASIC. After any refinements to the SMS methodology are completed, motor carriers will be able to see the SMS assessment of their violations through CSA. The purpose of this is to provide individual motor carriers the opportunity to view their data from the CSA perspective, and to use the time to identify and take actions to correct deficiencies in their operations that are leading to unsafe behavior.

CSA FACT SHEET

CSA is a major Federal Motor Carrier Safety Administration (FMCSA) initiative to improve the effectiveness of the agency's compliance and enforcement programs. Its goal is to achieve a greater reduction in large truck and bus crashes, injuries, and fatalities, while maximizing the resources of FMCSA and its state partners. For more information, visit www.csa2010.com/articles/FMCSA_CSA_2010_Fact_Sheet_Information.htm.

There are **four major elements** to CSA: 1—measurement, 2—intervention, 3—safety evaluation, and 4—COMPASS.

1. **The measurement system** would group the safety performance data of motor carriers and drivers into seven categories, called BASICs—Behavioral Analysis Safety Improvement Categories. The seven BASICs are:

   (1) Unsafe Driving

   (2) Fatigued Driving

   (3) Driver Fitness

   (4) Controlled Substances/Alcohol

(Continues)

CSA FACT SHEET (continued)

(5) Vehicle Maintenance

(6) Improper Loading/Cargo, and

(7) Crash Indicator

The data would be scored and weighted based on its relationship to crash causation. Based on a carrier's score within each BASIC, the measurement system would trigger when the agency should begin to intervene with a motor carrier, and when its performance has reached the proposed "unfit" threshold.

2. **Intervention**—Once the measurement system signals the need to intervene, CSA would draw upon a broad array of progressive interventions that are designed to advise the motor carrier or driver that their safety performance has come to the government's attention. These steps are meant to improve unsafe behavior early.

These include:

- Warning Letter
- Targeted Roadside Inspection
- Off-Site Investigation
- On-Site Investigation—Focused Cooperative Safety Plan Notice of Violation Increasing Severity On-Site Investigation
- Comprehensive Notice of Claim/Settlement Agreement

3. **Safety Evaluation**—Safety fitness determination would be based on performance data processed through the measurement system, and would not necessarily be tied to the current FMCSA compliance review. Depending on the motor carrier's BASIC scores, the safety fitness determination could be "continue to operate," "marginal" (with ongoing intervention), or proposed "unfit." Each motor carrier or driver for which there are sufficient data would receive a safety fitness determination that would be updated every 30 days.

4. **COMPASS**—CSA is closely aligned with COMPASS, an FMCSA-wide initiative that is leveraging new technology to transform the way that FMCSA does business. The ultimate goal is to implement an information technology (IT) solution that optimizes FMCSA's business processes and improves the Agency's ability to save lives.

Key objectives include:

- Creating a single source for crucial safety data via single sign-on access
- Improving data quality to ensure better, more informed decision making
- Providing actionable information as well as data

By optimizing FMCSA business processes and improving the agency's IT functionality, COMPASS will help FMCSA and state enforcement personnel make better decisions, identify high-risk carriers and drivers more effectively, and apply a wider range of interventions to correct high-risk behavior early.

CSA requirements that will be integrated into COMPASS include:

- Creation of a central, authoritative data source
- Incorporation of technical features that will allow the system to adapt to regulatory changes and improvements in business processes, with a minimum of programming and operational delay
- Incremental rollout of CSA-specified business processes through future COMPASS releases

WHAT DRIVERS NEED TO KNOW ABOUT CSA

CSA changes the way motor carriers are evaluated. Drivers will have more direct attention too—and it is important to know the ways CSA evaluates both carriers and drivers.

Primarily, CSA breaks down roadside activity into seven areas where previously four areas were used. Plus, before only out-of-service violations were counted in the calculations. Under CSA, *ALL* violations will be used in calculations.

Further, there are more intervention opportunities (chances to look at, educate, and improve operating policies) with specific element focus, so an investigator will have to look only at a problem area rather than all factors. This will allow more carriers to be visited. Another difference is that not all visits will be on-site. Some contacts will be off-site.

Another huge difference is that the former Safe-Stat way of measurement has no direct impact on the carrier's safety rating. However, under CSA,

▶ **Figure 36-5**

Carrier's rating may change monthly, depending on inspection volume.

the measurement tool (Safety Measurement System, SMS) feeds the safety fitness determination (rating). Therefore, the carrier's rating may change monthly, depending on inspection volume **(see Figure 36-5).**

In the past, drivers were rarely fined at roadside inspections. Under the new procedures, FMCSA can assess fines on problem drivers through intervention levels similar to motor carrier review. This means a driver's chances of receiving monetary fines will increase.

How Drivers Will Be Measured by CSA

CSA will not assess ratings to drivers. However, drivers with poor safety performance will be identified during an intervention. A driver-focused evaluation tool, **Driver Safety Measurement System (DSMS)** will be used by investigators, but this information will not be accessible by the industry.

Truck drivers will now have a **Pre-Employment Screening Program (PSP),** which is a screening tool that allows motor carriers and individual drivers to purchase driving records from the Federal Motor Carrier Safety Administration's (FMCSA) Motor Carrier Management Information System (MCMIS). Records are available for 24 hours a day via web request.

Driver Information Resource records purchased through PSP contain the most recent 5 years of crash data and 3 years of roadside inspection data from the FMCSA MCMIS system. Drivers will be able to see their individual safety information from the Driver Pre-Employment Screening Program. This program includes the driver's past history that inspectors are currently seeing. Access to these data requires driver consent.

FMCSA believes that making these driver data available to potential employers and operator-applicants will improve the quality of safety data and help employers make more informed decisions when hiring commercial drivers. The PSP provides more rapid access to commercial driver safety performance information than was previously available under Freedom of Information Act (FOIA) or Privacy Act requests.

CSA Interventions for Carriers

CSA interventions include:

Early Contact:

1. warning letter
2. carrier access to safety data and measurement information, and
3. targeted roadside inspection

Investigations:

1. off-site investigation
2. on-site focused investigation, and
3. on-site comprehensive investigation

Follow-on Interventions—Involving the Carrier:

1. cooperative safety plan
2. notice of violation
3. notice of claim, and
4. settlement agreement

How Interventions Happen. Interventions can be triggered by (1) one or more deficient BASICs, (2) a high crash indicator, or (3) a complaint or fatal crash.

As mentioned above, all violations count under CSA. However, violations are weighted, based on crash causation. By weighting violations, newer violations will be more damaging than older ones. There is a maximum level on the severity points any one violation charged against the driver or carrier can cause.

CSA Carrier Evaluation

Carriers are evaluated on size in CSA. Carriers will be broken into peer groups based on the number of power units in some basics and the number of inspections in other basics.

The evaluation data in SafeStat goes back 2-1/2 years. In CSA, there is a 24-month tracking period for carrier data. Driver data will be tracked three years.

A wider range of the industry will be assessed. By digging deeper within the evaluation areas, carriers will be assessed more stringently and may not appear as good as they have in the past.

FMCSA has put together a website devoted to CSA at www.csa2010.fmcsa.dot.gov. This site is being updated frequently. See the Frequently Asked Questions, the Safety Measurement System (SMS) document, the Driver Fact Sheet, Media Kit, Factsheets, Brochures, and other materials.

CAUTION!

CSA also retains some of the same elements of previous safety programs. As an example, carriers will still be evaluated and FMCSA field agents will still visit the motor carrier when performance suggests attention is needed.

SafeStat hides driver names and personal information to the general public and makes it available to the motor carrier. Under SafeStat, the motor carrier saw only a driver's activity that occurred while operating under their authority. This specific driver information is hidden from the general public view and will continue to be hidden under CSA.

DataQ is the Data Correction Request System that exists today and will continue. Carriers and drivers can request data be corrected through this system.

CSA ROADSIDE INSPECTION VIOLATIONS AND POINTS ASSIGNED

The Department of Transportation has assigned a **point value,** ranging from 1 to 10, to every violation that could be cited on a roadside inspection. These points are assigned even if no warning or citation is issued. If the problem (violation) appears on the Driver's Vehicle Inspection Report, but was not corrected before the trip began, points also are assigned.

The violations most likely to predict a future crash, as identified by the Department of Transportation, are assigned a value of 10 points and include some of the following:

- Use or possession of drugs or alcohol
- Reckless driving
- Operating a CMV while fatigued or ill
- Operating a CMV that has been issued an out-of-service order
- Possession of more than one license
- Most load securement violations

Other violations and their assigned point values:

- Wheel & tire violations **8 pts**
- Size & weight violations **7 pts**
- False log entries **7 pts**
- 70/14/11-hour violations **7 pts**

All of these violations and their assigned point values apply to both the carrier rating and the driver safety determination, as determined by the U.S. DOT.

> **NOTE**
>
> Prior to CSA, only out-of-service violations were used to rate carriers. With CSA, violations are now assigned to drivers, as well.

Violations that are more recent are given a higher weight rating. As an example, a violation for improper load securement that is less than 6 months old is assigned 3 points for a total value of 30. After 6 months, it's weighted only twice for a total value of 20, and after 12 months its value drops to 10.

According to FMCSA officials, CSA is designed to identify carriers and drivers with repeated violations involving behaviors designated as predictors of future involvement in highway crashes. Carriers and drivers who fail to correct these identified behaviors will receive increased monitoring as well as increasingly more intensive interventions.

Professional drivers as well as their employers should take time to learn more about CSA and implement training programs so all personnel, including drivers, will be able to reduce violations cited on roadside inspections.

In every case, putting safe and well-maintained rigs on the road, driven by educated and safety-aware professional drivers, is a team effort for every carrier and management team.

SUMMARY

The FMCSA's CSA initiative to make professional drivers safer on our continent's highways is an important step, one drivers should welcome and educate themselves about.

As anyone who has worked any length of time in the transportation industry knows, professional driving is a profession that involves many risks. Removing unsafe carriers and drivers from the road is not only the goal of CSA, but it should be a goal shared by every professional in the industry.

As you may be aware, it takes only one careless carrier or poorly trained or not rested driver to make banner headlines, should an accident occur. Not only do these headlines damage the reputations of all carriers and drivers, but they also tarnish the industry, regardless of individual efforts to meet every regulation and rule.

Taking safety shortcuts, believing that accidents only happen to other drivers, and skipping safety meetings only paves the roadway to disaster.

In the meantime, the sheer increase in the volume of data contained in CSA (all roadside violations cited) versus SafeStat (out-of-service violations only) is monumental—and as this program continues, there will be tweaks and major changes along the way. Yet, it is all for the safety of drivers, equipment, cargo, and the good name of the industry.

By way of example of the anticipated apathy and I-don't-care attitudes on the parts of carriers, the FMCSA recently revealed that only 13,000 carriers out of approximately 600,000 had even bothered to check out their CSA data.

As CSA continues to evolve and become more familiar within the industry, drivers and carriers will begin to see this program as a fair, performance-based tool that captures all violations of the Federal Motor Carrier Safety Regulations on roadside inspections. However, it also rewards carriers who "get it" and eliminate the violations because they reduce in value and eventually fall off their record.

When drivers and carriers address unsafe behaviors and practices, it's not only good for business, but it's good for the trucking transportation industry, as well.

KEY TERMS

BASIC
Compliance Review (CR)
Driver Safety Measurement
  System (DSMS)
Initiative

Intervention
Point value
Pre-Employment Screening
  Program (PSP)

SafeStat
Safety Measurement System
  (SMS)

REVIEW QUESTIONS

1. CSA is a U.S. government initiative to make roads safer by _____.

   a. hand-selected drivers

   b. taking trucks off roads

   c. identifying and correcting behaviors contributing to crashes

   d. distributing SMS cards to safe drivers

2. The U.S. Department of Transportation has assigned a value of 10 points when inspectors find the driver _____.

   a. is seriously ill

   b. is in training and driving without a trainer

   c. is in the lower 25 percent of his/her truck driving school

   d. is behind schedule for his/her destination

3. In CSA, there is a _____ tracking period for driver data.

   a. 18-month

   b. 24-month

   c. 3-year

   d. 2-year

4. Data gathered by inspectors for the Driver Safety Measurement System (DSMS) is not accessible by _____.

   a. the general public   **c.** law enforcement

   b. the industry *✔*   **d.** the ATA

5. The old safety rating system, SafeStat, was based on _____.

   a. the mechanical condition of the truck   **c.** hours-of-service record

   b. out-of-service *✔*   **d.** driver documents

6. In the early days of CSA, apathy in the industry was apparent by _____.

   a. the number of trucks put out of service   **c.** carriers that didn't check their CSA rating *✔*

   b. drivers that didn't check their SMS   **d.** the number of questions submitted to the CSA portal

7. The use or possession of drugs and alcohol, identified as a contributor to unsafe driving and/or a crash indicator, if found during roadside inspection, would be assigned a(n) _____ point total.

   a. 8   **c.** 12

   b. 10 *✔*   **d.** 15

8. CSA inventions for carriers include all but one of the following:

   a. warning letter   **c.** targeted roadside inspection

   b. driver fines *✔*   **d.** off-site investigation

9. An FMCSA-wide initiative that is leveraging new technology to transform the way that FMCSA does business is _____.

   a. CSA   **c.** SafeStat

   b. PRISM   **d.** COMPASS *✔*

10. All but one of the following are the seven BASICs:

   a. unsafe driving   **c.** driver fitness

   b. vehicle maintenance   **d.** overweight cargo *✔*

SUPPLEMENTAL LEARNING ACTIVITIES

1. Gather as much information about the CSA initiative as you can find on the Internet. Then, in a group, present a three-minute talk on what you think is the most important information for new drivers to know.

2. Look up the exact specifications of "Driver Fitness." Make a list of these specifications and discuss them in a small group.

3. Ask a safety director from a local carrier to come to your class and discuss CSA.

4. As a class, discuss what you should do if, as a professional driver, you are subjected to a roadside inspection. What information should you have? What documents? Who should you notify at your home terminal? What should you say to the inspector?

5. Find out how much drivers have been fined for an unacceptable roadside inspection in your area of the state.

FOR MORE INFORMATION

FMCSA CSA Information
csa2010.fmcsa.dot.gov/about

FMCSA Driver Pre-Employment Screening Program
www.psp.fmcsa.dot.gov

U.S. DOT CSA—Compliance, Safety, Accountability
csa.fmcsa.dot.gov/default.aspx

Note: In January 2012, CSA released a number of fact sheets, including topics such as driver fitness. These may be found at csa.fmcsa.dot.gov.

Troubleshooting Guide

Find out your company's rules for drivers doing any type of repairs to their equipment. Find out what they expect of you. Follow your company's policy. Do *not* do any type of repair work unless you have been authorized to do so.

Whatever you do, safety first—everywhere and always. And, if you see someone doing something that is unsafe or attempting something in an unsafe manner, don't hesitate to step up and say something. You may save a life . . . and remember, the most important thing is to get home safely after every run.

Warning.   Before you do anything regarding troubleshooting, always put on personal protective equipment including safety glasses, boots, safety vest, hat and gloves. Know what you're doing, and if you don't have the experience or training, leave these activities to the trained technicians. Nothing—time tables, traffic or even pride—is worth injury or your life.

If You See/Feel/Smell...	System Affected	What to Look For	What to Do
1. Ammeter shows continuous maximum charge	Electrical	Short circuit in wiring	Disconnect battery terminal until short has been repaired
		Points in voltage regulator or cutout sticking	Have mechanic repair
2. Ammeter shows discharge with motor running	Electrical	Loose connection or short in wiring	Tighten connection
		Battery installed wrong	Have checked by a mechanic
		Burned out or improperly adjusted generator or alternator	Have replaced or repaired by mechanic
		Loose or broken alternator	Replace or tighten belt
3. High engine temperature	Cooling	Low water level	Shut off engine, allow to cool to normal, add coolant/water
		Frozen radiator	Cover radiator, run motor slowly, add coolant/water as needed
		Broken fan belt	Replace fan belt
		Slow water or oil circulation	Have checked and repaired by mechanic
		Defective fan clutch or shutters	Have checked and repaired by mechanic
		Blocked radiator	Have checked and repaired by mechanic
		Defective thermostat or radiator hose suction side	Have checked and repaired by mechanic

If You See/Feel/Smell…	System Affected	What to Look For	What to Do
4. Coolant, oil, or fuel dripping	Cooling, lubricating, or fuel system	Check for source of leak	Have repaired by mechanic
5. Gauge reading out of proper range		Check the system that corresponds with the gauge	Have mechanic check gauge and appropriate system
6. Excessive exhaust smoke	Exhaust or turbo system	Air cleaner dirty Poor grade of fuel Return fuel link blocked, bent, or squeezed together Engine overfueled Fuel pump malfunctioning Pollution controls malfunctioning	Clean filter Let mechanic check and repair Have checked and repaired by mechanic
7. Black exhaust smoke	Engine, fuel system	Over-rich mixture due to restricted air supply, poor fuel spray distribution, improperly adjusted fuel control racks, or overloading or lugging the engine	Clean or change filters, let mechanic check Shift to lower gear to keep engine speed up
8. White (sometimes gray) exhaust smoke	Engine, fuel system	Due to incomplete combustion in cold engine; should clear up when engine warms If it does not, look for misfiring due to worn injector spray holes, low cylinder compression, faulty cooling system, or low fuel volatility	Have mechanic check
9. Blue exhaust smoke	Engine or fuel system	Due to the burning of large quantities of lubricating oil as a result of worn intake valve guides, poor oil control ring action, worn blower or turbo shaft seals, or overfilled oil bath air cleaner	Have mechanic check

If You See/Feel/Smell...	System Affected	What to Look For	What to Do
10. Low oil pressure warning indicator light on dash	Lubricating system	Oil has become diluted by fuel or coolant leaks High oil temperature Worn oil pump Wrong weight of oil for type of weather conditions Dirty filters Worn bearings Oil and filter needs changing Oil leak	Let mechanic check Let mechanic check Change oil Clean or replace Replace Change oil and filter Let mechanic check
11. Metallic click in time with wheel revolutions	Suspension, wheels, or tires	Wheel loose on axle Loose wheel or tire lugs Piece of metal in tire	Tighten axle nut Tighten lugs Remove metal or change tire
12. Dull thud in time with wheel revolutions	Wheels and tires	Flat tire Loose wheel or tire lugs Rock between duals	Change tire Tighten lugs Remove rock
13. Clanking noise in time with wheel	Tire on drive train system	Lock rim off tire Loose driveshaft	Change tire Have tightened by mechanic
14. Dull thud or loud rap in time with engine	Engine	Burned-out main or connecting rod bearing Piston slap	Shut off motor, contact garage for instructions
15. Air escaping	Tires, air system, or braking system	Punctured or damaged tire Open petcock on air Air lines or fittings leaking Brake application or relay valve sticking Ice on brake valves	Change tire Close petcock Repair lines, tighten or change fittings Apply air to brakes several times Apply heat if you have been taught how to do this
16. Snap or click when starting from dead stop	Drive train system Fifth wheel	Loose universal joint bolts Excessive wear in universal joint or differential Worn or broken fifth-wheel lock Loose or broken mounting bolts	Tighten bolts Report to mechanic
17. Under floor noises	Drive train	Clutch trouble Bad throw-out bearing Bent driveshaft Broken teeth in transmission	Have mechanic check

If You See/Feel/Smell...	System Affected	What to Look For	What to Do
18. Whine—harsh with high pitch	Drive train or engine system	Worn accessory drive gears Loose belts	Let mechanic check Tighten belts
19. Whine—short with high pitch	Engine	Ball bearing spinning in housing Generator or alternator malfunctioning Water pump malfunctioning	Have mechanic check Shut off engine immediately
20. Clicking sound in engine with loss of power, sluggishness, and overheating	Engine	Broken valve spring Worn timing gear	Have mechanic check
21. Sudden loss of power	Brake, drive train, engine, or fuel system	Brakes dragging Clutch slipping Spark plug wire disconnected Overheated engine Vapor lock Blocked fuel filter Fuel pedal linkage failure	Have adjusted by mechanic Have adjusted by mechanic Replace wire Determine cause of overheating and correct it Let cool Change filter or have it changed Check linkage connectors
22. Engine surges	Fuel or engine system	Air in fuel system Worn gear on fuel pump Throttle linkage loose Low fuel supply Buffer screw not properly set	Have mechanic check
23. Brakes grab	Braking system	Grease or brake lining Improperly adjusted brakes	Have grease removed by mechanic Have readjusted by mechanic
24. Brakes do not hold	Braking system	Brakes out of adjustment Grease on linings Water or ice on linings Low air pressure Air tanks full of oil or water Master cylinder low on fluid Worn brake linings Hydraulic line broken Broken air line or fitting leaking	Have readjusted by mechanic Have removed by mechanic Drive short distance with hand brake set Check for air leaks Bleed air tanks Fill master cylinder Have replaced by mechanic Repair or install new line Repair or install new air line or fitting

If You See/Feel/Smell...	System Affected	What to Look For	What to Do
25. Constant pull to right or left on steering	Tires, suspension, braking, or steering system	A soft tire A broken spring One front brake tight Misadjusted tandem or front axle alignment	Repair or change it Drive carefully until can be replaced or repaired Adjust or have adjusted by mechanic
26. Tractor does not want to come back straight after lane change or turn	Steering/fifth wheel	Dry fifth wheel	Grease fifth wheel
27. Vibration in engine	Engine system	One or more cylinders not firing caused by defective spark plugs, shortened spark plug wires, or wires off spark plug Sticky valve Broken valve Blown cylinder head gasket Vibration damper loose or worn Unbalanced or damaged fan Engine mounting loose or worn Engine out of line in frame Clutch out of balance Drive line out of balance or line Bad injectors Air in fuel	Change plugs or make necessary adjustments Have repairs made by mechanic
28. Vibration in steering in time with rotation of wheels	Tire, wheel, or rim	Wheels out of balance Bubble on side of tire Broken lock rim on tire Bent wheels or rims Uneven tire wear caused by other defects Tire mounted on wheel incorrectly Loose wheel lugs, broken studs	Have adjustments made by mechanic Change tire Change tire Change tire Have defects corrected by mechanic Loosen tire lugs and tighten evenly Tighten lugs, have broken studs replaced

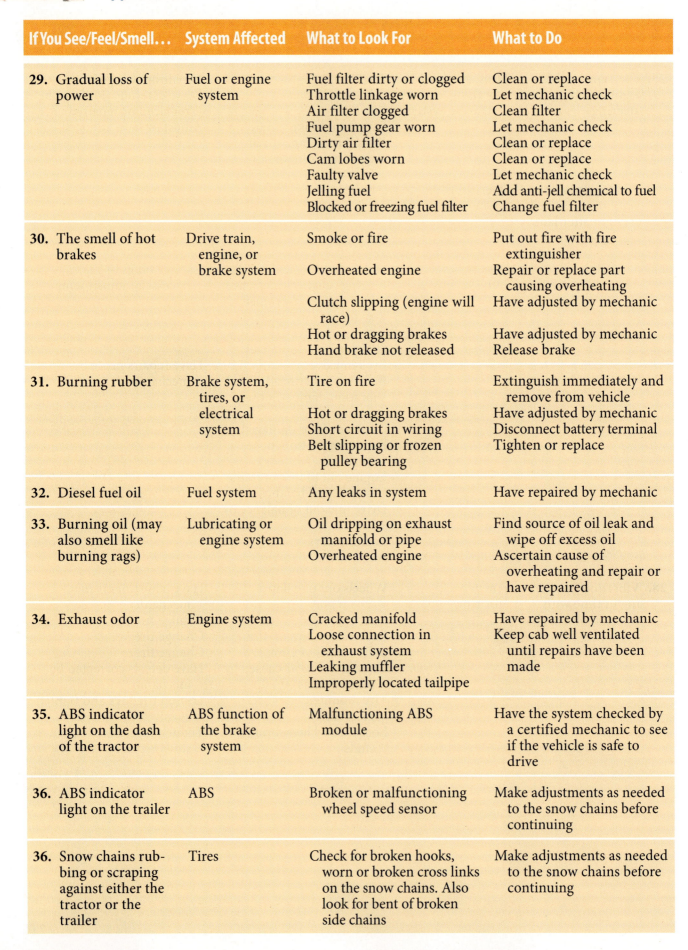

If You See/Feel/Smell...	System Affected	What to Look For	What to Do
29. Gradual loss of power	Fuel or engine system	Fuel filter dirty or clogged Throttle linkage worn Air filter clogged Fuel pump gear worn Dirty air filter Cam lobes worn Faulty valve Jelling fuel Blocked or freezing fuel filter	Clean or replace Let mechanic check Clean filter Let mechanic check Clean or replace Clean or replace Let mechanic check Add anti-jell chemical to fuel Change fuel filter
30. The smell of hot brakes	Drive train, engine, or brake system	Smoke or fire Overheated engine Clutch slipping (engine will race) Hot or dragging brakes Hand brake not released	Put out fire with fire extinguisher Repair or replace part causing overheating Have adjusted by mechanic Have adjusted by mechanic Release brake
31. Burning rubber	Brake system, tires, or electrical system	Tire on fire Hot or dragging brakes Short circuit in wiring Belt slipping or frozen pulley bearing	Extinguish immediately and remove from vehicle Have adjusted by mechanic Disconnect battery terminal Tighten or replace
32. Diesel fuel oil	Fuel system	Any leaks in system	Have repaired by mechanic
33. Burning oil (may also smell like burning rags)	Lubricating or engine system	Oil dripping on exhaust manifold or pipe Overheated engine	Find source of oil leak and wipe off excess oil Ascertain cause of overheating and repair or have repaired
34. Exhaust odor	Engine system	Cracked manifold Loose connection in exhaust system Leaking muffler Improperly located tailpipe	Have repaired by mechanic Keep cab well ventilated until repairs have been made
35. ABS indicator light on the dash of the tractor	ABS function of the brake system	Malfunctioning ABS module	Have the system checked by a certified mechanic to see if the vehicle is safe to drive
36. ABS indicator light on the trailer	ABS	Broken or malfunctioning wheel speed sensor	Make adjustments as needed to the snow chains before continuing
36. Snow chains rubbing or scraping against either the tractor or the trailer	Tires	Check for broken hooks, worn or broken cross links on the snow chains. Also look for bent of broken side chains	Make adjustments as needed to the snow chains before continuing

Website Reference List

Chapter One

American Trucking Associations campaign
www.trucksbringit.com

Federal Motor Carrier Safety Administration (FMCSA)—Find information about FMCSA's safety programs and the most up-to-date listing of rules and regulations
www.fmcsa.dot.gov

Bureau of Labor Statistics—Search transportation for information about occupations
www.bls.gov

NSC Standards—Learn details
www.ccmta.ca/english/producstandservices/
publications/publications.cfm#NSC

Chapter Two

FMCSA Commercial Driver's License Program
www.fmcsa.dot.gov/registration-licensing/cdl/cdl
.htm

Information on driver's licenses for each province or territory
www.servicecanada.gc.ca/eng/subjects/cards/
drivers_licence.shtml

Driver's licenses are issued by the provincial governments in Canada
canadaonline.about.com/od/driverslicence/Drivers
_Licences_in_Canada.htm

More information about 49 CFR Part 383
fmcsa.dot.gov

Chapter Three

Professional Truck Driver Institute Standards
www.ptdi.org/standards/index.aspx

PTDI—Read and Interpret Control Systems, Page 7, Click on Skill Standards
www.ptdi.org/standards

Chapter Four

PTDI—Check and Maintain Vehicle Systems and Components, Page 17, Click on Skill Standards
www.ptdi.org/standards

FMCSA Commercial Vehicle Tire Condition Sensors—Search for Tire Condition Sensors to view PDF
www.fmcsa.dot.gov

FMCSA Benefits and Costs of Roll Stability Control Systems—Search for Roll Stability Control Systems
www.fmcsa.dot.gov

Chapter Five

Technology for Reducing Idling Time
www.transportation.anl.gov/pdfs/TA/74.pdf

Transportation Technology Videos
americanhistory.si.edu/onthemove/themes/
story_50_1.html

Transportation Technology Used in Trucks
www.yousigma.com/technologyandarchitectures/
transportationtechnologyusedintrucks.pdf

On-Board Recorders Part 395.15—Search for Automatic On-board Recording Devices
www.fmcsa.dot.gov/

Chapter Six

PTDI—Perform Vehicle Inspections, Page 9, Click on Skill Standards
www.ptdi.org/standards

FMCSA Preventive Maintenance and Inspection Procedures—Search for Preventive Maintenance and Inspection Procedures
www.fmcsa.dot.gov/

CSA Inspection Standards—Search for North American Standard Driver/Vehicle Inspection Levels
www.fmcsa.dot.gov/

California Commercial Driver Handbook Truck or Combination Vehicle Inspection Guide
dmv.ca.gov/pubs/cdl_htm/sec10_trkguide.htm

CDL Pre-Trip Inspection and Skills Evaluation Score Sheet
dmv.ca.gov/forms/dl/dl65prt1.pdf

CCOHS Vehicle Start-Up, the Circle Check
www.ccohs.ca/oshanswers/safety_haz/landscaping/vehicle.html

Chapter Seven

PTDI—Exercise Basic Control, Page 10, Click on Skill Standards
www.ptdi.org/standards

PTDI—Manage and Adjust Vehicle Speed, Page 15, Click on Skill Standards
www.ptdi.org/standards

Controlling Sway
www.timberman.com/RIG/sway.htm

Chapter Eight

PTDI—Execute Shifting, Page 11, Click on Skill Standards
www.ptdi.org/standards

How to Shift a Tractor Trailer
www.ehow.com/how_5505283_shift-tractor-trailer.html

How to Double Clutch a Tractor Trailer
www.ehow.com/how_4852957_double-clutch-tractor-trailer.html

Chapter Nine

PTDI—Back and Dock Tractor-Trailer, Page 12, Click on Skill Standards
www.ptdi.org/standards

Backing a Tractor-Trailer
www.tpub.com/content/engine/14081/css/14081_176.htm

Backing Up Tractor-Trailer Rigs
www.gonefcon.com/trucktcom/backing.htm

Chapter Ten

PTDI—Couple Trailer, Page 12, Click on Skill Standards
www.ptdi.org/standards

California DMV—Coupling and Uncoupling
dmv.ca.gov/pubs/cdl_htm/sec7.htm

Coupling & Uncoupling
www.newbiedriver.com/abcsupdates/couplinguncoupling.htm

Chapter Eleven

Freight Management and Operations
www.ops.fhwa.dot.gov/freight/

Moving the Fifth Wheel on Your 18-Wheel Tractor Trailer
www.truck-drivers-money-saving-tips.com/fifth-wheel.html

Council of Ministers—A detailed description of legal weights per axle and for various tractor-trailer configurations across North America
www.comt.ca/english/programs/trucking/NAFTA%20Side%20by%20Side%20Update%20May%202001.pdf

Chapter Twelve

PTDI—Check and Maintain Vehicle Systems and Components, Page 17, Click on Skill Standards
www.ptdi.org/standards

Commercial Vehicle Safety Alliance—Roadcheck
www.cvsa.org/programs/int_roadcheck.php

U.S. DOT Roadcheck 2011
fastlane.dot.gov/2011/06/roadcheck-2011.html

Chapter Thirteen

PTDI—Diagnose and Report Malfunctions, Page 18, Click on Skill Standards
www.ptdi.org/standards

Driver Vehicle Inspection Report
www.fmcsa.dot.gov/rules-regulations/administration/fmcsr/fmcsrruletext.aspx?reg=396.11

How to Jump-Start a Big Rig Using the Rescue 2000
www.youtube.com/watch?v=_fLV3Jb62oo

Chapter Fourteen

Domestic Preparedness—Search on Highway Watch Program
www.domesticpreparedness.com/

Trucker CB Communications
www.truckercountry.com/trucker-communications.html

Sections of the Canadian Highway Traffic Act, Ontario
www.e-laws.gov.on.ca/html/statutes/english/elaws_statutes_90h08_e.htm#BK120 and www.e-laws.gov.on.ca/html/regs/english/elaws_regs_900596_e.htm

Chapter Fifteen

PTDI—Perform Visual Search, Page 14, Search on Skill Standards
www.ptdi.org/standards

Concave and Convex Mirrors and Lenses
faculty.virginia.edu/teach-present-bio/LightRefraction.html

Chapter Sixteen

PTDI—Manage and Adjust Vehicle Space Relations, Page 15, Click on Skill Standards
www.ptdi.org/standards

FMCSA Defensive Driving Tips for CMV Drivers
www.fmcsa.dot.gov/facts-research/research-technology/report/FMCSA-RRR-09-003.pdf

Keys To Safety
thekeystruckers.com/keys-to-safety/

Chapter Seventeen

PTDI—Manage and Adjust Vehicle Speed, Page 15, Click on Skill Standards
www.ptdi.org/standards

Safety Impacts on Differential Speed Limits on Rural Interstate Highways
www.fhwa.dot.gov/publications/research/safety/04156/index.cfm

FMCSA Large Truck Crash Causation Study
www.fmcsa.dot.gov/facts-research/research-technology/analysis/fmcsa-rra-07-017.htm

National Motorists Association State Speed Limit Chart
www.motorists.org/speed-limits/state-chart

Chapter Eighteen

PTDI—Identify and Adjust to Difficult and Extreme Driving Conditions, Page 20, Click on Skill Standards
www.ptdi.org/standards

Tips for Safe Night Driving, Road & Travel Magazine
www.roadandtravel.com/safetyandsecurity/safenightdrivingtips.htm

Hub Pages—Night Driving Tips
hubpages.com/hub/Night-Driving-Tips

FMCSA—Driver Fatigue
www.fmcsa.dot.gov/about/outreach/education/driverTips/Driver-fatigue.htm

Chapter Nineteen

PTDI—Identify and Adjust to Difficult and Extreme Driving Conditions, Page 20, Click on Skill Standards
www.ptdi.org/standards

PTDI—Deal with Environmental Issues, Page 24, Click on Skill Standards
www.ptdi.org/standards

Weather Channel, Driving Safety Tips
www.weather.com/activities/driving/drivingsafety/drivingsafetytips/snow.html

Washington State Department of Transportation—Guide for Cold Weather Driving
www.wsdot.wa.gov/winter

Chapter Twenty

Antilock Braking Systems
www.fmcsa.dot.gov/documents/fhwa-abs.pdf

Why Does a Tractor Trailer Jackknife?
www.cartaste.com/transport-safety/article-4-08022.html

Tractor Trailer Jackknife
www.marules.com/docs/expertreports/ExpertReport_TractorTrailerJackknife.pdf

How to Avoid Jackknifing
auto.howstuffworks.com/auto-parts/towing/vehicle-towing/maneuvers/how-to-avoid-jackknifing.htm/printable

Chapter Twenty-One

PTDI—Identify Potential Driving Hazards and Perform Emergency Maneuvers, Page 19, Click on Skill Standards
www.ptdi.org/standards

Alberta's Traffic Safety Amendment Act–2005
www.saferoads.com/drivers/constructionsfty_faq.html

British Columbia's Laws, as of Aug. 2011
www.bclaws.ca/EPLibraries/bclaws_new/document/ID/freeside/96318_05

Tractor Trailer Driving Tips
www.ehow.com/way_5610919_tractor-trailer-driving-tips.html

Chapter Twenty-Two

Operation Lifesaver—Canada
www.operationlifesaver.ca and www.TrainToDrive.net

Operation Lifesaver—U.S.
oli.org

U.S. DOT Compilation of State Laws Regarding Railroad Crossings
www.fra.dot.gov/rrs/pages/fp_2305.shtml

Highway–Rail Grade Crossing Safety Regulations
www.fmcsa.dot.gov/about/outreach/railcrossing/railregs.htm?printer=true

U.S. DOT Railway–Highway Grade Crossing
safety.fhwa.dot.gov/xings/

CDC—Railroad Crossing Safety for Emergency Responders
www.cdc.gov/niosh/docs/2003-121/

Chapter Twenty-Three

PTDI—Identify Potential Driving Hazards and Perform Emergency Maneuvers, Page 19, Click on Skill Standards
www.ptdi.org/standards

FMCSA—Required Knowledge and Skills, Search Required Knowledge
www.fmcsa.dot.gov

FMCSA—Preventive Maintenance and Inspection Procedures, Search Preventive Maintenance
www.fmcsa.dot.gov

Chapter Twenty-Four

PTDI—Deal with Accident Scenes and Reporting Procedures, Page 23, Click on Skill Standards
www.ptdi.org/standards

Canadian Emergency Response Guidebook
www.tc.gc.ca/eng/canutec/new-222.htm

Example of a Trucker's Accident Packet
www.thehortongroup.com/Files/86365175-6df5-f5d6-b78e-342151174129.pdf

FMCSA's "Smart Roadside Initiative"
www.fmcsa.dot.gov/facts-research/art-technology-smart-roadside-for-commercial.htm

Chapter Twenty-Five

FMCSA Cargo Securement
www.fmcsa.dot.gov/rules-regulations/truck/driver/education-material.htm

FMCSA Development of North American Standard for Protection Against Shifting and Falling Cargo
www.fmcsa.dot.gov/cargosecurement.pdf

OSHA Worker Safety Series Warehousing
www.osha.gov/Publications/3220_Warehouse.pdf

FMCSA Cargo Securement Rules
www.fmcsa.dot.gov/rules-regulations/truck/vehicle/cs-policy.htm

Oregon Motor Carrier Transportation Load Securement
www.oregon.gov/ODOT/MCT/SAFETY.shtml#Load_Securement

Chapter Twenty-Six

PTDI—Handle and Document Cargo, Page 22, Click on Skill Standards
www.ptdi.org/standards

Cabotage Rules for Canadian Drivers in the U.S.
www.fmcsa.dot.gov/intl-programs/intl-programs.htm

U.S. Customs and Border Protection
www.cbp.gov

FHWA's Office of Freight Management and Operations—Information on CMV weight and size Regulations in the U.S.
www.ops.fhwa.dot.gov/freight/sw/index.htm

Highway Traffic Act—Canadian Truck Weight
and Size Laws
www.e-laws.gov.on.ca/html/regs/english/elaws
_regs_050413_e.htm

Chapter Twenty-Seven

Tanker Driving Jobs
www.ehow.com/about_4795086_tanker-driving-jobs.html

NYS DMV Commercial Driver's Manual—Tank Vehicles
www.nydmv.state.ny.us/broch/cdl/cdl10sec08.pdf

Cattle Hauling Jobs
www.ehow.com/list_6851078_cattle-hauling-jobs.html

Big Rigs Around the World
en.wikipedia.org/wiki/Semi-trailer_truck

Ontario LCV Program
www.mto.gov.on.ca/english/trucks/lcv/program-conditions/overview-and-principles.shtml

Chapter Twenty-Eight

PTDI—Record and Maintain Hours of Service Requirements, Page 28, Click on Skill Standards
www.ptdi.org/standards

FMCSA Hours of Service Regulations
www.fmcsa.dot.gov/rules-regulations/truck/driver/hos/fmcsa-guide-to-hos.pdf

Sleep Apnea Disorder Information
sleepapneadisorder.info

Ontario Hours of Service
www.e-laws.gov.on.ca/html/regs/english/elaws
_regs_060555_e.htm

Department of Justice Canada—Hours of Service Regulations
laws-lois.justice.gc.ca/eng/regulations/SOR-2005-313/

Chapter Twenty-Nine

Plan Trips/Make Appropriate Decisions, Page 25
www.ptdi.org/errata/SKILLSTANDARDS_
ENTRYLEVEL1.pdf

Trucker Country—Trip Planning Center
www.truckercountry.com/trip-planning.html

CDL Jobs Trip Planning
www.cdljobs.com/tripplanning.htm

Longhauler Maps
www.longhauler-usa.com/bttrmaps.htm

Canadian Permits
www.bclaws.ca/EPLibraries/bclaws_new/document/ID/freeside/30_78

Ministry of Transportation Ontario—Guide to Oversize/Overweight Vehicles and Loads in Ontario
www.mto.gov.on.ca/english/trucks/oversize/guide.shtml

U.S. DOT Federal Highway Administration—Oversize/Overweight Load Permits
ops.fhwa.dot.gov/freight/sw/permit_report/index.htm

Chapter Thirty

FMCSA Limiting the Use of Wireless Communication Devices—Search on Limiting Wireless Communication
www.fmcsa.dot.gov/

NCTR UCF Intermodal Transportation Safety and Security Issues
www.nctr.usf.edu/jpt/pdf/JPT%208-4S%20Tarr.pdf

Trucking Security from the TSA
www.tsa.gov/what_we_do/grants/programs/tsp/2009/index.shtm

Road Transportation in Canadian Regions
www.tc.gc.ca/eng/regions-road.htm

U.S. DOT FMCSA Safety & Security
www.fmcsa.dot.gov/safety-security/safety-security.htm

Chapter Thirty-One

Mexican Laws and Regulations Available on MTO
mexicotrucker.com/en/translation-of-mexican-laws-and-regulations-available-on-mto

Mexico's Vehicle Height and Weight standards
mexicotrucker.com/wp-content/uploads/downloads/2010/09/Translated-Mexican-Transport-Rules-and-Regulation.pdf

Transport Canada CANUTEC
www.tc.gc.ca/eng/canutec/

Guide to the Agreement on Uniform Vehicle Weights and Dimensions Limits in Atlantic Canada
www.comt.ca/english/programs/trucking/Guide.PDF

Canadian Trucking—Trucking Regulations
www.articlesbase.com/industrial--articles/canadian-trucking-trucking-regulations-1189440.html

Chapter Thirty-Two

TSA Transportation Worker Identification Credential
www.tsa.gov/what_we_do/layers/twic/index.shtm

Transport Canada—CANUTEC
www.tc.gc.ca/eng/canutec/menu.htm

TSA HAZMAT Endorsement Threat Assessment Program
www.tsa.gov/what_we_do/layers/hazmat/index.shtm

British Columbia—Ministry of Environment
www.gov.bc.ca/env/

British Columbia—Ministry of Transportation and Infrastructure
www.gov.bc.ca/tran/

Environment Canada
www.ec.gc.ca/default.asp?lang=En&n=FD9B0E51-1

FMCSA—Hazardous Materials
www.fmcsa.dot.gov/safety-security/hazmat/hm-theme.htm

Chapter Thirty-Three

PTDI—Use Effective Communications, Page 26, Click on Skill Standards
www.ptdi.org/standards

Job Search Tips
jobsearch.about.com/cs/jobsearchhelp/a/jobtips.htm

Bureau of Labor Statistics—Job Interview Tips
www.bls.gov/oco/oco20045.htm

Public Relations Tips
www.mindtools.com/CommSkll/FirstImpressions.htm

Professional Driving Careers
www.ehow.com/list_6557208_professional-driving-careers.html

For additional job opportunities (and these are only a few sites of many):

Class A Drivers Jobs
classadrivers.com

National Truck Driving Jobs
www.nationaltruckdrivingjobs.com

Chapter Thirty-Four

PTDI—Manage Personal Resources While on the Road, Page 27, Click on Skill Standards
www.ptdi.org/standards

FMCSA Drug and Alcohol Program
www.fmcsa.dot.gov/rules-regulations/topics/drug/drug.htm

DOT Office of Drug and Alcohol Policy and Compliance Notice
www.fmcsa.dot.gov/documents/Medical-Marijuana-Notice.pdf

Risk Factors in Professional Driving
www.workhealth.org/OSI%20Index/OSI%20Introduction.html

Chapter Thirty-Five

Human Resources and Skills Development Canada
www.hrsdc.gc.ca/eng/labour/health_safety/overview.shtml

FMCSA Motor Carrier Employee Whistle Blower Protection
www.fmcsa.dot.gov/rules-regulations/administration/w-blower.htm

FMCSA—Rules and Regulations
www.fmcsa.dot.gov/rules-regulations/rules-regulations.htm

U.S. Department of Labor Whistleblower Protection
www.dol.gov/compliance/laws/comp-whistleblower.htm

U.S. DOT OIG Hotline Complaint Center
www.oig.dot.gov/Hotline

Chapter Thirty-Six

FMCSA CSA Information
csa2010.fmcsa.dot.gov/about/

FMCSA Driver Pre-Employment Screening Program
www.psp.fmcsa.dot.gov

U.S. DOT CSA—Compliance, Safety, Accountability
csa.fmcsa.dot.gov/default.aspx

Trucking Organizations

Training Standards and Course Certification

Professional Truck Driver Institute
555 E. Braddock Road
Alexandria, VA 22314
703-647-7015
www.ptdi.org

American Trucking Associations and Its Conferences and Councils

American Trucking Associations
950 North Glebe Road, Suite 210
Arlington, Virginia 22203-4181
703-838-1700
www.trucking.org

U.S. State Trucking Associations

Alabama Trucking Association
P. O. Box 242337
Montgomery, Alabama 36124-2337
334-834-3983
www.alabamatrucking.org

Alaska Trucking Association
3443 Minnesota Drive
Anchorage, Alaska 99503
907-276-1149
www.aktrucks.org

Arizona Trucking Association
7500 West Madison Street
Tolleson, Arizona 85353
602-850-6000
www.arizonatrucking.com

Arkansas Trucking Association
P. O. Box 3476
Little Rock, Arkansas 72203
501-372-3462
www.arkansastrucking.com

California Trucking Association
4148 E. Commerce Way
Sacramento, California 95834
916-373-3500
www.caltrux.com

Colorado Motor Carriers Association
4060 Elati Street
Denver, Colorado 80216-4814
303-433-3375
www.cmca.com

Motor Transport Association of Connecticut
60 Forest Street
Hartford, Connecticut
860-520-4455
www.mtac.us

Delaware Motor Transport Association
445 Pear Street
Dover, Delaware 19904
302-672-7763
www.dmta.org

Florida Trucking Association
359 East College Avenue
Tallahassee, Florida 32301-1565
850-222-9900
www.fltrucking.org

Georgia Motor Trucking Association
2060 Franklin Way, Suite 200
Marietta, Georgia 30067
770-444-9771
www.gmta.org

Hawaii Transportation Association
P. O. Box 30166
Honolulu, Hawaii 96820
808-833-6628
www.htahawaii.org

Idaho Trucking Association
3405 East Overland Road, Suite 175
Meridian, Idaho 83642
208-342-3521
www.idtrucking.org

Illinois Trucking Association
700 Adams, Suite 130
Willow Brook, IL 60527
630-654-0884
www.iltrucking.org

Indiana Motor Truck Association
One N. Capitol, Suite 460
Indianapolis, Indiana 46204
317-630-4682
www.imtaonline.net

Iowa Motor Truck Association
717 East Court Avenue
Des Moines, Iowa 50309
515-244-5193
www.iowamotortruck.com

Kansas Motor Carriers Association
P. O. Box 1673
Topeka, Kansas 66611
785-267-1641
www.kmca.org

Kentucky Motor Transport Association
617 Shelby Street
Frankfort, KY 40601
502-227-0848
www.kmta.net

Louisiana Motor Transport Association
4838 Bennington Avenue, P.O. Box 80278
Baton Rouge, LA 70898
225-928-5682
www.louisianatrucking.com

Maine Motor Transport Association
P. O. Box 857, 142 Whitten Road
Augusta, Maine 04332-0857
207-623-4128
www.mmta.com

Maryland Motor Truck Association
3000 Washington Boulevard
Baltimore, MD 21230
410-644-4600
www.mmtanet.com

Massachusetts Motor Transportation Association
10 Liberty Square, 5th Floor
Boston, Massachusetts 02109
617-695-3512
www.mass-truck.org

Michigan Trucking Association
1141 Centennial Way
Lansing, Michigan 48917
517-321-1951
www.mitrucking.org

Minnesota Trucking Association
2277 Hwy 36 West, #302
Roseville, Minnesota 55113
651-646-7351
www.mntruck.org

Mississippi Trucking Association
825 North President Street
Jackson, Mississippi 39202
601-354-0616
www.mstrucking.org

Missouri Trucking Association
102 East High Street
Jefferson City, MO 65203
573-634-3388
www.motrucking.org

Motor Carriers of Montana
501 N. Sanders, #201
Helena, MT 59601
406-442-6600
www.mttrucking.org

Nebraska Trucking Association
1701 K Street, P. O. Box 81010
Lincoln, Nebraska 68501-1010
402-476-8504
www.nebtrucking.com

Nevada Motor Transport Association
8745 Technology Way, Suite E
Reno, NV 89521
775-673-6111
www.nmta.com

New Hampshire Motor Transport Association
19 Henniker Street, P.O. Box 3898
Concord, NH 03302
603-224-7337
www.nhmta.org

New Jersey Motor Truck Association
160 Tices Lane
East Brunswick, NJ 08816
732-254-5000
www.njta.org

New Mexico Trucking Association
4809 Jefferson St. N.E.
Albuquerque, NM 87109
505-884-5575
www.nmtrucking.org

New York State Motor Truck Association
828 Washington Avenue
Albany, New York 12203
518-458-9696
www.nytrucks.org

North Carolina Trucking Association
219 West Martin Street
Raleigh, NC 27601
919-834-0387
www.nctrucking.com

North Dakota Motor Carriers Association
1031 East Interstate Avenue
Bismarck, ND 58502
701-223-2700
www.ndmca.org

Ohio Trucking Association
50 W. Broad St. Suite 1111
Columbus, Ohio 43215
614-221-5375
www.ohiotruckingassn.org

Oklahoma Trucking Association
3909 N. Lindsay Ave.
Oklahoma City, OK 73105
405-525-9488
www.oktrucking.org

Oregon Trucking Associations, Inc.
4005 SE Naef Road
Portland, OR 97267
503-513-0005 or 888-293-0005
www.ortrucking.org

Pennsylvania Motor Truck Association
910 Linda Lane
Camp Hill, PA 17011
717-761-7122
www.pmta.org

Rhode Island Trucking Association
660 Roosevelt Avenue
Pawtucket, RI 02860
401-729-5210
www.ritrucking.org

South Carolina Trucking Association
2425 Devine Street, P.O. Box 50166
Columbia, SC 29250-0166
803-799-4306
www.sctrucking.org

South Dakota Trucking Association
P.O. Box 89008
Sioux Falls, SD 57109-9008
605-223-8871
www.southdakotatrucking.com

Tennessee Trucking Association
4531 Trousdale Drive
Nashville, TN 37204
615-777-2882
www.tntrucking.org

Texas Motor Transportation Association
700 E. 11th Street
Austin, TX 78701
512-478-2541
www.tmta.com

Utah Trucking Association
3060 West California Avenue Suite A
Salt Lake City, Utah 84104
801-973-9370
www.utahtrucking.org

Vermont Trucking Association
192 South Main Street, 2nd Floor
Barre, Vermont 05641
802-479-1778
Email: vttruckandbus@aol.com

Virginia Trucking Association
1707 Summit Avenue Suite 110
Richmond, VA 23230
804-355-5371
www.vatrucking.org

Washington Trucking Associations
930 South 336th Street, Suite B
Federal Way WA 98003, U.S.A.
253-838-1650
www.wta.com

West Virginia Trucking Association
2506 Kanawha Blvd. East
Charleston, West Virginia 25311
304-345-2800
www.wvtrucking.com

Wisconsin Motor Carriers Association
P. O. Box 44849
Madison, Wisconsin 53744-4849
608-833-8200
www.witruck.org

Wyoming Trucking Association
555 N. Poplar
Casper, Wyoming 82602
877-878-2515
www.wytruck.org

Other U.S. Trucking Associations

American Association of Motor Vehicle Administrators
4301 Wilson Boulevard, Suite 400
Arlington, VA 22203
703-522-4200
www.aamva.org

Commercial Vehicle Safety Alliance
6303 Ivy Lane, Suite 310
Greenbelt, MD 20770-6319
301-830-6143
www.cvsa.org

Commercial Vehicle Training Association
7005 Backlick Ct. Suite 100
Springfield, VA 22151
703-642-9444
www.cvta.org

Intermodal Association of North America
11785 Beltsville Drive, Suite 1100
Calverton, MD 20705
301-982-3400
www.intermodal.org

Mid-West Truckers Association, Inc.
2727 North Dirksen Parkway
Springfield, IL 62704
217-525-0310
www.mid-westtruckers.com

National Association of Independent Truckers
800-821-8014
www.naitusa.com

National Association of Publicly Funded Truck Driving Schools
3 CT Circle
Drumright, OK 74030
918-352-7314
www.napftds.org

National Private Truck Council
950 N. Glebe Road, Suite 530
Arlington, VA 22203-4183
703-683-1300
www.nptc.org

National Tank Truck Carriers, Inc.
950 North Glebe Road, Suite #520
Arlington, Virginia 22203-4183
703-838-1960
www.tanktruck.org

Owner-Operator Independent Drivers Association
1 NW OOIDA Drive
Grain Valley, Missouri 64029
816-229-5791
www.ooida.com

Specialized Carriers & Rigging Association
2750 Prosperity Avenue, Suite 620
Fairfax, VA 22031-4312
703-698-0291
www.scranet.org

The Healthy Trucking Association of America
103 Technacenter Drive
Montgomery, AL 36117
800-800-1198
www.healthytruck.org

The National Association of Small Trucking Companies
104 Stuart Drive
Hendersonville, TN 37075
800-264-8580
615-451-4555
www.nastc.com

Trucker Buddy International
3200 Rice Mine Rd
Tuscaloosa, AL 35406
1-800-MY-BUDDY (692-8339)
www.truckerbuddy.org

Truckload Carriers Association
555 E. Braddock Road
Alexandria, VA 22314
703-838-1950
www.truckload.org

Women in Trucking
P.O. Box 400
Plover, WI 54467-0400
1-888-GO4-WITA (1-888-464-9482)
www.womenintrucking.org

Canadian Province Trucking Associations

Alberta Motor Transport Association
#1 - 285005 Wrangler Way Rocky View, AB T1X 0K3
800-267-1003
www.amta.ca

Atlantic Provinces Trucking Association
105 Englehart St., Suite 800
Dieppe, NB E1A 8K2
506-855-2782
www.apta.ca

British Columbia Trucking Association
#100–20111 93A Avenue
Langley, BC V1M 4A9
800-565-2282
www.bctrucking.com

Manitoba Trucking Association
25 Bunting Street
Winnipeg, Manitoba R2X 2P5
204-632-6600
www.trucking.mb.ca

Ontario Trucking Association
555 Dixon Road
Toronto, ON M9W 1H8
416-249-7401
www.ontruck.org

Quebec Trucking Association
6450 Notre-Dame West, Suite 200
Montreal, Quebec H4C 1V4
514-932-0377
www.carrefour-acq.org/

Saskatchewan Trucking Association
1335 Wallace Street
Regina, Saskatchewan S4N 3Z5
800-563-7632
www.sasktrucking.com

Other Canadian Trucking Associations

Canadian Association of Supply Chain and Logistics Management
7270 Woodbine Avenue, Suite 204
Markham, ON L3R 4B9
866-456-1231
www.sclcanada.org

Canadian Automobile Association
www.caa.ca

Canadian Council of Motor Transport Administrators
2323 St. Laurent Blvd.
Ottawa, Ontario K1G 4J8
613-736-1003
www.ccmta.ca

Canadian Courier & Logistics Association
Unit 119-660 Eglinton Avenue East, Box 333
Toronto, Ontario M4G 2K2
877-766-6604
canadiancourier.org

Canadian Crime Stoppers
888-222-8477
www.canadiancrimestoppers.org

Canadian Industrial Transportation Association
580 Terry Fox Drive, Suite 405
Ottawa, Ontario K2L 4C2
613-599-3283
www.cita-acti.ca

Canadian Institute of Traffic and Transportation
10 King Street East, Suite 400
Toronto, ON M5C 1C3
416-363-5696
www.citt.ca

Canadian International Freight Forwarders Association
170 Attwell Drive, Suite 480
Toronto, Ontario M9W 5Z5
416-234-5100
www.ciffa.com

Canadian Society of Customs Brokers
320, 55 Murray Street
Ottawa, Ontario K1N 5M3
613-562-3543
www.cscb.ca

Canadian Transportation Equipment Association (CTEA)
16 Barrie Blvd, Unit 3B
St. Thomas, Ontario N5P 4B9
519-631-0414
ctea.ca

Canadian Truckers
#217-96 Highfield Park Drive
Dartmouth, Nova Scotia B3A 4W4
902-434-7326
www.canadiantruckers.com

Canadian Trucking Alliance
555 Dixon Road
Toronto, ON M9W 1H8
613-236-9426
www.cantruck.ca

Canadian Trucking Human Resources Council
203-720, ch. Belfast Road
Ottawa, Ontario K1G OZ5
613-244-4800
www.cthrc.com

Freight Carriers Association of Canada
427 Garrison Road, Unit 3 & 4
Fort Erie, ON L2A 6E6
800-559-7421
www.fca-natc.org

OBAC
275 Slater Street, Suite 900
Ottawa, Ontario K1P 5H9
888-794-9990
www.obac.ca

Private Motor Truck Council of Canada
1660 North Service Road East, Suite 115
Oakville, Ontario L6H 7G3
877-501-PMTC
www.pmtc.ca

Transportation Association of Canada
2323 St. Laurent Blvd.
Ottawa, Ontario K1G 4J8
613-736-1350
www.tac-atc.ca

Truck Training Schools Association of Ontario
866-475-9436
www.ttsao.com

Mexican Trucking Associations

Instituto Mexicano del Transporte
www.imt.mx

Mexican Department of Transportation
www.sct.gov.mx

Program of Adjustment and/or Substitution of Panchuca Tankers
www.canacar.com.mx

Glossary

Accelerator or accelerator pedal located just under the steering wheel, you can operate this pedal with your right foot to control engine speed. Make sure there is no looseness or sticking.

Accident packet given by most companies to drivers to help them handle their responsibilities at the scene of an accident. Packets usually contain basic instructions for handling the scene of an accident, a preliminary accident report or memo, and witness cards.

Active railroad crossing usually attracts high traffic and is marked with the familiar white crossbuck with flashing lights or the crossbuck with flashing lights and a gate. These active warning devices activate only when a train is approaching the crossing, or intersection.

Aftercooler cools the intake air from the turbocharger and returns it to a safe temperature level.

Agent a person or company that acts as the official representative of another, such as a consignee's agent.

Air application pressure gauge shows the amount of air pressure being applied to the brakes. When the brakes are not in use, the gauge will read zero psi.

Air bag suspension air bags designed to provide a comfortable ride while increasing vehicle's "level load" capacity. Made with rugged, durable components, these adjustable air springs mount between the truck's frame and the suspension.

Air blockage when air cannot reach the brakes. This is usually caused by water freezing in the air system.

Air brake application gauge indicates in psi (pounds per square inch) the amount of air pressure used when the brake pedal is pushed.

Air brake system in an air brake system, pressure is used to increase the braking force. The compressed air can multiply the force of mechanical braking many times.

Air compressor squeezes the air into a smaller space. This increases the force the air exerts.

Air filter element keeps the air that flows through the vehicle clean and free of dirt particles.

Air intake system delivers fresh air to the cylinders. An air cleaner removes dirt, dust, and water from the fresh air.

Air operated release the device on a fifth wheel that allows you to release the locking mechanism on the sliding fifth wheel by moving the fifth-wheel release lever in the cab to the unlocked position.

Air pressure gauge tells the amount of pressure in the tanks. The maximum pressure is around 120 psi. The air compressor will build when the pressure falls below 90 psi (pounds per square inch).

Air reservoir provides air to your braking system. You should always bleed them each day to remove moisture.

Air starter using another vehicle's air supply to charge your starter.

Air suspension uses bags of air placed between the axle and frame.

Alcoholism a chronic disorder marked by excessive and usually compulsive drinking of alcohol leading to psychological and physical dependence or addiction.

Alley dock a freight pick-up or delivery dock that can be accessed only through an alley.

Alley dock backing The "alley dock" maneuver is a multi-part sequence of backing moves to bring a tractor-trailer up to a dock accessed only by the alley.

Alternators (see **Generators and alternators**)

Ammeter a gauge on the instrument panel that shows the current output of the alternator. It indicates whether the alternator is being charged by the battery or is discharging.

Antilock brake system (ABS) prevents the wheels from locking up by sensing the speed of each wheel electronically. The computer-operated system can apply the brakes 3 to 5 times faster than pumping the brakes manually. ABS keeps the rig from moving outside its lane while coming to a stop.

Arrester beds an escape ramp, 300 to 700 feet (91.4 to 213.4 m) long, made of loose material (usually pea gravel).

Articulated vehicle a rig that has several parts connected by joints.

Articulation movement between two separate parts, such as a tractor and a trailer.

Atlas consists of maps of states, major cities, and areas. Some atlases may also include the location of permanent scales, low underpasses, size and weight limits, fuel taxes, designated routes, and state laws for access to the designated highway system.

A-train a rig that uses an A-dolly (a converter with a draw bar with one eye that connects to the pintle hook on the back of the first trailer).

Automatic transmission one that, when set for a certain speed range, will not exceed that speed and the engine automatically shifts through the gears until it reaches that speed.

Auxiliary brakes or speed retarders devices that reduce the rig's speed without using the service brakes.

Auxiliary lights include reflectors, marker lights, clearance lights, tail lights, ID lights, and brake lights. When working, auxiliary lights make the rig visible to other highway users.

Auxiliary starter button available on some cab-over-engine (COE) models. It lets you start the engine with the cab tilted.

Average speed formula   Average Speed = Distance ÷ Time.

Aviation and Transportation Security Act (ATSA)   The Aviation and Transportation Security Act (ATSA) was enacted by the U.S. Congress as a result of the September 11, 2001 attacks. ATSA was created within the U.S. Department of Transportation and the Transportation Security Administration (TSA) to oversee civil aviation security. Hence, the central feature of ATSA is federalization of the nation's transportation security system through creation of TSA. The purpose of the Congress in enacting ATSA was to deploy ATSA's new security measures as rapidly as possible.

Axles   connect the wheels to the rest of the rig and support the weight of the vehicle and its cargo.

Axle temperature gauge   shows the temperature of the lubricant in the front and rear drive axles. The normal reading is 150 to 200 degrees, but it can reach higher readings, up to 230 to 250 degrees for a short period of time.

Axle weight   the load each axle is supporting. It can either be checked with portable scales by adding the weight of the wheel or at a weigh station by driving each axle over the scale.

Background checks   a background check or background investigation is the process of looking up and compiling criminal records, commercial records, and financial records (in certain instances such as employment screening) of an individual.

Backward serpentine   a weaving backward maneuver; one of the skills to be mastered in backing a tractor-trailer.

Baffle   a wall that has holes in it through which the liquid can flow in a tanker.

Bail-out area   emergency exits and other places you can use to avoid a crash.

BASIC   Within CSA 2010, motor carrier scores are calculated using the Safety Measurement System (SMS). The purpose of the scoring system is to identify candidates for interventions, to determine the specific safety problems exhibited by a carrier or driver, and to monitor whether safety problems are improving or worsening. The carrier SMS uses a motor carrier's data from roadside inspections, including all safety-based violations, State-reported crashes, and the Federal motor carrier census to quantify performance in the following Behavior Analysis Safety Improvement Categories (BASICS).

Basic controls skill test   A part of the Commercial Driver's License skills test, the Basic Controls Skills Test asks the applicant to demonstrate three of the following: straight-line backing, off-set backing right, off-set backing left, alley dock (driver side) parallel park (conventional), parallel park (sight side).

Battery   creates or receives and stores electrical energy.

Battery fluid   on some vehicles the fluid level in the batteries needs to be checked or maintained.

Behind-the-wheel test   the portion of the CDL where the applicant is tested by an inspector regarding his or her ability driving the tractor-trailer rig. This portion of the test is usually done on public roadways and in traffic.

Belly mount trailer   a refrigerated trailer that has the refrigeration unit under the trailer.

Belted bias tires   have body cords that run across the tread at an angle.

Bias-ply tires   have body cords running across the tire at an angle.

Bill of lading (BL)   a contract between a shipper and a carrier.

Binders   used to bind down loads on flatbed trailers. It is important to make sure that all cargo is packaged correctly.

Binding   something that confines, constrains, or restricts a moving part from operating.

BlackBerry   a hand-held multipurpose electronic communications system.

Black ice   a thin layer of ice clear enough to let you see the road underneath.

Bleeding tar   tar in the roads that rises to the top, causing the road to be slippery.

Blind-side   specific to the tractor-trailer, the "blind side" is the area around the rig which the driver cannot see, even if aided by side mirrors.

Blind-side backing   backing toward the right (blind) side of the rig.

Blocking   pieces of wood nailed to the floor.

Blood alcohol content (BAC)   the amount of alcohol in the bloodstream. Determines the level of intoxication.

Blowout   when a tire suddenly loses air.

Border crossing   patrolled stations at the borders between Mexico and the U.S. and the U.S. and Canada where tractor-trailers must present paperwork, representing their loads, before they are allowed to enter the country.

Braces and supports   methods used to prevent loads from moving. Whether flatbed or drybox, a load must be blocked or braced to prevent movement on all sides.

Bracing   pieces cut to fit and nailed or otherwise secured.

Brake controls   controls in the tractor's cab which allow the driver to control the rig's brakes.

Brake fade   occurs when the brakes overheat and lose their ability to stop the truck on a downgrade.

Brakes   used to stop the vehicle. Make sure that you maintain air pressure and prevent leaks in brake lines. If the brakes are pulling, have them checked right away. Bad brakes are dangerous to you and other motorists.

Braking system   used to slow or stop the rig. The braking system uses service brakes, secondary brakes, and parking brakes.

Bridge Formula   Congress enacted the Bridge Formula in 1975 to limit the weight-to-length ratio of a vehicle crossing a bridge. This is accomplished either by spreading weight over additional axles or by increasing the distance between axles. Compliance with Bridge Formula weight limits is determined by using the following formula:

$$W = 500 \left[\frac{LN}{N-1} + 12N + 36 \right]$$

W = the overall gross weight on any group of two or more consecutive axles to the nearest 500 pounds (227 kg).

L = the distance in feet between the outer axles of any group of two or more consecutive axles.

N = the number of axles in the group under consideration.

In addition to Bridge Formula weight limits, Federal law states that single axles are limited to 20,000 pounds (9,072 kg), and axles closer than 96 inches (244 cm) apart (tandem axles) are limited to 34,000 pounds (15,422 kg). Gross vehicle weight is limited to 80,000 pounds (36,287 kg) (23 U.S.C. 127).

B-train   a rig with two semitrailers pulled by a tractor.

Bulkhead   a solid wall or steel divider that divides a large tank into smaller tanks.

Buttonhook turn   a right turn that allows you to clear the corner by proceeding straight ahead until the trailer tires clear the corner then turning right.

Bypass system   filters a small amount of the oil flow. It is normally used with the full flow system.

Cab   the part of the vehicle where the driver sits. Keep it clean so that papers and trash do not obstruct your view or fall under the clutch, brake, or accelerator.

Cable antijackknife devices   are mounted on the trailer and connected to the tractor. They keep the trailer and tractor in line.

Cable-operated clutch control   is simple, lightweight and is the most common linkage and control. Normally, one end of the cable is connected to the clutch pedal and a spring is attached to the pedal assembly to keep the pedal in the "up" position. The other end of the cable is connected to the clutch release fork with a fitting that allows for free-play adjustments. When the clutch pedal is depressed, the cable pulls the clutch fork, causing the release bearing to move forward against the pressure plate. In a cable-operated clutch there is no self-adjusting mechanism and the throw out bearing is under no pressure except when you are changing gears. In these types of clutches, there is a possibility of the cable stretching or the clutch plate wearing out early and hence any adjustment should be done manually every few months.

Cabotage   trade or transport of goods between two countries.

Cab-over-engine (COE) tractor   has a flat face with the engine beneath the cab.

Camber   an alignment feature that is the amount the front wheels are tilted outward at the top. It is best for trucks to have positive camber.

Camshaft   a shaft to which a cam is fastened or of which a cam forms an integral part.

Canadian Council of Motor Transport Administrators (CCMTA)   the official organization in Canada that coordinates all aspects of highway safety and motor transportation.

Canadian Labour Code – Part II   The Canada Labour Code is an Act of Parliament of the Canadian government to consolidate certain statutes respecting labour. The objective of the code is to facilitate production by controlling strikes and lockouts, occupational safety and health, and some employment standards. Part II deals, specifically, with occupational health and safety.

Canadian Transport Emergency Centre (CANUTEC)   The center in Canada responsible for responding to all hazardous material emergencies, incidents, and questions.

Cargo compartment doors   at the back or side of trailer where cargo may be loaded or unloaded. All hinges should be secure and rust and damage free.

Cargo net   a net made of rope, plastic, or other material used on top of freight being carried on a flat top trailer to keep it secure. The cargo net is always used in tandem with tie downs.

Cargo retainer bars   used to secure cargo and keep loose cargo from moving.

Cargo securement devices   tie-downs, chains, tarps, and other methods of securing cargo in a flatbed. During inspection, make sure there is no damage and that they can withstand 1-1/2 times any pressure from the load.

Carrier (also see Common carrier, Contract carrier, Delivery carrier, For-hire carrier, Originating carrier, Private carrier)   an organization that hauls cargo by truck.

Carrier bearings   on trucks with a long wheel base, they join two driveshafts.

Carrier's time record   a record maintained by the carrier that records a driver's duty status.

Caster   an alignment feature that is the amount the axle kingpin is tilted backward at the top. It is measured in degrees. The axle should have a positive caster or tilt forward.

Cellular phone   a personal communications device operating on wireless technology.

Center of gravity   the point where weight acts as a force. Center of gravity affects the vehicle's stability. (Also see **High center of gravity**.)

Centers for Disease Control (CDC)   agency to be notified if a cargo spill is a disease-causing agent.

Centrifugal filter   a type of bypass filter in which the oil enters the permanent housing and spins the filter at a high speed, forcing the dirt and particles out of the oil for more efficient cleaning of the oil.

Centrifugal force   the force that pushes objects away from the center of rotation. This force has the ability to push a vehicle off the road in a curve.

Chain control area   a highway area on which it is illegal to drive without chains.

Chains   metal links, joined together to tie down and secure freight.

Chamfer   another word for groove.

Charging circuit   produces electricity to keep the battery charged and run the electrical circuits which include battery, alternator or generator, voltage regulator, ammeter or voltmeter, electrical wires, and battery cables.

Checklist   list of parts of the vehicle to check or inspect.

Chemical Transportation Emergency Center (CHEMTREC)   tells emergency personnel what they need to know to take care of a chemical problem. It also helps make the proper notifications and supplies the emergency personnel with expert technical assistance.

Chock   a block (usually a piece of wood) put in the front or back of a wheel to keep it from moving.

Circuit breaker   breaks an electrical circuit during an overload.

Class A fire   a fire in ordinary combustibles such as wood, paper, and cloth.

Class B fire   a fire in flammable or combustible liquids and gases such as gasoline, diesel fuel, alcohol, paint, acetylene, hydrogen.

Class C fire   a fire in live electrical equipment. You must put it out with something that does not conduct electricity. After the electricity is cut off, extinguishers suitable for Class A or Class B fires may be used.

Class D fire   a fire in combustible metals such as magnesium and sodium. These fires can be put out only with special chemicals or powders.

Clutch connects or disconnects the engine from the rest of the power train.

Clutch brake stops the gears from turning. To engage it, push the clutch pedal all the way to the floor.

Clutch pedal used when you start the engine or shift the gears. It has three basic positions—disengaged, free play, and engaged.

Cold metal in cold or freezing weather, many of the tractor-trailer's metal surfaces will be too cold to touch without the use of protective gloves. And, although it sounds trivial, avoid touching cold metal, especially with wet hands, because in freezing temperatures it will make you feel colder and may cause frostbite.

Collect on delivery (COD) shipments shipments in which the driver collects payment on delivery for freight or cargo and freight.

Combination bypass/full flow filter oil from the full flow filter goes to the bearings, and the oil from the bypass filter returns to the oil pan.

Combination ramp and arrester bed this escape ramp relies on loose surface material to stop a rig. It has a grade of 1.5% to 6% and is 500 to 2,200 feet (152.4 to 670.6 m) long.

Combination vehicle when you add a trailer to a tractor or a straight truck. It is also called a combination rig.

Combined axle weight the load of all axles (tandem or triple axles).

Combustible materials capable of combustion.

Combustion a usually rapid chemical process (as oxidation) that produces heat and usually light.

Commercial Driver's License (CDL) required to operate commercial motorized vehicles.

Commercial motor vehicle (CMV) a motor vehicle or combination of motor vehicles used in commerce to transport passengers or property if the vehicle has a gross combination weight rating of 29,001 pounds (13,152 kg) or more inclusive of a towed unit with a gross vehicle weight rating of more than 10,000 pounds (4,535 kg); or is designed to transport 15 or more passengers, including the driver.

Commercial Motor Vehicle Safety Act of 1986 (CMVSA/86) was passed to make sure all CMV drivers were qualified.

Commercial Vehicle Operator's Registration (CVOR) The Commercial Vehicle Operator's Registration (CVOR) system and the Carrier Safety Rating (CSR) program were developed by the Ministry of Transportation as part of Ontario's ongoing commitment to road safety. These programs promote the safe operation of trucks and buses on Ontario's roadways.

Commercial Vehicle Safety Alliance (CVSA) CVSA is an international not-for-profit organization comprised of local, state, provincial, territorial, and federal motor carrier safety officials and industry representatives from the United States, Canada, and Mexico. CVSA's mission is to promote commercial motor vehicle safety and security by providing leadership to enforcement, industry, and policy makers.

Common carrier a motor carrier that offers its services to all individuals and businesses.

Communication the ability to signal and share ideas. In transportation, horns and lights may be used to signal a driver's intention.

Compliance Review (CR) There are five important differences between Compliance, Safety, Accountability (CSA) interventions and FMCSA's former compliance reviews: (1) CSA provides a set of tools to address carriers' safety breakdowns; the CR is a one-size-fits-all tool. (2) CSA interventions provide the ability to focus on specific safety breakdowns, while the CR required a broad examination of the carrier. (3) CSA interventions focus on improving behaviors that are linked to crash risk; CR is focused on broad compliance based on a set of acute/critical violations. (4) CSA onsite-focused investigations and offsite investigations are less resource-intensive and less time consuming for the carrier; CRs are resource intensive. (5) CSA investigations may take place at a carrier's place of business or offsite; CRs are generally conducted onsite.

Compressor (see **Air compressor**)

Computerized idle timer a function of the engine's electronic controls, it will shut down the engine in a prescribed amount of time after the truck has come to a halt.

Connecting carrier any carrier that transports freight to an interchange location and then transfers the cargo to another company to continue the shipment.

Containment rules requirements for freight containers used to haul hazmat or dangerous goods.

Contract carrier a motor carrier that is under contract to customers to transport their freight. The contract sets the rates and other terms of service.

Control routines—start, warm-up, shutdown basic steps used to start, warm-up, or shutdown a tractor's engine.

Controlled braking putting on the brakes with a steady pressure just short of wheel lockup.

Conventional converter dollies used to change semitrailers into full trailers. The dolly becomes the front axle of the trailer.

Conventional tractors have a smoother ride because the driver sits between the front wheels and the rear wheels. Its main drawback is a longer wheelbase, making it difficult to maneuver in tight spaces.

Converter dolly a set of wheels with a fifth wheel used to connect a tractor to a trailer or a trailer to a trailer.

Converter dolly axle attaches to the front end of the trailer. This axle steers the second trailer in a set of doubles. The entire axle turns for steering.

Convex mirror a curved mirror that gives the driver a wide-angle view to the rear of the rig.

Coolant a fluid, usually a mixture of water and antifreeze, that circulates within the system. Coolant helps keep the engine cool and should be checked according to your truck's operator manual.

Coolant filter keeps the coolant system free of impurities.

Coolant level alarm lights up when the coolant level starts dropping, indicating a probable leak.

Coolant system a system that circulates coolant, incorporated into the engine of a tractor to keep it cool over long periods of use.

Coolant temperature gauge shows the temperature of the coolant in the engine block. The normal operating range is around 170 to 195 degrees F.

Coolant temperature warning lights up when the temperature is too high.

Cool-down the period after stopping a rig but before turning off the engine.

Cooling system keeps the temperature down in the engine.

Countersteering   turning sharply in one direction and then quickly turning back in the other direction.

Coupling   joining a tractor to a trailer.

Coupling device   device—called a converter gear or dolly—that makes it possible to attach one trailer to another or to a tractor. Check to make sure all parts are not damaged and are properly secured.

Coupling/uncoupling system   connects and disconnects the tractor to/from the trailer.

CR   (see **Compliance Review**)

Cranking circuit   sends electricity from the battery to a small starter motor.

Crankshaft   shaft consisting of a series of cranks and crankpins to which the connecting rods of an engine are attached.

Crossbuck sign   a railroad crossing sign, featuring two white crossed planks with "RAILROAD CROSSING" in black letters. This sign is usually positioned immediately before railroad tracks.

Crosswind   wind currents traveling from side to side—particularly dangerous on mountain roads.

Cruise control   an electronic device in a vehicle that controls the throttle so as to maintain a constant speed.

Curvature   used in this book to describe the amount of curve you'll often find in the roadway, specifically found in entrances to or exits from freeways and other major roadways. Technically, curvature is the rate of change of the angle through which the tangent to a curve turns in moving along the curve and for which a circle is equal to the reciprocal of the radius.

Custom trailer and dolly for hauling large-diameter and long items   has a drop frame and two rear axles.

Customer relations   how you, as a truck driver, get along with customers.

Customer service   a vital part of the professional driver's job—in most cases, the driver represents the carrier to every customer he or she serves.

Customs   duties, tolls, or imposts imposed by the sovereign law of a country on imports or exports.

Cybernetics   "cybernetics" comes from a Greek word meaning "the art of steering."

Danger zones   areas of the highway that present challenging navigation or extreme risk to a professional driver, the load he or she is hauling, and the rig.

"Dangerous" placard   a placard required on all four sides of a rig carrying dangerous materials or hazardous materials.

Dead axle   an axle that is not powered.

Defensive driving   driving to avoid or get out of problems that may be created by other drivers.

Defrosters   a mechanism on every tractor designed to warm the windshield enough to clear fog or ice.

Delivery (terminal) carrier   the carrier that delivers the shipment to the consignee.

Delivery receipt   a paper signed by the consignee or an agent of the consignee accepting the shipment from the driver. The driver keeps the receipt as proof of delivery.

Department of Homeland Security (DHS)   responsible for safety and security of all American citizens.

Department of Labor (DOL)   a department within the U.S. federal government with the mission of fostering, promoting, and developing the welfare of the wage earners, job seekers, and retirees of the United States; improve working conditions; advance opportunities for profitable employment; and assure work-related benefits and rights.

Department of Motor Vehicles (DMV)   assists in making state laws and regulations for motor carriers.

Department of Transportation (DOT)   administers federal regulations and interstate trucking operations.

Detention time or demurrage   detaining a vehicle beyond a given time. Payment is made to the carrier when delivery is delayed.

Diamond-shaped yellow advance warning signs   usually with black letters or symbols warn drivers of existing or possible hazards on the road.

Diesel engine   has fuel injectors to supply fuel to the cylinders. The air intake system supplies the air to the cylinders. It does not have a carburetor.

Diet   the food a person eats.

Differential   transfers driving power to the wheels through the drive axle shafts.

Differential warning   flashes when the interaxle differential is in the locked position.

Dipstick   a graduated rod used to indicate depth or capacity, such as oil in a crankcase.

Direct clutch control   electronic mechanism that activates hydraulic pressure to the clutch.

Disc brakes   a modern disc brake system usually has a fixed disc attached to the inside of the wheel. To slow down or stop, the linings are squeezed against each side of the disc. This looks something like a wide-jawed vice closing quickly on a spinning disk. It creates the friction that slows or stops the rig.

Disqualification   the loss of a commercial driver's license due to infractions of roadway laws and/or putting yourself, your rig, and others at risk. These infractions could include driving under the influence or failing to practice safe driving.

Distance formula   Distance ÷ Speed = Time.

Distracted driving   driving while your attention is on something besides driving, such as eating, talking to a passenger, drinking a beverage, or talking/texting on a cell phone.

Dock board, dock plate   the metal plate used to bridge the gap between a loading dock and the trailer being unloaded.

Documentation   the papers that accompany shipments and provide an accurate record of the cargo. It also serves as a contract for the transportation services.

Domestic cargo   cargo manufactured and loaded in the country of origin.

DOT physical examination   the physical examination required for professional drivers by the Department of Transportation, to be undergone every 24 months or less, if indicated by the medical examiner.

Double clutching   a method of shifting in which you shift to neutral, then shift to the desired gears to match the rpm.

Double drop deck (also called double drop frame)   low beds that can haul heavy and oversized equipment without going over the height limits. Since these trailers are low to the ground they may have bottom clearance problems at railroad crossings, curbs, and large potholes.

Doubles   a rig consisting of a tractor and two trailers.

Downgrade   a steep downward slant in the road, usually around mountains or hill country.

Downshifting   when the engine needs more power, moving down the gears increases engine power while giving up some speed.

Drag link   transfers movement from the Pitman arm to the left steering arm.

Drain cocks   valves used to drain moisture from the air brake system reservoirs; should be drained each day.

Drayage   the work or cost of hauling goods from one point to another.

Drift   the tendency for a trailer to move as it is pulled behind a tractor. In most cases, this is a minimum amount of off-tracking.

Drive axle   an axle that is driven by the engine.

Drive pinion gear   (see **Pinion gear**)

Drive time   all time spent at the controls of the rig. Written as a (D) on the log book.

Drive wheel skid (tractor jackknife)   a skid that occurs when the tractor drive wheels lose traction.

Driver awareness   a driver must be aware of his or her vehicle at all times and be constantly alert.

Driver error   a mistake in judgment, perception, or an omission that could account for lost time.

Driver fatigue   the result of lack of sleep, eating a heavy meal, or illness, driver fatigue is one of the primary reasons for truck crashes or lost time.

Driver image   the impression a truck driver makes on other people.

Driver reaction distance   the distance your rig travels during the time it takes to identify a hazard.

Driver Safety Measurement System (DSMS)   a part of CSA, the Driver Safety Measurement System is used to rate drivers using a formula based on BASICS.

Driver's daily log   a required record, to be completed daily by the professional driver—or each time a trip is completed in a vehicle—that shows the activities of the day, including miles driven, breaks taken, time for loading, repairs, and anything else a driver has spent time doing for the period he or she is "on the clock."

Driver's side   the side of the vehicle that includes the driver's seat and control panel.

Driver-side backing   backing toward the left (driver) side of the rig.

Driver's Vehicle Inspection Report (DVIR)   the form a professional driver completes prior to every trip and after every arrival.

Driveshaft   a steel shaft that runs from the transmission to the rear of the vehicle.

Drivetrain   takes the power generated by the engine and applies it to the tractor's rear wheels. As the wheels turn, the rig moves.

Driving experience   the weeks, months, or years the individual has spent behind the wheel, navigating the roadways in a specific vehicle.

Drug testing   required testing of personnel working for a carrier. These tests can come at any time and are also required after any incident. Drivers who decline tests will lose their jobs.

Drum brakes   a metal cylinder that looks something like a drum that is bolted to each end of the axle. To stop the vehicle, the brake shoe linings are forced against the inside surface of the brake drums which creates the friction that slows or stops the rig.

Drum truck   hand truck used to carry drums. Never roll drums to load them.

Dry bulk tankers   used to haul dry bulk cargo. Dry bulk tankers have a high center of gravity that requires careful speed control, particularly on curves.

DSMS   (see **Driver Safety Measurement System**)

Duals   wheels with tires mounted in pairs on each end of the axle.

Dunnage   filler material such as sheets of plywood, padding, or inflatable bags used to fill voids in the load.

Dunnage and return charges   the weight of the dunnage will be listed on the bill of lading. If the shipper wishes it to be returned, this will be stated on the bill of lading.

Dunnage bag   a bag used to fill in gaps between containers of loaded freight.

Dunnage box   box used to fill in gaps between containers of loaded freight.

Eaton Fuller 13 Speed, Nine Speed, Super 10, Top 2   types of CMV transmission.

18-wheeler   is the most familiar combination rig. The tractor has ten wheels and the semitrailer has eight.

Electric retarder   uses electromagnets to slow the rotors attached to the drive train. The driver turns it on or off with a switch in the cab.

Electrical system   provides electricity to power the charging, cranking, ignition, lighting, and accessory circuits.

Electronic control unit (ECU)   the generic term for any embedded system that controls one or more of the electrical systems or subsystems in a motor vehicle.

Electronic engine controls   a type of electronic control unit that controls a series of actuators on an internal combustion engine to ensure the optimum running. It does this by reading values from a multitude of sensors within the engine bay, interpreting the data using multidimensional performance maps (called Look-up tables), and adjusting the engine actuators accordingly.

Electronic stability control (ESC)   a computerized technology that improves the safety of a vehicle's stability by detecting and reducing loss of traction (*skidding*). When ESC detects loss of steering control, it automatically applies the brakes to help "steer" the vehicle where the driver intends to go. Braking is automatically applied to wheels individually, such as the outer front wheel to counter oversteer or the inner rear wheel to counter understeer. Some ESC systems also reduce engine power until control is regained. ESC does not improve a vehicle's cornering performance; instead, it helps to minimize the loss of control. According to Insurance Institute for Highway Safety and the U.S. National Highway Traffic Safety Administration, one-third of fatal accidents could have been prevented by the technology.

Emergency engine stop control   shuts down the engine. Use this control in emergency situations only. Many companies insist that it be reset by a mechanic after each use.

Emergency equipment   equipment needed during an emergency. For a CMV, the emergency equipment consists of a fire extinguisher, reflective emergency triangles, fuses if needed, tire change kit, accident notification kit, and a list of emergency numbers. It is also good to have extra food, drinking water, medicine, extra clothes, and cold weather outerwear.

Emergency relay valve   relays air from the trailer air tank to the brake chambers. If there is a break in the lines between the tractor and trailer, the valve sends air from the trailer reservoir to the brake chambers.

Emergency stopping   stopping quickly while keeping the vehicle under control.

Emergency triangles   reflective triangles to be carried on all current commercial vehicles and required by law under FMCSR 393.95.

Employer discrimination   when an employer obviously mistreats an employee or offers fewer opportunities or less attractive assignments to an employee.

Employer–employee relations   how you, as a truck driver, get along with your employer.

Engine block   houses the pistons.

Engine brake   retarder alters valve timing and turns the engine into an air compressor. It can be operated by hand with a switch on the dash or automatically when the foot is removed from the accelerator pedal.

Engine compartment   area where engine is kept. Check to see that it has been properly serviced. Look for signs of damage or possible problems with the engine, steering mechanism, and suspension system.

Engine controls   start the engine and shut it down.

Engine oil temperature gauge   indicates the temperature of the engine oil. The normal operating temperature for engine oil is 180 to 225 degrees F.

Engine shutdown   the period of time from stopping the rig until the engine is turned off. Shutting down an engine requires a cooling off period. This prevents damage if the engine has a turbocharger.

Engine stop control knob   used in some diesel engines to shut off the engine. You pull the knob out and hold it until the engine stops.

Engine warm-up   the period between starting a CMV's engine and driving it down the road.

Enhanced roll stability   (see **Electronic stability control**)

En route inspection   a rig's control and instrument check while driving and a check of critical items at each stop.

Environment (also see **External environment** and **Internal environment**)   the area around and within the rig that you must see, hear, feel, and sense when driving.

Environmental Protection Agency (EPA)   regulates hazardous materials.

Escape ramps   areas used to stop runaway rigs by either sinking the rig in loose gravel or sand or sending it up an incline. They are designed to stop a vehicle safely without injuring people or damaging the cargo.

Evasive steering   steering out of an emergency situation.

Exempt commodity carrier   carriers that haul commodities, intrastate or interstate, exempt from regulations, such as fresh fruit (except bananas) and vegetables.

Exercise   physical activity that elevates the heart rate, strengthens muscles, and burns calories.

Exhaust brake   a retarder that keeps the exhaust gases from escaping, which creates pressure that keeps the engine from increasing speed. It is controlled by an on/off switch in the cab or automatically by a switch on the accelerator or clutch pedal.

Exhaust pyrometer gauge   indicates the temperature of the gases in the exhaust manifold. Maximum safe operating temperatures may be shown on the pyrometer name plate or listed in the operator's manual.

Exhaust system   required on all motor vehicles and used to discharge gases created by the operation of the engine. These fumes could be deadly if they get into the cab or sleep berth. For safety, do not operate a vehicle with missing, loose, or broken exhaust pipes, mufflers, tailpipes, or vertical stacks.

Explosive   a material with the capacity to combust and create a violent reaction.

External environment   the area, temperature, and conditions outside a certain enclosed area, such as a tractor-trailer.

Extreme driving conditions   hazardous conditions created by weather such as snow, rain, or ice, or by difficult terrain such as mountains.

Eye lead time   the time it takes for a vehicle to travel from a fixed starting point to the farthest point of the driver's vision.

Fan belt   a belt from the engine that drives the fan.

Fatigue   being very tired from overwork, stress, or lack of sleep.

Fatigue management   the ability to know when your body is fully rested and at its highest functioning level and when you need to simply stop and rest before attempting another trip or task.

Federal Bridge Formula   a formula used to figure permissible gross loads. It also requires minimum distances between the tractor and trailer axles.

Federal Motor Carrier Safety Administration (FMCSA)   the federal entity in the U.S. charged with regulating and enforcing carrier, driver, and vehicle safety regulations.

Federal Motor Carrier Safety Regulations (FMCSR)   federal laws that regulate commercial vehicle operation.

Federal regulations for hazardous materials transport   federal laws that regulate the manner in which hazardous materials must be shipped.

Felony   formerly differing from a misdemeanor under English common law by involving forfeiture in addition to any other punishment.

Fender mirror   a mirror mounted on the fender of a regular long nose tractor. Requires less eye movement and makes it easier to watch ahead of you. Wide-angle fender mirrors let you see more when you are making right turns.

Field of view   the area that you can see either in front of you or behind you with your mirrors.

Field of vision   everything you can see (front and both sides) while looking straight ahead.

Fifth wheel   a flat disk mounted on the rear of the tractor that is used to connect the trailer to the tractor. The trailer kingpin fits into and is held in place by the fifth wheel.

Fifth-wheel antijackknife device   prevents a collision between the trailer and the cab. It is automatic and restricts the rotation of the kingpin.

Firearm   a deadly weapon from which a shot is discharged by gunpowder—usually small arms used for aggression or survival. Every state and province has its specific laws regarding firearms.

Fire extinguishers   used to put out fires, usually marked by a letter and symbol to indicate the classes of fires for which it can be used. Every truck or tractor-trailer with a gross vehicle weight rating (GVWR) of 10,001 pounds (4,535 kg) or more must have a fire extinguisher.

First aid   immediate and temporary care given to a victim until professional help arrives.

Fish-eye mirror   a mirror having a highly curved protruding front, that covers an angle of about 180 degrees, and that gives a circular image.

5-axle removable gooseneck lowbed with detachable two-axle dolly   this low-bed frame has three rear trailer axles. A two-axle dolly is attached to the rear of the trailer.

Fixed-mount fifth wheel   the fifth wheel that is secured in a fixed position behind the cab.

Fixed or stationary trailer tandem axle assembly   a tandem axle that is placed to get the best weight distribution between the tractor and the trailer, but cannot be moved. Weight adjustments between the tractor and the trailer are then made by moving, or shifting, the load inside the trailer.

Flammable   highly combustible material. Includes fuel as well as hazmat or dangerous materials.

FMCSR 392.4   prohibits driving while under the influence of any dangerous drug. These drugs include narcotics, morphine, heroin, codeine, and amphetamines.

FMCSR 392.9   the part of the federal law that protects the driver by prohibiting the operation of a truck that is not loaded or secured properly.

FMCSR 396.9c Motor Vehicle Declared Out of Service   motor vehicles and intermodal equipment declared "out-of-service." Authorized personnel shall declare and mark "out-of-service" any motor vehicle or intermodal equipment which by reason of its mechanical condition or loading would likely cause an accident or a breakdown. No motor carrier or intermodal equipment provider shall require or permit any person to operate nor shall any person operate any motor vehicle or intermodal equipment declared and marked "out-of-service" until all repairs required by the "out-of-service notice" have been satisfactorily completed.

FMCSR 397   regulations that deal with driving and parking vehicles with hazardous materials.

FMCSR 397.3   requires all vehicles carrying hazardous materials to comply with state and local restrictions on routes and parking.

FMCSR 397.5   the safe haven regulation that requires all vehicles carrying Class A or Class B explosives (Explosives 1.1 through 1.3) to be attended at all times.

FMCSR 397.9   controls the routes of hazmat carriers. Trips must be planned in the best interest of public safety.

Foot brake control valve (also called foot valve or treadle valve)   this valve operates the service brakes on both the tractor and trailer.

Force of motion   movement determined by the weight and speed of an object as it moves along.

For-hire carrier   an organization that has as its primary business hauling cargo by truck.

Forklift   used for loading pallets and heavy objects.

45-degree angle parking   an alley dock backing technique in which the rig is pulled forward at a 45-degree angle to the target, then backed in.

49 CFR Part 166   specification for hazardous materials that require special equipment or protection.

Forward stop   halting the forward movement of a vehicle.

4-axle, removable gooseneck, low bed with outriggers   a low-bed frame, four rear trailer axles, and a detachable gooseneck and outriggers for wide loads.

Four-way flashers   two amber lights at front and two amber lights or red lights at rear of vehicle. These are usually the front and rear turn signal lights, equipped to do double duty as warning lights. Make sure they are clean.

Frame   the metal infrastructure of any vehicle—creates the underpinnings to support the rest of the vehicle.

Frame rails   steel beams that run the length of the tractor and trailer.

Frameless construction   the exterior of the van or tank is the weight-carrying part instead of the frame.

Free and Secure Trade (FAST) program   cross-border trusted travel programs facilitate land border crossing of prescreened low-risk commercial truck drivers through exclusive dedicated lanes. Members in these voluntary programs must meet certain eligibility requirements and pay a 5-year membership fee.

Free play   easy movement vs. torque in a steering wheel.

Freight bills   bills prepared by the carrier from the bill of lading that must be signed by the consignee before the cargo can be unloaded and indicate whether the charges are prepaid or COD.

Freight broker   a person or company that arranges for transporting freight.

Freight forwarder   a person who gathers small shipments from various shippers and puts them together into larger shipments. These shipments then may go to a break-bulk facility where they are broken down for delivery to the consignees.

FreightWatch International   FreightWatch is the world leader in logistics security services, offering the only active monitoring solutions that provide organizations with complete cargo transparency and supply chain integrity from origin to destination.

Front axle   is a central shaft for a rotating wheel or gear. On wheeled vehicles, the axle may be fixed to the wheels, rotating with them, or fixed to its surroundings, with the wheels rotating around the axle. In the former case, bearings or bushings are provided at the mounting points where the axle is supported. In the latter case, a bearing or bushing sits inside the hole in the wheel to allow the wheel or gear to rotate around the axle. Sometimes, especially on bicycles, the latter type is referred to as a spindle. It may or may not be the drive axle.

Fuel filters   clean the fuel as it goes from the entry tube of the tank, through the tank and fuel lines, and into the injectors. To keep contaminants out of the fuel system.

Fuel gauge   shows how much fuel is in tanks. Since the gauge is not always accurate, a driver should check the tanks visually before each trip and at stopovers.

Fuel pedal   also called the accelerator in four-wheel vehicles, delivers a steady supply of fuel to the engine.

Fuel system regulates the amount of fuel that is sent to the engine and how often it is injected into the cylinders.

Fuel system heater keeps the fuel system from freezing.

Fuel tank holds the fuel.

Fuel use tax a tax that is paid by the carrier to each state; based on the number of miles driven in that state.

Full flow system all oil leaving the oil pump passes through an oil filter.

Full-stability system a system consisting of sensors and a computer that prevents rollovers.

Full trailer built so that no part of its weight rests upon the vehicle pulling and can fully support itself with its axles.

Fuse completes the electrical circuit and prevents overheating by breaking a circuit.

Gasoline engine a combustion engine fueled by gasoline.

Gear box temperature gauge shows the temperature of the lubricant in the transmission. The normal reading is 150 to 200 degrees F.

Gearshift lever the lever by which a driver shifts gears in a manual transmission.

General knowledge test (see **Knowledge test**)

Generators (and alternators) devices that recharge the battery when it loses electricity.

Glad hands connect the service and emergency air lines of the tractor to the trailer. The connections are secure when the glad hands lock.

Glare to shine or reflect a very harsh, bright light, such as "the glaring lights of oncoming traffic blinded me."

Global positioning system (GPS) is a space-based satellite navigation system that provides location and time information in all weather, anywhere on or near the Earth, where there is an unobstructed line of sight to four or more GPS satellites. It is maintained by the United States government and is freely accessible by anyone with a GPS receiver.

Good driving record an individual's record of any incidents (accidents) occurring while they are behind the wheel. A good driving record spans several years without any recorded incidents, attributed to their handling of their vehicle.

Gooseneck used to rest the trailer on the ground to load heavy equipment.

Governor regulates the air flow to maintain the desired pressure. When the air pressure approaches 125 psi (862 kPa) (pounds per square inch), the inlet valves open. They will close again when the pressure drops below 110 psi (784 kPa).

Gravity Isaac Newton defined gravity as a force—one that attracts all objects to all other objects. We know that Albert Einstein said gravity is a result of the curvature of space-time. These two theories are the most common and widely held (if somewhat incomplete) explanations of gravity. Gravity also keeps us grounded (rather than floating) on the earth.

Gravity ramp escape ramp that has a loose material surface with a grade of 5 percent to 43 percent.

Green Angels are a government-paid bilingual crew that patrol the toll roads throughout Mexico every day in green trucks. They carry tools and spare parts, looking for motorists in trouble. The Angeles Verdes will provide mechanical assistance, first aid, basic supplies, and towing. In addition they also have a communication network with different government offices and offer basic tourist information. The services they provide are FREE of charge unless your vehicle needs parts or fuel. Even though the services are free, tipping is extremely appreciated, however don't be offended if they do not accept except it.

Gross combination vehicle weight rating (GCVWR) the total weight of a tractor, trailer, and load.

Gross vehicle weight (GVW) the total weight of a straight truck and load.

Gross vehicle weight rating (GVWR) the total weight of a tractor and all trailers.

Hand truck used to carry small loads from the trailer to a storage area.

Hardship license in the U.S., there are no hardship licenses if a CDL is suspended or revoked. A hardship license is a restricted license issued administratively in accordance with statutes or by order of the court to an applicant whose driving privileges are under suspension. This license allows the applicant to drive during the period of suspension to earn a livelihood or to maintain the necessities of life. In many instances, the installation of an ignition interlock device will be required.

Hazard any road condition or road user (driver, cyclist, pedestrian, or animal) that presents a possible danger to you or your rig.

Hazard class every hazardous material is assigned to one of nine hazard classes as defined in 49 CFR 172.101 and 173. The nine hazard classes are as follows: Class 1: Explosives; Class 2: Gases; Class 3: Flammable and Combustible Liquids; Class 4: Flammable Solids; Class 5: Oxidizing Substances, Organic Peroxides; Class 6: Toxic Substances and Infectious Substances; Class 7: Radioactive Materials; Class 8: Corrosives; Class 9: Miscellaneous Hazardous Materials. Some of the nine classes are further separated into divisions based on their physical or chemical properties.

Hazardous material material that may pose a risk to health, safety, and property while being transported.

Hazardous materials endorsement an endorsement on a CDL that all drivers who transport hazardous materials must obtain.

Hazardous materials incident report a written report that must be filed within 15 days if there is an unintended release of hazardous materials.

Hazardous materials regulations standards set by the Research and Special Programs Administration (RSPA) Office of Hazardous Materials Transportation (OHMT) that regulate how hazardous materials are shipped.

Hazardous materials shipping papers a bill of lading that describes hazardous materials by the proper shipping name, hazard class, identification number, and the quantity being shipped. This form must be legible. These papers are required to accompany every hazmat load and lists each item by the proper shipping name, hazard class, identification number, and packing group.

Hazardous materials table found at Title 49 CFR 172.101 Table (*List of Hazardous Materials*). The Office of Hazardous Materials Safety maintains this data to enhance public access to the Department's information. The data contained in this Excel table is not intended to take the place of published agency regulations.

Hazardous waste waste of any type (nuclear, medical, human) that requires special processing and disposal. Trucks hauling hazardous waste must be placarded and the driver must have hazmat training and endorsement.

Hazardous waste manifest　a form (EPA-8700-22) that describes hazardous waste and identifies the shipper, carrier, and destination by name and by the identification numbers assigned by the Environmental Protection Agency. The shipper prepares, dates, and signs the manifest. All carriers of the shipment must sign the paper. It must also be signed by the consignee. The driver keeps a copy.

Hazmat endorsement　(see **Hazardous materials endorsement**).

Hazmat labels　labels resembling small placards that are placed on packages near the proper shipping name and identification number.

Hazmat Threat Assessment Program　TSA conducts a security threat assessment for any driver seeking to obtain, renew, or transfer a hazardous materials endorsement (HME) on a state-issued commercial driver's license (CDL). The program was implemented to meet the requirements of the USA PATRIOT Act, which prohibits states from issuing a license to transport hazardous materials in commerce unless a determination has been made that the driver does not pose a security risk. The Act further requires that the risk assessment include checks of criminal history records, legal status, and relevant international databases.

Headerboard (headache rack)　protects the driver from the freight shifting or crushing him or her during a sudden stop and/or accident.

Headlights　two white lights, one to the right and one to the left on the front of the tractor—required on buses, trucks, and tractor-trailer. Used to illuminate the vehicle to help the driver see and help others see the vehicle. During an inspection, make sure they are clean and both high and low beams work.

Helper service　a helper is to be provided for loading or unloading freight. The bill of lading specifies who will pay for the helper.

High blood pressure　blood pressure elevated beyond 130/70. There are, of course, drugs a physician may prescribe to lower the blood pressure. High blood pressure (anything above 130/70) is an indicator of the presence of heart disease or coronary artery disease in which the arteries serving the heart, itself, are clogged with cholesterol.

High center of gravity (see **Center of gravity**)　the bulk of the weight of the load is high off the ground.

Highway–rail grade crossing　is unique in that it is the intersection of two transportation modes, which differ in both the physical characteristics of their traveled ways and their operations. As of 2011, there were—in the U.S.—more than 250,000 public and private highway rail crossings. In Canada, there were more than 37,000 public, private, and pedestrian rail crossings.

Highway valve　allows air from the hand valve to flow through the air line to put on only the trailer brakes.

HMR 177.810　requires drivers of vehicles containing hazardous materials to obey state and local laws for the use of tunnels.

Hours of service　the amount of time you may spend on duty.

Hours of service (HOS) regulations　regulations to be followed by professional drivers on U.S. highways. For more information, go to www.fmcsa.dot.gov/rules-regulations/topics/hos/index.htm

Household goods bill of lading　used by moving companies for their shipments. This type of bill serves as a legal contract between the shipper and the carrier.

Hydraulic retarder　a type of driveline retarder, mounted on the drive line between the engine and the fly wheel or between the transmission and drive axles that reduces speed by directing a flow of oil against the stator vanes. It can be turned on by hand with a lever in the cab or automatically by an accelerator switch on the floor.

Hydroplaning　a road condition in which a thin film of water separates the tires from the road and the rig simply slides along on top of the water.

Identification (ID) number　four-digit numbers used to identify all hazardous materials.

Idling　letting the engine run while the rig is not moving.

Ignition circuit　The purpose of the ignition system is to create a spark that will ignite the fuel-air mixture in the cylinder of an engine. It must do this at exactly the right instant and do it at the rate of up to several thousand times per minute for each cylinder in the engine. If the timing of that spark is off by a small fraction of a second, the engine will run poorly or not run at all. The ignition system sends an extremely high voltage to the spark plug in each cylinder when the piston is at the top of its compression stroke. The tip of each spark plug contains a gap that the voltage must jump across in order to reach ground. That is where the spark occurs.

Imminent danger　situations in which danger is near and probable.

Independent trailer brake (trolley valve)　a hand valve that regulates the air flow to only the trailer unit and puts on the brakes. It is usually called the trolley valve and is normally on the right side of the steering column.

Individual wheel weight　the load each wheel is supporting. It is usually checked by state or local officials with a portable scale.

Inhalation hazard　a hazard involving a hazardous material that produces a vapor which can be inhaled. If the vapor—odorless or not—is inhaled, damage can result.

Initiative　a program or scheme to enhance a situation or resolve a problem.

Inner bridge　the distance between the center of the rearmost tractor axle and the center of the leading trailer axle. Determines weight limits.

Inside delivery　indicates the freight is to be delivered inside instead of unloaded at the curb.

Inspection routine　list of steps you go through each time you inspect your vehicle so you do not forget a step.

Instruments and gauges　make sure to check all instruments and gauges. In trucks with electronically controlled engines, the needles on all gauges will make a full sweep right after the engine is turned on to ensure all gauges are working.

Interaxle differential　(also called a power divider) is an integral shaft in the forward axle. That shaft is the input for the forward axle and also the rear axle with a differential separating the input from the output allowing for a difference in speed between the front and rear axle.

Interaxle differential lock control　locks and unlocks rear tandem axles. In the locked position, keeps the wheels from spinning. This position is used on slippery roads.

Interline carrier a carrier that accepts or delivers shipments for only part of the trip. Another carrier either begins or completes the trip.

Intermodal carrier a trucking company that usually picks up intermodal containers at a port and hauls them to the designated recipient.

Intermodal freight transport involves the transportation of freight in an intermodal container or vehicle, using multiple modes of transportation (rail, ship, and truck), without any handling of the freight itself when changing modes. The method reduces cargo handling, and so improves security, reduces damages and losses, and allows freight to be transported faster.

Internal combustion engine burns fuel within enclosed chambers called cylinders.

Internal environment the environment inside a tractor and/ or a trailer. The internal environment involves recirculating air, air or heat, noise (radio, CB), and other items required for the operation of the rig.

International Registration Plan (IRP) an agreement among the states and Canadian provinces for paying registration fees that are based on the percentage of miles operated in each state or province.

International transportation the movement of cargo from one nation to another.

Interpersonal communication one's ability to transmit a thought or idea through words, body language, and facial expression, to another. The purpose of interpersonal communication is to conduct business, express an idea, solve a problem, or provide information. Interpersonal communication skills are a requirement for a successful career in truck transportation.

Intersection the crossing point between two roadways, usually running from north and south and crossing a roadway running from east to west.

Interstate carrier operates between states.

Interstate Commerce Commission (ICC) was a regulatory body in the United States created by the Interstate Commerce Act of 1887. The agency's original purpose was to regulate railroads (and later trucking) to ensure fair rates, to eliminate rate discrimination, and to regulate other aspects of common carriers, including interstate bus lines and telephone companies. The agency was abolished in 1995, and its remaining functions were transferred to the Surface Transportation Board.

Interstate operating authority issued by the DOT.

Interstate routes these routes have separate opposing traffic, limited access, and bypass many small communities.

Intervention to interfere with the outcome or course especially of a condition or process (as to prevent harm or improve functioning). An intervention for an unskilled driver would be more education, training on the job, and the help of a veteran driver instructor.

Intrastate carrier operates within the state.

Invoice a bill from the shipper that lists the goods, prices, and total due. This may be mailed to the consignee, or the driver may have to give it to the consignee if it is a COD shipment.

Irregular route an irregular route describes long-distance transport between a combination of origin and destination points using any suitable route.

Jackknife a type of accident in which the tractor and trailer turn to make a V shape.

Jake brake a **compression release engine brake**, frequently called a **Jake brake** or **Jacobs brake**, is an engine braking mechanism installed on some diesel engines. When activated, it opens exhaust valves in the cylinders after the compression cycle, releasing the compressed air trapped in the cylinders, and slowing the vehicle. Although *Jake brake* properly refers to the Jacobs brand of engine brakes, the term has become a genericized trademark and is often used to refer to engine brakes or compression release engine brakes in general, especially on large vehicles or heavy equipment.

Jifflox converter dolly used in the eastern United States, it is hooked behind the axle of a single-axle tractor. This converts it to a tandem-axle tractor. The tractor then can pull a loaded trailer.

Job stress stress coming from a job situation.

Jug handle turn a right turn where you compensate for off-tracking by moving into another lane of traffic before entering the intersection. This type of turn is dangerous and sloppy.

Jump-starting using another vehicle battery to start a dead battery. You should always remember to observe safety rules, prepare the truck, and properly hook up the jumper cables when working on the battery.

Just-in-time (JIT) delivery system a method of shipping that gets rid of the costly overhead of warehousing stock.

Kingpin usually a 2-inch steel pin that is locked into the jaws of the fifth wheel to couple the tractor to the trailer.

Knowledge test the written test all CDL applicants must take to see how much they know about the laws regulating the trucking industry.

Labels (see **Hazmat labels**) for hazard class; look very much like small placards and should be placed near the proper shipping name and identification number.

Landing gear on a trailer, used to support the load while it is not attached to a tractor.

Laptop computers computers that are small enough to be portable.

Lateral acceleration the acceleration created when a vehicle corners that tends to push a vehicle sideways. For this reason, the driver needs to accelerate a little as the vehicle reaches the top of the curve to pull the vehicle through the curve. An inexperienced driver may panic in a curve as the lateral acceleration pushes his vehicle into the left lane and might hit the brakes to slow the motion only to find that the problem actually increases. The proper way to take a sharp corner is to slow down before the curve, then accelerate at the apex of it to bring the vehicle around the curve.

Leaf spring suspension narrow metal strips of varying lengths bolted together and attached to frame hangers.

Lift axle an axle, usually kept in the raised position, that can be lowered when the vehicle is loaded to spread the load over more axles, reducing tire and axle wear.

Lifting safety a sequence of prescribed steps to use when lifting heavy objects. Failure to follow this sequence may result in back strain or injury.

Lights illumination devices.

Liquid cargo tankers rigs, consisting of a tractor and a semi-trailer that is either oval, circular, or square shaped, that are used to transport liquid cargos such as gasoline, asphalt, milk, juices, and liquefied gas.

Liquid surge the wave action of the liquid cargo in a tanker.

Liquid tankers tankers that are specifically designed to transport liquids.

Live axle supports the vehicle weight, sends power to the wheels, and is hollow.

Livestock transport trailer a type of trailer used to carry live animals. These trailers have either a flat floor or double drop frame design. They can have side or rear doors, or both. Slots or holes in the sides allow the livestock to breathe. Depending on the size of the livestock being carried, these trailers can be converted to have two or three decks.

Local pick-up and delivery the driver operates in and around cities. He or she will usually be delivering freight to its final destination.

Local truck routes many cities and towns have designated routes for trucks.

Locking jaws in coupling and uncoupling, the locking jaws are the part of the fifth wheel that fit around the shank of the kingpin on the trailer to connect the tractor to the trailer.

Locking lever in coupling and uncoupling, the locking lever should be locked, once the locking jaws are around the trailer's kingpin.

Long-distance transport cargo is transported from a point of origin to one or more distant destinations.

Low air pressure warning alarm sounds or lights up when there is low pressure in the air brake system.

Low air pressure warning signal tells the driver the air pressure has dropped below 60 psi (414 kPa). A red warning light will turn on, a buzzer will sound, or both will happen.

Low ground clearance warning sign warns the professional driver that ground clearance is low between the railroad track and the undercarriage of the truck. These are most often found at railroad crossings.

Low-light an exterior environment where the natural daylight is minimal, usually just before dawn and just before sunset.

Lubrication system distributes oil between the moving parts to keep them from rubbing together.

Lug lever the device that unlocks locking lugs on a sliding tandem axle.

Lug tread deep grooves in the tire shoulders that run perpendicular to the sidewalls. These tires are best for the drive wheels.

Lugging occurs when the driver fails to downshift when the engine speed starts to fall below the normal operating range. In this condition, the tractor produces too little power and lugs, or struggles.

Maintenance policy guidelines companies set up that tell drivers and mechanics what their responsibilities are in servicing and maintaining their vehicles.

Malfunction when a part of system does not work properly.

Managing your speed adjusting your speed for the road, weather, and traffic conditions.

Maneuver to change direction while moving.

Maneuverability the ability of the tractor-trailer to change direction while moving.

Manifest specifically a "freight manifest" or "cargo manifest" is a list or invoice of cargo for any or several forms of transportation, usually containing marks of contents, consignee, and other pertinent information for use at terminals or a customs inspector.

Manual release the device on a fifth wheel that allows you to release, or unlock, the sliding mechanism by pushing or pulling a release handle.

Manual transmission one that must be shifted by the driver through the different gears. A clutch must be used.

Measured right turn a required maneuver for CDL candidates.

Meet and turn a type of relay run in which two drivers start toward each other from different points and meet at a chosen mid-point. At the meeting place, the drivers exchange complete units or only trailers. Then each driver goes back to his or her starting point.

Monetary exchange rate the daily rate of exchange between one country's money and another. As an example, the exchange rate between U.S. dollars and the Mexican peso or the Mexican peso and the Canadian dollar.

Motor carrier the person or company that is in the business of transporting goods.

Motor Carrier Safety Assistance Program (MCSAP) is a Federal grant program that provides financial assistance to states to reduce the number and severity of crashes and hazardous materials incidents involving commercial motor vehicles (CMV). The goal of the MCSAP is to reduce CMV-involved crashes, fatalities, and injuries through consistent, uniform, and effective CMV safety programs.

Multiarticulation the connection points on a tractor and two or more trailers. A tractor-trailer has one articulation point, between the tractor and the trailer. A tractor pulling "doubles" has articulation points between the tractor and the first trailer and the first and second trailer. This is a multiarticulated rig.

Multiple-axle assembly two or more dead axles together. They spread the rig's weight over more axles. This reduces the amount of weight on any one axle.

Multiwheel low-bed trailer with jeep dolly has a low bed frame and two rear trailer axles.

NAFTA (see **North American Free Trade Agreement**)

National network roadways that allow truck combinations to operate.

National Response Center helps coordinate the emergency forces in response to major chemical hazards.

National Safety Code (NSC) in 1987, the federal, provincial, and territorial ministers responsible for transportation and highway safety agreed to develop and implement a National Safety Code (NSC) to encourage trucking safety, promote efficiency in the motor carrier industry, and achieve consistent safety standards in this area across Canada. The NSC was based on a consolidation of existing provincial and territorial legislation and regulations, supplemented with new initiatives designed to further enhance safety across the country.

National System of Interstate Highways also known as the Designated System or National Network. Consists of the interstates and many additional multilane, divided highways, such as the U.S. routes.

National Transportation Safety Board (NTSB) investigates accidents and offers solutions to prevent future accidents.

Nonsynchronized transmission one that does not have thin plates between the gears to assist in shifting. The driver must double-clutch.

North American Free Trade Agreement (NAFTA) a trade agreement that allows the free movement of freight between Canada, the United States, and Mexico.

Nose mount trailer a refrigerated trailer that has the refrigeration unit at the upper front of the trailer.

No-zones areas around a tractor-trailer rig where the driver has difficulty seeing or no vision of other nearby vehicles. No-zones include behind the rig, to both sides of the trailer and, in some cases, in front of the rig.

Nuclear Regulatory Commission (NRC) regulates hazardous materials.

Occupational Safety and Health (OSH) Act is the primary federal law which governs occupational health and safety in the private sector and federal government in the United States. It was enacted by Congress in 1970 and was signed by President Richard Nixon on December 29, 1970. Its main goal is to ensure that employers provide employees with an environment free from recognized hazards, such as exposure to toxic chemicals, excessive noise levels, mechanical dangers, heat or cold stress, or unsanitary conditions.

Occupational Safety and Health Administration (OSHA) regulates hazardous materials.

Odometer shows how many miles or kilometers the rig has been driven.

Off-duty time illustrated as (OFF) on the log book. It is any time during which the driver is relieved of all on-duty time responsibilities.

Offense in terms of traffic citations is the law, rule or regulation that has been ignored or not followed. As an example, traveling at 60 mph (97 km/h) in a 40 mph (64 km/h) zone would be an offense that would be cited.

Office of Hazardous Materials Transportation (OHMT) part of the Research and Special Programs Administration (RSPA) that classifies hazardous materials.

Office of Motor Carriers (OMC) part of the Federal Highway Administration (FHWA) that issues and enforces the Federal Motor Carrier Safety Regulations.

Off-road recovery using the roadside as an escape path and safely returning to the highway.

Offset backing is the opposite of straight-line backing in that the tractor-trailer rig must line up to the right or the left of the destination point and then back the rig into that space.

Off-tracking when the rear wheels of a tractor-trailer follow a different path than the front wheels while making a turn.

Oil filter keeps the lubrication system free of impurities.

Oil level alarm lights up when the oil level becomes too low for normal operation.

Oil pan bolted to the bottom of the engine is a container, or reservoir.

Oil pressure gauge indicates the oil pressure within the system. If pressure is lost, it means there is not enough lubrication in the system.

Onboard recorder (OBR) is an electronic device attached to a commercial motor vehicle, which is used to record the amount of time a vehicle is being driven. This is similar to the tachograph, and is the American equivalent of the digital tachograph used in Europe. The driving hours of commercial drivers (truck and bus drivers) are regulated by a set of rules known as the hours of service (HOS). The HOS are rules intended to prevent driver fatigue, by limiting the amount of time drivers spend operating commercial vehicles.

On-duty time illustrated as (ON) in the log book; this is the time the driver begins work, or must be ready to go to work, until the time he or she is relieved from work of any kind.

One-way check valve prevents air from flowing back into the compressor from the reservoirs.

Open dispatch the driver goes from the point of origin to a distant point.

Order notify bill of lading a bill of lading that permits the shipper to collect payment before the shipment reaches the destination. The driver must pick up the consignee's copy of the bill of lading before he or she delivers the shipment.

Order notify shipment one in which payment for the goods is made when the driver gets a copy of the Order Notify Bill of Lading from the consignee.

Ordinary trailer axle connects the trailer wheels to the trailer body.

Originating, or pickup, carrier the carrier that first accepts the shipment from the shipper.

Outer bridge the distance from the center of the steering axle to the center of the last axle in the combination. Determines weight limits.

Outriggers used for extra support of wide loads.

Overdriving driving at a speed that will not let you stop within your sight distance.

Overlength load cargo that is longer than the legal limit permits.

Oversteering turning the wheels beyond the intended path of travel or more sharply than the vehicle can handle.

Over-the-counter drugs drugs that do not require a prescription, but still may have important side effects such as drowsiness.

Over-the-road trucking cargo is hauled on regular routes. Drivers may be away for a week or more.

Overweight load cargo that weighs more than the legal limit permits.

Overweight trucks trucks that are carrying more weight than specified on the manifest—or trucks that weigh more than the road's stated capacity.

Overwidth load cargo that is wider than the legal limit permits.

Packing slip a detailed list of packed goods that is prepared by the shipper.

Pallet jacks used for loading palletized cargo.

Parallel parking parking in a straight line behind one vehicle and in front of another vehicle.

Parking brake tool used when the vehicle is not running. To check that it is working, put on the brake and engage the transmission to see if it holds.

Parking brake control valve a flip switch or push-pull knob that lets the driver put on the parking brake. Use this valve only when the vehicle is parked.

Parking brake system is used to hold the rig in place when it is parked.

Partial-authority control systems where the operator has only partial authority on systems of the truck. A good example is the use of a governor to control speed.

Passive railroad crossings A passive railroad crossing does not have electric gates, signals, or sirens to notify motorists of approaching trains. Most passive crossings only have stop signs and railroad signs.

Pavement markings aside from lane definition, pavement markings provide the driver with information in addition to signs and/or traffic lights, particularly at intersections and rail-road crossing.

Peddle run local pick-up and delivery operation; the freight is usually hauled from the terminal to separate destinations in the nearby areas and freight is also picked up along the way and brought back to the terminal.

Peso the Mexican equivalent to a U.S. or Canadian dollar, depending on the exchange rate that day.

Pinion gear a short shaft at the rear end of the propeller shaft that has a small gear at the end.

Pipeline and Hazardous Materials Safety Administration (PHMSA) was created under the Norman Y. Mineta Research and Special Programs Improvement Act of 2004. The purpose of the Act was to provide the Department a more focused research organization and establish a separate operating administration for pipeline safety and hazardous materials transportation safety operations.

Pitman arm connected to and moves the drag link.

Placards 10-3/4 inches square and turned upright on a point in a diamond shape. Federal laws specify when placards must be displayed on vehicles transporting hazardous materials.

Plane mirror a flat mirror for seeing to the rear of the rig.

Point of reference a stationary object that you spot or use as a target when you are driving.

Pole trailer carries long, narrow cargo. A pole trailer can be telescoped, or made longer or shorter to fit the load. Cargo may be poles, timbers, logs, steel girders, or concrete beams. Be careful because you could have problems with visibility and location of the steering axle.

Port of entry locations where the driver must stop and prove the carrier has authority to operate in the state.

Posted bridges many bridges have special weight restrictions. Do not cross a bridge if your rig's weight is more than the weight that is posted. Some fines are as much as $10,000.

Posttrip inspection a thorough check of the rig at the end of a trip.

Power the rate at which energy is transferred, used, or transformed. Energy transfer can be used to do work, so power is also the rate at which this work is performed. The power expended to move a vehicle is the product of the traction force of the wheels and the velocity of the vehicle.

Power skid a skid that happens when the drive wheels spin and the rear of the tractor moves sideways.

Power steering lets the driver control the tractor with less effort and stress.

Power steering fluid makes the steering easier to turn and should be checked during regular maintenance.

Pre-Employment Screening Program is designed to assist the motor carrier industry in assessing individual operators' crash and serious safety violation history as a pre-employment condition.

Prepaid shipments shipments in which the transportation charges are paid at the shipping point.

Prescription drugs are drugs that are prescribed by a doctor.

Pressure points are arteries that supply blood to the body.

Pretrip inspection a systematic parts and system check made before each trip.

Preventive maintenance servicing that is done at regular intervals on a truck.

Primary provincial roads in Canada, all the provincial roads have been classified based on their mobility function, in order to differentiate maintenance standards. The classification is: Class A: Roads defined as national primary roads by the National Department of Transport; Class B: Provincial primary roads, which promote intra-provincial, inter-city, and inter-regional mobility; Class C: Provincial secondary roads, which promote intra-regional and inter-district mobility; Class D: Provincial tertiary roads with an intra-district mobility function; Class E: Local access roads to provide access to the higher-class road network for isolated communities and centres of economic activity. Classes A and B form 59 percent of the paved network and provide national and intra-provincial mobility. Classes C and D form 39 percent of the paved network and provide intra-regional and intra-district mobility. Only 2 percent of the paved network provides local access to the higher order road network.

Primary vehicle controls allow the driver to control the truck.

Principal place of business the main office of the carrier where all records are kept.

Private carrier an organization that uses trucks to transport its own goods in its own trucks.

Pro numbers preprinted numbers on freight bills that are often used to identify the freight bill.

Progressive shifting shifting before you reach the maximum governed rpm.

PSI pounds per square inch.

Public relations how you, as a truck driver, get along with the public.

Pusher axle nondriven axle mounted ahead of the drive axle.

Pusher tandem the rear axle is powered (live) and the forward axle is not powered (dead). The forward axle must have a drop center so the driveshaft can be attached to the live axle.

Pyrometer gauge that measures the temperature of exhaust gases.

Pyrometer warning lights up when exhaust temperatures are too high.

QualComm is an American global telecommunication corporation that designs, manufactures, and markets digital wireless telecommunications products and services based on its code division multiple access (CDMA) technology and other technologies. Its first products used satellite locating and messaging to assist long-haul truckers.

Quick-release valve allows the brakes to release swiftly. When you remove your foot from the brakes, air escapes from the chambers into the atmosphere.

Radial tires have body ply cords that run across the tire perpendicular to the tread.

Radiator cap located at the top of the radiator. It keeps the coolant from overflowing.

Radioactive materials substances that contain unstable radioactive atoms that give off radiation as they decay.

Railway crossing a point in the road where railroad tracks cross as a right-of-way.

Random alcohol and substance abuse testing the unannounced testing, using human urine, for the presence of alcohol or illegal substances. These tests are random and are not given to every employee.

Rear-view mirrors mirrors used to see on the sides and behind the vehicle. Should be at the proper angle and clean.

Recapped tires is a previously worn tire which has gone through a remanufacturing process designed to extend its useful service life. Recapping starts with a safety inspection of the tire. The old tread is then buffed away, and a new rubber tread is applied to the bare "casing" using specialized machinery. Recapped tires are significantly cheaper than new tires. As a result, they are widely used in large-scale operations such as trucking, busing, and commercial aviation. They are also the most environmentally friendly way of recycling used tires—in some applications, a tire can be retreaded up to 10 times. Recycled rubber from retreads can be shredded to make rubber mulch.

Receiver/consignee the person or company to whom the goods are being shipped or consigned.

Reflective triangle warning device carried on big rigs that is placed to warn other drivers when the rig is stopped. It is usually bright orange with red borders.

Refrigerated trailer used for hauling cargo that needs to be refrigerated.

Regrooved tires regrooving is the practice of carving out the rubber in the grooves of a tire to create additional tread depth so the tire with 2/32 (3.2 mm) of tread magically gets 4/32 (1.6 mm) or more. DOT still has regulations for regrooving on the books. According to 49 CFR 569.3 (c): "Regroovable tire means a tire, either original or retread, designed and constructed with sufficient tread material to permit renewal of the tread pattern in a manner which conforms to this part." Part 569.7 says: "After regrooving, cord material below the grooves shall have a protective covering of tread material at least 3/32nd-in. thick."

Regular route refers to line-haul transport between given origins and destinations using assigned highways.

Regular run the driver operates between the same points on each trip and may or may not have a regular starting and finishing time for each period of driving.

Regulations laws and rules which govern a certain group or area of industry. Regulations for the truck transportation industry are made and enforced by the Federal Motor Carrier Safety Administration.

Relaxation response a relaxation technique that calms the mind, body, and spirit. The relaxation response helps combat the ill effects of stress.

Relay run refers to a trip in which a driver drives for 10 hours and then goes off duty as prescribed by the hours-of-service laws. Another driver takes the unit on to the next point. This cycle may be repeated several times as the truck is driven from origin to final destination by several different drivers.

Relay valve makes up for brake lag on a long wheelbase vehicle.

Residential delivery The bill of lading will specify the address and method of collecting payment if the shipment is to a residence.

Restricted routes routes that you are not allowed to go on because the route is hazardous or prone to accidents.

Retention groove a groove in the fifth wheel designed to retain lubrication for the ease of turning of the fifth wheel.

Retread tires (see **Recapped Tires**)

Rib tread grooves in the tire tread that run parallel to the sidewalls. They are designed for highway speeds.

Right to know the ability to know what an individual is responsible for or is interacting with. In trucking, as an example, a professional driver has the right to know what he or she is hauling so that precautions may be taken—for the driver's safety, the safety of fellow highway users, and the safety of the rig.

Right to participate workers in Canada have the right to participate in decisions affecting workplace health and safety. Federal, provincial, and territorial laws state that workers can get elected as paid worker representatives on workplace health and safety committees. In smaller workplaces, workers can get elected as worker health and safety representatives. Workers participating in health and safety decision making work with management on controlling or eliminating dangers in the workplace.

Right to refuse When you believe working conditions are unsafe or unhealthful, you should call your employer's attention to the problem. If your employer does not correct the hazard or disagrees with you about the extent of the hazard, you also may file a complaint with OSHA. Refusing to do a job because of potentially unsafe workplace conditions is not ordinarily an employee right under the OSH Act. (Your union contract or state law may, however, give you this right, but OSHA cannot enforce it.) Refusing to work may result in disciplinary action by the employer. However, employees do have the right to refuse to do a job if they believe in good faith that they are exposed to an imminent danger. "Good faith" means that even if an imminent danger is not found to exist, the worker had reasonable grounds to believe that it did exist.

Rims part of the wheel that holds the tire in place. To prevent excess wear, loss of air pressure, or loss of a tire, rims should not be dented or damaged and should be rust free.

Ring gear sometimes called a starter ring or ring gear, is a medium carbon steel ring with teeth that is fitted on the periphery of a flexplate or flywheel of an internal combustion engine.

Road rage a term developed in the 1980s, road rage is an aggressive or angry behavior by a driver of a motor vehicle. Such behavior might include rude gestures, verbal insults, deliberately driving in an unsafe or threatening manner, or making threats. Road rage can lead to altercations, assaults, and collisions which result in injuries and even deaths. It can be thought of as an extreme case of aggressive driving.

Rocky Mountain double larger than a standard double, but smaller than a turnpike double. The lead trailer is typically longer than the second trailer. Overall length is 80 to 100 feet (24.4 to 30.5 m).

Roll and rest a single driver takes the truck from origin to destination.

Rolling traction the friction occurring when one surface rolls over another.

Roll stability control is an active vehicle safety system that automatically intervenes if a high rollover risk is detected while driving. If a rollover threat is occurring, the system intervenes and assists the driver in minimizing the rollover risk by automatically reducing vehicle speed. RSC continuously checks and updates the lateral acceleration of the tractor and compares it to a critical threshold where rollover may occur. When the critical threshold is exceeded, RSC intervenes by reducing engine torque, and engaging the engine retarder, while automatically applying drive axle and trailer brakes.

Route restrictions throughout North America, some routes are restricted for use by trucks. Some of these restrictions include weight capacities, times of use, type of load, number of axles and others.

Routine servicing tasks that can be done by drivers, such as add fuel, oil, and coolant, or drain the moisture from the fuel and air systems.

Safe Explosives Act Previous to the Safe Explosives Act of 2002, the manufacture and sale of explosives strictly within the borders of one state was regarded as outside the domain of the federal government. It was through the interstate commerce clause the federal government obtained its authority to regulate explosives.

Safe haven an area approved in writing by local, state, or federal officials in which unattended vehicles carrying Class A or Class B explosives may be parked.

SafeStat formerly used to measure the performance of professional drivers. With the introduction of CSA, SafeStat is now replaced by SMS.

Safety awareness training provided by a carrier's safety director to acquaint drivers, mechanics, and dock employees with best practices for loading, unloading, repairing, and driving trucks.

Safety equipment equipment with the purpose of maintaining a driver's safety. This equipment ranges from eye protection and gloves to the fire extinguisher in the tractor and safety triangles and sometimes flares for use in case of breakdown.

Safety Measurement System (SMS) as part of CSA and a tool used by FMCSA and State partners to evaluate a carrier's safety performance.

Safety valves keep the air pressure from rising to a dangerous level.

Sand piles mounds or ridges built high enough to drag the undercarriage of the rig.

Satellite radio radio transmissions assisted by orbiting satellite.

Scanning looking far ahead, just ahead of the rig, and on both sides.

Scene the surroundings, or environment, in which the driver operates. It includes the road conditions, weather, scenery, people, animals, and other road users.

Scheduled preventive maintenance servicing that is based on time or mileage since the last scheduled maintenance.

Seat belt safety harness that holds you in the seat. You should always put your seat belt on before you start the vehicle.

Secondary braking system can slow or even stop the rig if the service brake system fails.

Secondary collision a collision that results from either being involved in an accident or taking evasive action to avoid an emergency.

Secondary vehicle controls do not affect the rig's power or movement but help the driver's vision, communication, comfort, and safety.

Security the ability of a professional driver to protect him- or herself, the rig, and the cargo being hauled against terrorist activity, theft, accident, and injury.

Security seals seals shippers place on cargo containers that do not let the driver fully inspect the load.

Semiautomatic transmission one that is essentially a manual transmission, but uses electronic controls to automate some of the gear changes.

Semitrailer is the one most often used in a tractor-trailer combination. It has axles only at the rear of the trailer. The front of the trailer is supported by the tractor.

September 11, 2001 the date of terrorist attacks on U.S. soil. Three thousand Americans were killed, three airplanes were crashed, two skyscrapers were destroyed, and damage was done to the Pentagon building in Washington, D.C.

Service brake system normally used to slow down or stop the vehicle.

Shipper/consignor the person or company who offers the goods for shipment.

Shipping paper another word for "bills of lading" or "manifests," which list items being hauled, weight, point of origin, and destination. These papers are carried by the driver and given to the receiver of the load.

Shock happens when something reduces the flow of blood throughout the body and could kill a person. Keep the person warm and quiet.

Shock absorbers reduce the motion of the vehicle body as the wheels move over uneven surfaces.

Shuttle operations in transportation, shuttle operations are schedules where a driver hauls a load to one point, where another driver picks it up and moves it to its destination. The first driver, after dropping his or her load, usually either picks up another load and hauls it back to the point of origin or deadheads back home.

Sideswipe most often used when one vehicle strikes a glancing blow to the side of another vehicle. The vehicle being damaged is often parked but can be moving, as well.

Sight distance the objects you can see at night with your headlights. Your sight distance is limited to the range of your headlights.

Signal (or identification) lights truck lights on top, sides, and back to identify it as a large vehicle. It is important for these lights to be clean, working, and the proper color.

Single drive axles found on the rear of the tractor.

Single drop deck low beds that can haul heavy and oversized equipment without going over the height limits. Since these trailers are low to the ground, they may have bottom clearance problems at railroad crossings, curbs, and large potholes, but not as much of a problem as a double drop frame.

Skidding when the rig's tires lose grip or traction of the road.

Skills test the portion of the CDL testing process in which applicants are tested on their ability to control a tractor-trailer.

Sleep apnea   often seen as the cause of driver fatigue, sleep apnea is a sleep disorder characterized by abnormal pauses in breathing or instances of abnormally low breathing, during sleep. Each pause in breathing, called an apnea, can last from a few seconds to minutes, and may occur 5 to 30 times or more an hour. Similarly, each abnormally low breathing event is called a hypopnea. Sleep apnea is diagnosed with an overnight sleep test called a polysomnogram, or "sleep study."

Sleeper berth (SB)   a berth in the tractor cab in which the driver can sleep. Its size and other specifications are determined by law.

Sleeper operations   the driver of a rig that has a sleeper berth can accumulate the required off-duty time in two periods as long as neither period is less than 2 hours.

Slides   sliding assemblies for the fifth wheel and the tandem axle.

Sliding (adjustable) fifth wheel (slider)   slides backward and forward. It can be locked into place to adapt to different loads. It greatly increases the flexibility of the total rig.

Sliding fifth wheels   fifth wheels that are attached to sliding bracket assemblies and can be moved.

Sliding tandem   used on semitrailers. Allows the trailer axles to be moved forward and backward on a track.

Sliding traction   the friction occurring when one surface slides across another.

Sliding trailer tandem axle assembly   a tandem axle that allows the axle and suspension to slide, or move along, the frame rails of the trailer to make weight adjustments.

Smoothbore tank   a tank that has no bulkheads or baffles.

SMS   (see **Safety Measurement System**)

Social networking   the use of electronic communications, such as Facebook, Twitter, and others. Social networking can be for personal use as well as business.

Space management   keeping a cushion of air around the rig at all times.

Spare tire   additional tire used as a precaution in case something happens to the vehicle tires. Make sure they are properly secured, the right size, and inflated.

Special rig   any rig designed to haul specific commerce, such as hanging meat, livestock, liquids, gas, oversized loads, and more. Examples of special rigs are reefers, flatbeds, drop-deck trailers, etc.

Special routing   used with oversized, special, or hazmat loads. These routes are designed to eliminate driving in heavy traffic and often are used during off-peak hours as well.

Speed   the rate of motion of your rig.

Speeding   driving faster than the legal or posted speed limit or driving too fast for the conditions.

Speedometer   indicates road speed in miles and kilometers per hour and is required by law to work.

Speed retarders   are part of the transmission, cooled by the engine's cooling system and compatible with ABS. For mountain driving, use the speed retarder so you don't have to ride the brake. In traffic, use it to slow your vehicle the moment the accelerator is released.

Spider gears   Spider gears are an integral part of a tractor's differential. They are part of the gear set that allows the rear wheels to turn at different speeds, which is necessary in many instances. When your vehicle goes into a turn, the outer wheel turns at a faster rate than the inner wheel; this is accomplished through a series of gears, including spider gears.

Splash guards (mud flaps)   rubberized sheaths hanging behind the wheels that lessen the amount of water/mud kicked up in back of the trailer or truck. Make sure they are properly attached and not rubbing the wheels.

Splines   are ridges or teeth on a drive shaft that mesh with grooves in a mating piece and transfer torque to it, maintaining the angular correspondence between them.

Split shifting   A split shift is used in a truck with two transmissions, a main and an auxilary. The main has 4 or 5 forward and 1 reverse gear. The other box has 3 or 4 gears. When taking off in first gear in the main box you would be in first gear in the secondary box, then you would shift to second in the secondary, and third. The split comes when you shift the main box to second and the secondary box back to first, which would be the next higher gear, thus you split the gear.

Splitter valve   splits gears into direct or overdrive. This valve is controlled with a button on the top of the gear shift knob.

Spoke wheel made of two pieces   difficult to balance and align the tires and rims. Make sure you check lug nuts often for tightness.

Spring leaf suspension   (see **Leaf spring suspension**)

STAA Unsafe Conditions   (see **Surface Transportation Assistance Act**)

Stab braking   first, apply the brakes fully. Then release the pedal partly when the wheels lock. Put on the brakes again when the wheels start to roll.

Standard double   two semitrailers. The second trailer is converted into a full trailer by using a converter dolly.

Standard double rig   a single axle tractor pulling a 28-foot (8.5 m) semitrailer and a 28-foot (8.5 m) trailer.

Starting routine   steps used to start the engine.

Startup   the routine followed for starting an engine.

State primary routes   within each state, these are the major routes.

Stationary fifth wheel   a fifth wheel that is placed to get the best weight distribution between the tractor's steer axle and the drive axle(s) of a properly loaded trailer, and is fixed in that position.

Steering arm   the one on the right side attaches the tie rod to the wheels. The one on the left side is attached to the drag link.

Steering gear box   transfers the turning of the steering shaft to the Pitman arm.

Steering gear shaft   connects the steering wheel to the steering gear box.

Steering system   allows you to steer the vehicle and should not have more than 10 degrees of steering wheel play.

Steering wheel   connected to the steering shaft and controls the direction of the vehicle.

Steering wheel lash   the rebound of motion of the steering wheel after it has been turned its maximum rotations.

Storage and delay charges   an additional amount to be paid to the carrier if a delivery is postponed by the consignee or shipper or a shipment must be stored before it can be delivered. These terms are stated in the bill of lading.

Straight bill of lading   a contract that provides for delivery of a shipment to the consignee. The driver does not need to get a copy from the consignee when the goods are delivered.

Straight-line backing   the ability of a professional driver to back a tractor-trailer rig in a straight line, from start to finish.

Straight-line parking an alley dock backing technique in which the rig is pulled forward so that the rear is facing the target, then backed in.

Straight truck a single unit truck with the engine, cab, and cargo compartment all on the same frame.

Stress (also see **Job stress** and **stress management**) your body's response to difficulty, frustration, fatigue, or anger.

Stress management the process of maintaining calm and patience in emotionally uncomfortable situations. Because stress takes such a large toll on the human body, the ability to control stress in usually high stress situations will keep you healthy and able to function at the highest levels.

Supply/emergency brakes are spring brakes that require air pressure in order to be released. They are applied when air pressure is released from the system, and disengaged when air pressure is supplied. This is an emergency feature which ensures that if air pressure to either unit is lost, the trailer will stop to a grinding halt instead of not stopping and becoming uncontrollable.

Surface Transportation Assistance Act (STAA) provides the protection of the "whistleblower" accommodation to employees who may be asked by employers to ignore the laws, rules, and regulations of transportation and/or to drive vehicles which are not safe to drive.

Surging loads periodic increased rpms, caused by uneven power to engine.

Suspension springs used to support a vehicle and its axles. Failure can have tragic results.

Suspension system supports, distributes, and carries the weight of the truck.

Synchronized transmission one that has thin plates between the gears called synchronizers. Allows shifting without double-clutching.

Synchronizing requires the coordination of events to operate a system in unison. Systems with synchronized parts are said to be operating in synch.

Systematic search (or Systematic seeing) a driver's visual search pattern that helps him or her know what to look at, what to look for, and where to look.

Tachometer displays the engine speed in revolutions per minute (rpm). It is a guide to knowing when to shift gears. The tachometer helps you use the engine and transmission effectively during acceleration and deceleration.

Tag axle nondriven axle mounted behind the drive axle.

Tag tandem the forward axle is live and the rear axle is dead. The dead axle tags along behind the live axle.

Tailgate delivery the freight is unloaded and delivered at the tailgate (the back of the truck).

Tailgating following too close behind a vehicle.

Tailswing the movement of the last unit of a tractor-trailer rig during a turn.

Tandem axle tractor a tractor with two axles.

Tandem axles two axles that work together. There are three types of tandem axles.

Tanker endorsement (see **Tank vehicles endorsement**).

Tank vehicles endorsement an endorsement on a CDL that all drivers who transport liquids in bulk must obtain.

Tariff a tax on commodities coming into or going out of one country and into or out of another.

Tarp or tarpaulin is used to cover most freight and tied down with rope, webbing, or elastic hooks. To do its job properly it should be tightly secured.

Technology ever-improving and expanding frontier of new inventions, often electronic and wireless, affecting all aspects of transportation industry.

Terrorist activities planned, violent acts designed to disrupt transportation, commerce, and financial activities by enemies of a country. The crashing of airplanes into buildings in the U.S. in 2001, subway bombings in the UK, and poison gas explosions in Asia are examples of terrorist activities.

Texting using a cell phone or other handheld electronic device to send messages. Texting-while-driving, as well as use of a cell phone for conversations has been banned by the FMCSR.

The Infra-Red Traffic Logger (TIRTL) more commonly known simply by the acronym **TIRTL**, is a multi-purpose traffic sensor that can be used as a traffic counter, speed sensor, red light camera sensor, heavy vehicle tracker, overheight vehicle sensor, rail crossing sensor, and network management system. The initial development of the device started in 1997 and is currently in use in 16 countries.

Thermostat a valve in the water jacket located at the point where the coolant leaves the engine. It opens to let the coolant go to the radiator for cooling after the engine temperature exceeds 180 degrees F.

Third-party skills testing an organization, outside the state licensing department or the educational agency, that provides testing for candidates seeking to earn the CDL.

Through bill of lading a bill of lading used for shipments transported by more than one carrier that has a fixed rate for the service of all of the carriers.

Tie-downs chains, ropes, and other implements used to secure cargo. Cargo should have at least one tie-down for each 10 feet (3.0 m) of cargo.

Tie rod connects the front wheels together and adjusts their operating angle.

Tire chains chain grids used on tires to provide additional traction on snowy, icy roadways. Tire chains are required during bad weather in some states.

Tire pressure amount of air pressure enabling tires to support their maximum weight. Check the manufacturer's instructions for proper air pressure.

Tire slides occur when the forces from weight and acceleration of the rig are greater than the tires' ability to maintain traction.

Tire tread the part of the tire that makes contact with the road.

Tires provide traction and reduce road vibration, transferring braking and driving force to the road. During inspection check tread depth, air pressure, and general condition of the tires. Bald or worn tires can cause a blowout, hydroplaning, or make the vehicle hard to stop. Tires with low pressure make the rig hard to handle and cause unnecessary wear.

Toe-in Toe-in is the tendency for the wheels of a vehicle to be closer together at the front than at the back.

Toe-out inclination for the wheels of a tractor or other vehicle to be closer together at the back than at the front. Toe-in is the opposite.

Toll roads   except for having to pay a toll, these roads are similar to the interstates.

Torque   is a measure of the turning force on an object such as a bolt or a flywheel. For example, pushing or pulling the handle of a wrench connected to a nut or bolt produces a torque (turning force) that loosens or tightens the nut or bolt.

Total stopping distance   the driver reaction distance plus the vehicle braking distance.

Tracks Out of Service sign   a signal to traffic that railroad tracks are not in use, due to maintenance or defect. However, all truck traffic should stop and check both ways for train traffic, nonetheless, before attempting to cross these tracks.

Traction   the contact between the tires and the road surface.

Tractor   pulls the trailer and drives the vehicle.

Tractor-trailer   a vehicle used to pull one or more other vehicles, such as a semitrailer.

Tractor parking valve   a round blue knob you can push in to release the tractor parking brake.

Tractor protection system   secures the tractor's air pressure if the trailer should break away from the tractor and snap the air lines.

Tractor steering axle   supports and steers the front end of the tractor.

Trailer   the freight hauling part of the vehicle meant to be pulled by a tractor.

Trailer air supply valve (also called tractor protection valve)   in the open position, it provides air to the trailer brakes. In the closed position, it shuts off the air supply to the trailer.

Trailer brake control valve (also called hand valve, trolley valve, **or independent trailer brake**)   operates the service brakes on the trailer only.

Trailer emergency relay valve   used only in an emergency when the air supply is lost. If the air lines are crossed, the brakes will stay on.

Trailer hand valve brake   valve in the cab used to operate the service brake of the trailer. To check it, apply the brake and begin to drive. If the unit moves, you have a problem and should stop immediately.

Transmission   a case, or box, of gears located behind the clutch. It adjusts the power generated by the engine so it provides the right speed and torque for the job.

Transmission control unit   is a device that controls electronic automatic transmissions. A TCU generally uses sensors from the vehicle as well as data provided by the Engine Control Unit to calculate how and when to change gears in the vehicle for optimum performance, fuel economy, and shift quality.

Transport Canada   a Canadian governmental department that serves the public interest through the promotion of a safe, secure, efficient, and environmentally responsible transportation system throughout the provinces.

Transportation charges   fees for transportation services.

Transportation Security Administration (TSA)   in the U.S., this agency protects the nation's transportation systems, making it possible for people and commerce to move safely from origin to destination.

Treadle valve (foot brake)   controls the air that operates the brakes.

Tri-drive axles   three axles in the same assembly. They are used where a load carrying advantage is needed.

Trip time formula   Trip Time = Distance ÷ Average Speed.

Triple trailers (triples)   combination rigs that have three semitrailers pulled by a tractor.

Troubleshoot   search out the source of a problem and attempt to solve it.

Truck scales   roadside enforcement entities requiring CMVs to pull over and be weighed on their scales to assure their weight matches their manifests.

Turnaround run   a driver travels for about 5 hours to a point destination and then returns to his or her home terminal. At the turn-around point, the driver might switch units or trailers for the return trip.

Turnpike double   a three-axle tractor pulling two tandem-axle semitrailers—nine axles in all. Turnpikes are most commonly used in the eastern states.

Turn signal lights   lights used to signal to other drivers that you are turning.

Twin screws   the two drive axles of a tandem.

2-axle dolly   attached to the trailer using the actual cargo. One end of the cargo rests on the dolly. The other end rests on the trailer.

Two-axle, double drop low bed with outriggers   a double-top frame and two rear axles. Outriggers are attached to each side of the trailer to support wider loads.

Two-axle float   a flat-bed frame with two rear axles and no landing gear. It is used mostly in oil fields for hauling drilling equipment, pipes, and so on.

2-axle jeep dolly   can be attached to the fifth wheel. The fifth wheel is between the tractor and trailer.

2-axle truck with single drive axle   a truck or tractor with only one axle in the rear.

Uncoupling   separating a tractor from a trailer.

Under the influence   refers to any driver operating under the influence of alcohol or drugs.

Uniform straight bill of lading   a contract that the parties cannot change. The goods must be delivered to the consignee or an authorized representative.

Universal joints (U-joints)   allow the cab to move in any direction and let the drive shaft change its angle of operation.

Unscheduled maintenance and repair   occurs when unexpected breakdowns or emergencies require immediate maintenance.

Upgrade   a steepening of the road, usually found around mountainous terrain or in the hill country; the opposite of a downgrade.

Upshifting   allows the rig to gain speed. Moving up the gears provides more speed but less power.

U.S. Coast Guard National Response Center   helps coordinate emergency forces in response to chemical hazards.

U.S. Department of Transportation   a department within the U.S. government, charged with overseeing federal highway, air, railroad, and maritime and other transportation administration functions.

U.S. numbered routes   major through-routes. Those that parallel the interstates may be good alternatives in case of delays on the interstate.

USA Patriot Act is an Act of the U.S. Congress that stands for Uniting (and) Strengthening America (by) Providing Appropriate Tools Required (to) Intercept (and) Obstruct Terrorism *Act of 2001*. The act was passed in response to the terrorist attacks of 9/11 and dramatically increased vigilance in the U.S., even against domestic terrorist acts, including tampering with CMVs.

Valves in relation to the mechanical aspects of an engine, a valve is any of numerous mechanical devices by which the flow of liquid, gas, or loose material in bulk may be started, stopped, or regulated by a movable part that opens, shuts, or partially obstructs one or more ports or passageways.

Variable load suspension (VLS) axle allows adjustment of the weight carried by each axle. One type uses air or hydraulic suspension. The other type has springs.

Vehicle braking distance the distance your rig travels from the time you apply pressure to the brake pedal until the rig stops.

Vehicle condition report (VCR) a daily report filed with the supervisor by each driver that states the true condition of each truck he or she drove that day.

Visibility your ability to see in front of you.

Vision the ability to see, or sight.

Visual search the sequential process of checking mirrors, the road, and the space around a vehicle by the driver as he or she guides the vehicle down the highway.

Voltage regulator controls the voltage produced by the alternator or generator. The regulator keeps the battery voltage from getting too high.

Voltmeter gives an overview of the charging system. It tells the state of charge of the battery and whether the charging system is keeping up with the demands for electricity. During normal operation the meter needle should be between 13 and 14.5.

Walkie-talkie a combined transmitter-receiver, light enough to be carried by one person. Originally developed for use during World War II.

Warehouse receipt a receipt for goods shipped or received by a warehouse.

Water jacket a water-filled casing or compartment used to cool an engine or an engine component.

Weapons of mass destruction a term used frequently in the lead-up to the war in Iraq, referencing nuclear missiles and other weaponry.

Weight distance tax a tax levied on heavy trucks by some states (New Mexico and Kentucky) based on the mileage traveled within that state. The tax coincides with a permit allowing that vehicle to travel within the state.

Weight distribution how the weight of a load is distributed over each axle.

Wheel load how much weight, depending upon how freight is loaded on a trailer, each wheel and axle will carry.

Wheel lockup the suspension of motion of a wheel or wheels due to skids or defective parts.

Whistleblower complaint a complaint brought against an employer who is asking an employee to ignore a law or regulation in their day-to-day activities.

Winch mechanism, usually used by a wrecker to remove a vehicle or other heavy object from a ditch, sand, or other area.

Windshield wipers in-cab, controlled, and timed mechanisms mounted on the windshield of every vehicle, making it possible to operate that vehicle in inclement weather, such as rain or snow.

Wrist pin in internal combustion engines, the wrist pin (called the gudgeon pin in Canada) connects the piston to the connecting rod and provides a bearing for the connecting rod to pivot upon as the piston moves.

Yaw (directional stability) A yaw rotation is a movement around the yaw axis of a vehicle that changes the direction the vehicle is facing, to the left or right of its direction of motion. It is one of the main targets of the electronic stability control systems. Arrows, darts, rockets, and airships have tail surfaces to achieve stability. A road vehicle does not have elements specifically designed to maintain stability, but relies primarily on the distribution of mass.

Index